NINTH EDITION

Child Development

John W. Santrock

UNIVERSITY OF TEXAS AT DALLAS

McGraw-Hill

Boston Burr Ridge, IL Dubuque, IA Madison, WI New York San Francisco St. Louis
Bangkok Bogotá Caracas Lisbon London Madrid
Mexico City Milan New Delhi Seoul Singapore Sydney Taipei Toronto

McGraw-Hill Higher Education

A Division of The **McGraw-Hill** *Companies*

CHILD DEVELOPMENT, NINTH EDITION

Published by McGraw-Hill, an imprint of The McGraw-Hill Companies, Inc., 1221 Avenue of the Americas, New York, NY 10020. Copyright © 2001, 1998, 1996, 1994, 1992, 1989, 1987, 1982 by The McGraw-Hill Companies, Inc. All rights reserved. No part of this publication may be reproduced or distributed in any form or by any means, or stored in a database or retrieval system, without the prior written consent of The McGraw-Hill Companies, Inc., including, but not limited to, in any network or other electronic storage or transmission, or broadcast for distance learning.

Some ancillaries, including electronic and print components, may not be available to customers outside the United States.

This book is printed on recycled, acid-free paper containing 10% postconsumer waste.

4 5 6 7 8 9 10   QPD/ QPD   04 03 02

ISBN 0–697–36215–9
ISBN 0–07–118007–9 (ISE)

Vice president and editor-in-chief: *Thalia Dorwick*
Editorial director: *Jane E. Vaicunas*
Senior sponsoring editor: *Rebecca H. Hope*
Senior developmental editor: *Sharon Geary*
Marketing manager: *Chris Hall*
Senior project manager: *Marilyn Rothenberger*
Lead media producer: *David Edwards*
Senior production supervisor: *Sandra Hahn*
Coordinator of freelance design: *Michelle D. Whitaker*
Freelance cover/interior designer: *Diane Beasley*
Cover image: *Lisette LeBon/©SuperStock, Inc.*
Senior photo research coordinator: *Carrie K. Burger*
Photo research: *LouAnn K. Wilson*
Supplement coordinator: *Tammy Juran*
Compositor: *GTS Graphics, Inc.*
Typeface: *10.5/12 Minion*
Printer: *Quebecor Printing Book Group/Dubuque, IA*

The credits section for this book begins on page C-1 and is considered an extension of the copyright page.

Library of Congress Cataloging-in-Publication Data

Santrock, John W.
      Child development / John W. Santrock. — 9th ed.
          p. cm.
      Includes bibliographical references and index.
      ISBN 0–697–36215–9
      1. Child development.   2. Child psychology.   I. Title.

   RJ131 .S264   2001
   305.231—dc21   00–028271
                                                                               CIP

INTERNATIONAL EDITION ISBN 0-07-118007-9
Copyright © 2001. Exclusive rights by The McGraw-Hill Companies, Inc., for manufacture and export. This book cannot be re-exported from the country to which it is sold by McGraw-Hill. The International Edition is not available in North America.

www.mhhe.com

With special appreciation
to my wife Mary Jo, my children
Tracy and Jennifer, and my
granddaughter Jordan.

About the Author

John W. Santrock

John Santrock received his PH.D. from the
University of Minnesota in 1973. He taught at the
University of Charleston and the University of
Georgia before joining the psychology department
at the University of Texas at Dallas. He has been a
member of the editorial boards of *Child
Development* and *Developmental Psychology*. His
research on father custody is widely cited and used
in expert witness testimony to promote flexibility
and alternative considerations in custody disputes.
John has also authored these exceptional Brown &
Benchmark texts: Child Development, Sixth Edition,
Life-Span Development, Sixth Edition, Children,
Third Edition, and Adolescence, Fifth Edition. He is
co-author, with Jane Halonen, of Psychology, The
Contexts of Behavior, Second Edition.

Brief Contents

Contents

Section 2

Biological Processes, Physical Development, and Perceptual Development   67

Section 3

Cognition and Language   201

Chapter 9

Intelligence   281

Chapter 10

Language Development   309

Section 4

*S*ocioemotional Development 337

Chapter 11

Emotional Development   339

Chapter 12

The Self and Identity   371

Chapter 13

Gender   395

Chapter 14

Moral Development   419

Section 5

Social Contexts of Development 453

Chapter 15

Families 455

Chapter 16

Peers 487

Chapter 17

Schools   517

Chapter 18

Culture   553

The Ninth Edition: A Substantial Revision

This, the ninth edition, is the first edition of this book of the twenty-first century, some 23 years after the first edition was published in 1978. When a book reaches its ninth edition, it typically generates two reactions from instructors: (1) The book must be successful to have lasted this long, and (2) the ninth edition likely is not much different from the eighth edition.

We acknowledge the accuracy of the first impression—more than 300,000 students have used previous editions. However, to instructors who might have the second perception of *Child Development*, ninth edition, we optimistically challenge you to put it to the test. With the most extensive input from instructors, research experts, and students any edition of the book has ever received, the inclusion of many new topics, the deletion of others, a new illustration program, new learning and study aids, a new design, and line-by-line revision of material, *we are confident you will find that the ninth edition of* Child Development *is significantly different from the eighth edition and that you will be pleasantly surprised.*

What Did We Learn?

What do most instructors and students really want from a topical child development text? One of the comments we heard most repeatedly from instructors and students was that too many books written for the main undergraduate child development course are too high-level and unnecessarily complex. One of the most consistent statements we heard from instructors and students about *Child Development*, ninth edition, was that it is written at just the right level for undergraduates.

Another frequent comment from instructors and students was that *Child Development,* ninth edition, has a good balance of research and applications. They commented that some topical child development books do not adequately capture the real world of children and are too research oriented.

Thus, two important aspects of recent editions of *Child Development* that have made them successful and popular with instructors and students are the writing level and the balance of research and applications. Every effort was made in the ninth edition to ensure that these characteristics differentiate this book from other topical child development texts more than ever.

Chapter-by-Chapter Changes

To illustrate some to the substantial content changes in the ninth edition of *Child Development,* let's briefly examine each of the 18 chapters. Many of these changes are responses to requests by the expert consultants and individuals who teach the topical child development class. Among the most significant changes are increased coverage of the brain's development, learning and educational applications, emotional development, peers, and technology.

CHAPTER 1 Introduction

New Explorations in Child Development box with examination of recent research on children's resilience

CHAPTER 2 The Science of Child Development

Completely restructured and rewritten section on research methods that is easier to understand

New elaborate figure on a research study involving mentoring of children to illustrate how the scientific method works

New figures for Freud's, Erikson's, and Piaget's stages that stretch diagonally on the page to illustrate the staircase nature of the theories

New section on Vygotsky's theory

New section on research journals

CHAPTER 3 Biological Beginnings

Expanded, updated, contemporary discussion of the evolutionary psychology approach

Updated, expanded coverage of new reproductive technologies

Extensively revised examination of heredity-environment interaction

Discussion of Judith Harris' controversial book *The Nurture Assumption*

CHAPTER 4 Prenatal Development and Birth

New high-interest chapter-opening story: "The Story of Tanner Roberts' Birth: A Fantastic Voyage"

Recent research on links between a pregnant mother's stress and fetal development (Gupta, 1999; Wadhwa, 1999)

Recent research on prenatal alcohol exposure (Baer & others, 1998)

New section on caffeine and pregnancy

New section on paternal factors in prenatal development

New coverage of the newborn's ability to cope with the stress of the birth process (VonBeveren, 1999)

Updated research of Tiffany Field on the roles of touch and massage in infant development

CHAPTER 5 Physical Development in Infancy

Expanded coverage of brain research, including new section on early experience and the brain's development

Expanded, updated discussion of the left and right hemispheres and brain lateralization

New research by Hutenlocker (1997) on autopsies of infants' brains

Recent research on SIDS

New figure on sleep across the human life span

Recent conceptualization of perceiving objects and space when motion is involved

New Explorations in Child Development box: "A Healthy Start"

CHAPTER 6 Physical Development in Childhood and Puberty

Recent study of myelination using MRI scans (Paus & others, 1999)

New discussions of reasons for death of children under the age of 5

New section on cancer in children

Updated, contemporary data on adolescent sexuality

New research on gene damage to lungs due to early smoking (Wiencke & others, 1999)

New section on adolescent health

New Explorations in Child Development box: "Life Science and Life Skills Education"

CHAPTER 7 Cognitive Developmental Approaches

Expanded, updated treatment of educational applications of Piaget's theory to education

New discussion of infant cognition (Haith & Benson, 1998)

New photos of Piaget when he was 27 years old and with his wife and three children

Significantly expanded examination of Vygotsky's theory and link to introductory overview of his theory in chapter 2

Much-expanded coverage of Vygotsky and education

New discussion of scaffolding in Vygotsky's theory

New section on evaluating and comparing Vygotsky's theory and Piaget's theory

CHAPTER 8 Information Processing

Significant revision and restructuring, with many new applications to children's learning and education

New opening story, "The Story of Laura Bickford," in which Ms. Bickford describes how she guides children to develop their critical-thinking skills

New discussion of Siegler's recent ideas about what characterizes the information-processing approach

Completely rewritten memory section, with an initial discussion of encoding, storage, and retrieval

New research by Carolyn Rovee-Collier and her colleagues (1999) on infant memory

Recent research discussion by experts on differences between experts and novices (Committee on Developments in the Science of Learning, 1999)

Expanded coverage of schema theory

New section on retrieval and forgetting

New section on personal trauma in children and their memory

Updated material on repressed memories (Bruck & Ceci, 1999)

Added discussion of rethinking and redefining problems and solutions over time in problem-solving section

Expanded coverage of critical thinking

Extensively revised, updated examination of metacognition

New section on metacognitive strategies

New section on self-regulatory learning

New section on controversies in math education

New section on science education

CHAPTER 9 Intelligence

New chapter-opening story: "The Story of Project Spectrum" (an educational program based on Gardner's theory of multiple intelligences)

New discussion of concurrent and predictive validity

Expanded examination of Gardner's multiple-intelligences view and inclusion of the eighth intelligence: naturalist

Application of Sternberg's triarchic theory to education

New section on evaluating the multiple-intelligences approach

New Explorations in Child Development box: "The Abecedarian Project"

New material on the increase in IQ scores from 1932 to 1997

Expanded coverage of creativity, including strategies for improving children's creative thinking

CHAPTER 10 Language Development

New Explorations in Child Development box: "How Parents Can Facilitate Their Children's Language Development"

Added language milestones of cooing and fussing

New discussion of research on the role of experiences in children's vocabulary development

New section: "Overview of Early Language Development"

Extensively rewritten and updated coverage of reading, writing, and literacy

Updated discussion of approaches to reading, including conclusions of the National Research Council (1999)

New Explorations in Child Development box: "Technology Resources for Improving Phonological Awareness and Decoding Skills"

New section on children's writing

Extensively revised and updated discussion of bilingualism

CHAPTER 11 Emotional
Development

New chapter title to emphasize the increased coverage of emotional development in the chapter

Chapter restructured so that the core of emotional development is described in the first part of the chapter rather than at the end of the chapter

New chapter-opening story: "The Story of Tom's Fathering"

New section: "Relational Emotion"

New section on emotion in peer relations

New section: "Regulation of Emotion"

New section on stranger anxiety

New section on social referencing

New sections on the development of emotion in early childhood, middle and late childhood, and adoelscence

New section on coping with death

Updated, contemporary treatment of temperament categories (Rothbart & Bates, 1998)

New research by L. Alan Sroufe and his colleagues (1999) on attachment

Coverage of Type D attachment category

New section: "Caregiving Styles and Attachment Classification"

New cross-cultural research and attachment discussion

Updated, contemporary coverage of the NICHD child-care study

CHAPTER 12 The Self and
Identity

New Explorations in Child Development box: "Multiple Selves and Sociocultural Contexts"

New discussion of the domains of identity development

New material on multiple identities

Extensively revised, updated coverage of cultural and ethnic aspects of identity, including more material on biculturalism and immigration

CHAPTER 13 Gender

New high-interest opener: "The Story of Jerry Maguire: Gender, Emotion, and Caring"

Updated and expanded coverage of biological influences and gender

New section on evolutionary psychology and gender

New description of Alice Eagly's social-roles view of gender

Revised, updated discussion of socioemotional similarities and differences in gender

Deleted section on women's and men's issues

Deleted section on ethnicity and gender

CHAPTER 14 Moral
Development

New figure of Kohlberg's stages set diagonally on page to illustrate their staircase nature

New recent longitudinal study of Lawrence Walker and his colleagues (in press) on parents' and friends' influence on moral maturity

New organization of discussion of emotion, altruism, and parenting, with these now being examined under separate headings

Extensively rewritten, updated coverage of moral education

Updated, contemporary examination of service learning

New discussion of whether an adolescent who commits a crime should be tried as an adult

Extensively revised, updated exploration of violence and youth

New Explorations in Child Development box: "Why Youth Kill"

CHAPTER 15 Families

New high-interest chapter-opening story: "The Story of Jessica Dubroff, Child Pilot"

New research on continuity in development (Sroufe, Egeland, & Carlson, 1999)

New research on discontinuity in development (Collins & others, 1999)

New section: "The Roles of Cognition and Emotion in Family Relationships"

Extensively rewritten, updated discussion of attachment in adolescence, including attachment styles in adolescence

Recent research on latchkey children (Pettit & others, 1999)

Extensively revised, expanded coverage of the effects of divorce on children

New Explorations in Child Development box on strategies for divorced parents

Revised, updated discussion of cultural, ethnic, and socioeconomic influences on families

New research on father involvement (Yeung & others, 1999)

CHAPTER 16 Peers

Chapter restructured and more cohesive: Material on media moved to chapter 18, material on culture and peers significantly expanded

New chapter opener on adolescence, peers, and romantic relationships

New discussion of peer groups as heterogeneous rather than monolithic by Hartup (1999)

New section on bullying

New section on mixed-aged friendships

New discussion of Brad Brown's (1998) ideas on cliques and school achievement

New section on types of dating and developmental changes

New section on emotion and romantic relationships

CHAPTER 17 Schools

New discussion of the APA's learner-centered psychological principles

Deleted sections on preschools and school readiness

Extensively revised, updated coverage of poverty and education

New Explorations in Child Development box: "Savage Inequalities"

Extensively revised, updated coverage of children with disabilities

New discussion of dyslexia and reading problems in children with learning disabilities

New section on intervention strategies, in learning disabilities section

New section: "Educational Issues Involving Children with Disabilities"

Extensively revised, updated coverage of extrinsic and intrinsic motivation

Expanded examination of attribution

Updated, expanded coverage of goal-setting, planning, and self-monitoring

New discussion of schools that serve ethnic minority students (Eccles, Wigfield, & Shiefele, 1998)

CHAPTER 18 Culture

Chapter expanded to include media and technology
Extensively revised, updated material on socioeconomic status and poverty

Recent research on SES, parenting, and skill building (DeGarmo & others, 1998)

New discussion of two-generation poverty programs (McLloyd, 1998)

New material on immigration and ethnicity

New Explorations in Child Development box: "El Puente"

New discussion of the "browning" of America

New major section on technology

Recent research by Federman (1997) on TV violence and aggression

New data (1999) on adolescents' use of the Internet

New section on technology and sociocultural diversity

New Explorations in Child Development box: "Using the Internet in the Classroom"

New section on Technology and Education

Technology

We have significantly expanded the discussion of technology in this edition of *Child Development*. Not only is children's use of computers and the Internet discussed in chapter 18, "Culture," but this edition also has the important new addition of Internet icons in the margins of the text. The icons and their labels signal students that they can go to the website for *Child Development*, ninth edition, and be linked to further information about the topic. This allows for more in-depth exploration of a topic than often is possible in the text itself. Also, at the end of each chapter, in a new feature called "Taking It to the Net," students are presented with problem-solving exercises that require them to visit the websites listed.

Improved Instructor- and Student-Driven Pedagogy

Students not only should be challenged to study hard and think more deeply and productively about child development, but they also should be provided with a pedagogical framework to help them learn more. The learning and study aids that follow, some of which are unique to this text and many of which are new to this edition, have been class-tested with students and endorsed by them. As a consequence, we are more confident than ever before that your students will find this edition of *Child Development* to be very student friendly. Following are some of the new pedagogical features in the book.

Cross-Linkages   Reviewers recommended that we provide more connections and links with material across chapters. To accomplish this, we created a new pedagogical feature that is unique in the topical child development field. The new *cross-linkages* refer students to primary discussion of key concepts. Each time a key concept occurs in a chapter subsequent to its initial coverage, the page reference for its initial coverage is embedded in the text with a backward-pointing arrow.

Cognitive Maps   Instructor and student reviewers said they liked the cognitive map at the end of the chapter but thought that it also should be placed at the beginning of the chapter. We added a map at the beginning of the chapter and also added mini cognitive maps, which are unique in child development texts, throughout the chapters. Students now get many visual looks at the organization of material: Each chapter opens with a cognitive map of the entire chapter, and then several times within each chapter, mini cognitive maps provide students with an ongoing visual picture of what they will be reading next. Finally, in the chapter-ending review a cognitive map of the entire chapter once again is presented along with reminders to study the summary tables, which are page-referenced.

Revised Summary Tables   Summary tables have been a very popular pedagogical feature in *Child Development*. However, reviewers recommended that we modify them in two ways: (1) Make them shorter and less dense, and (2) use bullets to highlight important characteristics and descriptions of material. We made both of these changes in the summary tables and believe that they will be even more valuable to students in helping them get a handle on important concepts as they go through each chapter.

Through the Eyes of Children   Reviewers asked us to include more material on the real lives of children in the book. To this end, we created a new feature, *Through the Eyes of Children,* that provides a window in the lives of real children. Through their words, you will be able to obtain a better sense of how children think, feel, and behave at different developmental levels. Through the Eyes of Children boxes appear in every chapter.

Through the Eyes of Psychologists   Reviewers said they liked the use of quotations throughout the text but would like to see more quotations from leading developmental psychologists. To accomplish this, we developed a new feature. *Through the Eyes of Psychologists* appears multiple times in each chapter and lets you read the actual words of the world's leading developmental psychologists and also look at a photograph of them. These brief passages were especially chosen to stimulate you to think more deeply about a particular area of children's development.

Key People   Reviewers recommended that, at the end of each chapter, we list the most important theorists and researchers discussed in the chapter. We did this and page-referenced where the theorist and researcher materials are discussed.

The New Look and Design

The ninth edition of *Child Development* has a very different look and design. The new look is more colorful and attractive with more student-relevant features. The new design is single-column with more open space.

This new design allows quotations, web icons, and other features to be placed in the margins where they do not interrupt the text. The new look and design were developed at the recommendations of instructors and students.

Acknowledgments

I also owe a special thanks to the reviewers who teach the topical child development course. As indicated at the beginning of the preface, the substantial revision that was undertaken for this edition of the book was based on their detailed recommendations. I sincerely appreciate the time and effort that the following professors gave in this regard as it has made all the difference:

Ruth L. Ault, Davidson College
Mary Ballard, Appalachian State University
William H. Barber, Midwestern State University
Wayne Benenson, Illinois State University
Michael Bergmire, Jefferson College
David Bernhardt, Carleton University
Kathryn Norcross Black, Purdue University
Elaine Blakemore, Indiana University
Susan Bland, Niagara County Community College
Marc Bornstein, National Institute of Child Health and Human Development
Amy Booth, Northwestern University
Maureen Callahan, Webster University
D. Bruce Carter, Syracuse University
Elaine Cassel, Marymount University, Lord Fairfax Community College
Steven Ceci, Cornell University
Theodore Chandler, Kent State University
Dante Cicchetti, University of Rochester
Audrey E. Clark, California State University, Northridge
Debra E. Clark, SUNY–Cortland
Robert Cohen, The University of Memphis
John D. Coie, Duke University
Cynthia Garcia Coll, Wellesley College
Robert C. Coon, Louisiana State University
Roger W. Coulson, Iowa State University
Fred Danner, University of Kentucky
Denise M. DeZolt, Kent State University
K. Laurie Dickson, Northern Arizona University
Daniel R. DiSalvi, Kean College
Diane C. Draper, Iowa State University
Beverly Brown Dupré, Southern University at New Orleans
Glen Elder, Jr., University of North Carolina
Claire Etaugh, Bradley University

Dennis T. Farrell, Luzerne County Community College
Saul Feinman, University of Wyoming
Tiffany Field, University of Miami (Florida)
Jane Goins Flanagan, Lamar University
L. Sidney Fox, California State University–Long Beach
Janet Fuller, Mansfield University
Irma Galejs, Iowa State University
Mary Gauvain, University of California, Riverside
Colleen Gift, Highland Community College
Margaret S. Gill, Kutztown State College
Hill Goldsmith, University of Wisconsin
Cynthia Graber, Columbia University
Nira Grannott, University of Texas at Dallas
Donald E. Guenther, Kent State University
Robert A. Haaf, University of Toledo
Daniel Hart, Rutgers University
Elizabeth Hasson, Westchester University
Rebecca Heikkinen, Kent State University
Stanley Henson, Arkansas Technical University
Alice Honig, Syracuse University
Helen L. Johnson, Queens College
Seth Kalichman, Loyola University
Kenneth Kallio, SUNY–Geneseo
Maria Kalpidou, Assumption College
Daniel W. Kee, California State University, Fullerton
Melvyn B. King, SUNY–Cortland
Claire Kopp, UCLA
Deanna Kuhn, Columbia University
John W. Kulig, Northern Illinois University
Janice Kupersmidt, University of North Carolina
Michael Lamb, National Institute of Child Health and Human Development
Daniel K. Lapsley, University of Notre Dame
David B. Liberman, University of Houston
Marianna Footo Linz, Marshall University
Kevin MacDonald, California State University, Long Beach
Dottie McCrossen, University of Ottawa
Sheryll Mennicke, Concordia College, St. Paul
Carolyn Meyer, Lake Sumter Community College
Dalton Miller-Jones, NE Foundation for Children
Marilyn Moore, Illinois State University
Dara Musher-Eizenman, Bowling Green State University
Jose E. Nanes, University of Minnesota
Sherry J. Neal, Oklahoma City Community College
Larry Nucci, University of Illinois at Chicago
Daniel J. O'Neill, Bristol Community College
Margaret Owen, Timberlawn Research Foundation
Robert Pasnak, George Mason University
Elizabeth Pemberton, University of Delaware
Herb Pick, University of Minnesota
Kathy Lee Pillow, Arkansas State University, Beebe
Nan Ratner, University of Maryland
Brenda Reimer, Southern Missouri State
Cosby Steel Rogers, Virginia Polytechnic Institute and State University
Kimberly A. Gordon Rouse, Ohio State University

Douglas B. Sawin, University of Texas, Austin
Ed Scholwinski, Southwest Texas State University
Dale Schunk, Purdue University
Bill M. Seay, Louisiana State University
Matthew J. Sharps, University of Colorado
Marilyn Shea, University of Maine, Farmington
Robert Siegler, Carnegie Mellon University
Evelyn D. Silva, Cosumnes River College
Dorothy Justus Sluss, Virginia Polytechnic Institute and State University
Janet Spence, University of Texas, Austin
Melanie Spence, University of Texas at Dallas
Mark S. Strauss, University of Pittsburgh
Donna J. Tyler Thompson, Midland College
Cherie Valeithian, Kent State University
Lawrence Walker, University of British Columbia
Kimberlee L. Whaley, Ohio State University
Belinda M. Wholeben, Northern Illinois University

Ancillaries

For the Instructor:

Instructor's Manual

By Cosby Steele Rogers, Bonnie Graham, Virginia Polytechnic Institute and State University
This extensively revised and expanded flexible manual provides a variety of useful tools for both the seasoned instructors and those new to the Child Development course. New features include a chapter introduction, learning objectives, and cognitive map handouts for students highlighting key concepts, terms, and people, short situational questions, and a current research feature. Additionally, the new Total Teaching Reference Package features a fully integrated outline to help instructors better use the many resources for the course. Instructors will find that all of the course resources available have been correlated to the main concepts in each chapter. Classroom activities and demonstrations, critical-thinking exercises, and essay questions have been extensively revised, with new material and possible answers provided where appropriate. Research projects now take into account varying class sizes and provide a useful timeline for their completion. Other features of the Instructor's Manual include teaching tips, a guide for using the Internet in teaching, and comprehensive transparency, video, and film resources.

Printed Test Bank

By Marilyn Moore, Illinois State University
This comprehensive Test Bank has been extensively revised and expanded to include a wide range of multiple-choice, fill-in-the blank, critical thinking, and short essay questions for each of the text's eighteen chapters. In addition, for this edition there are new short situational questions and questions specifically related to the text's boxed items. Each item is designated as factual, conceptual, or applied as defined by Benjamin Bloom's taxonomy of educational objectives.

Computerized Test Bank (Mac/IBM)

The computerized test bank contains all of the questions in the print test bank and is available in both Macintosh and Windows platforms.

The McGraw-Hill Child Developmental Psychology Image Database

Overhead Transparencies and CD-ROM
This set of 174 full-color images was developed using the best selection of our child development illustrations and tables and is available in both print overhead transparency set as well as on a CD-ROM with a fully functioning editing feature. Instructors can add their own lecture notes to the CD-ROM as well as organize the images to correspond to their particular classroom needs. The author has also selected key images for each chapter, which are available via the text's website.

Presentation Manager CD-ROM

This resourceful tool offers instructors the opportunity to customize McGraw-Hill materials to create their lecture presentations. Resources for instructors includes the Instructor's Manual materials, PowerPoint presentation slides, and the Image Database for *Child Development*.

Website

This extensive website, designed specifically to accompany Santrock, *Child Development*, ninth edition, offers an array of resources for both instructor and student. Hotlinks can be found for the text's topical web links that appear in the margins as well as for the Taking It to the Net exercises that appear at the end of each chapter. These resources and more can be found by logging on to the website at http://www.mhhe.com/santrockc9. com.

The AIDS Booklet

Frank D. Cox
This brief but comprehensive text has been revised to provide the most up-to-date information about aquired immune deficiency syndrome (AIDS).

The Critical Thinker

Richard Mayer and Fiona Goodchild of the University of California, Santa Barbara, use excerpts from introductory psychology textbooks to show students how to think critically about psychology.

Annual Editions—Child Growth & Development

Dushkin/McGraw-Hill
This supplement provides a collection of articles on topics related to the latest research and thinking in child development. These editions are updated annually, and their helpful features include a topic guide, an annotated table of contents, unit overviews, and a topical index. An Instructor's Guide containing testing materials is also available.

Taking Sides—Childhood & Society

A debate-style reader designed to introduce students to controversial viewpoints on the field's most critical issues. Each issue is carefully framed for the student, and the pro and con essays represent the arguments of leading scholars and commentators in their fields. An Instructor's Guide containing testing materials is available.

For the Student:

Student Study Guide
By Wayne Benenson, Illinois State University
The Study Guide provides a complete introduction for students studying child development, beginning with the How to Use This Study Guide and Time Management features. This fully revised study guide includes key terms with definitions, blank and partially completed cognitive maps to help test key concepts, terms, and people, and an innovative annotated outline similar to the model established in the Instructor's Manual. In addition, a guided review, self-tests, and section tests provide a variety of study and quizzing opportunities for the student. Essay questions and activities specifically related to the text's boxed features provides students with project and paper ideas directly related to the course objectives.

Making the Grade CD-ROM—Child Development
This user-friendly CD-ROM gives students an opportunity to test their comprehension of the course material in the manner which is most comfortable and beneficial to them. The CD-ROM opens with a Learning Assessment questionnaire that the student can complete to find out what type of learner she or he is. Once the student's learning style is identified, the student can go to the testing component included specifically for that learning style. The student is not, however, limited to one type of testing. All testing components are available to students to help them complete practice tests of the course material.

BEGINNING OF CHAPTER

NEW!
Cognitive Map
This provides students
with a visual overview
of the entire chapter.

Quotations
These appear at the beginning of the chapter
and occasionally in the margins to stimulate
further thought about a topic.

Gender

*To be meek, patient,
tactful, modest, honorable,
brave, is not to be either
manly or womanly,
it is to be humane.*

Jane Harrison
English Writer, 20th Century

The Story of Jerry Maguire:
Gender, Emotion, and Caring

GENDER AND EMOTION researcher Stephanie Shields (1998) recently analyzed the movie *Jerry Maguire* in terms of how it reflects the role of gender in emotions and relationships. In brief, the movie is a "buddy" picture with sports agent Jerry Maguire (played by Tom Cruise) paired with two buddies: the too-short Arizona Cardinals running back Rod Tidwell (played by Cuba Gooding, Jr.) and 6-year-old Ray, son of Jerry's love interest, the accountant Dorothy Boyd (played by Renée Zellweger). Through his buddies, the thinking-but-not-feeling Jerry discovers the right path by connecting to Ray's emotional honesty and African American Rod's devotion to his family. Conversely, the emotionally flamboyant and self-centered Rod, through his White buddy, Jerry, discovers that he must bring passion back to his game to be successful.

The image of nurturing and nurtured males is woven throughout the movie. Jerry's relationship with Ray, the 6-year-old, is a significant theme in the film. Through discovering a caring relationship with Ray, Jerry makes his first genuine move toward emotional maturity. The boy is the guide to the man. Chad, Ray's baby-sitter, is a good example of appropriate caring by a male.

How are gender, emotion and caring portrayed in the movie Jerry Maguire?

Males are shown crying in the movie. Jerry sheds tears while writing his mission statement, when thinking about Dorothy's possible move to another city (which also means he would lose Ray), and at the success of his lone client (Rod). Rod is brought to tears when he speaks of his family. Historically, weeping, more than any emotional expression, has been associated with feminine emotion. However, it has increasingly taken on a more prominent role in the male's emotional makeup.

The movie *Jerry Maguire* reflects changes in gender roles as an increasing number of males show an interest in improving their social relationships and

395

"The Story of . . ."
Each chapter opens
with a high-interest
story that is linked to
the chapter's content.
Most of the chapter-
opening stories are
new in this edition.

WITHIN CHAPTER

NEW!
Mini Cognitive Maps

These mini maps appear
three to five times per
chapter and provide
students with a more
detailed, visual look at
the organization of the
chapter.

(Inset textbook page, p. 396 — Santrock • Child Development)

396   Santrock • Child Development

achieving emotional maturity. However, as we will see later in this chapter, experts on gender argue that overall females are more competent in their social relationships than males are and that large numbers of males still have a lot of room for improvement in dealing better with their emotions.

WHAT IS GENDER?   **INFLUENCES ON GENDER DEVELOPMENT**
Biological Influences   Social Influences   Cognitive Influences

What Is Gender?

What exactly do we mean by gender? **Gender** *is the sociocultural dimension of being female or male.* Two aspects of gender bear special mention: gender identity and gender role. **Gender identity** *is the sense of being female or male, which most children acquire by the time they are 3 years old.* A **gender role** *is a set of expectations that prescribe how females and males should think, act, and feel.*

gender
The sociocultural dimension of being male or female.

gender identity
The sense of being female or male, which most children acquire by the time they are 3 years old.

gender role
A set of expectations that prescribes how females and males should think, act, and feel.

Influences on Gender Development

How is gender influenced by biology? by children's social experiences? by cognitive factors?

Biological Influences

To understand biological influences, we need to consider heredity and hormones. We also will explore the theoretical views of Freud and Erikson, and the more recent view of evolutionary psychologists.

Heredity and Hormones   It was not until the 1920s that researchers confirmed the existence of human sex chromosomes, the genetic material that determines our sex. As we discussed in chapter 3, "Biological Beginnings," normally have 46 chromosomes arranged in pairs. The 23rd pair may have two X-shaped chromosomes, to produce a female, or it may have both an X-shaped and a Y-shaped chromosome to produce a male ◀ P. 73.

Sex hormones are powerful chemicals that are controlled by the master gland in the brain, the pituitary. The two main classes of sex hormones are estrogens and androgens. **Estrogens**, *the most important of which is estradiol, influence the development of female physical sex characteristics and help to regulate the menstrual cycle. Estrogens are produced by the ovaries.* **Androgens**, *the most important of which is testosterone, promote the development of male genitals and secondary sex characteristics.* They influence sexual motivation in both sexes. Androgens are produced by the adrenal glands in males and females, and by the testes in males.

In the first few weeks of gestation, female and male embryos look alike. Male sex organs start to differ from female sex organs when the Y chromosome in the male embryo triggers the secretion of androgens. Low levels of androgens in a female embryo allow the normal development of female sex organs.

Although rare, an imbalance in this system of hormone secretion can occur during fetal development. If there is insufficient androgen in a male embryo or an excess of androgen in the female embryo, the result is an individual with both male and female sex organs, a hermaphrodite. When genetically female (XX chromosomes) infants are born with masculine-looking genitals, surgery can achieve a genital/genetic match. At puberty, production of estrogens influences both physical development and behavior in these females. However, even prior to puberty, these females often behave in a more aggressive, "tomboyish" manner than most

estrogens
Hormones, the most important of which is estradiol, that influence the development of female physical sex characteristics and help regulate the menstrual cycle.

androgens
Hormones, the most important of which is testosterone, that promote the development of male genitals and secondary sex characteristics.

(Inset textbook page, p. 492 — Santrock • Child Development)

492   Santrock • Child Development

& Kochenderfer, in press). This study also found that parent-child relationships characterized by intense closeness were linked with higher levels of peer victimization in boys. Overly close and emotionally intense relationships between parents and sons might not foster assertiveness and independence. Rather, they might foster self-doubts and worries that are perceived as weaknesses when expressed in male peer groups. Recall from a study we discussed earlier in the chapter that both bullying and victim behavior are linked to parent-child relationships (Olweus, 1980). Bullies' parents were more likely to be rejecting, authoritarian, or permissive about their son's aggression, whereas victims' parents were more likely to be anxious and overprotective.

Another recent study found that third- and sixth-grade boys and girls who experienced internalizing problems (such as being anxious and withdrawn), physical weakness, and peer rejection increasingly were victimized over time (Hodges & Perry, 1999). Yet another study found that the relation between internalizing problems and victimization was reduced by a protective friendship (Hodges & others, 1999).

Victims of bullies can suffer both short-term and long-term effects (Limber, 1997). Short-term they can become depressed, lose interest in schoolwork, or even avoid going to school. The effects of bullying can persist into adulthood. A recent longitudinal study of male victims who were bullied during childhood found that in their twenties they were more depressed and had lower self-esteem than their counterparts who had not been bullied in childhood (Olweus, in press). Bullying also can indicate a serious problem for the bully as well as the victim. In the study just mentioned, about 60 percent of the boys who were identified as bullies in middle school had at least one criminal conviction (and about one-third had three or more convictions) in their twenties, a far higher percentage than for nonbullies. To reduce bullying, teachers can do the following (Limber, 1997):

Reducing Bullying

- Get older peers to serve as monitors for bullying and intervene when they see it taking place.
- Develop school-wide rules and sanctions against bullying and post them throughout the school.
- Form friendship groups for adolescents who are regularly bullied by peers.
- Incorporate the message of the antibullying program into church, school, and other community activities where adolescents are involved.

Next, we will turn our attention to the role of social cognition in peer relations. In part of this discussion, we will explore ideas about reducing the aggression of children in their peer encounters.

perspective taking
The ability to assume another person's perspective and understand his or her thoughts and feelings.

Social Cognition

How might children's thoughts contribute to their peer relations? Three possibilities are through their perspective-taking ability, social information-processing skills, and social knowledge.

As we discussed in chapter 14, "Moral Development," **perspective taking** *involves taking another's point of view* ◀ P. 434. As children enter the elementary school years, both their peer interaction and their perspective-taking ability increase. Reciprocity—playing games, functioning in groups, and cultivating friendships, for example—is especially important in peer interchanges at this point in development. One of the important skills that help elementary school children improve their peer relations is communication effectiveness. In one investigation, the communication exchanges among peers at kindergarten, first-, third-, and fifth-grade levels were evaluated (Krauss & Glucksberg, 1969). Children were asked to instruct a peer in how to stack a set of blocks. The peer sat behind a screen with blocks similar to those the other child was stacking (see figure 16.2). The kindergarten children made numerous errors in telling the peer how to duplicate the novel block stack. The older children, especially the fifth-graders, were much more efficient in communicating to a peer how to stack the blocks. They were sensitive to the communication demands of the task and were far superior at perspective taking and figuring out how they had

---

NEW!
Cross-Linkage

This system, unique to this text and
new in this edition, refers students
to the primary discussion of all key
concepts. A specific page reference
appears in the text with a
backward-pointing arrow each time
a key concept occurs in a chapter
subsequent to its initial coverage.

NEW!
Single-Column Design

The previous edition of *Child Development*
had a dense, two-column format. Instructors
and students told us to change this to a more
open, one-column design. They said this
makes the text material easier to read and
allows the wider margins to be used for many
pedagogical features, such as key term
definitions and Internet sites.

NEW!
Through the Eyes of Psychologists

This feature, appearing several times in each chapter, includes a photograph and quotation from leading psychologists to stimulate further thinking about the content.

New!
Web Icons

Web icons appear a number of times in each chapter. They signal students to go to the website for Santrock's *Child Development*, ninth edition, where they will find connecting links that provide additional information on the topic discussed in the text. The labels under the Internet icon appear as Web links at the Santrock website, under that chapter for easy access.

---

398 Santrock • Child Development

Through the Eyes of Psychologists
Alice Eagly, *Northwestern University*

"Sex differences are adaptations to the differing restrictions and opportunities that a society provides for its males and females."

Alice Eagly's Research

Critics of the evolutionary psychology view argue that humans have the decision-making ability to change their gender behavior and therefore are not locked into the evolutionary past. They also stress that the extensive cross-cultural variation in sex differences and mate preferences provides stronger evidence for the social construction of gender differences than for an evolutionary source. Next, we will explore what some of these social influences are.

An Interactionist View   No one questions the presence of genetic, biochemical, and anatomical differences between the sexes. Even child developmentalists with a strong environmental orientation acknowledge that boys and girls are treated differently because of their physical differences and their different roles in reproduction. The importance of biological factors is not at issue. What is at issue is the directness or indirectness of their effects on social behavior (Huston, 1983; Rose, 1997). For example, if a high androgen level directly influences the central nervous system, which in turn increases activity level, then the biological effect on behavior is direct. By contrast, if a child's high level of androgen produces strong muscle development, which in turn causes others to expect the child to be a good athlete and, in turn, leads the child to participate in sports, then the biological effect on behavior is indirect.

Although virtually everyone thinks that children's behavior as males or females is due to an interaction of biological and environmental factors, an interactionist position means different things to different people (Maccoby, 1997). For some, it suggests that certain environmental conditions are required before preprogrammed dispositions appear. For others, it suggests that a particular environment will have different effects, depending on the child's predispositions. For still others, it means that children shape their environments, including their interpersonal environment, and vice versa. The processes of influence and counterinfluence unfold over time. Throughout development, in this view, males and females actively construct their own versions of acceptable masculine and feminine behavior patterns.

Social Influences

Many social scientists, such as Alice Eagly (1997, 2000; Eagly & Wood, 1999), locate the cause of psychological sex differences not in biologically evolved dispositions but in the contrasting positions and social roles of women and men. In contemporary American society and in most cultures around the world, women have less power and status than men and control fewer resources. Women perform more domestic work than men and spend fewer hours in paid employment. Although most women are in the workforce, they receive lower pay than men and are thinly represented in the highest levels of organizations. Thus, from the perspective of social influences, gender hierarchy and sexual division of labor are important causes of sex-differentiated behavior. As women adapted to roles with less power and less status in society, they showed more cooperative, less dominant profiles than men.

Identification and Social Cognitive Theories   Two prominent theories address the way children acquire masculine and feminine attitudes and behaviors from their parents. **Identification theory** *stems from Freud's view that the preschool child develops a sexual attraction to the opposite-sex parent, then by approximately 5 or 6 years of age renounces this attraction because of anxious feelings, and subsequently identifies with the same-sex parent, unconsciously adopting the same-sex parent's characteristics.* However, today many child developmentalists do not believe that gender development proceeds on the basis of identification, at least in terms of Freud's emphasis on childhood sexual attraction. Children become gender-typed much earlier than 5 or 6 years of age, and they become

identification theory
A theory that stems from Freud's view that preschool children develop a sexual attraction to the opposite-sex parent, then at 5 to 6 years of age renounce the attraction because of anxious feelings, subsequently identifying with the same-sex parent and unconsciously adopting the same-sex parent's characteristics.

---

448 Santrock • Child Development

SUMMARY TABLE 14.4
Moral Education and Juvenile Delinquency

Concept	Processes/Related Ideas	Characteristics/Description
Moral Education	The Hidden Curriculum	• Originally proposed by John Dewey, the hidden curriculum refers to the moral atmosphere of a school.
	Character Education	• A direct education approach that advocates teaching students a basic moral literacy.
	Values Clarification	• Focuses on helping students to clarify what their lives are for and what is worth exploring.
	Cognitive Moral Education	• Emphasizes helping students develop such values as democracy and justice as their moral reasoning develops. • Kohlberg's theory has served as the basis for a number of cognitive moral education programs.
	Service Learning	• A form of education that promotes social responsibility and service to the community. • Service learning benefits youth in a number of ways.
	Rest's Four-Component Model	• Rest argues that moral development can best be understood by considering four components of morality—sensitivity, judgment, motivation, and character.
Juvenile Delinquency	What Is Juvenile Delinquency?	• Delinquency includes a broad range of behaviors, ranging from socially unacceptable behavior to status offenses. • Conduct disorder is a psychiatric category often used to describe delinquent-type behaviors. • Self-reported patterns suggest that about 20 percent of adolescents engage in delinquent behaviors.
	Antecedents of Delinquency	• Predictors of delinquency include a negative identity, low self-control, early initiation of delinquency, weak educational orientation, heavy peer influence, low parental monitoring, ineffective discipline, and living in an urban, high-crime area.
	Violence and Youth	• The high rate of violence in youth is an increasing problem. • Recommendations for reducing youth violence include effective parenting, prevention, support for schools, and forging effective partnerships among families, schools, and communities. • Conflict resolution programs are being used in attempts to reduce youth violence.

Summary Tables

Several times in each chapter, we review what has been discussed so far in that chapter by displaying the information in summary tables. This learning device helps students get a handle on material several times a chapter, so they don't have to wait until the end of a chapter and have too much information to digest.

NEW!

Explorations in Child Development

This new box, appearing one or more times in each chapter, focuses on applications that involve providing a more caring world for children.

412   Santrock • Child Development

EXPLORATIONS IN CHILD DEVELOPMENT
Gender Roles in Egypt and China

IN RECENT DECADES, roles assumed by males and females in the United States have become increasingly similar—that is, androgynous. In many countries, though, gender roles have remained more gender-specific. For example, in Egypt, the division of labor between Egyptian males and females is dramatic. Egyptian males are socialized to work in the public sphere, females in the private world of home and child rearing. The Islamic religion dictates that the man's duty is to provide for his family, the woman's to care for her family and household (Dickerscheid & others, 1988). Any deviations from this traditional gender-role orientation are severely disapproved of.

Egypt is not the only country in which males and females are socialized to behave, think, and feel in strongly gender-specific ways. Kenya and Nepal are two other cultures in which children are brought up under very strict gender-specific guidelines (Munroe, Himmin, & Munroe, 1984). In the People's Republic of China, the female's status has historically been lower than the male's. The teachings of the fifth-century B.C. Chinese philosopher Confucius were used to reinforce the concept of the female as an inferior being. Beginning with the 1949 revolution in China, women began to achieve more economic freedom and more-equal status in marital relationships. However, even with the sanctions of a socialist government, the old patriarchal traditions of male supremacy in China have not been completely uprooted. Chinese women still make considerably less money than Chinese men in comparable positions, and in rural China a tradition of male supremacy still governs many women's lives.

Thus, while in China, females have made considerable strides, complete equality remains a distant objective. And in many cultures, such as Egypt and other countries

where the Muslim religion predominates, gender-specific behavior is pronounced, and females are not given access to high-status positions.

In China, females and males are usually socialized to behave, feel, and think differently. The old patriarchal traditions of male supremacy have not been completely uprooted. Chinese women still make considerably less money than Chinese men do, and, in rural China (such as here in the Lixian Village of Sichuan) male supremacy still governs many women's lives.

At this point we have studied many ideas about gender-role classification. A review of these ideas is presented in summary table 13.3. Next, we will continue our exploration of gender by focusing on some developmental changes.

Developmental Windows of Gender Opportunity and Asymmetric Gender Socialization

Are children more prone to forming gender roles at some points in development than at others? Are the amount, timing, and intensity of gender socialization different for girls and boys?

Key Terms Definitions

Key terms appear in boldface type with their definitions immediately following in italic type and they also appear nearby in the margin. This provides you with a clear understanding of important concepts.

Western cultures includes behaviors that do not have social approval but nonetheless validate the adolescent boy's masculinity. That is, in the male adolescent culture, male adolescents perceive that they will be thought of as more masculine if they engage in premarital sex, drink alcohol and take drugs, and participate in illegal delinquent activities.

Gender-Role Transcendence

Some critics of androgyny say enough is enough and that there is too much talk about gender. They believe that androgyny is less of a panacea than originally envisioned (Paludi, 1999). An alternative is **gender-role transcendence**, *the view that when an individual's competence is at issue, it should be conceptualized on a personal basis, rather than on the basis of masculinity, femininity, or androgyny* (Pleck, 1983). That is, we should think about ourselves as people, not as masculine, feminine, or androgynous. Parents should rear their children to be competent boys and girls, not masculine, feminine, or androgynous, say the gender-role critics. They believe such gender-role classification leads to too much stereotyping.

Gender in Context

The concept of gender-role classification involves a personality-traitlike categorization of a person. However, it may be helpful to think of personality in terms of person-situation interaction rather than personality traits alone. Thus, in our discussion of gender-role classification, we describe how different gender roles might be more appropriate, depending on the context, or setting, involved.

To see the importance of considering gender in context, let's examine helping behavior and emotion. The stereotype is that females are better than males at helping. But it depends on the situation. Females are more likely than males to volunteer their time to help children with personal problems and to engage in caregiving behavior. However, in situations in which males feel a sense of competence and involve danger, males are more likely than females to help (Eagly & Crowley, 1986). For example, a male is more likely than a female to stop and help a person stranded by the roadside with a flat tire.

"She is emotional; he is not"—that is the master emotional stereotype. However, like differences in helping behavior, emotional differences in males and females depend on the particular emotion involved and the context in which it is displayed (Shields, 1991). Males are more likely to show anger toward strangers, especially male strangers, when they feel they have been challenged. Males also are more likely to turn their anger into aggressive action. Emotional differences between females and males often show up in contexts that highlight social roles and relationships. For example, females are more likely to discuss emotions in terms of relationships, and they are more likely to express fear and sadness.

The importance of considering gender in context is nowhere more apparent than when examining what is culturally prescribed behavior for females and males in different countries around the world. While there has been greater acceptance of androgyny and similarities in male and female behavior in the United States, in many countries gender roles remain gender-specific. To read about gender roles in two countries—Egypt and China—see the Explorations in Child Development box.

Chapter 13 • Gender   411

	Masculine	
	High	Low
Feminine Low | High	Androgynous	Feminine
	Masculine	Undifferentiated

Figure **13.5**
Gender-Role Classification

gender-role transcendence
The belief that, when an individual's competence is at issue, it should be conceptualized not on the basis of masculinity, femininity, or androgyny but, rather, on a personal basis.

Gender Around the World
Gender Socialization in Six Countries

ADVENTURES FOR THE MIND
Gender Roles, Parenting, and the Future

IN THE LAST TWO decades, dramatic changes in gender roles have taken place in the United States. How much change have you personally experienced? How do you think gender roles will be different in the twenty-first century? Or do you believe that gender roles will stay about the way they are now?

There is a practical side to considering such questions. How will you raise your children, in terms of gender matters? Will gender neutrality be your goal? Will you encourage more traditional gender distinctions?

"Adventures for the Mind"

These critical thinking boxes appear periodically in each chapter to challenge students to stretch their minds.

END OF CHAPTER

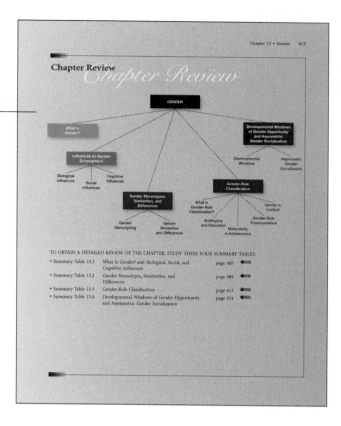

Chapter Review

The chapter review consists of a cognitive map of the entire chapter and a bulleted list of the summary tables, which are page-referenced with a backward-pointing arrow.

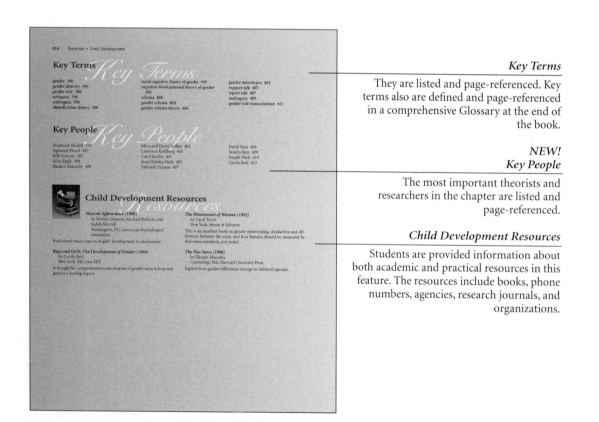

Key Terms

They are listed and page-referenced. Key terms also are defined and page-referenced in a comprehensive Glossary at the end of the book.

NEW!
Key People

The most important theorists and researchers in the chapter are listed and page-referenced.

Child Development Resources

Students are provided information about both academic and practical resources in this feature. The resources include books, phone numbers, agencies, research journals, and organizations.

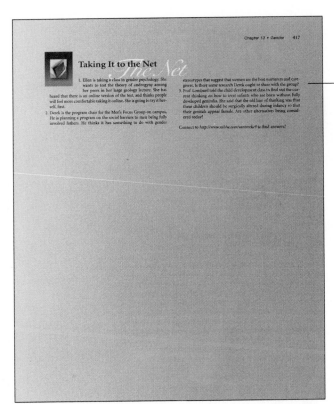

This presents students with questions to explore on the Internet that are related to the chapter. By going to the Santrock website under Taking It to the Net, students will be able to connect to other websites, where they can find information that will help them think more deeply about the questions posed.

END OF TEXT
Epilogue

Beginning on page 581, this montage of thoughts and images from the author provides an insightful capstone to the child development course.

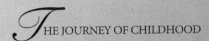

THE JOURNEY OF CHILDHOOD

I hope you can look back and say that you learned a lot in this course about children, not only other children, but yourself as a child and how your childhood contributed to who you are today. The insightful words of nineteenth-century Danish philosopher Søren Kierkegaard capture the importance of looking back to understand ourselves: "Life is lived forward but understood backwards." I also hope that those of you who become the parents of children or who work with children in some capacity—whether as teacher, as counselor, or as community leader—feel that you now have a better grasp of what children's development is all about.

Future generations depend on our ability to face our children. At some point in our adult lives, each one of us needs to examine the shape of our life and ask whether we have met the responsibility of competently and caringly carving out a better world for our children. Twenty-one centuries ago, Roman poet and philosopher Lucretius described one of adult life's richest meanings: grasping that the generations of living things pass in a short while and, like runners, pass on the torch of life. More than twenty centuries later, American writer James Agee acptured yet another of life's richest meaning: In every child who is born, the potentiality of the human species is born again.

As we come to the end of this book, I leave you with the following montage of thoughts and images that convey the beauty and complexity of children's development.

Prologue

If I Had My Child to Raise Over Again

If I had my child to raise all over again,

I'd finger paint more, and point the finger less.

I'd do less correcting, and more connecting.

I'd take my eyes off my watch, and watch with my eyes.

I would care to know less, and know to care more.

I'd take more hikes and fly more kites.

I'd stop playing serious, and seriously play

I would run through more fields, and gaze at more stars.

I'd do more hugging, and less tugging.

I would be firm less often, and affirm much more.

I'd build self-esteem first, and the house later.

I'd teach less about the love of power,

And more about the power of love.

DIANE LOOMANS

The Nature of Child Development

In every child who is born, under no matter what circumstances, and of no matter what parents, the potentiality of the human race is born again.

James Agee
American Writer, 20th Century

Examining the shape of childhood allows us to understand it better. Every childhood is distinct, the first chapter of a new biography in the world. This book is about children's development—its universal features, its individual variations, its nature at the beginning of the twenty-first century. *Child Development* is about the rhythm and meaning of children's lives, about turning mystery into understanding, and about weaving together a portrait of who each of us was, is, and will be. In Section 1, you will read two chapters: "Introduction" (chapter 1) and "The Science of Child Development" (chapter 2).

Chapter 1

```
                        ┌─────────────────┐
                        │  INTRODUCTION   │
                        └─────────────────┘
        ┌───────────────────┼───────────────────────┐
┌──────────────────┐        │              ┌──────────────────┐
│ Why Study        │        │              │    Careers in    │
│ Children?        │        │              │ Child Development│
└──────────────────┘        │              └──────────────────┘
              ┌─────────────┴──────────┐
    ┌──────────────────┐      ┌──────────────────┐
    │ Child Development—│      │   The Nature     │
    │Yesterday and Today│      │ of Development   │
    └──────────────────┘      └──────────────────┘
```

Child Development—Yesterday and Today

Historical Views of Childhood

The Modern Study of Child Development

Today's Children: Some Contemporary Concerns

Social Policy and Children's Development

The Nature of Development

Biological, Cognitive, and Socioemotional Processes

Periods of Development

Developmental Issues

Introduction

The Stories of Jeffrey Dahmer and Alice Walker

JEFFREY DAHMER had a troubled childhood. His parents constantly bickered before they divorced, his mother had emotional problems and doted on his younger brother, and he felt that his father neglected him. When he was 8 years old, Jeffrey was sexually abused by an older boy. But most individuals who suffer through such childhood pains never go on to commit Dahmer's grisly crimes.

In 1991, a man in handcuffs dashed out of Dahmer's bizarrely cluttered apartment in a tough Milwaukee neighborhood, called the police, and stammered that Dahmer had tried to kill him. At least 17 other victims did not get away.

Alice Walker was born in 1944. She was the eighth child of Georgia sharecroppers who earned $300 a year. When Walker was 8, her brother accidentally shot her in the left eye with a BB gun. By the time her parents got her to the hospital a week later (they had no car), she was blind in that eye and it had developed a disfiguring layer of scar tissue.

Despite the counts against her, Alice Walker went on to become an essayist, a poet, and an award-winning novelist. She won the Pulitzer Prize for her book *The Color Purple.* Like her characters, especially the women, Alice Walker overcame pain and anger to celebrate the human spirit. Walker writes about people who "make it, who come out of nothing. People who triumph."

What leads one child to grow up and commit brutal acts of violence and another to turn poverty and trauma into a rich literary harvest? How can we explain how one child picks up the pieces of a life shattered by tragedy, while another becomes unhinged by life's stress? Why is it that some children are whirlwinds—full of energy, successful in school, and able to get along well with their peers—while others hang out on the sidelines, mere spectators of life? If you ever have wondered about what makes children develop into who they are, you have asked yourself the central questions we will explore in this book.

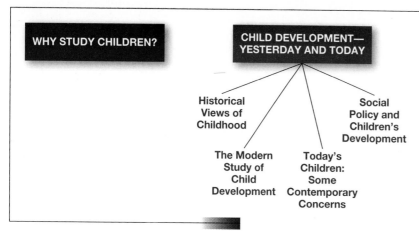

WHY STUDY CHILDREN?

CHILD DEVELOPMENT—
YESTERDAY AND TODAY

Historical Views of Childhood

Social Policy and Children's Development

The Modern Study of Child Development

Today's Children: Some Contemporary Concerns

Why Study Children?

Why study children? Perhaps you are or will be a parent or teacher. Responsibility for children is or will be a part of your everyday life. The more you learn about children, the better you can deal with them. Perhaps you hope to gain some insight into your own history—as an infant, as a child, and as an adolescent. Perhaps you just stumbled onto this course, thinking that it sounded interesting and that the topic of child development would raise some provocative and intriguing issues about how human beings grow and develop. Whatever your reasons, you will discover that the study of child development *is* provocative, *is* intriguing, and *is* filled with information about who we are and how we grew to be this way.

As you might imagine, understanding children's development, and our own personal journey through childhood, is a rich and complicated undertaking. You will discover that various experts approach the study of children in many different ways and ask many different questions. Amid this richness and complexity we seek to understand how children change as they grow up and the forces that contribute to this change.

History of Childhood

original sin view
Advocated during the Middle Ages, the belief that children were born into the world as evil beings and were basically bad.

tabula rasa view
The idea, proposed by John Locke, that children are like a "blank tablet."

Child Development—Yesterday and Today

Everywhere an individual turns in contemporary society, the development and well-being of children capture public attention, the interest of scientists, and the concern of policymakers. Historically, though, interest in the development of children has been uneven.

Historical Views of Childhood

Childhood has become such a distinct period that it is hard to imagine that it was not always thought of in that way. However, in medieval times, laws generally did not distinguish between child and adult offenses. After analyzing samples of art along with available publications, historian Philippe Ariès (1962) concluded that European societies did not accord any special status to children prior to 1600. In paintings, children were often dressed in adultlike clothing (see figure 1.1).

Were children actually treated as miniature adults with no special status in medieval Europe? Ariès' interpretation has been criticized. He primarily sampled aristocratic, idealized subjects, which might have been misleading. In medieval times, children did often work, and their emotional bond with parents might not have been as strong as it is for many children today. However, childhood probably was recognized as a distinct phase of life more than Ariès believed. Also, we know that the ancient Egyptians, Greeks, and Romans held rich conceptions of children's development.

Throughout history, philosophers have speculated at length about the nature of children and how they should be reared. Three such philosophical views portray children in terms of original sin, tabula rasa, and innate goodness. In the **original sin view,** *especially advocated during the Middle Ages, children were perceived as basically bad, being born into the world as evil beings.* The goal of child rearing was to provide salvation, to remove sin from the child's life. Toward the end of the seventeenth century, the **tabula rasa view**

Through the Eyes of Psychologists

Çiğdem Kağitçibaşi,
Koc University, Istanbul, Turkey

"*Human development is the core of societal development and psychology is centrally relevant to it.*"

was proposed by English philosopher John Locke. He argued that children are not innately bad but, instead, are like a "blank tablet," a tabula rasa. Locke believed that childhood experiences are important in determining adult characteristics. He advised parents to spend time with their children and to help them become contributing members of society. In the eighteenth century, the **innate goodness view** *was presented by Swiss-born philosopher Jean-Jacques Rousseau, who stressed that children are inherently good.* Because children are basically good, said Rousseau, they should be permitted to grow naturally, with little parental monitoring or constraint.

In the past century and a half, our view of children has changed dramatically. We now conceive of childhood as a highly eventful and unique period of life that lays an important foundation for the adult years and is highly differentiated from them. In most approaches to childhood, distinct periods are identified, in which children master special skills and confront new life tasks. Childhood is no longer seen as an inconvenient "waiting" period during which adults must suffer the incompetencies of the young. We now value childhood as a special time of growth and change, and we invest great resources in caring for and educating our children. We protect them from the excesses of the adult work world through tough child labor laws; we treat their crimes against society under a special system of juvenile justice; and we have governmental provisions for helping children when ordinary family support systems fail or when families seriously interfere with children's well-being.

The Modern Study of Child Development

The modern era of studying children has a history that spans only a little more than a century (Cairns, 1983, 1998). This era began with some important developments in the late 1800s. Why is this past century so special? During the past century, the study of child development has evolved into a sophisticated science. A number of major theories, along with elegant techniques and methods of study, help organize our thinking about children's development (Dixon & Lerner, 1999). New knowledge about children—based on direct observation and testing—is accumulating at a breathtaking pace.

During the last quarter of the nineteenth century, a major shift took place—from a strictly philosophical perspective on human psychology to a perspective that includes direct observation and experimentation. Most of the influential early psychologists were trained either in the natural sciences (such as biology or medicine) or in philosophy. In the field of child development, this was true of such influential thinkers as Charles Darwin, G. Stanley Hall, James Mark Baldwin, and Sigmund Freud. The natural scientists, even then, underscored the importance of conducting experiments and collecting reliable observations of what they studied. This approach had advanced the state of knowledge in physics, chemistry, and biology; however, these scientists were not at all sure that people, much less children or infants, could be profitably studied in this way. Their hesitation was due, in part, to a lack of examples to follow in studying children. In addition, philosophers of the time debated, on both intellectual and ethical grounds, whether the methods of science were appropriate for studying people.

The deadlock was broken when some daring thinkers began to study infants, children, and adolescents, trying new methods of study. For example, near the turn of the century, French psychologist Alfred Binet invented many tasks to study attention and memory. He used them to study his own daughters, other normal children, children with mental retardation, extremely gifted children, and adults. Eventually, he collaborated in the development of the first modern test of intelligence, which is named after him (the Binet test). At about the same time, G. Stanley Hall pioneered the use of questionnaires with large groups of children and popularized psychology's

Figure 1.1
Historical Perception of Children
This artistic impression shows how children were viewed as miniature adults earlier in history. Artists' renditions of children as miniature adults may have been too stereotypical.

innate goodness view
The idea, presented by Swiss-born philosopher Jean-Jacques Rousseau, that children are inherently good.

Ah! What would the world be to us
If the children were no more?
We should dread the desert behind us
Worse than the dark before.

Henry Wadsworth Longfellow
American Poet, 19th Century

$\mathscr{F}igure$ 1.2

Gesell's Photographic Dome

Cameras rode on metal tracks at the top of the dome and were moved as needed to record the child's activities. Others could observe from outside the dome without being seen by the child.

$\mathscr{T}$hrough the Eyes of Psychologists

Robert Cairns, *University of North Carolina–Chapel Hill*

"One hundred years after they began, developmental research and theory continue to be diverse, vigorous, contentious, fresh, and in many instances, brilliant."

findings. In one investigation, Hall tested 400 children in the Boston schools to find out how much they "knew" about themselves and the world, asking them such questions as "Where are your ribs?"

Later, during the 1920s, a large number of child development research centers were created (White, 1995), and their professional staffs began to observe and chart a myriad of behaviors in infants and children. The centers at the Universities of Minnesota, Iowa, California at Berkeley, Columbia, and Toronto became famous for their investigations of children's play, friendship patterns, fears, aggression and conflict, and sociability. This work became closely associated with the so-called child study movement, and a new organization, the Society for Research in Child Development, was formed at about the same time.

Another ardent observer of children was Arnold Gesell. With his photographic dome, Gesell (1928) could systematically observe children's behavior without interrupting them (see figure 1.2). The direct study of children, in which investigators directly observe children's behavior, conduct experiments, and obtain information about children by questioning their parents and teachers, had an auspicious start in the work of these child study experts. The flow of information about children, based on direct study, has not slowed since that time.

Gesell not only developed sophisticated observational strategies for studying children, but he also had some provocative views on the nature of children's development. He theorized that certain characteristics of children simply "bloom" with age because of a biological, maturational blueprint. Gesell strove for precision in charting what a child is like at a specific age. Gesell's views, as well as G. Stanley Hall's, were strongly influenced by Charles Darwin's evolutionary theory (Darwin had made the scientific study of children respectable when he developed a baby journal for recording systematic observations of children). Hall (1904) believed that child development follows a natural evolutionary course that can be revealed by child study. He also theorized that child development unfolds in stages, with distinct motives and capabilities at each stage. Hall had much to say about adolescence, arguing that it is full of "storm and stress."

Sigmund Freud's psychoanalytic theory was prominent in the early part of the twentieth century. Freud believed that children are rarely aware of the motives and reasons for their behavior and that the bulk of their mental life is unconscious. His ideas were compatible with Hall's, emphasizing conflict and biological influences on development, although Freud did stress that a child's experiences with parents in the first 5 years of life are important determinants of later personality development. Freud envisioned the child moving through a series of psychosexual stages, filled with conflict between biological urges and societal demands. Freud's theory has had a profound influence on the study of children's personality development and socialization, especially in the areas of gender, morality, family processes, and problems and disturbances.

During the 1920s and 1930s, John Watson's (1928) theory of behaviorism influenced thinking about children. Watson proposed a view of children very different from Freud's, arguing that children can be shaped into whatever society wishes by examining and changing the environment. One element of Watson's view, and of behaviorism in general, was a strong belief in the systematic observation of children's behavior under controlled conditions. Watson had some provocative views about child rearing as well. He claimed that parents are too soft on children; quit cuddling and smiling at babies so much, he told parents.

Whereas John Watson was observing the environment's influence on children's behavior and Sigmund Freud was probing the depths of the unconscious mind to discover clues about our early experiences with our parents, others were more concerned about the development of children's conscious thoughts—that is, the thoughts of which they are aware. James Mark Baldwin was a pioneer in the study of children's thought (Cairns, 1998). **Genetic epistemology** *was the term Baldwin gave to the study of how children's knowledge changes over the course of their development.* (The term *genetic* at that time was a synonym for "developmental," and the term *epistemology* means "the nature or study of knowledge.") Baldwin's ideas initially were proposed in the 1880s. Later, in the twentieth century, Swiss psychologist Jean Piaget adopted and elaborated on many of Baldwin's themes, keenly observing the development of thoughts in his own children and devising clever experiments to investigate how children think. Piaget became a giant in developmental psychology. Many of you, perhaps, are already familiar with his view that children pass through a series of cognitive, or thought, stages from infancy through adolescence. According to Piaget, children think in a qualitatively different manner than adults do.

Our introduction to several influential and diverse theories of children's development has been brief, designed to give you a glimpse of some of the different ways children have been viewed as the study of child development unfolded. You will read more about theoretical perspectives later in the text.

genetic epistemology
The study of how children's knowledge changes over the course of their development.

Today's Children: Some Contemporary Concerns

Consider some of the newspaper articles you might read every day on important dimensions of children's lives—such as their health and well-being, families and parenting, education, culture and ethnicity, and gender. What the experts are discovering in each of these areas has direct and significant consequences for understanding children and for improving their lives (Zigler & Finn-Stevenson, 1999). An important theme of this book is to provide up-to-date coverage of the roles that health and well-being, families and parenting, education, culture and ethnicity, and gender play in improving children's lives.

*C*hildren are the legacy we leave for the time we will not live to see.

Aristotle
Greek Philosopher, 4th Century B.C.

Health and Well-Being   Although we have become a nation obsessed with health and well-being, the health and well-being of our nation's children and children in many countries around the world are jeopardized by many factors, including

- poverty
- the AIDS epidemic
- starvation
- poor-quality health care
- inadequate nutrition and exercise
- alcohol and drug abuse in adolescence
- sexual abuse of children

Asian physicians around 2600 B.C. and Greek physicians around 500 B.C. recognized that good habits are essential for good health. They did not blame the gods for illness and think that magic would cure it. They realized that people have some control over their health and well-being. A physician's role was as guide, assisting patients in restoring a natural and emotional balance.

As we enter the twenty-first century, once again we recognize the power of lifestyles and psychological states in promoting health and well-being (Sallis, 2000; Weiss, 2000). We are returning to the ancient view that the ultimate responsibility for our health and well-being, both ours and our children's, rests in our hands. Parents, teachers, nurses, physicians, and other adults serve as important models of health and well-being for children. They also can communicate effective strategies for health and well-being to

Children's Issues
Prevention Programs

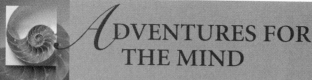

ADVENTURES FOR THE MIND

The Importance of Asking Questions—Exploring Your Own Development as a Child

OUR QUESTION ASKING reflects our active curiosity. Children—especially young children—are remarkable for their ability to ask questions. When my granddaughter, Jordan, was 3½ years old "Why?" was one of her favorite questions, and she used the word *why* relentlessly. As strong as question asking is early in our life, many of us ask far fewer questions as adults.

Asking questions can help you engage in critical thinking about children's development, including our own development as a child. As you go through this course, ask yourself questions about how you experienced a particular aspect of development. For example, consider your experiences in your family as you were growing up. Questions you can pose to yourself include the following: "How did my parents bring me up?" "How did the way they reared me influence what I'm like today?" "How did my relationship with my brothers or sisters affect my development?" Consider also questions about your experiences with peers and at school: "Did I have many close friends while I was growing up?" "How much time did I spend with my peers and friends at various points in childhood and adolescence compared with the time I spent with my parents?" "What were the schools I attended like?" "How good were my teachers?" "How did the schools and teachers affect my achievement orientation today?"

Be curious. Ask questions. Ask your friends and classmates about their experiences as they were growing up and compare them with yours. As you do this, though, keep in mind that, as we reconstruct our past, we may distort it, and it can reflect our biases.

children and monitor how effectively children are following these strategies (Weissberg & Greenberg, 1998).

Recognizing that adolescents are not getting adequate advice about health and well-being, the editors of the *Journal of the American Medical Association* devoted an entire issue (March, 1993) to encouraging doctors and nurses, who are used to curing with a stethoscope and prescription pad, to ask more personal questions of teenagers, to establish a doctor/teenager relationship instead of merely a doctor/parent relationship, and to explain that everything that goes on in the office is confidential, except when the teenagers are a danger to themselves or others.

Families and Parenting

Experts increasingly describe the pressures on contemporary families (Cowan, Powell, & Cowan, 1998; Hetherington, 1999, 2000). The number of families in which both parents work is increasing; at the same time, the number of one-parent families has risen over the past two decades as a result of a climbing divorce rate. With more children being raised by single parents or by two working parents, the time parents have to spend with their children is being squeezed and the quality of child care is of concern to many (Harvey, 1999; Scarr, 2000). Are working parents better using the decreased time with their children? Do day-care arrangements provide high-quality alternatives for parents? How troubled should we be about the increasing number of latchkey children—those at home alone after school, waiting for their parents to return from work? Answering these questions requires several different kinds of information obtained by experts in child development. For example, information comes from studies of the way working parents use time with their children, studies of the ways various day-care arrangements influence children's social and intellectual growth in relation to home-care arrangements, and examination of the consequences of a child being without adult supervision for hours every day after school (Gottfried, Gottfried, & Bathurst, 1995; Lamb, 1998; Lamb & others, 1999).

Twentieth-century Irish playwright George Bernard Shaw once commented that, although parenting is a very important profession, no test of fitness for it is ever imposed. If a test were imposed, some parents would turn out to be more fit than others. Parents want their children to grow into socially mature individuals, but they often are not sure about what to do to help their children reach this goal (Stenhouse, 1996). One reason for parents' frustration is that they often get conflicting messages about how to deal with their children. One "expert" might urge them to be more permissive with their children. Another might tell them to place stricter controls on them or they will grow up to be spoiled brats.

You might be a parent someday or might already be one. You should take seriously the importance of rearing your children, because they are the future of our society. Good parenting takes considerable time. If you plan to become a parent, commit yourself day after day, week after week, month after month, and year after year to providing your children with a warm, supportive, safe, and stimulating environment that will make them feel secure and allow them to reach their full potential as human beings.

We believe the children are the future . . . teach them well and let them lead the way . . . show them all the beauty they possess inside . . . give them a sense of pride . . . let the children's laughter remind us how we used to be.

George Benson
Contemporary American Singer

Understanding the nature of children's development can help you become a better parent. Many parents learn parenting practices and how to care for their children from their parents—some practices they accept but some they discard. Unfortunately, when parenting practices and child-care strategies are passed from one generation to the next, both desirable and undesirable ones are usually perpetuated. This book and your instructor's lectures in this course can help you become much more knowledgeable about children's development and sort through which practices in your own upbringing you should continue with your own children and which you should abandon.

If a community values its children, it must cherish their parents.

John Bowlby
Contemporary British Psychiatrist

AskERIC
Education Resources
Diversity
Trends in the Well-Being of Children and Youth
Children Now
Children and Advocacy

Education

Like parenting, education is an extremely important dimension of children's lives (Calfel, 2000; Gorman & Pollitt, 1996; Parkay & Stanford, 1999). Education takes place not only in schools. Children learn from their parents, from their siblings, from their peers, from books, from watching television, and from computers.

You might look back on your own education and think of ways it could have been a lot better. Some, or even most, of your school years might have been spent in classrooms in which learning was not enjoyable but boring, stressful, and rigid. Some of your teachers might have not adequately considered your unique needs and skills. On the other hand, you might remember some classrooms and teachers that made learning exciting, something you looked forward to each morning you got up. You liked the teacher and the subject, and you learned.

There is widespread agreement that something needs to be done to improve the education of our nation's children (Eccles & Roeser, 1999; Holtzman, 1992; Reynolds, 2000). What can we do to make the education of children more effective? What can we do to make schools more productive and enjoyable contexts for children's development? Should we make the school days longer or shorter? the school year longer or shorter? or keep it the same and focus more on changing the curriculum itself? Should we emphasize less memorization and give more attention to the development of children's ability to process information more efficiently? Have schools become too soft and watered down? Should they make more demands on and have higher expectations of children? Should schools focus only on developing the child's knowledge and cognitive skills, or should they pay more attention to the whole child and consider the child's socioemotional and physical development as well? Should more tax dollars be spent on schools, and should teachers be paid more to educate our nation's children? Should schools be dramatically changed so that they serve as a locus for a wide range of services, such as primary health care, child care, preschool education, parent education, recreation, and family counseling, as well as the traditional educational activities, such as learning in the classroom?

Culture and Ethnicity

The tapestry of American culture has changed dramatically in recent years. Nowhere is the change more noticeable than in the increasing ethnic diversity of America's citizens. Non-white ethnic minority groups—African American, Latino, Native American (American Indian), and Asian American, for example—made up 20 percent of all children and adolescents under the age of 17 in 1989. As we begin the twenty-first century, one-third of all school-age children fall into this category. This changing demography promises not only the richness that diversity produces but also difficult challenges in extending the American dream to individuals of all ethnic groups (McLoyd, 1999, 2000). Historically, immigrant and non-white ethnic minorities have found themselves at the bottom of the economic and social order. They have been disproportionately represented among the poor and the inadequately educated (Edelman, 1997). Half of all African American children and one-third of all Latino children live in poverty. School dropout rates for minority youth reach the alarming rate of 60 percent in some urban areas. These population trends and our nation's inability to prepare minority individuals for

Children learn to love when they are loved

Shown here are two Korean-born children on the day they became U.S. citizens. Asian American children are the fastest-growing group of ethnic minority children.

Children and Poverty

Social Policy

Children's Rights

UNICEF

context
The settings, influenced by historical, economic, social, and cultural factors, in which development occurs.

culture
The behavior patterns, beliefs, and all other products of a group that are passed on from generation to generation.

cross-cultural studies
Comparisons of one culture with one or more other cultures. These provide information about the degree to which children's development is similar, or universal, across cultures, and to the degree to which it is culture-specific.

ethnicity
A characteristic based on cultural heritage, nationality characteristics, race, religion, and language.

ethnic identity
A sense of membership in an ethnic group, based upon shared language, religion, customs, values, history, and race.

social policy
A national government's approach to influencing the welfare of its citizens.

full participation in American life have produced an imperative for the social institutions that serve minorities (Halonen & Santrock, 1999). Schools, social services, health and mental health agencies, juvenile probation services, and other programs need to become more sensitive to ethnic issues and to provide improved services to ethnic minority and low-income individuals (Hollins & Oliver, 1999; Hones & Cha, 1999).

An especially important idea in considering minority groups is that, not only is there ethnic diversity within a culture such as the United States, but there is also considerable diversity within each ethnic group (Leong, 2000; Wilson, 2000). Not all African American children come from low-income families. Not all Latino children are members of the Catholic church. Not all Asian American children are academically gifted. Not all Native American children drop out of school. It is easy to make the mistake of stereotyping the members of an ethnic minority group as all being the same. Keep in mind, as we describe children from ethnic groups, that each group is heterogeneous.

Sociocultural contexts of development involve three important concepts: contexts, culture, and ethnicity. These concepts are central to our discussion of children's development in this book, so we need to define them clearly. **Context** *refers to the setting in which development occurs, a setting that is influenced by historical, economic, social, and cultural factors.* To sense how important context is in understanding children's development, consider a researcher who wants to discover whether children today are more racially tolerant than children were a decade ago. Without reference to the historical, economic, social, and cultural aspects of race relations, students' racial tolerance cannot be fully understood. Every child's development occurs in numerous contexts (Greenfield & Suzuki, 1998; Valsiner, 2000). These contexts, or settings, include homes, schools, peer groups, churches, cities, neighborhoods, communities, countries—each with meaningful historical, economic, social, and cultural legacies (Cole, 1999; Kagitcibasi, 1996).

Two sociocultural contexts that many child development researchers believe merit special attention are culture and ethnicity. **Culture** *refers to the behavior patterns, beliefs, and all other products of a particular group of people that are passed on from generation to generation.* The products result from the interaction between groups of people and their environment over many years. A cultural group can be as large as the United States or as small as an African hunter-gatherer group. Whatever its size, the group's culture influences the identity, learning, and social behavior of its members (Bornstein, 1999; Goodnow, 1995). For example, the United States is an achievement-oriented culture with a strong work ethic, but comparisons of American and Japanese children revealed that the Japanese are better at math, spend more time working on math in school, and spend more time doing homework than do Americans (Stevenson, 1995).

Cross-cultural studies—*comparisons of one culture with one or more other cultures—provide information about the degree to which children's development is similar, or universal, across cultures and to what degree it is culture-specific.* A special concern in comparing the United States with other cultures is our nation's unsatisfactory record in caring for its children, especially in terms of poverty.

Ethnicity *(the word* ethnic *comes from the Greek word for "nation")* is based on cultural heritage, nationality characteristics, race, religion, and language. Ethnicity is central to the development of an **ethnic identity,** *which is a sense of membership in an ethnic group, based upon shared language, religion, customs, values, history, and race.* You are a member of one or more ethnic groups. Your ethnic identity reflects your deliberate decision to identify with an ancestor or ancestral group (Phinney, 2000). If you are of Native American and African slave ancestry, you might choose to align yourself with the traditions and history of Native Americans, although an outsider might believe that your identity is African American.

Social Policy and Children's Development

Social policy *is a national government's approach to influencing the welfare of its citizens.* A current trend is to conduct child development research that produces knowledge that will lead to wise and effective decision making in the area of social policy (Erwin, 1996; Sigel, 1998). When more than 20 percent of all children and more than half of all ethnic minority children are being raised in poverty, when between 40 and 50 percent of all children born today can expect to spend at least 5 years in a single-parent home, when children and young adolescents are giving birth, when the use and abuse of drugs are widespread, and when the specter and spread of AIDS is present, our nation needs a revised social policy related to children (Horowitz & O'Brien, 1989; Wilcox, 1999; Zigler & Hall, 2000).

The shape and scope of social policy related to children are heavily influenced by our political system, which is based on negotiation and compromise. The values held by individual lawmakers, the nation's economic strengths and weaknesses, and partisan politics all influence the policy agenda. Periods of comprehensive social policy are often the outgrowth of concern over broad social issues. Child labor laws were established in the early twentieth century to protect children and jobs for adults as well; federal day-care funding during World War II was justified by the need for women laborers in factories; and Head Start and other War on Poverty programs in the 1960s were implemented to decrease intergenerational poverty (Zigler & Styfco, 1994).

Among the groups that have worked to improve the lives of children are UNICEF in New York and the Children's Defense Fund in Washington, DC. At a United Nations convention, a number of children's rights were declared (Limber & Wilcox, 1996). Marian Wright Edelman, president of the Children's Defense Fund, has been a leading advocate of children's rights. Especially troubling to Edelman (1997) are the indicators that rank the United States as one of the worst industrialized nations in terms of social neglect of its children. Edelman says that we need a better health-care system for families, safer schools and neighborhoods, better parent education, and improved family support systems.

At the beginning of the twenty-first century, the well-being of children is one of America's foremost concerns. We all cherish the future of our children, because they are the future of any society. Children who do not reach their potential, who are unable to contribute effectively to society, and who do not take their place as productive adults diminish the power of society's future (Horowitz & O'Brien, 1989). To read about the characteristics that help children be resilient in the face of adversity, and about strategies for preventing problems and enhancing competency, see the Explorations in Child Development box.

At this point we have studied a number of ideas about the reasons for studying children's development and child development yesterday and today. A review of these ideas is presented in summary table 1.1. Next, we will further explore the basic nature of children's development.

ADVENTURES FOR THE MIND

Imagining What Your Development as a Child Would Have Been Like in Other Cultural Contexts

IMAGINE WHAT YOUR development as a child would have been like in a culture that offered fewer or distinctly different choices than your own. If you were raised in a large city, how might you have developed differently if you had been raised in a rural setting? If you were raised in this country, how might being raised in the city have affected your development? How might your development have been different if your family had been significantly richer or poorer than it was? Suppose you had grown up in a culture in which your career or marriage partner was selected for you, as has been the case in some cultures (such as India) throughout the past? How would that cultural difference likely have affected your development as a child?

Marian Wright Edelman, president of the Children's Defense Fund (shown here interacting with a young child), has been a tireless advocate of children's rights and has been instrumental in calling attention to the needs of children.

EXPLORATIONS IN CHILD DEVELOPMENT
Resilience, Prevention, and Competence

EVEN WHEN CHILDREN are faced with adverse conditions, such as poverty, there are buffers that help make them resilient and improve their chances of successful development. Some children do triumph over life's adversities (Garmezy, 1993; Markstrom & Tryon, 1997). Ann Masten (in press; Masten & Coatsworth, 1998; Masten & Coatsworth, 1995) analyzed the research literature on resilience and concluded that a number of individual factors (such as good intellectual functioning), family factors (close relationship to a caring parent), and extrafamilial factors (bonds to prosocial adults outside the family) characterize resilient children (see figure 1.3).

Norman Garmezy (1993) described a setting in a Harlem neighborhood of New York City to illustrate resilience. In the foyer of the walkup apartment building is a large frame that displays photographs of children who live in the building and a written request that if anyone sees any of the children endangered on the street to bring them back to the apartment house. Garmezy commented that this is an excellent example of adult competence and concern for the safety and well-being of children.

Among the prevention programs aimed at promoting children's competence are those that attempt to build a specific skill in children. These have included programs to teach children interpersonal problem-solving skills, assertiveness training, and other life skills. Recently, prevention programs aimed at improving children's competence have increasingly placed more emphasis on developmental issues, social contexts, and multiple causes (Masten & Coatsworth, 1998). A competence enhancement program might be two-generational (for example, working to help a child's parents find good jobs and health care, in addition to focusing on the child), include health education for the child, and seek to improve the child's socioemotional skills. For example, broadly applicable social skills such as self-

control, stress management, problem solving, decision making, communication, peer resistance, and assertiveness have been found to reduce children's aggressive behavior and improve their adjustment and competence (Weissberg & Greenberg, 1998). Such prevention programs support the concept that effective programs focus not just on a reduction of problems alone but also on competence enhancement.

Source	Characteristic
Individual	Good intellectual functioning Appealing, sociable, easygoing disposition Self-efficacy, self-confidence, high self-esteem Talents Faith
Family	Close relationship to caring parent figure Authoritative parenting: warmth, structure, high expectations Socioeconomic advantages Connections to extended supportive family networks
Extrafamilial context	Bonds to prosocial adults outside the family Connections to prosocial organizations Attending effective schools

Figure 1.3
Characteristics of Resilient Children and Their Contexts

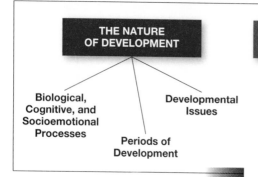
THE NATURE OF DEVELOPMENT — Biological, Cognitive, and Socioemotional Processes — Periods of Development — Developmental Issues

CAREERS IN CHILD DEVELOPMENT

The Nature of Development

Each of us develops in certain ways like all other individuals, like some other individuals, and like no other individuals. Most of the time, our attention is directed to a person's uniqueness, but psychologists who study development are drawn to our shared as well as our unique characteristics. As humans, each of us has traveled some common paths. Each of us—Leonardo da Vinci, Joan of Arc, George Washington, Martin Luther King, Jr., and you—walked at about the age of 1, engaged in fantasy play as a young child, and became more independent as a youth.

What do psychologists mean when they speak of an individual's development? **Development** *is the pattern of change that begins at conception and continues through the life span.* Most development involves growth, although it also includes decay (as

development
The pattern of change that begins at conception and continues through the life cycle.

SUMMARY TABLE 1.1

The Reasons for Studying Children's Development and Child Development—Yesterday and Today

Concept	Processes/Related Ideas	Characteristics/Description
Why Study Children?	Explanations	• Responsibility for children is or will be a part of our everyday lives. • The more we learn about children, the more we can better deal with them and support their journey to becoming competent human beings.
Child Development—Yesterday and Today	Historical Views of Childhood	• The history of interest in children is long and rich. • In the Renaissance, philosophical views were important. Three important philosophical views portrayed children in terms of original sin, *tabula rasa,* and innate goodness. • Today, we conceive of childhood as an important time of development.
	The Modern Study of Child Development	• The modern era of studying children spans a little more than a century, an era in which the study of child development has become a sophisticated science. • Methodological advances in observation and theoretical views—among them psychoanalytic, behavioral, and cognitive developmental—characterize this scientific theme.
	Today's Children: Some Contemporary Concerns	• Four important contemporary concerns in children's development are health and well-being, families and parenting, education, and culture and ethnicity.
	Social Policy and Children's Development	• Social policy is a national government's course of action designed to influence the welfare of its citizens. • The shape and scope of social policy is influenced by the political system.

in death and dying). The pattern of movement is complex because it is the product of several processes—biological, cognitive, and socioemotional.

Biological, Cognitive, and Socioemotional Processes

Biological processes *involve changes in an individual's body.* Genes inherited from parents, the development of the brain, height and weight gains, motor skills, and the hormonal changes of puberty all reflect the role of biological processes in development.

    Cognitive processes *involve changes in an individual's thought, intelligence, and language.* The tasks of watching a colorful mobile swinging above a crib, putting together a two-word sentence, memorizing a poem, solving a math problem, and imagining what it would be like to be a movie star all reflect developing cognitive processes.

    Socioemotional processes *involve changes in an individual's relationships with other people, changes in emotions, and changes in personality.* An infant's smile in response to her mother's touch, a young boy's aggressive attack on a playmate, a girl's development of assertiveness, and an adolescent's joy at the senior prom all reflect socioemotional development.

    Biological, cognitive, and socioemotional processes are intricately interwoven. Socioemotional processes shape cognitive processes, cognitive processes promote or restrict socioemotional processes, and biological processes influence cognitive processes. Although it is helpful to study the various processes involved in children's development in separate sections of the book, keep in mind that you are studying the development of an integrated human child who has only one interdependent mind and body (see figure 1.4).

biological processes
Changes in an individual's body.

cognitive processes
Changes in an individual's thought, intelligence, and language.

socioemotional processes
Changes in an individual's relationships with other people, emotions, and personality.

If our American way of life fails the child, it fails us all.

Pearl Buck
American Author, 20th Century

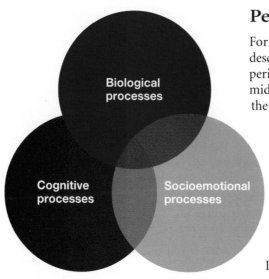

Figure 1.4

Biological, Cognitive, and Socioemotional Processes

Changes in development are the result of biological, cognitive, and socioemotional processes. These processes are interwoven as the child develops.

prenatal period
The time from conception to birth.

infancy The developmental period that extends from birth to 18 to 24 months.

early childhood
The developmental period that extends from the end of infancy to about 5 to 6 years, sometimes called the preschool years.

middle and late childhood
The developmental period that extends from about 6 to 11 years of age, approximately corresponding to the elementary school years, sometimes called the elementary school years.

adolescence
The developmental period of transition from childhood to early adulthood, entered at approximately 10 to 12 years of age and ending at 18 to 22 years of age.

maturation
The orderly sequence of changes dictated by the individual's genetic blueprint.

Periods of Development

For the purposes of organization and understanding, development is commonly described in terms of periods. The most widely used classification of developmental periods involves the following sequence: the prenatal period, infancy, early childhood, middle and late childhood, and adolescence. Approximate age ranges are placed on the periods to provide a general idea of when a period first appears and when it ends.

The **prenatal period** *is the time from conception to birth, roughly a 9-month period.* It is a time of tremendous growth—from a single cell to an organism, complete with a brain and behavioral capabilities.

Infancy *is the developmental period that extends from birth to 18 to 24 months.* Infancy is a time of extreme dependence on adults. Many psychological activities are just beginning—language, symbolic thought, sensorimotor coordination, and social learning, for example.

Early childhood *is the developmental period that extends from the end of infancy to about 5 or 6 years; sometimes the period is called the preschool years.* During this time, young children learn to become more self-sufficient and to care for themselves, they develop school readiness skills (following instructions, identifying letters), and they spend many hours in play and with peers. First grade typically marks the end of this period.

Middle and late childhood *is the developmental period that extends from about 6 to 11 years of age, approximately corresponding to the elementary school years; sometimes this period is called the elementary school years.* Children master the fundamental skills of reading, writing, and arithmetic, and they are formally exposed to the larger world and its culture. Achievement becomes a more central theme of the child's world, and self-control increases.

Adolescence *is the developmental period of transition from childhood to early adulthood, entered approximately at 10 to 12 years of age and ending at 18 to 22 years of age.* Adolescence begins with rapid physical changes—dramatic gains in height and weight; changes in body contour; and the development of sexual characteristics such as enlargement of the breasts, development of pubic and facial hair, and deepening of the voice. At this point in development, the pursuit of independence and an identity are prominent. Thought is more logical, abstract, and idealistic. More and more time is spent outside of the family during this period.

Today, developmentalists do not believe that change ends with adolescence (Baltes, Lindenberger & Staudinger, 1998; Santrock, 1999). They describe development as a lifelong process. However, the purpose of this text is to describe the changes in development that take place from conception through adolescence.

The periods of development from conception through adolescence are shown in figure 1.5, along with the processes of development—biological, cognitive, and socioemotional. The interplay of biological, cognitive, and socioemotional processes produces the periods of development.

Developmental Issues

Major issues raised in the study of children's development include the following: Is children's development due more to maturation (nature, heredity) or more to experience (nurture, environment)? Is development more continuous and smooth or more discontinuous and stagelike? To what extent is development permanently shaped by early experience, and to what extent does later experience influence development?

Maturation and Experience (Nature and Nurture) We can
think of development as produced not only by the interplay of biological, cognitive, and socioemotional processes but also by the interplay of maturation and experience. **Maturation** *is the orderly sequence of changes dictated by the individual's genetic blueprint.* Just as a sunflower tends to grow in an orderly way from its seed, so does a human being tend to grow in an orderly way, according to the maturational view. The range of environments can be vast, but the maturational approach argues that the genetic blueprint produces commonalities in our growth and development. We walk before we

talk, speak one word before two words, grow rapidly in infancy and less so in early childhood, experience a rush of sexual hormones in puberty after a lull in childhood, reach
the peak of our physical strength in late adolescence and early adulthood and then decline, and so on. The maturationists acknowledge that extreme environments—those
that are psychologically barren or hostile—can depress development, but they believe
that basic growth tendencies are genetically wired
into human beings.

By contrast, other psychologists emphasize the
importance of experiences in child development.
Experiences run the gamut from individuals' biological
environment (nutrition, medical care, drugs, and
physical accidents) to their social environment (family, peers, schools, community, media, and culture).

The debate about whether development is primarily influenced by maturation or by experience has been a part of psychology since its
beginning. This debate is often referred to as
the **nature-nurture controversy.** Nature *refers
to an organism's biological inheritance,* nurture
*to environmental experiences. The "nature"
proponents claim that biological inheritance is
the most important influence on development, the
"nurture" proponents claim that environmental experiences are the most important.*

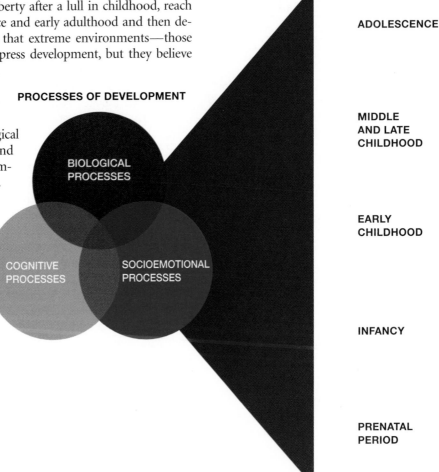

PROCESSES OF DEVELOPMENT

Continuity and Discontinuity
Think about your development for a moment. Did you gradually grow to become the
person you are, in the slow cumulative way
a seedling grows into a giant oak? Or did you
experience sudden, distinct changes in your
growth, the way a caterpillar changes into a
butterfly? (See figure 1.6.) For the most part,
developmentalists who emphasize experience have described development as a gradual, continuous process; those who
emphasize maturation have described development as a series of distinct stages.

Some developmentalists emphasize the
continuity of development, *the view that
development involves gradual, cumulative change from conception to death.* A child's
first word, while seemingly an abrupt, discontinuous event, is actually the result of
months of growth and practice. Puberty, while also seemingly an abrupt, discontinuous occurrence, is actually a gradual process occurring over several years.

Other developmentalists focus on the **discontinuity of development,** *the view
that development involves distinct stages in the life span.* This view sees each of us as
passing through a sequence of stages in which change is qualitative rather than quantitative. As an oak moves from seedling to giant tree, it becomes *more* oak—its development is continuous. As a caterpillar changes into a butterfly, it does not become
more caterpillar but, instead, becomes a *different kind* of organism—its development
is discontinuous. For example, at a certain point a child moves from not being able
to think abstractly about the world to being able to do so. This is a qualitative, discontinuous change in development, not a quantitative, continuous change.

Early and Later Experience
Another important developmental topic is the
early-later experience issue, *which focuses on the degree to which early experiences (especially in infancy) or later experiences are the key determinants of the child's development.*
That is, if infants experience negative, stressful circumstances in their lives, can those experiences be overcome by later, more-positive experiences? Or are the early experiences

Figure 1.5

Processes and Periods of Development
Development moves through the prenatal, infancy, early childhood, middle and late childhood, and adolescence periods. These periods of development are the result of biological,
cognitive, and socioemotional processes.

nature-nurture controversy
Nature refers to an organism's biological
inheritance, *nurture* to environmental influences.
The "nature" proponents claim biological
inheritance is the most important influence on
development; the "nurture" proponents claim that
environmental experiences are the most
important.

continuity of development
The view that development involves gradual,
cumulative change from conception to death.

discontinuity of development
The view that development involves distinct
stages in the life span.

early-later experience issue
The issue of the degree to which early
experiences (especially infancy) or later
experiences are the key determinants of the
child's development.

*T*hrough the Eyes of Psychologists

Jerome Kagan,
Harvard University

"It is becoming increasingly clear that children inherit certain biologies that, in turn, affect the manner in which environmental events influence their psychological growth."

so critical—possibly because they are the infant's first, prototypical experiences—that they cannot be overridden by a later, better environment?

The early-later experience issue has a long history and continues to be hotly debated among developmentalists. Some believe that, unless infants experience warm, nurturant caregiving in the first year or so of life, their development will never be optimal (Bowlby, 1989; Sroufe, Egeland, & Carlson, 1999; Waters & others, 1995). Plato was sure that infants who were rocked frequently become better athletes. Nineteenth-century New England ministers told parents in Sunday sermons that the way they handled their infants would determine their children's future character. The emphasis on the importance of early experience rests on the belief that each life is an unbroken trail on which a psychological quality can be traced back to its origin (Kagan, 1992, 1998).

The early-experience doctrine contrasts with the later-experience view, which states that, rather than statuelike permanence after change in infancy, development continues to be like the ebb and flow of an ocean. The later-experience advocates argue that children are malleable throughout development and that later sensitive caregiving is just as important as earlier sensitive caregiving. A number of life-span developmentalists, who focus on the entire life span rather than only on child development, stress that too little attention has been given to later experiences in development (Baltes, 1987). They accept that early experiences are important contributors to development, but no more important than later experiences. Jerome Kagan (1992, 1998) points out that even children who show the qualities of an inhibited temperament, which is linked to heredity, have the capacity to change their behavior. In his research, almost one-third of a group of children who had an inhibited temperament at 2 years of age were not unusually shy or fearful when they were 4 years of age (Kagan & Snidman, 1991).

People in Western cultures, especially those steeped in the Freudian belief that the key experiences in development are children's relationships with their parents in the first 5 years of life, have tended to support the idea that early experiences are more important than later experiences (Chan, 1963; Lamb & Sternberg, 1992). By contrast, the majority of people in the world do not share this belief. For example, people in many Asian countries believe that experiences occurring after about 6 to 7 years of age are more important aspects of development than are earlier experiences. This stance stems from the long-standing belief in Eastern cultures that children's reasoning skills begin to develop in important ways in the middle childhood years.

One recent book—*The Myth of the First Three Years* (Bruer, 1999)—supports the later-experience argument. The argument is made, based on the available research evidence, that learning and cognitive development do not occur only in the first 3 years of life but rather are lifelong. The author concludes that too many parents treat their children as if a switch goes off after age 3, after which further learning either does not take place or is greatly diminished. That is not to say that experiences in the first 3 years are unimportant, but rather that later experiences are too. We will have more to say about this fascinating topic in chapter 5, "Physical Development in Infancy."

Evaluating the Developmental Issues

Most developmentalists recognize that it is unwise to take an extreme position on the issues of nature and nurture, continuity and discontinuity, and early and later experiences. Development is not all nature or all nurture, not all continuity or all discontinuity, and not all early or later experiences (Horowitz, 1999; Keating & Hertzman, 1999). Nature and nurture, continuity and discontinuity, and early and later experiences all characterize our

*F*igure **1.6**

Continuity and Discontinuity in Development

Is human development more like that of a seedling gradually growing into a giant oak or more like that of a caterpillar suddenly becoming a butterfly?

development through the human life span. For example, in considering the nature-nurture issue, the key to development is the *interaction* of nature and nurture rather than either factor alone (Plomin, 1996). Thus, an individual's cognitive development is the result of heredity-environment interaction, not heredity or environment alone. Much more about the role of heredity- environment interaction appears in chapter 3.

Nonetheless, although most developmentalists do not take extreme positions on these three important issues, this consensus has not meant the absence of spirited debate about how strongly development is influenced by each of these factors. Are girls less likely to do well in math because of their "feminine" nature or because of society's masculine bias? If, as children, adolescents experienced a world of poverty, neglect by parents, and poor schooling, can enriched experiences in adolescence remove the "deficits" they encountered earlier in their development? The answers to these questions influence public policy decisions about children and how each of us lives through the human life span.

What is the nature of the early and later experience issue in development?

Careers in Child Development

A career in child development is one of the most rewarding vocational opportunities you can pursue. By choosing a career in child development, you will be able to help children who might not reach their potential as productive contributors to society or develop into physically, cognitively, and socially mature individuals. Adults who work professionally with children invariably feel a sense of pride in their ability to contribute in meaningful ways to the next generation.

If you decide to pursue a career related to children's development, a number of options are available to you. As a college or university professor you could teach courses in child development, education, family development, and nursing; you could become a counselor, clinical psychologist, pediatrician, psychiatrist, school psychologist, pediatric nurse, psychiatric nurse, or social worker and see children with problems and disorders; you could become a teacher and instruct children in kindergarten, elementary school, or secondary school. In pursuing a career related to child development, you can expand your opportunities (and income) considerably by obtaining a graduate degree, although an advanced degree is not absolutely necessary for some of these professions.

Most college professors in child development and its related areas of psychology, education, family and consumer sciences, nursing, and social work have a master's degree and/or doctorate degree that required 2 to 5 years of academic work beyond their undergraduate degree. Becoming a child clinical psychologist or counseling psychologist requires 5 to 6 years of graduate work to obtain the necessary Ph.D.; this includes both clinical and research training. School and career counselors pursue a master's or doctoral degree in counseling, often in graduate programs in education departments; these degrees require 2 to 6 years to complete. Becoming a pediatrician or psychiatrist requires 4 years of medical school, plus an internship and a residency in pediatrics or psychiatry, respectively; this career path takes 7 to 9 years beyond a bachelor's degree. School psychologists obtain either a master's degree (approximately 2 years) or a D.Ed. degree (approximately 4 to 5 years) in school psychology. School psychologists counsel children and parents when children have problems in school, often giving psychological tests to assess children's personality and intelligence. Social work positions can be obtained with an undergraduate degree in social work or related fields, but opportunities are expanded with an M.S.W. (master's of social work) or Ph.D., which require 2 and 4 to 5 years, respectively. Pediatric and psychiatric nursing positions can also be attained with an undergraduate R.N. degree; M.A. and Ph.D. degrees in nursing, which require 2 and 4 to 5 years of graduate training,

Careers
Nonacademic Careers in Psychology

Jobs/careers	Degree	Education required
Child clinical psychologist or counseling psychologist	Ph.D. or Psy.D.	5–7 years postundergraduate
Child life specialist	Undergraduate degree	4 years of undergraduate study
Child psychiatrist	M.D.	7–9 years postundergraduate
Child welfare worker	Undergraduate degree (minimum)	4 years minimum
College/university professor in child development, education, family development, nursing, social work	Ph.D. or master's degree	5–6 years for Ph.D. (or D.Ed.) postundergraduate; 2 years for master's degree postundergraduate
Day-care supervisor	Varies by state	Varies by state
Early childhood educator	Undergraduate degree (minimum)	4 years (minimum)
Elementary or secondary school teacher	Undergraduate degree (minimum)	4 years
Exceptional children teacher (special education teacher)	Undergraduate degree (minimum)	4 years or more (some states require a master's degree or passing a standardized exam to obtain a license to work with exceptional children)
Guidance counselor	Undergraduate degree (minimum); many have master's degree	4 years undergraduate; 2 years graduate
Pediatrician	M.D.	7–9 years medical school
Pediatric nurse	R.N.	2–5 years
Preschool/kindergarten teacher	Usually graduate degree	4 years
Psychiatric nurse	R.N.	2–5 years
School psychologist	Master's degree or Ph.D.	5–6 years of graduate work for Ph.D. or D.Ed.; 2 years for master's degree

Figure **1.7**

Jobs and Careers in Child Development and Related Fields

Nature of training	Description of work
Includes both clinical and research training; involves a 1-year internship in a psychiatric hospital or mental health facility.	Child clinical psychologists or counseling psychologists diagnose children's problems and disorders, administer psychological tests, and conduct psychotherapy sessions. Some work at colleges and universities, where they do any combination of teaching, therapy, and research.
Many child life specialists have been trained in child development or education but undergo additional training in child life programs that includes parent education, developmental assessment, and supervised work with children and parents.	Child life specialists are employed by hospitals and work with children and their families before and after the children are admitted to the hospital. They often develop and monitor developmentally appropriate activities for child patients. They also help children adapt to their medical experiences and their stay at the hospital. Child life specialists coordinate their efforts with physicians and nurses.
Four years of medical school, plus an internship and residency in child psychiatry are required.	The role of the child psychiatrist is similar to that of the child clinical psychologist, but the psychiatrist can conduct biomedical therapy (for example, using drugs to treat clients); the child clinical or counseling psychologist cannot.
Coursework and training in social work or human services	Child welfare workers are employed by the Child Protective Services Unit of each state to protect children's rights. They especially monitor cases of child maltreatment and abuse and make decisions about what needs to be done to help protect the abused child from further harm and to help the child cope with prior abuse.
Take graduate courses, learn how to conduct research, attend and present papers at professional meetings	College and university professors teach courses in child development, family development, education, or nursing; conduct research; present papers at professional meetings; write and publish articles and books; and train undergraduate and graduate students for careers in these fields.
The Department of Public Welfare in many states publishes a booklet with the requirements for a day-care supervisor.	Day-care supervisors direct day-care or preschool programs, being responsible for the operation of the center. They often make decisions about the nature of the center's curriculum, may teach in the center themselves, work with and consult with parents, and conduct workshops for the staff or parents.
Coursework in early childhood education and practice in day-care or early childhood centers with supervised training	Early childhood educators usually teach in community colleges that award associate or bachelor's degrees in early childhood education with specialization in day care. They train individuals for careers in the field of day care.
Wide range of courses, with a major or concentration in education	Elementary and secondary teachers teach one or more subjects; prepare the curriculum; give tests, assign grades, and monitor students' progress; interact with parents and school administrators; attend lectures and workshops involving curriculum planning or help on special issues; and direct extracurricular programs.
Coursework in education, with a concentration in special education	Exceptional children teachers (also called special education teachers) work with children who are educationally handicapped (those who are mentally retarded, have a physical handicap, have a learning disability, or have a behavioral disorder) or who are gifted. They develop special curricula for the exceptional children and help them adapt to their exceptional circumstances. Special education teachers work with other school personnel and with parents to improve the adjustment of exceptional children.
Coursework in education and counseling in a school of education; counselor training experience	The majority of guidance counselors work with secondary school students, assisting them in educational and career planning. They often give students aptitude tests and evaluate their interests, as well as their abilities. Guidance counselors also see students who are having school-related problems, including emotional problems, referring them to other professionals, such as school psychologists or clinical psychologists, when necessary.
Four years of medical school, plus an internship and residency in pediatrics	Pediatricians monitor infants' and children's health and treat their diseases. They advise parents about infant and child development and the appropriate ways to deal with children.
Courses in biological sciences, nursing care, and pediatrics (often in a school of nursing); supervised clinical experiences in medical settings	Pediatric nurses promote health in infants and children, working to prevent disease or injury, assisting children with handicaps or health problems so they can achieve optimal health, and treating children with health deviations. Some pediatric nurses specialize in certain areas (for example, the neonatal intensive care unit clinician cares exclusively for newborns; the new-parent educator helps the parents of newborns develop better parenting skills). Pediatric nurses work in a variety of medical settings.
Coursework in education with a specialization in early childhood education; state certification usually required	Preschool teachers direct the activities of prekindergarten children, many of whom are 4-year-olds. They develop an appropriate curriculum for the age of the children that promotes their physical, cognitive, and social development in a positive atmosphere. The number of days per week and hours per day varies from one program to another. Kindergarten teachers work with young children who are between the age of preschool programs and the first year of elementary school; they primarily develop appropriate activities and curricula for 5-year-old children.
Courses in biological sciences, nursing care, and mental health in a school of nursing; supervised clinical training in child psychiatric settings	Psychiatric nurses promote the mental health of individuals; some specialize in helping children with mental health problems and work closely with child psychiatrists to improve these children's adjustment.
Includes coursework and supervised training in school settings, usually in a department of educational psychology	School psychologists evaluate and treat a wide range of normal and exceptional children who have school-related problems; work in a school system and see children from a number of schools; administer tests, interview and observe children, and consult with teachers, parents, and school administrators; and design programs to reduce the child's problem behavior.

Summary Table 1.2
The Nature of Development, and Careers in Child Development

Concept	Processes/Related Ideas	Characteristics/Description
The Nature of Development	What Is Development?	• Development is the pattern of movement or change that occurs throughout the life span.
	Biological, Cognitive, and Socioemotional Processes	• Development is influenced by an interplay of biological, cognitive, and socioemotional processes.
	Periods of Development	• Development is commonly divided into the following periods from conception through adolescence: prenatal, infancy, early childhood, middle and late childhood, and adolescence.
	Developmental Issues	• The debate over whether development is due primarily to maturation or to experience is another version of the nature-nurture controversy. • Some developmentalists describe development as continuous (gradual, cumulative change), others describe it as discontinuous (a sequence of abrupt stages). • The early-later experience issue focuses on whether early experiences (especially in infancy) are more important in development than later experiences. • Most developmentalists recognize that extreme positions on the nature-nurture, continuity-discontinuity, and early-later experience issues are unwise. Despite this consensus, these issues continue to be spiritedly debated.
Careers in Child Development	Their Nature	• A wide range of opportunities are available to individuals who want to pursue a career related to child development. • Opportunities include jobs in college and university teaching/research, child clinical psychology and counseling, school teaching and school psychology, nursing, pediatrics, psychiatry, and social work.

respectively, are also available. To read further about jobs and careers that involve working with children, see figure 1.7. This list is not exhaustive but, rather, is meant to give you an idea of the many opportunities. Also keep in mind that majoring in child development or a related field can provide sound preparation for adult life.

At this point, we have discussed a number of ideas about the nature of development and careers in child development. An overview of these ideas is presented in summary table 1.2.

Chapter Review

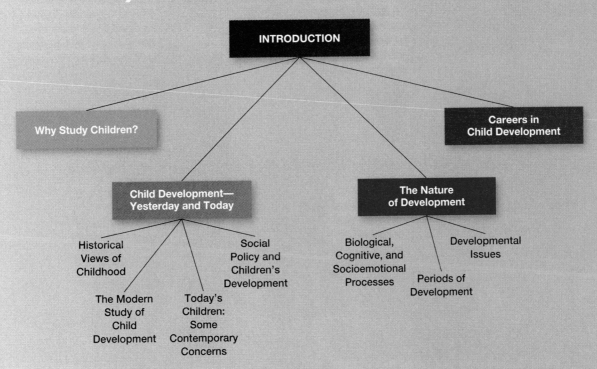

FOR A DETAILED REVIEW OF THE CHAPTER, STUDY THESE TWO SUMMARY TABLES:

- Summary Table 1.1   The Reasons for Studying Children's Development,   page 15 ◀||||||||
  and Child Development Yesterday and Today
- Summary Table 1.2   The Nature of Development, and Careers in   page 22 ◀||||||||
  Child Development

Key Terms

Key People

Child Development Resources

Child Development and Social Policy (2000)
     by Edward Zigler and Nancy Hall
An up-to-date analysis of what needs to be done to improve America's social policy for children.

Children's Defense Fund
     25 E Street
     Washington, DC 20001
     800-424-9602

The Children's Defense Fund exists to provide a strong and effective voice for children and adolescents who cannot vote, lobby, or speak for themselves. The Children's Defense Fund is especially interested in the needs of poor, minority, and handicapped children and adolescents. The fund provides information, technical assistance, and support to a network of state and local child and youth advocates. The Children's Defense Fund publishes a number of excellent books and pamphlets related to children's needs.

Handbook of Child Psychology (5th Ed., Vols. 1–4) (1998)
     Edited by Marc Bornstein
     New York: John Wiley

The *Handbook of Child Psychology* is the standard reference work for overviews of theory and research in this field. It has in-depth discussions of many topics that we will explore in this book.

Taking It to the Net

1. George is teaching fourth grade. He wants his students to learn about the difficulties and challenges of being a child in colonial America. What was life like for children in the early history of our country?

2. Janice thinks that better and stricter gun control laws will help decrease violent crime among children. Her husband, Elliott, disagrees. Janice found a March 2000 Department of Justice study that provides support for her argument. What facts in the report can she point to in order to convince Elliott?

3. For his political science class, Darren has to track federal funding appropriations in the most recent Congress for any issue of his choice. He has chosen children's issues. How did children and families fare in terms of congressional appropriations in the first half of the 106th Congress?

Connect to http://www.mhhe.com/santrockc9 to find the answers!

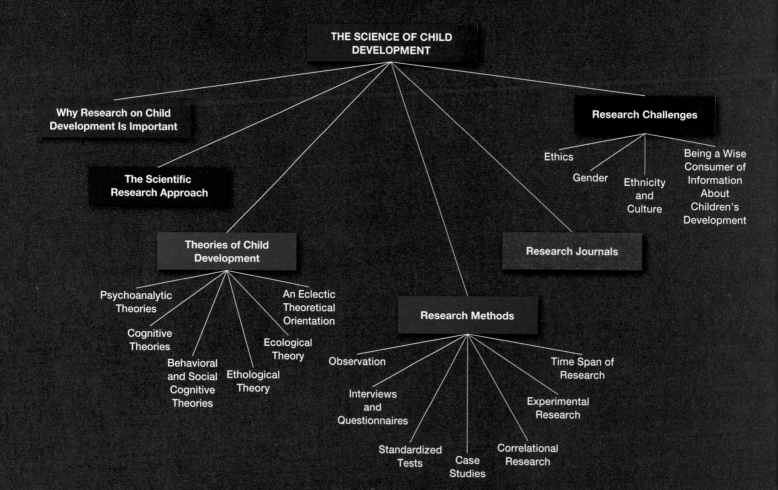

Chapter 2

THE SCIENCE OF CHILD DEVELOPMENT

Why Research on Child Development Is Important

The Scientific Research Approach

Theories of Child Development

Psychoanalytic Theories

Cognitive Theories

Behavioral and Social Cognitive Theories

Ethological Theory

An Eclectic Theoretical Orientation

Ecological Theory

Research Methods

Observation

Interviews and Questionnaires

Standardized Tests

Case Studies

Correlational Research

Experimental Research

Time Span of Research

Research Journals

Research Challenges

Ethics

Gender

Ethnicity and Culture

Being a Wise Consumer of Information About Children's Development

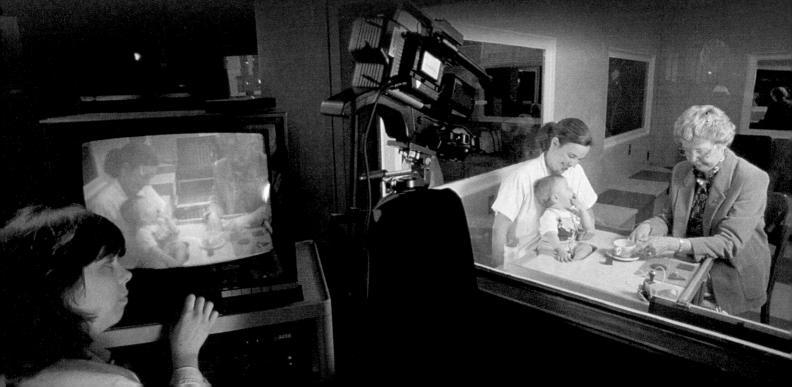

The Stories of Erik Erikson and Jean Piaget

IMAGINE THAT YOU have developed a major theory of child development. What would influence someone such as you to construct this theory? A person interested in developing such a theory usually goes through a long university training program that culminates in a doctoral degree. As part of the training, the future theorist is exposed to many ideas about a particular area of child development, such as biological, cognitive, or socioemotional development. Another factor that could explain why someone develops a particular theory is that person's life experiences. Two important developmental theorists, whose views will be described later in the chapter, are Erik Erikson and Jean Piaget. Let's examine a portion of their lives as they were growing up to discover how their experiences might have contributed to the theories they developed.

Erik Homberger Erikson (1902–1994) was born near Frankfurt, Germany, to Danish parents. Before Erik was born, his parents separated, and his mother left Denmark to live in Germany. At age 3, Erik became ill, and his mother took him to see a pediatrician named Homberger. Young Erik's mother fell in love with the pediatrician, married him, and named Erik after his new stepfather.

Erik attended primary school from the ages of 6 to 10 and then the gymnasium (high school) from 11 to 18. He studied art and a number of languages rather than science courses, such as biology and chemistry. Erik did not like the atmosphere of formal schooling, and this was reflected in his grades. Rather than go to college at age 18, the adolescent Erikson wandered around Europe, keeping a diary about his experiences. After a year of travel through Europe, he returned to Germany and enrolled in art school, became dissatisfied, and enrolled in another. Later he traveled to Florence, Italy. Psychiatrist Robert Coles described Erikson at this time:

> To the Italians he was . . . the young, tall, thin Nordic expatriate with long, blond hair. He wore a corduroy suit and was seen by his family and friends as not odd or "sick" but as a wandering artist who was trying to come to grips with himself, a not unnatural or unusual struggle. (Coles, 1970, p.15)

The second major theorist whose life we will examine is Jean Piaget. Piaget (1896–1980) was born in Neuchâtel, Switzerland. Jean's father was an intellectual who taught young Jean to think systematically. Jean's mother was also very bright. His father had an air of detachment from his mother, whom Piaget described as prone to frequent outbursts of neurotic behavior.

In his autobiography, Piaget detailed why he chose to study cognitive development rather than social or abnormal development:

> I started to forego playing for serious work very early. Indeed, I have always detested any departure from reality, an attitude which I relate to . . . my mother's poor health. It was this disturbing factor which at the beginning of my studies in psychology made me keenly interested in psychoanalytic and pathological psychology. Though this interest helped me to achieve independence and widen my cultural background, I have never since felt any desire to involve myself deeper in that particular direction, always much preferring the study of normalcy and of the workings of the intellect to that of the tricks of the unconscious. (Piaget, 1952a, p. 238)

These excerpts from Erikson's and Piaget's lives illustrate how personal experiences might influence the direction in which a particular theorist goes. Erikson's own wanderings and search for self contributed to his theory of identity development, and Piaget's intellectual experiences with his parents and schooling contributed to his emphasis on cognitive development.

WHY RESEARCH ON CHILD DEVELOPMENT IS IMPORTANT	THE SCIENTIFIC RESEARCH APPROACH

Why Research on Child Development Is Important

It sometimes is said that experience is the most important teacher. We get a great deal of knowledge from personal experience. We generalize from what we observe and frequently turn memorable encounters into lifetime "truths." But how valid are these conclusions? Sometimes we err in making these personal observations or misinterpret what we see and hear. Chances are, you can think of many situations in which you thought other people read you the wrong way, just as they may have felt that you misread them. When we base information only on personal experiences, we also aren't always completely objective, because sometimes we make judgments that protect our ego and self-esteem (McMillan, 2000).

We get information not only from personal experiences but also from authorities and experts. You may hear experts spell out a "best way" to parent children or educate them, but the authorities and experts don't always agree. You might hear one expert proclaim that one strategy for interacting with children is the best and, the next week, see that another expert touts another strategy as the best. How can you tell which one to believe? One way to clarify the situation is to carefully examine research that has been conducted on the topic.

Science refines everyday thinking.

Albert Einstein
German-born American Physicist, 20th Century

Generating Research Ideas

The Scientific Research Approach

Some individuals have difficulty thinking of child development as being a science in the same way that physics, chemistry, and biology are sciences. Can a discipline that studies how babies develop, how parents nurture children, how peers interact, and how children think be equated with disciplines that investigate the way gravity works and the molecular structure of a compound? Science is defined not by *what* it investigates but by *how* it investigates. Whether you are studying photosynthesis, butterflies, Saturn's moons, or human development, it is the *way* you study that makes the approach scientific or not.

Researchers take a skeptical, scientific attitude toward knowledge. When they hear someone claim that a particular method is effective in helping children cope with

Researchers use the scientific method to obtain accurate information about children's behavior and development. Data collection is part of the scientific method, demonstrated here by a researcher conducting a study of infant development.

stress, they want to know if the claim is based on *good* research. The science part of child development seeks to sort fact from fancy by using particular strategies for obtaining information.

Scientific research is objective, systematic, and testable. It reduces the likelihood that information will be based on personal beliefs, opinions, and feelings. Scientific research is based on the **scientific method,** *an approach that can be used to discover accurate information. It includes these steps: conceptualize the problem, collect data, draw conclusions, and revise research conclusions and theory.*

The first step, *conceptualizing a problem,* involves identifying the problem, it might include theory, and it consists of developing one or more hypotheses. For example, a team of researchers decide that they want to study ways to improve the achievement of children from impoverished backgrounds. The researchers have *identified a problem,* which, at a general level, might not seem like a difficult task. However, as part of the first step, they also must go beyond a general description of the problem by isolating, analyzing, narrowing, and focusing more specifically on what aspect of it they hope to study. Perhaps the researchers decide to discover if mentoring that involves sustained support, guidance, and concrete assistance to children from impoverished backgrounds can improve their academic performance. At this point, even more narrowing and focusing needs to take place. What specific strategies do the researchers want the mentors to use? How often will the mentors see the children? How long will the mentoring program last? What aspects of the children's achievement do the researchers want to assess?

As researchers formulate a problem to study, they often draw on *theories* and *develop hypotheses.* A **theory** *is an interrelated, coherent set of ideas that helps to explain and to make predictions.* For example, a theory on mentoring might attempt to explain and predict why sustained support, guidance, and concrete experience make a difference in the lives of children from impoverished backgrounds. The theory might focus on children's opportunities to model the behavior and strategies of mentors, or it might focus on the effects of individual attention, which might be missing in the children's lives. **Hypotheses** *are specific testable assumptions and predictions that are derived from theories.*

scientific method
An approach that can be used to discover accurate information. It includes these steps: conceptualize the problem, collect data, draw conclusions, and revise research conclusions and theory.

theory
An interrelated, coherent set of ideas that helps to explain and make predictions.

hypotheses
Specific testable assumptions and predictions that are derived from theories.

The next step is to *collect information (data)*. In the study of mentoring, the researchers might decide to conduct the mentoring program for six months. Their data might consist of classroom observations, teachers' ratings, and achievement tests given to the mentored children before the mentoring began and at the end of six months of mentoring.

Once data have been collected, child development researchers use *statistical procedures* to understand the meaning of the data. Then they try to draw *conclusions*. In the study of mentoring, statistics would help determine whether or not their own observations are due to chance. After data have been analyzed, researchers compare their findings with those others have found about the same topic.

The final step in the scientific method is *revising research conclusions and theory.* A number of theories have been generated to describe and explain children's development; Over time, some theories have been discarded, others revised. Shortly in this chapter and throughout the text you will read about a number of theories of child development. Figure 2.1 illustrates the steps in the scientific method applied to the study of mentoring we have been discussing.

At this point we have studied a number of ideas about why research on child development is important and the scientific research approach. A review of these ideas is presented in summary table 2.1. We have seen that theorizing is often a part of the scientific approach. Next, we will explore some of the major theories of child development.

Step 1: Conceptualize the problem

A researcher identifies this problem: Many children from impoverished backgrounds have lower achievement than children from higher socioeconomic backgrounds. The researcher develops the hypothesis that mentoring will improve the achievement of the children from impoverished backgrounds.

↓

Step 2: Collect information (data)

The researcher conducts the mentoring program for six months and collects data before the program begins and after its conclusion, using classroom observations, teachers' ratings, and achievement test scores.

↓

Step 3: Draw conclusions

The researcher statistically analyzes the data and finds that the children's achievement improved over the six months of the study. The researcher concludes that mentoring is likely an important reason for the increase in the children's achievement.

↓

Step 4: Revise research conclusions and theory

This research on mentoring, along with other research that obtains similar results, increases the likelihood that mentoring will be considered as an important component of theorizing about how to improve the achievement of children from low-income backgrounds.

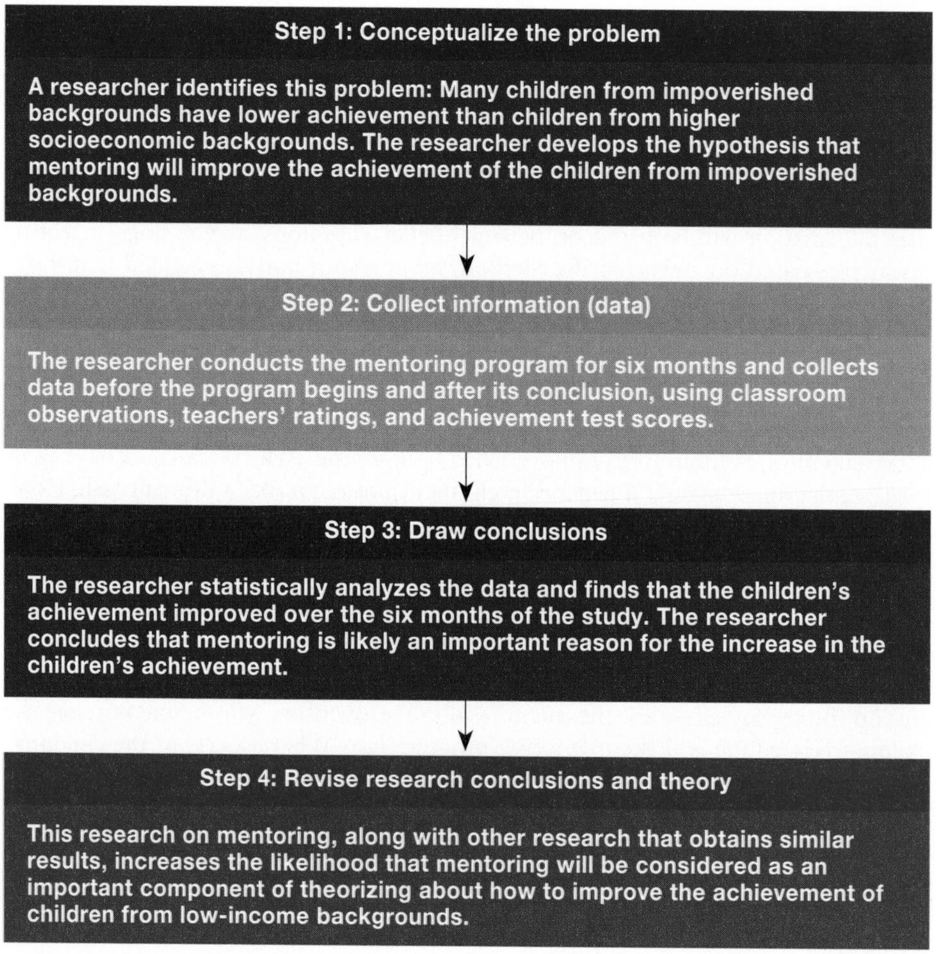

Figure **2.1**

The Scientific Method Applied to a Study of Mentoring

Summary Table 2.1
Why Research on Child Development is Important, and the Scientific Research Approach

Concept	Processes/ Related Ideas	Characteristics/Description
Why Research on Child Development is Important	Some Reasons	• When we base information on personal experience, we aren't always objective. • Research provides a vehicle for evaluating the accuracy of what experts and authorities say.
The Scientific Research Approach	Its Nature	• Scientific research is objective, systematic, and testable, reducing the probability that the information will be based on personal beliefs, opinions, or feelings. • Scientific research is based on the scientific method, which includes these steps: conceptualize the problem, collect data, draw conclusions, and revise theory. • A theory is a coherent set of ideas that helps to explain and to make predictions. Hypotheses are derived from theories.

Theories of Child Development

We will briefly explore five major theoretical perspectives on child development: psychoanalytic, cognitive, behavioral and social cognitive, ethological, and ecological. You will learn more about these theories at different points in later chapters in the book.

The diversity of theories makes understanding children's development a challenging undertaking. Just when you think one theory correctly explains children's development, another theory crops up and makes you rethink your earlier conclusion. To keep from getting frustrated, remember that children's development is a complex, multifaceted topic, and no single theory has been able to account for all its aspects. Each theory has contributed an important piece to the child development puzzle. Although the theories sometimes disagree about certain aspects of children's development, much of their information is *complementary* rather than contradictory. Together the various theories let us see the total landscape of children's development in all its richness.

In chapter 1, we described the three major processes involved in children's development: biological cognitive, and socioemotional ◀▥▥ P. 15. The theoretical approaches that we will describe here reflect these processes. Biological processes are very important in Freud's psychoanalytic theory and in ethological theory, and cognitive processes are important in Piaget's, Vygotsky's, information-processing, and social cognitive theories. Socioemotional processes are important in Freud's and Erikson's psychoanalytic theories, Vygotsky's sociocultural cognitive theory, behavioral and social cognitive theories, and ecological theory. To begin our exploration of theories of child development, we will examine the first of the theories proposed: Freud's psychoanalytic theory.

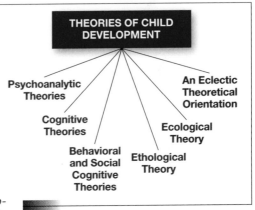

Psychoanalytic Theories

Psychoanalytic theory *describes development as primarily unconscious—that is, beyond awareness—and as heavily colored by emotion. Psychoanalytic theorists believe that behavior is merely a surface characteristic and that, to truly understand develop-*

psychoanalytic theory
According to this theory, development is primarily unconscious and heavily colored by emotion, behavior is merely a surface characteristic, it is important to analyze the symbolic meanings of behavior, and early experiences are important in development.

Sigmund Freud, the pioneering architect of psychoanalytic theory.

Freud's Theory

THE FAR SIDE   By GARY LARSON

"So, Mr. Fenton . . . Let's begin with your mother."

ment, we have to analyze the symbolic meanings of behavior and the deep inner workings of the mind. Psychoanalytic theorists also stress that early experiences with parents extensively shape our development. These characteristics are highlighted in the main psychoanalytic theory, that of Sigmund Freud.

Freud's Theory   Freud (1856–1939) developed his ideas about psychoanalytic theory from work with mental patients. He was a medical doctor who specialized in neurology. He spent most of his years in Vienna, though he moved to London near the end of his career because of the Nazis' anti-Semitism.

Freud (1917) believed that personality has three structures: the id, the ego, and the superego. The *id* is the Freudian structure of personality that consists of instincts, which are an individual's reservoir of psychic energy. In Freud's view, the id is totally unconscious; it has no contact with reality. As children experience the demands and constraints of reality, a new structure of personality emerges—the *ego,* the Freudian structure of personality that deals with the demands of reality. The ego is called the executive branch of personality because it uses reasoning to make decisions. The id and the ego have no morality. They do not take into account whether something is right or wrong. The *superego* is the Freudian structure of personality that is the moral branch of personality. The superego takes into account whether something is right or wrong. Think of the superego as what we often refer to as our "conscience." You probably are beginning to sense that both the id and the superego make life rough for the ego. Your ego might say, "I will have sex only occasionally and be sure to take the proper precautions because I don't want the intrusion of a child in the development of my career." However, your id is saying, "I want to be satisfied; sex is pleasurable." Your superego is at work too: "I feel guilty about having sex."

As Freud listened to, probed, and analyzed his patients, he became convinced that their problems were the result of experiences early in life. Freud believed that we go through five stages of psychosexual development, and that at each stage of development we experience pleasure in one part of the body more than in others. *Erogenous zones,* according to Freud, are parts of the body that have especially strong pleasure-giving qualities at particular stages of development.

Freud thought that our adult personality is determined by the way we resolve conflicts between these early sources of pleasure—the mouth, the anus, and then the genitals—and the demands of reality. When these conflicts are not resolved, the individual may become fixated at a particular stage of development. *Fixation* occurs when the individual remains locked in an earlier developmental stage because needs are under- or overgratified. For example, a parent might wean a child too early, be too strict in toilet training the child, punish the child for masturbation, or "smother" the child with too much attention.

The *oral stage* is the first Freudian stage of development, occurring during the first 18 months of life in which the infant's pleasure centers around the mouth. Chewing, sucking, and biting are the chief sources of pleasure. These actions reduce tension in the infant.

The *anal stage* is the second Freudian stage of development, occurring between 1½ and 3 years of age, in which the child's greatest pleasure involves the anus or the eliminative functions associated with it. In Freud's view, the exercise of anal muscles reduces tension.

The *phallic stage* is the third Freudian stage of development, which occurs between the ages of 3 and 6; its name comes from the Latin word *phallus,* which means "penis." During the phallic stage, pleasure focuses on the genitals as the child discovers that self-manipulation is enjoyable.

In Freud's view, the phallic stage has a special importance in personality development because it is during this period that the Oedipus complex appears. This name comes from Greek mythology, in which Oedipus, the son of the King of Thebes, unwittingly kills his father and marries his mother. The *Oedipus complex,* according to Freudian theory, is the young child's development of an intense desire to replace the same-sex parent and enjoy the affections of the opposite-sex parent.

How is the Oedipus complex resolved? At about 5 to 6 years of age, children recognize that their same-sex parent might punish them for their incestuous wishes. To reduce this conflict, the child identifies with the same-sex parent, striving to be like him or her. If the conflict is not resolved, though, the individual may become fixated at the phallic stage.

The *latency stage* is the fourth Freudian stage of development, which occurs between approximately 6 years of age and puberty; the child represses all interest in sexuality and develops social and intellectual skills. This activity channels much of the child's energy into emotionally safe areas and helps the child forget the highly stressful conflicts of the phallic stage.

The *genital stage* is the fifth and final Freudian stage of development, occurring from puberty on. The genital stage is a time of sexual reawakening; the source of sexual pleasure now becomes someone outside of the family. Freud believed that unresolved conflicts with parents reemerge during adolescence. When resolved, the individual is capable of developing a mature love relationship and functioning independently as an adult.

Freud's theory has undergone significant revisions by a number of psychoanalytic theorists. Many contemporary psychoanalytic theorists place less emphasis on sexual instincts and more emphasis on cultural experiences as determinants of an individual's development. Unconscious thought remains a central theme, but most contemporary psychoanalysts believe that conscious thought makes up more of the iceberg than Freud envisioned. Next, we will explore the ideas of an important revisionist of Freud's ideas—Erik Erikson.

Erikson's Theory

Erikson's Theory   Erik Erikson (1902–1994) recognized Freud's contributions but believed that Freud misjudged some important dimensions of human development. For one, Erikson (1950, 1968) said we develop in *psychosocial stages,* in contrast to Freud's psychosexual stages. For another, Erikson emphasized developmental change throughout the human life span, whereas Freud argued that our basic personality is shaped in the first five years of life. In **Erikson's theory,** *eight psychosocial stages of development unfold as we go through the life span* (see figure 2.2). *Each stage consists of a unique developmental task that confronts individuals with a crisis that must be faced.* According to Erikson, this crisis is a turning point of increased vulnerability and enhanced potential. The more an individual resolves the crises successfully, the healthier her or his development will be (Hopkins, 2000).

Trust versus mistrust is Erikson's first psychosocial stage, which is experienced in the first year of life. A sense of trust requires a feeling of physical comfort and a minimal amount of fear and apprehension about the future. Trust in infancy sets the stage for a lifelong expectation that the world will be a good and pleasant place to live.

Autonomy versus shame and doubt is Erikson's second stage of development, occurring in late infancy and toddlerhood (1–3 years). After gaining trust in their caregivers, infants begin to discover that their behavior is their own. They start to assert their sense of independence, or autonomy. They realize their *will.* If infants are restrained too much or punished too harshly, they are likely to develop a sense of shame and doubt.

Initiative versus guilt is Erikson's third stage of development, occurring during the preschool years. As preschool children encounter a widening social world, they are challenged more than when they were infants. Active, purposeful behavior is needed to cope with these challenges. Children are asked to assume responsibility for their bodies, their behavior, their toys, and their pets. Developing a sense of responsibility increases initiative. Uncomfortable guilt feelings may arise, though, if the child is irresponsible and is made to feel too anxious. Erikson has a positive outlook on this stage. He believes that most guilt is quickly compensated for by a sense of accomplishment.

Industry versus inferiority is Erikson's fourth developmental stage, occurring approximately in the elementary school years. Children's initiative brings them in contact with a wealth of new experiences. As they move into middle and late childhood, they direct their energy toward mastering knowledge and intellectual skills. At

Erikson's Theory

Erikson's theory
Erikson proposed eight stages of psychosocial development that unfold throughout the human life span. Each stage consists of a unique developmental task that confronts individuals with a crisis that must be faced.

Erik Erikson with his wife, Joan, an artist. Erikson generated one of the most important developmental theories of the twentieth century.

no other time is the child more enthusiastic about learning than at the end of early childhood's period of expansive imagination. The danger in the elementary school years is the development of a sense of inferiority—of feeling incompetent and unproductive. Erikson believes that teachers have a special responsibility for children's development of industry. Teachers should "mildly but firmly coerce children into the adventure of finding out that one can learn to accomplish things which one would never have thought of by oneself" (Erikson, 1968, p. 127).

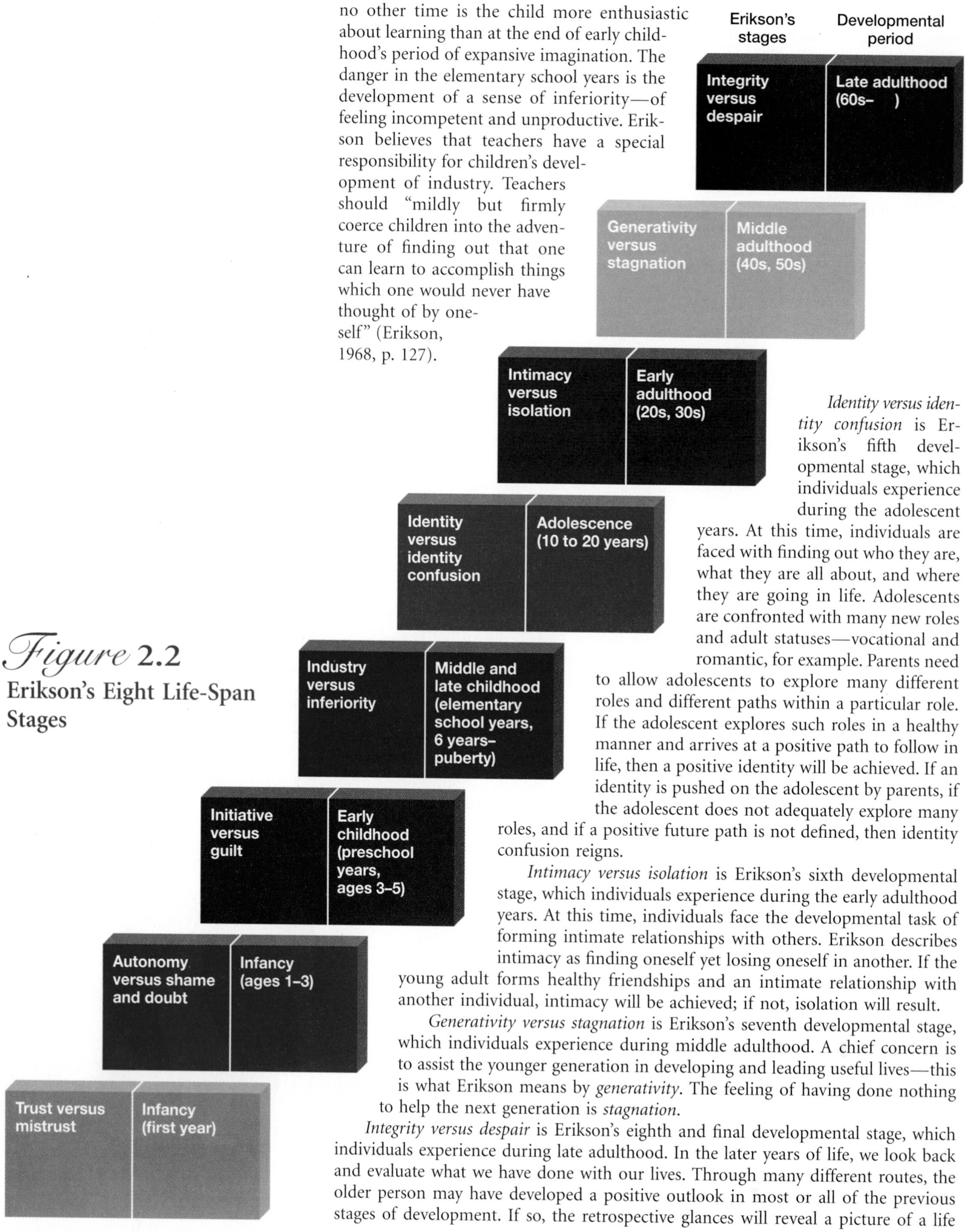

Figure 2.2
Erikson's Eight Life-Span Stages

Identity versus identity confusion is Erikson's fifth developmental stage, which individuals experience during the adolescent years. At this time, individuals are faced with finding out who they are, what they are all about, and where they are going in life. Adolescents are confronted with many new roles and adult statuses—vocational and romantic, for example. Parents need to allow adolescents to explore many different roles and different paths within a particular role. If the adolescent explores such roles in a healthy manner and arrives at a positive path to follow in life, then a positive identity will be achieved. If an identity is pushed on the adolescent by parents, if the adolescent does not adequately explore many roles, and if a positive future path is not defined, then identity confusion reigns.

Intimacy versus isolation is Erikson's sixth developmental stage, which individuals experience during the early adulthood years. At this time, individuals face the developmental task of forming intimate relationships with others. Erikson describes intimacy as finding oneself yet losing oneself in another. If the young adult forms healthy friendships and an intimate relationship with another individual, intimacy will be achieved; if not, isolation will result.

Generativity versus stagnation is Erikson's seventh developmental stage, which individuals experience during middle adulthood. A chief concern is to assist the younger generation in developing and leading useful lives—this is what Erikson means by *generativity*. The feeling of having done nothing to help the next generation is *stagnation*.

Integrity versus despair is Erikson's eighth and final developmental stage, which individuals experience during late adulthood. In the later years of life, we look back and evaluate what we have done with our lives. Through many different routes, the older person may have developed a positive outlook in most or all of the previous stages of development. If so, the retrospective glances will reveal a picture of a life well spent, and the person will feel a sense of satisfaction—integrity will be achieved. If the older adult resolved many of the earlier stages negatively, the retrospective glances likely will yield doubt or gloom—the despair Erikson talks about.

Erikson does not believe that the proper solution to a stage crisis is always completely positive. Some exposure or commitment to the negative end of the person's bipolar conflict is sometimes inevitable—you cannot trust all people under all circumstances and survive, for example. Nonetheless, in the healthy solution to a stage crisis, the positive resolution dominates.

Evaluating the Psychoanalytic Theories   The contributions of psychoanalytic theories include their emphases on these factors:

- Early experiences play an important part in development.
- Family relationships are a central aspect of development.
- Personality can be better understood if it is examined developmentally.
- The mind is not all conscious; unconscious aspects of the mind need to be considered.
- Changes take place in the adulthood as well as the childhood years (Erikson).

These are some of the criticisms of psychoanalytic theories:

- The main concepts of psychoanalytic theories have been difficult to test scientifically.
- Much of the data used to support psychoanalytic theories come from individuals' reconstruction of the past, often the distant past, and are of unknown accuracy.
- The sexual underpinnings of development are given too much importance (especially in Freud's theory).
- The unconscious mind is given too much credit for influencing development.
- Psychoanalytic theories present an image of humans that is too negative (especially Freud).
- Psychoanalytic theories are culture- and gender-biased.

Cognitive Theories

Whereas psychoanalytic theories stress the importance of children's unconscious thoughts, cognitive theories emphasize their conscious thoughts. Three important cognitive theories are Piaget's cognitive development theory, Vygotsky's sociocultural cognitive theory, and information-processing theory.

Piaget's Cognitive Developmental Theory   The famous Swiss psychologist Jean Piaget (1896–1980) proposed an important theory of cognitive development. **Piaget's theory** *states that children actively construct their understanding of the world and go through four stages of cognitive development* (See figure 2.3). Each of the stages is age-related and consists of distinct ways of thinking. Remember, it is the *different* way of understanding the world that makes one stage more advanced than another; knowing *more* information does not make a child's thinking more advanced, in the Piagetian view. This is what Piaget meant when he said the child's cognition is *qualitatively* different in one stage compared to another (Vidal, 2000). What are Piaget's four stages of cognitive development like?

The *sensorimotor stage,* which lasts from birth to about 2 years of age, is the first Piagetian stage. In this stage, infants construct an understanding of the world by coordinating sensory experiences (such as seeing and hearing) with physical, motoric actions—hence the term *sensorimotor.* At the beginning of this stage, newborns have little more than reflexive patterns with which to work. At the end of the stage, 2-year-olds have complex sensorimotor patterns and are beginning to operate with primitive symbols.

The *preoperational stage,* which lasts from approximately 2 to 7 years of age, is the second Piagetian stage. In this stage, children begin to represent the world with

Horney's Theory
Piaget's Theory

Piaget's theory
The theory that children actively construct their understanding of the world and go through four stages of cognitive development.

Jean Piaget, the famous Swiss developmental psychologist, changed the way we think about the development of children's minds. For Piaget, a child's mental development is a continuous creation of increasingly complex forms.

Figure **2.3**

Piaget's Four Stages of
Cognitive Development

words, images, and drawings. Symbolic thought goes beyond simple connections of sensory information and physical action. However, although preschool children can symbolically represent the world, according to Piaget, they still lack the ability to perform *operations,* the Piagetian term for internalized mental actions that allow children to do mentally what they previously did physically.

The *concrete operational stage,* which lasts from approximately 7 to 11 years of age, is the third Pia-

FORMAL OPERATIONAL STAGE

The adolescent reasons in more abstract, idealistic, and logical ways.

11 years of age through adulthood

CONCRETE OPERATIONAL STAGE

The child can now reason logically about concrete events and classify objects into different sets.

7–11 years of age

PREOPERATIONAL STAGE

The child begins to represent the world with words and images. These words and images reflect increased symbolic thinking and go beyond the connection of sensory information and physical action.

2–7 years of age

SENSORIMOTOR STAGE

The infant constructs an understanding of the world by coordinating sensory experiences with physical actions. An infant progresses from reflexive, instinctual action at birth to the beginning of symbolic thought toward the end of the stage.

Birth to 2 years of age

getian stage. In this stage, children can perform operations, and logical reasoning replaces intuitive thought as long as reasoning can be applied to specific or concrete examples. For instance, concrete operational thinkers cannot imagine the steps necessary to complete an algebraic equation, which is too abstract for thinking at this stage of development.

The *formal operational stage,* which appears between the ages of 11 and 15, is the fourth and final Piagetian stage. In this stage, individuals move beyond concrete experiences and think in abstract and more logical terms. As part of thinking more abstractly, adolescents develop images of ideal circumstances. They might think about what an ideal parent is like and compare their parents to this ideal standard. They begin to entertain possibilities for the future and are fascinated with what they can be. In solving problems, formal operational thinkers are more systematic, developing hypotheses about why something is happening the way it is, then testing these hypotheses in a deductive manner. We will further examine Piaget's cognitive developmental theory in chapter 7.

At this point we have discussed three major stage theories of human development—Freud's, Erikson's, and Piaget's. Figure 2.4 provides a comparison of these stage theories. Notice that Erikson's theory involves far greater change in the adult years than Freud's or Piaget's theories.

Vygotsky's Sociocultural Cognitive Theory

Like Piaget, Russian Lev Vygotsky (1896–1934) also believed that children actively construct their knowledge. **Vygotsky's theory** *is a sociocultural cognitive theory that emphasizes developmental analysis, the role of language, and social relations.* Vygotsky was born in Russia in the same year as Piaget, but he died much earlier, at the age of 37. Both Piaget's and Vygotsky's ideas remained virtually unknown to American scholars for many years, not being introduced to American audiences through English translations until the 1960s. In the past several decades, American psychologists and educators have shown increased interest in Vygotsky's (1962) views.

Three claims capture the heart of Vygotsky's view (Tappan, 1998): (1) The child's cognitive skills can be understood only when they are developmentally analyzed and

Vygotsky's theory
A sociocultural cognitive theory that emphasizes developmental analysis, the role of language, and social relations.

		Piaget's cognitive stages	Freud's psychosexual stages	Erikson's psychosocial stages	
Periods of Life-Span Development	Late adulthood			Ego integrity vs. despair	Adolescent and adult stages
	Middle adulthood			Generativity vs. stagnation	
	Early adulthood			Intimacy vs. isolation	
	Adolescence	Formal operational	Genital	Identity vs. identity confusion	
	Middle and late childhood	Concrete operational	Latency	Industry vs. inferiority	Middle and late childhood stages
	Early childhood	Preoperational	Phallic	Initiative vs. guilt	Early childhood stages
	Infancy	Sensorimotor	Anal Oral	Autonomy vs. shame/doubt Trust vs. mistrust	Infant stages

Figure **2.4**

Comparison of Piaget's, Freud's, and Erikson's Stages

interpreted, (2) cognitive skills are mediated by words, language, and forms of discourse, which serve as psychological tools for facilitating and transforming mental activity, and (3) cognitive skills have their origins in social relations and are embedded in a sociocultural backdrop.

For Vygotsky, taking a developmental approach means that, in order to understand any aspect of the child's cognitive functioning, one must examine its origins and transformations from earlier to later forms. Thus, a particular mental act, such as using private speech (speech-to-self), cannot be viewed accurately in isolation but should be evaluated as a step in a gradual developmental process.

Vygotsky's second claim, that to understand cognitive functioning it is necessary to examine the tools that mediate and shape it, led him to believe that language is the most important of these tools. Vygotsky argued that, in early childhood, language begins to be used as a tool that helps the child plan activities and solve problems.

Vygotsky's third claim was that cognitive skills originate in social relations and culture. Vygotsky portrayed the child's development as inseparable from social and cultural activities (Kozulin, 2000). He believed that the development of memory, attention, and reasoning involves learning to use the inventions of society, such as language, mathematical systems, and memory strategies. In one culture, this might consist of learning to count with the help of a computer. In another, it might consist of counting on one's fingers or using beads.

Vygotsky's theory has stimulated considerable interest in the view that knowledge is *situated* and *collaborative* (Greeno, Collins, & Resnick, 1996; Rogoff, 1998). That is, knowledge is distributed among people and environments, which include objects, artifacts, tools, books, and the communities in which people live. This suggests that knowing can best be advanced through interaction with others in cooperative activities.

Within these basic claims, Vygotsky articulated unique and influential ideas about the relation between learning and development. In chapter 7 "Cognitive Developmental Approaches," we will further explore Vygotsky's contributions to our understanding of children's development.

Lev Vygotsky
Vygotsky's Theory

There is considerable interest today in Lev Vygotsky's sociocultural cognitive theory of child development. What were Vygotsky's three basic claims about children's development?

information processing
How individuals process information about their world; how information enters the mind, how it is stored and transformed, and how it is retrieved to perform such complex activities as problem solving and reasoning.

The Information-Processing Approach
Information processing involves the ways in which individuals process information about their world—how information enters the mind, how it is stored and transformed, and how it is retrieved to perform such complex activities as problem solving and reasoning. A simple model of information processing is shown in figure 2.5.

Cognition begins when children detect information from the world through their sensory and perceptual processes. Then children store, transform, and retrieve the information through the processes of memory. Notice in our model that information can flow back and forth between memory and perceptual processes. For example, children are good at remembering the faces they see, yet their memory of a person's face may differ from the way the person actually looks. Keep in mind that our information-processing model is a simple one, designed to illustrate the main cognitive processes and their interrelations. We could have drawn other arrows—between memory and language, between thinking and sensory and perceptual processes, and between language and sensory and perceptual processes, for example. Also, it is important to know that the boxes in figure 2.5 do not represent sharp, distinct stages in processing information. There is continuity, flow, and overlap between the cognitive processes. We will explore children's information processing in much greater depth in chapter 8, "Information Processing."

Evaluating the Cognitive Theories
Among the contributions of the cognitive theories are these:

- The cognitive theories present a positive view of development, emphasizing individuals' conscious thinking.
- The cognitive theories (especially Piaget's and Vygotsky's) emphasize the individual's active construction of understanding.
- Piaget's and Vygotsky's theories underscore the importance of examining developmental changes in children's thinking.
- The information-processing approach offers detailed descriptions of cognitive processes.

Among the criticisms of the cognitive theories are these:

- It is implausible that developmental stages are as precise as Piaget thought.
- The cognitive theories do not give adequate attention to individual variations in cognitive development.
- The information-processing approach does not provide an adequate description of developmental changes in cognition.
- Psychoanalytic theorists argue that the cognitive theories do not give enough credit to unconscious thought.

At this point we have studied a number of ideas about psychoanalytic and cognitive theories. A review of these ideas is presented in summary table 2.2. Next, we continue our exploration of theories of development by examining the behavioral and social cognitive theories.

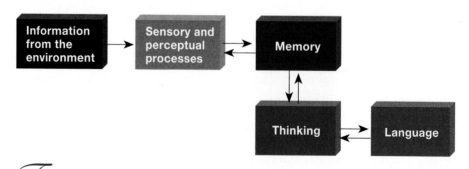

Figure **2.5**

A Model of Information Processing

$\mathscr{S}$UMMARY $\mathscr{T}$ABLE 2.2
Psychoanalytic Theories and Cognitive Theories

Concept	Processes/ Related Ideas	Characteristics/Description
Psychoanalytic Theories	Their Nature	• They describe development as primarily unconscious. • Early experiences are thought to be especially important.
	Freud's Theory	• Personality is made up of three structures—id, ego, and superego. The conflicting demands of these structures produce anxiety. Defense mechanisms are used to resolve this anxiety. • Most of children's thoughts are unconscious. • Freud was convinced that problems develop because of early experiences. • Individuals go through five psychosexual stages—oral, anal, phallic, latency, and genital. During the phallic stage, the Oedipus conflict is a major source of conflict.
	Erikson's Theory	• His theory emphasizes these eight psychosocial stages of development: trust vs. mistrust, autonomy vs. shame and doubt, initiative vs. guilt, industry vs. inferiority, identity vs. identity confusion, intimacy vs. isolation, generativity vs. stagnation, and integrity vs. despair.
	Evaluating the Psychoanalytic Theories	• Their contributions include emphases on early experiences, family relationships, a developmental framework, the unconscious mind, and changes in adulthood (Erikson). • Critics argue that these theories involve a lack of scientific support, data based on a reconstruction of the distant past, too much emphasis on sexuality, giving too much power to unconscious thought, an image of human development that is too negative, and being culture- and gender-biased.
Cognitive Theories	Piaget's Cognitive Developmental Theory	• Piaget said that children actively construct an understanding of the world. • Children go through four cognitive stages: sensorimotor, preoperational, concrete operational, and formal operational.
	Vygotsky's Sociocultural Cognitive Theory	• His theory includes three basic claims about development: (1) Cognitive skills need to be interpreted developmentally, (2) cognitive skills are mediated by language, and (3) cognitive skills have their origins in social relations and culture.
	The Information- Processing Approach	• This approach is concerned with how individuals process information about their world. • Includes how information gets into the child's mind, how it is stored and transformed, and how it is retrieved to think and solve problems.
	Evaluating the Cognitive Theories	• Contributions include emphases on a positive view of development, the active construction of understanding, the importance of developmental changes in children's thinking (Piaget and Vygotsky), and detailed descriptions of cognitive processes (information processing). • Critics argue that these theories involve implausibly precise stages (Piaget), too little attention to individual variations, lack of emphasis on developmental changes (information processing), and little interest in unconscious thought.

Behavioral and Social Cognitive Theories

Behaviorists believe we should examine only what can be directly observed and measured. At approximately the same time as Freud was interpreting his patients' unconscious minds through early childhood experiences, behaviorists such as Ivan Pavlov and John B. Watson were conducting detailed observations of behavior in controlled laboratory circumstances. Out of the behavioral tradition grew the belief that development

Behavioral and Social Cognitive Theories
Classical Conditioning

is observable behavior, learned through experience with the environment. We will explore three versions of the behavioral approach: Pavlov's classical conditioning, Skinner's operant conditioning, and Bandura's social cognitive theory.

Classical Conditioning

It is a nice spring day. A father takes his baby out for a walk. The baby reaches over to touch a pink flower and is badly stung by the bumblebee sitting on the petals. The next day, the baby's mother brings home some pink flowers. She removes a flower from the arrangement and takes it over for her baby to smell. The baby cries loudly as soon as she sees the pink flower. The baby's panic at the sight of the pink flower illustrates the learning process of **classical conditioning**, *in which a neutral stimulus becomes associated with a meaningful stimulus and acquires the capacity to elicit a similar response.*

In the early 1900s, the Russian physiologist Ivan Pavlov investigated the way the body digests food. As part of his experiments, he routinely placed meat powder in a dog's mouth, causing the dog to salivate. Pavlov began to notice that the meat powder was not the only stimulus that caused the dog to salivate. The dog salivated in response to a number of stimuli associated with the food, such as the sight of the food dish, the sight of the individual who brought the food into the room, and the sound of the door closing when the food arrived. Pavlov recognized that the dog's association of these sights and sounds with the food was an important type of learning, which came to be called classical conditioning.

Pavlov wanted to know *why* the dog salivated to various sights and sounds before eating the meat powder. He observed that the dog's behavior included both learned and unlearned components. The "unlearned" part of classical conditioning is based on the fact that some stimuli automatically produce certain responses apart from any prior learning; in other words, they are inborn or innate. *Reflexes* are automatic stimulus-response connections. They include salivation in response to food, nausea in response to bad food, shivering in response to low temperature, coughing in response to the throat being clogged, pupil constriction in response to light, and withdrawal in response to blows or burns. An *unconditioned stimulus (US)* is a stimulus that produces a response without prior learning; food was the US in Pavlov's experiments. An *unconditioned response (UR)* is an unlearned response that is automatically elicited by the US. In Pavlov's experiments, the saliva that flowed from the dog's mouth in response to food was the UR. In the case of the baby and the flower, the baby's learning and experience did not cause her to cry when the bee stung her. Her crying was unlearned and occurred automatically. The bee's sting was the US and the crying was the UR.

In classical conditioning, the *conditioned stimulus (CS)* is a previously neutral stimulus that eventually elicits the conditioned response after being associated with the unconditioned stimulus. The *conditioned response (CR)* is the learned response to the conditioned stimulus that occurs after CS-US pairing (Pavlov, 1927). In studying a dog's response to various stimuli associated with meat powder, Pavlov rang a bell before giving the meat powder to the dog. Until then, ringing the bell did not have a particular effect on the dog, except perhaps to wake the dog from a nap. The bell was a neutral stimulus. But the dog began to associate the sound of the bell with the food and salivated when it heard the bell. The bell had become a conditioned (learned) stimulus (CS) and the salivation a conditioned response (CR). Before conditioning (or learning), the bell and the food were not related. After their association, the conditioned stimulus (the bell) produced a conditioned response (salivation). For the unhappy baby, the flower was the baby's bell, or CS, crying was the CR after the sting (US) and the flower (CS) were paired. A summary of how classical conditioning works is shown in figure 2.6.

Since Pavlov's experiments, children have been conditioned in other experiments to respond to the sound of a buzzer, a glimpse of light, or the touch of a hand. Classical conditioning has a great deal of survival value for children. Because of classical conditioning, children jerk their hands away before they are burned by fire and they move out of the way of a rapidly approaching truck before it hits them. Classical con-

classical conditioning
The process in which a neutral stimulus becomes associated with a meaningful stimulus and acquires the capacity to elicit a similar response.

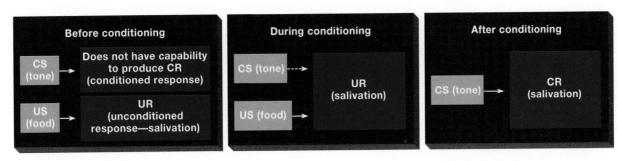

Figure 2.6
Classical Conditioning
At the start of conditioning, the US will evoke the UR, but the CS does not have this capacity. During conditioning, the CS and US are paired so that the CS comes to elicit the response. The key learning ingredient is the association of the US and CS.

ditioning is at work in words that serve as important signals. A boy walks into an abandoned house with a friend and yells, "Snake!" His friend bolts out the door. An adolescent imagines a peaceful, tranquil scene—an abandoned beach with waves lapping onto the sand—and relaxes as if she were actually lying on the beach.

Phobias are irrational fears. Classical conditioning provides an explanation of these and other fears. Behaviorist John Watson conducted an investigation to demonstrate classical conditioning's role in phobias. A little boy named Albert was shown a white laboratory rat to see if he was afraid of it. He was not. As Albert played with the rat, a loud noise was sounded behind his head. As you might imagine, the noise caused little Albert to cry. After only seven pairings of the loud noise with the white rat, Albert began to fear the rat even when the noise was not sounded. Albert's fear was generalized to a rabbit, a dog, and a sealskin coat (see figure 2.7). Today, we could not ethically conduct such an experiment. Especially noteworthy is the fact that Watson did not remove Albert's fear of rats, so presumably this phobia remained with him after the experiment. Many of our fears—fear of the dentist from a painful experience, fear of driving from being in an automobile accident, fear of heights from falling off a high chair when we were infants, and fear of dogs from being bitten, for example—can be learned through classical conditioning.

If we can produce fears by classical conditioning, we should be able to eliminate them. *Counterconditioning* is a classical conditioning procedure for weakening a CR by associating the stimuli with a new response incompatible with the CR. Though Watson did not eliminate little Albert's fear of white rats, an associate of Watson's, Mary Cover Jones (1924), did eliminate the fears of a 3-year-old boy named Peter. Peter had many of the same fears as Albert; however, Peter's fears were not produced by Jones. Among Peter's fears were white rats, fur coats, frogs, fish, and mechanical toys. To eliminate these fears, a rabbit was brought into Peter's view but kept far enough away that it would not upset him. At the same time the rabbit was brought into view, Peter was fed crackers and milk. On each successive day, the rabbit was moved closer to Peter as he ate crackers and milk. Eventually, Peter reached the point at which he could eat the food with one hand and pet the rabbit with the other.

Some of the behaviors we associate with health problems or mental disorders can involve classical conditioning. Certain physical complaints—asthma, headaches, ulcers, and high blood pressure, for example—might partly be the products of classical conditioning. We usually say that such health problems are caused by stress, but often what has happened is that certain stimuli, such as a teacher's critical attitude or fighting by parents,

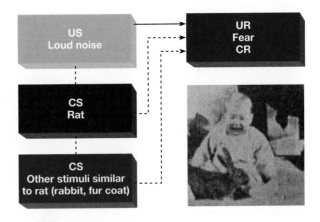

Figure 2.7
Little Albert's Generalized Fear
In 1920, to condition 9-month-old little Albert to fear a white rat, Watson paired the rat with a loud noise. When little Albert was subsequently placed with other stimuli similar to the white rat, such as the rabbit shown here with little Albert, he was afraid of them too. This illustrates the principle of stimulus generalization in classical conditioning.

Photo courtesy of Professor Benjamin Harris.

B. F. Skinner was a tinkerer who liked to make new gadgets. The younger of his two daughters, Deborah, was raised in Skinner's enclosed Air-Crib, which he invented because he wanted to control her environment completely. The Air-Crib was soundproofed and temperature controlled. Some critics accused Skinner of monstrous experimentation with his children; however, the early controlled environment has not had any noticeable harmful effects. Debbie, shown here as a child with her parents, is currently a successful artist, is married, and lives in London.

behaviorism
The scientific study of observable behavioral responses and their environmental determinants.

social cognitive theory
The theory that behavior, environment, and person/cognitive factors are important in understanding development.

Through the Eyes of Psychologists

Albert Bandura, *Stanford University*

"Humans have an unparalleled capacity to become many things."

are conditioned stimuli for children's physiological responses. Over time, the frequent presence of the physiological responses may produce health disorders.

Pavlov described all learning in terms of classical conditioning. In reality, children learn in many ways. Still, classical conditioning helps children learn about their environment and has been successful in eliminating children's fears. However, a view that describes children as *responding* to the environment fails to capture the *active* nature of children and their influence on the environment.

Skinner's Behaviorism
Behaviorism *emphasizes the scientific study of observable behavioral responses and their environmental determinants.* In Skinner's behaviorism, the mind, conscious or unconscious, is not needed to explain behavior and development. Development is behavior. For example, observations of Sam reveal that his behavior is shy, achievement-oriented, and caring. Why is Sam's behavior this way? For Skinner, rewards and punishments in Sam's environment have shaped him into a shy, achievement-oriented, and caring person. Because of interactions with family members, friends, teachers, and others, Sam has *learned* to behave in this fashion.

The concept of operant conditioning was developed by American psychologist B. F. Skinner (1938). *Operant conditioning* (or instrumental conditioning) is a form of learning in which the consequences of behavior produce changes in the probability of the behavior's occurrence. In operant conditioning, an organism acts, or operates, on the environment to produce a change in the probability of the behavior's occurrence; Skinner chose the label *operants* for the responses that are actively emitted because of the consequences for the organism. The consequences are *contingent,* or dependent, on the organism's behavior. For example, a simple operant might be the pressing of a lever that leads to the delivery of food (the consequence); the delivery of food is contingent on pressing the lever.

We just indicated that Skinner described operant conditioning as a form of learning in which the consequences of behavior lead to changes in the probability of that behavior's occurrence. The consequences—rewards or punishments—are contingent on the organism's behavior. *Reinforcement* (or reward) is a consequence that increases the probability a behavior will occur. By contrast, *punishment* is a consequence that decreases the probability that a behavior will occur. For example, if an adult smiles at a child, and the adult and child continue talking for some time, the smile reinforced the child's talking. However, if an adult meets a child and frowns at the child, and the child quickly leaves the situation, then the frown punished the child's talking with the adult.

Because behaviorists believe that development is learned and often changes according to environmental experiences, it follows that rearranging experiences can change development. For behaviorists, shy behavior can be transformed into outgoing behavior; aggressive behavior can be shaped into docile behavior; lethargic, boring behavior can be turned into enthusiastic, interesting behavior.

Social Cognitive Theory
Some psychologists believe that the behaviorists basically are right when they say development is learned and is influenced strongly by environmental experiences. However, they believe that Skinner went too far in declaring that cognition is unimportant in understanding development. **Social cognitive theory** *is the view of psychologists who emphasize behavior, environment, and cognition as the key factors in development.*

American psychologists Albert Bandura (1986, 1998, 2000) and Walter Mischel (1973, 1995) are the main architects of social cognitive theory's contemporary version, which Mischel (1973) initially labeled *cognitive* social learning theory. Both Bandura and Mischel believe that cognitive processes are important mediators of environment-behavior connections. Bandura's early research program focused heavily on observational learning, learning that occurs through observing what others do. Observational learning is also referred to as imitation or modeling. What is *cognitive* about observational learning in Bandura's view? Bandura (1925–) believes that people cognitively represent the behavior of others and then sometimes adopt this behavior themselves. For example, a young boy might observe his father's aggressive outbursts and hostile interchanges with people; when observed with his peers, the young boy's style of interaction is highly aggressive, showing the same characteristics as his father's behavior. A girl might adopt the dominant and sarcastic style of her teacher. When observed interacting with her younger brother, she says, "You are so slow. How can you do this work so slowly?" Social cognitive theorists believe that children acquire a wide range of such behaviors, thoughts, and feelings through observing others' behavior. These observations form an important part of children's development.

Bandura's (1986, 1998, 2000) most recent model of learning and development involves behavior, the person, and the environment. As shown in figure 2.8, behavior, personal (and cognitive), and environmental factors operate interactively. Behavior can influence personal factors and vice versa. The person's cognitive activities can influence the environment, the environment can change the person's cognition, and so on.

Like the behavioral approach of Skinner, social cognitive theorists such as Bandura emphasize the importance of empirical research in studying children's development. This research focuses on the processes that explain children's development—the social and cognitive factors that influence what children are like.

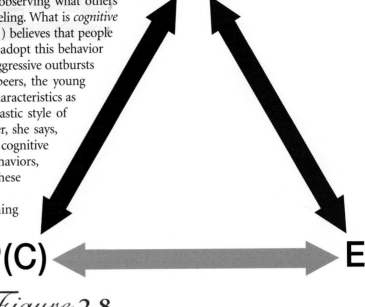

Figure 2.8
Bandura's Social Cognitive Model
P(C) stands for personal and cognitive factors, *B* for behavior, and *E* for environment. The arrows reflect how relations between these factors are reciprocal rather than unidirectional. Examples of personal factors include intelligence, skills, and self-control.

Albert Bandura

Evaluating the Behavioral and Social Cognitive Theories
These are some of the contributions of the behavioral and social cognitive theories:

- An emphasis on the importance of scientific research
- A focus on the environmental determinants of behavior
- An underscoring of the importance of observational learning (Bandura)
- An emphasis on person and cognitive factors (social cognitive theory)

These are some of the criticisms of the behavioral and social cognitive theories:

- Too little emphasis on cognition (Pavlov, Skinner)
- Too much emphasis on environmental determinants
- Inadequate attention to developmental changes
- Too mechanical and inadequate consideration of the spontaneity and creativity of humans

The behavioral and social cognitive theories emphasize the importance of environmental experiences in human development. Next we will turn our attention to a theory that underscores the importance of biological foundations of development—ethological theory.

Ethological Theory

Sensitivity to different kinds of experience varies over the life span. The presence or absence of certain experiences at particular times in the life span influences individuals well beyond the time they first occur. Ethologists believe that most psychologists underestimate the importance of these special time frames in early development. Ethologists also stress the powerful roles that evolution and biological foundations play in development (Hinde, 1992; Rosenzweig, 2000).

The tide of evolution carries everything before it, thoughts no less than bodies, and persons no less than nations.

George Santayana
Spanish-born American Philosopher, 20th Century

ethology
An approach that stresses that behavior is strongly influenced by biology, tied to evolution, and characterized by critical or sensitive periods.

Exploring Ethology

Ethology emerged as an important view because of the work of European zoologists, especially Konrad Lorenz (1903–1989). **Ethology** *stresses that behavior is strongly influenced by biology, is tied to evolution, and is characterized by critical or sensitive periods.*

Working mostly with greylag geese, Lorenz (1965) studied a behavior pattern that was considered to be programmed within the birds' genes. A newly hatched gosling seemed to be born with the instinct to follow its mother. Observations showed that the gosling was capable of such behavior as soon as it hatched. Lorenz proved that it was incorrect to assume that such behavior was programmed in the animal. In a remarkable set of experiments, Lorenz separated the eggs laid by one goose into two groups. One group he returned to the goose to be hatched by her. The other group was hatched in an incubator. The goslings in the first group performed as predicted. They followed their mother as soon as they hatched. However, those in the second group, which saw Lorenz when they first hatched, followed him everywhere, as though he were their mother. Lorenz marked the goslings and then placed both groups under a box. Mother goose and "mother" Lorenz stood aside as the box lifted. Each group of goslings went directly to its "mother" (see figure 2.9). Lorenz called this process *imprinting*, the rapid, innate learning within a limited critical period of time that involves attachment to the first moving object seen.

The ethological view of Lorenz and the European zoologists forced American developmental psychologists to recognize the importance of the biological basis of behavior. However, the research and theorizing of ethology still lacked some ingredients that would elevate it to the ranks of the other theories discussed so far in this chapter. In particular, there was little or nothing in the classical ethological view about the nature of social relationships across the human life span, something that any major theory of development must explain. Also, its concept of *critical period,* a fixed time period very early in development during which certain behaviors optimally emerge, was overdrawn when applied to humans. Classical ethological theory was weak in stimulating studies with humans. Recent expansion of the ethological view has improved its status as a viable developmental perspective. For example, current conceptions of infant attachment, which will be discussed in chapter 11, "Emotional Development," often have connections to ethological theory.

Figure **2.9**

Konrad Lorenz, a Pioneering Student of Animal Behavior, Is Followed Through the Water by Three Imprinted Greylag Geese

Lorenz described imprinting as rapid, innate learning within a critical period that involves attachment to the first moving object seen. For goslings, the critical period is the first 36 hours after birth.

Like behaviorists, ethologists are careful observers of behavior. Unlike behaviorists, ethologists believe that laboratories are not good settings for observing behavior. Rather, they meticulously observe behavior in its natural surroundings, in homes, playgrounds, neighborhoods, schools, hospitals, and so on.

Evaluating Ethological Theory

These are some of the contributions of ethological theory:

- An increased focus on the biological and evolutionary basis of development
- The use of careful observations in naturalistic settings
- An emphasis on sensitive periods of development

These are some of the criticisms of ethological theory:

- The critical and sensitive period concepts might be too rigid
- It might place too strong an emphasis on biological foundations
- It might give inadequate attention to cognition
- The theory has been better at generating research with animals than with humans

In addition to ethological theory, another theory that emphasizes the biological aspects of human development—evolutionary psychology—will be presented in chapter 3, "Biological Beginnings," along with views on the role of heredity in development.

Ecological Theory

While ethological theory stresses biological factors, ecological theory emphasizes environmental factors. One ecological theory that has important implications for understanding life-span development was created by Urie Bronfenbrenner (1917–).

Ecological theory is Bronfenbrenner's environmental system view of development. It consists of five environmental systems ranging from the fine-grained inputs of direct interactions with social agents to the broad-based inputs of culture. The five systems in Bronfenbrenner's ecological theory are the microsystem, mesosystem, exosystem, macrosystem, and chronosystem. Bronfenbrenner's (1986, 1995, 2000; Bronfenbrenner & Morris, 1998) ecological model is shown in figure 2.10. The *microsystem* in Bronfenbrenner's ecological theory is the setting in which the individual lives. These contexts include the person's family, peers, school, and neighborhood. It is in the microsystem that the most direct interactions with social agents take place—with parents, peers, and teachers, for example. The individual is not viewed as a passive recipient of experiences in these settings, but as someone who helps to construct the settings. Bronfenbrenner points out that most research on sociocultural influences has focused on microsystems.

The *mesosystem* in Bronfenbrenner's ecological theory involves relationships between microsystems or connections between contexts. Examples are the relation of family experiences to school experiences, school experiences to work experiences, and family experiences to peer experiences. For instance, children whose parents have rejected them may have difficulty developing positive relations with teachers. Developmentalists increasingly believe it is important to observe behavior in multiple settings—such as family, peer, and school contexts—to obtain a more complete picture of children's development (Booth & Dunn, 1996).

The *exosystem* in Bronfenbrenner's ecological theory is involved when experiences in another social setting—in which the individual does not have an active role—influence what the individual experiences in an immediate

THE FAR SIDE   By GARY LARSON

"When imprinting studies go awry . . ."

ecological theory
Bronfenbrenner's environmental system view of development, involving five environmental systems—microsystem, mesosystem, ecosystem, macrosystem, and chronosystem. These emphasize the role of social contexts in development.

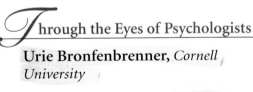

Through the Eyes of Psychologists

Urie Bronfenbrenner, *Cornell University*

"Perhaps even more in developmental science than in other fields, the pathways to discovery are not easy to find."

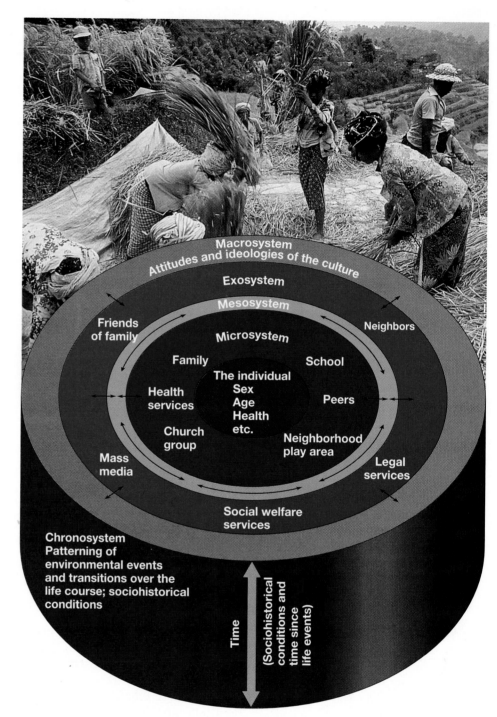

Figure **2.10**

Bronfenbrenner's Ecological Theory of Development

Bronfenbrenner's ecological theory consists of five environmental systems: microsystem, mesosystem, exosystem, macrosystem, and chronosystem.

context. For example, work experiences might affect a woman's relationship with her husband and their child. The mother might receive a promotion that requires more travel, which might increase marital conflict and change patterns of parent-child interaction. Another example of an exosystem is the city government, which is responsible for the quality of parks, recreation centers, and library facilities for children and adolescents. Yet another example is the federal government through its role in the quality of medical care and support systems for the elderly.

The *macrosystem* in Bronfenbrenner's ecological theory involves the culture in which individuals live. Remember from chapter 1 that *culture* refers to the behavior patterns, beliefs, and all other products of a group of people that are passed on from generation to generation ◀▥ P. 12. Remember also that *cross-cultural studies*—the comparison of one culture with one or more other cultures—provide information about the generality of development ◀▥ P. 12.

The *chronosystem* in Bronfenbrenner's ecological theory involves the patterning of environmental events and transitions over the life course, as well as sociohistorical circumstances. For example, in studying the effects of divorce on children, researchers have found that the negative effects often peak in the first year after the divorce. The effects also are more negative for sons than for daughters (Hetherington, 1989, 1995). By 2 years after the divorce, family interaction is less chaotic and more stable. With regard to sociocultural circumstances, women today are much more likely to be encouraged to pursue a career than they were 20 to 30 years ago. In ways such as these, the chronosystem has a powerful impact on our development.

Bronfenbrenner (1995, 2000; Bronfenbrenner & Morris, 1998) recently added biological influences to his theory and now describes it as a bioecological theory. Nonetheless, ecological, environmental contexts still predominate in Bronfenbrenner's theory. Bronfenbrenner (1999) recently got together with Glen Elder, Jr., who has developed a life-course theory of development. They talked about their theories and commented about each other's theories. To read about their thoughts, see Explorations in Child Development.

Bronfenbrenner's Theory

Bronfenbrenner and a Multicultural Framework

Evaluating Ecological Theory   These are some of the contributions of ecological theory:

• A systematic examination of macro and micro dimensions of environmental systems
• Attention to connections between environmental settings (mesosystem)
• Consideration of sociohistorical influences on development (chronosystem)

These are some of the criticisms of ecological theory:

• Even with the added discussion of biological influences in recent years, there is still too little attention to biological foundations of development.
• The theory gives inadequate attention to cognitive processes.

An Eclectic Theoretical Orientation

An **eclectic theoretical orientation** *does not follow any one theoretical approach but instead selects and uses from each theory whatever is considered the best in it.* No single theory described in this chapter is indomitable or capable of explaining entirely the rich complexity of child development. Each of the theories has made important contributions to our understanding of children's development. Psychoanalytic theory best explains the unconscious mind. Erikson's theory best describes the changes that occur in adult development. Piaget's theory, Vygotsky's theory, and the information-processing approach are the most complete descriptions of children's cognitive development. The behavioral and social cognitive and ecological theories have been the most adept at examining the environmental determinants of development.

eclectic theoretical orientation
An approach that does not follow any one theoretical approach, but instead selects and uses whatever is considered the best in many different theories.

EXPLORATIONS IN CHILD DEVELOPMENT
Bronfenbrenner and Elder Talk About Their Theories

URIE BRONFENBRENNER (1999) believes that the field of life-span development will move forward if we increase our investigation of connectedness across different domains—including biological, cognitive, emotional, social, and cultural domains. Too often, he says, our research focuses on a single domain (such as cognitive), without regard for how the other domains might be involved. These borders are increasingly being crossed in the field of life-span development, and Bronfenbrenner hopes this will happen even more in the future. To expand the field of life-span development, he recommends greater consideration of what is happening in fields like biology, history, and economics.

The increased interrelatedness that Bronfenbrenner advocates already characterizes his ecological theory and the life-course theory of Glen Elder, Jr. For more than two decades, Bronfenbrenner and Elder have been friends, discussed their views with each other in depth, and reviewed each other's manuscripts. Each gratefully acknowledges the other's contribution to his work. Bronfenbrenner believes it is important to point this out because too often students think that scientists work in isolation from each other and that once they create a theory they never modify it. An important property of science is that it involves the evolving product of a community of scholars working over extended periods of time. Bronfenbrenner also acknowledges the powerful influence of the Russian Lev Vygotsky on his own work. Vygotsky especially contributed to Bronfenbrenner's belief that sociocultural contexts and historical circumstances are key aspects of human development. Vygotsky's influence on Bronfenbrenner further underscores the fact that science advances when a community of scholars work across generations for an extended period of time. As can be seen, the creation of a major developmental theory like Bronfenbrenner's has its own life course, and, in Bronfenbrenner's words, "what counts the most is not the destination reached but the rich experiences of the journey."

Elder's influence on Bronfenbrenner is apparent in Bronfenbrenner's increased interest in the role that time plays in development. However, time is an area where Bronfenbrenner's and Elder's theories depart. Elder's life-course theory focuses primarily on the kinds of environments people live in over the long term, especially in terms of outcomes in the adult years. Thus, Elder's theory involves examining "macro environments" over "macro time," in some cases most of people's lives. By contrast, Bronfenbrenner's ecological theory (or "bioecological theory" in his most recent writings) primarily focuses on person-environment interaction in "micro environments" during briefer time frames in the child and adolescent years.

Elder has a Ph.D. in sociology, although his graduate training also included a number of courses in psychology. Elder's efforts have significantly contributed to the transport and integration of ideas across disciplines (such as psychology and sociology) in the field of life-span development. He acknowledges Bronfenbrenner's persistent efforts over the last two decades to get him to more directly address issues in developmental psychology. Elder believed that Bronfenbrenner's early formulations of ecological theory did not give adequate attention to how historical time and place linked people's lives over a lifetime. He applauds Bronfenbrenner's recent acknowledgment of how important time is in understanding people's lives. Elder says that one of the similarities in their views is that both highlight the social ecologies in which people live and work.

In terms of differences in their theories, Elder (1999) commented that his life-course theory emphasizes the importance of changes in adult development for children's development, whereas Bronfenbrenner's theory mainly focuses on the childhood years. He also believes that Bronfenbrenner's ecological theory does not have concepts that describe social trajectories or developmental pathways.

Ethological theory has made us aware of biology's role and the importance of sensitive periods in development. It is important to recognize that, although theories are helpful guides, relying on a single theory to explain children's development is probably a mistake.

In this chapter we attempted to present five theoretical perspectives objectively. The same eclectic orientation will be retained throughout the book. This will help you view the study of development as it actually exists—with different theorists making different assumptions, stressing different empirical problems, and using different strategies to discover information.

The theories that we have discussed were developed at different points in the twentieth century. To see when these theories were proposed, see figure 2.11.

These theoretical perspectives, along with research issues that were discussed in chapter 1 and methods that will be described shortly, provide a sense of development's scientific nature. Figure 2.12 compares the main theoretical perspectives in terms of how they view important developmental issues.

In addition to the grand theories discussed in this chapter, which serve as general frameworks for thinking about and interpreting many aspects of children's development, there are many more "local" theories, or mini-models, that guide research in specific areas (Kuhn, 1998; Parke & Buriel, 1998). For example, in chapter 5 you will read about the recently developed dynamic systems theory (Lewis, 2000; Thelen & Smith, 1998), which offers an explanation of infant perceptual-motor development; in chapter 11 you will read about the new functionalist approach to understanding infants' emotional development; and in chapter 15 you will read about the old and new approaches to parent-adolescent relationships.

The "micro" theories focus on a specific aspect or time frame of development, seeking precise explanations of that particular dimension. As you read the remaining chapters of this book, you will come across many of these more focused views. Together, the grand theories and the micro approaches give us a more complete view of how the fascinating journey of development unfolds.

At this point we have studied a number of ideas about the behavioral and social cognitive theories, ethological theory, ecological theory, and an eclectic theoretical orientation. A review of these ideas is presented in summary table 2.3. Next, we will explore the methods that scientists use to study development.

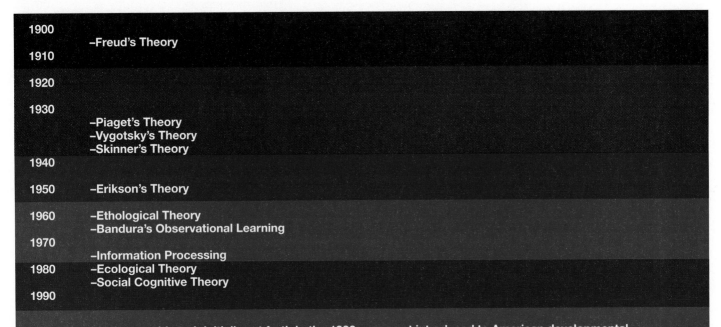

1900
—Freud's Theory
1910

1920

1930
—Piaget's Theory
—Vygotsky's Theory
—Skinner's Theory
1940

1950   —Erikson's Theory

1960   —Ethological Theory
—Bandura's Observational Learning
1970
—Information Processing
1980   —Ecological Theory
—Social Cognitive Theory
1990

Note: Piaget's theory, although initially set forth in the 1930s, was not introduced to American developmental psychologists until the late 1960s. Likewise, Vygotsky's theory, also initially conceptualized in the 1930s, started to be recognized by American developmentalists in the 1970s but only in the last decade has been given extensive attention. Bandura's initial theorizing took place in the early 1960s and focused on observational learning. In the late 1980s, Bandura expanded his earlier views by focusing more on person/cognitive factors and changed the name of his theory from social learning theory to social cognitive theory. In recent years, less attention has been given to Freud's theory, and more attention to Erikson's theory, Bandura's theory, Vygotsky's theory, information processing, and ecological theory.

Figure **2.11**
Time Line for Major Developmental Theories

Theory	Issues and methods		
	Continuity/discontinuity, early versus later experiences	*Biological and environmental factors*	*Importance of cognition*
Psychoanalytic	Discontinuity between stages—continuity between early experiences and later development; early experiences very important; later changes in development emphasized in Erikson's theory	Freud's biological determination interacting with early family experiences; Erikson's more balanced biological-cultural interaction perspective	Emphasized, but in the form of unconscious thought
Cognitive	Discontinuity between stages—continuity between early experiences and later development in Piaget's theory; has not been important to information-processing psychologists	Piaget's emphasis on interaction and adaptation; environment provides the setting for cognitive structures to develop; information-processing view has not addressed this issue extensively but mainly emphasizes biological-environmental interaction	The primary determinant of behavior
Behavioral and social cognitive	Continuity (no stages); experience at all points of development important	Environment viewed as the cause of behavior in both views	Strongly deemphasized in the behavioral approach but an important mediator in the social cognitive approach
Ethological	Discontinuity but no stages; critical or sensitive periods emphasized; early experiences very important	Strong biological view	Not emphasized
Ecological	Little attention to continuity/discontinuity; change emphasized more than stability	Strong environmental view	Not emphasized

Figure 2.12

A Comparison of Theories and Issues in Child Development

SUMMARY TABLE 2.3
Behavioral and Social Cognitive Theories, Ethological Theories, Ecological Theories, and an Eclectic Theoretical Orientation

Concept	Processes/ Related Ideas	Characteristics/Description
Behavioral and Social Cognitive Theories	Their Nature	• Emphasis is given to observable behavior, learned through experience.
	Classical Conditioning	• Pavlov's behaviorism emphasizes classical conditioning.
	Skinner's Behaviorism	• Development is observed behavior, which is determined by rewards and punishments.
	Social Cognitive Theory	• Bandura states that the environment is an important determinant of behavior but so are cognitive processes. • Bandura emphasizes reciprocal interactions among the person, behavior, and the environment.
	Evaluating the Behavioral and Social Cognitive Theories	• Contributions include emphases on scientific research, environmental determinants, observational learning, and person and cognitive factors (Bandura). • Critics argue there is too little emphasis on cognition (Skinner), too much emphasis on environmental determinants, and inadequate attention to developmental changes, and that the theories are too mechanical.
Ethological Theory	Its Nature	• Lorenz was one of the key figures in conceptualizing ethological theory. • Imprinting and critical periods are key concepts.
	Evaluating Ethological Theory	• Contributions include a focus on the biological and evolutionary basis of development, use of careful observations in naturalistic settings, and attention to sensitive periods in development. • Critics argue that the critical and sensitive period concepts are too rigid and that there is too much emphasis on biological foundations, inadequate attention to cognitive factors, and a lack of research on humans.
Ecological Theory	Their Nature	• In Bronfenbrenner's theory, five environmental systems are important: microsystem, mesosystem, exosystem, macrosystem, and chronosystem.
	Evaluating Ecological Theory	• Contributions include a systematic examination of macro and micro dimensions of environmental systems, attention to connections between environmental systems, and considerations of sociohistorical influences. • Critics argue there is inadequate attention to biological and cognitive factors.
An Eclectic Theoretical Orientation	Its Nature	• No single theory can explain the rich, complex nature of child development. Each of the theories has made a different contribution. • Many "local" theories, or mini-models, also guide research in specific areas of child development.

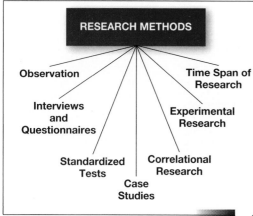

RESEARCH METHODS

Observation

Interviews and Questionnaires

Standardized Tests

Case Studies

Time Span of Research

Experimental Research

Correlational Research

Research Methods

Remember that, in addition to theories, the scientific study of child development also involves research. We will begin our research inquiry with an overview of the measures child developmentalists use to obtain information about children.

When researchers want to find out, for example, if cocaine taken by pregnant women will affect the fetus, if academic preschool programs place too much stress on young children, and if watching a lot of MTV detracts from adolescents' learning in school, they can choose from many methods. We will discuss these methods separately, but recognize that often more than one is used in a single study.

Observation

Sherlock Holmes chided his assistant, Watson, "You see but you do not observe." We look at things all the time; however, casually watching two children interacting is not the same as the type of observation used in scientific studies. Scientific observation is highly systematic. It requires knowing what you are looking for, conducting observations in an unbiased manner, accurately recording and categorizing what you see, and effectively communicating your observations.

A common way to record observations is to write them down, often using shorthand or symbols. In addition, tape recorders, video cameras, special coding sheets, one-way mirrors, and computers increasingly are being used to make observations more efficient.

Observations can be made in either laboratories or natural settings (Hartmann & George, 1999). A **laboratory** *is a controlled setting from which many of the complex factors of the real world have been removed.* Some researchers conduct studies in laboratories at the colleges or universities where they teach. Although laboratories often help researchers gain more control over the behavior of the participants, laboratory studies have been criticized as being artificial. In **naturalistic observation,** *behavior*

laboratory
A controlled setting from which many of the complex factors of the real world have been removed.

naturalistic observation
Observation that takes place out in the real world instead of in a laboratory.

In this research study, an observer is watching a preschool classroom. She is coding the interaction of the teacher and children using a number of precise, well-defined categories.

is observed outside of a laboratory, in the so-called real world. Researchers conduct naturalistic observations of adolescents in classrooms, at home, at youth centers, at museums, in neighborhoods, and in other settings.

Virtually all of the theories that we discussed in the first part of the chapter emphasize some form of observation to obtain information about children's development. The behavioral and social cognitive theories especially advocate the use of laboratory observation, whereas ethological theory emphasizes the importance of naturalistic observation.

Interviews and Questionnaires

Sometimes the quickest and best way to get information about children is to ask them or adults who know them for it. Researchers use interviews and questionnaires (surveys) to find out about children's experiences, beliefs, and feelings. Most interviews take place face-to-face, although they can be done over the phone or via the Internet. Questionnaires are usually given to individuals in printed form, and they are asked to fill them out. This can be done in person, by mail, or via the Internet.

Good interviews and surveys involve concrete, specific, and unambiguous questions and a means of checking the authenticity of the respondents' replies. However, interviews and surveys are not without problems. One crucial limitation is that many individuals give answers that they think are socially acceptable and desirable, rather than say what they truly think or feel. For example, when asked whether they cheat on tests in school, some adolescents might say that they don't even though they do, because it is socially undesirable to cheat. Skilled interviewing techniques and questions that increase forthright responses are critical in obtaining accurate information.

Of the theories discussed in the first part of this chapter, psychoanalytic theory, Piaget's theory, and Vygotsky's theory all use interviews. The behavioral and social cognitive theories and ethological theory are the least likely to use interviews.

Standardized Tests

Standardized tests *are commercially prepared tests that assess performance in different domains. A standardized test often allows a child's performance to be compared with those of other children at the same age, in many cases on a national level.* Standardized tests can be given to children to assess their intelligence, achievement, personality, career interests, and other skills (Embretton & Hershberger, 1999; Nezami, 2000). These tests may be given for a variety of purposes, including outcome measures in research studies, information that helps psychologists make decisions about individual children, or comparisons of students' performance across schools, states, and countries. In chapter 9, "Intelligence," we will further explore standardized tests of intelligence. None of the theories discussed in the first part of this chapter emphasize the use of standardized tests.

standardized tests
Commercially prepared tests that assess performance in different domains. A standardized test often allows a child's performance to be compared with the performance of other children at the same age, in many cases on a national level.

Case Studies

A **case study** *is an in-depth look at an individual.* It often is used when unique aspects of a person's life cannot be duplicated, for either practical or ethical reasons. A case study provides information about an individual's fears, hopes, fantasies, traumatic experiences, upbringing, family relationships, health, and anything else that helps a psychologist understand that person's development. Some vivid case studies appear at different points in this text, among them one about a modern-day "wild child" named Genie, who lived in near isolation during her childhood.

Although case studies provide dramatic, in-depth portrayals of people's lives, we need to exercise caution when generalizing from this information. The subject of a case study is unique, with a genetic makeup and experiences no one else shares. In addition, case studies involve judgments of unknown reliability, in that usually no check is made to see if other psychologists agree with the observations. Of the

case study
An in-depth look at an individual.

theories discussed in first part of this chapter, psychoanalytic theory is most likely to advocate the use of case studies.

Correlational Research

correlational research
Research in which the goal is to describe the strength of the relation between two or more events or characteristics.

In **correlational research,** *the goal is to describe the strength of the relation between two or more events or characteristics.* Correlational research is useful because, the more strongly two events are correlated (related or associated), the more effectively we can predict one from the other. For example, if researchers find that low-involved, permissive parenting is correlated with a child's lack of self-control, it suggests that low-involved, permissive parenting might be one source of the lack of self-control.

A caution is in order, however. *Correlation does not equal causation.* The correlational finding just mentioned does not mean that permissive parenting necessarily causes low self-control in children. It could mean that, but it also could mean that a child's lack of self-control caused the parents to simply throw up their arms in despair and give up trying to control the child. It also could mean that other factors, such as heredity or poverty, caused the correlation between permissive parenting and low self-control in children. Figure 2.13 illustrates these possible interpretations of correlational data. Correlational research is used by all of the theoretical approaches described in the first part of this chapter.

Correlational Research

Experimental Research

experimental research
Research involving experiments that permit the determination of cause. A carefully regulated procedure in which one or more of the factors believed to influence the behavior being studied are manipulated and all other factors are held constant.

Experimental research *allows researchers to determine the causes of behavior. They accomplish this task by performing an experiment, a carefully regulated procedure in which one or more of the factors believed to influence the behavior being studied are manipulated and all other factors are held constant. If the behavior under study changes when a factor is manipulated, we say the manipulated factor* causes *the behavior to change.* "Cause" is the event being manipulated. "Effect" is the behavior that changes because of the manipulation. Experimental research is the only truly reliable method of establishing cause and effect. Because correlational research does not involve the manipulation of factors, it is not a dependable way to isolate cause.

Observed correlation

| As permissive parenting increases, children's self-control decreases. |

Possible explanations for this correlation

Permissive parenting	causes	Children's lack of self-control
Children's lack of self-control	causes	Permissive parenting
Other factors, such as genetic tendencies, poverty, and sociohistorical circumstances	cause both	Permissive parenting and Children's lack of self-control

Figure 2.13

Possible Explanations for Correlational Data

An observed correlation between two events cannot be used to conclude that one event caused the other. Some possibilities are that the second event caused the first event or that a third, unknown event caused the correlation between the first two events.

Experiments involve at least one independent variable and one dependent variable. The **independent variable** *is the manipulated, influential, experimental factor.* The label "independent" indicates that this variable can be changed independently of any other factors. For example, suppose we want to design an experiment to study the effects of peer tutoring on children's achievement. In this example, the amount and type of peer tutoring could be independent variables. The **dependent variable** *is the factor that is measured in an experiment. It can change as the independent variable is manipulated.* The label *dependent* is used because this variable depends on what happens to the participants in an experiment as the independent variable is manipulated. In the peer tutoring study, achievement is the dependent variable. This might be assessed in a number of ways. Let's say in this study it is measured by scores on a nationally standardized achievement test.

In experiments, the independent variable consists of differing experiences that are given to one or more experimental groups and one or more control groups. An *experimental group* is a group whose experience is manipulated. A *control group* is a group that is treated in every way like the experimental group except for the manipulated factor. The control group serves as the baseline against which the effects of the manipulated condition can be compared. In the peer tutoring study, we need to have one group of adolescents that gets peer tutoring (experimental group) and one that doesn't (control group).

Another important principle of experimental research is **random assignment,** *which involves assigning participants to experimental and control groups by chance.* This practice reduces the likelihood that the experiment's results will be due to any preexisting differences between the groups (Kirk, 2000). In our study of peer tutoring, random assignment greatly reduces the probability that the two groups will differ on such factors as age, family background, initial achievement, intelligence, personality, and health.

To summarize the study on peer tutoring and achievement, children are randomly assigned to one of two groups: one (the experimental group) is given peer tutoring; the other (control group) is not. The independent variables consist of the differing experiences that the experimental and control groups receive. After the peer tutoring is completed, the adolescents are given a nationally standardized achievement test (dependent variable). Figure 2.14 illustrates the experimental research method applied to a different problem: the effects of aerobic exercise by pregnant women on their newborns' breathing and sleeping patterns.

Of the theories described in the first part of this chapter, the behavioral and social cognitive approaches and the information-processing approach are most likely to advocate the use of experimental research.

Time Span of Research

Another research decision involves the time span of the research. There are several options—we can study individuals all at one time or we can study the same individuals over time.

Cross-sectional research *involves studying people all at one time.* For example, a researcher might be interested in studying the self-esteem of 8-, 12-, and 16-year-olds. In a cross-sectional study, the participants' self-esteem would be assessed at one time. The cross-sectional study's main advantage is that the researcher does not have to wait for the children to grow older. However, this approach provides no information about the stability of the children's and adolescents' self-esteem or how it might change over time.

Longitudinal research *involves studying the same individuals over a period of time, usually several years or more.* In a longitudinal study of self-esteem, the researcher might examine the self-esteem of a group of 8-year-old children, then assess their self-esteem again when they are 12, and then again when they are 16. One of the great values of longitudinal research is that we can evaluate how individual children and adolescents change as they get older. However, because longitudinal research is time consuming and costly, most research is cross-sectional.

independent variable
The manipulated, influential, experimental factor in an experiment.

dependent variable
The factor that is measured as the result of an experiment.

Experimental Research

random assignment
In experimental research, the assignment of participants to experimental and control groups by chance.

cross-sectional research
Research that studies people all at one time.

longitudinal research
Research that studies the same people over a period of time, usually several years or more.

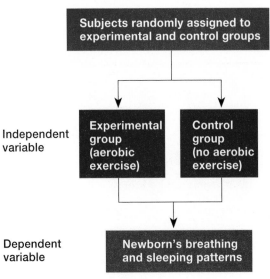

Figure 2.14

Principles of Experimental Strategy

The effects of aerobic exercise by pregnant women on their newborns' breathing and sleeping patterns.

RESEARCH METHOD	THEORY
Observation	• All theories emphasize some form of observation • Behavioral and social cognitive theories strongest emphasis on laboratory observation • Ethological theory strongest emphasis on naturalistic observation
Interview/Survey	• Psychoanalytic and cognitive (Piaget, Vygotsky) often use interviews • Behavioral and social cognitive, and ethological, theories are the least likely to use interview/survey
Standardized Test	• None of the theories discussed emphasize the use of this method
Case Study	• Psychoanalytic theories (Freud, Erikson) most likely to use this method
Correlational Research	• All of the theories use this research method, although psychoanalytic theories are the least likely to use it
Experimental Research	• The behavioral and social cognitive theories, and the information-processing approach, are most likely to use the experimental method • Psychoanalytic theories are the least likely to use it
Cross-Sectional/Longitudinal Research	• No theory described uses these methods more than any other

Figure **2.15**

Connections of Research Methods to Theories

Cross-sectional and longitudinal studies might be used by all of the theoretical approaches described in the first part of this chapter.

At the end of our discussion of each research method, we mentioned which theories were most or least likely to advocate the use of that particular method. Indeed, the particular research methods used by a researcher often are tied to the researcher's theoretical approach. A summary of the connections between research methods and theories is presented in figure 2.15.

At this point we have studied a number of ideas about research methods. A review of these ideas is presented in summary table 2.4. Next, we continue our exploration of research in child development by examining research journals and some research challenges.

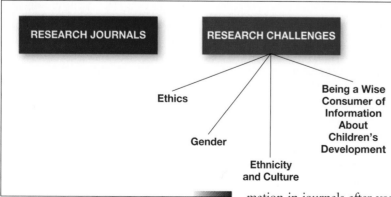

Research Journals

Regardless of whether you pursue a career in child development, education, psychology, nursing, or a related field, you can benefit by learning about research journals. Possibly as a student you will be required to look up original research in journals as part of writing a term paper. As a parent, teacher, or nurse you might want to consult journals to obtain information that will help you understand and work more effectively with children. And, as an inquiring person, you might want to look up information in journals after you have heard or read something that piqued your curiosity.

A *journal* publishes scholarly and academic information, usually in a specific domain, such as physics, math, sociology, or, in the case of our interest, child devel-

Summary Table 2.4
Research Methods

Concept	Processes/ Related Ideas	Characteristics/Description
Observation	Its Nature	• Observations need to be conducted systematically. • Observations can be made in laboratories or in naturalistic settings.
Interviews and Questionnaires	Their Nature	• Most interviews take place face-to-face. • Most questionnaires (surveys) are given to individuals in printed form to be filled out. • Social desirability and lying can be problematic for interviews and surveys.
Standardized Tests	Their Nature	• These are commercially prepared tests that assess performance in different domains.
Case Studies	Their Nature	• These are an in-depth look at an individual. • Generalizing from a case study to other persons is often not warranted.
Correlational Research	Its Nature	• The goal is to describe the relation between two or more events or characteristics. • Correlation does not equal causation.
Experimental Research	Its Nature	• This allows the determination of behavior's causes. • This research involves examining the influence of one at least one independent variable (the manipulated, influential, experimental factor) on one or more dependent variables (the measured factors). • Participants are randomly assigned to one or more experimental and one or more control groups.
Time Span of Research	Cross-Sectional	• Studying people all at one time.
	Longitudinal	• Studying the same people over time.

opment. Scholars in these fields publish most of their research in journals, which are the core information source in virtually every academic discipline.

Journal articles are usually written for other professionals in the same field as the journal's focus—such as geology, anthropology, or child development. Because the articles are written for other professionals, they often contain technical language and specialized terms related to a specific discipline that are difficult for nonprofessionals to understand. You have probably already had one or more courses in psychology, and you will be learning a great deal more about the specialized field of child development in this course, which should improve your ability to understand journal articles in this field.

An increasing number of journals publish information about children's development. Among the leading journals of child development are *Child Development, Developmental Psychology, Infant Behavior and Development, Pediatric Nursing, Pediatrics, Early Childhood Research Quarterly,* and *Journal of Research on Adolescence.* Also, a number of journals that do not focus solely on development include articles on children's development, such as *Journal of Educational Psychology, Sex Roles, Journal of Cross-Cultural Psychology, Journal of Marriage and the Family,* and *Journal of Consulting and Clinical Psychology.*

In psychology and the field of child development, most journal articles are reports of original research. Many journals also include review articles that present an overview of different studies on a particular topic, such as a review of day care, a review of the transition to elementary school, or a review of adolescent depression.

Many journals are highly selective about what they publish. Every journal has a board of experts that evaluates articles submitted for publication. One or more of the experts carefully examine the submitted paper and accept or reject it on such factors as its contribution to the field, its theoretical relevance, its methodological excellence, and its clarity of writing. Some of the most prestigious journals reject as many as 80 to 90 percent of the articles that are submitted because they fail to meet the journal's standards.

Where can you find research journals? Your college or university library likely has one or more of the journals listed. Some public libraries also carry journals. An increasing number of research journals can be accessed on the Internet.

An *abstract* is a brief summary that appears at the beginning of a journal article. The abstract lets readers quickly determine whether the article is relevant to their interests and if they want to read the entire article. The *introduction,* as its title suggests, introduces the problem or issue that is being studied. It includes a concise review of research relevant to the topic, theoretical ties, and one or more hypotheses to be tested. The *method* section consists of a clear description of the subjects evaluated in the study, the measures used, and the procedures followed. The method section should be sufficiently clear and detailed so that, by reading it, another researcher could repeat, or replicate, the study. The *results* section reports the analysis of the data collected. In most cases, the results section includes statistical analyses that are difficult for nonprofessionals to understand. The *discussion* section describes the author's conclusions, inferences, and interpretation of the findings. Statements are usually made about whether the hypotheses presented in the introduction were supported, the limitations of the study, and suggestions for future research. The last part of a journal article is called *references,* which lists bibliographic information for every source cited in the article. The references section is often a good source for finding other articles relevant to the topic you are interested in.

Research journals are the core of information in virtually every academic discipline. Those shown here are among the increasing number of research journals that publish information about child development. What are the main parts of a research article that presents findings from original research?

Child Development
Developmental Psychology
Ethics

Research Challenges

Research on children's development poses many challenges. These include ensuring that the research is ethical, taking into account gender and ethnicity, and developing a better understanding of the information derived from studies.

Ethics

Researchers must take steps to ensure the well-being of children participating in a study. Most colleges have review boards that evaluate whether the research is ethical.

The code of ethics adopted by the American Psychological Association (APA) instructs researchers to protect participants from mental and physical harm (Jones, 2000; Sieber, 2000). The best interests of the participants always must be kept foremost in the researcher's mind (Kimmel, 1996). All participants, if they are old enough (typically 7 years or older), must give their informed consent to participate. If they are not old enough, their parents' or guardians' consent must be obtained. Informed consent means that the participants (and/or their parents/legal guardians) have been told what their participation will entail and any risks that might be involved. For example, if researchers want to study the effects of conflict in divorced families on children's self-esteem, the participants should be informed that in some instances discussion of a family's experiences might improve family relationships, but in other cases might raise unwanted family stress. After informed consent is given, participants retain the right to withdraw at any time.

Gender

Traditionally, science has been presented as nonbiased and value-free. However, many experts on gender believe that psychological research often has entailed gender bias (Anselmi, 1998; Doyle & Paludi, 1998). They argue that for too long the female experience was subsumed under the male experience. For example, conclusions have been drawn routinely about females based on research conducted only with males.

Following are three broad questions that female scholars have raised regarding gender bias in psychological research (Tetreault, 1997):

- How might gender be a bias that influences the choice of theory, questions, hypotheses, participants, and research design?
- How might research on topics of primary interest to females, such as relationships, feelings, and empathy, challenge existing theory and research?
- How has research that heretofore has exaggerated gender differences between females and males influenced the way parents, teachers, and others think about and interact with female and male adolescents? For example, gender differences in mathematics often have been exaggerated and fueled by societal bias.

ADVENTURES FOR THE MIND

Isn't Everyone a Psychologist?

EACH OF US has theories about human behavior, and it is hard to imagine how we could get through life without them. In this sense, we are all psychologists. However, the theories of psychology that we carry around and the way we obtain support for our theories are often quite different from the way psychologists go about theorizing and collecting data about an issue or topic (Stanovich, 1998).

Look back over the various scientific theories that were described earlier in this chapter. Pick out one theory or part of a theory that surprised you or seemed different from one of your own current personal views (your own private psychology) about how children develop. Now think about your personal view. How did you arrive at it? Was there any personal bias involved? In what ways might it have resulted more from your own personal experiences, needs, or preferences, than from more objective observation?

Pick out another theory or part of a theory that immediately made sense and seemed right to you. Again, how did you arrive at your feeling that the theory is true? Is your feeling based mainly on personal experience? In what ways might scientific research be more reliable than your personal experience?

Ethnicity and Culture

More children from ethnic minority backgrounds need to be included in research (Graham, 1992). Historically, ethnic minority children essentially have been ignored in research or simply have been viewed as variations from the norm, or average. Their developmental and educational problems have been viewed as "confounds," or "noise" in data. Researchers have deliberately excluded these children from the samples they have selected to study (Ryan-Finn, Cauce, & Grove, 1995). Because ethnic minority children have been excluded from research for so long, there likely is more variation in children's real lives than research studies have indicated (Stevenson, 1995, 1998, in press).

Researchers also have tended to practice what is called "ethnic gloss" when they select and describe ethnic minority samples (Trimble, 1989). *Ethnic gloss* is using an ethnic label, such as African American or Latino, in a superficial way that makes an ethnic group look more homogeneous than it really is. For example, a researcher might describe a sample as "20 Latinos and 20 Anglo Americans," when a more precise description of the Latino group would need to state, "The 20 Latino participants were Mexican

Through the Eyes of Psychologists

Sandra Graham, *UCLA*

"Academic psychology cannot maintain its integrity by continuing to exclude ethnic minorities from mainstream research."

*T*hrough the Eyes of Psychologists

Keith Stanovich, *University of Toronto*

"Media presentations of psychology are just as misleading as they ever were."

Americans from low-income neighborhoods in the southwestern area of Los Angeles. Twelve were from homes in which Spanish is the dominant language spoken, 8 from homes in which English is the main spoken language. Ten were born in the United States, 10 in Mexico. Ten described themselves as Mexican American, 5 as Mexican, 3 as American, 2 as Chicano, and 1 as Latino." Ethnic gloss can cause researchers to obtain samples of ethnic groups that either are not representative or conceal the group's diversity, which can lead to overgeneralization and stereotyping.

Also, historically, when researchers have studied ethnic minority children, they have focused on the children's problems. It is important to study the problems, such as poverty, that many ethnic minority adolescents face, but it also is important to examine their strengths as well, such as their pride, self-esteem, improvised problem-solving skills, and extended family support systems. Fortunately, now, in the context of a more pluralistic view of our society, researchers are increasingly studying the positive dimensions of ethnic minority children (Swanson, 1997).

Being a Wise Consumer of Information About Children's Development

We live in a society that generates a vast amount of information about children in various media ranging from research journals to newspaper and television accounts. The information varies greatly in quality. How can you evaluate this information?

Be Cautious About What Is Reported in the Popular Media

Television, radio, newspapers, and magazines frequently report research on child development. Many researchers regularly supply the media with information about children. In some cases, this research has been published in professional journals or presented at national meetings and then is picked up by the popular media. And most colleges have a media relations department, which contacts the press about current faculty research.

However, not all research on children that appears in the media comes from professionals with excellent credentials and reputations. Journalists, television reporters, and other media personnel generally are not scientifically trained. It is not an easy task for them to sort through the avalanche of material they receive and to make sound decisions about which information to report.

Unfortunately, the media often tend to focus on sensational, dramatic findings. They want you to stay tuned or buy their publication. When the information they gather from research journals is not sensational, they may embellish it and sensationalize it, going beyond what the researcher intended.

Another problem with research reported in the media is a lack of time or space to go into important details about a study. They often have only a few lines or a few minutes to summarize as best they can what may be complex findings. Too often this means that what is reported is overgeneralized and stereotyped.

Don't Assume Group Research Applies to an Individual

Nomothetic research is research conducted at the level of the group. Most research on children is nomothetic research. Individual variations in how children behave is not a common focus. For example, if researchers are interested in the effects of divorce on children's self-esteem, they might conduct a study with 50 children from divorced families and 50 children from intact, never-divorced families. They might find that the children from divorced families, as a group, had lower self-esteem than did the children from intact families. That is a nomothetic finding that applies to children from divorced families as a group, and that is what is commonly reported in the media and in research journals. In this study, it likely was the case that some of the children from divorced families had higher school achievement than did the children from intact families—not as many, but some. Indeed, it is entirely possible that, of the 100 children in the study, the 2 or 3 children who had the highest school achievement were from divorced families, but that was never reported.

Nomothetic research provides valuable information about the characteristics of a group of children, revealing strengths and weaknesses of the group. However, in many instances, parents, teachers, and others want to know about how to help one particular child cope and learn more effectively. *Idiographic needs* are needs of an individual, not the group. Unfortunately, while nomothetic research can point up problems for certain groups of children, it does not always hold for an individual child.

Don't Overgeneralize About a Small or Clinical Sample

There often isn't space or time in media presentations to go into detail about the nature of the sample of the children on which a study was based. In many cases, samples are too small to let us generalize to a larger population. For example, if a study of children from divorced families is based on only 10 to 20 children, what is found in the study cannot be generalized to all children from divorced families. Perhaps the sample was drawn from families who have substantial economic resources, are Anglo-American, live in a small southern town, and are undergoing therapy. From this study, we clearly would be making unwarranted generalizations if we thought the findings also characterize children from low to moderate income families, are from other ethnic backgrounds, live in a different geographic region, and are not undergoing therapy.

Don't Generally Take a Single Study as the Defining Word

The media might identify an interesting research study and claim that it is something phenomenal with far-reaching implications. As a competent consumer of information, be aware that it is extremely rare for a single study to have earth-shattering, conclusive answers that apply to all children. In fact, where there are large numbers of studies that focus on a particular issue, it is not unusual to find conflicting results from one study to the next. Reliable answers about children's development usually emerge only after many researchers have conducted similar studies and have drawn similar conclusions. In our example of divorce, if one study reports that a counseling program for children from divorced families improved their self-esteem, we cannot conclude that the counseling program will work as effectively with all children from divorced families until many more studies have been conducted.

Don't Accept Causal Conclusions from Correlational Studies

Drawing causal conclusions from correlational studies is one of the most common mistakes made by the media. In nonexperimental studies (remember that, in an experiment, participants are randomly assigned to treatments or experiences), two variables or factors might be related to each other. However, causal conclusions cannot be drawn when two or more factors simply are correlated; we cannot say that one causes the other. In the case of divorce, the headline might read "Divorce Causes Children to Have Low Self-Esteem." We read the story and find out that the information is based on the results of a research study. Because obviously we cannot, for ethical and practical reasons, randomly assign children to families that either will become divorced or will remain intact, this headline is based on a correlational study, and the causal statements are unproved. It might well be, for example, that another factor, such as family conflict or economic problems, is typically responsible for both children's poor school performance and parents' divorce.

ADVENTURES FOR THE MIND

Reading and Analyzing Reports About Children's Development

INFORMATION ABOUT CHILDREN'S development appears in research journals and in magazines and newspapers. Choose one of the topics covered in this book and course—such as day care, adolescent problems, or parenting. Find an article in a research journal (for example, *Child Development* or *Developmental Psychology*) and an article in a newspaper or magazine on the same topic. How did the research article on the topic differ from the newspaper or magazine article? What did you learn from this comparison?

SUMMARY TABLE 2.5
Research Journals and Research Challenges

Concept	Processes/Related Ideas	Characteristics/Description
Research Journals	Their Nature	• A journal publishes scholarly and academic information, and an increasing number of journals publish information about child development. • Most journal articles are reports of original research. • Most research journal articles follow this format: abstract, introduction, methods, results, discussion, and references.
Research Challenges	Ethics	• Researchers recognize that a number of ethical concerns have to be met when conducting studies. • The best interests of the participants always have to be kept in mind.
	Gender	• Every effort should be made to make research equitable for both females and males. • In the past, research often was biased against females.
	Culture and Ethnicity	• We need to include more children from ethnic minority backgrounds in child development research. • A special concern is ethnic gloss.
	Being a Wise Consumer of Information About Child Development	• Be cautious about what is reported in the media. • Avoid assuming that group research applies to an individual. • Don't overgeneralize about a small or clinical sample. • Don't take a single study as the defining word. • Don't accept causal conclusions from correlational studies. • Always consider the source of the information and evaluate its credibility.

Always Consider the Source of the Information and Evaluate Its Credibility Studies are not automatically accepted by the research community. As discussed earlier in the chapter, researchers usually have to submit their findings to a research journal, where it is reviewed by their colleagues, who decide whether or not to publish the paper. Though the quality of research in journals is far from uniform, in most cases the quality of the research has undergone far more scrutiny and careful consideration than has research or other information that has not gone through the journal process. Within the media, we can distinguish between what is presented in respected newspapers and magazines, such as the *New York Times* and *Newsweek,* and what appears in much less respected tabloids, such as the *National Enquirer.*

At this point, we have discussed many ideas about research journals and research challenges. A review of these ideas is presented in summary table 2.5.

Chapter Review

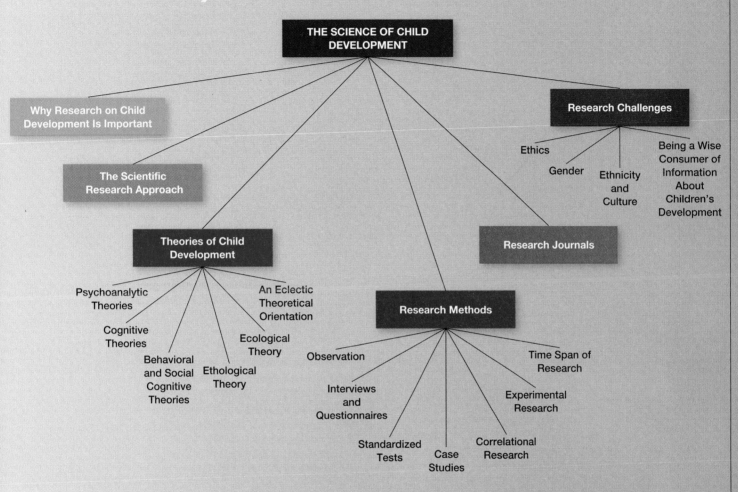

TO OBTAIN A DETAILED REVIEW OF THE CHAPTER, STUDY THESE FIVE SUMMARY TABLES:

- Summary Table 2.1   Why Research on Child Development is Important,   page 31
  and the Scientific Research Approach
- Summary Table 2.2   Psychoanalytic Theories and Cognitive Theories   page 39
- Summary Table 2.3   Behavioral and Social Cognitive Theories,   page 51
  Ethological Theories, Ecological Theories, and
  an Eclectic Theoretical Orientation
- Summary Table 2.4   Research Methods   page 57
- Summary Table 2.5   Research Journals and Research Challenges   page 62

Key Terms

scientific method 29
theory 29
hypotheses 29
psychoanalytic theory 31
Erikson's theory 33
Piaget's theory 35
Vygotsky's theory 36
information processing 38
classical conditioning 40

behaviorism 42
social cognitive theory 42
ethology 44
ecological theory 45
eclectic theoretical orientation 47
laboratory 52
naturalistic observation 52
standardized tests 53

case study 53
correlational research 54
experimental research 54
independent variable 55
dependent variable 55
random assignment 55
cross-sectional research 55
longitudinal research 55

Key People

Sigmund Freud 32
Erik Erikson 33
Jean Piaget 35
Lev Vygotsky 36
Ivan Pavlov 40

B. F. Skinner 42
Albert Bandura 42
Walter Mischel 42
Konrad Lorenz 44
Urie Bronfenbrenner 45

Glen Elder, Jr. 47
Sandra Graham 59
Keith Stanovich 59

Child Development Resources

Identity: Youth and Crisis (1968)
by Erik H. Erikson
New York: W. W. Norton

Erik Erikson was one of the leading theorists in the field of life-span development. In *Identity: Youth and Crisis,* he outlines his eight stages of life-span development and provides numerous examples from his clinical practice to illustrate the stages. Special attention is given to the fifth stage in Erikson's theory, identity versus identity confusion. Especially worthwhile are Erikson's commentaries about identity development in different cultures.

Observational Strategies of Child Study (1990)
by D. M. Irwin and M. M. Bushnell
Fort Worth, TX: Harcourt Brace

Being a good observer can benefit you a great deal in helping children reach their full potential. Observational skills can be learned. This practical book gives you a rich set of observational strategies that will help you become a more sensitive observer of children's behavior.

Taking It to the Net

1. Erika has never put much faith in Freud's theories, especially the one about the "Oedipus complex" and how it accounts for differences in male and female moral development. Her child development teacher challenged her to find out if there is any empirical evidence to back up Freud's claims.

2. Sean has to do a presentation in his psychology class on how ethological theories can be utilized to understand some aspects of child development. Sean found a report that compares and contrasts how and why nonhuman primates and human beings imitate others of their species.

3. For her senior psychology project, Doris wants to study the effect on self-esteem of mandatory school uniforms. She wants to limit her study to fourth-graders. She has located a school with a mandatory uniform policy and one without such a policy. What type of research design should she use?

Connect to *http://www.mhhe.com/santrockc9* to find the answers!

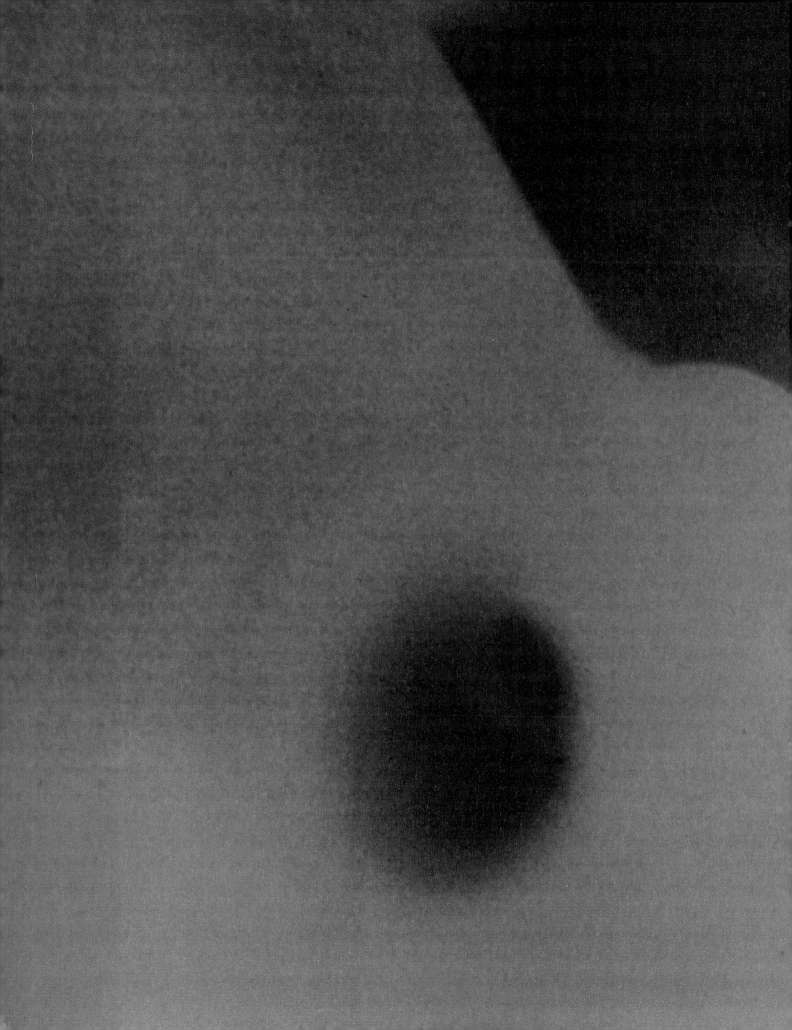

Biological Processes, Physical Development, and Perceptual Development

Section 2

What endless questions vex the thought, of whence and whither, when and how.

Sir Richard Burton
British Explorer, 19th Century

The rhythm and meaning of life involve beginnings. Questions are raised about how, from so simple a beginning, endless forms develop, grow, and mature. What was this organism, what is this organism, and what will this organism be? In Section 2, you will read four chapters: "Biological Beginnings" (chapter 3), "Prenatal Development and Birth" (chapter 4), "Physical Development in Infancy" (chapter 5), and "Physical Development in Childhood and Puberty" (chapter 6).

Chapter 3

```
                    BIOLOGICAL BEGINNINGS


    The Evolutionary                                    Heredity-Environment
    Perspective                                         Interaction


Natural          Evolutionary              Heredity-                    Conclusions
Selection        Psychology                Environment                 About
and Adaptive                               Correlations                Heredity-
Behavior                                                               Environment
                                                     Shared and        Interaction
                                                     Nonshared
                                                     Environmental
                                                     Experiences
           Heredity and                Genetic Principles,
           Reproduction                Methods, and Influences


What Are             Abnormalities          Genetic                 Heredity's
Genes?              in Genes and            Principles              Influence on
                    Chromosomes                        Methods      Development
      Reproduction                                     Used by
                    Adoption                           Behavior
                                                       Geneticists
```

There are one hundred and ninety-three living species of monkeys and apes. One hundred and ninety-two of them are covered with hair. The exception is the naked ape, self-named Homo sapiens.

Desmond Morris
British Zoologist, 20th Century

The Story of the Jim and Jim Twins

JIM SPRINGER AND JIM LEWIS are identical twins. They were separated at 4 weeks of age and did not see each other again until they were 39 years old. Both worked as part-time deputy sheriffs, vacationed in Florida, drove Chevrolets, had dogs named Toy, and married and divorced women named Betty. One twin named his son James Allan, and the other named his son James Alan. Both liked math but not spelling, enjoyed carpentry and mechanical drawing, chewed their fingernails down to the nubs, had almost identical drinking and smoking habits, had hemorrhoids, put on 10 pounds at about the same point in development, first suffered headaches at the age of 18, and had similar sleep patterns.

But Jim and Jim have some differences. One wears his hair over his forehead, the other slicks it back and has sideburns. One expresses himself best orally; the other is more proficient in writing. But, for the most part, their profiles are remarkably similar.

Another pair, Daphne and Barbara, are called the "giggle sisters" because, after being united, they were always making each other laugh. A thorough search of their adoptive families' histories revealed no gigglers. And the identical sisters handled stress by ignoring it, avoided conflict and controversy whenever possible, and showed no interest in politics.

Two other female identical twin sisters were separated at 6 weeks and reunited in their fifties. Both had nightmares, which they describe in hauntingly similar ways: both dreamed of doorknobs and fishhooks in their mouths as they smothered to death! The nightmares began during early adolescence and stopped in the past 10 to 12 years. Both women were bed wetters until about 12 or 13 years of age, and they report educational and marital histories that were remarkably similar.

Jim Jewis (left) and Jim Springer (right).

These sets of twins are part of the Minnesota Study of Twins Reared Apart, directed by Thomas Bouchard and his colleagues. The researchers bring identical twins (identical genetically because they come from the same fertilized egg) and fraternal twins (dissimilar genetically because they come from different fertilized eggs) from all over the world to Minneapolis to investigate their lives. The twins are given a number of personality tests, and detailed medical histories are obtained, including information about diet and smoking, exercise habits, chest X-rays, heart stress tests, and EEGs (brain-wave tests). The twins are interviewed and asked more than 15,000 questions about their family and childhood environment, personal interests, vocational orientation, values, and aesthetic judgments. They also are given ability and intelligence tests (Bouchard & others, 1990).

Critics of the Minnesota identical twins study point out that some of the separated twins were together several months prior to their adoption, that some of the twins had been reunited prior to their testing (in some cases, a number of years earlier), that adoption agencies often place twins in similar homes, and that even strangers who spend several hours together and start comparing their lives are likely to come up with some coincidental similarities (Adler, 1991). Still, even in the face of such criticism, the Minnesota study of identical twins indicates how scientists have recently shown an increased interest in the genetic basis of human development and that we need further research on genetic and environmental factors (Bouchard, 1995).

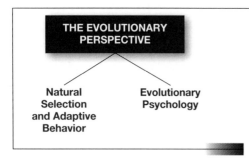

The Evolutionary Perspective

In evolutionary time, humans are relative newcomers to Earth, yet we have established ourselves as the most successful and dominant species. If we consider evolutionary time as a calendar year, humans arrived here in the last moments of December (Sagan, 1977). As our earliest ancestors left the forest to feed on the savannahs, and finally to form hunting societies on the open plains, their minds and behaviors changed. How did this evolution come about?

Natural Selection and Adaptive Behavior

Natural selection *is the evolutionary process that favors individuals of a species that are best adapted to survive and reproduce.* To understand natural selection, let's return to the middle of the nineteenth century, when Charles Darwin was traveling around the world, observing many different species of animals in their natural surroundings. Darwin, who published his observations and thoughts in *On the Origin of Species* (1859), observed that most organisms reproduce at rates that would cause enormous increases in the population of most species and yet populations remain nearly constant. He reasoned that an intense, constant struggle for food, water, and resources must occur among the many young born each generation, because many of the young do not survive. Those that do survive pass on their genes to the next generation. Darwin believed that those who do survive to reproduce are probably superior in a number of ways to those who do not. In other words, the survivors are better adapted to their world than are the nonsurvivors (Enger & others, 1996). Over the course of many generations, organisms with the characteristics needed for survival would comprise a larger percentage of the population. Over many, many generations, this could produce a gradual modification of the whole population. If environmental conditions change, however, other characteristics might become favored by natural selection, moving the process in a different direction (Zubay, 1996).

To understand the role of evolution in behavior we need to understand the concept of adaptive behavior (Crawford & Krebs, 1998; Knight, 1999). In evolutionary

natural selection
The evolutionary process that favors individuals of a species that are best adapted to survive and reproduce.

Evolution

Evolution and Behavior

Evolutionary Psychology

Handbook of Evolutionary Psychology

Evolutionary Psychology Resources

adaptive behavior
Behavior that promotes the organism's survival in its habitat.

evolutionary psychology
The theory that emphasizes the importance of adaptation, reproduction, and "survival of the fittest" in explaining behavior.

conceptions of psychology, **adaptive behavior** *is behavior that promotes an organism's survival in its habitat.* Adaptive behavior involves the organism's modification of its behavior to include its likelihood of survival. All organisms must adapt to particular places, climates, food sources, and ways of life. Natural selection designs adaptation to perform a certain function. An example of adaptation is an eagle's claws, designed by natural selection to facilitate predation. In the human realm, attachment is a system designed by natural selection to ensure an infant's closeness to the caregiver for feeding and protection from danger.

Evolutionary Psychology

Although Darwin introduced the theory of evolution by natural selection in 1859, his ideas about evolution only recently have emerged as a popular framework for explaining behavior. Psychology's newest approach, **evolutionary psychology,** *emphasizes the importance of adaptation, reproduction, and "survival of the fittest" in explaining behavior.* Evolution favors organisms that are best adapted to survive and reproduce in a particular environment. The evolutionary psychology approach focuses on conditions that allow individuals to survive or to fail (Geary & Bjorlund, 2000). In this view, the evolutionary process of natural selection favors behaviors that increase organisms' reproductive success and their ability to pass their genes to the next generation.

David Buss' (1995, 1998, 1999, 2000) ideas on evolutionary psychology have ushered in a whole new wave of interest in how evolution is involved in explaining human behavior. He believes that just as evolution shapes our physical features, such as body shape and height, it also pervasively influences how we make decisions, how aggressive we are, our fears, and our mating patterns.

Albert Bandura (1998), whose social cognitive theory was described in chapter 2, "The Science of Child Development," recently addressed the "biologizing" of psychology and evolution's role in social cognitive theory 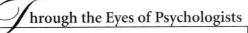 P.42. Bandura acknowledges the important influence of evolution on human adaptation and change. However, he rejects what he calls "one-sided evolutionism," according to which social behavior is the product of evolved biology. In the bidirectional view, evolutionary pressures created changes in biological structures for the use of tools, which enabled organisms to manipulate, alter, and construct new environmental conditions. Environmental innovations of increasing complexity, in turn, produced new selection pressures for the evolution of specialized biological systems for consciousness, thought, and language.

Human evolution gave us bodily structures and biological potentialities, yet it does not entirely dictate behaviors. Having evolved, advanced biological capacities can be used to produce diverse cultures—aggressive, pacific, egalitarian, or autocratic. As American scientist Steven Jay Gould (1981) concluded, in most domains of human functioning, biology allows a broad range of cultural possibilities. And Russian American Theodore Dobzhansky (1977) reminds us that the human species has been selected for the ability to learn and plasticity, allowing us to adapt to diverse contexts rather than being biologically fixed and inflexible in our behaviors. Bandura (1998) points out that the pace of social change gives testimony that biology does permit a range of possibilities.

At this point we have studied a number of ideas about the evolutionary perspective. A review of these ideas is presented in summary table 3.1. Next, we will continue our exploration of biological influences by examining heredity and reproduction.

Humans, more than any other mammal, adapt to and control most types of environments. Because of longer parental care, humans learn more complex behavior patterns, which contribute to adaptation.

Through the Eyes of Psychologists

David Buss, *University of Texas at Austin*

"In recent years there has been a scientific revolution in the form of evolutionary psychology. . . . Evolutionary psychology is not about genetic determination but is truly interactional because no behavior can be produced without input from evolved psychological mechanisms."

SUMMARY TABLE 3.1
The Evolutionary Perspective

Concept	Processes/Related Ideas	Characteristics/Description
Natural Selection and Adaptive Behavior	Natural Selection	• Natural selection is the process that favors the individuals of a species that are best adapted to survive and reproduce. • The process of natural selection was originally proposed by Charles Darwin.
	Adaptive Behavior	• In evolutionary theory, adaptive behavior is behavior that promotes the organism's survival in its habitat. • Biological evolution shaped human beings into a culture-making species.
Evolutionary Psychology	Its Nature	• This theory emphasizes the importance of adaptation, reproduction, and "survival of the fittest" in explaining behavior.
	Bandura's Evaluation	• Social cognitive theorist Albert Bandura acknowledges evolution's important role in human adaptation and change but argues for a bidirectional view according to which organisms alter and construct new environmental conditions.

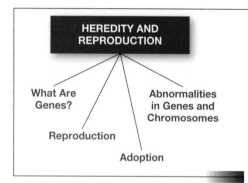

chromosomes
Threadlike structures that come in 23 pairs, one member of each pair coming from each parent. Chromosomes contain the genetic substance DNA.

DNA
A complex molecule that contains genetic information.

genes
Units of hereditary information composed of DNA. Genes act as a blueprint for cells to reproduce themselves and manufacture the proteins that maintain life.

mitosis
The process by which each chromosome in a cell's nucleus duplicates itself.

meiosis
The process of cell doubling and separation of chromosomes in which each pair of chromosomes in a cell separates, with one member of each pair going into each gamete.

Heredity and Reproduction

Every species must have a mechanism for transmitting characteristics from one generation to the next. This mechanism is explained by the principles of genetics. Each of us carries a genetic code that we inherited from our parents. This code is located within every cell in our bodies. Our genetic codes are alike in one important way—they all contain the human genetic code. Because of the human genetic code, a fertilized human egg cannot grow into an egret, eagle, or elephant.

What Are Genes?

Each of us began life as a single cell weighing about one twenty-millionth of an ounce! This tiny piece of matter housed our entire genetic code—information about who we would become. These instructions orchestrated growth from that single cell to a person made of trillions of cells, each containing a perfect replica of the original genetic code (Miller & Harley, 1996).

The nucleus of each human cell contains 46 **chromosomes,** *which are threadlike structures that come in 23 pairs, one member of each pair coming from each parent. Chromosomes contain the remarkable genetic substance deoxyribonucleic acid, or DNA.* **DNA** *is a complex molecule that contains genetic information.* DNA's "double helix" shape looks like a spiral staircase. **Genes,** *the units of hereditary information, are short segments composed of DNA. Genes act as a blueprint for cells to reproduce themselves and manufacture the proteins that maintain life.* Chromosomes, DNA, and genes can be mysterious. To help you turn mystery into understanding, see figure 3.1.

Mitosis *is the process by which each chromosome in the cell's nucleus duplicates itself.* The resulting 46 chromosomes move to the opposite sides of the cell, then the cell separates, and two new cells are formed with each now containing 46 chromosomes. Thus, the process of mitosis allows DNA to replicate itself.

Reproduction

A specialized division of chromosomes occurs during the formation of reproductive cells. **Meiosis** *is the process by which cells divide into gametes (human reproduction cells created in the testes of males and ovaries of females), which have half the genetic material of the parent cell.*

Figure 3.2 illustrates the basic transformations that occur during mitosis and meiosis. To understand the difference between mitosis and meiosis, remember:

- Meiosis only occurs for sexual reproduction, whereas mitosis is involved in cell growth and repair.
- In mitosis, the number of chromosomes present remains the same (the chromosomes copy themselves), whereas in meiosis the chromosomes are halved.
- Mitosis results in two daughter cells; meiosis produces four daughter cells.

Each human gamete has 23 unpaired chromosomes. The process of human **reproduction** *begins when a female gamete (ovum) is fertilized by a male gamete (sperm)* (see figure 3.3). A **zygote** *is a single cell formed through fertilization.* In the zygote, two sets of unpaired chromosomes combine to form one set of paired chromosomes—one member of each pair from the mother and the other member from the father. In this manner, each parent contributes 50 percent of the offspring's heredity.

An ovum is about 90,000 times as large as a sperm. Thousands of sperm must combine to break down the ovum's membrane barrier to allow even a single sperm to penetrate the membrane barrier. Ordinarily, females have two X chromosomes, and males have one X and one Y chromosome. Because the Y chromosome is smaller and lighter than the X chromosome, Y-bearing sperm can be separated from X-bearing sperm in a centrifuge. This raises the possibility that the offspring's sex can be controlled. Not only are the Y-bearing sperm lighter, but they are more likely than the X-bearing sperm to coat the ovum. This results in the conception of 120 to 150 males for every 100 females. However, males are more likely to die (spontaneously abort) at every stage of prenatal development, so only about 106 males are born for every 100 females.

Considerable interest has recently been generated by the findings reported by the Genetics and IVF Institute in Fairfax, Virginia (Fugger & others, 1998). The clinic reported a 93 percent success rate with the births of 13 girls from 14 pregnancies in which the goal was to have a girl, and a similar success rate when the goal was to have a boy. How did it achieve this? The clinic capitalized on the fact that sperm with a Y chromosome have about 2.8 percent less genetic material than sperm with an X chromosome. Based on this difference in the genetic material in X and Y chromosomes, the clinic sorted sperm and then artificially inseminated women with the sperm that had more genetic material in those cases in which parents wanted a girl. The first woman inseminated in this manner at the clinic wanted a daughter because the woman carried a gene for a rare disease that strikes boys almost exclusively.

The clinic has been criticized for its strategy of sperm sorting for selecting the sex of an offspring. Critics argue that the method should not be used for the family balancing of sex and that it interferes with nature's way of choosing sex with no medical benefit (Rosenwalks, 1998; Stillman, 1998). However, they acknowledge that it is appropriate to use when medical reasons are involved, as when there is a risk for a sex-linked disease, such as hemophilia. Critics also say the sample of 14 offspring is too small to determine whether the success rate will hold up over time. Also, since 1992 researchers have been able to remove a cell from an eight-cell pre-embryo created through in vitro fertilization (IVF) and determine its sex. Thus, for example, if parents are carriers of a genetic disease that affects boys, they can select a female pre-embryo for implantation. There is a cost differential in the sperm-sorting and IVF procedures: about $2,500 for sperm sorting and $10,000 for IVF.

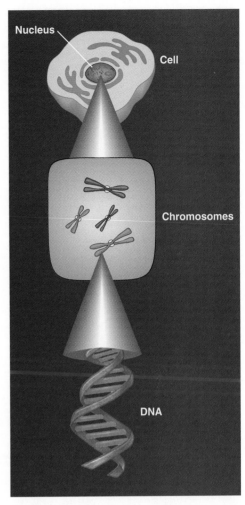

Figure 3.1
Cells, Chromosomes, Genes, and DNA

(Top) The body contains billions of cells, which are the basic structural units of life. Each cell contains a central structure, the nucleus. *(Middle)* Chromosomes and genes are located in the nucleus of the cell. Chromosomes are made up of threadlike structures composed mainly of DNA molecules. *(Bottom)* A gene, which is a segment of DNA that contains the hereditary code. The structure of DNA is a spiraled double chain of molecules.

reproduction
The process that, in humans, begins when a female gamete (ovum) is fertilized by a male gamete (sperm).

zygote
A single cell formed through fertilization.

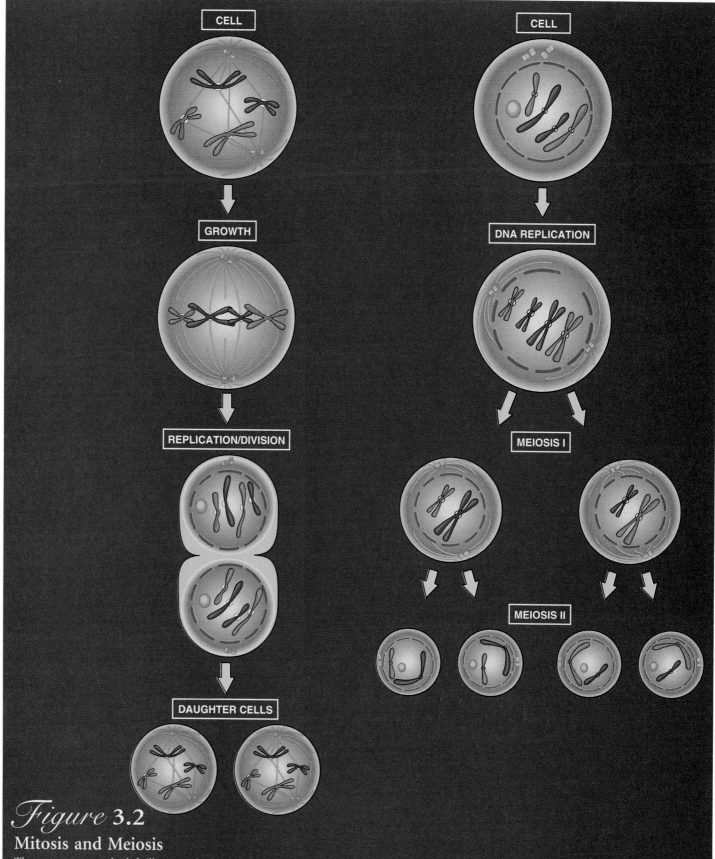

Figure 3.2
Mitosis and Meiosis

The sequences on the left illustrate the basic transformations that take place in mitosis, those on the right that take place in meiosis. In mitosis, the cell's nucleus duplicates itself. Notice in the third drawing from the top, on the left, how the chromosomes have moved to opposite sides and then in the fourth drawing how the cell has separated to form two daughter cells. In the meiosis transformations shown on the right side of the page, during meiosis I the chromosome pairs separate. During meiosis II, four daughter cells are formed. Note that the blue chromosomes were inherited from one parent, the red chromosomes from the other parent.

Infertility is another challenge involving reproduction. Approximately 10 to 15 percent of couples in the United States experience infertility, which is defined as the inability to conceive a child after 12 months of regular intercourse without contraception. The cause of infertility can rest with the woman or the man. The woman might not be ovulating, she may be producing abnormal ova, her fallopian tubes may be blocked, or she may have a disease that prevents implantation of the ova. The man may produce too few sperm, the sperm might lack motility (the ability to move adequately), or he may have a blocked passageway. In one study, long-term use of cocaine by men was related to low sperm count, low motility, and a higher number of abnormally formed sperm (Bracken & others, 1990). Cocaine-related infertility appears to be reversible if users stop taking the drug for at least one year. In some cases of infertility, surgery may correct the problem; in others, hormonal-based drugs can improve the probability of having a child. However, in some instances, fertility drugs have caused superovulation, producing three or more babies at a time. A summary of some of infertility's causes and solutions is presented in figure 3.4.

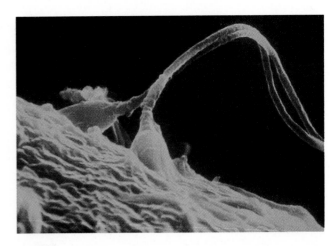

Figure **3.3**
Union of Sperm and Egg

Infertility Resources

Men		
Problem	**Possible Causes**	**Treatment**
Low sperm count	Hormone imbalance, varicose vein in scrotum, possibly environmental pollutants	Hormone therapy, surgery, avoiding excessive heat
	Drugs (cocaine, marijuana, lead, arsenic, some steroids and antibiotics)	
	Y chromosome gene deletions	
Immobile sperm	Abnormal sperm shape Infection Malfunctioning prostate	None Antibiotics Hormones
Antibodies against sperm	Problem in immune system	Drugs
Women		
Problem	**Possible Causes**	**Treatment**
Ovulation problems	Pituitary or ovarian tumor Underactive thyroid	Surgery Drugs
Antisperm secretions	Unknown	Acid or alkaline douche, estrogen therapy
Blocked fallopian tubes	Infection caused by IUD or abortion or by sexually transmitted disease	Surgical incision, cells removed from ovary and placed in uterus
Endometriosis (Tissue buildup in uterus)	Delayed parenthood until the thirties	Hormones, surgical incision

Figure **3.4**
Fertility Problems, Possible Causes, and Treatments

Figure 3.5

In Vitro Fertilization

Egg meets sperm in a laboratory dish.

In the United States, more than 2 million couples seek help for infertility every year. Of those, about 40,000 try high-tech assisted reproduction. The following are the five most common techniques:

- *In vitro fertilization (IVF)*. An egg and a sperm are combined in a laboratory dish. If the egg is fertilized, the resulting embryo is transferred into the woman's uterus (see figure 3.5). The success rate is just under 20 percent.
- *Gamete intrafallopian transfer (GIFT)*. A doctor inserts eggs and sperm directly into a woman's fallopian tube. The success rate is almost 30 percent.
- *Intrauterine insemination (IUI)*. Frozen sperm—that of the husband or another donor—is placed directly into the uterus, bypassing the cervix and upper vagina. The success rate is 10 percent.
- *Zygote intrafallopian transfer (ZIFT)*. This involves a two-step procedure. First, eggs are fertilized in the laboratory. Then, any resulting zygotes are transferred to a fallopian tube. The success rate is approximately 25 percent.
- *Intracytoplasmic sperm injection (ICSI)*. A doctor uses a microscopic pipette to inject a single sperm from a man's ejaculate into an egg. The zygote is returned to the uterus. The success rate is approximately 25 percent.

The creation of families by means of the new reproductive technologies raises important questions about the psychological consequences for children. In one study, the family relationship and socioemotional development of children were investigated in four types of families—two created by the most widely used reproductive technologies (in vitro fertilization and donor insemination) and two control groups (families with a naturally conceived child and adoptive families) (Golombok & others, 1995). There were no differences between the four types of families on any of the measures of children's socioemotional development. The picture of families created by the new reproductive technologies was a positive one.

One consequence of fertility treatments is an increase in multiple births. Twenty-five to 30 percent of pregnancies achieved by fertility treatments—including in vitro fertilization—now result in multiple births. While parents may be thrilled at the prospect of having children, they also face serious risks. Any multiple birth increases the likelihood that the babies will have life-threatening and costly problems, such as extremely low birthweight.

Adoption

Although surgery and fertility drugs can solve the infertility problem in some cases, another choice is to adopt a child (Gibbs, 2000). Adoption is the social and legal process by which a parent-child relationship is established between persons unrelated at birth. Researchers have found that adopted children and adolescents often show more psychological and school-related problems than nonadopted children (Brodzinsky & others, 1984; Brodzinsky, Lang, & Smith, 1995). Adopted adolescents are referred to psychological treatment two to five times as often as their nonadopted peers (Grotevant & McRoy, 1990).

In one large-scale study of 4,682 adopted adolescents and the same number of nonadopted adolescents, adoptees showed slightly lower levels of adjustment (Sharma, McGue, & Benson, 1996). However, adoptees actually showed higher levels of

The McCaughey septuplets, born in 1998. The increasing use of fertility drugs is producing greater numbers of multiple births.

prosocial behavior. Also, the later adoption occurred, the more problems the adoptees had. Infant adoptees had the fewest adjustment difficulties; those adopted after they were 10 years of age the most.

This result has policy implications, especially for the thousands of children who are relegated to the foster care system after infancy. Most often, older children are put up for adoption due to parental abuse or neglect. The process of terminating the birth parents' parental rights can be lengthy. In the absence of other relatives, children are turned over to the foster care system, where they must wait for months or even years to be adopted. In the recent large-scale adoption study by Ann Sharma, Matthew McGue, and Peter Bensen (1996), increasingly negative effects occurred if a child was adopted above the age of 2, but the effects were even more deleterious when adoption took place after the age of 10.

A question that virtually every adoptive parent wants answered is, "Should I tell my adopted child that he or she is adopted? If so, when?" Most psychologists believe that adopted children should be told that they are adopted, because they will eventually find out anyway. Many children begin to ask where they came from when they are approximately 4 to 6 years of age. This is a natural time to begin to respond in simple ways to children about their adopted status. Clinical psychologists report that one problem that sometimes surfaces is the desire of adoptive parents to make life too perfect for the adoptive child and to present a perfect image of themselves to the child. The result too often is that adopted children feel that they cannot release any angry feelings and openly discuss problems in this climate of perfection (Warshak, 1997).

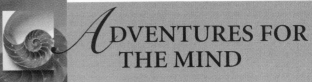

ADVENTURES FOR THE MIND

Who Am I? Identity and Adoption

MOST ADOPTIVE PARENTS are given little information about the child's birth parents or family history at the time of adoption. In turn, the birth parents are given little information about the adoptive parents (Brodzinsky, Schechter, & Henig, 1992). This strategy—followed by most adoption agencies—is thought to be in the best interest of both parties. A number of activist groups, such as the Adoptees Liberty Movement Association and Concerned United Birthmothers, challenge this strategy. These groups stress that sealing records at the time of adoption violates people's basic rights to know about themselves (and their offspring, in the case of the Concerned United Birthmothers). They also argue that sealing records about one's identity can set the stage for potential difficulties related to the adoption experience.

Develop an argument that sealing records and giving little information at the time of adoption is a wise strategy. Now argue the opposite side of this issue.

Abnormalities in Genes and Chromosomes

What are some abnormalities that can occur in genes and chromosomes? What tests can be used to determine the presence of these abnormalities?

Types of Abnormalities   Geneticists and developmentalists have identified a range of problems caused by major gene or chromosome defects (Baum, 2000). **Phenylketonuria (PKU)** *is a genetic disorder in which the individual cannot properly metabolize an amino acid. Phenylketonuria is now easily detected, but, if left untreated, mental retardation and hyperactivity result.* The disorder is treated by diet to prevent an excess accumulation of phenylalanine, an amino acid. Phenylketonuria involves a recessive gene and occurs about once in every 10,000 to 20,000 live births. Phenylketonuria accounts for about 1 percent of institutionalized mentally retarded individuals, and it occurs primarily in Whites.

Down syndrome *is a common genetically transmitted form of mental retardation, caused by the presence of an extra (47th) chromosome.* An individual with Down syndrome has a round face, a flattened skull, an extra fold of skin over the eyelids, a protruding tongue, short limbs, and retardation of motor and mental abilities. It is not known why the extra chromosome is present, but the health of the male sperm or female ovum may be involved (MacLean, 2000). Women between the ages of 18 and 38 are less likely to give birth to a child with Down syndrome than are younger or older women. Down syndrome appears approximately once in every 700 live births. African American children are rarely born with Down syndrome. Some individuals have developed special programs to help children with Down syndrome. One such individual is Janet Marchese, adoptive mother of a baby with Down syndrome. She began putting the parents of children with Down syndrome together with couples who wanted to adopt them. Her adoption network has placed

Genetic Disorders

Prenatal Testing and Down Syndrome

Genetic Counseling

phenylketonuria (PKU)
A genetic disorder in which an individual cannot properly metabolize an amino acid. PKU is now easily detected but, if left untreated, results in mental retardation and hyperactivity.

Down syndrome
A common genetically transmitted form of mental retardation, caused by the presence of an extra (47th) chromosome.

These athletes, many of whom have Down syndrome, are participating in a Special Olympics competition. Notice the distinctive facial features of the individuals with Down syndrome, such as round face and a flattened skull. Down syndrome is caused by the presence of an extra (47th) chromosome.

Figure **3.6**

Sickle-Cell Anemia

During a physical examination for a college football tryout, Jerry Hubbard, 32, learned that he carried the gene for sickle-cell anemia. Daughter Sara is healthy but daughter Avery (in the print dress) has sickle-cell anemia. The couple says that they won't try to have any more children.

sickle-cell anemia
A genetic disorder that affects the red blood cells and occurs most often in people of African descent.

Klinefelter syndrome
A genetic disorder in which males have an extra X chromosome, making them XXY instead of XY.

fragile X syndrome
A genetic disorder that results from an abnormality in the X chromosome, which becomes constricted and often breaks.

Turner syndrome
A genetic disorder in which females are missing an X chromosome, making them XO instead of XX.

XYY syndrome
A genetic disorder in which males have an extra Y chromosome.

more than 1,500 children with Down syndrome and has a waiting list of couples who want to adopt.

Sickle-cell anemia, *which occurs most often in people of African descent, is a genetic disorder affecting the red blood cells.* A red blood cell is usually shaped like a disk, but in sickle-cell anemia a change in a recessive gene modifies its shape to a hook-shaped "sickle." These cells die quickly, causing anemia and early death of the individual because of their failure to carry oxygen to the body's cells. About 1 in 400 African American babies is affected. One in 10 African Americans is a carrier, as is 1 in 20 Latinos (see figure 3.6).

Other disorders are associated with sex-chromosome abnormalities. Remember that normal males have an X chromosome and a Y chromosome, and normal females have two X chromosomes. **Klinefelter syndrome** *is a genetic disorder in which males have an extra X chromosome, making them XXY instead of XY.* Males with this disorder have undeveloped testes, and they usually have enlarged breasts and become tall. Klinefelter syndrome occurs approximately once in every 800 live male births.

Fragile X syndrome *is a genetic disorder that results from an abnormality in the X chromosome, which becomes constricted and often breaks.* Mental deficiency often is an outcome, but its form can vary considerably (mental retardation, learning disability, short attention span) (Lewis, 1999). This disorder occurs more frequently in males than in females; it is possible that the second X chromosome in females negates the disorder's negative effects (see figure 3.7).

Turner syndrome *is a genetic disorder in which females are missing an X chromosome, making them XO instead of XX.* These females are short in stature and have a webbed neck. They may be mentally retarded and sexually underdeveloped. Turner syndrome occurs approximately once in every 3,000 live female births.

XYY syndrome *is a genetic disorder in which the male has an extra Y chromosome. Early interest in this syndrome involved the belief that the Y chromosome found in males contributed to male aggression and violence.* It was then reasoned that if a male had an extra Y chromosome he would likely be extremely aggressive and possibly develop a violent personality. However, researchers subsequently found that XYY males are no more likely to commit crimes than are XY males (Witkin & others, 1976).

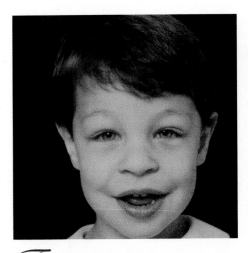
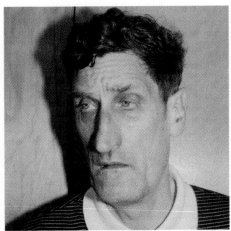

Figure 3.7
Fragile X Syndrome
A male child and a male adult with fragile X syndrome. The characteristic facial structure and features (a very long, narrow face and protruding ears) become more pronounced with age in this disorder. Children with the disorder do not show these characteristics.

We have discussed a number of genetic disorders. A summary of many of these as well as others is presented in figure 3.8 on page 80.

Each year in the United States, 100,000 to 150,000 infants are born with a genetic disorder or malformation. These infants comprise about 3 to 5 percent of the 3 million births and account for at least 20 percent of infant deaths. Prospective parents increasingly are turning to genetic counseling for assistance, wanting to know their risk of having a child born with a genetic defect or malformation. To read further about genetic counseling, see Explorations in Child Development on page 81.

The Human Genome Project (a *genome* is a complete set of genes), begun in the late 1970s, has as its goal the construction of the first detailed map of every human gene. Genetic engineers hope to use the knowledge derived from the project to reverse the course of many natural diseases (Olson, 1999; Sheffield, 1999). Recently, they isolated the genes for Huntington's disease, Lou Gehrig's disease, the so-called bubble-boy disease, and a common form of colon cancer, among others.

Human Genome Project
Genetics and Ethics

Tests to Determine Abnormalities
Scientists have developed a number of tests to determine whether a fetus is developing normally, among them amniocentesis, ultrasound sonography, the chorionic villus test, and the maternal blood test, each of which we discuss in turn.

Amniocentesis *is a prenatal medical procedure in which a sample of amniotic fluid is withdrawn by syringe and tested to discover if the fetus is suffering from any chromosomal or metabolic disorders. Amniocentesis is performed between the 12th and 16th weeks of pregnancy.* The later amniocentesis is performed, the better its diagnostic potential. The earlier it is performed, the more useful it is in deciding whether a pregnancy should be terminated.

Ultrasound sonography *is a prenatal medical procedure in which high-frequency sound waves are directed into the pregnant woman's abdomen.* The echo from the sounds is transformed into a visual representation of the fetus's inner structures. This technique has been able to detect such disorders as microencephaly, a form of mental retardation involving an abnormally small brain. Ultrasound sonography is often used in conjunction with amniocentesis to determine the precise location of the fetus in the mother's abdomen (see figure 3.9 on page 82).

amniocentesis
A prenatal medical procedure in which a sample of amniotic fluid is withdrawn by syringe and tested to discover if the fetus is suffering from any chromosomal or metabolic disorders. It is performed between the 12th and 16th weeks of pregnancy.

ultrasound sonography
A prenatal medical procedure in which high-frequency sound waves are directed into the pregnant woman's abdomen.

Name	Description	Treatment/ Prognosis	Incidence	Prenatal detection	Carrier detection
Cystic fibrosis	Glandular dysfunction that interferes with mucus production; breathing and digestion are hampered, resulting in a shortened life span.	Physical and oxygen therapy, synthetic enzymes, and antibiotics	1 in 2,000	Amniocentesis	Family history, DNA analysis
Diabetes	Body does not produce enough insulin, which causes abnormal metabolism of sugar.	Early onset can be fatal unless treated with insulin	1 in 2,500 births	No	No
Down syndrome	Extra or altered 21st chromosome causes mild to severe retardation and physical abnormalities.	Surgery, early intervention, infant stimulation, and special learning programs	1 in 800 women, 1 in 350 women over 35	AFP, CVS, amniocentesis	Family history, chromosomal analysis
Hemophilia	Lack of the clotting factor causes excessive internal and external bleeding.	Blood transfusions and/or injections of the clotting factor	1 in 10,000 males	CVS, amniocentesis	Family history, DNA analysis
Klinefelter syndrome	An extra X chromosome causes physical abnormalities.	Hormone therapy	1 in 800 males	CVS, amniocentesis	None
Phenylketonuria (PKU)	Metabolic disorder that, left untreated, causes mental retardation.	Special diet	1 in 14,000	CVS, amniocentesis	Family history, blood test
Sickle-cell anemia	Blood disorder that limits the body's oxygen supply; it can cause joint swelling, sickle-cell crises, heart and kidney failure.	Penicillin, medication for pain, antibiotics, and blood transfusions	1 in 400 African American children (lower among other groups)	CVS, amniocentesis	Blood test
Spina bifida	Neural-tube disorder that causes brain and spine abnormalities.	Corrective surgery, orthopedic devices, and physical/medical therapy	2 in 1,000	AFP, ultrasound, amniocentesis	None
Tay-Sachs disease	Deceleration of mental and physical development caused by an accumulation of lipids in the nervous system; few children live to age 5.	Medication and special diet	One in 30 American Jews is a carrier.	CVS, amniocentesis	Blood test

Figure 3.8
Genetic Disorders and Conditions

chorionic villi sampling
A prenatal medical procedure in which a small sample of the placenta is removed at a certain point in the pregnancy between the 8th and the 11th weeks of pregnancy.

As scientists have searched for more accurate, safer assessments of high-risk prenatal conditions, they have developed a new test. **Chorionic villi sampling** *is a prenatal medical procedure in which a small sample of the placenta is removed at some point between the 8th and 11th weeks of pregnancy.* Diagnosis takes approximately 10 days. Chorionic villi sampling allows a decision about abortion to be made near the end of the first trimester of pregnancy, a point when abortion is safer and less traumatic than after amniocentesis in the second trimester. These techniques provide valuable information about the presence of birth defects, but they also raise issues pertaining to whether an abortion should be obtained if birth defects are present. Figure 3.10 (on page 82) shows how the procedures of amniocentesis and chorionic villi sampling are carried out.

EXPLORATIONS IN CHILD DEVELOPMENT
Genetic Counseling

IN 1978, RICHARD DAVIDSON was an athletic 37-year-old. A slip on an icy driveway landed him in the hospital for minor surgery for a broken foot. The day after the operation, he died. The cause was malignant hyperthermia (MH), a fatal allergylike reaction to certain anesthetics. The condition is hereditary and preventable—if the anesthesiologist is aware of the patient's susceptibility, alternative drugs can be used. Richard's death inspired his parents, Owen and Jean Davidson, to search their family tree for others with the MH trait. They mailed 300 letters to relatives, telling them of their son's death and warning about the hereditary risk. The gene, it turned out, came from Jean's side of the family. When her niece, Suellen Gallamore, informed the hospital where she going to have infertility surgery about the MH in her bloodline, the doctors refused to treat her. In 1981, she cofounded the Malignant Hyperthermia Association to educate medical providers about MH, so that people at risk, like her sons, would not suffer as she had—or lose their lives, as her cousin had (Adato, 1995).

Consider also Bob and Mary Sims, who have been married for several years. They would like to start a family, but they are frightened. The newspapers and popular magazines are full of stories about infants who are born prematurely and don't survive, infants with debilitating physical defects, and babies found to have congenital mental retardation. The Simses feel that to have such a child would create a social, economic, and psychological strain on them and on society.

Accordingly, the Simses turn to a genetic counselor for help. Genetic counselors are usually physicians or biologists who are well versed in the field of medical genetics. They are familiar with the kinds of problems that can be inherited, the odds for encountering them, and helpful measures for offsetting some of their effects. The Simses tell their counselor that there has been a history of mental retardation in Bob's family. Bob's younger sister was born with Down syndrome, a form of mental retardation. Mary's older brother has hemophilia, a condition in which bleeding is difficult to stop. They wonder what the chances are that a child of theirs might also be retarded or have hemophilia and what measures they can take to reduce their chances of having a mentally or physically defective child.

The counselor probes more deeply, because she understands that these facts in isolation do not give her a complete picture of the possibilities. She learns that no other relatives in Bob's family are retarded and that Bob's mother was in her late forties when his younger sister was born. She concludes that the retardation was probably due to the age of Bob's mother and not to some general tendency for members of his family to inherit retardation. It is well known that women over 40 have a much higher probability of giving birth to retarded children than are younger women. Apparently, in women over 40 the ova (egg cells) are not as healthy as in women under 40.

In Mary's case, the counselor determines that there is a small but clear possibility that Mary might be a carrier of hemophilia and might transmit that condition to a son. Otherwise, the counselor can find no evidence from the family history to indicate genetic problems.

The decision is then up to the Simses. In this case, the genetic problem will probably not occur, so the choice is fairly easy. But what should parents do if they face the strong probability of having a child with a major birth defect? Ultimately, the decision depends on the couple's ethical and religious beliefs (Wilfond, 1999).

Suellen Gallamore with her sons, Scott and Greg Vincent. Among her immediate family, only Suellen has had the painful muscle biopsy for the MH gene. Scott, 24, and Greg, 26, assume that they carry the gene and protect against MH by alerting doctors about their family's medical history.

Amniocentesis

Obstetric Ultrasound

Chorionic Villi Sampling

Figure **3.9**

Ultrasound Sonography

A 6-month-old infant poses with the ultrasound sonography record taken 4 months into the baby's prenatal development.

Figure **3.10**

Amniocentesis and Chorionic Villi Sampling

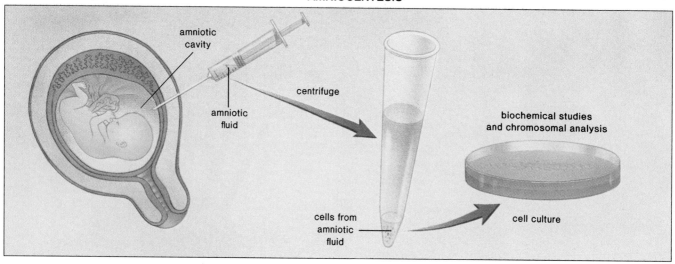

AMNIOCENTESIS

amniotic cavity

amniotic fluid

centrifuge

biochemical studies and chromosomal analysis

cells from amniotic fluid

cell culture

CHORIONIC VILLI SAMPLING

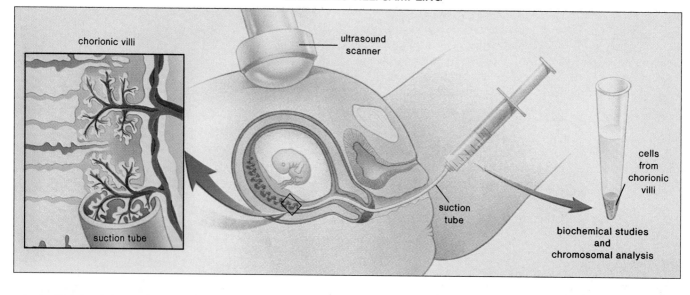

chorionic villi

ultrasound scanner

suction tube

cells from chorionic villi

suction tube

biochemical studies and chromosomal analysis

SUMMARY TABLE 3.2
Heredity and Reproduction

Concept	Processes/ Related Ideas	Characteristics/Description
What Are Genes?	Their Nature	• The nucleus of each human cell contains 46 chromosomes, which are composed of DNA. • Genes are short segments of DNA that act as a blueprint for cells to reproduce and manufacture proteins that maintain life. • Mitosis is the process by which chromosomes duplicate themselves.
Reproduction	Gene Transmission and Gametes	• Genes are transmitted from parents to offspring by gametes, or sex cells. • Gametes are formed by the splitting of cells in the process called meiosis. • Reproduction takes place when a female gamete (ovum) is fertilized by male gamete (sperm) to create a single-celled ovum.
	Infertility	• High-tech assisted reproduction has helped solve some infertility problems. • Approximately 10 to 15 percent of U.S. couples have infertility problems, some of which can be corrected through surgery or fertility drugs.
Adoption	Outcomes	• Adopted children and adolescents have more problems than their nonadopted counterparts. • When adoption occurs after the age of 10, it has more negative effects than when it happens in infancy.
Abnormalities in Genes and Chromosomes	Types of Abnormalities	• Among problems caused by gene or chromosome gene defects are PKU, Down syndrome, sickle-cell anemia, Klinefelter syndrome, fragile X syndrome, Turner syndrome, and XYY syndrome.
	Tests to Determine Abnormalities	• Genetic counseling has increased in popularity as couples desire information about their risk of having a child with genetic defects. • Amniocentesis, ultrasound sonography, chorionic villi sampling, and the maternal blood test are used to determine the presence of defects once pregnancy has begun.

The **maternal blood test** *(alpha-fetoprotein—AFP) is a prenatal diagnostic technique that is used to assess blood alphaprotein level, which is associated with neural-tube defects.* This test is administered to women 14 to 20 weeks into pregnancy only when they are at risk for bearing a child with defects in the formation of the brain and spinal cord.

At this point we have discussed a number of ideas about heredity and reproduction. A review of these ideas is presented in summary table 3.2. Next, we will continue our examination of heredity by exploring genetic principles, methods, and influences on behavior.

maternal blood test
A prenatal diagnostic technique that is used to assess blood alphaprotein level, which is associated with neural-tube defects. This technique is also called the alpha-fetoprotein test (AFP).

Genetic Principles, Methods, and Influences

Behavior geneticists study heredity's influence on behavior. What are some of the methods they use? How does heredity influence such aspects of children's development as their intelligence? How do heredity and environment interact to influence children's development?

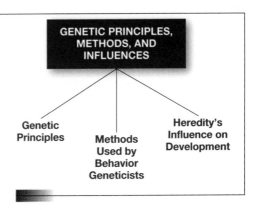

GENETIC PRINCIPLES, METHODS, AND INFLUENCES

Genetic Principles

Methods Used by Behavior Geneticists

Heredity's Influence on Development

Genetic Principles

Genetic determination is a complex affair, and much is unknown about the way genes work (Lewis, 1999). But a number of genetic principles have been discovered, among them those of dominant-recessive genes, sex-linked genes, polygenically inherited characteristics, reaction range, and canalization.

According to the **dominant-recessive genes principle,** *if one gene of a pair is dominant and one is recessive, the dominant gene exerts its effect, overriding the potential influence of the other, recessive gene. A recessive gene exerts its influence only if the two genes of a pair are both recessive.* If you inherit a recessive gene for a trait from each of your parents, you will show the trait. If you inherit a recessive gene from only one parent, you may never know you carry the gene. Brown eyes, farsightedness, and dimples rule over blue eyes, nearsightedness, and freckles in the world of dominant-recessive genes. Can two brown-eyed parents have a blue-eyed child? Yes, they can. Suppose that in each parent the gene pair that governs eye color includes a dominant gene for brown eyes and a recessive gene for blue eyes. Since dominant genes override recessive genes, the parents have brown eyes. But both are carriers of blueness and pass on their recessive genes for blue eyes. With no dominant gene to override them, the recessive genes can make the child's eyes blue. Figure 3.11 illustrates the dominant-recessive genes principles.

For thousands of years, people wondered what determined whether we become male or female. Aristotle believed that the father's arousal during intercourse determines the offspring's sex. The more excited the father was, the more likely it would be a son, he reasoned. Of course, he was wrong, but it was not until the 1920s that researchers confirmed the existence of human sex chromosomes, 2 of the 46 chromosomes human beings normally carry. As we saw earlier, ordinarily females have two X chromosomes, and males have an X and a Y. (Figure 3.12 shows the chromosomal makeup of a male and a female.)

Genetic transmission is usually more complex than the simple examples we have examined thus far (Hohnen & Stevenson, 1999; Weaver & Hedrick, 1999). **Polygenic inheritance** *is the genetic principle that many genes can interact to produce a particu-*

dominant-recessive genes principle
If one gene of a pair is dominant and one is recessive (goes back or recedes), the dominant gene exerts its effect, overriding the potential influence of the recessive gene. A recessive gene exerts its influence only if both genes in a pair are recessive.

polygenic inheritance
The genetic principle that many genes can interact to produce a particular characteristic.

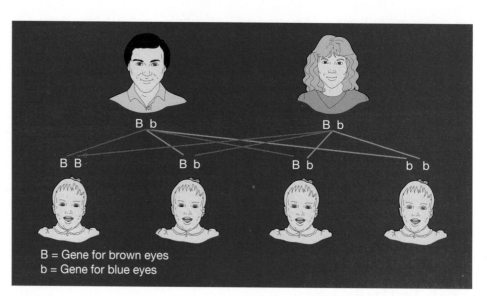

Figure **3.11**

How Brown-Eyed Parents Can Have a Blue-Eyed Child

Although both parents have brown eyes, each parent can have a recessive gene for blue eyes. In this example, both parents have brown eyes, but each parent carries the recessive gene for blue eyes. Therefore, the odds of their child having blue eyes is one in four—the probability the child will receive a recessive gene *(b)* from each parent.

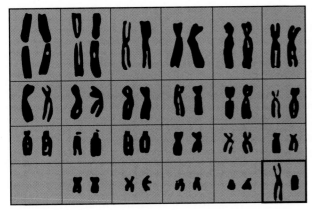

a.

b.

Figure **3.12**

The Genetic Difference Between Males and Females

Set (a) shows the chromosome structure of a male, and set (b) shows the chromosome structure of a female. The last pair of 23 pairs of chromosomes is in the bottom right box of each set. Notice that the Y chromosome of the male is smaller than that of the female. To obtain this kind of chromosomal picture, a cell is removed from a person's body, usually from the inside of the mouth. The chromosomes are stained by chemical treatment, magnified extensively, and then photographed.

lar characteristic. Few psychological characteristics are the result of single pairs. Most are determined by the interaction of many different genes. There are 50,000 or more genes, so you can imagine that possible combinations of these are staggering in number. Traits produced by this mixing of genes are said to be polygenically determined.

No one possesses all the characteristics that our genetic structure makes possible. A **genotype** *is the person's genetic heritage, the actual genetic material.* However, not all of this genetic material is apparent in our observed and measurable characteristics. A **phenotype** *is the way an individual's genotype is expressed in observed and measurable characteristics.* Phenotypes include physical traits (such as height, weight, eye color, and skin pigmentation) and psychological characteristics (such as intelligence, creativity, personality, and social tendencies).

For each genotype, a range of phenotypes can be expressed. Imagine that we could identify all of the genes that would make a person introverted or extraverted. Would measured introversion-extraversion be predictable from knowledge of the specific genes? The answer is no, because, even if our genetic model were adequate, introversion-extraversion is a characteristic that also is shaped by experience throughout life. For example, parents may push an introverted child into social situations and encourage the child to become more gregarious.

To understand how introversion might develop, think about a series of genetic codes that predispose the child to develop in a particular way, and imagine environments that are responsive or unresponsive to this development. For instance, the genotype of some persons may predispose them to be introverted in an environment that promotes a turning inward of personality, yet, in an environment that encourages social interaction and outgoingness, these individuals may become more extraverted. However, it would be unlikely for the individual with this introverted genotype to become a strong extravert. The **reaction range** *is the range of possible phenotypes for each genotype, suggesting the importance of an environment's restrictiveness or richness* (see figure 3.13).

Sandra Scarr (1984) explains reaction range this way: Each of us has a range of potential. For example, an individual with "medium-tall" genes for height who grows up in a poor environment may be shorter than average; however, in an excellent nutritional environment, the individual may grow up taller than average. No matter

genotype
A person's genetic heritage; the actual genetic material.

phenotype
The way an individual's genotype is expressed in observed and measurable characteristics.

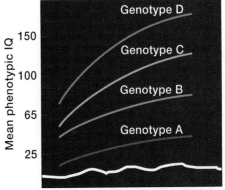

Figure **3.13**

Responsiveness of Genotypes to Environmental Influences

Although each genotype responds favorably to improved environments, some are more responsive than others to environmental deprivation and enrichment.

Identical twins develop from a single fertilized egg that splits into two genetically identical organisms. Twin studies compare identical twins with fraternal twins. Fraternal twins develop from separate eggs, making them genetically no more similar than nontwin siblings.

reaction range
The range of possible phenotypes for each genotype, suggesting the importance of an environment's restrictiveness or richness.

canalization
The process by which characteristics take a narrow path or developmental course. Apparently, preservative forces help to protect a person from environmental extremes.

behavior genetics
The study of the degree and nature of behavior's heredity basis.

twin study
A study in which the behavioral similarity of identical twins is compared with the behavioral similarity of fraternal twins.

identical twins
Twins who develop from a single fertilized egg that splits into two genetically identical replicas, each of which becomes a person.

fraternal twins
Twins who develop from separate eggs and separate sperm, making them genetically no more similar than nontwin siblings.

adoption study
A study in which investigators seek to discover whether, in behavior and psychological characteristics, adopted children are more like their adoptive parents, who provided a home environment, or more like their biological parents, who contributed their heredity. Another form of the adoption study is to compare adoptive and biological siblings.

how well fed the person is, though, someone with "short" genes will never be taller than average. Scarr believes that characteristics such as intelligence and introversion work the same way. That is, there is a range within which the environment can modify intelligence, but intelligence is not completely malleable. Reaction range gives us an estimate of how modifiable intelligence is.

Although some traits have a wide reaction range, other are somewhat immune to extensive changes in the environment. These characteristics seem to stay on a particular developmental course, regardless of the environmental assaults on them (Waddington, 1957). **Canalization** *is the term chosen to describe the narrow path, or developmental course, that certain characteristics take. Apparently, preservative forces help to protect, or buffer, a person from environmental extremes.* For example, American developmental psychologist Jerome Kagan (1984) points to his research on Guatemalan infants who had experienced extreme malnutrition as infants yet showed normal social and cognitive development later in childhood. And some abused children do not grow up to be abusers themselves.

Although the genetic influence of canalization exerts its power by keeping organisms on a particular developmental path, genes alone do not directly determine human behavior. Developmentalist Gilbert Gottlieb (1991; Gottlieb, Wahlsteni & Lickliter, 1998) points out that genes are an integral part of the organism but that their activity (genetic expression) can be affected by the organism's environment. For example, hormones that circulate in the blood make their way into the cell, where they influence the cell's activity. The flow of hormones themselves can be affected by environmental events, such as light, day length, nutrition, and behavior.

Methods Used by Behavior Geneticists

Behavior genetics *is the study of the degree and nature of behavior's hereditary basis.* Behavior geneticists assume that behaviors are jointly determined by the interaction of heredity and environment (Goldsmith, 1994). To study heredity's influence on behavior, behavior geneticists often study either twins or adoption situations (Wahlsten, 2000).

In a **twin study,** *the behavioral similarity of identical twins is compared with the behavioral similarity of fraternal twins.* **Identical twins** *(called monozygotic twins) develop from a single fertilized egg that splits into two genetically identical replicas, each of which becomes a person.* **Fraternal twins** *(called dizygotic twins) develop from separate eggs and separate sperm, making them genetically no more similar than nontwin siblings.* Although fraternal twins share the same womb, they are no more alike genetically than are nontwin brothers and sisters, and they may be of different sexes. By comparing groups of identical and fraternal twins, behavior geneticists capitalize on the basic knowledge that identical twins are more similar genetically than are fraternal twins. (Mitchell, 1999; Plomin & DeFries, 1998; Scarr, 1996). In one twin study, 7,000 pairs of Finnish identical and fraternal twins were compared on the personality traits of extraversion and neuroticism (psychological instability) (Rose & others, 1988). On both of these personality traits, the identical twins were much more similar than fraternal twins were, suggesting the role of heredity in both traits. However, several issues crop up as a result of twin studies. Adults might stress the similarities of identical twins more than those of fraternal twins, and identical twins might perceive themselves as a "set" and play together more than fraternal twins do. If so, observed similarities in identical twins could be environmentally influenced.

In an **adoption study,** *investigators seek to discover whether, in behavior and psychological characteristics, adopted children are more like their adoptive parents, who provided a home environment, or more like their biological parents, who contributed their heredity. Another form of the adoption study is to compare adoptive and biological siblings.* In one investigation, the educational levels attained by biological parents were better predictors of the adopted children's IQ scores than were the IQs of the children's adopted parents (Scarr & Weinberg, 1983). Because of the genetic relation between the adopted children and their biological parents, the implication is that heredity influences children's IQ scores.

THE WIZARD OF ID

By permission of Johnny Hart and Creators Syndicate, Inc.

Heredity's Influence on Development

Behavior Genetics
Twin Research

What aspects of development are influenced by genetic factors? They all are. However, behavior geneticists are interested in more precise estimates of a characteristic's variation than can be accounted for by genetic factors (Ganger & others, 1999). Intelligence is among the most widely investigated aspects of heredity's influence on development.

Arthur Jensen (1969) sparked a lively and, at times, hostile debate when he presented his thesis that intelligence is primarily inherited. Jensen believes that environment and culture play only a minimal role in intelligence. He examined several studies of intelligence, some of which involved comparisons of identical and fraternal twins. Remember that identical twins have identical genetic endowments, so their IQs should be similar. Fraternal twins and ordinary siblings are less similar genetically, so their IQs should be less similar. Jensen found support for his argument in these studies. Studies with identical twins produced an average correlation of .82; studies with ordinary siblings produced an average correlation of .50. Note the difference of .32. To show that genetic factors are more important than environmental factors, Jensen compared identical twins reared together with those reared apart; the correlation for those reared together was .89 and for those reared apart was .78 (a difference of only .11). Jensen argued that, if environmental influences were more important than genetic influences, then siblings reared apart, who experience different environments, should have IQs much further apart.

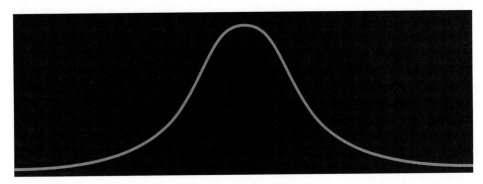

Figure **3.14**

The Bell Curve

The term *bell curve* is used to describe a normal distribution graph, a symmetrical shape that looks like a bell—bulging in the middle and thinning out at the edges.

Two Views of *The Bell Curve*

Sternberg's Critique of *The Bell Curve*

Many scholars have criticized Jensen's work. One criticism concerns the definition of intelligence itself. Jensen believes that IQ as measured by standardized intelligence tests is a good indicator of intelligence. Critics argue that IQ tests tap only a narrow range of intelligence. Everyday problem solving, work, and social adaptability, say the critics, are important aspects of intelligence not measured by the traditional intelligence tests used in Jensen's sources. A second criticism is that most investigations of heredity and environment do not include environments that differ radically. Thus, it is not surprising that many genetic studies show environment to be a fairly weak influence on intelligence.

Intelligence is influenced by heredity, but most developmentalists have not found as strong a relationship as Jensen found in his work. Other experts estimate heredity's influence on intelligence to be in the 50 percent range (Plomin, DeFries, & McClearn, 1990).

The most recent controversy about heredity and intelligence focuses on the book *The Bell Curve: Intelligence and Class Structure in Modern Life,* (1994) by Richard Herrnstein and Charles Murray. The authors argue that America is rapidly evolving a huge underclass of intellectually deprived individuals whose cognitive abilities will never match the future needs of most employers. The authors believe that members of this underclass, a large percentage of whom are African American, might be doomed by their shortcomings to welfare dependency, poverty, crime, and lives devoid of any hope of ever reaching the American dream.

Herrnstein and Murray believe that IQ can be quantitatively measured and that IQ test scores vary across ethnic groups. They point out that, in the United States, Asian Americans score several points higher than Whites, while African Americans score about 15 points lower than Whites. They also argue that these IQ differences are at least partly due to heredity and that government money spent on education programs such as Project Head Start is wasted, helping only the government's bloated bureaucracy.

Why do Herrnstein and Murray call their book *The Bell Curve?* A bell curve is a normal distribution graph, which has the shape of a bell—bulging in the middle and thinning out at the edges (see figure 3.14 on page 87). Normal distribution graphs are used to represent large numbers of people, who are sorted according to a shared characteristic, such as weight, exposure to asbestos, taste in clothing, or IQ.

Herrnstein and Murray often refer to bell curves to make a point: that predictions about any individual based exclusively on the person's IQ are useless. Weak correlations between intelligence and job success have predictive value only when they are applied to large groups of people. Within such large groups, say Herrnstein and Murray, the pervasive influence of IQ on human society becomes apparent.

Significant criticisms have been leveled at *The Bell Curve.* Experts on intelligence generally agree that African Americans score lower than Whites on IQ tests. However, many of these experts raise serious questions about the ability of IQ tests to accurately measure a person's intelligence. Among the criticisms of IQ tests is that the tests are cul-

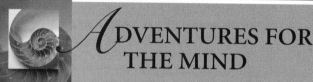

ADVENTURES FOR THE MIND

The Nobel Prize Sperm Bank

IN THE 1980s, Dr. Robert Graham founded the Repository for Germinal Choice in Escondido, California, as a sperm bank for Nobel Prize winners and other bright individuals with the intent of producing geniuses. The sperm is available to women of "good stock" whose husbands are infertile, according to Graham.

Dr. Graham with the frozen sperm of a donor who has won a Nobel Prize.

What are the odds that the sperm bank will yield that special combination of factors required to produce a creative genius? Twentieth-century Irish-born British playwright George Bernard Shaw once told a story about a beautiful woman who wrote him, saying that, with her body and his mind, they could produce marvelous offspring. Shaw responded by saying that, unfortunately, the offspring might get his body and her mind.

What do you think about the Nobel Prize sperm bank? Is it right to breed for intelligence? Does it raise visions of the German gene program of the 1930s and 1940s, in which the Nazis believed that certain traits are superior? They tried to breed children with such traits and killed people without them. Or does the sperm bank merely provide a social service for couples who cannot conceive a child, couples who want to maximize the probability that their offspring will have good genes?

Where do you stand on this controversial topic of breeding for intelligence? Do you think it is unethical? Can you see where it might bring hope for once childless couples?

SUMMARY TABLE 3.3
Genetic Principles, Methods, and Influences

Concept	Processes/ Related Ideas	Characteristics/Description
Genetic Principles	Their Nature	• Genetic transmission is complex, but a number of principles have been worked out. • Genetic principles include those involving dominant-recessive genes, sex-linked genes, polygenic inheritance, genotype-phenotype influences, reaction range, and canalization.
Methods Used by Behavior Geneticists	Behavior Genetics	• Behavior genetics is the field concerned with the degree and nature of behavior's hereditary basis.
	Range of Methods	• These include twin studies and adoption studies.
Heredity's Influence on Development	Scope of Influence	• All aspects of development are influenced by heredity.
	Intelligence	• Herrnstein, Murray, and Jensen argue that intelligence is mainly due to heredity. This has sparked a lively debate. • Intelligence is influenced by heredity but not as strongly as Jensen, Herrnstein, and Murray believe. • Most experts today accept that the environment plays an important role in intelligence.

turally biased against African Americans and Latinos. In 1971, the U.S. Supreme Court endorsed such criticisms and ruled that tests of general intelligence, in contrast to tests that solely measure fitness for a particular job, are discriminatory and cannot be administered as a condition of employment. Another criticism is that most investigations of heredity and environment do not include environments that differ radically.

Most experts today agree that the environment plays an important role in intelligence (Ceci & others, 1997). This means that improving children's environments can raise their intelligence. It also means that enriching children's environments can improve their school achievement and their acquisition of skills needed for employability. Craig Ramey and his associates (1988) found that high-quality early educational day care (through 5 years of age) significantly raised the tested intelligence of young children from impoverished backgrounds. Positive effects of this early intervention were still evident in the intelligence and achievement of these students when they were in middle school (Campbell & Ramey, 1994).

At this point we have discussed a number of ideas about genetic principles, methods, and influences. A review of these ideas is presented in summary table 3.3. Next, we continue our coverage of heredity by examining how it interacts with environmental influences.

Heredity-Environment Interaction

A common misconception is that behavior geneticists analyze only the effects of heredity on development. Although they believe heredity plays an important role in children's development, they are especially interested in the way that heredity and environment work together (Rowe & Jacobson, 1999; Waldman & Rhee, 1999).

Heredity-Environment Correlations

The notion of heredity-environment correlations involves the concept that individuals' genes influence the types of environments to which they are exposed. That

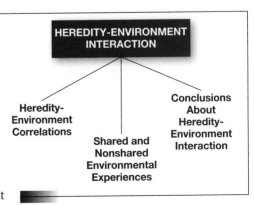

passive genotype-environment correlations
Correlations that exist when parents, who are genetically related to the child, provide a rearing environment for the child.

evocative genotype-environment correlations
Correlations that exist when the child's genotype elicits certain types of physical and social environments.

active (niche-picking) genotype-environment correlations
Correlations that exist when children seek out environments they find compatible and stimulating.

shared environmental experiences
Children's common environmental experiences that are shared with their siblings, such as their parents' personalities and intellectual orientation, the family's social class, and the neighborhood in which they live.

nonshared environmental experiences
The child's own unique experiences, both within the family and outside the family, that are not shared by another sibling. Thus, experiences occurring within the family can be part of the "nonshared environment."

is, individuals inherit environments that are related or linked to their genetic propensities (Plomin & others, 1994). Behavior geneticist Sandra Scarr (1993) described three ways that heredity and environment are correlated: passively, evocatively, and actively.

Passive genotype-environment correlations *occur when biological parents, who are genetically related to the child, provide a rearing environment for the child.* For example, the parents might have a genetic predisposition to be intelligent and read skillfully. Because they read well and enjoy reading, they provide their children with books to read. The likely outcome is that their children, given their own, inherited predispositions, will become skilled readers.

Evocative genotype-environment correlations *occur because a child's genotype elicits certain types of physical and social environments.* For example, active, smiling children receive more social stimulation than passive, quiet children do. Cooperative, attentive adolescents evoke more pleasant and instructional responses from the adults around them than uncooperative, distractible adolescents do. Athletically inclined youth tend to elicit encouragement to engage in school sports. As a consequence, these adolescents tend to be the ones who try out for sport teams and go on to participate in athletically oriented environments.

Active (niche-picking) genotype-environment correlations *occur when children and adolescents seek out environments they find compatible and stimulating.* Niche-picking refers to finding a niche or setting that is suited to one's abilities. Adolescents select from their surrounding environment some aspect that they respond to, learn about, or ignore. Their active selections of environments are related to their particular genotype. For example, attractive adolescents tend to seek out attractive peers. Adolescents who are musically inclined are likely to select musical environments in which they can successfully perform their skills.

Scarr believes that the relative importance of the three genotype-environment correlations changes as children develop from infancy through adolescence. In infancy, much of the environment that children experience is provided by adults. Thus, passive genotype-environment correlations are more common in the lives of infants and young children than they are for older children and adolescents who can extend their experiences beyond the family's influence and create their environments to a greater degree.

Shared and Nonshared Environmental Experiences

Behavior geneticists also believe that another way the environment's role in heredity-environment interaction can be carved up is to consider the experiences of children that are in common with those of other children living in the same home, as well as experiences that are not shared (Finkel, Whitfield, & McGue, 1995; Perusse, 1999). Behavior geneticist Robert Plomin (1993) has found that common rearing, or shared environment, accounts for little of the variation in children's personality or interests. In other words, even though two children live under the same roof with the same parents, their personalities are often very different.

Shared environmental experiences *are children's common experiences, such as their parents' personalities and intellectual orientation, the family's social class, and the neighborhood in which they live.* By contrast, **nonshared environmental experiences** *are a child's unique experiences, both within the family and outside the family, that are not shared with another sibling. Thus, experiences occurring within the family can be part of the "nonshared environment."* Parents often interact differently with each sibling, and siblings interact differently with parents (Hetherington, Reiss & Plomin, 1994). Siblings often have different peer groups, different friends, and different teachers at school.

Conclusions About Heredity-Environment Interaction

In sum, both genes and environment are necessary for a person to even exist. Without genes, there is no person; without environment, there is no person (Scarr & Weinberg, 1980). Heredity and environment operate together—or cooperate—to produce a person's intelligence, temperament, height, weight, ability to pitch a baseball, ability to read, and so on (Gottlieb, Wahlsten, & Lickliter, 1998; Kallio, 1999) ◀▥ P. 16. If an attractive, popular, intelligent girl is elected president of her senior class in high school, is her success due to heredity or to environment? Of course, the answer is both. Because the environment's influence depends on genetically endowed characteristics, we say the two factors *interact* (Mader, 1999, 2000).

The relative contributions of heredity and environment are not additive, as in such-and-such a percentage of nature, such-and-such a percentage of experience. That's the old view. Nor is it accurate to say that full genetic expression happens once, around conception or birth, after which we take our genetic legacy into the world to see how far it gets us. Genes produce proteins throughout the life span, in many different environments. Or they don't produce these proteins, depending on how harsh or nourishing those environments are.

The emerging view is that many complex behaviors likely have some genetic loading that gives people a propensity for a particular developmental trajectory. But the actual development requires more: an environment. And that environment is complex, just like the mixture of genes we inherit. Environmental influences range from the things we lump together under "nurture" (such as parenting, family dynamics, schooling, and neighborhood quality) to biological encounters (such as viruses, birth complications, and even biological events in cells) (Greenough, 1997, 1999, 2000).

Imagine for a moment that there is a cluster of genes somehow associated with youth violence (this is hypothetical because we don't know of any such combination). The adolescent who carries this genetic mixture might experience a world of loving parents, regular nutritious meals, lots of books, and a series of masterful teachers. Or the adolescent's world might consist of parental neglect, a neighborhood where gunshots and crime are everyday occurrences, and inadequate schooling. In which of these environments are the adolescent's genes likely to manufacture the biological underpinnings of criminality? Also note that growing up with all of the "advantages" does not necessarily guarantee success. Adolescents from wealthy families might have access to books, excellent schools, travel, and tutoring. But they might take such opportunities for granted and fail to develop the motivation to learn and achieve. In the same way, "poor" or "disadvantaged" does not equal "doomed"; many impoverished adolescents make the best of the opportunities available to them and learn to seek out advantages that can help them improve their lives.

The most recent nature-nurture controversy erupted when Judith Harris (1998) published *The Nurture Assumption.* In this provocative book, she argued that what parents do does not make a difference in their children's and adolescents' behavior. Yell at them. Hug them. Read to them. Ignore them. Harris says it won't influence how they turn out. She argues that genes and peers are far more important than parents in children's and adolescents' development.

Harris is right that genes matter and she is right that peers matter, although her descriptions of peer influences are too monolithic and do not take into account the complexity of peer contexts and developmental trajectories (Hartup, 1999). In addition to not adequately considering peer complexities, Harris is wrong that parents don't matter. To begin with, in the early child years parents play an important role in selecting children's peers and indirectly influencing children's development (Baumrind, 1999). There is a huge parenting literature with many research studies

What is the theme of Judith Harris' (1998) controversial book, The Nurture Assumption? *What is the nature of the controversy?*

$\mathcal{S}$UMMARY $\mathcal{T}$ABLE 3.4
Heredity-Environment Interaction

Concept	Processes/ Related Ideas	Characteristics/Description
Heredity-Environment Correlations	Scarr's View	• Sandra Scarr argues that the environments parents select for their children depend on the parents' genotypes.
	Three Correlations	• Passive genotype-environment correlations occur when parents who are genetically related to the child provide a rearing environment for the child. • Evocative genotype-environment correlations occur because a child's genotype elicits certain types of physical and social environments. • Active (niche-picking) genotype-environment correlations occur when children seek out environments they find compatible and stimulating. • Scarr believes that the relative importance of these three genotype-environment correlations changes as children develop.
Shared and Nonshared Environmental Influences	Shared Experiences	• These refer to siblings' common experiences, such as their parents' personalities and intellectual orientation, the family's socioeconomic status, and the neighborhood in which they live.
	Nonshared Experiences	• These refer to the child's unique experiences, both within a family and outside the family, that are not shared by another sibling. • Plomin argues that nonshared environmental experiences are the primary environmental reasons for one sibling's personality being different from another's.
Conclusions About Heredity-Environment Interaction	Their Nature	• Many complex behaviors have some genetic loading that gives people a propensity for a particular developmental trajectory. • Actual development also requires an environment, and that environment is complex. • The interaction of heredity and environment is extensive.

documenting the importance of parents in children's development. We will discuss parents' important roles throughout this book, giving them special attention in chapter 15, "Families." But for now, consider the research on just one area of development: child abuse. Many studies reveal that when parents abuse their children, the children have problems in regulating their emotions, becoming securely attached to others, developing competent peer relations, and adapting to school, and they tend to develop anxiety and depression disorders. In many instances these difficulties continue into adolescence (Cicchetti & Toth, 1998; Rogosch & others, 1995). Child development expert T. Berry Brazelton (1998) commented, "*The Nurture Assumption* is so disturbing it devalues what parents are trying to do.... Parents might say, 'If I don't matter, why should I bother?' That's terrifying and its coming when children and youth need a stronger home base." Even Jerome Kagan (1998), a champion of biological influences on development, when commenting about Harris' book, concluded that whether children are cooperative or competitive, achievement-oriented or not, they are strongly influenced by their parents for better or for worse.

A review of the main ways in which heredity and environment interact to produce development is presented in summary table 3.4. In the next chapter, we will continue to discuss biological beginnings, turning to the nature of prenatal development and birth.

Chapter Review

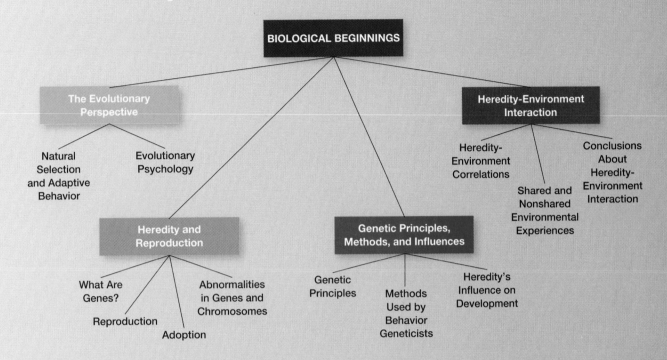

TO OBTAIN A DETAILED REVIEW OF THE CHAPTER, STUDY THESE FOUR SUMMARY TABLES:

Key Terms

natural selection 70
adaptive behavior 71
evolutionary psychology 71
chromosomes 72
DNA 72
genes 72
mitosis 72
meiosis 73
reproduction 73
zygote 73
phenylketonuria (PKU) 77
Down syndrome 77
sickle-cell anemia 78
Klinefelter syndrome 78

fragile X syndrome 78
Turner syndrome 78
XYY syndrome 78
amniocentesis 79
ultrasound sonography 79
chorionic villi sampling 80
maternal blood test 83
dominant-recessive genes principle 84
polygenic inheritance 84
genotype 85
phenotype 85
reaction range 85
canalization 86
behavior genetics 86

twin study 86
identical twins 86
fraternal twins 86
adoption study 86
passive genotype-environment correlations 90
evocative genotype-environment correlations 90
active (niche-picking) genotype-environment correlations 90
shared environmental experiences 90
nonshared environmental experiences 90

Key People

Thomas Bouchard 70
Charles Darwin 70
David Buss 71
Sandra Scarr 85

Gilbert Gottlieb 86
Arthur Jensen 87
Richard Herrnstein and Charles Murray 88

Robert Plomin 90
William Greenough 91
Judith Harris 91

Child Development Resources

American Fertility Society
2131 Magnolia Avenue
Birmingham, AL 35256
205-252-9764

This organization provides information about infertility and possible solutions to it.

Being Adopted (1992)
by David Brodzinsky,
Marshall Schecter, and
Robin Henig
New York: Doubleday

This book provides an excellent overview of how adoption influences people's lives throughout the human life span, including a discussion of how adoption ties in with Erikson's stages of the human life cycle.

How Healthy Is Your Family Tree? (1995)
by Carol Krause
New York: Simon & Schuster

In this book, you will learn how to create a family medical tree. Once you put together a medical family tree, a specialist or genetic counselor can help you understand it.

National Organization for Rare Disorders (NORD)
Fairwood Professional Building
100 Route 37
New Fairfield, CT 06812
203-746-6518

This foundation supports awareness and education about rare birth defects and genetic disorders.

The Twins Foundation
P.O. Box 9487
Providence, RI 02940
401-274-6910

For information about twins and multiple births, contact this foundation.

Taking It to the Net

1. Denita is going to do a book report for her English class on the *Nurture Assumption: Why Children Turn Out the Way They Do*, by Judith Rich Harris. As part of her report, she plans to address the controversy among children development experts about Harris's conclusions.

2. Warren is majoring in education and hopes to be involved in teaching mentally retarded children. He is interested in learning exactly what genetic defects cause fragile X syndrome, the most common inherited cause of mental retardation.

3. Joyce is considering becoming a genetic counselor for prospective parents. What issues involving genetic testing, reproduction decisions, and *in utero* gene therapy will Joyce likely address with her clients?

Connect to *http://www.mhhe.com/santrockc9* to find the answsers!

Chapter 4

```
                    PRENATAL DEVELOPMENT
                          AND BIRTH


    Prenatal Development                                    The Postpartum
                                                               Period

                                         The Nature
  The Course        Teratology            of the                          Bonding
  of Prenatal       and Hazards        Postpartum
  Development       to Prenatal    Birth   Period
                    Development                        Physical      Emotional and
                                                     Adjustments     Psychological
                                                                      Adjustments
                 The Birth
                  Process
                                      Measures
              Preterm Infants        of Neonatal
              and Age-Weight          Health and
              Considerations        Responsiveness
```

Prenatal Development and Birth

The Story of Tanner Roberts' Birth: A Fantastic Voyage

TANNER ROBERTS was born in a suite at St. Joseph's Medical Center in Burbank, California (Warrick, 1992). Let's examine what took place in the hours leading up to his birth. It is day 266 of his mother, Cindy's, pregnancy. She is in the frozen-food aisle of a convenience store and feels a sharp pain, starting in the small of her back and reaching around her middle, which causes her to gasp. For weeks, painless Braxton Hicks spasms (named for the gynecologist who discovered them) have been flexing her uterine muscles. But these practice contractions were not nearly as intense and painful as the one she just experienced. After 6 hours of irregular spasms, her uterus settles into a more predictable rhythm.

At 3 A.M., Cindy and her husband, Tom, are wide awake. They time Cindy's contractions with a stopwatch. The contractions are now only 6 minutes apart. It's time to call the hospital. At the hospital, Cindy goes to a labor-delivery suite. The nurse puts a webbed belt and fetal monitor around Cindy's middle to measure the labor. The monitor picks up the fetal heart rate. With each contraction of the uterine wall, Tanner's heartbeat jumps from its resting state of about 140 beats to 160–170 beats per minute. When the cervix is dilated to more than 4 centimeters, or almost half open, Cindy is given her first medication. As Demerol begins to drip into her veins, she becomes more relaxed. Tanner's heart rate dips to 130 and then 120.

Contractions are now coming every 3 to 4 minutes, each one lasting about 25 seconds. The Demerol does not completely obliterate Cindy's pain. She hugs her husband as the nurse urges her to "relax those muscles. Breathe deep. Relax. You are almost done."

Each contraction briefly cuts off Tanner's source of oxygen. However, the minutes of rest between each contraction resupply the oxygen, and Cindy's deep breathing helps rush fresh blood to the fetal heart and brain.

At 8 A.M., Cindy's obstetrician arrives and determines that her cervix is almost completely dilated. Using a tool made for the purpose, he reaches into the birth canal

germinal period
The period of prenatal development that takes place in the first 2 weeks after conception. It includes the creation of the zygote, continued cell division, and the attachment of the zygote to the uterine wall.

blastocyst
The inner layer of cells that develops during the germinal period. These cells later develop into the embryo.

trophoblast
The outer layer of cells that develops in the germinal period. These cells provide nutrition and support for the embryo.

implantation
The attachment of the zygote to the uterine wall, which takes place about 10 days after conception.

and tears the membranes of the amniotic sac, and about half a liter of clear fluid flows out. Contractions are now coming every 2 minutes, and each one is lasting a full minute.

By 9 A.M., the labor suite has been transformed into a delivery room. Tanner's body is compressed by his mother's contractions and pushes. As he nears his entrance into the world, the compressions help press the fluid from his lungs in preparation for his first breath.

Squeezed tightly in the birth canal, the top of Tanner's head emerges. His face is puffy and scrunched. Although fiercely squinting because of the sudden light, Tanner's eyes are open. Tiny bubbles of clear mucus are on his lips. Before any more of his body emerges, the obstetrician cradles Tanner's head and suctions his nose and mouth. Tanner takes his first breath, a large gasp followed by whimpering, and then a loud cry.

Tanner's trunk and head are luminescent pink. His limbs are still gray-blue from lack of oxygen. His fingers and toes are gray. His body is wet but only slightly bloody as the doctor lifts him onto his mother's abdomen.

The umbilical cord, still connecting Tanner with his mother, slows and stops pulsating. The obstetrician cuts it, severing Tanner's connection to his mother's womb. Now Tanner's blood flows not to his mother's blood for nourishment, but to his own lungs, intestines, and other organs.

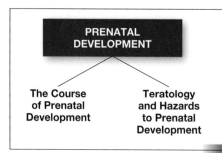

Prenatal Development

Imagine how Tanner Roberts came to be. Out of thousands of eggs and millions of sperm, one egg and one sperm united to produce him. Had a different sperm united with that egg instead, a different child would have come into being. Remember from chapter 3 that conception occurs when a single sperm cell from the male unites with an ovum (egg) in the female's fallopian tube in a process called fertilization. Remember also that the fertilized egg is called a zygote. By the time the zygote ends its 3- to 4-day journey through the fallopian tube and reaches the uterus, it has divided into approximately 12 to 16 cells.

The Course of Prenatal Development

Prenatal development is divided into three periods: germinal, embryonic, and fetal.

The Germinal Period   The **germinal period** *is the period of prenatal development that takes place in the first 2 weeks after conception. It includes the creation of the zygote, continued cell division, and the attachment of the zygote to the uterine wall.* By approximately 1 week after conception, the zygote is composed of 100 to 150 cells. The differentiation of cells has already commenced, as inner and outer layers of the organism are formed. The **blastocyst** *is the inner layer of cells that develops during the germinal period. These cells later develop into the embryo* (see figure 4.1). The **trophoblast** *is the outer layer of cells that develops during the germinal period. It later provides nutrition and support for the embryo.* **Implantation,** *the attachment of the zygote to the uterine wall, takes place about 10 days after conception.* Figure 4.2 illustrates some of the most significant developments during the germinal period.

The Embryonic Period   The **embryonic period** *is the period of prenatal development that occurs from 2 to 8 weeks after conception. During the embryonic period, the rate of cell differentiation intensifies, support systems for the cells form, and organs appear.* As the zygote attaches to the uterine wall, its cells form two layers. At this time, the name of the mass of cells changes from *zygote* to *embryo.* The embryo's **endoderm** *is the inner layer of cells, which will develop into the digestive and respiratory systems.* The outer layer of cells is divided into two parts. The **ectoderm** *is the outermost layer, which will become the nervous system, sensory receptors (ears, nose, and*

embryonic period
The period of prenatal development that occurs 2 to 8 weeks after conception. During the embryonic period, the rate of cell differentiation intensifies, support systems for the cells form, and organs appear.

endoderm
The inner layer of cells that develops into digestive and respiratory systems.

ectoderm
The outermost layer of cells, which becomes the nervous system, sensory receptors (ears, nose, and eyes, for example), and skin parts (hair and nails, for example).

mesoderm
The middle layer of cells, which becomes the circulatory system, bones, muscles, excretory system, and reproductive system.

placenta
A life-support system that consists of a disk-shaped group of tissues in which small blood vessels from the mother and offspring intertwine.

eyes, for example), and skin parts (hair and nails, for example). The **mesoderm** *is the middle layer, which will become the circulatory system, bones, muscles, excretory system, and reproductive system.* Every body part eventually develops from these three layers. The endoderm primarily produces internal body parts, the mesoderm primarily produces parts that surround the internal areas, and the ectoderm primarily produces surface parts.

As the embryo's three layers form, life-support systems for the embryo mature and develop rapidly. These life-support systems include the placenta, the umbilical cord, and the amnion. The **placenta** *is a life-support system that consists of a disk-shaped group of tissues in which small blood vessels from the mother and the offspring intertwine but do not join.* The **umbilical cord** *is a life-support system, containing two arteries and one vein, that connects the baby to the placenta.* Very small molecules—oxygen, water, salt, food from the mother's blood, as well as carbon dioxide and digestive wastes from the embryo's blood—pass back and forth between the mother and embryo. Large molecules cannot pass through the placental wall; these include red blood cells and harmful substances, such as most bacteria, maternal wastes, and hormones. The mechanisms that govern the transfer of substances across the placental barrier are complex and are still not entirely understood (Rosenblith, 1992). Figure 4.3 provides an illustration of the placenta, the umbilical cord, and the nature of blood flow in the expectant mother and developing child in the uterus. The **amnion,** *a bag or an envelope that contains a clear fluid in which the developing embryo floats,* is another important life-support system. Like the placenta and umbilical cord, the amnion develops from the fertilized egg, not from the mother's own body. At approximately 16 weeks, the kidneys of the fetus begin to produce urine. This fetal urine remains the main source of the amniotic fluid until the third trimester, when some of the fluid is excreted from the lungs of the growing fetus. Although the amniotic fluid increases in volume tenfold from the 12th to the 40th week of pregnancy, it is also removed in various ways. Some is swallowed by the fetus, and some is absorbed through the umbilical cord and the membranes covering the placenta. The amniotic fluid provides an environment that is temperature and humidity controlled, as well as shockproof.

Figure **4.1**

The Blastocyst

The blastocyst produces a mass of cells when the fertilized egg repeatedly divides after conception. The blastocyst is the inner layer of cells that develops during the germinal period. These cells later develop into the embryo.

umbilical cord
A life-support system containing two arteries and one vein that connects the baby to the placenta.

amnion
The life-support system that is a bag or envelope that contains a clear fluid in which the developing embryo floats.

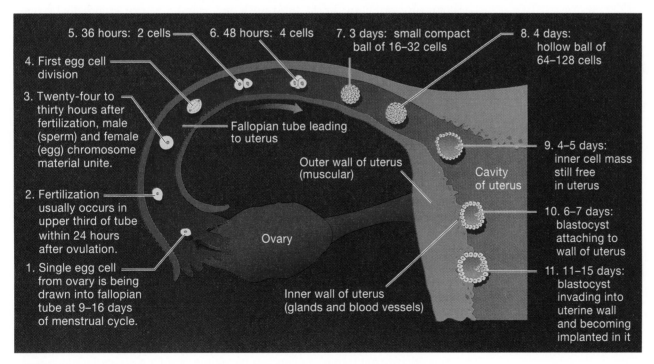

Figure **4.2**

Significant Developments in the Germinal Period

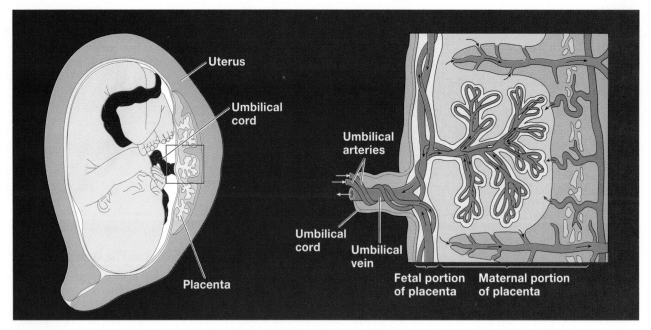

Figure 4.3
The Placenta and the Umbilical Cord

Maternal blood flows through the uterine arteries to the spaces housing the placenta, and it returns through the uterine veins to maternal circulation. Fetal blood flows through the umbilical arteries into the capillaries of the placenta and returns through the umbilical veins to the fetal circulation. The exchange of materials takes place across the layer separating the maternal and fetal blood supplies, so the bloods never come into contact. *Note:* The area bound by the square is enlarged in the right half of the illustration. Arrows indicate the direction of blood flow.

organogenesis
Organ formation that takes place during the first 2 months of prenatal development.

fetal period
The prenatal period of development that begins 2 months after conception and lasts for 7 months, on the average.

The history of man for nine months preceding his birth would, probably, is far more interesting, and contain even of greater moment than all three score and ten years that follow it.

Samuel Taylor Coleridge
English Poet, Essayist, 19th Century

Before most women even know they are pregnant, some important embryonic developments take place. In the third week, the neural tube that eventually becomes the spinal cord forms. At about 21 days, eyes begin to appear, and at 24 days the cells for the heart begin to differentiate. During the fourth week, the first appearance of the urogenital system is apparent, and arm and leg buds emerge. Four chambers of the heart take shape, and blood vessels surface. From the fifth to the eighth week, arms and legs differentiate further; at this time, the face starts to form but still is not very recognizable. The intestinal tract develops and the facial structures fuse. At 8 weeks, the developing organism weighs about 1/30 ounce and is just over 1 inch long. **Organogenesis** *is the process of organ formation that takes place during the first 2 months of prenatal development.* When organs are being formed, they are especially vulnerable to environmental changes. Later in the chapter, we will describe the environmental hazards that are harmful during organogenesis.

The Fetal Period   The **fetal period** *is the prenatal period of development that begins 2 months after conception and lasts for 7 months, on the average.* Growth and development continue their dramatic course during this time. Three months after conception, the fetus is about 3 inches long and weighs about 1 ounce. It has become active, moving its arms and legs, opening and closing its mouth, and moving its head. The face, forehead, eyelids, nose, and chin are distinguishable, as are the upper arms, lower arms, hands, and lower limbs. The genitals can be identified as male or female. By the end of the fourth month, the fetus has grown to 6 inches in length and weighs 4 to 7 ounces. At this time, a growth spurt occurs in the body's lower parts. Prenatal reflexes are stronger; arm and leg movements can be felt for the first time by the mother.

By the end of the fifth month, the fetus is about 12 inches long and weighs close to a pound. Structures of the skin have formed—toenails and fingernails, for example. The fetus is more active, showing a preference for a particular position in

SUMMARY TABLE 4.1
Prenatal Development

Concept	Processes/ Related Ideas	Characteristics/Description
The Germinal Period	Its Nature	• The period from conception until 10 to 14 days later. • A fertilized egg is called a zygote. • The period ends when the zygote attaches to the uterine wall.
The Embryonic Period	Its Nature	• The period that lasts approximately from the 2nd to the 8th week after conception. • The embryo differentiates into three layers, life-support systems develop, and organ systems form (organogenesis).
The Fetal Period	Its Nature	• The period that lasts from about 2 months after conception until 9 months, or when the infant is born. • Growth and development continue their dramatic course, and organ systems mature to the point at which life can be sustained outside of the womb.

the womb. By the end of the sixth month, the fetus is about 14 inches long and already has gained another half pound to a pound. The eyes and eyelids are completely formed, and a fine layer of hair covers the head. A grasping reflex is present and irregular breathing movements occur. By the end of the seventh month, the fetus is about 16 inches long and has gained another pound, now weighing about 3 pounds. During the eighth and ninth months, the fetus grows longer and gains substantial weight—about another 4 pounds. At birth, the average American baby weighs 7 pounds and is about 20 inches long. In these last two months, fatty tissues develop, and the functioning of various organ systems—heart and kidneys, for example—steps up.

We have described a number of developments in the germinal, embryonic, and fetal periods. An overview of some of the main developments we have discussed and some more specific changes in prenatal development are presented in figure 4.4. Notice in figure 4.4 that we have divided these changes into trimesters, or three equal time periods. The three trimesters are not the same as the three prenatal periods we have discussed—germinal, embryonic, and fetal. An important point that needs to be made is that the first time a fetus has a chance of surviving outside of the womb is the beginning of the third trimester (at about 7 months). An infant born in the seventh month usually needs assistance in breathing.

At this point we have studied a number of ideas about the course of prenatal development. A review of these ideas is presented in summary table 4.1. Next, we continue our exploration of prenatal development by discussing teratology.

The Visible Embryo
The Trimesters
Exploring Teratology
High-Risk Situations

Teratology and Hazards to Prenatal Development

Some expectant mothers carefully tiptoe about, in the belief that everything they do and feel has a direct effect on their unborn child. Others behave casually, assuming that their experiences will have little effect. The truth lies somewhere between these two extremes. Although living in a protected, comfortable environment, the fetus is not totally immune to the larger world surrounding the mother (McFarlane, Parker, & Soeken, 1996). The environment can affect the child in many well-documented ways. Thousands of babies are born deformed or mentally retarded every year as the result of events that occurred in the mother's life, as early as 1 or 2 months before conception.

First trimester (first 3 months)

	Conception to 4 weeks	8 weeks	12 weeks
Fetal growth	• Is less than $1/10$ inch long • Beginning development of spinal cord, nervous system, gastrointestinal system, heart, and lungs • Amniotic sac envelops the preliminary tissues of entire body • Is called an "ovum"	• Is less than 1 inch long • Face is forming with rudimentary eyes, ears, mouth, and tooth buds • Arms and legs are moving • Brain is forming • Fetal heartbeat is detectable with ultrasound • Is called an "embryo"	• Is about 3 inches long and weighs about 1 ounce • Can move arms, legs, fingers, and toes • Fingerprints are present • Can smile, frown, suck, and swallow • Sex is distinguishable • Can urinate • Is called a "fetus"

Second trimester (middle 3 months)

	16 weeks	20 weeks	24 weeks
Fetal growth	• Is about $5 1/2$ inches long and weighs about 4 ounces • Heartbeat is strong • Skin is thin, transparent • Downy hair (lanugo) covers body • Fingernails and toenails are forming • Has coordinated movements; is able to roll over in amniotic fluid	• Is 10 to 12 inches long and weighs $1/2$ to 1 pound • Heartbeat is audible with ordinary stethoscope • Sucks thumb • Hiccups • Hair, eyelashes, eyebrows are present	• Is 11 to 14 inches long and weighs 1 to $1 1/2$ pounds • Skin is wrinkled and covered with protective coating (vernix caseosa) • Eyes are open • Meconium is collecting in bowel • Has strong grip

Third trimester (last $3 1/2$ months)

	28 weeks	32 weeks	36 to 38 weeks
Fetal growth	• Is 14 to 17 inches long and weighs $2 1/2$ to 3 pounds • Is adding body fat • Is very active • Rudimentary breathing movements are present	• Is $16 1/2$ to 18 inches long and weighs 4 to 5 pounds • Has periods of sleep and wakefulness • Responds to sounds • May assume birth position • Bones of head are soft and flexible • Iron is being stored in liver	• Is 19 inches long and weighs 6 pounds • Skin is less wrinkled • Vernix caseosa is thick • Lanugo is mostly gone • Is less active • Is gaining immunities from mother

re **4.4**

e Trimesters of Prenatal Development

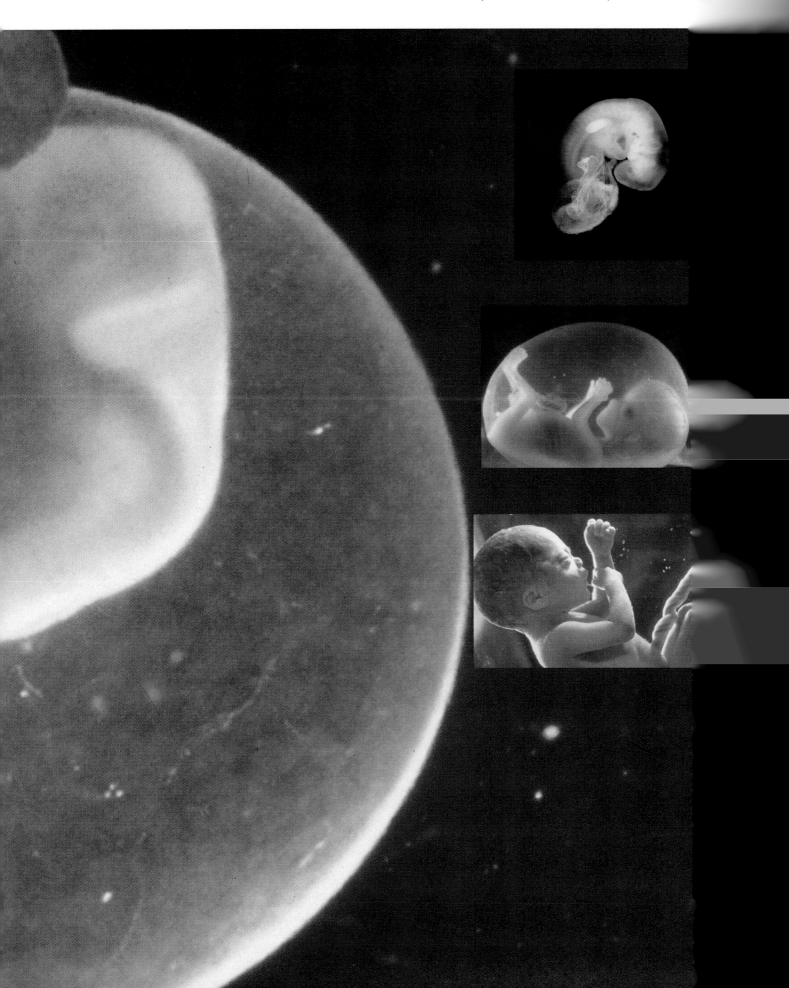

teratogen
From the Greek word *tera*, meaning "monster." Any agent that causes a birth defect. The field of study that investigates the causes of birth defects is called teratology.

Pregnancy and HIV

An explosion at the Chernobyl nuclear power plant in the Ukraine produced radioactive contamination that spread to surrounding areas. Thousands of infants were born with health problems and deformities as a result of the nuclear contamination, including this boy whose arm did not form.

Teratology   A **teratogen** (*the word comes from the Greek word* tera *meaning* "*monster*") *is any agent that causes a birth defect. The field of study that investigates the causes of birth defects is called teratology.* A specific teratogen (such as a drug) usually does not cause a specific birth defect (such as malformation of the legs). So many teratogens exist that practically every fetus is exposed to at least some teratogens. For this reason, it is difficult to determine which teratogen causes which birth defect. In addition, it can take a long time for the effects of a teratogen to show up. Only about half of all potential effects appear at birth.

Despite the many unknowns about teratogens, scientists have discovered the identity of some hazards to prenatal development and the particular point of fetal development at which they do their greatest damage. As figure 4.5 shows, sensitivity to teratogens begins about 3 weeks after conception. The probability of a structural defect is greatest early in the embryonic period, because this is when organs are being formed. After organogenesis is complete, teratogens are less likely to cause anatomical defects. Exposure later, during the fetal period, is more likely to stunt growth or to create problems in the way organs function. The precision of organogenesis is evident; teratologists point out that the vulnerability of the brain is greatest at 15 to 25 days after conception, the eyes at 24 to 40 days, the heart at 20 to 40 days, and the legs at 24 to 36 days.

Maternal Factors   Maternal characteristics that can affect prenatal development include maternal diseases and conditions and the mother's age, nutrition, emotional states, and stress.

Maternal Diseases and Conditions   Maternal diseases and infections can produce defects by crossing the placental barrier, or they can cause damage during the birth process itself (Lieberman & others, 2000). Rubella (German measles) is a maternal disease that can cause prenatal defects. A rubella outbreak in 1964–1965 resulted in 30,000 prenatal and neonatal (newborn) deaths, and more than 20,000 affected infants were born with malformations, including mental retardation, blindness, deafness, and heart problems. The greatest damage occurs when mothers contract rubella in the third and fourth weeks of pregnancy, although infection during the second month is also damaging. Elaborate preventive efforts ensure that rubella will never again have the disastrous effects it had in the mid 1960s. A vaccine that prevents German measles is now routinely administered to children, and women who plan to have children should have a blood test before they become pregnant to determine if they are immune to the disease.

Syphilis (a sexually transmitted disease) is more damaging later in prenatal development—4 months or more after conception. Rather than affecting organogenesis, as rubella does, syphilis damages organs after they have formed. Damage includes eye lesions, which can cause blindness, and skin lesions. When syphilis is present at birth, other problems, involving the central nervous system and gastrointestinal tract, can develop. Most states require that pregnant women be given a blood test to detect the presence of syphilis.

Another infection that has received widespread attention recently is genital herpes. Newborns contract this virus when they are delivered through the birth canal of a mother with genital herpes. About one-third of babies delivered through an infected birth canal die; another one-fourth become brain damaged. If an active case of genital herpes is detected in a pregnant woman close to her delivery date, a cesarean section can be performed (in which the infant is delivered through an incision in the mother's abdomen) to keep the virus from infecting the newborn.

AIDS   The importance of women's health to the health of the offspring is nowhere better exemplified than when the mother has AIDS (acquired immune deficiency syndrome) (Bates & others, 1999; D'Angelo & others, 2000). As the number of women with AIDS increases, more newborns are born exposed to and infected with HIV (Cohen & others, 1996).

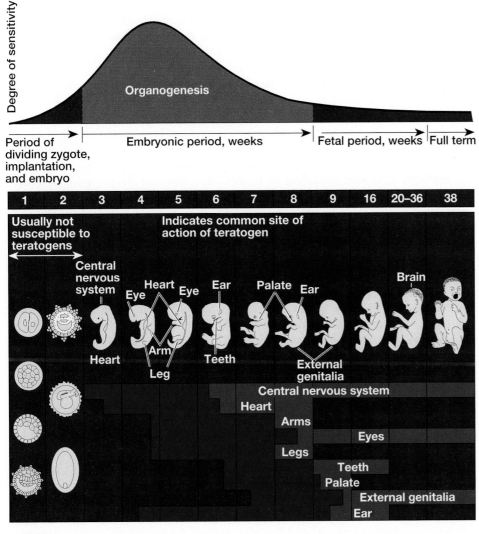

Figure 4.5

Teratogens and the Timing of Their Effects on Prenatal Development

The danger of structural defects caused by teratogens is greatest early in embryonic development. This is the period of organogenesis, and it lasts for several months. Damage caused by teratogens during this period is represented by the dark-colored bars. Later assaults by teratogens typically occur during the fetal period and, instead of causing structural damage, are more likely to stunt growth or cause problems of organ function.

AIDS is currently the sixth leading cause of death for children 1 to 4 years of age in the United States. Between 15 and 30 percent of infants born to HIV-infected women become infected with the virus. This results in 1,500 to 2,000 children born with HIV annually in the United States. Treatment can help reduce the rate of HIV transmission from an infected woman to her baby to less than 10 percent.

A mother with HIV infection can infect her offspring in three ways: (1) during gestation across the placenta; (2) during delivery through contact with maternal blood or fluids; and (3) postpartum through breast-feeding. Babies born to HIV-infected mothers can be (1) infected and symptomatic (show AIDS symptoms), (2) infected but asymptomatic (not show AIDS symptoms), or (3) not infected at all. An infant who is infected and asymptomatic can still develop HIV symptoms up until 15 months of age. One study documented a rare instance of HIV subsequently disappearing in an infant who was born infected with HIV (Bryon & others, 1995). This might have been an unusual transient or defective form of HIV.

The Mother's Age

In terms of possible harmful effects on the fetus and infant, two maternal ages are of special interest: adolescence and the thirties and beyond. Approximately one of every five births is to an adolescent; in some urban areas, the figure reaches as high as one in every two births. Infants born to adolescents are often premature. The mortality rate of infants born to adolescent mothers is double that of infants born to mothers in their twenties. Although such figures probably reflect the mother's immature reproductive system, they also may involve poor nutrition, lack of prenatal care, and low socioeconomic status. Prenatal care decreases the probability that a child born to an adolescent girl will have physical problems. However, adolescents are the least likely of women in all age groups to obtain prenatal assistance from clinics, pediatricians, and health services.

Increasingly, women seek to establish their careers before beginning a family, delaying childbearing until their thirties. Down syndrome, a form of mental retardation, is related to the mother's age. A baby with Down syndrome rarely is born to a mother under the age of 30, but the risk increases after the mother reaches 30. By age 40, the probability is slightly over 1 in 100, and, by age 50, it is almost 1 in 10. The risk is also higher before age 18.

Women also have more difficulty becoming pregnant after the age of 30. One study in a French fertility clinic focused on women whose husbands were sterile (Schwartz & Mayaux, 1982). To make it possible for the women to have a child, the women were artificially inseminated once a month for 1 year. Each woman had 12 chances to become pregnant. Seventy-five percent of the women in their twenties became pregnant, 62 percent of the women 31 to 35 years old became pregnant, and only 54 percent of the women over 35 years old became pregnant.

We still have much to learn about the role of the mother's age in pregnancy and childbirth. As women remain active, exercise regularly, and are careful about their nutrition, their reproductive systems may remain healthier at older ages than was thought possible in the past (Windridge, Cert, & Berryman, 1999). Indeed, as we will see next, the mother's nutrition influences prenatal development.

Infants born to adolescent mothers face developmental risks, including higher mortality rates and mental retardation than infants born to mothers in their twenties.

Nutrition

A developing fetus depends completely on its mother for nutrition, which comes from the mother's blood. Nutritional status is not determined by any specific aspect of diet. Among the important factors are the total number of calories and appropriate levels of protein, vitamins, and minerals. The mother's nutrition even influences her ability to reproduce. In extreme instances of malnutrition, women stop menstruating, thus precluding conception. Children born to malnourished mothers are more likely to be malformed.

One study of Iowa mothers documents the important role of nutrition in prenatal development and birth (Jeans, Smith, & Stearns, 1955). The diets of 400 pregnant women were studied, and the status of their newborns was assessed. The mothers with the poorest diets had offspring who weighed the least, had the least vitality, were born prematurely, or died. In another study, diet supplements given to malnourished mothers during pregnancy improved the performance of their offspring during the first three years of life (Werner, 1979).

Because the fetus depends entirely on its mother for nutrition, it is important for the pregnant woman to have good nutritional habits. In Kenya, this government clinic provides pregnant women with information about how their diet can influence the health of their fetus and offspring.

Emotional States and Stress

Tales abound about how a pregnant woman's emotional state affects the fetus. For centuries it was thought that frightening experiences—such as a severe thunderstorm or a family member's death—leave birthmarks on the child or affect the child in more serious ways. Today still we believe that the mother's stress can be transmitted to the fetus, but we have a better grasp of how this takes place (Parker & Barrett, 1992). We now know that, when a pregnant woman experiences intense fears, anxieties, and other emotions, physiological changes occur—among them, changes in respiration and glandular secretions. For example, producing adrenaline in response to fear restricts blood flow to the uterine area and may deprive the fetus of adequate oxygen.

The mother's emotional state during pregnancy can influence the birth process too. An emotionally distraught mother might have irregular contractions and a more difficult labor, which can cause irregularities in the baby's oxygen supply or can produce irregularities after birth. Babies born after extended labor also may adjust more slowly to their world and be more irritable.

Researchers have found that maternal anxiety during pregnancy is related to less than optimal outcomes (Stechler & Halton, 1982). In one study, maternal anxiety during pregnancy was associated with infants who were more hyperactive and irritable and who had more feeding and sleeping problems (Stanley, Soule, & Copens, 1979). Stresses during pregnancy that have been linked with maternal anxiety include marital discord, the death of a husband, and unwanted pregnancy (Field, 1990).

In one recent study of 156 fetuses several weeks before delivery, a tool was placed on a pregnant woman's abdomen to mildly stimulate the fetus (Wadhwa, 1999). Maternal blood samples were taken and the women filled out questionnaires on their mental health and social support. When the stimulus was active, fetal heart rates jumped significantly higher in expectant mothers who had the highest levels of stress hormones and who reported feeling the most anxiety and the least social support. The heart rates of the "stressed" mothers also stayed high the longest. In another recent study, 513 pregnant women were asked about the extent to which they recently had experienced stressful life events, and their stress hormone levels were assessed (Gupta, 1999). Ultrasound measurements of the fetus' head, abdomen, and bone were taken. High stress levels in the pregnant women were significantly related to a retardation in growth, seen as early as the second trimester of prenatal development. In this study, women with high levels of stress hormones were more likely to deliver premature babies.

In other research on stress and prenatal development, Christine Dunkel-Schetter and her colleagues (Dunkel-Schetter, 1998; Dunkel-Schetter & others, in press) have found that women under stress are about four times as likely to deliver their babies prematurely than are their low-stress counterparts. In another study, maternal stress increased corticotropin-releasing hormone (CRH) early in pregnancy (Hobel & others, 1999). This hormone is linked with stress. There also is a connection between stress and unhealthy behaviors, such as smoking, drug use, and poor prenatal care (Dunkel-Schetter, 1999). Further, researchers have found that pregnant women who are optimistic thinkers have less-adverse birth outcomes than pregnant women who are pessimistic thinkers (Loebel & Yali, 1999). Optimists believe that they have more control over the outcome of their pregnancy.

Tiffany Field and her colleagues (1985) attempted to reduce anxiety about pregnancy by giving video and verbal feedback during ultrasound assessments to assure the mother of the fetus's well-being. Compared with infants whose mothers did not receive such feedback, infants whose mothers got the intervention were less active in utero and had higher birthweights. As newborns, they were less irritable, and their performance on neonatal behavior assessments was superior. Thus, reassuring the mother of fetal well-being had positive outcomes for the infants in this study.

Drugs

How do drugs affect prenatal development? Some pregnant women take drugs, smoke tobacco, and drink alcohol without thinking about the possible effects on the fetus. Occasionally, an unusually high number of deformed babies are born, bringing to light the damage drugs can have on a developing fetus. This happened in 1961, when many pregnant

Later Life Pregnancy

Nutrition and Pregnancy

Exercise in Pregnancy

Through the Eyes of Psychologists

Christine Dunkel-Schetter, *UCLA*

"There appears to be a clear link between stress during pregnancy and premature delivery."

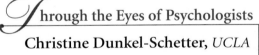

Figure **4.6**

Fetal Alcohol Syndrome

Notice the wide-set eyes, flat bones, and thin upper lip.

fetal alcohol syndrome (FAS)
A cluster of abnormalities that appear in the offspring of mothers who drink alcohol heavily during pregnancy.

*T*hrough the Eyes of Psychologists

Ann Streissguth, *University of Washington*

"Long-term negative effects of prenatal alcohol exposure have been demonstrated both in experimental studies with animals and in longitudinal studies of humans."

women took a popular tranquilizer, thalidomide, to alleviate their morning sickness. In adults, the effects of thalidomide are mild; in embryos, however, they are devastating. Not all infants were affected in the same way. If the mother took thalidomide on day 26 (probably before she knew she was pregnant), an arm might not grow. If she took the drug 2 days later, the arm might not grow past the elbow. The thalidomide tragedy shocked the medical community and parents into the stark realization that the mother does not have to be a chronic drug user for the fetus to be harmed. Taking the wrong drug at the wrong time is enough to physically handicap the offspring for life.

Alcohol   Heavy drinking by pregnant women can be devastating to offspring (Toth, Conner, & Streissguth, 1999)). **Fetal alcohol syndrome (FAS)** *is a cluster of abnormalities that appear in the offspring of mothers who drink alcohol heavily during pregnancy.* The abnormalities include facial deformities and defective limbs, face, and heart. Most of these children are below average in intelligence, and some are mentally retarded (Olson & Burgess, 1996). Although many mothers of FAS infants are heavy drinkers, many mothers who are heavy drinkers do not have children with FAS or have one child with FAS and other children who do not have it. Figure 4.6 shows a child with fetal alcohol syndrome. Although no serious malformations such as those produced by FAS are found in infants born to mothers who are moderate drinkers, in one study, the infants whose mothers drank moderately (one to two drinks a day) during pregnancy were less attentive and alert, with the effects still present at 4 years of age (Streissguth & others, 1984). In one recent study, prenatal alcohol exposure was a better predictor of adolescent alcohol use and its negative consequences than was family history of alcohol problems (Baer & others, 1998). And in another recent study, adults with fetal alcohol syndrome had a high incidence of mental disorders, such as depression or anxiety (Famy, Streissguth, & Unis, 1998).

Nicotine   Cigarette smoking by pregnant women can also adversely influence prenatal development, birth, and postnatal development. Fetal and neonatal deaths are higher among smoking mothers. There also are higher incidences of preterm births and lower birthweights (see figure 4.7).

In one recent study, urine samples from 22 of 31 newborns of smoking mothers had substantial amounts of one of the strongest carcinogens (NNK) in tobacco smoke; the urine samples of the newborns whose mothers did not smoke did not contain the carcinogen (Lackmann & others, 1999). In another study, prenatal exposure to cigarette smoking was related to poorer language and cognitive skills at 4 years of age (Fried & Watkinson, 1990). Respiratory problems and sudden infant death syndrome (also known as crib death) are more common among the offspring of mothers who smoked during pregnancy (Schoendorf & Kiely, 1992). Intervention programs designed to get pregnant women to stop smoking can reduce some of smoking's negative behaviors, especially by raising birth weights (Chomitz, Cheung, & Lieberman, 1995).

Caffeine   Can the caffeine that pregnant women take in by drinking coffee, tea, or cola, or by eating chocolate, be transmitted to the fetus? In one study, no relation between caffeine consumption and infertility was found when caffeine intake was low to moderate (less than 3 cups of coffee per day) (Grodstein, Goldman, & Cramer, 1993). However, with heavier consumption, caffeine users were more than twice as likely to become pregnant than women who consumed less caffeine.

Once a woman has become pregnant, the effects of her caffeine use might depend on her level of consumption (Pinger & others, 1998). In one study, even low doses of caffeine (as little as one cup of coffee a day) were associated with miscarriage (Infante-Rivard & others, 1993). However, in another study, drinking up to 3 cups of coffee a day did not increase the risk of miscarriage or have any adverse effects on the offspring (Mills & others, 1993). One review concluded that the small number of studies and the conflicting

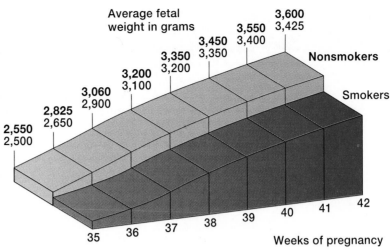

Average fetal weight in grams

2,550 / 2,500

2,825 / 2,650

3,060 / 2,900

3,200 / 3,100

3,350 / 3,200

3,450 / 3,350

3,550 / 3,400

3,600 / 3,425

Nonsmokers

Smokers

35 36 37 38 39 40 41 42

Weeks of pregnancy

Figure 4.7
The Effects of Smoking by Expectant Mothers on Fetal Weight

Throughout prenatal development, the fetuses of expectant mothers who smoke weigh less than the fetuses of expectant mothers who do not smoke.

results of those studies make it impossible to reach a conclusion about the effects of caffeine use by pregnant women at this time (Astrid & Derby, 1994). Taking into account such results, the U.S. Food and Drug Administration recommends that pregnant women either abstain from caffeine or ingest it sparingly.

Marijuana   Marijuana use by pregnant women has detrimental effects on a developing fetus. Marijuana use by pregnant women is associated with increased tremors and startles among newborns and poorer verbal and memory development at 4 years of age (Fried & Watkinson, 1990).

Cocaine   With the increased use of cocaine in the United States, there is growing concern about its effects on the embryos, fetuses, and infants of pregnant cocaine users (Hurt & others, 1999; Scher, Richardson & Day, 2000). Cocaine use during pregnancy has recently attracted considerable attention because of possible harm to the developing embryo and fetus (Eyler & others, 1998; Zelazo, Potter, & Valiante, 1995; Zeskind & others, 1999). In one recent study, deficits in information processing involving attentional and arousal systems were found in cocaine-exposed infants (Singer & others, 1999). The most consistent finding is that cocaine-exposed infants have reduced birth weight and length (Chasnoff & others, 1992). There are increased frequencies of congenital abnormalities in the offspring of cocaine users during pregnancy, but other factors in the drug addict's lifestyle, such as malnutrition and other substance abuse, might be responsible for the congenital abnormalities (Eyler, Behnke, & Stewart, 1990). For example, cocaine users are more likely than nonusers to smoke cigarettes and marijuana, drink alcohol, and take amphetamines. Teasing apart these potential influences from the effects of cocaine use itself has not yet been adequately accomplished (Lester, Freier, & LaGasse, 1995). Obtaining valid information about the frequency and type of drug use by mothers is complicated, since many mothers fear prosecution or loss of custody because of their drug use.

Fetal Alcohol Syndrome
Smoking and Pregnancy

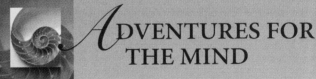

*A*DVENTURES FOR THE MIND
Intervention to Stop Pregnant Women from Smoking

SCIENTISTS HAVE KNOWN about the negative consequences of smoking for more than three decades, but they have made little progress in developing effective interventions to help pregnant women quit smoking or to keep young women from becoming addicted to smoking. What needs to be done to get pregnant women to not smoke? Consider the role of health-care providers and their training, the role of insurance companies, and specific programs targeted at pregnant women.

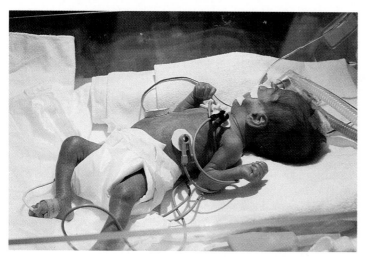

This baby was born addicted to cocaine because its mother was a cocaine addict. Researchers have found that the offspring of women who use cocaine during pregnancy often have hypertension and heart damage. Many of these infants face a childhood full of medical problems.

Heroin   It is well documented that infants whose mothers are addicted to heroin show several behavioral difficulties (Hans, 1989). The young infants of these mothers are addicted and show withdrawal symptoms characteristic of opiate abstinence, such as tremors, irritability, abnormal crying, disturbed sleep, and impaired motor control. Behavioral problems are still often present at the first birthday, and attention deficits might appear later in the child's development. The most common treatment for heroin addicts, methadone, is associated with very severe withdrawal symptoms in newborns.

The effects of various other drugs on offspring and some guidelines for safe use of these drugs are presented in figure 4.8.

Paternal Factors   So far, we have been considering maternal factors during pregnancy that can influence prenatal development and the development of the child. Might there also be some paternal factors that can have this influence? Men's exposure to lead, radiation, certain pesticides, and petrochemicals can cause abnormalities in sperm that lead to miscarriage or diseases, such as childhood cancer (Lindbohm, 1991; Taskinen, 1989). When fathers have a diet low in vitamin C, their offspring

Drug	Effects on fetus and offspring	Safe use of the drug
Alcohol	Small amounts increase risk of spontaneous abortion. Moderate amounts (one to two drinks a day) are associated with poor attention in infancy. Heavy drinking can lead to fetal alcohol syndrome. Some experts believe that even low to moderate amounts, especially in the first three months of pregnancy, increase the risk of FAS.	Avoid use.
Nicotine	Heavy smoking is associated with low-birthweight babies, which means the babies may have more health problems than other infants. Smoking may be especially harmful in the second half of pregnancy.	Avoid use.
Tranquilizers	Taken during the first three months of pregnancy, they may cause cleft palate or other congenital malformations.	Avoid use if you might become pregnant and during early pregnancy. Use only under a doctor's supervision.
Barbiturates	Mothers who take large doses may have babies who are addicted. Babies may have tremors, restlessness, and irritability.	Use only under a doctor's supervision.
Amphetamines	They may cause birth defects.	Use only under a doctor's supervision.
Cocaine	Cocaine may cause drug dependency and withdrawal symptoms at birth, as well as physical and mental problems, especially if the mother uses cocaine in the first three months of pregnancy. There is a higher risk of hypertension, heart problems, developmental retardation, and learning difficulties.	Avoid use.
Marijuana	It may cause a variety of birth defects and is associated with low birthweight and height.	Avoid use.

Figure **4.8**
Drug Use During Pregnancy

$\mathcal{E}$XPLORATIONS IN CHILD DEVELOPMENT
Prenatal Care and Classes

PRENATAL CARE VARIES enormously but usually involves a package of medical care services in a defined schedule of visits. In addition to medical care, prenatal care programs often include comprehensive educational, social, and nutritional services (Shiono & Behrman, 1995).

Prenatal care usually includes screening that can reveal manageable conditions and/or treatable diseases in the baby and the pregnant mother. The education the mother receives about pregnancy, labor and delivery, and caring for the newborn can be extremely valuable, especially for first-time mothers. Prenatal care is also very important for women in poverty because it links them with other social services. The legacy of prenatal care continues after the birth because women who experience this type of care are more likely to get preventive care for their infants (Bates & others, 1994).

Women sometimes receive inadequate prenatal care for reasons related to the health-care system, provider practices, and their own individual and social characteristics (Alexander & Korenbrot, 1995). In one national study, 71 percent of the low-income women experienced a problem in getting prenatal care (U.S. General Accounting Office, 1987). They cited finances, transportation, and child care as barriers. Motivating positive attitudes toward pregnancy is also important. Women who do not want to be pregnant, who have negative attitudes about being pregnant, or who unintentionally become pregnant are more likely to delay prenatal care or to miss appointments (Joseph, 1989).

Early prenatal classes may include couples in both early pregnancy and prepregnancy (Olds, London, & Ladewig, 1988). The classes often focus on topics such as these:

- Changes in the development of the embryo and the fetus
- Self-care during pregnancy
- Fetal development concerns and environmental dangers for the fetus
- Sexuality during pregnancy
- Birth setting and types of care providers
- Nutrition, rest, and exercise
- Common discomforts of pregnancy and relief measures
- Psychological changes in both the expectant mother and her partner
- Information needed to get the pregnancy off to a good start

Early classes also may include information about factors that place the expectant mother at risk for preterm labor and recognition of the possible signs and symptoms of preterm labor. Prenatal education classes also may include information on the advantages and disadvantages of breast- and bottle-feeding. Most expectant mothers (50 to 80 percent) make this infant feeding decision prior to the sixth month of pregnancy. Therefore, information about the issues involved in breast- versus bottle-feeding in an early prenatal education class is helpful.

So far, the prenatal education classes we have described focus on expectant couples in the first trimester of pregnancy. The later classes—those when the expectant mother is in the second or third trimester of pregnancy—focus on preparation for the birth, infant care and feeding, postpartum self-care, and birth choices.

Early prenatal education classes focus on such topics as changes in the development of the fetus, while many later classes focus on preparation for the birth and care of the newborn.

SUMMARY TABLE 4.2
Teratology and Hazards to Prenatal Development

Concept	Processes/ Related Ideas	Characteristics/Description
What Is Teratology?	Its Nature	• This field investigates the causes of congenital (birth) defects. • Any agent that causes birth defects is called a teratogen.
Maternal Factors	Diseases and Conditions	• Maternal diseases and infections can cause damage by crossing the placental barrier, or they can be destructive during the birth process. • Among the maternal diseases and conditions that can cause birth defects are rubella, syphilis, genital herpes, HIV, the mother's age, nutrition, and emotional state and stress.
	Drugs	• Alcohol, nicotine, caffeine, marijuana, cocaine, and heroin are drugs that can adversely affect prenatal and infant development.
Paternal Factors	Their Nature	• Paternal factors that can adversely affect prenatal development include exposure to lead, radiation, certain pesticides, and petrochemicals. • Vitamin C deficiencies, cocaine use, and smoking also can harm the fetus. • Older fathers, like older mothers, are linked with some birth defects.

Reproductive Health Links

Exploring Pregnancy

Childbirth Classes

Prenatal Care

Health Care Providers

have a higher risk of birth defects and cancer (Fraga & others, 1991). Also, it has been speculated that in fathers who use cocaine, the cocaine can attach itself to sperm and cause birth defects, but the evidence for this is not yet strongly established. In some studies, chronic marijuana use has been shown to reduce testosterone levels and sperm counts, although the results have been inconsistent (Fields, 1998; Nahas, 1984).

The father's smoking during the mother's pregnancy also can cause problems for the offspring. In one investigation, the newborns of fathers who smoked during their wives' pregnancy were 4 ounces lighter at birth for each pack of cigarettes smoked per day than were the newborns whose fathers did not smoke during their wives' pregnancy (Rubin & others, 1986). In another study, in China, the longer the fathers smoked, the stronger the risk was for their children to develop cancer (Ji & others, 1997). In such studies, it is very difficult to tease apart prenatal and postnatal effects.

As is the case with older mothers, older age in fathers is also associated with certain birth defects. These include Down syndrome (about 5 percent of these children have older fathers), dwarfism, and Marfan's syndrome, which involves head and limb deformities.

As can be seen, there are many things that parents can do to reduce the risks for their offspring. To read further about some positive parenting strategies in prenatal development, see the Explorations in Child Development box on page 111, where we examine prenatal care and classes.

At this point we have discussed a number of ideas about teratology and hazards to prenatal development. A review of these ideas is presented in summary table 4.2. Next, we explore the nature of the birth process itself.

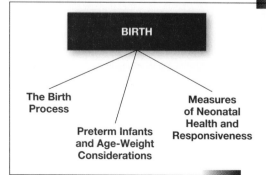

Birth

As we saw in the opening story about Tanner Roberts, many changes take place during the birth of a baby. Let's further explore the birth process.

The Birth Process

To learn more about the birth process, we will examine the stages of birth, the transition from fetus to newborn, childbirth strategies, preterm infants and age-weight considerations, and measures of neonatal health and responsiveness.

Stages of Birth   The birth process occurs in three stages. For a woman having her first child, the first stage lasts an average of 12 to 24 hours; it is the longest of the three stages. In the first stage, uterine contractions are 15 to 20 minutes apart at the beginning and last up to a minute. These contractions cause the woman's cervix to stretch and open. As the first stage progresses, the contractions come closer together, appearing every 2 to 5 minutes. Their intensity increases too. By the end of the first birth stage, contractions dilate the cervix to an opening of about 4 inches, so that the baby can move from the uterus to the birth canal.

The second birth stage begins when the baby's head starts to move through the cervix and the birth canal. It terminates when the baby completely emerges from the mother's body. This stage lasts approximately 1½ hours. With each contraction, the mother bears down hard to push the baby out of her body. By the time the baby's head is out of the mother's body, the contractions come almost every minute and last for about a minute.

Afterbirth *is the third stage, at which time the placenta, umbilical cord, and other membranes are detached and expelled.* This final stage is the shortest of the three birth stages, lasting only minutes.

The Transition from Fetus to Newborn

Being born involves considerable stress for the baby. During each contraction, when the placenta and umbilical cord are compressed as the uterine muscles draw together, the supply of oxygen to the fetus is decreased. **Anoxia** *is the condition in which the fetus/newborn has an insufficient supply of oxygen.* Anoxia can cause brain damage. If the delivery takes too long, anoxia can develop.

The baby has considerable capacity to withstand the stress of birth. Large quantities of adrenaline and nonadrenalin, hormones that are important in protecting the fetus in the event of oxygen deficiency, are secreted in stressful circumstances. These hormones increase the heart's pumping activity, speed up heart rate, channel blood flow to the brain, and raise blood-sugar level. Never again in life will such large amounts of these hormones be secreted. This circumstance underscores how stressful it is to be born but also how prepared and adapted the fetus is for birth (Von Beveren, 1999).

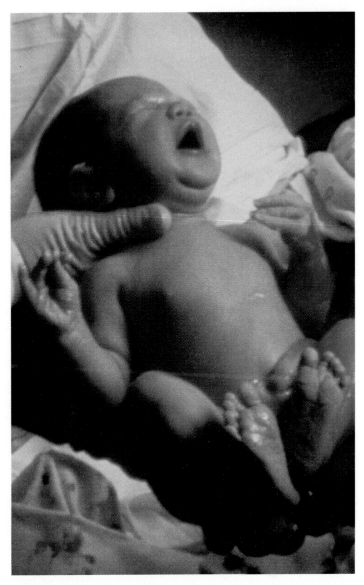

After the long journey of prenatal development, birth takes place. During birth the baby is on a threshold between two worlds.

As we saw in the case of Tanner Roberts at the beginning of the chapter, the umbilical cord is cut immediately after birth, and the baby is on its own. Now 25 million little air sacs in the lungs must be filled with air. Until now, these air sacs have held fluid, but this fluid is rapidly expelled in blood and lymph. The first breaths may be the hardest ones at any point in the life span. Until now, oxygen came from the mother via the umbilical cord, but now the baby has to be self-sufficient and breathe on its own. The newborn's blood is redirected through the lungs and to all parts of the body.

At the time of birth, the baby is covered with what is called *vernix caseosa,* a protective skin grease. This vernix consists of fatty secretions and dead cells, thought to protect the baby's skin against heat loss before and during birth. After the baby and mother have met and become acquainted with each other, the baby is taken to be cleaned, examined, weighed, and evaluated. Later in the chapter, we will discuss several measures that are used to examine the newborn's health and responsiveness.

afterbirth
The third stage of birth, when the placenta, umbilical cord, and other membranes are detached and expelled.

anoxia
The insufficient availability of oxygen to the fetus or newborn.

Preparing for Birth

We must respect this instant of birth, this fragile moment. The baby is between two worlds, on a threshold, hesitating...

Frederick Leboyer
French Obstetrician, 20th Century

Childbirth Strategies
Childbirth Setting and Attendants
Midwifery
Doula

doula
A caregiver who provides continuous physical, emotional, and educational support to the mother before, during, and just after childbirth.

analgesia
Drugs used to alleviate pain, such as tranquilizers, barbiturates, and narcotics.

anesthesia
Drugs used in late first-stage labor and during expulsion of the baby to block sensation in an area of the mother's body or to block the mother's consciousness.

oxytocics
Synthetic hormones designed to stimulate contractions.

Childbirth Strategies   Among the childbirth decisions that need to be made are what the setting will be and who the attendants will be, which childbirth technique will be used, and what the father's or sibling's role will be.

Childbirth Setting and Attendants   In the United States, 99 percent of births take place in hospitals, and more than 90 percent are attended by physicians (Ventura & others, 1997). Many hospitals now have birthing centers, where fathers or birth coaches may be with the mother during labor and delivery. Some people believe this so-called alternative birthing center offers a good compromise between a technological, depersonalized hospital birth (which cannot offer the emotional experience of a home birth) and a birth at home (which cannot offer the medical backup of a hospital). A birthing room approximates a home setting as much as possible. The birthing room allows for a full range of birth experiences, from a totally unmedicated, natural birth to the most complex, medically intensive care. Some women with good medical histories and low risk for problem delivery choose a home delivery or a delivery in a freestanding birthing center, which is usually staffed by nurse-midwives.

Approximately 6 percent of women who deliver a baby in the United States are attended by a midwife (Ventura & others, 1997). Most midwives are nurses who have been specially trained in delivering babies (Webster & others, 1999).

In many countries around the world, babies are more likely to be delivered at home than they are in the United States. For example, in Holland, 35 percent of the babies are born at home, and more than 40 percent are delivered by midwives rather than by doctors (Treffers & others, 1990).

In many countries, a doula attends a childbearing woman. *Doula* is a Greek word that means "a woman who helps." A **doula** *is a caregiver who provides continuous physical, emotional, and educational support for the mother before, during, and after childbirth.* Doulas remain with the mother throughout labor, assessing and responding to her needs. In one study, the mothers who received doula support reported less labor pain than the mothers who did not receive doula support (Klaus, Kennell, & Klaus, 1993). Doulas typically function as part of a "birthing team," serving as an adjunct to the midwife or the hospital obstetric staff (McGrath & others, 1999).

In the United States, most doulas work as independent providers hired by the expectant woman. Managed care organizations are increasingly offering doula support as a part of regular obstetric care. In many cultures, the practice of a knowledgeable woman helping a mother in labor is not officially labeled "doula" support but is simply an ingrained, centuries-old custom.

Methods of Delivery   Methods of delivery include medicated, natural and prepared, and cesarean.

The American Academy of Pediatrics recommends the least possible medication during delivery (Hotchner, 1997). There are three basic kinds of drugs that are used for labor: analgesia, anesthesia, and oxytocics. **Analgesia** *is used to relieve pain.* Analgesics include tranquilizers, barbiturates, and narcotics (such as Demerol). **Anesthesia** *is used in late first-stage labor and during expulsion of the baby to block sensation in an area of the body or to block consciousness.* There is a trend toward not using general anesthesia in normal births because it can be transmitted through the placenta to the fetus. However, an epidural anesthesia does not cross the placenta. An *epidural block* is regional anesthesia that numbs the woman's body from the waist down. Even this drug, thought to be relatively safe, has come under recent criticism because it is associated with fever, extended labor, and increased risk for cesarean delivery (Lieberman & others, 1997). **Oxytocics** *are synthetic hormones that are used to stimulate contractions.* Pitocin is the most commonly used oxytocic.

Predicting how a particular drug will affect an individual pregnant woman and the fetus is difficult. While we have many commonalities as human beings, we also vary a great deal. Thus, a particular drug may have only a minimal effect on one fetus

Lamaze
Labor Induction
Labor and Birth Resources
Cesarean Childbirth

yet have a much stronger effect on another fetus. The drug's dosage also is a factor, with stronger doses of tranquilizers and narcotics given to decrease the mother's pain having a potentially more negative effect on the fetus than mild doses. It is important for the mother to assess her level of pain and be an important voice in the decision of whether she should receive medication or not.

Though the trend at one time was toward a natural childbirth without any medication, today the emphasis is on using some medication but keeping it to a minimum when possible. The emphasis today also is on broadly educating the pregnant woman so that she can be reassured and confident. Next, we will consider natural and prepared childbirth, which reflect this emphasis on education.

Natural childbirth *was developed in 1914 by English obstetrician Grantley Dick-Read. It attempts to reduce the mother's pain by decreasing her fear through education about childbirth and by teaching her to use breathing methods and relaxation techniques during delivery.* Dick-Read also believed that the doctor's relationship with the mother is an important dimension of reducing her perception of pain. He said the doctor should be present during her active labor prior to delivery and should provide reassurance.

Prepared childbirth *was developed by French obstetrician Ferdinand Lamaze. This childbirth strategy is similar to natural childbirth but includes a special breathing technique to control pushing in the final stages of labor and a more detailed anatomy and physiology course.* The Lamaze method has become very popular in the United States. The pregnant woman's husband or a friend usually serves as a coach, who attends childbirth classes with her and helps her with her breathing and relaxation during delivery.

Many other prepared childbirth techniques also have been developed (Samuels & Samuels, 1996). They usually include elements of Dick-Read's natural childbirth or Lamaze's method, plus one or more new components. For instance, the Bradley method places special emphasis on the father's role as a labor coach. Virtually all of the prepared childbirth methods emphasize some degree of education, relaxation and breathing exercises, and support. In recent years, new ways of teaching relaxation have been offered, including guided mental imagery, massage, and meditation. In sum, the current belief in prepared childbirth is that, when information and support are provided, women *know* how to give birth.

In a **cesarean delivery,** *the baby is removed from the mother's uterus through an incision made in her abdomen. This also is sometimes called a cesarean section.* A cesarean section is usually performed if the baby is in a **breech position,** *which causes the baby's buttocks to be the first part to emerge from the vagina.* Normally, the crown of the baby's head comes through the vagina first, but in 1 of every 25 babies, the head does not come through first. Breech babies' heads are still in the uterus while the rest of their bodies are out, which can cause respiratory problems.

Cesarean deliveries also are performed if the baby is lying crosswise in the uterus, if the baby's head is too large to pass through the mother's pelvis, if the baby develops complications, or if the mother is bleeding vaginally.

The benefits and risks of cesarean sections continue to be debated. Cesarean deliveries are safer than breech deliveries, but they involve a higher infection rate, longer hospital stay, and greater expense and stress that accompany any surgery.

Some critics believe that in the United States too many babies are delivered by cesarean section. More cesarean sections are performed in the United States than in any other country in the world. In the 1980s, births by cesarean section increased almost 50 percent in the United States, with almost one-fourth of babies delivered in this way. In the 1990s, the growing use of vaginal birth after a previous cesarean, greater public awareness, and peer pressure in the medical community led to some decline in cesarean sections.

Now that we have explored the stages of birth and childbirth strategies, it is important to consider how the birth process unfolds when babies are born preterm or low birthweight.

natural childbirth
A method of childbirth, developed in 1914 by Dick-Read, intended to reduce the mother's pain by decreasing her fear through education about childbirth and relaxation techniques during delivery.

prepared childbirth
Developed by French obstetrician, Ferdinand Lamaze, this childbirth strategy is similar to natural childbirth but includes a special breathing technique to control pushing in the final stages of labor and a more detailed anatomy and physiology course.

cesarean delivery
A childbirth method in which the baby is removed from the mother's uterus through an incision made in her abdomen. This also is sometimes referred to as cesarean section.

breech position
A baby's position in the uterus that causes the buttocks to be the first part to emerge from the vagina.

Many husbands, or coaches, take childbirth classes with their wives or friends as part of prepared or natural childbirth. This is a Lamaze training session. Lamaze training is available on a widespread basis in the United States and usually consists of six weekly classes.

Neonatal Research

Preterm Infants and Age-Weight Considerations

How can we distinguish between a preterm infant and a low-birthweight infant? What are the developmental outcomes for low-birthweight infants? Do preterm infants have a different profile from that of full-term infants? What conclusions can we reach about preterm infants?

preterm infant
An infant born prior to 38 weeks after conception.

low-birthweight infant
An infant born after a regular period of gestation (the length of time between conception and birth) of 38 to 42 weeks but who weighs less than 5½ pounds.

Preterm and Low-Birthweight Infants   An infant is full-term when it has grown in the womb for the full 38 to 42 weeks between conception and delivery. A **preterm infant** *is one who is born prior to 38 weeks after conception.* A **low-birthweight infant** *is born after a regular gestation period (the length of time between conception and birth) of 38 to 42 weeks but weighs less than 5½ pounds.* Both preterm and low-birthweight infants are considered high-risk infants (Barton, Hodgman, & Pavlova, 1999; Malloy, 1999).

A short gestation period does not necessarily harm an infant. It is distinguished from retarded prenatal growth, in which the fetus has been damaged (Kopp, 1992). The neurological development of a short-gestation infant continues after birth on approximately the same timetable as if the infant still were in the womb. For example, consider an infant born after a gestation period of 30 weeks. At 38 weeks, approximately 2 months after birth, this infant shows the same level of brain development as a 38-week fetus who is yet to be born.

Some infants are born very early and have a precariously low birthweight. "Kilogram kids" weigh less than 2.3 pounds (which is 1 kilogram, or 1,000 grams) and are very premature. The task of saving such a baby is not easy. At the Stanford University Medical Center in Palo Alto, California, 98 percent of the preterm babies survive; however, 32 percent of those between 750 and 1,000 grams do not, and 76 percent of those below 750 grams do not. Approximately 250,000 preterm babies are born in the United States each year, and more than 15,000 of these weigh less than 1,000 grams.

Equal opportunity for life is an American ideal that is not fulfilled at birth (Paneth, 1995). African American babies are twice as likely as White babies to be born low-birthweight, to be born preterm, or to die at birth. Seventeen percent of all births are to African American families, yet 33 percent of all low-birthweight infants and 38 percent of all very low-birthweight infants are born to African American families.

A *"kilogram kid," weighing less than 2.3 pounds at birth. In the neonatal intensive care unit, banks of flashing lights, blinking numbers, and beeping alarms stand guard over kilogram kids, who are extremely preterm infants. They often lie on a water bed that gently undulates; the water bed is in an incubator that is controlled for temperature and humidity by the baby's own body. Such vital signs as brain waves, heartbeat, blood gases, and respiratory rate are constantly monitored. All of this care can be very expensive. Though the cost can usually be kept within five figures, 5 or 6 months of neonatal intensive care can result in expenses of as much as a million dollars or more.*

Long-Term Outcomes for Low-Birthweight Infants   Although most low-birthweight infants are normal and healthy, as a group they have more health and developmental problems than normal-birthweight infants (Chescheir & Hansen, 1999; Hack, Klein, & Taylor, 1995; Saigal & others, 2000). The number and severity of these problems increase as birth weight decreases (Barton, Hodgman, & Pavlova, 1999; Malloy, 1999). With the improved survival rates for infants who are born very early and very small come increases in severe brain damage. Cerebral palsy and other forms of brain injury are highly correlated with brain weight—the lower the brain weight, the greater the likelihood of brain injury. Approximately 7 percent of moderately low-birthweight infants (3 pounds 5 ounces to 5 pounds 8 ounces) have brain injuries. This figure increases to 20 percent for the smallest newborns (1 pound 2 ounces to 3 pounds 5 ounces). Low-birthweight infants are also more likely than normal-birthweight infants to have lung or liver diseases.

At school age, children who were born low in birth weight are more likely than their normal-birthweight counterparts to have a learning disability, attention deficit disorder, or breathing problems such as asthma (Taylor, Klein, & Hack, 1994). Children born very low in birth weight have more learning problems and lower levels of achievement in reading and math than moderately low birthweight children. These problems are reflected in much higher percentages of low-birthweight children being enrolled in special education programs. Approximately 50 percent of all low-birth-weight children are enrolled in special education programs.

Not all of these adverse consequences can be attributed solely to being born low in birth weight. Some of the less severe but more common developmental and physical delays occur because many low-birthweight children come from disadvantaged environments.

Some of the devastating effects of being born low in birth weight can be reversed (Blair & Ramey, 1996; Chescheir & Hansen, 1999; Shiono & Behrman, 1995). Intensive enrichment programs that provide medical and educational services for both the parents and the child have been shown to improve short-term developmental outcomes for low-birthweight children. Federal laws mandate that services for school-age children with disabilities (which include medical, educational, psychological, occupational, and physical care) be expanded to include family-based care for infants. At present, these services are aimed at children born with severe congenital disabilities. The availability of services for moderately low birthweight children who do not have severe physical problems varies from state to state, but generally these services are not available.

Preterm Infants
Low-Birthweight Infants
Social Factors and Low Birth Weight
Exploring Low Birth Weight
Touch Research Institute

Stimulation of Preterm Infants   Just three decades ago, preterm infants were perceived to be too fragile to cope well with environmental stimulation, and the recommendation was to handle such infants as little as possible. The climate of opinion changed when the adverse effects of maternal deprivation (mothers' neglect of their infants) became known and was interpreted to include a lack of stimulation. A number of research studies followed that indicated a "more is better" approach in the stimulation of preterm infants. Today, however, experts on infant development argue that preterm infant care is far too complex to be described only in terms of amount of stimulation.

Following are some conclusions about the stimulation of preterm infants (Lester & Tronick, 1990):

1. Preterm infants' responses to stimulation vary with their conceptual age, illness, and individual makeup. The immature brain of the preterm infant might be more vulnerable to excessive, inappropriate, or mistimed stimulation. The very immature infant should be protected from excessive stimulation because it might destabilize the baby's homeostatic condition.

2. As the healthy preterm infant becomes less fragile and approaches term, the issue of what is appropriate stimulation should be considered. Infants' behavioral cues can be used to determine appropriate interventions. An infant's signs of stress or avoidance behaviors indicate that stimulation should be terminated. Positive behaviors indicate that stimulation is appropriate.

3. Intervention with the preterm infant should be organized in the form of an individualized developmental plan. This plan should be constructed as a psychosocial intervention to include the parents and other immediate family members and to acknowledge the socioeconomic, cultural, and home environmental factors that will determine the social context in which the infant will be reared. The developmental plan should also include assessing the infant's behavior, working with the parents to help them understand the infant's medical and behavioral status, and helping the parents deal with their own feelings. The very immature infant should probably be protected from stimulation that could destabilize its homeostatic condition.

To read further about stimulating preterm infants, see the Explorations in Psychology box, where we discuss Tiffany Field's research on the power of massage in development. An important task is assessing the newborn's health and responsiveness. Next, we explore the main ways this is carried out.

EXPLORATIONS IN CHILD DEVELOPMENT
The Power of Touch and Massage in Development

THERE HAS BEEN a recent surge of interest in the roles of touch and massage in improving the growth, health, and well-being of infants and children. This interest has been stimulated by the research of Tiffany Field (1998), director of the Touch Research Institute at the University of Miami School of Medicine. In one investigation, 40 preterm infants who had just been released from an intensive care unit and placed in a transitional nursery were studied (Field, Scafidi, & Schanberg, 1987). Twenty of the preterm babies were given special stimulation with massage and exercise for three 15-minute periods at the beginning of 3 consecutive hours every morning for 10 weekdays. For example, each infant was placed on its stomach and gently stroked. The massage began with the head and neck and moved downward to the feet. It also moved from the shoulders down to the hands. The infant was then rolled over. Each arm and leg was flexed and extended; then both legs were flexed and extended. Next, the massage was repeated.

The massaged and exercised preterm babies gained 47 percent more weight than their preterm counterparts who were not massaged and exercised, even though both groups had the same number of feedings per day and averaged the same intake of formula. The increased activity of the massaged, exercised infants would seem to work against weight gain. However, similar findings have been discovered with animals. The increased activity may increase gastrointestinal and metabolic efficiency. The massaged infants were more active and alert, and they performed better on developmental tests. Also, their hospital stays were about six days shorter than those of the nonmassaged, nonexercised group, which saved about $3,000 per preterm infant. Field has recently replicated these findings with preterm infants in another study.

In another study, Field (1992) gave the same kind of massage (firm stroking with the palms of the hands) to preterm infants who were exposed to cocaine in utero. The infants also showed significant weight gain and improved scores on developmental tests. In another study, 28 newborns born to HIV-positive mothers were randomly assigned to massage therapy or to a control group (Scafidi & Field, 1996). The treatment-group infants were given three 15-minute massages daily for 10 days. The massaged group showed superior performance on a wide range of infant assessments, including daily weight gain. Field also has conducted a number of studies of infants born to depressed mothers. In one study, Field and her colleagues (Field, Grizzle, and others, 1996) investigated 1- to 3-month-old infants born to depressed adolescent mothers. The infants were given 15 minutes of either massage or rocking for 2 days per week for a 6-week pe-

riod. The infants who received massage therapy had lower stress, as well as improved emotionality, sociability, and soothability, when compared with the rocked infants. Field and her colleagues also have demonstrated the benefits of massage therapy with women in reducing their labor pain (Field, Hernandez-Reif, Taylor, and others, 1997), with children who have arthritis (Field, Hernandez-Reif, Seligman, and others, 1997), with children who have asthma (Field, Henteleff, and others, 1998), with autistic children's attentiveness (Field, Lasko, and others, 1997), with alleviating stress in children following a hurricane (Field, Seligman, and others, 1996), and with adolescents who have attention deficit hyperactivity disorder (Field, Quintino, and others, 1998). (Field & others, 1998b).

Field and her colleagues (Cigales & others, 1996) also are studying the amount of touch a child normally receives during school activities. They hope that positive forms of touch will return to school systems, where touching has been outlawed because of potential sexual abuse lawsuits.

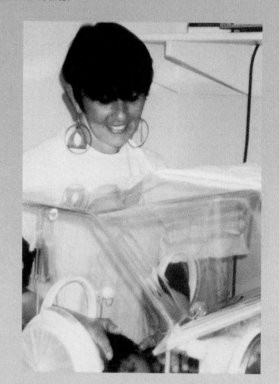

Shown here is Dr. Tiffany Field massaging a newborn infant. Dr. Field's research has clearly demonstrated the power of massage in improving the developmental outcome of at-risk infants. Under her direction, the Touch Research Institute in Miami, Florida, was developed to investigate the role of touch in a number of domains of health and well-being.

Measures of Neonatal Health and Responsiveness

The **Apgar Scale** *is widely used to assess the health of newborns at 1 and 5 minutes after birth. The Apgar Scale evaluates infants' heart rate, respiratory effort, muscle tone, body color, and reflex irritability.* An obstetrician or a nurse does the evaluation and gives the newborn a score, or reading, of 0, 1, or 2 on each of these five health signs (see figure 4.9). A total score of 7 to 10 indicates that the newborn's condition is good. A score of 5 indicates there may be developmental difficulties. A score of 3 or below signals an emergency and indicates that the baby might not survive. The Apgar Scale is especially good at assessing the newborn's ability to respond to the stress of delivery, labor, and the new environment (Butterfield, 1999). The Apgar Scale also identifies high-risk infants who need resuscitation.

To evaluate the newborn more thoroughly, the **Brazelton Neonatal Behavioral Assessment Scale** *is performed within 24 to 36 hours after birth to evaluate the newborn's neurological development, reflexes, and reactions to people.* When the Brazelton is given, the newborn is treated as an active participant, and the score attained is based on the newborn's best performance. Sixteen reflexes, such as sneezing, blinking, and rooting, are assessed, along with reactions to circumstances, such as the infant's reaction to a rattle. (We will have more to say about reflexes in the next chapter, when we discuss physical development in infancy.) The examiner rates the newborn on each of 27 categories (see figure 4.10). As an indication of how detailed the ratings are, consider item 15: "cuddliness." Nine categories are involved in assessing this item, with infant behavior scored on a continuum that ranges from the infant's being very resistant to being held to the infant's being extremely cuddly and clinging. The Brazelton scale not only is used as a sensitive index of neurological competence in the week after birth, but it also is used widely as a measure in many research studies on infant development. In scoring the Brazelton scale, T. Berry Brazelton and his colleagues (Brazelton, Nugent, & Lester, 1987) categorize the 27 items into four categories—physiological, motoric, state, and interaction. They also classify the baby in global terms, such as "worrisome," "normal," or "superior," based on these categories (Nugent & Brazelton, 2000).

A very low Brazelton score can indicate brain damage, or it can reflect stress to the brain that may heal in time. However, if an infant merely seems sluggish in responding to social circumstances, parents are encouraged to give the infant attention and become more sensitive to the infant's needs. Parents are shown how the newborn can respond to people and how to stimulate such responses. Researchers have found that the social interaction skills of both high-risk infants and healthy, responsive infants can be improved through such communication with parents (Worobey & Belsky, 1982).

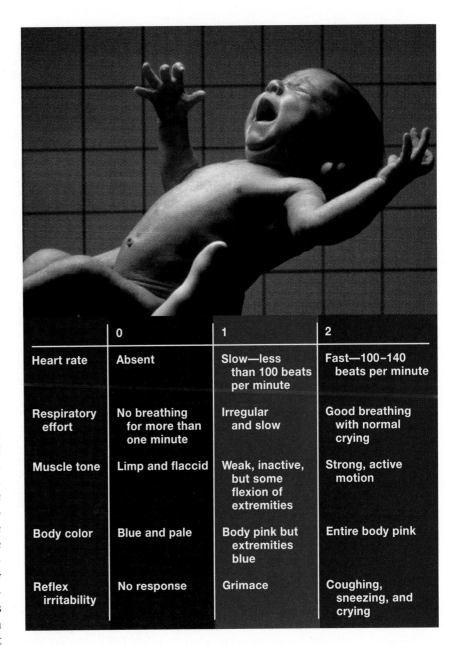

	0	1	2
Heart rate	Absent	Slow—less than 100 beats per minute	Fast—100–140 beats per minute
Respiratory effort	No breathing for more than one minute	Irregular and slow	Good breathing with normal crying
Muscle tone	Limp and flaccid	Weak, inactive, but some flexion of extremities	Strong, active motion
Body color	Blue and pale	Body pink but extremities blue	Entire body pink
Reflex irritability	No response	Grimace	Coughing, sneezing, and crying

Figure **4.9**
The Apgar Scale

Apgar Scale
A widely used method to assess the health of newborns at 1 and 5 minutes after birth. The Apgar Scale evaluates infants' heart rate, respiratory effort, muscle tone, body color, and reflex irritability.

Brazelton Neonatal Behavioral Assessment Scale
A test given several days after birth to assess newborns' neurological development, reflexes, and reactions to people.

1. Response decrement to repeated visual stimuli
2. Response decrement to rattle
3. Response decrement to bell
4. Response decrement to pinprick
5. Orienting response to inanimate visual stimuli
6. Orienting response to inanimate auditory stimuli
7. Orienting response to inanimate visual and auditory stimuli
8. Orienting response to animate visual stimuli—examiner's face
9. Orienting response to animate auditory stimuli—examiner's voice
10. Orienting response to animate visual and auditory stimuli
11. Quality and duration of alert periods
12. General muscle tone—in resting and in response to being handled, passive, and active
13. Motor activity
14. Traction responses as the infant is pulled to sit
15. Cuddliness—responses to being cuddled by examiner
16. Defensive movements—reactions to a cloth over the infant's face
17. Consolability with intervention by examiner
18. Peak of excitement and capacity to control self
19. Rapidity of buildup to crying state
20. Irritability during examination
21. General assessment of kind and degree of activity
22. Tremulousness
23. Amount of startling
24. Lability of skin color—measuring autonomic lability
25. Lability of states during entire examination
26. Self-quieting activity—attempts to console self and control state
27. Hand-to-mouth activity

Figure **4.10**

The 27 Categories on the Brazelton Neonatal Behavioral Assessment Scale (NBAS)

postpartum period
The period after childbirth when the mother adjusts, both physically and psychologically, to the process of childbirth. This period lasts for about 6 weeks, or until her body has completed its adjustment and returned to a near prepregnant state.

At this point we have studied a number of ideas about birth. A review of these ideas is presented in summary table 4.3. Next, we turn our attention to the period after the birth of the baby—the postpartum period.

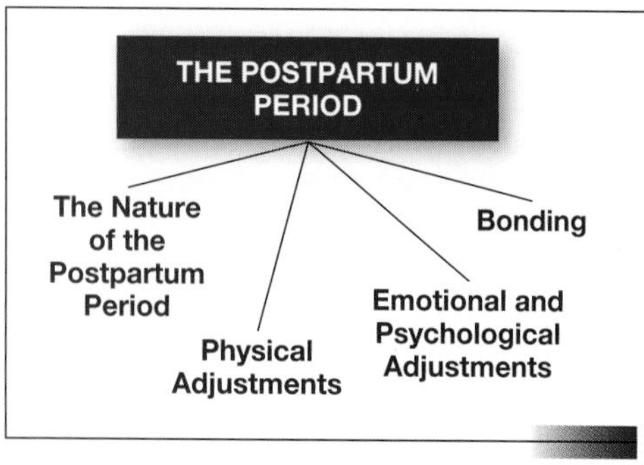

THE POSTPARTUM PERIOD
- The Nature of the Postpartum Period
- Physical Adjustments
- Emotional and Psychological Adjustments
- Bonding

The Postpartum Period

Many health professionals believe that the best postpartum care is family centered, using the family's resources to support an early and smooth adjustment to the newborn by all family members. What is the postpartum period?

The Nature of the Postpartum Period

The **postpartum period** *is the period after childbirth or delivery. It is a time when the woman's body adjusts, both physically and psychologically, to the process of childbearing. It lasts for about 6 weeks or until the body has completed its adjustment and has returned to a near prepregnant state.* Some health professionals refer to the postpartum period as the "fourth trimester." Though the time span of the postpartum period does not necessarily cover 3 months, the terminology of "fourth trimester" demonstrates the

SUMMARY TABLE 4.3
Birth

Concept	Processes/ Related Ideas	Characteristics/Description
The Birth Process	Stages of Birth	• The first stage lasts about 12 to 24 hours for a woman having her first child. The cervix dilates to about 4 centimeters. • The second stage begins when the baby's head moves through the cervix and ends with the baby's complete emergence. • The third stage is afterbirth.
	The Transition from Fetus to Newborn	• Being born involves considerable stress for the baby, but the baby is well prepared and adapted to handle the stress. • Anoxia—in which there is insufficient oxygen supply to the fetus/newborn—is a potential hazard.
	Childbirth Strategies	• Considerations include the childbirth setting and attendants. In many countries, a doula attends a childbearing woman. • Methods of delivery include medicated, natural and prepared, and cesarean.
Preterm Infants and Age-Weight Considerations	Preterm and Low-Birthweight Infants	• Preterm infants are those born before the end of the normal gestation period. • Infants who are born after a regular gestation period of 38 to 42 weeks but who weigh less than $5\frac{1}{2}$ pounds are called low-birthweight infants.
	Long-Term Outcomes	• Although most low-birthweight infants are normal and healthy, as a group they have more health and developmental problems than normal-birthweight infants.
	Stimulation of Preterm Infants	• Preterm infants' responses vary according to their conceptual age, illness, and individual makeup. • Stimulation should be organized in the form of an individualized developmental plan.
Measures of Neonatal Health and Responsiveness	Apgar Scale	• For many years, the Apgar Scale has been used to assess the newborn's health.
	Brazelton Neonatal Behavioral Assessment Scale	• This more recently developed scale is used for long-term neurological assessment. • This scale also assesses social responsiveness

idea of continuity and the importance of the first several months after birth for the mother.

The postpartum period is influenced by what preceded it. During pregnancy, the woman's body gradually adjusted to physical changes, but now it is forced to respond quickly. The method of delivery and circumstances surrounding the delivery affect the speed with which the woman's body readjusts during the postpartum period.

The postpartum period involves a great deal of adjustment and adaptation. The baby has to be cared for; the mother has to recover from childbirth; the mother has to learn how to take care of the baby; the mother needs to learn to feel good about herself as a mother; the father needs to learn how to take care of his recovering wife; the father needs to learn how to take care of the baby; and the father needs to learn how to feel good about himself as a father.

Physical Adjustments

The woman's body makes numerous physical adjustments in the first days and weeks after childbirth. She might have a great deal of energy or feel exhausted and let down.

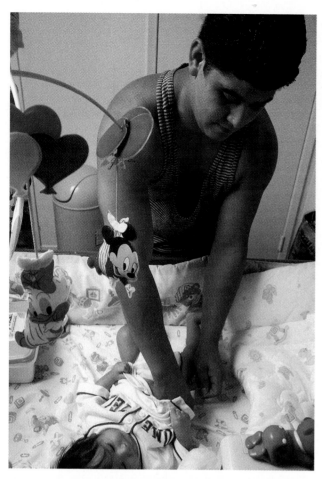

The postpartum period is a time of considerable adjustment and adaptation for both the mother and the father. Fathers can provide an important support system for mothers, especially in helping mothers care for young infants.

involution
The process by which the uterus returns to its prepregnant size.

Postpartum Adjustment
Postpartum Resources

Most new mothers feel tired and need rest. Though these changes are normal, the fatigue can undermine the new mother's sense of well-being and confidence in her ability to cope with a new baby and a new family life.

Involution *is the process by which the uterus returns to its prepregnant size 5 or 6 weeks after birth.* Immediately following birth, the uterus weighs 2 to 3 pounds. By the end of 5 or 6 weeks, the uterus weighs 2 to 3½ ounces. Nursing the baby helps to contract the uterus at a rapid rate.

After delivery, a woman's body undergoes sudden and dramatic changes in hormone production. When the placenta is delivered, estrogen and progesterone levels drop steeply and remain low until the ovaries start producing hormones again. The woman will probably begin menstruating again in 4 to 8 weeks if she is not breast-feeding. If she is breast-feeding, she might not menstruate for several months, though ovulation can occur during this time. The first several menstrual periods following delivery might be heavier than usual, but periods soon return to normal.

Some women and men want to resume sexual intercourse as soon as possible after the birth. Others feel constrained or afraid. A sore perineum (the area between the anus and vagina in the female), a demanding baby, lack of help, and extreme fatigue affect a woman's ability to relax and to enjoy making love. Physicians often recommend that women refrain from having sexual intercourse for approximately 6 weeks following the birth of the baby. However, it is probably safe to have sexual intercourse when the stitches heal, vaginal discharge stops, and the woman feels like it.

If the woman regularly engaged in conditioning exercises during pregnancy, exercise will help her to recover her former body contour and strength during the postpartum period. With a caregiver's approval, the woman can begin some exercises as soon as 1 hour after delivery. In addition to recommending exercise in the postpartum period for women, health professionals also increasingly recommend that women practice the relaxation techniques they used during pregnancy and childbirth. Five minutes of slow breathing on a stressful day in the postpartum period can relax and refresh the new mother, as well as the new baby.

Emotional and Psychological Adjustments

Emotional fluctuations are common on the part of the mother in the postpartum period (O'Hara, 2000). These emotional fluctuations can be due to any of a number of factors: hormonal changes, fatigue, inexperience or lack of confidence with newborn babies, or the extensive time and demands involved in caring for a newborn. For some women, the emotional fluctuations decrease within several weeks after the delivery and are a minor aspect of their motherhood. For others, they are longer-lasting and can produce feelings of anxiety, depression, and difficulty in coping with stress. Mothers who have such feelings, even when they are getting adequate rest, might benefit from professional help in dealing with their problems. Following are some of the signs that can indicate a need for professional counseling about postpartum adaptation:

• Excessive worrying
• Depression
• Extreme changes in appetite
• Crying spells
• Inability to sleep

A special concern of many new mothers is whether they should stay home with the baby or go back to work. Some mothers want to return to work as soon as possible after the infant is born; others want to stay home with the infant for several months, then return to work; others want to stay home for a year before they return to work; and yet others did not work outside the home prior to the baby's arrival and do not plan to do so in the future.

Many women, because of a variety of pressures—societal, career, financial—do not have the option of staying at home after their babies are born. However, for women who have to make the choice, the process of decision making is often difficult and agonizing.

The father also undergoes considerable adjustment in the postpartum period, although in many cases he will be away at work all day, whereas the mother will be at home, at least in the first few weeks. One of the most common reactions of the husband is the feeling that the baby comes first and gets all of the attention. In some marriages, the man might have come first with his wife and now feels that he has been replaced by the baby.

One strategy to help the man's postpartum reaction is for the parents to set aside some special time to be together with each other. The father's postpartum reaction also likely will be improved if he has taken childbirth classes with his wife and is an active participant in caring for the baby.

Important factors for both the mother and the father are the time and thought that go into being a competent parent of a young infant. It is important for both the mother and the father to become aware of the young infant's developmental needs— physical, psychological, and emotional. Both the mother and the father need to develop a sensitive, comfortable relationship with the baby.

ADVENTURES FOR THE MIND

Thinking About the Postpartum Period

GET TOGETHER with several other students in the class, making sure that the group includes at least one or more females and one or more males. After reading the material on the postpartum period, discuss your views on

- The most important adjustments the mother and father will have to make in their lives because of the newborn baby.
- Whether the mother should stay home with the baby or go back to work. If you think she should stay home, how long should she stay home with the baby before returning to work?
- The ways parents can help each other in adapting to the newborn baby in their lives.

Fathers and Childbirth
Siblings and Childbirth

Bonding

A special component of the parent-infant relationship is **bonding,** *the occurrence of close contact, especially physical, between parents and newborn in the period shortly after birth.* Some physicians believe that this period shortly after birth is critical in development. During this time, the parents and child need to form an important emotional attachment that provides a foundation for optimal development in years to come (Kennell & McGrath, 1999). Special interest in bonding came about when some pediatricians argued that the circumstances surrounding delivery often separate mothers and their infants, preventing or making difficult the development of a bond. The pediatricians further argued that giving the mother drugs to make her delivery less painful can contribute to the lack of bonding. The drugs might make the mother drowsy, thus interfering with her ability to respond to and stimulate the newborn. Advocates of bonding also assert that preterm infants are isolated from their mothers to an even greater degree than are full-term infants, thereby increasing their difficulty in bonding.

Is there evidence that such close contact between mothers and newborns is critical for optimal development later in life? Although some research supports the bonding hypothesis (Klaus & Kennell, 1976), a body of research challenges the significance of the first few days of life as a critical period (Bakeman & Brown, 1980; Rode & others, 1981). Indeed, the extreme form of the bonding hypothesis—that the newborn must have close contact with the mother in the first few days of life to develop optimally—simply is not true.

Nonetheless, the weakness of the maternal-infant bonding research should not be used as an excuse to keep motivated mothers from interacting with their infants in the postpartum period. Such contact brings pleasure to many mothers. In some mother-infant pairs—including preterm infants, adolescent mothers, or mothers

bonding
Close contact, especially physical, between parents and their newborn in the period shortly after birth.

SUMMARY TABLE 4.4
The Postpartum Period

Concept	Processes/Related Ideas	Characteristics/Description
The Nature of the Postpartum Period	Key Features	• This is the period after childbirth or delivery. • The woman's body adjusts physically and psychologically to having given birth. • This period lasts for about 6 weeks or until the body has completed its adjustment.
Physical Adjustments	Their Nature	• These include fatigue, involution (the process by which the uterus returns to its prepregnant size 5 to 6 weeks after birth), hormonal changes, when to resume sexual intercourse, and exercises to recover body contour and strength.
Emotional and Psychological Adjustments	Mother	• Emotional fluctuations are common for the mother in this period, and they can vary a great deal from one mother to the next.
	Father	• The father also goes through a postpartum adjustment.
Bonding	Its Nature	• Bonding involves close contact, especially physical contact, between parents and the newborn shortly after birth. • This has not been found to be critical in the development of a competent infant.

from disadvantaged circumstances—the practice of bonding may set in motion a climate for improved interaction after the mother and infant leave the hospital.

In recognition of the belief that bonding may have a positive effect on getting the parental-infant relationship off to a good start, many hospitals now offer a *rooming in* arrangement, in which the baby remains in the mother's room most of the time during its hospital stay. However, if parents choose not to use this rooming-in arrangement, the weight of the research evidence suggests that it will not harm the infant emotionally (Lamb, 1994).

At this point, we have discussed a number of ideas about the postpartum period. A review of these ideas is presented in summary table 4.4.

Chapter Review

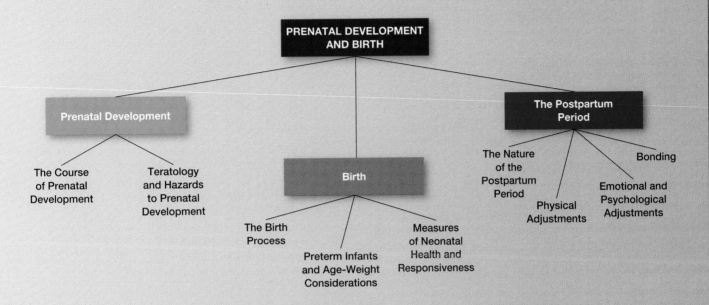

TO OBTAIN A DETAILED REVIEW OF THE CHAPTER, STUDY THESE FOUR SUMMARY TABLES:

Key Terms

germinal period 98
blastocyst 98
trophoblast 98
implantation 98
embryonic period 98
endoderm 98
ectoderm 98
mesoderm 99
placenta 99
umbilical cord 99
amnion 99

organogenesis 100
fetal period 100
teratogen 104
fetal alcohol syndrome (FAS) 108
afterbirth 113
anoxia 113
doula 114
analgesia 114
anesthesia 114
oxytocics 114
natural childbirth 115

prepared childbirth 115
cesarean delivery 115
breech position 115
preterm infant 116
low-birthweight infant 116
Apgar Scale 119
Brazelton Neonatal Behavioral Assessment
    Scale 119
postpartum period 120
involution 122
bonding 123

Key People

Ann Streissguth 108
Grantley Dick-Read 115
Ferdinand Lamaze 115

Tiffany Field 118
T. Berry Brazelton 119

Child Development Resources

ASPO/Lamaze
1840 Wilson Boulevard, Suite 204
Arlington, VA 22201

This organization provides information about the Lamaze method and taking or teaching Lamaze classes.

Birth: Issues in Perinatal Care

This multidisciplinary journal on perinatal care is written for health professionals and contains articles on research and clinical practice, review articles, and commentary.

National Center for Education in Maternal and Child Health
38th and R Streets NW
Washington, DC 20057
202-625-8400

This center answers questions about pregnancy and childbirth, high-risk infants, and maternal and child health programs. It also publishes a free guide, *Maternal and Child Health Publications.*

Prenatal Care Tips

Pregnant women can call this federal government toll-free number for prenatal care advice and referral to local health-care providers 800-311-2229.

What to Expect When You're Expecting
(1989, 2nd ed.) by Arlene Eisenberg, Heidi Murkoff, and Sandee Hathaway
New York: Workman

What to Expect When You're Expecting is a month-by-month, step-by-step guide to pregnancy and childbirth. The book tries to put expectant parents' normal fears into perspective by giving them comprehensive information and helping them enjoy this transition in their lives.

Taking It to the Net

1. Margaret's best friend, Sarah, suffered a miscarriage after several years of trying to become pregnant. Before Margaret goes to visit Sarah, she wants to understand more about the psychological trauma that Sarah may be experiencing as a result of the miscarriage.

2. Candice, age 28, has just learned that she is pregnant. She is proud of the fact that she weighs the same as she did in high school. She is terrified of getting fat and not being able to lose the weight after the baby is born. How can Candice eat properly to keep her and her baby healthy, while minimizing unnecessary and unhealthy weight gain?

3. Jackson and Diana have made an application with a foreign adoption agency to adopt a child from a former Soviet Union state. The agency told them the boy they have chosen might be suffering from a mild version of fetal alcohol syndrome. Jackson and Diana want to know more about FAS before their application is approved.

Connect to *http://www.mhhe.com/santrockc9* to find the answers!

Chapter 5

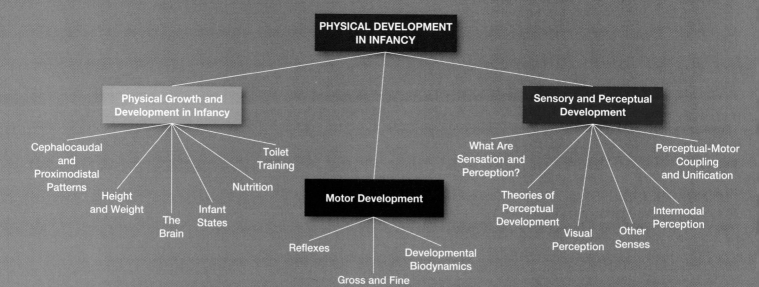

PHYSICAL DEVELOPMENT IN INFANCY

Physical Growth and Development in Infancy

- Cephalocaudal and Proximodistal Patterns
- Height and Weight
- The Brain
- Infant States
- Nutrition
- Toilet Training

Motor Development

- Reflexes
- Gross and Fine Motor Skills
- Developmental Biodynamics

Sensory and Perceptual Development

- What Are Sensation and Perception?
- Theories of Perceptual Development
- Visual Perception
- Other Senses
- Intermodal Perception
- Perceptual-Motor Coupling and Unification

abies are such a nice way to start people.

Don Herold
American Writer, 20th Century

The Stories of Latonya and Ramona: Bottle- and Breast-Feeding in Africa

LATONYA IS A NEWBORN BABY in the African country of Ghana. The culture of the area in which she was born discourages breast-feeding. She has been kept apart from her mother and bottle-fed in her first days of infancy. Manufacturers of infant formula provide the hospital where she was born with free or subsidized milk powder. Her mother has been persuaded to bottle-feed rather than breast-feed her.

When her mother bottle-feeds Latonya, she overdilutes the milk formula with unclean water. Latonya's feeding bottles also have not been sterilized. Latonya starts getting sick, very sick. She dies before her first birthday.

By contrast, Ramona lives in the African country of Nigeria. Her mother is breast-feeding her. Ramona was born at a Nigerian hospital where a "baby-friendly" program had been initiated. In this program, babies are not separated from their mothers when they are born, and the mothers are encouraged to breast-feed them. The mothers are told of the perils that bottle-feeding can bring because of unsafe water and unsterilized bottles. They also are informed about the advantages of breast milk, which include its nutritious and hygienic qualities, its ability to immunize babies against common illnesses, and its role in reducing the mother's risk of breast and ovarian cancer. At 1 year of age, Ramona is very healthy.

For the past 10 to 15 years, the World Health Organization and UNICEF have been trying to reverse the trend toward bottle-feeding of infants that emerged in many impoverished countries. They have instituted the "baby-friendly" program in many countries. They also have persuaded the International Association of Infant Formula Manufacturers to stop marketing their baby formulas to hospitals in countries where the governments support the baby-friendly initiatives. For the hospitals themselves, costs actually will be reduced as infant formula, feeding bottles, and separate nurseries become unnecessary. For example, the baby-friendly Jose Fabella Memorial Hospital in the Philippines already has reported saving 8 percent of its annual budget.

Hospitals play an important role in getting mothers to breast-feed their babies. For many years, maternity units were on the side of bottle-feeding babies and failed to give mothers adequate information about the benefits of breast-feeding. Fortunately, with the initiatives of the World Health Organization and UNICEF, that is beginning to change, but there still are many impoverished places in the world where the baby-friendly initiatives have not been implemented (Grant, 1993).

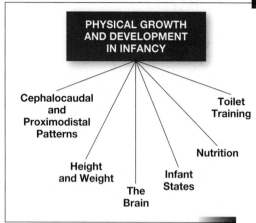

cephalocaudal pattern
The sequence in which the greatest growth occurs at the top—the head—with physical growth in size, weight, and feature differentiation gradually working from top to bottom.

proximodistal pattern
The sequence in which growth starts at the center of the body and moves toward the extremities.

Physical Growth and Development in Infancy

Infants' physical development in the first 2 years of life is extensive. At birth, neonates have a gigantic head (relative to the rest of the body), which flops around uncontrollably. They also possess reflexes that are dominated by evolutionary movements. In the span of 12 months, infants become capable of sitting anywhere, standing, stooping, climbing, and usually walking. During the second year, growth decelerates, but rapid increases in such activities as running and climbing take place. Let's now examine in greater detail the sequence of physical development in infancy.

Cephalocaudal and Proximodistal Patterns

The **cephalocaudal pattern** *is the sequence in which the greatest growth always occurs at the top—the head—with physical growth in size, weight, and feature differentiation gradually working its way down from top to bottom (neck, shoulders, middle trunk, and so on).* This same pattern occurs in the head area because the top parts of the head—the eyes and brain—grow faster than the lower parts, such as the jaw. An extraordinary proportion of the total body is occupied by the head during prenatal development and early infancy.

The **proximodistal pattern** *is the sequence in which growth starts at the center of the body and moves toward the extremities.* An example of this is the early maturation of muscular control of the trunk and arms, as compared with that of the hands and fingers.

Height and Weight

The average North American newborn is 20 inches long and weighs 7½ pounds. Ninety-five percent of full-term newborns are 18 to 22 inches long and weigh between 5½ and 10 pounds.

In the first several days of life, most newborns lose 5 to 7 percent of their body weight before they learn to adjust to neonatal feeding. Once infants adjust to sucking, swallowing, and digesting, they grow rapidly, gaining an average of 5 to 6 ounces per week during the first month. They have doubled their birthweight by the age of 4 months and have nearly tripled it by their first birthday. Infants grow about 1 inch per month during the first year, reaching approximately 1½ times their birth length by their first birthday.

Infants' rate of growth is considerably slower in the second year of life. By 2 years of age, infants weigh approximately 26 to 32 pounds, having gained a quarter to half a pound per month during the second year; now they have reached about one-fifth of their adult weight. At 2 years of age, the average infant is 32 to 35 inches in height, which is nearly one-half of their adult height.

The Brain

As an infant walks, talks, runs, shakes a rattle, smiles, and frowns, changes in its brain are occurring. Consider that the infant began life as a single cell and nine months later was born with a brain and nervous system that contained approximately 100 billion nerve cells, or neurons. A **neuron** *is a nerve cell that handles information processing at the cellular level* (see figure 5.1). Indeed, at birth the infant probably has all of the neurons it will ever have.

The Brain's Development
As the human embryo develops inside the womb, the central nervous system begins as a long, hollow tube on the embryo's back. About 3 weeks after conception, the brain forms into a large mass of neurons and loses its tubular appearance.

Scientists have identified three processes in the development of neurons: cell production, cell migration, and cell elaboration. Most neurons are produced between 10 and 26 weeks after conception. Amazingly, that means cells are generated at about 250,000 per minute in the human brain during this period. The second stage of neuron development involves cell migration, which occurs when cells move from the center of the brain, where neurons are produced, to their appropriate locations. Migration of neurons is completed 7 months after conception. The third stage of neuron development involves cell elaboration, which begins after cell migration. During cell migration, axons (the part of the neuron that carries information away from the cell to other neurons) and dendrites (the part of the neuron that collects information and routes it to the center of the cell) grow and form connections with other cells. Cell elaboration continues for years after birth and even has been documented in very old adults. As portrayed in figure 5.2, dendritic spreading in infancy is dramatic.

A myelin sheath, which is a layer of fat cells, encases most axons (review figure 5.1). Not only does the myelin sheath insulate nerve cells, but it also helps nerve impulses travel faster. Myelination, the process of encasing axons with fat cells, begins prenatally and continues after birth. Myelination for visual pathways occurs rapidly after birth, being completed in the first 6 months. Auditory myelination is not completed until 4 to 5 years of age. Some aspects of myelination continue even into adolescence.

At birth, the newborn's brain is about 25 percent of its adult weight. By the second birthday, the brain is about 75 percent of its adult weight. However, the brain's areas do not mature uniformly. Some areas, such as the primary motor areas, develop earlier than others, such as the primary sensory areas.

Studying the brain's development in infancy is not as easy as it might seem, because even the latest brain-imaging technologies can't make out fine details and they can't be used on babies. PET scans pose a radiation risk, and infants wriggle too much for an MRI (Marcus, Mulrine, & Wong, 1999).

However, one researcher who is making strides in finding out more about the brain's development in infancy is Charles Nelson (1999; deHaan & Nelson, 1999). He attaches up to 128 electrodes to babies' scalps and has found that even newborns produce distinctive brain waves that reveal they can distinguish their mother's voice from another woman's voice, even while they are asleep. Other research conducted by Nelson has found that by 8 months of age babies can distinguish the picture of a wooden toy they were allowed to feel, but not see, from pictures of other toys. This achievement coincides with the development of neurons in the brain's hippocampus (an important structure in memory), allowing the infant to remember specific items and events.

The Brain's Lobes and Hemispheres
The forebrain is the highest level of the brain. It consists of a number of structures, including the **cerebral cortex,** *which makes up about 80 percent of the brain's volume and covers the lower portions of*

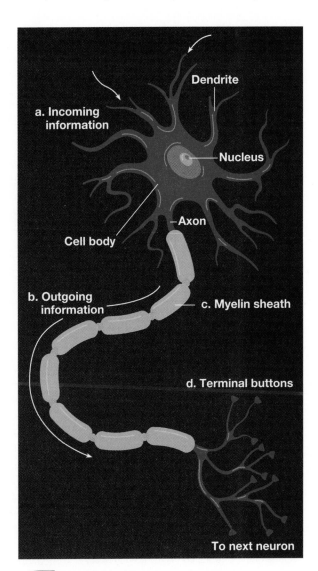

Figure 5.1
The Neuron
(a) The dendrites of the cell body receive information from other neurons, muscles, or glands through the axon. *(b)* Axons transmit information away from the cell body. *(c)* A myelin sheath covers most axons and speeds information transmission. *(d)* As the axon ends, it branches out into terminal buttons.

Neural Processes

neuron
A nerve cell that handles information processing at the cellular level.

cerebral cortex
An area of the forebrain that makes up about 80 percent of the brain's volume and plays critical roles in perception, language, thinking, and many other important functions.

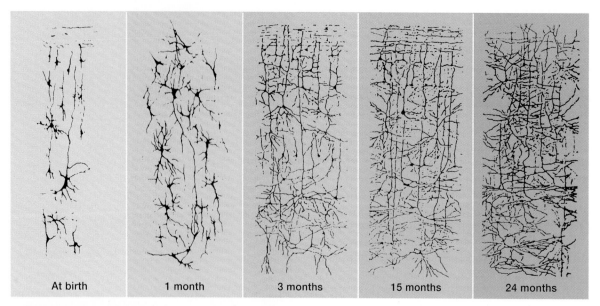

At birth   1 month   3 months   15 months   24 months

Figure 5.2
The Development of Dendritic Spreading
Note the increase in connectedness between neurons over the course of the first 2 years of life.

frontal lobe
An area of the cerebral cortex involved in
voluntary movement and thinking.

occipital lobe
An area of the cerebral cortex involved in vision.

temporal lobe
An area of the cerebral cortex involved in hearing.

parietal lobe
An area of the cerebral cortex involved in bodily
sensations, such as touch.

the brain like a cap. The cerebral cortex plays critical roles in many important human functions, such as perception, language, and thinking. Figure 5.3 shows an image of the cerebral cortex.

The cerebral cortex is divided into four main areas called lobes: the **frontal lobe** *is involved in voluntary movement and thinking.* The **occipital lobe** *is involved in vision.* The **temporal lobe** *is involved in hearing.* The **parietal lobe** *is involved in processing information about bodily sensations, such as touch.* Figure 5.4 shows the locations of the four lobes in the cerebral cortex.

The frontal lobes of the cerebral cortex are immature in the newborn. However, as neurons in the frontal lobes become myelinated and interconnected during the first year of life, infants develop an ability to regulate their physiological states (such as sleep) and gain more control over their reflexes. Cognitive skills that require deliberate thinking don't emerge until later (Bell & Fox, 1992). Indeed, the frontal lobes have the most prolonged development of any region in the human brain, with changes detectable at least into the adolescent years (Johnson, 1998). In general, the cerebral cortex is on a slower developmental pathway than other brain regions (Johnson, 1999).

The cerebral cortex is divided into two halves, or hemispheres (see figure 5.5 on page 134). The term **lateralization** *is used to describe specialization of functions in one hemisphere of the cerebral cortex or the other.* There continues to be considerable interest in the degree to which each is involved in various aspects of thinking, feeling, and behavior.

The most extensive research on the brain's hemispheres has focused on

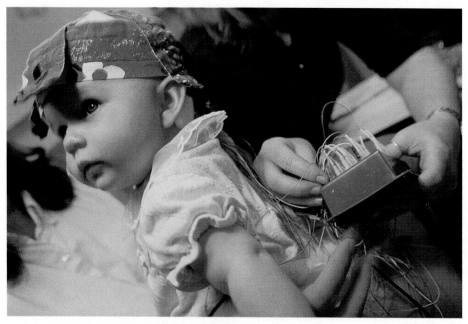

In Charles Nelson's research, electrodes are attached to a baby's scalp to measure the brain's activity to determine its role in the development of an infant's memory.

language. At birth, the hemispheres already have started to specialize, with newborns showing greater electrical brain activity in the left hemisphere than the right hemisphere when they are listening to speech sounds (Hahn, 1987). A common misconception is that virtually all language processing is carried out in the left hemisphere. Speech and grammar are localized to the left hemisphere in most people; however, the understanding of such aspects of language as appropriate language use in different contexts and the use of metaphor and humor involves the right hemisphere. Thus, language in general does not occur exclusively in the brain's left hemisphere (Johnson, 1998, 1999).

In the media and public, the left hemisphere has been described as the exclusive location of logical thinking and the right hemisphere the exclusive location of creative thinking. However, most neuroscientists point out that complex functions, such as reading, performing music, and creating art, involve both hemispheres. They believe labeling people as "left-brained" because they are logical thinkers and "right-brained" because they are creative thinkers does not correspond to the way the brain's hemispheres actually work. Such complex thinking in normal people is the outcome of communication between both sides of the brain.

Early Experience and the Brain

Until the middle of the twentieth century, scientists believed that the brain's development is determined almost exclusively by biological, hereditary factors. Researcher Mark Rosenzweig (1969) was curious about whether early experiences change the brain's development. He conducted a number of experiments with rats and other animals to investigate this possibility. Animals were randomly assigned to grow up in different environments. Animals in an enriched early environment lived in cages with stimulating features, such as wheels to rotate, steps to climb, levers to press, and toys to manipulate. In contrast, other animals had the early experience of growing up in standard cages or in barren, isolated conditions.

The results were stunning. The brains of the animals growing up in the enriched environment developed better than the brains of the animals reared in standard or isolated conditions. The brains of the "enriched" animals weighed more, had thicker layers, had more neuronal connections, and had higher levels of neurochemical activity.

Similar findings occurred when older animals were reared in vastly different environments, although the results were not as strong as for the younger animals. Such results give hope that enriching the lives of infants and young children who live in impoverished environments can produce positive changes in their development.

Scientists also now know that, starting shortly after birth, a baby's brain produces trillions more connections between neurons than it can possibly use. The brain eliminates connections that are seldom or never used. This pruning of brain connections continues at least until about 10 years of age.

Underlying the changes in visual perception during infancy are dramatic increases in synapses (connections between cells where chemical messengers called neurotransmitters carry information from one cell to the next) in the visual cortex. Pediatric neurologist Peter Hutenlocher (1997) carried out autopsies of the brains of infants who died unexpectedly. The number of synapses in one layer of the visual cortex rises from about 2,500 per neuron at birth to as many as 18,000 about 6 months later. These connections among neurons continue to form throughout life, but they reach their highest density (about 15,000 synapses per neuron) around 2 years of age and remain at that level until the age of 10 or 11. Similar synaptic growth occurs in other areas of the cerebral cortex, although on slightly different schedules.

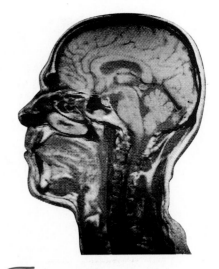

Figure 5.3
Cerebral Cortex
The cerebral cortex is located in the forebrain, the highest level of the brain. The cerebral cortex plays critical roles in important human functions, such as perception, thinking, and language.

lateralization
Specialization of functions in one hemisphere of the cerebral cortex or the other.

Development of the Brain
Early Development of the Brain
Early Experience and the Brain

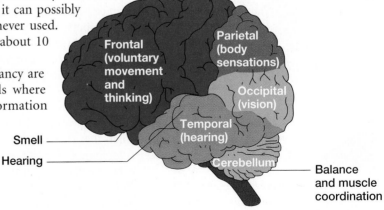

Figure 5.4
The Brain's Four Lobes
Shown here are the locations of the brain's four lobes: frontal, occipital, temporal, and parietal.

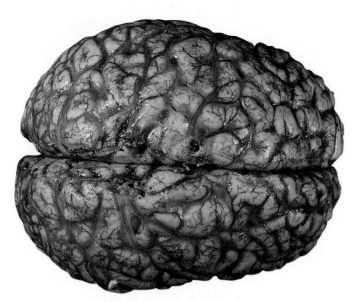

Figure 5.5

The Human Brain's Hemispheres

The two halves (hemispheres) of the human brain are clearly seen in this photograph.

Brandi Binder is evidence of the brain's hemispheric flexibility and resilience. Despite having the right side of her cortex removed because of a severe case of epilepsy, Brandi engages in many activities often portrayed as only "right-brain" activities. She loves music, math, and art, and is shown here working on one of her paintings.

The profusion of connections provides the growing brain with flexibility and resilience. Consider 13-year-old Brandi Binder, who developed such a severe case of epilepsy that surgeons at UCLA had to remove the right side of her cortex when she was 6. Binder lost virtually all the control she had established over muscles on the left side of her body, the side controlled by the right side of her brain, yet today, after years of therapy, ranging from leg lifts to math and music training, Binder is an A student. She loves music, math, and art—skills usually linked with the right side of the brain. Her recuperation is not 100 percent—for example, she never has regained the use of her left arm—however, her recovery is remarkable and shows that, if there is a way to compensate, the developing brain will find it.

Neuroscientists believe that what wires the brain—or rewires it, in the case of Brandi Binder—is repeated experience (Nash, 1997). Each time a baby tries to touch an attractive object or gazes intently at a face, tiny bursts of electricity shoot through the brain, knitting together neurons into circuits. The results are some of the behavioral milestones we discuss in this and other chapters. For example, at about 2 months of age, the motor-control centers of the brain develop to the point at which infants can suddenly reach out and grab a nearby object. At about 4 months, the neural connections necessary for depth perception begin to take form. And, at about 12 months, the brain's speech centers are poised to produce one of infancy's magical moments: when the infant utters its first word.

John Bruer (1999), in a recently published book that is being given considerable attention—*The Myth of the First Three Years*—argues that the evidence for the importance of early experience in development is far more scant than is commonly believed. He says that parents and educators have come to believe that early enrichment inoculates children against later academic shortcomings. He believes this involves an abuse of the neuroscience research literature and is misleading to parents and educators. Bruer argues that much of the evidence used to support the power of early experience grew out of research with rats (whose cages were "enriched" with wheels and other toys) in the 1970s. As we saw earlier, these rats had more neural connections and performed learning tasks better than their counterparts who lived in barren cages. The critics say there may be a huge gap between such findings for rats and what's critical for children. They also say that the difference between a barren and enriched environment is very different from the difference between a good and a great environment.

The critics of early experiences importance also worry about the proliferation of early learning programs for babies (Marcus, Mulrine, & Wong, 1999). In their quest for having a better and brighter child, parents can select from a dizzying list of "enrichment" products. They can purchase videos, such as *Brainy Baby*, which promise to make a parent's baby smarter. Educational software is available for babies as young as 6 months of age, called "lapware" because the babies are so small that they have to be held in a parent's lap at the computer. Such titles include *JumpStart Baby*. In Georgia and Tennessee, a classical music CD is sent home with every newborn. Florida requires public schools to play classical music for toddlers. *Baby Needs Mozart* is a best-selling CD. Ivy League preschools have sprung up across the United States. In Chicago, toddlers as young as 17 months of age can "work out" at the Children's Health and Executive Club. The workout includes tiny stair-climbing machines equipped with intellectually stimulating activities on a tray (such as Magna Doodles, a contemporary version of Etch-a-Sketch). Most developmental psychologists believe that these highly organized, intense programs do not benefit infants and in some cases can be harmful by overstimulating them and placing them in stressful circumstances (Bruer 1999; Sameroff, 1999; 2000).

Developmental psychology researcher Elizabeth Spelke (1999) said it would be unfortunate if Bruer's book is interpreted that all attempts to link brain development, cognition, and child rearing are a myth. We are still at a very early point in developing measures that effectively assess brain development in infancy. In coming decades, advances in brain science likely will allow more precise measurement in this area.

Conclusions   In sum, neural connections are formed early in life. The infant's brain literally is waiting for experiences to determine how connections are made (Greenough, 1999; Johnson, 1999, 2000a, b). Before birth, it appears that genes mainly direct how the brain establishes basic wiring patterns. Neurons grow and travel to distant places awaiting further instructions. After birth, environmental experiences are important in the brain's development. The inflowing stream of sights, sounds, smells, touches, language, and eye contact helps the brain's connections take shape. However, many experts believe that enriched early experiences have been overdramatized and that placing babies in highly enriched environments is not going to make them a lot smarter than if they experience their early years in merely good environments. The critics even argue that some babies in these environments might be overstimulated. That being said, everything we do know about infants tells us that although they should not be overstimulated, they should be provided with a very nurturant, supportive environment.

At this point we have studied a number of ideas about cephalocaudal and proximodistal patterns, height and weight, and the brain. A review of these ideas is presented in summary table 5.1. Next, we continue our exploration of physical development in infancy by discussing infant states.

THE MYTH OF THE FIRST THREE YEARS

A NEW UNDERSTANDING OF EARLY BRAIN DEVELOPMENT AND LIFELONG LEARNING

JOHN T. BRUER, PH.D.

What is the main theme of John Breur's controversial book, *The Myth of the First Three Years*?

Infant States

Not only do developmentalists chart infants' height and weight patterns, but they also examine the infants' states of consciousness, the levels of awareness that characterize individuals (Ingersoll & Thoman, 1999). One classification scheme describes eight infant states (Thoman & others, 1981):

1. *No **REM (rapid eye movement) sleep**, a recurring sleep stage during which vivid dreams commonly occur.* The infant's eyes are closed and still, and there is no motor activity other than occasional startle, rhythmic mouthing, or slight limb movement.
2. *Active sleep without REM.* The infant's eyes are closed and still; motor activity is present.
3. *REM sleep.* The infant's eyes are closed, although they may open briefly. Rapid eye movements can be detected through closed eyelids, and motor activity may or may not be present.
4. *Indeterminate sleep.* This category is reserved for all transitional states that cannot fit the above codes.
5. *Drowsy.* The infant's eyes might be opening and closing but they have a dull, glazed appearance. Motor activity is minimal.
6. *Inactive alert.* The infant is relatively inactive, although there may be occasional limb movements. The eyes are wide open and bright and shiny.
7. *Active awake.* The infant's eyes are open, and there is motor activity.
8. *Crying.* The infant's eyes can be open or closed, and motor activity is present. Agitated vocalizations are also present.

Using classification schemes such as the one just described, researchers have identified many aspects of infant development. One such aspect is the sleeping-waking cycle (Henderson & France, 1999). When we were infants, sleep consumed more of our time than it does now. Newborns sleep 16 to 17 hours a day, although some sleep more and others

REM (rapid eye movement) sleep
A recurring sleep stage during which vivid dreams commonly occur.

*T*hrough the Eyes of Psychologists

Ross Thompson,
University of Nebraska

"Whether you are using a megaphone to talk to your child in utero (before birth), or labeling everything in their little world with flashcards, you are not going to unleash some special brain potential."

SUMMARY TABLE 5.1
Cephalocaudal and Proximodistal Patterns, Height and Weight, and the Brain

Concept	Processes/ Related Ideas	Characteristics/Description
Cephalocaudal and Proximodistal Patterns	Cephalocaudal	• Growth from the top down.
	Proximodistal	• Growth from the center out.
Height and Weight	Nature of Changes	• The average North American newborn is 20 inches long and weighs 7½ pounds. • Infants grow about 1 inch per month in the first year and nearly triple their weight by their first birthday. • Infants' rate of growth slows in the second year.
The Brain	The Brain's Development	• Three processes include cell production, migration, and elaboration.
	The Brain's Lobes and Hemispheres	• The cerebral cortex has four lobes (frontal, occipital, temporal, and parietal) and two hemispheres (left and right). • Lateralization refers to specialization of the hemispheres.
	Early Experience and the Brain	• The brains of animals growing up in enriched early environments develop better than those living in standard or isolated early environments.
	Conclusions	• Neural connections are formed early in life. Before birth, genes mainly direct neurons to locations. After birth, the inflowing stream of sights, sounds, smells, touches, language, and eye contact help the brain's connections to take shape. • However, some critics believe that the importance of early experience in development has been exaggerated. They especially worry about highly organized, intense programs that parents use to enrich their babies' lives. Such programs can overstimulate babies.

Sleep that knits up the ravelled sleave of care. . . .

Balm of hurt minds, nature's second course.

Chief nourisher in life's feast.

William Shakespeare
English Playwright, 17th Century

less. The range is from a low of about 10 hours to a high of about 21 hours, although the longest period of sleep is not always between 11 P.M. and 7 A.M. Although total sleep remains somewhat consistent for young infants, their sleep during the day does not always follow a rhythmic pattern. An infant might change from sleeping several long bouts of 7 or 8 hours to three or four shorter sessions only several hours in duration. By about 1 month of age, most infants have begun to sleep longer at night, and, by about 4 months of age, they usually have moved closer to adultlike sleep patterns, spending their longest span of sleep at night and their longest span of waking during the day.

Researchers are intrigued by the various forms of infant sleep. They are especially interested in REM sleep. Most adults spend about one-fifth of their night in REM sleep, and REM sleep usually appears about 1 hour after non-REM sleep. However, about one-half of an infant's sleep is REM sleep, and infants often begin their sleep cycle with REM sleep rather than non-REM sleep. By the time infants reach 3 months of age, the percentage of time they spend in REM sleep falls to about 40 percent, and no longer does REM sleep begin their sleep cycle. The large amount of REM sleep might provide infants with added self-stimulation, because they spend less time awake than do older children. REM sleep also might promote the brain's development.

The amount of REM sleep changes over the life span. As indicated in figure 5.6, the percentage of total sleep made up of REM sleep is especially large in early infancy

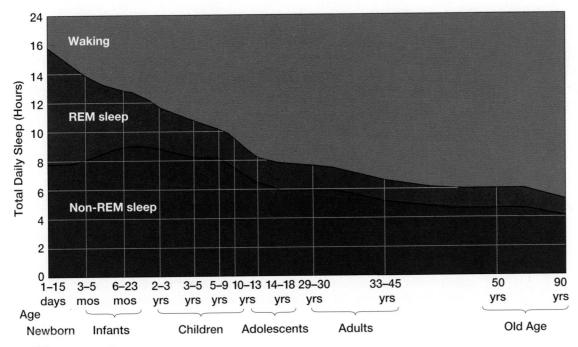

Figure 5.6
Sleep Across the Human Life Span

Reprinted with permission from H.P. Roffwarg, J.N. Muzio, & W.C. Dement, "Ontogenetic development of human-dream sleep cycle, "*Science*, 152, pp. 604–609. Copyright 1966 American Association for the Advancement of Science.

(almost 8 hours). Elderly adults engage in less than 1 hour of REM sleep a night. Figure 5.6 also reveals how the amount of total sleep changes from approximately 16 hours at the beginning of infancy to less than 6 hours in old age.

Of special concern is **sudden infant death syndrome (SIDS),** *a condition that occurs when an infant stops breathing, usually during the night, and suddenly dies without apparent cause.* SIDS is the leading cause of neonatal and infant death in the United States (Hunt, 1999; Lucey, 1999). Approximately 13 percent of all infant deaths are due to SIDS. It occurs in 1 to 2 of every 1,000 live births. It has not been determined whether the primary cause of death in SIDS is respiratory or cardiac failure (National Commission on Sleep Disorders Research, 1993).

Risk of SIDS is highest at 10 to 12 weeks of age. Unfortunately, at present there is no definitive way to predict the onset of the disorder. However, some infants are at particular risk (Maas, 1998):

- Low-birthweight infants are five to ten times more likely to die of SIDS than are their normal-weight counterparts.
- Twins and triplets, even at normal birthweight, are twice as likely to die of SIDS; after one twin dies, the surviving twin also has an increased risk of dying from SIDS.
- Infants whose siblings have died of SIDS are two to four times as likely to die of it.
- Six percent of infants with sleep apnea, a temporary cessation of breathing in which the airway is completely blocked, usually 10 seconds or longer, die of SIDS.
- African American and Eskimo infants are four to six times as likely as all others to die of SIDS.
- SIDS is more common in lower socioeconomic groups.
- SIDS is more common in infants who are passively exposed to cigarette smoke. (Klonoff-Cohen & others, 1995)

It is advisable that an infant be placed on its back, not on its side or stomach. This will make it less likely that its breathing will be obstructed.

sudden infant death syndrome (SIDS)
A condition that occurs when an infant stops breathing, usually during the night, and suddenly dies without an apparent cause.

SIDS

Nutrition

Four-month-old Robert lives in Bloomington, Indiana, with his middle-class parents. He is well nourished and healthy. By contrast, 4-month-old Nikita and his parents live in Ethiopia in impoverished conditions. Nikita is so poorly nourished that he has become emaciated and lies near death. The lives of Robert and Nikita reveal the vast diversity of nutritional status among today's children. Our coverage of infant nutrition begins with information about nutritional needs and eating behavior, then turns to the issue of breast- versus bottle-feeding, and concludes with an overview of malnutrition.

Nutritional Needs and Eating Behavior   The importance of adequate energy and nutrient intake consumed in a loving and supportive environment during the infant years cannot be overstated (Yip, 1995). From birth to 1 year of age, human infants triple their weight and increase their length by 50 percent. Individual differences among infants in terms of their nutrient reserves, body composition, growth rates, and activity patterns make defining actual nutrient needs difficult. However, because parents need guidelines, nutritionists recommend that infants consume approximately 50 calories per day for each pound they weigh—more than twice an adult's requirement per pound.

Some years ago, controversy surrounded the issue of whether a baby should be fed on demand or on a regular schedule. Famous behaviorist John Watson (1928) argued that scheduled feeding is superior because it increases the child's orderliness. An example of a recommended schedule for newborns is 4 ounces of formula every 6 hours. In recent years, demand feeding—in which the timing and amount of feeding are determined by the infant—has become more popular.

In the 1990s, we became extremely nutrition-conscious. Does the same type of nutrition that makes us healthy adults also make young infants healthy? Some affluent, well-educated parents almost starve their babies by feeding them the low-fat, low-calorie diet they eat themselves. Diets designed for adult weight loss and prevention of heart disease may actually retard growth and development in babies. Fat is very important for babies. Nature's food—breast milk—is not low in fat or calories. No child under the age of 2 should be consuming skim milk.

In one investigation, seven cases were documented in which babies 7 to 22 months of age were unwittingly undernourished by their health-conscious parents (Lifshitz & others, 1987). In some instances, the parents had been fat themselves and were determined that their child was not going to be. The well-meaning parents substituted vegetables, skim milk, and other low-fat foods for what they called junk food. However, for infants, broccoli is not always a good substitute for a cookie. For growing infants, high-calorie, high-energy foods are part of a balanced diet.

Breast- Versus Bottle-Feeding   Human milk, or an alternative formula, is the baby's source of nutrients and energy for the first 4 to 6 months. For years, developmentalists and nutritionists have debated whether breast-feeding an infant has substantial benefits over bottle-feeding. The growing consensus is that breast-feeding is better for the baby's health (Bier & others, 1999; Eiger, 1992). Breast-feeding provides milk that is clean and digestible and helps immunize the newborn from disease (Newman, 1995; Slusser & Powers, 1997). Breast-fed babies gain weight more rapidly than do bottle-fed babies. However, only about one-half of mothers nurse newborns, and even fewer continue to nurse their infants after several months. Mothers who work outside the home find it impossible to breast-feed their young infants for many months. Even though breast-feeding provides more ideal nutrition, some researchers argue that there is no long-term evidence of physiological or psychological harm to American infants when they are bottle-fed (Ferguson, Harwood, & Shannon, 1987). Despite these researchers' claims that no long-term negative consequences of bottle-feeding have been documented in American children, the American Academy of Pediatrics, the majority of physi-

Breast-Feeding
Feeding Infants

cians and nurses, and two leading publications for parents—the *Infant Care Manual* and *Parents* magazine—endorse breast-feeding as having physiological and psychological benefits (Young, 1990).

There is a consensus among experts that breast-feeding is the preferred practice, especially in developing countries where inadequate nutrition and poverty are common. In 1991, the Institute of Medicine, part of the National Academy of Sciences, issued a report that women should be encouraged to breast-feed their infants exclusively for the first 4 to 6 months of life. According to the report, the benefits of breast-feeding are protection against some gastrointestinal infections and food allergies for infants and possible reduction of osteoporosis and breast cancer for mothers. Nonetheless, while the majority of experts recommend breast-feeding, the issue of breast- versus bottle-feeding continues to be hotly debated. Many parents, especially working mothers, now follow a sequence of breast-feeding in the first several months and bottle-feeding thereafter. This strategy allows the mother's natural milk to provide nutritional benefits to the infant early in development and permits mothers to return to work after several months. Working mothers are also increasingly using a breast pump to extract breast milk that can be stored for later feeding of the infant when the mother is not present.

Malnutrition in Infancy

marasmus
A wasting away of bodily tissues in the infant's first year, caused by severe protein-calorie deficiency.

Malnutrition in Infancy

Marasmus is a wasting away of body tissues in the infant's first year, caused by severe protein-calorie deficiency. The infant becomes grossly underweight, and its muscles atrophy. The main cause of marasmus is early weaning from breast milk to inadequate nutrients, such as unsuitable and unsanitary cow's milk formula. Something that looks like milk, but is not, usually a form of tapioca or rice, also might be used. In many of the world's developing countries, mothers used to breast-feed their infants for at least 2 years. To become more modern, they stopped breast-feeding much earlier and replaced it with bottle-feeding. Comparisons of breast-fed and bottle-fed infants in such countries as Afghanistan, Haiti, Ghana, and Chile document that the death rate of bottle-fed infants is up to five times greater than that of breast-fed infants (Grant, 1997).

Even if not fatal, severe and lengthy malnutrition is detrimental to physical, cognitive, and social development (Mortimer, 1992). In some cases, even moderate malnutrition can produce subtle difficulties in development. In one investigation, two groups of extremely malnourished 1-year-old South African infants were studied (Bayley, 1970). The children in one group were given adequate nourishment during the next six years; no intervention took place in the lives of the other group. After the seventh year, the poorly nourished group of children performed much worse on tests of intelligence than did the adequately nourished group. In yet another investigation, the diets of rural Guatemalan infants were associated with their social development at the time they entered elementary school (Barrett, Radke-Yarrow, & Klein, 1982). Children whose mothers had been given

Human milk, or an alternative formula, is a baby's source of nutrients for the first 4 to 6 months. The growing consensus is that breast-feeding is better for the baby's health, although controversy still swirls about the issue of breast- versus bottle-feeding.

nutritious supplements during pregnancy and who themselves had been given more nutritious, high-calorie foods in their first two years of life were more active, more involved, more helpful with their peers, less anxious, and happier than their

EXPLORATIONS IN CHILD DEVELOPMENT
A Healthy Start

THE HAWAII FAMILY SUPPORT/HEALTHY START PROGRAM began in 1985 (Allen, Brown, & Finlay, 1992). It was designed by the Hawaii Family Stress Center in Honolulu, which already had been using home-visitor services to improve family functioning and reduce child abuse for more than a decade. Participation is voluntary. Families of newborns are screened for family risk factors, including unstable housing, histories of substance abuse, depression, parents' abuse as a child, late or no prenatal care, fewer than 12 years of schooling, poverty, and unemployment. Early identification workers screen and interview new mothers in the hospital. They also screen families referred by physicians, nurses, and others. Because the demand for services outstrips available resources, only families with a substantial number of risk factors can participate.

Each new participating family receives a weekly visit from a family support worker. Each of the program's eight home visitors works with approximately 25 families at a time. The worker helps the family cope with any immediate crises, such as unemployment or substance abuse. The family also is linked directly with a pediatrician to ensure that the children receive regular health care. Infants are screened for developmental delays and are immunized on schedule. Pediatricians have been educated about the program. They are notified when a child is enrolled in Healthy Start and when a family at risk stops participating.

The Family Support/Healthy Start Program recently hired a child development specialist to work with families of children with special needs. And, in some instances, the program's male family support worker also visits a father to talk specifically about his role in the family. The support workers encourage parents to participate in group activities held each week at the program center located in a neighborhood shopping center.

Over time, parents are encouraged to assume more responsibility for their family's health and well-being. Families can participate in Healthy Start until the child is 5 and enters public school.

The Hawaii Family Support/Healthy Start Program provides overburdened families of newborns and young children many home-visitor services. This program has been very successful in reducing abuse and neglect in families.

mildly undernourished counterparts, who had not been given nutritional supplements. The results suggest how important it is for parents to be attentive to the nutritional needs of their infants.

In further research on early supplementary feeding and children's cognitive development, Ernesto Pollitt and his colleagues (1993) conducted a longitudinal investigation over two decades in rural Guatemala. They found that early nutritional supplements in the form of protein and increased calories can have positive long-term effects on cognitive development. The researchers also found that the relation of nutrition to cognitive performance is moderated both by the time period during which the supplement is given and by the sociodemographic context. For example, the children in the lowest socioeconomic groups benefited more than did the children in higher socioeconomic groups. Although there still was a positive nutritional influence when supplementation began after 2 years of age, the effect on cognitive development was less powerful. To read about a program that gives infants a healthy start in life, see the Explorations in the Child Development box.

SUMMARY TABLE 5.2
Infant States, Nutrition, and Toilet Training

Concept	Processes/ Related Ideas	Characteristics/Description
Infant States	Categorization	• Researchers have crafted different classification systems. • One system has 8 different categories, including deep sleep, drowsy, alert and focused, and inflexibly focused.
	Sleep	• Newborns usually sleep 16 to 17 hours a day. By 4 months of age they approach adultlike sleeping patterns. • REM sleep—during which dreaming occurs—is present more in early infancy than in childhood and adulthood. • Sudden infant death syndrome (SIDS) is a condition that occurs when a sleeping infant stops breathing and suddenly dies without apparent cause.
Nutrition	Nutritional Needs and Eating Behavior	• Infants need to consume about 50 calories per day for each pound they weigh.
	Breast- Versus Bottle-Feeding	• The growing consensus is that breast-feeding is superior to bottle-feeding, but the increase in working mothers has meant fewer breast-fed babies.
	Malnutrition in Infancy	• Severe infant malnutrition is still prevalent in many parts of the world. • A special concern in impoverished countries is early weaning from breast milk. • Malnutrition in infancy can impair physical, cognitive, and socioemotional development.
Toilet Training	Its Nature	• Toilet training is expected to be attained by about 3 years of age in North America. • Toilet training should be carried out in a relaxed, supportive atmosphere. • Late toilet training can lead to confrontations with the autonomy-seeking toddler.

Toilet Training

In the North American culture, being toilet trained is a physical and motor skill that is expected to be attained by 3 years of age (Charlesworth, 1987). By the age of 3, 84 percent of children are dry throughout the day, and 66 percent are dry throughout the night. The ability to control elimination depends on both muscular maturation and motivation. Children must be able to control their muscles to eliminate at the appropriate time, and they must want to eliminate in the toilet or potty, rather than in their pants.

In actuality, there are no data on the optimal time of toilet training, but developmentalists argue that, when it is initiated, it should be accomplished in a warm, relaxed, supportive manner. Many of today's parents begin toilet training of their infants at about 20 months to 2 years of age.

One argument being made today against late toilet training is that the "terrible twos" may be encountered. The 2-year-old's strong push for autonomy can lead to battles with parents trying to toilet train the 2-year-old. Late toilet training can become such a battleground that it extends to 4 to 5 years of age. Another argument against late toilet training is that many toddlers go to day care, and a child in diapers or training pants can be stigmatized by peers.

At this point we have studied a number of ideas about infant states, nutrition, and toilet training. A review of these ideas is presented in summary table 5.2. Next, we turn our attention to the infant's motor development.

Toilet Training

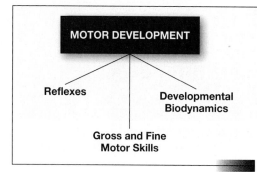

Motor Development

The study of motor development has seen a renaissance in the past decade. New insights are being made into the ways in which infants acquire motor skills. We will begin our exploration of motor development by examining reflexes and rhythmic movements, then turn our attention to gross and fine motor skills. To conclude, we will cover the fascinating field of developmental biodynamics, which is responsible for the awakened interest in the ways in which infants acquire motor skills.

Reflexes

The newborn is not an empty-headed organism. Among other things, it has some basic reflexes, which are genetically carried survival mechanisms. For example, the newborn has no fear of water, naturally holding its breath and contracting its throat to keep water out. Reflexes can serve as important building blocks for subsequent purposeful motor activity.

Reflexes govern the newborn's movements, which are automatic and beyond the newborn's control. They are built-in reactions to stimuli. In these reflexes, infants have adaptive responses to their environment before they have had the opportunity to learn. The **sucking reflex** *occurs when newborns automatically suck an object placed in their mouth. The sucking reflex enables newborns to get nourishment before they have associated a nipple with food.* The sucking reflex is an example of a reflex that is present at birth but later disappears. The **rooting reflex** *occurs when the infant's cheek is stroked or the side of the mouth is touched. In response, the infant turns its head toward the side that was touched in an apparent effort to find something to suck.* The sucking and rooting reflexes disappear when the infant is 3 to 4 months old. They are replaced by the infant's voluntary eating. The sucking and rooting reflexes have survival value for newborn mammals, who must find the mother's breast to obtain nourishment.

The **Moro reflex** *is a neonatal startle response that occurs in response to a sudden, intense noise or movement. When startled, the newborn arches its back, throws back its head, and flings out its arms and legs. Then the newborn rapidly closes its arms and legs to the center of its body.* The Moro reflex is a vestige from our primate ancestry, and it also has survival value. This reflex, which is normal in all newborns, also tends to disappear at 3 to 4 months of age. Steady pressure on any part of the infant's body calms the infant after it has been startled. Holding the infant's arm flexed at the shoulder will quiet the infant.

Some reflexes present in the newborn—coughing, blinking, and yawning, for example—persist throughout life. They are as important for the adult as they are for the infant. Other reflexes, though, disappear several months following birth, as the infant's brain functions mature, and voluntary control over many behaviors develops. The movements of some reflexes eventually become incorporated into more complex, voluntary actions. One important example is the **grasping reflex,** *which occurs when something touches the infant's palms. The infant responds by grasping tightly.* By the end of the third month, the grasping reflex diminishes, and the infant shows a more voluntary grasp, which is often produced by visual stimuli. For example, when an infant sees a mobile whirling above its crib, it may reach out and try to grasp it. As its motor development becomes smoother, the infant will grasp objects, carefully manipulate them, and explore their qualities.

An overview of the main reflexes we have discussed, along with others, is given in figure 5.7.

Sucking is an especially important reflex: it is the infant's route to nourishment. The sucking capabilities of newborns vary considerably. Some newborns are efficient at forceful sucking and obtaining milk; others are not as adept and get tired before they are full. Most newborns take several weeks to establish a sucking style that is coordinated with

sucking reflex
A newborn's built-in reaction of automatically sucking an object placed in its mouth. The sucking reflex enables the infant to get nourishment before it has associated a nipple with food.

rooting reflex
A newborn's built-in reaction that occurs when the infant's cheek is stroked or the side of the mouth is touched. In response, the infant turns its head toward the side that was touched, in an apparent effort to find something to suck.

Moro reflex
A neonatal startle response that occurs in reaction to a sudden, intense noise or movement. When startled, the newborn arches its back, throws its head back, and flings out its arms and legs. Then the newborn rapidly closes its arms and legs to the center of the body.

grasping reflex
A neonatal reflex that occurs when something touches the infant's palms. The infant responds by grasping tightly.

The experiences of the first three years of life are almost entirely lost to us, and when we attempt to enter into a small child's world, we come as foreigners who have forgotten the landscape and no longer speak the native tongue.

Selma Fraiberg
Developmentalist and Child Advocate, 20th Century

Reflex	Stimulation	Infant's response	Developmental pattern
Blinking	Flash of light, puff of air	Closes both eyes	Permanent
Babinski	Sole of foot stroked	Fans out toes, twists foot in	Disappears after nine months to one year
Grasping	Palms touched	Grasps tightly	Weakens after three months, disappears after one year
Moro (startle)	Sudden stimulation, such as hearing loud noise or being dropped	Startles, arches back, throws head back, flings out arms and legs and then rapidly closes them to center of body	Disappears after three to four months
Rooting	Cheek stroked or side of mouth touched	Turns head, opens mouth, begins sucking	Disappears after three to four months
Stepping	Infant held above surface and feet lowered to touch surface	Moves feet as if to walk	Disappears after three to four months
Sucking	Object touching mouth	Sucks automatically	Disappears after three to four months
Swimming	Infant put face down in water	Makes coordinated swimming movements	Disappears after six to seven months
Tonic neck	Infant placed on back	Forms fists with both hands and usually turns head to the right (sometimes called the "fencer's pose" because the infant looks like it is assuming a fencer's position)	Disappears after two months

Figure 5.7

Infant Reflexes

the way the mother is holding the infant, the way milk is coming out of the bottle or breast, and the infant's sucking speed and temperament.

A study by pediatrician T. Berry Brazelton (1956) involved observations of infants for more than a year to determine the incidence of their sucking when they were nursing and how their sucking changed as they grew older. Over 85 percent of the infants engaged in considerable sucking behavior unrelated to feeding. They sucked their fingers, their fists, and pacifiers. By the age of 1 year, most had stopped the sucking behavior.

Parents should not worry when infants suck their thumb, fist, or even a pacifier. Many parents, though, do begin to worry when thumb sucking persists into the preschool and elementary school years. As much as 40 percent of children continue to suck their thumbs after they have started school (Kessen, Haith, & Salapatek, 1970). Most developmentalists do not attach a great deal of significance to this behavior and are not aware of parenting strategies that might contribute to it. Individual differences in children's biological makeup may be involved to some degree in the continuation of sucking behavior.

Gross and Fine Motor Skills

Gross motor skills *involve large muscle activities, such as moving one's arms and walking.* **Fine motor skills** *involve more finely tuned movements, such as finger dexterity.* Let's examine the changes in gross and fine motor skills in the first two years of life.

gross motor skills
Motor skills that involve large muscle activities, such as walking.

fine motor skills
Motor skills that involve more finely tuned movements, such as finger dexterity.

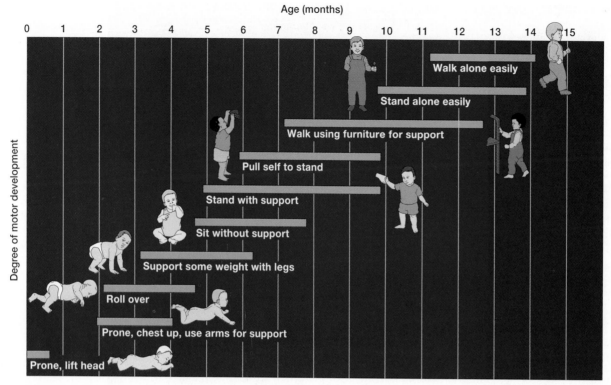

Age (months)

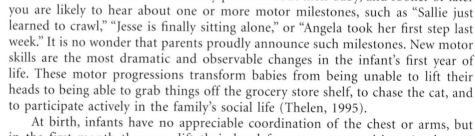

Figure **5.8**

Milestones in Gross Motor Development

Developmental Milestones

Physical Development in Infancy

A baby is an angel whose wings decrease as his legs increase.

French proverb

Gross Motor Skills Ask any parents about their baby, and sooner or later you are likely to hear about one or more motor milestones, such as "Sallie just learned to crawl," "Jesse is finally sitting alone," or "Angela took her first step last week." It is no wonder that parents proudly announce such milestones. New motor skills are the most dramatic and observable changes in the infant's first year of life. These motor progressions transform babies from being unable to lift their heads to being able to grab things off the grocery store shelf, to chase the cat, and to participate actively in the family's social life (Thelen, 1995).

At birth, infants have no appreciable coordination of the chest or arms, but in the first month they can lift their head from a prone position. At about 3 months, infants can hold their chest up and use their arms for support after being in a prone position. At 3 to 4 months, infants can roll over, and at 4 to 5 months they can support some weight with their legs. At about 6 months, infants can sit without support, and by 7 to 8 months they can crawl and stand without support. At approximately 8 months, infants can pull themselves up to a standing position, at 10 to 11 months they can walk using furniture for support (this is called cruising), and at 12 to 13 months they can walk without assistance. A summary of the developmental accomplishments in gross motor skills during the first year is shown in figure 5.8. The actual month at which the milestones occur varies by as much as 2 to 4 months, especially among older infants. What remains fairly uniform, however, is the sequence of accomplishments. An important implication of these infant motor accomplishments is the increasing degree of independence they bring. Older infants can explore their environment more extensively and initiate social interaction with caregivers and peers more readily than when they were younger.

In the second year of life, toddlers become more motorically skilled and mobile. They are no longer content with being in a playpen and want to move all over the place. Child development experts believe that motor activity during the second year is vital to the child's competent development and that few restrictions, except for safety purposes, should be placed on their motoric adventures (Fraiberg, 1959).

By 13 to 18 months, toddlers can pull a toy attached to a string, use their hands and legs to climb up a number of steps, and ride four-wheel wagons. By 18 to 24 months, toddlers can walk quickly or run stiffly for a short distance, balance on their feet in a squat position while playing with objects on the floor, walk backward without losing their balance, stand and kick a ball without falling, stand and throw a ball, and jump in place.

With the increased interest of today's adults in aerobic exercise and fitness, some parents have tried to give their infants a head start on becoming physically fit and physically talented. However, the American Academy of Pediatricians recently issued a statement that recommends against structured exercise classes for babies. Pediatricians are seeing more bone fractures and dislocations and more muscle strains in babies now than in the past. They point out that, when an adult is stretching and moving an infant's limbs, it is easy to go beyond the infant's physical limits without knowing it.

The physical fitness classes for infants range from passive fare—with adults putting infants through the paces—to programs called "aerobic" because they demand crawling, tumbling, and ball skills. However, exercise for infants is not aerobic. They cannot adequately stretch their bodies to achieve aerobic benefits.

Fine Motor Skills

Infants have hardly any control over fine motor skills at birth, although they have many components of what later become finely coordinated arm, hand, and finger movements (Rosenblith, 1992). The onset of reaching and grasping marks a significant achievement in infants' functional interactions with their surroundings (McCarty & Ashmead, 1999). For many years it was believed that reaching for an object is visually guided—that is, the infant must continuously have sight of the hand and the target (White, Castle, & Held, 1964). However, in one study, Rachel Clifton and her colleagues (1993) demonstrated that infants do not have to see their own hands when reaching for an object. They concluded that, because the infants could not see their hand or arm in the dark in the experiment, proprioceptive (muscle, tendon, joint sense) cues, not sight of limb, guided the early reaching of the 4-month-old infants. The development of reaching and grasping becomes more refined during the first 2 years of life. Initially, infants show only crude shoulder and elbow movements, but later they show wrist movements, hand rotation, and coordination of the thumb and forefinger. The maturation of hand-eye coordination over the first 2 years of life is reflected in the

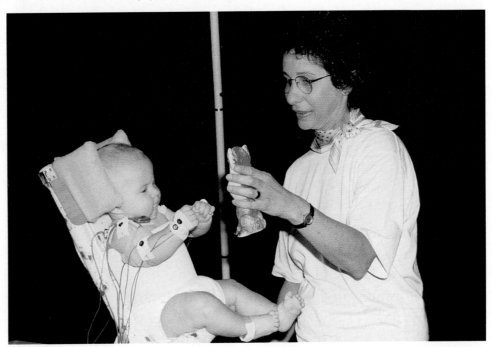

Esther Thelen is shown conducting an experiment to discover how infants learn to control their arms to reach and grasp for objects. A computer device is used to monitor the infants' arm movements and to track muscle patterns.

Birth to 6 months	
2 mo.	Holds rattle briefly
2 1/2 mo.	Glances from one object to another
3–4 mo.	Plays in simple way with rattle; inspects fingers; reaches for dangling ring; visually follows ball across table
4 mo.	Carries object to mouth
4–5 mo.	Recovers rattle from chest; holds two objects
5 mo.	Transfers object from hand to hand
5–6 mo.	Bangs in play; looks for object while sitting

6–12 months	
6 mo.	Secures cube on sight; follows adult's movements across room; immediately fixates on small objects and stretches out to grasp them; retains rattle
6 1/2 mo.	Manipulates and examines an object; reaches for, grabs, and retains rattle
7 mo.	Pulls string to obtain an object
7 1/2–8 1/2 mo.	Grasps with thumb and finger
8–9 mo.	Persists in reaching for toy out of reach on table; shows hand preference, bangs spoon; searches in correct place for toys dropped within reach of hands; may find toy hidden under cup
10 mo.	Hits cup with spoon; crude release of object
10 1/2–11 mo.	Picks up raisin with thumb and forefinger; pincer grasp; pushes car along
11–12 mo.	Puts three or more objects in a container

12–18 months
Places one 2-inch block on top of another 2-inch block (in imitation)
Scribbles with a large crayon on large piece of paper
Turns two to three pages in a large book with cardboard pages while sitting in an adult's lap
Places three 1-inch cube blocks in a 6-inch diameter cup (in imitation)
Holds a pencil and makes a mark on a sheet of paper
Builds a four-block tower with 2-inch cube blocks (in imitation)

18–24 months
Draws an arc on piece of unlined paper with a pencil after being shown how
Turns a doorknob that is within reach, using both hands
Unscrews a lid put loosely on a small jar after being shown how
Places large pegs in a pegboard
Connects and takes apart a pop bead string of five beads
Zips and unzips a large zipper after being shown how

Figure 5.9
The Development of Fine Motor Skills in Infancy

improvement of fine motor skills. Figure 5.9 provides an overview of the development of fine motor skills in the first 2 years of life.

Developmental Biodynamics

Traditional views of motor development have chronicled the stage-like changes in posture and movement that characterize the first several years of life (Gesell, 1928; Shirley, 1933). In the last decade, advances in a number of domains have generated a new perspective on infant motor development. Rather than describing the ages at which various motor achievements are reached and explaining them as a result of brain and nervous-system maturation, the new perspective—**developmental biodynamics**—*seeks to explain how motor behaviors are assembled for perceiving and acting.* This perspective is an outgrowth of developments in the neurosciences, biomechanics, and the behavioral sciences (Lockman & Thelen, 1993). The research of Rachel Clifton and her colleagues (1993), which was described earlier, illustrates the developmental biodynamics view. They found that proprioceptive cues play an important role in early guided reaching. Their research shows *how* perception *and* action are linked in early manual skill development.

The developmental biodynamics view of infant motor development has especially been advanced by the theorizing and research of Esther Thelen (1995). Following are some of the main concepts in her developmental biodynamics perspective.

The new view of motor development emphasizes the importance of exploration and selection in finding solutions to new task demands. This means that infants need to assemble adaptive patterns by modifying their current movement patterns. The first step is to get the infant into the "ball park" of the task demands—a tentative crawl or several stumbling steps. Then, the infant has to "tune" these configurations to make them smoother and more effective. Such tuning is achieved through repeated cycles of actions and perception of the consequences of those actions in relation to the goal.

The developmental biodynamics view contrasts with the traditional maturational view by proposing that even the universal milestones, such as crawling, reaching, and walking, are learned through a process of adaptation. Infants modulate their movement patterns to fit a new task by exploring and selecting various possible configurations. The assumption is that the infant is motivated by the new challenge—a desire to get a new toy into one's mouth or to cross the room to join other family members. It is the new task, the challenge of the context, not prescribed genetic instructions that represents the driving force for change (Lewis, 2000).

Consider the challenging task the infant faces when placed in a "Jolly Jumper" infant bouncer (see figure 5.10). The task for the infant is to first assemble the right movements to drive the spring and then to tune the spring to discover the "best bounce for the ounce." In one study involving an infant bouncer, infants began with only a few tentative bounces that varied considerably (Goldfield, Kay, & Warren, 1993). As weeks passed, they increased their bounces, but the variability of the bounces decreased. Studies such as those involving the infant bouncer are important because, rather than looking only for performance differences as a function of age, they emphasize discovering the processes involved in learning new motor skills.

At this point, we have discussed many ideas about motor development. Summary table 5.3 provides a review of these ideas. A key theme in the developmental

Figure **5.10**

Learning to Use an Infant Bouncer

Learning to use an infant bouncer is an excellent example of how the infant assembles the right movements over time to solve this challenging task.

developmental biodynamics
The new perspective on motor development in infancy that seeks to explain how motor behaviors are assembled for perceiving and acting.

SUMMARY TABLE 5.3
Motor Development

Concept	Processes/ Related Ideas	Characteristics/Description
Reflexes	Their Nature	• The newborn is no longer viewed as a passive, empty-headed organism. • Reflexes—automatic movements—govern the newborn's behavior. • For infants, sucking is an important means of obtaining nutrition.
Gross and Fine Motor Skills	Gross Motor Skills	• These involve large muscle activities, such as moving one's arms and walking. • A number of gross motor milestones occur in infancy.
	Fine Motor Skills	• These involve movements that are more finely tuned than gross motor skills. • A number of fine motor milestones occur in infancy.
Developmental Dynamics	Its Nature	• This approach seeks to explain how motor behaviors are assembled for perceiving and acting. • It emphasizes the importance of exploration and selection in finding solutions to new task demands. • A key theme is that perception and action are coupled when new skills are learned.

biodynamics view we just evaluated is that perception and action are coupled when new skills are learned. Let's now explore the nature of the infant's sensory and perceptual development.

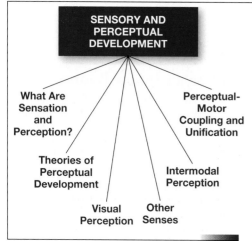

Sensory and Perceptual Development

What are sensation and perception? Can a newborn see? If so, what can it perceive? What about the other senses—hearing, smell, taste, touch, and pain? What are they like in the newborn, and how do they develop in infancy? Can an infant put together information from two different modalities, such as sight and sound, in perceiving its world? These are among the intriguing questions we will now explore.

What Are Sensation and Perception?

How does a newborn know that her mother's skin is soft rather than rough? How does a 5-year-old know what color his hair is? How does an 8-year-old know that summer is warmer than winter? How does a 10-year-old know that a firecracker is louder than a cat's meow? Infants and children "know" these things because of their senses. All information comes to the infant through the senses. Without vision, hearing, touch, taste, smell, and other senses, the infant's brain would be isolated from the world; the infant would live in a dark silence, a tasteless, colorless, feelingless void.

Sensation *occurs when information interacts with sensory receptors—the eyes, ears, tongue, nostrils, and skin.* The sensation of hearing occurs when waves of pulsating air are collected by the outer ear and transmitted through the bones of the inner ear to the auditory nerve. The sensation of vision occurs as rays of light contact the eyes and become focused on the retina.

Perception *is the interpretation of what is sensed.* The information about physical events that contacts the ears may be interpreted as musical sounds, for example. The physical energy transmitted to the retinas may be interpreted as a particular color, pattern, or shape.

sensation
Occurs when information interacts with the sensory receptors—the eyes, ears, tongue, nostrils, and skin.

perception
The interpretation of what is sensed.

Theories of Perceptual Development

Two main theoretical perspectives attempt to capture how the infant's perception develops: the constructivist view and the ecological view.

The Constructivist View

The **constructivist view,** *advocated by Piaget and information-processing psychologists, states that perception is a cognitive construction based on sensory input plus information retrieved from memory. In this view, perception is a representation of the world that builds up as the infant constructs an image of its experiences.*

The constructivist view argues that perception is the process of internally representing information from the world. As information from the world is processed, it undergoes a series of internal manipulations. For example, information-processing psychologists ask the question, What is the purpose of vision (Marr, 1982)? Some of the answers to this question include to navigate through the environment without bumping into things, to be able to grasp things, and eventually to create a representation of visual objects that can be compared with representations in memory.

The Ecological View

Much of the research on perceptual development in infancy in the past several decades has been guided by the ecological view of Eleanor and James J. Gibson (Gibson, 1982, 1989; Gibson, 1966, 1979). They believe, unlike Piaget, that we can directly perceive information that exists in the world around us. We do not have to build up representations of the world in our mind; information about the world is available out there in the environment. Thus, the **ecological view** *states that the perception has functional purposes of bringing the organism in contact with the environment and of increasing adaptation.* A key function of this perceptual adaptation is to detect perceptual invariants—those that remain stable—in a constantly changing world. A key feature of the ecological view is that even complex things (such as a spatial layout) can be perceived directly without constructive activity.

The Gibsons believe that, if complex things can be perceived directly, perhaps they can be perceived even by young infants. Thus, the ecological view has inspired investigators to search for the competencies that young infants possess (Bower, 1989). Of course, ecological theorists do not deny that perception develops as infants and children develop. In fact, the ecological theorists stress that, as perceptual processes mature, the child becomes more efficient at discovering the invariant properties of objects available to the senses.

For the Gibsons, all objects have many **affordances**—*opportunities for interaction offered by an object that are necessary to perform functional activities.* For example, adults immediately know when a chair is appropriate for sitting, a surface is appropriate for walking, or an object is within reach. We directly and accurately perceive these affordances by sensing information from the environment—the light or sound reflecting from the surfaces of the world—and from our own bodies through muscle receptors, joint receptors, and skin receptors, for example. The developmental question, though, is how these affordances are acquired. In one investigation, infants who were crawlers or walkers recognized the action-specific properties of surfaces (Gibson & others, 1987). When faced with a rigid plywood surface or a squishy waterbed, crawlers crossed both without hesitating. The toddlers, however, first stopped and explored the waterbed, then chose to crawl rather than walk across it.

Visual Perception

Can newborns see? How does visual perception develop in infancy?

Visual Acuity and Color

Psychologist William James (1890/1950) called the newborn's perceptual world a "blooming, buzzing"

constructivist view
Advocated by Piaget and the information-processing psychologists, this view states that perception is a cognitive construction based on sensory input plus information retrieved from memory. In this view, perception is a kind of representation of the world that builds up as the infant constructs an image of experiences.

Perceptual Development
Newborns' Senses
Richard Aslin's Research
International Society on Infant Studies

ecological view
Advocated by the Gibsons, this view states that the purpose of perception is to detect perceptual invariants—those that remain stable—in a constantly changing world.

affordances
The opportunities for interaction that an object offers us, allowing us to perform functional activities.

Through the Eyes of Psychologists

Herb Pick,
University of Minnesota

"The infant is by no means as helpless as it looks and is quite capable of some very complex and important actions."

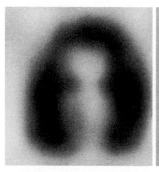

Figure **5.11**

Visual Acuity During the First Months of Life

The two photographs represent a computer estimation of what a picture of a face looks like to a 1-month-old child and a 1-year-old child (whose vision approximates that of an adult).

confusion. Was James right? A century later, we can safely say that he was wrong. The infant's perception of visual information is far more advanced than was previously thought.

Just how well can infants see? The newborn's vision is estimated to be 20/400 to 20/800 on the well-known Snellan chart, with which you are tested when you have your eyes examined (Haith, 1991). This is about 10 to 30 times lower than normal adult vision (20/20). By 6 months of age, though, vision is 20/100 or better, and, by about the first birthday, the infant's vision approximates that of an adult (Banks & Salapatek, 1983). (see figure 5.11).

Can newborns see color? At birth, babies can distinguish between green and red (Adams, 1989). And adultlike functioning in all three types (red, blue, green) of color-sensitive receptors (cones) is present by 2 months of age.

Visual Preferences   Robert Fantz (1963) is an important pioneer in the study of visual perception in infants. Fantz made an important discovery that advanced the ability of researchers to investigate infants' visual perception: infants look at different things for different lengths of time. Fantz placed infants in a "looking chamber," which had two visual displays on the ceiling above the infant's head. An experimenter viewed the infant's eyes by looking through a peephole. If the infant was fixating on one of the displays, the experimenter could see the display's reflection in the infant's eyes. This allowed the experimenter to determine how long the infant looked at each display. In figure 5.12 you can see Fantz's looking chamber and the results of his experiment. The infants preferred to look at patterns rather than at color or brightness. For example, they preferred to look at a face, a piece of printed matter, or a bull's-eye longer than at red, yellow, or white discs. In another experiment, Fantz found that younger infants—only 2 days old—look longer at patterned stimuli, such as faces and concentric circles, than at red, white, or yellow discs. Based on these results, it is likely that pattern perception has an innate basis, or at least is acquired after only minimal environmental experience. The newborn's visual world is not the blooming, buzzing confusion William James imagined.

Perception of Faces   The human face is perhaps the most important visual pattern for the newborn to perceive. The infant progresses through a sequence of steps to full perceptual appreciation of the face (Gibson, 1969). At about 3½ weeks, the infant is fascinated with the eyes, perhaps because the infant notices simple perceptual features such as dots, angles, and circles. At 1 to 2 months of age, the infant notices and perceives contour. At 2 months of age and older, the infant begins to differentiate facial features—it distinguishes eyes from other parts of the face, notices the mouth, and pays attention to movements of the mouth. By 5 months of age, the infant has detected other features of the face—its plasticity, its solid, three-dimensional surface, the oval shape of the head, and the orientation of the eyes and the mouth. Beyond 6 months of age, the infant distinguishes familiar faces from unfamiliar faces—mother from stranger, masks from real faces, and so on.

How do young infants scan the human face? In one study, researchers showed human faces to 1- and 2-month-old infants (Maurer & Salapatek, 1976). By use of a special mirror arrangement, the faces were projected as images in front of the infant's eyes so that the infant's eye movements could be photographed. Figure 5.13 shows the plotting of the eye fixations of a 1-month-old and a 2-month-old infant. Notice that the 1-month-old scanned only a few portions of the entire face—a narrow segment of the chin and two spots on the head. The 2-month-old scanned a much wider area of the figure—the mouth, the eyes, and a large portion of the head. The older infant spent more time examining the internal details of the face, while the younger infant concentrated on areas on the outer contour of the face.

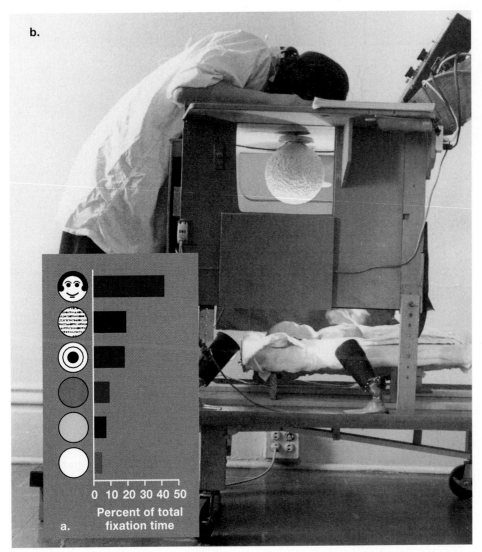

a.

b.

Figure **5.12**

Fantz's Experiment on Infants' Visual Perception

(a) Infants 2 to 3 months old preferred to look at some stimuli more than others. In Fantz's experiment, infants preferred to look at patterns rather than at color or brightness. For example, they looked longer at a face, a piece of printed matter, or a bull's-eye than at red, yellow, or white discs. *(b)* Fantz used a "looking chamber" to study infants' perception of stimuli.

size constancy
The recognition that an object remains the same size even though the retinal image of the object changes.

shape constancy
The recognition that an object remains the same shape even though its orientation to us changes.

Perceptual Constancy   Some perceptual accomplishments are especially intriguing because they seem to indicate that an infant's perception is better than it ought to be on the basis of sensory information. Such is the case for perceptual constancy, in which the sensory stimulation is changing but our perception (like the world) remains constant. Let's explore two types of perceptual constancy: size constancy and shape constancy.

Size constancy *is the recognition that an object remains the same size even though the retinal image of the object changes.* The size of an object on the retina is not sufficient to determine its actual size. The farther away from us an object is, the smaller its image is on our eyes. For example, a bicycle standing right in front of a child appears smaller than a car parked across the street, even though the bicycle casts a larger image on the child's eyes than the car does.

But what about babies? Do they have size constancy? Researchers have found that infants as young as 3 months of age show size constancy (Bower, 1966; Day & McKenzie, 1973). However, at 3 months of age, the ability is not full-blown and continues to develop. As infants' binocular vision develops between 4 and 5 months of age, their ability to perceive size constancy improves (Aslin, 1987). Further progress in perceiving size constancy continues until the age of 10 or 11 (Kellman & Banks, 1998).

Shape constancy *is the recognition that an object remains the same shape even though its orientation to us changes.* Look around the room while you are read-

Figure **5.13**

How 1- and 2-Month-Old Infants Scan the Human Face

Figure 5.14
Examining Infants' Depth Perception on the Visual Cliff

Eleanor Gibson and Richard Walk (1960) found that most infants would not walk out on the glass, which indicated that they had depth perception.

ADVENTURES FOR THE MIND
Measuring Infant Perception

BECAUSE YOUNG INFANTS are preverbal and have limited motor skills, it is a challenge to measure their perceptual development. One technique researchers have used to assess visual perception is to move a large object toward a newborn's head to determine whether it can see. The infant's head movement suggests that it has at least some vision.

Can you think of other techniques that could be used to study the young infant's perception? One simple method is to look for evidence that an infant prefers one stimulus to another. If you are studying visual perception, you might place two visual stimuli in front of an infant and determine which stimulus the infant looks at more. If you have a question about smell, you might place a different odorous substance on each side of the infant's head and see if the infant turns more toward one side than the other. To test for auditory perception, you might use a "conditional head-turning procedure." In this procedure, an infant sits on its mother's lap and a sound comes out of a speaker. If the infant turns toward the speaker, it sees a colorful mechanical toy in motion (the toy is switched on if the infant turns toward the sound). This is rewarding, and the infant soon learns to look at the speaker whenever a sound comes out of it. If you are interested in determining the infant's threshold for hearing, you might manipulate the loudness of the sound. Can you think of yet other ways the infant's perception could be assessed?

ing this book. You probably see objects of various shapes—chairs and tables, for example. If you walk around the room, you will see these objects from different sides and angles. Even though your retinal images of the objects change as you walk, you still perceive the objects as remaining the same shape.

Do babies have shape constancy? As with size constancy, researchers have found that babies as young as 3 months of age have shape constancy, at least for regularly shaped objects like toy blocks (Bower, 1966; Day & McKenzie, 1973). Three-month-old infants, however, do not seem to have shape constancy for irregularly shaped objects, such as those with tilted planes (Cook & Birch, 1984).

Why is it important for infants to develop these perceptual constancies early in their lives? If infants did not develop perceptual constancy, each time they saw an object at a different distance or in a different orientation, they would perceive it as a different object. Thus, the development of perceptual constancy allows the infant to perceive its world as stable.

Depth Perception   How early can infants perceive depth? To investigate this question, infant perception researchers Eleanor Gibson and Richard Walk (1960) conducted a classic experiment. They constructed a miniature cliff with a drop-off covered by glass. The motivation for this experiment arose when Gibson was eating a picnic lunch on the edge of the Grand Canyon. She wondered whether an infant looking over the canyon's rim would perceive the dangerous drop-off and back up. In their laboratory, Gibson and Walk placed infants on the edge of a visual cliff and had their mothers coax them to crawl onto the glass (see figure 5.14). Most infants would not crawl out on the glass, choosing instead to remain on the shallow side, indicating that they could perceive depth. However, because the 6- to 14-month-old infants had extensive visual experience, this research did not answer the question of whether depth perception is innate.

Exactly how early in life does depth perception develop? Since younger infants do not crawl, this question is difficult to answer. Research with 2- to 4-month-old infants shows differences in heart rate when they are placed directly on the deep side of the visual cliff instead of on the shallow side (Campos, Langer, & Krowitz, 1970). However, an alternative interpretation is that young infants respond to differences in some visual characteristics of the deep and shallow cliffs, with no actual knowledge of depth.

Many of the earliest-appearing abilities to perceive objects and space involve information carried by motion, such as the optical transformations in perceiving an approaching object (Bornstein & Arterberry, 1999; Kellman & Banks, 1998). Infants' sensitivity to motion-carried information before other types of depth information might be due to the early maturation of the brain's temporal lobe.

Visual Expectations   Infants not only see forms and figures at an early age but also develop expectations about future events in their world by the time they are 3 months of age. Marshall Haith and his colleagues (Canfield & Haith, 1991; Haith, Hazen, & Goodman, 1988) studied whether babies would form expectations about where an interesting picture would appear. The pictures were presented to the infants in either a regular alternating sequence—such as left, right, left, right—or an unpredictable sequence—such as right, right, left, right. When the sequence was predictable, the 3-month-old infants began to anticipate the location of the picture, looking at the side on which it was expected to appear. The young infants formed this visual expectation in less than one minute. However, younger infants did not develop expectations about where a picture would be presented.

Elizabeth Spelke (1988, 1991) also has demonstrated that young infants form visual expectations. She placed babies before a puppet stage and showed them a series of unexpected actions—for example, a ball seemed to roll through a solid barrier, another seemed to leap between two platforms, and a third appeared to hang in midair (Spelke, 1979) (see figure 5.15). Spelke measured the babies' looking times and recorded longer intervals for unexpected than expected actions. She concluded that, by 4 months of age, even though infants do not yet have the ability to talk about objects, move around objects, manipulate objects, or even see objects with high resolution, they can recognize where a moving object is when it has left their visual field and can infer where it should be when it comes into their sight again.

At this point we have studied a number of ideas about what sensation and perception are, theories of perceptual development, and visual perception. A review of these ideas is presented in summary table 5.4. Next, we continue our exploration of sensory and perceptual development by examining senses other than vision.

Figure 5.15
The Young Infant's Knowledge of the Perceptual World
A 4-month-old in Elizabeth Spelke's infant perception laboratory is tested to determine if it knows that an object in motion will not stop in midair. She found that babies looked longer at the ball when it stopped in midair, an unexpected action, than when it landed on the table, an expected action.

Other Senses

Considerable development also takes place in other sensory systems. We will explore development in hearing, touch and pain, smell, and taste.

Hearing   What is the nature of hearing in newborns? Can the fetus hear? What types of auditory stimulation should be used with infants at different points in the first year? We examine each of these questions.

Immediately after birth, infants can hear, although their sensory thresholds are somewhat higher than those of adults (Trehub & others, 1991). That is, a stimulus must be louder to be heard by a newborn than by an adult. Also, in one study, as infants aged from 8 to 28 weeks, they became more proficient at localizing sounds (Morrongiello, Fenwick, & Chance, 1990). Not only can newborns hear, but the possibility has been raised that the fetus can hear as it nestles within its mother's womb. Let's examine this possibility further.

In the last few months of pregnancy, the fetus can hear sounds: the mother's voice, music, and so on (Kisilevsky, 1995). Given that the fetus can hear sounds, two psychologists wanted to find out if listening to Dr. Seuss' classic story *The Cat in the Hat*, while still in the mother's womb, would produce a preference for hearing the story after birth (DeCasper & Spence, 1986). Sixteen pregnant women read *The Cat in the Hat* to their fetuses twice a day over the last 6 weeks of their pregnancies. When the babies were born, their mothers read *The Cat in the Hat* or a story with a different rhyme and pace, *The King, the Mice, and the Cheese*. The infants sucked on a nipple in a different way when the mothers read *The Cat in*

Elizabeth Spelke's Research

SUMMARY TABLE 5.4
The Nature of Sensation and Perception, Theories of Perceptual Development, and Visual Perception

Concept	Processes/ Related Ideas	Characteristics/Description
What Are Sensation and Perception?	Sensation	• Sensation occurs when information interacts with the sensory receptors—the eyes, ears, tongue, nostrils, and skin.
	Perception	• Perception is the interpretation of what is sensed.
Theories of Perceptual Development	The Constructivist View	• This view is advocated by Piaget and information-processing psychologists. • According to this view, perception is a cognitive construction based on sensory input plus information retrieved from memory.
	The Ecological View	• This view is advocated by the Gibsons. • According to this view, perception has the function of bringing organisms in contact with the environment and increasing adaptation. • A key aspect involves perceptual invariants. • For the Gibsons, objects have affordances.
Visual Perception	Visual Acuity and Color	• William James was wrong—the newborn's visual world is not a blooming, buzzing confusion. • Newborns can see and distinguish colors.
	Visual Preferences	• In Fantz's pioneering research, infants only 2 days old looked longer at patterned stimuli, such as faces, than at single-colored discs.
	Perception of Faces	• The human face is an important pattern for the newborn, and the infant gradually masters a sequence of steps in perceiving it.
	Perceptual Constancy	• Two types are size and shape constancy, both of which are present in infants by 3 months of age.
	Depth Perception	• A classic study by Gibson and Walk demonstrated through the use of the visual cliff that infants as young as 6 months of age have depth perception.
	Visual Expectations	• Spelke has demonstrated that infants develop expectations about future events in their world by the time they are 3 months of age.

the Hat, suggesting that the infants recognized its pattern and tone (to which they had been exposed prenatally) (see figure 5.16).

Two important conclusions can be drawn from this investigation. First, it reveals how ingenious scientists have become at assessing the development not only of infants but of fetuses as well, in this case discovering a way to "interview" newborn babies who cannot yet talk. Second, it reveals the remarkable ability of an infant's brain to learn even before birth.

Babies are born into the world prepared to respond to the sounds of any human language. Even very young infants can discriminate subtle phonetic differences, such as those between the speech sounds *ba* and *ga*. Young infants also will suck more on a nipple to hear a recording of their mother's voice than they will to hear the voice of an unfamiliar woman, and they will suck more to listen to their mother's native language than they will to listen to a foreign language (Mehler & others, 1988; Spence & DeCasper, 1987). And an interesting developmental change occurs during the first year: 6-month-old infants can discriminate phonetic sound contrasts from languages to which they have never been exposed, but they lose this discriminative ability by their first birthday, demonstrating that experience with a specific language is necessary for maintaining this ability (Werker & LaDonde, 1988).

well: the sound of the ball bouncing or being hit, the grunts and groans, and so on. There is good correspondence between much of the visual and auditory information: when you see the ball bounce, you hear a bouncing sound; when a player stretches to hit a ball, you hear a groan.

We live in a world of objects and events that can be seen, heard, and felt. When mature observers simultaneously look and listen to an event, they experience a unitary episode. All of this is so commonplace that it scarcely seems worth mentioning, but consider the task of very young infants with little practice at perceiving. Can they put vision and sound together as precisely as adults do?

Intermodal perception *is the ability to relate and integrate information about two or more sensory modalities, such as vision and hearing.* The two main theories described earlier address the question of whether young infants develop intermodal perception. The ecological view argues that infants have intermodal perception capabilities very early in infancy. In this view, infants only have to attend to the appropriate sensory information; they do not have to build up an internal representation of the information through months of sensorimotor experiences. In contrast, the contructivist view advocated by Piaget states that perceptual abilities, such as vision, hearing, and touch, are not coordinated early in infancy; therefore, young infants do not have intermodal perception. According to Piaget, only through months of sensorimotor interaction with the world is intermodal perception possible. For example, infants can coordinate touch and vision only when they learn to look at objects as their hands grasp them.

To test intermodal perception, Elizabeth Spelke (1979) showed 4-month-old infants two films simultaneously. In each film, a puppet jumped up and down, but in one of the films a sound track matched the puppet's dancing movements; in the other film, it did not. By measuring the infants' gaze, Spelke found that the infants looked more at the puppet whose actions were synchronized with the sound track, suggesting that they recognized the visual-sound correspondence. Young infants can also coordinate visual-auditory information involving people. In one study, as early as 3½ months old, infants looked more at their mother when they also heard her voice and longer at their father when they also heard his voice (Spelke & Owsley, 1979).

Might auditory-visual relations be coordinated even in newborns? Newborns do turn their eyes and their head toward the sound of a voice or rattle when the sound is maintained for several seconds (Clifton & others, 1981), but the newborn can localize a sound and look at an object only in a crude way (Bechtold, Bushnell, & Salapatek, 1979). Improved accuracy at auditory-visual coordination likely requires a sharpening through experience with visual and auditory stimuli. Nonetheless, although at a crude level, auditory-visual intermodal perception appears to be present at birth, likely having evolutionary value.

In sum, crude exploratory forms of intermodal perception exist in newborns. These exploratory forms of intermodal perception become sharpened with experience in the first year of life. In the first 6 months, infants have difficulty forming mental representations that connect sensory input from different modes, but in the second half of the first year they show an increased ability to make this connection mentally. Thus, babies are born into the world with some innate abilities to perceive relations among sensory modalities, but their intermodal abilities improve considerably through experience. As with all aspects of development, in perceptual development, nature and nurture interact and cooperate.

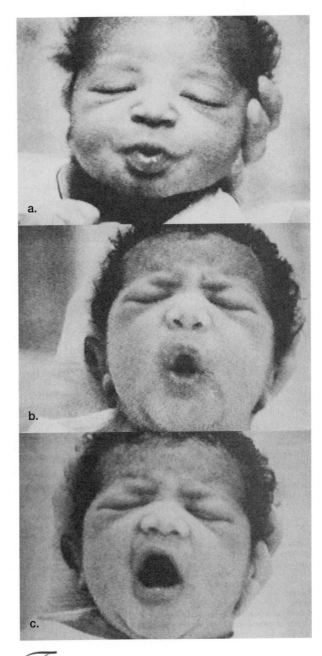

Figure 5.18

Newborns' Facial Responses to Basic Tastes

Facial expressions elicited by (*a*) a sweet solution, (*b*) a sour solution, and (*c*) a bitter solution.

intermodal perception
The ability to relate and integrate information about two or more sensory modalities, such as vision and hearing.

SUMMARY TABLE 5.5
Other Senses, Intermodal Perception, and Perceptual-Motor Coupling and Unification

Concept	Processes/ Related Ideas	Characteristics/Description
Other Senses	Hearing	• The fetus can hear several weeks before birth. • Immediately after birth, newborns can hear, although their sensory threshold is higher than that of adults.
	Touch and Pain	• Newborns respond to touch and can feel pain. • Research on circumcision shows that 3-day-old males experience pain and can adapt to stress.
Intermodal Perception	Its Nature	• This is the ability to relate and integrate information about two or more sensory modalities, such as vision and hearing. • The ecological view argues that young infants have intermodal perception; the constructivist view states that sensory modalities are not coordinated in early infancy. • Spelke's research demonstrates that infants as young as 3 months of age can connect visual and auditory stimuli. • Crude, exploratory forms of intermodal perception are present in newborns and become sharpened in the first year of life.
Perceptual-Motor Coupling and Unification	Their Nature	• Thelen argues that perceptual and motor development are coupled and unified. She says that individuals perceive in order to move and move in order to perceive.

Through the Eyes of Psychologists

Bennett Bertenthal,
University of Chicago

"The development of perception and action is mutual and reciprocal. Improvements in coordinating actions demand greater perceptual differentiation; likewise, greater perceptual differentiation that provides children with more precise information for coordinating their actions."

Perceptual-Motor Coupling and Unification

The main thrust of research in the Gibsonian tradition has been to discover how perception guides action. A less-well-studied but equally important issue is how action shapes perception. Motor activities may be crucial because they provide the means for exploring the world and learning about its properties. Only by moving one's eyes, head, hands, and arms and by traversing from one location to another can individuals fully experience their environment and learn effectively to adapt to it.

The distinction between perceiving and doing has been a time-honored tradition in psychology. However, Esther Thelen (1995) questions whether this distinction is real. She argues that individuals perceive in order to move and move in order to perceive. Thus, there is an increasing belief that perceptual and motor development do not develop in isolation from one another but, rather, are coupled (Bornstein & Arterberry, 1999; Lohman, 2000; Thelen, 2000). Babies are continually coordinating their movements with concurrent perceptual information to learn how to maintain balance, reach for objects in space, and locomote across various surfaces and terrains.

At this point we have studied a number of ideas about other senses, intermodal perception, and perceptual-motor coupling and unification. A review of these ideas is presented in summary table 5.5.

Chapter Review

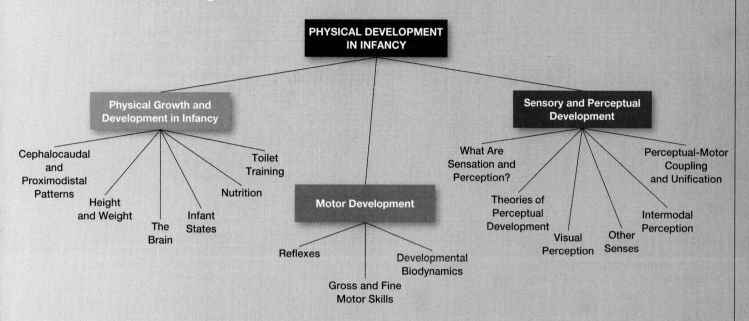

TO OBTAIN A DETAILED REVIEW OF THE CHAPTER, STUDY THESE FIVE SUMMARY TABLES:

Key Terms

cephalocaudal pattern 130
proximodistal pattern 130
neuron 131
cerebral cortex 131
frontal lobe 132
occipital lobe 132
temporal lobe 132
parietal lobe 132
lateralization 133

REM (rapid eye movement) sleep 135
sudden infant death syndrome (SIDS) 137
marasmus 139
sucking reflex 142
rooting reflex 142
Moro reflex 142
grasping reflex 142
gross motor skills 143
fine motor skills 143

developmental biodynamics 147
sensation 148
perception 148
constructivist view 149
ecological view 149
affordances 149
size constancy 151
shape constancy 151
intermodal perception 157

Key People

Mark Rosenzweig 133
Ross Thompson 135
Elizabeth Spelke 135, 153
Ernesto Pollitt 140
T. Berry Brazelton 143

Rachel Clifton 145
Esther Thelen 145, & 157
Jean Piaget 149
Eleanor and James J. Gibson 149
William James 149

Herb Pick 149
Robert Fantz 150
Richard Walk 152
Megan Gunnar 155
Bennett Bertenthal 158

Child Development Resources

Baby Steps
(1994) by Clair Kopp
New York: W. H. Freeman

Baby Steps is a guide to physical, cognitive, and socioemotional development in the first 2 years of life. The book is organized developmentally, with major sections divided into birth through 3 months, 4 through 7 months, 8 through 12 months, and the second year.

Infancy
(1990) by Tiffany Field
Cambridge, MA: Harvard University Press

This is an outstanding book on infant development, written by one of the world's leading researchers on the topic. The book accurately cap-

tures the flavor of the young infant as an active learner and one far more competent than once was believed.

Solve Your Child's Sleep Problems
(1985) by Richard Ferber
New York: Simon & Schuster

Solve Your Child's Sleep Problems helps parents recognize when their infant or child has a sleep problem and tells them what to do about it.

Taking It to the Net

1. Juan and Monika are first-time parents. Monika insists that their 2-month-old daughter, Carmen, can tell the difference between her mother's and her father's face, voice, and touch. Juan says that is ridiculous. Who is correct?

2. Aleysha's mother, Carolyn, has just arrived from out of town and is seeing her 3-month-old grandson, Cameron, for the first time. Carolyn exclaims, "What are you feeding this roly-poly hunk? He looks overweight to me." Aleysha is shocked. She didn't think a baby could be overweight. Should she cut back on his feedings?

3. Tina, who has three children, volunteers to baby-sit for her friend Natalie's 5-month-old boy, Dylan, so that Natalie can go on a job interview. As Tina is undressing Dylan, she thinks it's odd that he doesn't seem able to turn over in his crib. When she cradles him in her arm to bathe him, he feels "floppy" and appears to lack muscle strength. Is Dylan evidencing any motor developmental delays?

Connect to *http://www.mhhe.com/santrockc9* to find the answers!

Chapter 6

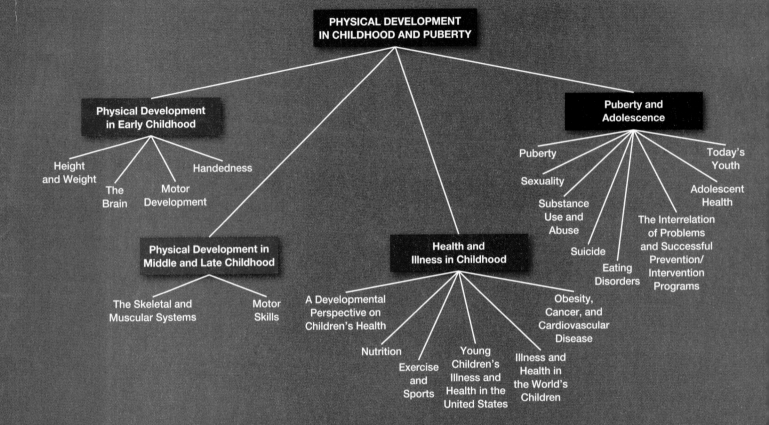

PHYSICAL DEVELOPMENT IN CHILDHOOD AND PUBERTY

Physical Development in Early Childhood

- Height and Weight
- The Brain
- Motor Development
- Handedness

Physical Development in Middle and Late Childhood

- The Skeletal and Muscular Systems
- Motor Skills

Health and Illness in Childhood

- A Developmental Perspective on Children's Health
- Nutrition
- Exercise and Sports
- Young Children's Illness and Health in the United States
- Illness and Health in the World's Children
- Obesity, Cancer, and Cardiovascular Disease

Puberty and Adolescence

- Puberty
- Sexuality
- Substance Use and Abuse
- Suicide
- Eating Disorders
- The Interrelation of Problems and Successful Prevention/ Intervention Programs
- Adolescent Health
- Today's Youth

Physical Development in Childhood and Puberty

That energy which makes a child hard to manage is the energy which afterward makes him a manager of life.

Henry Ward Beecher
American Author, 19th Century

The Story of Zhang Liyin

STANDING ON THE BALANCE BEAM at a sports school in Beijing, China, 6-year-old Zhang Liyin stretches her arms outward as she gets ready to perform a backflip. She wears the bright red gymnastic suit of the elite—a suit given to only the best 10 girls in her class of 6- to 8-year-olds. But her face wears a dreadful expression. She can't drum up enough confidence to do the flip. Maybe it is because she has had a rough week. A purple bruise decorates one leg, and a nasty gash disfigures the other. Her coach, a woman in her twenties, makes Zhang jump from the beam and escorts her to the high bar, where she is instructed to hang for three minutes. If Zhang falls, she must pick herself up and try again. But she does not fall, and she is escorted back to the beam, where her coach puts her through another tedious routine.

Zhang attends the sports school in the afternoon. The sports school is a privilege given to only 260,000 of China's 200 million students of elementary to college age. The Communist party has decided that sports is one avenue China can pursue to prove that China has arrived in the modern world. The sports schools designed to produce Olympic champions were the reason for China's success in the last three Olympics. These schools are the only road to Olympic stardom in China. There are precious few neighborhood playgrounds. And there is only one gymnasium for every 3.5 million people.

Many of the students who attend the sports schools in the afternoon live and study at the schools as well. Only a few attend a normal school and then go to a sports school in the afternoon. Because of her young age, Zhang stays at home during the mornings and goes to the sports school from noon until 6 P.M. A part-timer such as Zhang can stay enrolled until she

The training of future Olympians in the sports schools of China. Six-year-old Zhang Liyin (third from the left) hopes someday to become an Olympic gymnastics champion. Attending the sports school is considered an outstanding privilege; only 260,000 of China's 200 million children are given this opportunity.

no longer shows potential to move up to the next step. Any child who seems to lack potential is asked to leave.

Zhang was playing in a kindergarten class when a coach from a sports school spotted her. She was selected because of her broad shoulders, narrow hips, straight legs, symmetrical limbs, open-minded attitude, vivaciousness, and outgoing personality. If Zhang continues to show progress, she could be asked to move to full-time next year. At age 7, she would then go to school there and live in a dorm six days a week. If she becomes extremely competent at gymnastics, Zhang could be moved to Shishahai, where the elite gymnasts train and compete (Reilly, 1988).

PHYSICAL DEVELOPMENT IN EARLY CHILDHOOD

Height and Weight

The Brain

Handedness

Motor Development

Physical Development in Early Childhood

Remember from chapter 5 that the infant's growth in the first year is rapid and follows cephalocaudal and proximodistal patterns ◀‖‖ P. 130. At some point around the first birthday, most infants begin to walk. During the infant's second year, the growth rate begins to slow down, but both gross and fine motor skills progress rapidly ◀‖‖ P. 144. The infant develops a sense of mastery through increased proficiency in walking and running. Improvement in fine motor skills—such as being able to turn the pages of a book, one at a time—also contributes to the infant's sense of mastery in the second year. The growth rate continues to slow down in early childhood. Otherwise, we would be a species of giants.

Height and Weight

The average child grows 2½ inches in height and gains between 5 and 7 pounds a year during early childhood. As the preschool child grows older, the percentage of increase in height and weight decreases with each additional year. Figure 6.1 shows the average height and weight of children as they age from 2 to 6 years. Girls are only slightly smaller and lighter than boys during these years, a difference that continues until puberty. During the preschool years, both boys and girls slim down as the trunks of their bodies lengthen. Although their heads are still somewhat large for their bodies, by the end of the preschool years most children have lost their top-heavy look. Body fat also shows a slow, steady decline during the preschool years. The chubby baby often looks much leaner by the end of early childhood. Girls have more fatty tissue than boys; boys have more muscle tissue.

Growth patterns vary individually. Think back to your preschool years. This was probably the first time you noticed that some children were taller than you, some shorter; some were fatter, some thinner; some were stronger, some weaker. Much of the variation is due to heredity, but environmental experiences are involved to some extent. A review of the height and weight of children around the world concluded that the two most important contributors to height differences are ethnic origin and nutrition (Meredith, 1978). The urban, middle-SES, and firstborn children were taller than rural, lower-SES, and later-born children. The children whose mothers smoked during pregnancy were half an inch shorter than the children whose mothers did not smoke during pregnancy. In the United States, African American children are taller than White children.

Why are some children unusually short? The culprits are congenital factors (genetic or prenatal problems), a physical problem that develops in childhood, or an emotional difficulty. In many cases, children with congenital growth problems can be treated with hormones. Usually this treatment is directed at the pituitary, the body's master gland, located at the base of the brain. This gland secretes growth-related hormones. With regard to physical problems that develop during childhood, malnutrition and chronic infections can stunt growth. However, if the problems are properly treated, normal growth usually is attained. **Deprivation dwarfism** is a type of growth

Passing hence from infancy, I came to boyhood, or rather it came to me, displacing infancy, nor did that depart— and yet it was no more.

St. Augustine
Roman Clergyman and Philosopher, 5th Century

deprivation dwarfism
A type of growth retardation caused by emotional deprivation; when children are deprived of affection, they experience stress, which alters the release of hormones by the pituitary gland.

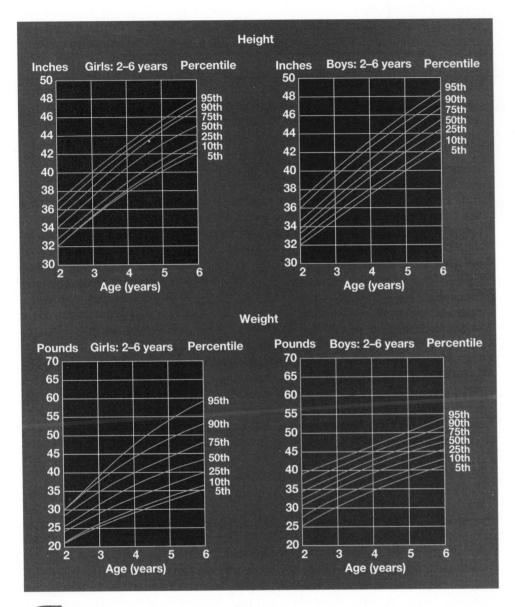

Figure 6.1
Average Height and Weight of Girls and Boys from 2 to 6 Years of Age

retardation caused by emotional deprivation; children are deprived of affection, which causes stress and alters the release of hormones by the pituitary gland. Some children who are not dwarfs may also show the effects of an impoverished emotional environment, although most parents of these children say they are small and weak because they have a poor body structure or constitution (Gardner, 1972).

Preschool Growth and Development
Developmental Milestones

The Brain

One of the most important physical developments during early childhood is the continuing development of the brain and nervous system. The brain continues to grow in early childhood, but it does not grow as rapidly as in infancy ◀▥ P. 130. By the time children have reached 3 years of age, the brain is three-quarters of its adult size. By age 5, the brain has reached about nine-tenths of its adult size.

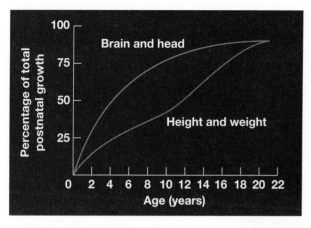

Figure 6.2

Growth Curves for the Head and Brain and for Height and Weight

The more rapid growth of the brain and head can easily be seen. Height and weight advance more gradually over the first two decades of life.

myelination
A process in which nerve cells are insulated with a layer of fat cells, which increases the speed at which information travels through the nervous system.

Swiftly the brain becomes an enchanted loom, where millions of flashing shuttles weave a dissolving pattern—always a meaningful pattern—though never an abiding one.

Sir Charles Sherrington
English Neuroscientist, 20th Century

The brain and the head grow more rapidly than any other part of the body. The top parts of the head, the eyes, and the brain grow faster than the lower portions, such as the jaw. Figure 6.2 reveals how the growth curve for the head and brain advances more rapidly than the growth curve for height and weight. At 5 years of age, when the brain has attained approximately 90 percent of its adult weight, the 5-year-old's total body weight is only about one-third of what it will be when the child reaches adulthood.

Some of the brain's increase in size is due to the increase in the number and size of nerve endings within and between areas of the brain. These nerve endings continue to grow at least until adolescence. Some of the brain's increase in size also is due to the increase in **myelination**, *in which nerve cells are covered and insulated with a layer of fat cells. This has the effect of increasing the speed of information traveling through the nervous system.* Some developmentalists believe myelination is important in the maturation of a number of children's abilities. For example, myelination in the areas of the brain related to hand-eye coordination is not complete until about 4 years of age. Myelination in the areas of the brain related to focusing attention is not complete until the end of the middle or late childhood.

In one recent study, magnetic resonance imaging (MRI) scans of 111 children and adolescents revealed age-related increases in the density of pathways in the areas of the brain involving motor and speech functions (Paus & others, 1999). The increasing maturation of the brain, combined with opportunities to experience a widening world, contribute to children's emerging cognitive abilities. Consider a child who is learning to read and is asked by a teacher to read aloud to the class. Input from the child's eyes is transmitted to the child's brain, then passed through many brain systems, which translate (process) the patterns of black and white into codes for letters, words, and associations. The output occurs in the form of messages to the child's lips and tongue. The child's own gift of speech is possible because brain systems are organized in ways that permit language processing.

Motor Development

Running as fast as you can, falling down, getting right back up and running just as fast as you can . . . building towers with blocks . . . scribbling . . . cutting paper with scissors. During your preschool years, you probably developed the ability to perform all of these activities.

Gross Motor Skills   The preschool child no longer has to make an effort simply to stay upright and to move around. As children move their legs with more confidence and carry themselves more purposefully, moving around in the environment becomes more automatic.

At 3 years of age, children enjoy simple movements, such as hopping, jumping, and running back and forth, just for the sheer delight of performing these activities. They delight in showing how they can run across a room and jump all of 6 inches. The run-and-jump will win no Olympic gold medals, but for the 3-year-old the activity is a source of considerable pride and accomplishment.

By 4 years of age, children are still enjoying the same kinds of activities, but they have become more adventurous. They scramble over low jungle gyms as they display their athletic prowess. Although they have been able to climb stairs with one foot on each step for some time now, they are just beginning to be able to come down the same way. They still often revert to marking time on each step.

By 5 years of age, children are even more adventuresome than when they were 4. Five-year-olds run hard and enjoy races with each other and their parents. A summary of development in gross motor skills during early childhood is shown in figure 6.3.

37–48 months	49–60 months	61–72 months
Throws ball underhanded (4´)	Bounces and catches ball	Throws ball (44´ boys; 25´ girls)
Pedals tricycle 10´	Runs 10´ and stops	Carries a 16-pound object
Catches large ball	Pushes/pulls a wagon/doll buggy	Kicks rolling ball
Completes forward somersault (aided)	Kicks 10″ ball toward target	Skips alternating feet
Jumps to floor from 12″	Carries 12-pound object	Roller skates
Hops three hops with both feet	Catches ball	Skips rope
Steps on footprint pattern	Bounces ball under control	Rolls ball to hit object
Catches bounced ball	Hops on one foot four hops	Rides two-wheel bike with training wheels

Figure **6.3**

The Development of Gross Motor Skills in Early Childhood

The skills are listed in the approximate order of difficulty within each age period.

You probably have arrived at one important conclusion about preschool children: They are very, very active. Indeed, 3-year-old children have the highest activity level of any age in the entire human life span. They fidget when they watch television. They fidget when they sit at the dinner table. Even when they sleep, they move around quite a bit. Because of their activity level and the development of large muscles, especially in the arms and legs, preschool children need daily exercise.

All the sun long I was running...

Dylan Thomas
Welsh Poet and Writer, 20th Century

Handedness

Fine Motor Skills   At 3 years of age, children are still emerging from the infant ability to place and handle things. Although they have had the ability to pick up the tiniest objects between their thumb and forefinger for some time, they are still somewhat clumsy at it. Three-year-olds can build surprisingly high block towers, each block placed with intense concentration but often not in a completely straight line. When 3-year-olds play with a form board or a simple jigsaw puzzle, they are rather rough in placing the pieces. Even when they recognize the hole a piece fits into, they are not very precise in positioning the piece. They often try to force the piece in the hole or pat it vigorously.

By 4 years of age, children's fine motor coordination has improved substantially and become much more precise. Sometimes 4-year-old children have trouble building high towers with blocks because, in their desire to place each of the blocks perfectly, they may upset those already stacked. By age 5, children's fine motor coordination has improved further. Hand, arm, and body all move together under better command of the eye. Mere towers no longer interest the 5-year-old, who now wants to build a house or a church, complete with steeple, though adults may still need to be told what each finished project is meant to be. A summary of the typical development of fine motor skills in early childhood is shown in figure 6.4.

Handedness

For centuries, left-handers have suffered discrimination in a world designed for right-handers. Even the devil himself has been portrayed as a left-hander. For many

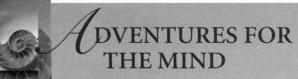

ADVENTURES FOR THE MIND

Explaining to Parents Why Most 3-Year-Olds Should Not Participate in Sports

ASSUME THAT YOU are the director of a preschool program and the parents ask you to develop a program to teach the children how to participate in sports. Think through how you would explain to the parents why most 3-year-olds are not ready for participation in sports programs. Include in your answer information about 3-year-olds' limited motor skills, as well as the importance of learning basic motor skills first.

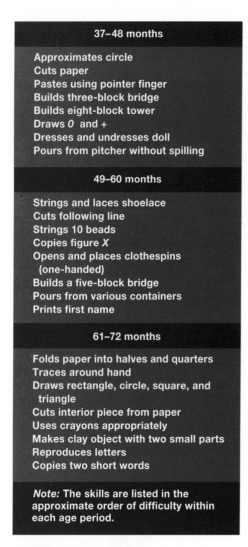

37–48 months
Approximates circle
Cuts paper
Pastes using pointer finger
Builds three-block bridge
Builds eight-block tower
Draws *0* and +
Dresses and undresses doll
Pours from pitcher without spilling

49–60 months
Strings and laces shoelace
Cuts following line
Strings 10 beads
Copies figure *X*
Opens and places clothespins (one-handed)
Builds a five-block bridge
Pours from various containers
Prints first name

61–72 months
Folds paper into halves and quarters
Traces around hand
Draws rectangle, circle, square, and triangle
Cuts interior piece from paper
Uses crayons appropriately
Makes clay object with two small parts
Reproduces letters
Copies two short words

Note: The skills are listed in the approximate order of difficulty within each age period.

Figure 6.4

The Development of Fine Motor Skills in Early Childhood

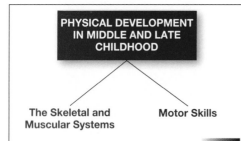

```
PHYSICAL DEVELOPMENT
IN MIDDLE AND LATE
CHILDHOOD
```

The Skeletal and Muscular Systems   Motor Skills

years, teachers forced all children to write with their right hand, even if they had a left-hand tendency. Fortunately, today most teachers let children write with the hand they favor.

Some children are still discouraged from using their left hand, even though many left-handed individuals have become very successful. Their ranks include Leonardo da Vinci, Benjamin Franklin, and Pablo Picasso. Each of these famous men was known for his imagination of spatial layouts, which might be stronger in left-handed individuals. Left-handed athletes also are often successful. Because there are fewer left-handed athletes, the opposition is not as accustomed to the style and approach of "lefties." Their tennis serve spins in the opposite direction, their curve ball in baseball swerves the opposite way, and their left foot in soccer is not the one children are used to defending against. Left-handed individuals also do well intellectually. In an analysis of the Scholastic Aptitude Test (SAT) scores of more than 100,000 students, 20 percent of the top-scoring group was left-handed, which is twice the rate of left-handedness found in the general population (Bower, 1985). Clearly, many left-handed people are competent in a wide variety of human activities.

When does hand preference develop? Adults usually notice a child's hand preference during early childhood, but researchers have found handedness tendencies in the infant years. Even newborns have some preference for one side of their body over the other. In one study, 65 percent of the infants turned their head to the right when they were lying on their stomachs in the crib (Michel, 1981). Fifteen percent preferred to face toward the left. These preferences for the right or left were related to later handedness. At about 7 months of age, infants prefer grabbing with one hand or the other, and this is also related to later handedness (Ramsay, 1980). By 2 years of age, about 10 percent of children favor their left hand. Many preschool children, though, use both hands, with a clear hand preference not completely distinguished until later in development. Some children use one hand for writing and drawing, and the other hand for throwing a ball. My oldest daughter, Tracy, confuses the issue even further. She writes left-handed and plays tennis left-handed, but she plays golf right-handed. During early childhood, her handedness was still somewhat in doubt. My youngest daughter, Jennifer, was left-handed from early in infancy.

What is the origin of hand preference? Genetic inheritance and environmental experiences have been proposed as causes. In one study, a genetic interpretation was favored. The handedness of adopted children was not related to the handedness of their adoptive parents but was related to the handedness of their biological parents (Carter-Saltzman, 1980).

Physical Development in Middle and Late Childhood

The period of middle and late childhood involves slow, consistent growth. This is a period of calm before the rapid growth spurt of adolescence. In middle and late childhood, important developmental changes occur in the skeletal system, the muscular system, and motor skills.

The Skeletal and Muscular Systems

During the elementary school years, children grow an average of 2 to 3 inches a year until, at the age of 11, the average girl is 4 feet 10¾ inches tall and the average boy is 4 feet 9 inches tall. Children's legs become longer and their trunks slimmer. During the middle and late childhood years, children gain about 5 to 7 pounds a year. The weight increase is due mainly to increases in the size of the skeleton and muscular systems, as well as the size of some body organs. Muscle mass and strength gradually increase as "baby fat" decreases. The loose movements and knock-knees of early childhood give way to improved muscle tone. The increase in muscular strength is due to heredity and to exercise. Children double their strength capabilities during these years. Because of their greater number of muscle cells, boys are usually stronger than girls. Changes in height and weight in middle and late childhood are summarized in figure 6.5.

Proportional changes are among the most pronounced physical changes in middle and late childhood. Head circumference, waist circumference, and leg length decrease in relation to body height (Wong, 2000).

Motor Skills

During middle and late childhood, children's motor development becomes much smoother and more coordinated than it was in early childhood. For example, only one child in a thousand can hit a tennis ball over the net at the age of 3, yet by the age of 10 or 11 most children can learn to play the sport. Running, climbing, skipping rope, swimming, bicycle riding, and skating are just a few of the many physical skills elementary school children can master. And, when mastered, these physical skills are a source of great pleasure and accomplishment for children. In gross motor skills involving large muscle activity, boys usually outperform girls.

As children move through the elementary school years, they gain greater control over their bodies and can sit and attend for longer periods of time. However, elementary school children are far from having physical maturity, and they need to be active. Elementary school children become more fatigued by long periods of sitting than by running, jumping, or bicycling. Physical action is essential for these children to refine their developing skills, such as batting a ball, skipping rope, or balancing on a beam. An important principle of practice for elementary school children, therefore, is that they should be engaged in *active,* rather than passive, activities.

As children move through the elementary school years, they gain greater control over their bodies. Physical action is essential for them to refine their developing skills.

Increased myelinization of the central nervous system is reflected in the improvement of fine motor skills during middle and late childhood. Children use their hands more adroitly as tools. Six-year-olds can hammer, paste, tie shoes, and fasten clothes. By 7 years of age, children's hands become steadier. At this age, children prefer a pencil to a crayon for printing, and reversal of letters is less common. Printing becomes smaller. Between 8 to 10 years of age, the hands can be used independently with more ease and precision. Fine motor coordination develops to the point where children can write rather than print words. Letter size continues to decrease and becomes more even. By 10 to 12 years of age, children's manipulative skills begin to approximate those of adults. Children begin to master complex, intricate, and rapid movements needed to produce fine-quality crafts or a difficult piece on a musical instrument can be mastered. One final point: Girls usually outperform boys in fine motor skills.

At this point we have studied a number of ideas about physical development in early and middle/late childhood. A review of these ideas is presented in summary table 6.1. Next, we will continue our exploration of physical development by examining health and illness in childhood.

SUMMARY TABLE 6.1
Physical Development in Early, Middle, and Late Childhood

Concept	Processes/Related Ideas	Characteristics/Description
Early Childhood	Height and Weight	• The average child grows 2½ inches in height and gains 5 to 7 pounds a year during early childhood. • Growth patterns, though, vary individually. • Some children are unusually short because of congenital (physical) problems, others possibly because of emotional problems.
	The Brain	• By age 5, the brain has reached nine-tenths of its adult size. • Some of the increase in size is due to increases in the size and number of nerve endings, some to myelination. • Increasing brain maturation contributes to improved cognitive abilities.
	Motor Development	• Gross and fine motor skills improve considerably in early childhood. • Young children's lives are extremely active.
	Handedness	• Today, it is recommended that children be allowed to use the hand they favor. • Left-handed children are as competent as right-handed children in motor skills and intellect. • Both genetic and environmental explanations of handedness have been given.
Physical Development in Middle and Late Childhood	Nature of Changes	• Children's motor development becomes much smoother and more coordinated. • Increased myelination of the nervous system is reflected in improved fine motor skills. • Boys are usually better at gross motor skills, girls are often better at fine motor skills.

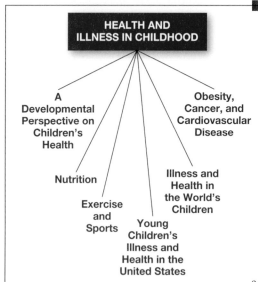

Health and Illness in Childhood

Although we have become a health-conscious nation, aware of the importance of nutrition and exercise in our lives, many of us still eat junk food, have extra flab hanging around our middles, and spend too much time as couch potatoes. All too often, this description fits children as well as adults (Hayman, Mahon, & Turner, 1999).

A Developmental Perspective on Children's Health

Although there has been great national interest in the psychological aspects of adult health, only recently has a developmental perspective on the psychological aspects of children's health been proposed (Bolen, Brand, Sacks, 1999; Raman, 1999; Tinsley, 1992). The uniqueness of young children's health-care needs is evident when we consider their motor, cognitive, and social development (Maddux & others, 1986). For example, think about the infant's and preschool child's motor development—it is inadequate to ensure personal safety while riding in an automobile. Adults must take preventive measures to restrain infants and young children in car seats. Young children might lack the intellectual skills—including reading ability—to discriminate between safe and unsafe household substances, and they might lack the impulse control to keep them from running out into a busy street while chasing after a ball or toy.

Playgrounds for young children need to be designed with their safety in mind (Frost & Wortham, 1988; Waltzman & others, in press). The initial step in ensuring children's safety is to walk with children through the existing playground or the site where the playground is to be developed, talking with them about possible safety hazards, letting them assist in identifying hazards, and indicating how they can use the playground safely. The outdoor play environment should enhance children's motor, cognitive, and social development.

Health education programs for preschool children need to be cognitively simple. There are three simple but important goals for health education programs for preschool children (Parcel & others, 1979): (1) to help children identify feelings of wellness and illness and be able to express them to adults, (2) to help children identify appropriate sources of assistance for health-related problems, and (3) to help children independently initiate the use of sources of assistance for health problems.

Caregivers have an important health role for young children (Gomel, Hanson, & Tinsley, 1999; Tinsley, Finley, & Ortiz, 1999). For example, by controlling the speed of the vehicles they drive, by decreasing their drinking, and by not smoking around children, caregivers enhance children's health (Gergen & others, 1998). In one investigation, it was found that if a mother smokes, her children are twice as likely to have respiratory ailments (Etzel, 1988). The young children of single, unemployed, smoking mothers are also three times more likely to be injured. Smoking may serve as a marker to identify mothers less able to supervise young children. In sum, caregivers can actively affect young children's health and safety by training them and monitoring their recreational safety, self-protection skills, proper nutrition, and dental hygiene.

Illnesses, especially those that are not life threatening, provide an excellent opportunity for young children to expand their development (Deluca, 1999). The preschool period is a peak time for such illnesses as respiratory infections (colds, flu) and gastrointestinal upsets (nausea, diarrhea). The illnesses usually are of short duration and are often handled outside the medical community through the family, day care, or school. Such minor illnesses can increase the young child's knowledge of health and illness and sense of empathy.

Nutrition

Feeding and eating habits are important aspects of development during early childhood. What children eat affects their skeletal growth, body shape, and susceptibility to disease. Recognizing that nutrition is important for the child's growth and development, the federal government provides money for school lunch programs. An average preschool child requires 1,700 calories per day. Figure 6.5 shows the increasing energy needs of children as they move from infancy through the childhood years. Energy requirements for individual children are determined by the **basal metabolism rate (BMR),** *which is the minimum amount of energy a person uses in a resting state.* Energy needs of individual children of the same age, sex, and size vary. Reasons for

**Pediatrics
Health Links
MEDLINE Plus
Harvard Center for Children's Health
Maternal and Child Health Resources**

basal metabolism rate (BMR)
The minimum amount of energy an individual uses in a resting state.

Age	Weight (kg)	Height (cm)	Energy needs (calories)	Calorie ranges
1–3	13	90	1,300	900–1,800
4–6	20	112	1,700	1,300–2,300
7–10	28	132	2,400	1,650–3,300

Figure **6.5**

Recommended Energy Intakes for Children Ages 1 Through 10

Eating Problems
Children and Exercise

these differences remain unexplained. Differences in physical activity, basal metabolism, and the efficiency with which children use energy are among the candidates for explanation.

Caregivers need to be aware of the appropriate amount of fat and sugar in young children's diets (Troiano & Flegal, 1998). While some health-conscious parents may be providing too little fat in their infants' and children's diets, other parents are raising their children on diets in which the percentage of fat is far too high. Our increasing tendency to eat on the run and pick up fast-food meals, contribute to the increased fat levels in children's diets. Most fast-food meals are high in protein, especially meat and dairy products. But the average American child does not need to be concerned about getting enough protein. What must be of concern is the vast number of young children who are being weaned on fast foods that are also high in fat. Eating habits become ingrained very early in life; unfortunately, it is during the preschool years that many people get their first taste of fast food (Poulton & Sexton, 1996). The American Heart Association recommends that the daily limit for calories from fat should be approximately 35 percent.

In the middle and late childhood years, children's average body weight doubles. And children exert considerable energy as they engage in many different motor activities. To support their growth and activity, children need to consume more food than they did in the early childhood years. As shown in figure 6.5, from 1 to 3 years of age, infants and toddlers only need to consume 1,300 calories per day on the average and only 1,700 calories per day at 4 to 6 years of age. However, at 7 to 10 years of age, children need to consume 2,400 calories per day on the average (the range being 1,650 to 3,300 calories, depending on the child's size) (Pipes, 1988).

One of the most common nutritional problems in childhood is iron deficiency anemia, which results in chronic fatigue. This is a problem that results from the failure to eat adequate amounts of quality meats and dark green vegetables. Children from low-income families are most likely to develop iron deficiency anemia.

Poor nutrition is a special concern in the lives of children from low-income families. In a review of hunger in the United States, it was estimated that 11 million preschool children are malnourished (Brown & Allen, 1988). Many of these children do not get essential amounts of iron, vitamins, or protein.

Exercise and Sports

How much exercise do children get? What are children's sports like?

Exercise   Many of our patterns of health and illness are long-standing. Our experiences as children contribute to our health practices as adults. Did your parents seek medical help at your first sniffle, or did they wait until your temperature reached 104 degrees? Did they feed you heavy doses of red meat and sugar or a more rounded diet with vegetables and fruit? Did they involve you in sports or exercise programs, or did you lie around watching television all the time?

Television could be at least partially to blame for the poor physical condition of some children. In one study, children who watched little television were significantly more physically fit than their heavy-television-viewing counterparts (Tucker, 1987). The more children watch television, the more they are likely to be overweight. No one is quite sure whether this is because children spend their leisure time in front of the television set instead of chasing each other around the neighborhood or because they tend to eat a lot of junk food they see advertised on television.

Some of the blame also falls on the nation's schools, many of which fail to provide daily physical education classes. In the 1985 School Fitness Survey, 37 percent of the children in the first through fourth grades took gym classes only once or twice a week. The investigation also revealed that parents are poor role models when it comes to physical fitness. Less than 30 percent of the parents of children in grades 1 through 4 exercised three days a week. Roughly half said they never get any vigorous exercise. In another study, observations of children's behavior in physical education classes at four elementary schools revealed how little vigorous exercise is done in these classes (Parcel & others, 1987). Children moved through space only 50 percent of the time they were in the class, and they moved continuously an average of only 2.2 minutes. In summary, not only do children's school weeks not include adequate physical education classes, but the majority of children do not exercise vigorously, even when they are in such classes.

Does it make a difference if we push children to exercise more vigorously in elementary school? One study says yes (Tuckman & Hinkle, 1988). One hundred fifty-four elementary school children were randomly assigned either to three 30-minute running programs per week or to regular attendance in physical education classes. Although the results sometimes varied according to sex, for the most part, the cardiovascular health as well as the creativity of children in the running program were enhanced. For example, the boys in this program had less body fat, and the girls had more creative involvement in their classrooms.

In addition to the school, the family plays an important role in a child's exercise program. A wise strategy is for the family to take up activities involving vigorous physical exercise that parents and children can enjoy together. Running, swimming, cycling, and hiking are especially recommended. In encouraging children to exercise more, parents should not push them beyond their physical limits or expose them to competitive pressures that take the fun out of sports and exercise. For example, long-distance running may be too strenuous for young children and could result in bone injuries. Recently, there has been an increase in the number of children competing in strenuous athletic events, such as marathons and triathlons. Doctors are beginning to see some injuries in children that they previously saw only in adults. Some injuries, such as stress fractures and tendonitis, stem from the overuse of young, still-growing bodies. If left to their own devices, how many 8-year-old children would want to prepare for a marathon? It is recommended that parents downplay cutthroat striving and encourage healthy sports that children can enjoy, a topic we discuss further in our examination of children's competitive sports.

Little League baseball, basketball, soccer, tennis, dance—as children's motor development becomes smoother and more coordinated, they are able to master these activities more competently in middle and late childhood than in early childhood.

Sports   In the story that opened the chapter, you read about 6-year-old Zhang Liyin, who attends a sports school that is designed to produce future Olympians. By American standards, Zhang's life sounds rigid and punitive. Even though sports has a lofty status in American society, children are not being trained with the intensity that characterizes Zhang Liyin's school. Still, sports have become an integral part of American culture. Thus, it is not surprising that more and more children become involved in sports every year. Both in public schools and in community agencies, children's sports programs that involve baseball, soccer, football, basketball, swimming, gymnastics, and other activities have grown to the extent that they have changed the shape of many children's lives.

Participation in sports can have both positive and negative consequences for children. Children's participation in sports can provide exercise, opportunities to learn how to compete, self-esteem, and a setting for developing peer relations and friendships. However, sports also can have negative outcomes for children: the pressure to achieve and win, physical injuries, a distraction from academic work, and unrealistic expectations for success as an athlete. Few people challenge the value of sports for children when conducted as part of a school physical education or intramural program. However, some critics question the appropriateness of highly competitive, win-oriented children's sports teams in schools and communities.

There is a special concern for children in high-pressure sports settings involving championship play with accompanying media publicity. Some clinicians and child developmentalists believe such activities not only put undue stress on the participants but also teach children the wrong values—namely, a win-at-all-costs philosophy. The

We are underexercised as a nation. We look instead of play. We ride instead of walk. Our existence deprives us of the minimum of physical activity essential for healthy living.

John F. Kennedy
American President, 20th Century

Cause	1949	1996
Birth immaturity/respiratory distress	1018.8	26.3
Birth defects (spina bifida, etc.)	443.9	36.8
Accidents	234.7	15.2
Cancer	45.7	2.7
Homicide	5.7	3.6
Heart disease	8.0	4.3

Figure **6.6**

Deaths per 100,000 Children Under 5 Years of Age in 1949 and 1996

Preschoolers' Health
Children's Health Resources
A Healthy Start

possibility of exploiting children through highly organized, win-oriented sports programs is an ever present danger. Overly ambitious parents, coaches, and community boosters can unintentionally create a highly stressful atmosphere in children's sports. When parental, agency, or community prestige becomes the central focus of the child's participation in sports, the danger of exploitation is clearly present. Programs oriented toward such purposes often require long and arduous training sessions over many months and years, frequently leading to sports specialization at too early an age. In such circumstances, adults often transmit a distorted view of the role of the sport in the child's life, communicating to the child that the sport is the most important aspect of the child's existence.

Young Children's Illness and Health in the United States

If a pediatrician stopped practicing 50 years ago and observed the illness and health of young children today, the sight might seem to be more science fiction than medical fact (Elias, 1998). The story of children's health in the past 50 years is a shift toward prevention and outpatient care.

In recent decades, vaccines have nearly eradicated disabling bacterial meningitis and have become available to prevent measles, rubella, mumps, and chicken pox. Figure 6.6 reveals the dramatic decline in deaths of children under the age of 5 that occurred from 1949 to 1996 for birth immaturity, birth defects, accidents, cancer, homicide, and heart disease. The disorders still most likely to be fatal during early childhood today are birth defects, cancer, and heart disease. Although the dangers of many diseases for children have been greatly diminished, it still is important for parents to keep young children on an immunization schedule.

A special concern about children's illness and health is exposure to parental smoking. Exposure to tobacco smoke increases children's risk for developing a number of medical problems, including pneumonia, bronchitis, middle ear infections, burns, and asthma. It also can lead to cancer in adulthood. As indicated in figure 6.7, more children under 5 years of age in the United States die from exposure to tobacco

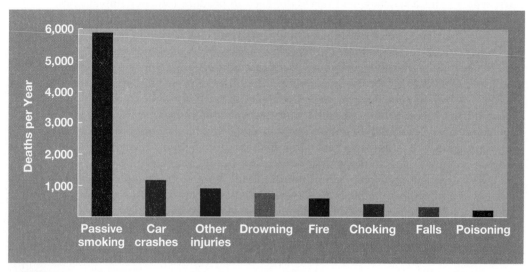

Figure **6.7**

Number of Deaths per Year in Children Under the Age of 5 Due to Passive Smoking and Accidents

Ten percent of all children born in Bangladesh die before reaching the age of 5 from dehydration and malnutrition brought about by diarrhea.

smoke (called passive smoking) than from car crashes and other injuries (Aligne & Stoddard, 1997). Because of such findings, most experts on children's health recommend that children be raised in a smoke-free environment.

Of special concern in the United States is the poor health status of many young children from low-income families. As we saw earlier in our discussion of nutrition and eating behavior, about 11 million preschool children in the United States are malnourished. Their malnutrition places their health at risk. Many have less resistance to diseases, including minor ones, such as colds, and major ones, such as influenza.

Illness and Health in the World's Children

Of every three deaths in the world, one is a child under the age of 5. Every week, more than a quarter of a million young children die in developing countries in a quiet carnage of infection and undernutrition (Grant, 1996).

What are the main causes of death and child malnutrition in the world?

- *Diarrhea* is the leading cause of childhood death. However, approximately 70 percent of the more than 4 million children killed by diarrhea in 1990 could have been saved if all parents had available a low-cost breakthrough known as **oral rehydration therapy (ORT)**. *This treatment encompasses a range of techniques designed to prevent dehydration during episodes of diarrhea by giving the child fluids by mouth.* When a child has diarrhea, dehydration can often be prevented by giving the child a large volume of water and other liquids.
- More than 3 million children were killed in 1990 by *measles, tetanus,* and *whooping cough.* Another 200,000 have been permanently disabled by *polio.* Immunization has become more available and the lives of many children have been saved by vaccination costing only about $5 a child. What is needed is improved communication to inform parents in developing countries and around the world of the importance of a course of vaccinations for their children.
- *Acute respiratory infections, mainly pneumonias,* killed 2 to 3 million children under the age of 5 in 1990. Most of these children could have been saved by 50 cents worth of antibiotics administered by a community health worker with a few months of training. Most of the children's parents could have sought out the low-cost help if they had known how to distinguish between a bad cough and a life-threatening lung infection.
- *Undernutrition* was a contributing cause in about one-third of the 14 million child deaths in the world in 1990. Though not having enough to eat is still a

Children's Health Around the World
Exploring the Health of the World's Children

oral rehydration therapy (ORT)
A treatment involving a range of techniques designed to prevent dehydration during episodes of diarrhea by giving children fluids by mouth.

A simple child
That lightly draws its breath,
What should it know of death?

William Wordsworth
English Poet, 19th Century

fundamental problem in some of the world's poorest countries, the major cause of undernutrition in the world is not a shortage of food in the home. Rather, it is a lack of basic services and a shortage of information about preventing infection and using food to promote growth. Making sure that parents know that they can protect their children's nutritional health by such means as birth spacing, care during pregnancy, breast-feeding, immunization, illness prevention, special feeding before and after illness, and regular checks of the child's weight gain can overcome many cases of malnutrition and poor growth in today's world.

• A contributing factor in at least one-fourth of today's child deaths is the *timing of births*. Births that are too numerous or too close, or mothers who are too young or too old, carry a much higher risk for both the mother and the child. Using this knowledge and today's low-cost ways of timing births is one of the most powerful and least expensive means of raising the child survival rate and improving children's health around the world.

• Also, more than half of all illnesses and deaths among children are associated with inadequate *hygiene*. In communities without a safe water supply and sanitation, it is very difficult to prevent the contamination of food and water. Some low-cost methods can prevent the spread of germs, and all families should be informed of these sanitation measures.

In summary, most child malnutrition, as well as most child deaths, can be prevented by parental actions that are almost universally affordable and are based on knowledge that is already available.

Obesity, Cancer, and Cardiovascular Disease

Obesity, cancer and cardiovascular disease are three major health problems in adulthood. They also represent health concerns in children.

Obesity   We will examine the definition of obesity, the causes of obesity, its consequences, and strategies for treating it.

Overweight Children
Helping an Overweight Child

When Is a Child Considered to Be Obese?   Defining when someone is obese is not a simple task. Weight for height is the most commonly used measure because it can be computed using a standard growth chart. If an individual is 20 percent over the expected weight for height, the individual is considered to be obese. Slightly more than 10 percent of 6- to 19-year-olds are considered to be obese (Wolfe & others, 1994). This represents a 15 percent increase in obesity from just a decade earlier.

Girls are more likely than boys to be obese. Obesity is less common in African American than in White children during childhood, but during adolescence this reverses. Obesity at 6 years of age results in approximately a 25 percent probability that the child will be obese as an adult; obesity at age 12 results in approximately a 75 percent chance that the adolescent will be obese as an adult.

What Causes Obesity?   Fat parents tend to have fat children, even if they are not living in the same household (Klish, 1998). Such characteristics as body type, height, body fat composition, and metabolism are inherited from parents. If both parents are obese, two-thirds of their children will become obese. If one parent is obese and the other is normal size, half of their children will become obese. If both parents are not obese, less than 10 percent of their children will become obese (Whitaker & others, 1997).

In 1994, the first rodent gene for obesity, the ob gene, was identified. The product of the ob gene is the substance *leptin*, named for the Greek word for "thin." Leptin is circulated through the bloodstream to the hypothalamus in the brain, which plays important roles in eating behavior. Obese humans typically have high leptin levels (Considine, Sinha, & Heiman, 1996).

A child's insulin level is another important factor in eating behavior and obesity. Judy Rodin (1984) argues that what children eat influences their insulin levels. When children eat complex carbohydrates, such as cereals, bread, and pasta, insulin levels go up and fall off gradually. When children consume simple sugars, such as candy bars and soft drinks, insulin levels rise and then fall sharply—producing the sugar low with which many of us are all too familiar. Glucose levels in the blood are affected by these complex carbohydrates and simple sugars. Children are more likely to eat within the next several hours after eating simple sugars than after eating complex carbohydrates. And the food children eat at one meal influences what they will eat at the next meal. Thus, consuming doughnuts and candy bars, in addition to providing minimal nutritional value, sets up an ongoing sequence of craving for similar foods at the next sitting.

Thus, Rodin's analysis suggests that the type of food children eat plays a role in obesity. Another factor that contributes to obesity is low activity level. A child's activity level is influenced by heredity but also by a child's motivation to engage in energetic activities and caregivers who model an active lifestyle or provide children with opportunities to be active.

Consequences of Obesity in Children   We already have mentioned an important consequence of obesity in children: 25 percent of obese children become obese adults, and 75 percent of obese young adolescents become obese adults. Obesity also is a risk factor for many medical and psychological problems (Hill & Trowbridge, 1995). Obese children can develop breathing problems that involve upper airway obstruction. Hip problems also are common in obese children. Obese children also are prone to have high blood pressure and elevated blood cholesterol levels. Low self-esteem and depression also are common outgrowths of obesity. Furthermore, obese children often are excluded from peer groups.

Treatment of Obesity   No evidence supports the use of surgical procedures in obese children. They should be used only when obesity is life-threatening (Klish, 1998). Diets only moderately deficient in calories are more successful over the long term than are those involving extreme deprivation of calories. Exercise is believed to be an extremely important component of a successful weight-loss program for overweight children (Kohl & Hobbs, 1999). Exercise increases the child's lean body mass, which increases the child's resting metabolic rate. This results in more calories being burned in the resting state. Many experts on childhood obesity recommend a treatment that involves a combination of diet, exercise, and behavior modification. In a typical behavior modification program, children are taught to monitor their own behavior, keeping a food diary while attempting to lose weight. The diary should record not only the type and amount of food eaten but also when, with whom, and where it was eaten. That is, do children eat in front of the TV, by themselves, or because they are angry or depressed? A diary identifies behaviors that need to be changed.

Cancer   Cancer is the second leading cause of death (injuries are the leading cause) in children 5 to 14 years of age. Three percent of all children's deaths in this age period are due to cancer. In the 15 to 24 age group, cancer accounts for 13 percent of all deaths. Currently, 1 in every 330 children in the United States develops cancer before the age of 19. Moreover, the incidence of cancer in children is increasing.

Child cancers have a different profile than adult cancers. Adult cancers attack mainly the lungs, colon, breast, prostate, and pancreas. Child cancers are mainly those of the white blood cells (leukemia), brain, bone, lymph system, muscles, kidneys, and nervous system. All are characterized by an uncontrolled proliferation of abnormal cells.

As indicated in figure 6.8, the most common cancer in children is leukemia, a cancer of the tissues that make blood cells. In leukemia, the bone marrow makes an abundance of white blood cells that don't function properly. They invade the marrow and crowd out normal cells, making the child susceptible to bruising and infection. Lymphomas are cancers that arise in the lymph system. Childhood lymphomas

Cancer in Children

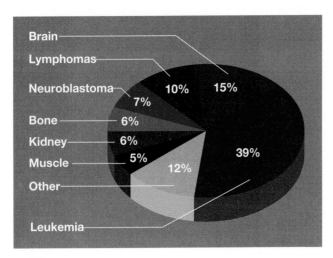

Figure **6.8**
Types of Cancer in Children

Heart Smart

spread to the central nervous system and bone marrow. Treatments have been developed that can cure many children with lymphoma.

When cancer strikes children, it behaves differently than it does when it attacks adults. Children frequently have a more advanced stage of cancer when they are first diagnosed. When cancer is first diagnosed in adults, it has spread to distant parts of the body in only about 20 percent of the cases; however, that figure is 80 percent in children. Most adult cancers result from lifestyle factors, such as smoking, diet, occupation, and exposure to other cancer-causing agents. By contrast, little is known about the causes of childhood cancers (National Childhood Cancer Foundation, 1998).

Most adult cancer patients are treated in their local community by their family physician, consulting surgeon, or cancer specialist. Children with cancer are rarely treated by family physicians or pediatricians. They typically are treated by teams of physicians in children's hospitals, university medical centers, or cancer centers.

Many children with cancer survive for a long period of time and experience problems associated with chronic illness or physical disability. Families initially might react with shock or denial when they find out that their child has cancer or any other type of terminal illness. Adjustment gradually follows and is usually characterized by an open admission that the illness exists. Most families move on to have realistic expectations for the child. A common pattern in parents of terminally ill children is chronic sorrow, in which acceptance of the child's illness is interspersed with periods of intense sorrow. Families with a terminally ill child benefit from the support of professionals and other families who have coped successfully with similar experiences.

Cardiovascular Disease   Cardiovascular disease is uncommon in children. Children with heart problems usually have one of the following, which often can be corrected by surgery: holes in the heart, abnormal connections of heart vessels, abnormally narrow heart vessels, or abnormal heart valves. Unlike in adulthood, in which cardiovascular disease commonly arises from environmental experiences and behavior, such as smoking, most cases of cardiovascular disease in children are unrelated to environmental experiences and behavior.

Nonetheless, environmental experiences and behavior in the childhood years can sow the seeds for cardiovascular disease in adulthood. The precursors of cardiovascular disease often appear at a young age, with many elementary-school-aged children already possessing one or more of the risk factors, such as hypertension and obesity.

One large-scale investigation designed to improve children's cardiovascular health is the Bogalusa Heart Study, also called "Heart Smart." It involves an ongoing evaluation of 8,000 boys and girls in Bogalusa, Louisiana (Friedman & others, 1999; Nicklas & others, 1995). The school is the focus of the Heart Smart intervention. Since 95 percent of children and adolescents aged 5 to 18 are in school, schools are an efficient context in which to educate individuals about health. Special attention is given to teachers, who serve as role models. Teachers who value the role of health in life and who engage in health-enhancing behavior present children and adolescents with positive models for health. Teacher in-service education is conducted by an interdisciplinary team of specialists, including physicians, psychologists, nutritionists, physical educators, and exercise physiologists. The school's staff is introduced to heart health education, the nature of cardiovascular disease, and risk factors for heart disease. Coping behavior, exercise behavior, and eating behavior are discussed with the staff, and a Heart Smart curriculum is explained. For example, the Heart Smart curriculum for grade 5 includes the content areas of cardiovascular health (such as risk factors associated with heart disease), behavior skills (for example, self-assessment and monitoring), eating behavior (for example, the effects of food on health), and exercise behavior (for example, the effects of exercise on the heart).

The physical education component of Heart Smart involves two to four class periods each week to incorporate a "Superkids-Superfit" exercise program. The physical education instructor teaches skills required by the school system plus aerobic activities aimed at cardiovascular conditioning, including jogging, racewalking, interval workouts, rope skipping, circuit training, aerobic dance, and games. Classes begin and end with 5 minutes of walking and stretching.

The school lunch program serves as an intervention site, where sodium, fat, and sugar levels are decreased. Children and adolescents are told reasons they should eat healthy foods, such as a tuna sandwich, and why they should not eat unhealthy foods, such as a hot dog with chili. The school lunch program includes a salad bar, where children and adolescents can serve themselves. The amount and type of snack foods sold on the school premises are monitored.

Heart Smart identifies high-risk children—those with elevated blood pressure, cholesterol, and weight. A multidisciplinary team of physicians, nutritionists, nurses, and behavioral counselors work with the high-risk boys and girls and their parents through group-oriented activities and individual-based family counseling. High-risk boys and girls and their parents receive diet, exercise, and relaxation prescriptions in an intensive 12-session program, followed by long-term monthly evaluations.

Extensive assessment is a part of this ongoing program, including short-term and long-term changes in children's knowledge about cardiovascular disease and changes in their behavior.

In one analysis in the Bogalusa Heart Study, more than half of the children exceeded the recommended intake of salt, fat, cholesterol, and sugar (Nicklas & others, 1995). Families with a history of heart disease have children with more risk factors than other families. Also, African American children have hormonal and renal factors that predispose them to develop hyptertension.

Other school health programs that are being evaluated include the Minnesota Heart Health Program (Kelder & others, 1995) and the Southwest Cardiovascular Curriculum Project (Davis & others, 1995).

At this point we have discussed many aspects of health and illness in childhood. A review of these ideas is presented in summary table 6.2. Next, we continue our examination of physical development by exploring puberty and adolescent development.

Puberty and Adolescence

After the slow, methodical growth of middle and late childhood, children grow more rapidly during pubertal change. In this section we explore the nature of pubertal change as well as some important dimensions of adolescent development.

Puberty

Imagine a toddler displaying all features of puberty. Think about a 3-year-old girl with fully developed breasts or a boy just slightly older with a deep male voice. That is what we will see by the year 2250 if the age at which puberty arrives continues to decrease the way it did for much of the twentieth century.

In Norway, **menarche,** *first menstruation,* now occurs at just over 13 years of age, as opposed to 17 years of age in the 1840s. In the United States—where children mature up to a year earlier than do children in European countries—the average age of menarche has declined from 14.2 years of age in 1900 to about 12.45 years of age today.

Fortunately, however, we are unlikely to see pubescent toddlers, since what has characterized the past century is special—most likely, a higher level of nutrition and health. The available information suggests that menarche began to occur earlier at about the time of the Industrial Revolution, a period associated with increased standards of living and advances in medical science.

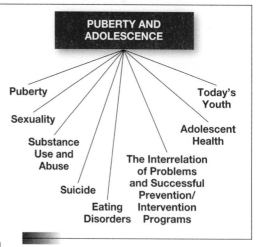

menarche
First menstruation.

SUMMARY TABLE 6.2
Health and Illness in Childhood

Concept	Processes/ Related Ideas	Characteristics/Description
A Developmental Perspective on Children's Health	Its Nature	• Only recently have researchers applied a developmental perspective to children's health. • Children's health-care needs involve their motor, cognitive, and social development.
Nutrition	Its Nature	• In the middle and late childhood years, children's average body weight doubles and children expend considerable energy in various motor activities. • To support their activity, children need to consume more calories than when they were younger. • Within recommended calorie range, it is important to impress on children the value of a balanced diet.
Exercise and Sports	Exercise	• Every indication is that North America's children are not getting enough exercise. • Television viewing, parents being poor role models for exercise, and the lack of adequate physical education classes might be the culprits.
	Sports	• Children's participation in sports can have positive and negative consequences.
Young Children's Illness and Health in the United States	Their Nature	• In recent decades, vaccines have eradicated many diseases that once were responsible for many child deaths. • The disorders most likely to be fatal for children today are birth defects, cancer, and heart disease.
Illness and Health in the World's Children	Their Nature	• One death of every three in the world is the death of a child under 5. • The main causes of death and child malnutrition in the world are diarrhea, measles, tetanus, whooping cough, acute respiratory infections, and undernutrition.
Obesity, Cancer, and Cardiovascular Disease	Obesity	• Obesity is an increasing problem in childhood. • Slightly more than one-fifth of all U.S. children are overweight and 10 percent are obese. • Heredity, insulin levels influenced by poor diet, and low activity levels are implicated in obesity. • Treatment of obesity focuses mainly on diet, exercise, and behavior modification.
	Cancer	• Childhood cancers have a different profile from adult cancers—they usually already have spread to other parts of the body and they are of a different type. • Leukemia is the most common childhood cancer.
	Cardiovascular Disease	• Cardiovascular disease is uncommon in children. • When it occurs, it usually is not due to experiences or behavior, which makes it different from cardiovascular disease in adults.

Menarche is one event that characterizes puberty, but there are others. What are puberty's markers? What are the psychological accompaniments of puberty's changes? What health-care issues are raised by early and late maturation?

puberty
A period of rapid skeletal and sexual maturation that occurs mainly in early adolescence.

Pubertal Change
Puberty *is a period of rapid skeletal and sexual maturation that occurs mainly in early adolescence.* However, puberty is not a single, sudden event. It is part of a gradual process. We know when a young person is going through puberty, but pinpointing its beginning and its end is difficult. Except for menarche, which occurs rather late in puberty, no single marker heralds puberty. For boys, the

From Penguin Dreams and Stranger Things *by Berke Breathed. Copyright © 1985 by The Washington Post Company. By permission of Little, Brown and Company.*

first whisker and first wet dream are events that could mark its appearance, but both might go unnoticed.

Behind the first whisker in boys and widening of hips in girls is a flood of hormones, powerful chemical substances secreted by the endocrine glands and carried through the body by the bloodstream. The concentrations of certain hormones increase dramatically during adolescence. **Testosterone** *is a hormone associated in boys with the development of genitals, an increase in height, and a change in voice.* **Estradiol** *is a hormone associated in girls with breast, uterine, and skeletal development.* In one investigation, testosterone levels increased eighteenfold in boys but only twofold in girls during puberty; estradiol increased eightfold in girls but only twofold in boys (Nottelmann & others, 1987).

The same influx of hormones that puts hair on a male's chest and imparts curvature to a female's breast may contribute to psychological development in adolescence. In one study of 108 normal boys and girls ranging in age from 9 to 14, a higher concentration of testosterone was present in boys who rated themselves as more socially competent (Nottelmann & others, 1987). In another investigation of 60 normal boys and girls in the same age range, girls with higher estradiol levels expressed more anger and aggression (Inoff-Germain & others, 1988). However, hormonal effects by themselves may account for only a small portion of the variance in adolescent development. For example, in one study, social factors accounted for two to four times as much variance as hormonal factors did in young adolescent girls' depression and anger (Brooks-Gunn & Warren, 1989).

Among the most noticeable physical changes during puberty are increases in height and weight, as well as sexual maturation. As indicated in figure 6.9, the growth spurt occurs approximately two years earlier for girls than for boys (Abbassi, 1998). The mean beginning of the growth spurt in girls is 9 years of age; for boys, it is 11 years of age. The peak rate of pubertal change occurs at 11.5 years for girls and 13.5 years for boys. During their growth spurt, girls increase in height about 3½ inches per year, boys about 4 inches.

Boys and girls who are shorter or taller than their peers before adolescence are likely to remain so during adolescence. In our society, there is a stigma attached to short boys. At the beginning of the adolescent period, girls tend to be as tall as or taller than boys of their age, but by the end of the middle school years most boys have caught up or, in many cases, have even surpassed girls in height. And, even though height in the elementary school years is a good predictor of height later in adolescence, there is still room for the individual's height to change in relation to the height of his or her peers. As much as 30 percent of the height of late adolescence is unexplained by height in the elementary school years.

Pubertal Changes

testosterone
A hormone associated in boys with the development of genitals, an increase in height, and a change in voice.

estradiol
A hormone associated in girls with breast, uterine, and skeletal development.

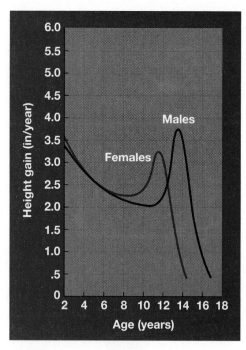

Figure **6.9**

Pubertal Growth Spurt

On the average, the pubertal growth spurt begins and peaks about 2 years earlier for girls (starts at 9, peaks at 11½) than for boys (starts at 11½, peaks at 13½).

The rate at which adolescents gain weight follows approximately the same developmental timetable as the rate at which they gain height. Marked weight gains coincide with the onset of puberty. During early adolescence, girls tend to outweigh boys, but, just as with height, by about age 14 boys begin to surpass girls.

Think back to the onset of your puberty. Of the striking changes that were taking place in your body, what was the first change that occurred? Researchers have found that male pubertal characteristics develop in this order: increase in penis and testicle size, appearance of straight pubic hair, minor voice change, first ejaculation (which usually occurs through masturbation or a wet dream), appearance of kinky pubic hair, onset of maximum growth, growth of hair in armpits, more detectable voice changes, and growth of facial hair.

What is the order of appearance of physical changes in females? First, either the breasts enlarge or pubic hair appears. Later, hair appears in the armpits. As these changes occur, the female grows in height, and her hips become wider than her shoulders. Her first menstruation comes rather late in the pubertal cycle. Initially, her menstrual cycles may be highly irregular. For the first several years, she might not ovulate every menstrual cycle. Some girls do not become fertile until 2 years after the period begins. No voice changes comparable to those in pubertal males occur in pubertal females. By the end of puberty, the female's breasts have become more fully rounded.

Body Image   One psychological aspect of physical change in puberty is certain: adolescents are preoccupied with their bodies and develop individual images of what their bodies are like. Perhaps you looked in the mirror on a daily and sometimes even hourly basis to see if you could detect anything different about your changing body. Preoccupation with one's body image is strong throughout adolescence, but it is especially acute during puberty, a time when adolescents are more dissatisfied with their bodies than in late adolescence (Wright, 1989).

There are gender differences in adolescents' perceptions of their bodies. In general, girls are less happy with their bodies and have more negative body images, compared with boys, throughout puberty (Brooks-Gunn & Paikoff, 1993; Henderson & Zivian, 1995). Also, as pubertal change proceeds, girls often become more dissatisfied with their bodies, probably because their body fat increases, whereas boys become more satisfied as they move through puberty, probably because their muscle mass increases (Gross, 1984).

Early and Late Maturation   You might have entered puberty early, late, or on time. When adolescents mature earlier or later than their peers, might they perceive themselves differently? In the Berkeley Longitudinal Study some years ago, early-maturing boys perceived themselves more positively and had more successful peer relations than did their late-maturing counterparts (Jones, 1965). The findings for early-maturing girls were similar but not as strong as for boys. When the late-maturing boys were in their thirties, however, they had developed a stronger sense of identity than the early-maturing boys had (Peskin, 1967). Possibly this occurred because the late-maturing boys had more time to explore life's options or because the early-maturing boys continued to focus on their advantageous physical status instead of on career development and achievement.

More recent research confirms, though, that at least during adolescence it is advantageous to be an early-maturing rather than a late-maturing boy (Simmons & Blythe, 1987). The more recent findings for girls suggest

Adolescents show a strong preoccupation with their changing bodies and develop individual images of what their bodies are like. Adolescent boys, as well as adolescent girls, rate body build as one of the most important dimensions of physical attractiveness.

that early maturation is a mixed blessing: these girls experience more problems in school but also more independence and popularity with boys. The time that maturation is assessed also is a factor. In the sixth grade, early-maturing girls show greater satisfaction with their figures than do late-maturing girls, but by the tenth grade late-maturing girls are more satisfied than the early-maturing girls. The reason for this is that, in late adolescence, early-maturing girls are shorter and stockier, whereas late-maturing girls are taller and thinner. In general, late-maturing girls in late adolescence have bodies that more closely approximate the current American ideal of feminine beauty—tall and thin.

In the past decade, an increasing number of researchers have found that early maturation increases girls' vulnerability to a number of problems (Brooks-Gunn & Paikoff, 1993; Sarigiani & Petersen, 2000). Early-maturing girls are more likely to smoke, drink, be depressed, have an eating disorder, request earlier independence from their parents, and have older friends; and their bodies are likely to elicit responses from males that lead to earlier dating and earlier sexual experiences. In one study, the early-maturing girls had lower educational and occupational attainment in adulthood (Stattin & Magnusson, 1990). Apparently as a result of their social and cognitive immaturity, combined with early physical development, early-maturing girls are easily lured into problem behaviors, not recognizing the possible long-term effects of these on their development (Petersen, 1993).

Sexuality

Adolescence wraps the lives of male and female in sexuality. Adolescence is a bridge between the asexual child and the sexual adult (Feldman, 1999). Adolescence is a time of sexual exploration and experimentation, of sexual fantasies and realities, of incorporating sexuality into one's identity. In some societies, adults clamp down and protect adolescent females from males by chaperoning them. Other societies promote early marriage. In yet other societies, such as the United States, some sexual experimentation is allowed but there is controversy about just how far this should be allowed to go. As we discuss adolescent sexuality, an important point to keep in mind is that sexual development and interest are normal and that the majority of adolescents have healthy sexual attitudes and engage in healthy sexual behaviors.

Heterosexual Attitudes and Behavior What is the current profile of the sexual activity of adolescents? Based on a national survey of adolescents, sexual intercourse is uncommon in early adolescence but becomes more common in the high school and college years (see figure 6.10) (Allan Guttmacher Institute, 1995, 1998). A summary of these findings includes

- Eight in 10 girls and 7 in 10 boys are virgins at age 15.
- The probability that adolescents will have sexual intercourse increases steadily with age, but 1 in 5 individuals has not yet had sexual intercourse by age 19.
- Initial sexual intercourse occurs in the mid- to late-adolescent years for most teenagers, about 8 years before they marry; more than one-half of 17-year-olds have had sexual intercourse.
- Most adolescent females' first voluntary sexual partners are either younger, the same age, or no more than 2 years older; 27 percent are 3 to 4 years older; 12 percent are 5 or more years older.

Most studies find that adolescent males are more likely than adolescent females to report that they have had sexual intercourse

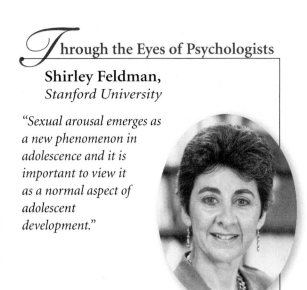

Through the Eyes of Psychologists

Shirley Feldman,
Stanford University

"*Sexual arousal emerges as a new phenomenon in adolescence and it is important to view it as a normal aspect of adolescent development.*"

The Kinsey Institute
Sexuality Research Information Service

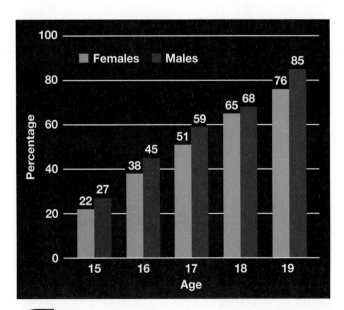

Figure **6.10**
Percentage of Youth Who Say They Have Had Sexual Intercourse

and are sexually active (Hayes, 1987). Males also say that sexual intercourse is a more enjoyable experience for them. Males also report that they are sexually active at an earlier age than females do. And African American adolescents report that they are more sexually active than White or Latino adolescents (Hayes, 1987).

In some areas of the United Sates, the percentages of sexually active young adolescents may be even greater. In an inner-city area of Baltimore, 81 percent of the males at age 14 said that they already had engaged in sexual intercourse. Other surveys in inner-city, low-income areas also reveal a high incidence of early sexual intercourse (Clark, Zabin, & Hardy, 1984).

In sum, by the end of adolescence, most individuals have had sexual intercourse. Male, African American, and inner-city adolescents report being the most sexually active. Sexual intercourse can be a meaningful experience for older, mature adolescents, but many adolescents are not emotionally prepared to handle sexual experiences, especially in early adolescence. In one study, the earlier in adolescence the boys and girls engaged in sexual intercourse, the more likely they were to show adjustment problems (Bingham & Crockett, 1996).

Homosexual Attitudes and Behavior

Although the development of gay or lesbian identity has been widely studied in adults, few researchers have investigated the gay or lesbian identity (often referred to as the coming-out process) in adolescents. In one study of gay male adolescents, coming out was conceptualized in three stages: sensitization; awareness with confusion, denial, guilt, and shame; and acceptance (Newman & Muzzonigro, 1993). The majority of the gay adolescents said they felt different from other boys as children. The average age at having their first crush on another boy was 12.7 years, and the average age at realizing they were gay was 12.5 years. Most of the boys said they felt confused when they first became aware that they were gay. About half of the boys said they initially tried to deny their identity as a gay. The parents who had strong traditional family values (belief in the importance of religion, emphasis on marriage and having children) were less accepting of their gay sons than were the parents who had weaker traditional family values.

Both the early and more recent surveys indicate that about 4 percent of males and 3 percent of females are exclusively homosexual (Hunt, 1974; Kinsey, Pomeroy, & Martin, 1948). In a recent comprehensive survey of adolescent sexual orientation in almost 35,000 junior and senior high school students in Minnesota, 4.5 percent reported predominantly homosexual attractions (Remafedi & others, in press). Homosexual identities, attractions, and behaviors increased with age. More than 6 percent of the 18-year-olds said they had predominantly homosexual attractions. How many of these youth later become gay is not known, although it is widely accepted that many adolescents who engage in homosexual behavior in adolescence do not continue the practice into adulthood.

An individual's sexual orientation—heterosexual, bisexual, or homosexual—is most likely determined by a combination of genetic, hormonal, and environmental factors (D'Augell, 2000; Herek, 2000; Savin-Williams & Rodriguez, 1993). Many experts on homosexuality believe that no one factor alone causes homosexuality and that the relative weight of each factor can vary from one individual to the next.

Adolescent Sexual Scripts

As adolescents explore their sexual identities, they tend to act out sexual scripts. A **sexual script** *is a stereotyped pattern of role prescriptions for how individuals should behave sexually.* Differences in the way females and males are socialized are wrapped up in the sexual scripts adolescents follow. Discrepancies in male/female scripting can cause problems and confusion for adolescents as they work out their sexual identities. Adolescent girls have learned to link sexual intercourse with love. Female adolescents often rationalize their sexual behavior by telling

National Gay and Lesbian Task Force

sexual script
A stereotyped pattern of role prescriptions for how individuals should behave sexually.

A sexual script is a stereotyped pattern of role prescriptions for how individuals should behave sexually. How do female and male sexual scripts differ?

themselves that they were swept away by love. A number of investigators have reported that adolescent females, more than adolescent males, report being in love as the main reason for being sexually active (Cassell, 1984). Far more females than males have intercourse with partners they love and would like to marry. Other reasons for females having sexual intercourse include giving in to male pressure, gambling that sex is a way to get a boyfriend, curiosity, and sexual desire unrelated to loving and caring. In one recent study, adolescent males said that boys do expect sex from girls (Crump & others, 1996). They also said that the typical adolescent male does not force sex but does put pressure on females to have sex. Adolescent males might be aware that their female counterparts have been socialized into a love ethic. They also might understand the pressure many of them feel to have a boyfriend. A classic male line shows how males understand female thinking about sex and love: "If you really loved me, you would have sex with me." The female adolescent who says "If you really loved me, you would not put so much pressure on me" reflects her insight about male sexual motivation.

Contraceptive Use   Adolescents are increasing their use of contraceptives. Adolescent girls' contraceptive use at first intercourse rose from 48 percent to 65 percent during the 1980s (Forrest & Singh, 1990). By 1995, use at first intercourse had reached 78 percent, with two thirds of that figure involving condom use. A sexually active adolescent who does not use contraception has a 90 percent chance of pregnancy within one year (Alan Guttmacher Institute, 1998). The method adolescent girls use most frequently is the pill (44 percent), followed by condoms (38 percent). About 10 percent rely on an injectable contraception, 4 percent on withdrawal, and 3 percent on an implant (Alan Guttmacher Institute, 1998). Approximately one third of adolescent girls who rely on condoms also take the pill or practice withdrawal.

Although adolescent contraceptive use is increasing, many sexually active adolescents still do not use contraceptives, or they use them inconsistently. Sexually active younger adolescents are less likely to take contraceptive precautions than older adolescents. Younger adolescents are more likely to use a condom or withdrawal, while older adolescents are more likely to use the pill or a diaphragm.

Sexually Transmitted Diseases (STDs)   Tammy, age 15, has just finished listening to a lecture in her health class. We overhear her talking to one of her girlfriends as she walks down the school corridor: "That was a disgusting lecture. I can't believe all the diseases you can get by having sex. I think she was probably trying to scare us. She spent a lot of time talking about AIDS, which I've heard that normal people don't get. Right? I've heard that only homosexuals and drug addicts get AIDS, and I've also heard that gonorrhea and most other sexual diseases can be cured, so what's the big deal if you get something like that?" Tammy's view of sexually transmitted diseases (formerly called venereal disease, or VD) is common among adolescents. Teenagers tend to believe that sexually transmitted diseases always happen to someone else, can be easily cured without any harm done, and are too disgusting for a nice young person to even hear about, let alone get. This view is wrong. Adolescents who are having sex *do* run a risk of getting sexually transmitted diseases. Sexually transmitted diseases are fairly common among today's adolescents. The greatest concern about STDs in recent years has focused on AIDS (Kelly, 2000).

AIDS (acquired immune deficiency syndrome) *is caused by the human immunodeficiency virus (HIV), which destroys the body's immune system.* Many germs that usually would not harm a person with a healthy immune system can produce devastation and death in persons with AIDS.

The number of AIDS cases reported in the 13-to-19 age group each year has increased from one case in 1981 to almost 2,184 cases in 1995 (Centers for Disease Control, 1998). However, the average latency time from viral infection to time of illness is about 5 to 7 years. Thus, most infected adolescents would not become ill until they are adults. Most individuals in their early twenties with an AIDS diagnosis likely were infected with HIV during adolescence—the early-twenties age group accounts for 17 percent of all AIDS cases in the United States.

The Alan Guttmacher Institute
CDC National Prevention Network
American Social Health Association
Preventing STDs in Adolescence
HIV/AIDS and Adolescents

AIDS (acquired immune deficiency syndrome)
A disease caused by a virus (HIV) that destroys the body's immune system. Consequently, germs that usually do not harm someone with a normal immune system produce devastating results and death.

There are some differences between AIDS in adolescents and AIDS in adults:

1. A higher percentage of adolescent AIDS cases are acquired by heterosexual transmission.
2. A higher percentage of adolescents are asymptomatic (they will become symptomatic in adulthood).
3. A higher percentage of African American and Latino cases occur in adolescence.
4. A special set of ethical and legal issues are involved in testing and informing partners and parents of adolescents.
5. There is less use and availability of contraceptives in adolescence.

Adolescent Pregnancy
Teen Pregnancy Prevention Initiative
P. Lindsay Chase-Lansdale

Adolescent Pregnancy   Angela is 15 years old and pregnant. She reflects, "I'm three months pregnant. This could ruin my whole life. I've made all of these plans for the future and now they are down the drain. I don't have anybody to talk to about my problem. I can't talk to my parents. There is no way they can understand." Pregnant adolescents were once practically invisible and unmentionable, but yesterday's secret has become today's national dilemma.

They are from different backgrounds and from different places, but their circumstances have the same stressfulness. Each year, more than 500,000 American teenagers became pregnant, more than 70 percent of them unmarried (*Child Trends,* 1996). They represent a flaw in America's social fabric. Like Angela, far too many become pregnant in their early or middle adolescent years. More than 200,000 females in the United States have a child before their 18th birthday. As one 17-year-old Los Angeles mother of a 1-year-old son said, "We are children having children." The bright spot in adolescent pregnancy statistics is that the teenage birthrate declined 18 percent from 1991 to 1998 after rising 25 percent from 1986 to 1991 (U.S. Department of Health and Human Services, 2000).

Despite the rise in the teenage birthrate that occurred in the late 1980s, the rate is lower now than it was in the 1950s and 1960s. What is different now, though, is the steady rise in the number of nonmarital teenage pregnancy. Dramatic changes have swept through the American culture in the past three decades, changes that involve sexual attitudes and social morals. Adolescents gave birth at a higher rate in 1950 than they do today, but that was a time of early marriage. Then, the vast majority of 15- to 19-year-olds married. The overwhelming majority of births to adolescent mothers in the 1950s occurred within a marriage and mainly involved females 17 years of age and older. Two or three decades ago, if an unwed adolescent girl became pregnant, her parents often had her swiftly married in a "shotgun" wedding. If marriage was impractical, the girl would discreetly disappear, the child would be put up for adoption, and the "predicament" would never be discussed again. Abortion was not a real option for most adolescent females until 1973, when the Supreme Court ruled that it could not be outlawed.

In today's world, if an adolescent girl does not choose to have an abortion (almost 40 percent do), she usually keeps the baby and raises it without the traditional involvement of marriage. With the stigma of illegitimacy less severe, adolescent girls are less likely to give up their babies for adoption. Fewer than 5 percent do, compared with approximately 35 percent in the early 1960s. But, while the stigma of illegitimacy has lessened, the lives of most pregnant adolescents is anything but rosy.

The adolescent pregnancy rate in the United States is much higher than in other industrialized countries (East & Felice, 1996). It is more than twice as high as the rates in England, France, and Canada; almost three times as high as the rate in Sweden; and seven times as high as the rate in the Netherlands (*Child Trends,* 1996; Jones & others, 1985; Kenney, 1987). Although American adolescents are no more sexually active than their counterparts in these other countries, they are many more times likely to become pregnant. Although the adolescent pregnancy rate in the United States is still very high, the adolescent birthrate fell an estimated 3 percent in 1997, con-

𝒯hrough the Eyes of Psychologists

P. Lindsay Chase-Lansdale,
Northwestern University

"Even though U.S. adolescents do not show significantly different patterns of sexual activity compared to adolescents in many industrialized countries, they contracept less consistently and effectively."

tinuing a six-year trend (U.S. Department of Health and Human Services, 1998). Since 1990, the sharpest drop (20 percent) in the adolescent birthrate has occurred in 15- to 17-year-old African Americans. Fear of sexually transmitted diseases, especially AIDS, school/community health center health classes, and a greater hope for the future are the likely reasons for this decrease.

The consequences of our nation's high adolescent pregnancy rate are of great concern (Brooks-Gunn & Chase-Lansdale, 1995; Luster & Brophy-Herb, 2000). Pregnancy in adolescence increases the health risks of both the child and the mother. Infants born to adolescent mothers are more likely to have low birthweights (a prominent cause of infant mortality), as well as neurological problems and childhood illnesses. Adolescent mothers often drop out of school, fail to gain employment, and become dependent on welfare. Although many adolescent mothers resume their education later in life, they generally do not catch up with women who postpone childbearing. In the National Longitudinal Survey of Work Experience of Youth, it was found that only half of the women 20 to 26 years old who first gave birth at age 17 had completed high school by their twenties. The percentage was even lower for those who gave birth at a younger age (Mott & Marsiglio, 1985). By contrast, among females who waited until age 20 to have a baby, more than 90 percent had obtained a high school education. Among the younger adolescent mothers, almost half had obtained a general equivalency diploma (GED), which does not often open up good employment opportunities. These educational deficits have negative consequences for the young women themselves and for their children. Adolescent parents are more likely than those who delay childbearing to have low-paying, low-status jobs or to be unemployed. The mean family income of White females who gave birth before age 17 is approximately half that of families in which the mother delays birth until her mid or late twenties.

Although the consequences of America's high adolescent pregnancy rate are cause for great concern, it often is not pregnancy alone that leads to negative consequences for an adolescent mother and her offspring (Brooks-Gunn & Paikoff, 1997; Feldman, 1999). Adolescent mothers are more likely to come from low-income than from middle- or high-income backgrounds. Many adolescent mothers were not good students before they became pregnant. Not every adolescent female who bears a child lives a life of poverty and low achievement. Thus, although adolescent pregnancy is a high-risk circumstance, and in general adolescents who do not become pregnant fare better than those who don't, some adolescent mothers do quite well in school and have positive developmental outcomes (Ahn, 1994).

At this point we have discussed a number of ideas about puberty and sexuality. A review of these ideas is presented in summary table 6.3. Next, we will continue our exploration of adolescence by examining substance use and abuse.

Substance Use and Abuse

The 1960s and 1970s were times of marked increase in the use of illicit drugs. During the social and political unrest of those years, many youth turned to marijuana, stimulants, and hallucinogens. Adolescent alcohol consumption also increased (Robinson & Greene, 1988). More precise data about drug use by adolescents have been collected in recent years. Each year since 1975, Lloyd Johnston, Patrick O'Malley, and Gerald Bachman (1999), working at the Institute of Social Research at the University of Michigan, have carefully monitored drug use by America's high school seniors in a wide range of public and private high schools. From time to time, they also sample the drug use of younger adolescents and adults.

The use of drugs among U.S. secondary school students declined in the 1980s but began to increase in the early 1990s (Johnston, O'Malley, & Bachman, 1999). For the first time in 6 years, the use of marijuana and other drugs did not increase among U.S. eighth-graders in 1998. And although marijuana use is still rising among tenth- and twelfth-graders, their use of other illicit drugs appears to be leveling off.

Nonetheless, even with the recent leveling off in use, the United States still has

National Clearinghouse for Alcohol and Drug Information
Monitoring the Future
National Institute of Drug Abuse

$\mathcal{S}$UMMARY $\mathcal{T}$ABLE 6.3
Puberty and Sexuality

Concept	Processes/Related Ideas	Characteristics/Description
Puberty	Pubertal Change	• Puberty is a period of rapid skeletal and sexual maturation that occurs mainly in early adolescence. • Testosterone plays an important role in male pubertal development; estradiol plays an important role in female pubertal development. • The initial onset of pubertal growth occurs, on the average, at 9½ years for girls, 11½ years for boys, reaching a peak change at 11½ for girls and 13½ for boys.
	Body Image	• Adolescents show a heightened interest in body image. • Girls have more negative body images in adolescence than boys do.
	Early and Late Maturation	• Early maturation favors boys over girls, at least during adolescence. • As adults, though, men who were late-maturing achieve more competent identities than men who were early-maturing. • Researchers are increasingly finding that early-maturing girls are vulnerable to a number of problems.
Sexuality	Heterosexual Attitudes and Behavior	• In the twentieth century, a major increase occurred in the number of adolescents reporting intercourse. • The percentage of females reporting intercourse has increased more rapidly than the percentage of males reporting intercourse.
	Homosexual Attitudes and Behavior	• Rates of homosexuality remained constant in the twentieth century. • No definitive conclusions have been reached about the causes of homosexuality.
	Adolescent Sexual Scripts	• As we develop our sexual attitudes, we follow certain scripts, which often are gender-based.
	Contraceptive Use	• Adolescent contraceptive use is increasing, but many sexually active adolescents (especially young adolescents and adolescents having their first intercourse experience) still do not use contraceptives.
	Sexually Transmitted Diseases	• Many adolescents underestimate their risk of getting an STD. • A special concern involves AIDS.
	Adolescent Pregnancy	• More than 500,000 American adolescents become pregnant each year. • The U.S. adolescent pregnancy rate is the highest in the industrialized world. • The consequences involve health risks for the mother and the offspring.

the highest rate of adolescent drug use of any industrialized nation. Also, the University of Michigan survey likely underestimates the percentage of adolescents who take drugs because it does not include high school dropouts, who have a higher rate of drug use than do students who are still in school. Johnston, O'Malley, and Bachman (1999) believe that "generational forgetting" contributed to the rise of adolescent drug use in the 1990s, with adolescents' beliefs about the dangers of drugs eroding considerably. Let's now consider separately a number of drugs that are used by adolescents.

Marijuana use by adolescents decreased in the 1980s. For example, in 1979, 37 percent of high school seniors said they had used marijuana in the last month, but in 1992 that figure had dropped to 12 percent. In one recent analysis, the increased use of marijuana in the 1990s was not related to such factors as religious commitment or grades but was linked with increased approval of using the drug and decreased perception that the drug is harmful (Johnston, Bachman, & O'Malley, 1998).

Alcohol use remains very high among adolescents and has not changed much in the last several years (Johnston, O'Malley, & Bachman, 1999). Although alcohol use is still high, it actually has shown a gradual decline—monthly prevalence among high school seniors was 72 percent in 1980 but declined to 51 percent in 1999. Binge drinking (defined in the University of Michigan surveys as having 5 or more drinks in a row in the last 2 weeks) fell from 41 percent to 33 percent in 1999. A consistent sex difference occurs in binge drinking, with males engaging in this more than females. In 1997, 39 percent of male high school seniors said they had been drunk in the last 2 weeks, compared to 29 percent of their female counterparts.

A special concern is the use of drugs by young adolescents. Also, it is important to note that the United States has the highest rate of adolescent drug use of all the world's industrialized nations.

Alcohol   Alcohol is the drug most widely used by adolescents in our society. For them, it has produced many enjoyable moments and many sad ones as well. Alcoholism is the third leading killer in the United States, with more than 13 million people classified as alcoholics, many of whom established their drinking habits during adolescence. Each year, approximately 25,000 people are killed and 1.5 million injured by drunk drivers. In 65 percent of aggressive male acts against females, the offender is under the influence of alcohol (Goodman & others, 1986). In numerous instances of drunken driving and assaults on females, the offenders are adolescents.

Cigarette Smoking   Cigarette smoking (in which the active drug is nicotine) is one of the most serious yet preventable health problems. Smoking is likely to begin in grades 7 through 9, although sizable portions of youth are still establishing regular smoking habits during high school and college. Since the national surveys by Johnston, O'Malley, and Bachman began in 1975, cigarettes have been the substance most frequently used on a daily basis by high school seniors.

Though adolescents' use of cigarettes dropped between 1976 and 1981 (from 39 percent to 29 percent for seniors in the last 30 days), it began increasing in 1994—and in 1999, 35 percent of high school seniors said that they had smoked cigarettes in the last 30 days. Similar percentages of male and female adolescents smoke cigarettes. Approximately 8 percent of high school seniors said that they use smokeless tobacco in the last 30 days, with male adolescents doing this overwhelmingly more than females (19 percent to 1 percent for females).

A special concern is that many young adolescents smoke cigarettes. In the University of Michigan survey, 17.5 percent of eighth-graders said they had smoked cigarettes in the last 30 days (Johnston, Johnston, O'Malley, & Bachman, 1999). This is a drop of 3.5 percent in the last 2 years, a drop that also appeared in tenth-graders and slightly less so in twelfth-graders. Despite these modest improvements, American adolescents have very high rates of smoking. One study found that the addictive properties of nicotine made it very difficult for adolescents to stop smoking (Melby & Vargas, 1996).

In the 1998 survey, the University of Michigan researchers asked adolescents for the first time which brands of cigarettes they smoked. Marlboro was easily the leader, chosen by nearly two-thirds of adolescent smokers. Just three brands accounted for nearly all adolecent smoking—Marlboro, Newport, and Camel.

Peer disapproval of cigarette smoking has dropped over the last several years, and the percentage of adolescents who see smoking as dangerous has been declining since 1993. Among eighth-graders, only one-half think there is great risk to smoking a pack or more a day.

What is the pattern of alcohol consumption among adolescents?

National Institute on Alcohol Abuse and Alcoholism

National Cancer Institute

Cigarette Brands and Adolescents

Addicted to Nicotine

Effective Prevention Programs for Tobacco Use

Cigarettes are readily available to these underage youth. Of the eighth-graders, most of whom are 13 to 14 years of age, three-fourths said that they can get cigarettes fairly easily if they want them. By the tenth grade, more than 90 percent say they can buy cigarettes easily.

The devastating effects of early smoking were brought home in a recent research study that found that smoking in the adolescent years causes permanent genetic changes in the lungs and forever increases the risk of lung cancer, even if the smoker quits (Weincke & others, 1999). Such damage was much less likely among smokers in the study who started in their twenties. One of the remarkable findings in the study was that the early age of onset of smoking was more important in predicting the genetic damage than how much the individuals smoked.

One comprehensive health approach that includes an attempt to curb cigarette smoking by adolescents was developed by clinical psychologist Cheryl Perry and her colleagues (1988). Three programs were developed based on peer group norms, healthy role models, and social skills training. Elected peer leaders were trained as instructors. In seventh grade, adolescents were offered "Keep It Clean," a six-session course emphasizing the negative effects of smoking. In eighth grade, students were involved in "Health Olympics," an approach that included exchanging greeting cards on smoking and health with peers in other countries. In ninth grade, students participated in "Shifting Gears," which included six sessions focused on social skills. In the social skills program, students critiqued media messages and created their own positive health videotapes. At the same time as the school intervention, a communitywide smoking cessation program, as well as a diet and health awareness campaign, was initiated. After 5 years, students who were involved in the smoking and health program were much less likely to smoke cigarettes, use marijuana, or drink alcohol than were their counterparts who were not involved in the program.

A Parent's Guide to Adolescent Drug Use

Suicide Facts

What Do You Know About Suicide?

Suicide and Homicide

Research on Suicidal Behavior

The Roles of Development, Parents and Peers in Adolescent Drug Abuse

Most adolescents become drug users at some point in their development, whether limited to alcohol, caffeine, and cigarettes or extended to marijuana, cocaine, and hard drugs. A special concern involves adolescents using drugs as a way of coping with stress, which can interfere with the development of competent coping skills and responsible decision making. Researchers have found that drug use in childhood or early adolescence has more detrimental long-term effects on the development of responsible, competent behavior than when drug use occurs in late adolescence (Newcomb & Bentler, 1988). When they use drugs to cope with stress, many young adolescents enter adult roles of marriage and work prematurely, without adequate socioemotional growth, and experience greater failure in adult roles.

How early are adolescents beginning drug use? National samples of eighth- and ninth-grade students were included for the first time in 1991 in the Institute for Social Research survey of drug use (Johnston, O'Malley, & Bachman, 1992). Early in the drug use increase in the United States (late 1960s, early 1970s), drug use was much higher among college students than among high school students, who in turn had much higher rates of drug use than middle or junior high school students. However, today the rates for college and high school students are similar, and the rates for young adolescents are not as different from those for older adolescents as might be anticipated.

Parents, peers, and social support play important roles in preventing adolescent drug abuse (Johnson & others, 1996; Pentz, 1994). Positive relationships with parents and others are important in reducing adolescents' drug use (Emshoff & others, 1996). In one study, social support (which consisted of good relationships with parents, siblings, adults, and peers) during adolescence substantially reduced drug abuse (Newcomb & Bentler, 1988). In another study, the adolescents were most likely to take drugs when both of their parents took drugs (such as tranquilizers, amphetamines, alcohol, or nicotine) and when their peers took drugs (Kandel, 1974).

Suicide

Suicide is a common problem in our society. Its rate has tripled in the past 30 years in the United States; each year, about 25,000 people take their own lives. Beginning with the 15-year-old age group, the suicide rate begins to rise rapidly.

Suicide is now the third leading cause of death in 15- to 24-year olds (Bell & Clark, 1998; Schneidman, 1996). Males are about three times as likely to commit suicide as females are; this may be because of their choice of more active methods for attempting suicide—shooting, for example. By contrast, females are more likely to use passive methods, such as sleeping pills, which are less likely to produce death. Although males commit suicide more frequently, females attempt it more frequently.

Estimates indicate that, for every successful suicide in the general population, 6 to 10 attempts are made. For adolescents, the figure is as high as 50 attempts for every life taken. As many as two in every three college students has thought about suicide on at least one occasion; their methods range from overdosing on drugs to crashing into the White House in an airplane.

Why do adolescents attempt suicide? There is no simple answer to this important question. It is helpful to think of suicide in terms of proximal and distal factors. Proximal, or immediate, factors can trigger a suicide attempt. Highly stressful circumstances, such as the loss of a boyfriend or girlfriend, poor grades at school, or an unwanted pregnancy, can trigger a suicide attempt. Drugs have been involved more often in recent suicide attempts than in attempts in the past (Wagner, Cole, & Schwartzman, 1993).

Distal, or earlier, experiences often are involved in suicide attempts as well. A long-standing history of family instability and unhappiness may be present (Reinherz & others, 1994). Just as a lack of affection and emotional support, high control, and pressure for achievement by parents during childhood are related to adolescent depression, such combinations of family experiences are also likely to show up as distal factors in suicide attempts. The adolescent might also lack supportive friendships. In a study of suicide among gifted women, previous suicide attempts, anxiety, conspicuous instability in work and in relationships, depression, or alcoholism also was present in the women's lives (Tomlinson-Keasey, Warren, & Elliot, 1986). These factors are similar to those found to predict suicide among gifted men.

Just as genetic factors are associated with depression, they are also associated with suicide. The closer a person's genetic relationship to someone who has committed suicide, the more likely that person is to also commit suicide.

What is the psychological profile of the suicidal adolescent? Suicidal adolescents often have depressive symptoms (Gadpaille, 1996). Although not all depressed adolescents are suicidal, depression is the most frequently cited factor associated with adolescent suicide. A sense of hopelessness, low self-esteem, and high self-blame are also associated with adolescent suicide (Harter & Marold, 1992). Figure 6.11 provides valuable information about what to do and what not to do when you suspect someone is contemplating suicide.

What to do

1. Ask direct, straightforward questions in a calm manner: "Are you thinking about hurting yourself?"

2. Assess the seriousness of the suicidal intent by asking questions about feelings, important relationships, who else the person has talked with, and the amount of thought given to the means to be used. If a gun, pills, a rope, or other means has been obtained and a precise plan developed, clearly the situation is dangerous. Stay with the person until help arrives.

3. Be a good listener and be very supportive without being falsely reassuring.

4. Try to persuade the person to obtain professional help and assist him or her in getting this help.

What not to do

1. Do not ignore the warning signs.

2. Do not refuse to talk about suicide if a person approaches you about it.

3. Do not react with humor, disapproval, or repulsion.

4. Do not give false reassurances by saying such things as "Everything is going to be OK." Also do not give out simple answers or platitudes, such as "You have everything to be thankful for."

5. Do not abandon the individual after the crisis has passed or after professional help has commenced.

Figure **6.11**

What to Do and What Not to Do When You Suspect Someone Is Likely to Commit Suicide

Eating Disorders

A tall, slender, 16-year-old girl goes into the locker room of a fitness center, throws her towel across the bench, and looks squarely in the mirror. She yells, "You fat pig.

Anorexia nervosa has become an increasing problem for adolescent females.

anorexia nervosa
An eating disorder that involves the relentless pursuit of thinness through starvation.

bulimia
An eating disorder that involves a binge-and-purge sequence on a regular basis.

Eating Disorders

Anorexia Nervosa and Other Eating Disorders

Anorexia Nervosa

There is no easy path leading out of life, and few are the easy ones that lie within it.

Walter Savage Landor
English Poet, 20th Century

You are nothing but a fat pig." America is a nation obsessed with food, spending extraordinary amounts of time thinking about, eating, and avoiding food. Eating disorders are complex, involving genetic inheritance, physiological factors, cognitive factors, and environmental experiences. In one study, girls who in early adolescence felt most negatively about their bodies were more likely to develop eating problems two years later (Attie & Brooks-Gunn, 1989). In another study, adolescent girls who had positive relationships with both parents tended to have healthier eating patterns (Swarr & Richards, 1996). In yet another study, the girls who were both sexually active with their boyfriends and in pubertal transition were the most likely to be dieting or engaging in disordered eating patterns (Cauffman, 1994). The three most prominent eating disorders are obesity, anorexia nervosa, and bulimia. We discussed many aspects of obesity earlier in the chapter. Here, we will focus on anorexia nervosa and bulimia.

Fifteen-year-old Jane gradually eliminated foods from her diet to the point at which she subsisted by eating *only* applesauce and eggnog. She spent hours observing her body, wrapping her fingers around her waist to see if it was getting any thinner. She fantasized about becoming a beautiful fashion model who would wear designer bathing suits. Even when she reached 85 pounds, Jane still felt fat. She continued to lose weight, eventually emaciating herself. She was hospitalized and treated for **anorexia nervosa,** *an eating disorder that involves the relentless pursuit of thinness through starvation.* Eventually, anorexia nervosa can lead to death, as it did for popular gymnast Christy Henrich.

Most anorexics are White adolescent or young adult females from well-educated, middle- and upper-income families. They distort their body image, perceiving themselves as overweight even when they become skeletal. Numerous causes of anorexia nervosa have been proposed. One is the current fashion image of thinness, reflected in the saying "You can't be too rich or too thin." Many anorexics grow up in families with high achievement demands. Unable to meet these high expectations and control their grades, they turn to something they can control: their weight.

Bulimia *is an eating disorder in which the individual consistently follows a binge-and-purge eating pattern.* The bulimic goes on an eating binge and then purges by inducing vomiting or using a laxative. Sometimes the binges alternate with fasting, at other times with normal eating. Like anorexia nervosa, bulimia is primarily a female disorder.

The Interrelation of Problems and Successful Prevention/Intervention Programs

We have described some of the major adolescent problems in this chapter: substance abuse, adolescent pregnancy and sexually transmitted diseases, and suicide. We also will discuss depression in chapter 11, "Emotional Development," examine juvenile delinquency in chapter 14, "Moral Development," and explore school-related problems in chapter 17, "Schools."

The most at-risk adolescents have more than one problem. Researchers are increasingly finding that problem behaviors in adolescence are interrelated (Tubman & Windle, 1995). For example, heavy substance abuse is related to early sexual activity, lower grades, dropping out of school, and delinquency. Early initiation of sexual activity is associated with the use of cigarettes and alcohol, the use of marijuana and other illicit drugs, lower grades, dropping out of school, and delinquency. Delinquency is related to early sexual activity, early pregnancy, substance abuse, and dropping out of school. As many as 10 percent of all adolescents in the United States have serious multiple-problem behaviors (for example, adolescents who have dropped out of school, are behind in their grade level, are users of heavy drugs, regularly use cigarettes and marijuana, and are sexually active but do not use contraception). Many, but not all, of these very high-risk youth "do it all." Another 15 percent of adolescents participate in many of these behaviors but with slightly lower frequency and less deleterious consequences. These high-risk youth often engage in two- or three-problem behaviors (Dryfoos, 1990).

In addition to understanding that many adolescents engage in multiple-problem behaviors, it also is important to develop programs that reduce adolescent problems.

In a review of the programs that have been successful in preventing or reducing adolescent problems, adolescent researcher Joy Dryfoos (1990) described the common components of these successful programs:

1. *Intensive individualized attention.* In successful programs, high-risk children are attached to a responsible adult, who gives the child attention and deals with the child's specific needs. This theme occurs in a number of programs. In a successful substance-abuse program, a student assistance counselor is available full-time for individual counseling and referral for treatment.
2. *Community-wide multiagency collaborative approaches.* The basic philosophy of community-wide programs is that a number of different programs and services have to be in place. In one successful substance-abuse program, a community-wide health promotion campaign has been implemented that uses local media and community education, in concert with a substance-abuse curriculum in the schools.
3. *Early identification and intervention.* Reaching children and their families before children develop problems, or at the beginning of their problems, is a successful strategy (Botvin, 1999; Hill & others, 1999). One preschool program serves as an excellent model for the prevention of delinquency, pregnancy, substance abuse, and dropping out of school. Operated by the High Scope Foundation in Ypsilanti, Michigan, the Perry Preschool has had a long-term positive impact on its students. This enrichment program, directed by David Weikart, serves disadvantaged African American children. They attend a high-quality two-year preschool program and receive weekly home visits from program personnel. Based on official police records, by age 19, individuals who had attended the Perry Preschool program were less likely to have been arrested and reported fewer adult offenses than a control group. The Perry Preschool students also were less likely to drop out of school, and teachers rated their social behavior as more competent than that of a control group who had not received the enriched preschool experience.

Adolescent Health

Adolescence is a critical juncture in the adoption of behaviors relevant to health (Maggs, Schulenberg, & Hurrelmann, 1997). Many of the factors linked to poor health habits and early death in the adult years begin during adolescence.

The early formation of healthy behavioral patterns, such as eating foods low in fat and cholesterol and engaging in regular exercise, not only has immediate health benefits but contributes to the delay or prevention of major causes of premature disability and mortality in adulthood—heart disease, stroke, diabetes, and cancer (Jessor, Turbin, & Costa, 1998; in press).

Many adolescents often reach a level of strength and energy that they will never match during the remainder of their lives. They also have a sense of uniqueness and invulnerability that leads them to think that poor health will never enter their lives, or that if it does, they will quickly recoup from

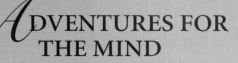

ADVENTURES FOR THE MIND

Why Is Risk Taking in Adolescence Likely to Have More Serious Consequences Today Than in the Past?

THE WORLD IS dangerous and unwelcoming for too many of America's teenagers, especially those from low-income families, neighborhoods, and schools. Many adolescents are resilient and cope with the challenges of adolescence without too many setbacks. Others struggle unsuccessfully to find jobs, are written off as losses by their schools, become pregnant before they are ready to become parents, or risk their health through drug abuse. Adolescents in virtually every era have been risk takers, testing limits and making shortsighted judgments. But why are the consequences of choosing a course of risk taking possibly more serious today than they have ever been?

Youth Risk Behavior
Prevention Research
Adolescent Health
National Longitudinal Study of Adolescent Health

Through the Eyes of Psychologists

Susan Millstein, *University of California, San Francisco*

"Identifying adolescents' unmet needs and setting goals for health promotion are important steps to take in maximizing adolescent development."

EXPLORATIONS IN CHILD DEVELOPMENT
Life Science and Life Skills Education

EARLY ADOLESCENCE IS a time when many health-compromising behaviors—drug abuse, unprotected sex, poor dietary habits, and lack of exercise, for example—either occur for the first time or intensify. As children move through puberty and often develop a feeling that they should be able to engage in adultlike behaviors, they essentially ask, "How should I use my body?" According to David Hamburg and his colleagues (1993), any responsible education must answer that basic question with a substantial life science curriculum that provides adolescents with accurate information about their own bodies, including what the consequences are for engaging in health-compromising behaviors.

Most adolescent health experts believe that a life science education program should be an important part of the curriculum in all middle schools (Hamburg, 1990; Kolbe, Collins, & Cortese, 1997). This education involves providing adolescents with a better understanding of adolescent development, including puberty (its biological and social ramifications), the reproductive system, sexual behavior, sexually transmitted diseases, nutrition, diet, and exercise. In addition, young adolescents should have readily accessible health services, nutritious food in the cafeteria, a smoke-free and physically safe environment, and appropriate physical fitness activities.

Many adolescent health experts also believe that life skills training should be part of the life science curriculum (Hamburg, 1990; Hamburg & others, 1993). Life skills training programs teach young adolescents how to make informed, deliberate, and constructive decisions that will reduce their health-compromising behaviors. Life skills training programs also can improve the interpersonal skills of young adolescents, helping them relate better with others and solve interpersonal problems more effectively.

One new school-based model for enhancing the life opportunities of adolescents is the full-service school, which encompasses school-based primary health clinics, youth service programs, and other innovative services to improve access to health and social services. These programs have in common the use of school facilities for delivering services through partnerships with community agencies, a shared vision of youth development, and financial support from sources outside of school systems, especially states and foundations. Organizing a full-service school requires careful planning to involve school personnel, community agencies, parents, and students. Evaluation of the full-service school's effectiveness is still scattered, although some recent results are encouraging with regard to adolescents' health and mental health care, dropout rates, substance abuse, pregnancy prevention, and improved attendance (Dryfoos, 1995).

It is also important to remember that health promotion in adolescence should not be solely the responsibility of schools. Adolescent health can benefit from the cooperation and integration of a number of societal institutions: the family, schools, the health-care system, the media, and community organizations (Hamburg & others, 1993).

Profile of America's Youth

Trends in the Well-Being of American Youth

Youth Information Directory

it. Given this combination of physical and cognitive factors, it is not surprising that many adolescents have poor health habits. To read further about improving adolescents' health habits, see Explorations in Child Development.

In a recent comparison of adolescent health behavior in 28 countries, U.S. adolescents exercised less and ate more junk food than their counterparts in most countries (World Health Organization, 2000). Just two-thirds of U.S. adolescents exercised at least twice a week, compared to 80 percent or more adolescents in Ireland, Austria, Germany, and the Slovak Republic. U.S. adolescents were more likely to eat fried food and less likely to eat fruits and vegetables than adolescents in most other countries studied. U.S. adolescents' eating choices were similar to those of adolescents in England. U.S. eleven-year-olds were as likely as European 11-year-olds to smoke, but by age 15, U.S. adolescents were less likely to smoke.

Many health experts believe that improving adolescent health involves far more than trips to a doctor's office when sick. The health experts increasingly recognize that whether adolescents will develop a health problem or be healthy is primarily based on their behavior. The goals are to (1) reduce adolescents' *health-compromising behaviors,* such as drug abuse, violence, unprotected sexual intercourse, and dangerous driving, and (2) increase *health-enhancing behaviors,* such as eating nutritiously, exercising, and wearing seat belts.

Today's Youth

Today's adolescents face demands and expectations, as well as risks and temptations, that appear to be more numerous and complex than those faced by adolescents only a generation ago. Nonetheless, contrary to the popular stereotype of adolescents as highly stressed and incompetent, the vast majority of adolescents successfully negotiate the path from childhood to adulthood. By some criteria, today's adolescents are doing better than their counterparts from a decade or two earlier. Today, more adolescents complete high school, especially African American adolescents. The majority of adolescents today have a positive self-concept and positive relationships with others.

A cross-cultural study by Daniel Offer and his colleagues (1988) supported the contention that most adolescents have positive images of themselves and contradicted the stereotype that most adolescents have problems or are disturbed in some way. The self-images of adolescents around the world were sampled—in the United States, Australia, Bangladesh, Hungary, Israel, Italy, Japan, Taiwan, Turkey, and West Germany. A healthy self-image characterized at least 73 percent of the adolescents studied. They appeared to be moving toward adulthood with a healthy integration of previous experiences, self-confidence, and optimism about the future. Although there were some differences among the adolescents, they were happy most of the time, they enjoyed life, they perceived themselves as able to exercise self-control, they valued work and school, they expressed confidence about their sexual selves, they expressed positive feelings toward their families, and they felt they had the capability to cope with life's stresses: not exactly a storm-and-stress portrayal of adolescence.

According to adolescent researchers Shirley Feldman and Glen Elliott (1990), public attitudes about adolescence emerge from a combination of personal experience and media portrayals, neither of which produce an objective picture of how normal adolescents develop. Some of the readiness to assume the worst about adolescents likely involves the short memories of adults. Many adults measure their current perceptions of adolescents by their memories of their own adolescence. Adults may portray today's adolescents as more troubled, less respectful, more self-centered, more assertive, and more adventurous than they were.

However, in matters of taste and manners, the young people of every generation have seemed radical, unnerving, and different from adults—different in how they look, in how they behave, in the music they enjoy, in their hairstyles, and in the clothing they choose. It is an enormous error, though, to confuse adolescents' enthusiasm for trying on new identities and enjoying moderate amounts of outrageous behavior with hostility toward parental and societal standards. Acting out and boundary testing are time-honored ways in which adolescents move toward accepting, rather than rejecting, parental values.

Although the majority of adolescents experience the transition from childhood to adulthood more positively than is portrayed by many adults and the media, too many adolescents today are not provided with adequate opportunities and support to become competent adults. In many ways, today's adolescents are presented with a less stable environment than adolescents of a decade or two ago. High divorce rates, high adolescent pregnancy rates, and increased geographic mobility of families contribute to this lack of stability in adolescents' lives. Today's adolescents are exposed to a complex menu of lifestyle options through the media, and, although the rate of adolescent drug use is beginning to show signs of decline, the rate of adolescent drug use in the United States is higher than that of any other country in the industrialized Western world. Many of today's adolescents face these temptations, as well as sexual activity, at increasingly younger ages.

American Youth Policy Forum

SUMMARY TABLE 6.4
Substance Use and Abuse, Suicide, Eating Disorders, the Interrelation of Problems and Successful Prevention/Intervention Programs, Adolescent Health, and Today's Youth

Concept	Processes/ Related Ideas	Characteristics/Description
Substance Use and Abuse	Their Nature	• The United States has the highest adolescent drug-use rate of any industrialized country. • The 1960s and 1970s were times of marked increase in adolescent drug use. • In the 1980s there was a decrease in adolescent drug use, but beginning in 1993 an upward trend began to take place again. Recently, a leveling off has occurred. • Alcohol is the drug most widely used by adolescents, and adolescent alcohol abuse is a major problem.
Suicide	Its Nature	• The rate of adolescent suicide has tripled in the last 30 years. • The suicide rate dramatically increases at about age 15. • Both proximal and distal factors are involved in understanding suicide.
Eating Disorders	Anorexia Nervosa and Bulimia	• Anorexia nervosa is an increasing problem. • Societal, psychological, and physiological causes of these disorders have been proposed.
The Interrelation of Problems and Successful Prevention/ Intervention Programs	Interrelation Prevention/ Intervention	• At-risk adolescents often have more than one problem. • Common components of successful programs include individualized attention, community-wide intervention, and early identification and intervention.
Adolescent Health	Its Nature	• Adolescence is a critical juncture in the adoption of positive health behaviors. • Health goals for adolescents include (1) reducing health-compromising behaviors and (2) increasing health-enhancing behaviors.
Today's Youth	Stereotypes	• Many stereotypes of adolescents are too negative. • The majority of adolescents successfully negotiate the path from childhood to adulthood.
	Support	• Too many of today's youth, though, are not provided with adequate opportunities and support.
	Heterogeneity	• Different portraits of adolescents emerge depending on the particular set of adolescents being described.

Our discussion underscores an important point about adolescents: they do not make up a homogeneous group (Galambos & Tilton-Weaver, 1996). Most adolescents negotiate the lengthy path to adult maturity successfully, but too large a group does not. Ethnic, cultural, gender, socioeconomic, age, and lifestyle differences influence the actual life trajectory of every adolescent. Different portrayals of adolescence emerge, depending on the particular group of adolescents being described.

At this point we have discussed many aspects of substance use and abuse, suicide, eating disorders, adolescent health, and today's youth. A review of these ideas is presented in summary table 6.4.

Chapter Review

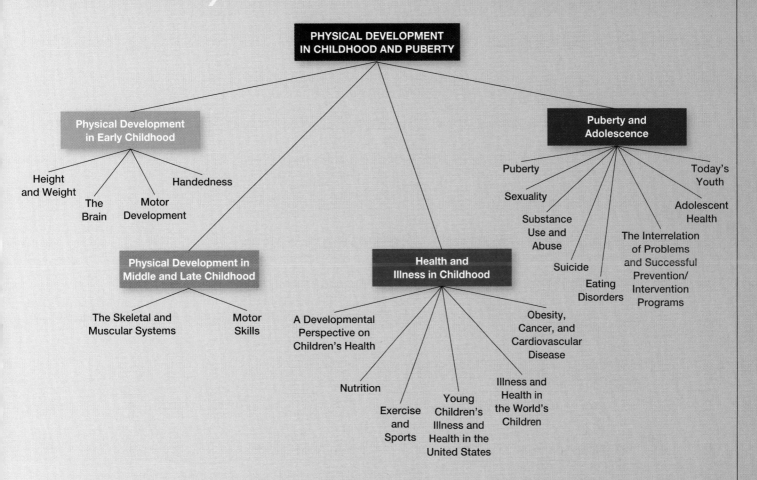

TO OBTAIN A DETAILED REVIEW OF THE CHAPTER, STUDY THESE FOUR SUMMARY TABLES:

Key Terms

Key People

Child Development Resources

Children's Aid International
P.O. Box 83220
San Diego, CA 92138
619-694-0095
800-942-2810

This multinational charitable organization provides nutritional, medical, and educational assistance to needy children in Southeast Asia, Africa, Latin America, Eastern Europe, and the United States.

Great Transitions
(1995) by the Carnegie Council on Adolescent Development
New York: Carnegie Foundation

This report by the Carnegie Council on Adolescent Development covers a wide range of topics. A number of discussions evaluate ways to reduce adolescent risk and enhance their opportunities.

Journal of School Health
This journal covers research and programs that involve school-related dimensions of health, including a number of health education programs.

Search Institute
Thresher Square West
700 South Third Street, Suite 210
Minneapolis, MN 55415
612-376-8955

The Search Institute has a large number of resources available for improving the lives of adolescents.

Taking It to the Net

1. Janice and Derek are both left-handed. What are the chances that their son, Kyle, will be left-handed?

2. Rashad and Gloria are overcome with guilt over the news that their 5-year-old daughter, Briana, has leukemia. They can't stop thinking that they had it in their genes and passed it on to her. Their friends, Tom and Nancy, want to find some facts to reassure Rashad and Gloria that they aren't responsible for Briana's cancer.

3. Dana's part-time job involves helping in a community center's after-school program for inner-city elementary school children. Many of the children eat too much junk food, have low energy levels, and are overweight. She wants to institute an exercise program as part of each day's activities. What are some things that Dana should keep in mind?

Connect to *http://www.mhhe.com/santrockc9* to find the answers!

Cognition and Language

Learning is an ornament in prosperity, a refuge in adversity.

Aristotle
Greek Philosopher, 4th Century B.C.

Children thirst to know and understand. In their effort to know and understand, they construct their own ideas about the world around them. They are remarkable for their curiosity and their intelligence. In Section 3, you will read four chapters: "Cognitive Developmental Approaches" (chapter 7), "Information Processing" (chapter 8), "Intelligence" (chapter 9), and "Language Development" (chapter 10).

Chapter 7

COGNITIVE DEVELOPMENTAL APPROACHES

Piaget's Cognitive Developmental Theory

- Jean Piaget and His Place in Developmental Psychology
- Cognitive Developmental Theory and Processes

Piaget's Stages of Cognitive Development

- Sensorimotor Thought
- Preoperational Thought
- Concrete Operational Thought
- Formal Operational Thought

Applying and Evaluating Piaget's Theory

- Piaget and Education
- Evaluating Piaget's Theory

Vygotsky's Theory of Cognitive Development

- The Zone of Proximal Development
- Scaffolding
- Language and Thought
- Vygotsky and Education
- Evaluating and Comparing Vygotsky's and Piaget's Theories

Cognitive Developmental Approaches

We are born capable of learning.

Jean-Jacques Rousseau
Swiss-Born French Philosopher, 18th Century

The Stories of Laurent, Lucienne, and Jacqueline

JEAN PIAGET, the famous Swiss psychologist, was a meticulous observer of his three children—Laurent, Lucienne and Jacqueline. His books on cognitive development are filled with these observations. Following are a few of Piaget's observations of his children's cognitive development in infancy (Piaget, 1952).

- At 21 days of age, Laurent finds his thumb after three attempts; once he finds his thumb, prolonged sucking begins. But, when he is placed on his back, he doesn't know how to coordinate the movement of his arms with that of his mouth; his hands draw back, even when his lips seek them.

- During the third month, thumb sucking becomes less important to Laurent because of new visual and auditory interests. But, when he cries, his thumb goes to the rescue.

- Toward the end of Lucienne's fourth month, while she is lying in her crib, Piaget hangs a doll above her feet. Lucienne thrusts her feet at the doll and makes it move. Afterward, she looks at her motionless foot for a second, then kicks at the doll again. She has no visual control of her foot because her movements are the same whether she only looks at the doll or it is placed over her head. By contrast, she does have tactile control of her foot; when she tries to kick the doll and misses, she slows her foot movements to improve her aim.

- At 11 months, while seated, Jacqueline shakes a little bell. She then pauses abruptly so she can delicately place the bell in front of her right foot; then she kicks the bell hard. Unable to recapture the bell, she grasps a ball and places it in the same location where the bell was. She gives the ball a firm kick.

- At 1 year, 2 months, Jacqueline holds in her hands an object that is new to her: a round, flat box that she turns over and shakes; then she rubs it against her crib. She lets it go and tries to pick it up again. She succeeds only in touching it with her index finger, being unable to fully reach and grasp it. She keeps trying to grasp it and presses to the edge of her crib. She makes the box tilt up, but it nonetheless falls again. Jacqueline shows an interest in this result and studies the fallen box.

- At 1 year, 8 months, Jacqueline arrives at a closed door with a blade of grass in each hand. She stretches her right hand toward the doorknob but detects that she cannot turn it without letting go of the grass, so she puts the grass on the floor, opens the door, picks up the grass again, and then enters. But, when she wants to leave the room, things get complicated. She puts the grass on the floor

203

and grasps the doorknob. Then she perceives that, by pulling the door toward her, she simultaneously chases away the grass that she had placed between the door and the threshold. She then picks up the grass and places it out of the door's range of movement.

For Piaget, these observations reflect important changes in the infant's cognitive development. Later in the chapter, you will learn that Piaget believed that infants go through six substages of development and that the behaviors you have just read about characterize those substages.

PIAGET'S COGNITIVE DEVELOPMENTAL THEORY

Jean Piaget and His Place in Developmental Psychology

Cognitive Developmental Theory and Processes

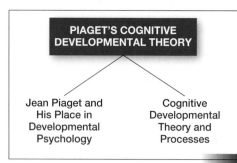

The Jean Piaget Society

Piaget's Cognitive Developmental Theory

What is Piaget's place in developmental psychology? What is the basic nature of his theory?

Jean Piaget and His Place in Developmental Psychology

In discussing Sigmund Freud's contribution to psychology, Edwin Boring (1950) remarked that it is not likely that a history of general psychology could be written in the next three centuries without mention of Freud's name and still claim to be a general history of psychology. Indeed, the best criterion of greatness might be posthumous fame. Four decades after Boring published his book, it seems likely that his judgment was accurate—Freud is still a dominating presence in psychology. However, Jean Piaget's contribution to developmental psychology may be as important as Freud's contribution to personality and abnormal behavior. Piaget's death was rather recent (he died in 1980), so it may be too early to judge, but Piaget's contributions will be strongly felt for the foreseeable future. He truly is a giant in the field of developmental psychology.

Shortly after Piaget's death, John Flavell (1980, p. 1), a leading Piagetian scholar, described what we owe Piaget:

> First, we owe him a host of insightful concepts of enduring power and fascination . . . concepts of object permanence, conservation, assimilation, accommodation, and decentration, for example. Second, we owe him a vast conceptual framework that has highlighted key issues and problems in human cognitive development. This framework is the now-familiar vision of the developing child, who, through its own active and creative commerce with its environment, builds an orderly succession of cognitive structures en route to intellectual maturity. These two debts add up to a third, more general one: We owe him the present field of cognitive development. . . . Our task is now to extend and go beyond what he began so well.

Cognitive Developmental Theory and Processes

What is the basic nature of cognitive developmental theory? What cognitive processes are responsible for changes in a child's development?

Piaget stressed that children actively construct their own cognitive worlds; information is not just poured into their minds from the environment. Two processes underlie an individual's construction of the world: organization and adaptation. To make sense of our world,

Jean Piaget, the famous Swiss developmental psychologist, dramatically changed the way we think about children's cognitive development.

we organize our experiences. For example, we separate important ideas from less important ideas. We connect one idea to another. We not only organize our observations and experiences; however, we also *adapt* our thinking to include new ideas because additional information furthers understanding. Piaget (1954) believed that we adapt in two ways: through assimilation and accommodation.

Assimilation *occurs when children incorporate new information into their existing knowledge.* **Accommodation** *occurs when children adjust to new information.* Consider a circumstance in which an 8-year-old girl is given a hammer and nails to hang a picture on the wall. She has never used a hammer, but from experience and observation she realizes that a hammer is an object to be held, that it is swung by the handle to hit the nail, and that it is usually swung a number of times. Recognizing each of these things, she fits her behavior into information she already has (assimilation). However, the hammer is heavy, so she holds it near the top. She swings too hard and the nail bends, so she adjusts the pressure of her strikes. These adjustments reveal her ability to alter her conception of the world slightly (accommodation).

Piaget thought that assimilation and accommodation operate even in a very young infant's life. Newborns reflexively suck everything that touches their lips; by sucking different objects, infants learn about the nature of these objects—their taste, texture, shape, and so on (assimilation). After several months of experience, though, they construct their understanding of the world differently. Some objects, such as fingers and the mother's breast, can be sucked, and others, such as fuzzy blankets, should not be sucked (accommodation).

Piaget also emphasized that, to make sense out of their world, children cognitively organize their experiences. **Organization** *is Piaget's concept of grouping isolated behaviors into a higher-order, more smoothly functioning cognitive system. Every level of thought is organized.* Continual refinement of this organization is an inherent part of development. A boy who has only a vague idea about how to use a hammer might also have a vague idea about how to use other tools. After learning how to use each one, he must interrelate these uses, or organize his knowledge, if he is to become skilled in using tools. In the same way, children continually integrate and coordinate the many other branches of knowledge that often develop independently. Organization occurs within stages of development as well as across them.

Equilibration *is a mechanism that Piaget proposed to explain how children shift from one stage of thought to the next. The shift occurs as children experience cognitive conflict or a disequilibrium in trying to understand the world. Eventually, the child resolves the conflict and reaches a balance, or equilibrium, of thought.* Piaget believed there is considerable movement between states of cognitive equilibrium and disequilibrium as assimilation and accommodation work in concert to produce cognitive change. For example, if a child believes that an amount of liquid changes simply because it is poured into a container with a different shape (from a container that is short and wide into a container that is tall and narrow), she might be puzzled by such issues as where the "extra" liquid came from and whether there is actually more liquid to drink. The child will eventually resolve these puzzles as her thought becomes more advanced. In the everyday world, the child is constantly faced with such counterexamples and inconsistencies.

Piaget also believed that we go through four stages in understanding the world. Each of the stages is age related and consists of distinct ways of thinking ◀IIII P. 35. Remember, it is the *different* way of understanding the world that makes one stage more advanced than another; knowing *more* information does not make a child's thinking more advanced, in the Piagetian view. This is what Piaget meant when he said a child's cognition is *qualitatively* different in one stage compared with another.

At this point we have discussed a number of ideas about Piaget's place in developmental psychology and cognitive processes in Piaget's theory. A review of these ideas is presented in summary table 7.1. Now let's explore Piaget's stages of cognitive development in greater depth.

assimilation
Piagetian concept of the incorporation of new information into existing knowledge.

accommodation
Piagetian concept of adjustment to new information.

organization
Piaget's concept of grouping isolated behaviors into a higher-order, more smoothly functioning cognitive system; the grouping or arranging of items into categories. The use of organization improves long-term memory.

equilibration
A mechanism that Piaget proposed to explain how children shift from one stage of thought to the next. The shift occurs as children experience cognitive conflict or disequilibrium in trying to understand the world. Eventually, they resolve the conflict and reach equilibrium of thought.

*T*hrough the Eyes of Psychologists

Rochel Gelman, *UCLA*

"All learners have a shared set of innate, skeletal knowledge structures with which to find, interpret, and learn about environments. . . . Individuals interpret environments with reference to what they already know."

Summary Table 7.1
Piaget's Place in Developmental Psychology, and Cognitive Developmental Theory and Processes

Concept	Processes/ Related Ideas	Characteristics/Description
Piaget's Place in Developmental Psychology	Adaptation	• Piaget's contribution to developmental psychology might be as important as Freud's to abnormal psychology. • We owe to Piaget the present field of cognitive development.
Cognitive Developmental Theory and Processes	Cognitive Developmental Theory	• The development of the child's rational thinking and stages of thought are emphasized. • Thoughts are the primary determinant of the child's actions.
	Adaptation	• This refers to effective interaction with the environment. • Cognitive adaptation involves assimilation and accommodation.
	Assimilation and Accommodation	• Assimilation occurs when children incorporate new information into existing knowledge. • Accommodation refers to children's adjustment to new information.
	Organization	• Piaget believed that children group isolated behaviors into a higher-order, more smoothly functioning cognitive system. • Every level of thought is organized.
	Equilibration	• This is a mechanism Piaget proposed to explain how children shift from one cognitive stage to the next. • The shift occurs as the child experiences cognitive conflict or disequilibrium in trying to understand the world. • Eventually the child resolves the conflict and reaches a new balance of thought.

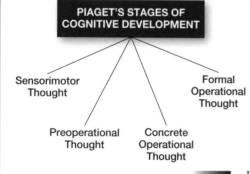

PIAGET'S STAGES OF COGNITIVE DEVELOPMENT

Sensorimotor Thought

Formal Operational Thought

Preoperational Thought

Concrete Operational Thought

Piaget's Stages

Sensorimotor Development

Cognitive Milestones

Piaget's Stages of Cognitive Development

Piaget proposed that cognitive development consists of four main stages: sensorimotor, preoperational, concrete operational, and formal operational. We briefly discussed these four stages in chapter 2, "The Science of Child Development." Here we will cover the stages in greater depth.

Sensorimotor Thought

Poet Nora Perry asked, "Who knows the thoughts of the child?" As much as anyone, Piaget knew. Through careful, inquisitive interviews and observations of his own three children—Laurent, Lucienne, and Jacqueline—Piaget changed our perceptions of the way infants think about their world. Two of the most important features of sensorimotor thought involve the child's coordination of sensation and action and the nonsymbolic aspects of the period.

According to Piaget, the sensorimotor stage lasts from birth to about 2 years of age, corresponding to the period of infancy. During this time, mental development is characterized by considerable progression in the infant's ability to organize and coordinate sensations with physical movements and actions—hence the name *sensorimotor* (Piaget, 1952).

At the beginning of the sensorimotor stage, the infant has little more than reflexive patterns with which to work. By the end of the stage, the 2-year-old has complex sensorimotor patterns and is beginning to operate with a primitive system of symbols. Unlike other stages, the sensorimotor stage is subdivided into six substages, each of which involves qualitative changes in sensorimotor organization.

The term **scheme (or schema)** *refers to the basic unit (or units) for an organized pattern of sensorimotor functioning.* Within a substage, there can be different schemes. For example, substage 1 includes sucking, rooting, and blinking. In substage 1, the schemes are basically reflexive. From substage to substage, the schemes change in organization. This change is at the heart of Piaget's description of the stages. The six substages of sensorimotor development are (1) simple reflexes; (2) first habits and primary circular reactions; (3) secondary circular reactions; (4) coordination of secondary circular reactions; (5) tertiary circular reactions, novelty, and curiosity; and (6) internalization of schemes.

Simple reflexes *is Piaget's first sensorimotor substage, which corresponds to the first month after birth. In this substage, the basic means of coordinating sensation and action is through reflexive behaviors. These include rooting and sucking, which the infant has at birth.* In substage 1, the infant exercises these reflexes. More important, the infant develops an ability to produce behaviors that resemble reflexes in the absence of obvious reflexive stimuli. The newborn may suck when a bottle or nipple is only nearby, for example. When the baby was just born, the bottle or nipple would have produced the sucking pattern only when placed directly in its mouth or touched to the lips. Reflexlike actions in the absence of a triggering stimulus are evidence that the infant is initiating action and is actively structuring experiences in the first month of life.

First habits and primary circular reactions *is Piaget's second sensorimotor substage, which develops between 1 and 4 months of age. In this substage, the infant learns to coordinate sensation and types of schemes or structures—that is, habits and primary circular reactions.* A *habit* is a scheme based on a simple reflex, such as sucking, that has become completely separated from its eliciting stimulus. For example, an infant in substage 1 might suck when orally stimulated by a bottle or when visually shown the bottle. However, an infant in substage 2 might exercise the sucking scheme even when no bottle is present. A **primary circular reaction** *is a scheme based on the infant's attempt to reproduce an interesting or a pleasurable event that initially occurred by chance.* In a popular Piagetian example, a child accidentally sucks his fingers when they are placed near his mouth. Later, he searches for his fingers to suck them again, but the fingers do not cooperate in the search because the infant cannot coordinate visual and manual actions. Habits and circular reactions are stereotyped, in that the infant repeats them the same way each time. The infant's own body remains the center of attention. There is no outward pull by environmental events. Next, you will see that Piaget's second substage of infant development also involves the concept of "circular reaction," which Piaget used to describe repetitive actions that take different forms.

Secondary circular reactions *is Piaget's third sensorimotor substage, which develops between 4 and 8 months of age. In this substage, the infant becomes more object-oriented or focused on the world, moving beyond preoccupation with the self in sensorimotor interactions.* The chance shaking of a rattle, for example, may fascinate the infant. The infant will repeat this action for the sake of experiencing fascination. The infant imitates some simple actions of others, such as the baby talk or burbling of adults, and some physical gestures. However, these imitations are limited to actions the infant is already able to produce. Although directed toward objects in the world, the infant's schemes lack an intentional, goal-directed quality.

Coordination of secondary circular reactions *is Piaget's fourth sensorimotor substage, which develops between 8 and 12 months of age. In this substage, several significant changes take place that involve the coordination of schemes and intentionality.* Infants readily combine and recombine previously learned schemes in a *coordinated way.* They might look at an object and grasp it simultaneously, or they might visually inspect a toy, such as a rattle, and finger it simultaneously in obvious tactile exploration. Actions are even more outwardly directed than before. Related to this coordination is the second achievement—the presence of *intentionality,* the separation of means and goals in accomplishing simple feats. For example, infants might manipulate a stick (the means) to bring a desired toy within reach (the goal). They might knock over one block to reach and play with another one.

---

scheme (or schema)
The basic unit of an organized pattern of sensorimotor functioning.

simple reflexes
Piaget's first sensorimotor substage, which corresponds to the first month after birth. The basic means of coordinating sensation and action is through reflexive behaviors, such as rooting and sucking, which infants have at birth.

first habits and primary circular reactions
Piaget's second sensorimotor substage, which develops between 1 and 4 months of age. Infants learn to coordinate sensation and types of schemes or structures—that is, habits and primary circular reactions.

primary circular reactions
Schemes based on the infant's attempt to reproduce an interesting or pleasurable event that initially occurred by chance.

secondary circular reactions
Piaget's third sensorimotor substage, which develops between 4 and 8 months of age. Infants become more object oriented or focused on the world, moving beyond preoccupation with the self in sensorimotor interactions.

coordination of secondary circular reactions
Piaget's fourth sensorimotor substage, which develops between 8 and 12 months of age. In this substage, several significant changes take place involving the coordination of schemes and intentionality.

tertiary circular reactions, novelty, and curiosity
Piaget's fifth sensorimotor substage, which develops between 12 and 18 months of age. Infants become intrigued by the variety of properties that objects possess and by the multiplicity of things they can make happen to objects.

tertiary circular reactions
Schemes in which the infant purposely explores new possibilities with objects, continually changing what is done to them and exploring the results.

internalization of schemes
Piaget's sixth sensorimotor substage, which develops between 18 and 24 months of age. In this substage, infants' mental functioning shifts from a purely sensorimotor plane to a symbolic plane, and they develop the ability to use primitive symbols.

object permanence
The Piagetian term for one of an infant's most important accomplishments: understanding that objects and events continue to exist even when they cannot directly be seen, heard, or touched

There was a child who went forth every day. And the first object he looked upon, that object he became. And that object became part of him for the day, or a certain part of the day, or for many years, or stretching cycles of years.

Walt Whitman
American Poet, 19th Century

Tertiary circular reactions, novelty, and curiosity *is Piaget's fifth sensorimotor substage, which develops between 12 and 18 months of age. In this substage, infants become intrigued by the variety of properties that objects possess and by the many things they can make happen to objects.* A block can be made to fall, spin, hit another object, and slide across the ground. **Tertiary circular reactions** *are schemes in which the infant purposely explores new possibilities with objects, continually changing what is done to them and exploring the results.* Piaget says that this stage marks the developmental starting point for human curiosity and interest in novelty. Previous circular reactions have been devoted exclusively to reproducing former events, with the exception of imitation of novel acts, which occurs as early as substage 4. The tertiary circular act is the first to be concerned with novelty.

Internalization of schemes *is Piaget's sixth and final sensorimotor substage, which develops between 18 and 24 months of age. In this substage, the infant's mental functioning shifts from a purely sensorimotor plane to a symbolic plane, and the infant develops the ability to use primitive symbols.* For Piaget, a *symbol* is an internalized sensory image or word that represents an event. Primitive symbols permit the infant to think about concrete events without directly acting them out or perceiving them. Moreover, symbols allow the infant to manipulate and transform the represented events in simple ways. In a favorite Piagetian example, Piaget's young daughter saw a matchbox being opened and closed. Sometime later, she mimicked the event by opening and closing her mouth. This was an obvious expression of her image of the event. In another example, a child opened a door slowly to avoid disturbing a piece of paper lying on the floor on the other side. Clearly, the child had an image of the unseen paper and what would happen to it if the door opened quickly. However, developmentalists have debated whether 2-year-olds really have such representations of action sequences at their command (Corrigan, 1981).

Object Permanence

Object permanence *is the Piagetian term for one of an infant's most important accomplishments: understanding that objects and events continue to exist, even when they cannot directly be seen, heard, or touched.* Imagine what thought would be like if you could not distinguish between yourself and your world. Your thought would be chaotic, disorganized, and unpredictable. This is what the mental life of a newborn is like, according to Piaget. There is no self-world differentiation and no sense of object permanence. By the end of the sensorimotor period, however, both are present.

The principal way that object permanence is studied is by watching an infant's reaction when an interesting object or event disappears (see figure 7.1). If infants

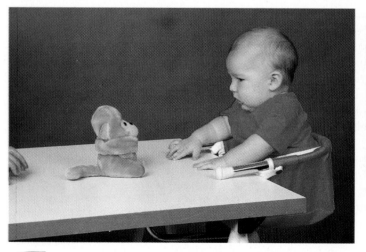 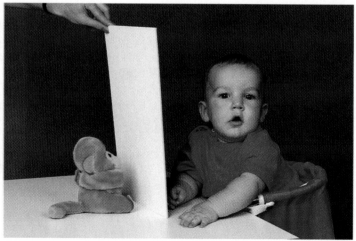

Figure **7.1**   Object Permanence

Piaget thought that object permanence is one of infancy's landmark cognitive accomplishments. For this 5-month-old boy, "out-of-sight" is literally out of mind. The infant looks at the toy monkey *(left)*, but, when his view of the toy is blocked *(right)*, he does not search for it. Several months later, he will search for the hidden toy monkey, reflecting the presence of object permanence.

show no reaction, it is assumed they believe the object no longer exists. By contrast, if infants are surprised at the disappearance and search for the object, it is assumed they believe it continues to exist.

According to Piaget, object permanence develops in a series of substages that correspond to the six substages of sensorimotor development. Figure 7.2 shows how the six substages of object permanence reflect Piaget's substages of sensorimotor development.

Although Piaget's stage sequence is the best summary of what might happen as an infant fathoms the permanence of things in the world, some contradictory findings have emerged (Baillargeon, 1995; Xu & Carey, 1995). Piaget's stages broadly describe the interesting changes reasonably well, but an infant's life is not neatly packaged into distinct areas of organization as Piaget believed. Some of Piaget's explanations for the causes of change are debated.

Piaget claimed that certain processes are crucial in stage transitions, but the data do not always support his explanations. For example, according to Piaget the critical requirement for an infant to progress into sensorimotor substage 4 is the coordination of vision and the sense of touch, or hand-eye coordination. Another important feature in the progression into substage 4 is an infant's inclination to search for an object hidden in a familiar location rather than to look for the object in a new location. The **AB error** *is the Piagetian object-permanence concept in which an infant progressing into substage 4 makes frequent mistakes, selecting the familiar hiding place (A) rather than new hiding places ($\bar{B}$).* Researchers have found, however, that the AB error does not show up consistently (Ahmed & Ruffman, 2000; Corrigan, 1981; Sophian, 1985). There is also accumulating evidence that AB errors are sensitive to the delay between hiding an object at $\bar{B}$ and the infant's attempt to find it (Diamond, 1985). Thus, the AB error might be partly due to the failure of memory. And the AB error might be due to a lack of maturation of the frontal cortex of the brain (Diamond, 1995; Diamond & Goldman-Rakic, 1989).

At this point, we have discussed a number of characteristics of Piaget's stage of sensorimotor thought. To help you remember Piaget's description of the main characteristics of sensorimotor thought, turn to figure 7.3.

Sensorimotor Stage	Behavior
Substage 1	There is no apparent object permanence. When a spot of light moves across the visual field, an infant follows it but quickly ignores its disappearance.
Substage 2	A primitive form of object permanence develops. Given the same experience, the infant looks briefly at the spot where the light disappeared, with an expression of passive expectancy.
Substage 3	The infant's sense of object permanence undergoes further development. With the newfound ability to coordinate simple schemes, the infant shows clear patterns of searching for a missing object, with sustained visual and manual examination of the spot where the object apparently disappeared.
Substage 4	The infant actively searches for a missing object in the spot where it disappeared, with new actions to achieve the goal of searching effectively. For example, if an attractive toy has been hidden behind a screen, the child may look at the screen and try to push it away with a hand. If the screen is too heavy to move or is permanently fixed, the child readily substitutes a secondary scheme—for example, crawling around it or kicking it. These new actions signal that the infant's belief in the continued existence of the missing object is strengthening.
Substage 5	The infant now is able to track an object that disappears and reappears in several locations in rapid succession. For example, a toy may be hidden under different boxes in succession in front of the infant, who succeeds in finding it. The infant is apparently able to hold an image of the missing object in mind longer than before.
Substage 6	The infant can search for a missing object that disappeared and reappeared in several locations in succession, as before. In addition, the infant searches in the appropriate place even when the object has been hidden from view as it is being moved. This activity indicates that the infant is able to "imagine" the missing object and to follow the image from one location to the next.

Figure **7.2**

The Six Substages of Object Permanence

Evaluating Piaget's Sensorimotor Stage

Piaget opened up a whole new way of looking at infants by describing how their main task is to coordinate their sensory impressions with their motor activity. His view is a good summary of the general way that infants come to fathom the permanence of things in their world. However, the infant's cognitive world is not as neatly packaged as Piaget portrayed it, and some of Piaget's explanations for the cause of change are debated.

Piaget constructed his view of infancy mainly by observing the development of his own three children. Few laboratory techniques were available at the time. In the past several decades, sophisticated experimental techniques have been devised to study infants, and there have been a large number of research studies on infant development. Much of the new research suggests that Piaget's view of sensorimotor

AB error
The Piagetian object-permanence concept in which an infant progressing into substage 4 makes frequent mistakes, selecting the familiar hiding place (A) rather than the new hiding place ($\bar{B}$).

Ability to organize and coordinate sensations with physical movements

Is nonsymbolic through most of its duration

Consists of six substages of cognitive development

Object permanence develops

Figure 7.3
The Main Characteristics of Sensorimotor Thought, According to Piaget

*T*hrough the Eyes of Psychologists

Renée Baillargeon,
University of Illinois

"Infants know that objects are substantial and permanent at an earlier age than Piaget envisioned."

development needs to be modified (Gounin-Decarie, 1996). The two research areas that have led researchers to a somewhat different understanding of infant development are (1) perceptual development and (2) conceptual development.

In chapter 5, we said that a number of theorists, such as Eleanor Gibson (1989), Elizabeth Spelke (1991; Spelke & Newport, 1998), and Tom Bower (1996), believe that infants' perceptual abilities are highly developed very early in infancy ◀▭ Pp. 149, 152. For example, Spelke has demonstrated that infants as young as 4 months of age have intermodal perception—the ability to coordinate information from two or more sensory modalities, such as vision and hearing. Other research, by Renée Baillargeon (1995), documented that infants as young as 4 months expect objects to be substantial (in the sense that other objects cannot move through them) and permanent (in the sense that objects continue to exist when they are hidden). In sum, researchers believe that infants see objects as bounded, unitary, solid, and separate from their background, possibly at birth or shortly thereafter, but definitely by 3 to 4 months of age. Young infants still have much to learn about objects, but the world appears both stable and orderly to them and, thus, capable of being conceptualized. Infants are continually trying to structure and make sense of their world (Meltzoff, 2000; Meltzoff & Gopnik, 1997).

It is more difficult to study what infants are thinking about than to study what they see. Still, researchers have devised ways to assess whether or not infants are thinking. One strategy is to look for symbolic activity, such as using a gesture to refer to something. Piaget (1952) used this strategy to document infants' motor recognition. For example, he observed his 6-month-old daughter make a gesture when she saw a familiar toy in a new location. She was used to kicking at the toy in her crib. When she saw it across the room, she made a brief kicking motion. However, Piaget did not consider this to be true symbolic activity because it was a motor movement, not a purely mental act. Nonetheless, Piaget suggested that his daughter was referring to, or classifying, the toy through her actions (Mandler, 1992). In a similar way, infants whose parents use sign language have been observed to start using conventional signs at about 6 to 7 months of age (Bonvillian, Orlansky, & Novack, 1983).

In summary, the recent research on infants' perceptual and conceptual development suggests that infants have more sophisticated perceptual abilities and can begin to think earlier than Piaget envisioned (Baillargeon, 2000). These researchers believe that infants either are born with or acquire these abilities early in their development (Mandler, 1990, 1998).

It is clear from the new look at infant cognition that Piaget's view of sensorimotor development requires considerable revision (Lutz & Sternberg, 1999; Meltzoff & Moore, 1999). Piaget's view is a general, unifying story of how biology and experience sculpt the infant's cognitive development: assimilation and accommodation always take the infant to higher ground through a series of substages. And, for Piaget, the motivation for change is general, an internal search for equilibrium. Many of today's researchers believe that Piaget wasn't specific enough about how infants learn about their world and that infants are far more competent than Piaget envisioned.

However, according to infant development experts Marshall Haith and Janette Benson (1998), today it is difficult to tell such a unifying story of infant cognition. Many key questions are matters of debate. How much of the infant's cognitive development is innate? How much has strong biological foundations but requires considerable environmental input? How much is more perceptual than cognitive? How much emerges full-blown rather than gradually?

Like much of the modern world, the field of infant cognition is very specialized. There are many researchers working on different questions, with no general theory emerging that can connect all of the different findings (Nelson, 1999). Their theories are local theories, focused on specific research questions, rather than grand theories like Piaget's (Kuhn, 1998). If there are unifying themes, they are that investigators in infant development struggle with the big issues of nature and nurture, cognition and perception.

Some developmentalists, such as Haith (1993), believe that the following Piagetian ideas should not be discarded: that infants acquire knowledge about their world in a gradual rather than full-blown fashion and that each level of understanding builds on previous ones. They argue that the most accurate story of infant development is one of partial, graded accomplishments along the route to acquiring a concept.

I wish I could travel by the road that crosses the baby's mind, and out beyond all bounds; where messengers run errands for no cause between the kingdoms of kings of no history; where reason makes kites of her laws and flies them, and truth sets facts free from its fetters.

Rabindranath Tagore
Bengali Poet, Essayist, 20th Century

Preoperational Thought

The cognitive world of the preschool child is creative, free, and fanciful. The imagination of preschool children works overtime and their mental grasp of the world improves. When Piaget described the preschool child's cognition as *preoperational*, what did he mean?

Because this stage of thought is called preoperational, it might seem that not much of importance occurs until full-fledged operational thought appears. Not so. The preoperational stage stretches from approximately 2 to 7 years of age. It is a time when stable concepts are formed, mental reasoning emerges, egocentrism begins strongly and then weakens, and magical beliefs are constructed. Preoperational thought is anything but a convenient waiting period for concrete operational thought. However, the label *preoperational* emphasizes that the child at this stage does not yet think in an operational way. What are operations? **Operations** *are internalized sets of actions that allow the child to do mentally what before she did physically.* Operations are highly organized and conform to certain rules and principles of logic. The operations appear in one form in concrete operational thought and in another form in formal operational thought. Thought in the preoperational stage is flawed and not well organized. Preoperational thought is the beginning of the ability to reconstruct at the level of thought what has been established in behavior. Preoperational thought also involves a transition from primitive to more sophisticated use of symbols. Preoperational thought can be divided into two substages: the symbolic function substage and the intuitive thought substage.

operations
Internalized sets of actions that allow children to do mentally what before they had done physically.

Symbolic Function Substage   The **symbolic function substage** *is the first substage of preoperational thought, occurring roughly between the ages of 2 and 4. In this substage, the young child gains the ability to mentally represent an object that is not present.* The ability to engage in such symbolic thought is called symbolic function, and it vastly expands the child's mental world. Young children use scribbled designs to represent people, houses, cars, clouds, and so on. Other examples of symbolism in early childhood are language and the prevalence of pretend play. In sum, the ability to think symbolically and to represent the world mentally predominates in this early substage of preoperational thought. However, although young children make distinct progress during this substage, their thought still has several important limitations, two of which are egocentrism and animism.

Egocentrism *is a salient feature of preoperational thought. It is the inability to distinguish between one's own perspective and someone else's perspective.* The following

symbolic function substage
The first substage of preoperational thought, occurring roughly between the ages of 2 and 4. In this substage, the young child gains the ability to represent mentally an object that is not present.

egocentrism
A salient feature of preoperational thought, the inability to distinguish between one's own and someone else's perspective.

Symbolic Thinking

animism
A facet of preoperational thought, the belief that inanimate objects have "lifelike" qualities and are capable of action.

intuitive thought substage
The second substage of preoperational thought, occurring approximately between 4 and 7 years of age. Children begin to use primitive reasoning and want to know the answers to all sorts of questions.

telephone conversation between 4-year-old Mary, who is at home, and her father, who is at work, typifies Mary's egocentric thought:

Father: Mary, is Mommy there?
Mary: (Silently nods)
Father: Mary, may I speak to Mommy?
Mary: (Nods again silently)

Mary's response is egocentric in that she fails to consider her father's perspective before replying. A nonegocentric thinker would have responded verbally.

Piaget and Barbel Inhelder (1969) initially studied young children's egocentrism by devising the three mountains task (see figure 7.4). The child walks around the model of the mountains and becomes familiar with what the mountains look like from different perspectives, and they can see that there are different objects on the mountains. The child is then seated on one side of the table on which the mountains are placed. The experimenter moves a doll to different locations around the table, at each location asking the child to select, from a series of photos, the one photo that most accurately reflects the view the doll is seeing. Children in the preoperational stage often pick their view from where they are sitting, rather than the doll's view. Perspective taking does not develop uniformly in preschool children, who frequently show perspective skills on some tasks but not others.

Animism, *another limitation within preoperational thought, is the belief that inanimate objects have "lifelike" qualities and are capable of action.* A young child might show animism by saying, "That tree pushed the leaf off, and it fell down," or "The sidewalk made me mad; it made me fall down." A young child who uses animism fails to distinguish the appropriate occasions for using human and nonhuman perspectives.

Possibly because young children are not very concerned about reality, their drawings are fanciful and inventive. Suns are blue, skies are yellow, and cars float on clouds in their symbolic, imaginative world. One 3½-year-old looked at a scribble he had just drawn and described it as a pelican kissing a seal (see figure 7.5a). The symbolism is simple but strong, like abstractions found in some modern art. As Picasso commented, "I used to draw like Raphael but it has taken me a lifetime to draw like young children." In the elementary school years, a child's drawings become more realistic, neat, and precise (see figure 7.5b). Suns are yellow, skies are blue, and cars travel on roads (Winner, 1986).

Intuitive Thought Substage   Tommy is 4 years old. Although he is starting to develop his own ideas about the world he lives in, his ideas are still simple, and he is not very good at thinking things out. He has difficulty understanding events he knows are taking place but which he cannot see. His fantasized thoughts bear little resemblance to reality. He cannot yet answer the question "What if . . . ?" in any reliable way. For example, he has only a vague idea of what would happen if a car were to hit him. He also has difficulty negotiating traffic because he cannot do the mental calculations necessary to estimate whether an approaching car will hit him when he crosses the road.

The **intuitive thought substage** *is the second substage of preoperational thought, occurring between approximately 4 and 7 years of age. In this substage, children begin to use primitive reasoning and want to know the answers to all sorts of questions.* Piaget called this time period *intuitive* because, on the one hand, young children seem so

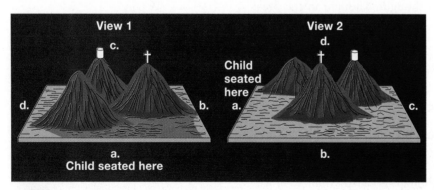

Figure 7.4
The Three Mountains Task
View 1 shows the child's perspective from where he or she is sitting. View 2 is an example of the photograph the child would be shown, mixed in with others from different perspectives. To correctly identify this view, the child has to take the perspective of a person sitting at spot (b). Invariably, a preschool child who thinks in a preoperational way cannot perform this task. When asked what a view of the mountains looks like from position (b), the child selects a photograph taken from location (a), the child's view at the time.

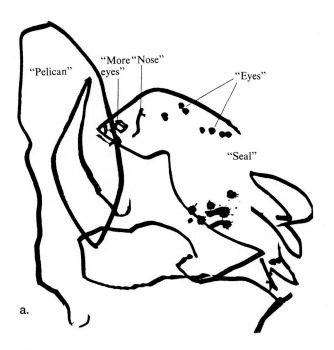

Figure 7.5
The Symbolic Drawings of Young Children
(*a*) A 3½-year-old's symbolic drawing. Halfway into this drawing, the 3½-year-old artist said it was "a pelican kissing a seal." (*b*) This 11-year-old's drawing is neater and more realistic but also less inventive.

sure about their knowledge and understanding, yet they are so unaware of how they know what they know. That is, they say they know something but know it without the use of rational thinking.

An example of young children's reasoning ability is the difficulty they have putting things into correct categories. Faced with a random collection of objects that can be grouped together on the basis of two or more properties, preoperational children are seldom capable of using these properties consistently to sort the objects into appropriate groupings. Look at the collection of objects in figure 7.6a. You would respond to the direction "Put the things together that you believe belong together" by sorting according to the characteristics of size and array. Your sorting might look something like that shown in figure 7.6b. In the social realm, a 4-year-old girl might be given the task of dividing her peers into groups according to whether they are friends and whether they are boys or girls. She would be unlikely to arrive at the following classification: friendly boys, friendly girls, unfriendly boys, unfriendly girls. Another example of classification shortcomings involves the preoperational child's understanding of religious concepts (Elkind, 1976). When asked "Can you be a Protestant and an American at the same time?" 6- and 7-year-olds usually say no. Nine-year-olds often say yes, understanding that objects can be cross-classified simultaneously.

Many of these examples show a characteristic of preoperational thought called **centration**—*the focusing, or centering, of attention on one characteristic to the exclusion of all others.* Centration is most clearly evidenced in young children's lack of **conservation**—*the idea that an amount stays the same regardless of how its container changes.* To adults, it is obvious that a certain amount of liquid stays the same, regardless of a container's shape.

centration
The focusing of attention on one characteristic to the exclusion of all others.

conservation
The idea that an amount stays the same regardless of how its container changes.

"*Mrs. Hammond! I'd know you anywhere from little Billy's portrait of you.*"

Figure 7.6
Arrays
(a) A random array of objects. *(b)* An ordered array of objects.

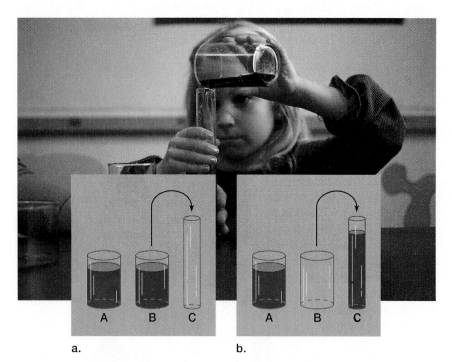

Figure 7.7
Piaget's Conservation Task
The beaker test is a well-known Piagetian test to determine whether a child can think operationally—that is, can mentally reverse actions and show conservation of the substance. *(a)* Two identical beakers are presented to the child. Then, the experimenter pours the liquid from B into C, which is taller and thinner than A or B. *(b)* The child is asked if these beakers (A and C) have the same amount of liquid. The preoperational child says no. When asked to point to the beaker that has more liquid, the preoperational child points to the tall, thin beaker.

But this is not at all obvious to young children. Instead, they are struck by the height of the liquid in the container. In the conservation task—Piaget's most famous test—a child is presented with two identical beakers, each filled to the same level with liquid (see figure 7.7). The child is asked if these beakers have the same amount of liquid, and she usually says yes. Then the liquid from one beaker is poured into a third beaker, which is taller and thinner than the first two. The child is then asked if the amount of liquid in the tall, thin beaker is equal to that which remains in one of the original beakers. Children who are less than 7 or 8 years old usually say no and justify their answers in terms of the differing height or width of the beakers. Older children usually answer yes and justify their answers appropriately ("If you poured the milk back, the amount would still be the same").

In Piaget's theory, failing the conservation of liquid task is a sign that children are at the preoperational stage of cognitive development. Passing this test is a sign that they are at the concrete operational stage. In Piaget's view, the preoperational child fails to show conservation not only of liquid but also of number, matter, length, volume, and area (see figure 7.8).

The child's inability to mentally reverse actions is an important characteristic of preoperational thought. For example, in the conservation of matter task shown in figure 7.8, preoperational children say that the longer shape has more clay because they assume that "longer is more." Preoperational children cannot mentally reverse the clay-rolling process to see that the amount of clay is the same in both the shorter ball shape and the longer stick shape.

Some developmentalists do not believe Piaget was entirely correct in his estimate of when children's conservation skills emerge. For example, Rochel Gelman (1969) showed that, when the child's attention to relevant aspects of the conservation task is improved, the child is more likely to conserve. Gelman has also demonstrated that attentional training on one dimension, such as number, improves the preschool child's performance on another dimension, such as mass. Thus, Gelman believes that conservation appears earlier than Piaget thought and that attention is especially important in explaining conservation.

Yet another characteristic of preoperational children is that they ask a barrage of questions. Children's earliest questions appear around the age of 3, and by the age of 5 they have just about exhausted the adults around them with "why" questions. The child's questions yield clues about mental development and reflect intellectual

Type of conservation	Initial presentation	Manipulation	Preoperational child's answer
Number	Two identical rows of objects are shown to the child, who agrees they have the same number.	One row is lengthened and the child is asked whether one row now has more objects.	Yes, the longer row.
Matter	Two identical balls of clay are shown to the child. The child agrees that they are equal.	The experimenter changes the shape of one of the balls and asks the child whether they still contain equal amounts of clay.	No, the longer one has more.
Length	Two sticks are aligned in front of the child. The child agrees that they are the same length.	The experimenter moves one stick to the right, then asks the child if they are equal in length.	No, the one on the top is longer.
Volume	Two balls are placed in two identical glasses, with an equal amount of water. The child sees the balls displace equal amounts of water.	The experimenter changes the shape of one of the balls and asks the child if it still will displace the same amount of water.	No, the longer one on the right displaces more.
Area	Two identical sheets of cardboard have wooden blocks placed on them in identical positions. The child agrees that the same amount of space is left on each piece of cardboard.	The experimenter scatters the blocks on one piece of cardboard and then asks the child if one of the cardboard pieces has more space covered.	Yes, the one on the right has more space covered up.

Figure 7.8

Some Dimensions of Conservation: Number, Matter, Length, Volume, and Area

curiosity. These questions signal the emergence of the child's interest in reasoning and figuring out why things are the way they are. Following are some samples of the questions children ask during the questioning period of 4 to 6 years of age (Elkind, 1976):

- "What makes you grow up?"
- "What makes you stop growing?"
- "Why does a lady have to be married to have a baby?"
- "Who was the mother when everybody was a baby?"
- "Why do leaves fall?"
- "Why does the sun shine?"

"I still don't have all the answers, but I'm beginning to ask the right questions."

Rochel Gelman's Research

At this point we have discussed a number of characteristics of preoperational thought. To help you remember these characteristics, see figure 7.9.

Earlier, we mentioned that Gelman's research demonstrated that children may fail a Piagetian task because they do not attend to relevant dimensions of the task—length, shape, density, and so on. Gelman and other developmentalists also believe that many of the tasks used to assess cognitive development may not be sensitive to the child's cognitive abilities. Thus, any apparent limitations on cognitive development may be due to the tasks used to assess that development. Gelman's research reflects the thinking of information-processing psychologists who place considerable importance on the tasks and procedures involved in assessing children's cognition.

At this point, we have discussed a number of ideas about Piaget's first two stages—sensorimotor and preoperational. A review of these ideas is presented in summary table 7.2. Next, we will explore Piaget's third stage of cognitive development.

Concrete Operational Thought

In the well-known test of reversibility of thought involving conservation of matter, a child is presented with two identical balls of clay. An experimenter rolls one ball into a long, thin shape; the other remains in its original ball shape. The child is then asked if there is more clay in the ball or in the long, thin piece of clay. By the time children reach the age of 7 or 8, most answer that the amount of clay is the same. To answer this problem correctly, children have to imagine that the clay ball is rolled out into a long, thin strip and then returned to its original round shape—imagination that involves a reversible mental action. Thus, a concrete operation is a reversible mental action on real, concrete objects. Concrete operations allow children to coordinate several characteristics

| More symbolic than sensorimotor thought | Inability to engage in operations; can't mentally reverse actions; lacks conservation skills | Egocentric (inability to distinguish between own perspective and someone else's) | Intuitive rather than logical |

Figure **7.9**

Characteristics of Preoperational Thought

SUMMARY TABLE 7.2
Sensorimotor Thought and Preoperational Thought

Concept	Processes/Related Ideas	Characteristics/Description
Sensorimotor Thought	Basic Features	• The infant is able to organize and coordinate sensations with physical movements. • The stage lasts from birth to about 2 years of age and is nonsymbolic throughout, according to Piaget.
	Substages	• Sensorimotor thought has six substages: simple reflexes; first habits and primary circular reactions; secondary circular reactions; coordination of secondary circular reactions; tertiary circular reactions, novelty, and curiosity; and internalization of schemes.
	Object Permanence	• This is the ability to understand that objects and events continue to exist even though the infant is no longer in contact with them. • Piaget believed this ability develops over the course of the six substages of sensorimotor thought.
	Evaluating Piaget's Sensorimotor Stage	• Piaget opened up a whole new way of looking at infant development in terms of coordinating sensory input with motoric actions. • However, in the past two decades, many research studies have suggested that revision of Piaget's view is needed. • In perceptual development, researchers have found that a stable and differentiated perceptual world is established earlier than Piaget envisioned. • In conceptual development, researchers have found that memory and other forms of symbolic activity occur at least by the second half of the first year of life, also much earlier than Piaget believed. • Some developmentalists argue that it is hard to tell a unifying story about infant cognitive development today the way Piaget did many years ago. • Debate flourishes about many issues, such as whether a concept is innate and whether a concept emerges full-blown or gradually.
Preoperational Thought	Its Nature	• This is the beginning of the ability to reconstruct at the level of thought what has been established in behavior. • It involves a transition from a primitive to a more sophisticated use of symbols. • The child does not yet think in an operational way.
	Symbolic Function Substage	• This substage occurs roughly from 2 to 4 years of age and is characterized by symbolic though, egocentrism, and animism.
	Intuitive Thought Substage	• This substage stretches from 4 to 7 years of age. • It is called intuitive because, on the one hand, children seem so sure about their knowledge, yet, on the other hand, they are unaware of how they know what they know. • The child lacks conservation and asks a barrage of questions.

rather than focus on a single property of an object. In the clay example, a preoperational child is likely to focus on height or width; a concrete operational child coordinates information about both dimensions. We can get a better understanding of concrete operational thought by considering further ideas about conservation and the nature of classification.

We already have highlighted some of Piaget's basic ideas on conservation in our discussion of preoperational children's failure to answer questions correctly about such circumstances as the beaker task. Remember that conservation involves the recognition that the length, number, mass, quantity, area, weight, and volume of objects and substances do not change by transformations that alter their appearance.

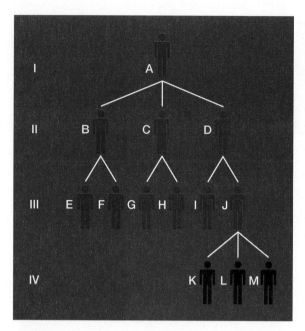

Figure 7.10

Classification: An Important Ability in Concrete Operational Thought

A family tree of four generations *(I to IV):* The preoperational child has trouble classifying the members of the four generations; the concrete operational child can classify the members vertically, horizontally, and obliquely (up and down and across). For example, the concrete operational child understands that a family member can be a son, a brother, and a father, all at the same time.

horizontal décalage
Piaget's concept that similar abilities do not appear at the same time within a stage of development.

seriation
The concrete operation that involves ordering stimuli along a quantitative dimension (such as length).

transitivity
In concrete operational thought, a mental concept that underlies the ability to logically combine relations to understand certain conclusions. It focuses on reasoning about the relations between classes.

An important point that needs to be made about conservation is that children do not conserve all quantities or on all tasks simultaneously. The order of their mastery is number, length, liquid quantity, mass, weight, and volume. **Horizontal décalage** *is Piaget's concept that similar abilities do not appear at the same time within a stage of development.* As we have just seen, during the concrete operational stage, conservation of number usually appears first and conservation of volume last. Also, an 8-year-old child might know that a long stick of clay can be rolled back into a ball but not understand that the ball and the stick weigh the same. At about 9 years of age, the child recognizes that they weigh the same, and eventually, at about 11 to 12 years of age, the child understands that the clay's volume is unchanged by rearranging it. Children initially master tasks in which the dimensions are more salient and visible, only later mastering those not as visually apparent, such as volume.

Many of the concrete operations identified by Piaget involve the ways children reason about the properties of objects. One important skill that characterizes concrete operational children is the ability to classify or divide things into sets or subsets and to consider their interrelationships. An example of concrete operational classification skills involves a family tree of four generations (Furth & Wachs, 1975) (see figure 7.10). This family tree suggests that the grandfather (A) has three children (B, C, and D), each of whom has two children (E through J), and that one of these children (J) has three children (K, L, and M). The concrete operational child understands that person J can, at the same time, be father, brother, and grandson. A child who comprehends this classification system can move up and down a level (vertically), across a level (horizontally), and up and down and across (obliquely) within the system.

Some Piagetian tasks require children to reason about relations between classes. One such task is **seriation,** *the concrete operation that involves ordering stimuli along a quantitative dimension (such as length).* To see if students can serialize, a teacher might haphazardly place eight sticks of different lengths on a table. The teacher then asks the students to order the sticks by length. Many young children end up with two or three small groups of "big" sticks or "little" sticks, rather than a correct ordering of all eight sticks. Another mistaken strategy they use is to evenly line up the tops of the sticks but ignore the bottoms. The concrete operational thinker simultaneously understands that each stick must be longer than the one that precedes it and shorter than the one that follows it.

Another aspect of reasoning about the relations between classes is **transitivity.** *This involves the ability to logically combine relations to understand certain conclusions.* In this case, consider three sticks (A, B, and C) of differing lengths. A is the longest, B is intermediate in length, and C is the shortest. Does the child understand that, if A > B and B > C, then A > C? In Piaget's theory, concrete operational thinkers do; preoperational thinkers do not.

Although concrete operational thought is more advanced than preoperational thought, it has its limitations. Logical reasoning replaces intuitive thought as long as the principles can be applied to specific or *concrete* examples. For example, a concrete operational child cannot imagine the steps necessary to complete an algebraic equation, which is too abstract for thinking at this stage of cognitive development. A summary of the characteristics of concrete operational thought is shown in figure 7.11.

Formal Operational Thought

Adolescents' developing power of thought opens up new cognitive and social horizons. Their thought becomes more abstract, logical, and idealistic. Adolescents are more capable of examining their own thoughts, others' thoughts, and what others are thinking about them, and more likely to interpret and monitor the social world.

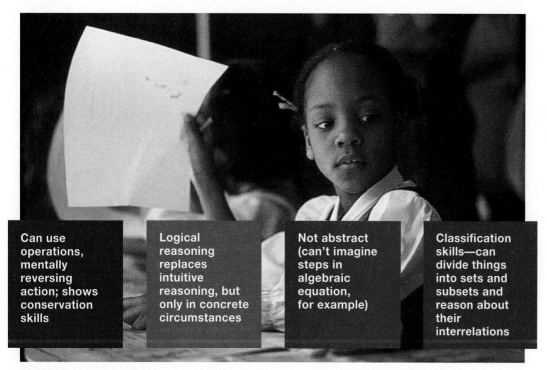

Can use operations, mentally reversing action; shows conservation skills

Logical reasoning replaces intuitive reasoning, but only in concrete circumstances

Not abstract (can't imagine steps in algebraic equation, for example)

Classification skills—can divide things into sets and subsets and reason about their interrelations

Figure 7.11
Characteristics of Concrete Operational Thought

Characteristics of Formal Operational Thought   Piaget believed that formal operational thought comes into play between the ages of 11 and 15. Formal operational thought is more *abstract* than a child's thinking. Adolescents are no longer limited to actual, concrete experiences as anchors for thought. They can conjure up make-believe situations, events that are purely hypothetical possibilities or strictly abstract propositions, and can try to reason logically about them.

The abstract quality of the adolescent's thought at the formal operational level is evident in the adolescent's verbal problem-solving ability. Whereas the concrete operational thinker needs to see the concrete elements A, B, and C to be able to make the logical inference that, if A = B and B = C, then A = C, the formal operational thinker can solve this problem when it is merely presented verbally.

Another indication of the abstract quality of adolescents' thought is their increased tendency to think about thought itself. One adolescent commented, "I began thinking about why I was thinking what I was. Then I began thinking about why I was thinking about what I was thinking about what I was." If this sounds abstract, it is, and it characterizes the adolescent's enhanced focus on thought and its abstract qualities.

Accompanying the abstract nature of formal operational thought in adolescence is thought full of idealism and possibilities. Whereas children frequently think in concrete ways, or in terms of what is real and limited, adolescents begin to engage in extended speculation about ideal characteristics—qualities they desire in themselves and in others. Such thoughts often lead adolescents to compare themselves with others in regard to such ideal standards. And adolescents' thoughts are often fantasy flights into future possibilities. It is not unusual for the adolescent to become impatient with these newfound ideal standards and to become perplexed over which of many ideal standards to adopt.

At the same time that adolescents think more abstractly and idealistically, they also think more logically. Adolescents begin to think more as a scientist thinks, devising plans to solve problems and systematically testing solutions. This type of

*T*he thoughts of youth are long, long thoughts.

Henry Wadsworth Longfellow
American Poet, 19th Century

"*. . . and give me good abstract-reasoning ability, interpersonal skills, cultural perspective, linguistic comprehension, and a high sociodynamic potential.*"

ADVENTURES FOR THE MIND

Piaget, Children, Adolescents, and Political Conventions

SUPPOSE AN 8-YEAR-OLD and a 16-year-old are watching a political convention on television. In view of where each child is likely to be in terms of Piaget's stages of cognitive development, how would their perceptions of the proceedings likely differ? What would the 8-year-old "see" and comprehend? What Piagetian changes would these differences reflect?

hypothetical-deductive reasoning
Piaget's formal operational concept that adolescents have the cognitive ability to develop hypotheses about ways to solve problems and can systematically deduce which is the best path to follow in solving the problem.

The error of youth is to believe that intelligence is a substitute for experience, while the error of age is to believe that experience is a substitute for intelligence.

Lyman Bryson
American Author, 20th Century

problem solving has an imposing name. **Hypothetical-deductive reasoning** *is Piaget's formal operational concept that adolescents have the cognitive ability to develop hypotheses, or best guesses, about ways to solve problems, such as an algebraic equation. Then they systematically deduce, or conclude, which is the best path to follow in solving the equation.* By contrast, children are more likely to solve problems in a trial-and-error fashion.

One example of hypothetical-deductive reasoning involves a modification of the familiar game Twenty Questions. Individuals are shown a set of 42 color pictures, displayed in a rectangular array (six rows of seven pictures each) and are asked to determine which picture the experimenter has in mind (that is, which is "correct"). The subjects are allowed to ask only questions to which the experimenter can answer yes or no. The object of the game is to select the correct picture by asking as few questions as possible. Adolescents who are deductive hypothesis testers formulate a plan and test a series of hypotheses, which considerably narrows the field of choices. The most effective plan is a "halving" strategy (*Q:* Is the picture in the right half of the array? *A:* No. *Q:* OK. Is it in the top half? And so on.). A correct halving strategy guarantees the answer in seven questions or less. By contrast, concrete operational thinkers may persist with questions that continue to test some of the same possibilities that previous questions could have eliminated. For example, they may ask whether the correct picture is in row 1 and are told that it is not. Later, they ask whether the picture is *x*, which is in row 1.

Thus, formal operational thinkers test their hypotheses with judiciously chosen questions and tests. By contrast, concrete operational thinkers often fail to understand the relation between a hypotheses and a well-chosen test of it, stubbornly clinging to ideas that already have been discounted.

Piaget believed that formal operational thought is the best description of how adolescents think. A summary of formal operational thought's characteristics is shown in figure 7.12. As we will see next, though, formal operational thought is not a homogeneous stage of development.

Some of Piaget's ideas on formal operational thought are being challenged (Overton & Byrnes, 1991). There is much more individual variation in formal operational thought than Piaget envisioned. Only about one in three young adolescents is a formal operational thinker. Many American adults never become formal operational thinkers, and neither do many adults in other cultures. Consider the following conversation between a researcher and an illiterate Kpelle farmer in the West African country of Liberia (Scribner, 1977):

Researcher: All Kpelle men are rice farmers. Mr. Smith is not a rice farmer. Is he a Kpelle man?
Kpelle farmer: I don't know the man. I have not laid eyes on the man myself.

Members of the Kpelle culture who had gone through formal schooling answered the researcher in a logical way. As with our discussion of concrete operational thought in chapter 10, we find that cultural experiences influence whether individuals reach a Piagetian stage of thought. Education in the logic of science and mathematics is an important cultural experience that promotes the development of formal operational thinking.

Also, for adolescents who become formal operational thinkers, assimilation (incorporating new information into existing knowledge) dominates the initial development of formal operational thought, and the world is perceived subjectively and idealistically. Later in adolescence, as intellectual balance is restored, these individuals accommodate (adjust to new information) to the cognitive upheaval that has occurred.

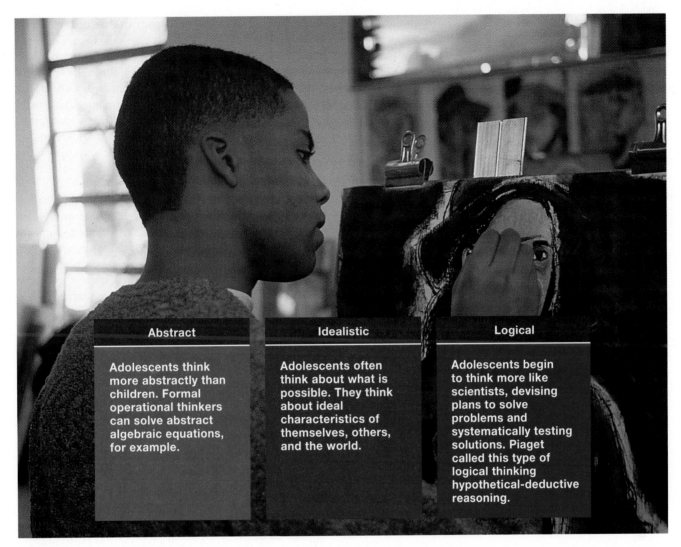

Abstract	Idealistic	Logical
Adolescents think more abstractly than children. Formal operational thinkers can solve abstract algebraic equations, for example.	Adolescents often think about what is possible. They think about ideal characteristics of themselves, others, and the world.	Adolescents begin to think more like scientists, devising plans to solve problems and systematically testing solutions. Piaget called this type of logical thinking hypothetical-deductive reasoning.

Figure **7.12**

Characteristics of Formal Operational Thought

Adolescents begin to think more as scientists think, devising plans to solve problems and systematically testing solutions. Piaget gave this type of thinking the imposing name *hypothetical-deductive reasoning.*

In addition to thinking more logically, abstractly, and idealistically, which characterize Piaget's formal operational thought stage, what other ways does adolescent cognition change? One important way involves adolescent egocentrism.

Adolescent Egocentrism   "Oh, my gosh! I can't believe it. Help! I can't stand it!" Tracy desperately yells. "What is wrong? What is the matter?" her mother asks. Tracy responds, "Everyone in here is looking at me." The mother queries, "Why?" Tracy says, "Look, this hair just won't stay in place," as she rushes to the rest room of the restaurant. Five minutes later, she returns to the table in the restaurant after she has depleted an entire can of hair spray.

During a conversation between two 14-year-old girls, the one named Margaret says, "Are you kidding, I won't get pregnant." And, 13-year-old Adam describes himself, "No one understands me, particularly my parents. They have no idea of what I am feeling."

Adolescent egocentrism *is the heightened self-consciousness of adolescents, which is reflected in adolescents' belief that others are as interested in them as the adolescents are in themselves, and in adolescents' sense of personal uniqueness and invulnerability.*

adolescent egocentrism
The heightened self-consciousness of adolescents, which is reflected in their belief that others are as interested in them as the adolescents are in themselves, and in adolescents' sense of personal uniqueness and vulnerability.

imaginary audience
An adolescent's belief that others are as preoccupied with her as she is.

personal fable
An adolescent's sense of personal uniqueness and indestructibility.

David Elkind (1978) believes that adolescent egocentrism can be dissected into two types of social thinking—imaginary audience and personal fable. The term **imaginary audience** *refers to the heightened self-consciousness of adolescents that is reflected in their belief that others are as interested in them as they themselves are. The imaginary audience involves attention-getting behavior—the attempt to be noticed, visible, and "on stage."* Tracy's comments and behavior above reflect the imaginary audience. Another adolescent might think that others are as aware of a small spot on his trousers as he is, possibly knowing that he has masturbated. Another adolescent, an eighth-grade girl, walks into her classroom and thinks that all eyes are riveted on her complexion. Adolescents especially sense that they are "on stage" in early adolescence, believing they are the main actors and all others are the audience.

According to Elkind, the **personal fable** *is the part of adolescent egocentrism involving an adolescent's sense of uniqueness.* The comments of Margaret and Adam above reflect the personal fable. Adolescents' sense of personal uniqueness makes them feel that no one can understand how they really feel. For example, an adolescent girl thinks that her mother cannot possibly sense the hurt she feels because her boyfriend has broken up with her. As part of their effort to retain a sense of personal uniqueness, adolescents might craft a story about the self that is filled with fantasy, immersing themselves in a world that is far removed from reality. Personal fables frequently show up in adolescent diaries.

Developmentalists have increasingly studied adolescent egocentrism in recent years. The research interest focuses on what the components of egocentrism really are, the nature of self-other relationships, the reasons egocentric thought emerges in adolescence, and the role of egocentrism in adolescent problems. For example, Elkind (1985) believes that adolescent egocentrism is brought about by formal operational thought. Others, however, argue that adolescent egocentrism is not entirely a cognitive phenomenon. Rather, they think the imaginary audience is due both to the ability to think hypothetically (formal operational thought) and to the ability to step outside oneself and anticipate the reactions of others in imaginative circumstances (perspective taking) (Lapsley, 1991).

Early and Late Formal Operational Thought

Formal operational thought has been conceptualized as occurring in two phases. In the first phase, the increased ability to think hypothetically produces unconstrained thoughts with unlimited possibilities. This early formal operational thought submerges reality (Broughton, 1983). Reality is overwhelmed. Idealism and possibility dominate. During the middle years of adolescence, an intellectual balance is restored; adolescents test the products of their reasoning against experience and develop a consolidation of formal operational thought.

Piaget's (1952) early writings seemed to indicate that the onset and consolidation of formal operational thought is completed during early adolescence, from about 12 to 15 years of age. Later, Piaget (1972) concluded that formal operational thought is not achieved until later in adolescence, between approximately 15 and 20 years of age.

Piaget's concepts of assimilation and accommodation help us understand the two phases of formal operational thought. Remember that *assimilation* occurs when adolescents incorporate new information into their existing knowledge; *accommodation* occurs when adolescents adjust to new information. During early adolescence, there is an excess of assimilation as the world is perceived too subjectively and idealistically. In the middle years of adolescence, an intellectual balance is restored, as the individual accommodates to the cognitive change that has taken place. In this view, the assimilation of formal operational thought marks the transition to adolescence; accommodation marks a later consolidation of thought (Lapsley, 1989).

Variations in Adolescent Cognition

Piaget's theory emphasizes universal and consistent patterns of formal operational thought; his

*T*hrough the Eyes of Psychologists

Daniel Keating,
University of Toronto

"In any consideration of adolescent cognition it is important to recognize the wide variation in performance among them."

theory does not adequately account for the unique differences that characterize the cognitive development of adolescents. These individual variations in adolescents' cognitive development have been documented in a number of investigations (Neimark, 1982).

Some individuals in early adolescence are formal operational thinkers; others are not. A review of formal operational thought investigations revealed that only about one of every three eighth-grade students is a formal operational thinker (Strahan, 1983). Some investigators have found that formal operational thought increases with age in adolescence (Martorano, 1977); others have not (Strahan, 1987). Many college students and adults do not think in formal operational ways, either. For example, investigators have found that from 17 percent to 67 percent of all college students think in formal operational ways (Elkind, 1961; Tomlinson-Keasey, 1972).

Many young adolescents are at the point of consolidating their concrete operational thought, using it more consistently than in childhood. At the same time, many young adolescents are just beginning to think in a formal operational manner. By late adolescence, many adolescents have begun to consolidate their formal operational thought, using it more consistently, and there often is variation across the content areas of formal operational thought, just as there is in concrete operational thought in childhood. A 14-year-old might reason at the formal operational level when it comes to analyzing algebraic equations but not do so with verbal problem solving or when reasoning about interpersonal relations.

Formal operational thought is more likely to be used in areas in which adolescents have the most experience and knowledge (Carey, 1988). Children and adolescents gradually build up elaborate knowledge through extensive experience and practice in various sports, games, hobbies, and school subjects such as math, English, and science. The development of expertise in different domains of life may make possible high-level, developmentally mature-looking thought. In some instances, the sophisticated reasoning of formal operational thought might be responsible. In other instances, however, the thought might be largely due to the accumulation of knowledge that allows more automatic, memory-based processes to function. Some developmentalists wonder if the acquisition of knowledge accounts for all cognitive growth. Most, however, argue that *both* cognitive changes in such areas as concrete and formal operational thought *and* the development of expertise through experience are at work in understanding the adolescent's cognitive world. More about the role of knowledge in the adolescent's thinking appears in the next chapter.

At this point we have studied a number of ideas about concrete operational and formal operational thought. A review of these ideas is presented in summary table 7.3.

Applying and Evaluating Piaget's Theory

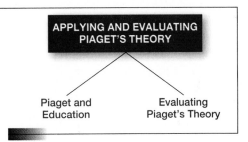

What are some applications of Piaget's theory to education? What are the main contributions and criticisms of Piaget's theory?

Piaget and Education

Piaget was not an educator and never pretended to be. However, he provided a sound conceptual framework from which to view learning and education. Following are some ideas in Piaget's theory that can be applied to teaching (Elkind, 1976; Heuwinkel, 1996):

1. *Take a constructivist approach.* In a constructivist vein, Piaget emphasized that children learn best when they are active and seek solutions for themselves. Piaget opposed teaching methods which imply that children are passive receptacles. The educational implication of Piaget's view is that, in all subjects, students

Piaget and Education

SUMMARY TABLE 7.3
Concrete Operational Thought and Formal Operational Thought

Concept	Processes/ Related Ideas	Characteristics/Description
Concrete Operational Thought	Its Nature	• This stage occurs roughly from 7 to 11 years of age. • It involves operations, conservation, classification, seriation, and transitivity. • Thought is not as abstract as later in development.
Formal Operational Thought	Characteristics	• Piaget believed that formal operational thought appears between 11 and 15 years of age. • Formal operational thought is more abstract, idealistic, and logical than concrete operational thought. • Piaget believes that adolescents become capable of engaging in hypothetical-deductive reasoning.
	Adolescent Egocentrism	• Adolescents develop a special kind of egocentrism that involves an imaginary audience and a personal fable about being unique and invulnerable.
	Early and Late Formal Operational Thought	• Formal operational thought has two phases—an assimilation phase in which reality is overwhelmed (early adolescence) and an accommodation phase in which intellectual balance is restored (late adolescence).
	Variations in Adolescent Cognition	• Piaget did not give adequate attention to individual variation in adolescent thinking. • Many young adolescents do not think in hypothetical-deductive ways but rather are consolidating their concrete operational thinking.

learn best by making discoveries, reflecting on them, and discussing them, rather than blindly imitating the teacher or doing things by rote.

2. *Facilitate rather than direct learning.* Effective teachers design situations that allow students to learn by doing. These situations promote students' thinking and discovery. Teachers listen, watch, and question students to help them gain better understanding. Don't just examine *what* students think and the product of their learning. Rather, carefully observe them as they find out *how* they think. Ask relevant questions to stimulate their thinking and ask them to explain their answers.

3. *Consider the child's knowledge and level of thinking.* Students do not come to class with empty heads. They have many ideas about the physical and natural world. They have concepts of space, time, quantity, and causality. These ideas differ from the ideas of adults. Teachers need to interpret what a student is saying and respond in a mode of discourse that is not too far from the student's level.

4. *Use ongoing assessment.* Individually constructed meanings cannot be measured by standardized tests. Evaluate students' progress with such tools as math and language portfolios (which contain work in progress as well as finished products), individual conferences in which students discuss their thinking strategies, and students' written and verbal explanations of their reasoning can be used to evaluate progress.

5. *Promote the student's intellectual health.* When Piaget came to lecture in the United States, he was asked, "What can I do to get my child to a higher cognitive stage sooner?" He was asked this question so often here compared with other countries that he called it the American question. For Piaget, children's learning

should occur naturally. Children should not be pushed and pressured into achieving too much too early in their development, before they are maturationally ready. Some parents spend long hours every day holding up large flash cards with words on them to improve their baby's vocabulary. In the Piagetian view, this is not the best way for infants to learn. It places too much emphasis on speeding up intellectual development, involves passive learning, and will not work.

6. *Turn the classroom into a setting of exploration and discovery.* What do actual classrooms look like when the teachers adopt Piaget's views? Several first- and second-grade math classrooms provide some good examples (Kamii, 1985, 1989). The teachers emphasize students' own exploration and discovery. The classrooms are less structured than what we think of as a typical classroom. Workbooks and predetermined assignments are not used. Rather, the teachers observe the students' interests and natural participation in activities to determine what the course of learning will be. For example, a math lesson might be constructed around counting the day's lunch money or dividing supplies among students. Often, games are prominently used in the classroom to stimulate mathematical thinking. For example, a version of dominoes teaches children about even-numbered combinations. A variation on tic-tac-toe involves replacing Xs and Os with numbers. Teachers encourage peer interaction during the lessons and games because students' different viewpoints can contribute to advances in thinking.

Through the Eyes of Psychologists

John Flavell, *Stanford University*

"We owe to Piaget the present field of cognitive development with its image of the developing child, who through its own active and creative commerce with its environment, builds an orderly succession of cognitive structures enroute to intellectual maturity."

Evaluating Piaget's Theory

What were Piaget's main contributions? Has his theory withstood the test of time?

Contributions   Piaget was a giant in the field of developmental psychology, the founder of the present field of children's cognitive development. Psychologists owe him a long list of masterful concepts of enduring power and fascination: assimilation, accommodation, object permanence, egocentrism, conservation, and others. Psychologists also owe him the current vision of children as active, constructive thinkers (Vidal, 2000).

Piaget also was a genius when it came to observing children. His careful observations showed us inventive ways to discover how children act on and adapt to their world. Piaget showed us some important things to look for in cognitive development, such as the shift from preoperational to concrete operational thinking. He also showed us how children need to make their experiences fit their schemas (cognitive frameworks) yet simultaneously adapt their schemas to experience. Piaget also revealed how cognitive change is likely to occur if the context is structured to allow gradual movement to the next higher level and that a concept does not emerge suddenly, full-blown but, rather, through a series of partial accomplishments that lead to increasingly comprehensive understanding (Haith & Benson, 1998).

Criticisms   Piaget's theory has not gone unchallenged. Questions are raised about his estimates of children's competence at different developmental levels; his view of stages; his ideas about the training of children to reason at higher levels; and his downplayed views of culture and education.

• *Estimates of children's competence.* Some cognitive abilities emerge earlier than Piaget thought (Meltzoff, 2000). For example, as previously noted, some aspects of object permanence emerge earlier than he believed. Even 2-year-olds are nonegocentric in some contexts. When they realize that another person will not see an object, they investigate whether the person is blindfolded or looking in a different direction. Conservation of number has been demonstrated as early as age 3, although Piaget did not think it emerged until 7. Young children are not

Jean Piaget, the main architect of the field of cognitive development, at age 27.

Piaget with his wife and three children; he often used his observations of his children to provide examples of his theory.

neo-Piagetians
Developmentalists who have elaborated on Piaget's theory, believing that children's cognitive development is more specific in many respects than he thought.

Challenges to Piaget

as uniformly "pre-" this and "pre-" that (precausal, preoperational) as Piaget thought. Other cognitive abilities also can emerge later than Piaget thought. Many adolescents still think in concrete operational ways or are just beginning to master formal operations. Even many adults are not formal operational thinkers. In sum, recent theoretical revisions highlight more cognitive competencies of infants and young children and more cognitive shortcomings of adolescents and adults (Flavell, Miller, & Miller, 1993).

• *Stages.* Piaget conceived of stages as unitary structures of thought. Thus, his theory assumes developmental synchrony; that is, various aspects of a stage should emerge at the same time. However, some concrete operational concepts do not appear in synchrony. For example, children do not learn to conserve at the same time they learn to cross-classify. Thus, most contemporary developmentalists agree that children's cognitive development is not as stagelike as Piaget thought.

• *The training of children to reason at higher levels.* Some children who are at one cognitive stage (such as preoperational) can be trained to reason at a higher cognitive stage (such as concrete operational). This poses a problem for Piaget's theory. He argued that such training is only superficial and ineffective, unless the child is at a maturational transition point between the stages (Gelman & Williams, 1998).

• *Culture and education.* Culture and education exert stronger influences on children's development than Piaget believed (Gelman & Brenneman, 1994). The age at which children acquire conservation skills is related to the extent to which their culture provides relevant practice. An outstanding teacher and education in the logic of math and science can promote concrete and formal operational thought.

Still, some developmental psychologists believe we should not throw out Piaget altogether. These **neo-Piagetians** *argue that Piaget got some things right but that his theory needs considerable revision. In their revision of Piaget, more emphasis is given to how children process information through attention, memory, and strategy use* (Case, 1987, 1999). They especially believe that a more accurate vision of children's thinking requires more emphasis on strategies, the speed at which children process information, the particular cognitive task involved, and the division of cognitive problems into smaller, more precise steps.

Now that we have examined Piaget's ideas about how children think, we will turn to the ideas of another important theorist, Lev Vygotsky.

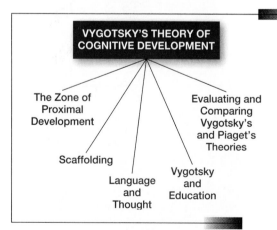

Vygotsky's Theory of Cognitive Development

In chapter 2, we described the basic principles of Vygotsky's theory (Tappan, 1998): (1) The child's cognitive skills can be understood only when they are developmentally analyzed and interpreted; (2) cognitive skills are mediated by words, language, and forms of discourse, which serve as psychological tools for facilitating and transforming mental activity; and (3) cognitive skills have their origins in social relations and are embedded in a sociocultural background ◀ P. 36. Here we expand on Vygotsky's theory of development, beginning with his unique ideas about the zone of proximal development.

The Zone of Proximal Development

zone of proximal development (ZPD)
Vygotsky's term for the range of tasks that are too difficult for children to master alone but that can be mastered with the guidance and assistance of adults or more highly skilled children.

Zone of proximal development (ZPD) *is Vygotsky's term for the range of tasks too difficult for children to master alone but which can be learned with the guidance and assistance of adults or more-skilled children.* Thus, the lower limit of the ZPD is the level of problem solving reached by the child working independently. The upper limit is the level of additional responsibility the child can accept with the assistance of an able instructor (see figure 7.13). Vygotsky's emphasis on the ZPD underscores his belief in the importance of social influences, especially instruction, on children's cognitive development.

The ZPD captures the child's cognitive skills that are in the process of maturing and can be accomplished only with the assistance of a more skilled person (Kozulin, 2000; Panofsky, 1999). Vygotsky (1962) called these the "buds" or "flowers" of development, to distinguish them from the "fruits" of development, which the child already can accomplish independently.

Scaffolding

Closely linked to the idea of zone of proximal development is the concept of **scaffolding.** *Scaffolding means changing the level of support. Over the course of a teaching session, a more skilled person (teacher or more advanced peer of the child) adjusts the amount of guidance to fit the student's current performance level.* When the task the student is learning is new, the more skilled person may use direct instruction. As the student's competence increases, less guidance is given.

Dialogue is an important tool of scaffolding in the zone of proximal development (Tappan, 1998). Vygotsky viewed children as having rich but unsystematic, disorganized, and spontaneous concepts. These meet with the skilled helper's more systematic, logical, and rational concepts. As a result of the meeting and dialogue between the child and the skilled helper, the child's concept become more systematic, logical, and rational.

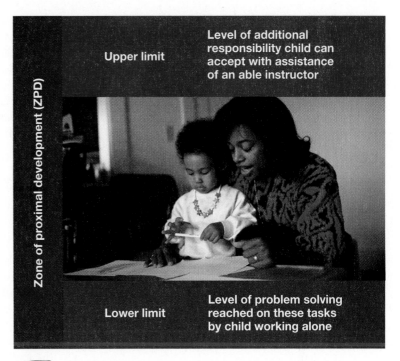

Figure 7.13
Vygotsky's Zone of Proximal Development
Vygotsky's zone of proximal development has a lower limit and an upper limit. Tasks in the ZPD are too difficult for the child to perform alone. They require assistance from an adult or a more-skilled child. As children experience the verbal instruction or demonstration, they organize the information in their existing mental structures, so they can eventually perform the skill or task alone.

scaffolding
Changing the level of support over the course of a teaching session in which a more-skilled individual (teacher or more advanced peer of the child) adjusts the amount of guidance to fit the child's current performance level.

Vygotsky on Language and Thought

Language and Thought

Vygotsky (1962) believed that young children use language not only for social communication but also to plan, guide, and monitor their behavior in a self-regulatory fashion. The use of language for self-regulation is called inner speech or private speech. For Piaget private speech is egocentric and immature, but for Vygotsky it is an important tool of thought during the early childhood years.

Vygotsky believed that language and thought initially develop independently of each other and then merge. He said that all mental functions have external, or social, origins. Children must use language to communicate with others before they can focus inward on their own thoughts. Children also must communicate externally and use language for a long period of time before the transition from external to internal speech takes place. This transition period occurs between the ages of 3 and 7 years of age and involves talking to oneself. After a while, the self-talk becomes second nature to children, and they can act without verbalizing. When this occurs, children have internalized their egocentric speech in the form of inner speech, which becomes their thoughts. Vygotsky believed that children who use a lot of private speech are more socially competent than those who don't. He argued that private speech represents an early transition in becoming more socially communicative.

Lev Vygotsky (1896–1934), shown here with his daughter, believed that children's cognitive development is advanced through social interaction with skilled individuals embedded in a sociocultural backdrop.

Vygotsky's view challenged Piaget's ideas on language and thought. Vygotsky said that language, even in its earliest forms, is socially based (Kozulin, 2000). By contrast, Piaget emphasized young children's egocentric and nonsocial speech. For Vygotsky, when young children talk to themselves, they are using language to govern their behavior and guide themselves. Piaget believed that such self-talk reflects immaturity. However, researchers have found support for Vygotsky's view of the positive role of private speech in children's development (Winsler, Diaz, & Montero, 1997).

Vygotsky and Education

Following are some ways that Vygotsky's theory can be incorporated in the classroom:

1. *Use the child's zone of proximal development in teaching.* Teaching should begin toward the zone's upper limit, where the child is able to reach the goal only through close collaboration with the instructor. With adequate continuing instruction and practice, the child organizes and masters the behavioral sequences required to perform the target skill. As the instruction continues, the performance transfers from the teacher to the child. The teacher gradually reduces the explanations, hints, and demonstrations until the student is able to perform the skill alone. Once the goal is achieved, it may become the foundation for the development of a new ZPD.

2. *Use scaffolding.* Look for opportunities to use scaffolding when children need help with self-initiated learning activities (Elicker, 1996). Also use scaffolding to help children move to a higher level of skill and knowledge. Offer just enough assistance. You might ask, "What can I do to help you?" Or simply observe the child's intentions and attempts, smoothly providing support when needed. When the child hesitates, offer encouragement. And encourage the child to practice the skill. You may watch and appreciate the child's practice or offer support when the child forgets what to do.

3. *Use more-skilled peers as teachers.* It is not just adults that Vygotsky believed are important in helping children learn important skills. Children also benefit from the support and guidance of more-skilled children.

4. *Monitor and encourage children's use of private speech.* Be aware of the developmental change from externally talking to oneself when solving a problem during the preschool years to privately talking to oneself in the early elementary school years. In the elementary school years, encourage children to internalize and self-regulate their talk to themselves.

5. *Asses the child's ZPD, not IQ.* Like Piaget, Vygotsky did not believe that formal, standardized tests are the best way to assess children's learning. Rather, Vygotsky argued that assessment should focus on determining the child's zone of proximal development. The skilled helper presents the child with tasks of varying difficulty to determine the best level at which to begin instruction. The ZPD is a measure of learning potential. IQ, also a measure of learning potential, emphasizes that intelligence is a property of the child. By contrast, ZPD emphasizes that learning is interpersonal. It is inappropriate to say that the child *has* a ZPD. Rather, a child *shares* a ZPD with a more-skilled individual.

6. *Transform the classroom with Vygotskian ideas.* What does a Vygotskian classroom look like? The Kamehameha Elementary Education Program (KEEP) is based on Vygotsky's theory (Tharp, 1994). The zone of proximal development is the key element of instruction in this program. Children might read a story and then interpret its meaning. Many of the learning activities take place in small groups. All children spend at least 20 minutes each morning in an activity setting called "Center One." In this context, scaffolding is used to improve children's literary skills. The instructor asks questions, responds to students' queries, and builds on the ideas that students generate. Thousands of low-income children have attended KEEP public schools in Hawaii, on an Arizona Navajo Indian reservation, and in Los Angeles. Compared with a control group of non-KEEP children, the KEEP children participate more actively in classroom discussion, are more attentive in class, and have higher reading achievement (Tharp & Gallimore, 1988).

Through the Eyes of Psychologists

Barbara Rogoff, *University of California–Santa Cruz*

"Cognitive development occurs as new generations collaborate with older generations in varying forms of interpersonal engagement and institutional practices."

Evaluating and Comparing Vygotsky's and Piaget's Theories

Vygotsky's theory became known later than Piaget's theory, so it has not yet been evaluated as thoroughly. However, Vygotsky's theory already has been embraced by many teachers and has been successfully applied to education. His view of the importance of sociocultural influences on children's development fits with the current belief that it is important to evaluate contextual factors in learning (Gojdamascho, 1999). To read further about some strategies for working with children that have ties to Vygotsky's views on culture, see Explorations in Child Development. Criticisms of Vygotsky's approach have surfaced. For example, some critics say that he overemphasizes the role of language in thinking.

We already have mentioned several comparisons of Vygotsky's and Piaget's theories, such as Vygotsky's emphasis on the importance of inner speech in development and Piaget's view that such speech is immature. We also said earlier that both Vygotsky's and Piaget's theories are constructivist, emphasizing that children actively construct knowledge and understanding, rather than being passive receptacles.

Although both theories are constructivist, Vygotsky's is a **social constructivist approach,** *which emphasizes the social contexts of learning and the fact that knowledge is mutually built and constructed.* Moving from Piaget to Vygotsky, the conceptual shift is from the individual to collaboration, social interaction, and sociocultural activity (Rogoff, 1998). For Piaget, children construct knowledge by transforming, organizing, and reorganizing previous knowledge. For Vygotsky, children construct knowledge through social interaction with others (Hogan & Tudge, 1999). The implication of Piaget's theory for teaching is that children need support to explore their world and discover knowledge. The main implication of Vygotsky's theory for teaching is that students need many opportunities to learn with the teacher and more-skilled peers. In both Piaget's and Vygotsky's theories, teachers serve as facilitators and guides, rather than as directors and molders of learning. Figure 7.14 compares Vygotsky's and Piaget's theories.

At this point we have studied many ideas about the theories of Piaget and Vygotsky. A review of these ideas is presented in summary table 7.4.

Lev Vygotsky: Revolutionary Scientist

Vygotsky Links

Scaffolding

Cognitive Apprenticeship

social constructivist approach
Emphasizes the social contexts of learning and that knowledge is mutually built and constructed.

EXPLORATIONS IN CHILD DEVELOPMENT
Apprenticeship Training

BARBARA ROGOFF (1990, 1998) believes that children's cognitive development is an apprenticeship that occurs through participation in social activity, guided by companions who stretch and support children's understanding of and skill in using the "tools" of the culture. Some of the technologies that are important tools for handling information in a culture are (1) language systems that organize categories of reality and structure ways of approaching situations, (2) literate practices to record information and transform it through written exercises, (3) mathematical systems that handle numerical and spatial problems, and (4) memory strategies to preserve information in memory over time. Some of these technologies have material supports, such as pencil and paper, word-processing programs, alphabets, calculators, abacus and slide rule, notches on sticks, and knots on ropes. These tools provide a mechanism for transmitting information from one generation to the next.

In presenting her ideas on apprenticeship in thinking, Rogoff draws heavily on Vygotsky's theory. Rogoff argues that guided participation is widely used around the world, but with important variations in activities for and communication with children in different cultures. The most salient differences focus on the goals of development—what lessons are to be learned—and the means available for children either to observe and participate in culturally important activities or to receive instruction outside the context of skilled activity (Morelli, Rogoff, & Angelillo, 1992).

The general processes of guided participation appear around the world. Caregivers and children arrange children's activities and revise children's responsibilities as they gain skill and knowledge. With guidance, children participate in cultural activities that socialize them into skilled activities. For example, Mayan mothers in Guatemala help their daughters learn to weave in a process of guided participation. In the United States and in many other nations, the development of prominent and creative thinkers is promoted through interaction with a knowledgeable person as well as by studying books and attending classes and exhibits.

Children begin to practice the skills for using cultural tools, such as literacy, even before the children have contact with the technology. For example, most middle-class American parents involve their children in extensive conversation long before they go to kindergarten or elementary school, and they provide their young children with picture books and read stories to them at bedtime as part of their daily routine. Most middle-class American parents embed their children in a way of life in which reading and writing are integral parts of communication, recreation, and livelihood (Rogoff, 1990).

By contrast, consider the practices of two communities whose children have trouble reading (Heath, 1989). Parents in an Appalachian mill town taught their children respect for the written word but did not involve book characters or information in the children's everyday lives. Their children did well in the first several years of learning to read but had difficulty when required to *use* these literate skills to express themselves or interpret text. Children of rural origin in another mill town learned the skillful and creative use of language but were not taught about books or the style of communication and language used in school. These children had difficulty learning to read, which kept them from using their creative skills with language in the school setting. Early childhood in both of these communities did not include school-style reading and writing in the context of daily life and, not surprisingly, the children experienced difficulties with literacy in school.

In sum, Rogoff argues that guided participation—the participation of children in skilled cultural activities with other people of varying levels of skill and status—is an important aspect of children's development.

At about 7 years of age, Mayan girls in Guatemala are assisted in beginning to learn to weave a simple belt, with the loom already set up for them. The young girl shown here is American developmental psychologist Barbara Rogoff's daughter, being taught to weave by a Mayan woman.

Topic	Vygotsky	Piaget
Constructivism	Social constructivist	Cognitive constructivist
Stages	No general stages of development proposed	Strong emphasis on stages (sensorimotor, preoperational, concrete operational, and formal operational)
Key processes	Zone of proximal development, language, dialogue, tools of the culture	Schema, assimilation, accommodation, operations, conservation, classification, hypothetical-deductive reasoning
Role of language	A major role; language plays a powerful role in shaping thought	Language has a minimal role; cognition primarily directs language
View on education	Education plays a central role, helping children learn the tools of the culture.	Education merely refines the child's cognitive skills that already have emerged.
Teaching implications	Teacher is a facilitator and guide, not a director; establish many opportunities for children to learn with the teacher and more-skilled peers	Also views teacher as a facilitator and guide, not a director; provide support for children to explore their world and discover knowledge

Figure **7.14**

Comparison of Vygotsky's and Piaget's Theories

SUMMARY TABLE 7.4
Applying and Evaluating Piaget's Theory; Vygotsky's Theory of Cognitive Development

Concept	Processes/ Related Ideas	Characteristics/Description
Applying and Evaluating Piaget's Theory	Piaget and Education	• Piaget was not an educator, but his constructivisit views have been applied to teaching.
	Contributions and Criticisms	• We owe to Piaget the field of cognitive development, he was a genius at observing children, and he gave us a number of masterful concepts. • Critics question his estimates of competence at different developmental levels, his stage concept, and other ideas. • Neo-Piagetians believe that children's cognition is more specific than Piaget thought.
Vygotsky's Theory of Cognitive Development	The Zone of Proximal Development (ZPD)	• This is Vygotsky's term for the range of tasks that are too difficult for children to master alone but that can be learned with the guidance and assistance of more-skilled adults and peers.
	Scaffolding	• Scaffolding involves changing support over the course of a teaching session, with the more-skilled person adjusting guidance to fit the child's current performance level. • Dialogue is an important aspect of scaffolding.
	Language and Thought	• Vygotsky believed that language plays a key role in cognition. • Language and thought initially develop independently, but then children internalize their egocentric speech in the form of inner speech, which becomes their thoughts. • This transition to inner speech occurs from 3 to 7 years of age. • Vygotsky's view contrasts with Piaget's view that young children's speech is immature and egocentric.
	Vygotsky and Education	• Applications to education include using the child's zone of proximal development, using scaffolding, monitoring and encouraging children's use of private speech, assessing the ZPD instead of IQ, and transforming the classroom with Vygotskian ideas.
	Evaluating and Comparing Vygotsky's and Piaget's Theories	• Vygotsky's view increasingly has been applied to education. • Especially important are Vygotsky's ideas related to sociocultural influences on children's development. • Some critics say Vygotsky overestimated the role of the language. • Comparison of Vygotsky's and Piaget's theories involves constructivism, stages, key processes, role of language, views on education, and teaching implications.

Chapter Review

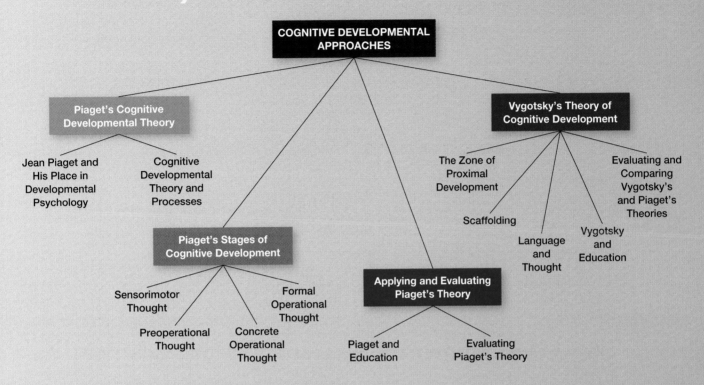

Key Terms

Key Terms

assimilation 205
accommodation 205
organization 205
equilibration 205
scheme (schema) 207
simple reflexes 207
first habits and primary circular reactions 207
primary circular reaction 207
secondary circular reactions 207
coordination of secondary circular reactions 207

tertiary circular reactions, novelty, and curiosity 208
tertiary circular reactions 208
internalization of schemes 208
object permanence 208
AB error 209
operations 211
symbolic function substage 211
egocentrism 211
animism 212
intuitive thought substage 212
centration 213

conservation 213
horizontal décalage 218
seriation 218
transitivity 218
hypothetical-deductive reasoning 220
adolescent egocentrism 221
imaginary audience 222
personal fable 222
neo-Piagetians 226
zone of proximal development (ZPD) 226
scaffolding 227
social constructivist approach 229

Key People

Key People

Jean Piaget 204
Renée Baillargeon 210
Marshall Haith 210
Barbel Inhelder 212

Rochel Gelman 205, 214
David Elkind 222
Daniel Keating 222
John Flavell 225

Lev Vygotsky 226
Barbara Rogoff 229, 230

Child Development Resources

Resources

The First Three Years of Life
(1990, rev. ed.) by Burton White.
New York: Prentice Hall.

The First Three Years of Life presents a broad-based approach to how parents can optimally rear their infants and young children. White strongly believes that most parents in America fail to provide an adequate intellectual and social foundation for their child's development, especially between the ages of 8 months and 3 years.

Raising Kids Who Want to Learn
Sesame Street
P.O. Box 40
Vernon, NH 07462

This 220-page book gives parents practical strategies for encouraging their children to learn without pushing them.

Taking It to the Net

1. Francesca is surveying Time magazine's list of the top 100 people of the twentieth century. She notices that Piaget made the list. Why would Piaget be on the list?

2. Ellen is majoring in interdisciplinary studies. She is preparing a report on famous thinkers who engaged in cross-disciplinary study and teaching and how this influenced their theories. She has heard that Piaget was adept at several disciplines. She wants to know what they were and how they might have influenced his theory of cognitive development.

3. Theo has to write a compare-and-contrast paper for his English class. His teacher has encouraged the class to write about something they are studying in another class. Theo thinks it would be interesting to compare and contrast Vygotsky's and Piaget's theories of cognitive development. Would a paper on their beliefs about how culture influences cognitive development be a good choice?

Connect to *http://www.mhhe.com/santrockc9* to find the answers!

Chapter 8

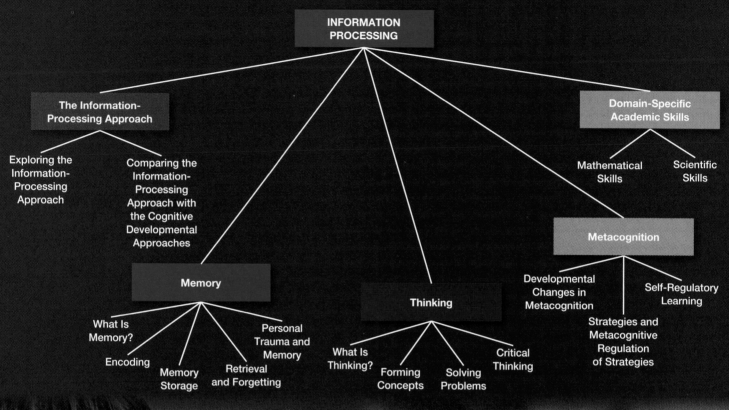

INFORMATION PROCESSING

The Information-Processing Approach

- Exploring the Information-Processing Approach
- Comparing the Information-Processing Approach with the Cognitive Developmental Approaches

Memory

- What Is Memory?
- Encoding
- Memory Storage
- Retrieval and Forgetting
- Personal Trauma and Memory

Thinking

- What Is Thinking?
- Forming Concepts
- Solving Problems
- Critical Thinking

Domain-Specific Academic Skills

- Mathematical Skills
- Scientific Skills

Metacognition

- Developmental Changes in Metacognition
- Strategies and Metacognitive Regulation of Strategies
- Self-Regulatory Learning

Information Processing

The Story of Laura Bickford

LAURA BICKFORD is a master teacher and chairs the English Department at Nordoff High School in Ojai, California. She recently spoke about how she encourages her students to think:

I believe the call to teach is a call to teach students how to think. In encouraging critical thinking, literature itself does a good bit of work for us but we still have to be guides. We have to ask good questions. We have to show students the value in asking their own questions, in having discussions and conversations. In addition to reading and discussing literature, the best way to move students to think critically is to have them write. We write all the time in a variety of modes: journals, formal essays, letters, factual reports, news articles, speeches, or other formal oral presentations. We have to show students where they merely scratch the surface in their thinking and writing. I call these moments "hits and runs." When I see this "hit and run" effort, I draw a window on the paper. I tell them it is a "window of opportunity" to go deeper, elaborate, and clarify. Many students don't do this kind of thinking until they are prodded to do so.

I also use metacognitive strategies all the time—that is, helping students know about knowing. These include: asking students to comment on their learning after we have finished particular pieces of projects and asking them to discuss in advance what we might be seeking to learn as we *begin* a new project or activity. I also ask them to keep reading logs so they can observe their own thinking as it happens. For example, they might copy a passage from a reading selection and comment on it. Studying a passage from J. D. Salinger's *A Catcher in the Rye*, a student might write: "I've never thought about life the way that Holden Caulfield does. Maybe I see the world differently than he does. He always is so depressed. I'm not depressed. Salinger is good at showing us someone who is usually depressed. How does he manage to do that?" In addition, I ask students to comment on their own learning by way of grading themselves. This year a student gave me one of the most insightful lines about her growth as a reader I have ever seen from a student. She wrote, "I no longer think in a monotone when I'm reading." I don't know if she grasps the magnitude of that thought or how it came to be that she made that change. It is magic when students see themselves growing like this.

*T*he mind is an
enchanting thing.

Marianne Moore
American Poet, 20th Century

237

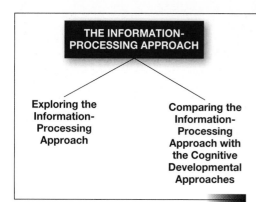

THE INFORMATION-PROCESSING APPROACH

Exploring the Information-Processing Approach

Comparing the Information-Processing Approach with the Cognitive Developmental Approaches

information-processing approach
The approach that focuses on the ways children process information about their world—how they manipulate information, monitor it, and strategize about it.

Strategies

encoding
The mechanism by which information gets into memory.

automaticity
The ability to process information with little or no effort.

strategy construction
The process of discovering a new procedure for processing information.

generalization
Generalizing or applying information to other problems or situations. This also has been discussed in the context of transfer.

metacognition
Cognition about cognition, or "knowing about knowing."

The Information-Processing Approach

What are some of the basic ideas in the information-processing approach? How is it similar to and different from the cognitive developmental approaches we described in chapter 7? ◀▥ P. 204.

Exploring the Information-Processing Approach

The **information-processing approach** *focuses on the ways children process information about their world—how they manipulate the information, monitor it, and strategize about it.* Central to this approach are the processes of memory and thinking. According to the information-processing approach, children develop a gradually increasing capacity for processing information, which allows them to acquire increasingly complex knowledge and skills (Stevenson, Hofer, & Randel, 1999) ◀▥ P. 38.

Leading theorist and researcher Robert Siegler (1998) described three main characteristics of information processing according to this approach:

- *Thinking.* In Siegler's view, thinking is information processing. In this regard, Siegler presents a broad perspective on thinking. He says that when children perceive, encode, represent, store, and retrieve information from the world, they are engaging in thinking. Siegler believes that thinking is highly flexible, allowing individuals to adapt to and adjust to changes in circumstances, task requirements, and goals. However, our remarkable thinking abilities have some constraints. Individuals can attend to only a limited amount of information at one point in time. Also, we are constrained by how fast we can process information, a challenge for children that we will explore later in the chapter.
- *Change mechanisms.* Siegler (2000) argues that in studying information processing, the main focus should be on the role that mechanisms of change play in development. He believes that four main mechanisms work together to create changes in children's cognitive skills: encoding, automatization, strategy construction, and generalization. **Encoding** *is the mechanism by which information gets into memory.* Siegler states that a key aspect of solving problems is the ability to encode relevant information and ignore irrelevant information.
- *Automaticity.* The term **automaticity** *refers to the ability to process information with little or no effort.* With age and experience, information processing becomes increasingly automatic on many tasks, allowing children to detect connections among ideas and events they otherwise would miss. The third and fourth change mechanisms are strategy construction and generalization. **Strategy construction** *involves the discovery of a new procedure for processing information.* Siegler says that children need to encode key information about a problem and coordinate the information with relevant prior knowledge to solve the problem (Chen & Siegler, 2000; Siegler, 2000). **Generalization** *involves generalizing or applying information to other problems or situations* (Crowley & Siegler, 1999).
- *Self-modification.* The information-processing approach also emphasizes self-modification. That is, children play an active role in their own development. They use knowledge and strategies that they have learned in previous circumstances to adapt their responses to a new learning situation. In this manner, children build newer and more sophisticated responses from their established knowledge and strategies. An important facet of self-modification is **metacognition,** *which means cognition about cognition, or "knowing about knowing"* (Flavell, 1999; Flavell & Miller, 1998). We will study metacognition toward the end of this chapter and especially will emphasize how children's self-awareness can enable them to adapt and manage their strategies during thinking and problem solving.

SUMMARY TABLE 8.1
The Information-Processing Approach

Concept	Processes/ Related Ideas	Characteristics/Description
Exploring the Information-Processing Approach	Its Nature	• This approach emphasizes that children manipulate information, monitor it, and strategize about it.
	Siegler's View	• Siegler described 3 main characteristics of the information-processing approach: (1) thinking, (2) change mechanisms (include encoding, automaticity, strategy construction, and generalization, and (3) self-modification.
Comparing the Information-Processing Approach with the Cognitive Developmental Approaches	Comparisons	• Both the information-processing and cognitive developmental approaches try to identify children's cognitive capacities and limits at various points in development. • The information-processing approach places more emphasis on processing limitations, strategies for overcoming limitations, knowledge about specific content, and precise analysis of change. • Piaget's theory underscores the importance of cognitive stages and Vygotsky's theory the social construction of knowledge, while the information-processing approach does not.

Comparing the Information-Processing Approach with the Cognitive Developmental Approaches

The information-processing and cognitive developmental approaches have quite a bit in common. Both try to identify children's cognitive capabilities and limits at various points in development. Both try to describe ways in which children do and do not understand important concepts at different points in life and try to explain how later, more advanced understandings grow out of earlier, more primitive ones. Both also emphasize the impact that existing understandings can have on children's ability to acquire new understandings.

However, the two approaches differ in some important ways. The information-processing approach places greater emphasis on the role of processing limitations, strategies for overcoming the limitations, and knowledge about specific content. It also focuses on more precise analysis of change and on the contribution of ongoing cognitive activity to that change. These differences have led to a greater use of formal descriptions, such as computer simulations and flow diagrams, that allow information-processing theorists to determine in detail how thinking proceeds.

The information-processing approach does not describe cognition as unfolding in stages like Piaget did ◀▥ P. 35. Rather, for information-processing psychologists, development is more continuous. Also, for information-processing psychologists, children socially construct knowledge to a lesser degree than Vygotsky suggests.

At this point we have introduced the information-processing approach and compared it with the cognitive developmental approaches. These ideas are reviewed in summary table 8.1. Next, we will turn our attention to some of the main areas of children's information processing, beginning with memory.

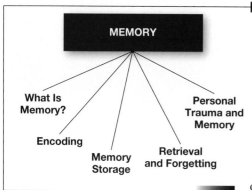

Memory Links

memory
The retention of information over time, involving encoding, storage, and retrieval.

storage
The retention of information over time.

retrieval
Taking information out of storage.

attention
Concentrating and focusing mental resources.

Memory

Twentieth-century playwright Tennessee Williams once commented that life is all memory except for that one present moment that goes by so quickly that you can hardly catch it going. But just what is memory?

What Is Memory?

Memory *is the retention of information over time and involves encoding, storage, and retrieval. Encoding* is the mechanism by which information gets into memory. **Storage** *consists of the retention of information over time.* And **retrieval** *takes place when information is taken out of storage.* Memory anchors the self in continuity. Without memory children would not be able to connect what happened to them yesterday with what is going on in their lives today. Contemporary developmentalists and educators emphasize that it is important not to view memory in terms of how children add something to it but rather underscore how children actively construct their memory (Mayer, 1999; Schneider & Bjorklund, 1998). Thinking about memory in terms of encoding, storage, and retrieval should help you to understand it better (see figure 8.1).

Encoding

Encoding clearly is a critical process for memory (Craik & Brown, 2000). We will explore a number of aspects of encoding, beginning with attention.

Attention   In everyday language, encoding has much in common with attention and learning. When a child is listening to a teacher, watching a movie, listening to music, or talking with a friend, he or she is encoding information into memory. Although children can perform some activities automatically, many others require them to pay **attention**, *which refers to concentrating and focusing mental resources.* One critical skill in paying attention is doing it *selectively*. As the teacher gives instructions for completing a task, students need to pay attention to what she is saying and not be distracted by other students who are talking. As students study for a test, they need to focus selectively on the book they are reading and tune out or eliminate other stimuli, such as the sound of a television. In one research study, 8-year-old children tended to use exhaustive attentional searches to find information, whereas 11-year-olds used more selective attentional strategies in searching for information (Davidson, 1996).

Being able to *shift* from one activity to another when called for is another challenge related to attention. For example, learning to write good stories requires shifting among the competing tasks of forming letters, composing grammar, structuring paragraphs, and conveying the story as a whole. Older children and adolescents are better than younger children at shifting attention when it is required.

Another problem for many young children is that they focus too much on the attention-grabbing aspects of a task or situation rather than on what is important. That is, they focus more on the *salient* aspects of the situation than on the *relevant* aspects. For example, if a clown is giving directions for solving a problem on a video display, preschoolers often focus more on the clown's attention-grabbing appearance than on the instructions he is giving. Researchers have found that by the middle of elementary school, children are better at focusing their attention on the relevant dimensions of a task (Paris & Lindauer, 1982). This change often signals greater reflection and less impulsive-

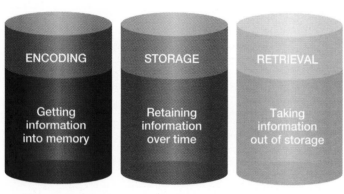

Figure 8.1
Processing Information in Memory
As you read about the many aspects of memory in this chapter, it should help you to think about the organization of memory in terms of these three main activities.

ness. Of course, there are individual differences in attention, and some elementary school children need help in attending to the relevant dimensions of a task.

One reason older children are better than younger children at deploying attention is that they are more likely to construct a plan of action to guide their attentional efforts when they are trying to solve a problem. However, younger children often can use attention-focusing strategies when such strategies are provided to them. Possibly school experiences help children become more aware of their own attentional capabilities; or as children develop, perhaps they come to understand that their mind works best when it is active and constructive (Lovett & Pillow, 1996). Thus, attending to something relevant is an active, effortful process that draws on mental resources rather than a passive process of receiving the available information.

Habituation, Dishabituation, and Infant Memory

If a stimulus—a sight or sound—is presented to infants several times in a row, they usually pay less attention to it each time. This suggests they become bored with it. This is the process of **habituation**—*repeated presentation of the same stimulus that causes reduced attention to the stimulus.* **Dishabituation** *is an infant's renewed interest in a stimulus.* Among the measures researchers use to study whether habituation is occurring are sucking behavior (sucking behavior stops when the young infant attends to a novel object), heart and respiration rates, and the length of time the infant looks at an object. Newborn infants can habituate to repetitive stimulation in virtually every stimulus modality—vision, hearing, touch, and so on (Rovee-Collier, 1987). However, habituation becomes more acute over the first three months of life. The extensive assessment of habituation in recent years has resulted in its use as a measure of an infant's maturity and well-being. Infants who have brain damage or have suffered birth traumas, such as lack of oxygen, do not habituate well and may later have developmental and learning problems.

The usefulness of the habituation paradigm for studying infant memory is evident in studies of individual differences in infants. Infants who are destined to have higher IQs when they are 6 to 9 years of age habituate more rapidly as 6-month-olds, and dishabituate more completely in response to new stimuli, than do infants destined to have lower IQs (Bornstein & Sigman, 1986). This link might reflect more-intelligent infants' encoding stimuli more effectively and thus recognizing earlier that they have seen a certain stimulus but that they have not seen the new, somewhat different stimulus presented in the dishabituation trials.

In one study of habituation, Carolyn Rovee-Collier (1987) placed a baby in a crib underneath an elaborate mobile, tied one of the baby's ankles to the mobile with a ribbon, then observed as the baby kicked to make the mobile move. Weeks later, the baby was returned to the crib, under the mobile, but its foot was not tied to the mobile. The baby tried to move the mobile again by kicking its foot, apparently remembering the earlier effects of its kicking (see figure 8.2). However, if the mobile's configuration is changed even slightly, the baby does not kick at it. Then as soon as the familiar and expected configuration is brought back into the context, the baby remembers and begins kicking.

In another study, infants were laid in large black boxes where they looked up at television screens and viewed a sequence of colorful objects (Canfield & Haith, 1991). The babies' eye movements were monitored with an infrared camera linked to a computer. After only five tries the babies anticipated where the next object would appear. With just a little more practice, they predicted a four-step sequence, and most could remember it up to 2 weeks later!

*M*an is the only animal that can be bored.

Erich Fromm
American Psychotherapist, 20th Century

habituation
Repeated presentation of the same stimulus, which causes reduced attention to the stimulus.

dishabituation
Renewed interest in a stimulus.

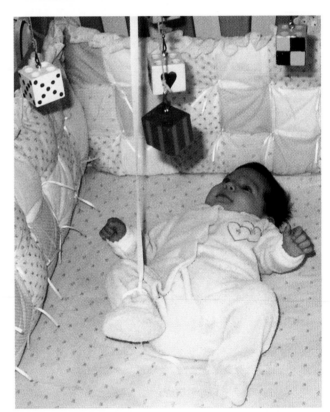

Figure 8.2

The Technique Used in Rovee-Collier's Investigation of Infant Memory

The mobile is connected to the infant's ankle by a ribbon and moves in direct proportion to the frequency and vigor of the infant's kicks. This infant is in a reinforcement period. During this period, the infant can see the mobile, but, because the ribbon is attached to a different stand, she cannot make the mobile move. Baseline activity is assessed during a nonreinforcement period prior to training, and all retention tests are also conducted during periods of nonreinforcement. As can be seen, this infant already has learned and is attempting to make the mobile move by kicking her leg with the ribbon attachments.

Figure **8.3**

The Toy Train Task Used to Study Infant Memory

Shown here is a 6-month-old infant pressing a lever to move the toy train and turn the lights on and off for 2 seconds.

Infant Memory Research

hrough the Eyes of Psychologists

Carolyn Rovee-Collier,
Rutgers University

"The memory processing of infants and adults is essentially the same."

Two recent studies from Carolyn Rovee-Collier's laboratory have demonstrated that periodic nonverbal reminders can maintain the memory of an event from early infancy (2 and 6 months of age) through 1½ to 2 years. Previously, this was thought to be impossible and all of infancy described as a period of "infantile amnesia." In one of these studies, 8-week-olds learned the mobile task shown in figure 8.2 (Rovee-Collier, Hartshorn, & DiRubbio, 1999). Every 3 weeks thereafter through 26 weeks of age, they were given a preliminary retention test followed by a 3-minute visual reminder. Their final retention test came at 29 weeks of age. Eight-week-old infants forgot after 1 or 2 days, but after exposure to the triweekly periodic reminders, they still showed significant retention 4½ months later and most remembered 5¼ months later. In the other study (Hartshorn, 1998), 6-month-olds learned the "train task" (see figure 8.3). In the train task, infants learn to move a miniature train around a circular track by pushing a lever. Infants shown the train when the lever is deactivated indicate that they recognize it by pressing the lever above their baseline rate. The infants were briefly reminded about it at 7, 8, 9, and 12 months of age, and were tested at 18 months of age. Although 6- to 8-month-old infants typically forgot after 2 weeks, when briefly reminded on a periodic basis they still showed significant retention 1 year later (at 18 months of age). Further, five of six infants who were reminded immediately after the 18-month test still remembered when tested at 24 months of age, 1½ years after the original event. They had been given only one reminder (at 18 months) in the previous year.

These studies, as well as others (Klein & Meltzoff, 1999; Meltzoff, 1995), raise serious doubts about the generality of infantile amnesia. Neither the immaturity of the brain nor the inability to talk limits how long young infants can remember an event as long as they experience periodic reminders of it (Rovee-Collier, 1997, in press).

Rehearsal   Rehearsal is the conscious repetition of information over time that increases the length of time that information stays in memory. Rehearsal does not hold more information in memory, it just keeps the same information in memory longer. Rehearsal works best when individuals need to remember a list of items over a brief period of time. When they must retain information over long periods of time, as when studying for a test the next week, other strategies usually work better than rehearsal. A main reason rehearsal does not work well for retaining information over the long term is that rehearsal often involves just rotely repeating information without imparting any meaning to it. When children construct their memory in meaningful ways, they remember better.

A classic study by John Flavell and his colleagues (Flavell, Beach, & Chinsky, 1966) illustrates the importance of rehearsal and developmental changes in its use. Children from 5 to 10 years old were given the task of remembering the names of a set of two to five pictures for 15 seconds. The novel feature of the experiment was that the experimenter was a trained lip-reader. Although not many children said anything aloud, a number of children made lip movements that indicated rehearsal of names and pictures. The percentage of children making lip movements increased with age: 10 percent of the 5-year-olds, 60 percent of the 7-year-olds, and 85 percent of the 10-year-olds made lip movements. In a later study of 6-year-olds, the research team found that children who rehearsed showed better recall than those who did not. When nonrehearsers were taught to rehearse, their performance rivaled that of the spontaneous rehearsers (Keeney, Cannizzo, & Flavell, 1967).

Subsequent investigations made the interesting point that rudimentary, rehearsal-like processes begin to appear at very young ages (DeLoache, Cassidy, & Brown, 1985). In one study, 3- and 4-year-old children watched a toy dog being hidden under one of three cups. Instructed to remember where the dog was hidden, the children looked at, pointed to, and touched the appropriate cup (Wellman, Ritter, & Flavell, 1985). Even 1½-year-olds, under certain circumstances, use rehearsal—when they see an object hidden in a room, they will point to it, touch it, and repeat its name while they wait to be able to retrieve it (DeLoache, 1984).

If using rehearsal is so helpful in short-term remembering, why do young children so often not rehearse? One simple reason is that young children both benefit less and incur greater costs by using the strategy than do older children. When children begin to use rehearsal (and other new strategies), executing the new strategy requires greater mental resources than it will later (Kee & Howell, 1988). Similarly, when the experimental procedure makes it easier to execute the strategy, the difference between the performances produced by older and younger children's use of the strategy decreases (DeMarie-Dreblow & Miller, 1988). The point is that children need a reasonable amount of experience with a strategy before they can gain the full potential benefit from using it.

A second reason why young children tend not to rehearse, even when they have been taught to do so and have benefited from doing so, is that they often attribute their success to other factors—luck, greater effort, or being smart. Those children who attribute their success to the new strategy they used tend to use it again in the future, but those who think other factors were responsible tend not to use the new approach again (Fabricius & Hagen, 1984).

Deep Processing   Following the discovery that rehearsal is not an efficient way to remember information over the long term, Fergus Craik and Robert Lockhart (1972) proposed that individuals process information at different levels. Their theory, *levels of processing theory,* states that memory is on a continuum from shallow to deep, with deeper processing producing better memory. The sensory or physical features of stimuli are analyzed first at a *shallow* level. This might involve detecting the lines, angles, and contours of a printed word's letters, or a spoken word's frequency, duration, and loudness. At an *intermediate* level of processing, the stimulus is recognized and given a label. For example, a four-legged, barking object is identified as a dog. Then, at the *deepest* level, information is processed semantically, in terms of its meaning. For example, if a child sees the word *boat,* at the shallow level she might notice the shapes of the letters, at the intermediate level she might think of the characteristics of the word (such as it rhymes with *coat*), and at the deepest level she might think about the last time she went fishing with her dad on a boat and the kind of boat it was. Researchers have found that individuals remember information better when they process it at a deeper level (Hunt & Ellis, 1999).

Exploring Memory Models

Elaboration   Cognitive psychologists soon recognized, however, that there is more to good memory than just depth of processing. They discovered that individuals have better memory if they use elaboration in their encoding of information. *Elaboration* involves more extensive information processing. Thus, when a teacher presents the concept of democracy to students, they likely will remember it better if they come up with good examples of it. Thinking of examples is a good way to elaborate information. Self-reference is also an effective way to elaborate information. A person will be more likely to remember the concept of fairness if he can generate personal examples of inequities and equities he has personally experienced; a person will be more likely to remember the concept of a symphony if she associates it with the last time she attended a symphony concert rather than merely rehearses the words that define what a symphony is. Thinking about personal associations with information makes the information more meaningful and helps students remember it.

One reason elaboration works so well in producing good memory is that it adds to the *distinctiveness* of memory code (Ellis, 1987). To remember a piece of information such as a name, an experience, or a fact about geography, children need to search for the code that contains this information among the mass of codes in long-term memory. The search process is easier if the memory code is unique (Hunt & Kelly, 1996). The situation is not unlike searching for a friend at a crowded airport. A friend who is 6 feet 3 inches tall and has flaming red hair will be easier to find in the crowd than someone who has more common features. Also, as a person elaborates information, more information is stored, making it easier to differentiate the memory from others. For example, if a child witnesses another child being hit by a car that speeds away, the child's memory of the car will be far better if she deliberately encodes that the car is a red 1995 Pontiac with tinted windows and spinners on the wheels than if she encodes only that it is a red car.

As children get older, they are more likely to use elaboration without being instructed to do so (Schneider & Bjorklund, 1998). There are especially impressive increases in the use of elaboration from late childhood to late adolescence (Schneider & Pressley, 1989). Elementary-school-age children are less likely to use elaboration spontaneously, but they benefit considerably from being taught to use it to remember.

Constructing Images   When we construct an image of something, we are elaborating the information. For example, think of a house or apartment where you have spent a lot of time—do you know how many windows are in it? Few of us ever memorize this information, but you probably can come up with a good answer, especially if you reconstruct a mental image of each room. Take a "mental walk" through the house or apartment, counting the windows as you go.

Allan Paivio (1971, 1986) believes that memories are stored in two ways: as a verbal code or as an image code. For example, you can remember a picture by a label (*The Last Supper,* a verbal code) or by a mental image. Paivio says that the more detailed and distinctive the image code, the better your memory of the information will be.

The *keyword method* is a method in which vivid imagery is attached to specific words to improve memory. This method has been used to practical advantage in teaching children how to rapidly master new information, such as foreign vocabulary words, the states and capitals of the United States, and the names of presidents of the United States (Levin, 1980). For example, in teaching children that Annapolis is the capital of Maryland, instructors taught the children the keywords for the states, such that when a state (Maryland) was given, the children could supply the keyword *(marry).* Then, children were given the reverse type of keyword practice with the capitals. That is, they had to respond with the capital (Annapolis) when given a keyword *(apple).* Finally, an illustration was provided (see figure 8.4). The keyword strategy's use of vivid mental imagery, such as the image in figure 8.4, was effective in increasing children's memory of state capitals. Developmentalists today encourage the use of imagery in our nation's schools, believing it helps increase children's memory (McDaniel & Pressley, 1987).

Organization   If children organize information when they are encoding it, their memory benefits. To understand the importance of organization in encoding, complete the following exercise. Recall the 12 months of the year as quickly as you can. How long did it take you? What was the order of your recall? Your probable answer: a few seconds and in natural order (January, February, March, and so on). Now try to remember the months in alphabetical order. Did you make any errors? How long did it take you? There is a clear distinction between recalling the months in natural order and alphabetically. This exercise is a good one to use with children to help them understand the importance of organizing their memories in *meaningful* ways.

Mnemonics

Figure **8.4**

The Keyword Method

To help children remember the state capitals, the keyword method was used. A special component of the keyword method is the use of mental imagery, which was stimulated by presenting the children with a vivid visual image, such as two apples being married. The strategy is to help the children associate *apple* with Annapolis and *marry* with Maryland.

©FRANK & ERNEST reprinted by permission of Newspaper Enterprise Associaton, Inc.

The more adults present information in an organized way, the easier it will be for children to remember it. This is especially true if adults organize information hierarchically or outline it. Also, simply encouraging children to organize information helps them to remember it better than if they are given no instructions about organizing (Mandler, 1980).

Children show increased organization in middle and late childhood. In one investigation, children were presented with a circular array of pictures from four categories: clothing, furniture, animals, and vehicles (Moely & others, 1969). The children were told to study the pictures so that later they could say their names back to the experimenter. They also were told they could move the pictures around to remember them better. The 10- and 11-year-olds performed such groupings; the younger children did not. When younger children were put through a brief training procedure that encouraged grouping, they were able to follow this strategy, and their memory for the pictures improved.

The development of organizational strategies in many ways parallels that of rehearsal. Organization is used far less often by 5- and 6-year-olds than by 9- and 10-year-olds and older children. The quality of the younger children's execution of the strategy is also lower than that of older ones. Executing the strategy also requires more of the younger children's cognitive resources, so it often yields poorer recall among younger than among older children (Bjorklund & Harnishfeger, 1987). Thus, it is not altogether surprising that young children use these strategies less often than older children do—they have more difficulty executing the strategies, and realize smaller benefits from using them.

Chunking is an organizational strategy that benefits memory. Chunking involves grouping or "packing" information into "higher-order units" that can be remembered as single units. Chunking works by making large amounts of information more manageable and more meaningful. For example, consider this simple list of words: *hot, city, book, forget, tomorrow,* and *smile.* Try to hold these in memory for a moment, then write them down. If you recalled all seven words, you succeeded in holding 34 letters in your memory.

Memory Storage

After children encode information, they need to retain or store the information. The most prominent aspects of memory storage include the three main stores that vary according to time: sensory memory, working (or short-term) memory, and long-term memory.

Memory Time Frames   Children remember some information for less than a second, some for about half a minute, and other information for minutes, hours, years, even a lifetime. The three types of memory that vary according to their

"Can we hurry up and get to the test? My short-term memory is better than my long-term memory."

© 1999: reprinted courtesy of Bunny Hoest and Parade Magazine.

sensory memory
The memory system that holds information from the world in its original sensory form for only an instant.

Short-Term Memory

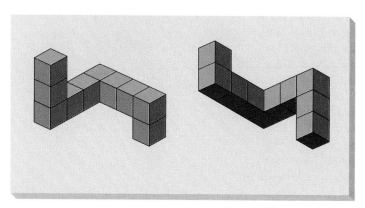

Figure **8.5**

Cubes Used to Study Mental Rotation Abilities

Both children and adults attempt to determine whether the Lego-like figures are identical by rotating one of them into the same orientation as the other. For all age groups, the more discrepant the initial position of the two figures, the longer this rotation process takes. However, from age 5 to adulthood, the older the individual, the faster their rate of mental rotation.

time frames are *sensory memory* (which lasts a fraction of a second to several seconds); *working memory, or short-term memory,* (which lasts about 30 seconds); and *long-term memory* (which lasts up to a lifetime).

Sensory Memory   **Sensory memory** *holds information from the world in its original sensory form for only an instant, not much longer than the brief time a child is exposed to the visual, auditory, and other sensations.* Its information is quickly lost unless the child engages in mental processes like rehearsal to transfer it into short-term or long-term memory.

Children have a sensory memory for sounds up to several seconds, sort of like a brief echo. However, their sensory memory for visual images lasts only for about one-fourth of a second. Because sensory information lasts for only a fleeting moment or two, an important task for the child is to attend to the sensory information that is important for learning.

The sensory memories of children as young as 5 years old have the same capacity as those of adults (Morrison, Holmes, & Haith, 1974). However, young children form sensory-level representations at a slower speed than adults do. Under ideal viewing conditions, adults can represent objects at a sensory level for a tenth of a second, while 7-year-olds take about one-seventh of a second to form similar representations (Hoving & others, 1978). Although this difference is small, when multiplied by the huge amount of sensory-level processing that people do every day, the differences likely have large cumulative effects.

Working (Short-Term) Memory   **Working (short-term) memory** *is a limited-capacity memory system in which information is retained for as long as 30 seconds, unless the information is rehearsed or otherwise processed further, in which case it can be retained longer.* Compared to sensory memory, short-term memory is limited in capacity but relatively longer in duration.

One way to illustrate the growth of working, or short-term, memory is to present children of different ages with memory tasks. If you have taken an intelligence test, you probably were exposed to one of these tasks. A short list of stimuli, usually digits, is presented at a rapid pace (for example, one item per second). Using this type of memory-span task, researchers have found that short-term memory increases over time in childhood (Case, 1985; Dempster, 1981). The increase is from about two digits in 2- to 3-year-old children, to about five digits in 7-year-old children, to about seven digits in 12- to 13-year-old children. Not every child of a given age has the same short-term memory capacity, however, which is why these items are often used on intelligence tests. In general, children who have larger short-term memory spans do better in school than do their counterparts of the same age who have smaller spans (Siegler, 1998).

Just as the capacity of short-term memory increases with age, so does the speed of processing (Pressley & Schneider, 1997). This has been the finding with virtually every task that has been used to study memory. For example, children are sometimes shown two shapes, such as those in figure 8.5, and asked whether the shape on the left is just a rotated form of the shape on the right or whether they are different shapes. For children and adults of all ages, the greater the amount of rotation, the longer it takes to tell that the shapes are the same (on trials in which they are the same). However, the rate of rotation is slower for younger children and gradually increases with age, reaching adultlike levels only at about 15 years of age.

Because the growth of processing speed is similar on many different tasks, some investigators have concluded that the speedup reflects a basic maturation of the central nervous system (Hale, 1990; Kail, 1993). Other researchers have reviewed the same data and concluded that they reflect the greater amount of practice that older children engage in, rather than changes in physiological maturation (Stigler, Nusbaum, & Chalip, 1988).

Developmental changes in processing speed are intertwined with changes in processing capacity. For example, in one study, the faster that 6-year-olds repeated auditorially presented words, the longer their memory spans for those words were (Case, Kurland, & Goldberg, 1982). When speed of word presentation was controlled, though, the memory spans of the 6-year-olds were equal to those of young adults. Thus, the greater memory spans usually observed in older children might be due in large part to the fact that older children can process the material more quickly.

Earlier we said that short-term memory is also called working memory. Indeed, most cognitive psychologists today prefer the term *working memory*. Working memory is a kind of mental "workbench" where students manipulate and assemble information when they make decisions, solve problems, and comprehend written and spoken language (Baddeley, 1990, 1998).

Long-Term Memory   **Long-term memory** *is a type of memory that holds enormous amounts of information for a long period of time in a relatively permanent fashion.* A typical human's long-term-memory capacity is staggering. The distinguished computer scientist John von Neumann put the size at 2.8 × 10 (280 quintillion) bits, which in practical terms means that long-term memory storage is virtually unlimited. Even more impressive is the efficiency with which individuals can retrieve information. It often takes only a moment to search through this vast storehouse to find the information we want. Think about your own long-term memory. Who wrote the Gettysburg Address? Who was your first-grade teacher? When were you born? Where do you live? You can answer thousands of such questions instantly. Of course, not all information is retrieved so easily from long-term memory.

Now that we have studied memory's time frames, let's examine the contents of long-term memory in more depth.

Memory's Contents   Just as memory can be distinguished by how long it lasts, it can also be differentiated on the basis of its *content*. For long-term memory, many contemporary psychologists accept the hierarchy of contents described in figure 8.6 (Squire, 1987). In this hierarchy, long-term memory is divided into the subtypes of declarative memory and procedural memory. Declarative memory is subdivided into episodic memory and semantic memory.

Declarative Memory and Procedural Memory   *Declarative memory* is the conscious recollection of information, such as specific facts or events that can be verbally communicated. Declarative memory has been called "knowing that," and more recently has been labeled "explicit memory." Demonstrations of children's declarative memory could include recounting an event they have witnessed or describing a basic principle of math. However, children do not need to be talking to be using

ADVENTURES FOR THE MIND

Developmental Changes in Information Processing

SELECT A TOPIC, construct some questions about the topic, and then talk with a 5-year-old, 9-year-old, and 14-year-old about it. What kind of developmental changes can you detect in how the children processed information in the course of your conversations? Did the adolescent process information more automatically and faster than the younger children?

working (short-term) memory
The limited-capacity memory system in which information is retained for as long as 30 seconds, unless the information is rehearsed, in which case it can be retained longer.

long-term memory
A type of memory that holds enormous amounts of information for a long period of time in a relatively permanent fashion.

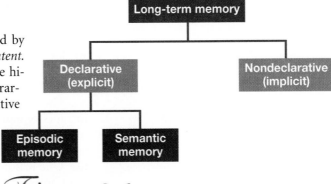

Figure 8.6

Classification of Long-Term Memory's Contents

From L.R. Squire, "Declarative and Non Declarative Memory: Multiple Brain Systems Supporting Learning and Memory," Memory Systems by Schacter, Daniel, & Endel (eds.), 1994. Used by permission of the MIT Press.

Although in many ways children are universal novices, some children have high levels of skill in chess and can be considered experts.

declarative memory. If children simply sit and reflect on an experience, their declarative memory is involved.

Procedural memory refers to knowledge in the form of skills and cognitive operations (Schacter, 2000). Procedural memory cannot be consciously recollected, at least not in the form of specific events or facts. This makes procedural memory difficult, if not impossible, to communicate verbally. Procedural memory is sometimes called "knowing how," and recently it also has been described as "implicit memory." When children apply their abilities to perform a dance, ride a bicycle, or type on a computer keyboard, their procedural memory is at work. It also is at work when they speak grammatically correct sentences without having to think about how to do it.

Episodic and Semantic Memory   Cognitive psychologist Endel Tulving (1972) distinguishes between two subtypes of declarative memory: episodic and semantic. *Episodic memory* is the retention of information about the where and when of life's happenings. Children's memories of the first day of school, who they had lunch with, or the guest who came to talk with their class last week are all episodic.

Semantic memory is a child's general knowledge about the world. It includes:

• Knowledge of the sort learned in school (such as knowledge of geometry)
• Knowledge in different fields of expertise (such as knowledge of chess, for a skilled chess player)
• "Everyday" knowledge about meanings of words, famous people, important places, and common things (such as what being "street smart" means or who Nelson Mandela or Mohandas Ghandi is)

Semantic memory knowledge is independent of the person's identity with the past. For example, children might access a fact—such as "Lima is the capital of the country of Peru"—and not have the foggiest idea of when and where they learned it.

Content Knowledge and How It Is Represented in Long-Term Memory
Does what children already know about a subject affect their ability to remember new information about it? How do children represent information in their memory?

Content Knowledge   Our ability to remember new information about a subject does depend considerably on what we already know about it. For example, a child's ability to recount what she has seen on a trip to the library is largely governed by what she already knows about libraries, such as where books on certain topics are located, how to check books out, and so on. With little knowledge of libraries, the child would have a much harder time recounting what she saw there.

The contribution of content knowledge to memory is especially evident in the memory of individuals who are experts or novices in a particular knowledge domain. An expert is the opposite of a novice (someone who is just beginning to learn a content area). Experts demonstrate especially impressive memory in their areas of expertise. One reason children remember less than adults is that they are far less expert in most areas.

In areas where children are experts, their memory is often extremely good. In fact, it often exceeds that of adults who are novices in that content area. This was documented in a study of 10-year-old chess experts (Chi, 1978). These children were excellent chess players, but not especially brilliant in other ways. When their memory spans for digits were contrasted with those of adults, they, like most 10-year-olds, remem-

*K*nowledge is power.

Frances Bacon
English Philosopher, 17th Century

bered fewer of the numbers. However, when they were presented chess boards, they remembered the configurations far better than did the adults who were novices at chess.

How do experts acquire such a rich knowledge base? Their expertise is developed over a long period of time in which they show considerable motivation to learn more about a topic. Expert knowledge in areas like chess, music, tennis, and many other domains often requires considerable amounts of practice over many years (Schneider & Bjorklund, 1998).

We have seen that, compared to novices, experts are more likely to have better content knowledge and memory in a particular domain, and be more motivated to learn the material over a long period of time. What are some other ways that experts differ from novices? They include these (Committee on Developments in the Science of Learning, 1999):

- Experts are more likely to notice features and meaningful patterns of information.
- Experts' knowledge is more likely to be organized in ways that reflect a deep understanding of their subject matter.
- Experts are more likely to flexibly retrieve important aspects of their knowledge with less effort.

Network Theories   *Network theories* describe how information in memory is organized and connected. They emphasize nodes in the memory network. The nodes stand for labels or concepts. Consider the concept "bird." One of the earliest network theories described memory representation as being hierarchically arranged, with more concrete concepts ("canary," for example) nestled under more abstract concepts (like "bird"). However, it soon was realized that such hierarchical networks are too neat to fit the way memory representation really works. For example, students take longer to answer the question "Is an ostrich a bird?" than to answer the question "Is a canary a bird?" Thus, today memory researchers envision the memory network as more irregular and distorted. A *typical bird,* such as a canary, is closer to the node or center of the category *bird* than is the atypical *ostrich.*

Experts in a particular area usually have far more elaborate networks of information about it than do novices (see figure 8.7). The information they represent in

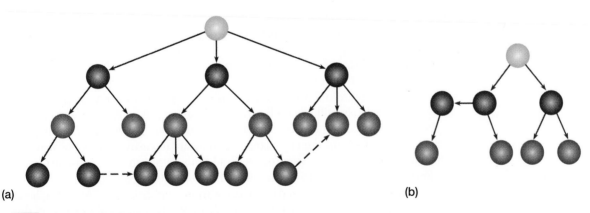

(a)   (b)

𝓕*igure* **8.7**

An Example of How Information Is Organized in the Minds of an Expert and a Novice

(A) An expert's knowledge is based on years of experience in which small bits of information have been linked with many other small pieces, which together are placed in a more general category. This category is in turn placed in an even more general category of knowledge. The dotted lines show associations between specific elements of knowledge that connect the lower branches and provide mental shortcuts in the expert's mind. *(B)* The novice's knowledge shows far fewer connections, shortcuts, and levels than an expert's knowledge.

memory has more nodes, more interconnections, and better hierarchical organization. It's not that experts have a better memory than novices in general, just in a particular domain.

Schema Theories   Long-term memory has been compared to a library of books. The idea is that our memory stores information just as a library stores books. In this analogy, the way children retrieve information is said to be similar to the process they use to locate and check out a book. However, the process of retrieving information from long-term memory is not as precise as the library analogy suggests. When children search through their long-term memory storehouse, they don't always find the *exact* "book" they want, or they might find the "book" they want but discover that only "several pages" are intact. They have to *reconstruct* the rest.

Schema theories state that when individuals reconstruct information, they fit it into information that already exists in their minds (Fiske, 2000). A *schema* is information—concepts, events, knowledge—that already exists in a person's mind. You might recall our description of schemas in Piaget's theory (chapter 7, "Cognitive Developmental Approaches"). Schemas from prior experiences influence the way children encode, make inferences about, and retrieve information (Chi, 2000). Unlike network theories, which assume that retrieval involves specific facts, schema theory claims that long-term memory searches are not very exact. Children often don't find precisely what they want. Hence, as we just indicated, children have to reconstruct the rest. Often when asked to retrieve information, they fill in the gaps between their fragmented memories with varying accuracies and inaccuracies (Grant & Ceci, 2000).

Children have schemas for all sorts of information. If a teacher tells a story to a class and then asks the students to write down what the story was about, she likely will get many different versions. That is, the students won't remember every detail of the story the teacher told and will reconstruct stories with their own particular stamps on them. For example, imagine that a teacher tells a class a story about two men and two women who were involved in a train crash in France. One student might reconstruct the story as being about a plane crash, another might say it involved three men and three women, another might say it took place in Germany, and so on. The reconstruction and distortion of memory is nowhere more apparent than in the memories given by people involved in a trial. In criminal court trials like that of O. J. Simpson, the variations in people's memories of what happened underscores the fact that we reconstruct the past rather than take an exact photograph of it.

A *script* is a schema for an event. Scripts often have information about physical features, people, and typical occurrences. This kind of information is helpful when children need to figure out what is happening around them. In a script for an art activity, children likely will remember that the teacher has told them what to draw, that they are supposed to put on smocks over their clothes, that they must get the art paper and paints from the cupboard, that they are to clean the brushes when they are finished, and so on. For example, a child who comes in late to the art activity likely knows much of what to do because of his art activity script.

As children develop, their scripts become more sophisticated. For example, a 4-year-old's script for a restaurant might include only information about sitting down and eating food. In middle and late childhood, the child adds information to the restaurant script about the types of people who serve food, about paying the cashier, and so on. The process of elaborating this type of information in long-term memory continues throughout life.

Retrieval and Forgetting

After children have encoded information and then represented it in memory, they might be able to retrieve some of it but might also forget some of it.

Retrieval   When children retrieve something from their mental "data bank," they search their store of memory to find the relevant information. Just as with encoding, this search can be automatic or it can require effort. For example, if children are asked what month it is, the answer might immediately spring to their lips. That is, the retrieval might be automatic. But if children are asked to name the guest speaker who came to the class 2 months earlier, the retrieval process likely will require more effort.

An item's position on a list also affects how easy or difficult the item will be to remember. The *serial position effect* is that recall is better for items at the beginning and end of a list than for items in the middle (see figure 8.8). Suppose a child is given these directions about where to go to get tutoring help:

"Left on Mockingbird, right on Central, left on Balboa, left on Sandstone, and right on Parkside." The child likely will remember "Left on Mockingbird" and "Right on Parkside" better than "Left on Balboa." The *primacy effect* is that items at the beginning of a list tend to be the easiest to remember. The *recency effect* is that items at the end of the list tend to be remembered the easiest.

Yet another aspect of retrieval is the nature of the retrieval task itself. *Recall* is a memory task in which individuals must retrieve previously learned information, as when students are given fill-in-the-blank or essay questions. *Recognition* is a memory task in which individuals only have to identify ("recognize") learned information, as is often the case on multiple-choice tests. Many students prefer multiple-choice items because they have good retrieval cues, whereas fill-in-the-blank and essay items don't.

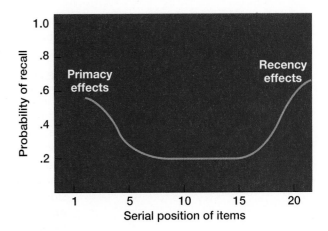

Figure 8.8
The Serial Position Effect
When a child is asked to memorize a list of words, the child usually remembers the words memorized last the best, those at the beginning next best, and those in the middle least efficiently.

Forgetting   One form of forgetting involves the cues we just discussed. *Cue-dependent forgetting* is retrieval failure caused by a lack of effective retrieval cues. Cue-dependent forgetting explains why students might fail to retrieve a needed fact for an exam even when the student is sure she "knows" the information. For example, if you are studying for a test in this course and are asked a question about a distinction between recall and recognition in retrieval, you likely will remember the distinction better if you possess the cues of fill-in-the-blank and multiple-choice, respectively.

The principle of cue-dependent forgetting is consistent with *interference theory*, which states that we forget not because we actually lose memories from storage, but rather because other information gets in the way of what we are trying to remember. Thus, if a student studies for a biology test, then studies for a history test, and then takes the biology test, the information about history will interfere with remembering the information about biology. Thus, interference theory implies that a good study strategy is to study last what you are going to be tested on next if you have multiple courses to study for. That is, the student taking the biology test would have benefited from studying history first, then biology just before taking the biology test. This strategy also fits with the recency effect we described earlier. Take a moment and think about how you might use your knowledge of interference theory in terms of reviewing for students what you plan to test them on next.

Another source of forgetting is memory decay. *Decay theory* states that when something new is learned, a neurochemical "memory trace" is formed that will disintegrate. Thus, decay theory suggests that the passage of time is responsible for forgetting. Memories decay at different speeds. Some memories are vivid and last for long periods of time, especially when they have emotional ties. These "flashbulb" memories—such as memory of a car accident you were in or witnessed, the night of your high school graduation, an early romantic experience, where you were when you heard about Princess Diana's death—can have considerable accuracy and vivid imagery, and chances are you can retrieve such information even when the events happened a long time ago.

Personal Trauma and Memory

In 1890, American psychologist William James said that an experience can be so arousing emotionally as to almost leave a scar on the brain's tissue. Personal traumas can have such an effect. Some psychologists argue that memory for emotionally traumatic events is accurately retained, possibly forever, in considerable detail (Langer, 1991). There is good evidence that memory for traumatic events is usually more accurate than memory for ordinary events (Schacter, 1996). But consider the traumatic experience of children who were kidnapped at gunpoint on a school bus in Chowchilla, California, then buried underground for 16 hours before escaping. On the one hand, the children had the classic signs of traumatic memory—detailed and vivid recollections. On the other hand, when a child psychiatrist interviewed them 4 or 5 years after the chilling episode, she noted some striking errors and distortions in half of the children's memories of it (Terr, 1988).

How can a traumatic memory be so vivid and detailed, yet at the same time have inaccuracies? A number of factors can be involved. Some children might have made perceptual errors at the time of encoding information because the episode was so shocking. Others might have distorted the information and recalled the episode as being less traumatic than it actually was, in order to reduce their anxiety about what happened. Others, in discussing the traumatic event with various people, might have incorporated bits and pieces of these persons' recollections of what happened into their own version of the event.

In sum, memories of real-life traumas are usually more accurate and long-lasting than everyday events. However, memories of traumas are subject to some deterioration and distortion. In traumatic memories, the central part of the memory is almost always effectively remembered. Where distortion often arises is in the details of the traumatic episode.

Some cases of memory for personal trauma involve a mental disorder called *post-traumatic stress disorder,* which includes severe anxiety symptoms that can immediately follow the trauma or be delayed by months or even years until onset. This mental disorder can emerge as a consequence of exposure to any of several traumatic events, such as war, severe abuse (as in rape), and accidental disasters (such as a plane crash). The symptoms of this disorder can include "flashbacks" in which the individual relives the traumatic event in nightmares, or in an awake but dissociative-like state. They also can include difficulties with memory and concentration.

The emotional blows of personal trauma can produce distortions of memory or vivid reenactments of the event in memory. In the case of post-traumatic stress disorder, the event might be pushed beneath awareness only to reappear in vivid flashbacks months or even years later. Repression takes place when something shocking happens and the mind pushes all memory of the occurrence into some inaccessible part of the unconscious mind. At some later point, the memory might emerge in consciousness, as in the case of post-traumatic stress disorder.

In psychoanalytic theory, which we initially discussed in chapter 2, repression's main function is to protect the individual from threatening information ◀▥ P. 32. Repression doesn't erase a memory, it just makes it extremely difficult to remember consciously. To read further about repressed memories, see the Explorations in Child Development box.

At this point we have discussed many aspects of memory. A review of these ideas is presented in summary table 8.2. Next, we will continue our exploration of how children process information by focusing on thinking.

EXPLORATIONS IN CHILD DEVELOPMENT
Repressed Memories, Child Abuse, and Reality

THERE HAS BEEN a dramatic increase in reported memories of childhood sexual abuse that were allegedly repressed for many years. With recent changes in legislation, people with recently discovered memories are suing alleged perpetrators for events that occurred 20, 30, even 40 or more years earlier.

In 1991, popular actress Roseanne was on the cover of *People* magazine. She reported that her mother had abused her from the time Roseanne was an infant until she was 6 or 7 years of age, but that she had become aware of the abuse only recently during therapy. Other highly publicized cases of repressed memories of child abuse coming into awareness during therapy dot the pages of popular magazines and self-help books.

There is little doubt that actual childhood abuse is tragically common. Memory experts such as Elizabeth Loftus (1993) and others (Kutchinsky, 1992) don't dispute that child abuse is a serious problem. What they take issue with is the way therapists get their clients to recall abuse. Therapists might help their clients to reconstruct a memory that is not real. Some clients who originally claimed they were abused later have recanted their accusations, blaming their abuse report on the therapist's leading inquiries.

Roseanne said that her mother abused her from the time she was an infant until she was 6 or 7 years old. Why have many psychologists questioned some of the reports of activation of repressed memories, such as Roseanne's?

In recent years, there has been an increasing number of court cases entailing allegations of sexual improprieties involving children. Many cases that end up in the legal system likely involve true claims of sexual abuse but questions are raised about whether children's reports are reliable.

Is there a time in childhood when children are especially susceptible to misleading suggestions? Recent studies have confirmed that preschool children are disproportionately vulnerable to suggestive influences about such things as bodily touching, emotional events, and participatory events (Bruck & Ceci, 2000). Nonetheless, concerns remain about the reliability of older children's, adolescents', and even adults' testimony when they are subjected to suggestive interviews (Poole & Lindsey, 1996). Also, individual variations in preschool children suggest that some preschool children are resistant to interviewers' suggestions.

Few research studies offer convincing evidence about the extent to which repression of abuse actually occurs. At present, there are no satisfactory methods that can help us discover the answer. Although Loftus has demonstrated the ease with which memories can be implanted in unsuspecting individuals, her critics say that her research might not accurately capture the actual trauma that occurs in abuse episodes.

Therapists and their clients are left with the chilling possibility that not all abuse memories recovered in therapy are real. In the absence of corroboration, some recollections might be authentic and others might not be.

According to Loftus (1993), psychotherapists, counselors, social service agencies, and law enforcement personnel need to be careful about probing for horrors on the other side of some amnesiac barrier. They should be cautious in their interpretation of uncorroborated repressed memories that return. Clarification, compassion, and gentle confrontation along with a demonstration of empathy are techniques that can be used to help individuals in their painful struggle to come to grips with their personal truths.

There is a final tragic risk involved in suggestive probing and uncritical acceptance of all allegations made by clients. These activities increase the probability that society in general will disbelieve the actual cases of child abuse that deserve extensive attention and evaluation. In general, any careless or uncritical acceptance of unreplicated findings in psychology, especially when they have a colorful element that attracts media attention, harms public attitudes toward the contributions of psychological research.

SUMMARY TABLE 8.2
Memory

Concept	Processes/ Related Ideas	Characteristics/Description
What Is Memory?	Its Nature	• Memory is the retention of information over time. • Memory involves encoding (how information gets into memory), storage (how the information is stored over time), and retrieval (taking information out of memory).
Encoding	Its Nature	• In everyday language, encoding has much in common with attention and learning.
	Attention	• Two important aspects of attention are selectivity and the ability to shift attention.
	Other Processes	• Habituation, rehearsal, deep processing, elaboration, constructing images, and organization are other processes that are involved in encoding.
Memory Storage	Memory Time Frames	• One way that memory varies involves the time frames of sensory memory, working (or short-term) memory, and long-term memory. • Many contemporary psychologists prefer the term *working memory* to *short-term memory* because of its active, constructivist nature and because it fits the research results better.
	Memory's Contents	• Many cognitive psychologists accept this hierarchy of long-term memory's contents: division into declarative and procedural subtypes, with declarative memory further subdivided into episodic and semantic memory.
	Content Knowledge and How It Is Represented in Long-Term Memory	• Children's ability to remember new information about a subject depends extensively on what they already know about it. • The contribution of content knowledge is especially relevant in the memory of experts. • Two major approaches to how memory is represented are in terms of networks and schemas. • A script is a schema for an event.
Retrieval and Forgetting	Retrieval	• Retrieval is influenced by the serial position effect, how effective retrieval cues are, and the memory task.
	Forgetting	• Forgetting can be explained in terms of cue-dependent forgetting, interference theory, and decay theory.
Personal Trauma and Memory		• Some cases of personal trauma involve post-traumatic stress disorder. • Personal trauma can cause children to repress emotionally laden information. • Repression doesn't erase memory, it just makes it extremely hard to remember consciously. • Controversy surrounds the accuracy of recovered memories in such situations as when child abuse has allegedly occurred.

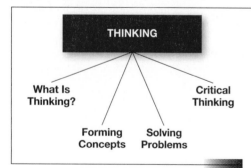

Thinking

What does it mean to "think"? What are some good strategies for helping children become better thinkers?

What Is Thinking?

Thinking *involves manipulating and transforming information in memory.* This often is done to form concepts, reason, think critically, and solve problems—topics that we will explore shortly. Children can think about the concrete, such as a vacation at the beach or how to win at a video game; as adolescents, they can think in more abstract ways, such as pondering the meaning of freedom or identity. They can think about the past (what happened to them last month) and the future (what will their life be like next year). They can think about reality (such as how to do better on the next test in a subject area) and fantasy (what it might be like to meet Elvis Presley or land a spacecraft on Mars).

Forming Concepts

Forming concepts is an important aspect of constructing information (Ross, 2000).

What Are Concepts?

Concepts *are categories used to group objects, events, and characteristics on the basis of common properties.* Concepts are elements of cognition that help to simplify and summarize information (Medin, Profitt, & Schwartz, 2000). In a world without concepts, each object would be unique, no generalization would be possible. Without concepts, the most trivial problem would be time-consuming and even impossible. Consider the concept of a book. If a child were not aware that a book is sheets of paper of uniform size, all bound together along one edge, and full of printed words and pictures in some meaningful order, each time the child encountered a new book she would have to figure out what it was. In a way, then, concepts keep us from "reinventing the wheel" each time we come across a new piece of information.

Concepts also aid the process of remembering, making it more efficient. When children group objects to form a concept, they can remember the concept, then retrieve the concept's characteristics. Thus, when a teacher assigns math homework, she probably doesn't need to go through the details of what math is or what homework is. Children will have embedded in their memory a number of associations with concepts of math and homework. In ways such as this, concepts not only help to jog memory, they also make communication more efficient. If a teacher says, "It's time for art," students know what this concept means. One doesn't have to go into a lengthy explanation of what art is. Thus, concepts help children to simplify and summarize information, as well as improve the efficiency of memory, communication, and time use.

Many of children's concepts embody implicit theories about the world (Carey & Gelman, 1991). Children often are not able to state these theories explicitly, but their use of the concepts shows many of the features characteristic of concepts within the theories of adult scientists.

Just as scientific theories are organized hierarchically, with some applying very broadly and others more narrowly, so might children's theories be. Thus, although children might possess many specific theories, they might also possess a few very general ones that apply to broad ranges of phenomena. Henry Wellman and Susan Gelman (1992) proposed that children begin life with three grand theories—a theory of the mind (naive psychology), a theory of the physical world (naive physics), and a theory of living things (naive biology). They further proposed that much of early conceptual development involves elaborating these three theories. Let's now further explore these theories.

The Child's Theory of Mind

From early in infancy, children interact differently with people than with animals, plants, or inanimate objects in their environment (DelCielo & others, 1993). This suggests that they might have an emerging understanding of the human mind (Ritblatt, 1995; Slaughter, 1995). As might be expected, however, their conceptual understanding increases considerably as they develop (Gopnik, 1997; Gopnik & Astington, 2000).

One of the most basic understandings relevant to the mind is that of *agency,* the idea that people cause events to happen through motivation that is entirely internal. Even infants in their first year of life appear to understand that people are agents of their own actions (Poulin-Doubois & Shultz,

thinking
Manipulating and transforming information in memory.

concepts
Categories used to group objects, events, and characteristics on the basis of common properties.

Forming Concepts

Through the Eyes of Psychologists

Henry Wellman, *University of Michigan*

"The importance of theory of mind is demonstrated both by its early appearance and its ubiquity in children's explanations."

1988). This makes them different from inanimate objects such as tables or cars. The very different ways in which infants interact with people, compared with how they interact with other animals, also suggest that they have implicit knowledge that people differ from other animals.

Children's understanding of the human mind grows extensively in early childhood (Wellman, 1997, 2000). By the age of 3, children turn some of their thoughts inward and understand that they and others have internal mental states (Flavell, Green, & Flavell, 1995). Beginning at about 3 years of age, children also show an understanding that the internal beliefs and desires of a person are connected to that person's actions (Wellman & Gelman, 1992).

How do children come to have this understanding of their own minds and those of other people? Henry Wellman (1990) proposed that from about 3 years of age children have a naive theory of how the mind works. He labeled this the belief-desire theory. He classified it as a theory because it divides the world into coherent categories, because it explains why events occur, and because it identifies the causal relations between mental states and actions.

In particular, Wellman proposed that from age 3 onward, children have four types of understanding that provide a foundation for their theory of mind:

1. That minds are different from other objects in the world
2. That the mind generates both beliefs and desires
3. That different types of mental states are related
4. That the mind is used to represent external reality

Regarding the first point, Wellman demonstrated that most 3-year-olds understand that thoughts, memories, and dreams differ from physical objects and from other insubstantial entities such as smoke and sounds. When 3-year-olds were asked to explain why they could not touch their thoughts, they often advanced explanations such as "Because it's in my mind." They did not explain the difficulty of touching sounds or smoke in this way. The 3-year-olds also knew that beliefs and desires were motivators of action, and that they could lead people to act even when they were incorrect (Wellman & Bartsch, 1988). They also knew that mental entities such as images usually corresponded to an external reality that could be touched, even though the images themselves could not be.

This belief-desire theory of mind appears to develop from an earlier understanding of desire without an understanding of belief. Two-year-olds know that desires influence what people do, but they do not understand that having a belief can lead to an action even when the belief is mistaken (Wellman & Wooley, 1990).

Development of the child's theory of mind also continues beyond 3 years of age (Flavell, 1999; Wellman & Gelman, 1998). One of the most interesting later developments involves children's distinction between appearance and reality (that is, between what seems to be true and what really is true). In one study, 3- to 5-year-olds were shown sponge-like objects that looked like rocks; then they were encouraged to play with them so that they knew that the sponge rocks were not actual rocks (Flavell, Flavell, & Green, 1983). The preschoolers were then asked what the object looked like and what it "really, really was," and also what the object would look like to another child and what it would "really, really be."

In a series of studies, 3- to 5-year old children could distinguish thinking from seeing, talking, touching, and knowing (Flavell, Green, & Flavell, 1995). The young children appear to know that thinking is an internal, mental activity that can refer to either real or imagined objects or events.

Most 4- and 5-year-olds could distinguish between appearances and reality regarding the objects. They knew that the object looked like a rock to them, that it was not really a rock, and that another child who had not played with it would think it was a rock because it looked like one. In contrast, most 3-year-olds confused the appearance with the reality, regarding the rock and other objects that were presented in the same way. For example, they often claimed that a model of an orange that smelled like an orange "really, really" was an orange. Many 3-year-olds also claim that the images on television represent real objects inside the television rather than transmitted images.

Yet another aspect of the child's theory of mind is what mental life is like when one is unconscious as opposed to conscious. In one recent study, John Flavell and his colleagues (1999) found that the recognition that people do not engage in conscious mental activities when unconscious is still developing in the middle and late childhood years.

What difference does it make how well people understand their own minds and those of other people? Considering the way we play games can help illustrate just how important it is. Regardless of whether we are playing chess, football, poker, or tennis, we analyze our opponents' intentions and beliefs, and vary our own behavior to take advantage of their expectations. Of course, they are doing the same with us, which is what makes playing such games so challenging. Without a theory not only of how minds in general work, but of how the minds of particular opponents work, such games would not be nearly as interesting, and probably would not be played at all.

The Child's Theory of Living Things

Children of all ages are fascinated by living things. Such words as *doggie* and *kitty* regularly are among the first words that they learn. Even before they learn language, infants will intently watch people and other animals. Part of this is due to their general interest in things that move. However, even compared with inanimate moving things, such as cars and trucks, children appear to be especially interested in things that move and that are living as well. Already during the first year of life, infants distinguish between the types of motion that biological entities tend to make and the types of motion characteristic of things that are not alive; they show special interest in the biological motion (Bertenthal, 1993).

Biological knowledge is complex, and young children have a great deal to learn about it. One key characteristic is growth—unlike nonliving things, biological entities often grow in size in regular, predictable ways. Another key characteristic is consumption of food; all living beings must ingest nutrients in order to produce energy. Another is that despite massive changes in appearance, biological entities keep their identity; the caterpillar before the metamorphosis is the same thing as the butterfly after it. Still another is the consistency of the innards of biological entities; two sofas may have within them entirely different materials, but two cats always have the same basic things inside them.

Even 3- and 4-year-olds have fairly sophisticated biological concepts. They in general realize that plants and animals grow and that other things do not (Inagaki, 1995). They also know that living things inherit many of their properties from their parents, and that subsequent environmental events that alter their appearance do not change these basic properties (Keil, 1989). They also know that animals and plants always have offspring that are of the same species—dogs always have puppies and never kittens. These offspring retain their basic characteristics even if they are raised by another type of animal. For example, 3- and 4-year-olds believe that a rabbit raised by a monkey family will still prefer lettuce rather than bananas (Springer & Keil, 1991).

A great deal of conceptual development occurs beyond this initial understanding of biology. For example, until the early years of schooling, many children do not know that plants as well as animals are living things. The age at which children realize which types of objects are living and which are not depends greatly on the particular culture in which they grow up.

The Child's Theory of the Physical World

Infants know not only that objects continue to exist even when they cannot be seen, but also that all parts of an object move together, that solid objects cannot pass through each other, and that objects do not spontaneously move without being acted on by some external force (Spelke, 1988).

Understanding of the physical world, of course, goes well beyond understanding of the properties of objects. Another important type of understanding involves knowledge of space. We live in a world of locations and distances, paths and barriers, enclosed and open space. Our ability to move around in this world and to pursue our goals depends critically on our ability to represent such spatial information accurately.

Like their understanding of the human mind, older children's understanding of space builds on rudimentary early understanding. Even infants have some understanding of space, largely in relation to themselves. As time passes, they represent space in an increasingly objective way that is decreasingly dependent on where they themselves are within the space.

Forming concepts is an important aspect of thinking. As we see next, so is solving problems.

Solving Problems

Let's examine what problem solving means and some steps involved in problem solving.

problem solving
Finding an appropriate way to attain a goal.

Exploring Problem Solving   **Problem solving** *involves finding an appropriate way to attain a goal.* Consider these problems that require students to engage in problem solving: creating a project for a science fair, writing a paper for an English class, getting a community to be more environmentally responsive, or giving a talk on the factors that cause people to be prejudiced.

Efforts have been made to specify the steps that individuals go through in effectively solving problems. Following are four such steps.

(1) Find and Frame Problems   Before a problem can be solved, it has to be recognized. In the past, most problem-solving exercises given to students have involved well-defined problems with well-defined solutions and operations for attaining the solutions. Schools need to place more emphasis on encouraging students to identify problems instead of just trying to solve well-defined textbook problems. Many real life problems are ill-defined: They are vague and don't have clearly defined ways of being solved. Consider a child's problem of having to get to a club meeting that is being held at a new location an hour after the last class at school. First, the child needs to identify the existence of a problem to be solved, such as what time to leave to make the club meeting on time. To solve this general problem the child has to solve several subproblems, such as these: Where is the new location? How far away is it? Can I get there in time by riding my bike? Will I have to take a bus? And so on.

(2) Develop Good Problem-Solving Strategies   Once children find a problem and clearly define it, they need to develop strategies for solving it. Effective strategies include setting subgoals, using algorithms, and calling on heuristics.

subgoaling
Setting intermediate goals that put one in a better position to reach the final goal or solution.

Subgoaling *involves setting intermediate goals that put students in a better position of reaching the final goal or solution.* Children might do poorly at solving problems because they don't generate subproblems or subgoals. Let's return to the science fair project of the reliability of people's memory for traumatic events they have experienced. What might be some subgoaling strategies? One might be locating the right books and research journals on thinking, another might be interviewing teachers about the strategies they use to encourage deep thinking. At the same time as this subgoaling strategy is taking place, the child likely will benefit from establishing further subgoals in terms of what she needs to accomplish along the way to her final goal of a finished science project. If the science project is due in 3 months, she might set a subgoal of finishing the first draft of the project 2 weeks before it is due, another subgoal of completing the research a month before the project is due, being halfway through the research 2 months before the project is due, having three teacher interviews done 2 weeks from today, and starting library research tomorrow.

Notice that in establishing the subgoals, we worked backward in time. Working backward in establishing subgoals is often a good strategy. Children first create a subgoal that is closest to the final goal and then work backward to the subgoal that is closest to the beginning of the problem-solving effort.

Algorithms *are strategies that guarantee an answer to a problem.* When children solve a multiplication problem by a set procedure, they are using an algorithm. When they follow the directions for diagramming a sentence, they are using an algorithm. Life would be easy if all its problems could be solved by algorithms. But many real-world problems are not so straightforward. They require the use of heuristics.

Heuristics *are strategies or rules of thumb that can suggest a solution to a problem but don't guarantee a solution.* Consider an adolescent who has just gotten his driver's license. He is going to drive over to a friend's house he has never been to before. He drives through an unfamiliar part of town and soon realizes that he is lost. If he knows that the correct direction to turn is north, he might use the heuristic of turning onto the road that goes in that direction. This strategy might work, but it also might fail. The road might end or it might veer east.

Means-end analysis *is the heuristic in which the goal (end) of a problem is identified, the current situation is assessed, and what needs to be done (means) to decrease the difference between the two conditions is evaluated.* Another name for the means-end analysis is "difference reduction." Means-end analysis also can involve the use of subgoaling, which we described earlier. Means-end analysis is commonly used in solving problems. Consider a 14-year-old girl who must do a science project (the end). She assesses her current state, in which she is just starting to think about the project. Then she maps out a plan to reduce the difference between her current state and the goal (end). Her "means" include talking to several scientists in the community about potential projects, going to the library to study about the topic she chooses, and exploring the Internet for potential projects and ways to carry them out.

Infants less than 1 year of age exhibit such means-end analysis in some situations. For example, in one study, 9-month-olds were presented with a foam-rubber barrier, behind which was hidden a cloth (Willatts, 1990). Some of the babies saw a small toy on the far end of the cloth, others saw the toy beside, rather than on top of, the cloth. When the toy was on the cloth rather than beside it, the 9-month-olds were much more likely to knock down the barrier and pull the cloth to them. Means-end analysis later is extended to much more complex situations, involving more numerous and complex subgoals and requiring the discipline to resist the lure of short-term goals to pursue longer-term ones.

(3) Evaluate Solutions   Once we think we have solved a problem, we won't really know how effective our solution is until we find out if it actually works. It helps to have in mind a clear criterion for effectiveness. For example, what will be the child's criterion for the science fair project? Will it be simply getting it completed? receiving positive feedback about the project? winning an award? winning first place? the self-satisfaction of having set a goal, planned for it, and reached it?

(4) Rethink and Redefine Problems and Solutions over Time   An important final step in problem solving is to continually rethink and redefine problems and solutions over time (Bereiter & Scardamalia, 1993). People who are good at problem solving are motivated to improve on their past performances and to make original contributions. Thus, the child who completed the science fair project can look back at the project and think about ways that the project can be improved. The child might use feedback from judges or information from others who talked with the child about the project to tinker with and fine-tune it.

Using Rules to Solve Problems   Much of information-processing research on problem solving has been aimed at identifying the rules children use to solve problems. The balance scale problem is useful for illustrating this research. The type of balance scale that has been used to examine children's understanding is shown in figure 8.9. The scale includes a fulcrum and an arm that can rotate around it. The arm can tip left or right or remain level, depending on how weights (metal disks with holes in the center) are arranged on the pegs on each side of the fulcrum. The child's task is to look at the configuration of weights on the pegs on each problem and then

algorithms
Strategies that guarantee a solution to a problem.

heuristics
Strategies or rules of thumb that can suggest a solution to a problem but don't guarantee a solution.

means-end analysis
A heuristic in which one identifies the goal (end) of a problem, assesses the current situation, and determines what needs to be done (means) in order to attain the goal.

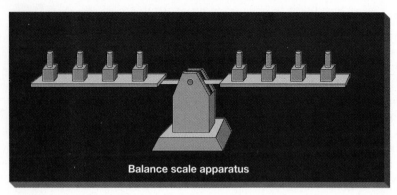

Balance scale apparatus

Figure 8.9
The Type of Balance Scale Used by Siegler (1976)

Weights could be placed on pegs on each side of the fulcrum; the torque (the weight on each side times the distance of that weight from the fulcrum) determined which side would go down.

predict whether the left side will go down, the right side will go down, or the arm will balance.

Robert Siegler (1976) hypothesized that children would use one of the four rules depicted in figure 8.10.

Rule I. If the weight is the same on both sides, predict that the scale will balance. If the weight differs, predict that the side with more weight will go down.

Rule II. If the weight is greater on one side, say that that side will go down. If the weights on the two sides are equal, choose the side on which the weight is farther from the fulcrum.

Rule III. Act as in Rule II, except that if one side has more weight and the weight on the other side is farther from the fulcrum, then guess.

Rule IV. Proceed as in Rule III, unless one side has more weight and the other more distance. In that case, calculate torques by multiplying weight times distance on each side. Then predict that the side with the greater torque will go down.

But how could it be determined which rule, if any, a given child was using? Siegler reasoned that presenting problems on which different rules would generate different outcomes would allow assessment of each child's rules. For example, suppose there were four weights on the third peg to the left of the fulcrum and three weights on the fourth peg to the right of the fulcrum. A child using Rule I or Rule II would say that the left side will go down, because it has more weight; a child using Rule III would guess and therefore sometimes say one answer and sometimes another; and a child using Rule IV would compute torques and realize that the two sides would balance. Through a child's pattern of correct answers and errors on a set of such problems, that child's underlying rule could be inferred.

This *rule assessment approach* demonstrated that almost 90 percent of children aged 5 to 17 years used one of the four rules. Almost all 5-year-olds used Rule I, almost all 9-year-olds used either Rule II or Rule III, and both 13-year-olds and 17-year-olds generally used Rule III. Interestingly, despite the 17-year-olds' having studied balance scales in their physics course, almost none of them used the only rule that generated consistently correct answers, Rule IV. Discussions with their teachers revealed why; the balance scale the students had studied was a pan balance, on which small pans could be hung from various locations along the arm, rather than an arm balance, with pegs extending upward. Retesting the children showed that most could consistently solve the problems when the familiar pan balance was used. The example illustrates a set of lessons that frequently has emerged from studies of problem solving—learning is often quite narrow, generalization beyond one's existing knowledge is difficult, and even analogies that seem straightforward are often missed.

The development of problem solving does not start at age 5. Certain basic problem-solving abilities are already present in infancy. Below we consider some of these, as well as the subsequent development of a number of other key problem-solving capabilities.

Using Analogies to Solve Problems
When people encounter new problems, often they interpret them with reference to better-understood, previously encountered ones. For example, in one study college students were presented with a problem in which a physician needed to destroy a patient's tumor, and the only way to do so was with massive amounts of radiation (Duncker, 1945). However, the amount of radiation was sufficiently large that it would also destroy healthy tissue on the way to the tumor. Half the dosage of radiation would not kill the healthy tissue, though it also would not destroy the tumor. What should the physician do?

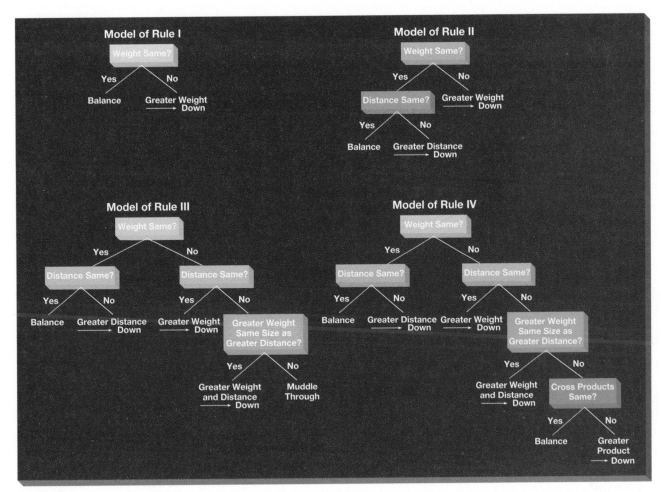

Figure 8.10
Four Rules for Solving the Balance Scale Task

Children following Rule I would always pick the side with more weight as the one that would go down, and would say that the scale would balance whenever the two sides had the same amount of weight. Children using Rule II would do the same, except that if the two sides had the same amount of weight, they would base their judgments on the distance of the weights from the fulcrum. Children using Rule III would always consider both weight and distance, and would respond correctly if one or both were equal. However, they would muddle through or guess if one side had more weight and the other had its weight farther from the fulcrum. Finally, children using Rule IV would act the same as those using Rule III, except that they would compute torques when one side had more weight and the other had its weight farther from the fulcrum.

Most people find this problem difficult. They are more likely to solve it, how-ever, if they first learn the solution to another problem in which an attacking army cannot travel in one large group, because the attack route is too narrow, but instead must divide into separate units, come from different directions, and converge at a central location. This suggests to many the idea of sending half the desired amount of radiation from each of two directions, with the two converging at the site of the tumor. Such extrapolation from better-understood to less-understood problems is the key to analogical problem solving.

The development of analogical problem solving resembles that of scientific rea-soning. Even very young children can draw reasonable analogies under some cir-cumstances and use them to solve problems (Freeman & Gehl, 1995). Under other circumstances, even college students fail to draw seemingly obvious analogies (as in the example of the high school students' difficulty in extrapolating from the familiar pan balance to the unfamiliar arm balance, described earlier). This resemblance is not coincidental, since scientific reasoning often depends on drawing useful analogies.

Judy DeLoache (left) has conducted research that focuses on young children's developing cognitive abilities. She has demonstrated that children's symbolic representation between 2½ and 3 years of age enables them to find a toy in a real room that is a much bigger version of the scale model.

Ann Brown and her collaborators (Brown, 1990; Brown, Kane, & Echols, 1986) have demonstrated some of the types of analogical reasoning that occur at ages 1 through 5 years. When 1- and 2-year-olds are shown that a curved stick can be used as a tool to pull in a toy that is too far away to be reached unaided, they draw the correct analogy in choosing which stick to use the next time. They do not choose sticks on the basis of their being of the same color as the stick they used before. They also do not just choose objects that look exactly like the tool they saw demonstrated to be effective (such as a curved cane); instead they identify the essential property and will choose whichever objects have it (they will choose a straight rake as well as the curved cane). The 2-year-olds were more likely than the 1-year-olds to learn the initial task without any help, but once they learned the task, both 1- and 2-year-olds drew the right analogy to new problems.

Successful analogical problem solving often involves tools more abstract than curved sticks for hauling in objects that are beyond one's reach. Maps and verbal descriptions of routes, for example, often help us to figure out how to get where we want to go (DeLoache, Miller, & Pierroutakos, 1997). Recent studies of toddlers' abilities to use scale models to guide their problem-solving activities show that dramatic developments occur in such tool use quite early in development.

Judy DeLoache (1989) created a situation in which 2½- and 3-year-olds were shown a small toy hidden within a scale model of a room. The child was then asked to find the toy in a real room that was a bigger version of the scale model. If the toy was hidden under the armchair in the scale model, it was also hidden under the armchair in the real room. Considerable development occurred between 2½ and 3 years of age on this task. Thirty-month-old children rarely could solve the problem; by 36 months they generally could.

What was the source of the 2½-year-olds' difficulty on the task? It was not inability to understand how any type of symbol could represent another situation. Shown line drawings or photographs of the larger room, 2½-year-olds had no difficulty finding the object. Instead, the difficulty seemed to come from the toddlers' simultaneously viewing the scale model as a symbol of the larger room and as an object in itself. Surprising consequences followed from this insight. Allowing children to play with the scale model before using it as a symbol worsened their performance, presumably because playing with it made them think of it more as an object in itself. Conversely, putting the scale model in a glass case, where the children could not handle it at all, resulted in the children's more often being able to use it successfully to find the object hidden in the larger room. The general lesson is that young children can use a variety of tools to draw analogies, but they easily can forget that an object is being used as a symbol of something else and instead take it as being of interest as an object in its own right.

We have studied a number of ways infants and young children learn and solve problems. Next we explore another very important way infants, as well as children and adults, solve problems—by imitation.

Infant Imitation   One of the most important ways to solve problems is to imitate the actions of more-knowledgeable others who are confronted with similar problems (Call, 1995). This is especially true for young children, who have less experience solving problems and fewer general problem-solving strategies than older individuals have. Copying its mother's problem-solving strategies has, clearly, survival value for an infant. Thus, it is not surprising that basic imitative abilities are present from early in life.

Just how early certain imitative capacities are present became apparent in an intriguing experiment conducted by Tiffany Field and her colleagues (1982). They examined the capabilities of newborns within 36 hours of their birth. An adult held each newborn in front of her, with its head upright, 10 inches from herself. With her face she expressed one of the three emotions: happiness, sadness, or surprise. Infants were most likely to imitate the model's display of surprise by widely opening their mouths. When the infants observed a happy expression, they frequently widened their lips. When the adult's face looked sad, the infant's lips moved into a pouting expression.

Infant development researcher Andrew Meltzoff (1990) has conducted numerous studies of infants' imitative abilities. He believes that these abilities are biologically based, because infants can imitate a facial expression within the first few days after birth, before they have had the opportunity to observe social agents in their environment engage in tongue protrusion and other behaviors. He also believes that infants' imitative abilities do not fit the ethologists' concept of a hardwired, reflexive, innate releasing mechanism, but rather that these abilities are flexible and adaptable to the demands of particular situations (Meltzoff, 2000). In Meltzoff's observations of infants in the first 72 hours of life, the infants gradually displayed a full imitative response to an adult's facial expressions, such as tongue protrusion or a wide opening of the mouth (see figure 8.11). Initially, a young infant might only get its tongue

> *We are in truth, more than half what we are by imitation.*
>
> Lord Chesterfield
> *English Statesman, 18th Century*

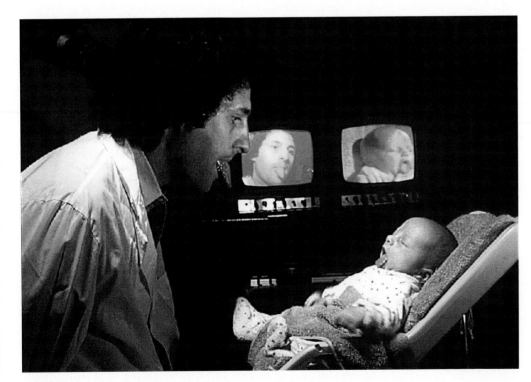

Figure 8.11

Infants' Ability to Imitate

Shown here is infant development researcher Andrew Meltzoff displaying tongue protrusion, prompting an infant to imitate his behavior. Researchers have demonstrated that infants can imitate adults' behavior far earlier than formerly believed.

to the edge of its lips, but after a number of attempts and observations of adult behavior, the infant displays a more full-blown imitation.

Meltzoff also has studied deferred imitation, imitation that occurs hours or days after the original event. In one investigation, Meltzoff (1988) demonstrated that 9-month-old infants can imitate actions they saw performed 24 hours earlier. Each action consisted of an unusual gesture, such as pushing a recessed button in a box (which produced a beeping sound). Piaget had concluded that deferred imitation was impossible until about 18 months of age, because he believed that until then infants lacked basic representational abilities needed to maintain the memory of the earlier event. Meltzoff's research suggests that infants can form such representations much earlier in development.

Current debate focuses on what is implied by the rich initial state of early imitation. One view is that the innate psychological structures involved in early imitation are adultlike. This approach argues that newborns remain virtually unchanged during the course of development. However, Meltzoff and his colleague M. Keith Moore (1999) argue that evolution equipped infants not with adult concepts but with early mental structures that allow imitation to be deployed as a discovery mechanism for understanding persons.

Now let's turn our attention to one final topic in problem solving: Let's examine the increasing interest in having students engage in problem-based learning in schools.

problem-based learning
An approach that emphasizes solving authentic problems, like those that occur in daily life.

Problem-Based Learning   **Problem-based learning** *emphasizes solving authentic problems like those that occur in daily life* (Jones, Rasmussen, & Moffitt, 1997). An example of problem-based learning involves the program called YouthALIVE! at the Children's Museum of Indianapolis (Schauble & others, 1996). Students solve problems related to conceiving, planning, and installing exhibits; designing videos; creating programs to help visitors understand and interpret museum exhibits; and brainstorming about strategies for building bridges into the community.

The Cognition and Technology Group at Vanderbilt (1997) developed a program of problem-based learning called *The Jasper Project. Jasper* consists of 12 videodisc-based adventures that are designed to improve the mathematical thinking of students in grades 5 and up, as well as help students to make connections with other disciplines, including science, history, and social studies. *Jasper*'s creators argue that too often math and other subjects are taught as isolated skills. One of the *Jasper* adventures, *The Right Angle,* can be used not only in geometry classes but also in geography (topography) and history (Native American cultures).

The Jasper Project

The adventures focus on a character named Jasper Woodbury and others, who encounter a number of real-life problems that need to be solved. Figure 8.12 profiles one of the *Jasper* problem-solving adventures.

As we saw earlier, finding and framing a problem is an important aspect of problem solving. The *Jasper* adventures end with challenges that motivate students to generate new problems to solve. Also, the *Jasper* series stimulates students to identify a number of subproblems or subgoals on their own.

The *Jasper* series also encourages collaborative problem solving among students. As students work together over a number of class periods, they have numerous opportunities to communicate about math, share their problem-solving strategies, and get feedback that helps them refine their thinking. Groups of students present their ideas to the class, discussing the strengths and weaknesses of their strategies and solutions.

Through the Eyes of Psychologists

John Bransford,
Vanderbilt University

"An important goal of curriculum design is to teach content and skills in the context of attempts to solve authentic problems."

Each videodisc-based adventure includes extension problems. These help students to engage in "what if" thinking by revisiting the original adventures from new points of view. Thus, after finding a way to rescue a wounded eagle in *Rescue at Boone's Meadow* (most students solve the problem with an ultralight airplane that is featured in this adventure), students are presented with a revised problem in which they must rethink how the presence of headwinds or tailwinds might affect their original solution.

The *Jasper Project* also encourages teachers to develop actual problem-solving projects after students have worked with a *Jasper* adventure. For example, in one school, after creating a business plan for the adventure *The Big Splash,* students were given the opportunity to gather relevant data to create a business plan to present to the principal. In this instance, the creation of a business plan led to a fun fair being held for the entire school (Barron & others, 1996). In another school, students who had spent time solving problems in the adventure *Blueprints for Success* were given the opportunity to design a playhouse for preschools. Well-designed playhouses were actually built and donated to the preschools in the students' names.

An optional feature of the *Jasper* series is the video-based SMART Challenge series. Its goal is to connect classes of students to form a community of learners that tries to solve *Jasper*-related challenges. SMART stands for Special Multimedia Arenas for Refining Thinking. These arenas use telecommunications, television technology, and Internet technology to give students feedback about other groups' problem-solving efforts. For example, students who are working on *Blueprint for Success* can see data from 60 other students about links between the length of legs for A-frame swing sets and the desired height of the swing sets.

The *Jasper Project* not only represents the use of problem-based learning, it also provides an example of how to encourage children to think critically, which we explore in greater detail next.

"Blueprint for Success"

Christina and Marcus, two students from Trenton, visit an architectural firm on Career Day. While learning about the work of architects, Christina and Marcus hear about a vacant lot being donated in their neighborhood for a playground. This is exciting news because there is no place in their downtown neighborhood for children to play. Recently, several students have been hurt playing in the street. The challenge is for students to help Christina and Marcus design a playground and ballfield for the lot.

Figure 8.12
Problem-Solving Adventures in the *Jasper Project*

Critical Thinking

Currently, there is considerable interest in critical thinking among psychologists and educators, although it is not an entirely new idea. The famous educator John Dewey (1933) proposed a similar idea when he talked about the importance of getting students to think reflectively. The well-known psychologist Max Wertheimer (1945) talked about the importance of thinking productively rather than just guessing at a correct answer. **Critical thinking** *involves thinking reflectively and productively, and evaluating the evidence.* In this book, the Adventures for the Mind boxes that appear in every chapter challenge you to think critically about a topic or issue related to the discussion. We can consciously build critical thinking in children by modeling or encouraging the following behaviors:

critical thinking
Thinking reflectively and productively, and evaluating the evidence.

- Asking not only *what* happened but *how* and *why* it happened
- Examining supposed "facts" to determine if there is evidence to support them
- Arguing in a reasoned way rather than through emotions
- Recognizing that there is sometimes more than one good answer or explanation
- Comparing various answers to a question and judging which is really the best answer
- Evaluating and possibly questioning what other people say rather than immediately accepting it as the truth
- Asking questions and speculating beyond what we already know to create new ideas and new information

Jacqueline and Martin Brooks (1993) lament that so few schools really teach students to think critically. In their view, schools spend too much time getting students to give a single correct answer in an imitative way rather than encouraging students to expand their thinking by coming up with new ideas and rethinking earlier conclusions. They believe that too often teachers ask students to recite, define, describe, state, and list—rather than to analyze, infer, connect, synthesize, criticize, create, evaluate, think, and rethink.

Brooks and Brooks point out that many successful students complete their assignments, do well on tests, and get good grades, yet don't ever learn to think critically

THINK

"We did that last year—how come we have to do it again this year?"

Used by permission of the Estate of W. A. Vanselow

and deeply. They believe our schools turn out students who think too superficially, staying on the surface of problems rather than stretching their minds and becoming deeply engaged in meaningful thinking.

Daniel Perkins and Sarah Tishman (1997) work with teachers to incorporate critical thinking into classrooms. The following are some of the critical-thinking skills they encourage teachers to help their students develop.

- *Open-mindedness.* This involves getting students to avoid narrow thinking and to explore options. For example, when teaching American literature, teachers might ask students to generate multiple critiques of Aldous Huxley's *Brave New World.*
- *Intellectual curiosity.* This involves encouraging students to wonder, probe, question, and inquire. Getting students to recognize problems and inconsistencies also is an aspect of intellectual curiosity. In history class, this might mean looking beyond culturally biased views of American history by reading British or Native American views on the American Revolution.
- *Planning and strategy.* Teachers can work with students to help them develop plans, set goals, find direction, and seek outcomes. In physical education, this might involve determining the best strategy for winning a basketball or softball game.
- *Intellectual carefulness.* Teachers can encourage students to check for inaccuracies and errors, to be precise, and to be organized. For example, when students write a paper, they can learn to structure the content and check the facts that they include.

For many years, the major debate in teaching critical thinking has been whether it should involve teaching critical thinking skills as general entities or in the context of specific subject matter instruction (math, English, or science, for example). A number of experts on children's thinking believe the evidence has come down on the side of instruction in critical thinking embedded in a rich subject matter (Kuhn, 1999).

Today, another debate regarding critical thinking has emerged. On the one side are traditionalists who see critical thinking as a set of mental competencies that reside in children's heads. On the other side are advocates of a situated-cognition approach to critical thinking, who regard intellectual skills as social entities that are exercised and shared within a community (Rogoff, 1998). This ongoing debate has not yet been resolved.

An innovative program that encourages critical thinking, Fostering a Community of Learners (FCL), was created by Anne Brown and Joe Campione (1996; Brown, 1997, 1998). The program focuses on literacy development and biology. As currently established, it is set in inner-city elementary schools and is appropriate for 6- to 12-year-old children. Reflection and discussion are key dimensions of the program. Constructive commentary, questioning, querying, and criticism are the mode rather than the exception. Three strategies that encourage reflection and discussion are (1) Having children teach children, (2) Implementing online computer consultation, and (3) using adults as role models.

- *Children Teaching Children*

  Brown says that children as well as adults enrich the classroom learning experience by contributing their particular expertise. Cross-age teaching, in which older students teach younger students, is used in FCL. This occurs both face-to-face and via electronic mail (e-mail). Older students often serve as discussion leaders. Cross-age teaching provides students with invaluable opportunities to talk about learning, gives students responsibility and purpose, and fosters collaboration among peers.

  Reciprocal teaching, *in which students take turns leading a small-group discussion,* is used in FCL. Reciprocal teaching requires students to discuss complex passages, collaborate, and share their individual expertise and perspectives on a particular topic. Reciprocal teaching can involve a teacher and a student as well as student-student interaction.

  FCL also uses a modified version of the jigsaw classroom (students cooperate by doing different parts of a project to reach a common goal). As students

Schools for Thought
Odyssey of the Mind

reciprocal teaching
A teaching method in which students take turns leading small-group discussions.

create preliminary drafts of reports, they participate in "cross-talk" sessions. These are whole-class activities in which groups periodically summarize where they are in their learning activity and get input from the other groups. "Mini-jigsaws" (small groups) also are used. At both the whole-class level and mini-jigsaw level, if group members can't understand what someone is saying or writing about, the students have to revise their product and present it again later. Students are then grouped into reciprocal teaching seminars in which each student is an expert on one subtopic, teaches the part to the others, and also participates in constructing test questions based on the subunit.

• *Online Computer Consultation*

Face-to-face communication is not the only way to build community and expertise. FCL classrooms also use electronic mail. Through e-mail, experts provide coaching and advice, as well as commentary about what it means to learn and understand. Online experts function as role models of thinking. They wonder, query, and make inferences based on incomplete knowledge.

• *Adults as Role Models*

Visiting experts and classroom teachers introduce the big ideas and difficult principles at the beginning of a unit. The adult models how to think and reflect in the process of finding a topic or reasoning with given information. The adults continually ask students to justify their opinions and then support them with evidence, to think of counterexamples to rules, and so on.

One example of a teaching theme used in the FCL program is "changing populations." Outside experts and/or teachers introduce this lesson and ask students to generate as many questions about it as possible—it is not unusual for students to come up with more than a hundred questions. The teacher and the students categorize the questions into subtopics according to the type of population they refer to (usually about five categories), such as extinct, endangered, artificial, assisted, and urbanized populations. About six students make up a learning group, and each group takes responsibility for one of the subtopics.

A culture of learning, negotiating, sharing, and producing work that is displayed to others is at the heart of FCL. The educational experience involves an interpretive community that encourages active exchange and reciprocity. This approach has much in common with what Jerome Bruner (1996) recommended for improving the culture of education. Research evaluation of the Fostering a Community of Learners approach suggests that it benefits students' understand-

A Fostering a Community of Learners classroom. What is the nature of this approach to education?

ᎦUMMARY ᏁABLE 8.3
Thinking

Concept	Processes/Related Ideas	Characteristics/Description
What Is Thinking?	Its Nature	• Thinking involves manipulating and transforming information in memory. • Thinking is often carried out to form concepts, reason, think critically, and solve problems.
Forming Concepts	What Are Concepts?	• They are categories used to group objects, events, and characteristics on the basis of common properties. • Concepts are elements of cognition that help to simplify and summarize information. They also improve memory, communication, and time use. • Many of children's concepts embody implicit theories about the world.
	The Child's Theory of Mind	• Wellman proposed that children have a naive theory of how the mind works—he labeled it "belief-desire theory."
	The Child's Theory of Living Things	• Even 3- and 4-year-olds have fairly sophisticated biological concepts.
	The Child's Theory of the Physical World	• Older children's understanding of space builds on rudimentary early understanding.
Solving Problems	Exploring Problem Solving	• Problem solving involves finding an appropriate way to attain a goal. • Four steps in problem solving are (1) finding and framing problems, (2) developing good problem-solving strategies, (3) evaluating solutions, and (4) rethinking and redefining problems over time.
	Using Rules to Solve Problems	• Much of the information-processing research on problem solving has focused on identifying the rules that children use in solving problems.
	Using Analogies to Solve Problems	• Even very young children can draw reasonable analogies in some circumstances.
	Infant Imitation	• Infants can imitate facial expressions in the first few days of life.
	Problem-Based Learning	• This approach emphasizes solving authentic problems like those in daily life. • The *Jasper Project* is an example of this type of learning.
Critical Thinking	Its Nature	• This involves thinking reflectively and productively, and evaluating the evidence. • Fostering a Community of Learners is an example of a program that seeks to improve children's critical-thinking skills.

ing and flexible use of content knowledge, resulting in improved achievement in reading, writing, and problem solving.

At this point we have studied a number of ideas about children's thinking. A review of these ideas is presented in summary table 8.3.

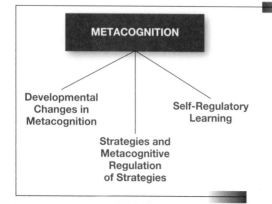

Metacognition

At the beginning of the chapter we defined *metacognition* as cognition about cognition, or "knowing about knowing" (Flavell, 1999; Flavell & Miller, 1998). One expert on children's thinking, Deanna Kuhn (1999), believes that metacognition should be a stronger focus of efforts to help children become better critical thinkers, especially at the middle school and high school levels. She distinguishes between first-order cognitive skills that enable children to know about the world (which have been the main focus of critical thinking programs) and second-order cognitive skills—*meta-knowing skills*—that entail knowing about one's own (and others') knowing.

A distinction can be made between metacognitive knowledge and metacognitive activity (Ferrari & Sternberg, 1998). **Metacognitive knowledge** *involves monitoring and reflecting on one's current or recent thoughts* (Flavell, Miller, & Miller, 1993). This includes both *factual knowledge,* such as knowledge about the task, one's goals, or oneself, and *strategic knowledge,* such as how and when to use specific procedures to solve problems. **Metacognitive activity** *occurs when students use self-awareness to adapt and manage strategies during actual problem-solving and thinking* (Ferrari & Sternberg, 1998; Kuhn & others, 1995). Thus, a student's awareness and use of self-regulatory learning strategies involve metacognition.

Developmental Changes in Metacognition

The majority of developmental studies classified as "metacognitive" have focused on metamemory, or knowledge about memory. This includes general knowledge about memory, such as knowing that recognition tests are easier than recall tests. It also encompasses knowledge about one's own memory, such as a student's ability to monitor whether she has studied enough for a test that is coming up next week.

By 5 or 6 years of age, children usually know that easy items are harder to learn than unfamiliar ones, that short lists are easier than long ones, that recognition is easier than recall, and that forgetting is more likely to occur over time (Lyon & Flavell, 1993). However, in other ways young children's metamemory is limited. They don't understand that related items are easier to remember than unrelated ones or that remembering the gist of a story is easier than remembering information verbatim (Kreutzer, Leonard, & Flavell, 1975). By fifth grade, students understand that gist recall is easier than verbatim recall. Young children also have an inflated opinion of their memory abilities. For example, in one study a majority of young children predicted that they would be able to recall all 10 items of a list of 10 items. When tested for this, none of the young children managed this feat (Flavell, Friedrichs, & Hoyt, 1970). As they move through the elementary school years, children give more realistic evaluations of their memory skills (Bjorklund & Rosenblum, 2000; Schneider & Pressley, 1997).

Young children also have little appreciation for the importance of "cognitive cueing," for memory. Cognitive cueing involves being reminded of something by an external cue or phrase, such as "Don't you remember, it helps you to learn a concept when you can think of an example of it." By 7 or 8 years of age, children better appreciate the importance of such cognitive cueing in memory.

Strategies and Metacognitive Regulation of Strategies

In Michael Pressley's view (Pressley, 1983; McCormick & Pressley, 1997), the key to education is helping students learn a rich repertoire of strategies that result in solutions of problems (Kuhn, 2000). Good thinkers routinely use strategies and effective planning to solve problems. Good thinkers also know when and where to use strategies (they have metacognitive knowledge about strategies). Understanding when and where to use strategies often results from the learner's monitoring of the learning situation.

Pressley argues that when students are given instruction about effective strategies, they often can apply these strategies that they previously have not used on their own. However, some strategies are not effective for young children. For example, young children cannot competently use mental imagery. Pressley emphasizes that students benefit when the teacher models the appropriate strategy and overtly

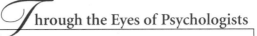

metacognitive knowledge
Monitoring and reflecting on one's current or recent thoughts.

metacognitive activity
Using self-awareness to adapt to and manage strategies during problem solving and thinking.

Metacognition
Metacognition and Reading

verbalizes the steps in the strategy. Then, students subsequently practice the strategy. Their practice of the strategy is guided and supported by the teacher's feedback until the students can effectively execute the strategy autonomously. When instructing students about employing the strategy, it also is a good idea to tell them how using the strategy will benefit them.

Practice alone will not guarantee that students will continue to use the new strategy and transfer it to new situations. For effective maintenance and transfer, encourage students to monitor the effectiveness of the new strategy relative to their use of old strategies by comparing their performance on tests and other assessments. Pressley says that it is not enough to say "Try it, you will like it"; you need to say "Try it and compare."

Learning how to effectively use strategies often takes time. Initially, executing the strategies is usually slow and requires guidance and support from the teacher. With practice, strategies are executed faster and more competently. This means using the effective strategy over and over again until it is automatically performed. For learners to execute the strategies effectively, they need to have the strategies in long-term memory, and extensive practice makes this possible. Learners also need to be motivated to use the strategies.

Let's examine an example of how strategy instruction can be effective. Good readers extract the main ideas from text and summarize them. In contrast, novice readers (for example, most children) usually don't store the main ideas of what they read. One intervention based on what is known about the summarization strategies of good readers consisted of instructing children to (1) ignore trivial information, (2) ignore redundant information, (3) replace less inclusive terms with more inclusive ones, (4) combine a series of events with a more inclusive action term, and (5) choose a topic sentence (Brown & Day, 1983). Researchers have found that instructing elementary school students to use these summarization strategies benefits their reading performance (Rinehart, Stahl, & Erickson, 1986).

Do children use one strategy or multiple strategies in memory and problem solving? They often use more than one strategy (Schneider & Bjorklund, 1998; Siegler, 1998). Most children benefit from generating a variety of alternative strategies and experimenting with different approaches to a problem, discovering what works well, when, and where (Schneider & Bjorklund, 1998). This is especially true for children from the middle elementary school grades on, although some cognitive psychologists believe that even young children should be encouraged to practice varying strategies (Siegler, 1998).

In this discussion, we have indicated that self-monitoring and self-regulatory skills are important aspects of metacognition. Next, we will explore self-regulatory skills in greater detail.

Self-Regulatory Learning

self-regulatory learning
Generating and monitoring thoughts, feelings, and behaviors to reach a goal.

Self-regulatory learning *consists of the self-generation and self-monitoring of thoughts, feelings, and behaviors to reach a goal.* These goals might be academic (improving comprehension while reading, becoming a more organized writer, learning how to do multiplication, asking relevant questions) or they might be socioemotional (controlling one's anger, getting along better with peers). What are some of the characteristics of self-regulated learners? Self-regulatory learners (Winne, 1995, 1997):

- Set goals for extending their knowledge and sustaining their motivation
- Are aware of their emotional makeup and have strategies for managing their emotions
- Periodically monitor their progress toward a goal

- Fine-tune or revise their strategies based on the progress they are making
- Evaluate obstacles that arise and make the necessary adaptations

Researchers have found that high-achieving students are often self-regulatory learners (Pressley, 1995; Schunk & Zimmerman, 1994; Zimmerman, 1998, 2000). For example, compared with low-achieving students, high-achieving students set more-specific learning goals, use more strategies to learn, self-monitor their learning more, and more systematically evaluate their progress toward a goal.

Figure **8.13**
A Model of Self-Regulatory Learning

A Model of Self-Regulatory Learning

Teachers, tutors, mentors, counselors, and parents can help children become self-regulatory learners. Barry Zimmerman, Sebastian Bonner, and Robert Kovach (1996) developed a model for turning low-self-regulatory students into students who engage in these multistep strategies: (1) self-evaluation and self-monitoring, (2) goal setting and strategic planning, (3) putting a plan into action and monitoring it, and (4) monitoring outcomes and refining strategies (see figure 8.13).

Self-Regulatory Learning

They describe a seventh-grade student who is doing poorly in history and apply their self-regulatory model to her situation. In step 1, she self-evaluates her studying and test preparation by keeping a detailed record of them. The teacher gives her some guidelines for keeping these records. After several weeks, the student turns the records in and traces her poor test performance to low comprehension of difficult reading material.

In step 2, the student sets a goal, in this case of improving her reading comprehension, and plans how to achieve the goal. The teacher helps her break down the goal into components such as locating main ideas and setting specific goals for understanding a series of paragraphs in her textbook. The teacher also provides the student with strategies, such as focusing initially on the first sentence of each paragraph and then scanning the others as a means of identifying main ideas. Another support the teacher might offer the student is adult or peer tutoring in reading comprehension if it is available.

In step 3, the student puts the plan into action and begins to monitor her progress. Initially, she might need help from the teacher or tutor in identifying main ideas in the reading. This feedback can help her monitor her reading comprehension more effectively on her own.

In step 4, the student monitors her improvement in reading comprehension by evaluating whether it has had any impact on her learning outcomes. Most importantly: Has her improvement in reading comprehension led to better performance on history tests?

Self-evaluations reveal that the strategy of finding main ideas has only partly improved her comprehension and only when the first sentence contained the paragraph's main idea. So the teacher recommends further strategies. Figure 8.14 describes how teachers can apply the self-regulatory model to homework.

ADVENTURES FOR THE MIND

Exploring Self-Regulatory Skills

LETITIA IS A high school student who doesn't have adequate self-regulatory skills and this is causing her to have serious academic problems. She doesn't plan or organize, has poor study strategies, and uses ineffective time management. Using Zimmerman's four-step strategy, design an effective self-regulation program for Letitia.

1. Self-Evaluation and Monitoring

- The teacher distributes forms so that students can monitor specific aspects of their studying.
- The teacher gives students daily assignments to develop their self-monitoring skills and a weekly quiz to assess how well they have learned the methods.
- After several days, the teacher begins to have students exchange their homework with their peers. The peers are asked to evaluate the accuracy of the homework and how effectively the student engaged in self-monitoring. Then the teacher collects the homework for grading and reviews the peers' suggestions.

2. Goal Setting and Strategic Planning

- After a week of monitoring and the first graded exercise, the teacher asks students to give their perceptions of the strengths and weaknesses of their study strategies. The teacher emphasizes the link between learning strategies and learning outcomes.
- The teacher and peers recommend specific strategies that students might use to improve their learning. Students may use the recommendations or devise new ones. The teacher asks students to set specific goals at this point.

3. Putting a Plan into Action and Monitoring It

- The students monitor the extent to which they actually enact the new strategies.
- The teacher's role is make sure that the new learning strategies are openly discussed.

4. Monitoring Outcomes and Refining Strategies

- The teacher continues to give students opportunities to gauge how effectively they are using their new strategies.
- The teacher helps students summarize their self-regulatory methods by reviewing each step of the self-regulatory learning cycle. She also discusses with students the hurdles the students had to overcome and the self-confidence they have achieved.

Figure **8.14**
Applying the Self-Regulatory Model to Homework

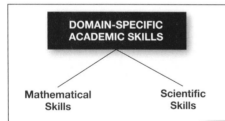

Domain-Specific Academic Skills

Children's information processing also has been studied in specific academic areas such as reading, writing, mathematics, and science. In chapter 10, "Language Development," we will further explore children's reading and writing skills. Here we examine their mathematical and science skills.

Mathematical Skills

Children already have a substantial understanding of numbers before they enter first grade (Winn, 2000). Most middle-socioeconomic-status kindergartners can count past 20; many can count as high as 100 or more, can accurately count the number of objects in a set, can solve small-number addition and subtraction problems (such as 3 + 2), and know the relative magnitudes of single-digit numbers (such as, Which is bigger, 8 or 6?) (Siegler & Robinson, 1982).

When they go to school, children learn many more-advanced kinds of numerical skills (Ginsburg, Klein, & Starkey, 1997). People often think that children just either learn or fail to learn what they are taught. In fact, what they learn often reflects their own thinking as much as anything they are taught. This is true even in the case of basic addition and subtraction, which might be thought to involve only the simplest of learning procedures, memorization.

Arithmetic   In most instruction aimed at helping children learn basic arithmetic facts (such as, How much is 3 plus 9?), the goal is to teach children how to retrieve the answer from memory. For a period of several years after they enter school, however, children use a mix of strategies, including ones that no one ever taught them. Thus, on a problem such as 3 + 9, some first-, second-, and third-graders will retrieve the answer from memory, some will count from 1, some will count from 9, and some will reason that 9 is 1 less than 10, that 3 + 10 is 13, and therefore 3 + 9 must be 12. These last two strategies are rarely taught by teachers or parents, yet children frequently use them anyway.

The fact that first-, second-, and third-graders use all of these arithmetic strategies to solve single-digit problems does not mean that no development occurs over the period. Children become both much faster and more accurate, in part because they increasingly use the faster and more accurate strategies, such as retrieval, and in part because they execute each of the strategies more quickly and accurately. Eventually, they solve all of these problems consistently, correctly, and very quickly.

As they move toward the end of the elementary school period, children learn to solve multidigit arithmetic problems and problems involving fractions. Much of what's involved in learning these more advanced arithmetic skills is overcoming misconceptions. For example, in learning multidigit subtraction, children need to overcome "buggy" rules (named for the "bugs" that appear in faulty computer programs). Suppose a third-grader is given the following four problems and generates the answers shown here:

$$
\begin{array}{rrrr}
306 & 453 & 204 & 370 \\
-43 & -274 & -177 & -89 \\
\hline
343 & 179 & 177 & 281
\end{array}
$$

Can you figure out what the student was doing wrong?

Analysis of the problems indicates that the child was following a "buggy" rule, similar to the partially correct balance scale rules discussed earlier (figure 8.9). The difficulty with these subtraction problems arose only when the problem involved borrowing across a zero; the child answered correctly on the problem that did not involve a zero and on the problem in which the zero was in the rightmost column. When it was necessary to borrow across a zero, the child proceeded in a consistent, but wrong, way that involved subtracting the zero from the number beneath it, rather than the reverse, and then not decrementing the number next to the zero (presumably because nothing had been borrowed from it). Such buggy algorithms are quite common in third-, fourth-, and fifth-graders' subtraction (VanLehn, 1986).

Making teachers aware of the bugs that interfere with their students' learning can lead to better mathematics instruction. For example, in one study a group of student teachers were taught how to design problems that would tell them the precise nature of the bugs in each student's performance (since different children show different bugs) (Brown & Burton, 1978). The precise assessment of children's difficulties promises to allow us to go well beyond standard written comments (such as "60 percent correct—You can do better!") to gear teaching to the needs of individual children.

Algebra   Children develop far more powerful mathematical reasoning when they learn algebra. A single equation can represent an infinite variety of situations. Even many students who get A's and B's in algebra classes, however, do so without understanding what they are learning—they simply memorize the equations. This approach might work well in the classroom, but it limits these students' ability to use algebra in real-world contexts.

This difficulty does not affect just junior high and high school students getting their first exposure to algebra—it also extends to the college level. Fewer than 30 percent of engineering students at a high-quality state university correctly solved the following problem:

Write an equation using the variables $\underline{C}$ and $\underline{S}$ to represent the following statement: "At Mindy's restaurant, for every four people who order cheesecake, there are five people who order strudel." Let $\underline{C}$ represent the number of cheesecakes and $\underline{S}$ the number of strudels. (Clement, Lockhead, & Soloway, 1979, p. 46)

Most of the students represented this problem as $4\underline{C} = 5\underline{S}$. Although this might initially seem logical, this equation says that multiplying two smaller quantities (4 and the number of people ordering cheesecake) yields a result equal to multiplying two larger quantities (5 and the number of people ordering strudel). The underlying difficulty is that even college students at fine universities often do not connect their mathematical equations to what the equations mean. Without such connections, algebra becomes a meaningless exercise in symbol manipulation. Clearly, successful instruction in algebra, as in other areas of mathematics, requires not only teaching students how to solve problems, but also leading students to a deeper understanding of how the solution procedures yield the solutions.

The Math Forum
Math and Science Clearinghouse
Psychology and Math/Science Education

Controversy in Math Education   Mathematics education is currently swirled in controversy over whether a cognitive or a practice approach should be followed (Stevenson, Hofer, & Randel, 1999). Some proponents of the cognitive approach argue against memorization and practice in teaching mathematics. They emphasize a constructivist approach to mathematical problem solving. Others assume that speed and automaticity are fundamental to effective mathematics achievement and emphasize that such skills can be acquired only through practice. In recent years, the constructivist approach has become increasingly popular. In this approach, effective instruction focuses on involving children in solving a problem or developing a concept, and in exploring the efficiency of alternative solutions.

The field of mathematics education is undergoing dramatic change. Shopkeepers' paper-and-pencil math of the low-tech past is no longer adequate in the high-tech age of computers and other electronic challenges that require new ways of understanding math. To meet these new challenges, the National Council of Teachers of Mathematics (1989) published *Curriculum and Evaluation Standards for School Mathematics.* These standards emphasize that teaching math should involve giving students opportunities to

- solve meaningful math problems,
- develop critical reasoning skills,
- make connections to prior knowledge, and
- discuss math concepts with each other.

In general, these standards emphasize that teachers should guide students in making sense of math problems rather than directing them to just do math computational drills.

Scientific Skills

Let's explore the extent to which children engage in scientific thinking and the nature of science education.

Children's Scientific Thinking   Children's problem solving is often compared to that of scientists. Both children and scientists ask fundamental questions about the nature of reality. Both also seek answers to problems that seem utterly trivial or unanswerable to other people (such as, Why is the sky blue?). Both also are granted by society the time and freedom to pursue answers to the problems they find interesting. This "child as scientist" metaphor has led researchers to ask whether children generate hypotheses, perform experiments, and reach conclusions concerning the meaning of their data in ways resembling those of scientists (Clinchy, Mansfield, & Schott, 1995).

Scientific reasoning often is aimed at identifying causal relations. In some ways, children's causal inferences are similar to those of scientists. For example, like scientists, they place a great deal of emphasis on causal mechanisms (Frye & others, 1996). Their understanding of how events are caused weighs more heavily in their causal inferences than do even such strong influences as whether the cause happened immediately before the effect (Shultz & others, 1986).

There also are important differences between the reasoning of children and the reasoning of scientists, however. This is true even of preadolescents who have had some instruction in school regarding the scientific method. One difference comes in the preadolescents' much greater difficulty in separating their prior theories from the evidence that they have obtained. Often, when they try to learn about new phenomena, they maintain their old theories regardless of the evidence (Kuhn, Schauble, & Garcia-Mila, 1992). Another difference is that they are more influenced by happenstance events than by the overall pattern of occurrences (Kuhn, Amsel, & O'Laughlin, 1988). They also have difficulty designing new experiments that can distinguish conclusively among alternative causes. Instead, they tend to bias the experiments in favor of whichever hypothesis they began with, and sometimes they will see the results as supporting their original hypothesis even when the results directly contradict it (Schauble, 1990). Thus, although there are important similarities between children and scientists, in their basic curiosity and in the kinds of questions they ask, there are also important differences in their ability to design conclusive experiments and in the degree to which they can separate theory and evidence (Schauble, 1996).

Science Resources for Teachers
Science Learning Network

Science Education   With an emphasis on discovery and hands-on laboratory investigation, many science teachers now help their students to construct their knowledge of science. Constructivist teaching emphasizes that children have to build their own scientific knowledge and understanding. At each step in science learning, they need to interpret new knowledge in the context of what they already understand. Rather than putting fully formed knowledge into children's minds, in the constructivist approach teachers help children to construct scientifically valid interpretations of the world and guide them in altering their scientific misconceptions (Resnick & Chi, 1988).

Most students are far more interested in science that addresses problems relevant to their lives than they are in discussing abstract theories. One elementary school program that reflects this emphasis is the Science for Life and Living (SLL) project funded by the National Science Foundation (Biological Sciences Curriculum Study, 1989). It emphasizes inquiry, structured groups, and technology.

Some critics argue that such constructivist approaches give too much attention to inquiry skills and not enough to discipline-specific information (American Association for the Advancement of Science, 1993).

The Fostering a Community of Learners Project (Brown, 1998; Brown & Campione, 1996), discussed earlier in the chapter, reflects an emphasis on the social contexts of science. Teacher-student and student-student collaborative interaction are stressed. Students investigate environmental science problems, create group or individual reports, and support each other as part of a community of science learners.

Another program that captures the social contexts of science theme is the Kids as Global Scientists Project. This project focuses on networked communication, incorporating students' perspectives from different countries on issues involving climate change.

At this point we have discussed a number of ideas about metacognition and domain-specific academic skills in mathematics and the sciences. A review of these ideas is presented in summary table 8.4. In the next chapter, we will continue to explore children's cognition by focusing on their intelligence.

SUMMARY TABLE 8.4
Metacognition and Domain-Specific Academic Skills

Concept	Processes/Related Ideas	Characteristics/Description
Metacognition	What Is It?	• Metacognition is cognition about cognition, or knowing about knowing. • Metacognition involves both metacognitive knowledge and metacognitive activity.
	Developmental Changes in Metacognition	• Most studies focus on metamemory, or what children know about how memory works. • Children's metamemory improves considerably during the elementary school years.
	Strategies and Metacognitive Regulation of Strategies	• In Pressley's view, the key to education is helping children learn a rich repertoire of strategies that result in solutions to problems. • Students benefit when teachers model effective strategies and give students opportunities to practice strategies, when students are encouraged to monitor the effectiveness of their new strategy, and when students are motivated to use the strategy. • It takes considerable time to learn a new strategy and use it independently. • Most children benefit from using multiple strategies, exploring when and where they work well.
	Self-Regulatory Learning	• This consists of the self-generation and self-monitoring of thoughts, feelings, and behaviors to reach a goal. • High-achieving students are often self-regulatory learners. • One model of self-regulatory learning involves these components: self-evaluation and self-monitoring; goal setting and strategic planning; putting a plan into action; and monitoring outcomes and refining strategies. • Self-regulatory learning gives children responsibility for their learning.
Domain-Specific Academic Skills	Mathematical Skills	• Children have a substantial understanding of numerical concepts before they enter first grade. • When children go to school, they learn many more-advanced types of numerical skills. • Currently, there is controversy about whether math education should be more cognitive or more practical.
	Scientific Skills	• Children's thinking skills share certain characteristics with those of scientists, but also differ in some ways. • Many science teachers use discovery and hands-on laboratory investigations to help students construct a knowledge of science.

Chapter Review

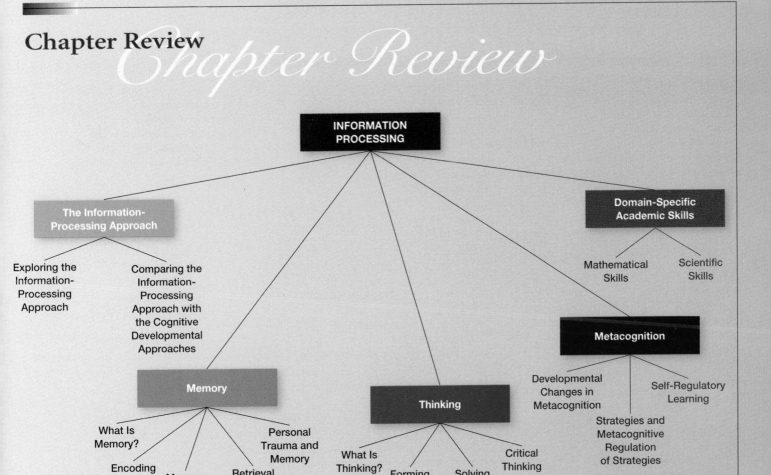

Key Terms

information-processing approach 238
encoding 238
automaticity 238
strategy construction 238
generalization 238
metacognition 238
memory 240
storage 240
retrieval 240
attention 240

habituation 241
dishabituation 241
sensory memory 246
working (short-term) memory 247
long-term memory 247
thinking 255
concepts 255
problem solving 258
subgoaling 258
algorithms 259

heuristics 259
means-end analysis 259
problem-based learning 264
critical thinking 265
reciprocal teaching 266
metacognitive knowledge 269
metacognitive activity 269
self-regulatory learning 270

Key People

Robert Siegler 238
Carolyn Rovee-Collier 241
John Flavell 242
Fergus Craik and Robert Lockhart 243
Allan Paivio 244
Endel Tulving 248
Elizabeth Loftus 253

Henry Wellman and Susan Gelman 255
Judy DeLoache 262
Andrew Meltzoff and Keith Moore 264
John Bransford 264
John Dewey 265
Max Wertheimer 265
Jacqueline and Martin Brooks 265

Daniel Perkins and Sarah Tishman 266
Ann Brown and Joe Campione 266
Deanna Kuhn 268
Michael Pressley 269
Barry Zimmerman, Sebastian Bonner, and Robert Kovach 271

Child Development Resources

Children's Thinking (3rd ed.), 1998
by Robert Siegler
Upper Saddle River, NJ: Prentice Hall

In-depth coverage of information processing by one of the field's leading experts.

Handbook of Child Psychology (5th ed., Vol. 2), (1998)
by Deanna Kuhn and Robert Siegler (Eds.)
New York: John Wiley

Leading developmental psychologists in many areas of children's cognition examine theory and research.

How People Learn (1999)
by the Committee on Developments in the Science of Learning
Washington, DC: National Academy Press

A prestigious panel headed by John Bransford and Anne Brown describe the current state of knowledge about how children think and learn.

The Jasper Project (1997)
by the Cognition and Technology Group at Vanderbilt
Mahwah, NJ: Erlbaum

An innovative, problem-based learning approach is discussed; includes a CD of one of the *Jasper* adventures.

Taking It to the Net

1. Nancy, who is 14, is talking to her older sister, Joanne, age 20. Joanne insists that when Nancy was 6, she got lost at the circus and Joanne and their parents searched frantically for her for 2 hours. Joanne says that they finally found her hanging out by the concession stand, just watching the people. At first, Nancy had no recollection of this, but the more Joanne talked about it, the more Nancy started to recall some of the details. Is it possible that Nancy is imaging a false "memory"?

2. A group of parents have called a special PTA meeting to discuss the math curriculum at their children's elementary school. Apparently students are using computers and calculators, and working in groups on math "projects." The parents are alarmed that their children don't seem to be learning old-fashioned arithmetic. What happened to multiplication tables and long division?

3. Bill Harris, grandfather to fourth-grader Kevin and sixth-grader Jocelyn, is looking for a volunteer opportunity at Kevin and Jocelyn's school. A retired chemical engineer, he would like to help the school beef up its science education program. How could he help?

Connect to *http://www.mhhe.com/santrockc9* to find the answers!

Chapter 9

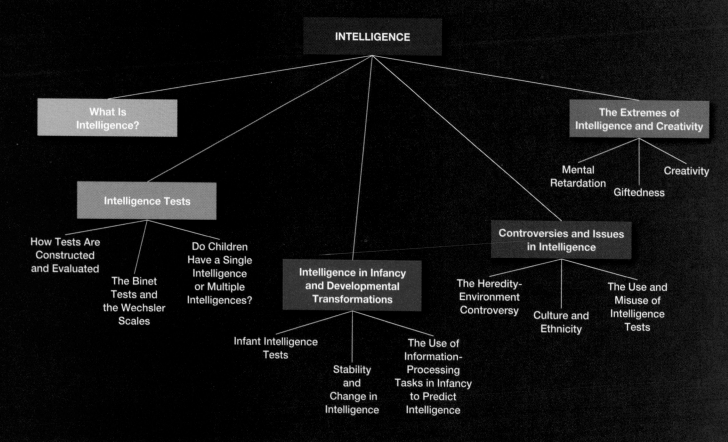

INTELLIGENCE

- What Is Intelligence?
  - Intelligence Tests
    - How Tests Are Constructed and Evaluated
    - The Binet Tests and the Wechsler Scales
    - Do Children Have a Single Intelligence or Multiple Intelligences?
- Intelligence in Infancy and Developmental Transformations
  - Infant Intelligence Tests
  - Stability and Change in Intelligence
  - The Use of Information-Processing Tasks in Infancy to Predict Intelligence
- The Extremes of Intelligence and Creativity
  - Mental Retardation
  - Giftedness
  - Creativity
- Controversies and Issues in Intelligence
  - The Heredity-Environment Controversy
  - Culture and Ethnicity
  - The Use and Misuse of Intelligence Tests

As many people,
as many minds;
everyone his own way.

Terence
Roman Playwright, 2nd Century B.C.

The Story of Project Spectrum

PROJECT SPECTRUM is an innovative educational attempt by Howard Gardner (1993) to encourage the development of a range of intelligences in young children. Spectrum begins with the basic idea that every child has the potential to develop strengths in one or more areas. It provides a context in which to see the strengths and weaknesses of individual children more clearly.

What is a Spectrum classroom like? The classroom has rich and engaging materials that can stimulate a range of intelligences. Teachers do not try to evoke an intelligence directly by using materials that are separated under labels like *sensory* or *verbal*. Rather, materials that relate to a combination of intelligence domains are used. For example, a naturalist corner houses biological specimens that children can explore and compare. This area elicits children's sensory capacities, logical analytic skills, and naturalist skills. In a storytelling area, children create imaginative tales with stimulating props and design their own storyboards. This area encourages children to use their skills in language, drama, and imagery. In a building corner, children can construct a model of their classroom and arrange small-scale photographs of the children and teachers in their class. This area encourages the use of spatial and personal skills. In all, the Spectrum classroom has twelve such areas designed to improve children's multiple intelligences.

The Spectrum classroom can identify skills that are typically missed in a regular classroom. In one first-grade Spectrum classroom, a boy who was the product of a highly conflicted home was at risk for school failure. However, when Project Spectrum was introduced, the boy was identified as the best student in the class at taking apart and putting together common objects, like a food grinder or a doorknob. His teacher became encouraged when she found that he possessed this skill, and his overall school performance began to improve.

In addition to identifying unexpected strengths in children, Project Spectrum also can identify weaknesses. Gregory was doing very well in first grade, being especially skilled in math computation and conceptual knowledge. However, he performed poorly in a number of Spectrum areas. He did well only in the areas in which he needed to give the correct answer and a person in authority gave it to him. As a result of the Spectrum program, Gregory's teacher began to search for ways to encourage him to take risks on more open-ended tasks, to try things out in innovative ways, and to realize that it is okay to make mistakes.

Project Spectrum has evolved to include the development of theme-related kits that tap a range of intelligences. Two such themes are "Night and Day" and "About Me." Children experience the basics of reading, writing, and calculating in the context of the themes and materials with which they are motivated to work. Later in the chapter we will further explore Howard Gardner's ideas about multiple intelligences.

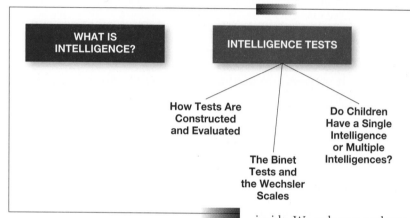

What Is Intelligence?

Twentieth-century English novelist Aldous Huxley said that children are remarkable for their intelligence. What do people mean when they use the term *intelligence?*

Intelligence is one of our most prized possessions, yet it is a concept that even the most intelligent people have not been able to agree on. Unlike such characteristics as height, weight, and age, intelligence cannot be directly measured. We can't peel back a child's scalp and observe the intelligence going on inside. We only can evaluate a child's intelligence *indirectly* by studying the intelligent acts that children generate. For the most part, intelligence tests have been relied on to provide an estimate of a child's intelligence (Kail & Pellegrino, 1985).

Some experts describe intelligence as including verbal ability and problem-solving skills. Others describe it as the ability to adapt to and learn from life's everyday experiences. Combining these ideas, we arrive at a definition of **intelligence** *as verbal ability, problem-solving skills, and the ability to adapt to and learn from life's everyday experiences.*

The primary components of intelligence are very close to the mental processes (such as memory, thinking, and problem solving) that we discussed in chapter 8 ◀◀◀◀ P. 238. The differences in how we described mental processes and how we will discuss intelligence lie in the degree of emphasis placed on individual differences and assessment. **Individual differences** *are the stable, consistent ways in which people are different from each other.* As individual assessment tools, intelligence tests are designed to tell us whether a child can reason better than other children who have taken the test.

intelligence
Verbal ability, problem-solving skills, and the ability to adapt to and learn from life's everyday experiences.

individual differences
The stable, consistent ways in which people are different from one another.

Mental Measurements Yearbook

Intelligence Tests

At some point in your life you probably have taken an intelligence test. Psychologist Robert Sternberg (1997) remembers his early, highly anxious experiences with intelligence tests. Sternberg eventually overcame his anxieties about IQ tests. Thereafter, he not only began performing better on them but when he was 13 he devised his own intelligence test and began using it to assess classmates—that is, until the school principal found out and scolded him. Sternberg became so fascinated by intelligence that he made its study one of his lifelong pursuits. Later in the chapter we will discuss his approach to intelligence. To begin, though, we need to explore how tests are constructed and evaluated, then examine the most widely used tests of intelligence.

How Tests Are Constructed and Evaluated

Measurement and testing have been involved in assessing human thought and behavior for centuries. The Chinese first developed formal oral tests of knowledge as early as 2200

B.C. The Chinese emperor Ta Yü conducted a 3-year cycle of "competency testing" of government officials. After three examinations, the officials were either promoted or fired (Sax, 1997). Tests have become commonplace in today's world as psychologists have sought more precise measurement of psychology's concepts (Embretson & McCollam, 2000; Kaufman, 2000). Any good test must meet three criteria—it must be reliable, it must be valid, and it must be standardized. We will consider each of these criteria.

Reliability

If a test that measures a characteristic is stable and consistent, scores should not significantly fluctuate because of chance factors, such as how much sleep you get the night before the test, who the examiner is, the temperature in the room where you take the test, and so on. **Reliability** *is the extent to which a test yields a consistent, reproducible measure of performance.* Reliability can be measured in several ways (Segal, 2000). **Test-retest reliability,** *is the extent to which a test yields the same measure of performance when an individual is given the same test on two different occasions.* Thus, if we gave an intelligence test to a group of high school students today and then gave them the same test in 6 months, the test would be considered reliable if those who scored high on the test today generally scored high on the test in 6 months. One limitation of test-retest reliability is that individuals sometimes do better the second time they take the test because they are familiar with it.

Alternative forms reliability *involves giving alternate forms of the same test on two different occasions.* The test items on the two forms of the test are similar but not identical. This strategy eliminates the chance of children performing better due to familiarity with the items, but it does not eliminate a child's familiarity with the procedures and strategies involved in the testing. One difficulty with alternate forms reliability is creating two truly parallel alternative forms.

A third method of measuring reliability is **split-half reliability.** *It involves dividing the items into two halves, such as the first half of the test and second half of the test. Individuals' scores on the two halves of the test are compared to determine how consistently they performed.* When split-half reliability is high, we say that a test is *internally consistent.* For example, if we gave an intelligence test in which vocabulary items made up the first half of the test and logical reasoning items made up the second half, to be internally consistent children's scores would have to be similar on each half of the test. Sometimes psychologists compare children's scores on odd-numbered and even-numbered items as another means of establishing the internal consistency of a test.

Validity

A test might give consistent results and yet not truly measure the attribute that it is intended to measure. A test of intelligence might actually measure something else, such as anxiety. The test might consistently measure how anxious a child is and, thus, have high reliability but not measure the child's intelligence, which it purports to measure. **Validity** *is the extent to which a test measures what it is intended to measure.*

Like reliability, there are a number of methods to measure validity. One method is **content validity,** *which refers to the test's ability to test a broad range of the content that is to be measured.* For example, a final test in this class, if it is over the entire book, should sample items from each of the chapters rather than just two or three chapters. If an intelligence test purports to measure both verbal ability and problem-solving ability, the items should include a liberal sampling of items that reflects both of these domains. The test would not have high content validity if it asked a child to define several vocabulary items but did not require the child to reason logically in solving a number of problems.

One of the most important methods of measuring validity is **criterion validity,** *which is the test's ability to predict an individual's performance when assessed by other measures, or criteria, of the attribute.* For example, a psychologist might validate an intelligence test by asking the employers of the individuals who took the intelligence test how intelligent they are at work. The employers' perceptions would be another criterion for measuring intelligence. It is not unusual for the validation of an intelligence test to be another intelligence test. When the scores on the two measures

reliability
The extent to which a test yields a consistent, reproducible measure of performance.

test-retest reliability
The extent to which a test yields the same measure of performance when an individual is given the same test on two different occasions.

alternate forms reliability
Giving alternate forms of the same test on two different occasions.

split-half reliability
Dividing the items into two halves, such as the first half of the test and the second half of the test. Individuals' scores on the two halves of the test are compared to determine how consistently they performed.

Reliability and Validity

validity
The extent to which a test measures what it is intended to measure.

content validity
The test's ability to test a broad range of the content that is to be measured.

criterion validity
The test's ability to predict an individual's performance when assessed by other measures, or criteria, of the attribute.

overlap substantially, we say the test has high criterion validity. Of course, we may use more than one other measure to establish criterion validity. We might give the individuals a second intelligence test, get their employers' perceptions of their intelligence, and observe their behavior in real-life problem-solving situations ourselves.

Criterion validity can follow one of two courses, concurrent or predictive (Krueger & Kling, 2000). **Concurrent validity** *is a form of criterion validity that assesses the relation of a test's scores to a criterion that is presently available (concurrent).* For example, a test might assess children's intelligence. Concurrent validity might be established by analyzing how the scores on the intelligence test correspond to the children's grade in school at this time.

Predictive validity *is a form of criterion validity that assesses the relation of a test's scores to an individual's performance at a point in the future.* For example, scores on an intelligence test might be used to predict whether the individual will be successful in college. The SAT test is used for that purpose (though it is not intended as a test of intelligence). Tests might also be developed to determine success as a police officer or pilot. Individuals take the test and then are evaluated *later* to see if they are indeed able to perform effectively in these jobs (Lubinski, 2000).

A test that is valid is necessarily reliable, but a test that is reliable is not necessarily valid. Children can respond consistently on a test but the test might not be measuring what it purports to measure. To understand this, imagine that you have three darts to throw. If all three fall close together, you have reliability. However you have validity only if three hit the bull's-eye (see figure 9.1).

concurrent validity
A form of criterion validity that assesses the relation of a test's scores to a criterion that is presently available (concurrent).

predictive validity
A form of criterion validity that assesses the relation of a test's scores to the individual's performance at a point in the future.

standardization
Developing uniform procedures for administering and scoring a test, as well as creating norms for the test.

norms
Established standards of performance for a test. Norms are created by giving the test to a large group of individuals representative of the population for whom the test is intended. This allows the test constructor to determine the distribution of the test scores. Norms tell us which scores are considered high, low, or average.

Standardization   Good tests are not only reliable and valid, they are standardized as well. **Standardization** *involves developing uniform procedures for administering and scoring a test, as well as creating norms for the test.* Uniform testing procedures require that the testing environment be as similar as possible for all individuals. Without standardization, it is difficult to compare scores across individuals. If individuals take the SAT in a room where loud music is playing, they are disadvantaged compared to others who take the test in a quiet room. The test directions and the amount of time allowed to complete the test should be the same, for example. **Norms** *are established standards of performance for a test. Norms are created by giving the test to a large group of individuals representative of the population for whom the test is intended. This allows the test constructor to determine the distribution of test scores. Norms inform us which scores are considered high, low, or average.* For example, suppose a child attains a score of 120 on an intelligence test; that number alone has little meaning. The score takes on meaning when we compare it with the other scores. If only 20 percent of the standardized group scored above 120, then we can interpret the child's score as high rather than low or average. Many tests of intelligence are designed for children from diverse groups. So that the tests are applicable to such different groups, many of them have norms—established standards of performance for children of different ages, socioeconomic statuses, and ethnic groups (Cohen, Swerdlik, & Phillips, 1996). Figure 9.2 summarizes the main themes of our discussion of how tests are constructed and evaluated.

Valid and reliable   Reliable but not valid

Figure **9.1**

Links Between Reliability and Validity

A test that is valid is reliable, but a test that is reliable is not necessarily valid. This is illustrated by the dart-throwing analogy. All three darts might land far away from the bull's-eye but land in about the same place (reliability or consistency). To be valid, though, all three darts have to hit the bull's-eye (which also means they have to be reliable, or consistent).

The Binet Tests and the Wechsler Scales

Intelligence tests can be administered to people on an individual basis or in a group. The two most widely used individual tests of intelligence are the Binet tests and Wechsler scales.

The Binet Tests   In 1904 the French Ministry of Education asked psychologist Alfred Binet to devise a method that would determine which students did not profit from typical school instruction. School officials wanted to reduce overcrowding by placing those who

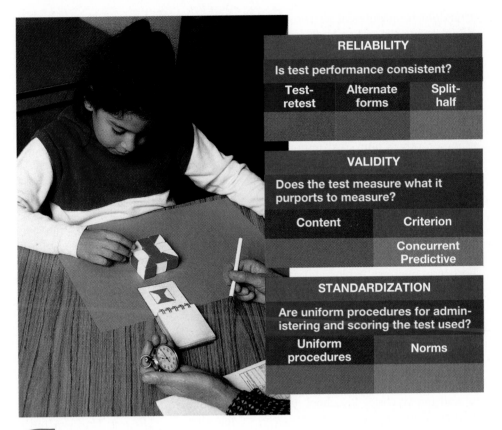

RELIABILITY

Is test performance consistent?

Test-retest	Alternate forms	Split-half

VALIDITY

Does the test measure what it purports to measure?

Content	Criterion
	Concurrent Predictive

STANDARDIZATION

Are uniform procedures for administering and scoring the test used?

Uniform procedures	Norms

Figure **9.2**

Test Construction and Evaluation

did not benefit from regular classroom teaching in special schools. Binet and his student Theophile Simon developed an intelligence test to meet this request. The test is referred to as the 1905 Scale and consisted of 30 items ranging from the ability to touch one's nose or ear when asked to the ability to draw designs from memory and define abstract concepts.

Binet developed the concept of **mental age (MA),** *which is an individual's level of mental development relative to others.* Binet reasoned that a child who is mentally retarded would perform like a normal child of a younger age. He developed norms for intelligence by testing 50 nonretarded children from the ages of 3 to 11. Children suspected of mental retardation were given the test and their performance was compared with children of the same chronological age in the normal sample. Average mental age (MA) scores correspond to chronological age (CA), which is age from birth. A bright child has an MA considerably above CA; a dull child has an MA considerably below CA.

mental age (MA)
An individual's level of mental development relative to others.

The term **intelligence quotient (IQ)** *was devised in 1912 by William Stern. IQ consists of an individual's mental age divided by chronological age multiplied by 100:*

intelligence quotient (IQ)
Devised in 1912 by William Stern, this consists of an individual's mental age divided by chronological age multiplied by 100.

$$IQ = \frac{MA}{CA} \times 100$$

If mental age is the same as chronological age, then the individual's IQ is 100; if mental age is above chronological age, the IQ is more than 100; if mental age is below chronological age, the IQ is less than 100. Scores noticeably above 100 are considered above average; those considerably below are considered below average. For example, a 6-year-old child with a mental age of 8 would have an IQ of 133, whereas a 6-year-old child with a mental age of 5 would have an IQ of 83.

Over the years, extensive effort has been expended to standardize the Binet test, which has been given to thousands of children and adults of different ages selected

normal distribution
A symmetrical distribution with a majority of the cases falling in the middle of the possible range of scores and few scores appearing toward the extremes of the range.

Alfred Binet

at random from different parts of the United States (Paolitto & Naglieri, 2000). By administering the test to large numbers of individuals and recording the results, it has been found that intelligence measured by the Binet approximates a normal distribution (see figure 9.3). A **normal distribution** *is symmetrical, with a majority of cases falling in the middle of the possible range of scores and few scores appearing toward the extremes of the range.*

The current Stanford-Binet is administered individually to people from the age of 2 through the adult years. It includes a variety of items, some of which require verbal responses, others nonverbal responses. For example, items that reflect a 6-year-old's performance on the test include the verbal ability to define at least six words, such as *orange* and *envelope,* as well as the nonverbal ability to trace a path through a maze. Items that reflect an average adult's intelligence include defining such words as *disproportionate* and *regard,* explaining a proverb, and comparing idleness and laziness.

The fourth edition of the Stanford-Binet was published in 1985. One important addition to this version was the analysis of the individual's responses in terms of four content areas: verbal reasoning, quantitative reasoning, abstract/visual reasoning, and short-term memory. A general composite score is still obtained to reflect overall intelligence. The Stanford-Binet continues to be one of the most widely used tests to assess a student's intelligence.

The Wechsler Scales   Besides the Stanford-Binet, the other most widely used intelligence tests are the Wechsler scales, developed by David Wechsler. They include the Wechsler Adult Intelligence Scale–Revised (WAIS-R); the Wechsler Intelligence Scale for Children–III (WISC-III), to test children between the ages of 6 and 16; and the Wechsler Preschool and Primary Scale of Intelligence (WPPSI), to test children from the ages of 4 to 6½.

The Wechsler scales not only provide an overall IQ score but the items are grouped according to eleven subscales, six of which are verbal and five of which are nonverbal. This allows the examiner to obtain separate verbal and nonverbal IQ scores and to see quickly the areas of mental performance in which the individual is below average, average, or above average (Naglieri, 2000). The inclusion of a number

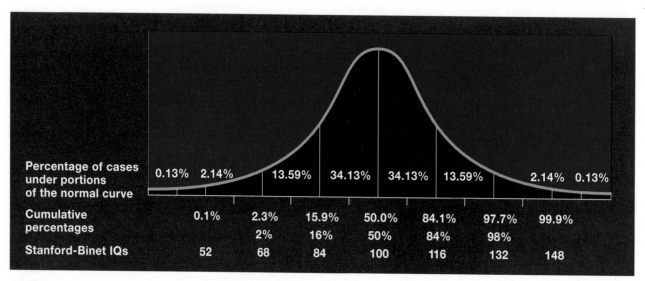

Figure 9.3

The Normal Curve and Stanford-Binet IQ Scores

The distribution of IQ scores approximates a normal curve. Most of the population falls in the middle range of scores. Notice that extremely high and extremely low scores are very rare. Slightly more than two-thirds of the scores fall between 84 and 116. Only about 1 in 50 individuals has an IQ of more than 132 and only about 1 in 50 individuals has an IQ of less than 68.

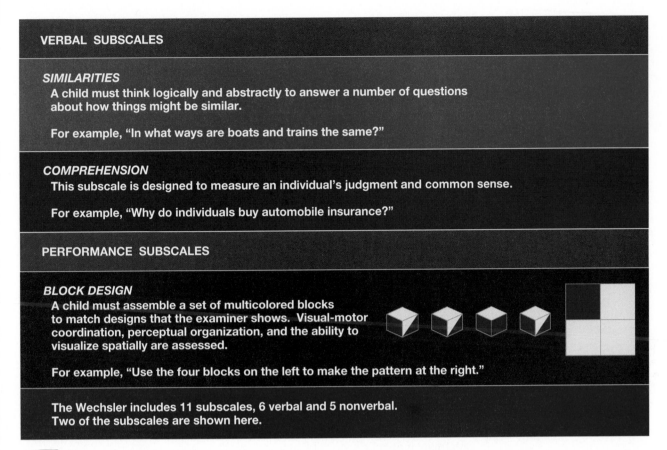

Figure **9.4**
Sample Subscales of the Wechsler Intelligence Scale for Children–Revised

of nonverbal subscales makes the Wechsler test more representative of verbal and non-verbal intelligence; the Stanford-Binet test includes some nonverbal items but not as many as the Wechsler scales. Several of the Wechsler subscales are shown in figure 9.4.

At this point we have discussed a number of ideas about the nature of intelligence and intelligence tests. A review of these ideas is presented in summary table 9.1. Next, we will explore whether children have a single intelligence or multiple intelligences.

Do Children Have a Single Intelligence or Multiple Intelligences?

Is it more accurate to describe intelligence as a general ability, or is intelligence made up of a number of specific abilities?

Early Views   The concept of mental age and IQ fits with the view of intelligence as a general ability. So although the early Binet tests tapped some different cognitive skills (such as memory and comprehension), individual's performance on these skills was lumped together to describe their general intellectual ability. The Wechsler scales provide an indication of a person's general ability and skills in a number of specific areas.

ADVENTURES FOR THE MIND

Should Parents Be Testing Their Own Child's IQ?

A CD-ROM, *Children's IQ and Achievement Test,* now lets parents test their child's IQ and how he or she is performing in relation to his or her grade in school. The company that make the CD-ROM says that it helps to get parents involved in a constructive way with children's education.

What might be some problems with parents giving their children an IQ test? In constructing your answer, consider whether intelligence is much more than just IQ, whether parents can objectively test their own child, and other cautions.

SUMMARY TABLE 9.1
The Nature of Intelligence and Intelligence Tests

Concept	Processes/ Related Ideas	Characteristics/Description
What Is Intelligence?	Its Nature	• Intelligence involves verbal ability, problem-solving skills, and the ability to adapt to and learn from life's everyday experiences. • Interest in intelligence has focused on individual differences and assessment.
Intelligence Tests	How Tests are Constructed and Evaluated	• A good test is reliable, valid, and standardized. • Reliability is how consistently an individual performs on a test. Three forms of reliability are test-retest, alternate forms, and split-half. • Validity is the extent to which a test measures what it is intended to measure. Two forms of validity are content and criterion. • Standardization focuses on uniform procedures for administering and scoring a test; it also involves norms.
	The Binet Tests and the Wechsler Scales	• Alfred Binet developed the first intelligence test, known as the 1905 Scale. • William Stern developed the concept of IQ. • The Binet has been standardized and revised a number of times. The many revisions are now called the Stanford-Binet. • The Stanford-Binet is given to individuals from 2 years of age through adulthood. • Besides the Stanford-Binet, the other most widely used tests of intelligence are the Wechsler scales, created by David Wechsler. • The Wechsler scales provide an overall IQ, verbal and performance IQs, and information about eleven subtests.

two-factor theory
Spearman's theory that individuals have both general intelligence, which he called *g,* and a number of specific intelligences, referred to as *s.*

multiple-factor theory
L. L. Thurstone's theory that intelligence consists of seven primary mental abilities: verbal comprehension, number ability, word fluency, spatial visualization, associative memory, reasoning, and perceptual speed.

Long before David Wechsler analyzed intelligence in terms of general and specific abilities (giving the individual an overall IQ but also providing information about specific subcomponents of intelligence), Charles Spearman (1927) proposed that intelligence has two factors. **Two-factor theory** *is Spearman's theory that individuals have both general intelligence, which he called* g, *and a number of specific intelligences, which he called* s. Spearman believed that these two factors accounted for a person's performance on an intelligence test.

However, some researchers abandoned the idea of a general intelligence and searched for specific factors only. **Multiple-factor theory** *is L. L. Thurstone's (1938) theory that intelligence consists of seven primary mental abilities: verbal comprehension, number ability, word fluency, spatial visualization, associative memory, reasoning, and perceptual speed.*

Contemporary Approaches
Two contemporary approaches that emphasize our multiple intellectual abilities have been proposed by Howard Gardner and Robert Sternberg.

Gardner's Eight Frames of Mind
Howard Gardner (1983, 1993) believes there are eight types of intelligence. These are described below, followed by examples of the types of vocations in which they are reflected as strengths (Campbell, Campbell, & Dickinson, 1999):

• *Verbal skills:* the ability to think in words and to use language to express meaning (authors, journalists, speakers)
• *Mathematical skills:* the ability to carry out mathematical operations (scientists, engineers, accountants)
• *Spatial skills:* the ability to think three-dimensionally (architects, artists, sailors)

- *Bodily-kinesthetic skills:* the ability to manipulate objects and be physically skilled (surgeons, craftspeople, dancers, athletes)
- *Musical skills:* Sensitivity to pitch, melody, rhythm, and tone (composers, musicians, and sensitive listeners)
- *Interpersonal skills:* the ability to understand and effectively interact with others (teachers, mental health professionals)
- *Intrapersonal skills:* the ability to understand oneself and effectively direct one's life (theologians, psychologists)
- *Naturalist skills:* the ability to observe patterns in nature and understand natural and human-made systems (farmers, botanists, ecologists, landscapers)

The Key School in Indianapolis immerses students in activities that closely resemble Gardner's frames of mind (Goleman, Kaufman, & Ray, 1993). Each day, every student is exposed to materials that are designed to stimulate a range of human abilities, including art, music, computing, language skills, math skills, and physical games. In addition, attention is given to students' understanding of themselves and others.

Like other public schools, the Key School is open to any child in Indianapolis, but it is so popular that its students have to be chosen by lottery. The teachers are selected with an eye toward their special abilities in certain domains. For example, one teacher is competent at signing for the deaf, a skill in both linguistic and kinesthetic domains.

The Key School's goal is to allow students to discover where they have natural curiosity and talent, then let them explore these domains. Gardner says that if teachers give students the opportunity to use their bodies, imaginations, and different senses, almost every student will find that he or she is good at something. Even students who are not outstanding in some area will find that they have relative strengths (Solomon, Powell, & Gardner, 1999).

Through the Eyes of Psychologists

Howard Gardner,
Harvard University

"If by 2013 [the 30th anniversary of the publication of Gardner's Frames of Mind*] there is a wider acceptance of the notion that intelligence deserves to be pluralized, I will be pleased."*

An Interview with Howard Gardner
Multiple Intelligence Links
Multiple Intelligences and Education

Children in the Key School form "pods," in which they pursue activities of special interest to them. Every day, each child can choose from activities that draw on Gardner's eight frames of mind. The school has pods that range from gardening to architecture to gliding to dancing.

Through the Eyes of Psychologists

Robert J. Sternberg,
Yale University

"My view of intelligence is quite different from the conventional one. Successful intelligence, as I view it, involves analytical, creative, and practical aspects."

triarchic theory
Sternberg's theory that intelligence consists of compotential intelligence, experiental intelligence, and contextual intelligence.

Sternberg's Theory

"You're wise, but you lack tree smarts."

Every 9 weeks, the school emphasizes a different theme, such as the Renaissance in sixteenth-century Italy and "Renaissance Now" in Indianapolis. Students develop projects related to the theme. The projects are not graded. Instead, students present them to their classmates, explain them, and answer questions. Collaboration and teamwork are emphasized in the theme projects and in all areas of learning.

Sternberg's Triarchic Theory   While Gardner believes there are eight types of intelligence, Robert J. Sternberg (1986, 1999) thinks there are three. **Triarchic theory** *is Sternberg's theory that intelligence consists of componential intelligence, experiential intelligence, and contextual intelligence.* Consider Ann, who scores high on traditional intelligence tests such as the Stanford-Binet and is a star analytical thinker. Consider Todd, who does not have the best test scores but has an insightful and creative mind. And consider Art, a street-smart person who has learned to deal in practical ways with his world, although his scores on traditional IQ tests are low.

Sternberg calls Ann's analytical thinking and abstract reasoning "componential intelligence"; it is the closest to what we call intelligence in this chapter and what is commonly measured by intelligence tests. Todd's insightful and creative thinking is called "experiential intelligence," by Sternberg. And Art's street smarts and practical know-how is called "contextual intelligence" by Sternberg.

In Sternberg's view of componential intelligence, the basic unit in intelligence is a component, simply defined as a basic unit of information processing. Sternberg believes such components include the ability to acquire or store information; to retain or retrieve information; to transfer information; to plan, make decisions, and solve problems; and to translate our thoughts into performance.

The second part of Sternberg's model focuses on experience. According to Sternberg, intellectual people have the ability to solve new problems quickly, but they also learn how to solve familiar problems in an automatic, rote way so their minds are free to handle other problems that require insight and creativity.

The third part of the model involves practical intelligence—such as how to get out of trouble, how to replace a fuse, and how to get along with people. Sternberg describes this practical or contextual intelligence as all of the important information about getting along in the real world that you are not taught in school. He believes contextual intelligence is sometimes more important than the "book knowledge" that is often taught in school.

Sternberg (1997) says that students with different triarchic patterns "look different" in school. Students with high analytic ability tend to be favored in conventional schooling. They often do well in direct instruction classes in which the teacher lectures and students are given objective tests. They often are considered "smart" students. They typically get good grades, do well on traditional IQ tests and the SAT, and later get admitted to competitive colleges. Students who are high in creative intelligence often are not in the top rung of their class. Sternberg says that many teachers have expectations about how assignments should be done and creatively intelligent students might not conform to those expectations. Instead of giving conformist answers, they give unique answers, for which they might get reprimanded or marked down. Like students high in creative intelligence, students who are practically intelligent often do not relate well to the demands of school. However, these students frequently do well outside of the classroom's walls. They may have excellent social skills and good common sense. As adults, they sometimes become successful managers, entrepreneurs, or politicians, yet have undistinguished school records.

SUMMARY TABLE 9.2
Do Children Have a Single Intelligence or Multiple Intelligences?

Concept	Processes/ Related Ideas	Characteristics/Description
Early Views	Their Nature	• The concept of mental age and IQ fits with the view of intelligence as a general ability. • The Wechsler scales assess general intelligence and skills in specific areas. • Spearman proposed the two-factor theory, which says that people have a general ability (g) and specific abilities (s). • Thurstone abandoned the idea of general intelligence. His multiple-factor theory proposed seven primary mental abilities.
Contemporary Approaches	Gardner's Eight Frames of Mind	• Gardner argues that intelligence consists of eight frames of mind (verbal, math, spatial, movement, music, insight about self, insight about others, and naturalist). • Currently there is considerable interest in applying Gardner's approach to education.
	Sternberg's Triarchic Theory	• His triarchic theory states that intelligence comes in three forms: componential, experiential, and practical.
	Evaluating the Multiple-Intelligences Approach	• There is much to offer in this approach, although insufficient research has been done to support it.

Sternberg believes that few tasks are purely analytic, creative, or practical. Most tasks require some combination of these skills. For example, when students write a book report, they might (1) analyze the book's main themes, (2) generate new ideas about how the book could have been written better, and (3) think about how the book's themes can be applied to people's lives. Sternberg argues that what is important in teaching is to balance instruction related to all three types of intelligence. That is, students should be given opportunities to learn through analytical, creative, and practical thinking, in addition to the conventional strategy of having students memorize material.

Evaluating the Multiple-Intelligences Approach

Gardner's and Sternberg's approaches have much to offer. They have stimulated us to think more broadly about what makes up people's intelligence (Torff, 2000; Wagner, 2000). And they have motivated educators to develop programs that instruct students in different domains. However, some critics say that classifying such domains as musical skills (in Gardner's approach) is off base. They ask whether there are possibly other skills domains that Gardner has left out. For example, there are outstanding chess players, prizefighters, writers, politicians, lawyers, ministers, and poets. Yet we don't refer to chess intelligence, prizefighter intelligence, and so on. Other critics say that insufficient research has been done to support the three intelligences of Sternberg and the eight intelligences of Gardner as the best way to characterize intelligence.

At this point we have discussed a number of ideas about whether children have a single intelligence or multiple intelligences. A review of these ideas is presented in summary table 9.2. Next, we will continue our exploration of intelligence by examining intelligence in infancy and developmental transformations.

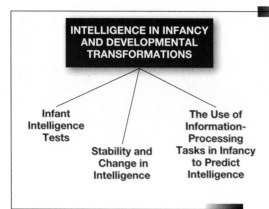

INTELLIGENCE IN INFANCY
AND DEVELOPMENTAL
TRANSFORMATIONS

Infant Intelligence Tests

Stability and Change in Intelligence

The Use of Information-Processing Tasks in Infancy to Predict Intelligence

Intelligence in Infancy and Developmental Transformations

In chapter 7, "Cognitive Developmental Approaches," we saw that Piaget characterized infants as being at the sensorimotor stage of development. Let's now explore the kinds of questions that have been posed on tests of infant intelligence and the extent to which intelligence changes or remains stable throughout the childhood years.

Infant Intelligence Tests

In chapter 4, we discussed the Brazelton Neonatal Behavioral Assessment Scale, which is widely used to evaluate newborns ◀▥ P. 119. Developmentalists want to know how development proceeds during the course of infancy as well. If an infant advances at an especially slow rate, then enrichment may be necessary. If an infant develops at an advanced pace, parents may be advised to provide toys that on average would stimulate cognitive growth in slightly older infants.

The infant-testing movement grew out of the tradition of IQ testing with older children. However, the measures that assess infants are necessarily less verbal than IQ tests that assess the intelligence of older children. The infant developmental scales contain far more items related to perceptual motor development. They also include measures of social interaction.

The most important early contributor to the developmental testing of infants was Arnold Gesell (1934). He developed a measure that served as a clinical tool to help sort out potentially normal babies from abnormal ones. This was especially useful to adoption agencies, which had large numbers of babies awaiting placement. Gesell's examination was used widely for many years and still is frequently employed by pediatricians in their assessment of normal and abnormal infants. The current version of the Gesell test has four categories of behavior: motor, language, adaptive, and personal-social. The **developmental quotient (DQ)** *is an overall developmental score that combines subscores in the motor, language, adaptive, and personal-social domains in the Gesell assessment of infants.* Overall scores on such tests as the Gesell do not correlate highly with IQ scores obtained later in childhood. This is not surprising, since the nature of the items on the developmental scales is considerably less verbal than the items on intelligence tests given to older children.

The **Bayley Scales of Infant Development** *are widely used in assessing infant development. They have three components: a Mental Scale, a Motor Scale, and the Behavior Rating Scale.* Initially created by Nancy Bayley (1969), the second edition of the Bayley Scales was recently developed (Black & Matula, 1999). The Behavior Rating Scale, which assesses the infant's behavior during testing, was formerly called the Infant Behavior Record. Among the uses of the scales are the diagnosis of developmental delays and the planning of intervention strategies. The Bayley Scales can be used to assess infants from 1 to 42 months of age.

According to the Bayley scales, at approximately 6 months of age an average baby should be able to do the following:

- Accept a second cube—the baby holds one cube, while the examiner places a second cube within easy reach of the infant
- Grasp the edge of a piece of paper when it is presented
- Vocalize pleasure and displeasure
- Persistently reach for objects placed just out of immediate reach
- Turn her or his head toward a spoon the experimenter suddenly drops on the floor
- Approach a mirror when the examiner places it in front of the infant

At approximately 12 months of age, an average baby should be able to do the following:

developmental quotient (DQ)
An overall developmental score that combines subscores on motor, language, adaptive, and personal-social domains in the Gesell assessment of infants.

Bayley Scales of Infant Development
Developed by Nancy Bayley, these scales are widely used in assessing infant development. The current version has three parts: Mental Scale, Motor Scale, and Behavior Rating Scale.

Bayley Scales of Infant Development (2nd ed.)

- Inhibit behavior when commanded to do so—for example, when the infant puts a block in his or her mouth and the examiner says, "No, no," the infant should cease the activity
- Repeat an action if she or he is laughed at
- Imitate words the experimenter says, such as *mama* and *dada*
- Imitate the experimenter's actions—for example, if the experimenter rattles a spoon in a cup, the infant should imitate this action
- Respond to simple requests, such as "Take a drink"

Stability and Change in Intelligence

In one study conducted by Nancy Bayley, no relation was found between the Bayley scales and intelligence as measured by the Stanford-Binet at the ages of 6 and 7 (Bayley, 1943). Another investigation found correlations of only .01 between intelligence measured at 3 months and at 5 years of age and .05 between measurements at 1 year and at 5 years (Anderson, 1939). These findings indicate virtually no relation between infant development scales and intelligence at 5 years of age. Again, it should be remembered that one of the reasons for this finding is that the components of intelligence tested in infancy are not the same as the components of intelligence tested at the age of 5.

There is a strong relation between IQ scores obtained at the ages of 6, 8, and 9 and IQ scores obtained at the age of 10. For example, in one study, the correlation between IQ at the age of 8 and IQ at the age of 10 was .88. The correlation between IQ at the age of 9 and IQ at the age of 10 was .90. These figures show a very high relation between IQ scores obtained in these years. The correlation of IQ in the preadolescent years and IQ at the age of 18 is slightly less but still statistically significant. For example, the correlation between IQ at the age of 10 and IQ at the age of 18 was .70 in one study (Honzik, MacFarlane, & Allen, 1948).

What has been said so far about the stability of intelligence has been based on measures of groups of individuals. The stability of intelligence also can be evaluated through studies of individuals. As we will see next, there can be considerable variability in an individual's scores on IQ tests.

Let's look at an example of the absence of a relation between intelligence in infancy and intelligence in later years for two children in the same family. The first child learned to speak at a very early age. She displayed the characteristics of an extravert, and her advanced motor coordination was indicated by her ability to walk at a very early age. The second child learned speech very late, saying very few words until she was 2½ years old. Both children were given standardized tests of intelligence during infancy and then later, during the elementary school years. In the earlier test, the first child's scores were higher than her sister's. In the later test, their scores were reversed. What are some of the possible reasons for the reversal in the IQ scores of the two girls? When the second child did begin to speak, she did so prolifically, and the complexity of her language increased rapidly, undoubtedly as a result of her biological readiness to talk. Her sensorimotor coordination had never been as competent as the first child's, perhaps also accounting in part for her lower scores on the infant intelligence tests. The parents recognized that they had initially given the first child extensive amounts of their time. They were not able to give the second child as much of their time, but when the second child was about 3 years old, they made every opportunity to involve her in physical and academic activities. They put her in a Montessori preschool program, gave her dancing and swimming lessons, and frequently invited other children of her age in to play with her. There may have been other reasons as well for the changes in scores, but these demonstrate that infant intelligence tests may not be good predictors of intelligence in later years.

Robert McCall and his associates (McCall, Applebaum, & Hogarty, 1973) studied 140 children between the ages of 2½ and 17. They found that the average range of IQ scores was more than 28 points. The scores of one out of three children changed by as much as 30 points and one out of seven by as much as 40 points.

SUMMARY TABLE 9.3
Intelligence in Infancy and Developmental Transformations

Concept	Processes/ Related Ideas	Characteristics/Description
Infant Intelligence Tests	Their Nature	• Many standardized intelligence tests do not assess infant intelligence. • Intelligence tests designed to assess infant intelligence are often called "developmental scales," the most widely used being the Bayley Scales. • Gesell was an important early contributor to the developmental testing of infants. • The developmental quotient (DQ) is an overall score in the Gesell assessment of infants.
Stability and Change in Intelligence	Their Nature	• Although intelligence is more stable across the childhood years than many other attributes are, many children's scores on intelligence tests fluctuate considerably.
The Use of Information-Processing Tasks in Infancy to Predict Intelligence	Linkages	• Developmentalists have found that infant information-processing tasks that involve attention—especially habituation and dishabituation—are related to scores on standardized intelligence tests in childhood.

These data suggest that intelligence test scores can fluctuate dramatically across the childhood years and that intelligence is not as stable as the original intelligence theorists envisioned.

The Use of Information-Processing Tasks in Infancy to Predict Intelligence

The explosion of interest in infant development has produced many new measures, especially tasks that evaluate the ways infants process information (Rose, Feldman, & Wallace, 1992). Evidence is accumulating that measures of habituation and dishabituation predict intelligence in childhood and adolescence (Bornstein, 1989; Bornstein & Sigman, 1986; Sigman, Cohen & Beckwith, 2000). Quicker decays or less cumulative looking in the habituation situation and greater amounts of looking in the dishabituation situation reflect more-efficient information processing ◀▦ P. 241. Both types of attention—decrement and recovery—when measured in the first 6 months of infancy, are related to higher IQ scores on standardized intelligence tests given at various times between infancy and adolescence. In sum, more-precise assessment of infant cognition with information-processing tasks involving attention has led to the conclusion that continuity between infant and childhood intelligence is greater than was previously believed (Bornstein & Krasnegor, 1989).

What can we conclude about the nature of stability and change in childhood intelligence? Children are adaptive beings. They have the capacity for intellectual changes but they do not become entirely new intelligent beings. In a sense, children's intelligence changes but has connections to earlier points in development—amid intellectual changes is some underlying coherence and continuity.

At this point we have discussed a number of ideas about intelligence in infancy and developmental transformations. A review of these ideas appears in summary table 9.3. Next, we will continue our exploration of intelligence by examining some controversies and issues.

Controversies and Issues in Intelligence

In chapter 3, "Biological Beginnings," we explored the controversial issue of how extensively intelligence is determined by heredity or environment. We will briefly revisit this issue and examine several others involving intelligence.

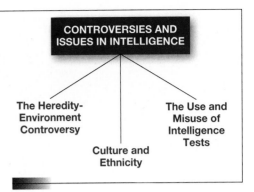

The Heredity-Environment Controversy

You might want to study again the section of chapter 3 that focuses on the roles of heredity and environment in children's intelligence to get a sense of this important issue. We will briefly summarize the controversy here ◀💴 P. 89.

We concluded that many complex behaviors, such as intelligence, have some genetic loading that gives children a propensity for a particular developmental trajectory. However, the actual development requires more: an environment. And that environment is complex, just like the mixture of 80,000 genes we receive from each parent (Detterman, 2000; Grigorenko, 2000). Environmental influences range from the things we typically lump together under "nurture" (such as parenting, family dynamics, schooling, and neighborhood quality) to biological encounters (such as viruses, birth complications, and even biological events in cells).

It no longer is believed that the relative contributions of heredity and environment to intelligence are additive, as in such-and-such a percentage of nature, and such-and-such a percentage of nurture. Nor is it accurate to say that full genetic expression happens once, around conception or birth, after which children take their genetic legacy into the world to see how far it gets them. Genes produce proteins throughout the human life span, in many different environments. Or they don't produce these proteins, depending on how harsh or nourishing those environments are.

Researchers increasingly are interested in manipulating the early environment of children who are at risk for impoverished intelligence (Blair & Ramey, 1996). The emphasis is on prevention rather than remediation. Many low-income parents have difficulty providing an intellectually stimulating environment for their children. Programs that educate parents to be more sensitive caregivers and train them to be better teachers, as well as support services, such as high quality Head Start programs, can make a difference in a child's intellectual development. The current trend is to conduct two-generation poverty interventions by working to improve the quality of life and skills of parents, as well as providing the child with an enriched environment (McLoyd, 1998).

In one study, 483 low-birthweight premature White and African American children were assessed with the Wechsler Preschool and Primary Scale of Intelligence when they reached 5 years of age (Brooks-Gunn, Klebanov, & Duncan, 1996). These children had been followed since birth, and information about their neighborhood and family income, family structure, family resources, maternal characteristics, and home environment had been obtained over the first 5 years of their lives. The African American children's IQ scores were one standard deviation lower than those of the White children. Adjustments for economic and social differences in the lives of the African American and White children virtually eliminated differences in the IQ scores of the two groups. Especially powerful in reducing the group IQ differences between African American and White children were adjustments for poverty, maternal education, and home environment. To read further about early intervention and children's intelligence, see the Explorations in Child Development box.

Another argument for the importance of environment in intelligence involves the increasing scores of IQ tests around the world (Flynn, 1999). Scores on these tests have been increasing so fast that a high percentage of people regarded as having average intelligence at the turn of the century

𝒯hrough the Eyes of Psychologists

Craig Ramey, *University of Alabama—Birmingham*

"The highest-risk children often benefit the most cognitively when they experience early interventions."

EXPLORATIONS IN CHILD DEVELOPMENT
The Abecedarian Project

EACH MORNING a young mother waited with her child for the bus that would take the child to school. The unusual part of this was that the child was only 2 months old and "school" was an experimental program at the University of North Carolina at Chapel Hill. There the child experienced a number of interventions designed to improve her intellectual development—everything from bright objects dangled in front of her eyes while she was a baby to language instruction and counting activities when she was a toddler (Wickelgren, 1999).

Without this early start, the child's intellectual development likely would never have fared as well as it has, because the child's mother had an IQ of 40 and could not read signs or determine how much change she should receive from a cashier. Her grandmother had a similarly low IQ. Today that child is 20 years old, and her IQ is 80 points higher than her mother's was when the child was just 2 months old.

Although this child's case is admittedly a dramatic one, researchers increasingly are demonstrating that the environment, especially early in life, exerts a powerful influence on IQ. They are showing that IQs can be changed, for better or for worse, depending on such environmental factors as how parents talk with their infants, the availability and quality of infant and toddler day-care programs, and the schooling the child experiences.

Not everyone agrees that IQ can be affected this extensively. However, even behavior geneticists such as Robert Plomin (1999) acknowledge that environment can make a substantial difference in a child's intelligence. As Plomin says, even something that is highly heritable (like intelligence) may be malleable through interventions.

The Abecedarian intervention program at the University of North Carolina at Chapel Hill was started in 1972 by Craig Ramey and his colleagues (Ramey & Campbell, 1984; Ramey & Ramey, 1998). They randomly assigned 111 young children from low-income, poorly educated families to either an intervention group, which experienced full-time, year-round day care along with medical and social work services, or a control group, which got medical and social benefits but no day care. The day-care program included gamelike learning activities aimed at improving language, motor, social, and cognitive skills. The success of the program in improving IQ was evident by the time the children were 3 years old, at which time the children in the experimental group showed normal IQs averaging 101, a 17-point advantage over the control group. Recent follow-up results suggest that the effects are longlasting. More than a decade later, at age 15, children from the intervention group still maintained an IQ advantage of 5 points over the control group children (97.7, compared to 92.6) (Ramey & others, in press; Ramey, Campbell, & Ramey, in press). They also did better on standardized tests of reading and math, and were less likely to be held back a year in school. Also, the greatest IQ gains were by the children whose mothers had especially low IQs—below 70. At age 15, these children showed a 10-point advantage over a group of children whose mothers had IQs below 70 but did not experience the day-care intervention.

would be considered below average in intelligence today (Hall, 1998) (see figure 9.5). If a representative sample of people today took the Stanford-Binet test used in 1932, about one-fourth would be defined as having very superior intelligence, a label usually accorded to fewer than 3 percent of the population. Because the increase has taken place in a relatively short period of time, it can't be due to heredity, but rather may be due to such environmental factors as the explosion in information people are exposed to as well as a much greater percentage of the population experiencing more education.

Although environmental factors contribute substantially to the development of intelligence, we do not completely understand which environmental factors are the most important or how they work (Neisser & others, 1996). Schooling is definitely related to individual differences in intelligence, but we still do not know which aspects of schooling are critical.

Culture and Ethnicity

Are there cultural and ethnic differences in intelligence? Are standard intelligence tests biased? If so, can we develop tests that are culturally fair?

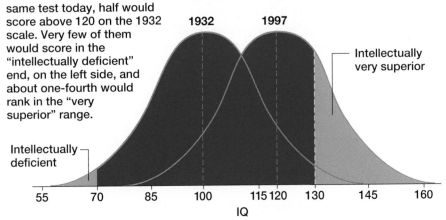

As measured by the Stanford-Binet intelligence test, American children seem to be getting smarter. Scores of a group tested in 1932 fell along a bell-shaped curve with half below 100 and half above. Studies show that if children took that same test today, half would score above 120 on the 1932 scale. Very few of them would score in the "intellectually deficient" end, on the left side, and about one-fourth would rank in the "very superior" range.

Figure 9.5

The Increase in IQ Scores from 1932 to 1997

Cultural and Ethnic Comparisons   In the United States, children from African American and Latino families score below children from White families on standardized intelligence tests. On the average, African American schoolchildren score 10 to 15 points lower on standardized intelligence tests than White American schoolchildren do (Lynn, 1996). We are talking about average scores, though. Estimates also indicate that 15 to 25 percent of all African American schoolchildren score higher than half of all White schoolchildren do, and many Whites score lower than most African Americans. This is because the distribution of scores for African Americans and Whites overlap.

How extensively are ethnic differences in intelligence influenced by heredity and environment? There is no evidence to support a genetic interpretation (Neisser & others, 1996). For example, as African Americans have gained social, economic, and educational opportunities, the gap between African American and White children on standardized intelligence tests has begun to narrow. Also, when children from disadvantaged African American families are adopted into more-advantaged middle-SES families, their scores on intelligence tests more closely resemble national averages for middle-SES children than for low-SES children (Scarr & Weinberg, 1983).

Cultural Bias and Culture-Fair Tests   Many of the early intelligence tests were culturally biased, favoring people who were from urban rather than rural environments, middle-SES rather than low-SES, and White rather than African American (Miller-Jones, 1989). For example, a question on an early test asked what should be done if you find a 3-year-old child in the street. The "correct" answer was "call the police." But children from inner-city families who perceive the police as adversaries are unlikely to choose this answer. Similarly, children from rural areas might not choose this answer if there is no police force nearby. Such questions clearly do not measure the knowledge necessary to adapt to one's environment or to be "intelligent" in an inner-city neighborhood or in rural America

"You can't build a hut, you don't know how to find edible roots and you know nothing about predicting the weather. In other words, you do terribly on our I.Q. test."

(Scarr, 1984). Also, members of minority groups often do not speak English or may speak nonstandard English. Consequently, they may be at a disadvantage in trying to understand verbal questions that are framed in standard English, even if the content of the test is appropriate (Gibbs & Huang, 1989).

Cultures also vary in the way they define intelligence (Rogoff, 1998; Serpell, 2000). Most European Americans, for example, think of intelligence in terms of technical skills, but people in Kenya consider responsible participation in family and social life an integral part of intelligence. Similarly, an intelligent person in Uganda is someone who knows what to do and then follows through with appropriate action. Intelligence to the Iatmul people of Papua, New Guinea, involves the ability to remember the names of 10,000 to 20,000 clans, and the islanders in the widely dispersed Caroline Islands incorporate the talent of navigating by the stars into their definition of intelligence.

Another example of possible cultural bias in intelligence tests can be seen in the life of Gregory Ochoa. When Gregory was a high school student, he and his classmates took an IQ test. When Gregory looked at the test questions, he understood only a few words, since he did not speak English very well and spoke Spanish at home. Several weeks later, Gregory was placed in a special class for mentally retarded students. Many of the students in the class, it turns out, had last names such as Ramirez and Gonzales. Gregory lost interest in school, dropped out, and eventually joined the Navy. In the Navy, Gregory took high school courses and earned enough credits to attend college later. He graduated from San Jose City College as an honor student, continued his education, and became a professor of social work at the University of Washington in Seattle.

As a result of such cases, researchers have tried to develop tests that accurately reflect a person's intelligence. **Culture-fair tests** *are intelligence tests that are intended to not be culturally biased.* Two types of culture-fair tests have been devised. The first includes questions that are familiar to people from all socioeconomic and ethnic backgrounds. For example, a child might be asked how a bird and a dog are different, on the assumption that virtually all children are familiar with birds and dogs. The second type of culture-fair test removes all verbal questions. Figure 9.6 shows a sample question from the Raven Progressive Matrices Test. Even though tests such as the Raven Progressive Matrices are designed to be culture-fair, people with more education still score higher than those with less education do.

One test that takes into account the socioeconomic background of children is the SOMPA, which stands for System of Multicultural Pluralistic Assessment (Mercer & Lewis, 1978). This test can be given to children from 5 to 11 years of age, and was especially designed for children from low-income families. Instead of relying on a single test, SOMPA is based on information from four different areas of the child's life: (1) verbal and nonverbal intelligence, assessed by the WISC-III; (2) social and economic background, obtained through a one-hour parent interview; (3) social adjustment to school, determined through a questionnaire that parents complete; and (4) physical health, assessed by a medical examination.

Why is it so hard to create a culture-fair test? Most tests tend to reflect what the dominant culture thinks is important (Sax, 1997). If tests have time limits, that will bias the test against groups not concerned with time. If languages differ, the same words might have different meanings for different language groups. Even pictures can produce bias because some cultures have less experience with drawings and photographs (Anastasi & Urbina, 1996). Even within the same culture, different groups could have different attitudes, values, and motivation, and this could affect their performance on intelligence tests. Items that ask why buildings should be made of brick are biased against children who have little or no experience with brick houses. Questions about railroads, furnaces, seasons of the year, distances between cities, and so on can be biased against groups who have less experience than others with these circumstances.

Cultural Bias and Testing

culture-fair tests
Intelligence tests that are intended to not be culturally biased.

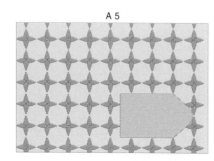

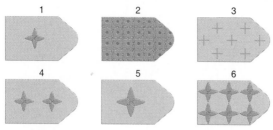

Figure **9.6**

Sample Item from the Raven Progressive Matrices Test

Individuals are presented with a matrix arrangement of symbols, such as the one at the top of this figure, and must then complete the matrix by selecting the appropriate missing symbol from a group of symbols.

The Use and Misuse of Intelligence Tests

Psychological tests are tools. Like all tools, their effectiveness depends on the knowledge, skill, and integrity of the user. A hammer can be used to build a beautiful kitchen cabinet or it can be used as a weapon of assault. Like a hammer, psychological tests can be used for positive purposes or they can be badly abused. It is important for both the test constructor and the test examiner to be familiar with the current state of scientific knowledge about intelligence and intelligence tests.

Even though they have limitations, tests of intelligence are among psychology's most widely used tools (Brody, 2000). To be effective, though, intelligence tests must be viewed realistically. They should not be thought of as unchanging indicators of intelligence. They should be used in conjunction with other information about an individual, not relied on as the sole indicator of intelligence. For example, an intelligence test should not solely determine whether a child is placed in a special education or gifted class. The child's developmental history, medical background, performance in school, social competencies, and family experiences should be taken into account too.

The single number provided by many IQ tests can easily lead to stereotypes and misguided expectations about an individual (Rosenthal, 2000; Rosnow & Rosenthal, 1996). Many people do not know how to interpret the results of intelligence tests, and sweeping generalizations are too often made on the basis of an IQ score. For example, imagine that you are a teacher in the teacher's lounge the day after school has started in the fall. You mention a student—Johnny Jones—and a fellow teacher remarks that she had Johnny in class last year; she comments that he was a real dunce and points out that his IQ is 78. You cannot help but remember this information, and it might lead to thoughts that Johnny Jones is not very bright so it is useless to spend much time teaching him. In this way, IQ scores are misused and stereotypes are formed (Rosenthal & Jacobsen, 1968).

Ability tests can help a teacher group together children who function at roughly the same level in math or reading so they can be taught the same concepts together. However, when children are placed in tracks, such as "advanced," "intermediate," and "low," extreme caution is advised. Periodic assessment of the groups is needed, especially with the "low" group. Ability tests measure current performance, and maturational changes or enriched environmental experiences may advance a child's intelligence, requiring that she be moved to a higher group.

Despite their limitations, when used judiciously by a competent examiner, intelligence tests provide valuable information about individuals. There are not many alternatives to these tests. Subjective judgments about individuals simply reintroduce the bias the tests were designed to eliminate.

At this point we have discussed a number of controversies and issues in intelligence. A review of these ideas is presented in summary table 9.4. An aspect of intelligence that needs to be explored further involves the extremes of intelligence.

"How are her scores?"

The Extremes of Intelligence and Creativity

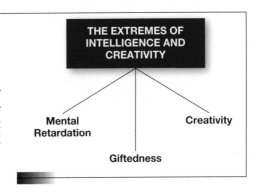

Intelligence tests have been used to discover indications of mental retardation or intellectual giftedness, the extremes of intelligence. At times intelligence tests have been misused for this purpose. As we explore intellectual extremes, keep in mind that an intelligence test should not be used as the sole indicator of mental retardation and giftedness.

Mental Retardation

The most distinctive feature of mental retardation is inadequate intellectual functioning. Long before formal tests were developed to assess intelligence, the individual with mental retardation was identified by a lack of age-appropriate skills in learning and

SUMMARY TABLE 9.4
Controversies and Issues in Intelligence

Concept	Processes/ Related Ideas	Characteristics/Description
The Heredity-Environment Controversy	Its Nature	• Controversy swirls about whether intelligence is based more on heredity or environment. • Intelligence, like other complex behaviors, has a genetic loading, but environmental factors make important contributions to children's intelligence. • Evidence for the environment's influence is that American children's IQ scores increased substantially in the twentieth century.
Culture and Ethnicity	Cultural and Ethnic Comparisons	• There are cultural and ethnic differences in scores on intelligence tests, but the evidence suggests that they are not genetically based. • In recent years the gap between African American and Whites on intelligence tests has narrowed as African Americans have experienced more socioeconomic opportunities.
	Cultural Bias and Culture-Fair Tests	• Early intelligence tests favored White, middle-SES, urban individuals. • These are intended to not be culturally biased. • Most psychologists do not believe these can replace traditional intelligence tests.
The Use and Misuse of Intelligence Tests	Their Nature	• Despite limitations, when used by a judicious examiner, tests can be valuable tools for assessing intelligence. The tests should be used with other information about the child. • IQ tests can produce unfortunate stereotypes and expectations. • Ability tests can be used to divide children into homogeneous groups, but periodic testing should be done.

mental retardation
A condition of limited mental ability in which the individual has a low IQ, usually below 70 on a traditional intelligence test, has difficulty adapting to everyday life, and has an onset of these characteristics during the so-called developmental period—by age 18.

American Association of Mental Retardation (AAMR)

Mental Retardation Resources

Mental Retardation Links

caring for themselves. Once intelligence tests were developed, numbers were assigned to indicate degrees of mental retardation. It is not unusual to find that, of two individuals with mental retardation with the same low IQ, one is married, employed, and involved in the community and the other requires constant supervision in an institution. These differences in social competence led psychologists to include deficits in adaptive behavior in their definition of mental retardation (Detterman, Gabriel, & Ruthsatz, 2000). **Mental retardation** *is a condition of limited mental ability in which the individual has low IQ, usually below 70 on a traditional intelligence test, has difficulty adapting to everyday life, and has an onset of these characteristics during the so-called developmental period— by age 18.* The reason for including developmental period in the definition of mental retardation is that we don't usually think of a college student who suffers massive brain damage in a car accident, resulting in an IQ of 60 as "mentally retarded." The low IQ and low adaptiveness should be evident in childhood, not following a long period of normal functioning that is interrupted by an insult of some form. About 5 million Americans fit this definition of mental retardation.

There are several classifications of mental retardation (Das, 2000). About 89 percent of individuals with mental retardation fall into the mild category, with IQs of 55 to 70. About 6 percent are classified as moderately retarded, with IQs of 40 to 54; these people can attain a second-grade level of skills and may be able to support themselves as adults through some type of labor. About 3.5 percent of individuals with mental retardation are in the severe category, with IQs of 25 to 39; these individuals learn to talk and engage in very simple tasks but require extensive supervision. Less than 1 percent have IQs below 25; they fall into the profoundly mentally retarded classification and are in constant need of supervision. (Drew & Hardman, 2000).

Mental retardation may have an organic cause, or it may be social and cultural in origin. **Organic retardation** *is mental retardation caused by a genetic disorder or by brain damage; organic refers to the tissues or organs of the body, so there is some physical damage in organic retardation.* Most people who suffer from organic retardation have IQs that range between 0 and 50. Down syndrome (discussed initially in chapter 3, "Biological Beginnings"), one form of mental retardation, occurs when an extra chromosome is present in the individual's genetic makeup (see figure 9.7) ◀▥▥ P. 78. It is not known why the extra chromosome is present, but it may involve the health or age of the female ovum or male sperm (MacLean, 2000).

Cultural-familial retardation *is a mental deficit in which no evidence of organic brain damage can be found; individuals' IQs range from 55 to 70.* Psychologists suspect that such mental deficits result from the normal variation that distributes people along the range of intelligence scores above 55, combined with growing up in a below-average intellectual environment. As children, those who are familially retarded can be detected in schools, where they often fail, need tangible rewards (candy rather than praise), and are highly sensitive to what others—both peers and adults—want from them (Feldman, 1996). However, as adults, the familially retarded are usually invisible, perhaps because adult settings don't tax their cognitive skills as sorely. It may also be that the familially retarded increase their intelligence as they move toward adulthood.

Giftedness

There have always been people whose abilities and accomplishments outshine others—the whiz kid in class, the star athlete, the natural musician. People who are **gifted** *have above-average intelligence (an IQ of 120 or higher) and/or superior talent for something.* When it comes to programs for the gifted, most school systems select children who have intellectual superiority and academic aptitude. Children who are talented in the visual and performing arts (arts, drama, dance), athletics, or other special aptitudes tend to be overlooked (Davidson, 2000).

Until recently, giftedness and emotional distress were thought to go hand in hand. English novelist Virgina Woolf suffered from severe depression, for example, and eventually committed suicide. Sir Isaac Newton, Vincent van Gogh, Ann Sexton, Socrates, and Sylvia Plath all had emotional problems. However, these are the exception rather than the rule; in general, no relation between giftedness and mental disorder has been found. Research studies support the conclusion that gifted people tend to be more mature and have fewer emotional problems than others (Feldman & Piirto, 1995). In one study, gifted children were more intrinsically motivated than were nongifted children.

Lewis Terman (1925) has followed the lives of approximately 1,500 children whose Stanford-Binet IQs averaged 150 into adulthood; the study will not be complete until the year 2010. Terman has found that this remarkable group is an accomplished lot. Of the 800 males, 78 have obtained doctorates (they include two past presidents of the American Psychological Association),

organic retardation
Mental retardation caused by a genetic disorder or by brain damage; "organic" refers to the tissues or organs of the body, so there is some physical damage in organic retardation.

cultural-familial retardation
A mental deficit in which no evidence of organic brain damage can be found; individuals' IQs range from 55 to 70.

gifted
Having above-average intelligence (an IQ of 120 or higher) and/or superior talent for something.

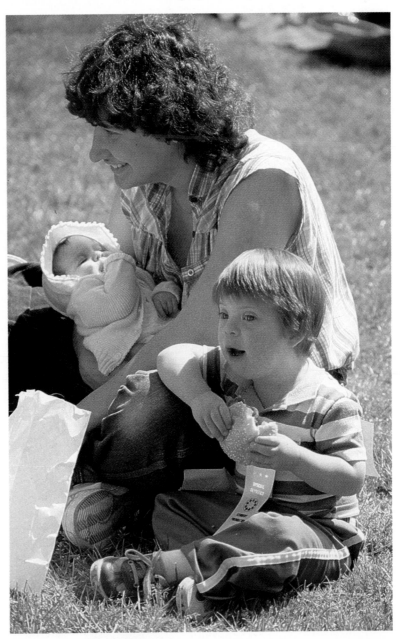

Figure **9.7**
A Child with Down Syndrome

What causes a child to develop Down syndrome? In which major classification of mental retardation does the condition fall?

creativity
The ability to think in novel and unusual ways and come up with unique solutions to problems.

convergent thinking
Thinking that produces one correct answer and is characteristic of the kind of thinking required on conventional intelligence tests.

divergent thinking
Thinking that produces many answers to the same question and is characteristic of creativity.

48 have earned M.D.s, and 85 have been granted law degrees. Most of these figures are 10 to 30 times greater than those found among the 800 men of the same age chosen randomly as a comparison group. These findings challenge the commonly held belief that the intellectually gifted are emotionally disordered or socially maladjusted.

The 672 gifted women studied by Terman (Terman & Oden, 1959) underscore the importance of relationships and intimacy in women's lives. Two-thirds of these exceptional women graduated from college in the 1930s, and one-fourth of them attended graduate school. Despite their impressive educational achievements, when asked to order their life's priorities, the gifted women placed families first, friendships second, and careers last. Such undivided commitments to the family are less true of women today. Terman's gifted women represent a cohort who reached midlife prior to the women's movement and the current pervasiveness of the dual-career couple and the single-parent family (Tomlinson-Keasey, 1993, 1997). For the women in Terman's study, having a career often meant not having children. Of the 30 most successful women, 25 did not have any children. Many of the highly gifted women in Terman's study questioned their intelligence and concluded that their cognitive skills had waned in adulthood. Studies reveal that today gifted women have a stronger confidence in their cognitive skills and intellectual abilities than did the gifted women in Terman's study (Tomlinson-Keasey, 1990).

Ellen Winner (1996) described three characteristics of gifted children, whether in the artistic, musical, or academic domain:

1. *Precocity.* Gifted children are precocious. They begin to master an area earlier than their peers. Learning in their domain is more effortless for them than for ordinary children. In most instances, these gifted children are precocious because they have an inborn high ability in a particular domain or domains (Howe, 2000).
2. *Tendency to march to their own drummer.* Gifted children learn in a qualitatively different way than ordinary children. One way that they march to a different drummer is that they need minimal help, or scaffolding, from adults to learn. In many instances, they resist any kind of explicit instruction. They also make discoveries on their own and solve problems in unique ways.
   3. *A passion to master.* Gifted children are driven to understand the domain in which they have high ability. They display an intense, obsessive interest and an ability to focus their motivation. They are not children who need to be pushed by their parents. They motivate themselves, says Winner.

Alexandra Nechita burst onto the child prodigy scene at age 10. She paints quickly and impulsively on large canvases, some as large as 5 feet by 9 feet. It is not unusual for her to complete several of these large paintings in a week's time. Her paintings—in the modernist tradition—sell for up to $80,000 a piece. Alexandra used to color in coloring books for hours when she was only 2 years old. She had no interest in dolls or friends. Once she started school, as soon as she got home in the evening she painted. And she continues to paint—relentlessly and passionately. It is, she says, what she loves to do.

Creativity

Creativity is the ability to think in novel and unusual ways and to come up with unique solutions to problems. Thus, intelligence and creativity are not the same thing (Csikszentmihalyi, 2000; Sternberg & O'Hara, 2000). This was recognized in Sternberg's account of intelligence earlier in this chapter and by J. P. Guilford (1967). Guilford distinguished between **convergent thinking**, which produces one correct answer and is characteristic of the kind of thinking required on conventional intelligence tests, and **divergent thinking**, which produces many different answers to

Alexandra Nechita, shown here at age 10, is a gifted child in the domain of art. She is precocious, marches to the tune of a different drummer, and has a passion to master her domain.

the same question and is more characteristic of creativity. For example, a typical item on a conventional intelligence test is "How many quarters will you get in return for 60 dimes?" By contrast, the following question has many possible answers: "What image comes to mind when you hear the phrase 'Sitting alone in a dark room' or 'Can you think of some unique uses for a paper clip?'"

Are intelligence and creativity related? Although most creative children are quite intelligent, the reverse is not necessarily true. Many highly intelligent children (as measured by high scores on conventional intelligence tests) are not very creative. And, if Sternberg were to have his way, creative thinking would become part of the broader criteria for intelligence.

An important goal is to help children become more creative (Rickards, 1999). What are the best strategies for accomplishing this goal?

- *Have children engage in brainstorming and come up with as many ideas as possible.* **Brainstorming** *is a technique in which children are encouraged to come up with creative ideas in a group, play off each other's ideas, and say practically whatever comes to mind* (Sternberg & Lubart, 1995). Children are usually told to hold off from criticizing others' ideas at least until the end of the brainstorming session. Whether in a group or individually, a good creativity strategy is to come up with as many new ideas as possible. Famous twentieth-century Spanish artist Pablo Picasso produced more than 20,000 works of art. Not all of them were masterpieces. The more ideas children produce, the better their chance of creating something unique (Rickards, 1999). Creative children are not afraid of failing or getting something wrong. They may go down twenty dead-end streets before they come up with an innovative idea. They recognize that it's okay to win some and lose some. They are willing to take risks, just as Picasso was.
- *Provide children with environments that stimulate creativity.* Some settings nourish creativity; others depress it. People who encourage children's creativity often rely on their natural curiosity. They provide exercises and activities that stimulate children to find insightful solutions to problems, rather than asking a lot of questions that require rote answers. Adults also encourage creativity by taking children to locations where creativity is valued. Howard Gardner (1993) believes that science, discovery, and children's museums offer rich opportunities to stimulate children's creativity.
- *Don't overcontrol.* Teresa Amabile (1993) says that telling children exactly how to do things leaves them feeling that any originality is a mistake and any exploration is a waste of time. Letting children select their interests and supporting their inclinations are less likely to destroy their natural curiosity than dictating which activities they should engage in. Amabile also believes that, when adults constantly hover over children, the children feel they are being watched while they are working. When children are under constant surveillance, their creative risktaking and adventurous spirit wane. Another strategy that can harm creativity is to have grandiose expectations for a child's performance and expect the child to do something perfectly, according to Amabile.
- *Encourage internal motivation.* The excessive use of prizes, such as gold stars, money, or toys, can stifle creativity by undermining the intrinsic pleasure children derive from creative activities. Creative children's motivation is the satisfaction generated by the work itself. Competition for prizes and formal evaluations often undermine intrinsic motivation and creativity (Amabile & Hennessey, 1992).
- *Foster flexible and playful thinking.* Creative thinkers are flexible and play with problems, which gives rise to a paradox. Although creativity takes effort, the effort goes more smoothly if students take it lightly. In a way, humor can grease the wheels of creativity (Goleman, Kaufman, & Ray, 1993). When children are joking around, they are more likely to consider unusual solutions to problems. Having fun helps disarm the inner censor that can condemn a child's ideas as off-base.

Through the Eyes of Psychologists

Mihaly Csikszentmihalyi,
University of Chicago

"A genuinely creative accomplishment is almost never the result of a sudden insight, a lightbulb flashing in the dark, but comes after years of hard work."

brainstorming
A technique in which participants are encouraged to come up with creative ideas in a group, play off each other's ideas, and say practically whatever comes to mind.

Teresa Amabile's Research

SUMMARY TABLE 9.5
The Extremes of Intelligence and Creativity

Concept	Processes/ Related Ideas	Characteristics/Description
Mental Retardation	Its Nature	• This is a condition of limited mental ability in which an individual has a low IQ (usually below 70 on a traditional intelligence test), has difficulty in adapting to everyday life, and has these characteristics in the so-called developmental period—by age 18.
	Classifications	• These range from mild (IQ of 55 to 70) to profound (an IQ below 25).
	Causes	• May have an organic cause (organic retardation) or be social and cultural in origin (cultural-familial retardation).
Giftedness	Its Nature	• Children are described as gifted when they have above-average intelligence (an IQ of 120 or higher) and/or a special talent for something.
	Terman's Study	• In Terman's study, children who were gifted were academically successful and socially well adjusted.
	Characteristics of Gifted Individuals	• Winner believes that children who are gifted are characterized by precocity, marching to the tune of a different drummer, and a passion to master.
Creativity	Its Nature	• This is the ability to think in novel and unusual ways and come up with unique solutions to problems.
	Guilford's View	• It is important to distinguish between convergent thinking and divergent thinking.
	Encouraging Children's Creativity	• Some good strategies are techniques like brainstorming, providing environments that stimulate creativity, not overcontrolling and criticizing, encouraging internal motivation, fostering flexible and playful thinking, and introducing children to creative people.

Through the Eyes of Psychologists

Teresa Amabile,
Harvard University

"Creative thinking skills include the ability to turn things over in your mind, like trying to make the strange familiar and the familiar strange."

As one clown named Wavy Gravy put it, "If you can't laugh about it, it just isn't funny anymore."

• *Introduce children to creative people.* You may not know a clown named Wavy Gravy whom you can ask to stimulate a child's creativity, but it is a good strategy to think about the identity of the most creative people in your community. Teachers can invite these people to their classrooms and ask them to describe what helps them become creative or to demonstrate their creative skills. A writer, poet, musician, scientist, and many others can bring their props and productions to the class, turning it into a theater for stimulating students' creativity. Poet Richard Lewis (1997) visits classrooms in New York City. He brings with him only a large clear glass marble. He lifts it above his head, so that every student can see the spectrum of colors the marble produces. He asks, "Who can see something playing inside?" Then he asks students to write about what they see. One student named Snigdha wrote that she sees the rainbow rising, the sun moving a lot, and the sun sleeping with the stars. She also wrote that she saw the rain dropping on the ground, stems breaking, apples falling from trees, and wind blowing the leaves.

At this point we have discussed a number of ideas about the extremes of intelligence and creativity. An overview of these ideas is presented in summary table 9.5.

Chapter Review

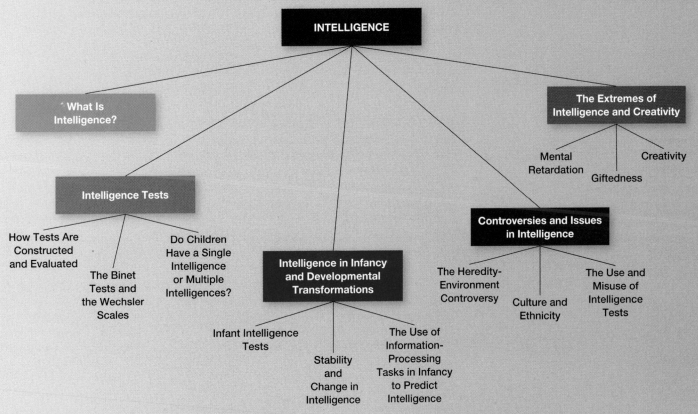

TO OBTAIN A DETAILED REVIEW OF THE CHAPTER, STUDY THESE FIVE SUMMARY TABLES:

Key Terms

intelligence 282
individual differences 282
reliability 283
test-retest reliability 283
alternate forms reliability 283
split-half reliability 283
validity 283
content validity 283
criterion validity 283
concurrent validity 284

predictive validity 284
standardization 284
norms 284
mental age (MA) 285
intelligence quotient (IQ) 285
normal distribution 286
two-factor theory 288
multiple-factor theory 288
triarchic theory 290
developmental quotient (DQ) 292

Bayley Scales of Infant Development 292
culture-fair tests 298
mental retardation 300
organic retardation 301
cultural-familial retardation 301
gifted 301
creativity 302
convergent thinking 302
divergent thinking 302
brainstorming 303

Key People

Alfred Binet 284
William Stern 285
David Wechsler 286
Charles Spearman 288
L. L. Thurstone 288
Howard Gardner 288

Robert J. Sternberg 290
Arnold Gesell 292
Nancy Bayley 292
Robert McCall 293
Craig Ramey 295
Lewis Terman 301

Ellen Winner 302
J. P. Guilford 302
Mihaly Csikszentmihalyi 303
Teresa Amabile 304

Child Development Resources

American Association on Mental Retardation
1719 Kalorama Road, NW
Washington, DC 20009
202-387-1968
800-424-3688

This organization works to promote the well-being of children and adults who are mentally retarded.

Encyclopedia of Creativity (Vols. 1 & 2) (1999)
by Mark Runco & Steven Pritzker (Eds.)
San Diego: Academic Press

A wealth of information about virtually every imaginable aspect of creativity written by leading experts.

Gifted Children: Myths and Realities (1996)
by Ellen Winner
New York: Basic Books.

Ellen Winner has studied gifted children for many years. In this book, she distinguishes the myths from the realities of gifted children.

Teaching and Learning Through Multiple Intelligences (2nd ed.) (1999)
by Linda Campbell, Bruce Campell, and Dee Dickenson
Boston: Allyn & Bacon

This book describes applications of Gardner's eight intelligences to classrooms.

Taking It to the Net

1. Terry and Lauren are on a debating team. They have to argue for the proposition "Intelligence is hereditary." Another pair of members will argue for the opposite proposition, "Intelligence is not related to heredity." What facts do Terry and Lauren need to know as they prepare for the debate?

2. Motabi is from the Congo. He is arguing with his developmental psychology classmates about the meaning of intelligence. Motabi insists that different cultures construct their own paradigms of intelligence and that intelligence in the Congo is a very different concept from intelligence in Illinois. Is there any evidence to support Motabi's argument?

3. Maureen and Harry received a letter from the elementary school principal suggesting that they enroll their daughter, Jasmine, in the gifted program. They know that Jasmine's IQ score is 125—certainly not in the genius category. Is there more to giftedness than IQ score? What talents might Jasmine's teachers have noticed in her that might qualify her as being gifted?

Connect to *http://www.mhhe.com/santrockc9* to find the answers!

Chapter 10

LANGUAGE DEVELOPMENT

What Is Language?
- Defining Language
- Language's Rule Systems

Biological and Environmental Influences
- Biological Influences
- Behavioral and Environmental Influences
- An Interactionist View of Language

Language and Cognition

How Language Develops
- Language Development in Infancy
- Language Development in Early Childhood
- Overview of Early Language Development
- Language Development in Middle and Late Childhood

Bilingualism

Language Development

The Story of Helen Keller

ONE OF THE MOST STUNNING portrayals of children isolated from the mainstream of language is the case of Helen Keller (1880–1968). At 18 months of age, Helen was an intelligent toddler in the process of learning her first words. Then she developed an illness that left her both deaf and blind, suffering the double affliction of sudden darkness and silence. For the next 5 years she lived in a world she learned to fear because she could not see or hear.

Even with her fears, Helen spontaneously invented a number of gestures to reflect her wants and needs. For example, when she wanted ice cream, she turned toward the freezer and shivered. When she wanted bread and butter, she imitated the motions of cutting and spreading. But this homemade language system severely limited her ability to communicate with the surrounding community, who did not understand her idiosyncratic gestures.

Alexander Graham Bell, the famous inventor of the telephone, suggested to her parents that they hire a tutor named Anne Sullivan to help Helen overcome her fears. By using sign language, Anne was able to teach Helen to communicate. Anne realized that language learning needs to occur naturally, so she did not force Helen to memorize words out of context as in the drill methods that were in vogue at the time. Sullivan's success depended not only on the child's natural ability to organize language according to form and meaning but also on introducing language in the context of communicating about objects events, and feelings about others.

Helen Keller eventually graduated from Radcliffe with honors, became a very successful educator, and crafted books about her life and experiences. She had this to say about language: "Whatever the process, the result is wonderful. Gradually from naming an object we advance step by step until we have traversed the vast distance between our first stammered syllable and the sweep of thought in a line of Shakespeare."

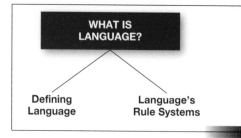

language
A form of communication, whether spoken, written, or signed, that is based on a system of symbols.

infinite generativity
The ability to produce an endless number of meaningful sentences using a finite set of words and rules.

phonology
A language's sound system.

Figure **10.1**

Language's Rule Systems

What Is Language?

In 1799, a nude boy was observed running through the woods in France. The boy was captured when he was 11 years old. He was called the Wild Boy of Aveyron and was believed to have lived in the woods alone for 6 years (Lane, 1976). When found, he made no effort to communicate. Even after a number of years, he never learned to communicate effectively. Sadly, a modern-day wild child named Genie was discovered in Los Angeles in 1970. Despite intensive intervention, Genie has never acquired more than a primitive form of language. We will discuss Genie's development in greater detail later in the chapter. Both cases—the Wild Boy of Aveyron and Genie—raise questions about the biological and environmental determinants of language, topics that we also will examine in greater detail later in the chapter. First, though, we need to define language.

Defining Language

Language *is a form of communication, whether spoken, written, or signed, that is based on a system of symbols.* Think how important language is in our everyday lives. We need language to speak with others, listen to others, read, and write. Our language enables us to describe past events in detail and to plan for the future. Language lets us pass down information from one generation to the next and create a rich cultural heritage.

All human languages have some common characteristics. These include infinite generativity and organizational rules. **Infinite generativity** *is the ability to produce an endless number of meaningful sentences using a finite set of words and rules.* This quality makes language a highly creative enterprise. Language is characterized by a number of organizational rules that include phonology, morphology, syntax, and semantics, which we will discuss next.

Language's Rule Systems

When nineteenth-century American writer Ralph Waldo Emerson said, "The world was built in order and the atoms march in tune," he must have had language in mind. The truly elegant system of language is highly ordered and organized (Gleason, 2000). What are this order and organization like? The order and organization of language involve five rule systems: phonology, morphology, syntax, semantics, and pragmatics (see figure 10.1).

Phonology   Language is made up of basic sounds, or phonemes. **Phonology** *refers to a language's sound system.* Phonological rules ensure that certain sound sequences occur (for example, *sp, ba,* or *ar*) and others do not (for example, *zx* or *qp*) (Booij, 2000). A good example of a phoneme in the English language is /k/, the sound represented by the letter *k* in the word *ski* and the letter *c* in the word *cat.* Although the /k/ sound is slightly different in these two words, the variation is not distinguished, and the /k/ sound is described as a single phoneme. In some languages, such as Arabic, this kind of variation represents separate phonemes.

Imagine what language would be like if there were no phonology. Each word in the language would have to be represented by a signal—a sound, for example—that differed from the signals of all other words. The obvious consequence is that the number of words could be no larger than the number of different signals that an individual could efficiently produce and perceive. We do not know precisely what that number is, but we do know that it is very small, especially in the case of speech, in contrast to the hundreds of thousands of words that commonly constitute a language. An increasing number of researchers believe that speech is an infant's gateway to language (Eimas, 1995; Morgan & Demuth, 1995). In their speech perception and processing, infants find cues in the speech stream that allow them to abstract out irregularities in words and how words are combined (Ratner, 1993).

Phonology provides a basis for constructing a large and expandable set of words—all that are or ever will be in that language—out of two or three dozen phonemes. We do not need 500,000 phonemes, we need only a few dozen.

Patricia Kuhl's (1993) research reveals that, long before they actually begin to learn words, infants can sort through a number of spoken sounds in search of the ones that have meaning. Kuhl argues that from birth to about 4 months of age, infants are "universal linguists" who are capable of distinguishing each of the 150 sounds that make up human speech. But by about 6 months of age, they have started to specialize in the speech sounds of their native language.

In one experiment, babies listened to a tape-recorded voice that repeated vowel and consonant combinations (see figure 10.2). Each time the sounds changed from *ah* to *oooh*, for instance, a toy bear in a box lit up and danced. The babies quickly learned to look at the bear when they heard sounds that were new to them. When Kuhl studied American and Swedish 6-month-old babies, she found that they ignored subtle variations in the pronunciation of their own language's sounds, but they heard similar variations in a foreign language as separate sounds. The implication of this research is that 6-month-old infants can already distinguish the sounds they will need for later speech.

By 8 to 9 months of age, comprehension is more noticeable. For example, babies look at a ball when their mothers say "ball." Language experts say that it is impossible to determine how many words babies understand at this point, but research with only slightly older children suggests that comprehension might outpace expression by a factor of as much as one hundred to one. Researchers have found that although some babies are slow in beginning to talk, comprehension is often about equal between the early and late talkers (Bates & Thal, 1991).

Morphology

Morphology *refers to word formation.* A *morpheme* is a unit of sound that conveys a specific meaning. Every word in the English language is made up of one or more morphemes. Some words consist of a single morpheme (for example, *help*), whereas others are made up of more than one morpheme (for example, *helper,* which has two morphemes, *help + er,* with the morpheme *-er* meaning "one who," in this case "one who helps"). Thus, not all morphemes are words by themselves (for example, *pre-, -tion,* and *-ing*). Just as the rules that govern phonemes ensure that certain sound sequences occur, the rules that govern morphemes ensure that certain strings of sounds occur in meaningful sequences.

Syntax

Syntax *involves the ways words are combined to form acceptable phrases and sentences.* If someone says to you, "Bob slugged Tom" or "Bob was slugged by Tom," you know who did the slugging and who was slugged in each case because you have a syntactic understanding of these sentence structures. You also understand that the sentence "You didn't stay, did you?" is a grammatical sentence but that "You didn't stay, didn't you?" is unacceptable and ambiguous.

If you learn another language, it will soon be clear to you that your English syntax will not get you very far. For example, in English an adjective usually precedes a noun (as in *blue sky*), whereas

Patricia Kuhl,
University of Washington

"*Infants have learned the sounds of their native language by the age of six months.*"

morphology
Word formation.

syntax
The ways words are combined to form acceptable phrases and sentences.

Figure 10.2
Infants' Recognition of Speech Sounds
In Patricia Kuhl's research, babies at 7 months of age show an ability to read lips, connecting vowel sounds with lip movements.

in Spanish the adjective usually follows the noun *(cielo azul)*. In fact, the difficulty of learning new syntactic patterns is one of the main complaints of a second-language learner. Despite the differences in their syntactic structures, however, the world's languages have much in common. For example, consider the following short sentences:

> *The cat killed the mouse.*
> *The mouse ate the cheese.*
> *The farmer chased the cat.*

In many languages it is possible to combine these sentences into more-complex sentences. For example:

> *The farmer chased the cat that killed the mouse.*
> *The mouse the cat killed ate the cheese.*

However, no language in the world permits sentences like the following one:

> *The mouse the cat the farmer chased killed ate the cheese.*

Can you make sense of this sentence? If you can, you probably can do it only after wrestling with it for several minutes. You likely could not understand it at all if someone uttered it during a real conversation. It appears that language users cannot process subjects and objects arranged in too complex a fashion in a sentence. That is good news for language learners, because it means there is some common ground that all syntactic systems adhere to. Such findings are also considered important by researchers who are interested in the universal properties of syntax (Clifton, 2000; Maratos, 1998).

Semantics   **Semantics** *refers to the meaning of words and sentences.* Every word has a set of semantic features. *Girl* and *woman,* for example, share many of the semantic features as the word *female,* but differ semantically in regard to age. Words have semantic restrictions on how they can be used in sentences. The sentence *The bicycle talked the boy into buying a candy bar* is syntactically correct but semantically incorrect. The sentence violates our semantic knowledge that bicycles do not talk.

Pragmatics   A final set of language rules involves **pragmatics,** *the use of appropriate conversation and knowledge underlying the use of language in context.* The domain of pragmatics is broad, covering such circumstances as (a) taking turns in discussions instead of everyone talking at once; (b) using questions to convey commands ("Why is it so noisy in here?" "What is this, Grand Central Station?"); (c) using words like *the* and *a* in a way that enhances understanding ("I read *a* book last night. *The* plot was boring"); (d) using polite language in appropriate situations (for example, when talking to one's teacher); and (e) telling stories that are interesting, jokes that are funny, and lies that convince.

*T*he maker of a sentence launches out into the infinite and builds a road into chaos and old night, and is followed by those who hear him with something of a wild, creative light.

Ralph Waldo Emerson
American Poet, Essayist, 19th Century

semantics
The meanings of words and sentences.

pragmatics
The use of appropriate conversation and knowledge underlying the use of language in context.

FRANK & ERNEST reprinted by permission of Newspaper Enterprise Association, Inc.

SUMMARY TABLE 10.1
The Nature of Language and Language's Rule Systems

Concept	Processes/ Related Ideas	Characteristics/Description
Defining Language	Its Nature	• Language is a form of communication, whether spontaneous, written, or signed, that is based on a system of symbols.
	Infinite Generativity	• The ability to produce an endless number of meaningful sentences using a finite set of words and rules.
Language's Rule Systems	Phonology	• A language's sound system.
	Morphology	• Word formation.
	Syntax	• The way words are combined to form acceptable phrases and sentences.
	Semantics	• The meaning of words and sentences.
	Pragmatics	• The use of appropriate conversation and knowledge underlying the use of language in context.

Pragmatic rules can be complex and differ from one culture to another. If you were to study the Japanese language, you would come face-to-face with countless pragmatic rules about conversing with individuals of various social levels and with various relationships to you. Some of these pragmatic rules concern the ways of saying thank you. Indeed, the pragmatics of saying thank you are complex even in our own culture. Preschoolers' use of the phrase *thank you* varies with sex, socioeconomic status, and the age of the individual they are addressing. Through pragmatics, children learn to convey meaning with words, phrases, and sentences. Pragmatics helps children communicate more smoothly with others (Didow, 1993).

At this point we have discussed a number of ideas about what language is and language's rule systems. A review of these ideas is presented in summary table 10.1. Next, we will turn our attention to biological and environmental influences on language.

Pragmatic Language

Biological and Environmental Influences

Is the ability to generate rules for language and then use them to create an infinite number of words the product of biological factors and evolution? Or is language learned and influenced by the environment?

Biological Influences

The strongest evidence for the biological basis of language is that children all over the world reach language milestones at about the same time developmentally and in about the same order, despite the vast variation in the language input they receive. For example, in some cultures adults never talk to children under 1 year of age, yet these infants still acquire language. Also, there is no other convincing way to explain how *quickly* children learn language than through biological foundations.

With these thoughts in mind, let's now explore these questions about biological influences on language. How strongly is language sculpted by biological evolution?

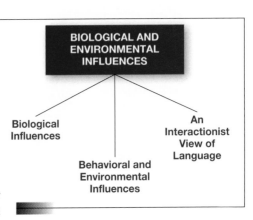

What is the brain's role in language? Are children biologically prewired to learn language? Is there a critical period for language acquisition?

Biological Evolution

Estimates vary as to how long ago humans acquired language—but many experts pick a period of about 100,000 years ago. In evolutionary time, then, language is a very recent acquisition. A number of experts believe that biological evolution undeniably shaped humans into linguistic creatures (Chomsky, 1957). The brain, nervous system, and vocal apparatus of our predecessors changed over hundreds of thousands of years. Physically equipped to do so, *Homo sapiens* went beyond grunting and shrieking to develop abstract speech. Language clearly gave humans an enormous edge over other animals and increased the chances of human survival (Pinker, 1994).

The Brain's Role in Language

There is evidence that the brain contains particular regions that are predisposed to be used for language (Tallal & Patterson, 2000). For example, accumulating evidence suggests that language processing occurs in the brain's left hemisphere (Gazzaniga, 1986). Studies of language in brain-damaged individuals have pinpointed two areas of the left hemisphere that are especially critical. In 1861, a patient of Paul Broca, a French surgeon and anthropologist, received an injury to the left side of his brain. The patient became known as Tan, because that was the only word he could speak after his brain injury. Tan suffered from **aphasia,** *a language disorder, resulting from brain damage, that involves a loss of the ability to use words.* Tan died several days after Broca evaluated him, and an autopsy revealed the location of the injury. Today, we refer to the part of the brain in which Broca's patient was injured as **Broca's area,** *an area of the left frontal lobe of the brain that directs the muscle movements involved in speech production.* Another place in the brain where an injury can seriously impair language is **Wernicke's area,** *an area of the brain's left hemisphere involved in language comprehension.* Individuals with damage to Wernicke's area often babble words in a meaningless way. The locations of Broca's area and Wernicke's area are shown in figure 10.3. Although the brain's left hemisphere is especially important in language, keep in mind that in most activities there is an interplay between the brain's two hemispheres (Hellige, 1990). For example, in reading, the left hemisphere comprehends syntax and grammar, which the right hemisphere does not. However, the right hemisphere is better at understanding a story's intonation and emotion.

Biological Prewiring

Linguist Noam Chomsky (1957) believes humans are biologically prewired to learn language at a certain time and in a certain way. He said that children are born into the world with a **language acquisition device (LAD),** *a biological endowment that enables the child to detect certain language categories, such as phonology, syntax, and semantics.* The LAD is a theoretical construct that flows from evidence about the biological basis of language.

Is there evidence for the existence of a LAD? Supporters of the LAD concept cite the uniformity of language milestones across languages and cultures, biological substrates for language, and evidence that children create language even in the absence of well-formed input. With regard to the last argument, most deaf children are the offspring of hearing parents. Some of these parents choose not to expose their deaf child to sign language, in order to motivate the child to learn speech while providing the child with a supportive social environment. Susan Goldin-Meadow (1979) has found that these children develop spontaneous gestures that are not based on their parents' gestures.

In the wild, chimps communicate through calls, gestures, and expressions, which evolutionary psychologists believe might be the roots of true language.

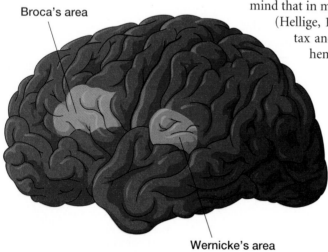

Broca's area

Wernicke's area

Figure **10.3**

Broca's Area and Wernicke's Area

Damage to Broca's area often causes problems in speech production, whereas damage to Wernicke's area often causes problems in language comprehension. These areas are in the left hemisphere of the brain.

Is There a Critical Period for Learning Language?   Have you ever encountered young children serving as unofficial "translators" for their non-English-speaking parents? Doctors and nurses sometimes encounter this when treating patients. Does this indicate that young children are able to easily learn language, while their parents have lost this ability? Such an explanation fits the view that there is a **critical period,** *a period in which there is a learning readiness. Beyond this period, learning is difficult or impossible.* The concept of a critical period applies nicely to certain varieties of songbirds. For example, baby white-crowned sparrows learn the song of their species quite well if they are exposed to it during a specific time as a chick. After this time, they can never develop a fully formed song pattern. But whether this notion can be extended to humans learning language is much less certain.

Almost all children learn one or more languages during their early years of development, so it is difficult to determine whether there is a critical period for language development (Obler, 1993). In the 1960s, Eric Lenneberg (1967) proposed a biological theory of language acquisition. He said that language is a maturational process and that there is a critical period between about 18 months of age and puberty, during which a first language must be acquired. Central to Lenneberg's thesis is the idea that language develops rapidly and with ease during the preschool years as a result of maturation. Lenneberg provided support for the critical-period concept from studies of several atypical populations. These included children with left-hemisphere brain damage, deaf children, and children with mental retardation (Tager-Flusberg, 1994). With regard to brain damage, Lenneberg believed that adults had already passed the critical period during which plasticity of brain function allows language skills to be relearned.

Remember from chapter 2, "The Science of Child Development," that a case study involves an in-depth study of a single individual ◀▥ P. 53. The case study of Genie, a modern-day "wild child" with stunted language development, supports the concept of a critical period in language. In 1970, a California social worker made a routine visit to the home of a partially blind woman who had applied for public assistance. The social worker discovered that the woman and her husband had kept their 13-year-old daughter, Genie, locked away in almost total isolation during her childhood. Genie could not speak or stand erect. She had spent every day bound naked to a child's potty seat. She could move only her hands and feet. At night she was placed in a kind of straightjacket and caged in a crib with wire mesh sides and a cover. Whenever Genie made a noise, her father beat her. He never communicated with her in words but growled and barked at her instead (Rymer, 1992).

After she was rescued from her parents, Genie spent a number of years in extensive rehabilitation programs, such as speech and physical therapy (Curtiss, 1977). She eventually learned to walk, although with a jerky motion, and to use the toilet. Genie also learned to recognize many words and to speak in rudimentary sentences. At first, she spoke in one-word utterances. Later she was able to string together two-word combinations, such as "Big teeth," "Little marble," and "Two hand." Consistent with the language development of most children, three-word combinations (such as "Small two cup") followed. Unlike normal children, Genie has not learned to ask questions, and she does not understand grammar. She is not able to distinguish among pronouns or between passive and active verbs. Four years after she began stringing words together, Genie's speech still sounded like a garbled telegram. As an adult, she speaks in short, mangled sentences, such as "Father hit leg," "Big wood," and "Genie hurt."

Children like Genie, "Wild" Peter of Germany, and Kamala (the wolf-girl), who are abandoned, abused, and not exposed to language for many years, rarely speak normally. Such tragic evidence supports the critical-period hypothesis in language development. However, because these children also suffer severe emotional trauma and possible neurological deficits, the issue is still far from clear.

Let's go back to our "child translator" example. Why is it that children seem to do better than older people in learning language? Many researchers have proposed that the preschool years (until age 5) may be a critical period for language acquisition. Evidence for this notion comes from studies of brain development in young

MIT linguist Noam Chomsky was one of the early architects of the view that children's language development cannot be explained by environmental input. In Chomsky's view, language has strong biological underpinnings, with children biologically prewired to learn language at a certain time and in a certain way.

Brain and Language Development

aphasia
A language disorder, resulting from brain damage, that involves a loss of the ability to use words.

Broca's area
An area of the brain's left frontal lobe that directs the muscle movements involved in speech production.

Wernicke's area
An area of the brain's left hemisphere that is involved in language comprehension.

language acquisition device (LAD)
Chomsky's theoretical concept of a biological endowment enables the child to detect certain language categories, such as phonology, syntax, and semantics.

critical period
A period in which there is learning readiness. Beyond this period, learning is difficult or impossible.

What were Genie's experiences like? What implications do they have for language acquisition?

Critical Period Hypothesis in Language

Genie

*T*hrough the Eyes of Psychologists

Lois Bloom, *Columbia University*

"The linguistics problems children have to solve are always embedded in personal and interpersonal contexts."

children, and from the amount of language learned by preschool children. However, other evidence suggests that we do not have a critical period for language learning. First of all, although much language learning takes place during the preschool years, learning continues well into the later school years and adulthood. Also, with respect to second-language learning, adults can do as well as or better than young children, provided they are motivated and spend equivalent amounts of learning time. In other words, young children's proficiency in language, while impressive, does not seem to involve a biologically salient critical period that older children and adults have passed.

Behavioral and Environmental Influences

Behaviorists view language as just another behavior, such as sitting, walking, and running. They argue that language represents chains of responses (Skinner, 1957) or imitation (Bandura, 1977). The difficulty with this argument is that many of the sentences we produce are novel; we have not heard them or spoken them before. For example, a child hears the sentence "The plate fell on the floor" and then says, "My mirror fell on the blanket," after dropping the mirror on the blanket. The behavioral mechanisms of reinforcement and imitation cannot completely explain this.

While spending long hours observing parents and their young children, child language researcher Roger Brown (1973) searched for evidence that parents reinforce their children for speaking in grammatical ways. He found that parents sometimes smile and praise their children for sentences they like. However, they also reinforce sentences that are ungrammatical. Brown concluded that no evidence exists that reinforcement is responsible for language's rule systems.

Another criticism of the behavioral view is that it fails to explain the extensive orderliness of language. The behavioral view predicts that vast individual differences should appear in children's speech development because of each child's unique learning history. But, as we have seen, a compelling fact about language is its orderly development. All infants coo before they babble. All toddlers produce one-word utterances before two-word utterances. All state sentences in the active form before they state them in a passive form.

However, we do not learn language in a social vacuum. Most children are bathed in language from a very early age (Hart & Risley, 1995). We need this early exposure to language to acquire competent language skills. The Wild Boy of Aveyron did not learn to communicate effectively after living in social isolation for years. Genie's language is rudimentary, even after years of extensive training.

Today most language acquisition researchers believe that children from a wide variety of cultural contexts acquire their native language without explicit teaching. In some cases, they do so without apparent encouragement. Thus, there appear to be very few aids that are necessary for learning a language. However, the support and involvement of caregivers and teachers greatly facilitate a child's language learning (MacWhinney, 1999; Snow, 1999). Of special concern are children who grow up in poverty areas and are not exposed to guided participation in language.

Betty Hart and Todd Risley (1995) observed the language environments and language development of children from middle-income professional backgrounds and from welfare backgrounds. All of the children developed normally in terms of learning to talk and acquiring all of the forms of English and basic vocabulary. However, there were enormous differences in the sheer amount of language the children were exposed to and the level of the children's language development. For example, in a typical hour, the middle-income professional parents spent almost twice as much time communicating with their children as the welfare parents did. The children from the middle-income professional families heard about 2,100 words an hour, their child counterparts in welfare families only 600 words an hour. The researchers estimated that by 4 years of age, the average welfare family child would have 13 million fewer words of cumulative language experience than the child in the average middle-income professional family. Amazingly, some of the 3-year-old children from middle-class professional families had a recorded vocabulary that exceeded the recorded vocabulary of some of the welfare parents!

One intriguing component of the young child's linguistic environment is **motherese,** *the kind of speech often used by mothers and other adults to talk to babies—in a higher pitch than normal and with simple words and sentences.* It is hard to talk in motherese when not in the presence of a baby. But, as soon as you start talking to a baby, you immediately shift into motherese. Much of this is automatic and something most parents are not aware they are doing. Motherese has the important functions of capturing the infant's attention and maintaining communication. When parents are asked why they use baby talk, they point out that it is designed to teach their baby to talk. Older peers also talk baby talk to infants, but observations of siblings indicate that the affectional features are dropped when sibling rivalry is sensed (Dunn & Kendrick, 1982).

Are there strategies other than motherese that adults use to enhance the child's acquisition of language? Four candidates are recasting, echoing, expanding, and labeling. **Recasting** *is rephrasing something the child has said in a different way, perhaps turning it into a question.* For example, if the child says, "The dog was barking," the adult can respond by asking, "When was the dog barking?" The effects of recasting fit with suggestions that "following in order to lead" helps a child learn language. That is, letting a child initially indicate an interest and then proceeding to elaborate that interest—commenting, demonstrating, and explaining—improve communication and help language acquisition. In contrast, an overly active, directive approach to communicating with the child may be harmful.

Echoing *is repeating what a child says, especially if it is an incomplete phrase or sentence.* **Expanding** *is restating, in a linguistically sophisticated form, what a child has said.* **Labeling** *is identifying the names of objects.* Young children are forever being asked to identify the names of objects. Roger Brown (1986) identified this as "the great word game" and claimed that much of the early vocabulary acquired by children is motivated by this adult pressure to identify the words associated with objects.

The strategies just described—recasting, echoing, expanding, and labeling—are used naturally and in meaningful conversations. Parents do not (and should not) use any deliberate method to teach their children to talk. Even for children who are slow in learning language, the experts agree that intervention should occur in natural ways, with the goal of being able to convey meaning.

It is important to recognize that children vary in their ability to acquire language and that this variation cannot be readily explained by differences in environmental input alone (Rice, 1996). For children who are slow in developing language skills, opportunities to talk and be talked with are important. Remember, though, that the encouragement of language development, not drill and practice, is the key (de Villiers, 1996; Snow, 1996). Language development is not a simple matter of imitation and reinforcement, a fact acknowledged even by most behaviorists today. To read further about ways that parents can facilitate children's language development, see the Explorations in Child Development box.

An Interactionist View of Language

We have seen that language has very strong biological foundations. The view that language has a biological base was especially promoted by Chomsky (1957), who, as we have noted, proposed the existence of a language acquisition device (LAD) to account for the complexity and speed of young children's understanding of grammar. We have

motherese
The kind of speech often used by mothers and other adults to talk to babies—in a higher pitch than normal and with simple words and sentences.

recasting
Rephrasing a statement that a child has said, perhaps turning it into a question.

echoing
Repeating what a child says, especially if it is an incomplete phrase or sentence.

expanding
Restating, in a linguistically sophisticated form, what a child has said.

labeling
Identifying the names of objects.

Communicating with Babies

EXPLORATIONS IN CHILD DEVELOPMENT
How Parents Can Facilitate Children's Language Development

IN *Growing Up with Language*, linguist Naomi Baron (1992) provides a number of ideas to help parents facilitate their child's language development. A summary of her ideas follows:

Infants

- *Be an active conversational partner.* Initiate conversation with the infant. If the infant is in a daylong childcare program, ensure that the baby gets adequate language stimulation from adults.
- *Talk as if the infant understands what you are saying.* Parents can generate self-fulfilling prophecies by addressing their young children as if they understand what is being said. The process may take four to five years, but children gradually rise to match the language model presented to them.
- *Use a language style with which you feel comfortable.* Don't worry about how you sound to other adults when you talk with your child. Your affect, not your content, is more important when talking with an infant. Use whatever type of baby talk you with which you feel comfortable.

Toddlers

- *Continue to be an active conversational partner.* Engaging toddlers in conversation, even one-sided conversation, is the most important thing a parent can do to nourish a child linguistically.
- *Remember to listen.* Since toddlers' speech is often slow and laborious, parents are often tempted to supply words and thoughts for them. Be patient and let toddlers express themselves, no matter how painstaking the process is or how great a hurry you are in.
- *Use a language style with which you are comfortable, but consider ways of expanding your child's language abilities and horizons.* For example, using long sentences need not be problematic. Don't be afraid to use ungrammatical language to imitate the toddler's novel forms (such as "No eat"). Use rhymes. Ask questions that encourage answers other than "Yes" and "No." Actively repeat, expand, and recast the child's utter-

ances. Introduce new topics. And use humor in your conversation.
- *Adjust to your child's idiosyncrasies instead of working against them.* Many toddlers have difficulty pronouncing words and making themselves understood. Whenever possible, make toddlers feel that they are being understood.
- *Avoid sexual stereotypes.* Don't let the toddler's sex unwittingly determine your amount or style of conversation. Many American mothers are more linguistically supportive of girls than of boys, and many fathers talk less with their children than mothers do. Active and cognitively enriching initiatives from both mothers and fathers benefit both boys and girls.
- *Resist making normative comparisons.* Be aware of the ages at which your child reaches specific milestones (first word, first 50 words, first grammatical combination). However, be careful not to measure this development rigidly against children of neighbors or friends. Such social comparisons can bring about unnecessary anxiety.

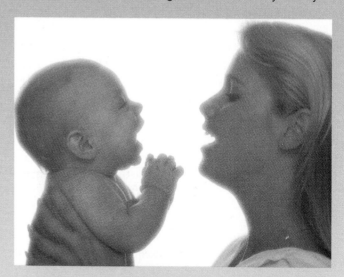

It is a good idea for parents to begin talking to their babies at the start. The best language teaching occurs when the talking is begun before the infant becomes capable of its first intelligible speech.

also seen that children all over the world acquire language milestones at about the same time developmentally and in about the same order, despite the vast variation in language input they receive, which is also evidence for a strong biological influence in language development.

However, children do not learn language in a social vacuum. American psychologist Jerome Bruner (1983, 1989, 1997) recognized this important point when he proposed that the sociocultural context is extremely important in understanding children's language development. Like Vygotsky, Bruner stresses the role of parents and teachers in constructing a child's communication environment. Bruner developed the concept of a language acquisition support system (LASS) to describe the behaviors of a language-skilled individual, especially a parent, in structuring and supporting the child's language development. Bruner's concept has much in common with Vygotsky's concept of a zone of proximal development, which was discussed in chapter 7 ◀▥ P. 226.

In sum, children are neither exclusively biological linguists nor exclusively social architects of language (Clifton, 2000; Gleason & Ratner, 1998). No matter how long you converse with a dog, it won't learn to talk, and unfortunately some children fail to develop good language skills even in the presence of very good role models and social stimulation. An interactionist view emphasizes the contributions of both biology and experience in language: It sees children as biologically prepared to learn language as they and their caregivers communicate.

Think for a moment about the longitudinal study described earlier that was conducted by Betty Hart and Todd Risley (1995). They observed the language environments of children from middle-income and welfare backgrounds. All of the children heard the basic forms and functions of English. Furthermore, all of the children acquired the basic forms and functions of the English language and the universals of language. However, there was extensive variation in the sheer amount of language they were exposed to and the level of language development they attained.

At this point we have discussed a number of ideas about biological and environmental influences on language. A review of these ideas is presented in summary table 10.2. Next, we explore the linkages between language and cognition.

ADVENTURES FOR THE MIND

Parental Strategies for Promoting Children's Language Development

HOW SHOULD PARENTS respond to children's grammatical mistakes in conversation? Should parents allow the mistakes to continue and assume that their young children will grow out of them, or should they closely monitor their children's grammar and correct mistakes whenever they hear them?

Should you also as a parent:

- Be an active conversation partner with your infant or child?
- Talk as if the infant understands what you are saying?
- Use a language style with which you feel comfortable?

Language and Cognition

There are essentially two basic and separate issues involved in exploring connections between language and cognition. The first is this: Is cognition necessary for language? Although some researchers have noted that certain aspects of language development typically follow mastery of selected cognitive skills in both normally developing children and children

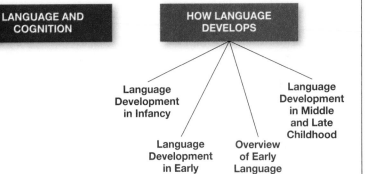

with mental retardation (Mundy, Seibert, & Hogan, 1984), it is not clear that language development depends upon any specific aspect of cognitive abilities (Lenneberg, 1967). Some experts believe that it is more likely that language and cognitive development occur in parallel but dissociated fashions (Cromer, 1987; Ratner, 1993). Thus, according to research and experts' judgments, cognition is not necessary for language development.

The second issue is this: Is language necessary for (or important to) cognition? This issue is addressed by studies of deaf children. On a variety of thinking and problem-solving skills, deaf children perform at the same level as children of the same age who have no hearing problems. Some of the deaf children in these studies do not even have command of written or sign language (Furth, 1973). Thus, based on studies of deaf children, language is not necessary for cognitive development.

$\mathcal{S}$UMMARY $\mathcal{T}$ABLE 10.2
Biological and Environmental Influences

Concept	Processes/ Related Ideas	Characteristics/Description
Biological Influences	Strongest Evidence	• Children all over the world reach language milestones at about the same time developmentally, despite vast variation in language input.
	Biological Evolution	• In evolution, language clearly gave humans an enormous edge over other animals and increased their chance of survival.
	The Brain's Role in Language	• A substantial portion of language processing occurs in the brain's left hemisphere, with Broca's area and Wernicke's area being important left-hemisphere locations.
	Biological Prewiring	• Chomsky's concept of language acquistion device (LAD) flows from the evidence about the biological foundations of language.
	Is There a Critical Period for Learning Language?	• The stunted growth of "wild children" such as Genie support the concept of a critical period in language acquisition. • However, the idea that there is a critical period in language development is still controversial.
Behavioral and Environmental Influences	The Behavioral View	• This view—that language reinforcement and imitation are the factors in language acquisition—has not been supported.
	Environmental Influences	• Among the ways that adults teach language to children are motherese, recasting, echoing, expanding, and labeling. • Parents should talk extensively with an infant, especially about what the baby is attending to. Talk primarily should be live talk, not mechanical talk.
An Interactionist View of Language	Its Nature	• One interactionist view is that both Chomsky's LAD and Bruner's LASS are involved in language acquisition. • An interactionist view emphasizes the contributions of both biology and experience in language.

Overall, though, there is considerable evidence of related activity in the cognitive and language worlds of children (de Villiers & de Villiers, 1999; Goldin-Meadow, 2000). Piaget's concept of object permanence has been the focus of some research that links cognitive and language development. Infants may need a concept of object permanence before they start to use words for disappearance, such as *all gone* (Gopnik & Meltzoff, 1997).

How Language Develops

In the thirteenth century, the Holy Roman Emperor Frederick II had a cruel idea. He wanted to know what language children would speak if no one talked to them. He selected several newborns and threatened their caregivers with death if they ever talked to the infants. Frederick never found out what language the children spoke because they all died. As we move forward in the twenty-first century, we are still curious about infants' development of language, although our experiments and observations are, to say the least, far more humane than the evil Frederick's.

Language Development in Infancy

When does an infant utter her first word? This event usually occurs at about 10 to 13 months of age, though some infants wait longer. Many parents view the onset of language development as coincident with this first word, but some significant accomplishments are attained earlier.

A newborn's cries are a form of reflexive communication. By 2 months of age, babies often utter a range of meaningful noises, such as cooing and fussing. These noises gradually become more varied over the first 6 months of life and might include squeals, grunts, and yells. Babbling begins at about 3 to 6 months of age. The start is determined mainly by biological maturation, not reinforcement or the ability to hear (Locke & others, 1991). Even deaf babies babble for a time (Lenneberg, Rebelsky, & Nichols, 1965). Babbling exercises the baby's vocal apparatus and facilitates the development of articulation skills that are useful in later speech. The purpose of a baby's earliest communication, however, is to attract attention from parents and others in the environment. Infants engage the attention of others by making or breaking eye contact, by vocalizing sounds, and by performing manual actions such as pointing. All of those behaviors involve pragmatics.

A child's first words include those that name important people *(dada)*, familiar animals *(kitty)*, vehicles *(car)*, toys *(ball)*, food *(milk)*, body parts *(eye)*, clothes *(hat)*, household items *(clock)*, or greeting terms *(bye)*. These were the first words of babies 50 years ago and they are the first words of babies today (Clark, 1983). At times, it is hard to tell what these one-word utterances mean. One possibility is that they stand for an entire sentence in the infant's mind. Because of the infant's limited cognitive or linguistic skills, possibly only one word comes out instead of the whole sentence. The **holophrase hypothesis** *is the theory that, in infants' first words, a single word is used to imply a complete sentence.*

Children sometimes overextend or underextend the meanings of the words they use (Woodward & Markman, 1998). **Overextension** *is the tendency of children to misuse words by extending one word's meaning to include objects that are not related to, or are inappropriate for, the word's meaning.* For example, when children learn to say the word *dada* for "father," they often apply the word beyond the individual it was intended to represent, using it for other men, strangers, or boys. With time, such overextensions decrease and eventually disappear. **Underextension** *occurs when children fail to use a word to name a relevant event or object.* For example, a child might learn to use the word *boy* to describe a 5-year-old neighbor but not apply the word to a male infant or a 9-year-old male.

By the time children are 18 to 24 months of age, they usually have begun to utter two-word statements. During this two-word stage, they quickly grasp the importance of expressing concepts and the role that language plays in communicating with others. To convey meaning with two-word utterances, the child relies heavily on gesture, tone, and context. Children can communicate a wealth of meaning with two words; for instance:

Identification: *See doggie.*
Location: *Book there.*
Repetition: *More milk.*
Nonexistence: *Allgone thing.*
Negation: *Not wolf.*
Possession: *My candy.*
Attribution: *Big car.*
Agent-action: *Mama walk.*
Action-direct-object: *Hit you.*
Action-indirect-object: *Give papa.*
Action-instrument: *Cut knife.*
Question: *Where ball?* (Slobin, 1972)

These examples are from children whose first languages were English, German, Russian, Finnish, Turkish, and Samoan. Although these two-word sentences omit many parts of speech, they are remarkably succinct in conveying many messages. In fact, a child's first combination of words has this economical quality in every language. **Telegraphic speech** *is the use of short and precise words to communicate; it is*

Babbling
Language Milestones
The Naming Explosion

holophrase hypothesis
The theory that, in infants' first words, a single word is used to stand for a complete sentence.

overextension
The tendency of children to misuse words by extending one word's meaning to include objects that are not related to, or are inappropriate for, the word's meaning.

underextension
A child's failure to apply a new word she is learning to a relevant object or event.

telegraphic speech
The use of short and precise words to communicate; it characterizes young children's two- or three-word combinations.

Around the world, young children learn to speak in two-word utterances, in most cases at about 18 to 24 months of age. What implications does this have for the biological basis of language?

mean length of utterance (MLU)
An index of language development based on the number of morphemes per sentence a child produces in a sample of about 50 to 100 sentences.

characteristic of young children's two- or three-word combinations. When we send a telegram, we try to be short and precise, excluding any unnecessary words. As a result, articles, auxiliary verbs, and other connectives usually are omitted. Of course, telegraphic speech is not limited to two-word phrases. "Mommy give ice cream" or "Mommy give Tommy ice cream" also are examples of telegraphic speech. As children leave the two-word stage, they move rather quickly into three-, four-, and five-word combinations.

In expanding this concept of classifying children's language development in terms of number of utterances, Roger Brown (1973) has proposed that **mean length of utterance (MLU),** *an index of language development based on the number of morphemes per sentence a child produces in a sample of about 50 to 100 sentences,* is a good index of language maturity. In computations of MLU, "Baby crawl" contains two morphemes whereas "Baby crawled" has three because the addition of *-ed* changes the meaning of the statement.

Brown identified five stages based on MLU:

Stage	MLU
1	1 + to 2.0
2	2.5
3	3.0
4	3.5
5	4.0

The first stage begins when a child generates sentences consisting of more than one morpheme, such as the examples of two-morpheme utterances mentioned earlier. The 1+ designation suggests that the average number of morphemes in each utterance is greater than one but not yet two, because some of the child's utterances are still holophrases. This stage continues until the child averages two morphemes per utterance. Subsequent stages are marked by increments of .5 in mean length of utterance.

Brown's stages are important for several reasons. First, children who differ in chronological age by as much as ½ to ¼ year still have similar speech patterns. Second, children with similar mean lengths of utterance seem to have similar rule systems that characterize their language. In some ways, then, MLU is a better indicator of language development than is chronological age. Figure 10.4 shows the individual variation in chronological age that characterizes children's MLU. In one study of communicative development from 8 to 30 months of age, there was extensive variability in the rate of lexical, gestural, and grammatical development, which challenged the concept of the modal child (Fenson & others, 1994).

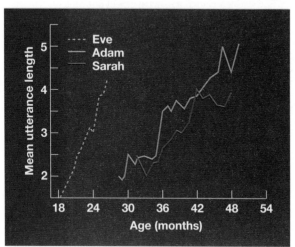

Figure 10.4
An Examination of MLU in Three Children

Shown here is the average length of utterances generated by three children who range in age from 1½ to just over 4 years.

From R. Brown et al, "The Child's Grammar from 1–3," Minnesota Symposium on Child Psychology, Vol. 2 by J.P. Hill (ed.), 1969. Used by permission of the University of Minnesota Press.

Language Development in Early Childhood

Young children's understanding sometimes gets way ahead of their speech. One 3-year-old, laughing with delight as an abrupt summer breeze stirred his hair and tickled his skin, commented, "It did winding me!" Adults would be understandably perplexed if a young child ventured, "Anything is not to break, only plates and glasses," when she meant, "Nothing is breaking except plates and glasses." Many of the oddities of young children's language sound like mistakes to adult listeners. From the children's point of view, however, they are not.

During the preschool years, most children gradually become sensitive to the sounds of spoken words (National Research Council, 1999). They show this phonological awareness in such ways as noticing rhymes, enjoying poems, making up silly names for things by substituting one sound for another (such as *bubblegum, bubblebum, bubbleyum*), breaking long words into syllables or clapping along with each syllable in a phrase, and noticing that the pronunciations of several words (such as *dog, dark,* and *dusty*) all begin the same way.

Regarding morphology, there is clear evidence that, as they move beyond two-word utterances, children know morphological rules. Children begin using the plural and possessive forms of nouns (*dogs* and *dog's*); putting appropriate endings on verbs (*-s* when the subject is third-person singular, *-ed* for the past tense, and *-ing* for the present progressive tense); and using prepositions (*in* and *on*), articles (*a* and *the*), and various forms of the verb *to be* ("I *was going* to the store"). Some of the best evidence for morphological rules appears in the form of *overgeneralizations* of these rules. Have you ever heard a preschool child say "foots" instead of "feet" or "goed" instead of "went"? If you do not remember having heard such things, talk to some parents who have young children or to the young children themselves. You will hear some interesting errors in the use of morphological rule endings.

In a classic experiment, children's language researcher Jean Berko (1958) presented preschool and first-grade children with cards such as the one shown in figure 10.5. Children were asked to look at the card while the experimenter read the words on it aloud. Then the children were asked to supply the missing word. This might sound easy, but Berko was interested not just in the children's ability to recall the right word but also in their ability to say it "correctly" (with the ending that was dictated by morphological rules). *Wugs* would be the correct response for the card in figure 10.5. Although the children were not perfectly accurate, they were much better than chance would dictate. Moreover, they demonstrated their knowledge of morphological rules not only with the plural forms of nouns ("There are two wugs") but also with possessive forms of nouns and with the third-person singular and past-tense forms of verbs. And Berko's study demonstrated not only that the children relied on rules, but also that they had *abstracted* the rules from what they had heard and could apply them to novel situations. What makes Berko's study impressive is that all of the words were fictional; they were created especially for the experiment. Thus, the children could not base their responses on remembering past instances of hearing the words. It seems, instead, that they were forced to rely on *rules*. Their performance suggested that they did so successfully.

Similar evidence that children learn and actively apply rules can be found at the level of syntax (Budwig, 1993). After advancing beyond two-word utterances, the child speaks word sequences that show a growing mastery of complex rules for how words should be ordered. Consider the case of *wh-* questions: "Where is Daddy going?" and "What is that boy doing?" for example. To ask these questions properly, the child has to know two important differences between *wh-* questions and simple affirmative statements (for instance, "Daddy is going to work" and "That boy is waiting on the school bus"). First, a *wh-* word must be added at the beginning of the sentence. Second, the auxiliary verb must be "inverted"—that is, exchanged with the subject of the sentence. Young children learn quite early where to put the *wh-* word, but they take much longer to learn the auxiliary-inversion rule. Thus, it is common to hear preschool children asking such questions as "Where daddy is going?" and "What that boy is doing?"

As children move into the elementary school years, they become skilled at using syntactical rules to construct lengthy and complex sentences. Utterances such as "The man who fixed the house went home" and "I don't want you to use my bike" are impressive demonstrations of how the child can use syntax to combine ideas into a single sentence. Just how a young child achieves the mastery of such complex rules, while at the same time she may be struggling with relatively simple arithmetic rules, is a mystery we have yet to solve.

Language Development in Early Childhood

Figure **10.5**

Stimuli in Berko's Study of Young Children's Understanding of Morphological Rules

In Jean Berko's (1958) study, young children were presented cards such as this one with a "wug" on it. Then the children were asked to supply the missing word and say it correctly. "Wugs" is the correct response here.

Regarding semantics, as children move beyond the two-word stage, their knowledge of meanings also rapidly advances. The speaking vocabulary of a 6-year-old child ranges from 8,000 to 14,000 words (Carey, 1977; Clark, 2000). Assuming that word learning began when the child was 12 months old, this translates into a rate for new word meanings of 5 to 8 words a day between the ages of 1 and 6. After 5 years of word learning, the 6-year-old child does not slow down. According to some estimates, the average child of this age is moving along at the awe-inspiring rate of 22 words a day (Miller, 1981). How would you fare if you were given the task of learning 22 new words every day? It is truly miraculous how quickly children learn language (Fenson & others, 1994).

Until recently, the wide variation in children's vocabulary was attributed to their inborn, hereditary abilities to learn language (Wickelgren, 1999). However, in recent research conducted by Janellen Huttenlocher and her colleagues (Huttenlocher, Levine, & Vevea, 1998), the importance of environmental input in children's vocabulary development was revealed. They taped extensive conversations between 22 toddlers and their mothers during the children's typical daily activities. Tapings were carried out every 2 to 4 months, when the children were 16 to 26 months of age. They found a remarkable link between the size a child's vocabulary and the talkativeness of her or his mother. The mothers varied as much as tenfold in how much they talked. The toddlers of the most talkative mother had a vocabulary more than four times the size of the vocabulary of the child with the quietest mother. Possibly this link might be due at least partly to genes for verbal ability shared by the mother and the child. However, Huttenlocher believes that is not the case, because the mothers in the study did not vary much in terms of their verbal IQs. Also, the children clearly were picking up what their mothers were saying, because the words each child used the most often mirrored those favored by the mother. In another recent study, 18- to 30-month-old African American children from more stimulating and responsive homes were reported to have larger vocabularies and longer utterances than those from less responsive homes (Roberts, Burchinal, & Durham, 1999).

In other recent research, socioeconomic differences in vocabulary have been documented. In one study, high-socioeconomic-status 2-year-old children used more different words in their spontaneous speech than middle-socioeconomic-status children, even when the size of the speech sample was held constant (Hoff-Ginsberg & Lerner, 1999). Researchers have found that this type of difference is due to differences in the quantity and nature of language input that children experience (Hoff-Ginsberg, 1998, 1999). This research provides similar conclusions to the research of Betty Hart and Todd Risley (1995) with welfare and professional families—that the socioeconomic status and the language environment experienced by the children strongly influence their language development.

In yet another recent study, the importance of the language environment in the home was documented for speech syntax, or grammar, an aspect thought to develop similarly in all children due to the shared mental machinery of language (Huttenlocher & Cymerman, 1999). The speech of 34 parents and their 4-year-old children was taped to determine the proportion of complex, multiclause sentences, such as "I am going to go to the store because we need to get some food," versus simple, single-clause ones, such as "Go to your room." A significant relation was found between the proportion of complex sentences spoken by the parents and the proportion of such sentences spoken by the children (both at home and at school). Although, as in the previous study, parents and children shared some language genes, the researchers concluded that a syntax gene alone is unlikely to account for the close similarity in the language use of the child and his or her parents. Such research demonstrates the important effect that early speech input can have on the development of a child's language skills (Jusczyk, 1999).

Changes in pragmatics also characterize young children's language development (Ninio & Snow, 1996). A 6-year-old is simply a much better conversationalist than a 2-year-old is. What are some of the improvements in pragmatics that are made in the preschool years? At about 3 years of age, children improve in their ability to talk

How do children's language abilities develop during early childhood?

about things that are not physically present: that is, they improve their command of an aspect of language known as *displacement*. Displacement is revealed in games of pretend. Although a 2-year-old might know the word *table*, he is unlikely to use this word to refer to an imaginary table that he pretends is standing in front of him. A child over 3 years of age is more likely to do so. There are large individual differences in preschoolers' talk about imaginary people and things.

At about 4 years of age, children develop a remarkable sensitivity to the needs of others in conversation. One way in which they show such sensitivity is their use of the articles *the* and *an* (or *a*). When adults tell a story or describe an event, they generally use *an* (or *a*) when they first refer to an animal or an object, and then use *the* when referring to it later (for example, "Two boys were walking through the jungle when *a* fierce lion appeared. *The* lion lunged at one boy while the other ran for cover."). Even 3-year-olds follow part of this rule (they consistently use the word *the* when referring to previously mentioned things). However, the use of the word *a* when something is initially mentioned develops more slowly. Although 5-year-old children follow this rule on some occasions, they fail to follow it on others.

Another pragmatic ability that appears around 4 to 5 years of age involves speech style. As adults, we have the ability to change our speech style in accordance with social situations and persons with whom we are speaking. An obvious example is that adults speak in a simpler way to a 2-year-old child than to an older child or to an adult. Interestingly, even 4-year-old children speak differently to a 2-year-old than to a same-aged peer (they "talk down" to the 2-year-old, using shorter utterance lengths). They also speak differently to an adult than to a same-aged peer, using more polite and formal language with the adult (Shatz & Gelman, 1973).

Overview of Early Language Development

As we have just seen, language unfolds sequentially. Language expert Lois Bloom (1998) concluded that three sequential frameworks help us better understand early language development:

SUMMARY TABLE 10.3
Language and Cognition; Language Development in Infancy and Early Childhood

Concept	Processes/Related Ideas	Characteristics/Description
Language and Cognition	Nature of Linkages	• Two basic and separate issues are these: (1) Is cognition necessary for language? (2) Is language necessary for cognition? • At an extreme, the answer likely is no to the above questions, but for the most part there is evidence of considerable linkages between language and cognition.
Language Development in Infancy and Early Childhood	Infancy	• Vocalization begins with babbling at about 3 to 6 months of age. • A baby's earliest communications are pragmatic. • One word utterances occur at about 10 to 13 months of age; the holophrase hypothesis describes this one-word utterance stage. • By 18 to 24 months, most infants have begun to use two-word utterances; language at this point is often referred to as "telegraphic." • Roger Brown developed the concept of mean length of utterance (MLU). • Five stages of MLU have been identified, providing an indicator of language maturity.
	Early Childhood	• Advances in phonology, morphology, syntax, semantics, and pragmatics continue in early childhood.
	Overview of Early Language Development	• Three important sequential frameworks are these: (1) the emergence of words and basic vocabulary (toward end of first year and through second year); (2) the transition to combining words and phrases into simple sentences (end of second year); and (3) the transition to complex sentences (begins at 2 or 3 years and continues through the elementary school years).

- The emergence of words and a basic vocabulary, which begins toward the end of the first year and continues through the second year
- The transition from saying one word at a time to combining words and phrases into simple sentences, which begins to take place toward the end of the second year
- The transition from simple sentences expressing a single proposition to complex sentences, which begins between 2 and 3 years of age and continues into the elementary school years

At this point we have discussed a number of ideas about language and cognition, and about how language develops in infancy and early childhood. A review of these ideas is presented in summary table 10.3. Next, we continue to explore the development of language, examining changes in middle and late childhood.

Language Development in Middle and Late Childhood

As children develop during middle and late childhood, changes take place in their vocabulary and grammar. Reading assumes a prominent role in their language world, as do writing and the importance of literacy. An increasingly important consideration is bilingualism.

Language Growth

Vocabulary and Grammar   During middle and late childhood, a change occurs in the way children think about words. They become less tied to the actions and perceptual dimensions associated with words, and they become more analytical in their approach to words. For example, when asked to say the first thing that comes to mind when they hear a word, such as *dog,* preschool children often respond with a word related to the immediate context of a dog. A child might associate *dog* with a word that indicates its appearance *(black, big)* or to an action associated with it *(bark, sit).* Older children more frequently respond to "dog" by associating it with an appropriate category *(animal)* or to information that intelligently expands the context *(cat, veterinarian).* The increasing ability of elementary school children to analyze words helps them understand words that have no direct relation to their personal experiences. This allows children to add more abstract words to their vocabulary. For example, *precious stones* can be understood by understanding the common characteristics of *diamonds* and *emeralds.* Also, children's increasing analytical abilities allow them to distinguish between such similar words as *cousin* and *nephew,* or *city, village,* and *suburb.*

Children make similar advances in grammar. The elementary school child's improvement in logical reasoning and analytical skills helps in the understanding of such constructions as the appropriate use of comparatives *(shorter, deeper)* and subjunctives *("If* I *were* president, . . .").* By the end of the elementary school years, children can usually apply most of the appropriate rules of grammar.

We have discussed many milestones in our coverage of language development. A summary of language milestones, from birth through adolescence, is presented in figure 10.6.

Reading, Writing, and Literacy
In the twenty-first century, literacy (the ability to read and write) will become even more critical than it was in the previous century. The biggest increase in jobs and the best jobs will be in the professional and technical sectors. These jobs require good reading, writing, and communication skills.

A Developmental Model of Reading
One view of reading skills describes their development in five stages (Chall, 1979). The age boundaries are approximate and do not apply to every child. For example, some children learn to read before they enter first grade. Nonetheless, the stages convey a general sense of the developmental changes involved in learning to read.

- *Stage 0.* From birth to first grade, children master several prerequisites for reading. Many learn the left-to-right progression and order of reading, how to identify the letters of the alphabet, and how to write their names. Some learn to read some words that appear on signs. As a result of TV shows like *Sesame Street* and attending preschool and kindergarten programs, many young children today develop greater knowledge about reading earlier than in the past.
- *Stage 1.* In first and second grades, many children learn to read. In doing so, they acquire the ability to sound out words (that is, translate letters into sounds and blend sounds into words). They also complete their learning of letter names and sounds during this stage.
- *Stage 2.* In second and third grades, children become more fluent at retrieving individual words and other reading skills. However, at this stage reading is still not used much for learning. The mechanical demands of learning to read are so taxing at this point that children have few resources left over to process the content.
- *Stage 3.* In fourth through eighth grade, children become increasingly able to obtain new information from print. In other words, they read to learn. They still have difficulty understanding information presented from multiple perspectives within the same story. When children don't learn to read, a downward spiral unfolds that leads to serious difficulties in many academic subjects.
- *Stage 4.* In the high school years, many students become fully competent readers. They develop the ability to understand material told from many different perspectives. This allows them to engage in sometimes more sophisticated discussions of literature, history, economics, and politics. It is no accident that great novels are not presented to students until high school, because understanding the novels requires advanced reading comprehension.

AGE PERIOD	CHILD'S DEVELOPMENT/BEHAVIOR
0–6 Months	Cooing Discrimination of vowels Babbling present by end of period
6–12 Months	Babbling expands to include sounds of spoken language Gestures used to communicate about objects
12–18 Months	First words spoken Understand vocabulary 50+ words, on the average
18–24 Months	Vocabulary increases to an average of 200 words Two-word combinations
2 Years	Vocabulary rapidly increases Correct use of plurals Use of past tense Use of some prepositions
3–4 Years	Mean length of utterances increases to 3–4 morphemes per sentence Use of yes/no questions, *wh-* questions Use of negatives and imperatives Increased awareness of pragmatics
5–6 Years	Vocabulary reaches an average of about 10,000 words at entry to first grade Coordination of simple sentences
6–8 Years	Vocabulary continues to increase rapidly More-skilled use of syntactical rules Conversational skills improve
9–11 Years	Word definitions include synonyms Conversational strategies continue to improve
11–14 Years	Vocabulary increases with addition of more abstract words Understanding of complex grammar forms Increased understanding of function a word plays in a sentence Understands metaphor and satire
15–20 Years	Can understand adult literary works

Figure 10.6

Language Milestones

Note: This list is not meant to be exhaustive but rather to highlight some of the main language milestones. Also keep in mind that there is a great deal of variation in the age at which children reach these milestones and still be considered within the normal range of language development.

reading
The ability to understand written discourse.

whole-language approach
An approach that stresses that reading instruction should parallel children's natural language learning. Reading materials should be whole and meaningful.

basic-skills-and-phonetics approach
An approach that emphasizes that reading instruction should teach phonetics and its basic rules for translating written symbols into sounds.

Approaches to Reading   As the previous discussion has implied, **reading** *is the ability to understand written discourse.* Children cannot be said to read if they just can respond to flash cards, as in some early child training programs. Early reading requires mastering the basic language rules of phonology, morphology, syntax, and semantics (Fields & Spangler, 2000). A child who has poor grammatical skills for speech and listening and does not understand what is meant by "The car was pushed by the truck" when it is spoken cannot understand its meaning in print either. Likewise, a child who cannot determine what pronouns refer to (as in "John went to the store with his dog. It was closed") will not do well in reading comprehension.

Education and language experts continue to debate how children should be taught to read. The debate focuses on the whole-language approach versus the basic-skills-and-phonetics approach. The **whole-language approach** *stresses that reading instruction should parallel children's natural language learning. Reading materials should be whole and meaningful.* That is, in early reading instruction, children should be presented with materials in their complete form, such as stories and poems. In this way, say the whole-language advocates, children learn to understand language's communicative function.

In the whole-language approach, reading is connected with listening and writing skills. Although whole-language programs vary, most share the premise that reading should be integrated with other skills and subjects, such as science and social studies, and that it should focus on real-world, relevant material. Thus, a class might read newspapers, magazines, or books, then write about them and discuss them.

By contrast, the **basic-skills-and-phonetics approach** *emphasizes that reading instruction should teach phonetics and its basic rules for translating written symbols into sounds.* According to this view, early reading instruction should involve controlled materials. Only after they have learned phonological rules should children be given complex reading materials such as books and poems.

Advocates of the basic-skills-and-phonetics approach often point to low reading achievement scores occurring as an outgrowth of the recent emphasis on holistic, literature-based instruction and the consequent lack of attention to basic skills and phonetics (Baumann & others, 1998). In California, a task force recently has recommended that children's reading skills be improved by pursuing a balanced approach which includes teaching phonemic awareness (sounds in words). To read about some technology resources for improving phonological awareness and decoding skills, see the Explorations in Child Development box.

EXPLORATIONS IN CHILD DEVELOPMENT
Technology Resources for Improving Phonological Awareness and Decoding Skills

TWO RESOURCES that can be used to improve students' phonological awareness and decoding skills are *Read-Along Books* and *Word Picker* (Cognition and Technology Group at Vanderbilt, 1997).

Read-Along Books are easy-to-read books written with short, decodable words that combine to form rhythm and rhyme patterns to improve students' sound-letter skills. Computer versions of the books include tools that pronounce sentences and words as needed. After students become competent at sound-letter skills, they can record the stories in their own voice.

Word Picker is a software tool that helps students build on their letter-sound knowledge to discover conventional spellings for words that they want to write. As the children work on creating their own books in a multimedia format, they can click on *Word Picker.* Scrolling through a list of words, they search for words that start with the same letter as the word they want to write. Then they click on different words to hear them pronounced and to observe how they are divided into syllables. When they find the word they want, they type it out.

After students write their own books, they can read the printed versions of their books in class to others. *Read-Along Books* and *Word Picker* are part of the Young Children's Literacy Project at Vanderbilt University. The current versions are most appropriate for grade 1. Future projects are planned for preschool to grade 3.

Reading and writing also are combined in IBM's *Writing to Read* program for kindergarten and first-grade students. Five learning stations are coordinated to provide an active learning environment: computer, work journal, writing/typing, listening library, and making words.

These students are participating in IBM's Writing to Read *program, which uses a variety of learning stations to improve children's literacy.*

The term *balanced instruction* is now being used to describe combinations of reading approaches (Au, Carroll, & Scueu, in press; Freppon & Dahl, 1998; Pressley, in press; Tompkins, 1997; Weaver, in press). However, "balance" often means different things to different researchers and teachers. For some, balanced means a primary emphasis on phonics instruction with minimal whole language emphasis, for others the reverse.

Which approach is best? Researchers have not been able to consistently document that one approach is better than the other. A recently convened national panel of seventeen reading experts concluded that a combination of the two approaches is the best strategy (National Research Council, 1999). The panel recommended that beginning readers be taught to sound out letters as the main way to identify unfamiliar words, the cornerstone of the basic-skills-and-phonetics approach. But the panel also endorsed several aspects of the whole-language approach: encourage children, as they begin to recognize words, to predict what might happen in a story, draw inferences about stories, and write their own stories.

Reading Research
Reading
Promoting Children's Reading Success
Children's Writing
Supporting Young Children's Writing

Writing Children's writing emerges out of their early scribbles, which appear at around 2 to 3 years of age. In early childhood, children's motor skills usually develop to the point at which they can begin printing letters. Most 4-year-olds can print their first name. Five-year-olds can reproduce letters and copy several short words. As they develop their printing skills, they gradually learn to distinguish between the distinctive characteristics of letters, such as whether the lines are curved or straight, open

Through the Eyes of Psychologists

Catherine Snow, *Harvard University*

"Children most at risk for reading difficulties in the first grade are those who began school with less verbal skill, less phonological awareness, less letter knowledge, and less familiarity with the basic purposes and mechanisms of reading."

Literacy
Children's Literature

or closed, and so on. Through the early elementary grades, many children continue to reverse letters such as *b* and *d* and *p* and *q* (Temple & others, 1993). At this point in development, if other aspects of the child's development are normal these letter reversals are not a predictor of literacy problems.

As they begin to write, children often invent spellings of words. They usually do this by relying on the sounds of words they hear and using those as the basis of forming the words they write.

Parents and teachers should encourage children's early writing but not be overly concerned about the proper formation of letters or correct conventional spelling. I (your author) once had a conference with my youngest daughter's first-grade teacher when she brought home a series of papers with her printing of words all marked up and sad faces drawn on the paper. Fortunately, the teacher agreed to reduce her criticism of Jennifer's print skills. Such printing errors should be viewed as a natural part of the child's growth. Spelling and printing corrections can be made selectively in positive ways and in the context of maintaining early writing and spontaneity.

Like becoming a good reader, becoming a good writer takes many years and lots of practice. Children should be given many writing opportunities in the elementary and secondary school years. As their language and cognitive skills improve with good instruction, so will their writing skills. For example, developing a more sophisticated understanding of syntax and grammar serves as an underpinning for better writing.

So do such cognitive skills as organization and logical reasoning. Through the course of elementary, middle, and high school, students develop increasingly sophisticated methods of organizing their ideas. In early elementary school, they narrate and describe or write short poems. In late elementary and middle school, they move to projects such as book reports that combine narration with more reflection and analysis. In high school, they become more skilled at forms of exposition that do not depend on narrative structure.

Literacy   Learning to both read and write should occur in a supportive environment in which children can generate a positive perception of themselves and develop a positive attitude toward both skills (Miller, 1999; Pianta, 1999). The National Association for the Education of Young Children (NAEYC) (the leading organization of early childhood educators) believes that, unfortunately, in the push to develop a nation of literate people, too many preschool children are being subjected to rigid, formal prereading programs with expectations and experiences that are too advanced (Bredekamp & Rosegrant, 1996). Learning to read and continuing to read should be an enjoyable experience for children, not a stressful one. So should writing.

Teachers and parents should take time to read to children from a wide variety of poetry, fiction, and nonfiction. They should present models for children to emulate by using language appropriately, listening and responding to children's talk, and engaging in their own reading and writing (Mathes & Torgesen, 1999; Slavin, 1999).

For children who have participated extensively in print-related interactions in their homes and communities, literacy often comes quickly in school. However, many children who have not participated extensively in lap reading and similar literacy events in the preschool years will take longer to develop literacy skills (Hiebert & Raphael, 1996). A positive school-home partnership provides teachers with opportunities to involve parents in helping children improve their literacy skills.

Bilingualism

Octavio's parents moved to the United States before he was born. They do not speak English fluently and always have spoken to Octavio in Spanish. At age 6, Octavio has just entered first grade in San Antonio. He speaks no English. What is the best way to teach Octavio?

As many as 10 million children in the United States come from homes in which English is not the primary language. Often, like Octavio, they live in a community in which English is not the main form of communication. But to be successful in the larger U.S. society, they have to master English.

Bilingual education, which has been the preferred strategy of schools for the last two decades, aims to teach academic subjects to immigrant children in their native languages (most often Spanish) while slowly and simultaneously adding English instruction. Researchers have found that bilingualism does not interfere with performance in either language (Hakuta, 2000; Hakuta & Garcia, 1989; Oller, 1999). Indeed, researchers have demonstrated that bilingualism has a positive effect on children's cognitive development. Children who are fluent in two languages perform better than their single-language counterparts on tests of attentional control, concept formation, analytical reasoning, cognitive flexibility, and cognitive complexity (Bialystok, 1999). They also are more conscious of spoken and written language structure and better at noticing errors of grammar and meaning, skills that benefit their reading ability (Bialystok, 1993, 1997).

A common fear is that early exposure to English will lead to children's loss of their native language. In recent studies of Latino American children, there was no evidence of a loss in Spanish proficiency (productive language, receptive language, and language complexity) for children attending a bilingual preschool (Rodriguez & others, 1995; Winsler & others, 1999). Children who attended bilingual preschool, compared to those who remained at home, showed significant and parallel gains in both English and Spanish.

Researchers have found that bilingual children in a number of countries (such as Canada, Israel, Singapore, and Switzerland) do better than monolingual children on tests of intelligence (Lambert & others, 1993). Based on these findings, a Canadian program was developed to immerse English-speaking children in French for much of their early elementary school education in Quebec. Their English does not appear to have been harmed and their math scores, aptitude scores, and appreciation of French culture have benefited.

Proponents of bilingual education argue that teaching immigrants in their native language values their family and community culture and increases their self-esteem, thus making their academic success more likely. By contrast, critics stress that, in actual practice, bilingual education harms immigrant children by failing to instruct them adequately in English, which will leave them behind in the workplace. In rebuttal, supporters of bilingual education say it aims to teach English. Some states recently have passed laws declaring English to be their official language, creating conditions in which schools are not obligated to teach minority children in languages other than English (Rothstein, 1998). In California, in 1998 voters repealed bilingualism altogether. Supporters of the appeal claimed that most Spanish-speaking voters opposed bilingual education, though polling after the election did not bear out this contention. Ironically, test scores released shortly after the election revealed that the scores of children in bilingual programs in several large school districts were higher on average than scores of children who are native speakers of English.

Linked to our earlier discussion of critical period is this question: Is it better to learn a second language as a child or as an adult? Adults make faster initial progress but their eventual success in the second language is not as great as children's. For example, in one study Chinese and Korean adults who immigrated to the United States at different ages were given a test of grammatical knowledge (Johnson & Newport, 1989). Those who began learning English from 3 to 7 years of age scored as well as native speakers on the test, but those who arrived in the United States (and therefore started learning English) in later childhood or adolescence had lower test scores. Children's ability to pronounce a second language with the correct accent also decreases with age, with an especially sharp decline occurring after the age of about 10 to 12 (Asher & Garcia, 1969). Adolescents and adults can become competent at a second language but this is a more difficult task than learning it as a child.

Bilingual Education

Bilingualism and Bilingual Education

Multilingual Multicultural Research

Improving Schooling for Language-Minority Children: A Research Agenda

Summary Table 10.4
Language Development in Middle and Late Childhood; Bilingualism

Concept	Processes/ Related Ideas	Characteristics/Description
Language Development in Middle and Late Childhood	Vocabulary and Grammar	• Children become more analytical and logical in their approach to words and grammar.
	Reading, Writing, and Literacy	• Chall's model proposes five stages in reading, ranging from birth/first grade to high school. • Current debate focuses on the whole-language approach versus the basic-skills-and-phonics approach. • Many experts today recommend a balance of these two approaches in teaching children to read. • Children's writing follows a developmental timetable, emerging out of scribbling. • Advances in children's language and cognitive development provide the underpinnings for improved writing. • Literacy involves learning to read and write; this should occur in a supportive atmosphere.
Bilingualism	Its Nature	• Bilingual education aims to teach academic subjects to immigrant children in their native languages (most often in Spanish) while gradually adding English instruction. • Researchers have found that bilingualism does not interfere with performance in either language. • Success in learning a second language is greater in childhood than in adolescence.

The United States is one of the few countries in the world in which most students graduate from high school knowing only their own language. For example, in Russia schools have 10 grades, called forms, which roughly correspond to the 12 grades in American schools. Children begin school at age 7 in Russia and begin learning English in the third form. Because of the emphasis on teaching English in Russian schools, most Russian citizens under the age of 40 today are bilingual, able to speak at least some English in addition to their native language.

Following are some recommendations for working with linguistically and culturally diverse children (National Association for the Education of Young Children, 1996):

• Recognize that all children are cognitively, linguistically, and emotionally connected to the language and culture of their home.
• Understand that second-language learning can be difficult. It takes time to become linguistically competent in any language. Although verbal proficiency in a second language can be attained in 2 to 3 years, the skills needed to understand academic content through reading and writing can take 4 or more years. Children who do not become proficient in their second language after 2 or 3 years usually are not proficient in their first language either.
• Recognize that children can and will acquire the use of English even when their home language is respected.

At this point we have discussed a number of ideas about how language develops in middle and late childhood and about bilingualism. A summary of these ideas is presented in summary table 10.4.

Chapter Review

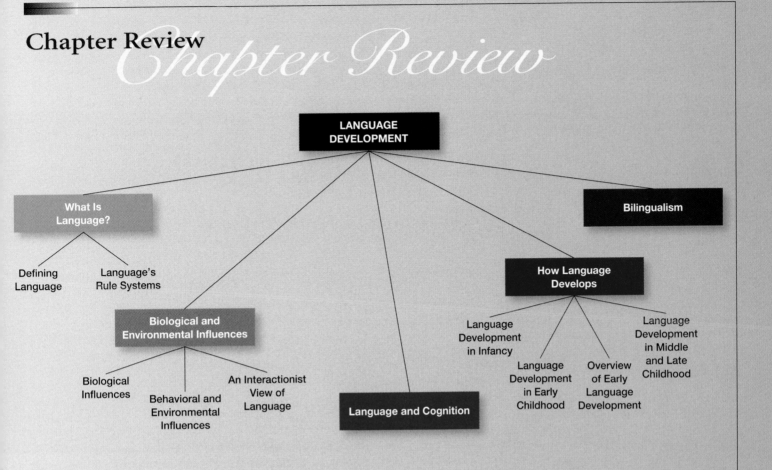

TO OBTAIN A DETAILED REVIEW OF THE CHAPTER, STUDY THESE FOUR SUMMARY TABLES:

Key Terms

Key People

Child Development Resources

Genie (1993)
by Russ Rymer
New York: HarperCollins

In this book, Russ Rymer tells the poignant story of Genie, a child who grew up without language or any form of social training.

Growing Up With Language (1992)
by Naomi Baron
Reading, MA: Addison-Wesley

This book does an excellent job of conveying the appropriate role of parents in children's language development.

Improving Schooling for Language-Minority Children (1997)
by National Research Council
Washington, DC: National Academy Press

An excellent book on bilingual education by a leading panel of experts.

Language Development in Its Developmental Context (1998)
by Lois Bloom. In W. Damon (Ed.), *Handbook of Child Psychology* (5th ed., Vol. 2).
New York: Wiley

Child language expert Lois Bloom provides an authoritative examination of research on children's language.

Starting Out Right: A Guide to Promoting Children's Reading Success (1999)
by National Research Council
Washington, DC: National Academy Press

An outstanding book written by leading experts on children's language development.

Taking It to the Net

1. Clarissa wants to be a speech therapist. In her child development class, she learned that Vygotsky believed that linguistic and cognitive development go hand in hand after a certain age. She wants to know more about his theory, because it might give her insight into children's language problems.

2. Todd is working in a day-care center after school. He notices that there is a wide range in the children's use of language, even within age groups. He wonders if there are guidelines that can indicate whether a child is delayed in language development.

3. Jared is concerned because his 7-year-old son, Damion, does not like to read. Damion's second-grade teacher says he is about average for his age, but she has to prod him to do his reading assignments at school. What can Jared do to help Damion become a better reader?

Connect to *http://www.mhhe.com/santrockc9* to find the answers!

Socioemotional Development

*I am what I hope
and give.*

Erik Erikson
*European-Born American Psychotherapist,
20th Century*

As children develop, they need the
meeting eyes of love. They split the
universe into two halves: "me" and "not
me." They juggle the need to curb their
own will with becoming what they can
will freely. They also want to fly but
discover that first they have to learn to
stand and walk and climb and dance. As
they become adolescents, they try on
one face after another, looking for a face
of their own. In Section 4 you will read
four chapters: "Emotional Development" (chapter 11), "The Self and
Identity" (chapter 12), "Gender"
(chapter 13), and "Moral Development"
(chapter 14).

Chapter 11

EMOTIONAL
DEVELOPMENT

Exploring
Emotion

Defining
Emotion

Functionalism
in Emotion

Regulation
of Emotion

Relational
Emotion

Development
of Emotion

Infancy

Early Childhood

Middle and
Late Childhood

Adolescence

Emotional Problems,
Stress, and Coping

Depression

Stress and
Coping

Emotional Intelligence

Attachment

What Is
Attachment?

Individual
Differences

Caregiving
Styles and
Attachment
Classification

Measurement
of Attachment

Day Care

Fathers as
Caregivers
for Infants

Attachment,
Temperament,
and the Wider
Social World

Temperament

Defining and
Classifying
Temperament

Parenting and
the Child's
Temperament

Emotional Development

*Blossoms are scattered by the wind
And the wind cares nothing, but
The blossoms of the heart
No wind can touch.*

Youshida Kenko
Buddhist Monk, 14th Century

Many fathers are spending more time with their infants.

The Story of Tom's Fathering

TOM IS A 1-year-old infant who is being reared by his father during the day. His mother works full-time at her job away from home, and his father is a writer who works at home; they prefer this arrangement over putting Tom in day care. Tom's father is doing a great job of caring for him. Tom's father keeps Tom nearby while he is writing and spends lots of time talking to him and playing with him. From their interactions, it is clear that they genuinely enjoy each other.

Tom's father is a far cry from the emotionally distant, conformist, traditional-gender-role fathers of the 1950s. He looks to the future and imagines the Little League games Tom will play in and the many other activities he can enjoy with Tom. Remembering how little time his own father spent with him, he is dedicated to making sure that Tom has an involved, nurturing experience with his father.

When Tom's mother comes home in the evening, she spends considerable time with him. Tom shows a positive attachment to both his mother and his father. His parents have cooperated and have successfully juggled their careers and work schedules to provide 1-year-old Tom with excellent child care. Later in this chapter we will explore many aspects of fathering and child care. To begin, though, we will examine the nature of children's emotions.

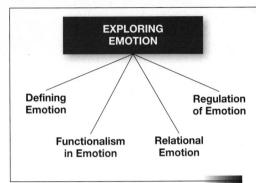

Exploring Emotion

Emotion plays a powerful role in children's development (Bruce, Olen, & Jensen, 1999). But just what is emotion?

Defining Emotion

Defining *emotion* is difficult because it is not easy to tell when a child or an adult is in an emotional state. Is a child in an emotional state when her heart beats fast, her palms sweat, and her stomach churns? Is she in an emotional state when she smiles or grimaces? The body and face play important roles in understanding children's emotion (Keltner & Ekman, 2000). However, psychologists debate how important each is in determining whether a child is in an emotional state. For our purposes, we will define **emotion** *as feeling or affect that involves a mixture of physiological arousal (a fast heartbeat, for example) and overt behavior (a smile or grimace, for example).*

When we think about children's emotions, a few dramatic feelings, such as rage, fear, and glorious joy, usually spring to mind. But emotions can be subtle as well—the feeling a mother has when she holds her baby, the mild irritation of boredom, or the uneasiness of being in a new situation.

Psychologists classify emotions in many different ways, but one characteristic of almost all classifications is the designation of an emotion as positive or negative. **Positive affectivity (PA)** *refers to the range of positive emotions, from high energy, enthusiasm, and excitement to being calm, quiet, and withdrawn. Joy, happiness, and laughter involve positive affectivity.* **Negative affectivity (NA)** *refers to emotions that are negatively toned, such as anxiety, anger, guilt, and sadness.* PA and NA are independent dimensions in that a child can be high along both dimensions at the same time (for example, in a high-energy state and enthusiastic yet angry).

An important aspect of emotional development is emotional regulation (Fabes & others, 1999; Saarni, Mume, & Campos, 1998). During the first year of life, the infant gradually develops an ability to inhibit, or minimize, the intensity and duration of emotional reactions. At the same time, infants acquire a greater diversity of emotional responses. Examples of early emotional regulation are infants' soothing themselves by sucking and their withdrawing from excessive stimulation. Equally important is caregivers' assisting infants in learning how to regulate their emotions by attending to their distress and providing them with comfort (Kochanska, 1999).

emotion
Feeling, or affect, that involves a mixture of physiological arousal and overt behavior.

positive affectivity (PA)
A range of positive emotions—from high energy, enthusiasm, and excitement to being calm, quiet, and withdrawn—that includes joy, happiness, and laughter.

negative affectivity (NA)
Emotions that are negatively toned, such as anxiety, anger, guilt, and sadness.

Exploring Emotion
International Society
for Research on Emotions

Functionionalism in Emotion

A number of developmentalists view the nature of emotion differently today than their predecessors did (Campos, 1994). The new view proposes that emotion is relational rather than intrapsychic, that there is a close link between emotion and the person's goals and effort, that emotional expressions can serve as social signals, and that the physiology of emotion involves much more than homeostasis and the person's interior. Emotion also includes the ability to regulate and be regulated by social processes.

The new approach is called "functionalism"—not because it focuses on evolutionary survival but because it links emotion with what the person is trying to do. In this view, the person and an environmental event constitute a whole. Emotion, thus, involves person-event transactions, in this perspective (see figure 11.1).

More needs to be said about goals and emotion. Goals are related to emotion in a variety of ways. Regardless of what the goal is, an individual who overcomes an obstacle to attain a goal experiences happiness. By contrast, a person who must relinquish a goal as unattainable experiences sadness. And a person who faces difficult obstacles in pursuing a goal often experiences

Through the Eyes of Psychologists

Nancy Eisenberg,
Arizona State University

"For many years emotion was a neglected aspect of the study of children's development. Today, emotion plays a central role in conceptualizations of development."

Figure 11.1

Functionalism in Emotion

Researcher Nathan Fox measured the brain waves of infants, such as this 4-month-old, who are stimulated with toys to elicit different emotional states. Fox demonstrated that very inhibited babies show a distinctive brain-wave pattern (as measured by the electroencephalogram [EEG] helmet in the photograph). Fox's research fits within the functionalist view of emotion, which argues that the physiology of emotion involves much more than homeostasis or an internal milieu. In functionalism, emotions are modes of adaptation to the environment.

anger. The specific nature of the goal can affect the experience of a given emotion. For example, the avoidance of threat is linked with fear, the desire to atone is related to guilt, and the wish to avoid the scrutiny of others is associated with shame. Many of the functionalists focus their work on goal-related emotions (Hakim-Larson, 1995).

Relational Emotion

In our description of the functionalist view of emotion, we underscored the links between emotion, relationships, and development. Let's explore the role of emotion in parent-child and peer relationships.

Parent-Child Relationships   Expressions of emotion are the first language with which parents and infants communicate before the infant acquires speech (Maccoby, 1992). Infants react to their parents' facial expressions and tone of voice. In return, parents "read" what the infant is trying to communicate, responding appropriately when their infants are either distressed or happy.

The initial aspects of infant attachment to parents are based on affectively toned interchanges, as when an infant cries and the caregiver sensitively responds. By the end of the first year, a mother's facial expression—either smiling or fearful—

The experiences of the first three years of life are almost entirely lost to us, and when we attempt to enter into a small child's world, we come as foreigners who have forgotten the landscape and no longer speak the native tongue.

Selma Fraiberg
American Child Psychiatrist, 20th Century

influences whether an infant will explore an unfamiliar environment. And, when children hear their parents quarreling, they often react with distressed facial expressions and inhibited play (Cummings, 1987). Exceptionally well-functioning families often include humor in their interactions, sometimes making each other laugh and developing light, pleasant mood states to defuse conflicts. When a positive mood has been induced in the child, the child is more likely to comply with a parent's directions.

Infant and adult affective communicative capacities make possible coordinated infant-adult interactions. The face-to-face interactions of even 3-month-old infants and their adults are bidirectional (mutually regulated). That is, infants modify their affective displays and behaviors on the basis of their appreciation of their parents' affective displays and behaviors. This coordination has led to characterizations of the mother-infant interaction as "reciprocal" or "synchronous." These terms are attempts to capture the quality of interaction when all is going well.

Parents differ in how they talk with their children about emotion. In this regard, parents can be described as having an *emotion-coaching* or an *emotion-dismissing* philosophy (Katz, 1999). Emotion-coaching parents monitor their children's emotions, view their children's negative emotions as opportunities for teaching, assist them in verbally labeling emotions, and coach them in how to effectively deal with emotions. In contrast, emotion-dismissing parents view their role as needing to deny, ignore, or change negative emotions. Researchers have found that emotion-coaching parents showed less hostility in their marital relationship, and their marriage was less likely to end in a divorce (Gottman, Katz, & Hooven, 1997). When interacting with their children, they were less rejecting, used more scaffolding and praise, and were more nurturant than were emotion-dismissing parents. The children of emotion-coaching parents were better at physiologically soothing themselves when they got upset, were better at regulating their negative affect, could focus their attention better, and had fewer behavior problems than the children of emotion-dismissing parents.

Peer Relationships

Emotions play an important role in whether a child's peer relationships are successful or not. Emotional regulation is an important aspect of getting along with peers (Cummings & Cummings, 1988; Workman & others, 2000). Moody and emotionally negative children experience greater rejection by peers, whereas emotionally positive peers are more popular (Sroufe & others, 1983; Stocker & Dunn, 1990). Children who have effective self-regulatory skills can modulate their emotional expressiveness in contexts that evoke intense emotions, as when a peer says something negative to a child or takes something away from the child. Popular children can regulate their excitability and make the transition to less active and arousing play, thus continuing the play activities.

In one recent study conducted in the natural context of young children's everyday peer interactions, Richard Fabes and his colleagues (1999) revealed that self-regulatory skills enhance children's social competence. Children who made an effort to control their emotional responses were more likely to respond in socially competent ways when an intense peer situation arose. In sum, the ability to modulate and control one's emotions is an important self-regulatory skill that benefits children in their relationships with peers.

Regulation of Emotion

The ability to control one's emotions is increasingly recognized as a key dimension of development. Among the developmental trends in regulating emotion are these (Eisenberg, 1998):

- With increasing age in infancy and early childhood, regulation of emotion shifts gradually from external sources in the world (for example, parents) to self-initiated, internal resources. Caregivers soothe young children, manage young

Healthy Emotional Development in Children

SUMMARY TABLE 11.1
Exploring Emotion

Concept	Processes/ Related Ideas	Characteristics/Description
Defining Emotion	Its Nature	• Emotion is feeling, or affect, that involves a mixture of physiological arousal and overt behavior. • Emotions can be classified in terms of positive affectivity and negative affectivity.
Functionalism in Emotion	Its Nature	• The three main functions of emotion are (1) adaptation and survival, (2) regulation, and (3) communication.
Relational Emotion	Parent-Child Relationships	• Emotions are the first information that parents and infants communicate before the infant acquires speech. • Infant and adult communicative capacities make possible coordinated infant-adult interaction. • Children benefit from having emotion-coaching rather than emotion-dismissing parents.
	Peer Relationships	• Emotions play an important role in whether a child's peer relations are successful or unsuccessful. • Children who show effortful control of their emotions when intense situations arise get along better with their peers and are more socially competent than children who are low in emotional self-regulation.
Regulation of Emotion	Its Nature	• The ability to regulate emotions is increasingly recognized as a key aspect of development. • With increasing age, children gradually shift from external sources for controlling their emotion to self-initiated sources. • Also with increasing age, children are more likely to increase their use of cognitive strategies for regulating emotion, modulate their emotional arousal, become more adept at managing situations to minimize negative emotion, and choose effective ways to cope with stress.

children's emotion by choosing the contexts in which they behave, and provide children with information (facial cues, narratives, and so on) to help them interpret events. With age and advances in cognitive development, children are better equipped to manage emotion themselves.

• Cognitive strategies for regulating emotions, such as thinking about situations in a positive light, cognitive avoidance, and the ability to shift the focus of one's attention, increase with age.

• With greater maturity, children develop greater capacity to modulate their emotional arousal (such as controlling angry outbursts).

• With age, individuals become more adept at selecting and managing situations and relationships in ways that minimize negative emotion.

• With age, children become more capable of selecting effective ways to cope with stress.

In thinking about these developmental trends in emotional regulation, keep in mind that there are wide individual variations in children's ability to modulate their emotions and that older children and adolescents with problems often have difficulty controlling their emotions.

At this point we have explored many ideas about emotion. To review these ideas, see summary table 11.1. Next, we will further examine a number of developmental changes in emotion.

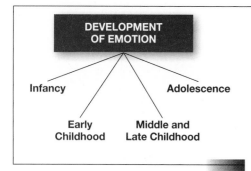

Development of Emotion

What is the course of development for children's emotion? Let's explore some of the key developmental changes in emotion in infancy, early childhood, middle/late childhood, and adolescence.

Infancy

What are infants' first emotional experiences? When is the first smile? the first expression of anger?

Maximally Discriminative Facial Movement Coding System (MAX)
Izard's system of coding infants' facial expressions related to emotion. MAX coders watch slow-motion and stop-action videotapes of infants' facial reactions to stimuli.

basic cry
A rhythmic pattern usually consisting of a cry, a briefer silence, a shorter inspiratory whistle that is higher pitched than the main cry, and then a brief rest before the next cry.

anger cry
A cry similar to the basic cry but with more air forced through the vocal cords (associated with exasperation or rage).

pain cry
A sudden appearance of loud crying without preliminary moaning and a long initial cry followed by an extended period of breath holding.

Developmental Timetable of Emotions   To determine whether infants are actually expressing a particular emotion, we need a system for measuring emotions. Carroll Izard (1982) developed such a system. The **Maximally Discriminative Facial Movement Coding System (MAX)** *is Izard's system of coding infants' facial expressions related to emotion. Using MAX, coders watch slow-motion and stop-action videotapes of infants' facial reactions to stimuli.* Among the stimulus conditions are giving an infant an ice cube, putting tape on the backs of the infant's hands, handing the infant a favorite toy and then taking it away, separating the infant from the mother and then reuniting them, having a stranger approach the infant, restraining the infant's head, placing a ticking clock next to the infant's ear, popping a balloon in front of the infant's face, and giving the infant camphor to sniff and lemon rind and orange juice to taste. To give just one example of how an emotion is coded, anger is indicated when the infant's brows are sharply lowered and drawn together, eyes are narrowed or squinted, and mouth is open in an angular, square shape. Based on Izard's classification system, interest, distress, and disgust are present at birth; a social smile appears at about 4 to 6 weeks; anger, surprise, and sadness emerge at about 3 to 4 months; fear is displayed at about 5 to 7 months; shame and shyness are displayed at about 6 to 8 months; and contempt and guilt don't appear until 2 years of age. An approximate timetable for the emergence of the facial expression of emotions is shown in figure 11.2.

Emotional expression	Approximate time of emergence
Interest, neonatal smile (a sort of half smile that appears spontaneously for no apparent reason),* startled response,* distress,* disgust	Present at birth
Social smile	4 to 6 weeks
Anger, surprise, sadness	3 to 4 months
Fear	5 to 7 months
Shame/shyness	6 to 8 months
Contempt, guilt	2 years

* These expressions are precursors of the social smile and the emotions of surprise and sadness, which appear later. No evidence exists to suggest that they are related to inner feelings when they are observed in the first few weeks of life.

Figure **11.2**

The Developmental Course of the Facial Expressions of Emotions

Crying   Crying is the most important mechanism newborns have for communicating with their world (Gustafson, Green, & Kalinowski, 1993). This is true for the first cry, which tells the mother and doctor the baby's lungs have filled with air. Cries also may tell physicians and researchers something about the central nervous system.

Babies don't have just one type of cry. They have at least three (Wolff, 1969). The **basic cry** *is a rhythmic pattern that usually consists of a cry, followed by a briefer silence, then a shorter inspiratory whistle that is somewhat higher in pitch than the main cry, then another brief rest before the next cry.* Some infancy experts believe that hunger is one of the conditions that incite the basic cry. The **anger cry** *is a variation of the basic cry. However, in the anger cry, more excess air is forced through the vocal cords.* The **pain cry,** *which is stimulated by high-intensity stimuli, differs from other types of cries. It is characterized by the sudden appearance of loud crying without preliminary moaning and a long initial cry followed by an extended holding of breath.*

Most parents, and adults in general, can determine whether an infant's cries signify anger or pain (Zeskind, Klein, & Marshall, 1992). Parents also can distinguish the cries of their own baby better than those of a strange baby. There is little consistent evidence to support the idea that females are more innately disposed to respond nurturantly to an infant's crying.

To soothe or not to soothe—should a crying baby be given attention and soothed, or does this spoil the infant? Many years ago, famous behaviorist John Watson (1928) argued that parents spend too much time responding to infant crying. As a consequence, he said, parents are actually rewarding infant crying and increasing its incidence. More recently, by contrast, infancy experts Mary Ainsworth (1979) and John Bowlby (1989) stress that you can't respond too much to infant crying in the first year of life. They believe that the caregiver's quick, comforting response to the infant's cries is an important ingredient in the development of secure attachment. In one of Ainsworth's studies, the mothers who responded quickly to their infants when they cried at 3 months of age had infants who cried less later in the first year of life (Bell & Ainsworth, 1972). On the other hand, behaviorist Jacob Gerwirtz (1977) found that a caregiver's quick, soothing response to crying increased subsequent crying.

Controversy, then, still swirls about the issue of whether parents should respond to an infant's cries. However, developmentalists increasingly argue that an infant cannot be spoiled in the first year of life, which suggests that parents should soothe a crying infant rather than be unresponsive; in this manner, infants will likely develop a sense of trust and secure attachment to the caregiver in the first year of life.

Smiling

Smiling is another important communicative affective behavior of the infant. Two types of smiling can be distinguished in infants—reflexive and social. A **reflexive smile** *does not occur in response to external stimuli. It appears during the first month after birth, usually during irregular patterns of sleep, not when the infant is in an alert state.* By contrast, a **social smile** *occurs in response to an external stimulus, which, early in development, typically is a face.* Social smiling does not occur until 2 to 3 months of age (Emde, Gaensbauer, & Harmon, 1976), although some researchers believe that infants grin in response to voices as early as 3 weeks of age (Sroufe & Waters, 1976). The power of the infant's smiles was appropriately captured by British attachment theorist John Bowlby (1969): "Can we doubt that the more and better an infant smiles the better he is loved and cared for? It is fortunate for their survival that babies are so designed by nature that they beguile and enslave mothers."

Stranger Anxiety

The most frequent expression of an infant's fear involves **stranger anxiety,** *an infant's fear of and wariness toward strangers.* This tends to appear in the second half of the first year of life. There are individual variations in stranger anxiety, and not all infants display it. Stranger anxiety usually emerges gradually, first appearing at about 6 months of age in the form of wary reactions. By age 9 months, the fear of strangers is often more intense and continues to escalate through the infant's first birthday (Emde, Gaensbauer, & Harmon, 1976).

A number of factors can influence whether an infant shows stranger anxiety, including the social context and the characteristics of the stranger. Infants show less stranger anxiety when they are in familiar settings. For example, in one study, 10-month-olds showed little stranger anxiety when they met a stranger in their own home but much greater fear when they encountered a stranger in a research laboratory (Sroufe, Waters & Matas, 1974). Also, infants show less stranger anxiety when they are sitting on their mothers' laps than when placed in an infant seat several feet away from their mothers (Bohlin & Hagekull, 1993). Thus, it appears that, when infants have a sense of security, they are less likely to show stranger anxiety.

Who the stranger is and how the stranger behaves also influence stranger anxiety in infants. Infants are less fearful of child strangers than adult strangers. They also are less fearful of friendly, outgoing, smiling strangers than of passive, unsmiling strangers (Bretherton, Stolberg, & Kreye, 1981).

Social Referencing

Social referencing *involves "reading" emotional cues in others to help determine how to act in a particular situation.* The development of social referencing especially helps infants interpret ambiguous situations more accurately, as when they encounter a stranger and need to know whether to fear the person. In social referencing, infants often look to their mother for cues about how

Infant Crying
Learning from Infants' Cries
Exploring Infant Crying

*H*e who binds himself to joy
Does the winged life destroy;
But he who kisses the joy as it
Flies lives in eternity's sun rise.

William Blake
English Poet, 19th Century

reflexive smile
A smile that does not occur in response to external stimuli. It happens during the first month after birth, usually during irregular patterns of sleep, not when the infant is in an alert state.

social smile
A smile in response to an external stimulus, which, early in development, typically is in response to a face.

stranger anxiety
An infant's fear of and wariness toward strangers; it tends to appear in the second half of the first year of life.

social referencing
"Reading" emotional cues in others to help determine how to act in a particular situation.

Approximate age of child	Description
2–3 years	Increase emotion vocabulary most rapidly
	Correctly label simple emotions in self and others and talk about past, present, and future emotions
	Talk about the causes and consequences of some emotions and identify emotions associated with certain situations
	Use emotion language in pretend play
4–5 years	Show increased capacity to reflect verbally on emotions and to consider more complex relations between emotions and situations
	Understand that the same event may call forth different feelings in different people and that feelings sometimes persist long after the events that caused them
	Demonstrate growing awareness about controlling and managing emotions in accord with social standards

Figure 11.3

Some Characteristics of Young Children's Language for Talking About Emotion and Their Understanding of It

to react or behave (Mumme, Fernald, & Herrera, 1996). Infants especially become better at social referencing in this manner during the second year of life. In their second year, infants show an increasing tendency to "check" with their mother before they act. That is, they check to see if she is happy, angry, or fearful. For example, in one study, 14- to 22-month-old infants were more likely to look at their mother's face as a source of information about how to react in a situation than were 6- to 9-month-old infants (Walden, 1991).

Early Childhood

Young children, like adults, experience many emotions during the course of a day. At times, young children also try to make sense of other people's emotional reactions and feelings. The most important changes in emotional development in early childhood include an increased ability to talk about emotion and an increased understanding of emotion (Kuebli, 1994). Preschoolers become more adept at talking about their own and others' emotions. Between 2 and 3 years of age, children considerably increase the number of terms they use to describe emotion (Ridgeway, Waters, & Kuczaj, 1985). However, in the preschool years, children are learning more than just the "vocabulary" of emotion terms, they also are learning about the causes and consequences of feelings.

At 4 to 5 years of age, children show an increased ability to reflect on emotions. At this age, they also begin to understand that the same event can elicit different feelings in different people. Moreover, they show a growing awareness about controlling and managing emotions to meet social standards. Figure 11.3 summarizes the characteristics of young children's talk about emotion and their understanding of it.

Parents, teachers, and other adults can help children understand emotions (Saarni, 1999). They can talk with children to help them cope with their feelings of distress, sadness, anger, or guilt. By being sensitive to children's emotional feelings and needs, adults can help children control their emotions and understand them. Learning to express some feelings and mask others are common, everyday lessons in children's lives. This has been called learning how to do "emotion work" (Hochschild, 1983).

Getting along with others often means handling emotions in a socially acceptable way. Children who get angry because they have to wait their turn or who laugh at a crying child who has fallen and skinned his knee can be encouraged to consider other children's feelings. Children who boast about winning something can be reminded how sad it feels to lose.

Middle and Late Childhood

Following are some important developmental changes in emotions during the middle and late childhood years (Kuebli, 1994; Wintre & Vallance, 1994):

- An increased ability to understand such complex emotions as pride and shame (Kuebli, 1994). These emotions become more internalized and integrated with a sense of personal responsibility
- Increased understanding that more than one emotion can be experienced in a particular situation
- An increased tendency to take into fuller account the events leading to emotional reactions
- Marked improvements in the ability to suppress or conceal negative emotional reactions
- The use of self-initiated strategies for redirecting feelings

Adolescence

Adolescence has long been described as a time of emotional turmoil (Hall, 1904). In its extreme form, this view is too stereotypical because adolescents are not constantly in a state of "storm and stress." Nonetheless, early adolescence is a time when emotional highs and lows increase. Young adolescents can be on top of the world one moment and down in the dumps the next. In many instances, the intensity of their emotions seems out of proportion to the events that elicit them (Steinberg & Levine, 1997). Young adolescents might sulk a lot, not knowing how to adequately express their feelings. With little or no provocation, they might blow up at their parents or siblings, which could involve using the defense mechanism of displacing their feelings onto another person. It is important for adults to recognize that moodiness is a *normal* aspect of early adolescence and most adolescents make it through these moody times to become competent adults. Nonetheless, for some children and adolescents, such emotions can be serious problems.

At this point we have discussed a number of ideas about the development of emotion. A review of these ideas is presented in summary table 11.2. In our discussion of emotional development we indicated that when problems arise they often involve emotion. Next, we will explore emotional problems, stress, and coping.

Emotional Problems, Stress, and Coping

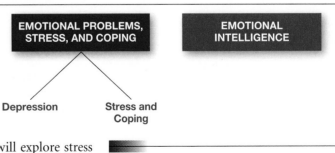

In chapter 6, "Physical Development in Childhood and Puberty," we described some problems in adolescence and some programs that have been used to effectively prevent or intervene in these problems ◀║║ P. 187. Here we focus on another problem that surfaces in childhood as well as adolescence—depression. We also will explore stress in children's lives and ways they can effectively cope with it.

Depression

Depression is a mood disorder in which the individual is unhappy, demoralized, self-derogatory, and bored. The individual does not feel well, loses stamina easily, often has a poor appetite, and is listless and unmotivated.

SUMMARY TABLE 11.2
Development of Emotion

Concept	Processes/ Related Ideas	Characteristics/Description
Infancy	Developmental Timetable of Emotions	• Izard developed the Maximally Discriminative Facial Coding System (MAX) for coding infant emotions. • Based on this system, interest, distress, and disgust are present at birth, and a number of other emotions first appear later in the first 2 years of life.
	Crying	• Crying is the most important mechanism newborns have for communicating with their world. • Babies have at least three types of cries—basic, anger, and pain cries. • Controversy swirls about whether babies should be soothed when they cry, although increasingly experts recommend immediately responding in a caring way in the first year.
	Smiling	• Two types of smiling are: reflexive and communicative.
	Stranger Anxiety	• Appears in the second half of the first year of life, intensifying toward the end of the first year. • The social context and characteristics of the stranger influence stranger anxiety.
	Social Referencing	• Increases considerably in the second year of life.
Early Childhood	Nature of Changes	• Preschoolers become more adept at talking about their own and others' emotions. • Two- and 3-year-olds substantially increase the number of terms they use to describe emotion and learn more about the causes and consequences of feelings. • At 4 to 5 years of age, children increasingly reflect on emotions and understand that a single event can elicit different emotions in different people. • Children show a growing awareness about controlling and managing emotions to meet social standards.
Middle and Late Childhood	Nature of Changes	• Children increasingly understand that complex emotions such as pride and shame and that more than one emotion can be expressed in a particular situation. • They also increasingly take into account the events that led up to an emotional reaction, suppress and conceal their emotions, and initiate strategies to redirect their emotions.
Adolescence	Nature of Change	• Early adolescence is a time when emotional highs and lows increase. • It is important for adults to recognize that moodiness is a *normal* aspect of early adolescence.

Depression in Childhood In childhood, the features of depression are often mixed with a broader array of behaviors than in adulthood. During childhood, depression is often associated with aggression, school failure, anxiety, antisocial behavior, and poor peer relations, which makes its diagnosis more difficult (Weiner, 1980). Depression is more likely to occur during adolescence than during childhood and is more pervasive among females than among males (Peterson, Leffert, & Miller, 1993).

Why does depression occur in childhood? Biogenetic, cognitive, and environmental causes have been proposed. Among the views currently being given special attention are Bowlby's developmental theory, Beck's cognitive theory, and Seligman's learned helplessness theory.

John Bowlby (1969, 1989) believes that insecure attachment, a lack of love and affection in child rearing, or the actual loss of a parent in childhood leads to a negative cognitive schema. The schema that is built up during early experiences causes children to interpret later losses as yet other failures in producing enduring and close positive relationships. In Bowlby's view, early experiences, especially those involving loss, create cognitive schemas that are carried forward to influence the way later experiences are interpreted. When the later experiences involve further loss, the loss precipitates depression.

In Aaron Beck's (1973) cognitive view, individuals become depressed because early in their development they acquire cognitive schemas that are characterized by self-devaluation and lack of confidence about the future. These habitual negative thoughts magnify and expand a depressed person's negative experiences. Depressed children blame themselves far more than is warranted, in Beck's view. In one expansion of Beck's view, depression in children is viewed as an outgrowth of attending to negative cues in the environment and identifying the source of negative outcomes as being within one's self (Quiggle & others, 1992).

Martin Seligman's theory is that depression is **learned helplessness**—*when individuals are exposed to negative experiences, such as prolonged stress or pain, over which they have no control, they are likely to become depressed* (Seligman, 1975). In a reformulation of this view, depression follows the experience of a negative event when the individual explains the event with self-blaming attributions (Abramson, Metalsky, & Alloy, 1989). This explanatory style results in the expectation that no action will control the outcome of similar events in the future, resulting in helplessness, hopelessness, passivity, and depression.

Depression in Parents

Depression has traditionally been perceived as a problem of the individual, but today we believe that this view is limited. Researchers have found an interdependence between depressed persons and their social contexts—this is especially true in the case of parents' depression and children's adjustment (Downey & Coyne, 1990; Field, 1995; Sheeber & others, 1997). Depression is a highly prevalent disorder—so prevalent it has been called the "common cold of mental disorders." It occurs often in the lives of women of childbearing age—at a rate of about 8 percent; the rate is 12 percent for women who have recently given birth. As a result, large numbers of children are exposed to depressed parents.

Research on the children of depressed parents clearly documents that depression in parents is associated with problems of adjustment and disorders, especially depression, in their children (Downey & Coyne, 1990; Radke-Yarrow & others, 1992). Depressed mothers show lower rates of behavior and show constricted affect, adopt less-effortful control strategies with their children, and sometimes act hostile and negative toward them as well. In considering the effects of parental depression on children, it is important to evaluate the social context of the family (Hammen, 1993). For example, marital discord and stress may precede, precipitate, or co-occur with maternal depression. In such instances, it may be marital turmoil that is the key factor that contributes to children's adjustment problems, not parental depression per se (Gelfand, Teti, & Fox, 1992).

Depression in Adolescence

In adolescence, pervasive symptoms of depression may lead adolescents to wear black clothes, write poetry with morbid themes, or be preoccupied with music that has depressive themes. Sleep problems may be linked with difficulty in getting up for school or sleeping during the day. Lack of motivation and energy may show up in missed classes. Boredom may be a result of feeling depressed. Adolescent depression also may occur in conjunction with conduct disorder, substance abuse, or an eating disorder, which were described in chapter 6, "Physical Development in Childhood and Puberty" ◀▥ P. 187.

How serious a problem is depression in adolescence? Surveys have found that approximately one-third of adolescents who go to a mental health clinic suffer from depression (Fleming, Boyle, & Offord, 1993). Estimates indicate that depression is twice as common in adolescence as in childhood (Compas & Grant, 1993). And

learned helplessness
Seligman's theory of depression—that it occurs when individuals are exposed to negative experiences, especially prolonged stress or pain, over which they have no control.

Depression Research

Depression Treatments

Exploring Adolescent Depression

Pathways to Depression in Adolescent Girls

adolescent girls have a much higher rate of depression than their male counterparts. Reasons proposed for this sex difference include these:

- Females tend to ruminate in their depressed mood and amplify it.
- Females' self-images, especially their body images, are more negative than males'.
- Females face more discrimination than males.

Treatment of adolescent depression has been carried out through drug therapy and psychotherapy. Antidepressant drugs, such as Elavil, reduce the symptoms of depression in about 60 to 70 percent of cases, taking about 2 to 4 weeks to improve mood. Cognitive therapy also has been effective in treating adolescent depression (Beck, 1993).

Stress and Coping

stress
The response of individuals to the circumstances and events (called stressors) that threaten them and tax their coping abilities.

Stress *is the response of individuals to the circumstances and events (called stressors) that threaten them and tax their coping abilities.* Let's explore the roles of cognitive factors, life events and daily hassles, and sociocultural factors in children's stress, as well as how children can effectively cope with stress or the death of someone close to them.

Cognitive Factors   Most of us think of stress as environmental events that place demands on an individual's life, events such as an approaching test, being in a car wreck, or losing a friend. While these are some common sources of stress, not everyone perceives the same events as stressful or experiences stress in the same way. For example, one child might perceive an approaching test as threatening, another child might perceive it as challenging. To some degree, then, what is stressful for children depends on how they cognitively appraise and interpret events. This view has been presented most clearly by stress researcher Richard Lazarus (1996). **Cognitive appraisal** *is Lazarus' term for children's interpretations of events in their lives as harmful, threatening, or challenging, and their determination of whether they have the resources to effectively cope with the event.*

cognitive appraisal
Lazarus' term for children's interpretations of events in their lives as harmful, threatening, or challenging, and their determination of whether they have the resources to effectively cope with the event.

In Lazarus' view, events are appraised in two steps: primary appraisal and secondary appraisal. In **primary appraisal,** *individuals interpret whether an event involves harm or loss that has already occurred, a threat that involves some future danger, or a challenge to be overcome.* Harm is the child's appraisal of the damage the event has already inflicted. For example, if a child failed a test in school yesterday, the harm has already been done. *Threat* is the child's appraisal of potential future damage an event may bring. For example, failing the test may lower the teacher's opinion of the child and increase the probability the child will get a low grade at the end of the year. *Challenge* is the child's appraisal of the potential to overcome the adverse circumstances of an event and ultimately profit from the event. After failing a test in school, the child may develop a commitment to never get into that situation again and become a better student.

primary appraisal
Lazarus' concept that individuals interpret whether an event involves harm or loss that already has occurred, a threat that involves some future danger, or a challenge to be overcome.

After children cognitively appraise an event for its harm, threat, or challenge, Lazarus says, they engage in secondary appraisal. In **secondary appraisal,** *individuals evaluate their resources and determine how effectively they can cope with the event.* This appraisal is called *secondary* because it comes after primary appraisal and depends on the degree to which the event has been appraised as harmful, threatening, or challenging. Coping involves a wide range of potential strategies, skills, and abilities for effectively managing stressful events. In the example of failing the exam, children who learn that their parents will get a tutor to help them likely will be more confident in coping with the stress than if their parents provide no support.

secondary appraisal
Lazarus' concept that individuals evaluate their resources and determine how effectively they can cope with an event.

Lazarus believes a child's experience of stress is a balance of primary and secondary appraisal. When harm and threat are high, and challenge and resources are low, stress is likely to be high; when harm and threat are low, and challenge and resources are high, stress is more likely to be moderate or low.

BAD EVENTS	
Pessimistic	**Optimistic**
• Teachers are unfair. • I'm a total clod at sports. • Tony hates me and will never hang out with me again. • Nobody will ever want to be friends with me here. • I got grounded because I'm a bad kid. • I got a C because I'm stupid.	• Mrs. Carmine is unfair. • I stink at kickball. • Tony is mad at me today. • It takes time to make a new best friend when you're at a new school. • I got grounded because I hit Michelle. • I got a C because I didn't study enough.

GOOD EVENTS	
Pessimistic	**Optimistic**
• I'm smart at math. • I was voted safety patrol captain because the other kids wanted to do a nice thing for me. • Dad is spending time with me because he's in a good mood. • The only reason I won the spelling bee is because I practiced hard this time.	• I'm smart. • I was voted safety patrol captain because the other kids like me. • Dad loves to spend time with me. • I won because I'm a hard worker and I study my lessons.

Figure 11.4
Optimistic and Pessimistic Children's Interpretations of Bad and Good Events

Martin Seligman (1995) also believes that cognitive factors play an important role in coping with stress. He distinguishes between optimistic and pessimistic children. Compared to optimistic children, pessimistic children are more likely to become depressed, feel hopeless, underachieve at school, and have poor health. Young pessimists believe there are permanent reasons why bad things happen to them. Young optimists perceive bad experiences as temporary. If self-blame is appropriate, the optimists blame their behavior, which is changeable; pessimists are more likely to say that their negative experiences are due to innate qualities in themselves. Figure 11.4 shows how some experiences are interpreted differently by pessimistic and optimistic children.

Seligman believes that pessimistic children can be turned into optimistic ones by adults who model optimistic ways of handling themselves. Also, when pessimistic children falter, adults should provide explanations that encourage further effort. Seligman has developed a program to correct distorted explanations of problems and teach realistic ways of interpreting setbacks. The program includes role playing and discussion. In Seligman's research, this program has been very effective in turning pessimistic thinkers into optimistic ones.

Life Events and Daily Hassles   Children can experience a spectrum of stresses, ranging from ordinary to severe (Kostelecky, 1997). At the ordinary end are experiences that occur in most children's lives and for which there are reasonably well-defined coping patterns. For example, most parents are aware that siblings are jealous of each other and that when one sibling does well at something the other sibling(s) will be jealous. They know how jealousy works and know ways to help children cope with it. More severe stress occurs when children become separated from their parents. Healthy coping patterns for this stressful experience are not as well spelled out. Some children are well cared for; others are ignored when there is a separation caused by divorce, death, illness, or foster placement. Even more severe are the experiences of children who have lived for years in situations of neglect or abuse (Pfeffer, 1996). Victims of incest also experience severe stress, with few coping guidelines.

It's not the large things that send a man to the madhouse. . . . No, it's the continuing series of small tragedies that send a man to the madhouse. . . . Not the death of his love but a shoelace that snaps with no time left.

Charles Bukowski

acculturation
Cultural change that results from continuous, firsthand contact between two distinctive cultural groups. Acculturative stress is the negative consequence of acculturation.

Recently, psychologists have emphasized that life's daily experiences as well as life's major events may be the culprits in stress (Crnic, 1996; Sorensen, 1993). Enduring a tense family life and living in poverty do not show up on scales of major life events in children's development, yet the everyday pounding children take from these living conditions can add up to a highly stressful life and, eventually, psychological disorders or physical illnesses (Folkman & Lazarus, 1991; Pillow, Zautra, & Sandler, 1996).

Sociocultural Factors   Sociocultural factors involved in stress include acculturative stress and poverty.

Acculturation *is cultural change that results from continuous, firsthand contact between two distinctive cultural groups. Acculturative stress is the negative consequence of acculturation.* Members of ethnic minority groups have historically encountered hostility, prejudice, and lack of effective support during crises, which contributes to alienation, social isolation, and heightened stress (Huang & Gibbs, 1989). As upwardly mobile ethnic minority families have attempted to penetrate all-White neighborhoods, interracial tensions often mount. Similarly, racial tensions and hostility often emerge among the various ethnic minorities as they each struggle for limited housing and employment opportunities, seeking a fair share of a limited market. Clashes become inevitable as Latino family markets spring up in African American urban neighborhoods; as Vietnamese extended families displace Puerto Rican apartment dwellers; as the increasing enrollment of Asian students on college campuses is perceived as a threat to affirmative action policies by other non-White ethnic minority students. While race relations in the United States have historically been conceptualized as Black/White, this is no longer the only combination producing ethnic animosity.

As the number of Latinos and Asians has increased dramatically, and as Native Americans have crossed the boundaries of their reservations, the visibility of these groups has brought them in contact not only with mainstream White society, but with one another as well. Depending on the circumstances, this contact has been sometimes harmonious, sometimes antagonistic.

Poverty imposes considerable stress on children and their families (Aber, 1993; McLoyd, 1993, 2000). Chronic life conditions such as inadequate housing, dangerous neighborhoods, burdensome responsibilities, and economic uncertainties are potent stressors in the lives of the poor (Brooks-Gunn, Klebanov, & McCarton, 1997; Sameroff & Bartko, 1997). The incidence of poverty is especially pronounced among ethnic minority children and their families (Braham, Rattansi, & Skellington, 1992). For example, African American women heading families face a risk of poverty that is more than 10 times that of White men heading families. Puerto Rican female family heads face a poverty rate that is almost 15 times that found among White male family heads (National Advisory Council on Economic Opportunity, 1980). Many individuals who become poor during their lives remain poor for 1 or 2 years. However, African Americans and female family heads are at risk for experiencing persistent poverty. The average poor African American child experiences poverty that will last almost 20 years (Wilson & Neckerman, 1986).

Poverty is related to threatening and uncontrollable events in children's lives (Russo, 1990). For example, poor females are more likely to experience crime and violence than middle-class females are. Poverty also undermines sources of social support that can help buffer the effects of stress.

Coping with Stress   An important aspect of children's emotional lives is learning how to cope effectively with stress. Also important is for caregivers to help children cope more effectively. Two effective strategies are to (1) remove at least one stressor from the child's life and (2) teach the child how to cope effectively.

Based on Michael Rutter's (1979) research on the multiple effects of stress, it makes sense that removing one stress or hassle can help children feel stronger and more competent. For example, consider Lisa, who had been coming to school hungry each morning. Her teacher arranged for Lisa to have hot breakfasts at school, which improved her concentration in school. This in turn helped Lisa suppress for a time her anxieties about her parents' impending divorce.

Children who have a number of coping techniques have the best chance of adapting and functioning competently in the face of stress. By learning new coping techniques, children might no longer feel as incompetent, and their self-confidence may improve. For example, Kim was relieved when a clinical psychologist helped her anticipate what it would be like to visit her seriously ill sister. She was frightened by the hospital and used withdrawal to cope. She said she did not want to see her sister, even though she missed her a great deal. Children tend to apply their coping strategies only in the situations in which stress develops. Adults can show children how to use these coping skills to their best advantage in many other situations as well. For example, Jennifer used altruism to cope when her mother was hospitalized for cancer. She coped with the separation by mothering her father, her little brother, and her classmates. Her classmates quickly became annoyed with her and began to tease her. Jennifer's teacher at school recognized the problem and helped Jennifer express her altruism by taking care of the class's pet animals and by being responsible for some daily cleanup chores. Her mothering of the children stopped, and so did the teasing.

Coping with Death   Children who have healthy and positive relationships with their parents before a parent dies cope with the death more effectively than children with unhappy prior relationships with the parent. The years of warmth and caring have probably taught the child effective ways of coping with such a traumatic event. Also, children who are given high-quality care by surviving family members during the mourning period, or who are effectively helped by caregivers in other contexts, experience less separation distress.

Sometimes the death of a sibling is even more difficult for children to understand and accept than the loss of a parent. Many children believe that only old people die, so the death of a child can stimulate children to think about their own immortality. The majority of children, though, seem to be able to cope with a sibling's death effectively if they are helped through a mourning period.

Knowing what children think about death can help adults understand their behavior in the period following the loss of a parent or sibling. When a 3-year-old boy creeps from his bed every night and runs down the street, searching for his mother who has just died, is he mourning for her? When a 6-year-old girl spends an entire afternoon drawing pictures of graveyards and coffins, is she grieving? When a 9-year-old boy can't wait to go back to school after the funeral so he can tell his classmates about how his sister died, is he denying grief? All of these are ways in which children cope with death. And all follow children's logic.

Children 3 to 5 years old think that dead people continue to live, but under changed circumstances. The missing person is simply missing, and young children expect the person to return at some point. When the person does not come back, they might feel hurt or angry at being abandoned. They might declare that they want to go to heaven to bring the dead person home. They might ask their caregivers where the dead person's house is, where the dead person eats, and why the dead person won't be cold if the person is buried without a coat and hat in winter.

Though children vary somewhat in the age at which they begin to understand death, the limitations of preoperational thought make it difficult for a child to comprehend death before the age of 7 or 8. Young children blame themselves for the death of someone they knew well, believing that the event may have happened because they disobeyed the person who died. Children under 6 rarely understand that death is universal, inevitable, and final. Instead, young children usually think that only people who want to die, or who are bad or careless, actually do die. At some point around the middle of the elementary school years, children begin to grasp the concept that death is the end of life and is not reversible. They come to realize that they, too, will die someday.

Emotional Intelligence

Exploring Emotional Intelligence in Children

emotional intelligence
A form of social intelligence that involves the ability to monitor one's own and others' feelings and emotions, to discriminate among them, and to use this information to guide one's thinking and action.

Emotional Intelligence

Both Sternberg's and Gardner's views, which we discussed in chapter 9, "Intelligence," include categories of social intelligence ◀▮▮▮ Pp. 288, 290. In Sternberg's theory the category is called "practical intelligence" and in Gardner's theory the categories are "insights about self" and "insights about others." However, the greatest interest in recent years in the social aspects of intelligence has focused on the concept of emotional intelligence. The concept of **emotional intelligence** *initially was proposed in 1990 as a form of social intelligence that involves the ability to monitor one's own and others' feelings and emotions, to discriminate among them, and to use this information to guide one's thinking and action* (Salovy & Mayer, 1990). However, the main interest in emotional intelligence was ushered in with the publication of Daniel Goleman's (1995) book *Emotional Intelligence*. Goleman believes that when it comes to predicting an individual's competence, IQ, as measured by standardized intelligence tests, matters less than emotional intelligence. In Goleman's view, emotional intelligence involves these four main areas:

- Developing emotional self-awareness (such as the ability to separate feelings from actions)
- Managing emotions (such as being able to control anger)
- Reading emotions (such as taking the perspective of others)
- Handling relationships (such as the ability to solve relationship problems)

Some schools have begun to develop programs that are designed to help children with their emotional lives. For example, one private school near San Francisco, the Nueva School, has a class in what is called "self science." The subject in self science is feelings—the child's own and those involved in relationships. Teachers speak to real issues, such as hurt over being left out, envy, and disagreements that could disrupt into a schoolyard battle. The list of the contents for self science matches up with many of Goleman's components of emotional intelligence. The topics in self science include these:

- Having self-awareness (in the sense of recognizing feelings and building a vocabulary for them); seeing the links between thoughts, feelings, and reactions
- Knowing if thoughts or feelings are ruling a decision
- Seeing the consequences of alternative choices
- Applying these insights to decisions about such issues as drugs, smoking, and sex
- Recognizing strengths and weaknesses, and seeing oneself in a positive but realistic light
- Managing emotions; realizing what is behind a feeling (such as the hurt that triggers anger); learning ways to handle anxieties, anger, and sadness
- Taking responsibility for decisions and actions, as well as following through on commitments
- Understanding that empathy, understanding others' feelings, and respecting differences in how people feel about things are key dimensions of getting along in the social world
- Recognizing the importance of relationships and learning how to be a good listener and question asker; being assertive rather than passive or aggressive; learning how to cooperate, resolve conflicts, and negotiate

Names for these classes range from "social development" to "life skills" to "social and emotional learning." Their common goal is to raise every child's emotional competence as part of regular education, rather than focus on emotional skills as something to be taught only remedially to children who are faltering and are identified as "troubled."

Measures of emotional intelligence are being developed, but as yet none has reached the point of wide acceptance (Goleman, 1995; Rockhill & Greener, 1999;

ᏚUMMARY ᎢABLE 11.3
Emotional Problems, Stress, and Coping; Emotional Intelligence

Concept	Processes/Related Ideas	Characteristics/Description
Emotional Problems, Stress, and Coping	Depression	• Depression is more likely to occur in adolescence than in childhood and in girls more than in boys. • In childhood, the features of depression often are mixed with a broader array of behaviors than in adulthood. • Bowlby's developmental view, Beck's cognitive view, and Seligman's learned helplessness view provide explanations of depression. • Depression is especially prominent in women of childbearing age. • Depression in parents is linked with children's adjustment problems. • Depression in adolescence can be manifested in boredom, sleep problems, and eating problems.
	Stress and Coping	• Lazarus believes that children's stress depends on how they cognitively appraise and interpret events. • Seligman argues that an important aspect of coping with stress is whether the child is optimistic or pessimistic. • Sociocultural influences, such as acculturative stress and poverty, can generate stress. • Two good strategies for caregivers in helping children cope with stress are to (1) remove at least one stressor from the child's life and (2) help the child learn to use effective coping strategies. • Young children do not understand the nature of death, believing it is not final. In the middle of the elementary school years, they comprehend its final, irreversible nature.
Emotional Intelligence	Its Nature	• This is a form of social intelligence that involves the ability to monitor one's own and others' feelings and emotions, to discriminate among them, and to use this information to guide one's own thinking and action.
	Goleman's View	• He believes emotional intelligence involves four main areas: emotional self-awareness, managing emotions, reading emotions, and handling relationships.

Salovy & Woolery, 2000). Especially lacking is research on the predictive validity of these measures (Mayer, Salovey, & Carsuso, 2000).

At this point we have discussed many aspects of emotional problems, stress, coping, and emotional intelligence. A review of these ideas is presented in summary table 11.3. Some children show tendencies to be very emotional, others are calmer. Next, we will explore how these aspects of emotion might be influenced by the child's temperament.

Temperament

Infants show different emotional responses. One infant may be cheerful and happy much of the time; another baby may cry a lot and more often display a negative mood. These behaviors reflect differences in their temperament. Let's explore a definition of *temperament,* the ways in which it can be classified, and the implications of temperamental variations for parenting.

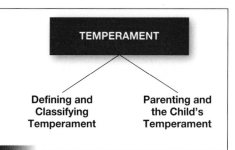

temperament
An individual's behavioral style and characteristic emotional response.

easy child
A temperament style in which the child is generally in a positive mood, quickly establishes regular routines, and adapts easily to new experiences.

difficult child
A temperament style in which the child tends to react negatively and cry frequently, engages in irregular daily routines, and is slow to accept new experiences.

slow-to-warm-up child
A temperament style in which the child has a low activity level, is somewhat negative, shows low adaptability, and displays a low intensity of mood.

Defining and Classifying Temperament

Temperament *is an individual's behavioral style and characteristic emotional response.* Developmentalists are especially interested in the temperament of infants (Bornstein, 2000).

The dimensions of temperament are widely debated. Psychiatrists Alexander Chess and Stella Thomas (Chess & Thomas, 1977; Thomas & Chess, 1991) believe there are three basic types, or clusters, of temperament—easy, difficult, and slow to warm up.

1. An **easy child** *is generally in a positive mood, quickly establishes regular routines, and adapts easily to new experiences.*
2. A **difficult child** *tends to react negatively and cry frequently, engages in irregular daily routines, and is slow to accept new experiences.*
3. A **slow-to-warm-up child** *has a low activity level, is somewhat negative, shows low adaptability, and displays a low intensity of mood.*

Various dimensions make up these three basic clusters of temperament. In their longitudinal investigation, Chess and Thomas found that 40 percent of the children they studied could be classified as easy, 10 percent as difficult, and 15 percent as slow to warm up. Researchers have found that these three basic clusters of temperament are moderately stable across the childhood years.

Children who have a difficult temperament or a temperament that reflects lack of control are at risk for problem behavior. In one study, a "difficult" temperament in adolescence was associated with higher levels of depression, drug use, and stressful life events, as well as lower levels of perceived family support (Tubman & Windle, 1995). In a longitudinal study, a temperament factor labeled "lack of control" (irritable, distractible) in early childhood (3 and 5 years of age) was related to externalized behavior problems (acting out, delinquent behavior) and less competent behavior in early adolescence (13 and 15 years of age) (Caspi & others, 1995). Across the same age span, a temperament factor labeled "approach" (friendliness, eagerness to explore new situations) was associated with fewer internalized problems (anxiety, depression) in boys. In an extension of this study, undercontrolled and inhibited 3-year-old children grew up to have more problem behaviors at 21 years of age than well-adjusted, reserved, and confident children (Newman & Caspi, 1996).

New classifications of temperament continue to be forged (Rothbart, 1999). In a recent review of temperament, Mary Rothbart and John Bates (1998) concluded that, based on current research, the best framework for classifying temperament involves a revision of Chess and Thomas' categories of easy, difficult, and slow to warm up. The general classification of temperament now focuses more on (1) positive affect and approach (much like the personality trait of extraversion/introversion), (2) negative affectivity, and (3) effortful control (self-regulation).

A number of scholars conceive of temperament as a stable characteristic of newborns, which comes to be shaped and modified by the child's later experiences. This raises the question of heredity's role in temperament (Goldsmith, 1988). Twin and adoption studies have been conducted to answer this question (Plomin & others, 1994). The researchers have found a heritability index in the range of .50 to .60, suggesting a moderate influence of heredity on temperament. However, the strength of the association usually declines as infants become older (Goldsmith & Gottesman, 1981). This finding supports the belief that temperament becomes more malleable with experience. Alternatively, it may be that, as a child becomes older, behavior indicators of temperament are more difficult to spot.

What are some ways that developmentalists have classified infants' temperaments? Which classification makes the most sense to you, based on your observations of infants?

Parenting and the Child's Temperament

Infant Temperament

Many parents don't become believers in temperament's importance until the birth of their second child. Many parents view the first child's behavior as being solely a result of how they socialized the child. However, management strategies that worked with the first child might not be as effective with the second child. Problems experienced with the first child (such as those involved in feeding, sleeping, and coping with strangers) might not exist with the second child, but new problems might arise. Such experiences strongly suggest that nature as well as nurture influence the child's development, that children differ from each other from very early in life, and that these differences have important implications for parent-child interaction (Kwak & others, 1999).

What are the implications of temperamental variations for parenting? Although answers to this question necessarily are speculative because of the incompleteness of the research literature, the following conclusions were reached by temperament experts Ann Sanson and Mary Rothbart (1995):

- *Attention to and respect for individuality.* An important implication of taking children's individuality seriously is that it becomes difficult to generate prescriptions for "good parenting," other than possibly specifying that parents need to be sensitive and flexible. Parents need to be sensitive to the infant's signals and needs. A goal of parenting might be accomplished in one way with one child and in another way with another child, depending on the child's temperament.

  Parents might react differently to a child's temperament, depending on whether the child is a girl or a boy and on the culture in which they live. For example, in one study, mothers were more responsive to the crying of irritable girls than to the crying of irritable boys (Crockenberg, 1986). Also, an active temperament might be valued in some cultures (such as the United States) but not in other cultures (such as China). Parents should respect each child's temperament, rather than try to fit all children into the same mold.

- *Structuring the child's environment.* Crowded, noisy environments can pose greater problems for some children (such as a "difficult child") than others (such as an "easygoing" child). We might also expect that a fearful, withdrawing child would benefit from slower entry into new contexts.

- *The "difficult child" and packaged parenting programs.* Some books and programs for parents focus specifically on temperament (Cameron, Hansen, & Rosen, 1989; Turecki & Tonner, 1989). These programs usually focus on children with "difficult" temperaments. Acknowledgment that some children are harder to parent is often helpful, and advice on how to handle particular difficult temperament characteristics can also be useful.

Whether a particular characteristic is difficult depends on its fit with the environment, whereas the notion of difficult temperament suggests that the problem rests solely with the child. To label a child "difficult" also has the danger of becoming a self-fulfilling prophecy. If a child is identified as "difficult," the labeling may maintain that categorization.

However, weighted against these potential advantages are several disadvantages.

Children's temperament needs to be taken into account when considering caregiving behavior. Research does not yet allow for many highly specific recommendations, but, in general, caregivers should (1) be sensitive to the individual characteristics of the child, (2) be flexible in responding to these characteristics, and (3) avoid negative labeling of the child.

At this point we have discussed a number of ideas about temperament. A review of these ideas is presented in summary

ADVENTURES FOR THE MIND

Temperament and You

CONSIDER YOUR OWN temperament. Does it fit one of Chess and Thomas' three styles—difficult, easy, or slow to warm up? Or do you have difficulty placing yourself in one of those three categories? Has your temperament changed as you have gotten older, or is it about the same as when you were a child and an adolescent? If your temperament has changed, what factors contributed to the changes? If you have siblings, is your temperament similar to or different from theirs? If your temperament is different from theirs, do you believe the difference is due more to nature and biology or to nurture and the way you were brought up by your parents?

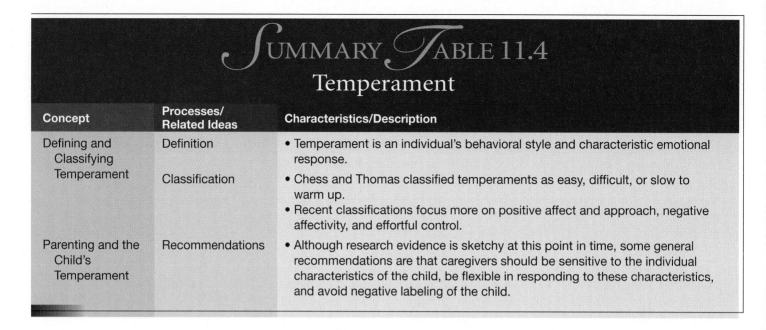

SUMMARY TABLE 11.4
Temperament

Concept	Processes/ Related Ideas	Characteristics/Description
Defining and Classifying Temperament	Definition	• Temperament is an individual's behavioral style and characteristic emotional response.
	Classification	• Chess and Thomas classified temperaments as easy, difficult, or slow to warm up.
		• Recent classifications focus more on positive affect and approach, negative affectivity, and effortful control.
Parenting and the Child's Temperament	Recommendations	• Although research evidence is sketchy at this point in time, some general recommendations are that caregivers should be sensitive to the individual characteristics of the child, be flexible in responding to these characteristics, and avoid negative labeling of the child.

table 11.4. In our discussion of functionalism in emotion earlier in the chapter, we indicated that emotion is relational. Next, we will explore an important aspect of the relational dimension of emotion: attachment.

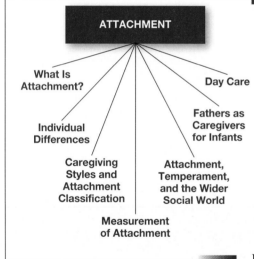

Attachment

A small curly-haired girl named Danielle, age 11 months, begins to whimper. After a few seconds, she begins to wail. The psychologist observing Danielle is conducting a research study on the nature of attachment between infants and their mothers. Subsequently, the mother reenters the room, and Danielle's crying ceases. Quickly, Danielle crawls over to where her mother is seated and reaches out to be held. The situation is one of the main ways that psychologists study the nature of attachment during infancy.

What Is Attachment?

In everyday language, attachment is a relationship between two individuals who feel strongly about each other and do a number of things to continue the relationship. Many pairs of people are attached: relatives, lovers, a teacher and student. In the language of developmental psychology, though, attachment is often restricted to a relationship between particular social figures and a particular phenomenon that is thought to reflect unique characteristics of the relationship. In this case, the developmental period is infancy, the social figures are the infant and one or more adult caregivers, and the phenomenon is a bond (Bowlby, 1969, 1989). To summarize, **attachment** *is a close emotional bond between the infant and the caregiver.*

There is no shortage of theories about infant attachment. Freud believed that infants become attached to the person or object that provides oral satisfaction. For most infants, this is the mother, since she is most likely to feed the infant.

Is feeding as important as Freud thought? A classic study by Harry Harlow and Robert Zimmerman (1959) reveals that the answer is no. These researchers evaluated whether feeding or contact comfort was more important to infant attachment. Infant monkeys were removed from their mothers at birth and reared for six months by surrogate (substitute) "mothers." One of the mothers was made of wire, the other of cloth (see figure 11.5). Half of the infant monkeys were fed by the wire mother, half by the cloth mother. Periodically, the amount of time the infant monkeys spent with

attachment
A close emotional bond between the infant and the caregiver.

either the wire or the cloth monkey was computed. Regardless of whether they were fed by the wire or the cloth mother, the infant monkeys spent far more time with the cloth mother. This study clearly demonstrated that feeding is not the crucial element in the attachment process and that contact comfort is important.

Most toddlers develop a strong attachment to a favorite soft toy or blanket. Toddlers may carry the toy or blanket with them everywhere they go, just as Linus does in the "Peanuts" cartoon strip. Or they may run for the toy or blanket only in moments of crisis, such as after an argument or a fall. By the time they have outgrown the security object, all that may be left is a small fragment of the blanket, or a stuffed animal that is hardly recognizable, having had a couple of new faces and all its seams resewn half a dozen times. If parents try to replace the security object with something newer, the toddler will resist. There is nothing abnormal about a toddler carrying around a security blanket. Children know that the blanket or teddy bear is not their mother, yet they react affectively to these objects and derive comfort from them as if they were their mother. Eventually, they abandon the security object as they grow up and become more sure of themselves.

Might familiarity breed attachment? A famous study by ethologist Konrad Lorenz (1965) revealed that the answer is yes. Remember from our description of this study in chapter 2 that newborn goslings became attached to "father" Lorenz rather than to their mother because he was the first moving object they saw ◀IIII P. 44. The time period during which familiarity is important for goslings is the first 36 hours after birth; for human beings, it is more on the order of the first year of life.

Erik Erikson (1968) believed that the first year of life is the key time frame for the development of attachment. Recall his proposal—also discussed in chapter 2—that the first year of life represents the stage of trust versus mistrust ◀IIII P. 33. A sense of trust requires a feeling of physical comfort and a minimal amount of fear and apprehension about the future. Trust in infancy sets the stage for a lifelong expectation that the world will be a good and pleasant place to be. Erikson also believed that responsive, sensitive parenting contributes to an infant's sense of trust.

The ethological perspective of British psychiatrist John Bowlby (1969, 1989) also stresses the importance of attachment in the first year of life and the responsiveness of the caregiver. Bowlby believes that an infant and its mother instinctively form an attachment (Weizmann, 2000). He argues that the newborn is biologically equipped to elicit the mother's attachment behavior. The baby cries, clings, coos, and smiles. Later, the infant crawls, walks, and follows the mother. The infant's goal is to keep the mother nearby. Research on attachment supports Bowlby's view that, at about 6 to 7 months of age, the infant's attachment to the caregiver intensifies (Sroufe, 1985).

Individual Differences

Isn't it likely that some babies have a more positive attachment experience than others? Mary Ainsworth (1979) thinks so. She says that, in **secure attachment,** *infants use the caregiver, usually the mother, as a secure base from which to explore the environment. Ainsworth believes that secure attachment in the first year of life provides an important foundation for psychological development later in life.* The caregiver's sensitivity to the infant's signals increases secure attachment (De Wolff & van Ijzendoorn, 1997). The securely attached infant moves

Figure **11.5**
Harlow's Classic "Contact Comfort" Study
Regardless of whether they were fed by a wire mother or by a cloth mother, the infant monkeys overwhelmingly preferred to be in contact with the cloth mother, demonstrating the importance of contact comfort in attachment.

Attachment theorists argue that early experiences play an important role in a child's later social development. For example, Bowlby and Ainsworth argue that secure attachment to the caregiver in infancy is related to the development of social competence during the childhood years.

secure attachment
The infant uses the caregiver as a secure base from which to explore the environment. Ainsworth believes that secure attachment in the first year of life provides an important foundation for psychological development later in life.

type B babies
Infants who use the caregiver as a secure base from which to explore the environment.

type A babies
Infants who show insecurity by avoiding their caregiver (for example, by ignoring the caregiver, averting their gaze, or failing to seek proximity).

type C babies
Infants who show insecurity by resisting the caregiver (for example, by clinging to the caregiver but at the same time kicking and pushing away).

type D babies
Infants who show insecurity by being disoriented or afraid. This type of behavior is described as disorganized.

Attachment Theory and Research
Mary Ainsworth
Recent Attachment Research
Responsive Care and Attachment

*T*hrough the Eyes of Psychologists

L. Alan Sroufe,
University of Minnesota

"Early attachment experiences do not directly or solely cause later problems but yet have special roles in framing subsequent experiences."

freely away from the mother but processes her location through periodic glances. The securely attached infant responds positively to being picked up by others and, when put back down, freely moves away to play. An insecurely attached infant, by contrast, avoids the mother or is ambivalent toward her, fears strangers, and is upset by minor, everyday separations (Main, 2000).

Ainsworth believes that insecurely attached infants can be classified as either anxious-avoidant or anxious-resistant, making four main attachment categories: secure (type B), avoidant (type A), ambivalent-resistant (type C), and disorganized (type D). **Type B babies** *use the caregiver as a secure base from which to explore the environment.* **Type A babies** *exhibit insecurity by avoiding the mother (for example, ignoring her, averting their gaze, and failing to seek proximity).* **Type C babies** *exhibit insecurity by resisting the mother (for example, by clinging to her but at the same time fighting against the closeness, perhaps by kicking and pushing away).* **Type D babies** *are disorganized and disoriented. They may look dazed, show confusion, and be afraid.*

If early attachment to a caregiver is important, it should relate to a child's social behavior later in development. Research by Alan Sroufe (1985, 1996) documents this connection. In one study, infants who were securely attached to their mothers early in infancy were less frustrated and happier at 2 years of age than were insecurely attached counterparts (Matas, Arend, & Sroufe, 1978). In other research, anxiety problems in adolescence were linked to ambivalent/resistant attachment in infancy, while conduct disorder (aggression problems) was related to avoidant attachment in infancy (Sroufe & Warren, 1999).

In recent research by Alan Sroufe and his colleagues (Sroufe, Egeland, & Carlson, 1999), attachment history and early care were related to peer competence in adolescence, up to 15 years after the infant assessments. In interviews with adolescents, those who formed couple relationships during camp retreats had been securely attached in infancy. Also, ratings of videotaped behavior revealed that adolescents with secure attachment histories were more socially competent, which included having confidence in social situations and showing leadership skills. For most children, there was a cascading effect in which early family relationships provided the necessary support for effectively engaging in the peer world, which in turn provided the foundation for more extensive, complex peer relationships.

Caregiving Styles and Attachment Classification

Attachment is defined as a close emotional bond between the infant and caregiver. Is the parent's caregiving style linked with this close emotional bond called attachment? Securely attached babies have caregivers who are sensitive to their signals and are consistently available to respond to their infants' needs. These caregivers often let their babies have an active part in determining the onset and pacing of interaction in the first year of life (Cassidy & Shaver, 1999).

How do the caregivers of insecurely attached babies interact with them? Caregivers of avoidant babies tend to be unavailable or rejecting (Cassidy & Berlin, 1994). They often don't respond to their babies' signals and have little physical contact with them. When they do interact with their babies, they may behave in an angry and irritable way toward them. Caregivers of ambivalent-resistant babies tend to be inconsistently available to their babies (Berlin & Cassidy, 2000). That is, sometimes they respond to their babies' needs, and sometimes they don't. In general, they tend not to be very affectionate with their babies and show little synchrony when interacting with them. Caregivers of disorganized babies often neglect or physically abuse their babies (Main & Solomon, 1990). In some cases, these caregivers also have depression (Barnett, Ganiban, & Cicchetti, 1999; Field, 1995). We will have more to say about child abuse in chapter 15, "Families."

Measurement of Attachment

Much of the early research on attachment relied on caregivers' impressions rather than on direct observation of caregivers interacting with their infants. However, interview data might be flawed and unreliably related to what actually takes place when parents interact with their infant. In the past several decades, researchers have increasingly observed infants with their caregivers. The main setting that has been used to observe attachment in infancy is the Strange Situation developed by attachment researcher Mary Ainsworth (1967). The **Strange Situation** *is an observational measure of infant attachment that requires the infant to move through a series of introductions, separations, and reunions with the caregiver and an adult stranger in a prescribed order* (see figure 11.6).

Although the Strange Situation has been used in a large number of studies of infant attachment, some critics believe that the isolated, controlled events of the setting might not necessarily reflect what would happen if infants were observed with their caregiver in a natural environment. The issue of using controlled, laboratory assessments versus naturalistic observations is widely debated in child development circles.

A child forsaken, waking suddenly,
Whose gaze affeared on all things round
doth rove,
And seeth only that it cannot see
The meeting eyes of love.

George Eliot
English Novelist, 19th Century

Strange Situation
Ainsworth's observational measure of infant attachment to a caregiver that requires the infant to move through a series of introductions, separations, and reunions with the caregiver and an adult stranger in a prescribed order.

Episode	Persons present	Duration of episode	Description of setting
1	Caregiver, baby, and observer	30 seconds	Observer introduces caregiver and baby to experimental room, then leaves. (Room contains many appealing toys scattered about.)
2	Caregiver and baby	3 minutes	Caregiver is nonparticipant while baby explores; if necessary, play is stimulated after 2 minutes.
3	Stranger, caregiver, and baby	3 minutes	Stranger enters. First minute: stranger is silent. Second minute: stranger converses with caregiver. Third minute: stranger approaches baby. After 3 minutes caregiver leaves unobtrusively.
4	Stranger and baby	3 minutes or less	First separation episode. Stranger's behavior is geared to that of baby.
5	Caregiver and baby	3 minutes or more	First reunion episode. Caregiver greets and/or comforts baby, then tries to settle the baby again in play. Caregiver then leaves, saying "bye-bye."
6	Baby alone	3 minutes or less	Second separation episode.
7	Stranger and baby	3 minutes or less	Continuation of second separation. Stranger enters and gears behavior to that of baby.
8	Caregiver and baby	3 minutes	Second reunion episode. Caregiver enters, greets baby, then picks baby up. Meanwhile, stranger leaves unobtrusively.

Figure 11.6
The Ainsworth Strange Situation
Mary Ainsworth developed the Strange Situation to assess whether infants are securely or insecurely attached to their caregiver.

In the Hausa culture, siblings and grandmothers provide a significant amount of care for infants.

Attachment, Temperament, and the Wider Social World

Not all research reveals the power of infant attachment to predict subsequent development (Fox, 1997). In one longitudinal study, attachment classification in infancy did not predict attachment classification at 18 years of age (Lewis, 1997). In this study, the best predictor of attachment classification at 18 was the occurrence of parent divorce in intervening years.

Thus, not all developmentalists believe that attachment in infancy is the only path to competence in life (Thompson & Colman, 2000). Indeed, some developmentalists believe that too much emphasis is placed on the importance of the attachment bond in infancy. Jerome Kagan (1987), for example, believes that infants are highly resilient and adaptive; he argues that they are evolutionarily equipped to stay on a positive developmental course, even in the face of wide variations in parenting. Kagan and others stress that genetic and temperament characteristics play more important roles in a child's social competence than the attachment theorists, such as Bowlby, Ainsworth, and Sroufe, are willing to acknowledge (Chauhuri & Williams, 1999; Young & Shahinfar, 1995). For example, infants may have inherited a low tolerance for stress. This, rather than an insecure attachment bond, may be responsible for their inability to get along with peers.

Also, researchers have found cultural variations in attachment. German and Japanese babies often show different patterns of attachment than American babies. German babies are more likely than American babies to be categorized as avoidant, possibly because caregivers encourage them to be more independent (Grossman & others, 1995). Japanese babies are more likely than American babies to be categorized as resistant-ambivalent. This may have more to do with the Ainsworth Strange Situation as a measure of attachment than with attachment insecurity itself. Japanese mothers rarely let anyone unfamiliar with their babies care for them. Thus, the Ainsworth Strange Situation may create considerably more stress for Japanese infants than for American infants, who are more accustomed to separation from their mothers (Takahashi, 1990). Even though there are cultural variations in attachment classification, the most frequent classification in every culture studied so far is secure attachment (van Ijzendoorn & Kroonenberg, 1988).

Another criticism of attachment theory is that it ignores the diversity of socializing agents and contexts that exists in an infant's world (Lamb, 2000). In some cultures, infants show attachments to many people. Among the Hausa (who live in Nigeria), both grandmothers and siblings provide a significant amount of care for infants (Harkness & Super, 1995). Infants in agricultural societies tend to form attachments to older siblings, who are assigned a major responsibility for younger siblings' care. The attachments formed by infants in group care in Israeli kibbutzim provide another challenge to the singular attachment thesis.

Researchers recognize the importance of competent, nurturant caregivers in an infant's development. At issue, though, is whether or not secure attachment, especially to a single caregiver, is critical (Lamb, 2000).

Fathers as Caregivers for Infants

Can fathers take care of infants as competently as mothers can? Observations of fathers and their infants suggest that fathers have the ability to act sensitively and responsively with their infants (McHale & others, 1995; Parke & Buriel, 1998). The strongest evidence of the plasticity of male caregiving abilities is based on male primates, that are notoriously low in their interest in offspring. When forced to live with infants whose female caregivers are absent, the adult male competently rears the infants. Remember, however, that, although fathers can be active, nurturant, involved caregivers with their infants, many do not choose to follow this pattern.

The Fatherhood Project
Online Resources for Fathers

Do fathers behave differently toward infants than mothers do? Maternal interactions usually center around child-care activities—feeding, changing diapers, bathing. Paternal interactions are more likely to include play. Fathers engage in more rough-and-tumble play. They bounce infants, throw them up in the air, tickle them, and so on (Lamb, 1986). Mothers do play with infants, but their play is less physical and arousing than that of fathers.

In stressful circumstances, do infants prefer their mother or father? In one study, 20 12-month-olds were observed interacting with their parents (Lamb, 1977). With both parents present, the infants preferred neither their mother nor their father. The same was true when the infants were alone with the mother or the father. However, the entrance of a stranger, combined with boredom and fatigue, produced a shift in the infants' social behavior toward the mother. In stressful circumstances, then, infants show a stronger attachment to the mother.

Might the nature of parent-infant interaction be different in families that adopt nontraditional gender roles? This question was investigated by Michael Lamb and his colleagues (1982). They studied Swedish families in which the fathers were the primary caregivers of their firstborn, 8-month-old infants. The mothers were working full-time. In all observations, the mothers were more likely to discipline, hold, soothe, kiss, and talk to the infants than were the fathers. These mothers and fathers dealt with their infants differently, along the lines of American fathers and mothers following traditional gender roles. Having fathers assume the primary caregiving role did not substantially alter the way they interacted with their infants. This may be for biological reasons or because of deeply ingrained socialization patterns in cultures.

In Sweden, mothers or fathers are given paid maternity or paternity leave for up to 18 months. In Sweden, fathers are required to take at least 1 month off from work to be involved in infant care. Sweden and many other European countries have well-developed child-care policies. To learn about these policies, turn to the Explorations in Child Development box. In Sweden, day care for infants under 1 year of age is usually not a major concern because one parent is on paid leave for child care. As we will see, since the United States does not have a policy of paid leave for child care, day care in the United States has become a major national concern.

Day Care

Each weekday at 8 A.M., Ellen Smith takes her 1-year-old daughter, Tanya, to the day-care center at Brookhaven College in Dallas. Then Mrs. Smith goes to work and returns in the afternoon to take Tanya home. After 3 years, Mrs. Smith reports that her daughter is adventuresome and interacts confidently with peers and adults. Mrs. Smith believes that day care has been a wonderful way to raise Tanya.

In Los Angeles, however, day care has been a series of horror stories for Barbara Jones. After 2 years of unpleasant experiences with sitters, day-care centers, and day-care homes, Mrs. Jones has quit her job as a successful real estate agent to stay home and take care of her 2½-year-old daughter, Gretchen. "I didn't want to sacrifice my baby for my job," said Mrs. Jones, who was unable to find good substitute day-care homes. When she put Gretchen into a day-care center, she said that she felt her daughter was being treated like a piece of merchandise—dropped off and picked up.

Many parents worry whether day care will adversely affect their children. They fear that day care will reduce their infants' emotional attachment to them, retard the infants' cognitive development, fail to teach them how to control anger, and allow them to be unduly influenced by their peers. How extensive is day care? Are the worries of these parents justified?

Today, far more young children are in day care than at any other time in history; about 2 million children currently receive formal, licensed day care, and more than 5 million children attend kindergarten. Also, uncounted millions of children are cared for by unlicensed baby-sitters.

The type of day care that young children receive varies extensively (Burchinal & others, 1996; Dewey, 1999). Many day-care centers house large groups of children and have elaborate facilities. Some are commercial operations; others are nonprofit

EXPLORATIONS IN CHILD DEVELOPMENT
Child-Care Policy Around the World

SHEILA KAMERMAN (1989) surveyed the nature of child-care policies around the world with special attention given to European countries. Maternity and paternity policies for working parents include paid, job-protected leaves, which are sometimes supplemented by unpaid, job-protected leaves. Child-care policy packages also often include full health insurance. An effective child-care policy is designed to get an infant off to a competent start in life and to protect maternal health while maintaining income. More than a hundred countries around the world have such child-care policies, including all of Europe, Canada, Israel, and many developing countries. Infants are assured of at least two to three months of maternal/paternal care and in most European countries five to six months.

The maternity policy as now implemented in several countries involves a paid maternity leave that begins 2 to 6 weeks prior to expected childbirth and lasts from 8 weeks to as long as 18 months after birth. This traditional maternal policy stems from an effort to protect the health of pregnant working women, new mothers, and their infants. Only since the 1960s has the maternity policy's link with employment become strong. A second child-care policy emphasizes the importance of parenting and rec-

ognizes the potential of fathers as well as mothers to care for their infants. In Sweden, a parent insurance benefit provides protection to the new mother before birth and for 6 to 12 weeks after birth but then allows the father to participate in the postchildbirth leave. Approximately one-fourth of Swedish fathers take further postchildbirth leave, in addition to the 4 weeks of paid leave all fathers are currently required to take. In a typical pattern in Sweden, the working mother might take off 3 months, after which she and her husband might share child-care between them, each working half-time for 6 months. In addition, Swedish parents have the option of taking an unpaid but fully protected job leave until their child is 18 months old and working a 6-hour day (without a reduction in pay) from the end of the parental leave until their child is 8 years old.

These policies are designed to let parents take maternity/paternity leave without losing employment or income. In sum, almost all the industrialized countries other than the United States have recognized the importance of developing maternity/paternity policies that allow working parents some time off after childbirth to recover physically, to adapt to parenting, and to improve the well-being of the infant.

National Child-Care Information Center
NICHD Study of Early Child Care

centers run by churches, civic groups, and employers. Child care is frequently provided in private homes, at times by child-care professionals, at others by mothers who want to earn extra money.

What constitutes high-quality day care? To read about the recommendations for high-quality care from the National Association for the Education of Young Children, see figure 11.7.

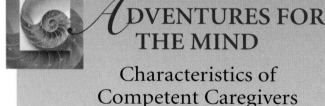

ADVENTURES FOR THE MIND
Characteristics of Competent Caregivers

MUCH OF THE health and well-being of infants is in the hands of caregivers. Whether the caregivers are parents or day-care personnel, these adults play significant roles in children's lives. What are the characteristics of competent caregivers? For one thing, competent caregivers enjoy caregiving. They reflect these positive feelings as they interact with infants and children. Try to come up with a list of five other characteristics of competent caregivers.

Aware of the growing use of child-care, the National Institute of Child Health and Human Development (NICHD) set out to develop a comprehensive, longitudinal study (a study that follows the same individuals over time, usually several years or more) that focuses on the child-care experiences of children and their development. (NICHD Early Child Care Research Network, 1997; Peth-Pierce, 1998). The study began in 1991, and data were collected on a diverse sample of almost 1,400 children and their families at 10 locations across the United States. Researchers are assessing children over seven years of their lives using multiple methods (trained observers, interviews, questionnaires, and testing) and measuring many facets of children's development, including physical health, cognitive development, and socioemotional development. Following are some of the results of this extensive study to date:

• The infants from low-income families were more likely

What constitutes quality child care? The following recommendations were made by the National Association for the Education of Young Children (1986). They are based on a consensus arrived at by experts in early childhood education and child development. It is especially important for parents to meet the adults who will care for their child. They are responsible for every aspect of the program's operation.

1. The adult caregivers

   - The adults should enjoy and understand how infants and young children grow.

   - There should be enough adults to work with a group and to care for the individual needs of children. The recommended ratios of adult caregivers for children of different ages are as follows (Kontos & Wilcox-Herzog, 1997):

Age of children	Adult:children ratio
0–1 Year	1:3
1–2 Years	1:5
2–3 Years	1:6
3–4 Years	1:8
4–5 Years	1:10

   - Caregivers should observe and record each child's progress and development.

2. The program activities and equipment

   - The environment should foster the growth and development of young children working and playing together.

   - A good center should provide appropriate and sufficient equipment and play materials and make them readily available.

   - Infants and children should be helped to increase their language skills and to expand their understanding of the world.

3. The relation of staff to families and the community

   - A good program should consider and support the needs of the entire family. Parents should be welcome to observe, discuss policies, make suggestions, and work in the activities of the center.

   - The staff in a good center should be aware of and contribute to community resources. The staff should share information about community recreational and learning opportunities with families.

4. The design of the facility and the program to meet the varied demands of infants and young children, their families, and the staff

   - The health of children, staff, and parents should be protected and promoted. The staff should be alert to the health of each child.

   - The facility should be safe for children and adults.

   - The environment should be spacious enough to accommodate a variety of activities and equipment. More specifically, there should be a minimum of 35 square feet of usable playroom floor space indoors per child and 75 square feet of play space outdoors per child.

Figure 11.7
What Is High-Quality Day Care?

to receive low-quality child-care than were their higher-income counterparts. Quality of care was based on such characteristics as group size, child–adult ratio, physical environment, caregiver characteristics (such as formal education, specialized training, and child-care experience), and caregiver behavior (such as sensitivity to children).

- Child-care in and of itself neither adversely affected nor promoted the security of infants' attachments to their mothers. Certain child-care conditions, in combination with certain home environments, did increase the probability that

Concept	Processes/ Related Ideas	Characteristics/Description
What Is Attachment?	Its Nature Views	• Attachment is a close emotional bond between the infant and the caregiver. • Feeding is not the critical element in attachment that Freud thought it was. • Contact comfort, familiarity, and trust are important in attachment. • Bowlby's ethological theory stresses that the caregiver and infant instinctively trigger attachment and that attachment to the caregiver intensifies at about 6 or 7 months of age.
Individual Differences	Ainsworth's View and Types of Attachment	• She believes that secure attachment (type B babies) in the first year of life is optimal. • In secure attachment, infants use the caregiver as a secure base from which to explore the environment. • Three types of insecure attachment are found in type A babies (avoidant), type C babies (ambivalent-resistant), and type D babies (disorganized).
Caregiving Styles and Attachment Classification	Their Nature	• Caregivers of secure babies are sensitive to their signals and are consistently available to meet their needs. • Caregivers of avoidant babies tend to be unavailable and rejecting. • Caregivers of ambivalent-resistant babies are inconsistently available and are usually not very affectionate. • Caregivers of disorganized babies often neglect or physically abuse them.
Attachment, Temperament, and the Wider Social World	Exploring Linkages Cultural Variations	• Some critics argue that attachment theorists and researchers have not given adequate attention to biological factors such as heredity and temperament on the one hand and not enough attention to the diversity of social agents and contexts on the other hand. • Cultural variations in attachment have been found, but in all cultures studied so far secure attachment is the most common type.
Measurement of Attachment	A Protocol	• The main way that attachment has been measured is by using the Ainsworth Strange Situation, although it has been criticized for being too unnatural.
Fathers as Caregivers for Infants	Involvement	• Fathers have increased their interaction with children, but they still lag far behind mothers, even when mothers are employed. • The mother's role is often caregiving, the father's playful interaction. • In stressful circumstances, infants often prefer their mother than their father.
Day Care	Its Nature NICHD Study	• Day care has become a basic need of the American family. • A special concern is the quality of day care that many American infants receive. • The extensive, ongoing NICHD study of day care reveals that infants from low-income families receive inferior day care, that quality day care is related to fewer child problems, and that certain child-care conditions, in combination with certain home environments, increases insecure attachment to mothers.

We have all the knowledge necessary to provide absolutely first-rate child care in the United States. What is missing is the commitment and the will.

Edward Zigler
Contemporary American Developmental Psychologist

infants would be insecurely attached to their mothers. The infants who received either poor quality of care or more than 10 hours per week of care or were in more than one setting in the first 15 months of life, were more likely to be insecurely attached, but only if their mothers were less sensitive in responding to them.

• Child-care quality, especially sensitive and responsive attention from caregivers, was linked with fewer child problems. The higher the quality of child-care over the first three years of life (more positive language stimulation and interaction between the child and the provider), the greater the child's language and cognitive abilities. No cognitive benefits were found for the children in the exclusive care of their mother.

At this point we have discussed many ideas about attachment. A review of these ideas is presented in summary table 11.5.

Chapter Review

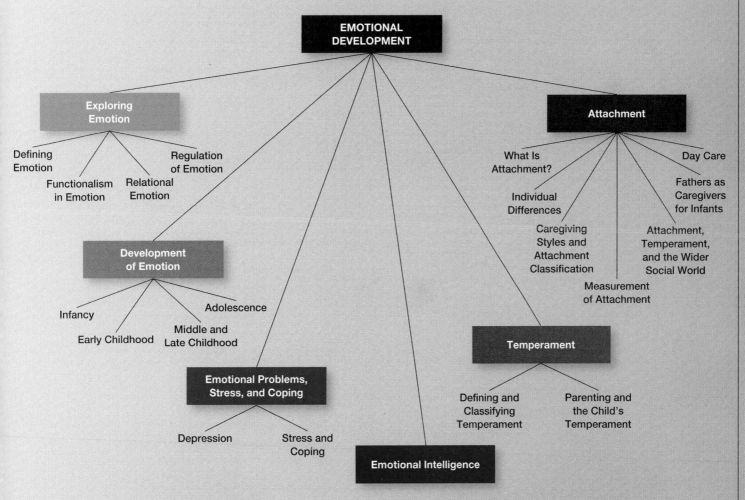

FOR A DETAILED REVIEW OF THE CHAPTER, STUDY THESE FIVE SUMMARY TABLES:

Key Terms

emotion 340
positive affectivity (PA) 340
negative affectivity (NA) 340
Maximally Discriminative Facial
   Movement Coding System (MAX) 344
basic cry 344
anger cry 344
pain cry 344
reflexive smile 345
social smile 345

stranger anxiety 345
social referencing 345
learned helplessness 349
stress 350
cognitive appraisal 350
primary appraisal 350
secondary appraisal 350
acculturation 352
emotional intelligence 354
temperament 356

easy child 356
difficult child 356
slow-to-warm-up child 356
attachment 358
secure attachment 360
type B babies 360
type A babies 360
type C babies 360
type D babies 360
Strange Situation 361

Key People

Nancy Eisenberg 340
Carroll Izard 344
John Watson 345
John Bowlby 345, 348
Aaron Beck 349
Martin Seligman 349, 351
Richard Lazarus 350

Michael Rutter 352
Daniel Goleman 354
Alexander Chess and Stella Thomas 356
Mary Rothbart 356
Harry Harlow and Robert Zimmerman 359
Konrad Lorenz 359

Erik Erikson 359
Mary Ainsworth 360
L. Alan Sroufe 360
Ross Thompson 362
Jerome Kagan 362
Michael Lamb 363

Child Development Resources

Daycare (1993, rev. ed.)
   by Alison Clarke-Stewart
   Cambridge, MA: Harvard University Press

This book draws on extensive research to survey the social, political, and economic contexts of day care. The author discusses options and consequences to help parents make informed choices.

The Development of Emotional Competence (1999)
   by Carolyn Saarni
   New York: Guilford

An excellent, up-to-date examination of the skills that lead to emotional competence.

Handbook of Child Psychology (5th ed., Vol. 3) (1998)
   Edited by Nancy Eisenberg
   New York: John Wiley

Written by leading experts in child development, this volume has many chapters that address emotion in children.

The Optimistic Child
   by Martin Seligman
   Boston: Houghton Mifflin

Seligman provides descriptions of optimistic and pessimistic children and strategies for turning the pessimists into optimists.

Touchpoints (1992)
   by T. Berry Brazelton
   Reading, MA: Addison-Wesley

Covering the period from pregnancy to first grade, Brazelton focuses on the concerns and questions parents have about the child's feelings, behavior, and development.

Taking It to the Net

1. David is a counselor at a juvenile detention center for children and adolescents aged 10 to 14. Each child has a full psychological evaluation upon admittance. David notices that far more girls than boys are diagnosed with depression. He can't accept that it is all due to "raging hormones," as the other counselors say. What factors help explain this gender difference in diagnosis?

2. Jasmine is interning at a child development center during the summer. She is going to be responsible for planning a program to help kids become more aware of their own emotions as well as the feelings of others. What should she know about Daniel Goleman's theory of emotional intelligence?

3. Liz wonders why she and her sister, Trish, have such different relationships with their mother. Liz is very outgoing, unlike her mother, and feels that her mother shows favoritism for Trish, who is quiet and shy like their mother. Could the mother/daughter difference in temperament have contributed to their mother treating Liz differently?

Connect to *http://www.mhhe.com/santrockc9* to find the answers!

Chapter 12

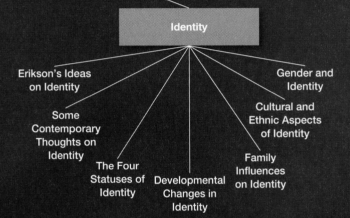

THE SELF AND IDENTITY

The Self

Self-Understanding

Self-Esteem and Self-Concept

Identity

Erikson's Ideas on Identity

Some Contemporary Thoughts on Identity

The Four Statuses of Identity

Developmental Changes in Identity

Family Influences on Identity

Cultural and Ethnic Aspects of Identity

Gender and Identity

The Self and Identity

The Story of a 15-Year-Old Girl's Self-Description

HOW DO ADOLESCENTS describe themselves? How would you have described yourself when you were 15 years old? What features would you have emphasized? The following is a self-portrait of one 15-year-old girl:

What am I like as a person? Complicated! I'm sensitive, friendly, outgoing, popular, and tolerant, though I can also be shy, self-conscious, and even obnoxious. Obnoxious! I'd *like* to be friendly and tolerant all of the time. That's the kind of person I *want* to be, and I'm disappointed when I'm not. I'm responsible, even studious now and then, but on the other hand, I'm a goof-off, too, because if you're too studious, you won't be popular. I don't usually do that well at school. I'm a pretty cheerful person, especially with my friends, where I can even get rowdy. At home I'm more likely to be anxious around my parents. They expect me to get all A's. It's not fair! I worry about how I probably *should* get better grades. But I'd be mortified in the eyes of my friends. So I'm usually pretty stressed-out at home, or sarcastic, since my parents are always on my case. But I really don't understand how I can switch so fast. I mean, how can I be cheerful one minute, anxious the next, and then be sarcastic? Which one is the *real* me? Sometimes, I feel phony, especially around boys. Say I think some guy might be interested in asking me out. I try to act different, like Madonna. I'll be flirtatious and fun-loving. And then everybody, I mean *everybody* else is looking at me like they think I'm totally weird. Then I get self-conscious and embarrassed and become radically introverted, and I don't know who I really am! Am I just trying to impress them or what? But I don't really care what they think anyway. I don't *want* to care, that is. I just want to know what my close friends think. I can be my true self with my close friends. I can't be my real self with my parents. They don't understand me. What do *they* know about what it's like to be a teenager? They still treat me like I'm still a kid. At least at school people treat you more like you're an adult. That gets confusing, though. I mean, which am I, a kid or an adult? It's scary, too, because I don't have any idea what I want to be when I grow up. I mean, I have lots of *ideas*. My friend Sheryl and I talk about whether we'll be stewardesses, or teachers, or nurses, veterinarians, maybe mothers, or actresses. I know I *don't* want to be a waitress or a secretary. But how do you decide all of this? I really don't know. I mean, I think about it a lot, but I can't resolve it. There are days when I wish I could just become immune to myself. (Harter, 1990, pp. 352–353)

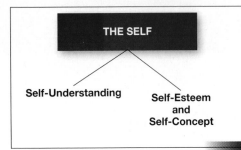

Self-Understanding

Self-Esteem
and
Self-Concept

self-understanding
A child's cognitive representation of the self, the substance and content of a child's self-conceptions.

Concepts of Person and Self

Recent and Forthcoming Books on the Self

International Society for Self and Identity

Self Development in Infancy

*K*now thyself, for once we know ourselves, we may learn how to care for ourselves, but otherwise we never shall.

Socrates
Greek Philosopher, 5th Century B.C.

The Self

In recent years, developmentalists have given special attention to two aspects of the self and self-conceptions: self-understanding and self-esteem.

Self-Understanding

What is self-understanding? When do children initially develop a self-understanding? How does self-understanding develop during the childhood and adolescent years? What is the role of perspective taking in self-understanding? We will examine each of these questions.

What Is Self-Understanding?   **Self-understanding** *is a child's cognitive representation of the self, the substance and content of the child's self-conceptions.* For example, an 11-year-old boy understands that he is a student, a boy, a football player, a family member, a video game lover, and a rock music fan. A 13-year-old girl understands that she is a middle school student, in the midst of puberty, a girl, a cheerleader, a student council member, and a movie fan. A child's self-understanding is based, in part, on the various roles and membership categories that define who children are (Harter, 1990, 1999). Though not the whole of personal identity, self-understanding provides its rational underpinnings (Damon & Hart, 1988).

Three facets of self-understanding are (a) personal memories, (b) representations of the self, and (c) theories of the self (Garcia, Hart, & Johnson-Ray, 1998). *Personal memories* are autobiographical episodes that are especially important in thoughts about oneself. These might include memories of a fight with one's parents, a day spent with a friend, a teacher saying how good your work is, and so on.

Representations of the self include the generalized ascriptions individuals make about their selves. For example, individuals have representations of their actual selves (such as "I am big, smart, and socially awkward"), their ideal selves ("I want to be a teacher and be respected by the community"), and their past selves ("I used to be very shy").

Theories of the self enable individuals to identify which characteristics of the self are relevant, arrange these characteristics in hierarchical order of importance, and make claims about how these characteristics are related to each other (Dweck, 2000). Theories of the self provide an individual with a sense of identity and a source of orientation to the world.

Infancy   Infants are not just "given" a self by their parents or the culture; rather, they find and construct selves (Garcia, Hart, & Johnson-Ray, 1998). Studying the self in infancy is difficult mainly because of infants' inability to describe with language their experiences of themselves. Two aspects of self-understanding that have been studied in infancy are self-awareness and self-recognition.

Self-Awareness   John Watson (1994) believes that although infants can distinguish between the self and others in the first few days of life, they actively work to elaborate and consolidate boundaries between self and others through the first 3 or 4 months of infancy. Watson's claims are based on his research, in which he has demonstrated that infants younger than 4 months of age show a preference for *perfect contingency,* which is typical only of the self's own actions. For example, leg-kicking when accompanied by visual attention directed toward the feet always results in visual perceptions of kicking legs. Watson says that the young infant's attentional bias toward perfect contingency reflects categorization of the self as distinct from other objects.

After the first 3 or 4 months of age, Watson found, infants show a preference for *imperfect contingency,* which is uncharacteristic of the self's actions but typical of interactions with both others and the natural world. For example, when interacting

Figure 12.1

The Development of Self-Recognition in Infancy

The graph gives the findings of two studies in which infants of different ages showed recognition of rouge by touching, wiping, or verbally referring to it. Notice that self-recognition did not occur extensively until the second half of the second year of life.

with another person, the infant might smile with the reasonable—but not certain—expectation that the other person will smile back. The preference for imperfect contingency draws attention away from the self and toward the social and natural world.

Self-Recognition   Infants cannot verbally express their views on the nature of the self. They also cannot understand the complex instructions required to engage in a child developmentalist's tasks. Given these restrictions, how can researchers study infants' self-understanding? They test infants' *visual self-recognition* by presenting them with images of themselves in mirrors, pictures, and other visual media. For example, let's examine how the mirror technique works. An infant's mother puts a dot of rouge on the infant's nose. An observer watches to see how often the infant touches its nose. Next, the infant is placed in front of a mirror, and observers detect whether nose touching increases. In two separate investigations, in the second half of the second year of life, infants recognized their own images in the mirror and coordinated the images they saw with the actions of touching their own bodies (Amsterdam, 1968; Lewis & Brooks-Gunn, 1979) (see figure 12.1). In sum, human infants initially develop a sense of rudimentary self-understanding called self-recognition at approximately 18 months of age (Hart & Karmel, 1996; Lewis & others, 1989).

Early Childhood   Because children can verbally communicate their ideas, research on self-understanding in childhood is not limited to visual self-recognition,

Reprinted with special permission of North America Syndicate.

as it is during infancy. Mainly through interviews, researchers have probed children's conceptions of many aspects of self-understanding, including mind and body, self in relation to others, and pride and shame in self. In early childhood, children usually conceive of the self in physical terms. Most young children conceive of the self as part of the body, which usually means the head. Young children generally confuse self, mind, and body (Broughton, 1978). For them, because the self is a body part, it can be described along many material dimensions, such as size, shape, and color. Young children distinguish themselves from others through many different physical and material attributes. Says 4-year-old Sandra, "I'm different from Jennifer because I have brown hair and she has blonde hair." Says 4-year-old Ralph, "I am different from Hank because I am taller and I am different from my sister because I have a bicycle."

Researchers also believe that the *active dimension* is a central component of the self in early childhood (Keller, Ford, & Meacham, 1978). If we define the category "physical" broadly enough, we can include physical actions as well as body image and material possessions. For example, preschool children often describe themselves in terms of activities such as play. In sum, in early childhood, children often describe themselves in terms of a physical self or an active self.

Another aspect of self-development in early childhood involves young children's awareness of how their present selves are causally bound to previous states of the self (Povinelli, 1995; Povinelli, Perilloux, & Landau, 1996; Povinelli & Simon, 1998). For example in one study, the reactions of 2-, 3-, and 4-year-old children to briefly displayed video images of themselves were examined (Povinelli, Perilloux, & Landau, 1996). The images showed the children playing an unusual game and revealed that one of the experimenters had covertly placed a large sticker on their head in the context of praising them. Few 2- and 3-year-olds reached up to their heads to remove the sticker while a majority of the 4- and 5-year-olds did so immediately after the delayed tape revealed that the experimenter had placed it there.

Middle and Late Childhood

In middle and late childhood, self-understanding increasingly shifts from defining oneself through external characteristics to defining oneself through internal characteristics. Also, elementary-school-age children are more likely to define themselves in terms of social characteristics and social comparison.

In middle and late childhood, children not only recognize differences between inner and outer states, but they are also more likely to include subjective inner states in their definition of self. In one investigation, second-grade children were much more likely than younger children to name psychological characteristics (such as preferences or personality traits) in their self-definition and less likely to name physical characteristics (such as eye color or possessions) (Aboud & Skerry, 1983). For example, 8-year-old Todd includes in his self-description, "I am smart and I am popular." Ten-year-old Tina says about herself, "I am pretty good about not worrying most of the time. I used to lose my temper but I'm better about that now. I also feel proud when I do well in school."

In addition to the increase of psychological characteristics in self-definition during the elementary school years, the *social aspects* of the self also increase at this point in development. In one investigation, elementary school children included references to social groups in their self-description (Livesly & Bromley, 1973). For example, some children referred to themselves as Girl Scouts, as Catholics, or as someone who has two close friends.

Children's self-understanding in the elementary school years also includes increasing reference to *social comparison*. At this point in development, children are more likely to distinguish themselves from others in comparative rather than in absolute terms. That is, elementary-school-age children are no longer as likely to think about what I do or do not do, but are more likely to think about what I can do *in comparison with others*. This developmental shift provides an increased tendency of establishing one's differences as an individual apart from others. In a series of studies, Diane Ruble (1983) investigated children's use of social comparison in their self-evaluations. Children were given a difficult task and then offered feedback on their performance, as well as information about the performances of other children their age. The children were then asked for self-evaluations. Children younger than 7 made virtually no reference to the information about other children's performances. However, many children older than 7 included socially comparative information in their self-descriptions.

Adolescence   The development of self-understanding in adolescence is complex and involves a number of aspects of the self (Harter, 1998, 1999). Let's examine how the adolescent's self-understanding differs from the child's.

Abstract and Idealistic   Remember from our discussion of Piaget's theory of cognitive development in chapters 2 and 7 that many adolescents begin to think in more *abstract* and *idealistic* ways ◀▥ PP. 36, 219. When asked to describe themselves, adolescents are more likely than children to use abstract and idealistic labels. Consider 14-year-old Laurie's abstract description of herself: "I am a human being. I am indecisive. I don't know who I am." Also consider her idealistic description of herself: "I am a naturally sensitive person who really cares about people's feelings. I think I'm pretty good-looking." Not all adolescents describe themselves in idealistic ways, but most adolescents distinguish between the real self and the ideal self.

Differentiated   Adolescents' self-understanding becomes increasingly *differentiated*. Adolescents are more likely than children to describe themselves with contextual or situational variations (Harter & others, 1998). For example, 15-year-old Amy describes herself with one set of characteristics in relation to her family and another set of characteristics in relation to her peers and friends. Yet another set of characteristics appears in self-description regarding her romantic relationship. In sum, adolescents are more likely than children to understand that one possesses different selves, depending on one's role or particular context.

The Fluctuating Self   Given the contradictory nature of the self in adolescence, it is not surprising that the self fluctuates across situations and across time (Harter, 1990). The 15-year-old girl quoted at the beginning of the chapter remarked that she could not understand how she could switch so fast—from being cheerful one moment, to being anxious the next, and then sarcastic a short time later. One researcher described the fluctuating nature of the adolescent's self with the metaphor of "the barometric self" (Rosenberg, 1986). The adolescent's self continues to be characterized by instability until the adolescent constructs a more unified theory of self, usually not until late adolescence or even early adulthood.

*T*hrough the Eyes of Psychologists

Susan Harter, *University of Denver*

"The contemporary perspective on the self emphasizes the construction of multiple self-representations across different relational contexts."

possible self
What an individual might become, what the person will be like, and what the person is afraid of becoming.

Hazel Markus Talks About Selfways

Culture and the Self

Contradictions Within the Self   After adolescence ushers in the need to differentiate the self into multiple roles in different relational contexts, this naturally leads to potential contradictions between these differentiated selves. In one study, Susan Harter (1986) asked seventh-, ninth-, and eleventh-graders to describe themselves. She found that the number of contradictory self-descriptions (moody *and* understanding, ugly *and* attractive, bored *and* inquisitive, caring *and* uncaring, introverted *and* fun-loving, and so on) dramatically increased between the seventh and ninth grades. The contradictory self-descriptions declined in the eleventh grade but still were higher than in the seventh grade. Adolescents develop the cognitive ability to detect these inconsistencies in the self as they strive to construct a general theory of the self or of their personality (Harter & Monsour, 1992).

Real and Ideal, True and False Selves   The adolescent's emerging ability to construct ideal selves in addition to actual ones can be perplexing to the adolescent. The capacity to recognize a discrepancy between *real* and *ideal* selves represents a cognitive advance, but humanistic theorist Carl Rogers (1950) believed that when the real and ideal selves are too discrepant, it is a sign of maladjustment. Depression can result from a substantial discrepancy between one's actual self and one's ideal self (the person one wants to be) because an awareness of this discrepancy can produce a sense of failure and self-criticism (Hart & others, in press).

While, as just mentioned, some theorists consider a strong discrepancy between the ideal and real selves as maladaptive, others argue that this is not always true, especially in adolescence. For example, in one view, an important aspect of the ideal or imagined self is the **possible self,** *what individuals might become, what they would like to become, and what they are afraid of becoming* (Markus & Nurius, 1986). Thus, adolescents' possible selves include both what adolescents hope to be as well as what they dread they will become (Cota-Robles, Neiss, & Hunt, 2000; Martin, 1997). In this view, the presence of both hoped-for as well as dreaded selves is psychologically healthy, providing a balance between positive, expected selves and negative, feared selves. The attributes of future positive selves (getting into a good college, being admired, having a successful career) can direct future positive states, while attributes of future negative selves (being unemployed, being lonely, not getting into a good college) can identify what is to be avoided in the future. To read further about the important concept of multiple selves in adolescence, see the Explorations in Child Development box.

Can adolescents distinguish between their *true* and *false* selves? In one research study, they could (Harter & Lee, 1989). Adolescents are most likely to show their false self in romantic or dating situations, and with classmates; they are least likely to show their false self with close friends. Adolescents display a false self to impress others, to try out new behaviors or roles, because others force them to behave in false ways, and because others do not understand their true self. Some adolescents report that they do not like their false-self behavior, but others say that it does not bother them. Harter and her colleagues (1996) found that experienced authenticity of the self is highest among adolescents who say they receive support from their parents.

Social Comparison   Some developmentalists believe that adolescents are more likely than children to use *social comparison* to evaluate themselves (Ruble & others, 1980). However, adolescents' willingness to admit that they engage in social comparison to evaluate themselves declines in adolescence because they view social comparison as socially undesirable. They think that acknowledging their social comparison motives will endanger their popularity. Relying on social comparison information in adolescence may be confusing because of the large number of reference groups. For example, should adolescents compare themselves to classmates in general? to friends? to their own gender? to popular adolescents? to good-looking adolescents? to athletic adolescents? Simultaneously considering all of these social comparison groups can get perplexing for adolescents.

EXPLORATIONS IN CHILD DEVELOPMENT

Multiple Selves and Sociocultural Contexts

ONE OF THE MOST IMPORTANT shifts in the study of the self-system in the last several decades has been toward conceptualizing the self as a multidimensional framework (Harter 1999). Differentiation of the self increases with age, so that the number of domains of the self that can be evaluated increase across the childhood, adolescence, and adult periods of development.

The increasing proliferation of selves in adolescence can vary across relationships with people, social roles, and sociocultural contexts (Kashima, Kashima, & Aldridge, 2000; Kitayama & Markus, 2000). Researchers have found that adolescents' portraits of themselves can change depending on whether they describe themselves when they are with their mother, father, close friend, romantic partner, or peer. They also can change depending on whether they describe themselves in roles as a student, athlete, or on the job. And adolescents can create different selves depending on their ethnic and cultural background and experiences.

The multiple selves of ethnic minority youth can reflect their efforts to bridge multiple worlds (Cooper, in press; Cooper & others, 1995). Many ethnic minority youth must move between multiple contexts, some of which are populated by members of their own ethnic group, others of which are populated by members of the majority culture

who might not share the values of their family of origin. Some youth, especially those whose values are similar to those of the majority culture, move smoothly across these multiple worlds. Others, for whom there is less compatibility across cultures, might adopt strong bicultural or multicultural selves.

Hazel Markus and her colleagues (Markus & Kitayama, 1994; Markus, Mullally, & Kitayama, 1999) believe that it is important to understand how multiple selves emerge through participation in cultural practices. They argue that all selves are culture-specific selves that emerge as individuals adapt to their cultural environments. In North American contexts (especially middle-SES), individuality is promoted and maintained. North Americans, when given the opportunity to describe themselves, often provide not only portraits of their current selves but notions of their future selves as well. They also frequently show a need for having multiple selves that are stable and consistent. In Japan, multiple selves are often described in terms of relatedness to others. Self-improvement also is an important aspect of the multiple selves of many Japanese. Markus and her colleagues recognize that cultural groups are characterized by diversity but nonetheless conclude that it is helpful to understand the dominant aspects of multiple selves within a culture.

Self-Conscious   Adolescents are more likely than children to be *self-conscious* about and *preoccupied* with their self-understanding. As part of their self-conscious and preoccupied self-exploration, adolescents become more introspective. However, the introspection is not always done in social isolation. Sometimes, adolescents turn to their friends for support and self-clarification, obtaining their friends' opinions of an emerging self-definition. As one researcher on self-development commented, adolescents' friends are often the main source of reflected self-appraisals, becoming the social mirror into which adolescents anxiously stare (Rosenberg, 1979). This self-consciousness and self-preoccupation reflect the concept of adolescent egocentrism, which we discussed in chapter 7 ◀▉▉▉ P. 221.

Self-Protective   In adolescence, self-understanding includes more mechanisms to *protect the self*. Although adolescents often display a sense of confusion and conflict stimulated by introspective efforts to understand themselves, they also call on mechanisms to protect and enhance the self. In protecting the self, adolescents are prone to denying their negative characteristics. For example, in Harter's investigation of self-understanding, positive self-descriptions, such as *attractive, fun-loving, sensitive, affectionate,* and *inquisitive,* were more likely to be ascribed to the core of the self, indicating more importance, whereas negative self-descriptions, such as *ugly, mediocre, depressed, selfish,* and *nervous,* were more likely to be ascribed to the periphery of the self, indicating less importance (Harter, 1986). Adolescents' tendency to protect themselves fits with the earlier description of adolescents' tendency to describe themselves in idealistic ways.

Unconscious   In adolescence, self-understanding involves greater recognition that the self includes *unconscious,* as well as conscious, components, a recognition not likely to occur until late adolescence (Selman, 1980). That is, older adolescents are more likely than younger adolescents to believe that certain aspects of their mental experience are beyond their awareness or control.

Self-Integration   In adolescence, self-understanding becomes more *integrative,* with the disparate parts of the self more systematically pieced together, especially in late adolescence. Older adolescents are more likely to detect inconsistencies in their earlier self-descriptions as they attempt to construct a general theory of self, an integrated sense of identity.

Because the adolescent creates multiple self-concepts, the task of integrating these varying self-conceptions becomes problematic. At the same time that adolescents are faced with pressures to differentiate the self into multiple roles, the emergence of formal operational thought presses for *integration* and the development of a consistent, coherent theory of self. These budding formal operational skills initially present a liability because they first allow adolescents to *detect* inconsistencies in the self across varying roles, only later providing the cognitive capacity to *integrate* such apparent contradictions. In the narrative that opened this chapter, the 15-year-old girl could not understand how she could be cheerful yet depressed and sarcastic, wondering "which is the real me." Researchers have found that 14- to 15-year-olds not only detect inconsistencies across their various roles (with parents, friends, and romantic partners, for example) but are much more troubled by these contradictions than younger (11- to 12-year-old) and older (17- to 18-year-old) adolescents are (Damon & Hart, 1988).

Conclusions   As we have seen, the development of self-understanding in adolescence is complex and involves a number of aspects of the self. Rapid changes that occur in the transition from childhood to adolescence result in heightened self-awareness and consciousness. This heightened self-focus leads to consideration of the self and the many changes that are occurring in it, which can produce doubt about who the self is and which facets of the self are "real" (Hart, 1996).

At this point, we have discussed a number of characteristics of adolescents' self-understanding. A summary of these characteristics is presented in figure 12.2.

Figure **12.2**

Characteristics of Adolescents' Self-Understanding

perspective taking
The ability to assume another person's perspective and understand his or her thoughts or feelings.

The Role of Perspective Taking in Self-Understanding   In Piaget's theory, which we discussed in chapters 2 "The Science of Child Development" and 7 "Cognitive Developmental Approaches," young children are egocentric ◀‖‖ P. 211. As they develop, they move away from this self-centeredness. These ideas of Piaget served as a foundation for the contemporary belief that perspective taking plays an important role in self-understanding. **Perspective taking** *is the ability to assume another person's perspective and understand his or her thoughts and feelings.* Robert Selman (1980) has proposed a developmental theory of perspective taking that has been given considerable attention. He believes perspective taking involves a series of five stages, ranging from 3 years of age through adolescence (see figure 12.3). These stages begin with the egocentric viewpoint in early childhood and end with in-depth perspective taking in adolescence.

To study children's perspective taking, Selman interviews individual children, asking them to comment on such dilemmas as the following:

> Holly is an 8-year-old girl who likes to climb trees. She is the best tree climber in the neighborhood. One day while climbing down from a tall tree, she falls, . . . but does not hurt herself. Her father sees her fall. He is upset and asks her to promise not to climb trees anymore. Holly promises.
>
>   Later that day, Holly and her friends meet Shawn. Shawn's kitten is caught in a tree and can't get down. Something has to be done right away or the kitten may fall. Holly is the only one who climbs trees well enough to reach the kitten and get it down but she remembers her promise to her father. (Selman, 1976, p. 302)

Stage	Perspective-taking stage	Ages	Description
0	Egocentric viewpoint	3–5	Child has a sense of differentiation of self and other but fails to distinguish between the social perspective (thoughts, feelings) of other and self. Child can label other's overt feelings but does not see the cause-and-effect relation of reasons to social actions.
1	Social-informational perspective taking	6–8	Child is aware that other has a social perspective based on other's own reasoning, which may or may not be similar to child's. However, child tends to focus on one perspective rather than coordinating viewpoints.
2	Self-reflective perspective taking	8–10	Child is conscious that each individual is aware of the other's perspective and that this awareness influences self's and other's view of each other. Putting self in other's place is a way of judging other's intentions, purposes, and actions. Child can form a coordinated chain of perspectives but cannot yet abstract from this process to the level of simultaneous mutuality.
3	Mutual perspective taking	10–12	Adolescent realizes that both self and other can view each other mutually and simultaneously as subjects. Adolescent can step outside the two-person dyad and view the interaction from a third-person perspective.
4	Social and conventional system perspective taking	12–15	Adolescent realizes mutual perspective taking does not always lead to complete understanding. Social conventions are seen as necessary because they are understood by all members of the group (the generalized other), regardless of their position, role, or experience.

Figure 12.3
Selman's Stages of Perspective Taking

Subsequently, Selman asks each child a series of questions about the dilemma, such as the following:

- Does Holly know how Shawn feels about the kitten?
- How will Holly's father feel if he finds out she climbed the tree?
- What does Holly think her father will do if he finds out she climbed the tree?
- What would you do in this situation?

By analyzing children's responses to these dilemmas, Selman (1980) concluded that children's perspective taking follows the developmental sequence described in figure 12.3.

Children's perspective taking not only can increase their self-understanding, but it can also improve their peer group status and the quality of their friendships. For example, one investigation found that the most popular children in the third and eighth grades had competent perspective-taking skills (Kurdek & Krile, 1982). Children who are competent at perspective taking are better at understanding the needs of their companions, so they likely can communicate more effectively with them (Hudson, Forman, & Brion-Meisels, 1982).

At this point, we have studied a number of developmental changes in self-understanding. Remember from our introduction to the self that self-conception involves not only self-understanding but also self-esteem and self-concept. That is, not only

SUMMARY TABLE 12.1
Self-Understanding

Concept	Processes/ Related Ideas	Characteristics/Description
What Is Self-Understanding?	Its Nature	• Self-understanding is a child's cognitive representation of the self, the substance and content of the child's self-conceptions. • It provides the rational underpinnings for identity.
Infancy	Self-Awareness	• Watson's research demonstrated that self-awareness emerges very early in infancy and develops over the first 3 or 4 months.
	Self-Recognition	• Infants develop a rudimentary form of self-recognition at approximately 18 months of age.
Early Childhood	Nature of Changes	• The physical and active self becomes a part of self-understanding.
Middle and Late Childhood	Nature of Changes	• The internal self, the social self, and the socially comparative self become more prominent.
Adolescence	Nature of Changes	• Dimensions of adolescents' self-understanding include abstract and idealistic; differentiated; the fluctuating self; contradictions within the self; real and ideal, true and false selves; social comparison; self-conscious; self-protective; unconscious; and self-integration.
The Role of Perspective Taking in Self-Understanding	Its Nature	• The ability to assume another person's perspective and understand his/her thoughts and feelings.
	Selman's View	• He proposed a developmental theory of perspective taking that has 5 stages, ranging from 3 years of age through adolescence. • The first stage in early childhood involves an egocentric viewpoint; the last stage in adolescence consists of having an in-depth perspective-taking ability.

It is difficult to make people miserable when they feel worthy of themselves.

Abraham Lincoln
American President, 19th Century

self-esteem
The global evaluative dimension of the self; also called self-worth or self-image.

self-concept
Domain-specific self-evaluations.

do children try to define and describe attributes of the self (self-understanding), but they also evaluate these attributes (self-esteem and self-concept).

At this point we have discussed a number of ideas about self-understanding. A review of these ideas is presented in summary table 12.1. Next, we will continue our exploration of the self by examining self-esteem and self-concept.

Self-Esteem and Self-Concept

What are self-esteem and self-concept? How are they measured? How do parent-child relationships contribute to self-esteem? What are the consequences of children's low self-esteem? And how can children's self-esteem be enhanced?

What Are Self-Esteem and Self-Concept? **Self-esteem** *is the global evaluative dimension of the self. Self-esteem is also referred to as self-worth or self-image.* For example, a child might perceive that she is not merely a person but a *good* person. Of course, not all children have an overall positive image of themselves. **Self-concept** *refers to domain-specific evaluations of the self.* Children can make self-evaluations in many domains of their lives—academic, athletic, physical appearance, and so on. In sum, self-esteem refers to global self-evaluations, self-concept to more domain-specific evaluations.

Investigators have not always made clear distinctions between self-esteem and self-concept, sometimes using the terms interchangeably or not precisely defining them (Tesser, 2000). As you read the remaining discussion of self-esteem and self-concept, the distinction between self-esteem as global self-evaluation and self-concept as domain-specific self-evaluation should help you to keep the terms straight.

Measuring Self-Esteem and Self-Concept   Measuring self-esteem and self-concept hasn't always been easy, especially when assessing adolescents (Wylie, 1979). Recently, different measures have been developed to assess children and adolescents.

Susan Harter's (1985) Self-Perception Profile for Children is a revision of her original instrument, the Perceived Competence Scale for Children (Harter, 1982). The Self-Perception Profile for Children taps five specific domains of self-concept—scholastic competence, athletic competence, social acceptance, physical appearance, and behavioral conduct—plus general self-worth. Harter's scale does an excellent job of separating children's self-evaluations in different skill domains, and when general self-worth is assessed, questions focus on the overall self-evaluations rather than on specific skill domains.

The Self-Perception Profile for Children is designed to be used with third-grade through sixth-grade children. Harter also has developed a separate scale for adolescents, recognizing important developmental changes in self-perceptions. The Self-Perception Profile for Adolescents (Harter, 1989) taps eight domains—scholastic competence, athletic competence, social acceptance, physical appearance, behavioral conduct, close friendship, romantic appeal, and job competence—plus global self-worth. Thus the adolescent version has three skill domains not present in the children's version—job competence, romantic appeal, and close friendship.

Parent-Child Relationships and Self-Esteem   In the most extensive investigation of parent-child relationships and self-esteem, the following parenting attributes were associated with boys' high self-esteem (Coopersmith, 1967):

- Expression of affection
- Concern about the child's problems
- Harmony in the home
- Participation in joint family activities
- Availability to give competent, organized help to the boys when they need it
- Setting clear and fair rules
- Abiding by these rules
- Allowing the children freedom within well-prescribed limits

Remember that these findings are correlational, and so, we cannot say that these parenting attributes *cause* children's high self-esteem. Such factors as parental acceptance and allowing children freedom within well-prescribed limits probably are important determinants of children's self-esteem, but we still must say that they *are related* to rather than that they *cause* children's self-esteem, based on the available research data.

Consequences of Low Self-Esteem   For most children and adolescents, low self-esteem results only in temporary emotional discomfort (Damon, 1991). But in some children and adolescents, low self-esteem can translate into other problems (DuBois, Felner, & Brand, 1997; Usher & others, 2000). It has been implicated in depression, suicide, anorexia nervosa, and delinquency (Harter & Marold, 1992). The seriousness of the problem depends not only on the nature of the child's and adolescent's low self-esteem but on other conditions as well. When low self-esteem is compounded by difficult school transitions or family life, or by other stressful events, the child's problems can intensify (Rutter & Garmezy, 1983).

Increasing Children's Self-Esteem   Four ways children's self-esteem can be improved are through (1) identification of the causes of low self-esteem and the domains of competence important to the self, (2) emotional support and social approval, (3) achievement, and (4) coping (see figure 12.4).

College of Positive Self-Image 7.
University of Low Self-Esteem 0.

An Adolescent Talks About Self-Esteem

Exploring Self-Esteem Research

Self-Esteem Websites

Figure 12.4

Four Key Aspects of Improving Self-Esteem

Building Self-Esteem
Improving Young Adolescents' Self-Esteem

Identifying children's sources of self-esteem—that is, competence in domains important to the self—is critical to improving self-esteem. Susan Harter (1990) points out that the self-esteem enhancement programs of the 1960s, in which self-esteem itself was the target and individuals were encouraged to simply feel good about themselves, were ineffective. Rather, Harter believes that intervention must occur at the level of the *causes* of self-esteem if the individual's self-esteem is to improve significantly. Children have the highest self-esteem when they perform competently in domains that are important to them. Therefore, children should be encouraged to identify and value areas of competence.

Emotional support and social approval in the form of confirmation from others also powerfully influence children's self-esteem. Some children with low self-esteem come from conflicted families or conditions in which they experienced abuse or neglect—situations in which support was unavailable. In some cases, alternative sources of support can be implemented either informally through the encouragement of a teacher, a coach, or another significant adult or, more formally, through programs such as Big Brothers and Big Sisters. While peer approval becomes increasingly important during adolescence, both adult and peer support are important influences on the adolescent's self-esteem.

Achievement also can improve children's self-esteem (Bednar, Wells, & Peterson, 1995). For example, the straightforward teaching of real skills to children often results in increased achievement and, thus, in enhanced self-esteem. Children develop higher self-esteem because they know the important tasks to achieve goals, and they have experienced performing them or similar behaviors. The emphasis on the importance of achievement in improving self-esteem has much in common with Bandura's social cognitive concept of *self-efficacy,* which refers to individuals' beliefs that they can master a situation and produce positive outcomes.

Self-esteem also is often increased when children face a problem and try to cope with it, rather than avoid it. If coping rather than avoidance prevails, children often face problems realistically, honestly, and nondefensively. This produces favorable self-evaluative thoughts, which lead to the self-generated approval that raises self-esteem. The converse is true of low self-esteem. Unfavorable self-evaluations trigger denial, deception, and avoidance in an attempt to disavow that which has already been

<table>
</table>

SUMMARY TABLE 12.2
Self-Esteem and Self-Concept

Concept	Processes/ Related Ideas	Characteristics/Description
What Are Self-Esteem and Self-Concept?	Self-Esteem	• The global, evaluative dimension of the self; also referred to as self-worth or self-image.
	Self-Concept	• Domain-specific evaluations of the self.
Measuring Self-Esteem Self-Concept	Harter's Measures	• They assess self-evaluations in different skill domains as well as general self-worth.
Parent-Child Relationships and Self-Esteem	Linkages	• In Coopersmith's study, children's self-esteem was associated with parental acceptance and allowing children freedom within well-prescribed limits.
Consequences of Low Self-Esteem	Their Nature	• For most children, low self-esteem only translates into temporary emotional discomfort, but for others, low self-esteem can result in depression, suicide, eating disorders, and delinquency.
Increasing Children's Self-Esteem	Strategies	• Four ways to increase children's self-esteem are to (1) identify the causes of low self-esteem and which domains are important to the self, (2) provide emotional support and social approval, (3) help the child achieve, and (4) improve the child's coping skills.

glimpsed as true. This process leads to self-generated disapproval as a form of feedback to the self about personal adequacy.

At this point, we have discussed a number of ideas about self-esteem and self-concept. A review of these ideas is presented in summary table 12.2. Next, we turn our attention to an important concept related to the self—identity.

Identity

By far the most comprehensive and provocative theory of identity development is Erik Erikson's. Some experts on adolescence consider Erikson's ideas to be the single most influential theory of adolescent development. Erikson's theory was introduced in chapter 2 ◄IIII P. 33. Here that introduction is expanded, beginning with reanalysis of his ideas on identity. Then we examine some contemporary thoughts on identity, the four statuses of identity, developmental changes, family influences on identity, cultural and ethnic aspects of identity, and gender and identity development.

Erikson's Ideas on Identity

Who am I? What am I all about? What am I going to do with my life? What is different about me? How can I make it on my own? Not usually considered during childhood, these questions surface as common, virtually universal, concerns during adolescence. Adolescents clamor for solutions to these questions that revolve around the concept of identity, and it was Erik Erikson (1950, 1968) who first understood how central such questions are to understanding adolescent development. That today identity is believed to be a key concept in adolescent development is a result of Erikson's masterful thinking and analysis.

Revisiting Erikson's Views on Identity and the Human Life Span   **Identity versus identity confusion** *is Erikson's fifth developmental*

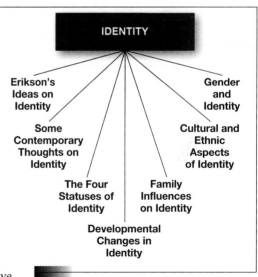

identity versus identity confusion
Erikson's fifth developmental stage, which individuals experience during the adolescent years. At this time, adolescents examine who they are, what they are all about, and where they are going in life.

psychosocial moratorium
Erikson's term for the gap between childhood security and adult autonomy that adolescents experience as part of their identity exploration.

*W*ho are you?" said the caterpillar. Alice replied rather shyly, "I—I hardly know, sir, just at present—at least I know who I was when I got up this morning, but I must have changed several times since then."

Lewis Carroll
English Writer, 19th Century

Exploring Identity

The Society for Research on Identity Development

Identity Development in Literature

*E*xplore thyself. Herein are demanded the eye and the nerve.

Henry David Thoreau
American Poet and Essayist, 19th Century

stage, which individuals experience during the adolescent years. At this time, adolescents examine who they are, what they are all about, and where they are going in life. Adolescents are confronted with many new roles, such as vocational and romantic roles. **Psychosocial moratorium** *is Erikson's term for the gap between childhood security and adult autonomy that adolescents experience as part of their identity exploration.* As adolescents explore and search their culture's identity files, they often experiment with different roles. Youths who successfully cope with these conflicting identities emerge with a new sense of self that is both refreshing and acceptable. Adolescents who do not successfully resolve this identity crisis suffer what Erikson calls identity confusion. The confusion takes one of two courses: Individuals withdraw, isolating themselves from peers and family, or they immerse themselves in the world of peers and lose their identity in the crowd.

Erikson's ideas about adolescent identity development reveal rich insights into adolescents' thoughts and feelings. Reading one or more of his original writings is worthwhile. A good starting point is *Identity: Youth and Crisis* (1968). Other works that portray identity development are *Young Man Luther* (1962) and *Gandhi's Truth* (1969)—the latter won a Pulitzer Prize.

Personality and Role Experimentation

Two core ingredients in Erikson's theory of identity development are personality and role experimentation. As indicated earlier, Erikson believes that adolescents face an overwhelming number of choices and at some point during youth enter a period of psychological moratorium. During this moratorium, they try out different roles and personalities before they reach a stable sense of self. They may be argumentative one moment, cooperative the next moment. They may dress neatly one day, sloppily the next day. They may like a particular friend one week, despise the friend the next week. This personality experimentation is a deliberate effort on the part of adolescents to find out where they fit in the world.

As they gradually come to realize that they will be responsible for themselves and their own lives, adolescents search for what those lives are going to be. Many parents and other adults, accustomed to having children go along with what they say, may be bewildered or incensed by the wisecracks, the rebelliousness, and the rapid mood changes that accompany adolescence. It is important for these adults to give adolescents the time and the opportunities to explore different roles and personalities. In turn, most adolescents eventually discard undesirable roles.

There are literally hundreds of roles for adolescents to try out, and probably just as many ways to pursue each role. Erickson believes that, by late adolescence, vocational roles are central to identity development, especially in a highly technological society like the United States. Youth who have been well trained to enter a workforce that offers the potential of reasonably high self-esteem will experience the least stress during the development of identity. Some youth have rejected jobs offering good pay and traditionally high social status, choosing instead to work in situations that allow them to be more genuinely helpful to their fellow humans, such as in the Peace Corps, in mental health clinics, or in schools for children from low-income backgrounds. Some youth prefer unemployment to the prospect of working at a job they feel they would be unable to perform well or at which they would feel useless. To Erikson, this attitude reflects the desire to achieve a meaningful identity through being true to oneself, rather than burying one's identity in that of the larger society.

Identity is a self-portrait composed of many pieces, including these:

- The career and work path the person wants to follow (vocational/career identity)
- Whether the person is conservative, liberal, or middle-of-the road (political identity)
- The person's spiritual beliefs (religious identity)
- Whether the person is single, married, divorced, and so on (relationship identity)
- The extent to which the person is motivated to achieve and is intellectual (achievement, intellectual identity)
- Whether the person is heterosexual, homosexual, or bisexual (sexual identity)

- Which part of the world or country a person is from and how intensely the person identifies with his/her cultural heritage (cultural/ethnic identity)
- The kind of things a person likes to do, which can include sports, music, hobbies, and so on (interest)
- The individual's personality characteristics (such as being introverted or extraverted, anxious or calm, friendly or hostile, and so on) (personality)
- The individual's body image (physical identity)

Some Contemporary Thoughts on Identity

Contemporary views of identity development suggest several important considerations. First, identity development is a lengthy process, in many instances a more gradual, less cataclysmic transition than Erikson's term *crisis* implies (Baumeister, 1991). Second, as just indicated, identity development is extraordinarily complex (Marcia, 1989). Identity formation neither begins nor ends with adolescence. It begins with the appearance of attachment, the development of a sense of self, and the emergence of independence in infancy, and reaches its final phase with a life review and integration in old age. What is important about identity development in adolescence, especially late adolescence, is that, for the first time, physical development, cognitive development, and social development advance to the point at which the individual can sort through and synthesize childhood identities and identifications to construct a viable path toward adult maturity. Resolution of the identity issue at adolescence does not mean that identity will be stable through the remainder of life. An individual who develops a healthy identity is flexible and adaptive, open to changes in society, in relationships, and in careers (Adams, Gulotta, & Montemayor, 1992). This openness assures numerous reorganizations of identity's contents throughout the identity-achieved individual's life.

Just as there is an increasing tendency to describe the adolescent's self-system in terms of multiple selves, so have experts on adolescence begun to characterize the adolescent's identity system in terms of multiple identities (Brooks-Gunn & Graber, 1999; Deaux, 2000). While identities during the adolescent years are preceded by childhood identities, central questions such as "Who am I?" and "What aspects of my identities come out in different contexts?" are asked more frequently in the adolescent years. It is during adolescence that identities are more strongly characterized by the search for balance between the needs for autonomy and connectedness (Graber & Brooks-Gunn, in press).

Identity formation does not happen neatly, and it usually does not happen cataclysmically. At the bare minimum, it involves commitment to a vocational direction, an ideological stance, and a sexual orientation. Synthesizing the identity components can be a long and drawn-out process, with many negations and affirmations of various roles and faces. Identity development gets done in bits and pieces. Decisions are not made once and for all, but have to be made again and again. And the decisions might seem trivial at the time: whom to date, whether or not to break up, whether or not to have intercourse, whether or not to take drugs, whether or not to go to college or finish high school and get a job, which major, whether to study or whether to play, whether or not to be politically active, and so on. Over the years of adolescence, the decisions begin to form a core of what the individual is all about as a human being—what is called his or her identity.

The Four Statuses of Identity

Eriksonian researcher James Marcia (1980, 1994) believes that Erikson's theory of identity development contains four statuses of identity, or ways of resolving the identity crisis: identity diffusion, identity foreclosure, identity moratorium, and identity achievement. The extent of an adolescent's crisis and commitment are used to classify the individual according to one of the four identity statuses. **Crisis** *is defined as a period of identity development during which the adolescent is exploring meaningful alternatives.* Most researchers use the term *exploration* rather than *crisis*, although, in the spirit of

Through the Eyes of Psychologists

James Marcia, *Simon Fraser University*

"Once formed, an identity furnishes individuals with a historical sense of who they have been, a meaningful sense of who they are now, and a sense of who they might become in the future."

The thoughts of youth are long, long thoughts.

Henry Wadsworth Longfellow
American Poet, 19th Century

Identity Status Research

crisis
A period of identity development during which the adolescent is choosing among meaningful alternatives.

commitment
The part of identity development in which adolescents show a personal investment in what they are going to do.

identity diffusion
Marcia's term for the state adolescents are in when they have not yet experienced a crisis (that is, they have not yet explored meaningful alternatives) or made any commitments.

identity foreclosure
Marcia's term for the state adolescents are in when they have made a commitment but have not experienced a crisis.

identity moratorium
Marcia's term for the state of adolescents who are in the midst of a crisis, but whose commitments either are absent or are only vaguely defined.

identity achievement
Marcia's term for an adolescent's having undergone a crisis and made a commitment.

Marcia's formulation, the term *crisis* is used here. **Commitment** *is a part of identity development in which adolescents show a personal investment in what they are going to do.*

Identity diffusion *is Marcia's term for the state adolescents are in when they have not yet experienced a crisis (that is, they have not yet explored meaningful alternatives) or made any commitments.* Not only are they undecided about occupational and ideological choices, they are also likely to show little interest in such matters. **Identity foreclosure** *is Marcia's term for the state adolescents are in when they have made a commitment but have not experienced a crisis.* This occurs most often when parents hand down commitments to their adolescents, usually in an authoritarian way. In these circumstances, adolescents have not had adequate opportunities to explore different approaches, ideologies, and vocations on their own. **Identity moratorium** *is Marcia's term for the state of adolescents who are in the midst of a crisis, but whose commitments either are absent or are only vaguely defined.* **Identity achievement** *is Marcia's term for an adolescent's having undergone a crisis and having made a commitment.* Marcia's four statuses of identity development are summarized in figure 12.5.

The identity status approach has been sharply criticized by some researchers and theoreticians (Blasi, 1988; Cote & Levine, 1988; Lapsley & Power, 1988). They believe that the identity status approach distorts and trivializes Erikson's notions of crisis and commitment. For example, concerning crisis, Erikson emphasized youth's questioning the perceptions and expectations of one's culture and developing an autonomous position with regard to one's society. In the identity status approach, these complex questions are dealt with by simply evaluating whether a youth has thought about certain issues and has considered alternatives. Erikson's idea of commitment loses the meaning of investing oneself in certain lifelong projects and is interpreted simply as having made a firm decision or not. Others still believe that the identity status approach is a valuable contribution to understanding identity (Archer, 1989; Marica, 1994; Waterman, 1989).

Developmental Changes in Identity

In Marcia's terms, young adolescents are primarily in the identity statuses of diffusion, foreclosure, or moratorium. At least three aspects of the young adolescent's development are important in identity formation (Marcia, 1987, 1996): Young adolescents must be confident that they have parental support, must have an established sense of industry, and must be able to adopt a self-reflective stance toward the future.

Some researchers believe the most important identity changes take place in youth rather than earlier in adolescence. For example, Alan Waterman (1985, 1989, 1992) has found that from the years preceding high school through the last few years of college, there is an increase in the number of individuals who are identity achieved, along with a decrease in those who are identity diffused. College upperclassmen are more likely to be identity achieved than college freshmen or high school students are. Many young adolescents are identity diffused. These developmental changes are especially true for vocational choice. For religious beliefs and political ideology, fewer college students have reached the identity-achieved status, with a substantial number characterized by foreclosure and diffusion. Thus, the timing of identity may depend on the particular life area involved, and many college students are still wrestling with ideological commitments (Arehart & Smith, 1990; Harter, 1990).

Many identity status researchers believe that a common pattern of individuals who develop positive identities

Identity status				
Position on occupation and ideology	**Identity moratorium**	**Identity foreclosure**	**Identity diffusion**	**Identity achievement**
Crisis	Present	Absent	Absent	Present
Commitment	Absent	Present	Absent	Present

Figure **12.5**

Marcia's Four Statuses of Identity

SUMMARY TABLE 12.3
Erikson's Ideas on Identity, and Developmental Changes in Identity

Concept	Processes/ Related Ideas	Characteristics/Description
Erikson's Ideas on Identity	Identity Versus Identity Confusion	• Erikson argues that identity versus identity confusion is the fifth stage of the human life span, occurring at about the same time as adolescence. • This stage involves entering a psychological moratorium between the security of childhood and the autonomy of adulthood.
	Personality and Role Experimentation	• Personality and role experimentation are important aspects of identity development. • In technological societies like those in North America, the vocational role is especially important.
	Some Contemporary Thoughts on Identity	• Identity development is lengthy, in many cases more gradual than Erikson implied. • Identity development is extraordinarily complex and is done in bits and pieces.
	The Four Statuses of Identity	• James Marcia proposed four identity statuses—identity diffusion, foreclosure, moratorium, and achievement—that are based on crisis (exploration) and commitment. • Some experts believe the identity status approach oversimplifies Erickson's ideas.
Developmental Changes in Identity	Their Nature	• Some experts argue the main changes in identity occur in the college years rather than earlier in adolescence. • College juniors and seniors are more likely to be identity achieved than freshmen or high school students, although many college students are still wrestling with ideological commitments.
	MAMA cycles	• Individuals often follow moratorium–achievement–moratorium–achievement (MAMA) cycles in their lives.

is to follow what are called "MAMA" cycles of *moratorium–achievement–moratorium–achievement* (Archer, 1989). These cycles may be repeated throughout life (Francis, Fraser, & Marcia, 1989). Personal, family, and societal changes are inevitable, and as they occur, the flexibility and skill required to explore new alternatives and develop new commitments are likely to enhance an individual's coping skills. Regarding commitment, Marcia (1996) believes that the first identity is just that—it is not, and should not be expected to be, the final product.

At this point we have studied a number of concepts related to Erikson's ideas on identity and developmental changes. A review of these ideas is presented in summary table 12.3. Next, we will continue our exploration of identity by examining family influences.

As long as one keeps searching, the answers come.

Joan Baez
American Folk Singer, 20th Century

Family Influences on Identity

Parents are important figures in the adolescent's development of identity. In studies that relate identity development to parenting styles, democratic parents, who encourage adolescents to participate in family decision making, foster identity achievement. Autocratic parents, who control the adolescent's behavior without giving the adolescent an opportunity to express opinions, encourage identity foreclosure. Permissive parents, who provide little guidance to adolescents and allow them to make their own decisions, promote identity diffusion (Enright & others, 1980).

ADVENTURES FOR THE MIND

Exploring Your Identity

THINK DEEPLY about your exploration and commitment in the areas listed below. For each area, check whether your identity status is diffused, foreclosed, moratorium, or achieved.

IDENTITY COMPONENT	IDENTITY STATUS			
	Diffused	Foreclosed	Moratorium	Achieved
Vocational (Career)				
Political				
Religious				
Relationship				
Achievement				
Sexual				
Gender				
Ethnic/Cultural				
Interests				
Personality				
Physical				

If you checked "diffused" or "foreclosed" for any areas, take some time to think about what you need to do to move into a moratorium identity status in those areas. How much has your identity in each of the areas listed changed in recent years?

individuality
An important element in adolescent identity development. It consists of two dimensions: self-assertion, the ability to have and communicate a point of view; and separateness, the use of communication patterns to express how one is different from others.

connectedness
An important element in adolescent identity development. It consists of two dimensions: mutuality, sensitivity to and respect for others' views; and permeability, openness to others' views.

ethnic identity
An enduring, basic aspect of the self that includes a sense of membership in an ethnic group and the attitudes and feelings related to that membership.

Researchers also have examined the role of individuality and connectedness in the development of identity. Developmentalist Catherine Cooper and her colleagues (Carlson, Cooper & Hsu, 1990; Cooper & Grotevant, 1989; Grotevant & Cooper, 1985, in press) believe that the presence of a family atmosphere that promotes both individuality and connectedness are important in the adolescent's identity development. **Individuality** *consists of two dimensions: self-assertion, the ability to have and communicate a point of view; and separateness, the use of communication patterns to express how one is different from others.* **Connectedness** *also consists of two dimensions: mutuality, sensitivity to and respect for others' views; and permeability, openness to others' views.* In general, Cooper's research findings reveal that identity formation is enhanced by family relationships that are both individuated, which encourages adolescents to develop their own point of view, and connected, which provides a secure base from which to explore the widening social worlds of adolescence. However, when connectedness is strong and individuation weak, adolescents often have an identity foreclosure status; by contrast, when connectedness is weak, adolescents often reveal an identity confusion status (Archer & Waterman, 1994).

Stuart Hauser and his colleagues (Hauser & Bowlds, 1990; Hauser & others, 1984) also have illuminated family processes that promote the adolescent's identity development. They have found that parents who use *enabling* behaviors (such as explaining, accepting, and giving empathy) facilitate the adolescent's identity development more than do parents who use *constraining* behaviors (such as judging and devaluing). In sum, family interaction styles that give the adolescent the right to question and to be different, within a context of support and mutuality, foster healthy patterns of identity development (Harter, 1990, 1999).

Cultural and Ethnic Aspects of Identity

Erikson was especially sensitive to the role of culture in identity development. He pointed out that, throughout the world, ethnic minority groups have struggled to maintain their cultural identities while blending into the dominant culture (Erikson, 1968). Erikson said that this struggle for an inclusive identity, or identity within the larger culture, has been the driving force in the founding of churches, empires, and revolutions throughout history.

For ethnic minority individuals, adolescence is often a special juncture in their development (Bat-Chava & others, 1997; Kurtz, Cantu, & Phinney, 1996; Spencer & Dornbusch, 1990; Swanson, Spencer, & Petersen, 1998). Although children are aware of some ethnic and cultural differences, most ethnic minority individuals consciously confront their ethnicity for the first time in adolescence. In contrast to children, adolescents have the ability to interpret ethnic and cultural information, to reflect on the past, and to speculate about the future (Wong, 1997).

Jean Phinney (1996) defined **ethnic identity** *as an enduring, basic aspect of the self that includes a sense of membership in an ethnic group and the attitudes and feelings related to that membership.* Thus, for adolescents from ethnic minority groups, the process of identity formation has an added dimension due to exposure to alternative sources of identification—their own ethnic group and the mainstream or dominant culture (Phinney, 2000). Researchers have found that ethnic identity increases with age and that higher levels of ethnic identity are linked with more positive attitudes not only toward one's own ethnic group but toward members of other ethnic groups as well (Phinney, Ferguson, & Tate, 1997). Many ethnic minority adolescents have bicultural identities—identifying in some ways with their ethnic minority group, in other ways with the majority culture (Phinney & Devich-Navarro, 1997).

The ease or difficulty with which ethnic minority adolescents achieve healthy identities depends on a number of factors (Phinney & Rosenthal, 1992; Sidhu, 2000; Tupuola, 2000). Many ethnic minority adolescents have to confront issues of prejudice and discrimination, and barriers to the fulfillment of their goals and aspirations.

In one investigation, ethnic identity exploration was higher among ethnic minority than among White American college students (Phinney & Alipuria, 1990). In this same investigation, ethnic minority college students who had thought about and resolved issues involving their ethnicity had higher self-esteem than did their ethnic minority counterparts who had not. In another investigation, the ethnic identity development of Asian American, African American, Latino, and White American tenth-grade students in Los Angeles was studied (Phinney, 1989). Adolescents from each of the three ethnic minority groups faced a similar need to deal with their ethnic-group identification in a predominantly White American culture. In some instances, the adolescents from the three ethnic minority groups perceived different issues to be important in their resolution of ethnic identity. For Asian American adolescents, pressures to achieve academically and concerns about quotas that make it difficult to get into good colleges were salient issues. Many African American adolescent females discussed their realization that White American standards of beauty (especially hair and skin color) did not apply to them; African American adolescent males were concerned with possible job discrimination and the need to distinguish themselves from a negative societal image of African American male adolescents. For Latino adolescents, prejudice was a recurrent theme, as was the conflict in values between their Latino culture heritage and the majority culture.

The contexts in which ethnic minority youth live influence their identity development (Spencer, 1999). Many ethnic minority youth in the United States live in low-income urban settings where support for developing a positive identity is absent. Many of these youth live in pockets of poverty, are exposed to drugs, gangs, and criminal activities, and interact with other youth and adults who have dropped out of school and/or are unemployed. In such settings, effective organizations and programs for youth can make important contributions to developing a positive identity.

Shirley Heath and Milbrey McLaughlin (1993) studied sixty youth organizations that involved 24,000 adolescents over a period of 5 years. They found that these organizations were especially good at building a sense of ethnic pride in inner-city ethnic youth. Heath and McLaughlin believe that many inner-city youth have too much time on their hands, too little to do, and too few places to go. Inner-city youth want to participate in organizations that nurture them and respond positively to their needs and interests. Organizations that perceive youth as fearful, vulnerable, and lonely, but also frame them as capable, worthy, and eager to have a healthy and productive life contribute in positive ways to the identity development of ethnic minority youth.

"Do you have any idea who I am?"

Exploring Ethnic Identities

An Adolescent Talks About Ethnic Identity

Ethnic Identity Research

Cultural Identity in Canada

Identity, Ethnicity, Religion, and Political Violence

*T*hrough the Eyes of Psychologists

Catherine Cooper, *University of California, Santa Cruz*

"Many ethnic minority youth must bridge 'multiple worlds' in constructing their identities."

Gender and Identity

In Erikson's (1968) classic presentation of identity development, the division of labor between the sexes was reflected in his assertion that males' aspirations were mainly oriented toward career and ideological commitments, while females' were centered around marriage and childbearing. In the 1960s and 1970s researchers found support for Erikson's assertion about gender differences in identity. For example, vocational concerns were more central to the identity of males, and affiliative concerns were more important in the identity of females (La Voie, 1976). However, in the last decade, as females have

SUMMARY TABLE 12.4
Family, Cultural, Ethnic, and Gender Aspects of Identity

Concept	Processes/ Related Ideas	Characteristics/Description
Family Influences on Identity	Their Nature	• Parents are important figures in adolescents' identity development. • Democratic parenting facilities identity development; autocratic and permissive parenting do not. • Both individuality and connectedness in family relations are related to identity development. • Enabling behaviors promote identity development, constraining behaviors restrict it.
Cultural and Ethnic Aspects of Identity	Erikson's View	• Erikson is especially sensitive to culture's role in identity, underscoring that throughout the world ethnic minority groups have struggled to maintain their identities while blending into the majority culture.
	Adolescence as a Special Juncture	• Adolescence is a special juncture in the identity development of ethnic minority individuals because for the first time they consciously confront their ethnic identity.
Gender and Identity	Erikson's View	• In Erikson's view, adolescent males have a stronger vocational identity, adolescent females a stronger social identity involving marriage and family roles.
	Contemporary Research and Theory	• Some researchers have found no sex differences in identity while others argue that relationships and emotional bonds are more central to female than to male identity development.

Some Developmental Models of Girls and Women

developed stronger vocational interests, these gender differences are disappearing (Madison & Foster-Clark, 1996; Waterman, 1985).

Some investigators believe that females and males go through Erikson's stages in different order. One view is that for males, identity formation precedes the stage of intimacy, while for females, intimacy precedes identity (Douvan & Adelson, 1966). These ideas are consistent with the belief that relationships and emotional bonds are more important concerns of females, while autonomy and achievement are more important concerns of males (Gilligan, 1992). In one study, the development of a clear sense of self by adolescent girls was related to their concerns about care and response in relationships (Rogers, 1987). In another investigation, a strong sense of self in college women was associated with their ability to solve problems of care in relationships while staying connected with both self and others (Skoe & Marcia, 1988). Indeed, conceptualization and measurement of identity development in females should include interpersonal content (Patterson, Sochting, & Marcia, 1992).

The task of identity exploration might be more complex for females than for males, in that females might try to establish identities in more domains than males do. In today's world, the options for females have increased and thus can at times be confusing and conflicting, especially for females who hope to successfully integrate family and career roles (Archer, 1994; Josselson, 1994; Streitmatter, 1993).

At this point we have studied a number of ideas about family, cultural, ethnic, and gender aspects of identity. A review of these ideas is presented in summary table 12.4.

Chapter Review

Chapter Review

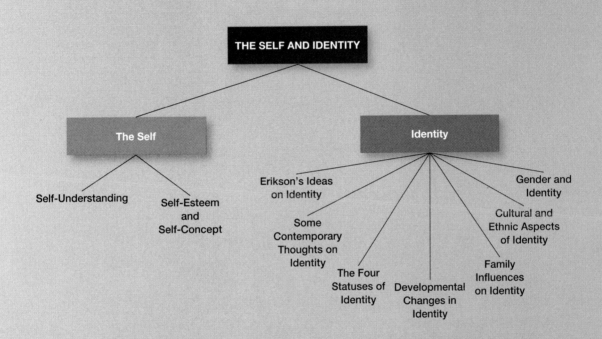

TO OBTAIN A DETAILED REVIEW OF THE CHAPTER, STUDY THESE FOUR SUMMARY TABLES:

- Summary Table 12.1   Self-Understanding   page 380 ◀▥
- Summary Table 12.2   Self-Esteem and Self-Concept   page 383 ◀▥
- Summary Table 12.3   Erikson's Ideas on Identity, and Developmental   page 387 ◀▥
  Changes in Identity
- Summary Table 12.4   Family, Cultural, Ethnic, and Gender Aspects   page 390 ◀▥
  of Identity

Key Terms

self-understanding 372
possible self 376
perspective taking 378
self-esteem 380
self-concept 380
identity versus identity confusion 383

psychosocial moratorium 384
crisis 386
commitment 386
identity diffusion 386
identity foreclosure 386
identity moratorium 386

identity achievement 386
individuality 388
connectedness 388
ethnic identity 388

Key People

John Watson 372
Susan Harter 376
Carl Rogers 376
Hazel Markus 377
Robert Selman 378

Erik Erikson 383
James Marcia 385
Alan Waterman 386
Catherine Cooper 388
Stuart Hauser 388

Jean Phinney 388
Shirley Heath and Milbrey McLaughlin 389

Child Development Resources

***Adolescent Psychological Development:
Rationality, Morality, and Identity (1999)***
by David Moshman
Mahwah, NJ: Erlbaum

A contemporary analysis of several important dimensions of adolescent development, including identity.

The Construction of the Self (1999)
by Susan Harter
New York: Guilford

Leading self theorist and researcher, Susan Harter, provides a contemporary look at how children and adolescents see themselves.

Gandhi (1969)
by Erik Erikson
New York: Norton

The Pulitzer Prize–winning book by Erik Erikson, who developed the concept of identity as a central aspect of adolescent development, analyzes the life of Mahatma Gandhi, the spiritual leader of India in the middle of the twentieth century.

Taking It to the Net

1. Rita's child development teacher wants each student to depict some aspect of child development from infancy to age 6 as a chronological time line represented by descriptions or illustrations. Rita has chosen the development of the self. What behaviors at 6, 12, and 18 months, and at 2, 3, 4, 5, and 6 years of age represent milestones in self-awareness, self-concept, self-understanding, and self-esteem.

2. Thirteen-year-old Amy was adopted out of a Korean orphanage by Americans when she was 4 years old. She is now struggling with an identity crisis. Is she Korean or American? She doesn't feel that she is either. How can Amy best resolve this ethnic identity crisis?

3. Frank is going to write a paper about how boys and girls differ in their identity development. He is looking for a central theme around which to construct his paper. What are the most salient identity issues for boys that are not so salient for girls?

Connect to *http://www.mhhe.com/santrockc9* to find the answers!

Chapter 13

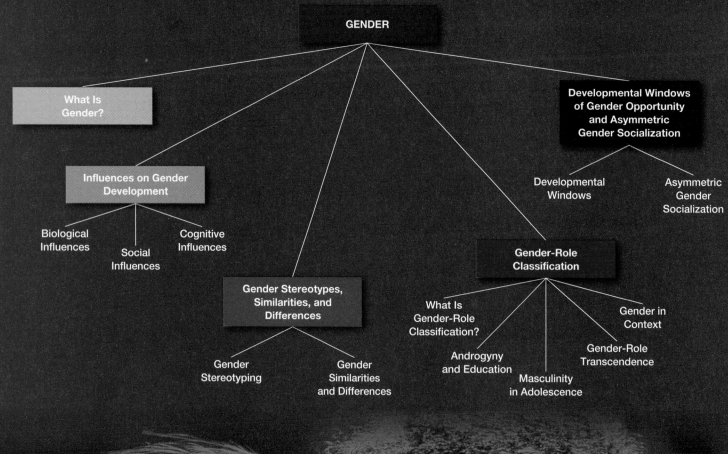

GENERED

What Is
Gender?

Influences on Gender
Development

Biological
Influences

Social
Influences

Cognitive
Influences

Gender Stereotypes,
Similarities, and
Differences

Gender
Stereotyping

Gender
Similarities
and Differences

Developmental Windows
of Gender Opportunity
and Asymmetric
Gender Socialization

Developmental
Windows

Asymmetric
Gender
Socialization

Gender-Role
Classification

What Is
Gender-Role
Classification?

Androgyny
and Education

Masculinity
in Adolescence

Gender-Role
Transcendence

Gender in
Context

To be meek, patient, tactful, modest, honorable, brave, is not to be either manly or womanly, it is to be humane.

Jane Harrison
English Writer, 20th Century

The Story of Jerry Maguire: Gender, Emotion, and Caring

GENDER AND EMOTION researcher Stephanie Shields (1998) recently analyzed the movie *Jerry Maguire* in terms of how it reflects the role of gender in emotions and relationships. In brief, the movie is a "buddy" picture with sports agent Jerry Maguire (played by Tom Cruise) paired with two buddies: the too-short Arizona Cardinals running back Rod Tidwell (played by Cuba Gooding, Jr.) and 6-year-old Ray, son of Jerry's love interest, the accountant Dorothy Boyd (played by Renée Zellweger). Through his buddies, the thinking-but-not-feeling Jerry discovers the right path by connecting to Ray's emotional honesty and African American Rod's devotion to his family. Conversely, the emotionally flamboyant and self-centered Rod, through his White buddy, Jerry, discovers that he must bring passion back to his game to be successful.

The image of nurturing and nurtured males is woven throughout the movie. Jerry's relationship with Ray, the 6-year-old, is a significant theme in the film. Through discovering a caring relationship with Ray, Jerry makes his first genuine move toward emotional maturity. The boy is the guide to the man. Chad, Ray's babysitter, is a good example of appropriate caring by a male.

Males are shown crying in the movie. Jerry sheds tears while writing his mission statement, when thinking about Dorothy's possible move to another city (which also means he would lose Ray), and at the success of his lone client (Rod). Rod is brought to tears when he speaks of his family. Historically, weeping, more than any emotional expression, has been associated with feminine emotion. However, it has increasingly taken on a more prominent role in the male's emotional makeup.

The movie *Jerry Maguire* reflects changes in gender roles as an increasing number of males show an interest in improving their social relationships and

How are gender, emotion and caring portrayed in the movie Jerry Maguire?

achieving emotional maturity. However, as we will see later in this chapter, experts on gender argue that overall females are more competent in their social relationships than males are and that large numbers of males still have a lot of room for improvement in dealing better with their emotions.

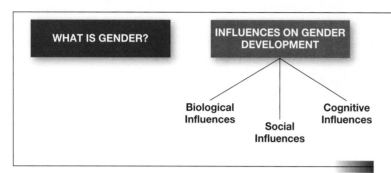

What Is Gender?

What exactly do we mean by gender? **Gender** *is the sociocultural dimension of being female or male.* Two aspects of gender bear special mention: gender identity and gender role. **Gender identity** *is the sense of being female or male, which most children acquire by the time they are 3 years old.* A **gender role** *is a set of expectations that prescribe how females and males should think, act, and feel.*

Influences on Gender Development

How is gender influenced by biology? by children's social experiences? by cognitive factors?

Biological Influences

To understand biological influences, we need to consider heredity and hormones. We also will explore the theoretical views of Freud and Erikson, and the more recent view of evolutionary psychologists.

Heredity and Hormones   It was not until the 1920s that researchers confirmed the existence of human sex chromosomes, the genetic material that determines our sex. As we discussed in chapter 3, "Biological Beginnings," normally have 46 chromosomes arranged in pairs. The 23rd pair may have two X-shaped chromosomes, to produce a female, or it may have both an X-shaped and a Y-shaped chromosome to produce a male ◀▥ P. 73.

Sex hormones are powerful chemicals that are controlled by the master gland in the brain, the pituitary. The two main classes of sex hormones are estrogens and androgens. **Estrogens,** *the most important of which is estradiol, influence the development of female physical sex characteristics and help to regulate the menstrual cycle. Estrogens are produced by the ovaries.* **Androgens,** *the most important of which is testosterone, promote the development of male genitals and secondary sex characteristics.* They influence sexual motivation in both sexes. Androgens are produced by the adrenal glands in males and females, and by the testes in males.

In the first few weeks of gestation, female and male embryos look alike. Male sex organs start to differ from female sex organs when the Y chromosome in the male embryo triggers the secretion of androgens. Low levels of androgens in a female embryo allow the normal development of female sex organs.

Although rare, an imbalance in this system of hormone secretion can occur during fetal development. If there is insufficient androgen in a male embryo or an excess of androgen in the female embryo, the result is an individual with both male and female sex organs, a hermaphrodite. When genetically female (XX chromosomes) infants are born with masculine-looking genitals, surgery can achieve a genital/genetic match. At puberty, production of estrogens influences both physical development and behavior in these females. However, even prior to puberty, these females often behave in a more aggressive, "tomboyish" manner than most

gender
The sociocultural dimension of being male or female.

gender identity
The sense of being female or male, which most children acquire by the time they are 3 years old.

gender role
A set of expectations that prescribes how females and males should think, act, and feel.

estrogens
Hormones, the most important of which is estradiol, that influence the development of female physical sex characteristics and help regulate the menstrual cycle.

androgens
Hormones, the most important of which is testosterone, that promote the development of male genitals and secondary sex characteristics.

girls. They also dress and play in ways that are more characteristic of boys than girls (Ehrhardt, 1987).

Is the "boyish" behavior of these surgically corrected girls due to their prenatal hormones? Or is it the result of their social experiences? Experiments with different animal species reveal that when male hormones are injected into female embryos, the females develop masculine physical traits and behave more aggressively (Hines, 1982). However, as we move from animals to humans, hormones exert less control over behavior. Perhaps, because these girls looked more masculine, they were treated more like boys and so adopted their tomboyish ways.

Sex hormone levels also are related to some cognitive abilities in females and males, especially spatial ability. For example, girls whose glands overproduce testosterone have spatial abilities more similar to those of the average boy than to those of the average girl (Hines, 1990). Boys whose glands underproduce testosterone, and thus are late maturing, have spatial abilities more similar to those of the average girl than to those of the average boy (Kimura, 1989).

Sex hormones are also related to aggression. Violent male criminals have above-average levels of testosterone (Dabbs & others, 1987), and professional football players have higher levels of testosterone than ministers do (Dabbs & Morris, 1990). Researchers have been able to increase the aggressiveness of animals in different species by giving them testosterone.

Freud and Erikson—Anatomy Is Destiny

Both Sigmund Freud and Erik Erikson argued that an individual's genitals influence his or her gender behavior and, therefore, that anatomy is destiny. One of Freud's basic assumptions was that human behavior and history are directly related to reproductive processes. From this assumption arose his belief that gender and sexual behavior are essentially unlearned and instinctual. Erikson (1968) extended Freud's argument, claiming that the psychological differences between males and females stem from their anatomical differences. Erikson argued that, because of genital structure, males are more intrusive and aggressive, females more inclusive and passive. Critics of the anatomy-is-destiny view believe that experience is not given enough credit. The critics say that females and males are more free to choose their gender roles than Freud and Erikson allow. In response to the critics, Erikson modified his view, saying that females in today's world are transcending their biological heritage and correcting society's overemphasis on male intrusiveness.

Gender Resources

Evolutionary Psychology and Gender

Evolutionary psychologists view emphasizes that evolutionary adaptations produced psychological sex differences (Buss, 1995; Buss & Kendrick, 1998) ◀|||| P. 71. Evolutionary psychologists argue that women and men faced different evolutionary pressures in primeval environments when the human species was evolving and that the sexes' different roles in reproduction was the key feature that framed different adaptive problems for females and males.

To support this view of behavior, evolutionary psychologists focus on sexual selection. They suggest that sex-typed features evolved through male competition and led to a reproductive advantage for dominant males. Men sought short-term mating strategies because this allowed them to increase their reproductive advantage by fathering more children. Women also devoted more time to parenting.

Because men competed with other men for access to women, men evolved dispositions that favor violence, competition, and risk taking. Women in turn developed a preference for long-term mates who could protect and support a family. As a consequence, men strived to acquire more resources than other men in order to attract women, and women developed preferences for successful, ambitious men who could provide these resources.

Through the Eyes of Psychologists

Alice Eagly, *Northwestern University*

"Sex differences are adaptations to the differing restrictions and opportunities that a society provides for its males and females."

Alice Eagly's Research

identification theory
A theory that stems from Freud's view that preschool children develop a sexual attraction to the opposite-sex parent, then at 5 to 6 years of age renounce the attraction because of anxious feelings, subsequently identifying with the same-sex parent and unconsciously adopting the same-sex parent's characteristics.

Critics of the evolutionary psychology view argue that humans have the decision-making ability to change their gender behavior and therefore are not locked into the evolutionary past. They also stress that the extensive cross-cultural variation in sex differences and mate preferences provides stronger evidence for the social construction of gender differences than for an evolutionary source. Next, we will explore what some of these social influences are.

An Interactionist View   No one questions the presence of genetic, biochemical, and anatomical differences between the sexes. Even child developmentalists with a strong environmental orientation acknowledge that boys and girls are treated differently because of their physical differences and their different roles in reproduction. The importance of biological factors is not at issue. What is at issue is the directness or indirectness of their effects on social behavior (Huston, 1983; Rose, 1997). For example, if a high androgen level directly influences the central nervous system, which in turn increases activity level, then the biological effect on behavior is direct. By contrast, if a child's high level of androgen produces strong muscle development, which in turn causes others to expect the child to be a good athlete and, in turn, leads the child to participate in sports, then the biological effect on behavior is indirect.

Although virtually everyone thinks that children's behavior as males or females is due to an interaction of biological and environmental factors, an interactionist position means different things to different people (Maccoby, 1997). For some, it suggests that certain environmental conditions are required before preprogrammed dispositions appear. For others, it suggests that a particular environment will have different effects, depending on the child's predispositions. For still others, it means that children shape their environments, including their interpersonal environment, and vice versa. The processes of influence and counterinfluence unfold over time. Throughout development, in this view, males and females actively construct their own versions of acceptable masculine and feminine behavior patterns.

Social Influences

Many social scientists, such as Alice Eagly (1997, 2000; Eagly & Wood, 1999), locate the cause of psychological sex differences not in biologically evolved dispositions but in the contrasting positions and social roles of women and men. In contemporary American society and in most cultures around the world, women have less power and status than men and control fewer resources. Women perform more domestic work than men and spend fewer hours in paid employment. Although most women are in the workforce, they receive lower pay than men and are thinly represented in the highest levels of organizations. Thus, from the perspective of social influences, gender hierarchy and sexual division of labor are important causes of sex-differentiated behavior. As women adapted to roles with less power and less status in society, they showed more cooperative, less dominant profiles than men.

Identification and Social Cognitive Theories   Two prominent theories address the way children acquire masculine and feminine attitudes and behaviors from their parents. **Identification theory** *stems from Freud's view that the preschool child develops a sexual attraction to the opposite-sex parent, then by approximately 5 or 6 years of age renounces this attraction because of anxious feelings, and subsequently identifies with the same-sex parent, unconsciously adopting the same-sex parent's characteristics.* However, today many child developmentalists do not believe that gender development proceeds on the basis of identification, at least in terms of Freud's emphasis on childhood sexual attraction. Children become gender-typed much earlier than 5 or 6 years of age, and they become masculine or feminine even when the same-sex parent is not present in the family.

The **social cognitive theory of gender** *emphasizes that children's gender development occurs through observation and imitation of gender behavior, and through the rewards and punishments children experience for gender-appropriate and -inappropriate behavior.* Unlike identification theory, social cognitive theory argues that sexual attraction to parents is not involved in gender development. (A comparison of identification and social cognitive views is presented in figure 13.1.) Parents often use rewards and punishments to teach their daughters to be feminine ("Karen, you are being a good girl when you play gently with your doll") and masculine ("Keith, a boy as big as you is not supposed to cry"). Peers also extensively reward and punish gender behavior. And by observing adults and peers at home, at school, in the neighborhood, and on television, children are widely exposed to a myriad of models who display masculine and feminine behavior. Critics of the social cognitive view argue that gender development is not as passively acquired as it indicates. Later we will discuss the cognitive views of gender development, which stress that children actively construct their gender world.

Parental Influences   Once the label *girl* or *boy* is assigned by the obstetrician, virtually everyone, from parents to siblings to strangers, begins treating the infant differently.

In one study, an infant girl, Avery, was dressed in a neutral outfit of overalls and a T-shirt (Brooks-Gunn & Matthews, 1979). People responded to her differently if they thought she was a girl rather than a boy. People who thought she was a girl made comments like "Isn't she cute. What a sweet little, innocent thing." By contrast, people who thought the baby was a boy made remarks like "I bet he is a tough little customer. He will be running around all over the place and causing trouble in no time."

In general, parents even hope that their offspring will be a boy. In one investigation in the 1970s, 90 percent of the men and 92 percent of the women wanted their

Theory	Processes	Outcome
Freud's identification theory	Sexual attraction to opposite-sex parent at 3–5 years of age; anxiety about sexual attraction and subsequent identification with same-sex parent at 5–6 years of age	Gender behavior similar to that of same-sex parent
Social learning theory	Rewards and punishments of gender-appropriate and -inappropriate behavior by adults and peers; observation and imitation of models' masculine and feminine behavior	Gender behavior

Figure **13.1**

Parents influence their children's gender development by action and example.

social cognitive theory of gender
This theory emphasizes that children's gender development occurs through observation and imitation of gender behavior, and through rewards and punishments they experience for gender-appropriate and -inappropriate behavior.

ADVENTURES FOR THE MIND

Gender Expectations

First imagine that this is a photograph of a baby girl. What expectations would you have for her? Then imagine that this is a photograph of a baby boy. What expectations would you have for him?

Through the Eyes of Psychologists

Eleanor Maccoby, *Stanford University*

"In childhood, boys and girls tend to gravitate toward others of their own sex. Boys' and girls' groups develop distinct cultures with different agendas."

firstborn child to be a boy (Peterson & Peterson, 1973). In a more recent study, parents still preferred a boy as the firstborn child—75 percent of the men and 79 percent of the women had that preference (Hamilton, 1991).

In some countries, a male child is so preferred over a female child that many mothers will abort a female fetus after fetal testing procedures, such as amniocentesis and sonograms, that reveal the fetus' sex. For example, in South Korea, where fetal testing to determine sex is common, male births exceed female births by 14 percent, in contrast to a worldwide average of 5 percent.

Both mothers and fathers are psychologically important in children's gender development. Mothers are more consistently given responsibility for nurturance and physical care; fathers are more likely to engage in playful interaction and be given responsibility for ensuring that boys and girls conform to existing cultural norms. And whether or not they have more influence on them, fathers are more involved in socializing their sons than in socializing their daughters (Lamb, 1986). Fathers seem to play an especially important part in gender-role development—they are more likely to act differently toward sons and daughters than mothers are, and thus contribute more to distinctions between the genders (Huston, 1983).

Many parents encourage boys and girls to engage in different types of play and activities (Fagot, 1995; Fisher-Thompson & others, 1993). Girls are more likely to be given dolls to play with during childhood and, when old enough, are more likely to be assigned babysitting duties. Girls are encouraged to be more nurturant and emotional than boys, and their fathers are more likely to engage in aggressive play with their sons than with their daughters. As adolescents increase in age, parents permit boys more freedom than girls, allowing them to be away from home and stay out later without supervision. When parents place severe restrictions on their adolescent sons, it has been found to be especially disruptive to the sons' development (Baumrind, 1989).

In recent years, the idea that parents are the critical socializing agents in gender-role development has come under fire (Huston, 1983). Parents are only one of many sources through which the individual learns gender roles. Culture, schools, peers, the media, and other family members are others. Yet it is important to guard against swinging too far in this direction because—especially in the early years of development—parents are important influences on gender development.

Peer Influences   Parents provide the earliest discrimination of gender roles in development, but before long, peers join the societal process of responding to and modeling masculine and feminine behavior. Children who play in sex-appropriate activities tend to be rewarded for doing so by their peers. Those who play in cross-sexed activities tend to be criticized by their peers or left to play alone. Children show a clear preference for being with and liking same-sex peers (Buhrmester, 1993; Maccoby, 1998), and this tendency usually becomes stronger during the middle and late childhood years (Hayden-Thomson, Rubin, & Hymel, 1987). After extensive observations of elementary school playgrounds, two researchers characterized the play settings as "gender school," pointing out that boys teach one another

As reflected in this tug-of-war battle between boys and girls, the playground in elementary school is like going to "gender school."
Elementary school children show a clear preference for being with and liking same-sex peers. Eleanor Maccoby has studied children's
gender development for many years. She believes peers play especially strong roles in socializing each other about gender roles.

the required masculine behavior and enforce it strictly (Luria & Herzog, 1985). Girls also pass on the female culture and mainly congregate with one another. Individual "tomboy" girls can join boys' activities without losing their status in the girls' groups, but the reverse is not true for boys, reflecting our society's greater sex-typing pressure for boys.

Peer demands for conformity to gender role become especially intense during adolescence. While there is greater social mixing of males and females during early adolescence, in both formal groups and in dating, peer pressure is strong for the adolescent boy to be the very best male possible and for the adolescent girl to be the very best female possible.

School and Teacher Influences

In certain ways, both girls and boys might receive an unfair education (Sadker & Sadker, 1994). For example:

- Girls' learning problems are not identified as often as boys' are.
- Boys are given the lion's share of attention in schools.
- Girls start school testing higher than boys in every academic subject, yet they graduate from high school scoring lower than boys do on the SAT exam.
- Pressure to achieve is more likely to be heaped on boys than on girls.

Consider the following research study (Sadker & Sadker, 1986). Observers were trained to collect data in more than 100 fourth-, sixth-, and eighth-grade classrooms. At all three grade levels, male students were involved in more interactions with teachers than female students were, and male students were given more attention than their female counterparts were. Male students were also given more remediation, more criticism, and more praise than female students. Further,

Shortchanging Girls,
Shortchanging America
Positive Expectations for Girls
War on Boys
Center for Gender Equity

girls with strong math abilities are given lower-quality instruction than their male counterparts are (Eccles, 1993).

Myra and David Sadker (1994), who have been studying gender discrimination in schools for more than two decades, believe that many educators are unaware of the subtle ways in which gender infiltrates the school's environment. Their hope is that sexism can be eradicated in the nation's schools.

A special concern is that most middle and junior high schools consist of independent, masculine learning environments, which appear better suited to the learning style of the average adolescent boy than to that of the average adolescent girl (Huston & Alvarez, 1990). Compared to elementary schools, middle and junior high schools provide a more impersonal environment, which meshes better with the autonomous orientation of male adolescents than with the relationship, connectedness orientation of female adolescents.

Gender and the Media

The messages carried by the media about what is appropriate or inappropriate for males and for females also are important influences on gender development (Calvert, 1999).

A special concern is the way females are pictured on television. In the 1970s, it became apparent that television was portraying females as less competent than males. For example, about 70 percent of the prime-time characters were males, men were more likely to be shown in the workforce, women were more likely to be shown as housewives and in romantic roles, men were more likely to appear in higher-status jobs and in a greater diversity of occupations, and men were presented as more aggressive and constructive (Sternglanz & Serbin, 1974).

Television networks have become more sensitive to how males and females are portrayed on television shows. Consequently, many programs now focus on divorced families, cohabitation, and women in high-status roles. Yet with this shift in programming, researchers continued to find that television portrayed males as more competent than females (Durkin, 1985). In one investigation, young adolescent girls indicated that television occupations were more extremely stereotyped than real-life occupations were (Wroblewski & Huston, 1987).

Television directed at adolescents might be the most extreme in its portrayal of the sexes, especially of teenage girls (Beal, 1994). In one study, teenage girls were shown as primarily concerned with dating, shopping, and their appearance (Campbell, 1988). They were rarely depicted as interested in school or career plans. Attractive girls were often portrayed as "airheads" and intelligent girls as unattractive.

Another highly stereotyped form of programming specifically targeted for teenage viewers is rock music videos. What adolescents see on MTV and rock music videos is highly stereotyped and slanted toward a male audience (for example, the *Beavis and Butt-Head* show). In music videos, females are twice as likely as in prime-time programming to be dressed provocatively, and aggressive acts are often perpetrated by females; for example, in one scene a woman pushes a man to the ground, holds him down, and kisses him. MTV has been described as a teenage boy's "dreamworld," filled with beautiful, aroused women who outnumber men, who seek out and even assault men to have sex, and who always mean yes even when they say no.

If television can communicate sexist messages and influence adolescents' gender behavior, might nonstereotyped gender messages on television reduce sexist behavior? One major effort to reduce gender stereotyping was the television series *Freestyle* (Johnston, Etteman, & Davidson, 1980; Williams, LaRose, & Frost, 1981). The series was designed to counteract career stereotypes in 9- to 12-year-olds. After watching *Freestyle*, both girls and boys were more open to nontraditional career possibilities. The benefits of *Freestyle* were greatest for students who viewed the TV series in the classroom and who participated in discussion groups about the show led by their teacher. Classroom discussion was especially helpful in altering boys' beliefs, which were initially more stereotyped than girls'.

Gender and Television
Girls and Technology
Telementoring for Girls

However, in one study with 12- to 13-year-olds, the strategy of showing non-stereotyped television programming backfired (Durkin & Hutchins, 1984). The young adolescents watched sketches that portrayed people with nontraditional jobs, such as a male secretary, a male nurse, and a female plumber. After viewing the series, the adolescents still held traditional views about careers, and in some cases were more disapproving of the alternative careers than they had been before watching the TV sketches. Thus, once stereotypes are strongly in place, they are difficult to change.

Gender stereotyping also appears in the print media. Females and males are portrayed with different personalities, and perform different tasks, in children's books (Matlin, 1993). Males are described and pictured as clever, industrious, and brave. They acquire skills, earn fame and fortune, and explore. By contrast, females tend to be passive, dependent, and kind. They cook and clean up (Bordelon, 1985; Marten & Matlin, 1976).

In one study, 150 children's books were analyzed for gender-role content (Kortenhaus & Demarest, 1993). It was found that the frequency with which females and males are depicted in the stories has become more equal over the past 50 years. The roles played by females and males in the books have changed in a more subtle way. Girls are now being pictured in more instrumental activities (behavior that is instrumental in attaining a goal), but in the portrayals they are as passive and dependent as they were depicted as being 50 years ago! Boys are occasionally shown as passive and dependent today, but the activities they are pictured in are no less instrumental than they were 50 years ago.

Today, with effort, parents and teachers can locate interesting books in which girls and women are presented as appropriate models. And it is worth the effort (Matlin, 1993).

Cognitive Influences

So far we have explored biological and social influences on gender. Cognitive factors also influence gender.

Cognitive Developmental Theory

In the **cognitive developmental theory of gender,** *children's gender typing occurs after they have developed a concept of gender. Once they consistently conceive of themselves as male or female, children often organize their world on the basis of gender.* Initially developed by psychologist Lawrence Kohlberg (1966), this theory argues that gender development proceeds in the following way: A child realizes, "I am a girl; I want to do girl things; therefore, the opportunity to do girl things is rewarding." Having acquired the ability to categorize, children then strive toward consistency in the use of categories and behavior. Kohlberg based his ideas on Piaget's cognitive developmental theory. As children's cognitive development matures, so does their understanding of gender. Although 2-year-olds can apply the labels *boy* and *girl* correctly to themselves and others, their concept of gender is simple and concrete. Preschool children rely on physical features, such as dress and hairstyle, to decide who falls into which category. Girls are people with long hair, they think, whereas boys are people who never wear dresses. Many preschool children believe that people can change their own gender at will by getting a haircut or a new outfit. They do not yet have the cognitive machinery to think of gender as adults do. According to Kohlberg, all the reinforcement in the world won't modify that fact. However, by the concrete operational stage (the third stage in Piaget's theory, entered at about 6 or 7 years of age), children understand gender constancy—that a male is still a male regardless of whether he wears pants or a skirt, or his hair is short or long (Tavris & Wade, 1984). When their concept of gender constancy is clearly established, children are motivated to become a competent, or "proper," girl or boy. Consequently, she or he finds female or male activities rewarding and imitates the behavior of same-sex models.

cognitive developmental theory of gender
In this view, children's gender-typing occurs after they have developed a concept of gender. Once they begin to consistently conceive of themselves as male or female, children often organize their world on the basis of gender.

schema
A cognitive structure or network of associations that organizes and guides an individual's perception.

gender schema
A cognitive structure that organizes the world in terms of male and female.

gender schema theory
According to this theory, an individual's attention and behavior are guided by an internal motivation to conform to gender-based sociocultural standards and stereotypes.

Theory	Processes	Emphasis
Cognitive developmental theory	Development of gender constancy, especially around 6–7 years of age, when conservation skills develop; after children develop the ability to consistently conceive of themselves as male or female, children often organize their world on the basis of gender, such as selecting same-sex models to imitate	Cognitive readiness facilitates sex typing
Gender schema theory	Sociocultural emphasis on gender-based standards and stereotypes; children's attention and behavior are guided by an internal motivation to conform to these gender-based standards and stereotypes, allowing children to interpret the world through a network of gender-organized thoughts	Gender schemas reinforce gender typing

Figure **13.2**

The Development of Gender-Typed Behavior According to the Cognitive Developmental and Gender Schema Theories of Gender Development

Gender Schema Theory   Remember from our discussion in chapter 8, "Information Processing," that a **schema** *is a cognitive structure, or network of associations, that organizes and guides a child's perceptions* ◀▥ P. 250. A **gender schema** *organizes the world in terms of female and male.* **Gender schema theory** *states that an individual's attention and behavior are guided by an internal motivation to conform to gender-based sociocultural standards and stereotypes* (Bem, 1981; Levy & Carter, 1989; Rodgers, 2000; Rose & Martin, 1993). Gender schema theory suggests that "gender typing" occurs when individuals are ready to encode and organize information along the lines of what is considered appropriate or typical for males and females in a society. Whereas Kohlberg's cognitive developmental theory argues that a particular cognitive prerequisite—gender constancy—is necessary for gender typing, gender schema theory states that a general readiness to respond to and categorize information on the basis of culturally defined gender roles fuels children's gender-typing activities. A comparison of the cognitive developmental theory and gender schema theory is presented in figure 13.2.

While researchers have shown that the appearance of gender constancy in children is related to their level of cognitive development, especially the acquisition of conservation skills (which supports the cognitive developmental theory of gender) (Serbin & Sprafkin, 1986). But researchers have also shown that young children who are pre-gender-constant have more gender-role knowledge than the cognitive developmental theory of gender predicts (which supports gender schema theory) (Carter & Levy, 1988).

The Role of Language in Gender Development
Gender is present in the language children use and encounter (Hort & Leinbach, 1993). The nature of the language children hear can be sexist. That is, the English language contains gender bias, especially through the use of *he* and *man* to refer to everyone. For example, in one investigation, mothers and their 1- to 3-year-old children looked at popular children's books, such as *The Three Bears,* together (DeLoache, Cassidy, & Carpenter, 1987). The three bears were almost always referred to as boys: 95 percent of all characters of indeterminate gender were referred to by mothers as males.

At this point we have studied a number of ideas about what gender is and biological, cognitive, and social influences. A review of these ideas is presented in summary table 13.1. Next, we will continue our examination of gender by focusing on stereotypes, similarities, and differences.

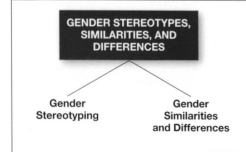

Gender Stereotypes, Similarities, and Differences

How pervasive is gender stereotyping? What are the real differences between boys and girls?

Gender Stereotyping

Gender stereotypes *are broad categories that reflect impressions and beliefs about what behavior is appropriate for females and males.* All stereotypes, whether they are based

SUMMARY TABLE 13.1
What Is Gender? and Biological, Social, and Cognitive Influences

Concept	Processes/ Related Ideas	Characteristics/Description
What Is Gender?	Its Nature	• Gender is the social dimension of being male or female. • A gender role is a set of expectations that prescribes how females or males should think, act, and feel.
Influences on Gender Development	Biological Influences	• The 23rd pair of chromosomes determines our sex. Ordinarily, females have two X chromosomes, males one X and one Y. • Chromosomes determine anatomical sex differences, but culture and society strongly influence gender. • The two main classes of hormones are androgens and estrogens. • The hormones from the testes (androgens) determine whether the organism will have male genitals (if androgens are secreted) or female genitals (if androgens are not secreted). • Erikson's theory promotes the idea that anatomy is destiny. • In the evolutionary psychology view, evolutionary adaptations produced psychological sex differences that are especially present in sexual selection.
	Social Influences	• In the social roles view, women have less power and status than men and control fewer resources. In this view, gender hierarchy and sexual division of labor are important causes of sex-differentiated behavior. • Both identification and social cognitive theory emphasize the adoption of parents' gender characteristics. • Parents and other adults also might assign gender roles to children and reward or punish behavior along gender lines. • Peers are especially adept at rewarding gender-appropriate behavior. • There is still concern about gender equity in education. • Despite improvements, TV still portrays males as more competent than females.
	Cognitive Influences	• Both cognitive developmental and gender schema theories emphasize the role of cognition in gender development. • Gender is present in the language children use and encounter. This language is often sexist.

on gender, ethnicity, or other groupings, refer to an image of what the typical member of a particular social category is like. The world is extremely complex. Every day we are confronted with thousands of different stimuli. The use of stereotypes is one way we simplify this complexity. If we simply assign a label (such as *soft*) to someone, we then have much less to consider when we think about the individual. However, once labels are assigned they are remarkably difficult to abandon, even in the face of contrary evidence.

Many stereotypes are so general they are very ambiguous. Consider the stereotypes for "masculine" and "feminine." Diverse behaviors can be called on to support each stereotype, such as scoring a touchdown or growing facial hair for "masculine" and playing with dolls or wearing lipstick for "feminine." The stereotype may be modified in the face of cultural change. At one point in history, muscular development may be thought of as masculine; at another point, masculinity might be associated with a more lithe, slender physique. The behaviors popularly agreed upon as reflecting a stereotype may also fluctuate according to socioeconomic circumstances. For example, lower socioeconomic groups might be more likely than higher socioeconomic groups to include "rough and tough" as part of a masculine stereotype.

gender stereotypes
Broad categories that reflect impressions and beliefs about what behavior is appropriate for females and males.

If you are going to generalize about women, you will find yourself up to here in exceptions.

Dolores Hitchens
American Mystery Writer, 20th Century

Gender Stereotyping

Even though the behaviors that are supposed to fit the stereotype often do not, the label itself can have significant consequences for the individual. Labeling a male "feminine" and a female "masculine" can produce significant social reactions to the individuals in terms of status and acceptance in groups, for example.

How widespread is feminine and masculine stereotyping? According to a far-ranging study of college students in thirty countries, stereotyping of females and males is pervasive (Williams & Best, 1982). Males were widely believed to be dominant, independent, aggressive, achievement oriented, and enduring, while females were widely believed to be nurturant, affiliative, less esteemed, and more helpful in times of distress.

In a more recent investigation, women and men who lived in more highly developed countries perceived themselves as being more similar to each other than did women and men who lived in less-developed countries (Williams & Best, 1989). In the more highly developed countries, women were more likely to attend college and be gainfully employed. Thus, as sexual equality increases, male and female stereotypes, as well as actual behavioral differences, may diminish. In this investigation, women were more likely to perceive similarity between the sexes than men were (Williams & Best, 1989). And the sexes were perceived more similarly in Christian than in Muslim societies.

Gender stereotyping also changes developmentally. Stereotypic gender beliefs increase during the preschool years, peak in the early elementary school years, and then decrease in the middle and late elementary school years (Bigler, Liben, & Yekel, 1992). In one recent study, age-related decreases in gender stereotyping were related to the acquisition of cognitive skills (Bigler & Liben, in press). Next, we go beyond stereotyping and examine the similarities and differences between the sexes.

There is more difference within the sexes than between them.

Ivy Compton-Burnett
English Novelist, 20th Century

Gender Similarities and Differences

As we examine some differences between the sexes, keeping in mind that (a) the differences are averages—not all females versus all males; (b) even when differences are reported, there is considerable overlap between the sexes; and (c) the differences may be due primarily to biological factors, sociocultural factors, or both.

Physical/Biological   From conception on, females are less likely than males to develop physical or mental disorders. Estrogen strengthens the immune system, making females more resistant to infection, for example. Female hormones also signal the liver to produce more "good" cholesterol, which makes their blood vessels more elastic than males'. Testosterone triggers the production of low-density lipoprotein, which clogs blood vessels. Males have twice the risk of coronary disease as females. Higher levels of stress hormones cause faster clotting in males, but also higher blood pressure than in females. Adult females have about twice the body fat of their male counterparts, most of it concentrated around breasts and hips. In males, fat is more likely to go to the abdomen. On the average, males grow to be 10 percent taller than females. Male hormones promote the growth of long bones; female hormones stop such growth at puberty.

Similarity was the rule rather than the exception in a recent study of metabolic activity in the brains of females and males (Gur & others, 1995). The exceptions involved areas of the brain that are linked with emotional expression and physical expression (which are more active in females). Overall, though, there are many physical differences between females and males. Are there as many cognitive differences?

"So according to the stereotype, you can put two and two together, but I can read the handwriting on the wall."

Cognitive   According to a classic review of gender differences in 1974, Eleanor Maccoby and Carol Jacklin (1974) concluded that males have better math skills and better visuospatial ability (the kind of skills an architect needs to design a building's angles and dimensions), while females have better verbal abilities. More recently, Maccoby (1987) revised her conclusions about several gender dimensions. She said that the accumulation of research evidence now suggests that differences in verbal ability between females and males have virtually disappeared, but that the math and visuospatial differences still exist. However, in recent analyses involving the National Assessment of Educational Progress (1996, 1997), there were no differences in the average math scores of eighth- and twelfth-grade females and males, although at the fourth grade, boys did outperform girls in math.

Some experts in the gender area, such as Janet Shibley Hyde (1993), believe that the cognitive differences between females and males have been exaggerated. For example, Hyde observes that there is considerable overlap in the distributions of females' and males' scores on math and visuospatial tasks. Figure 13.3 shows that although males outperform females on visuospatial tasks, the scores overlap substantially. Thus, while the *average* difference favors males, many females have higher scores on visuospatial tasks than most males do.

Socioemotional   Four areas of socioemotional development in which gender has been studied are relationships, aggression, emotion, and achievement. Sociolinguist Deborah Tannen (1990) distinguishes between rapport talk and report talk. **Rapport talk** *is the language of conversation and a way of establishing connections and negotiating relationships.* **Report talk** *is talk that gives information. Public speaking is an example of report talk.* Males hold center stage through report talk with such verbal performances as story telling, joking, and lecturing with information. By contrast, females enjoy private rapport talk more and conversation that is relationship-oriented.

Tannen says that boys and girls grow up in different worlds of talk—parents, siblings, peers, teachers, and others talk to boys and girls differently. The play of boys and girls is also different. Boys tend to play in large groups that are hierarchically structured, and their groups usually have a leader who tells the others what to do and how to do it. Boys' games have winners and losers and often are the subject of arguments. And boys often boast of their skill and argue about who is best at what. In contrast, girls are more likely to play in small groups or pairs and at the center of a girl's world is often a best friend. In girls' friendships and peer groups, intimacy is pervasive. Turn taking is more characteristic of girls' games than of boys' games. And much of the time, girls simply like to sit and talk with each other, concerned more about being liked by others than jockeying for status in some obvious way.

In sum, Tannen, like other gender experts such as Carol Gilligan, whose ideas you will read about in the next chapter, "Moral Development," believes that girls are more relationship-oriented than boys—and that this relationship orientation should be prized as a skill in our culture more than it currently is.

One of the most consistent gender differences is that boys are more physically aggressive than girls. Boys also are more active than girls. The difference in physical aggression is especially pronounced when adolescents are provoked. These differences occur across cultures and appear very early in children's development. However, researchers have found fewer gender differences in verbal aggression and in some cases no differences.

An important skill is to be able to regulate and control your emotions and behavior. Males usually show less self-regulation than females (Eisenberg, Martin, & Fabes, 1996), and this low self-control can translate into behavioral problems.

For some areas of achievement, gender differences are so large they can best be described as nonoverlapping. For example, no major league baseball players are female;

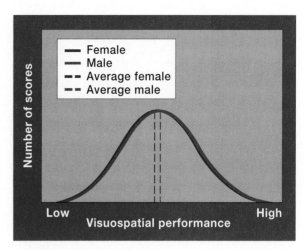

Figure **13.3**

Visuospatial Performance of Males and Females

Notice that, although an average male's visuospatial performance is higher than an average female's, the overlap between the sexes is substantial. Not all males have better visuospatial performance than all females— the substantial overlap indicates that, although the average score of males is higher, many females outperform many males on such tasks.

rapport talk
The language of conversation and a way of establishing connections and negotiating relationships; more characteristic of females than of males.

report talk
Talk that conveys information; more characteristic of males than of females.

Gender and Communication

*W*hat are little boys made of?
Frogs and snails
and puppy dogs' tails.
What are little girls made of?
Sugar and spice
And all that's nice

J.O. Halliwell
English Author, 19th Century

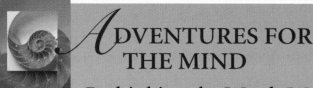

ADVENTURES FOR THE MIND

Rethinking the Words We Use in Gender Worlds

SEVERAL DECADES AGO, the word *dependency* was used to describe the relational orientation of femininity. Dependency took on negative connotations for females—for instance, that families can't take care of themselves and males can. Today, the term *dependency* is being replaced by the term *relational abilities,* which has much more positive connotations (Caplan & Caplan, 1999). Rather than being thought of as dependent, women are now more often described as skilled in forming and maintaining relationships. Make up a list of words that you associate with masculinity and a list of words you associate with femininity. Do these words have any negative connotations for males or females? For the words that do have negative connotations, think about replacements for them that have more positive connotations.

and 96 percent of all registered nurses are female. In contrast, many measures of achievement-related behaviors do not reveal gender differences. For example, girls show just as much persistence at tasks. The question of whether males and females differ in their expectations for success at various achievement tasks is not yet settled.

Gender Controversy Not all psychologists agree that psychological differences between females and males are rare or small. Alice Eagly (1996) stated that such a belief arose from a feminist commitment to similarity between the sexes as a route to political equality, and from piecemeal and inadequate interpretations of relevant empirical research. Many feminists express a fear that differences between females and males will be interpreted as deficiencies in females and as biologically based, which could promote the old stereotypes that women are inferior to men (Unger & Crawford, 2000). According to Eagly, contemporary psychology has produced a large body of research that reveals that behavior is sex differentiated to varying extents and that the differences are socially induced.

Evolutionary psychologist David Buss (1995) argues that men and women differ psychologically in those domains in which they have faced different adaptive problems across their evolutionary history. In all other domains, predicts Buss, the sexes will be found to be psychologically similar. He cites males' superiority in the cognitive domain of spatial rotation. This ability is essential for hunting, in which the trajectory of a projectile must anticipate the trajectory of a prey animal as each moves through space and time. Buss also cites a sex difference in casual sex, with men engaging in this behavior more than women do. In one study, men said that ideally they would like to have more than eighteen sex partners in their lifetime, whereas women stated that ideally they would like to have only four or five (Buss & Schmitt, 1993). In another study, 75 percent of the men but none of the women approached by an attractive stranger of the opposite sex consented to a request for sex (Clark & Hatfield, 1989). Such sex differences, says Buss, are exactly the type predicted by evolutionary psychology, since multiple sexual liaisons improve the likelihood that the male will pass on his genes. A woman's contribution to the gene pool is improved by securing resources for her offspring, which is promoted more effectively by a monogamous relationship.

In sum, controversy continues over whether sex differences are rare and small or common and large. Such controversy is evidence that gender is a political issue.

At this point, we have studied a number of ideas about gender stereotypes, similarities, and differences. A review of these ideas is presented in summary table 13.2. Next, we will continue our exploration of gender by examining how gender roles can be classified.

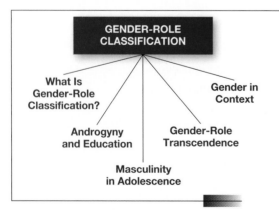

Gender-Role Classification

Not very long ago, it was accepted that boys should grow up to be masculine and girls to be feminine, that boys are made of "frogs and snails" and girls are made of "sugar and spice and all that is nice." Let's further explore such gender classifications of boys and girls as "masculine" and "feminine."

What Is Gender-Role Classification?

In the past, a well-adjusted boy was supposed to be independent, aggressive, and powerful. A well-adjusted girl was supposed to be dependent, nurturant, and

SUMMARY TABLE 13.2
Gender Stereotypes, Similarities, and Differences

Concept	Processes/ Related Ideas	Characteristics/Description
Gender Stereotyping	The Nature of Gender Stereotypes	• Gender stereotypes are widespread around the world, especially emphasizing the male's power and the female's nurturance.
Gender Similarities and Differences	Physical/Biological	• Physical and biological differences between males and females are substantial.
	Cognitive	• Males are often better at math and visuospatial skills. However, some experts, such as Hyde, argue that cognitive differences between males and females have been exaggerated.
	Socioemotional	• Males are more physically aggressive and active than females, while females are often more likely to focus on social relationships.
	Gender Controversy	• There is considerable controversy about how similar or different females and males are in a number of areas.

uninterested in power. The masculine characteristics were considered to be healthy and good by society; the feminine characteristics were considered undesirable.

In the 1970s, as both females and males became dissatisfied with the burdens imposed by their stereotypic roles, alternatives to femininity and masculinity were proposed. Instead of describing masculinity and femininity as a continuum in which more of one means less of the other, it was proposed that individuals could have both masculine and feminine traits. This thinking led to the development of the concept of **androgyny,** *the presence of desirable masculine and feminine characteristics in the same person* (Bem, 1977; Spence & Helmreich, 1978). The androgynous boy might be assertive (masculine) and nurturant (feminine). The androgynous girl might be powerful (masculine) and sensitive to others' feelings (feminine).

Measures have been developed to assess androgyny. One of the most widely used measures is the Bem Sex-Role Inventory. To see whether your gender-role classification is masculine, feminine, or androgynous, see figure 13.4. Based on their responses to the items in the Bem Sex-Role Inventory, individuals are classified as having one of four gender-role orientations: masculine, feminine, androgynous, or undifferentiated (see figure 13.5). The androgynous individual is simply a female or a male who has a high degree of both feminine (expressive) and masculine (instrumental) traits. No new characteristics are used to describe the androgynous individual. A feminine individual is high on feminine (expressive) traits and low on masculine (instrumental) traits; a masculine individual shows the reverse of these traits. An undifferentiated person is not high on feminine or masculine traits.

Gender experts, such as Sandra Bem, argue that androgynous individuals are more flexible, competent, and mentally healthy than their masculine or feminine counterparts. To some degree, though, deciding on which gender-role classification is best depends on the context involved. For example, in close relationships, feminine and androgynous orientations might be more desirable because of the expressive nature of close relationships. However, masculine and androgynous orientations might be more desirable in traditional academic and work settings because of the achievement demands in these contexts.

androgyny
The presence of desirable masculine and feminine characteristics in the same person.

Androgyny

The following items are from the Bem Sex-Role Inventory. To find out whether you score as androgynous, first rate yourself on each item, on a scale from 1 (never or almost never true) to 7 (always or almost always true).

1. self-reliant	21. reliable	41. warm
2. yielding	22. analytical	42. solemn
3. helpful	23. sympathetic	43. willing to take a stand
4. defends own beliefs	24. jealous	44. tender
5. cheerful	25. has leadership abilities	45. friendly
6. moody	26. sensitive to the needs of others	46. aggressive
7. independent	27. truthful	47. gullible
8. shy	28. willing to take risks	48. inefficient
9. conscientious	29. understanding	49. acts as a leader
10. athletic	30. secretive	50. childlike
11. affectionate	31. makes decisions easily	51. adaptable
12. theatrical	32. compassionate	52. individualistic
13. assertive	33. sincere	53. does not use harsh language
14. flatterable	34. self-sufficient	54. unsystematic
15. happy	35. eager to soothe hurt feelings	55. competitive
16. strong personality	36. conceited	56. loves children
17. loyal	37. dominant	57. tactful
18. unpredictable	38. soft-spoken	58. ambitious
19. forceful	39. likable	59. gentle
20. feminine	40. masculine	60. conventional

Scoring

(a) Add up your ratings for items 1, 4, 7, 10, 13, 16, 19, 22, 25, 28, 31, 34, 37, 40, 43, 46, 49, 55, and 58. Divide the total by 20. That is your masculinity score.

(b) Add up your ratings for items 2, 5, 8, 11, 14, 17, 20, 23, 26, 29, 32, 35, 38, 41, 44, 47, 50, 53, 56, and 59. Divide the total by 20. That is your femininity score.

(c) If your masculinity score is above 4.9 (the approximate median for the masculinity scale), and your femininity score is above 4.9 (the approximate femininity median), then you would be classified as androgynous on Bem's scales.

Figure 13.4

The Bem Sex-Role Inventory: Are You Androgynous?

Androgyny and Education

Can and should androgyny be taught to students? In general, it is easier to teach androgyny to girls than to boys and easier to teach it before the middle school grades. For example, in one study, a gender curriculum was put in place for one year in the kindergarten, fifth, and ninth grades (Guttentag & Bray, 1976). It involved books, discussion materials, and classroom exercises with an androgynous bent. The program was most successful with the fifth-graders, least successful with the ninth-graders. The ninth-graders, especially the boys, showed a boomerang effect, in which they had more traditional gender-role attitudes after the year of androgynous instruction than before it.

Despite such mixed findings, the advocates of androgyny programs believe that traditional sex-typing is harmful for all students and especially has prevented many girls from experiencing equal opportunity. The detractors argue that androgynous educational programs are too value-laden and ignore the diversity of gender roles in our society.

Psychological Study of Males

Male Issues

Exploring Masculinity

Masculinity in Adolescence

There is a special concern about boys who adopt a strong masculine role in adolescence, because this is increasingly being found to be associated with problem behaviors. Joseph Pleck (1995) believes that what defines traditional masculinity in many

Western cultures includes behaviors that do not have social approval but nonetheless validate the adolescent boy's masculinity. That is, in the male adolescent culture, male adolescents perceive that they will be thought of as more masculine if they engage in premarital sex, drink alcohol and take drugs, and participate in illegal delinquent activities.

Gender-Role Transcendence

Some critics of androgyny say enough is enough and that there is too much talk about gender. They believe that androgyny is less of a panacea than originally envisioned (Paludi, 1999). An alternative is **gender-role transcendence,** *the view that when an individual's competence is at issue, it should be conceptualized on a personal basis, rather than on the basis of masculinity, femininity, or androgyny* (Pleck, 1983). That is, we should think about ourselves as people, not as masculine, feminine, or androgynous. Parents should rear their children to be competent boys and girls, not masculine, feminine, or androgynous, say the gender-role critics. They believe such gender-role classification leads to too much stereotyping.

Gender in Context

The concept of gender-role classification involves a personality-traitlike categorization of a person. However, it may be helpful to think of personality in terms of person-situation interaction rather than personality traits alone. Thus, in our discussion of gender-role classification, we describe how different gender roles might be more appropriate, depending on the context, or setting, involved.

To see the importance of considering gender in context, let's examine helping behavior and emotion. The stereotype is that females are better than males at helping. But it depends on the situation. Females are more likely than males to volunteer their time to help children with personal problems and to engage in caregiving behavior. However, in situations in which males feel a sense of competence and involve danger, males are more likely than females to help (Eagly & Crowley, 1986). For example, a male is more likely than a female to stop and help a person stranded by the roadside with a flat tire.

"She is emotional; he is not"—that is the master emotional stereotype. However, like differences in helping behavior, emotional differences in males and females depend on the particular emotion involved and the context in which it is displayed (Shields, 1991). Males are more likely to show anger toward strangers, especially male strangers, when they feel they have been challenged. Males also are more likely to turn their anger into aggressive action. Emotional differences between females and males often show up in contexts that highlight social roles and relationships. For example, females are more likely to discuss emotions in terms of relationships, and they are more likely to express fear and sadness.

The importance of considering gender in context is nowhere more apparent than when examining what is culturally prescribed behavior for females and males in different countries around the world. While there has been greater acceptance of androgyny and similarities in male and female behavior in the United States, in many countries gender roles remain gender-specific. To read about gender roles in two countries—Egypt and China—see the Explorations in Child Development box.

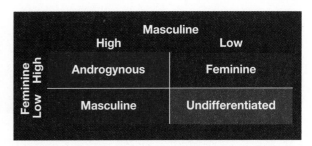

Figure **13.5**
Gender-Role Classification

gender-role transcendence
The belief that, when an individual's competence is at issue, it should be conceptualized not on the basis of masculinity, femininity, or androgyny but, rather, on a personal basis.

Gender Around the World
Gender Socialization in Six Countries

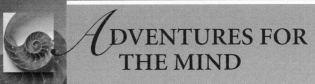

ADVENTURES FOR THE MIND
Gender Roles, Parenting, and the Future

IN THE LAST TWO decades, dramatic changes in gender roles have taken place in the United States. How much change have you personally experienced? How do you think gender roles will be different in the twenty-first century? Or do you believe that gender roles will stay about the way they are now?

There is a practical side to considering such questions. How will you raise your children, in terms of gender matters? Will gender neutrality be your goal? Will you encourage more traditional gender distinctions?

EXPLORATIONS IN CHILD DEVELOPMENT
Gender Roles in Egypt and China

IN RECENT DECADES, roles assumed by males and females in the United States have become increasingly similar—that is, androgynous. In many countries, though, gender roles have remained more gender-specific. For example, in Egypt, the division of labor between Egyptian males and females is dramatic: Egyptian males are socialized to work in the public sphere, females in the private world of home and child rearing. The Islamic religion dictates that the man's duty is to provide for his family, the woman's to care for her family and household (Dickerscheid & others, 1988). Any deviations from this traditional gender-role orientation are severely disapproved of.

Egypt is not the only country in which males and females are socialized to behave, think, and feel in strongly gender-specific ways. Kenya and Nepal are two other cultures in which children are brought up under very strict gender-specific guidelines (Munroe, Himmin, & Munroe, 1984). In the People's Republic of China, the female's status has historically been lower than the male's. The teachings of the fifth-century B.C. Chinese philosopher Confucius were used to reinforce the concept of the female as an inferior being. Beginning with the 1949 revolution in China, women began to achieve more economic freedom and more-equal status in marital relationships. However, even with the sanctions of a socialist government, the old patriarchal traditions of male supremacy in China have not been completely uprooted. Chinese women still make considerably less money than Chinese men in comparable positions, and in rural China a tradition of male supremacy still governs many women's lives.

Thus, while in China, females have made considerable strides, complete equality remains a distant objective. And in many cultures, such as Egypt and other countries where the Muslim religion predominates, gender-specific behavior is pronounced, and females are not given access to high-status positions.

In China, females and males are usually socialized to behave, feel, and think differently. The old patriarchal traditions of male supremacy have not been completely uprooted. Chinese women still make considerably less money than Chinese men do, and, in rural China (such as here in the Lixian Village of Sichuan) male supremacy still governs many women's lives.

At this point we have studied many ideas about gender-role classification. A review of these ideas is presented in summary table 13.3. Next, we will continue our exploration of gender by focusing on some developmental changes.

DEVELOPMENTAL WINDOWS OF GENDER OPPORTUNITY AND ASYMMETRIC GENDER SOCIALIZATION

Developmental Windows

Asymmetric Gender Socialization

Developmental Windows of Gender Opportunity and Asymmetric Gender Socialization

Are children more prone to forming gender roles at some points in development than at others? Are the amount, timing, and intensity of gender socialization different for girls and boys?

SUMMARY TABLE 13.3
Gender-Role Classification

Concept	Processes/ Related Ideas	Characteristics/Description
What Is Gender-Role Classification?	Traditional Gender Roles	• In the past, the well-adjusted male was supposed to show instrumental traits, the well-adjusted female expressive traits.
	Androgyny	• In the 1970s, alternatives to traditional gender roles were introduced. It was proposed that competent individuals could show both masculine and feminine traits. • This thinking led to the development of the concept of androgyny, the presence of desirable masculine and feminine traits in one individual. • Gender role measures often categorize individuals as masculine, feminine, androgynous, or undifferentiated. • Most androgynous individuals are flexible and mentally healthy, although the particular context and the individual's culture also determine the adaptiveness of a gender-role orientation.
Androgyny and Education	Its Nature	• Androgyny education programs have been more successful with females than males and more successful with children than adolescents.
Masculinity in Adolescence	Its Nature	• Some experts believe that gender-role intensification occurs in early adolescence because of increased pressure to conform to traditional gender roles. • Researchers have found that problem behaviors often characterize highly masculine adolescents.
Gender-Role Transcendence	An Alternative to Androgyny	• One alternative to androgyny which states that there has been too much emphasis on gender and that a better strategy is to think about competence in terms of people rather than gender.
Gender in Context	Situational Variation	• In thinking about gender, it is important to keep in mind the context in which gender behavior is displayed.
	Culture	• In many countries around the world, such as Egypt and China, traditional gender roles are still dominant.

Developmental Windows

Do gender lessons have to be hammered into children's heads year after year? Apparently not, according to gender expert Carole Beal (1994). Instead, what girls and boys learn about gender seems to be learned quickly at certain points in development, especially when new abilities first emerge. For example, toddlers learn a lot about gender when they make their first bids for autonomy and begin to talk. Children form many ideas about what the sexes are like from about 1½ to 3 years of age. Many parents don't really start to think about gender issues involving their child until preschool or kindergarten, but at that point children have already altered their gender behavior and learned to think of themselves as a girl or a boy. Few parents have to tell their little boys not to wear pink pants to the first grade!

Early adolescence is another transitional point that seems to be especially important in gender development. Young adolescents have to cope with the enormous changes of puberty, changes that are intensified by their expanding cognitive abilities that make them acutely aware of how they appear to others ◀◀◀ P. 182. Relations with others change extensively as dating relationships begin and sexuality is experienced.

We are born twice over; the first time for existence, the second time for life; once as human beings and later as men or as women.

Jean-Jacques Rousseau
French-Born Swiss Philosopher, 18th Century

SUMMARY TABLE 13.4
Developmental Windows of Gender Opportunity and Asymmetric Gender Socialization

Concept	Processes/ Related Ideas	Characteristics/Description
Developmental Windows of Gender Opportunity	Their Nature	• Two especially important transition points in learning gender roles are the toddler years and early adolescence.
Asymmetric Gender Socialization	Its Nature	• The amount, timing, and intensity of gender socialization are different for boys and girls. • Boys receive earlier and more intense gender socialization than girls do. • Boys often have a more difficult time learning the masculine gender role because (1) male models are less accessible to boys than female models are to girls, and (2) the messages from adults about the male role are not always consistent.

Adolescents often cope with the stress of these changes by becoming more conservative and traditional in their gender thinking and behavior, a tendency that is heightened by media stereotypes of females and males.

Asymmetric Gender Socialization

The amount, timing, and intensity of gender socialization is different for girls and boys (Beal, 1994). Boys receive earlier and more intense gender socialization than girls do. The social cost of deviating from the expected male role is higher for boys than is the cost for girls of deviating from the expected female role, in terms of peer rejection and parental disapproval. Imagine a girl who is wearing a toy holster, bandanna, and cowboy hat, running around in the backyard pretending to herd cattle. Now imagine a boy who is wearing a flowered hat, ropes of pearls, and lipstick, pretending to cook dinner on a toy stove. Which of these do you have a stronger reaction to—the girl's behavior or the boy's? Probably the boy's. Researchers have found that "effeminate" behavior in boys elicits much more negative reactions than does "masculine" behavior in girls (Feinman, 1981; Martin, 1990).

Boys might have a more difficult time learning the masculine gender role, because male models are less accessible to young children and messages from adults about the male role are not always consistent. For example, most mothers and teachers would like for boys to behave in masculine ways, but also to be neat, well-mannered, and considerate. However, fathers and peers usually want boys to behave in another way—independent and engaging in rough-and-tumble play. The mixed messages make it difficult for boys to figure out which gender role they should follow. According to Beal (1994), although gender roles have become more flexible in recent years, the flexibility has occurred more for girls than for boys. Girls can now safely be ambitious, competitive, and interested in sports, but relatively few adults are equally supportive of boys' being gentle, interested in fashion, and motivated to sign up for ballet classes.

At this point we have studied a number of ideas about developmental windows of gender opportunity and asymmetric gender socialization. A review of these ideas is presented in summary table 13.4.

Chapter Review

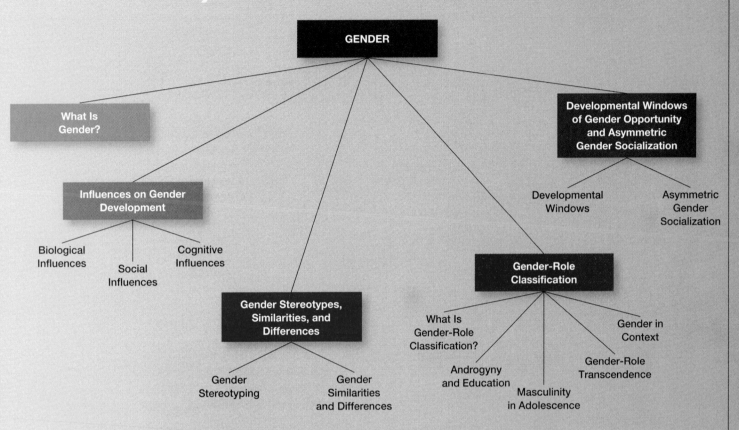

TO OBTAIN A DETAILED REVIEW OF THE CHAPTER, STUDY THESE FOUR SUMMARY TABLES:

Key Terms

gender 396
gender identity 396
gender role 396
estrogens 396
androgens 396
identification theory 398

social cognitive theory of gender 399
cognitive developmental theory of gender 403
schema 404
gender schema 404
gender schema theory 404

gender stereotypes 404
rapport talk 407
report talk 407
androgyny 409
gender-role transcendence 411

Key People

Stephanie Shields 395
Sigmund Freud 397
Erik Erikson 397
Alice Eagly 398
Eleanor Maccoby 400

Myra and David Sadker 401
Lawrence Kohlberg 403
Carol Jacklin 407
Janet Shibley Hyde 407
Deborah Tannen 407

David Buss 408
Sandra Bem 409
Joseph Pleck 410
Carole Beal 413

Child Development Resources

Beyond Appearance (1999)
 by Norine Johnson, Michael Roberts, and
 Judith Worrell
 Washington, DC: American Psychological
 Asociation

Read about many aspects of girls' development in adolescence.

Boys and Girls: The Development of Gender (1994)
 by Carole Beal
 New York: McGraw-Hill

A thoughtful, comprehensive examination of gender roles in boys and girls by a leading expert.

The Mismeasure of Woman (1992)
 by Carol Tavris
 New York: Simon & Schuster

This is an excellent book on gender stereotyping, similarities and differences between the sexes, and how females should be measured by their own standards, not males'.

The Two Sexes (1998)
 by Eleanor Maccoby
 Cambridge, MA: Harvard University Press

Explore how gender differences emerge in children's groups.

Taking It to the Net

1. Ellen is taking a class in gender psychology. She wants to test the theory of androgyny among her peers in her large geology lecture. She has heard that there is an online version of the test, and thinks people will feel more comfortable taking it online. She is going to try it herself, first.

2. Derek is the program chair for the Men's Focus Group on campus, He is planning a program on the social barriers to men being fully involved fathers. He thinks it has something to do with gender stereotypes that suggest that women are the best nurturers and caregivers. Is there some research Derek ought to share with the group?

3. Prof. Lombard told the child development class to find out the current thinking on how to treat infants who are born without fully developed genitalia. She said that the old line of thinking was that these children should be surgically altered during infancy so that their genitals appear female. Are other alternatives being considered today?

Connect to *http://www.mhhe.com/santrockc9* to find answers!

Chapter 14

MORAL DEVELOPMENT

What Is Moral Development?

Moral Thoughts

Piaget's Theory

Kohlberg's Theory

Moral Behavior

Basic Processes

Resistance to Temptation and Self-Control

Social Cognitive Theory

Moral Feelings

Psychoanalytic Theory

Empathy

The Contemporary Perspective on the Role of Emotions in Moral Development

Altruism

Juvenile Delinquency

What Is Juvenile Delinquency?

Antecedents of Delinquency

Violence and Youth

Moral Education

The Hidden Curriculum

Character Education

Values Clarification

Cognitive Moral Education

Service Learning

Rest's Four-Component Model

Parenting and Moral Development

Parental Discipline

Some Conclusions About Parenting and Moral Development

Moral Development

The Story of Pax, the Make-Believe Planet

CAN CHILDREN understand such concepts as discrimination, economic inequality, affirmative action, and comparable worth? Probably not, if we use those terms, but might we be able to construct circumstances involving those concepts that they are able to understand? Phyllis Katz (1987) asked elementary-school-age children to pretend that they had taken a long ride on a spaceship to a make-believe planet called Pax. She asked for their opinions about various situations in which they found themselves. The situations involved conflict, socioeconomic inequality, and civil-political rights. For example, regarding conflict she asked them what a teacher should do when two students were tied for a prize or when they have been fighting. The economic equality dilemmas included a proposed field trip that not all students could afford, a comparable-worth situation in which janitors were paid more than teachers, and an employment situation that discriminated against those with dots on their noses instead of stripes. The rights items dealt with minority rights and freedom of the press.

The elementary school children did indeed recognize injustice and often came up with interesting solutions to problems. For example, all but two children believed that teachers should earn as much as janitors—the holdouts said teachers should make less because they stay in one room or because cleaning toilets is more disgusting and therefore deserves higher wages. Children were especially responsive to the economic inequality items. All but one thought that not giving a job to a qualified applicant who had different physical characteristics (a dotted rather than a striped nose) was unfair. The majority recommended an affirmative action solution—giving the job to the one from the discriminated-against minority. None of the children verbalized the concept of freedom of the press or seemed to understand that a newspaper has the right to criticize a mayor in print without being punished. What are our schools teaching children about democracy? Some of the courses of action suggested were intriguing. Several argued that the reporters should be jailed. One child said that, if she were the mayor being criticized, she would worry, make speeches, and say, "I didn't do anything wrong," not unlike what American presidents have done in recent years. Another said that the mayor should not put the newspaper people out of work, because that might make them print more bad things. "Make them write comics instead," he said. The children believed that poverty exists on Earth but mainly in Africa, big cities, or Vietnam. War was mentioned as the biggest problem on Earth, although children were not certain whether it is presently occurring. Other problems mentioned were crime, hatred, school, smog, and meanness. Overall, the types of rules the children believed a society should abide by were quite sensible—almost all included the need for equitable sharing of resources and work and prohibitions against aggression.

WHAT IS MORAL DEVELOPMENT?

What Is Moral Development?

Moral development is one of the oldest topics of interest to those who are curious about human nature. In prescientific periods, philosophers and theologians heatedly debated children's moral status at birth, which they felt had important implications for how children should be reared. Today, most people have very strong opinions about acceptable and unacceptable behavior, ethical and unethical conduct, and the ways in which acceptable and ethical behaviors are to be fostered in children.

moral development
Age-related thoughts, feelings, and behaviors regarding rules, principles, and values that guide what people should do.

Moral development *involves age-related thoughts, feelings, and behaviors regarding rules, principles, and values that guide what people should do.* Moral development has an *intrapersonal* dimension (a person's basic values and sense of self) and an *interpersonal* dimension (a focus on what people should do in their interactions with other people) (Walker, 1996: Walker & Pitts, 1998). The intrapersonal dimension regulates a person's activities when she or he is not engaged in social interaction. The interpersonal dimension regulates people's social interactions and arbitrates conflict. Let's now further explore some basic ideas about moral thoughts, feelings, and behaviors.

First, how do children *reason* or *think* about rules for ethical conduct? For example, consider cheating. A child can be presented with a story in which someone has a conflict about whether or not to cheat in a particular situation, such as when taking a test in school. The child is asked to decide what is appropriate for the character to do and why. The focus is on the reasoning children use to justify their moral decisions.

Second, how do children actually *behave* in moral circumstances? In our example of cheating, emphasis is on observing the child's cheating and the environmental circumstances that produced and maintain the cheating. Children might be presented with some toys and asked to select which one they believe is the most attractive. Then, the experimenter tells the young child that the particular toy selected is someone else's and is not to be played with. Observations of different conditions under which the child deviates from the prohibition or resists temptation are conducted.

Third, how does the child *feel* about the moral matters? In the example of cheating, does the child feel enough guilt to resist temptation? If children cheat, do feelings of guilt after the transgression keep them from cheating the next time they face temptation?

Exploring Moral Development

MORAL THOUGHTS

```
MORAL THOUGHTS
      /        \
Piaget's    Kohlberg's
 Theory       Theory
```

Moral Thoughts

How do children think about the standards of right and wrong? Piaget had some thoughts about this question, and so did Lawrence Kohlberg.

Piaget's Theory

Interest in how children think about moral issues was stimulated by Piaget (1932), who extensively observed and interviewed children from the ages of 4 through 12. Piaget watched children play marbles to learn how they used and thought about the game's rules. He also asked children questions about ethical issues—theft, lies, punishment, and justice, for example. Piaget concluded that children think in two distinct ways about morality, depending on their developmental maturity. **Heteronomous morality** *is the first stage of moral development in Piaget's theory, occurring from 4 to 7 years of age. Justice and rules are conceived of as unchangeable properties of the world, removed from the control of people.* **Autonomous morality** *is the second stage of moral development in Piaget's theory, displayed by older children (about 10 years of age and older). The child becomes aware that rules and laws are created by people and that, in judging an action, one should consider the actor's intentions as well as the consequences.* Children 7 to 10 years of age are in a transition between the two stages, evidencing some features of both.

Let's consider Piaget's two stages of moral development further. A heteronomous thinker judges the rightness or goodness of behavior by considering the consequences of the behavior, not the intentions of the actor. For example, the heteronomous thinker says that breaking 12 cups accidentally is worse than breaking 1 cup intentionally while trying to steal a cookie. For the moral autonomist, the reverse is true. The actor's intentions assume paramount importance. The heteronomous thinker also believes that rules are unchangeable and are handed down by all-powerful authorities. When Piaget suggested to a group of young children that new rules be introduced into the game of marbles, they resisted. They insisted that the rules had always been the same and could not be altered. In contrast, older children—who are moral autonomists—accept change and recognize that rules are merely convenient, socially agreed-upon conventions, subject to change by consensus.

The heteronomous thinker also believes in **immanent justice,** *the concept that, if a rule is broken, punishment will be meted out immediately.* The young child somehow believes that the violation is connected automatically to the punishment. Thus, young children often look around worriedly after committing a transgression, expecting inevitable punishment. Immanent justice also implies that if something unfortunate happens to someone it must be because the person had transgressed earlier. Older children, who are moral autonomists, recognize that punishment is socially mediated and occurs only if a relevant person witnesses the wrongdoing and that, even then, punishment is not inevitable.

Piaget argued that, as children develop, they become more sophisticated in thinking about social matters, especially about the possibilities and conditions of cooperation. Piaget believed that this social understanding comes about through the mutual give-and-take of peer relations. In the child's peer group, where others have power and status similar to the child's, plans are negotiated and coordinated, and disagreements are reasoned about and eventually settled. Parent-child relations, in which parents have the power and children do not, are less likely to advance moral reasoning, because rules are often handed down in an authoritarian way.

Remember that Piaget believed adolescents usually become formal operational thinkers ◀‖‖ P. 219. Thus, they are no longer tied to immediate and concrete phenomena but are more logical, abstract, and deductive reasoners. Formal operational thinkers frequently compare the real to the ideal; create contrary-to-fact propositions; are cognitively capable of relating the distant past to the present; understand their roles in society, in history, and in the universe; and can conceptualize their own thoughts and think about their mental constructs as objects. For example, it usually is not until about the age of 11 or 12 that boys and girls spontaneously introduce concepts of belief, intelligence, and faith into their definitions of their religious identities.

Kohlberg's Theory

The most provocative view of moral development in recent years was crafted by Lawrence Kohlberg (Kohlberg, 1958, 1976, 1986). We will explore Kohlberg's concept of moral stages, influences on the Kohlberg stages, and Kohlberg's critics.

heteronomous morality (Piaget)
The first stage of moral development in Piaget's theory, occurring at 4 to 7 years of age. Justice and rules are conceived of as unchangeable properties of the world, removed from the control of people.

autonomous morality (Piaget)
The second stage of moral development in Piaget's theory, displayed by older children (about 10 years of age and older). The child becomes aware that rules and laws are created by people and that, in judging an action, one should consider the actor's intentions as well as the consequences.

immanent justice
Piaget's concept that if a rule is broken, punishment will be meted out immediately.

Childhood innocence

Through the Eyes of Psychologists

Lawrence Kohlberg *(1927–1987)*

"Moral development consists of a sequence of qualitative changes in the way an individual thinks."

internalization
The developmental change from behavior that is externally controlled to behavior that is controlled by internal standards and principles.

preconventional reasoning
The lowest level in Kohlberg's theory of moral development. The individual shows no internalization of moral values—moral reasoning is controlled by external rewards and punishment.

heteronomous morality (Kohlberg)
The first stage in Kohlberg's theory. At this stage, moral thinking is often tied to punishment.

individualism, instrumental purpose, and exchange
The second Kohlberg stage of moral development. At this stage, individuals pursue their own interests but also let others do the same.

conventional reasoning
The second, or intermediate, level in Kohlberg's theory of moral development. Internalization is intermediate. Individuals abide by certain standards (internal), but they are the standards of others (external), such as parents or the laws of society.

mutual interpersonal expectations, relationships, and interpersonal conformity
Kohlberg's third stage of moral development. At this stage, individuals value trust, caring, and loyalty to others as a basis of moral judgments.

social system morality
The fourth stage in Kohlberg's theory of moral development. Moral judgments are based on understanding the social order, law, justice, and duty.

Kohlberg's Stages   Kohlberg believed that moral development is primarily based on moral reasoning and unfolds in a series of stages. He arrived at his view after extensively interviewing children about moral dilemmas. In the interview, children are presented with a series of stories in which characters face moral dilemmas. The following is the most popular of the Kohlberg dilemmas:

> In Europe a woman was near death from a special kind of cancer. There was one drug that the doctors thought might save her. It was a form of radium that a druggist in the same town had recently discovered. The drug was expensive to make, but the druggist was charging ten times what the drug cost him to make. He paid $200 for the radium and charged $2,000 for a small dose of the drug. The sick woman's husband, Heinz, went to everyone he knew to borrow the money, but he could only get together $1,000, which is half of what it cost. He told the druggist that his wife was dying and asked him to sell it cheaper or let him pay later. But the druggist said, "No, I discovered the drug, and I am going to make money from it." So Heinz got desperate and broke into the man's store to steal the drug for his wife. (Kohlberg, 1969, p. 379)

This story is one of eleven that Kohlberg devised to investigate the nature of moral thought. After reading the story, interviewees answer a series of questions about the moral dilemma. Should Heinz have stolen the drug? Was stealing it right or wrong? Why? Is it a husband's duty to steal the drug for his wife if he can get it no other way? Would a good husband steal? Did the druggist have the right to charge that much when there was no law setting a limit on the price? Why?

From the answers interviewees gave for this and other moral dilemmas, Kohlberg hypothesized three levels of moral development, each of which is characterized by two stages. A key concept in understanding moral development is **internalization,** *the developmental change from behavior that is externally controlled to behavior that is controlled by internal standards and principles.* As children and adolescents develop, their moral thoughts become more internalized. Let's look further at Kohlberg's three levels of moral development (see figure 14.1).

Kohlberg's Level 1: Preconventional Reasoning   Preconventional reasoning *is the lowest level in Kohlberg's theory of moral development. At this level, the individual shows no internalization of moral values—moral reasoning is controlled by external rewards and punishments.*

- Stage 1. **Heteronomous morality** *is the first stage in Kohlberg's theory. At this stage, moral thinking is often tied to punishment.* For example, children and adolescents obey adults because adults tell them to obey.
- Stage 2. **Individualism, instrumental purpose, and exchange** *is the second Kohlberg stage of moral development. At this stage, individuals pursue their own interests but also let others do the same.* Thus, what is right involves an equal exchange. People are nice to others so that they will be nice to them in return.

Kohlberg's Level 2: Conventional Reasoning   Conventional reasoning *is the second, or intermediate, level in Kohlberg's theory of moral development. At this level, internalization is intermediate. Individuals abide by certain standards (internal), but they are the standards of others (external), such as parents or the laws of society.*

- Stage 3. **Mutual interpersonal expectations, relationships, and interpersonal conformity** *is Kohlberg's third stage of moral development. At this stage, individuals value trust, caring, and loyalty to others as a basis of moral judgments.* Children and adolescents often adopt their parents' moral standards at this stage, seeking to be thought of by their parents as a "good girl" or a "good boy."

Kohlberg's Theory of Moral Development
Kohlberg's Moral Dilemmas
Kohlberg's Moral Stages

- Stage 4. **Social systems morality** *is the fourth stage in Kohlberg's theory of moral development. At this stage, moral judgments are based on understanding the social order, law, justice, and duty.* For example, adolescents may say that, for a community to work effectively, it needs to be protected by laws that are adhered to by its members.

Kohlberg's Level 3: Postconventional Reasoning

Postconventional reasoning *is the highest level in Kohlberg's theory of moral development. At this level, morality is completely internalized and is not based on others' standards. The individual recognizes alternative moral courses, explores the options, and then decides on a personal moral code.*

- Stage 5. **Social contract or utility and individual rights** *is the fifth Kohlberg stage. At this stage, individuals reason that values, rights, and principles undergird or transcend the law.* A person evaluates the validity of actual laws and social systems can be examined in terms of the degree to which they preserve and protect fundamental human rights and values.
- Stage 6. **Universal ethical principles** *is the sixth and highest stage in Kohlberg's theory of moral development. At this stage, the person has developed a moral standard based on universal human rights.* When faced with a conflict between law and conscience, the person will follow conscience, even though the decision might involve personal risk.

Kohlberg believed that these levels and stages occur in a sequence and are age related: Before age 9, most children reason about moral dilemmas in a preconventional way; by early adolescence, they reason in more conventional ways; and, by early adulthood, a small number of people reason in postconventional ways. In a 20-year longitudinal investigation, the uses of stages 1 and 2 decreased. Stage 4, which did not appear at all in the moral reasoning of the 10-year-olds, was reflected in the moral thinking of 62 percent of the 36-year-olds. Stage 5 did not appear until the age of 20 to 22 and never characterized more than 10 percent of the individuals. Thus, the moral stages appeared somewhat later than Kohlberg initially envisioned, and the higher stages, especially stage 6, were extremely elusive (Colby & others, 1983). Recently, stage 6 was removed from the Kohlberg scoring manual but is still considered to be theoretically important in the Kohlberg scheme of moral development.

postconventional reasoning
The highest level in Kohlberg's theory of moral development. Morality is completely internalized.

social contract or utility and individual rights
Kohlberg's fifth stage of moral development. At this stage, individuals reason that values, rights, and principles undergird or transcend the law.

universal ethical principles
The sixth and highest stage in Kohlberg's theory of moral development. Individuals develop a moral standard based on universal human rights.

Figure **14.1**
Kohlberg's Three Levels and Six Stages of Moral Development

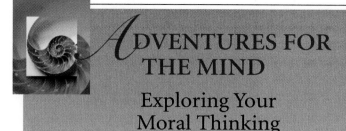

Adventures for the Mind

Exploring Your Moral Thinking

WHAT DO YOU THINK about the following circumstances?

• A man who had been sentenced to serve 10 years for selling a small amount of marijuana walked away from a prison camp after serving only 6 months of his sentence. Twenty-five years later he was caught. He is now in his fifties and has been a model citizen. Should he be sent back to prison? Why or why not? At which Kohlberg stage should your response be placed?

• A young woman who had been in a tragic accident is "brain dead" and has been kept on life support systems for 4 years without ever regaining consciousness. Should the life support systems be removed? Explain your response. At which Kohlberg stage should your response be placed?

Influences on the Kohlberg Stages

Kohlberg believed that children's moral orientation unfolds as a consequence of their cognitive development. Children construct their moral thoughts as they pass from one stage to the next rather than passively accepting a cultural norm of morality (Brabeck, 2000). Investigators have sought to understand the factors that influence children's movement through the moral stages, among them modeling, cognitive conflict, peer relations, and perspective-taking opportunities (Turiel, 1998).

Several investigators have attempted to advance individuals' levels of moral development by having a model present arguments that reflect moral thinking one stage above the individuals' established levels. These studies are based on the cognitive developmental concepts of equilibrium and conflict. By presenting moral information slightly beyond the children's cognitive level, a disequilibrium is created that motivates them to restructure their moral thought. The resolution of the disequilibrium and conflict should be toward increased competence, but the data are mixed. In one of the pioneer studies on this topic, Eliot Turiel (1966) discovered that children prefer a moral judgment stage one stage above their current stage over two stages above it. However, in the study, they chose one stage below their stage more often than one stage above it. Apparently, the children were motivated more by security needs than by the need to reorganize their thought to a higher level. Other studies indicate children prefer a more advanced stage over a less advanced stage (Rest, Turiel, & Kohlberg, 1969).

Since the early studies of stage modeling, a number of investigations have attempted to determine more precisely the effectiveness of various forms of stage

Both Piaget and Kohlberg believed that peer relations are a critical part of the social stimulation that challenges children to advance their moral reasoning. The mutual give-and-take of peer relations provides children with role-taking opportunities that give them a sense that rules are generated democratically.

modeling and argument (Lapsley & Quintana, 1985). The upshot of these studies is that virtually any plus-stage discussion format, for any length of time, seems to promote more advanced moral reasoning. For example, in one investigation (Walker, 1982), exposure to plus-two-stage reasoning (arguments two stages above the child's current stage of moral thought) was just as effective in advancing moral thought as plus-one-stage reasoning. Exposure to plus-two-stage reasoning did not produce more plus-two-stage reasoning but rather, like exposure to plus-one-stage reasoning, increased reasoning at one stage above the current stage. Other research has found that exposure to reasoning only one third of a stage higher than the individual's current level of moral thought advances that person's moral thought (Berkowitz & Gibbs, 1983). In sum, current research on modeling and cognitive conflict reveals that moral thought can be moved to a higher level through exposure to models or discussion that is more advanced than the child's level.

Kohlberg believed that peer interaction is a critical part of the social stimulation that challenges children to change their moral orientation. Whereas adults characteristically impose rules and regulations on children, the mutual give-and-take in peer interaction provides children with an opportunity to take the perspective of another person and to generate rules democratically. Kohlberg stressed that perspective-taking opportunities can, in principle, be engendered by any peer group encounter. Although Kohlberg believed that such perspective-taking opportunities are ideal for moral development, he also believed that certain types of parent-child experiences can induce the child to think at more advanced levels of moral thinking. In particular, parents who allow or encourage conversation about value-laden issues promote more advanced moral thought in their children; however, many parents do not systematically provide their children with such perspective-taking opportunities. Nonetheless, in one recent study, children's moral development was related to their parents' discussion style, which involved questioning and supportive interaction (Walker & Taylor, 1991). There is an increasing emphasis on the role of parenting in moral development (Eisenberg & Murphy, 1995).

In a recent longitudinal study conducted by Lawrence Walker and his colleagues over a 4-year period, both parent-child and friendship relationships were linked with children's moral maturity, as assessed by Kohlberg stories and scoring (Walker, Hennig, & Krettenauer, in press). A general Socratic style of eliciting the other's opinion and checking for understanding (as when using appropriate probes) was effective in advancing in both parent/child and peer contexts. However, excessive information giving was associated with lower rates of moral growth, possibly being interpreted as overly opinionated lecturing. Parents provided a more cognitively stimulating environment than did children's friends, while friends engaged in more simple sharing of information.

Kohlberg's Critics   Kohlberg's provocative theory of moral development has not gone unchallenged (Gilligan, 1982, 1992; Lapsley, 1996; Rest & others, 1999). The criticisms involve the link between moral thought and moral behavior, the quality of the research, inadequate consideration of culture's role in moral development, underestimation of the care perspective, and inadequate consideration of social conventions.

Moral Thought and Moral Behavior   Kohlberg's theory has been criticized for placing too much emphasis on moral thought and not enough emphasis on moral behavior. Moral reasons can sometimes be a shelter for immoral behavior. Bank embezzlers and presidents endorse the loftiest of moral virtues when commenting about moral dilemmas, but their own behavior may be immoral. No one wants a nation of cheaters and thieves who can reason at the postconventional level. The cheaters and thieves may know what is right, yet still do what is wrong.

In evaluating the relation between moral thought and moral behavior, consider the corrupting power of rationalizations and other defenses that

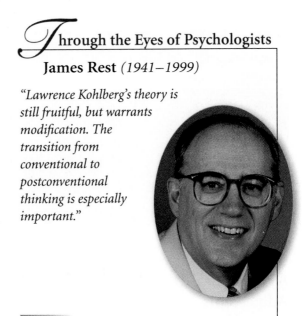

Through the Eyes of Psychologists

James Rest *(1941–1999)*

"Lawrence Kohlberg's theory is still fruitful, but warrants modification. The transition from conventional to postconventional thinking is especially important."

disengage us from self-blame; these include reconstrual of the situation, euphemistic labeling, and attribution of blame to authorities, circumstances, or victims (Bandura, 1991). One area in which a link between moral judgment and behavior has been found is where higher Kohlberg-stage reasoning acts as a buffer against criminal activity (Taylor & Walker, 1997).

Assessment of Moral Reasoning   Some developmentalists fault the quality of Kohlberg's research and believe that more attention should be paid to the way moral development is assessed (Boyes, Giordano, & Galperyn, 1993). For example, James Rest (1986) argued that alternative methods should be used to collect information about moral thinking instead of relying on a single method that requires individuals to reason about hypothetical moral dilemmas. Rest also said that Kohlberg's stories are extremely difficult to score. To help remedy this problem, Rest developed his own measure of moral development, called the Defining Issues Test (DIT).

The DIT attempts to determine which moral issues individuals feel are more crucial in a given situation by presenting them with a series of dilemmas and a list of definitions of the major issues involved (Kohlberg's procedure does not make use of such a list). In the dilemma of Heinz and the druggist, individuals might be asked whether a community's laws should be upheld or whether Heinz should be willing to risk being injured or caught as a burglar. They might also be asked to list the most important values that govern human interaction. They are given six stories and asked to rate the importance of each issue involved in deciding what ought to be done. Then they are asked to list what they believe are the four most important issues. Rest argued that this method provides a more valid and reliable way to assess moral thinking than Kohlberg's method (Rest & others, 1999).

Researchers also have found that the hypothetical moral dilemmas posed in Kohlberg's stories do not match the moral dilemmas many children and adults face in their everyday lives (Walker, de Vries, & Trevethan, 1987). Most of Kohlberg's stories focus on the family and authority. However, when one researcher invited adolescents to write stories about their own moral dilemmas, the adolescents generated dilemmas that were broader in scope, focusing on friends, acquaintances, and other issues, as well as family and authority (Yussen, 1977). The adolescents' moral dilemmas also were analyzed in terms of their content. As shown in figure 14.2, the moral issue that concerned adolescents more than any other was interpersonal relationships.

Some moral development researchers believe that a valuable method is to have research participants recall and discuss real-life dilemmas from their own experience (Walker & others, 1987). This strategy can provide a valid assessment not only of their moral stage but also of how they interpret moral situations that are relevant to them.

Culture and Moral Development   Yet another criticism of Kohlberg's view is that it is culturally biased (Banks, 1993; Jensen, 1995; Miller, 1991, 1995). A review of research on moral development in twenty-seven countries concluded that moral reasoning is more culture-specific than Kohlberg envisioned and that Kohlberg's scoring system does not recognize higher-level moral reasoning in certain cultural groups (Snarey, 1987). Examples of higher-level moral reasoning that would not be scored as such by Kohlberg's system are values related to communal equity and collective happiness in Israel, the unity and sacredness of all life-forms in India, and the relation of the individual to the community in New Guinea. These examples of moral reasoning would not be scored at the highest level in Kohlberg's system because they do not emphasize the individual's rights and abstract principles of justice. One study assessed the moral development of twenty adolescent male Buddhist monks in Nepal (Huebner & Garrod, 1993). The issue of justice, a basic theme in Kohlberg's theory, was not of paramount importance in the monks' moral views, and their concerns about prevention of suffering and the role of compassion are not captured by Kohlberg's theory. More about cultural variations in adolescents' moral thought appears in the

Figure 14.2
Actual Moral Dilemmas Generated by Adolescents

Story subject	Grade 7	Grade 9	Grade 12
	Percentage		
Alcohol	2	0	5
Civil rights	0	6	7
Drugs	7	10	5
Interpersonal relations	38	24	35
Physical safety	22	8	3
Sexual relations	2	20	10
Smoking	7	2	0
Stealing	9	2	0
Working	2	2	15
Other	11	26	20

From R. Shweder et al, "Culture and Moral Development," in J. Kagan and S. Lamb (eds.), *The Emergence in Morality in Young Children*, 1987. Used by permission of the Oxford University of Chicago Press.

EXPLORATIONS IN CHILD DEVELOPMENT
Children's Moral Reasoning in the United States and India

CULTURAL MEANING SYSTEMS vary around the world, and these systems shape children's morality (Miller & Bersoff, 1993; Shweder & others, 1998). Consider a comparison of American and Indian Hindu Brahman children (Shweder, Mahapatra, & Miller, 1987). Like people in many other non-Western societies, Indians view moral rules as part of the natural world order. This means that Indians do not distinguish between physical, moral, and social regulation, as Americans do. For example, in India, violations of food taboos and marital restrictions can be just as serious as acts intended to cause harm to others. In India, social rules are seen as inevitable, much like the law of gravity.

As shown here, there is some, but not much, overlap in the moral concerns of children in Indian and American cultures. For Americans accustomed to viewing morality as a freely chosen social contract, Indian beliefs pose a different worldview, one that is not easy to reconcile with such treasured ideas as the autonomy of an individualized conscience. The interviews conducted by Richard Shweder and his colleagues (Shweder, Mahapatra, & Miller, 1987) with Indian and American children revealed sharp cultural differences in what people judge to be right and wrong. For example, Indian and American children disagree about eating beef. On the other hand, there are areas of overlap between the two cultures. For example, both think that breaking promises and ignoring beggars is wrong.

According to William Damon (1988), where culturally specific practices take on profound moral and religious significance, as in India, the moral development of children focuses extensively on their adherence to custom and convention. In contrast, Western moral doctrine tends to elevate abstract principles, such as justice and welfare, to a higher moral status than customs or conventions. As in India, socialization practices in many Third World countries actively instill in children a great respect for their culture's traditional codes and practices (Edwards, 1987).

Disagreement: Brahman children think it is right; American children think it is wrong.

—Hitting an errant child with a cane
—Eating with one's hands
—Father opening a son's letter

Disagreement: Brahman children think it is wrong; American children think it is right.

—Addressing one's father by his first name
—Eating beef
—Cutting one's hair and eating chicken after father's death

Agreement: Brahman and American children think it is wrong.

—Ignoring a beggar
—Destroying another's picture
—Kicking a harmless animal
—Stealing flowers

Agreement: Brahman and American children think it is right.

—Men holding hands

Agreements/Disagreements Between American and Indian Hindu Brahman Children About Right and Wrong

Through the Eyes of Psychologists

Carol Gilligan,
Harvard University

"Many girls seem to fear, most of all, being alone—without friends, family, or relationships."

justice perspective
A moral perspective that focuses on the rights of the individual; individuals independently make moral decisions.

Explorations in Child Development box. In sum, although Kohlberg's approach does capture much of the moral reasoning voiced in various cultures around the world, as we have just seen, there are some important moral concepts in particular cultures that his approach misses or misconstrues (Haidt, 1997; Walker, 1996).

Gender and the Care Perspective

Carol Gilligan (1982, 1992, 1996) believes that relationships and connections to others are critical aspects of female development. Gilligan also has criticized Kohlberg's theory of moral development. She believes that his theory does not adequately reflect relationships and concern for others. The **justice perspective** *is a moral perspective that focuses on the rights of the individual; individuals stand alone and independently make moral decisions. Kohlberg's theory is a justice perspective.* By contrast, the **care perspective** *is a moral perspective that views people in terms of their connectedness with others and emphasizes interpersonal communication, relationships with others, and concern for others. Gilligan's theory is a care perspective.* According to Gilligan, Kohlberg greatly underplayed the care perspective in moral development. She believes that this may have happened because he was a male, because most of his research was with males rather than females, and because he used male responses as a model for his theory.

In extensive interviews with girls from 6 to 18 years of age, Gilligan and her colleagues found that girls consistently interpret moral dilemmas in terms of human relationships and base these interpretations on listening and watching other people (Gilligan, Brown, & Rogers, 1990). According to Gilligan, girls have the ability to sensitively pick up different rhythms in relationships and often are able to follow the pathways of feelings. Gilligan believes that girls reach a critical juncture in their development when they reach adolescence. Usually around 11 to 12 years of age, girls become aware that their intense interest in intimacy is not prized by the male-dominated culture, even though society values women as caring and altruistic. The dilemma is that girls are presented with a choice that makes them look either selfish or selfless. Gilligan believes that, as adolescent girls experience this dilemma, they increasingly silence their "distinctive voice."

Contextual variations influence whether adolescent girls silence their "voice." In one study, Susan Harter and her colleagues (Harter, Waters, & Whitesell, 1996) found evidence for a refinement of Gilligan's position in that feminine girls reported lower levels of voice in public contexts (at school with teachers and classmates) but not in more private interpersonal relationships with close friends and parents. However, androgynous girls reported a strong voice in all contexts. Harter and her colleagues also found that adolescent girls who buy into societal messages that females should be seen and not heard are at most risk in their development of a self. The greatest liabilities occurred for females who not only lacked a "voice" but emphasized the importance of appearance. In focusing on their outer selves, these girls face formidable challenges in meeting the punishing cultural standards of attractiveness.

Researchers have found support for Gilligan's claim that females' and males' moral reasoning often centers around different concerns and issues (Galotti, Kozberg, & Appleman, in press; Garmon, Basinger, & Gibbs, 1995; Wark & Krebs, 1996). However, one of Gilligan's initial claims—that traditional Kohlbergian measures of moral development are biased against females—has been extensively disputed. For example, most research studies using the Kohlberg stories and scoring system do not find sex differences (Walker, 1984). Thus, the strongest support for Gilligan's claims comes from studies that focus on items and

ADVENTURES FOR THE MIND

Mixed Justice/Care Responses to Moral Dilemmas

NOT ALL RESPONSES to moral dilemmas are either justice responses or care responses. Sometimes we respond to moral dilemmas with a mixture of justice and care responses. For example, the following involves mixed justice/care considerations:

Last year, some friends and I went out, and we were having a little celebration. . . . One girl met a friend of hers and she wanted to stay longer and talk. . . . The next morning we realized our friend had gotten busted. . . . I didn't know if I should turn myself in or what. In the end, I had a real hard time deciding on what to do because I felt it was really unfair. . . . She had gotten busted and we hadn't. And the problem was, if I turned myself in, I would have been responsible for four other people.

Can you think of other moral dilemmas and responses to them that might involve a combination of justice/care considerations?

SUMMARY TABLE 14.1
The Nature of Moral Development and Moral Thoughts

Concept	Processes/Related Ideas	Characteristics/Description
What Is Moral Development?	Its Nature	• Moral development involves thoughts, feelings, and behaviors regarding standards of right and wrong. • Moral development consists of intrapersonal and interpersonal dimensions.
Moral Thoughts	Piaget's Theory	• Piaget distinguishes between the heteronomous morality of younger children and the autonomous morality of older children. • His ideas about formal operational thought have implications for understanding adolescents' moral development.
	Kohlberg's Theory	• Kohlberg developed a provocative theory of moral reasoning. Kohlberg argued that moral development consists of 3 levels—preconventional, conventional, and postconventional—and six stages (two at each level). • Increased internalization characterizes movement to levels 2 and 3. • Influences on the stages include cognitive development, imitation and cognitive conflict, peer relations, and perspective taking. • Criticisms of Kohlberg's theory involve inadequate attention to moral behavior, failure to include the care perspective, underestimation of culture's role, and inadequate consideration of social conventional reasoning. • Gilligan advocates a stronger care perspective and says that early adolescence is a critical juncture in the development of girls.

scoring systems pertaining to close relationships, pathways of feelings, sensitive listening, and the rhythm of interpersonal behavior (Galotti, Kozberg, & Farmer, 1990).

While females often articulate a care perspective and males a justice perspective, the gender difference is not absolute, and the two orientations are not mutually exclusive (Lyons, 1990; Rothbart, Hanley, & Albert, 1986). For example, in one study, 53 of 80 females and males showed either a care or a justice perspective, but 27 subjects used both orientations, with neither predominating (Gilligan & Attanucci, 1988).

Social Conventional Reasoning   Some theorists and researchers argue that it is important to distinguish between moral reasoning and social conventional reasoning, something they believe Kohlberg did not adequately do (Turiel, 1998; Lapsley, 1996). **Social conventional reasoning** *focuses on thoughts about social consensus and convention.* In contrast, moral reasoning emphasizes ethical issues. Conventional rules are created to control behavioral irregularities and maintain the social system. Conventional rules are arbitrary and subject to individual judgment. For example, not eating food with one's fingers is a social conventional rule, as is raising one's hand in class before speaking.

In contrast, moral rules are not arbitrary and determined by whim. They also are not created by social consensus. Rather, moral rules are obligatory, widely accepted, and somewhat impersonal (Turiel, 1998). Thus, rules pertaining to lying, cheating, stealing, and physically harming another person are moral rules because violation of these rules affronts ethical standards that exist apart from social consensus and convention. In sum, moral judgments involve concepts of justice, whereas social conventional judgments are concepts of social organization.

At this point we have studied a number of ideas about what moral development is and moral thoughts. A review of these ideas is presented in summary table 14.1. Next, we will continue our exploration of moral development by examining moral behavior.

care perspective
The moral perspective, emphasized by Carol Gilligan, that views people in terms of their connectedness with others and emphasizes interpersonal communication, relationships with others, and concern for others.

social conventional reasoning
Thoughts about social consensus and convention.

In a Different Voice
Exploring Girls' Voices

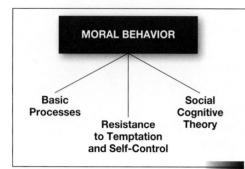

Moral Behavior

What are the basic processes that behaviorists believe are responsible for children's moral behavior? What is the nature of resistance to temptation and self-control? How do social cognitive theorists view children's moral development?

Basic Processes

Behavioral views emphasize the importance of studying children's moral behavior and its environmental determinants. The familiar processes of reinforcement, punishment, and imitation have been invoked to explain how and why children learn certain responses and why their responses differ from one another; the general conclusions to be drawn are the same as elsewhere. When children are reinforced for behavior that is consistent with laws and social conventions, they are likely to repeat that behavior. When provided with models who behave "morally," children are likely to adopt their actions. Finally, when children are punished for "immoral" or unacceptable behaviors, those behaviors can be eliminated, but at the expense of sanctioning punishment by its very use and of causing emotional side effects for the child.

To these general conclusions are added some qualifiers. The effectiveness of reward and punishment depends on the consistency with which they are administered and the schedule (for example, continuous or partial) that is adopted. The effectiveness of modeling depends on the characteristics of the model (such as esteem or power) and the presence of symbolic codes to enhance retention of the modeled behavior.

What kind of adult moral models are children being exposed to in our society? Do such models usually do what they say? There is evidence that the adult models children are exposed to often display a double standard, with their moral thinking not always corresponding to their actions. A poll of 24,000 Americans sampled their views on a wide variety of moral issues. Eight detailed scenarios of everyday moral problems were developed to test moral decision making. A summary of the responses to these moral dilemmas is shown in figure 14.3. Consider the example of whether the person queried would knowingly buy a stolen color television set. More than 20 percent of the respondents said they would, even though 87 percent said that such an act is probably morally wrong. Further, approximately 31 percent of the adults said that, if they knew they would not get caught, they would be more likely to buy the stolen television. Although moral thought is a very important dimension of moral development, these data glaringly point out that what people believe about right and wrong does not always predict how they will act in moral situations.

In addition to emphasizing the role of reinforcement, punishment, and imitation in determining moral behavior, behaviorists make a strong claim that moral behavior is situationally dependent. That is, from the behavioral perspective, children do not consistently display moral behavior in different situations. In a classic investigation of moral behavior, one of the most extensive ever conducted, Hugh Hartshorne and Mark May (1928–1930) observed the moral responses of 11,000 children who were given the opportunity to lie, cheat, and steal in a variety of circumstances—at home, at school, at social events, and in athletics. A completely honest or a completely dishonest child was difficult to find. Situation-specific behavior was the rule. Children were more likely to cheat when their friends put pressure on them to do so and when the chance of being caught was slim. Other analyses of the consistency of moral behavior suggest that, although moral behavior is influenced by situational determinants, some children are more likely than others to cheat, lie, and steal (Burton, 1984).

Resistance to Temptation and Self-Control

A key ingredient of moral development from the social cognitive perspective is a child's ability to resist temptation and to develop self-control (Bandura, 1986; Mischel, 1987). When pressures mount for children to cheat, lie, or steal, it is important

Would You:	Percentage Who Said Yes, or Probably:	Percentage Who Said It Is, or Probably Is, Unethical:	Percentage Who Would, or Probably Would, Be More Likely to If Sure They Would Not Get Caught:
Drive away after scratching a car without telling the owner?	44%	89%	52%
Cover for a friend's secret affair?	41	66	33
Cheat on your spouse?	37	68	42
Keep $10 extra change at a local supermarket?	26	85	33
Knowingly buy a stolen color television set?	22	87	31
Try to keep your neighborhood segregated?	13	81	8
Drive while drunk?	11	90	24
Accept praise for another's work?	4	96	8

Figure 14.3

The Hypocrisy of Adult Moral Models

to ask whether they have developed the ability to control themselves and to resist such temptations.

Developmentalists have invented a number of ways to investigate such temptations. In one procedure, children are shown attractive toys and told that the toys belong to someone else, who has requested that they not be touched. Children then experience social influence, perhaps in the form of a discussion of virtues about respecting other people's property or in the form of a model resisting or giving in to the temptation to play with prohibited objects. Children are left alone in the room to amuse themselves when the experimenter departs (under a pretext), announcing that he or she will return in 10 to 15 minutes. The experimenter then watches through a one-way mirror to see whether children resist or give in to the temptation to play with the toys.

There has been considerable interest in the effects of punishment on children's ability to resist temptation (Parke, 1972, 1977). For the most part, offering children cognitive rationales enhances most forms of punishment, such as reasons why a child should not play with a forbidden toy. Cognitive rationales have been more effective in getting children to resist temptation over a period of time than have strategies that do not use reasoning, such as when parents place children in their rooms without explaining the consequences for others of the children's deviant behavior.

The ability to resist temptation is closely tied to delay of gratification. Self-control is involved in both the ability to resist temptation and the ability to delay gratification. In the case of resisting temptation, children must overcome their impulses to get something that is desired but is known to be prohibited. Similarly, children must show a sense of patience and self-control in delaying gratification for a desirable future reward rather than succumbing to the immediate pressure of pursuing a smaller reward.

Considerable research has been conducted on children's self-control. Walter Mischel (1974) believes that self-control is strongly influenced by cognitive factors.

Researchers have shown that children can instruct themselves to be more patient and, in the process, show more self-control. In one investigation, preschool children were asked to perform a very dull task (Mischel & Patterson, 1976). Close by was a very enticing talking mechanical clown that tried to persuade the children to play with it. The children who had been trained to say to themselves, "I'm not going to look at Mr. Clown when Mr. Clown says to look at him" were more likely to control their behavior and continue working on the dull task than were children who were not given the self-instructional strategy.

Interest in the cognitive factors in resistance to temptation, delay of gratification, and self-control reflects the increasing interest among social cognitive theorists in the ways in which such cognitions mediate the link between environmental experiences and moral behavior. Next, we will examine a view that captures this cognitive trend.

Social Cognitive Theory

social cognitive theory of morality
The theory that distinguishes between *moral competence* (the ability to perform moral behaviors) and *moral performance* (performing those behaviors in specific situations).

The **social cognitive theory of morality** *emphasizes a distinction between a child's* moral competence *(the ability to perform moral behaviors) and* moral performance *(performing those behaviors in specific situations)* (Mischel & Mischel, 1975). Moral competence, or acquisition of moral knowledge, depends primarily on cognitive-sensory processes; it is the outgrowth of these processes. Competencies include what children are capable of doing, what they know, their skills, their awareness of moral rules and regulations, and their cognitive ability to construct behaviors. Children's moral performance, or behavior, however, is determined by their motivation and the rewards and incentives to act in a specific moral way. Albert Bandura (1991) also believes that moral development is best understood by considering a combination of social and cognitive factors, especially those involving self-control.

In general, social cognitive theorists have been critical of Kohlberg's theory of moral development. Among other reasons, they believe he placed too little emphasis on moral behavior and the situational determinants of morality. However, although Kohlberg argued that moral judgment is an important determinant of moral behavior, he, like the Mischels, stressed that an individual's interpretation of both the moral and the factual aspects of a situation leads to a moral decision (Kohlberg & Candee, 1979). For example, Kohlberg mentioned that "extra-moral" factors, such as the desire to avoid embarrassment, may cause children to avoid doing what they believe to be morally right. In sum, according to both the Mischels and Kohlberg, moral action is influenced by complex factors. Overall, the findings are mixed with regard to the association of moral thought and behavior (Arnold, 1989), although in one investigation with college students, individuals with both highly principled moral reasoning and high ego strength were less likely to cheat in a resistance-to-temptation situation than were their low-principled and low-ego-strength counterparts (Hess, Lonky, & Roodin, 1985).

At this point, we have discussed a number of ideas about moral behavior. A review of these ideas is presented in summary table 14.2. Now that we have studied children's moral thinking and moral behavior, we turn our attention to a third important dimension of moral development—moral feelings.

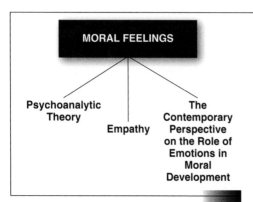

Moral Feelings

Think about when you do something you sense is wrong—does it affect you emotionally? Maybe you get a twinge of guilt. And when you give someone a gift, you might feel joy. Let's further explore the nature of moral feelings.

Psychoanalytic Theory

In chapter 2, we discussed Sigmund Freud's psychoanalytic theory, which describes the *superego* as one of the three main structures of personality (the id and ego are the other two) ◀‖‖ P. 32. In Freud's classical psychoanalytic theory, a child's super-

SUMMARY TABLE 14.2
Moral Behavior

Concept	Processes/ Related Ideas	Characteristics/Description
Basic Processes	Reinforcement, Punishment, and Imitation	• Behaviorists argue that children's moral behavior is determined by the processes of reinforcement, punishment, and imitation.
	Situational Variations	• Situational variability in moral behavior is stressed by behaviorists. • In Hartshorne and May's classic study, considerable situational variation in moral behavior was found.
Resistance to Temptation and Self-Control	Their Nature	• Behaviorists who study children's moral behavior often examine resistance to temptation and the development of self-control. • The use of rationales and self-instruction helps children to increase their self-control.
Social Cognitive Theory	Its Nature	• Social cognitive theory emphasizes a distinction between moral competence (the ability to perform moral behaviors) and moral performance (performing those behaviors in specific situations). • Social cognitive theorists believe Kohlberg gave inadequate attention to moral behavior and situational variations.

ego—the moral branch of personality—develops as the child resolves the Oedipus conflict and identifies with the same-sex parent in the early childhood years. One reason children resolve the Oedipus conflict is to alleviate the fears of losing their parents' love and of being punished for their unacceptable sexual wishes toward the opposite-sex parent. To reduce anxiety, avoid punishment, and maintain parental affection, children form a superego by identifying with the same-sex parent. Through this identification, children internalize the parent's standards of right and wrong that reflect societal prohibitions. Also, the child turns inward the hostility that was previously aimed externally at the same-sex parent. This inwardly directed hostility is then experienced self-punitively (and unconsciously) as guilt. In the psychoanalytic account of moral development, self-punitiveness of guilt keeps children from committing transgressions. That is, children conform to societal standards to avoid guilt.

In Freud's view, the superego consists of two main components, the ego-ideal and conscience, which promote children's development of moral feelings. The *ego ideal* is the component of the superego that involves ideal standards approved of by parents, whereas *conscience* is the component of the superego that involves behaviors disapproved of by parents. A child's ego-ideal rewards the child by conveying a sense of pride and personal value when the child acts according to moral standards. The conscience punishes the child for acting immorally by making the child feel guilty and worthless. In this way, self-control replaces parental control.

What is moral is what you feel good after and what is immoral is what you feel bad after.

Ernest Hemingway
American Author, 20th Century

Empathy

Positive feelings, such as empathy, contribute to the child's moral development. Feeling **empathy** *means reacting to another's feelings with an emotional response that is similar to the other's feelings* (Damon, 1988). Although empathy is experienced as an emotional state, it often has a cognitive component—the ability to discern another's inner psychological states, or what we have previously called *perspective taking* (Eisenberg, 2000; Eisenberg & others, 1991). Infants have the capacity for some purely empathic responses, but, for effective moral action, children need to learn to identify a wide range of emotional states in others and to anticipate what kinds of action will improve another person's emotional state.

empathy
Reacting to another's feelings with an emotional response that is similar to the other's feelings.

What are the main milestones in children's development of empathy? According to an analysis by child developmentalist William Damon (1988), changes in empathy take place in early infancy, at 1 to 2 years in age, in early childhood, and at 10 to 12 years of age. *Global empathy* is the young infant's empathic response in which clear boundaries between the feelings and needs of the self and those of another have not yet been established. For example, one 11-month-old infant fought off her own tears, sucked her thumb, and buried her head in her mother's lap after she had seen another child fall and hurt himself. Not all infants cry every time someone else is hurt, though. Many times, an infant will stare at another's pain with curiosity. Although global empathy is observed in some infants, it does not consistently characterize all infants' behavior.

Between 1 and 2 years of age, the infant's undifferentiated feelings of discomfort at another's distress grow into more genuine feelings of concern. The infant realizes that others are independent persons in their own right, with their own unhappy feelings. The infant may sense that these unhappy feelings in others need attention and relief, but the infant cannot translate this realization into effective behavior. For example, toddlers may offer a beloved blanket or doll for comfort to an unhappy-looking adult. In one study, empathy appeared more regularly after 18 months (Lamb, 1993).

In the early childhood years, children become aware that every person's perspective is unique and that someone else may have a reaction to a situation that is different from their own. Such awareness permits the child to respond more appropriately to another's distress. For example, at the age of 6, a child may realize that, in some instances, an unhappy person may best be left alone rather than helped, or the child may learn to wait for just the right time to give comfort. In sum, at this point, children make more objective assessments of others' distress and needs.

Toward the end of the elementary school years, at about 10 to 12 years of age, children develop empathy for people who live in unfortunate circumstances. Children's concerns are no longer limited to the feelings of particular persons in situations the child observes directly (Shorr & Shorr, 1995). Instead, children expand their concerns to the general problems of people in unfortunate situations—the poor, the handicapped, and the socially outcast, for example. This newfound sensitivity may lead to altruistic behavior by the older elementary school child and later, in adolescence, give a humanitarian flavor to the adolescent's development of ideological and political views. A summary of Damon's description of empathy development is shown in figure 14.4.

Although everyone may be capable of responding with empathy, not all individuals do. There is considerable variation in individual empathic behavior. For example, in older children and adolescents, empathic dysfunctions can contribute to antisocial behavior. Some delinquents convicted of violent crimes show a lack of feeling for their victims' distress. A 13-year-old boy convicted of violently mugging a number of elderly people, when asked about the pain he had caused for one blind woman, said, "What do I care? I'm not her" (Damon, 1988).

Not only is there individual variation in adolescents' empathy and concern about the welfare of others, but sociohistorical influences also may be involved. Over the past two decades, adolescents have shown an increased concern for personal well-being and a decreased concern for the welfare of others, especially for the dis-

**Developing Empathy
in Children and Youth**

**Moral Development, Empathy,
and Violent Boys**

Age period	Nature of empathy
Early infancy	Characterized by global empathy, the young infant's empathic response does not distinguish between feelings and needs of self and others.
1 to 2 years of age	Undifferentiated feelings of discomfort at another's distress grow into more genuine feelings of concern, but infants cannot translate realization of other's unhappy feelings into effective action.
Early childhood	Children become aware that every person's perspective is unique and that someone else may have a different reaction to a situation. This awareness allows the child to respond more appropriately to another person's distress.
10 to 12 years of age	Children develop an emergent orientation of empathy for people who live in unfortunate circumstances—the poor, the handicapped, and the socially outcast. In adolescence, this newfound sensitivity may give a humanitarian flavor to the individual's ideological and political views.

Figure **14.4**
Damon's Description of Developmental Changes in Empathy

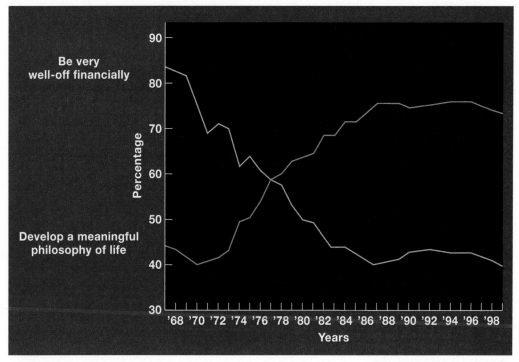

Figure 14.5
Changing Freshman Life Goals, 1968–1999

In the last three decades, a significant change has occurred in freshmen students' life goals. A far greater percentage of today's college freshmen state that a "very important" life goal is to be well-off financially, and far fewer state that developing a meaningful philosophy of life is a "very important" life goal.

advantaged. As shown in figure 14.5, today's college freshmen are more strongly motivated to be well-off financially and less motivated to develop a meaningful philosophy of life than were their counterparts 20 or even 10 years ago (Sax & others, 1999). Among high school seniors, increasing numbers are motivated by the opportunity to make a considerable amount of money (Bachman, Johnston, & O'Malley, 1987).

However, two values that increased during the 1960s continue to be important to today's youth: self-fulfillment and self-expression. As part of their motivation for self-fulfillment, many adolescents show great interest in their physical health and well-being. Greater self-fulfillment and self-expression can be laudable goals, but if they become the only goals, self-destruction, loneliness, or alienation may result. Young people also need to develop a corresponding sense of commitment to others' welfare (Yates, 1996). Encouraging adolescents to have a strong commitment to others, in concert with an interest in self-fulfillment, is a major task for our nation at the beginning of the twenty-first century.

Values of American College Freshmen

The Contemporary Perspective on the Role of Emotions in Moral Development

We have seen that classical psychoanalytic theory emphasizes the power of unconscious guilt in moral development but that other theorists, such as Damon, emphasize the role of empathy. Today, many child developmentalists believe that both positive feelings, such as empathy, sympathy, admiration, and self-esteem, and negative feelings, such as anger, outrage, shame, and guilt, contribute to children's moral development (Damon, 1988; Eisenberg & Fabes, 1998; Roberts & Strayer, 1996). When strongly experienced, these emotions influence children to act in accord with standards of right and wrong. Such emotions as empathy, shame, guilt, and anxiety over other people's violations of standards are present early in development and undergo developmental change throughout childhood and beyond (Damon, 1988). These emotions provide a natural base for children's acquisition of moral values, both orienting children toward moral events and motivating them to pay close attention to such events. However, moral emotions do not operate in a vacuum to build a child's moral awareness, and they are not sufficient in themselves to generate moral responsivity. They do not give the "substance" of moral regulation—the rules, values, and standards of behavior that children need to understand and act on. Moral emotions are inextricably interwoven with the cognitive and social aspects of children's development.

In one study of fifth-, eighth-, and eleventh-graders, parents were the individuals most likely to evoke guilt (Williams & Bybee, 1994). With development, guilt evoked by family members was less prevalent, but guilt engendered by girlfriends or boyfriends was more frequent. At the higher grade levels, the percentage of students reporting guilt about aggressive, externalizing behaviors declined, whereas those mentioning guilt over internal thoughts and inconsiderateness increased. Males were more likely to report guilt over externalizing behaviors, while females reported more guilt over violating norms of compassion and trust.

The web of feeling, cognition, and social behavior is also experienced in altruism—the aspect of children's moral development we will discuss next.

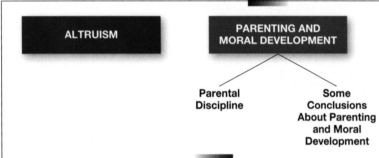

altruism
Unselfish interest in helping another person.

But you cannot give to people what they are incapable of receiving.

Agatha Christie
English Mystery Writer, 20th Century

Altruism

Altruism *is an unselfish interest in helping another person.* Human acts of altruism are plentiful—the hardworking laborer who places $5 in a Salvation Army kettle; rock concerts to feed the hungry, help farmers, and fund AIDS research; and the child who takes in a wounded cat and cares for it. How do psychologists account for such acts of altruism?

Reciprocity and exchange often are involved in altruism (Clark, 2000). Reciprocity is found throughout the human world. Not only is it the highest moral principle in Christianity, but it is also present in every widely practiced religion in the world—Judaism, Hinduism, Buddhism, and Islam. Reciprocity encourages children to do unto others as they would have others do unto them. Human sentiments are wrapped up in this reciprocity. Trust is probably the most important principle, over the long run, in altruism. Guilt surfaces if the child does not reciprocate, and anger may result if someone else does not reciprocate. Not all altruism is motivated by reciprocity and exchange, but self-other interactions and relationships help us understand altruism's nature. The circumstances most likely to involve altruism are empathic emotion for an individual in need or a close relationship between benefactor and recipient (Batson, 1989).

In addition to presenting a developmental sequence of children's empathy, which we discussed earlier, Damon (1988) has also described a developmental sequence of children's altruism, especially of sharing. Most sharing during the first 3 years of life is done for nonempathic reasons, such as for the fun of the social play ritual or out of mere imitation. Then, at about 4 years of age, a combination of empathic awareness and adult encouragement produces a sense of obligation on the part of the child to share with others. This obligation forces the child to share, even though the child may not perceive this as the best way to have fun. Most 4-year-olds are not selfless saints, however. Children believe they have an obligation to share but do not necessarily think they should be as generous to others as they are to themselves. Neither do their actions always support their beliefs, especially when the object of contention is coveted. What is important developmentally is that the child has developed an internal belief that sharing is an obligatory part of a social relationship and that this involves a question of right and wrong. However, a preschool child's sense of reciprocity does not constitute a moral duty but, rather, is a pragmatic means of getting one's way. Despite their shortcomings, these ideas about justice formed in early childhood set the stage for giant strides that children make in the years that follow.

By the start of the elementary school years, children genuinely begin to express more objective ideas about fairness. These notions about fairness have been used throughout history to distribute goods and to resolve conflicts. They involve the principles of equality, merit, and benevolence. *Equality* means that everyone is treated the same. *Merit* means giving extra rewards for hard work, a talented performance, or other laudatory behavior. *Benevolence* means giving special consideration to individuals in a disadvantaged condition. Equality is the first of these principles used regularly by elementary school children. It is common to hear 6-year-old children use the word *fair* as synonymous with *equal* or *same.* By the mid to late elementary school years, children also believe that equity means special treatment for those who deserve it—the principles of merit and benevolence.

Missing from the factors that guide children's altruism is one that many adults might expect to be the most influential of all: the motivation to obey adult authority figures. Surprisingly, a number of studies have shown that adult authority has only a small influence on children's sharing. For example, when Nancy Eisenberg (1982) asked children to explain their own altruistic acts, they mainly gave empathic and pragmatic reasons for their spontaneous acts of sharing. Not one of the children referred to the demands of adult authority. Parental advice and prodding certainly foster standards of sharing, but the give-and-take of peer requests and arguments provide the most immediate stimulation of sharing. Parents can set examples that children carry into peer interaction and communication, but parents are not present during all of their children's peer exchanges. The day-to-day construction of fairness standards is done by children in collaboration and negotiation with each other. Over the course of many years and thousands of encounters, children's understanding of altruism deepens. With this conceptual elaboration that involves such notions as equality, merit, benevolence, and compromise come a greater consistency and generosity in children's sharing behavior (Damon, 1988).

Without civic morality communities perish; without personal morality their survival has no value.

Bertrand Russell
English Philosopher, 20th Century

Parenting and Moral Development

Both Piaget and Kohlberg held that parents do not provide any unique or essential inputs to children's moral development. They do believe that parents are responsible for providing general role-taking opportunities and cognitive conflict, but they reserve the primary role in moral development for peers (Walker, 1996). Earlier in the chapter we discussed recent research that revealed how both parents and peers contribute to children's moral maturity (Walker, Hennig, & Krettenauer, in press). A general Socratic style of eliciting the other's opinion and checking for understanding was effective in advancing both moral maturity in both parent and peer contexts. Here we will focus more on parental discipline and its role in moral development and then draw some conclusions about parenting and moral development.

Parental Discipline

In Freud's psychoanalytic theory, the aspects of child rearing that encourage moral development are practices that instill the fears of punishment and of losing parental love. Child developmentalists who have studied child-rearing techniques and moral development have focused on parents' discipline techniques. These include love withdrawal, power assertion, and induction (Hoffman, 1970). Love withdrawal comes closest to the psychoanalytic emphasis on fear of punishment and of losing parental love. **Love withdrawal** *is a discipline technique in which a parent withholds attention or love from the child,* as when the parent refuses to talk to the child or states a dislike for the child. For example, the parent might say, "I'm going to leave you if you do that again," or "I don't like you when you do that." **Power assertion** *is a discipline*

love withdrawal
A discipline technique in which a parent withholds attention or love from the child.

power assertion
A discipline technique in which a parent attempts to gain control over the child or the child's resources.

induction
A discipline technique in which a parent uses reason and explanation of the consequences for others of the child's actions.

technique in which a parent attempts to gain control over the child or the child's resources. Examples include spanking, threatening, or removing privileges. **Induction** *is the discipline technique in which a parent uses reason and explanation of the consequences for others of the child's actions.* Examples of induction include, "Don't hit him. He was only trying to help" and "Why are you yelling at her? She didn't mean to trip you."

Moral development theorist and researcher Martin Hoffman (1970) believes that any discipline produces arousal on the child's part. Love withdrawal and power assertion are likely to evoke a very high level of arousal, with love withdrawal generating considerable anxiety and power assertion considerable hostility. Induction is more likely to produce a moderate level of arousal in children, a level that permits them to attend to the cognitive rationales parents offer. When a parent uses power assertion and love withdrawal, the child may be so aroused that, even if the parent gives accompanying explanations about the consequences for others of the child's actions, the child might not attend to them. Power assertion presents parents as weak models of self-control—as individuals who cannot control their feelings. Accordingly, children may imitate this model of poor self-control when they face stressful circumstances. The use of induction, however, focuses the child's attention on the action's consequences for others, not on the child's own shortcomings. For these reasons, Hoffman (1988) believes that parents should use induction to encourage children's moral development. In research on parenting techniques, induction is more positively related to moral development than is love withdrawal or power assertion, although the findings vary according to children's developmental level and socioeconomic status. Induction works better with elementary-school-age children than with preschool children (Brody & Shaffer, 1982) and better with middle-SES than with lower-SES children (Hoffman, 1970). Older children are probably better able to understand the reasons given to them and are better at perspective taking. Some theorists believe that the internalization of society's moral standards is more likely among middle-SES than among lower-SES individuals, because internalization is more rewarding in the middle-SES culture (Kohn, 1977).

Some Conclusions About Parenting and Moral Development

Parental discipline does contribute to children's moral development, but there are other aspects of parenting that also play an important role, such as providing opportunities for perspective taking and modeling moral behavior and thinking. Nancy Eisenberg and Bridget Murphy (1995) recently summarized the findings from the research literature on ways in which parenting can influence children's moral development. They concluded that, in general, moral children tend to have parents who

• Are warm and supportive rather than punitive
• Use inductive discipline
• Provide opportunities for the children to learn about others' perspectives and feelings
• Involve children in family decision making and in the process of thinking about moral decisions
• Model moral behaviors and thinking themselves and provide opportunities for their children to model such moral behaviors and thinking

Parents who show this configuration of behaviors likely foster the development of concern and caring about others in their children, and create a positive parent-child relationship. These parents also provide information about what behaviors are expected of the child and why, and promote an internal rather than an external sense of morality.

At this point we have studied a number of ideas about moral feelings, altruism, and the role of parenting in moral development. A review of these ideas is presented

SUMMARY TABLE 14.3
Moral Feelings, Altruism, and Parenting

Concept	Processes/ Related Ideas	Characteristics/Description
Moral Feelings	Psychoanalytic Theory	• In Freud's theory, the superego—the moral branch of personality—is one of personality's three main structures. • Through identification, children internalize a parent's standards of right and wrong. • Children conform to moral standards to avoid guilt. • The two main components of the superego are ego ideal and conscience.
	Empathy	• Feeling empathy means reacting to another's feelings with an emotional response that is similar to the other's feelings. • Empathy often has a cognitive component—perspective taking. • Empathy changes developmentally.
	The Contemporary Perspective	• Both positive feelings (such as empathy) and negative feelings (such as guilt) contribute to children's moral development. • Emotions are interwoven with the cognitive and social dimensions of moral development.
Altruism	Its Nature	• Altruism is an unselfish interest in helping another person. • Reciprocity and exchange are involved in altruism. • Damon described a developmental sequence of altruism that highlights sharing.
Parenting and Moral Development	Parental Discipline	• Discipline can involve love withdrawal, power assertion, or induction. • Induction has been the most effective technique, especially with middle-SES children.
	Some Conclusions About Parenting and Moral Development	• Children's moral development is advanced when parents are warm and supportive rather than punitive, provide opportunities for their children to learn about others' perspectives and feelings, involve children in family decision making, and model moral behavior and thinking.

in summary table 14.3. Now that we have studied the role of parents in children's moral development, let's turn our attention to another social context in which children learn about moral development—schools.

Moral Education

Moral education is hotly debated in educational circles. We will study one of the earliest analyses of moral education, then turn to some contemporary views.

The Hidden Curriculum

More than 60 years ago, educator John Dewey (1933) recognized that even when schools do not have specific programs in moral education, they provide moral education through a "hidden curriculum." The **hidden curriculum** *is conveyed by the moral atmosphere that is a part of every school.* The moral atmosphere is created by school and classroom rules, the moral orientation of teachers and school administrators, and text materials. Teachers serve as models of ethical or unethical behavior. Classroom rules and peer relations at school transmit attitudes about cheating, lying, stealing, and consideration of others. And through its rules and regulations, the school administration infuses the school with a value system.

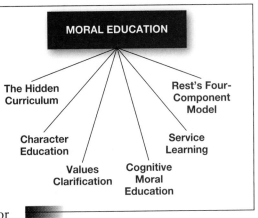

hidden curriculum
The moral atmosphere that is part of every school.

Character Education

Character education *is a direct approach that involves teaching students a basic moral literacy to prevent them from engaging in immoral behavior and doing harm to themselves or others.* The argument is that such behaviors as lying, stealing, and cheating are wrong and students should be taught this throughout their education. Every school should have an explicit moral code that is clearly communicated to students. Any violations of the code should be met with sanctions (Bennett, 1993). Instruction in specified moral concepts, like cheating, can take the form of example and definition, class discussions and role-playing, or rewarding students for proper behavior.

Some character education movements are the Character Education Partnership, the Character Education Network, the Aspen Declaration on Character Education, and the publicity campaign "Character Counts." Books that promote character education include William Bennett's (1993) *Book of Virtues* and William Damon's (1995) *Greater Expectations.*

Variations in Moral Education

Association for Moral Education

Moral Education in Japan

Values Clarification

Values clarification *means helping people to clarify what their lives are for and what is worth working for.* In this approach, students are encouraged to define their own values and understand the values of others. Values clarification differs from character education in not telling students what their values should be.

In the following values clarification example, students are asked to select from among 10 people the 6 who will be admitted to a safe shelter because a third world war has broken out (Johnson, 1990):

> You work for a government agency in Washington and your group has to decide which six of the following ten people will be admitted to a small fallout shelter. Your group has only 20 minutes to make the decision. These are your choices:
> • A 30-year-old male bookkeeper
> • The bookkeeper's wife, who is 6 months pregnant
> • A second-year African American male medical student who is a political activist
> • A 42-year-old male who is a famous historian-author
> • A Hollywood actress who is a singer and dancer
> • A female biochemist
> • A 54-year-old male rabbi
> • A male Olympic athlete who is good in all sports
> • A female college student
> • A policeman with a gun

In this type of values clarification exercise, there are no right or wrong answers. The clarification of values is left up to the individual student. Advocates of values clarification say it is value-free. However, critics argue that its controversial content offends community standards. They also say that because of its relativistic nature, values clarification undermines accepted values and fails to stress right behavior.

Cognitive Moral Education

Cognitive moral education *is a concept based on the belief that students should learn to value things like democracy and justice as their moral reasoning develops.* Kohlberg's theory has been the basis for a number of cognitive moral education programs. In a typical program, high school students meet in a semester-long course to discuss a number of moral issues. The instructor acts as a facilitator rather than as a director of the class. The hope is that students will develop more advanced notions of such concepts as cooperation, trust, responsibility, and community. Toward the end of his career, Kohlberg (1986) recognized that the moral atmosphere of the school is more important than he initially envisioned. For example, in one study, a semester-long moral education class based on Kohlberg's theory was successful in advancing moral thinking in three democratic schools but not in three authoritarian schools (Higgins, Power, & Kohlberg, 1983).

In our coverage of moral education, we have examined John Dewey's concept of the hidden curriculum, character education, values clarification, and cognitive moral education. As we see next, there is increasing interest in including service learning in education, especially at the secondary school level.

Service Learning

Service learning *is a form of education that promotes social responsibility and service to the community.* In service learning, adolescents might engage in tutoring, help the elderly, work in a hospital, assist at a day-care center, or clean up a vacant lot to make a play area. An important goal of service learning is for adolescents to become less self-centered and more strongly motivated to help others (Waterman, 1997).

Service learning takes education out into the community (Levesque & Prosser, 1996). One eleventh-grade student worked as a reading tutor for students from low-income backgrounds with reading skills well below their grade levels. She commented that until she did the tutoring she did not realize how many students had not experienced the same opportunities that she had when she was growing up. An especially rewarding moment was when one young girl told her, "I want to learn to read like you so I can go to college when I grow up." Thus, service learning not only can benefit adolescents but also the recipients of their help.

Researchers have found that service learning benefits adolescents in a number of ways:

- Their grades improve, they become more motivated, and set more goals (Johnson & others, 1998; Search Institute, 1999; Serow, Ciechalski, & Daye, 1990).
- Their self-esteem improves (Hamburg, 1997; Johnson & others, 1998).
- They have an improved sense of being able to make a difference for others (Search Institute, 1999).
- They become less alienated (Calabrase & Schumer, 1986).
- They increasingly reflect on society's political organization and moral order (Yates, 1995).

Required community service has increased in high schools. In one survey, 15 percent of the nation's largest school districts had such a requirement (National Community Service Coalition, 1995). Even though required community service has increased in high schools, in one survey of 40,000 adolescents, two-thirds said that they had never done any volunteer work to help other people (Benson, 1993). The benefits of service learning, both for the volunteer and the recipient, suggest that more adolescents should be required to participate in such programs.

Now that we have discussed a number of ideas about moral education, we will turn our attention to James Rest's model of moral development and its implications of moral education.

Rest's Four-Component Model

James Rest (Rest, 1995; Rest & others, 1999) believes that moral development builds upon four basic processes: moral sensitivity, moral judgment, moral motivation, and moral character.

ADVENTURES FOR THE MIND

Exploring Your Values

WHAT ARE YOUR VALUES? What is really important to you in life? To help explore your values, ask yourself to what extent you agree with the following:

- The federal government can do more to control handguns.
- It is okay to cheat on your taxes.
- Family is the most important aspect of life.
- Work is the most important aspect of life.
- Legal-status should be given to same-sex couples.
- Marijuana should be legalized.
- Racial discrimination no longer is a problem.
- A woman's best place is in the home.
- It is okay for people to have sex if they like each other.

Now that you have thought about some aspects of values, write down the five most important values to you:

1. _____
2. _____
3. _____
4. _____
5. _____

Spend a few minutes thinking about how you got these values. Were they influenced by your parents, friends, teachers? Did some event or experience lead you to adopt a particular value? How deeply have you thought about which values are most important to you?

service learning
A form of education that promotes social responsibility and service to the community.

National Service Learning Clearinghouse

Give Five

Kids Who Care

Volunteer Matching Online

Exploring Character Education

The Center for the Fourth and Fifth RS

Character Education Topics

Exploring Values Education

More than just about anything else, 12-year-old Katie Bell (at bottom) wanted a playground in her New Jersey town. She knew that other kids also wanted one so she put together a group, which generated fundraising ideas for the playground. They presented their ideas to the town council. Her group got more youth involved. They helped raise money by selling candy and sandwiches door-to-door. Katie says, "We learned to work as a community. This will be an important place for people to go and have picnics and make new friends." Katie's advice, "You won't get anywhere if you don't try."

Moral sensitivity involves interpreting situations and being aware of how our actions affect other people. It involves being aware of the different possible lines of action and how each line of action could affect the parties concerned, including oneself. Moral sensitivity consists of imaginatively constructing possible scenarios (often from limited cues and partial information), envisioning consequent chains of events in the real world, and empathy and role-taking skills. Moral sensitivity is needed to become aware that there is a moral issue in a situation.

Moral judgment involves making decisions about which actions are right and which are wrong. Once the person is aware that these various lines of action are possible, the question becomes, Which line of action has greater moral justification? This is the process emphasized by Piaget and Kohlberg. Even at an early age people have intuitions about what is fair and moral and make moral judgments about even the most complex human activities. The psychologist's job is to understand how these intuitions arise and determine what governs their application to real-world events.

Moral motivation involves prioritizing moral values over other personal values. People have many values, including those related to careers, affectionate relationships, aesthetic preferences, institutional loyalties, hedonistic pleasures, excitement, and so on. Why place a higher priority on moral values than on other values? The behavior of the most evil people the world has ever known, such as Hitler and Stalin, can be explained in terms of the low priority they gave to moral values and need not be explained as due to deficiencies in moral sensitivity and moral judgment. Further, people like Hitler and Stalin probably rated high on the next component of moral development.

Moral character involves having the strength of your convictions, persisting, and overcoming distractions and obstacles. An individual might have all of the first three components (might be sensitive to moral issues, have good judgment, and give high priority to moral values), but if the person does not have moral character, he or she might wilt under pressure or fatigue, fail to follow through, or become distracted or discouraged, and fail to produce moral behavior. Moral character presupposes that the person has set goals and that achieving those goals involves the strength and skills to act in accord with those goals. The individual with moral character does not act impulsively and has considerable self-discipline. Rest, as well as others, believes that Kohlberg's theory does not adequately focus on moral character (Walker & Pitts, 1998).

Rest's four-component model is useful in comparing different approaches to moral education (see figure 14.6):

1. The dilemma discussion approach, promoted in Kohlberg's earlier writings, emphasizes moral judgment. This cognitive moral education approach is still widely used with individuals in college or professional schools; it assumes that students are already advanced in basic socialization (by virtue of having made it through so much schooling). Here the main social concern is to prepare professionals to make decisions that will be morally right.
2. The character education approach emphasizes the fourth component—moral character—and the development of self-discipline consistent with living in a civilized society. Children, especially those prone to juvenile delinquency, are special targets of character education. The main social concern in character education is to eliminate the destructive behavior of youth (such as violence, drugs, and adolescent pregnancy).

3. Sensitivity approaches—such as sensitivity training for improved face-to-face communication, sensitivity to cultural diversity, sensitivity to sexual harassment, and sensitivity to physical and psychological abuse—emphasize the first component: moral sensitivity. The sensitivity approaches are aimed at individuals of all ages.

4. The communitarian approach suggests that students, usually middle school and secondary school students, should be involved in community service. The main social concern is to strengthen ties to social units larger than just the family. By emphasizing the importance of rootedness in the community, this approach is aimed at the third component of moral development—moral motivation.

At this point we have explored many aspects of moral development. When individuals engage in juvenile delinquency or commit violent acts, such as killing someone, questions often are raised about whether the adolescents have an adequate sense of morality—that is, of what is right and what is wrong. Let's now explore the nature of juvenile delinquency.

COMPONENT	EDUCATION
Moral sensitivity	Sensitivity approaches
Moral judgment	Cognitive moral education
Moral motivation	Communitarian approach
Moral character	Character education

Figure **14.6**

Rest's Components of Moral Development and Their Application to Education

Juvenile Delinquency

What is a juvenile delinquent? What are the antecedents of delinquency? What types of interventions have been used to prevent or reduce delinquency?

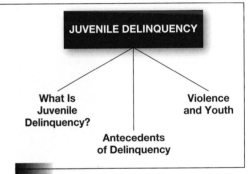

What Is Juvenile Delinquency?

The term **juvenile delinquency** *refers to a broad range of behaviors, ranging from socially unacceptable behavior (such as acting out in school) to status offenses (such as running away) to criminal acts (such as burglary).* For legal purposes, a distinction is made between index offenses and status offenses. **Index offenses** *are criminal acts, whether they are committed by juveniles or adults. They include such acts as robbery, aggravated assault, rape, and homicide.* **Status offenses,** *such as running away, truancy, underage drinking, sexual promiscuity, and uncontrollability, are less serious acts. They are performed by youth under a specified age, which classifies them as juvenile offenses.* States often differ in the age used to classify an individual as a juvenile or an adult. Approximately three-fourths of the states have established age 18 as a maximum for defining juveniles. Two states use age 19 as the cutoff, seven states use age 17, and four states use age 16. Thus, running away from home at age 17 may be an offense in some states but not others.

How many adolescents are arrested each year for committing juvenile delinquency offenses? In 1997, law enforcement agencies made an estimated 2.8 million arrests of individuals under the age of 18 in the United States (Office of Juvenile Justice and Prevention, 1998). This represents about 10 percent of adolescents 10 to 18 years of age in the United States. Note that this figure reflects only adolescents who have been arrested and does not include those who committed offenses but were not apprehended. In 1997, 26 percent of all juvenile arrests involved a female.

In addition to the legal classifications of index offenses and status offenses, many of the behaviors considered delinquent are included in widely used classifications of abnormal behavior. **Conduct disorder** *is the psychiatric diagnostic category used when multiple behaviors occur over a 6-month period. These behaviors include truancy, running away, fire setting, cruelty to animals, breaking and entering, excessive fighting, and others. When three or more of these behaviors co-occur before the age of 15 and the child or adolescent is considered unmanageable or out of control, the clinical diagnosis is conduct disorder.*

In sum, most children or adolescents at one time or another act out or do things that are destructive or troublesome for themselves or others. If these behaviors occur often in childhood or early adolescence, psychiatrists diagnose them as conduct

juvenile delinquency
A broad range of behaviors, ranging from socially unacceptable behavior (such as acting out in school) to status offenses (such as running away) to criminal acts (such as burglary).

index offenses
Criminal acts, whether they are committed by juveniles or adults. They include such acts as robbery, aggravated assault, rape, and homicide.

status offenses
Less serious acts (than index offenses). Status offenses include truancy, underage drinking, sexual promiscuity, and uncontrollability. They are performed by youth under a specified age, which make them juvenile offenses.

conduct disorder
The psychiatric diagnosis category used when multiple behaviors occur over a 6-month period. These behaviors include truancy, running away, fire setting, cruelty to animals, breaking and entering, excessive fighting, and others. When three or more of these behaviors co-occur before the age of 15 and the child or adolescent is considered unmanageable or out of control, the clinical diagnosis is conduct disorder.

**Office of Juvenile Justice
and Delinquency Prevention**

Justice Information Center

Preventing Crime

disorders. If these behaviors result in illegal acts by juveniles, society labels them *delinquents.*

One issue in juvenile justice is whether an adolescent who commits a crime should be tried as an adult. In a recent study, trying adolescent offenders as adults increased their crime rate rather than reducing it (Myers, 1999). In the study, more than 500 violent youths in Pennsylvania, which has adopted a "get tough" policy, were evaluated. Although these 500 offenders had been given harsher punishment than a comparison group retained in juvenile court, they were more likely to be rearrested—and rearrested more quickly—for new offenses once they were returned to the community. This suggests that the price of short-term public safety attained by prosecuting juveniles as adults might actually increase long-term criminal offenses.

Antecedents of Delinquency

Predictors of delinquency include identity (negative identity), self-control (low degree), age (early initiation), sex (male), expectations for education (low expectations, little commitment), school grades (low achievement in early grades), peer influence (heavy influence, low resistance), socioeconomic status (low), parental role (lack of monitoring, low support, and ineffective discipline), and neighborhood quality (urban, high crime, high mobility). A summary of these antecedents of delinquency is presented in figure 14.7.

Antecedent	Association with delinquency	Description
Identity	Negative identity	Erikson believes delinquency occurs because the adolescent fails to resolve a role identity.
Self-control	Low degree	Some children and adolescents fail to acquire the essential controls that others have acquired during the process of growing up.
Age	Early initiation	Early appearance of antisocial behavior is associated with serious offenses later in adolescence. However, not every child who acts out becomes a delinquent.
Sex	Male	Boys engage in more antisocial behavior than girls do, although girls are more likely to run away. Boys engage in more violent acts.
Expectations for education and school grades	Low expectations and low grades	Adolescents who become delinquents often have low educational expectations and low grades. Their verbal abilities are often weak.
Parental influences	Monitoring (low), support (low), discipline (ineffective)	Delinquents often come from families in which parents rarely monitor their adolescents, provide them with little support, and ineffectively discipline them.
Peer influences	Heavy influence, low resistance	Having delinquent peers greatly increases the risk of becoming delinquent.
Socioeconomic status	Low	Serious offenses are committed more frequently by lower-class males.
Neighborhood quality	Urban, high crime, high mobility	Communities often breed crime. Living in a high-crime area, which also is characterized by poverty and dense living conditions, increases the probability that a child will become a delinquent. These communities often have grossly inadequate schools.

Figure **14.7**

The Antecedents of Juvenile Delinquency

Let's look in more detail at several of these factors that are related to delinquency. Erik Erikson (1968) believes that adolescents whose development has restricted their access to acceptable social roles or made them feel that they cannot measure up to the demands placed on them may choose a negative identity. Adolescents with a negative identity may find support for their delinquent image among peers, reinforcing the negative identity. For Erikson, delinquency is an attempt to establish an identity, although it is a negative identity.

Although delinquency is less exclusively a lower-SES phenomenon than it was in the past, some characteristics of lower-SES culture can promote delinquency. The norms of many low-SES peer groups and gangs are antisocial, or counterproductive, to the goals and norms of society at large. Getting into and staying out of trouble are prominent features of life for some adolescents in low-income neighborhoods. Adolescents from low-income backgrounds may sense that they can gain attention and status by performing antisocial actions. Being "tough" and "masculine" are high-status traits for low-SES boys, and these traits are often measured by the adolescent's success in performing and getting away with delinquent acts. A community with a high crime rate also lets the adolescent observe many models who engage in criminal activities. These communities may be characterized by poverty, unemployment, and feelings of alienation toward higher-SES individuals. Quality schooling, educational funding, and organized neighborhood activities may be lacking in these communities.

Family support systems are also associated with delinquency (Feldman & Weinberger, 1994). Parents of delinquents are less skilled in discouraging antisocial behavior and in encouraging skilled behavior than are parents of nondelinquents. Parental monitoring of adolescents is especially important in determining whether an adolescent becomes a delinquent (Patterson, DeBarshye, & Ramsey, 1989). "It's 10 P.M.; do you know where your children are?" seems to be an important question for parents to answer affirmatively. Family discord and inconsistent and inappropriate discipline are also associated with delinquency. Peer relations also are involved in delinquency. Having delinquent peers greatly increases the risk of becoming delinquent.

Violence and Youth

An increasing concern is the high rate of violence displayed by adolescents. In a recent school year, 57 percent of elementary and secondary school principals reported that one or more incidents of crime or violence occurred in their school and were reported to law enforcement officials (National Center for Educational Statistics, 1998). Ten percent of all public schools experience one or more serious violent crimes (murder, rape, physical attack or fight with a weapon, robbery) each year (National Center for Education Statistics, 1998). Physical attacks or fights with a weapon lead the list of reported crimes. Yearly, more than 6,000 students are expelled for bringing firearms or explosives to school.

The following factors often are present in at-risk youths and seem to propel them toward violent acts (Walker, 1998):

- Early involvement with drugs and alcohol
- Easy access to weapons, especially handguns
- Association with antisocial, deviant peer groups
- Pervasive exposure to violence in the media

Many at-risk youths also are easily provoked to rage, reacting aggressively to real or imagined slights and acting upon them, sometimes with tragic consequences. They might misjudge the motives and intentions of others toward them because of the hostility and agitation they carry (Coie & Dodge, 1998). Consequently, they frequently engage in hostile confrontations with peers and teachers. It is not unusual to find anger-prone youth issuing threats of bodily harm to others.

Through the Eyes of Psychologists

Gerald Patterson, *University of Oregon*

"Common parenting weaknesses in the families of antisocial boys include a lack of supervision, poor disciplining skills, limited problem-solving abilities, and a tendency to be uncommunicative with sons."

Oregon Social Learning Center
National Youth Gang Center

A current, special concern in low-income areas is escalating gang violence.

Center for the Prevention of School Violence

A Guide for Safe Schools

School Shootings

Lost Boys

Through the Eyes of Psychologists

James Garbarino, *Cornell University*

"Youth who kill often have a distorted perspective on what is right and wrong. This distorted perspective can become a self-justifying rationale for violence."

These are some of the Oregon Social Learning Center's recommendations for reducing youth violence (Walker, 1998):

- *Recommit to raising children safely and effectively.* This includes engaging in parenting practices that have been shown to produce healthy, well-adjusted children. Such practices include consistent, fair discipline that is not harsh or severely punitive, careful monitoring and supervision, positive family management techniques, involvement in the child's daily life, daily debriefings about the child's experiences, and teaching problem-solving strategies.
- *Make prevention a reality.* Too often lip service is given to prevention strategies without investing in them at the necessary levels to make them effective.
- *Give more support to schools, which are struggling to educate a population that includes many at-risk children.*
- *Forge effective partnerships among families, schools, social service systems, churches, and other agencies to create the socializing experiences that will provide all youth with the opportunity to develop in positive ways.*

There recently has been a rash of murders committed by adolescents, with the targets of their violence being classmates or school personnel. To read further about adolescent murderers, see the Explorations in Child Development box.

At this point we have studied a number of ideas about moral education and juvenile delinquency. A review of these ideas is presented in summary table 14.4.

EXPLORATIONS IN CHILD DEVELOPMENT
Why Youth Kill

IN THE LATE 1990S, a series of school shootings gained national attention. In April 1999, two Columbine High School (in Littleton, Colorado) students, Eric Harris (age 18) and Dylan Klebold (age 17), shot and killed 12 students and a teacher, wounded 23 others, and then killed themselves. In May 1998, slightly-built Kip Kinkel strode into a cafeteria at Thurston High School in Springfield, Oregon, and opened fire on his fellow students, murdering two and injuring many others. Later that day, police went to Kip's home and found his parents lying dead on the floor, also victims of Kip's violence. In 1997, three students were killed and five others wounded in a hallway at Heath High School in West Paducah, Kentucky, by a 14-year-old student. These are but three of many school shooting incidents that have occurred in recent years.

Is there any way psychologists can predict whether a youth will turn violent? It's a complex task, but they have pieced together some clues (Cowley, 1998). Violent youth are overwhelmingly male, and many are driven by feelings of powerlessness. Violence seems to infuse these youth with a sense of power. Sixteen-year-old Luke Woodham was known as a chubby nerd at his school in Pearl, Mississippi. But in the fall of 1997, he shed that image by stabbing his mother to death and shooting nine of his classmates, killing two of them. Woodham wrote in a letter, "I killed because people like me are mistreated every day. Murder is not weak and slow-witted. Murder is gutsy and daring."

Small-town shooting sprees attract attention, but there is far more youth violence in poverty-infested areas of inner cities. Urban poverty fosters powerlessness and the rage that goes with it. Living in poverty is frustrating, and many inner-city neighborhoods provide almost daily op-

portunities to observe violence. Many urban youth who live in poverty also lack adequate parent involvement and supervision.

University of Virginia psychologist Dewey Cornell (1998) says that many youth give clear indications of their future violence but aren't taken seriously. Cornell University psychologist James Garbarino (1999) says there is a lot of ignoring that goes on in these kinds of situations. Parents often don't want to acknowledge what might be a very upsetting reality. Harris and Klebold were members of the "Trenchcoat Mafia" clique of Columbine outcasts. The two even had made a video for a school video class the previous fall that depicted them walking down the halls at the school, shooting other students. Allegations were made that a year earlier the sheriff's department had been given information that Harris had bragged openly on the Internet that he and Klebold had built four bombs. Kip Kinkel had an obsession with guns and explosives, a history of abusing animals, and a nasty temper when crossed. When police examined his room, they found two pipe bombs, three larger bombs, and bomb-making recipes that Kip had downloaded from the Internet. Clearly, some signs were present in these students' lives to suggest some serious problems, but it is still very difficult to predict whether youth like these will actually act on their anger and sense of powerlessness to commit murder.

Garbarino (1999) has interviewed a number of youth who are killers. He concludes that nobody really knows precisely why a tiny minority of youth kill, but that it might be a lack of a spiritual center. In the youthful killers he interviewed, Garbarino often found a spiritual or emotional emptiness in which the youth sought meaning on the dark side of life.

What are some of the reasons psychologists give to explain why youth like Eric Harris kill?

SUMMARY TABLE 14.4
Moral Education and Juvenile Delinquency

Concept	Processes/ Related Ideas	Characteristics/Description
Moral Education	The Hidden Curriculum	• Originally proposed by John Dewey, the hidden curriculum refers to the moral atmosphere of a school.
	Character Education	• A direct education approach that advocates teaching students a basic moral literacy.
	Values Clarification	• Focuses on helping students to clarify what their lives are for and what is worth exploring.
	Cognitive Moral Education	• Emphasizes helping students develop such values as democracy and justice as their moral reasoning develops. • Kohlberg's theory has served as the basis for a number of cognitive moral education programs.
	Service Learning	• A form of education that promotes social responsibility and service to the community. • Service learning benefits youth in a number of ways.
	Rest's Four-Component Model	• Rest argues that moral development can best be understood by considering four components of morality—sensitivity, judgment, motivation, and character.
Juvenile Delinquency	What Is Juvenile Delinquency?	• Delinquency includes a broad range of behaviors, ranging from socially unacceptable behavior to status offenses. • Conduct disorder is a psychiatric category often used to describe delinquent-type behaviors. • Self-reported patterns suggest that about 20 percent of adolescents engage in delinquent behaviors.
	Antecedents of Delinquency	• Predictors of delinquency include a negative identity, low self-control, early initiation of delinquency, weak educational orientation, heavy peer influence, low parental monitoring, ineffective discipline, and living in an urban, high-crime area.
	Violence and Youth	• The high rate of violence in youth is an increasing problem. • Recommendations for reducing youth violence include effective parenting, prevention, support for schools, and forging effective partnerships among families, schools, and communities. • Conflict resolution programs are being used in attempts to reduce youth violence.

Chapter Review

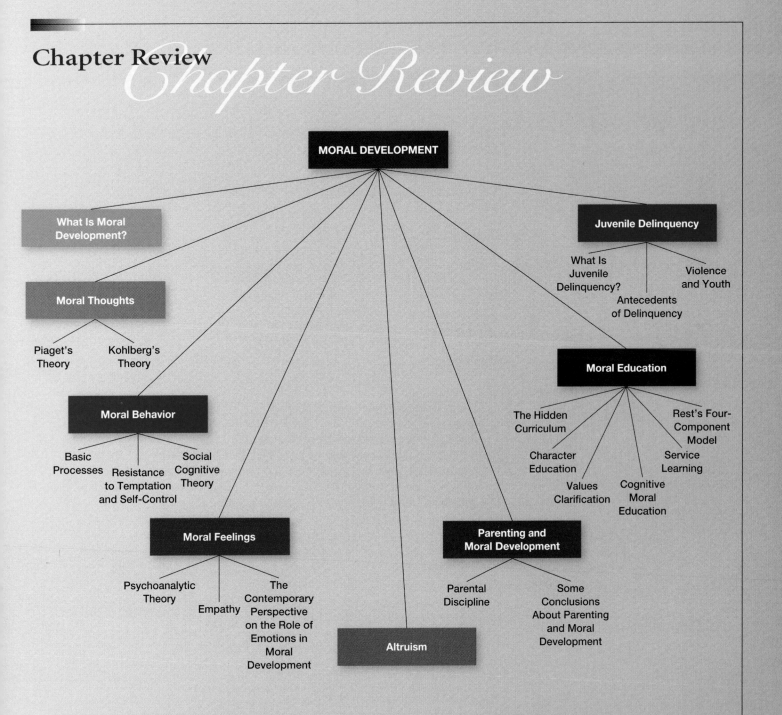

TO OBTAIN A DETAILED SUMMARY OF THE CHAPTER, STUDY THESE FOUR SUMMARY TABLES:

Key Terms

moral development 420
heteronomous morality (Piaget) 421
autonomous morality (Piaget) 421
immanent justice 421
internalization 422
preconventional reasoning 422
heteronomous morality (Kohlberg) 422
individualism, instrumental purpose, and
    exchange 422
conventional reasoning 422
mutual interpersonal expectations,
    relationships, and interpersonal
    conformity 422

social system morality 422
postconventional reasoning 423
social contract or utility and individual
    rights 423
universal ethical principles 423
justice perspective 428
care perspective 428
social conventional reasoning 429
social cognitive theory of morality 432
empathy 433
altruism 436
love withdrawal 437
power assertion 437

induction 438
hidden curriculum 439
character education 440
values clarification 440
cognitive moral education 440
service learning 441
juvenile delinquency 443
index offenses 443
status offenses 443
conduct disorder 443

Key People

Jean Piaget 420
Lawrence Kohlberg 421
James Rest 426, 441
Carol Gilligan 428
Hugh Hartshorne and Mark May 430

Walter Mischel 431
Albert Bandura 432
Sigmund Freud 432
William Damon 434
Nancy Eisenberg 437

Martin Hoffman 438
John Dewey 439
Gerald Patterson 445
James Garbarino 446

Child Development Resources

Lost Boys (1999)
    by James Garbarino
    New York: Free Press

This book explores why youth kill and what can be done to prevent
this.

Meeting at the Crossroads (1992)
    by Lyn Mikel Brown and Carol Gilligan
    Cambridge, MA: Harvard University Press

This book provides a vivid portrayal of how adolescent girls are often
ignored and misunderstood as they make their passage through adolescence.

Postconventional Thinking (1999)
    by James Rest, Darcia Narvaez,
    Muriel Bebeau, and Stephen Thoma
    Hillsdale, NJ: Erlbaum

James Rest and his colleagues provide a neo-Kohlbergian analysis of
moral development.

Service Learning (1997)
    by Alan Waterman (Ed.)
    Mahwah, NJ: Erlbaum

A number of leading experts discuss many aspects of service learning.

Taking It to the Net

1. Geraldine is giving a report on Kohlberg's theory of moral development. She is having a hard time thinking of an example of moral reasoning that would demonstrate each of the six Kohlberg stages of moral development. What examples would best demonstrate the six stages of moral development?

2. Kirk is planning to be a fifth-grade teacher. He is interested in the new approach to disciplining students that is designed to strengthen a child's character and impart moral values. How can Kirk begin to use this approach in the classroom?

3. Justin and his father are having a heated discussion over the factors that may have contributed to a young boy's shooting and killing a schoolmate. Justin thinks that the boy may have witnessed, or been a victim of, violence in his home. Justin's father says that if all people who have seen violence were themselves violent, we would all be locked up. How should Justin respond?

Connect to *http://www.mhhe.com/santrockc9* to find the answers!

Social Contexts of Development

Section 5

I *t is not enough for parents to understand children. They must also accord children the privilege of understanding them.*

Milton Sapirstein
American Psychiatrist and Writer, 20th Century

Parents cradle children's lives, but children's growth is also shaped by successive choirs of siblings, peers, friends, and teachers. Children's small worlds widen as they discover new refuges and new people. In the end there are but two lasting bequests that parents can leave children: one being roots, the other wings. In this section, we will study four chapters: "Families" (chapter 15), "Peers" (chapter 16), "Schools" (chapter 17), and "Culture"(chapter 18).

Chapter 15

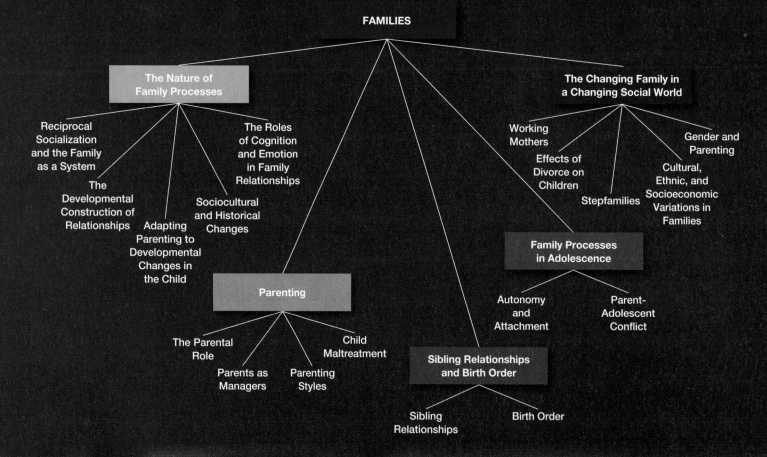

FAMILIES

- **The Nature of Family Processes**
  - Reciprocal Socialization and the Family as a System
  - The Developmental Construction of Relationships
  - Adapting Parenting to Developmental Changes in the Child
  - The Roles of Cognition and Emotion in Family Relationships
  - Sociocultural and Historical Changes
  - **Parenting**
    - The Parental Role
    - Parents as Managers
    - Parenting Styles
    - Child Maltreatment
- **Sibling Relationships and Birth Order**
  - Sibling Relationships
  - Birth Order
- **The Changing Family in a Changing Social World**
  - Working Mothers
  - Effects of Divorce on Children
  - Stepfamilies
  - Gender and Parenting
  - Cultural, Ethnic, and Socioeconomic Variations in Families
  - **Family Processes in Adolescence**
    - Autonomy and Attachment
    - Parent-Adolescent Conflict

There's no vocabulary for love within a family, love that's lived in but not looked at, love within the light of which all else is seen, the love within which all other love finds speech. This love is silent.

T.S. Eliot
American-Born English Poet, 20th Century

Some critics argue that Jessica Dubroff was not allowed to be a child. Was she given too much freedom and choice? Did her parents act irresponsibly?

The Story of Jessica Dubroff, Child Pilot

THINK FOR A MOMENT about how your parents reared you. Were they permissive or controlling? Warm or cold? Later in the chapter we will examine styles of parenting based on such characteristics, but for now to encourage you to think about parenting, let's examine the tragic story of Jessica Dubroff.

In 1996, Jessica Dubroff took off in cold rain and died when her single-engine Cessna nosedived into a highway. Seven-year-old Jessica was only 4 feet, 2 inches tall and weighed just 55 pounds. What was she doing flying an airplane, especially in a quest of being the youngest person ever to fly across the continent?

Jessica had been urged on by overzealous parents, by media drawn to a natural human-interest story, and by a Federal Aviation Administration that looked the other way. Jessica's feet did not even reach the rudder pedals. Overnight Jessica's death resulted in her becoming the poster child of parental and media exploitation. Some thought she had been granted too much freedom and had not been allowed to be a child.

Jessica's parents seemed determined to give their daughter independence from the beginning. She was delivered in a birthing tub without the benefit of a doctor or midwife. Her parents' philosophy was that real life is the best tutor, experience the best preparation for life. As a result, they kept Jessica and her brother (age 9) and sister (age 3) at home without filing a home-schooling plan with local authorities. Jessica had no dolls, only tools. Instead of studying grammar, she did chores and sought what her mother called "mastery." Jessica had few, if any, boundaries. Parenting mainly consisted of cheerleading.

Jessica became interested in flying after her parents gave her an airplane ride for her sixth birthday, only 23 months before her fatal crash. Her father admitted that the cross-country flight was his idea, but claimed that he had presented it to Jessica as a choice. The father became her press agent, courting TV, radio, and newspapers to publicize her flight.

After the crash, TV viewers were treated to a spectacle almost as disturbing as the accident itself. Jessica's mother said that if she had it to do over again, she would have done nothing differently. She also commented that she did everything she could to give Jessica freedom and choice. Developmental psychologists would counter that children should be given freedom and choice, but within the bounds of responsibility (Stengel, 1996).

Jessica's story is rare and tragic. However, the dangers of overachieving, of growing up too soon, of intensely focusing on a single activity, often show up in many different ways. The child actor grows up without an education. The adolescent tennis star mysteriously drops off the circuit to become a teenager. The young figure skater plots to club an opponent. Child athletes might ruin their bodies: ballerinas develop anorexia, teenage football players take steroids. Too many children have lives that are overscheduled, moving from one lesson to the next. They are being robbed of the time to develop coping skills that they need to deal with life's realities.

A vicious cycle has been set in motion. Parents who live vicariously through their children produce children who grow up feeling they have missed out on childhood, a time when play and its unstructured freedom should be prominent. Children should be allowed to have a well-rounded life, one that is not focused on achievement in a single domain.

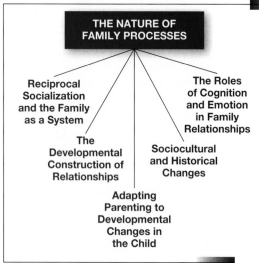

reciprocal socialization
The process by which children socialize parents just as parents socialize them.

Children, Youth, and Families Education and Research Network

Children, Youth, and Family Services

scaffolding
Parental behavior that supports children's efforts, allowing children to be more skillful than they would be if they relied only on their own abilities.

The Nature of Family Processes

Among the important considerations in studying children and their families are reciprocal socialization and the family system; how children construct relationships and how such relationships influence developmental changes in the child; sociocultural and historical influences on the family; and the roles of cognition and emotion in family relationships.

Reciprocal Socialization and the Family as a System

For many years, socialization between parents and children was viewed as a one-way process: Children were considered to be the products of their parents' socialization techniques. Today, however, we view parent-child interaction as reciprocal. **Reciprocal socialization** *is socialization that is bidirectional; children socialize parents just as parents socialize children.* For example, the interaction of mothers and their infants is sometimes symbolized as a dance or dialogue in which successive actions of the partners are closely coordinated. This coordinated dance or dialogue can assume the form of mutual synchrony (each person's behavior depending on the partner's previous behavior), or it can be reciprocal in a more precise sense; the actions of the partners can be matched, as when one partner imitates the other or when there is mutual smiling (Cohn & Tronick, 1988).

When reciprocal socialization has been investigated in infancy, mutual gaze or eye contact has been found to play an important role in early social interaction (Fogel, Toda, & Kawai, 1988). In one investigation, the mother and infant engaged in a variety of behaviors while they looked at each other; by contrast, when they looked away from each other, the rate of such behaviors dropped considerably (Stern & others, 1977). In sum, the behaviors of mothers and infants involve substantial interconnection and synchronization. And in one investigation, synchrony in parent-child relationships was positively related to children's social competence (Harrist, 1993).

Scaffolding *refers to parental behavior that serves to support children's efforts, allowing them to be more skillful than they would be if they relied only on their own abilities.* Parents' efforts to time interactions in such a way that the infant experiences turn taking with the parent illustrates an early parental scaffolding behavior. For example, in the game peek-a-boo, mothers initially cover their babies, then remove the covering, and finally register "surprise" at the reappearance. As infants become more skilled at peek-a-boo, they do the covering and uncovering. In addition to peek-a-boo, pat-a-cake and so-big are other caregiver games that exemplify scaffolding and turn-taking sequences. In one investigation, infants who had more-extensive scaffolding experiences with their parents, especially in the form of turn taking, were more likely to engage in turn taking as they interacted with their peers (Vandell & Wilson, 1988). Scaffolding is not just confined to parent-infant interaction but can be used by parents to support children's efforts at any age (Stringer & Neal, 1993). For example, parents can support children's achievement-related efforts in school by modifying the amount and type of support they provide to best suit the child's level of development.

As a social system, the family can be thought of as a constellation of subsystems defined in terms of generation, gender, and role (Davis, 1996). Divisions of labor among family members define particular subunits, and attachments define others. Each family member is a participant in several subsystems—some dyadic (involving two people), some polyadic (involving more than two people). The father and child represent one dyadic subsystem, the mother and father another; the mother-father-child represent one polyadic subsystem, the mother and two siblings another (Piotrowski, 1997).

An organizational scheme that highlights the reciprocal influences of family members and family subsystems is shown in figure 15.1 (Belsky, 1981). As the arrows in the figure show, marital relations, parenting, and infant/child behavior can have both direct and indirect effects on each other. For example, in one study, when marriages were less intimate and more distant during prenatal development, mothers were less sensitive, and fathers invested less time in parenting, when the infants were 3 months old (Cox & others, 1989).

The Developmental Construction of Relationships

Developmentalists have shown an increased interest in understanding how we construct relationships as we grow up (Cassidy & Shaver, 1999; Shaver, 1993). Psychoanalytic theorists have always been interested in how this process works in families. However, the current explanations of how relationships are constructed are virtually stripped of Freud's psychosexual stage terminology and also are not always confined to the first 5 years of life, as has been the case in classical psychoanalytic theory. Today's **developmental construction views** *share the belief that as individuals grow up they acquire modes of relating to others. There are two main variations within this view, one of which emphasizes continuity and stability in relationships through the life span and one of which emphasizes discontinuity and change in relationships through the life span.*

The Continuity View   The **continuity view** *emphasizes the role that early parent-child relationships play in constructing a basic way of relating to people throughout the life span.* These early parent-child relationships are carried forward to influence later points in development and all subsequent relationships (with peers, with friends, with teachers, and with romantic partners, for example) (Ainsworth, 1979; Bowlby, 1989; Sroufe, Egeland, & Carlson, 1999). In its extreme form, this view states that the basic components of social relationships are laid down and shaped by the security or insecurity of parent-infant attachment relationships in the first year or two of the infant's life (remember our discussion of attachment in chapter 11) ◄▉▉▉ P. 358.

Close relationships with parents also are important in the child's development, because these relationships function as models or templates that are carried forward over time to influence the construction of new relationships. Clearly, close relationships do not repeat themselves in an endless fashion over the course of the child's development. And the quality of any relationship depends to some degree on the specific individual with

developmental construction views
Views sharing the belief that as individuals grow up, they acquire modes of relating to others. There are two main variations of this view. One emphasizes continuity and stability in relationships throughout the life span; the other emphasizes discontinuity and changes in relationships throughout the life span.

continuity view
A developmental view that emphasizes the role of early parent-child relationships in constructing a basic way of relating to people throughout the life span.

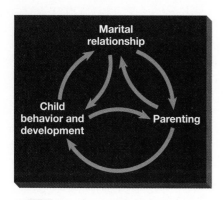

Figure 15.1

Interaction Between Children and Their Parents: Direct and Indirect Effects

discontinuity view
A developmental view that emphasizes change and growth in relationships over time.

whom the relationship is formed. However, the nature of earlier relationships that are developed over many years often can be detected in later relationships, both with those same individuals and in the formation of relationships with others at a later point in time (Gjerde, Block, & Block, 1991). Thus, the nature of parent-adolescent relationships does not depend only on what happens in the relationship during adolescence. Relationships with parents over the long course of childhood are carried forward to influence, at least to some degree, the nature of parent-adolescent relationships. And the long course of parent-child relationships also could be expected to influence, again at least to some degree, the fabric of the adolescent's peer relationships, friendships, and dating relationships.

In chapter 11, "Emotional Development," we described the longitudinal study of Alan Sroufe and his colleagues that supported the importance of continuity in development (Sroufe, Egeland, & Carlson, 1999). Recall that attachment history and early care were linked with peer competence in adolescence, up to 15 years after the infant assessments. For most children, there was a cascading effect in which early family relationships provided the necessary support for effectively engaging in the peer world, which in turn provided the foundation for more extensive, complex peer relationships.

The Discontinuity View   The **discontinuity view** *emphasizes change and growth in relationships over time.* As people grow up, they develop many different types of relationships (with parents, with peers, with teachers, and with romantic partners, for example). Each of these relationships is structurally different. With each new type of relationship, individuals encounter new modes of relating (Buhrmester & Furman, 1987; Furman & Wehner, in press; Piaget, 1932; Sullivan, 1953; Youniss, 1980). For example, Jean Piaget (1932) argued that parent-child relationships are strikingly different from children's peer relationships. Parent-child relationships, he said, are more likely to consist of parents' having unilateral authority over children. By contrast, peer relationships are more likely to consist of participants who relate to each other on a much more equal basis. In parent-child relationships, since parents have greater knowledge and authority, their children often must learn how to conform to rules and regulations laid down by parents. In this view, we use the parental-child mode when relating to authority figures (such as with teachers and experts) and when we ourselves become authority figures (when we become parents, teachers, and experts).

In contrast, relationships with peers have a different structure and require a different mode of relating to others. This more egalitarian mode is later called upon in relationships with romantic partners, friends, and coworkers. Because two peers possess relatively equal knowledge and authority (their relationship is reciprocal and symmetrical), children learn a democratic mode of relating that is based on mutual influence. With peers, children learn to formulate and assert their own opinions, appreciate the perspectives of peers, cooperatively negotiate solutions to disagreements, and evolve standards for conduct that are mutually acceptable. Because peer relationships are voluntary (rather than obligatory, as in the family), children and adolescents who fail to become skillful in the symmetrical, mutual, egalitarian, reciprocal mode of relating have difficulty being accepted by peers.

Evidence for the discontinuity view of relationships was found in the longitudinal study conducted by Andrew Collins and his colleagues (Collins, Hennighausen, & Sroufe, 1998). Quality of friendship interaction (based on observations of coordinated behavior, such as turn taking, sharing, eye contact, and touching, and their duration) in middle childhood was related to security with dating, and disclosure and intimacy with a dating partner, at age 16.

The discontinuity view does not deny that prior close relationships (such as with parents) are carried forward to influence later relationships, but it stresses that each new type of relationship that children and adolescents encounter (such as with peers, with friends, and with romantic partners) requires the construction of different and ever more sophisticated modes of relating to others. In the change-and-growth view, each period of development uniquely contributes to the construction of relationship knowledge; development across the life span is not solely determined by a sensitive or critical period during infancy.

Adapting Parenting to Developmental Changes in the Child

Children change as they grow from infancy to early childhood and on through middle and late childhood and adolescence. In the view of Eleanor Maccoby (1984), a competent parent adapts to the child's developmental changes. Parents should not treat a 5-year-old the same as a 2-year-old. The 5-year-old and 2-year-old have different needs and abilities. In the first year, parent-child interaction moves from a heavy focus on routine caretaking—feeding, changing diapers, bathing, and soothing—to later include more noncaretaking activities, such as play and visual-vocal exchanges. During the child's second and third years, parents often handle disciplinary matters by physical manipulation: They carry the child away from a mischievous activity to the place they want the child to go to; they put fragile and dangerous objects out of reach; they sometimes spank. As the child grows older, however, parents increasingly turn to reasoning, moral exhortation, and giving or withholding special privileges. As children move toward the elementary school years, parents show them less physical affection.

Parent-child interactions during early childhood focus on such matters as modesty, bedtime regularities, control of temper, fighting with siblings and peers, eating behavior and manners, autonomy in dressing, and attention seeking. Although some of these issues—fighting and reaction to discipline, for example—are carried forward into the elementary school years, many new issues appear by the age of 7. These include whether children should be made to perform chores and, if so, whether they should be paid for them, how to help children learn to entertain themselves rather than relying on parents for everything, and how to monitor children's lives outside the family in school and peer settings.

As children move into the middle and late childhood years, parents spend considerably less time with them. In one investigation, parents spent less than half as much time with their children aged 5 to 12 in caregiving, instruction, reading, talking, and playing as when the children were young (Hill & Stafford, 1980). This drop in parent-child interaction may be even more extensive in families with little parental education. Although parents spend less time with their children in middle and late childhood than in early childhood, parents continue to be extremely important socializing agents in their children's lives (Collins, Harris, & Susman, 1995). Children also must learn to relate to adults outside the family on a regular basis—adults who interact with the child much differently than parents do. During middle and late childhood, interactions with adults outside the family involve more formal control and achievement orientation.

CALVIN AND HOBBES © Watterson. Reprinted with permission of UNIVERSAL PRESS SYNDICATE. All rights reserved.

Discipline during middle and late childhood is often easier for parents than it was during early childhood; it may also be easier than during adolescence. In middle and late childhood, children's cognitive development has matured to the point where it is possible for parents to reason with them about resisting deviation and controlling their behavior. By adolescence, children's reasoning has become more sophisticated, and they may be less likely to accept parental discipline. Adolescents also push more strongly for independence, which contributes to parenting difficulties. Parents of elementary school children use less physical discipline than do parents of preschool children. By contrast, parents of elementary school children are more likely to use deprivation of privileges, appeals directed at the child's self-esteem, comments designed to increase the child's sense of guilt, and statements indicating to the child that she is responsible for her actions.

During middle and late childhood, some control is transferred from parent to child, although the process is gradual and involves *coregulation* rather than control by either the child or the parent alone (Maccoby, 1984). The major shift to autonomy does not occur until about the age of 12 or later. During middle and late childhood, parents continue to exercise general supervision and exert control while children are allowed to engage in moment-to-moment self-regulation. This coregulation process is a transition period between the strong parental control of early childhood and the increased relinquishment of general supervision of adolescence.

During this coregulation, parents should

- monitor, guide, and support children at a distance;
- effectively use the times when they have direct contact with the child; and
- strengthen in their children the ability to monitor their own behavior, to adopt appropriate standards of conduct, to avoid hazardous risks, and to sense when parental support and contact are appropriate.

To be a competent parent, further adaptation is required as children become adolescents, which will be discussed later in the chapter. Next, we will explore another important consideration in understanding families: sociocultural and historical changes.

Sociocultural and Historical Changes

Family development does not occur in a social vacuum. Important sociocultural and historical influences affect family processes (Parke, 1993; Parke & Buriel, 1998). Family changes may be due to great upheavals in a nation, such as war, famine, or mass immigration. Or they may be due more to subtle transitions in ways of life. The Great Depression in the early 1930s had some negative effects on families. During its height, the Depression produced economic deprivation, adult discontent, depression about living conditions, marital conflict, inconsistent child rearing, and unhealthy lifestyles—heavy drinking, demoralized attitudes, and health disabilities—especially in fathers (Elder, 1980). Subtle changes in a culture that have significant influences on the family were described by the famous anthropologist Margaret Mead (1978). The changes focus on the longevity of the elderly and the role of the elderly in the family, the urban and suburban orientation of families and their mobility, television, and a general dissatisfaction and restlessness.

Fifty years ago, the older people who survived were usually hearty and still closely linked to the family, often helping to maintain the family's existence. Today, older people live longer, which means that their middle-aged children are often pressed into a caretaking role for their parents or the elderly parents may be placed in a nursing home. Elderly parents may have lost some of their socializing role in the family during the twentieth century as many of their children moved great distances away.

Many of these family moves were away from farms and small towns to urban and suburban settings. In the small towns and farms, individuals were surrounded by lifelong neighbors, relatives, and friends. Today, neighborhood and extended-family support systems are not nearly as prevalent. Families now move all over the country, often uprooting the child from a school and peer group he or she has known for a considerable length of time. And for many families, this type of move occurs every year or two, as one or both parents are transferred from job to job.

The media and technology also plays a major role in the changing family. Many children who watch television find that parents are too busy working to share this experience with them. Children increasingly experience a world their parents are not a part of. Instead of participating in neighborhood peer groups, children come home after school and plop down in front of the television set or a computer screen. And television allows children and their families to see new ways of life. Lower-SES families can look into the family lives of middle-SES families by simply pushing a button.

Another subtle change in families has been an increase in general dissatisfaction and restlessness. Women have become increasingly dissatisfied with their way of life, which has resulted in great strain in many marriages. With fewer elders and long-term friends close by to help and advise young people during the initial difficult years of marriage and childbearing, marriages begin to fracture at the first signs of disagreement. Divorce has become epidemic in our culture. As women move into the labor market, men simultaneously become restless and look for stimulation outside of family life. The result of such restlessness and the tendency to divorce and remarry has been a hodgepodge of family structures, with far greater numbers of single-parent and step-parent families than ever before in history. Later in the chapter, we discuss such aspects of the changing social world of the child and the family in greater detail.

*T*hrough the Eyes of Psychologists

Ross Parke, *University of California—Riverside*

"Cognition and emotion are increasingly viewed as important socialization processes in families."

The Roles of Cognition and Emotion in Family Relationships

Cognitive processes are increasingly believed to be central to understanding socialization in the family (Bugental & Goodnow, 1998; Parke & Buriel, 1998). The role of cognition in family socialization comes in many forms, including parents' cognitions, beliefs, and values about their parental role, as well as how parents perceive, organize, and understand their children's behaviors and beliefs.

In one study, a link was found between mothers' beliefs and their preschool children's social problem-solving skills (Rubin, Mills, & Rose-Krasnor, 1989). Mothers who placed higher values on such skills as making friends, sharing with others, and leading or influencing other children had children who were more assertive, prosocial, and competent problem solvers.

Emotion also is increasingly viewed as central to understanding family processes (Parke & Buriel, 1998). Aspects of emotion in family processes that have been studied include the development of emotional regulation, the development of emotional production and understanding, and the role of emotion in carrying out the parental role.

Especially important in effective parenting is helping children learn to manage their emotions. Children's social competence is often linked to the emotional lives of their parents. For example, in one study, parents who displayed positive emotional expressiveness had children who were high in social competence (Boyum & Parke, 1995). Through interactions with parents, children learn to express their emotions in socially appropriate ways.

Researchers also are finding that parental support and acceptance of children's emotions is related to children's ability to manage their emotions in positive ways (Parke & Buriel, 1998). Parental comforting of children when they experience negative emotion is linked with constructive anger reactions (Eisenberg & Fabes, 1994). Also, parental motivation to discuss emotions with their children is related to children's awareness and understanding of others' emotions (Denham, Cook, & Zoller, 1992; Dunn & Brown, 1994). In another study, fathers' acceptance and assistance with children's sadness and anger at 5 years of age was linked with children's social competence with peers at 8 years of age (Gottman, Katz, & Hooven, 1996).

SUMMARY TABLE 15.1
The Nature of Family Processes

Concept	Processes/ Related Ideas	Characteristics/Description
Reciprocal Socialization and the Family as a System	Reciprocal Socialization	• Children socialize parents just as parents socialize children. • Scaffolding is an important aspect of reciprocal socialization.
	The Family as a System	• The family is a system of interacting individuals with different subsystems—some dyadic, some polyadic. • Belsky's model describes direct and indirect effects.
The Developmental Construction of Relationships	Its Nature	• The developmental construction views share the belief that as individuals grow up they acquire modes of relating to others. • There are two main variations within this view, one that emphasizes continuity and stability in relationships (the continuity view) and one that focuses on discontinuity and change in relationships (the discontinuity view).
Adapting Parenting to Developmental Changes in the Child	Nature of Adaptation	• Parents need to adapt their parenting as children grow older, using less physical manipulation and more reasoning in the process. • Parents spend less time in caregiving, instruction, reading, talking, and playing with children in middle childhood than earlier in the child's development. • In middle childhood, control becomes more coregulatory.
Sociocultural and Historical Changes	Their Nature	• Changes in families may be due to great upheavals, such as war, or more subtle changes, such as television and the mobility of families.
The Roles of Cognition and Emotion in Family Relationships	Cognition	• The role of cognition includes parents' cognitions, beliefs, and values about their parental role, as well as the way they perceive, organize, and understand their children's behaviors and beliefs.
	Emotion	• The role of emotion includes the regulation of emotion in children, the development of production and understanding of emotion in children, and emotion in carrying out the parenting role.

Underlying much of the current research on socialization processes in families is the belief that cognition and emotion generally operate together in determining parenting practices (Dix, 1991).

At this point we have studied a number of ideas about the nature of family processes. A review of these ideas is presented in summary table 15.1. Next, we will continue our exploration of families by examining the parental role, parents as managers, and parenting styles.

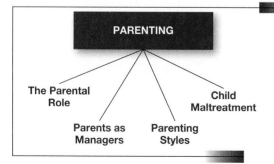

Parenting

What is the parent's role in the child's development? How can parents effectively manage children's lives? What parenting styles do parents use when they interact with their children?

The Parental Role

For many adults, the parental role is well planned and coordinated with other roles in life and is developed with the individual's economic situation in mind. For others, the discovery that they are about to become parents is a startling

CHEEVERWOOD © 1986 Michael Fry. Used by permission of Michael Fry.

surprise. In either event, the prospective parents may have mixed emotions and romantic illusions about having a child. Parenting consists of a number of interpersonal skills and emotional demands, yet there is little in the way of formal education for this task. Most parents learn parenting practices from their own parents—some of these practices they accept, some they discard. Husbands and wives may bring different viewpoints of parenting practices to the marriage. Unfortunately, when methods of parents are passed on from one generation to the next, both desirable and undesirable practices are perpetuated.

The needs and expectations of parents have stimulated many myths about parenting, such as these (Okun & Rappaport, 1980):

- The birth of a child will save a failing marriage.
- As a possession or extension of the parent, the child will think, feel, and behave like the parents did in their childhood.
- Children will take care of parents in old age.
- Parents can expect respect and get obedience from their children.
- Having a child means that the parents will always have someone who loves them and is their best friend.
- Having a child gives the parents a "second chance" to achieve what they should have achieved.
- If parents learn the right techniques, they can mold their children into what they want.
- It's always the parents' fault when children fail.
- Mothers are naturally better parents than fathers.
- Parenting is an instinct and requires no training.

Parents as Managers

In our discussion of the increased interest in studying the roles of cognition and emotion in family processes, we indicated that an important aspect of parenting is helping children manage their emotions. Likewise, an increasing trend in conceptualizing and researching parent-child relationships is to think of parents as managers of children's lives.

Parents can play important roles as managers of children's opportunities, as monitors of children's social relationships, and as social initiators and arrangers (Parke & Buriel, 1998). Parents serve as regulators of opportunities for social contact with peers, friends, and adults. From infancy through adolescence, mothers are more likely than fathers to have a managerial role in parenting. In infancy, this might involve taking a child to a doctor, and arranging for day care; in early childhood, it might involve a

For years we have given scientific attention to the care and rearing of plants and animals, but we have allowed babies to be raised chiefly by tradition.

Edith Belle Lowry
False Modesty (1912)

Parenting

Through the Eyes of Psychologists

Diana Baumrind, *University of California–Berkeley*

"Children from authoritative families are competent and prosocial."

I looked on child rearing not only as a work of love and duty but as a profession that was fully as interesting and challenging as any honorable profession in the world and one that demanded the best that I could bring to it.

Rose Kennedy
U.S. Public Figure and Philanthropist, 20th Century

authoritarian parenting
This is a restrictive, punitive style in which the parent exhorts the child to follow the parent's directions and to respect work and effort. Firm limits and controls are placed on the child, and little verbal exchange is allowed. This style is associated with children's socially incompetent behavior.

authoritative parenting
This style encourages children to be independent but still places limits and controls on their actions. Extensive verbal give-and-take is allowed, and parents are warm and nurturant toward the child. This style is associated with children's socially competent behavior.

neglectful parenting
A style in which the parent is very uninvolved in the child's life. It is associated with children's social incompetence, especially a lack of self-control.

decision about which preschool the child should attend; in middle and late childhood, it might include directing the child to take a bath, to match their clothes and wear clean clothes, and to put away toys; in adolescence, it could involve participating in a parent-teacher conference and subsequently managing the adolescent's homework activity.

An important aspect of the managerial role of parenting is effective monitoring of the child. This is especially important as children move into the adolescent years. Monitoring includes supervising a child's choice of social settings, activities, and friends. As we saw in chapter 14, "Moral Development," a lack of adequate parental monitoring is the parental factor that is related to juvenile delinquency more than any other (Patterson & Stouthamer-Loeber, 1984). ◀▥ P. 445.

Parents have an important role in facilitating their children's development by initiating contact between their children (especially when they are young) and potential play partners. In one study, children of parents who arranged peer contacts had a larger number of playmates outside of their school than children of parents were less active in arranging these contacts (Ladd, LeSeiur, & Profilet, 1993).

Parenting Styles

Parents want their children to grow into socially mature individuals, and they may feel frustrated in trying to discover the best way to accomplish this. Developmentalists have long searched for the ingredients of parenting that promote competent social development in children. For example, in the 1930s, John Watson argued that parents were too affectionate with their children. In the 1950s, a distinction was made between physical and psychological discipline, with psychological discipline, especially reasoning, emphasized as the best way to rear a child. In the 1970s and beyond, the dimensions of competent parenting have become more precise.

Especially widespread is the view of Diana Baumrind (1971), who believes parents should be neither punitive nor aloof, but should instead develop rules for their children and be affectionate with them. She emphasizes three types of parenting that are associated with different aspects of the child's social behavior: authoritarian, authoritative, and laissez-faire (permissive). More recently, developmentalists have argued that permissive parenting comes in two different forms: neglectful and indulgent. What are these forms of parenting like?

Authoritarian parenting *is a restrictive, punitive style in which the parents exhort the child to follow their directions and to respect work and effort. The authoritarian parent places firm limits and controls on the child and allows little verbal exchange. Authoritarian parenting is associated with children's social incompetence.* For example, an authoritarian parent might say, "You do it my way or else. There will be no discussion!" Children of authoritarian parents are often anxious about social comparison, fail to initiate activity, and have poor communication skills. In one study, early harsh discipline was associated with child aggression (Weiss & others, 1992).

Authoritative parenting *is a style in which the parents encourage children to be independent but still place limits and controls on their actions. Extensive verbal give-and-take is allowed and parents are warm and nurturant toward the child. Authoritative parenting is associated with children's social competence.* An authoritative parent might put his arm around the child in a comforting way and say, "You know you should not have done that; let's talk about how you can handle the situation better next time." Children whose parents are authoritative are socially competent, self-reliant, and socially responsible.

Permissive parenting comes in two forms: neglectful and indulgent (Maccoby & Martin, 1983). **Neglectful parenting** *is a style in which the parent is very uninvolved in the child's life; it is associated with children's social incompetence, especially a lack of self-control.* This parent cannot answer the question, "It is 10 P.M. Do you know where your child is?" Children have a strong need for their parents to care about them; children whose parents are permissive-indifferent develop the sense that other aspects of the parents' lives are more important than they are. Children whose parents are neglectful are socially incompetent—they show poor self-control and do not handle independence well.

Indulgent parenting *is a style of parenting in which parents are highly involved with their children but place few demands or controls on them. Indulgent parenting is associated with children's social incompetence, especially a lack of self-control.* They let their children do what they want, and the result is the children never learn to control their own behavior and always expect to get their way. Some parents deliberately rear their children in this way because they believe the combination of warm involvement with few restraints will produce a creative, confident child. One boy I knew whose parents deliberately reared him in an indulgent manner moved his parents out of their bedroom suite and took it over for himself. He is now 18 years old and has not learned to control his behavior; when he can't get something he wants, he still throws temper tantrums. As you might expect, he is not very popular with his peers. Children whose parents are indulgent rarely learn respect for others and have difficulty controlling their behavior.

The four classifications of parenting just discussed involve combinations of acceptance and responsiveness on the one hand, and demand and control on the other. How these dimensions combine to produce authoritarian, authoritative, neglectful, and indulgent parenting is shown in figure 15.2.

ADVENTURES FOR THE MIND

Evaluating the Parenting Styles of Both Parents

IN OUR DISCUSSION of parenting styles, authoritative parenting was associated with social competence in children. In some cases, though, a child's parents differ in their parenting styles. Consider all four styles of parenting—authoritarian, authoritative, neglectful, and indulgent—on the parts of the mother and the father. A best case is when both parents are authoritative. What might the effects on the child be if the father is authoritarian and the mother is indulgent, or the father is authoritarian and the mother is authoritative, and so on? Is it better for the child if both parents have the same parenting style, even if the styles both are authoritarian, both are indulgent, or both neglectful, or is it better for the child to have at least one authoritative parent when the other parent is authoritarian, indulgent, or neglectful?

In thinking about parenting styles, consider also what style or styles your father and mother used in rearing you. Were they both authoritative; one authoritarian, the other indulgent; and so on? What effects do you think their parenting styles had on your development?

Child Maltreatment

Unfortunately, parenting sometimes leads to the abuse of infants and children. Child abuse is an increasing problem in the United States. Estimates of its incidence vary, but some authorities say that as many as 500,000 children are physically abused every year. Laws in many states now require doctors and teachers to report suspected cases of child abuse, yet many cases go unreported, especially those of battered infants.

Child abuse is such a disturbing circumstance that many people have difficulty understanding or sympathizing with parents who abuse or neglect their children. Our response is often outrage and anger directed at the parent. This outrage focuses our attention on parents as bad, sick, monstrous, sadistic individuals who cause their children to suffer. Experts on child abuse believe that this view is too simple and deflects attention away from the social context of the abuse and parents' coping skills. It is especially important to recognize that child abuse is a diverse condition, that it is usually mild to moderate in severity, and that it is only partially caused by the individual personality characteristics of parents.

The Multifaceted Nature of Maltreatment   Whereas the public and many professionals use the term *child abuse* to refer to both abuse and neglect, developmentalists increasingly use the term *child maltreatment.* This term does not have quite the emotional impact of the term *abuse* and acknowledges that maltreatment includes several different conditions. Among the different types of maltreatment are physical and sexual abuse; the fostering of delinquency; lack of supervision; medical, educational, and nutritional neglect; and drug or alcohol abuse. In one large survey, approximately 20 percent of the reported cases involved abuse alone, 46 percent neglect alone, 23 percent both abuse and neglect, and 11 percent sexual abuse (American Association for Protecting Children, 1986).

indulgent parenting
A style in which parents are highly involved with their children but place few demands or controls on them. This is associated with children's social incompetence, especially a lack of self-control.

National Clearinghouse on Child Abuse and Neglect

Child Abuse Prevention Network

International Aspects of Child Abuse

Parenting is a very important profession, but no test of fitness for it is ever imposed in the interest of children.

George Bernard Shaw
Irish Playwright, 20th Century

	Accepting, responsive	Rejecting, unresponsive
Demanding, controlling	Authoritative	Authoritarian
Undemanding, uncontrolling	Indulgent	Neglectful

Figure 15.2

Classification of Parenting Styles

The four types of parenting styles (authoritative, authoritarian, indulgent, and neglectful) involve the dimensions of acceptance and responsiveness on the one hand and demand and control on the other. For example, authoritative parenting involves being both accepting/responsive and demanding/controlling.

Severity of Maltreatment   The concern about child abuse began with the identification of "battered child syndrome," which continues to be associated with severe, brutal injury for several reasons. First, the media tend to underscore the most bizarre and vicious incidents. Second, much of the funding for child abuse prevention, identification, and treatment depends on the public's perception of the horror of child abuse and the medical profession's lobby for funds to investigate and treat abused children and their parents. The emphasis is often on the worst cases. These horrific cases do exist and are indeed terrible. However, they make up only a small minority of maltreated children. Less than 1 percent of maltreated children die. Another 11 percent suffer life-threatening, disabling injuries (American Association for Protecting Children, 1986). By contrast, almost 90 percent suffer temporary physical injuries. These milder injuries, though, are likely to be experienced repeatedly in the context of daily hostile family exchanges. Similarly, neglected children, who suffer no physical injuries, often experience extensive, long-term psychological harm.

The Cultural Context of Maltreatment   The extensive violence that takes place in the American culture is reflected in the occurrence of violence in the family. A regular diet of violence appears on television screens, and parents often resort to power assertion as a disciplinary technique. In China, where physical punishment is rarely used to discipline children, the incidence of child abuse is reported to be very low. In the United States, many abusing parents report that they do not have sufficient resources or help from others. This may be a realistic evaluation of the situation experienced by many low-income families, who do not have adequate preventive and supportive services.

Community support systems are especially important in alleviating stressful family situations, thereby helping prevent child abuse. An investigation of the support systems in 58 counties in New York State revealed a relation between the incidence of child abuse and the absence of support systems available to the family (Garbarino, 1976). Both family resources—relatives and friends, for example—and such formal community support systems as crisis centers and child abuse counseling were associated with a reduction in child abuse.

Family Influences   To understand abuse in the family, the interactions of all family members need to be considered, regardless of who actually performs the violent acts against the child (Margolin, 1994). For example, even though the father may be the one who physically abuses the child, contributions by the mother, the child, and siblings also should be evaluated. Many parents who abuse their children come from families in which physical punishment was used. These parents view physical punishment as a legitimate way of controlling the child's behavior. Physical punishment might be a part of this sanctioning. Children themselves might unwittingly contribute to child abuse. An unattractive child might receive more physical punishment than an attractive child. A child from an unwanted pregnancy might be especially vulnerable to abuse (Harter, Alexander, & Neimeyer, 1988). Husband-wife violence and financial problems can result in displaced aggression toward a defenseless child. Displaced aggression is commonly involved in child maltreatment.

Developmental Consequences of Maltreatment   Among the developmental consequences of child maltreatment are poor emotion regulation, attachment problems, problems in peer relations, difficulty in adapting to school, and other psychological problems (Rogosch & others, 1995). Difficulties in initiating and modulating positive and negative affect have been observed in maltreated infants (Cicchetti, Ganiban, & Barnett, 1991). Maltreated infants also may show excessive negative affect or blunted positive affect.

Not only do maltreated infants show insecure patterns of attachment, but they also might show a form of attachment not often found in normal children. As we saw earlier in the chapter, maltreated children tend to display an attachment pattern referred to as *disorganized,* which involves high avoidance and high resistance (Main & Solomon, 1990). In one study, the disorganized attachment pattern was found in 80 percent of the maltreated infants observed (Carlson & others, 1989).

Maltreated children appear to be poorly equipped to develop successful peer relations, due to their aggressiveness, avoidance, and aberrant responses to both distress and positive approaches from peers (Mueller & Silverman, 1989). Two patterns of social behavior are common in maltreated children. Sometimes maltreated children show excessive physical and verbal aggression, while at other times maltreated children show a pattern of avoidance. These patterns have been described in terms of "fight or flight."

Maltreated children's difficulties in establishing effective relationships may show up in their interactions with teachers. Maltreated children might expect teachers to be unresponsive or unavailable, based on their relationships with their parents. For maltreated children, dealing with fears about abuse and searching for security in relationships with adults can take precedence over performing competently at academic tasks.

Being physically abused has been linked with children's anxiety, personality problems, depression, conduct disorder, and delinquency (Toth, Manley, & Cicchetti, 1992). Later, during the adult years, maltreated children show increased violence toward other adults, dating partners, and marital partners, as well as increased substance abuse, anxiety, and depression (Malinosky-Rummell & Hansen, 1993). In sum, maltreated children are at risk for developing a wide range of problems and disorders.

So far our coverage of families has taken us through the nature of family processes, the parenting role, parents as managers of children's lives, and parenting styles. Next, we explore another important aspect of family life for many children—siblings.

Sibling Relationships and Birth Order

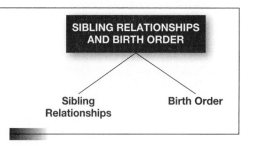

Sandra describes to her mother what happened in a conflict with her sister:

> We had just come home from the ball game. I sat down on the sofa next to the light so I could read. Sally (the sister) said, "Get up, I was sitting there first. I just got up for a second to get a drink." I told her I was not going to get up and that I didn't see her name on the chair. I got mad and started pushing her. Her drink spilled all over her. Then she got really mad; she shoved me against the wall, hitting and clawing at me. I managed to grab a handful of hair.

Sibling Relationships

Any of you who have grown up with siblings probably have a rich memory of aggressive, hostile interchanges. But sibling relationships also have many pleasant, caring

Big sisters are the crab grass in the lawn of life.

Charles Schulz, "Peanuts"
American Cartoonist, 20th Century

moments. Children's sibling relationships include helping, sharing, teaching, fighting, and playing. Children can act as emotional supports, rivals, and communication partners (Carlson, 1995). More than 80 percent of American children have one or more siblings (brothers or sisters). Because there are so many possible sibling combinations, it is difficult to generalize about sibling influences. Among the factors to consider are the number of siblings, the ages of siblings, birth order, age spacing, the sex of siblings, and whether sibling relationships are different from parent-child relationships.

Is sibling interaction different from parent-child interaction? There is some evidence that it is. Observations indicate that children interact more positively and in more varied ways with their parents than with their siblings (Baskett & Johnson, 1982). Children also follow their parents' dictates more than those of their siblings, and they behave more negatively and punitively with their siblings than with their parents.

In some instances, siblings may be stronger socializing influences on the child than parents are (Cicirelli, 1994). Someone close in age to the child—such as a sibling—may be able to understand the child's problems and communicate more effectively than parents can. In dealing with peers, coping with difficult teachers, and discussing such taboo subjects as sex, siblings may be more influential than parents in the socialization process.

Is sibling interaction the same around the world? In industrialized societies, such as the United States, the delegation of responsibility for younger siblings to older siblings tends to be carried out informally by parents. This is done primarily to give the parents freedom to pursue other activities. However, in nonindustrialized countries, such as Kenya, a much greater degree of importance is attached to the older sibling's role as a caregiver to younger siblings. In industrialized countries, the older sibling's caregiving role is often discretionary; in nonindustrialized countries, it is more obligatory (Cicirelli, 1994).

Birth Order

Birth order is a special interest of sibling researchers. When differences in birth order are found, they usually are explained by variations in interactions with parents and siblings associated with the unique experiences of being in a particular position in the family. This is especially true in the case of the firstborn child (Teti & others, 1993). The oldest child is the only one who does not have to share parental love and affection with other siblings—until another sibling comes along. An infant requires more attention than an older child; this means that the firstborn sibling now gets less attention than before the newborn arrived. Does this result in conflict between parents and the firstborn? In one research study, mothers became more negative, coercive, and restraining and played less with the firstborn following the birth of a second child (Dunn & Kendrick, 1982). Even though a new infant requires more attention from parents than does an older child, an especially intense relationship is often maintained between parents and firstborns throughout the life span. Parents have higher expectations for firstborn children than for later-born children. They put more pressure on them for achievement and responsibility. They also interfere more with their activities (Rothbart, 1971).

Birth order is also associated with variations in sibling relationships. The oldest sibling is expected to exercise self-control and show responsibility in interacting with younger siblings. When the oldest sibling is jealous or hostile, parents often protect the younger sibling. The oldest sibling is more dominant, competent, and powerful than the younger siblings. The oldest sibling is also expected to assist and teach younger siblings. Indeed, researchers have shown that older siblings are both more antagonistic—hitting, kicking, and biting—and more nurturant toward their younger siblings than vice versa (Abramovitch & others, 1986). There is also something unique about same-sex sibling relationships. Aggression and dominance occur more in same-sex relationships than in opposite-sex sibling relationships (Minnett, Vandell, & Santrock, 1983).

Given the differences in family dynamics involved in birth order, it is not surprising that firstborns and later-borns have different characteristics. Firstborn children are more adult-oriented, helpful, conforming, anxious, and self-controlled than their siblings. Parents give more attention to firstborns and this is related to firstborns' nurturant behavior (Stanhope & Corter, 1993). Parental demands and high standards established for firstborns result in these children's excelling in academic and professional endeavors. Firstborns are overrepresented in *Who's Who* and Rhodes scholars, for example. However, some of the same pressures placed on firstborns for high achievement may be the reason they also have more guilt, anxiety, and difficulty in coping with stressful situations, as well as higher admission to child guidance clinics.

What is the only child like? The popular conception is that the only child is a "spoiled brat," with such undesirable characteristics as dependency, lack of self-control, and self-centered behavior. But researchers present a more positive portrayal of the only child, who often is achievement-oriented and displays a desirable personality, especially in comparison with later-borns and children from large families (Falbo & Poston, 1993; Jiao, Ji, & Jing, 1996).

So far, our consideration of birth-order effects suggests that birth order might be a strong predictor of behavior. However, an increasing number of family researchers believe that birth order has been overdramatized and overemphasized. The critics argue that, when all of the factors that influence behavior are considered, birth order itself shows limited ability to predict behavior. Consider sibling relationships alone. They vary not only in birth order but also in number of siblings, age of siblings, age spacing of siblings, and sex of siblings.

Consider also the temperament of siblings. Researchers have found that siblings' temperamental traits ("easy" and "difficult," for example), as well as differential treatment of siblings by parents, influence how siblings get along (Stocker & Dunn, 1991). Siblings with "easy" temperaments who are treated in relatively equal ways by parents tend to get along with each other the best. By contrast, siblings with "difficult" temperaments, or whose parents have given one of them preferential treatment, get along the worst.

Beyond temperament and differential treatment of siblings by parents, think about some of the other important factors in children's lives that influence their behavior beyond birth order. They include heredity, models of competency or incompetency that parents present to children on a daily basis, peer influences, school influences, socioeconomic factors, sociohistorical factors, and cultural variations. When someone says firstborns are always like this but last-borns are always like that, you now know that the person is making overly simplistic statements that do not adequately take into account the complexity of influences on a child's behavior. Keep in mind, though, that, although birth order itself may not be a good predictor of children's behavior, sibling relationships and interaction are important dimensions of family processes.

Family Processes in Adolescence

Some of the most important issues and questions that need to be raised about family relationships in adolescence are these: What roles do attachment and autonomy play in parent-adolescent relationships? How intense is parent-adolescent conflict?

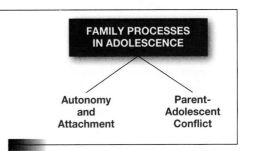

FAMILY PROCESSES IN ADOLESCENCE

Autonomy and Attachment — Parent-Adolescent Conflict

Autonomy and Attachment

The adolescent's push for autonomy and responsibility puzzles and angers many parents. Parents see their teenager slipping from their grasp. They may have an urge to take stronger control as the adolescent seeks autonomy and responsibility. Heated emotional exchanges may ensue, with either side calling names, making threats, and doing whatever seems necessary to gain control. Parents may seem frustrated because

Parents' and Adolescents' Expectations

Parenting Adolescents

Exploring Parent-Adolescent Relationships

they *expect* their teenager to heed their advice, to want to spend time with the family, and to grow up to do what is right. Most parents anticipate that their teenager will have some difficulty adjusting to the changes that adolescence brings, but few parents can imagine and predict just how strong an adolescent's desires will be to spend time with peers or how much adolescents will want to show that it is they—not their parents—who are responsible for their successes and failures.

The ability to attain autonomy and gain control over one's behavior in adolescence is acquired through appropriate adult reactions to the adolescent's desire for control (Keener & Boykin, 1996; Urberg & Wolowicz, 1996). At the onset of adolescence, the average individual does not have the knowledge to make appropriate or mature decisions in all areas of life. As the adolescent pushes for autonomy, the wise adult relinquishes control in those areas in which the adolescent can make reasonable decisions but continues to guide the adolescent to make reasonable decisions in areas in which the adolescent's knowledge is more limited. Gradually, adolescents acquire the ability to make mature decisions on their own.

Recall from chapter 11, "Emotional Development," that one of the most widely used concepts regarding the socioemotional development of infants is the concept of secure or insecure attachment. ◀||||| P. 360. In the past decade, developmentalists also have begun to explore the role of secure attachment, and related concepts such as connectedness to parents, in adolescence (Allen, Hauser, & Borman-Spurrell, 1996; Cassidy & Shaver, 1999). They believe that secure attachment to parents in adolescence may facilitate the adolescent's social competence and well-being, as reflected in such characteristics as self-esteem, emotional adjustment, and physical health (Cooper, Shaver, & Collins, 1998; Juang & Nyuyen, 1997). In the research of Joseph Allen and his colleagues (Allen & Hauser, 1994; Allen & Kuperminc, 1995), securely attached adolescents had somewhat lower probabilities of engaging in problem behaviors.

Many studies that assess secure and insecure attachment in adolescence use the Adult Attachment Interview (AAI) (George, Main, & Kaplan, 1984). This measure examines an individual's memories of significant attachment relationships. Based on the responses to questions on the AAI, individuals are classified as *secure-autonomous* (which corresponds to secure attachment in infancy) or one of three following insecure categories.

Dismissing/avoidant attachment *is an insecure category in which individuals deemphasize the importance of attachment. This category is associated with consistent experiences of the rejection of attachment needs by caregivers.* One possible outcome of dismissing/avoidant attachment is that parents and adolescents may mutually distance themselves from each other, which lessens parents' influence. In one study, dismissing/avoidant attachment was related to violent and aggressive behavior on the part of the adolescent.

Preoccupied/ambivalent attachment *is an insecure category in which adolescents are hypertuned to attachment experiences. This is thought to occur mainly when parents are inconsistently available to the adolescent.* This may result in a high degree of attachment-seeking behavior, mixed with angry feelings. Conflict between parents and adolescents in this type of attachment may be too high for healthy development.

Unresolved/disorganized attachment *is an insecure category in which the adolescent has an unusually high level of fear and is disoriented. This may result from such traumatic experiences as a parent's death or abuse by parents.*

Secure attachment, or connectedness to parents, promotes competent peer relations and positive, close relationships outside of the family (Cassidy, 1999, Kobak, 1999). In one investigation in which attachment to parents and peers was assessed, adolescents who were securely attached to parents also were securely attached to peers; those who were insecurely attached to parents also were more likely to be insecurely attached to peers (Armsden & Greenberg, 1984). There are times when adolescents reject closeness, connection, and attachment to their parents as they assert their ability to make decisions and to develop an identity. But, for the most

dismissing/avoidant attachment
An insecure attachment category in which individuals deemphasize the importance of attachment. This category is associated with consistent experiences of rejection of attachment needs by caregivers.

preoccupied/ambivalent attachment
An insecure attachment category in which adolescents are hypertuned to attachment experiences. This is thought to mainly occur because parents are inconsistently available to the adolescents.

unresolved/disorganized attachment
An insecure category in which the adolescent has an unusually high level of fear and is disoriented. This may result from such traumatic experiences as a parent's death or abuse by parents.

part, the worlds of parents and peers are coordinated and connected, not uncoordinated and disconnected.

Parent-Adolescent Conflict

While attachment to parents remains strong during adolescence, the connectedness is not always smooth. Early adolescence is a time when conflict with parents escalates beyond childhood levels. This increase may be due to a number of factors: the biological changes of puberty, cognitive changes involving increased idealism and logical reasoning, social changes focused on independence and identity, maturational changes in parents, and expectations that are violated by parents and adolescents. The adolescent compares her parents to an ideal standard and then criticizes their flaws. A 13-year-old girl tells her mother, "That is the tackiest-looking dress I have ever seen. Nobody would be caught dead wearing that." The adolescent demands logical explanations for comments and discipline. A 14-year-old boy tells his mother, "What do you mean I have to be home at 10 P.M. because it's the way we do things around here? Why do we do things around here that way? It doesn't make sense to me."

Many parents see their adolescent changing from a compliant child to someone who is noncompliant, oppositional, and resistant to parental standards. When this happens, parents tend to clamp down and put more pressure on the adolescent to conform to parental standards. Parents often expect their adolescents to become mature adults overnight, instead of understanding that the journey takes 10 to 15 years. Parents who recognize that this transition takes time handle their youth more competently and calmly than those who demand immediate conformity to adult standards. The opposite tactic—letting adolescents do as they please without supervision—is also unwise.

In one study, Reed Larson and Marsye Richards (1994) had mothers, fathers, and adolescents carry electronic pagers for a week and report their activities and emotions at random times. The result was a portrait of the hour-by-hour emotional realities lived by families with adolescents. Differences between the fast-paced daily realities lived by each family member created considerable potential for misunderstanding and conflict. Because each family member was often attending to different priorities, needs, and stressors, their realities were often out of sync. Even when they wanted to share leisure activity, their interests were at odds. One father said that his wife liked to shop, his daughter liked to play video games, and he liked to stay home. Although the main theme of this work was the hazards of contemporary life, some families with adolescents were buoyant, and their lives were coordinated.

Conflict with parents increases in early adolescence, but it does not reach the tumultuous proportions G. Stanley Hall envisioned at the beginning of the twentieth century (Holmbeck, 1996; Holmbeck, Paikoff, & Brooks-Gunn, 1995). Rather, much of the conflict involves the everyday events of family life, such as keeping a bedroom clean, dressing neatly, getting home by a certain time, and not talking forever on the phone. The conflicts rarely involve major dilemmas, such as drugs and delinquency.

It is not unusual to hear parents of young adolescents ask, "Is it ever going to get better?" Things usually do get better as adolescents move from early to late adolescence. Conflict with parents often escalates during early adolescence, remains somewhat stable during the high school years, and then lessens as the adolescent reaches 17 to 20 years of age. Parent-adolescent relationships become more positive if adolescents go away to college than if they stay at home and go to college (Sullivan & Sullivan, 1980).

The everyday conflicts that characterize parent-adolescent relationships may actually serve a positive developmental function. These minor disputes and negotiations facilitate the adolescent's transition from being dependent on parents to becoming an autonomous individual. For example, in one study, adolescents who expressed disagreement with their parents explored identity development more actively than

Parent-Adolescent Conflict
Families as Asset Builders
Prevention of Adolescent Problems
Reengaging Families with Adolescents

*A*dolescence is like cactus.

Anaïs Nin
French Novelist, 20th Century

*W*hen I was a boy of 14, my father was so ignorant I could hardly stand to have the man around. But when I got to be 21, I was astonished at how much he had learnt in 7 years.

Mark Twain
American Writer and Humorist, 19th Century

Old model	
Autonomy detachment from parents; parent and peer worlds are isolated	Intense, stressful conflict throughout adolescence; parent-adolescent relationships are filled with storm and stress on virtually a daily basis

New model	
Attachment and autonomy; parents are important support systems and attachment figures; adolescent-parent and adolescent-peer worlds have some important connections	Moderate parent-adolescent conflict common and can serve a positive developmental function; conflict greater in early adolescence, especially during the apex of puberty

Figure 15.3

Old and New Models of Parent-Adolescent Relationships

did adolescents who did not express disagreement with their parents (Cooper & others, 1982). As previously mentioned, one way for parents to cope with the adolescent's push for independence and identity is to recognize that adolescence is a 10- to 15-year transitional period in the journey to adulthood, rather than an overnight accomplishment. Recognizing that conflict and negotiation can serve a positive developmental function can tone down parental hostility too. Understanding parent-adolescent conflict, though, is not simple (Conger & Ge, 1999).

In sum, the old model of parent-adolescent relationships suggested that as adolescents mature they detach themselves from parents and move into a world of autonomy apart from parents. The old model also suggested that parent-adolescent conflict is intense and stressful throughout adolescence. The new model emphasizes that parents serve as important attachment figures and support systems as adolescents explore a wider, more complex social world. The new model also emphasizes that, in most families, parent-adolescent conflict is moderate rather than severe and that the everyday negotiations and minor disputes are normal and can serve the positive developmental function of helping the adolescent make the transition from childhood dependency to adult independence (see figure 15.3).

Still, a high degree of conflict characterizes some parent-adolescent relationships. One estimate of the proportion of parents and adolescents who engage in prolonged, intense, repeated, unhealthy conflict is about one in five families (Montemayor, 1982). While this figure represents a minority of adolescents, it indicates that 4 to 5 million American families encounter serious, highly stressful parent-adolescent conflict. And this prolonged, intense conflict is associated with a number of adolescent problems—movement out of the home, juvenile delinquency, school dropout, pregnancy and early marriage, membership in religious cults, and drug abuse (Brook & others, 1990).

At this point we have studied many ideas about parenting, sibling relationships and birth order, and parent-adolescent relationships. A review of these ideas is presented in summary table 15.2. Next, we will continue our exploration of families by examining the changing family in a changing world.

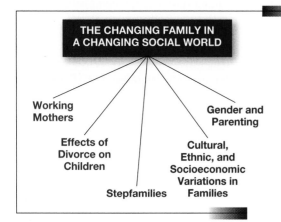

The Changing Family in a Changing Social World

More children are growing up in a greater variety of family structures than ever before. Many mothers spend the greatest part of their day away from their children, even their infants. More than one of every two mothers with a child under the age of 5 is in the labor force; more than two of every three with a child from 6 to 17 years of age is. And the increasing number of children growing up in single-parent families is staggering. As shown in figure 15.4 (on page 474), the United States has the highest percentage of single-parent families, compared with virtually all other countries.

Working Mothers

Because household operations have become more efficient and family size has decreased in America, it is not certain that children with mothers working outside the home actually receive less attention than children in the past whose mothers were not employed. Outside employment—at least for mothers with school-age children—may simply be filling time previously taken up by added household burdens and more children. It also cannot be assumed that, if the mother did not go to

SUMMARY TABLE 15.2
Parenting, Sibling Relationships, and Family Processes in Adolescence

Concept	Processes/Related Ideas	Characteristics/Description
The Parental Role, Parents as Managers, Parenting Styles, and Child Maltreatment	The Parental Role	• For some, the parental role is well planned and coordinated. For others, there is surprise and sometimes chaos. • There are many myths about parenting, including the myth that the birth of a child will save a failing marriage.
	Parents as Managers	• An increased trend is to conceptualize parents as managers of children's lives. • Parents play important roles as managers of children's opportunities, in monitoring children's relationships, and as social initiators and arrangers.
	Parenting Styles	• Authoritarian, authoritative, neglectful, and indulgent are the four main categories of parenting styles. • Authoritative parenting is associated with socially competent child behavior more than the other styles.
	Child Maltreatment	• This is an increasing problem in the United States and is a multifaceted problem. • Understanding child maltreatment requires information about the cultural context and family influences. • Child maltreatment places the child at risk for a number of developmental problems.
Sibling Relationships and Birth Order	Sibling Relationships	• Siblings interact with each other in more negative and less varied ways than parents and children interact.
	Birth Order	• This is related in certain ways to child characteristics, but some critics believe it has been overestimated as a predictor of child behavior.
Family Relationships in Adolescence	Autonomy and Attachment	• Many parents have a difficult time handling the adolescent's push for autonomy. • Attachment to parents increases the likelihood that the adolescent will be socially competent. • Researchers increasingly are classifying as secure-autonomous and breaking down insecure attachment into different categories.
	Parent-Adolescent Conflict	• Conflict with parents often increases in early adolescence but this conflict is often moderate rather than severe. • The increase in conflict probably serves the positive developmental functions of increasing adolescent autonomy and identity. • A small subset of adolescents experience high parent-adolescent conflict and this is linked with negative outcomes for adolescents.

work, the child would benefit from the time freed up by streamlined household operations and smaller families. Mothering does not always have a positive effect on the child. The educated, nonworking mother may overinvest her energies in her children. This can foster an excess of worry and discourage the child's independence. In such situations, the mother may give more parenting than the child can profitably handle.

Lois Hoffman (1989, 2000; Hoffman & Youngblade, 1999) believes that maternal employment is a part of modern life. It is not an aberrant aspect of it but a response to other social changes. It meets needs that cannot be met by the previous family ideal of a full-time mother and homemaker. Not only does it meet the parent's needs, but in many ways it may be a pattern better suited to socializing

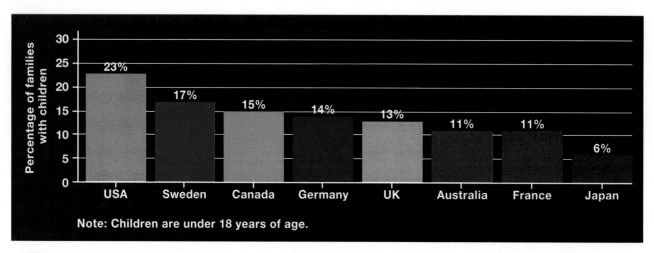

Figure 15.4
Single-Parent Families in Different Countries

Working Mothers
Family and the Workplace

children for the adult roles they will occupy. This is especially true for daughters, but it is also true for sons. The broader range of emotions and skills that each parent presents is more consistent with this adult role. Just as his father shares the breadwinning role and the child-rearing role with his mother, so the son, too, may be more willing to share these roles. The rigid gender stereotyping perpetuated by the divisions of labor in the traditional family is not appropriate for the demands that will be made on children of either sex as adults. The needs of the growing child require the mother to loosen her hold on the child. This task may be easier for the working woman, whose job is an additional source of identity and self-esteem. Overall, researchers have found no detrimental effects of maternal employment on children's development (Gottfried, Gottfried, & Bathurst, 1995; Richards & Duckett, 1994).

A common experience of working mothers (and working fathers) is feeling guilty about being away from their children. The guilt may be triggered by parents who miss their child, worry that their child is missing them, are concerned about the implications of working (such as whether the child is receiving good child care), and worry about the long-term effects of working (such as whether they are jeopardizing the child's future). To reduce guilt, the guilt needs to be acknowledged. Pediatrician T. Berry Brazelton (1983) believes that parents respond to guilt either by admitting it and working through it or by denying it and rationalizing it away. The latter tendency is not recommended. Working parents' guilt can also be reduced if they pay closer attention to how their children are doing.

A subset of children from working-mother families deserves further scrutiny: latchkey children. These children typically do not see their parents from the time they leave for school in the morning until about 6 or 7 P.M. They are called "latchkey" children because they are given the key to their home, take the key to school, and then use it to let themselves into the home while their parents are still at work. Latchkey children are largely unsupervised for 2 to 4 hours a day during each school week. During the summer months, they might be unsupervised for entire days, 5 days a week.

In one study, more than 1,500 latchkey children were interviewed (Long & Long, 1983). A slight majority of these children had had negative latchkey experiences. Some latchkey children may grow up too fast, hurried by the responsibilities placed on them. How do latchkey children handle the lack of limits and structure during the latchkey hours? Without limits and parental supervision, latchkey children find their way into trouble more easily, possibly stealing, vandalizing or abusing a sibling. Ninety percent of the juvenile delinquents in Montgomery County, Maryland, are latchkey children.

Joan Lipsitz (1983), in testifying before the Select Committee on Children, Youth, and Families, called the lack of adult supervision of children in the after-school hours one of today's major problems. Lipsitz called it the "three-to-six o'clock problem" because it was during this time that the Center for Early Adolescence in North Carolina, when Lipsitz was director, experienced a peak of referrals for clinical help. And, in a 1987 national poll, teachers rated the latchkey children phenomenon the number one reason that children have problems in schools (Harris, 1987).

While latchkey children may be vulnerable to problems, the experiences of latchkey children vary enormously, as do the experiences of all children with working mothers (Belle, 1999). Parents need to give special attention to the ways in which their latchkey children's lives can be effectively monitored. Variations in latchkey experiences suggest that parental monitoring and authoritative parenting help the children cope more effectively with latchkey experiences, especially in resisting peer pressure (Galambos & Maggs, 1989; Steinberg, 1986). In one recent study of children in the after-school hours, unsupervised peer contact, lack of neighborhood safety, and low monitoring were linked with externalizing problems (such as acting out problems, delinquency) in children (Pettit & others, 1999). In another study, attending a formal after-school program that included academic, recreational, and remedial activities was associated with better academic achievement and social adjustment, in comparison with other types of after-school care (such as informal adult supervision or self-care) (Posner & Vandell, 1994). Researchers and policy makers recommend that after-school programs have warm and supportive staff, a flexible and relaxed schedule, multiple activities, and opportunities for positive interactions with staff and peers (Pierce, Hamm, & Vandell, 1997; Vandell & Pierce, 1999).

Effects of Divorce on Children

These are the questions that we will explore that focus on the effects of divorce: Are children better adjusted in intact, never divorced families than in divorced families? Should parents stay together for the sake of their children? How much do parenting skills matter in divorced families? What factors are involved in the child's individual risk and vulnerability in a divorced family? What role does socioeconomic status play in the lives of children in divorced families?

Children and Divorce
Divorce and Family Ties
Divorce Resources

Children's Adjustment in Divorced Families   Most researchers agree that children from divorced families show poorer adjustment than their counterparts in nondivorced families (Amato & Keith, 1991). Those that have experienced multiple divorces are at greater risk (Kurdek, Fine, & Sinclair, 1995). Children in divorced families are more likely than children in nondivorced families to have academic problems, to show externalized problems (such as acting out and delinquency) and internalized problems (such as anxiety and depression), to be less socially responsible, to have less competent intimate relationships, to drop out of school, to become sexually active at an early age, to take drugs, to associate with antisocial peers, and to have low self-esteem (Conger & Chao, 1996; McLanahan & Sandefur, 1994).

Although there is a consensus that children from divorced families show these adjustment problems to a greater extent than do children from nondivorced families, there is less agreement about the size of the effects (Hetherington, Bridges, & Insabella, 1998). Some researchers report that the divorce effects are modest and have become smaller as divorce has become more commonplace in society (Amato & Keith, 1991). However, others argue that approximately 20 to 25 percent of children in divorced families have these types of adjustment problems, in contrast to only 10 percent of children in nondivorced families, which is a notable two-fold increase (Hetherington & Jodl, 1994). Nonetheless, the majority of children in divorced families do not have these problems (Buchanan, 2000; Hetherington, 1999, 2000). The weight of the research evidence underscores that most children competently cope with their parents' divorce but that significantly more children from divorced families have adjustment problems (20 to 25 percent) than children from nondivorced families (10 percent).

Should Parents Stay Together for the Sake of Their Children?

Whether parents should stay in an unhappy or conflicted marriage for the sake of their children is one of the most commonly asked questions about divorce (Hetherington, 1999, 2000). If the stresses and disruptions in family relationships associated with an unhappy, conflictual marriage that erode the well-being of children are reduced by the move to a divorced, single-parent family, divorce may be advantageous. However, if the diminished resources and increased risks associated with divorce also are accompanied by inept parenting and sustained or increased conflict, not only between the divorced couple but also between the parents, children, and siblings, the best choice for the children would be for an unhappy marriage to be retained. These are "ifs," and it is difficult to determine how these will play out when parents either remain together in an acrimonious marriage or become divorced.

How Much Do Family Processes Matter in Divorced Families?

Family processes matter a lot. When divorced parents' relationship with each other is harmonious and when they use authoritative parenting, the adjustment of children improves (Hetherington, Bridges, & Insabella, 1998). A number of researchers have shown that a disequilibrium, which includes diminished parenting skills, occurs in the year following the divorce but that, by two years after the divorce, restabilization has occurred and parenting skills have improved (Hetherington, 1989). About one-fourth to one-third of children in divorced families, compared with 10 percent in nondivorced families, become disengaged from their families, spending as little time as possible at home and in interaction with family members (Hetherington & Jodl, 1994). This disengagement is higher for boys than girls in divorced families. However, if there is a caring adult outside the home, such as a mentor, the disengagement may be a positive solution to a disrupted, conflicted family circumstance.

What Roles Do Noncustodial Parents Play in the Lives of Children in Divorced Families?

Father Custody

Most nonresidential fathers have a friendly, companionate relationship with their children, rather than a traditional parental relationship (Munsch, Woodward, & Darling, 1995). They want their visits to be pleasant and entertaining, so they are reluctant to assume the role of a disciplinarian or teacher. They are less likely than nondivorced fathers to criticize, control, and monitor their child's behavior or to help them with such tasks as homework (Bray & Berger, 1993). The frequency of contact with noncustodial fathers and children's adjustment is usually found to be unrelated (Amato & Keith, 1991). The quality of the contact matters more. Under conditions of low conflict, when noncustodial fathers participate in a variety of activities with their offspring and engage in authoritative parenting, children, especially boys, benefit (Lindner-Gunnoe, 1993). We know less about noncustodial mothers than fathers, but these mothers are less adept than custodial mothers are at controlling and monitoring their child's behavior (Furstenberg & Nord, 1987). Noncustodial mothers' warmth, support, and monitoring can improve children's adjustment (Lindner-Gunnoe, 1993). To read about effective ways of communicating with children about divorce, see the Explorations in Child Development box.

What Factors Are Involved in the Child's Individual Risk and Vulnerability in a Divorced Family?

Among the factors involved in the child's risk and vulnerability are the child's adjustment prior to the divorce, as well as the child's personality and temperament, developmental status, gender, and custody situation. Children whose parents later divorce show poorer adjustment before the breakup (Amato & Booth, 1996). When antecedent levels of problem behaviors are controlled, differences in the adjustment of children in divorced and nondivorced families are reduced (Cherlin & others, 1991).

$\mathscr{E}$XPLORATIONS IN CHILD DEVELOPMENT
Communicating with Children About Divorce

ELLEN GALINSKY AND JUDY DAVID (1988) developed a number of guidelines for communicating with young children about divorce.

Explain the Separation

As soon as the daily activities in the home make it obvious that one parent is leaving, tell the children. If possible, both parents should be present when the children are made aware of the separation to come. The reasons for the separation are very difficult for young children to understand. No matter what parents tell children, children can find reasons to argue against the separation. A child may say something like, "If you don't love each other anymore, you need to start trying harder." One set of parents told their 4-year-old, "We both love you. We will both always love you and take care of you, but we aren't going to live in the same house anymore. Daddy is moving to an apartment near the stores where we shop." It is extremely important for parents to tell the children who will take care of them and to describe the specific arrangements for seeing the other parent.

Explain That the Separation Is Not the Child's Fault

Young children often believe their parents' separation or divorce is their own fault. Therefore, it is important to tell children that they are not the cause of the separation. Parents need to repeat this a number of times.

Explain That It May Take Time to Feel Better

It is helpful to tell young children that it's normal to not feel good about what is happening, and that lots of other children feel this way when their parents become separated. It is also okay for divorced parents to share some of their emotions with children, by saying something like, "I'm having a hard time since the separation, just like you, but I know it's going to get better after a while." Such statements are best kept brief and should not criticize the other parent.

Keep the Door Open for Further Discussion

Tell your children that, anytime they want to talk about the separation, to come to you. It is healthy for children to get out their pent-up emotions in discussions with their parents and to learn that the parents are willing to listen to their feelings and fears.

Provide as Much Continuity as Possible

The less children's worlds are disrupted by the separation, the easier their transition to a single-parent family will be. This means maintaining as much as possible the rules already in place. Children need parents who care enough to not only give them warmth and nurturance but also set reasonable limits. If the custodial parent has to move to a new home, it is important to preserve as much of what is familiar to the child as possible. In one family, the child helped arrange her new room exactly as it had been prior to the divorce. If children must leave friends behind, it is important for parents to help the children stay in touch by phone or by letter. Keeping the child busy and involved in the new setting can also keep their minds off the stressful thoughts about the separation.

Provide Support for Your Children and Yourself

After a divorce or separation, parents are as important to children as before the divorce or separation. Divorced parents need to provide children with as much support as possible. Parents function best when other people are available to give them support as adults and as parents. Divorced parents can find people who provide practical help and with whom they can talk about their problems. Too often, divorced parents criticize themselves and say they feel that they don't deserve help. One divorced parent commented, "I've made a mess of my life. I don't deserve anybody's help." However, seeking out others for support and feedback about problems can make the transition to a single-parent family more bearable.

Personality and temperament also play a role in children's adjustment in divorced families. ◀▥ P. 356. Children who are socially mature and responsible, who show few behavioral problems, and who have an easy temperament are better able to cope with their parents' divorce. Children with a difficult temperament often have problems in coping with their parents' divorce (Hetherington, 1995).

Focusing on the developmental status of the child involves taking into account the age of onset of the divorce and the time when the child's adjustment is assessed. In most studies, these factors are confounded with the length of time since the divorce occurred. Some researchers have found that preschool children whose parents divorce are at greater risk for long-term problems than are older children (Zill & others, 1993). The explanation for this focuses on their inability to realistically appraise the

Through the Eyes of Psychologists

E. Mavis Hetherington, *University of Virginia*

"As marriage has become a more optional, less permanent institution in contemporary America, children and adolescents are encountering stresses and adaptive challenges associated with their parents' marital transitions."

Stepfamily Resources
Stepfamily Support
Stepfathers

causes and consequences of divorce, their anxiety about the possibility of abandonment, their self-blame for the divorce, and their inability to use extrafamilial protective resources. However, adolescence may be a period in which problems in adjustment emerge or increase, even when divorce has occurred much earlier.

Earlier studies reported gender differences in response to divorce, with divorce being more negative for boys than for girls in mother-custody families. However, more recent studies have shown that gender differences are less pronounced and consistent than was previously believed. Some of the inconsistency may be due to the increase in father custody, joint custody, and increased involvement of noncustodial fathers, especially in their sons' lives. However, female adolescents in divorced families are more likely to drop out of high school and college than are their male counterparts. Male and female adolescents from divorced families are similarly affected in the likelihood of becoming teenage parents, but single parenthood more adversely affects girls.

In recent decades, an increasing number of children have lived in father custody and joint-custody families (Maccoby, 1999). What is their adjustment like, compared with that of children in mother-custody families? Although there have been few thorough studies of the topic, there appear to be few advantages of joint custody over custody by one parent (Hetherington, Bridges, & Insabella, 1998). Some studies have shown that boys adjust better in father-custody families, girls in mother-custody families, while other studies have not. In one study, the adolescents in father-custody families had higher rates of delinquency, believed to be due to less competent monitoring by the fathers (Maccoby & Mnookin, 1992).

What Role Does Socioeconomic Status Play in the Lives of Children in Divorced Families? Custodial mothers experience the loss of about one-fourth to one-half of their predivorce income, in comparison with a loss of only one-tenth by custodial fathers (Emery, 1994). This income loss for divorced mothers is accompanied by increased workloads, high rates of job instability, and residential moves to less desirable neighborhoods with inferior schools.

Stepfamilies

The number of remarriages involving children has grown steadily in recent years, although the rate of remarriage actually has declined as the divorce rate has increased in the past several decades. Also, divorces occur at a 10 percent higher rate in remarriages than in first marriages (Cherlin & Furstenberg, 1994). As a result of their parents' successive marital transitions, about half of all children whose parents divorce will have a stepfather within four years of parental separation.

As in divorced families, children in stepfamilies have more adjustment problems than their counterparts in nondivorced families (Hetherington, Bridges, & Insabella, 1998). The adjustment problems of stepfamily children are much like those of children in divorced families—academic problems, externalizing and internalizing problems, lower self-esteem, early sexual activity, delinquency, and so on (Anderson & others, 1999). There is an increase in adjustment problems of children in newly remarried families (Hetherington & Clingempeel, 1992). Early adolescence seems to be an especially difficult time in which to have a remarriage occur, possibly because it exacerbates normal early adolescent concerns about autonomy, identity, and sexuality (Hetherington, 1995). Restabilization may take longer in stepfamilies, up to 5 years or more, than in divorced families, which often occurs in 1 to 2 years.

Boundary ambiguity, *the uncertainty in stepfamilies about who is in or out of the family and who is performing or responsible for certain tasks in the family system,* can present problems in stepfamilies. In the early stages of remarriage, stepfathers have been described as behaving like polite strangers, trying to win over their stepchildren by reducing negative behaviors and trying to control them less than do fathers in nondivorced families (Bray & Berger, 1993; Bray, Berger, & Boethel, 1999). In longer established stepfamilies, a distant, disengaged parenting style predominates for stepfathers, although conflict can remain high between stepfather and children. Stepmothers have a more difficult time integrating themselves into stepfamilies than do stepfathers. Children's relationships with custodial parents (biological father in stepmother families, biological mother in stepfather families) tend to be better than with stepparents (Santrock, Sitterle, & Warshak, 1998). Also, children in complex (or blended) stepfamilies (in which both parents bring offspring from previous marriages to live in the newly constituted stepfamily) show more adjustment problems than do children in simple stepfamilies (in which only one parent brings offspring into the stepfamily) (Hetherington, 1995; Santrock & Sitterle, 1987).

Cultural, Ethnic, and Socioeconomic Variations in Families

Cultures vary on a number of issues involving families, such as what the father's role in the family should be, the extent to which support systems are available to families, and the ways in which children should be disciplined. Although there are cross-cultural variations in parenting (Whiting & Edwards, 1988), in one study of parenting behavior in 186 cultures around the world, the most common pattern was a warm and controlling style, one that was neither permissive nor restrictive (Rohner & Rohner, 1981). The investigators commented that the majority of cultures have discovered, over many centuries, a "truth" that only recently emerged in the Western world—namely, that children's healthy social development is most effectively promoted by love and at least some moderate parental control.

What are some characteristics of families within different ethnic groups?

Families within different ethnic groups in the United States differ in their size, structure, composition, reliance on kinships networks, and levels of income and education (Parke & Buriel, 1998). Large and extended families are more common among minority groups than among the White majority. For example, 19 percent of Latino families have three or more children, compared with 14 percent of African American and 10 percent of White families. African American and Latino children interact more with grandparents, aunts, uncles, cousins, and more-distant relatives than do White children.

Single-parent families are more common among African Americans and Latinos than among White Americans. In comparison with two-parent households, single parents often have more limited resources of time, money, and energy. Ethnic minority parents also are less educated and more likely to live in low-income circumstances than their White counterparts. Still, many impoverished ethnic minority families manage to find ways to raise competent children (Gordon, 2000).

boundary ambiguity
The uncertainty in stepfamilies about who is in or out of the family and who is performing or responsible for certain tasks in the family system.

Family Diversity

Some aspects of home life can help protect ethnic minority children from injustice. The community and the family can filter out destructive racist messages, and parents can present alternative frames of reference to those presented by the majority. The extended family also can serve as an important buffer to stress (McAdoo, 1999; Wakschlag, Chase-Lansdale, & Brooks-Gunn, 1996).

In America and most Western cultures, differences have been found in child rearing among different socioeconomic groups. Low-income parents often place a high value on external characteristics, such as obedience and neatness. By contrast, middle- and upper-income families frequently place a high value on internal characteristics, such as self-control and delay of gratification. Middle- and upper-income parents are more likely to explain something, praise, use reasoning to accompany their discipline, and ask their children questions. By contrast, low-income parents are more likely to use physical punishment and criticize their children (Hoff-Ginsburg & Tardif, 1995).

There also are socioeconomic differences in the way that parents think about education (Lareau, 1996). Middle- and upper-income parents more often think of education as something that should be mutually encouraged by parents and teachers. By contrast, low-income parents are more likely to view education as the teacher's job. Thus, increased school-family linkages especially can benefit students from low-income families.

Gender and Parenting

What is the mother's role in the family? the father's role? How can mothers and fathers become cooperative, effective partners in parenting?

**Issues Involving Mothers
The Mother's Role**

The Mother's Role   What do you think of when you hear the word *motherhood*? If you are like most people, you associate motherhood with a number of positive images, such as warm, selfless, dutiful, and tolerant (Matlin, 1993). And while most women expect that motherhood will be happy and fulfilling, the reality is that motherhood has been accorded relatively low prestige in our society. When stacked up against money, power, and achievement, motherhood unfortunately doesn't fare too well, and mothers rarely receive the appreciation they warrant. When children don't succeed or develop problems, our society has had a tendency to attribute the lack of success or the development of problems to a single source—mothers. One of psychology's most important lessons is that behavior is multiply determined. So it is with children's development—when development goes awry, mothers are not the single cause of the problems even though our society stereotypes them in this way.

The reality of motherhood today is that while fathers have increased their child-rearing responsibilities somewhat, the main responsibility for children still falls on the mother's shoulders (Barnard & Martell, 1995). Mothers do far more family work than fathers do—two to three times more (Thompson & Walker, 1989). A few "exceptional" men do as much family work as their wives; in one study the figure was 10 percent of the men (Berk, 1985). Not only do women do more family work than men, the family work most women do is unrelenting, repetitive, and routine, often involving cleaning, cooking, child care, shopping, laundry, and straightening up. The family work most men do is infrequent, irregular, and nonroutine, often involving household repairs, taking out the garbage, and yard work. Women report that they often have to do several tasks at once, which helps to explain why they find domestic work less relaxing and more stressful than men do (Shaw, 1988).

Because family work is intertwined with love and embedded in family relations, it has complex and contradictory meanings (Villani, 1997). Many women feel that family tasks are mindless but essential. They usually enjoy tending to the needs of their loved ones and keeping the family going, even if they do not find the activities themselves enjoyable and fulfilling. Family work is both positive and negative for women. They are unsupervised and rarely criticized, they plan and control their own work, and they have only their own standards to meet. However, women's family work is often worrisome, tiresome, menial, repetitive, isolating, unfinished, inescapable, and often unappreciated. It is not surprising that men report that they are more satisfied with their marriage than women do.

In sum, the role of the mother brings with it benefits as well as limitations. Although motherhood is not enough to fill most women's entire lives, for most mothers, it is one of the most meaningful experiences in their lives (Hoffnung, 1984).

The Father's Role   The father's role has undergone major changes (Cabrera & others (in press); Lamb, 1997; Lambert, 1997). During the colonial period in America, fathers were primarily responsible for moral teaching. Fathers provided guidance and values, especially through religion. With the Industrial Revolution, the father's role changed; he gained the responsibility as the breadwinner, a role that continued through the Great Depression. By the end of World War II, another role for fathers emerged, that of being a gender-role model. Although being a breadwinner and moral guardian continued to be important father roles, attention shifted to his role as a male, especially for sons. Then, in the 1970s, the current interest in the father as an active, nurturant, caregiving parent emerged. Rather than being responsible only for the discipline and control of older children and for providing the family's economic base, the father now is being evaluated in terms of his active, nurturant involvement with his children (McBride, 1991; Perry-Jenkins, Payne & Hendricks, 1999).

Children can significantly benefit from interaction with a caring, accessible, and dependable father who fosters a sense of trust and confidence.

Fathering
The Fatherhood Project
Online Resources for Fathers

How much time do children spend with fathers? In one recent study, a nationally representative sample of more than 1,700 children up to 12 years of age spent an average of 2.5 hours a day with their fathers on weekdays and 6.2 hours a day on weekends (Yeung & others, 1999). For about half that time, fathers are directly engaged with their children—playing, eating, shopping, watching TV, or working together around the house. The rest of the time they are nearby or available to their children if needed. In this study, mothers still shouldered the lion's share of parenting, especially on weekdays. Research conducted in the 1970s suggested that fathers spent about one-third as much time with their children as mothers did. In the early 1990s, that proportion had jumped to approximately 43 percent. In the most recent study just mentioned, fathers spent about 65 percent as much time with children as mothers did on weekdays and about 87 percent as much time as mothers did on weekends (Yeung & others, 1999).

In the study just described, the entire sample was drawn from intact, nondivorced families (Yeung & others, 1999). Other studies that include mother-custody single-parent families often find that fathers spend less time with children. For example, a typical finding is that American fathers spend about an average of 45 minutes a day caring for children by themselves.

Family responsibility was a major theme of the Million Man March in Washington, DC, in 1995. It also is the theme of the revival-style meetings of the Promise Keepers, an evangelical group that has been filling stadiums with men across the United States. Men today appear to be better fathers—when they are around. However, too many children growing up today see little of their fathers. In 1994, 16.3 million children in the United States were living with their mothers. Forty percent of these children had not seen their father in the past year.

Partners in Parenting   When parents show cooperation, mutual respect, balanced communication, and attunement to each other's needs, this helps the child develop positive attitudes toward both males and females (Biller, 1993; Tamis-LeMonda & Cabrera, 1999). It is much easier for working parents to cope with changing family circumstances when the father and mother equitably share child-

SUMMARY TABLE 15.3
The Changing Family in a Changing Social World

Concept	Processes/ Related Ideas	Characteristics/Description
Working Mothers	Nature of Effects	• Overall, the mother's working outside the home does not have an adverse effect on children's development.
	Latchkey Children	• Latchkey experiences do not have a uniform effect on children. • Parental monitoring and participation in structured activities with competent supervision are important influences on latchkey children's adjustment.
Effects of Divorce on Children	Their Nature	• Children in divorced families show more adjustment problems than their counterparts in nondivorced families. • Whether parents should stay together for the sake of the children is difficult to determine. • Children show better adjustment in divorced families when parents' relationships with each other are harmonious and authoritative parenting is used. • Factors to be considered in the adjustment of children in divorced families are adjustment prior to the divorce, personality and temperament, developmental status, gender, and custody. • Income loss for divorced mothers may be linked with a number of stresses that can affect the child's adjustment.
Stepfamilies	Their Nature	• Like in divorced families, children in stepfamilies have more problems than their counterparts in nondivorced families. • Adolescence is especially a difficult time for remarriage of parents to occur. • Restabilization often takes longer stepfamilies than divorced families. • Children have better relationships with their biological parents than their stepparents and show more problems in complex, blended families than simple ones.
Cultural, Ethnic, and Socioeconomic Variations in Families	Cultures	• Cultures vary on a number of issues regarding families.
	Ethnic Variations	• African American and Latino children are more likely than White American children to live in single-parent families, larger families, and families with extended connections.
	Socioeconomic Status	• Higher-income families are more likely to use discipline that promotes internalization; low-income families are more likely to use discipline that encourages externalization.
Gender and Parenting	The Mother's Role	• Most people associate motherhood with a number of positive images, but the reality is that motherhood is accorded a relatively low status in our society.
	The Father's Role	• Over time, the father's role in the child's development has evolved from moral teacher to breadwinner to gender-role model to nurturant caregiver. Fathers are much less involved in child rearing than mothers are.
	Partners in Parenting	• Father-mother cooperation and mutual respect help the child to develop positive attitudes toward both males and females.

rearing responsibilities. Mothers feel less stress and have more positive attitudes toward their husbands when the husband is a supportive partner. Researchers have found that egalitarian marital relationships have positive effects on adolescent development, fostering their trust and encouraging communication (Yang & others, 1996).

At this point we have discussed a number of ideas about the changing family in a changing social world. A review of these ideas is presented in summary table 15.3.

Chapter Review

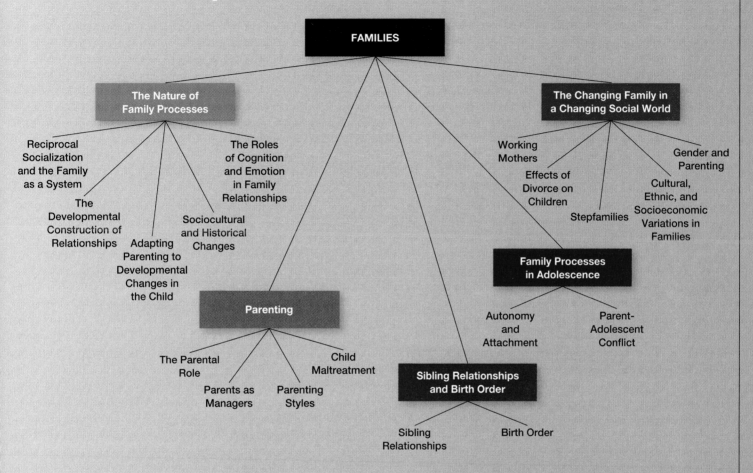

TO OBTAIN A DETAILED REVIEW OF THE CHAPTER, STUDY THESE THREE SUMMARY TABLES:

Key Terms

Key People

Child Development Resources

Growing Up With Divorce (1990)
> by Neal Kalter
> New York: The Free Press

This book gives divorced parents excellent advice about communicating with their children.

Raising Black Children (1992)
> by James P. Comer and Alvin E. Poussaint
> New York: Plume

This is an excellent book for African American parents that includes wise suggestions that are not in most child-rearing books.

Socialization in the Family: Ethnic and Ecological Perspectives (1998)
> by Ross Parke and Raymond Buriel in W. Damon (Ed.),
> *Handbook of Child Psychology* (5th ed., Vol. 3)
> New York: Wiley

An in-depth examination of research on parent-child relationships.

You and Your Adolescent (2nd ed.) (1997)
> by Laurence Steinberg and Ann Levine
> New York: HarperCollins

This book gives excellent recommendations for parenting adolescents.

Taking It to the Net

1. Frieda is the middle child in a family with five children. She is interested in what researchers have to say about the effect of birth order on sibling relationships. How does being a middle child contribute to the dynamics between Frieda and her brothers and sisters?

2. Mary and Peter are the parents of 13-year-old Cameron and 15-year-old Suzanne. They had heard that the adolescent years could be difficult, but they were not prepared for the constant conflict and bickering. They don't feel that they are doing a very good job as parents. Are there some guidelines that will help them restore some peace and sanity to their family?

3. Bruce and Caitlin are planning to separate and divorce. Both are miserable, and their household is like an armed camp. Unfortunately, they have three children, ages 6, 8, and 12. What should they tell the children, and how and when should they tell them?

Connect to *http://www.mhhe.com/santrockc9* to find the answers!

Chapter 16

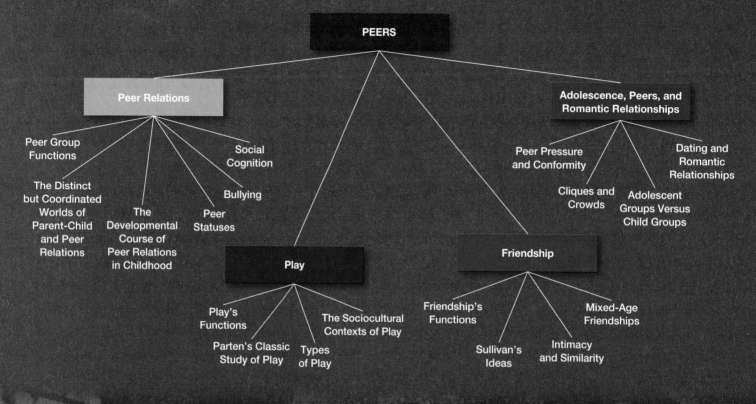

PEERS

Peer Relations

Peer Group Functions

The Distinct but Coordinated Worlds of Parent-Child and Peer Relations

The Developmental Course of Peer Relations in Childhood

Peer Statuses

Bullying

Social Cognition

Play

Play's Functions

Parten's Classic Study of Play

Types of Play

The Sociocultural Contexts of Play

Friendship

Friendship's Functions

Sullivan's Ideas

Intimacy and Similarity

Mixed-Age Friendships

Adolescence, Peers, and Romantic Relationships

Peer Pressure and Conformity

Cliques and Crowds

Adolescent Groups Versus Child Groups

Dating and Romantic Relationships

Peers

*Y*ou are troubled at seeing him spend his early years in doing nothing. What! Is it nothing to be happy? Is it nothing to skip, to play, to run about all day long? Never in his life will he be so busy as now.

Jean-Jacques Rousseau
Swiss-Born French Philosopher, 18th Century

The Stories of Young Adolescent Girls' Friends and Relational Worlds

LYNN BROWN AND CAROL GILLIGAN (1992) conducted in-depth interviews of one hundred 10- to 13-year-old girls who were making the transition to adolescence. They listened to what these girls were saying about how important friends were to them. The girls were very curious about the human world they lived in and kept track of what was happening to their peers and friends. The girls spoke about the pleasure they derived from the intimacy and fun of human connection, and about the potential for hurt in relationships. They especially highlighted the importance of clique formation in their lives.

One girl, Noura, said that she learned about what it feels like to be the person that everyone doesn't like and that it was very painful. Another girl, Gail, reflected on her life over the last year and said that she was getting along better with people, probably because she was better at understanding how they think and at accepting them. A number of the girls talked about the "whitewashing" of the adolescent relational world. That is, many girls say nice and kind things to be polite but they often don't really mean them. They know the benefits of being perceived as the perfect, happy girl, at least on the surface. Suspecting that people prefer the "perfect girl," they experiment with her image and the happiness she might bring. The perfectly nice girl seems to gain popularity with other girls, and as many girls strive to become her, jealousies and rivalries break out. Cliques can provide emotional support for girls who are striving to be perfect but know they are not. One girl, Victoria, commented that some girls like her, who weren't very popular, nonetheless were accepted into a "club" with three other girls. She now felt that when she was sad or depressed she could count on the "club" for support. Though they were "leftovers" and did not get into the most popular cliques, these four girls said they knew they were liked and it felt great.

Another girl, Judy, at age 13, spoke about her interest in romantic relationships. She said that although she and her girl friends were only 13, they wanted to be romantic. She covered her bodily desires and sexual feelings with romantic ideals. She described a girl who went out with guys and went farther than most girls would and said the girl's behavior is "disgusting." Rather than sex, Judy said she was looking for a really good relationship with a guy.

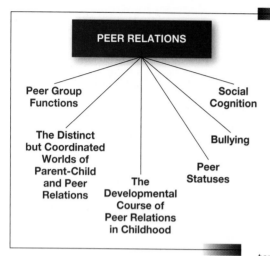

peers
Children of about the same age or maturity level.

Peer Relations

Peer Relations

As children grow older, peer relations consume increasing amounts of their time. What is the function of a child's peer group?

Peer Group Functions

Peers *are children of about the same age or maturity level.* Same-age peer interaction fills a unique role in our culture (Hartup, 1976). Age grading would occur even if schools were not age graded and children were left alone to determine the composition of their own societies. One of the most important functions of the peer group is to provide a source of information and comparison about the world outside the family. Children receive feedback about their abilities from their peer group. Children evaluate what they do in terms of whether it is better than, as good as, or worse than what other children do. It is hard to do this at home because siblings are usually older or younger.

Are peers necessary for development? When peer monkeys who have been reared together are separated, they become depressed and regress socially (Suomi, Harlow, & Domek, 1970). The human development literature contains a classic example of the importance of peers in social development. Anna Freud (Freud & Dann, 1951) studied six children from different families who banded together after their parents were killed in World War II. Intensive peer attachment was observed; the children formed a tightly knit group, dependent on one another and aloof with outsiders. Even though deprived of parental care, they became neither delinquent nor psychotic.

Thus, good peer relations may be necessary for normal social development. Special concerns focus on children who are withdrawn and aggressive (Coie, 1999; Ladd, 1999). Withdrawn children who are rejected by peers and/or victimized and feeling lonely are at risk for depression. Children who are aggressive with their peers are at risk for developing a number of problems, including deliquency and dropping out of school.

As you might have detected from our discussion of peer relations thus far, peer influences can be both positive and negative (Rubin, Bukowski, & Parker, 1998; Urberg, 1999). Both Jean Piaget (1932) and Harry Stack Sullivan (1953) were influential theorists who stressed that it is through peer interaction that children and adolescents learn the symmetrical reciprocity mode of relationships discussed in chapter 15. Children explore the principles of fairness and justice by working through disagreements with peers. They also learn to be keen observers of peers' interests and perspectives in order to smoothly integrate themselves into ongoing peer activities. In addition, Sullivan argued that adolescents learn to be skilled and sensitive partners in intimate relationships by forging close friendships with selected peers. These intimacy skills are carried forward to help form the foundation of later dating and marital relationships, according to Sullivan (Buhrmester, 1999).

In contrast, some theorists have emphasized the negative influences of peers on children's and adolescents' development. Being rejected or overlooked by peers leads some children to feel lonely or hostile. Further, such rejection and neglect by peers are related to an individual's subsequent mental health and criminal problems. Some theorists have also described the children's peer culture as a corrupt influence that undermines parental values and control. Further, peers can introduce adolescents to alcohol, drugs, delinquency, and other forms of behavior that adults view as maladaptive.

As you read about peers, also keep in mind that although peer experiences have important influences on children's development, those influences vary according to the way peer experience is measured, the outcomes specified, and the developmental trajectories traversed (Hartup, 1999). "Peers" and "peer group" are global concepts. These can be beneficial concepts in understanding peer influences as long as they are considered in terms of the specific type of setting or peer context in which the child participates, such as "acquaintance," "clique," "neighborhood associates," "friendship network," or "activity group." For example, one analysis of the peer group describes these aspects of the youth culture: membership crowd, neighborhood crowd, reference crowd, church crowd, sports team, friendship group, and friend (Brown, 1999).

The Distinct but Coordinated Worlds of Parent-Child and Peer Relations

What are some of the similarities and differences between peer and parent-child relationships? Children touch, smile, frown, and vocalize when they interact with both parents and peers. However, rough-and-tumble play occurs mainly with other children, not with adults, and, in times of stress, children often move toward their parents rather than toward their peers.

In addition to evaluating whether children engage in similar or dissimilar behaviors when interacting with parents and peers, it is also important to examine whether children's peer relations develop independently of parent-child relationships or are wedded to them (Hartup & Laursen, 1999). Recall our discussion of the developmental construction of relationships in chapter 15, which affords two different views. In the continuity view, early parent-child relationships strongly influence children's subsequent peer relations and friendships. By contrast, in the discontinuity view, peer relations and friendships have a more independent developmental path.

A number of theorists and researchers argue that parent-child relationships serve as emotional bases for exploring and enjoying peer relations (Allen & others, in press; Ladd, 1999; Mize, Petit, & Brown, 1995; Rubin, Bukowski, & Parker, 1998). In one study, the parent-child relationship history of each peer helped to predict the nature of peer interaction (Olweus, 1980) (see figure 16.1). Some boys were highly aggressive ("bullies") and other boys were the recipients of aggression ("whipping boys") throughout their preschool years. The bullies and the whipping boys had distinctive relationship histories. The bullies' parents frequently rejected them, were authoritarian, and were permissive about their sons' aggression, and the bullies' families were characterized by discord. By contrast, the whipping boys' parents were anxious and overprotective, taking special care to have their sons avoid aggression. The well-adjusted boys in the study were much less likely to be involved in aggressive peer interchanges than were the bullies and whipping boys. Their parents did not sanction aggression, and their responsive

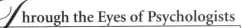

Through the Eyes of Psychologists

Gary Ladd, *University of Illinois at Urbana-Champaign*

"The premise that family processes influence children's social competence continues to be an important aspect of research on peer relations."

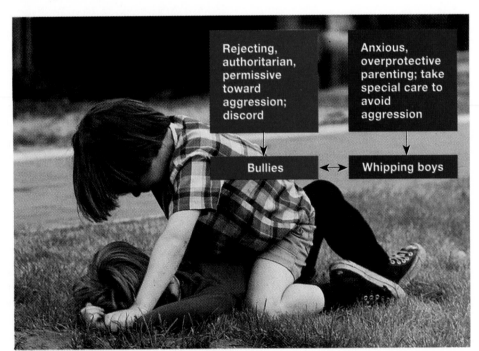

Figure 16.1
Peer Aggression
Children's peer behavior is influenced by their parent-child relationship histories.

involvement with their sons promoted the development of self-assertion rather than aggression or wimpish behavior. We will further discuss bullying later in the chapter.

Parents also can model or coach their children in the ways of relating to peers (Updegraff, 1999). In one investigation, parents indicated they recommended specific strategies to their children regarding peer relations (Rubin & Sloman, 1984). For example, parents told their children how to mediate disputes or how to become less shy with others. They also encouraged them to be tolerant and to resist peer pressure. In another study, parents who frequently initiated peer contacts for their preschool children had children who were more accepted by their peers and higher levels of prosocial behavior (Ladd & Hart, 1992).

A key aspect of peer relations can be traced to basic lifestyle decisions by parents (Cooper & Ayers-Lopez, 1985). Parents' choices of neighborhoods, churches, schools, and their own friends largely determine the pool from which their children might select possible friends. For example, the chosen schools can lead to specific grouping policies, as well as particular academic and extracurricular activities. In turn, such facts affect which students their children meet, their purpose in interacting, and eventually who become friends. For example, classrooms in which teachers encourage more cooperative peer interchanges have fewer isolates.

In sum, parent-child and peer worlds are coordinated and connected (Brown & Huang, 1995; Ladd, 1999; Maccoby, 1996). But they also are distinct. Earlier we indicated that rough-and-tumble play occurs mainly with other children, not in parent-child interaction. And, in times of stress, children often turn to parents, not peers, for support. Peer relations also are more likely to consist of interaction on a much more equal basis than parent-child relations. In parent-child relations, since parents have greater knowledge and authority, their children must often learn how to conform to rules and regulations laid down by parents. With peers, children learn to formulate and assert their own opinions, appreciate the perspective of peers, cooperatively negotiate solutions to disagreements, and evolve standards of conduct that are mutually acceptable.

The Developmental Course of Peer Relations in Childhood

Although we generally think of peer relations as not assuming an important role until early childhood, some researchers believe that the quality of peer interaction in infancy provides valuable information about social development (Vandell, 1985). For example, in one investigation, positive affect in infant peer relations was related to easy access to peer play groups and to peer popularity in early childhood (Howes, 1985). As increasing numbers of children attend day care, peer interaction in infancy takes on a more important developmental role.

The frequency of peer interaction, both positive and negative, picks up considerably during early childhood (Hartup, 1983). Although aggressive interaction and rough-and-tumble play increase, the *proportion* of aggressive exchanges, compared to friendly exchanges, decreases. Children tend to abandon their immature and inefficient social exchanges with age and acquire more mature ways of relating to peers.

Children spend an increasing amount of time in peer interaction during middle and late childhood and adolescence. In one investigation, children interacted with peers 10 percent of their day at age 2, 20 percent at age 4, and more than 40 percent between the ages of 7 and 11. In a typical school day, episodes with peers totaled 299 times per day (Barker & Wright, 1951).

ADVENTURES FOR THE MIND

Parent-Peer Linkages in Your Adolescence

THINK BACK to your middle school/junior high and high school years. What was your relationship with your parents like? Were you securely attached or insecurely attached to them? How do you think your relationship with your parents affected your friendship and peer relations in adolescence? Consider also dating and romantic relationships. How do adolescents' observations of their parents' marital lives and their own relationships with their parents influence their dating and romantic relationships?

Peer Statuses

Children often think, "What can I do to get all of the kids at school to like me?" or "What's wrong with me? Something must be wrong or I would be more popular." What makes a child popular with peers? **Popular children** *are frequently nominated as a best friend and are rarely disliked by their peers.* Researchers have found that popular children give out reinforcements, listen carefully, maintain open lines of communication with peers, are happy, act like themselves, show enthusiasm and concern for others, and are self-confident without being conceited (Hartup, 1983).

Developmentalists have distinguished three other types of peer statuses: neglected, rejected, and controversial (Wentzal & Asher, 1995). **Neglected children** *are infrequently nominated as a best friend but are not disliked by their peers.* **Rejected children** *are infrequently nominated as someone's best friend and are actively disliked by their peers.* **Controversial children** *are frequently nominated both as someone's best friend and as being disliked.*

The controversial peer status had not been studied until recently. In one study, girls who had a controversial peer status in the fourth grade were more likely to become adolescent mothers than were girls of other peer statuses (Underwood, Kupersmidt, & Coie, 1996). Also, aggressive girls had more children than nonaggressive girls.

Rejected children often have more serious adjustment problems than those who are neglected (Parker & Asher, 1987). For example, in one study, 112 fifth-grade boys were evaluated over a period of 7 years until the end of high school (Kupersmidt & Coie, 1990). The best predictor of whether rejected children would engage in delinquent behavior or drop out of school later during adolescence was aggression toward peers in elementary school.

Not all rejected children are aggressive (Bierman, Smoot, & Aumiller, 1993; Ladd, 1999). Aggression and its related characteristics of impulsiveness and disruptiveness underlie rejection about half the time, but approximately 10 to 20 percent of rejected children are shy (Cillessen & others, 1992).

An important question to ask is, How can neglected children and rejected children be trained to interact more effectively with their peers? (Coie & Dodge, 1998). The goal of training programs with neglected children is often to help them attract attention from their peers in positive ways and to hold their attention by asking questions, by listening in a warm and friendly way, and by saying things about themselves that relate to the peers' interests. They also are taught to enter groups more effectively (Duck, 1988).

The goal of training programs with rejected children is often to help them listen to peers and "hear what they say" instead of trying to dominate peer interactions. Rejected children are trained to join peers without trying to change what is taking place in the peer group.

Children may need to be persuaded or motivated that these strategies work effectively and are satisfying. In some programs, children are shown videotapes of appropriate peer interaction; then they are asked to comment on them and to draw lessons from what they have seen. In other training programs, popular children are taught to be more accepting of neglected or rejected peers.

popular children
Children who are frequently nominated as a best friend and are rarely disliked by their peers.

neglected children
Children who are infrequently nominated as a best friend but are not disliked by their peers.

rejected children
Children who are infrequently nominated as a best friend and are actively disliked by their peers.

controversial children
Children who are frequently nominated both as someone's best friend and as being disliked.

Peer Conflicts
Aggressive Boys, Friendships, and Adjustment

*T*hrough the Eyes of Psychologists

John Coie, *Duke University*

"Peer rejection contributes to subsequent problems of adaptation, including antisocial behavior."

Bullying

Significant numbers of students are victimized by bullies (Slee & Taki, 1999; Smith & others, 1999). In one recent survey of bullying in South Carolina middle schools, 1 of every 4 students reported that they had been bullied several times in a 3-month period; 1 in 10 said they were chronically bullied (at least once a week) (Institute for Families in Society, 1997).

Victims of bullying have been found to have certain characteristics (Pellegrini, 2000). In one recent study, victims of bullies had parents who were intrusive and demanding but low in responsiveness with their children (Ladd

& Kochenderfer, in press). This study also found that parent-child relationships characterized by intense closeness were linked with higher levels of peer victimization in boys. Overly close and emotionally intense relationships between parents and sons might not foster assertiveness and independence. Rather, they might foster self-doubts and worries that are perceived as weaknesses when expressed in male peer groups. Recall from a study we discussed earlier in the chapter that both bullying and victim behavior are linked to parent-child relationships (Olweus, 1980). Bullies' parents were more likely to be rejecting, authoritarian, or permissive about their son's aggression, whereas victims' parents were more likely to be anxious and overprotective.

Another recent study found that third- and sixth-grade boys and girls who experienced internalizing problems (such as being anxious and withdrawn), physical weakness, and peer rejection increasingly were victimized over time (Hodges & Perry, 1999). Yet another study found that the relation between internalizing problems and victimization was reduced by a protective friendship (Hodges & others, 1999).

Victims of bullies can suffer both short-term and long-term effects (Limber, 1997). Short-term they can become depressed, lose interest in schoolwork, or even avoid going to school. The effects of bullying can persist into adulthood. A recent longitudinal study of male victims who were bullied during childhood found that in their twenties they were more depressed and had lower self-esteem than their counterparts who had not been bullied in childhood (Olweus, in press). Bullying also can indicate a serious problem for the bully as well as the victim. In the study just mentioned, about 60 percent of the boys who were identified as bullies in middle school had at least one criminal conviction (and about one-third had three or more convictions) in their twenties, a far higher percentage than for nonbullies. To reduce bullying, teachers can do the following (Limber, 1997):

- Get older peers to serve as monitors for bullying and intervene when they see it taking place.
- Develop school-wide rules and sanctions against bullying and post them throughout the school.
- Form friendship groups for adolescents who are regularly bullied by peers.
- Incorporate the message of the antibullying program into church, school, and other community activities where adolescents are involved.

Next, we will turn our attention to the role of social cognition in peer relations. In part of this discussion, we will explore ideas about reducing the aggression of children in their peer encounters.

Social Cognition

How might children's thoughts contribute to their peer relations? Three possibilities are through their perspective-taking ability, social information-processing skills, and social knowledge.

As we discussed in chapter 14, "Moral Development," **perspective taking** *involves taking another's point of view* ◀▥▥ P. 434. As children enter the elementary school years, both their peer interaction and their perspective-taking ability increase. Reciprocity—playing games, functioning in groups, and cultivating friendships, for example—is especially important in peer interchanges at this point in development. One of the important skills that help elementary school children improve their peer relations is communication effectiveness. In one investigation, the communication exchanges among peers at kindergarten, first-, third-, and fifth-grade levels were evaluated (Krauss & Glucksberg, 1969). Children were asked to instruct a peer in how to stack a set of blocks. The peer sat behind a screen with blocks similar to those the other child was stacking (see figure 16.2). The kindergarten children made numerous errors in telling the peer how to duplicate the novel block stack. The older children, especially the fifth-graders, were much more efficient in communicating to a peer how to stack the blocks. They were sensitive to the communication demands of the task and were far superior at perspective taking and figuring out how they had

Reducing Bullying

perspective taking
The ability to assume another person's perspective and understand his or her thoughts and feelings.

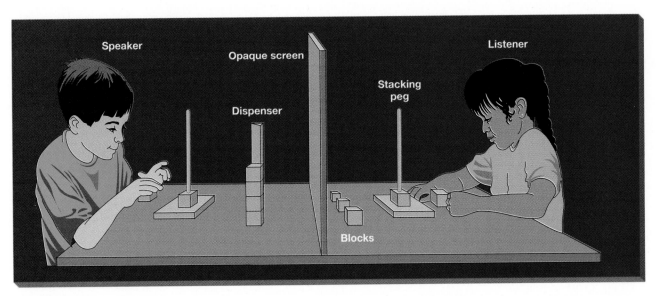

Figure 16.2

The Development of Communication Skills

This is an experimental arrangement of speaker and listener in the investigation of the development of communication skills.

to talk for the peer to understand them. In elementary school, children also become more efficient at understanding complex messages, so the listening skills of the peer in this experiment probably helped the communicating peer as well. Other researchers have documented the link between perspective-taking skills and the quality of peer relations, especially in the elementary school years (LeMare & Rubin, 1987).

Of special interest is how children process information about peer relations (Burgess & Rubin, 2000; Dodge, 1993; Quiggle & others, 1992). For example, a boy accidentally trips and knocks a peer's soft drink out of his hand. The peer misinterprets the encounter as hostile, which leads him to retaliate aggressively against the boy. Through repeated encounters of this kind, other peers come to perceive the aggressor as habitually acting inappropriately. Peer relations researcher Kenneth Dodge (1993) argues that children go through five steps in processing information about their social world: decoding social cues, interpreting, searching for a response, selecting an optimal response, and enacting it. Dodge has found that aggressive boys are more likely to perceive another child's actions as hostile when the child's intention is ambiguous, and when aggressive boys search for clues to determine a peer's intention, they respond more rapidly, less efficiently, and less reflectively than nonaggressive children.

Social knowledge also is involved in children's ability to get along with peers. An important part of children's social life involves choosing which goals to pursue in poorly defined or ambiguous situations. Social relationship goals are also important, such as how to initiate and maintain a social bond. Children need to know what scripts to follow to get children to be their friends. For example, as part of the script for getting friends, it helps to know that saying nice things, regardless of what the peer does or says, will make the peer like the child more.

The social cognitive perspective views children who are maladjusted as lacking social cognitive skills to interact effectively with others (Rabiner & others, 1991). One investigation explored the possibility that maladjusted children do not have the social cognitive skills necessary for positive social interaction (Asarnow & Callan, 1985). Boys with and without peer adjustment difficulties were identified, and their social cognitive skills were assessed. Boys without peer adjustment problems generated more alternative solutions to problems, proposed more assertive and mature solutions, gave less-

Social Cognition

SUMMARY TABLE 16.1
Peer Relations

Concept	Processes/ Related Ideas	Characteristics/Description
Peer Group Functions	Defining Peers	• Peers are individuals who are at about the same age or maturity level.
	Functions	• Peers provide a means of social comparison and a source of information about the world outside the family. • Good peer relations may be necessary for normal social development. The inability to "plug in" to a social network is associated with a number of problems. • Peer relations can be both positive and negative.
	Piaget and Sullivan	• They stressed that peer relations provide the context for learning the symmetrical reciprocity mode of relationships.
	Complexity	• Peer relations vary according to the way peer experience is measured, the outcomes specified, and the developmental trajectories traversed.
Distinct but Coordinated World of Parent-Child and Peer Relations	Exploring Common and Unique Characteristics	• Children touch, smile, and vocalize when they interact with parents and peers. • Healthy family relations usually promote healthy peer relations. • Parents can model or coach their children in ways of relating to peers. Parents' choices of neighborhoods, churches, schools, and their own friends influence the pool from which their children might select possible friends. • Rough-and-tumble play occurs mainly in peer relations rather than in parent-child relations. In times of stress, children usually turn to parents rather than peers. • Peer relations have a more equal basis than parent-child relations.
	Infancy	• Some researchers believe that the quality of social interaction with peers in infancy provides valuable information about social development. • As increasing numbers of infants have attended day care, infant peer relations have increased.
The Developmental Course of Peer Relations in Childhood	Childhood/ Adolescence	• The frequency of peer interaction, both positive and negative, increases in the preschool years. • Children spend even more time with peers in the elementary and secondary school years.
Peer Statuses	Their Nature	• Popular children are frequently nominated as a best friend and are rarely disliked by their peers. • Neglected children are infrequently nominated as a best friend but are not disliked by their peers. • Rejected children are rarely nominated as a best friend and are disliked by their peers. • Controversial children are frequently nominated both as one's best friend and as being disliked by peers.
Bullying	Its Nature	• Significant numbers of students are bullied, and this can result in short-term and long-term negative effects for the victim.
Social Cognition	Its Nature	• Perspective taking, social information-processing skills, and social knowledge are important dimensions of social cognition in peer relations.

intense aggressive solutions, showed more adaptive planning, and evaluated physically aggressive responses less positively than did the boys with peer adjustment problems.

At this point we have discussed a number of ideas about peer relations. A review of these ideas is presented in summary table 16.1. Next, we will explore another key dimension of children's development that often involves the world of peers: play.

Play

An extensive amount of peer interaction during childhood involves play; however, social play is but one type of play. **Play** *is pleasurable activity that is engaged in for its own sake.*

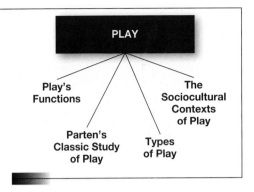

Play's Functions

Play is essential to a young child's health. As today's children continue to experience pressure in their lives, play becomes even more crucial. Play increases affiliation with peers, releases tension, advances cognitive development, and increases exploration. Play increases the probability that children will converse and interact with each other. During this interaction, children practice the roles they will assume later in life.

According to Freud and Erikson, play is an especially useful form of human adjustment, helping the child master anxieties and conflicts. Because tensions are relieved in play, the child can cope with life's problems. Play permits the child to work off excess physical energy and to release pent-up tensions. **Play therapy** *allows children to work off frustrations and is a medium through which therapists can analyze children's conflicts and ways of coping with them. Children may feel less threatened, and be more likely to express their true feelings, in the context of play* (Waas & Kleckler, 2000).

Piaget (1962) saw play as a medium that advances children's cognitive development. At the same time, he said that children's cognitive development constrains the way they play. Play permits children to practice their competencies and acquired skills in a relaxed, pleasurable way. Piaget believed that cognitive structures need to be exercised, and play provides the perfect setting for this exercise. For example, children who have just learned to add or multiply begin to play with numbers in different ways as they perfect these operations, laughing as they do so.

Vygotsky (1962), whose developmental theory was discussed in chapter 7, also believed that play is an excellent setting for cognitive development. He was especially interested in the symbolic and make-believe aspects of play, as when a child rides a stick as if it were a horse. For young children, the imaginary situation is real. Parents should encourage such imaginary play because it advances the child's cognitive development, especially creative thought.

Daniel Berlyne (1960) described play as exciting and pleasurable in itself because it satisfies the exploratory drive each of us possesses. This drive involves curiosity and a desire for information about something new or unusual. Play is a means whereby children can safely explore and seek out new information—something they might not otherwise do. Play encourages this exploratory behavior by offering children the possibilities of novelty, complexity, uncertainty, surprise, and incongruity.

Parten's Classic Study of Play

Many years ago, Mildred Parten (1932) developed one of the most elaborate attempts to categorize children's play. Based on observations of children in free play at nursery school, Parten arrived at the following play categories:

1. **Unoccupied play** *occurs when the child is not engaging in play as it is commonly understood and may stand in one spot, look around the room, or perform random movements that do not seem to have a goal.* In most nursery schools, unoccupied play is less frequent than other forms.
2. **Solitary play** *occurs when the child plays alone.* In this type of play, children seem engrossed in what they are doing and do not care much about what others are doing. Two- and 3-year-olds engage more frequently in solitary play than older preschoolers do.

play
A pleasurable activity that is engaged in for its own sake.

play therapy
Therapy that allows the child to work off frustrations and is a medium through which the therapist can analyze the child's conflicts and ways of coping with them. Children may feel less threatened and be more likely to express their true feelings in the context of play.

Play

*A*nd that park grew up with me; that small world widened as I learned its secret boundaries, as I discovered new refuges in the woods and jungles: hidden homes and lairs for the multitudes of imagination, for cowboys and devon-facing seashore, hoping for gold watches or the skull of a sheep or a message in a bottle to be washed up by the tide.

Dylan Thomas
Welsh Poet, 20th Century

unoccupied play
Play in which the child is not engaging in play as it is commonly understood and might stand in one spot, look around the room, or perform random movements that do not seem to have a goal.

solitary play
Play in which the child plays alone and independently of others.

Mildred Parten classified play into six categories. Study the photograph and determine which of her categories are reflected in the behavior of the children pictured.

onlooker play
Play in which the child watches other children play.

parallel play
Play in which the child plays separately from others, but with toys like those the others are using or in a manner that mimics their play.

associative play
Play that involves social interaction with little or no organization.

cooperative play
Play that involves social interaction in a group with a sense of group identity and organized activity.

3. **Onlooker play** *occurs when the child watches other children play.* The child may talk with other children and ask questions but does not enter into their play behavior. The child's active interest in other children's play distinguishes onlooker play from unoccupied play.
4. **Parallel play** *occurs when the child plays separately from others, but with toys like those the others are using or in a manner that mimics their play.* Young preschool children engage in this type of play more often than do older preschool children, but even older preschool children engage in parallel play quite often.
5. **Associative play** *occurs when play involves social interaction with little or no organization.* In this type of play, children seem to be more interested in each other than in the tasks they are performing. Borrowing or lending toys and following or leading one another in line are examples of associative play.
6. **Cooperative play** *involves social interaction in a group with a sense of group identity and organized activity.* Children's formal games, completion aimed at winning, and groups formed by the teacher for doing things together are examples of cooperative play. Cooperative play is the prototype for the games of middle childhood. Little cooperative play is seen in the preschool years.

Types of Play

Parten's categories represent one way of thinking about the different types of play. However, today researchers and practitioners who are involved with children's play believe other types of play are important in children's development (Sutton-Smith, 2000). Whereas Parten's categories emphasize the role of play in the child's social world, the contemporary perspective on play emphasizes both the cognitive and social aspects of play. Among the types of children's play most widely studied today are sensorimotor/practice play, pretend/symbolic play, social play, constructive play, and games.

Sensorimotor/Practice Play

Sensorimotor play *is behavior engaged in by infants to derive pleasure from exercising their existing sensorimotor schemas.* The development of sensorimotor play follows Piaget's description of sensorimotor thought, which we discussed in chapter 7. Infants initially engage in exploratory and playful visual and motor transactions in the second quarter of the first year of life. By 9 months of age, infants begin to select novel objects for exploration and play, especially those that are responsive, such as toys that make noise or bounce. By 12 months of age, infants enjoy making things work and exploring cause and effect. At this point in development, children like toys that perform when they act on them.

In the second year, infants begin to understand the social meaning of objects and their play reflects this awareness. And 2-year-olds may distinguish between exploratory play that is interesting but not humorous, and "playful" play, which has incongruous and humorous dimensions. For example, a 2-year-old might "drink" from a shoe or call a dog "cow." When 2-year-olds find these deliberate incongruities funny, they are beginning to show evidence of symbolic play and the ability to play with ideas.

Practice play *involves the repetition of behavior when new skills are being learned or when physical or mental mastery and coordination of skills are required for games or sports.* Sensorimotor play, which often involves practice play, is primarily confined to infancy, while practice play can be engaged in throughout life. During the preschool years, children often engage in play that involves practicing various skills. Estimates indicate that practice play constitutes about one-third of the preschool child's play activities, but less than one-sixth of the elementary school child's play activities (Rubin, Fein, & Vandenberg, 1983). Practice play contributes to the development of coordinated motor skills needed for later game playing. While practice play declines in the elementary school years, practice play activities such as running, jumping, sliding, twirling, and throwing balls or other objects are frequently observed on the playgrounds at elementary schools. While these activities appear similar to the earlier practice play of the preschool years, practice play in the elementary school years differs from earlier practice play because much of it is ends rather than means related. That is, elementary school children often engage in practice play for the purpose of improving motor skills needed to compete in games or sports.

Pretend/Symbolic Play

Pretend/symbolic play *occurs when the child transforms the physical environment into a symbol* (Doyle & others, 1992; Fein, 1986; Rogers & Sawyers, 1988). Between 9 and 30 months of age, children increase their use of objects in symbolic play. They learn to transform objects, that is, substituting them for other objects and acting toward them as if they were these other objects. For example, a preschool child treats a table as if it is a car and says, "I'm fixing the car" as he grabs a leg of the table.

Many experts on play consider the preschool years the "golden age" of pretend/symbolic play that is dramatic or sociodramatic in nature (Singer & Singer, 1988). This type of make-believe play often appears at about 18 months of age and reaches a peak at 4 to 5 years of age, then gradually declines. In the early elementary school years, children's interests often shift to games. In one observational study of nine children, at 4 years of age the children spent more than 12 minutes per hour in pretend play (Haight & Miller, 1993). In this study, a number of parents agreed with Piaget and Vygotsky that pretending helps to develop children's imagination.

Catherine Garvey (1977) has spent many years observing young children's play. She indicates that three elements are found in almost all of the pretend play she has observed: props, plot, and roles. Children use objects as *props* in their pretend play. Children can pretend to drink from a real cup or from a seashell. They can even create a make-believe cup from thin air, if nothing else is available. Most pretend play also has a story line, though the *plot* may be quite simple. Pretend play themes often reflect what children see going on in their lives, as when they play family, school, or

sensorimotor play
Behavior engaged in by infants to derive pleasure from exercising their existing sensorimotor schemas.

practice play
Play that involves repetition of behavior when new skills are being learned or when physical or mental mastery and coordination of skills are required for games or sports. Sensorimotor play, which often involves practice play, is primarily confined to infancy, while practice play can be engaged in throughout life.

pretend/symbolic play
Play that occurs when a child transforms the physical environment into a symbol.

doctor. Fantasy play can also take its theme from a story children have heard or a show they have seen. In pretend play, children try out many different *roles*. Some roles, like mother or teacher, are derived from reality. Other roles, like wonder woman or superman, come from fantasy.

Carolee Howes (1992) believes that the function of pretend play from 3 to 36 months is the mastery of the communication of meaning. As social pretend play becomes possible through increases in cognitive and language abilities, children engage in pretend play with parents, older siblings, and peers. During the earliest period, the scaffold provided by the parent or older sibling increases the child's ability to engage in more-complex social pretend play. As children become able to self-regulate their pretenses, their social pretend play with their peers becomes more complex.

social play
Play that involves social interactions with peers.

Social Play   **Social play** *is play that involves social interaction with peers.* Parten's categories, which we described earlier, are oriented toward social play. Social play with peers increases dramatically during the preschool years. In addition to general social play with peers and group pretense or sociodramatic play, another form of social play is rough-and-tumble play. The movement patterns of rough-and-tumble play are often similar to those of hostile behavior (running, chasing, wrestling, jumping, falling, hitting), but in rough-and-tumble play these behaviors are accompanied by signals such as laughter, exaggerated movement, and open rather than closed hands, which indicates this is play.

constructive play
Play that combines sensorimotor/practice repetitive activity with symbolic representation of ideas. Constructive play occurs when children engage in self-regulated creation or construction of a product or a problem solution.

Constructive Play   **Constructive play** *combines sensorimotor/practice repetitive activity with symbolic representation of ideas. Constructive play occurs when children engage in self-regulated creation or construction of a product or a problem solution.* Constructive play increases in the preschool years as symbolic play increases and sensorimotor play decreases. In the preschool years, some practice play is replaced by constructive play. For example, instead of moving their fingers around and around in finger paint (practice play), children are more likely to draw the outline of a house or a person in the paint (constructive play). Some researchers have found that constructive play is the most common type of play during the preschool years (Rubin, Maioni, & Hornung, 1976). Constructive play is also a frequent form of play in the elementary school years, both in and out of the classroom. Constructive play is one of the few playlike activities allowed in work-centered classrooms. For example, having children create a play about a social studies topic involves constructive play. Whether such activities are considered play by children usually depends on whether they get to choose whether to do it (it is play) or whether the teacher imposes (it is not play), and also whether it is enjoyable (it is play) or not (it is not play) (King, 1982).

A preschool "superhero" at play.

Constructive play can also be used in the elementary school years to foster academic skill learning, thinking skills, and problem solving. Many educators plan classroom activities that include humor, encourage playing with ideas, and promote creativity (Bergen, 1988). Educators also often support the performance of plays, the writing of imaginative stories, the expression of artistic abilities, and the playful exploration of computers and other technological equipment. However, distinctions between work and play frequently become blurred in the elementary school classroom.

Games   **Games** *are activities engaged in for pleasure that include rules and often competition with one or more individuals.* Preschool children may begin to participate in social game play that involves simple rules of reciprocity and turn taking, but games take on a much more salient role in the lives of elementary school children. In one investigation, the highest incidence of game playing occurred between 10 and 12 years of age (Eiferman, 1971). After age 12, games decline in popularity, often being replaced by practice play, conversations, and organized sports (Bergen, 1988).

games
Activities engaged in for pleasure that include rules and often competition with one or more individuals.

In the elementary years, games feature the meaningfulness of a challenge (Eiferman, 1971). This challenge is present if two or more children have the skills required to play and understand the rules of the game. Among the types of games children engage in are steady or constant games, such as tag, which are played consistently; recurrent or cyclical games, such as marbles or hopscotch, which seem to follow cycles of popularity and decline; sporadic games, which are rarely played; and one-time games, such as Hula Hoop contests, which rise to popularity once and then disappear.

In sum, play is a multidimensional, complex concept. It ranges from an infant's simple exercise of a newfound sensorimotor talent to a preschool child's riding a tricycle to an older child's participation in organized games. It is also important to note that children's play can involve a combination of the play categories we have described. For example, social play can be sensorimotor (rough-and-tumble), symbolic, or constructive.

The Sociocultural Contexts of Play

American children's freewheeling play once took place in rural fields and city streets, using equipment largely made by children themselves. Today, play is becoming confined to back yards, basements, playrooms, and bedrooms and

The little ones leaped, and shouted, and laugh'd and all the hills echoed.

William Blake
English Poet, 19th Century

SUMMARY TABLE 16.2
Play

Concept	Processes/ Related Ideas	Characteristics/Description
Play's Functions	Their Nature	• These include affiliation with peers, tension release, advances in cognitive development, and exploration.
Parten's Classic Study of Play	Categories of Social Play	• Parten examined these categories of social play: unoccupied, onlooker, parallel, associative, and cooperative.
	Developmental Changes	• Three-year-olds engaged in more solitary and parallel play, 5-year-olds in more cooperative and associative play.
Types of Play	Social and Cognitive	• The contemporary perspective emphasizes both social and cognitive aspects of play. • The most widely studied types of play include sensorimotor and practice play, pretend/symbolic play, social play, constructive play, and games.
Sociocultural Contexts of Play	Their Nature	• Modern children spend a large of part of their play with toys, and their play increasingly is confined to backyards, basements, playrooms, and bedrooms rather than rural fields and city streets. • The form and content of children's play are influenced by cultural and socioeconomic factors.

derives much of its content from video games, television dramas, and Saturday morning cartoons (Sutton-Smith, 1985). Modern children spend a large part of their lives alone with their toys, which was inconceivable several centuries earlier. Childhood was once part of collective village life. Children did not play separately but joined adults in seasonal festivals that intruded on the work world with regularity and boisterousness.

One of the most widely debated issues in the sociocultural contexts of play is whether children from low socioeconomic groups and traditional, non-Western societies have underdeveloped skills in the imaginative and sociodramatic aspects of pretense play (Johnson, Christie, & Yawkey, 1987). Some researchers believe there are developmental deficiencies in the imaginative and sociodramatic play of children from low socioeconomic groups and traditional, non-Western societies, whereas others believe that many methodological shortcomings in this research cloud the results. For example, many of these studies do not adequately measure socioeconomic status, do not systematically measure classroom and school variables, and in some cases do not use statistical analysis (McLoyd, 1982).

Some children may be capable of high-level imaginative play but require adult prompting and encouragement to overcome their initial shyness (Johnson, Christie, & Yawkey, 1987). Before expecting high-level play from children, teachers should determine if the children have had adequate time to become familiar with the materials and routines in their day-care center or preschool classroom. This familiarity is especially important for children whose main language is not English or for any child who comes from a home environment that is in marked contrast with the school environment.

At this point we have discussed a number of ideas about play. A review of these ideas is presented in summary table 16.2. Next, we will explore another very important dimension of children's peer worlds: friendship.

Friendship

The world of peers is one of varying acquaintances; children interact with some children they barely know, and with others they know well, for hours every day. It is to the latter type—friends—that we now turn.

Friendship's Functions

Friendships serve six functions (Gottman & Parker, 1987):

1. *Companionship.* Friendship provides children with a familiar partner, someone who is willing to spend time with them and join in collaborative activities.
2. *Stimulation.* Friendship provides children with interesting information, excitement, and amusement.
3. *Physical support.* Friendship provides resources and assistance.
4. *Ego support.* Friendship provides the expectation of support, encouragement, and feedback that helps children to maintain an impression of themselves as competent, attractive, and worthwhile individuals.
5. *Social comparison.* Friendship provides information about where children stand vis-à-vis others and whether children are doing okay.
6. *Intimacy/affection.* Friendship provides children with a warm, close, trusting relationship with another individual, a relationship that involves self-disclosure.

Each friend represents a world in us, a world possibly not born until they arrive, and it is only by this meeting that a new world is born.

Anaïs Nin
French-Born American Writer, 20th Century

Sullivan's Ideas

Harry Stack Sullivan (1953) was the most influential theorist to discuss the importance of friendships. He argued that there is a dramatic increase in the psychological importance and intimacy of close friends during early adolescence. In contrast to other psychoanalytic theorists' narrow emphasis on the importance of parent-child relationships, Sullivan contended that friends also play important roles in shaping children's and adolescents' well-being and development. In terms of well-being, he argued that all people have a number of basic social needs, including the need for tenderness (secure attachment), playful companionship, social acceptance, intimacy, and sexual relations. Whether or not these needs are fulfilled largely determines our emotional well-being. For example, if the need for playful companionship goes unmet, then we become bored and depressed; if the need for social acceptance is not met, we suffer a lowered sense of self-worth. During adolescence, individuals increasingly depend on friends, and thus the ups and downs of experiences with friends increasingly shape adolescents' state of well-being. In particular, Sullivan believed that the need for intimacy intensifies during early adolescence, motivating teenagers to seek out close friends. He felt that, if adolescents failed to forge such close friendships, they would experience painful feelings of loneliness coupled with a reduced sense of self-worth.

Research findings support many of Sullivan's ideas. For example, adolescents report more often disclosing intimate and personal information to their friends than do younger children (Buhrmester & Furman, 1987). Adolescents also say they depend more on friends than on parents to satisfy needs for companionship, reassurance of worth, and intimacy (Furman & Buhrmester, 1992). In one study, daily interviews with 13- to 16-year-old adolescents over a 5-day period were conducted to find out how much time they spent engaged in meaningful interactions with friends and parents (Carbery & Buhrmester, 1993). Adolescents spent an average of 103 minutes per day in meaningful interactions with friends, compared to just 28 minutes per day with parents. The quality of friendship is more strongly linked to feelings of well-being during adolescence than during childhood. Teenagers with superficial friendships, or no

"Friendships contribute importantly to a sense of self and feeling of self-worth in children and adolescents."

close friendships at all, report feeling lonelier and more depressed, and they have a lower sense of self-esteem than teenagers with intimate friendships (Buhrmester, 1990; Yin, Buhrmester, & Hibbard, 1996). In another study, friendship in early adolescence was a significant predictor of self-worth in early adulthood (Bagwell, Newcomb, & Bukowski, 1994).

In addition to the role they play in the socialization of social competence, friendship relationships are often important sources of support (Berndt, 1999; Berndt, Hawkins, & Jiao, 1999; Fehr, 2000). Sullivan described how adolescent friends support one another's sense of personal worth. When close friends disclose their mutual insecurities and fears about themselves, they discover that they are not "abnormal" and that they have nothing to be ashamed of. Friends also act as important confidants that help children and adolescents work through upsetting problems (such as difficulties with parents or the breakup of romance) by providing both emotional support and informational advice. Friends can also protect "at risk" adolescents from victimization by peers (Bukowski, Sippola, & Boivin, 1995). In addition, friends can become active partners in building a sense of identity. During countless hours of conversation, friends act as sounding boards as teenagers explore issues ranging from future plans to stances on religious and moral issues.

Willard Hartup (1996), who has studied peer relations across four decades, has concluded that children often use friends as cognitive and social resources on a regular basis. Hartup also commented that normative transitions, such as moving from elementary to middle school, are negotiated more competently by children who have friends than by those who don't. The quality of friendship is also important to consider. Supportive friendships between socially skilled individuals are developmentally advantageous, whereas coercive and conflict-ridden friendships are not (Hartup & Collins, 2000). Being able to forgive also is important in maintaining friendships (Rose & Asher, 1999). Friendship and its developmental significance can vary from one child to another. Children's characteristics, such as temperament ("easy" versus "difficult" for example), likely influence the nature of their friendships. To read about appropriate and inappropriate strategies for making friends, see figure 16.3.

Intimacy and Similarity

In the context of friendship, *intimacy* has been defined in different ways. For example, it has been defined broadly to include everything in a relationship that makes the relationship seem close or intense. In most research studies, though, **intimacy in friendship** *is defined narrowly as self-disclosure or sharing of private thoughts.* Private or personal knowledge about a friend has been used as an index of intimacy (Selman, 1980; Sullivan, 1953).

The most consistent finding in the last two decades of research on adolescent friendships is that intimacy is an important feature of friendship (Berndt & Perry, 1990; Bukowski, Newcomb, & Hoza, 1987). When young adolescents are asked what they want from a friend or how they can tell someone is their best friend, they frequently say that a best friend will share problems with them, understand them, and listen when they talk about their own thoughts or feelings. When young children talk about their friendships, they rarely comment about intimate self-disclosure or mutual understanding. In one investigation, friendship intimacy was more prominent in 13- to 16-year-olds than in 10- to 13-year-olds (Buhrmester, 1989).

Are the friendships of adolescent girls more intimate than the friendships of adolescent boys? When asked to describe their best friends, girls refer to intimate conversations and faithfulness more than boys do. For example, girls are more likely to describe their best friend as "sensitive just like me" or "trustworthy just like me" (Duck, 1975). The assumption behind this gender difference is that girls are more oriented toward interpersonal relationships. Boys may discourage one another from

intimacy in friendship
Self-disclosure and the sharing of private thoughts.

Category	Examples
Strategies appropriate for making friends	
Initiate interaction.	Learn about friend: ask for his or her name, age, favorite activities. Prosocial overtures: introduce self, start conversation, invite him or her to do things.
Be nice.	Be nice, kind, considerate.
Show prosocial behavior.	Be honest and trustworthy: tell the truth, keep promises. Be generous, sharing, cooperative.
Show respect for self and others.	Respect others, have good manners: be polite and courteous. Listen to what others say. Have a positive attitude and personality: be open to others, be friendly, be funny. Be yourself. Enhance your own reputation: be clean, dress neatly, be on best behavior.
Provide social support.	Be supportive: help, give advice, show you care. Engage in activities together: study or play, sit next to one another, be in same group. Enhance others: compliment them.
Strategies inappropriate for making friends	
Be psychologically aggressive.	Show disrespect, bad manners: be prejudiced and inconsiderate, use others, curse, be rude. Be exclusive, uncooperative: don't invite them to do things, ignore them, isolate them, don't share with or help them. Hurt their reputation or feelings: gossip, spread rumors, embarrass them, criticize them.
Present yourself negatively.	Be self-centered: be snobby, conceited, and jealous; show off, care only about yourself. Be mean, have bad attitude or affect: be mean, cruel, hostile, a grouch, angry all the time. Hurt own reputation: be a slob, act stupidly, throw temper tantrums, start trouble, be a sissy.
Behave antisocially.	Be physically aggressive: fight, trip, spit, cause physical harm. Be verbally aggressive or controlling: yell at others, pick on them, make fun of them, call them names, be bossy. Be dishonest, disloyal: steal, cheat, tell secrets, break promises. Break school rules: skip school, drink alcohol, use drugs.

Figure **16.3**

Appropriate and Inappropriate Strategies for Making Friends at School

openly disclosing their problems, as part of their masculine, competitive nature (Maccoby, 1996). Boys make themselves vulnerable to being called "wimps" if they can't handle their own problems and insecurities.

Another predominant characteristic of friendship is that, throughout the childhood and adolescent years, friends are generally similar—in terms of age, sex, ethnicity, and many other factors (Luo, Fang, & Aro, 1995). Friends often have similar attitudes toward school, similar educational aspirations, and closely aligned achievement orientations. Friends like the same music, wear the same kind of clothes, and prefer the same leisure activities (Berndt, 1982). If friends have different attitudes about schools, one of them may want to play basketball or go shopping rather than

Friendships

do homework. If the other friend insists on completing homework, the conflict may weaken the friendship, and the two may drift apart.

Mixed-Age Friendships

Although most adolescents develop friendships with individuals who are close to their own age, some adolescents become best friends with younger or older individuals. A common fear, especially among parents, is that adolescents who have older friends will be encouraged to engage in delinquent behavior or early sexual behavior. Researchers have found that adolescents who interact with older youths do engage in these behaviors more frequently, but it is not known whether the older youths guide younger adolescents toward deviant behavior or whether the younger adolescents were already prone to deviant behavior before they developed the friendship with the older youths (Billy, Rodgers, & Udry, 1984).

In a longitudinal study of eight-grade girls, early-maturing girls developed friendships with girls who were chronologically older but biologically similar to them (Magnusson, 1988). Because of their associations with older friends, the early-maturing girls were more likely than their peers to engage in a number of deviant behaviors, such as being truant from school, getting drunk, and stealing. Also, as adults (26 years of age), the early-maturing girls were more likely to have had a child and were less likely to be vocationally and educationally oriented than their later-maturing counterparts. Thus, parents do seem to have reason to be concerned when their adolescents become close friends with individuals who are considerably older than they are.

At this point we have studied a number of ideas about friendship. A review of these ideas is presented in summary table 16.3. In our discussion of friendship, we saw that intimacy in friendship increases in adolescence and that mixed-age friendships can bring vulnerability in adolescence. Next, we further explore the peer worlds of adolescence.

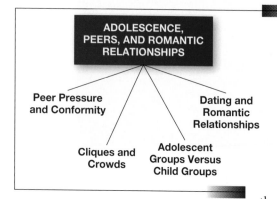

Each of you, individually; walkest with the tread of a fox, but collectively ye are geese.

Solon
Greek Statesman and Poet, 7th Century B.C.

Adolescence, Peers, and Romantic Relationships

Peer relations play powerful roles in the lives of adolescents. When you think back to your adolescent years, many of your most enjoyable moments probably were spent with peers—on the telephone, in school activities, in the neighborhood, at dances, or just hanging out. Peer relations undergo important changes in adolescence. In childhood, the focus of peer relations is on being liked by classmates and being included in games or lunchroom conversations. Being overlooked or, worse yet, being rejected can have damaging effects on children's development that sometimes are carried forward to adolescence. Beginning in early adolescence, teenagers typically prefer to have a smaller number of friendships that are more intense and intimate than those of young children. Cliques are formed and shape the social lives of adolescents as they begin go "hang out" together. Dating and romantic relationships become important in the social lives of most older adolescents.

Peer Pressure and Conformity

Consider the following statement made by an adolescent girl:

Peer pressure is extremely influential in my life. I have never had very many friends, and I spend quite a bit of time alone. The friends I have are older. . . . The closest friend I have had is a lot like me in that we are both sad and depressed a lot. I began to act even more depressed than before when I was with her. I would call her up and try to act even more depressed than I was because that is what I thought she liked. In that relationship, I felt pressure to be like her.

SUMMARY TABLE 16.3
Friendship

Concept	Processes/ Related Ideas	Characteristics/Description
Functions of Friendships	Their Nature	• These include companionship, stimulation, physical support, ego support, social comparison, and intimacy/affection.
Sullivan's Ideas	Importance of Adolescence	• Sullivan argued that there is a dramatic increase in the psychological importance and intimacy of close friends in adolescence. Research findings support his view.
Intimacy and Similarity	Key Aspects of Friendship	• These are two of the most common characteristics of friendships.
Mixed-Age Friendships	Potential Problems	• Children and adolescents who become close friends with older individuals engage in more deviant behaviors than their counterparts with same-age friends. • Early-maturing girls are more likely than late-maturing girls to have older friends, which can contribute to their problem behaviors.

Conformity to peer pressure in adolescence can be positive or negative (Wall, 1993). Teenagers engage in all sorts of negative conformity behavior—for instance, they use seedy language, steal, vandalize, and make fun of parents and teachers. However, a great deal of peer conformity, such as dressing like one's friends and wanting to spend huge chunks of time with members of a clique, is not negative and reflects the desire to be involved in the peer world.

Most adolescents conform to the mainstream standards of their peers. However, the rebellious or anticonformist adolescent reacts counter to the mainstream peer group's expectations, deliberately moving away from the actions or beliefs this group advocates.

During adolescence, especially early adolescence, we conformed more to peer standards than we did in childhood. Investigators have found that, around the eighth and ninth grades, conformity to peers—especially to their antisocial standards—peaks (Berndt, 1979; Leventhal, 1994). At this point in development, an adolescent is most likely to go along with a peer to steal hubcaps off a car, draw graffiti on a wall, or steal cosmetics from a store counter.

Cliques and Crowds

Most peer group relationships in adolescence can be categorized in one of three ways: the crowd, the clique, or individual friendships. The **crowd** *is the largest and least personal of adolescent groups.* Members of the crowd meet because of their mutual interest in activities, not because they are mutually attracted to each other. **Cliques** *are smaller, involve greater intimacy among members, and have more group cohesion than crowds.*

Allegiance to cliques, clubs, organizations, and teams exerts powerful control over the lives of many adolescents (Tapper, 1996). Group identity often overrides personal identity. The leader of a group might place a group member in a position of considerable moral conflict by asking, in effect, "What's more important, our code or your parents'?" or "Are you looking out for yourself, or the members of the group?" Such labels as *brother* and *sister* sometimes are adopted and used in the members' conversations with each other. These labels symbolize the bond between the members and suggest the high status of group membership.

One of the most widely cited studies of adolescent cliques and crowds is that of James Coleman (1961). Students from 10 high schools were asked to identify the leading crowds in their schools. They also were asked to identify the students who were the most outstanding in athletics, popularity, and various school activities. Regardless of the school sampled, the leading crowds were composed of athletes and popular girls. Much less power in the leading crowd was attributed to bright students.

Think about your high school years. What were the cliques, and which one were you in? Although the names of cliques change, we could go to almost any high school in the United States and find three to six well-defined cliques or crowds. In one investigation, six peer group structures emerged: populars, unpopulars, jocks, brains, druggies, and average students (Brown & Mounts, 1989). The proportion of students placed in these cliques was much lower in multiethnic schools because of the additional existence of ethnically based crowds.

In one study, Bradford Brown and Jane Lohr (1987) examined the self-esteem of 221 seventh- through twelfth-graders. The adolescents were either associated with one of the five major school cliques or were relatively unknown by classmates and not associated with any school clique. Cliques included the following: jocks (athletically oriented), populars (well-known students who lead social activities), normals (middle-of-the-road students who make up the masses), druggies/toughs (known for illicit drug use or other delinquent activities), and nobodies (low in social skills or intellectual abilities). The self-esteem of the jocks and the populars was highest, while that of the nobodies was lowest. But one group of adolescents not in a clique had self-esteem equivalent to the jocks and the populars. This group was the independents, who indicated that clique membership was not important to them. Keep in mind that these data are correlational—self-esteem could increase an adolescent's probability of becoming a clique member just as clique membership could increase the adolescent's self-esteem.

One of the main factors that distinguishes cliques is group norms regarding school orientation (Brown & Theobald, 1998). In one study of adolescents in nine midwestern and west coast high schools, grade-point differences of almost two full letter grades were found between the highest (brains) and lowest achievers (druggies) (Brown & others, 1993). The norms of particular cliques can place adolescents on a trajectory for school failure. Members of deviantly oriented cliques are more likely to drop out of school early (Cairns & Cairns, 1994).

crowd
The largest and least personal of adolescent groups.

cliques
Smaller groups that involve greater intimacy among members and have more cohesion than crowds.

Adolescent Peer Relationships
Peer Pressure

I didn't belong as a kid, and that always bothered me. If only I'd known that one day my differentness would be an asset, then my early life would have been much easier.

Bette Midler
Contemporary American Actress

Clique membership is also associated with drug use and sexual behavior. In one study, five adolescent cliques were identified: jocks (athletes), brains (students who enjoy academics), burnouts (adolescents who get into trouble), populars (social, student leaders), nonconformists (adolescents who go against the norm), as well as a none/average group (Prinstein, Fetter, & La Green, 1996). Burnouts and nonconformists were the most likely to smoke cigarettes, drink alcohol, and use marijuana; brains were the least likely. Jocks were the most sexually active clique.

Adolescent Groups Versus Child Groups

Child groups differ from adolescent groups in several important ways. The members of child groups often are friends or neighborhood acquaintances, and their groups usually are not as formalized as many adolescent groups. During the adolescent years, groups tend to include a broader array of members. In other words, adolescents other than friends or neighborhood acquaintances often are members of adolescent groups. Try to recall the student council, honor society, or football team at your junior high school. If you were a member of any of these organizations, you probably remember that they were made up of many people you had not met before and that they were a more heterogeneous group than your childhood peer groups. For example, peer groups in adolescence are more likely to have a mixture of individuals from different ethnic groups than are peer groups in childhood. To read further about ethnic minority adolescents' peer groups, see the Explorations in Child Development box. Also, in adolescent peer groups, rules and regulations are usually defined more precisely than in children's peer groups. For example, captains or leaders are often formally elected or appointed in adolescent peer groups.

A well-known observational study by Dexter Dunphy (1963) supports the notion that mixed-sex participation in groups increases during adolescence. In late childhood, boys and girls participate in small, same-sex cliques. As they move into the early adolescent years, the same-sex cliques begin to interact with each other. Gradually, the leaders and high-status members form further cliques based on mixed-sex relationships. Eventually, the newly created mixed-sex cliques replace the same-sex cliques. The mixed-sex cliques interact with each other in large crowd activities, too—at dances and athletic events, for example. In late adolescence, the crowd begins to dissolve as couples develop more-serious relationships and make long-range plans that may include engagement and marriage (see figure 16.4).

Dating and Romantic Relationships

While many adolescent boys and girls have social interchanges through formal and informal peer groups, it is through dating that more serious contacts between the sexes occur (Feiring, 1995; Furman, Brown & Feiring, in press; Shulman & Collins, in press). Many agonizing moments are spent by male adolescents worrying about whether they should call a certain girl and ask her out: "Will she turn me down?" "What if she says yes, what do I say next?" "How am I going to get her to the dance? I don't want my mother to take us!" "I want to kiss her, but what if she pushes me away?" "How can I get to be alone with her?" And, for the adolescent female: "What if no one asks me to the dance?" "What do I do if he tries to kiss me?" Or, "I really don't want to go with him. Maybe I should wait two more days and see if he will call me."

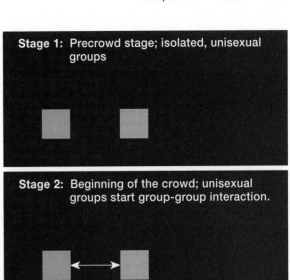

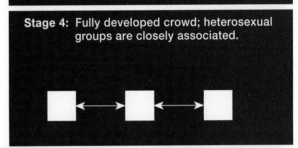

Boys   Girls   Boys and girls

Figure 16.4
Dunphy's Progression of Peer Group Relations in Adolescence

EXPLORATIONS IN CHILD DEVELOPMENT
Ethnic Minority Adolescents' Peer Relations

As ETHNIC MINORITY CHILDREN move into adolescence and enter schools with more heterogeneous school populations, they become more aware of their ethnic minority status (Phinney & Cobb, 1993). Ethnic minority adolescents may have difficulty joining peer groups and clubs in predominantly White schools. Similarly, White adolescents may have peer relations difficulties in predominantly ethnic minority schools. However, schools are only one setting in which peer relations take place; they also occur in the neighborhood and in the community (Jones & Costin, 1997).

Ethnic minority adolescents often have two sets of peer relationships, one at school, the other in the community. Community peers are more likely to be from their own ethnic group in their immediate neighborhood. Sometimes, they go to the same church and participate in activities together, such as Black History Week, Chinese New Year's, or Cinco de Mayo Festival. Because ethnic group adolescents usually have two sets of peers and friends, when researchers ask about their peers and friends, questions should focus on both relationships at school and in the neighborhood and community. Ethnic minority group adolescents who are social isolates at school may be sociometric stars in their segregated neighborhood. Also, because adolescents are more mobile than children, inquiries should be made about the scope of their social networks.

In one investigation the school and neighborhood friendship patterns of 292 African American and White adolescents who attended an integrated junior high school were studied (DuBois & Hirsch, 1990). Most students reported having an other-ethnic school friend, but only 28 percent of the students saw such a friend frequently outside school. Reports of an interethnic school friendship that extended to nonschool settings were more common among African American adolescents than among White adolescents and among adolescents who lived in an integrated rather than a segregated neighborhood. African American adolescents were more likely than White adolescents to have extensive neighborhood friendship networks, but African American adolescents said they talked with fewer friends during the school day.

Of special interest to investigators is the degree of peer support for an ethnic minority adolescent's achievement orientation. Some researchers argue that peers often dissuade African American adolescents from doing well in school (Fordham & Ogbu, 1986; Fuller, 1984). However, in one investigation, peer support of achievement was relatively high among Asian American adolescents, moderate among African American and Latino adolescents, and relatively low among Anglo-American adolescents (Brown & others, 1990). The low peer support of achievement among Anglo-American adolescents possibly is due to their strong individualistic, competitive, and social comparison in orientation.

Adolescent peer relations take place in a number of settings—at school, in the neighborhood, and in the community, for example. Ethnic minority adolescents often have two sets of peer relationships—one at school, the other in the community. A special interest is the degree to which peers support an ethnic minority adolescent's achievement orientation.

In the first half of the twentieth century, dating served mainly as courtship for marriage.

Today, the functions of dating include courtship but also many others. What are some of these other functions of dating?

Functions of Dating   Dating is a relatively recent phenomenon. It wasn't until the 1920s that dating as we know it became a reality, and even then, its primary role was for the purpose of selecting and winning a mate. Prior to this period, mate selection was the sole purpose of dating, and "dates" were carefully monitored by parents, who completely controlled the nature of any heterosexual companionship. Often, parents bargained with each other about the merits of their adolescents as potential marriage partners and even chose mates for their children. In recent times, of course, adolescents have gained much more control over the dating process and who they go out with. Furthermore, dating has evolved into something more than just courtship for marriage.

Dating today can serve at least eight functions (Paul & White, 1990):

1. Dating can be a form of recreation. Adolescents who date seem to have fun and see dating as a source of enjoyment and recreation.
2. Dating is a source of status and achievement. Part of the social comparison process in adolescence involves evaluating the status of the people one dates: are they the best looking, the most popular, and so forth.
3. Dating is part of the socialization process in adolescence: It helps the adolescent to learn how to get along with others and assists in learning manners and sociable behavior.
4. Dating involves learning about intimacy and serves as an opportunity to establish a unique, meaningful relationship with a person of the opposite sex.
5. Dating can be a context for sexual experimentation and exploration.
6. Dating can provide companionship through interaction and shared activities in an opposite-sex relationship.
7. Dating experiences contribute to identify formation and development; dating helps adolescents to clarify their identity and to separate from their families of origin.
8. Dating can be a means of mate sorting and selection, in keeping with its original courtship function.

Exploring Dating
Teen Chat

Types of Dating and Developmental Changes

In their early romantic relationships, many adolescents are not motivated to fulfill attachment or even sexual needs. Rather, early romantic relationships serve as a context for adolescents to explore how attractive they are, how they should romantically interact with someone, and how all of this looks to the peer group (Brown, in press). Only after adolescents acquire some basic competencies in interacting with romantic partners does the fulfillment of attachment and sexual needs become a central function of these relationships (Furman & Wehner, in press).

In their early exploration of romantic relationships, today's adolescents often find comfort in numbers and begin hanging out together in heterosexual groups. Sometimes they just hang out at someone's house or get organized enough to get someone to drive them to a mall or a movie (Peterson, 1997).

One new term on the adolescent dating scene is *hooking up,* which describes two individuals who casually see each other—usually only once or twice—and mainly just kiss and make out. *Seeing each other* also refers to a casual form of dating, but it lasts longer than hooking up. When seeing each other, adolescents aren't tied down to one person. This allows an adolescent to see one person but still date others. *Going out* describes a dating relationship in which adolescents stop seeing other people and see each other exclusively. Going out can still involve the couple in a lot of group dates or it can involve more private dates.

Yet another form of dating recently has been added. *Cyberdating* is dating over the Internet (Thomas, 1998). One 10-year-old girl posted this ad on the net:

> Hi! I'm looking for a Cyber Boyfriend! I'm 10. I have brown hair and brown eyes. I love swimming, playing basketball, and think kittens are adorable!!!

Cyberdating is especially becoming popular among middle school students. By the time they reach high school and are able to drive, dating usually has evolved into a more traditional real-life venture.

In one study of 15-year-olds' romantic relationships, although most said that they had had a girlfriend or boyfriend in the past 3 years, most were not currently dating (Feiring, 1996). Most of the 15-year-olds had had short-term dating relationships, averaging 4 months. Less than 10 percent had had a dating relationship that lasted for a year or longer. Although the length of their dating relationships was relatively brief, contact was very frequent. The adolescents reported seeing each other in person and talking on the phone almost daily. Dating occurred more in a group than in a couples-alone context. What did adolescents say they did when they were on a date? The most frequent dating activities were going to a movie, dinner, hanging out at a mall or school, parties, and visiting each other's home. In another study, the average length of a dating relationship for tenth-graders was 5 to 6 months, increasing to more than 8 months for twelfth-graders (Dowdy & Kliewer, 1996). In this study, dating-related conflict between adolescents and parents was less frequent for twelfth-graders than for tenth-graders.

A special concern is early dating and "going with" someone, which is associated with adolescent pregnancy and problems at home and school (Degirmencioglu, Saltz, & Ager, 1995; Downey & Bonica, 1997; Neemann, Hubbard, & Master, 1995).

In one recent study, fifth- to eighth-grade adolescents carried electronic pagers for one week and completed self-report forms in response to signals received at random times (Richards & others, 1998). Four years later the participants underwent the same procedure. Time with and thoughts about the opposite sex occupied more of the adolescents' week in high school than in fifth and sixth grade. Fifth- and sixth-grade girls spent approximately one hour a week in the presence of a boy, and their male counterparts spent even less time in the presence of a girl. Although more time was spent thinking about an individual of the opposite sex, it still added up to less than 2 hours a week for girls and less than 1 hour per week for boys in fifth and sixth grade. By eleventh and twelfth grade, girls were spending about 10 hours a week with a boy, boys about half that time with a girl. Frequency of thoughts had increased as well. The high school girls spent about 8 hours a week thinking about a boy, the high school boys about 5 or 6 hours thinking about a girl.

In sum, during early adolescence, individuals spent more time thinking about the opposite sex than they actually spent with them. In seventh and eighth grade, they spent 4 to 6 hours a week thinking about them but only about 1 hour actually with them. By eleventh and twelfth grade, this had shifted to more time spent in their actual presence than just thinking about them.

Male and Female Dating Scripts

Do male and female adolescents bring different motivations to the dating experience? In one study they did (Feiring, 1996). Fifteen-year-old girls were more likely to describe romance in terms of interpersonal qualities, boys in terms of physical attraction. For young adolescents, the affiliative qualities of companionship, intimacy, and support were frequently mentioned as positive dimensions of romantic relationships, but love and security were not. Also, the young adolescents described physical attraction more in terms of being cute, pretty, or handsome than in terms of sexuality (such as being a good kisser). Possibly the failure to discuss sexual interests was due to the adolescents' discomfort in talking about such personal feelings with an unfamiliar adult.

Dating scripts *are the cognitive models that adolescents and adults use to guide and evaluate dating interactions.* In one recent study, first dates were highly scripted along gender lines (Rose & Frieze, 1993). Males followed a proactive dating script, females a reactive one. The male's script involved initiating the date (asking for and planning it), controlling the public domain (driving and opening doors), and initiating sexual interaction (making physical contact, making out, and kissing). The female's script focused on the private domain (concern about appearance, enjoying the date), participating in the structure of the date provided by the male (being picked up, having doors opened), and responding to his sexual gestures. These gender differences give males more power in the initial stage of a relationship.

Emotion and Romantic Relationships

Romantic emotions can envelop adolescents' lives (Larson, Clore, & Wood, in press; Larson & Richards, in press). A 14-year-old reports feeling in love and can't think about anything else. A 15-year-old is distressed that "everyone else has a boyfriend but me." As we just saw, adolescents spend a lot of time thinking about romantic involvement. Some of this thought can involve positive emotions of compassion and joy, but it also can include negative emotions such as worry, disappointment, and jealousy (Richards & others, 1998).

Romantic relationships often are involved in an adolescent's emotional experiences. In one study of ninth- to twelfth-graders, girls have real and fantasized heterosexual relationships as the explanation for more than one-third of their strong emotions, and boys gave this reason for 25 percent of their strong emotions (Wilson-Shockley, 1995). Strong emotions were attached far less to school (13 percent, family 9 percent), and same-sex peer relations (8 percent). The majority of the emotions were reported as positive, but a substantial minority (42 percent) were reported as negative, including feelings of anxiety, anger, jealousy, and depression.

Adolescents who had a boyfriend or girlfriend reported wider daily emotional swings than their counterparts who did not (Larson, Csikszentmihalyi, & Graef, 1980; Richards & Larson, 1990). In a period of 3 days, one eleventh-grade girl went

*T*hrough the Eyes of Psychologists

Candice Feiring, *Rutgers University*

"Gender is a key component for understanding romantic relationships in adolescence."

dating scripts
The cognitive models that adolescents and adults use to guide and evaluate dating interactions.

SUMMARY TABLE 16.4
Adolescence, Peers, and Romantic Relationships

Concept	Processes/ Related Ideas	Characteristics/Description
Peer Pressure and Conformity	Their Nature	• The pressure to conform to peers is strong during adolescence, especially in eighth and ninth grade.
Cliques and Crowds	Their Nature	• There usually are three to six well-defined cliques in every secondary school.
	Cliques and Self-Esteem	• Membership in certain cliques—especially jocks and populars—is associated with higher self-esteem. Independents also show high self-esteem.
Adolescent Groups Versus Child Groups	Comparisons	• Children's groups are less formal, less heterogeneous, and less mixed-sex than adolescent groups.
Dating and Romantic Relationships	Functions of Dating	• In the first half of the twentieth century, dating mainly served a courtship function. • Today, dating serves many functions, including status, learning about intimacy, sexual experimentation, and identity formation.
	Types of Dating and Developmental Changes	• Younger adolescents hang out in heterosexual groups. • Hooking up, seeing each other, and going out represent different variations of commitment. • Early dating is linked with developmental problems. • In early adolescence, individuals spend more time thinking about the opposite sex than actually being with them, but this reverses in the high school years.
	Male and Female Dating Scripts	• Male dating scripts are proactive, those of females reactive.
	Emotion and Romantic Relationships	• Romantic relationships can envelop adolescents' lives. Sometimes these emotions are positive, sometimes negative, and the emotions often change quickly.
	Culture and Dating	• Culture can exert a powerful influence on dating with many adolescents from immigrant families facing conflicts with their parents about dating.

from feeling "happy because I'm with Dan," to upset because they had a "huge fight" and "he won't listen to me and keeps hanging on me," to feeling "suicidal because of the fight," to feeling "happy because everything between me and Dan is fine."

Culture and Dating   The sociocultural context exerts a powerful influence on adolescent dating patterns and on mate selection (Xiaohe & Whyte, 1990). Values and religious beliefs of people in various cultures often dictate the age at which dating begins, how much freedom in dating is allowed, whether dates must be chaperoned by adults or parents, and the roles of males and females in dating. For example, Latino and Asian American cultures have more conservative standards regarding adolescent dating than the Anglo-American culture. Dating may be a source of cultural conflict for many immigrants and their families who have come from cultures in which dating begins at a late age, little freedom in dating is allowed, dates are chaperoned, and adolescent girls' dating is especially restricted.

At this point we have studied a number of ideas about adolescence, peers, and romantic relationships. A review of these ideas is presented in summary table 16.4.

Chapter Review

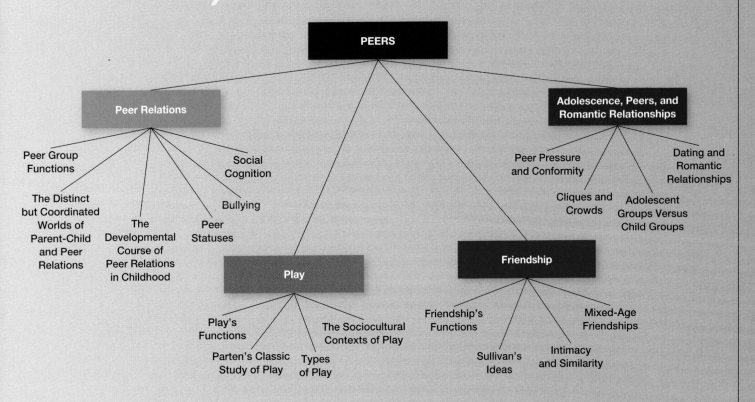

TO OBTAIN A DETAILED REVIEW OF THE CHAPTER, STUDY THESE FIVE SUMMARY TABLES:

Key Terms

peers 488
popular children 491
neglected children 491
rejected children 491
controversial children 491
perspective taking 492
play 495
play therapy 495

unoccupied play 495
solitary play 495
onlooker play 496
parallel play 496
associative play 496
cooperative play 496
sensorimotor play 497
practice play 497

pretend/symbolic play 497
social play 498
constructive play 498
games 499
intimacy in friendship 502
crowd 506
clique 506
dating scripts 511

Key People

Anna Freud 488
Gary Ladd 489
John Coie 491
Kenneth Dodge 493
Erik Erikson 495
Sigmund Freud 495

Jean Piaget 495
Lev Vygotsky 495
Daniel Berlyne 495
Mildred Parten 495
Carolee Howes 498
Harry Stack Sullivan 501

Willard Hartup 502
James Coleman 506
Brad Brown and Jane Lohr 506
Dexter Dunphy 507
Candice Feiring 511

Resources for Improving the Lives of Adolescents

Just Friends (1985)
  by Lilian Rubin
  New York: Harper

Just Friends explores the nature of friendship and intimacy.

Peer Interactions, Relationships, and Groups (1998)
  by Kenneth Rubin, William Bukowski, and Jeffrey Parker
  in W. Damon (Ed.), *Handbook of Child Psychology* (5th ed., Vol. 3)
  New York: Wiley

This article provides an in-depth examination of many areas of peer relations research by leading experts.

Peer Relationships and Social Competence in Early and Middle Childhood (1999)
  by Gary Ladd
  Annual Review of Psychology, Vol. 50
  Palo Alto, CA: Annual Reviews

An up-to-date, authoritative review of peer relations research from the 1970s to the present.

National Peer Helpers Association
  818-240-2926

This association has publications and information on peer programs across the United States.

Taking It to the Net

1. Barbara is going to lead a discussion in her child development class about peer relationships and friendships in early childhood. What should Barbara tell the class about how peer relationships develop between the ages of 3 and 6 years?

2. Darla, 13, has been living in foster homes since she was 4 years old. As a result of being abandoned by her parents and moved from foster home to foster home, she doesn't trust anyone. She is in counseling to help her adjust to her latest home and her new middle school. Her therapist brings up the importance of making and having friends, a concept alien to Darla. Why does Darla need to learn, in order to have a friend and be one.

3. Kristin is getting intense pressure from her friends at school to go out and drink with them. She wants to hang out with them, but has no interest in drinking. Because she can't turn to her friends to help her, she hopes her mother can give her some pointers for dealing with this pressure. What can Kristin's mother say to help?

Connect to *http://www. mhhe.com/santrockc9* to find the answers!

Chapter 17

SCHOOLS

The Nature of Children's Schooling

- Contemporary Approaches to Student Learning
- Schools' Changing Social Developmental Contexts

Schools and Developmental Status

- Early Childhood Education
- The Transition to Elementary School
- Schools for Adolescents

Socioeconomic Status and Ethnicity in Schools

- The Education of Students from Low-Socioeconomic-Status Backgrounds
- Ethnicity in Schools

Achievement

- Need for Achievement
- Extrinsic and Intrinsic Motivation
- Attribution
- Mastery Orientation
- Self-Efficacy
- Goal Setting, Planning, and Self-Monitoring
- Ethnicity and Culture

Children with Disabilities

- Who Are Children with Disabilities?
- Learning Disabilities
- Attention Deficit Hyperactivity Disorder
- Educational Issues Involving Children with Disabilities

> *The whole art of teaching is only the art of awakening the natural curiosity of young minds.*
>
> Anatole France
> *French Novelist, 20th Century*

The Story of Reggio Emilia's Children

THE REGGIO EMILIA approach is an educational program for young children that was developed in the northern Italian city of Reggio Emilia. Children of single parents and children with disabilities have priority in admission; other children are admitted according to a scale of needs. Parents pay on a sliding scale based on income.

The children are encouraged to learn by investigating and exploring topics that interest them. A wide range of stimulating media and materials is available for children to use as they learn—music, movement, drawing, painting, sculpting, collages, puppets and disguises, and photography, for example.

In this program, children often explore topics in a group, which fosters a sense of community, respect for diversity, and a collaborative approach to problem solving. Two co-teachers are present to serve as guides for children. The Reggio Emilia teachers consider a project as an adventure, which can start from an adult's suggestion, from a child's idea, or from an event, such as a snowfall or something else unexpected. Every project is based on what the children say and do. The teachers allow children enough time to think and craft a project.

At the core of the Reggio Emilia approach is the image of children who are competent and have rights, especially the right to outstanding care and education (Bredekamp, 1993). Parent participation is considered essential, and cooperation is a major theme in the schools (Gandini, 1993). Many early childhood education experts believe the Reggio Emilia approach provides a supportive, stimulating context in which children are motivated to explore their world in a competent and confident manner (Firlik, 1996).

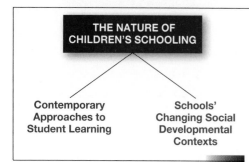

THE NATURE OF CHILDREN'S SCHOOLING

Contemporary Approaches to Student Learning

Schools' Changing Social Developmental Contexts

direct instruction approach
A teacher-centered approach that is characterized by teacher direction and control, mastery of academic material, high expectations for students' progress, and maximum time spent on learning tasks.

cognitive constructivist approaches
Approaches that emphasize the child's active, cognitive construction of knowledge and understanding; Piaget's theory is an example of this approach.

social constructivist approaches
Approaches that focus on collaboration with others to produce knowledge and understanding; Vygotsky's theory is an example of this approach.

National Education Research Centers

Pathways to School Improvement

APA's Education Directorate

Phi Delta Kappan

Constructivist Teaching and Learning

APA's Learner-Centered Psychological Principles

The Nature of Children's Schooling

Two of the important questions we will explore regarding children's schooling are these: What are some contemporary approaches to student learning? How do the school contexts of their schools change as children age?

Contemporary Approaches to Student Learning

There is much controversy over what the best way is for children to learn in school. The back-to-basics movement still has strong advocates, who believe that children should mainly be taught in a **direct instruction approach,** *a teacher-centered approach that is characterized by teacher direction and control, mastery of academic skills, high expectations for students' progress, and maximum time spent on learning, tasks.* This approach has much in common with the behavioral approach we discussed in chapter 2, "The Science of Child Development" ◀|||| P. 39.

In the 1990s there was a wave of interest in constructivist approaches to school reform (Santrock, 2001). **Cognitive constructivist approaches** *emphasize the child's active, cognitive construction of knowledge and understanding.* Piaget's theory (discussed in chapters 2 and 7) *is an example of a cognitive constructivist approach* ◀|||| Pp. 35, 204. The implications of Piaget's theory are that teachers should provide support for students to explore their world and develop understanding. **Social constructivist approaches** *focus on collaboration with others to produce knowledge and understanding.* Vygotsky's theory (also discussed in chapters 2 and 7) *is an example of a social constructivist approach.* The implications of Vygotsky's theory are that teachers should create many opportunities for students to learn with the teacher and with peers in co-constructing understanding ◀|||| Pp. 36, 226.

Advocates of the cognitive and social constructivist approaches argue that the direct instruction approach turns children into passive learners and does not adequately challenge them to think in critical and creative ways. The direct instruction enthusiasts say that the constructivist approaches often do not give enough attention to the content of a discipline, such as history or science. They also say that many constructivist approaches are too relativistic and vague.

A constructivist theme is evident in what are called learner-centered principles, which move instruction away from the teacher and toward the student. Increased interest in learner-centered principles resulted in the publication of *Learner-Centered Psychological Principles: A Framework for School Reform and Redesign* (Presidential Task Force on Psychology in Education, 1992; Work Group of the American Psychological Association's Board of Affairs, 1995; Learner-Centered Principles Work Group, 1997). This statement of principles was constructed and is periodically revised by a prestigious group of scientists and educators from a wide range of disciplines and interests. The principles have important implications for the way teachers instruct students.

The fourteen learner-centered principles involve cognitive and metacognitive factors, motivational and affective factors, developmental and social factors, and individual difference factors. To read more about these learner-centered principles, see figure 17.1 on page 520.

Schools' Changing Social Developmental Contexts

The social context differs at the preschool, elementary, and secondary level. The preschool setting is a protected environment, whose boundary is the classroom. In this limited social setting, preschool children interact with one or two teachers, almost always female, who are powerful figures in the young child's life. The preschool child also interacts with peers in a dyadic relationship or in small groups. Preschool children have little concept of the classroom as an organized social system, although they are learning how to make and maintain social contacts and communicate their needs. The preschool serves to modify some patterns of behavior developed through family experiences. Greater self-control may be required in the preschool than earlier in development.

The classroom is still the major context for the elementary school child, although it is more likely to be experienced as a social unit than in the preschool. The network of social expression also is more complex now. Teachers and peers have a prominent influence on children during the elementary school years. The teacher symbolizes authority, which establishes the climate of the classroom, conditions of social inter-action, and the nature of group functioning. The peer group becomes more salient, with increased interest in friendship, belonging, and status. And the peer group also becomes a learning community in which social roles and standards related to work and achievement are formed.

As children move into middle or junior high schools, the school environment increases in scope and complexity. The social field is the school as a whole rather than the classroom. Adolescents socially interact with many different teachers and peers from a range of social and ethnic backgrounds. Students are often exposed to a greater mix of male and female teachers. And social behavior is heavily weighted toward peers, extracurricular activities, clubs, and the community. The student in sec-ondary school is usually aware of the school as a social system and may be motivated to conform and adapt to the system or challenge it (Minuchin & Shapiro, 1983).

Schools and Developmental Status

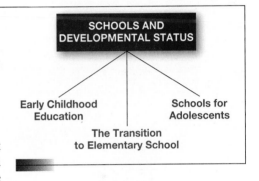

What is the nature of early childhood education? How do children make the transi-tion to elementary school? What is the nature of schools for adolescents?

Early Childhood Education

There are many variations in the way young children are educated. In the story that opened this chapter, you read about the Reggio Emilia program in northern Italy, a promising strategy that is receiving increased attention. First, we will explore the nature of the child-centered kindergarten, then turn our attention to Maria Montes-sori's approach. Next, we will examine the important concepts of developmentally appropriate and inappropriate education, followed by a discussion of what early childhood education's effects are.

The Child-Centered Kindergarten   Kindergarten programs vary a great deal (Roopnarine & Johnson, 2000). Some approaches place more emphasis on young children's social development, others on their cognitive development. Some experts on early childhood education believe that the curriculum of too many of today's kindergarten and preschool programs place too much emphasis on achieve-ment and success, putting pressure on young children too early in their development (Charlesworth, 1996; Elkind, 1988). Kindergartens were not originally intended to be factories of achievement.

A special worry of early childhood educators is that the back-to-basics move-ment that has recently characterized educational reform is filtering down to kinder-garten. Another worry is that many parents want their children to go to school earlier than kindergarten for the purpose of getting a "head start" in achievement.

In the 1840s, Friedrich Froebel's concern for quality education for young chil-dren led to the founding of the kindergarten—literally, "a garden for children." The founder of the kindergarten understood that, like growing plants, children require careful nurturing. Unfortunately, too many of today's kindergartens have forgotten the importance of careful nurturing for our nation's young children.

In the **child-centered kindergarten,** *education involves the whole child and includes concern for the child's physical, cognitive, and social development.* Instruction is organized around the child's needs, interests, and learning styles. Emphasis is on

Ask ERIC

American Educational Research Association (AERA)

Early Childhood Education

Reggio Emilia

child-centered kindergarten
Education that involves the whole child by considering both the child's physical, cognitive, and social development and the child's needs, interests, and learning styles.

COGNITIVE AND METACOGNITIVE FACTORS

1. **Nature of the Learning Process**
   The learning of complex subject matter is most effective when it is an intentional process of constructing meaning and experience.

2. **Goals of the Learning Process**
   Successful learners, over time and with support and instructional guidance, can create meaningful, coherent representations of knowledge.

3. **Construction of Knowledge**
   Successful learners can link new information with existing knowledge in meaningful ways.

4. **Strategic Thinking**
   Successful learners can create a repertoire of thinking and reasoning strategies to achieve complex goals.

5. **Thinking about Thinking**
   Higher order strategies for selecting and monitoring mental operations facilitate creative and critical thinking.

6. **Context of Learning**
   Learning is influenced by environmental factors, including culture, technology, and instructional practices.

MOTIVATIONAL AND INSTRUCTIONAL FACTORS

7. **Motivational and Emotional Influences on Learning**
   What and how much is learned is influenced by the learner's motivation. Motivation to learn, in turn, is influenced by the learner's emotional states, beliefs, interests, goals, and habits of thinking.

8. **Intrinsic Motivation to Learn**
   The learner's creativity, higher order thinking, and natural curiosity all contribute to motivation to learn. Instrinsic (internal, self-generated) motivation is stimulated by tasks of optimal novelty and difficulty, tasks that are relevant to personal interests, and when learners are provided personal choice and control.

9. **Effects of Motivation on Effort**
   Acquiring complex knowledge and skills requires extended learner effort and guided practice. Without learners' motivation to learn, the willingness to exert this effort is unlikely without coercion.

DEVELOPMENTAL AND SOCIAL FACTORS

10. **Developmental Influences on Learning**
    As individuals develop, there are different opportunities and constraints for learning. Learning is most effective when development within and across physical, cognitive, and socioemotional domains is taken into account.

11. **Social Influences on Learning**
    Learning is influenced by social interactions, interpersonal relations, and communication with others.

INDIVIDUAL DIFFERENCE FACTORS

12. **Individual Differences in Learning**
    Learners have different strategies, approaches, and capabilities for learning that are a function of prior experience and heredity.

13. **Learning and Diversity**
    Learning is most effective when differences in learners' linguistic, cultural, and social backgrounds are considered.

14. **Standards and Assessment**
    Setting appropriately high and challenging standards and assessing the learner as well as learning progress are integral aspects of the learning experience.

Figure 17.1
Learner-Centered Psychological Principles

the process of learning rather than on what is learned (White & Coleman, 2000). Each child follows a unique developmental pattern, and young children learn best through firsthand experiences with people and materials. Play is extremely important in the child's total development. *Experimenting, exploring, discovering, trying out, restructuring, speaking, and listening* are all words that describe the activities in excellent kindergarten programs. Such programs are closely attuned to the developmental status of 4- and 5-year-old children. They are based on a state of being, not on a state of becoming.

The Montessori Approach

Montessori schools are patterned after the educational philosophy of Maria Montessori, an Italian physician-turned-educator, who crafted a revolutionary approach to young children's education at the beginning of the twentieth century (Wentworth, 1999). Her work began in Rome with a group of children who were mentally retarded. She was successful in teaching them to read, write, and pass examinations designed for normal children. Some time later, she turned her attention to poor children from the slums of Rome and had similar success in teaching them. Her approach has since been adopted extensively in private nursery schools in the United States.

The **Montessori approach** *is a philosophy of education in which children are given considerable freedom and spontaneity in choosing activities. They are allowed to move from one activity to another as they desire.* The teacher acts as a facilitator rather than a director of learning. The teacher shows the child how to perform intellectual activities, demonstrates interesting ways to explore curriculum materials, and offers help when the child requests it.

Some developmentalists favor the Montessori approach, but others believe that it neglects children's social development (Chattin-McNichols, 1992). For example, while Montessori fosters independence and the development of cognitive skills, it deemphasizes verbal interaction between the teacher and child and peer interaction. Montessori's critics also argue that it restricts imaginative play.

Developmentally Appropriate and Inappropriate Practices in the Education of Young Children

It is time for number games in a kindergarten class at the Greenbrook School in South Brunswick, New Jersey. With little prodding from the teacher, 23 5- and 6-year-old children fetch geometric puzzles, playing cards, and counting equipment from the shelves lining the room. At one round table, some young children fit together brightly colored shapes. One girl forms a hexagon out of triangles. Other children gather around her to count up how many parts were needed to make the whole. After about half an hour, the children prepare for story time. They put away their counting equipment and sit in a circle around one young girl. She holds up a giant book about a character named Mrs. Wishywashy, who insists on giving the farm animals a bath. The children recite the whimsical lines, clearly enjoying one of their favorite stories. The hallway outside the kindergarten is lined with drawings depicting the children's own interpretations of the book. After the first reading, volunteers act out various parts of the book. There is not one bored face in the room.

This is not reading, writing, and arithmetic the way most individuals remember it. A growing number of educators and psychologists believe that preschool and young elementary school children learn best through active, hands-on teaching methods such as games and dramatic play. They know that children develop at varying rates and that schools need to allow for these individual differences (Henninger, 1999; Jalongo & Isenberg, 2000). They also believe that schools should focus on improving children's social development, as well as their cognitive development. Educators refer to this type of schooling as **developmentally appropriate practice,** *which is based upon knowledge of the typical development of children within an age span (age appropriateness) as well as the uniqueness of the child (individual appropriateness). Developmentally appropriate practice contrasts with developmentally inappropriate practice, which ignores the concrete, hands-on approach to learning. Direct teaching largely through abstract paper-and-pencil activities presented to large groups of young children is believed to be developmentally inappropriate.*

One of the most comprehensive documents addressing the issue of developmentally appropriate practice in early childhood programs is the position statement by the National Association for the Education of Young Children (NAEYC) (Bredekamp, 1987, 1997; National Association for the Education of Young Children, 1986). This document represents the expertise of many of the foremost experts in the field of early childhood education. In figure 17.2, you can examine some of the NAEYC recommendations for developmentally appropriate and inappropriate practice. In one study, the children who attended developmentally appropriate kindergartens displayed more appropriate classroom behavior and had better conduct records and better work and study habits in the first grade than did the children who attended developmentally inappropriate kindergartens (Hart & others, 1993).

How common are programs that use developmentally appropriate practice? Unfortunately, as few as one-third to one-fifth of all early childhood programs follow this educational strategy. Even fewer elementary schools do. Child-initiated activities, divergent questioning, and small-group instruction are the exception rather than the rule (Dunn & Kontos, 1997).

Education for Children Who Are Disadvantaged

For many years, children from low-income families did not receive any education before they entered the first grade. In the 1960s, an effort was made to try to break the cycle of poverty and poor education for young children in the United States through compensatory education. **Project Head Start** *is a compensatory education program designed to provide children from low-income families the opportunity to acquire the skills and experiences important for success in school.* Project Head Start began in the summer of 1965, funded by the Economic Opportunity Act, and it continues to serve disadvantaged children today.

Initially, Project Head Start consisted of many different types of preschool programs in different parts of the country. Little effort was made to find out whether

Montessori approach
An educational philosophy in which children are given considerable freedom and spontaneity in choosing activities and are allowed to move from one activity to another as they desire.

developmentally appropriate practice
Education that focuses on the typical developmental patterns of children (age appropriateness) and the uniqueness of each child (individual appropriateness). Such practice contrasts with developmentally inappropriate practice, which ignores the concrete, hands-on approach to learning. Direct teaching largely through abstract paper-and-pencil activities presented to large groups of young children is believed to be developmentally inappropriate.

NAEYC
High/Scope: Active Learning
Head Start Resources

Project Head Start
Compensatory education designed to provide children from low-income families the opportunity to acquire the skills and experiences important for school success.

Component	Appropriate practice	Inappropriate practice
Curriculum goals	Experiences are provided in all developmental areas—physical, cognitive, social, and emotional.	Experiences are narrowly focused on cognitive development without recognition that all areas of the child's development are interrelated.
	Individual differences are expected, accepted, and used to design appropriate activities.	Children are evaluated only against group norms, and all are expected to perform the same tasks and achieve the same narrowly defined skills.
	Interactions and activities are designed to develop children's self-esteem and positive feelings toward learning.	Children's worth is measured by how well they conform to rigid expectations and perform on standardized tests.
Teaching strategies	Teachers prepare the environment for children to learn through active exploration and interaction with adults, other children, and materials.	Teachers use highly structured, teacher-directed lessons almost exclusively.
	Children select many of their own activities from among a variety the teacher prepares.	The teacher directs all activity deciding what children will do and when.
	Children are expected to be mentally and physically active.	Children are expected to sit down, be quiet, and listen or do paper-and-pencil tasks for long periods of time. A major portion of time is spent passively sitting, watching, and listening.
Guidance of socioemotional development	Teachers enhance children's self-control by using positive guidance techniques, such as modeling and encouraging expected behavior, redirecting children to a more acceptable activity, and setting clear limits.	Teachers spend considerable time enforcing rules, punishing unacceptable behavior, demeaning children who misbehave, making children sit and be quiet, and refereeing disagreements.
	Children are provided many opportunities to develop social skills, such as cooperating, helping, negotiating, and talking with the person involved to solve interpersonal problems.	Children work individually at desks and tables most of the time and listen to the teacher's directions to the total group.

Figure **17.2**   NAEYC Recommendations for Developmentally Appropriate

Component	Appropriate practice	Inappropriate practice
Language development, literacy, and cognitive development	Children are provided many opportunities to see how reading and writing are useful before they are instructed in letter names, sounds, and word identification. Basic skills develop when they are meaningful to children. An abundance of these activities is provided to develop language and literacy: listening to and reading stories and poems; taking field trips; dictating stories; participating in dramatic play; talking informally with other children and adults; and experimenting with writing.	Reading and writing instruction stresses isolated skill development, such as recognizing single letters, reading the alphabet, singing the alphabet song, coloring within predefined lines, and being instructed in correct formation of letters on a printed line.
	Children develop an understanding of concepts about themselves, others, and the world around them through observation, interaction with people and real objects, and the seeking of solutions to concrete problems. Learning about math, science, social studies, health, and other content areas is integrated through meaningful activities.	Instruction stresses isolated skill development through memorization. Children's cognitive development is seen as fragmented in content areas, such as math or science, and times are set aside for each of these.
Physical development	Children have daily opportunities to use large muscles, including running, jumping, and balancing. Outdoor activity is planned daily so children can freely express themselves.	Opportunity for large muscle activity is limited. Outdoor time is limited because it is viewed as interfering with instructional time, rather than as an integral part of the children's learning environment.
	Children have daily opportunities to develop small muscle skills through play activities, such as puzzles, painting, and cutting.	Small motor activity is limited to writing with pencils, coloring predrawn forms, and engaging in similar structured lessons.
Aesthetic development and motivation	Children have daily opportunities for aesthetic expression and appreciation through art and music. A variety of art media are available.	Art and music are given limited attention. Art consists of coloring predrawn forms or following adult-prescribed directions.
	Children's natural curiosity and desire to make sense of their world are used to motivate them to become involved in learning.	Children are required to participate in all activities to obtain the teacher's approval; to obtain extrinsic rewards, such as stickers or privileges; or to avoid punishment.

and Inappropriate Educational Practices

Project Follow Through
An adjunct to Project Head Start, in which the enrichment programs are carried through the first few years of elementary school.

some programs worked better than others, but it eventually became apparent that some programs did work better than others. **Project Follow Through** *was implemented in 1967 as an adjunct to Project Head Start. In Project Follow Through, different types of educational programs were devised to determine which programs were the most effective. In the Follow Through programs, the enriched programs were carried through the first few years of elementary school.*

Were some Follow Through programs more effective than others? Many of the variations were able to produce the desired effects on children. For example, children in academically oriented, direct-instruction approaches did better on achievement tests and were more persistent on tasks than were children in the other approaches. Children in affective education approaches were absent from school less often and showed more independence than children in other approaches. Thus, Project Follow Through was important in demonstrating that variation in early childhood education does have significant effects in a wide range of social and cognitive areas (Stallings, 1975).

The effects of early childhood compensatory education continue to be studied, and recent evaluations support the positive influence on both the cognitive and social worlds of disadvantaged young children (Reynolds, 1999; Schweinhart, 1999). Of special interest are the long-term effects such intervention might produce. Model preschool programs lead to lower rates of placement in special education, dropping out of school, grade retention, delinquency, and use of welfare programs. Such programs might also lead to higher rates of high school graduation and employment. For every dollar invested in high-quality, model preschool programs, taxpayers receive about $1.50 in return by the time the participants reach the age of 20. The benefits include savings on public school education (such as special-education services), tax payments on additional earnings, reduced welfare payments, and savings in juvenile justice system costs. Predicted benefits over a lifetime are much greater to the taxpayer, a return of $5.73 on every dollar invested.

One long-term investigation of early childhood education involved pooling data from eleven different early education studies that focused on children ranging in age from 9 to 19 years (Lazar, Darlington, & others, 1982). The early education models varied substantially, but all were carefully planned and executed by experts in early childhood education. Outcome measures included indicators of school competence (such as special education and grade retention), abilities (as measured by standardized intelligence and achievement tests), attitudes and values, and impact on the family. The results indicated substantial benefits of competent preschool education with low-income children on all four dimensions investigated. In sum, ample evidence indicates that well-designed and well-implemented early childhood education programs are successful with low-income children.

Although educational intervention in impoverished young children's lives is important, Head Start programs are not all created equal. One estimate is that 40 percent of the 1,400 Head Start programs are of questionable quality (Zigler & Styfco, 1994). More attention needs to be given to developing consistently high-quality Head Start programs (Bronfenbrenner, 1995; Parker & others, 1995). One high-quality early childhood education program (although not a Head Start program) is the Perry Preschool program in Ypsilanti, Michigan, designed by David Weikart (1982). The Perry Preschool program is a 2-year program that includes weekly home visits from program personnel. In an analysis of the long-term effects of the program, as young adults the Perry Preschool children have higher high school graduation rates, more are in the workforce, fewer need welfare, crime rates are lower among them, and there are fewer teen pregnancies than in

ADVENTURES FOR THE MIND

Observing Children in Preschool and Kindergarten

TO LEARN ABOUT CHILDREN, there is no substitute for interacting with them and observing them. Try to visit at least one preschool and one kindergarten. When I was trying to develop a meaningful idea for a master's thesis some years ago, my advisor suggested that I spend several weeks at different Head Start programs in Miami, Florida. The experience was invaluable and contributed significantly to my further pursuit of a career in the field of child development.

When you conduct your observations, consider whether the programs meet the criteria of developmentally appropriate education. Are the programs play- and child-centered or academics-centered?

a control group from the same background who did not get the enriched early childhood education experience (Weikart, 1993).

Too many young children go to substandard early childhood programs (Morrison, 2000). In a report by the Carnegie Corporation (1996), four out of five early childhood programs did not meet quality standards. Early childhood education should encourage adequate preparation for learning, varied learning activities, trusting relationships between adults and children, and increased parental involvement (Hildebrand, Phenice, & Hines, 2000).

Poverty and Learning

Early Childhood Care and Education Around the World

Early Childhood Education Resources

The Effects of Early Childhood Education   Because kindergarten and preschool programs are so diverse, it is difficult to make overall conclusions about their effects on children's development. Nonetheless, in one review of early childhood education's influence (Clarke-Stewart & Fein, 1983), it was concluded that children who attend preschool or kindergarten

- interact more with peers, both positively and negatively
- are less cooperative with and responsive to adults than home-reared children
- are more socially competent and mature, in that they are more confident, extraverted, assertive, self-sufficient, independent, verbally expressive, knowledgeable about the social world, comfortable in social and stressful circumstances, and better adjusted when they go to school (exhibiting more task persistence, leadership, and goal direction, for example)
- are less socially competent, in that they are less polite, less compliant to teacher demands, louder, and more aggressive and bossy, especially if the school or family supports such behavior

In sum, early childhood education generally has a positive effect on children's development, since the behaviors just mentioned—while at times negative—seem to be in the direction of developmental maturity, in that they increase as the child ages through the preschool years.

As children make the transition to elementary school, they interact and develop relationships with new and significant others. School provides them with a rich source of new ideas to shape their sense of self.

The Transition to Elementary School

For most children, entering the first grade signals a change from being a "homechild" to being a "schoolchild"—a situation in which new roles and obligations are experienced. Children take up a new role (being a student), interact and develop relationships with new significant others, adopt new reference groups, and develop new standards by which to judge themselves. School provides children with a rich source of new ideas to shape their sense of self.

A special concern about children's early school experiences is emerging. Evidence is mounting that early schooling proceeds mainly on the basis of negative feedback. For example, children's self-esteem in the latter part of elementary school is lower than it is in the earlier part, and older children rate themselves as less smart, less good, and less hardworking than do younger ones (Blumenfeld & others, 1981).

In school as well as out of school, children's learning, like children's development, is *integrated* (NAEYC, 1988). One of the main pressures on elementary teachers has been the need to "cover the curriculum." Frequently, teachers have tried to do so by tightly scheduling discrete time segments for each subject. This approach ignores the fact that children often do not need to distinguish learning by subject area. For example, they advance their knowledge of reading and writing when they work on social studies projects; they learn mathematical concepts through music and physical education (Katz & Chard, 1989). A curriculum can be facilitated by providing learning areas in which children plan and select their activities. For example, the classroom may include a fully equipped publishing center, complete with materials for writing, illustrating, typing, and binding student-made books; a science area, with animals and plants for observation and books to study; and other similar areas. In this type of classroom, children learn reading as they discover information about science; they learn writing as they work together on interesting projects. Such classrooms also provide opportunities for spontaneous play, recognizing that elementary school children continue to learn in all areas through unstructured play, either alone or with other children.

Education experts Lillian Katz and Sylvia Chard (1989) recently described two elementary school classrooms. In one, children spent an entire morning making identical pictures of traffic lights. The teacher made no attempt to get the children to relate the pictures to anything else the class was doing. In the other class, the children were investigating a school bus. They wrote to the district's school superintendent and asked if they could have a bus parked at their school for a few days. They studied the bus, discovered the functions of its parts, and discussed traffic rules. Then, in the classroom, they built their own bus out of cardboard. The children had fun, but they also practiced writing, problem solving, and even some arithmetic. When the class had their parents' night, the teacher was ready with reports on how each child was doing. However, all the parents wanted to see was the bus because their children had been talking about it at home for weeks. Many contemporary education experts believe that this is the kind of education all children deserve. That is, they believe that children should be active, constructivist learners and taught through concrete, hands-on experience (Bonk & Cunningham, 1999).

At this point we have studied a number of ideas about the nature of children's schooling, early childhood education, and the transition to elementary school. A review of these ideas is presented in summary table 17.1. Next, we will continue our developmental analysis of schools by focusing on schools for adolescents.

Schools for Adolescents

These are some of the questions regarding schools for adolescents that we will explore: What is the nature of the transition from elementary or middle or junior high school? What are effective schools for young adolescents like? Why do adolescents drop out of school?

Elementary Education

The world rests on the breath of the children in the schoolhouse.

The Talmud
Palestinian and Babylonian Source of Jewish Law and Schools, 4th Century

SUMMARY TABLE 17.1
The Nature of Children's Schooling, Early Childhood Education, and the Transition to Elementary School

Concept	Processes/ Related Ideas	Characteristics/Description
The Nature of Children's Schooling	Approaches to Educating Students	• Contemporary approaches to student learning include the direct instruction and constructivist (cognitive and social) approaches. • The American Psychological Association has proposed 14 learner-centered psychological principles to guide children's education.
Early Childhood Education	Variations	• These include the child-centered kindergarten, the Montessori approach, the Reggio Emilia approach, and developmentally appropriate and inappropriate education.
	Education for Children Who Are Disadvantaged	• Compensatory education has tried to break through the poverty cycle with programs like Project Head Start. • Long-term studies reveal that model preschool programs have positive effects on children's development.
	Effects of Early Childhood Education	• It is difficult to evaluate these effects, but overall they appear to be positive.
Transition to Elementary School	Its Nature	• A special concern is that early elementary education proceeds mainly on the basis of negative feedback to children. • Many education experts believe that early elementary school children should involve active, constructivist learning.

The Transition to Middle or Junior High School   The emergence of junior high schools in the 1920s and 1930s was justified on the basis of physical, cognitive, and social changes that characterize early adolescence, as well as the need for more schools for the growing student population. Old high schools became junior high schools, and new regional high schools were built. In most systems, the ninth grade remained a part of the high school in content, although physically separated from it in a 6-3-3 system. Gradually, the ninth grade was restored to the high school, as many school systems developed middle schools that include the seventh and eighth grades, or sixth, seventh, and eighth grades. Middle schools were created partly because of the earlier onset of puberty in recent decades.

One worry of educators and psychologists is that junior high and middle schools have simply become watered-down versions of high schools, mimicking their curricular and extracurricular schedules. The critics argue that unique curricular and extracurricular activities reflecting a wide range of individual differences in biological and psychological development in early adolescence should be incorporated into our junior high and middle schools. The critics also stress that many high schools foster passivity rather than autonomy and that schools should create a variety of pathways for students to achieve an identity.

The transition to middle school or junior high school from elementary schools can be stressful. Why? The transition takes place at a time when many changes—in the individual, in the family, and in school—are occurring simultaneously. These changes include puberty and related concerns about body image; the emergence of at least some aspects of formal operational thought, including accompanying changes in social cognition; increased responsibility and independence in association with

The transition from elementary to middle or junior high school occurs at the same time as a number of other developmental changes. Biological, cognitive, and socioemotional changes converge with this schooling transition to make it a time of considerable adaptation.

top-dog phenomenon
The circumstance of moving from the top position in elementary school to the lowest position in middle or junior high school.

decreased dependency on parents; change from a small, contained classroom structure to a larger, more impersonal school structure; change from one teacher to many teachers and from a small, homogeneous set of peers to a larger, more heterogeneous set of peers; and an increased focus on achievement and performance and their assessment. This list includes a number of negative, stressful features, but there can be positive aspects to the transition. Students are more likely to feel grown up, have more subjects from which to select, have more opportunities to spend time with peers and to locate compatible friends, and enjoy increased independence from direct parental monitoring, and they may be more challenged intellectually by academic work.

When students make the transition from elementary school to middle or junior high school, they experience the **top-dog phenomenon,** *the circumstance of moving from the top position (in elementary school, being the oldest, biggest, and most powerful students in the school) to the lowest position (in middle or junior high school, being the youngest, smallest, and least powerful students in the school).* Researchers who have charted the transition from elementary to middle or junior high school find that the first year of middle or junior high school can be difficult for many students (Hawkins & Berndt, 1985). For example, in one study of the transition from sixth grade in an elementary school to the seventh grade in a junior high school, adolescents' perceptions of the quality of their school life plunged in the seventh grade (Hirsch & Rapkin, 1987). In the seventh grade, the students were less satisfied with school, were less committed to school, and liked their teachers less. The drop in school satisfaction occurred regardless of how academically successful the students were.

Effective Schools for Young Adolescents   What makes a successful middle school? Joan Lipsitz (1984) and her colleagues searched the nation for the best middle schools. Extensive contacts and observations were made. Based on the recommendations of education experts and observations in schools in different parts of the United States, four middle schools were chosen for their outstanding ability to educate young adolescents. What were these middle schools like? The most striking feature was their willingness and ability to adapt all school practices to their students' individual differences in physical, cognitive, and social development. The schools took seriously the knowledge we have developed about young adolescents. This seriousness was reflected in the decisions about different aspects of school life. For example, one middle school fought to keep its schedule of minicourses on Friday, so that every student could be with friends and pursue personal interests. Two other middle schools expended considerable energy on a complex school organization, so that small groups of students worked with small groups of teachers who could vary the tone and pace of the school day, depending on the students' needs. Another middle school developed an advisory scheme, so that each student had daily contact with an adult who was willing to listen, explain, comfort, and prod the adolescent. Such school policies reflect thoughtfulness and personal concern about individuals who have compelling developmental needs.

Another aspect of the effective middle schools was that early in their existence—the first year in three of the schools and the second year in the fourth school—they emphasized the importance of creating an environment that was positive for the adolescents' social and emotional development. This goal was established not only because such environments contribute to academic excellence but also because social and emotional development were valued as intrinsically important in adolescents' schooling.

Recognizing that the vast majority of middle schools do not approach the excellent schools described by Joan Lipsitz (1984), in 1989 the Carnegie Corporation issued an extremely negative evaluation of our nation's middle schools. In the report, *Turning Points: Preparing American Youth for the 21st Century,* the conclusion was put forth that most young adolescents attend massive, impersonal schools, learn from seemingly irrelevant curricula, trust few adults in school, and lack access to health care and counseling. The Carnegie Corporation (1989) report recommended the following:

- Develop smaller "communities" or "houses" to lessen the impersonal nature of large middle schools.
- Lower student-to-counselor ratios from several hundred-to-1 to 10-to-1.
- Involve parents and community leaders in schools.
- Develop curricula that produce students who are literate, understand the sciences, and have a sense of health, ethics, and citizenship.
- Have teachers team teach in more flexibly designed curriculum blocks that integrate several disciplines, instead of presenting students with disconnected, rigidly separated 50-minute segments.
- Boost students' health and fitness with more in-school programs and help students who need public health care to get it.

Many of these recommendations were echoed in a report from the National Governor's Association (*America in Transition,* 1989), which stated that the very structure of middle school education in America neglects the basic developmental needs of young adolescents. Many educators and psychologists strongly support these recommendations (Wigfield & Eccles, 1994, 1995). The Edna McConnell Clark Foundation's Program for Disadvantaged Youth is an example of a multiyear, multisite effort designed to implement many of the proposals for middle school improvement.

Middle School Resources
Middle Schools
Educating Young Adolescents

*W*hat does education often do? It makes a straight-cut ditch of a free, meandering brook.

Henry David Thoreau
American Poet, Essayist, 19th Century

*A*DVENTURES FOR THE MIND

Evaluating Your Own Middle or Junior High School

WHAT WAS YOUR OWN middle or junior high school like? How did it measure up to Lipsitz's criteria for effective schools for young adolescents? Did the school characteristically take individual differences into account? Did the administrators and teachers adequately address the unique needs of young adolescents as separate from those of children and older adolescents? Was socioemotional development emphasized as much as cognitive development? Suppose you could redesign the middle school you attended in one or two significant ways to improve students' socioemotional development. What changes would you make?

The foundation has engaged the Center for Early Adolescence at the University of North Carolina to guide five urban school districts in their middle school reform (Scales, 1992). In sum, middle schools throughout the nation need a major redesign if they are to be effective in educating adolescents for becoming competent adults in the twenty-first century.

Reducing the Dropout Rate

High School Education

High School Dropouts

For many decades, dropping out of high school has been viewed as a serious educational and societal problem. By leaving high school before graduating, many dropouts take with them educational deficiencies that severely curtail their economic and social well-being throughout their adult lives. We will study the scope of the problem, the causes of dropping out, and ways to reduce dropout rates. While dropping out of high school has negative consequences for youth, the picture is not entirely bleak. Over the past 40 years, the proportion of adolescents who have not finished high school has decreased considerably. In 1940, more than 60 percent of all individuals 25 to 29 years of age had not completed high school. By 1998, this proportion had dropped to less than 12 percent.

Despite the decline in overall high school dropout rates, a major concern is the higher dropout rate of minority-group and low-income students, especially in the large cities (Evans & others, 1995; Romo, 2000). The student dropout rates of most minority groups have been declining, but remain above those of White youth. In 1970, 15 percent of non-Latino White individuals 16-24 years of age were high school dropouts, but by 1998 that figure had fallen to 8 percent (Digest of Education Statistics, 1999). In 1970, 29 percent of African American individuals 16-24 years of age were high school dropouts. By 1998, that figure had been cut more than in half—to 14 percent. The high school dropout rate for Latinos is still precariously high—30 percent (dropping only 4 percent since 1970).

Dropout rates are also high for Native Americans (fewer than 10 percent graduate from high school). In some inner-city areas, the dropout rate for ethnic minority students is especially high, reaching more than 50 percent in Chicago, for example.

Students drop out of schools for many reasons (Jacobs, Garnier, & Weisner, 1996). In one study, almost 50 percent of the dropouts cited school-related reasons for leaving school, such as not liking school or being expelled or suspended (Rumberger, 1983). Twenty percent of the dropouts (but 40 percent of the Latino students) cited economic reasons for leaving school. One third of the female students dropped out for personal reasons, such as pregnancy or marriage.

Most research on dropouts has focused on high school students. One study focused on middle school dropouts (Rumberger, 1995). The observed differences in dropout rates among ethnic groups were related to differences in family background—especially socioeconomic status. Lack of parental academic support, low parental supervision, and low parental educational expectations for their adolescents were also related to dropping out of middle school.

To help reduce the dropout rate, community institutions, especially schools, need to break down the barriers

These adolescents participate in the "I Have a Dream" (IHAD) program, a comprehensive, long-term dropout prevention program that has been very successful.

Local IHAD projects around the country "adopt" entire grades (usually the third or fourth) from public elementary schools, or corresponding age-cohorts from public housing developments. These children—"Dreamers"—are then provided with a program of academic, social, cultural, and recreational activities throughout their elementary, middle school, and high school years. An important part of this program is that it is personal rather than institutional: IHAD sponsors and staff develop close long-term relationships with the children. When participants complete high school, IHAD provides the tuition assistance necessary for them to attend a state or local college or vocational school.

The IHAD Program was created in 1981, when philanthropist Eugene Lang made an impromptu offer of college tuition to a class of graduating sixth-graders at P.S. 121 in East Harlem. Statistically, 75 percent of the students should have dropped out of school; instead, 90 percent graduated and 60 percent went on to college. Since the National IHAD Foundation was created in 1986, it has grown to number over 150 Projects in 57 cities and 28 states, serving some 12,000 children.

between work and school. Many youth step off the education ladder long before reaching the level needed for a professional career, often with nowhere to step next, and are left to their own devices to search for work. These youth need more assistance than they are now receiving. Among the approaches worth considering are these (William T. Grant Foundation Commission, 1988):

- Monitored work experiences, such as through cooperative education, apprenticeships, internships, preemployment training, and youth-operated enterprises
- Community and neighborhood services, including voluntary and youth-guided services
- Redirected vocational education, the principal thrust of which should not be preparation for specific jobs but acquisition of basic skills needed for a wide range of jobs
- Guarantees of continuing education, employment, or training, especially in conjunction with mentor programs
- Career information and counseling to expose youth to job opportunities and career options, as well as to successful role models
- School volunteer programs, not only for tutoring but also for access to adult friends and mentors

Socioeconomic Status and Ethnicity in Schools

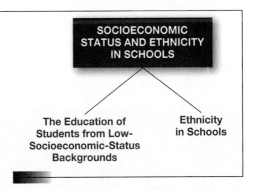

Children from low-income, ethnic minority backgrounds have more difficulties in school than do their middle-socioeconomic status, White counterparts. Why? Critics argue that schools have not done a good job of educating low-income, ethnic minority students to overcome the barriers to their achievement (Scott-Jones, 1995). Let's further explore the roles of socioeconomic status and ethnicity in schools.

The Education of Students from Low-Socioeconomic-Status Backgrounds

Many children in poverty face problems at home and at school that present barriers to their learning (Phillips & others, 1999; Wertheimer, 1999). At home, they may have parents who don't set high educational standards for them, who are incapable of reading to them, and who don't have enough money to pay for educational materials and experiences, such as books and trips to zoos and museums. They may experience malnutrition and live in areas where crime and violence are a way of life (Ceballo, 1999; DuRant, 1999).

Many of the schools that children from impoverished backgrounds attend have fewer resources than do the schools in higher-income neighborhoods (Shade, Kelly, & Oberg, 1997). Schools in low-income areas are likely to have more students with lower achievement test scores, lower graduation rates, and smaller percentages of students going to college. And they are more likely to have young teachers with less experience than do schools in higher-income neighborhoods. In some instances, though, federal aid has provided a context for improved learning in schools located in low-income areas.

Schools in low-income areas also are more likely to encourage rote learning, while schools in higher-income areas are more likely to work with children to improve their thinking skills (Spring, 1998). Thus far too many schools in low-income neighborhoods provide students with environments that are not conducive to effective learning, and many of the schools' buildings and classrooms are old, crumbling, and poorly maintained. To read a vivid description of poverty and schools, see the Explorations in Child Development box.

EXPLORATIONS IN CHILD DEVELOPMENT
Savage Inequalities

JONATHAN KOZOL (1991) vividly described some of the problems that children of poverty face in their neighborhood and at school in *Savage Inequalities*. Following are some of his observations in one inner-city area. East St. Louis, Illinois, which is 98 percent African American, has no obstetric services, no regular trash collection, and few jobs. Nearly one third of the families live on less than $7,500 a year, and 75 percent of its population lives on welfare of some form. Blocks upon blocks of housing consist of dilapidated, skeletal buildings. Residents breathe the chemical pollution of nearby Monsanto Chemical Company. Raw sewage repeatedly backs up into homes. Lead from nearby smelters poisons the soil. Child malnutrition and fear of violence are common. The problems of the streets spill over into the schools, where sewage also backs up from time to time. Classrooms and hallways are old and unattractive, athletic facilities inad-

equate. Teachers run out of chalk and paper, the science labs are 30–50 years out of date, and the school's heating system has never worked correctly. A history teacher has 110 students but only 26 books.

Kozol says that anyone who visits places like East St. Louis, even for a brief time, comes away profoundly shaken. After all, these are innocent children who have done nothing wrong. Kozol's interest was in describing what life is like in the nation's inner-city neighborhoods and schools, which are predominantly African American and Latino. However, as indicated earlier, there are many non-Latino White children who live in poverty, although they often are in suburban or rural areas. Kozol argues that many inner-city schools are still segregated, are grossly underfunded, and do not provide adequate opportunities for children to learn effectively.

James Comer (left) is shown with some of the inner-city African American children who attend a school that became a better learning environment because of Comer's intervention. Comer is convinced that a strong, familylike atmosphere is a key to improving the quality of inner-city schools.

Ethnicity in Schools

School segregation is still a factor in the education of children of color in the United States (Simons, Finlay, & Yang, 1991). Almost one third of all African American and Latino students attend schools in which 90 percent or more of the students are from ethnic minority groups.

The school experiences of students from different ethnic groups vary considerably (Hollins & Oliver, 1999). African American and Latino students are much less likely than non-Latino White or Asian American students to be enrolled in academic, college preparatory programs and are much more likely to be enrolled in remedial and special education programs. Asian American students are far more likely than other ethnic minority groups to take advanced math and science courses in high school. African American students are twice as likely as Latinos, Native Americans, or Whites to be suspended from school. Ethnic minorities of color constitute the majority in 23 of the 25 largest school districts in the United States, a trend that is increasing (Banks, 1995). However, 90 percent of the teachers in America's schools are non-Latino White, and the percentage of minority teachers is projected to decrease even further in the coming years.

American anthropologist John Ogbu (1989) proposed the view that ethnic minority students are placed in a position of subordination and exploitation in the American educational system. He believes that students of color, especially African Americans and Latinos, have inferior educational opportunities, are exposed to teachers and school administrators who have low academic expectations for them, and encounter negative stereotypes about ethnic minority groups. In one study of middle schools in predominantly Latino areas of Miami, Latino and White teachers rated African American students as having more behavioral problems than African American teachers rated the same students as having (Zimmerman & others, 1995).

SUMMARY TABLE 17.2
Schools for Adolescents;
Socioeconomic Status, and Ethnicity in Schools

Concept	Processes/ Related Ideas	Characteristics/Description
Schools for Adolescents	The Transition to Middle or Junior High School	• Middle schools have become more popular than junior high schools in recent years to coincide with puberty's earlier arrival. • The transition to middle/junior high school occurs at the same time as many physical, cognitive, and socioemotional changes involved in the transition to adolescence. • This transition is often stressful and involves moving from being a "top dog" to the least powerful position in a school.
	Effective Schools for Young Adolescents	• They take individual differences seriously, show a deep concern for what is known about early adolescence, and stress the importance of socioemotional development at least as much as cognitive development. • The Carnegie Foundation has recommended a major overhaul of America's middle schools.
	High School Dropouts	• This has been a serious problem for decades. • Some progress has been made in reducing dropout rates for African American students, but the dropout rates for Native American and Latino students are still extremely high. • Dropping out of school is associated with demographic, family-related, peer-related, school-related, economic, and individual factors.
Socioeconomic Status and Ethnicity in Schools	Socioeconomic Status	• Children in poverty face problems at home and at school that present barriers to their learning. • Schools in low-income neighborhoods often have fewer resources, have less experienced teachers, and are more likely to encourage rote learning rather than thinking skills.
	Ethnicity	• The school experiences of students from different ethnic groups vary considerably. • It is important for teachers to have positive expectations for students of color. • Comer believes a community, team approach is the best way to educate children. • Aronson created the jigsaw classroom to reduce racial tension.

Like Ogbu, educational psychologist Margaret Beale Spencer (1990, 1999) says that a form of institutional racism permeates many American schools. That is, well-meaning teachers, acting out of misguided liberalism, fail to challenge children of color to achieve. Such teachers prematurely accept a low level of performance from these children, substituting warmth and affection for high standards of academic success.

James Comer (1988; Comer & others, 1996) believes that a community team approach is the best way to educate children. Three important aspects of the Comer Project for Change are (1) a governance and management team that develops a comprehensive school plan, assessment strategy, and staff development plan; (2) a mental health or school support team; and (3) a parent's program. Comer believes that the entire school community should have a cooperative rather than an adversarial attitude. The Comer program is currently operating in more than 600 schools in 26 states.

Teachers can play a powerful role as a cultural mediator by being sensitive to racist content in materials and classroom interactions, learning more about different ethnic groups, being sensitive to children's ethnic attitudes, viewing students of color

Interview with Jonathan Kozol
Exploring Multicultural Education
Multicultural Education Resources
The Comer School Development Program

positively, and thinking of positive ways to get parents of color more involved as partners with teachers in educating children (Banks, 1997; Cushner, 1999).

When Eliot Aronson was a professor at the University of Texas as Austin, the school system contacted him for ideas on how to reduce the increasing racial tension in classrooms. Aronson (1986) developed the concept of "jigsaw classroom," in which students from different cultural backgrounds are placed in a cooperative group in which they have to construct different parts of a project to reach a common goal. Aronson used the term *jigsaw* because he saw the technique as much like a group of students cooperating to put different pieces together to complete a jigsaw puzzle. How might this work? Consider a class of students, some White, some African American, some Latino, and some Asian American. The lesson to be learned by the groups focuses on the life of Joseph Pulitzer. The class might be broken up into groups of six students each, with the groups being as equal as possible in terms of ethnic composition and achievement level. The lesson about Pulitzer's life is divided into six parts, with each part given to a member of each six-person group. The parts might be paragraphs from Pulitzer's biography, such as how the Pulitzer family came to the United States, Pulitzer's childhood, and his early work. All the students in each group are given an allotted time to study their parts. Then the groups meet, and each member tries to teach a part to the group. Learning depends on the students' interdependence and cooperation in reaching the same goal. Sometimes the jigsaw classroom strategy is referred to as creating a superordinate goal or common task for students. Team sports, drama productions, and music performances are examples of contexts in which students cooperatively participate to reach a superordinate goal.

At this point we have discussed a number of ideas about schools for adolescents and about socioeconomic status and ethnicity in schools. A review of these ideas is presented in summary table 17.2 on page 533. Next, we will continue our exploration of schools by examining children with disabilities and their education.

Children with Disabilities

Children with a disability are especially sensitive about their differentness and how it is perceived by others. Life is not always fair for children with a disability. Adjusting to school and to peers is often difficult for them.

Who Are Children with Disabilities?

Approximately 10 percent of all children in the United States receive special education or related services (Reschly, 1996). Figure 17.3 shows the approximate percentages of children with various disabilities who received special education services in the 1994–1995 school year (U.S. Department of Education, 1996).

Within this group, a little more than half have a learning disability. Substantial percentages of children also have speech or language impairments (21 percent of those with disabilities), mental retardation (12 percent), and serious emotional disturbance (9 percent).

Educators now prefer to speak of "children with disabilities" rather than "disabled children" to emphasize the person, not the disability (Culatta & Tompkins, 1999). The term *handicapping conditions* is still used to describe impediments to the learning and functioning of individuals with a disability that have been imposed by society. For example, when children who use a wheelchair do not have adequate access to a bathroom, transportation, and so on, this is referred to as a handicapping condition.

In chapter 9, we discussed one disability: mental retardation. Our further discussion of disabilities here focuses on learning disabilities, attention deficit hyperactivity disorder (ADHD), and the education of children with disabilities.

Learning Disabilities

Paula doesn't like kindergarten and can't seem to remember the names of her teacher and classmates. Bobby's third-grade teacher complains that his spelling is awful. Eleven-year-old Tim says reading is really hard for him, and a lot of times the words don't make much sense. Each of these students has a learning disability.

Characteristics   Children with a **learning disability** *(1) are of normal intelligence or above, (2) have difficulties in at least one academic area and usually several, and (3) have a difficulty that is not attributable to any other diagnosed problem or disorder, such as mental retardation.* The global concept of learning disabilities includes problems in listening, concentrating, speaking, thinking.

About three times as many boys as girls are classified as having a learning disability (U.S. Department of Education, 1996). Among the explanations for this gender difference are a greater biological vulnerability of boys, as well as referral bias (boys are more likely to be referred by teachers for treatment because of their disruptive, hyperactive behavior).

By definition, children do not have a learning disability unless they have an academic problem. Among the most common academic areas in which children with a learning disability have problems are reading, written language, and math (Hallahan & Kaufmann, 2000).

About 5 percent of all school-age children in the United States receive special education or related services because of a learning disability. In the federal classification of children receiving special education and related services, attention deficit hyperactivity disorder (ADHD) is included in the learning disabilities category. Because of the significant interest in ADHD today, we will discuss it by itself following learning disabilities.

In the past two decades, the percentage of children classified as having a learning disability has increased substantially—from less than 30 percent of all children receiving special education and related services in 1977–1978 to a little more than 50 percent today. Some experts say that the dramatic increase reflects poor diagnostic practices and overidentification. They believe that teachers sometimes are too quick to label children with the slightest learning problem as having a learning disability, instead of recognizing that the problem may rest in their ineffective teaching. Other experts say the increase in children being labeled with a "learning disability" is justified (Hallahan & Kaufmann, 2000).

The most common problem that characterizes children with a learning disability involves reading (Kamphaus, 2000; Torgesen, 1999). Such children especially show problems with phonological skills (recall from chapter 10, "Language Development," that these involve being able to understand how sounds and letters match up to make words) (Lyon, 1996). **Dyslexia** *is a category that is reserved for individuals who have a severe impairment in their ability to read and spell.*

Children with a learning disability often have difficulties in handwriting, spelling, or composition. Their writing may be extremely slow, their writing products may be virtually illegible, and they may make numerous spelling errors because of their inability to match up sounds and letters.

Diagnosing whether a child has a learning disability is a difficult task. A learning disability often encompasses co-occurring conditions that can include problems in listening, concentrating, speaking, reading, writing, reasoning, math, or social interaction. Thus, individual children with a learning disability can have very different profiles. Learning disabilities often appear in association with such medical

Exploring Disabilities
Learning Disabilities
Learning Disabilities Association

learning disability
A disability that involves (1) having normal intelligence or above, (2) having difficulties in at least one academic area and usually several, and (3) having no other problem or disorder, such as mental retardation, that can be determined as causing the difficulty.

dyslexia
A category of learning disabilities involving a severe impairment in the ability to read and spell.

Disability	Total[a]	Percentage of Total[b]
Specific learning disabilities	2,513,977	51.1
Speech or language impairments	1,023,665	20.8
Mental retardation	570,855	11.6
Serious emotional disturbance	428,168	8.7
Multiple disabilities	89,646	1.8
Hearing impairments	65,568	1.3
Orthopedic impairments	60,604	1.2
Other health impairments	106,509	2.2
Visual impairments	24,877	0.5
Autism	22,780	0.5
Deaf-blindness	1,331	0.0
Traumatic brain injury	7,188	0.1
All disabilities	4,915,168	100.0

Figure 17.3
The Diversity of Children with Disabilities

[a]The total number of children and adolescents with this disability who received special education services in the 1994–1995 school year. Children with multiple disabilities also have been counted under various single disabilities.
[b]Of all children and adolescents who received special education services in the 1994–1995 school year, the percentage who had this disability.

conditions as lead poisoning and fetal alcohol syndrome (American Psychiatric Association, 1994). And learning disabilities can occur with other disabilities, such as communication disorders and emotional/behavioral disorders (Polloway & others, 1997).

Intervention Strategies   Many interventions have focused on improving the child's reading ability (Lyon & Moats, 1997). For example, in one study, instruction in phonological awareness at the kindergarten level had positive effects on reading development when the children reached the first grade (Blachman & others, 1994).

Unfortunately, not all children who have a learning disability that involves reading problems have the benefit of appropriate early intervention. Most children whose reading disability is not diagnosed until the third grade or later and who receive standard interventions fail to show noticeable improvement (Lyon, 1996). However, intensive instruction over a period of time by a competent teacher can remediate the deficient reading skills of many children. For example, in one study, 65 severely dyslexic children were given 65 hours of individual instruction in addition to group instruction in phonemic awareness and thinking skills (Alexander & others, 1991). The intensive intervention significantly improved the dyslexic children's reading skills.

Children with severe phonological deficits that lead to poor decoding and word recognition skills respond to intervention more slowly than do children with mild to moderate reading problems (Torgesen, 1999). Also, the success of even the best-designed reading intervention depends on the training and skills of the teacher.

Disability in basic reading skills has been the most common target of intervention studies because it is the most common form of learning disability, it is identifiable, and it represents the area of learning disabilities about which there is the most knowledge (Lyon, 1996). Interventions for other types of learning disabilities have been created but have not been extensively researched.

Improving outcomes for children with a learning disability is a challenging task and generally has required intensive intervention for even modest improvement in outcomes. However, no model program has proven to be effective for all children with learning disabilities (Terman & others, 1996).

Attention Deficit Hyperactivity Disorder

Matthew has attention deficit hyperactivity disorder, and the outward signs are typical. He has trouble attending to the teacher's instructions and is easily distracted. He can't sit still for more than a few minutes at a time, and his handwriting is messy. His mother describes him as very fidgety.

Attention deficit hyperactivity disorder (ADHD) *is a disability in which children consistently show one or more of the following characteristics over a period of time: (1) inattention, (2) hyperactivity, and (3) impulsivity.* Children who are inattentive have difficulty focusing on any one thing and may get bored with a task after only a few minutes. Children who are hyperactive show high levels of physical activity, almost always seeming to be in motion. Children who are impulsive have difficulty curbing their reactions and don't do a good job of thinking before they act. Depending on the characteristics that children with ADHD display, they can be diagnosed as (1) ADHD with predominantly inattention, (2) ADHD with predominantly hyperactivity/impulsivity, or (3) ADHD with both inattention and hyperactivity/impulsivity.

The U.S. Office of Education figures on children with a disability that were shown in figure 17.3 include children with ADHD in the category of children with specific learning disabilities, an overall category that comprises slightly more than one-half of all children who receive special education services. The number of children diagnosed and treated for ADHD has increased substantially, by some estimates doubling in the 1990s. The disorder occurs as much as four to nine times more in boys than in girls. There is controversy about the increased diagnosis of ADHD (Terman & others, 1996), however. Some experts attribute the increase mainly to heightened awareness of the disorder. Others are concerned that many children are being diagnosed without undergoing extensive professional evaluation based on input from multiple sources.

ADHD

attention deficit hyperactivity disorder (ADHD)
A disability in which children consistently show one or more of the following characteristics: (1) inattention, (2) hyperactivity, and (3) impulsivity.

Many children with ADHD show impulsive behavior, such as this child who is jumping out of his seat and throwing a paper airplane at other children. How would you handle this situation if this were to happen to your classroom?

Signs of ADHD may be present in the preschool years. Parents and preschool or kindergarten teachers may notice that the child has an extremely high activity level and a limited attention span. They may say the child is "always on the go," "can't sit still even for a second," or "never seems to listen." Many children with ADHD are difficult to discipline, have a low frustration tolerance, and have problems in peer relations. Other common characteristics of children with ADHD include general immaturity and clumsiness.

Although signs of ADHD are often present in the preschool years, their classification often doesn't take place until the elementary school years (Pueschel & others, 1995; Whalen, 2000). The increased academic and social demands of formal schooling, as well as stricter standards for behavioral control, often illuminate the problems of the child with ADHD. Elementary school teachers typically report that this type of child has difficulty in working independently, completing seat work, and organizing work. Restlessness and distractibility also are often noted. These problems are more likely to be observed in repetitive or taxing tasks, or tasks the child perceives to be boring (such as completing worksheets or doing homework).

It used to be thought that ADHD decreased in adolescence, but now it is believed that this often is not the case. Estimates suggest that ADHD decreases in only about one-third of adolescents. Increasingly, it is being recognized that these problems may continue into adulthood.

Definitive causes of ADHD have not been found. For example, scientists have not been able to identify cause-related sites in the brain. However, a number of causes have been proposed, such as low levels of certain neurotransmitters (chemical messengers in

Increasingly, children with disabilities are being taught in the regular classroom, as is this child with mild mental retardation.

the brain), prenatal and postnatal abnormalities, and environmental toxins, such as lead. Heredity also may play a role, as 30 to 50 percent of children with ADHD have a sibling or parent who has the disorder (Woodrich, 1994).

Students with ADHD have a failure rate in school that is two to three times that of other students. About one-half of students with ADHD have repeated a grade by adolescence and more than one-third eventually drop out of school.

Many experts recommend a combination of academic, behavioral, and medical interventions to help students with ADHD learn and adapt more effectively (Appalachia Educational Laboratory, 1998). This intervention requires cooperation and effort on the part of the parents of students with ADHD, school personnel (teachers, administrators, special educators, and school psychologists), and health-care professionals.

It is estimated that about 85 to 90 percent of students with ADHD are taking stimulant medication such as Ritalin to control their behavior (Tousignant, 1995). A child should be given medication only after a complete assessment that includes a physical examination. Typically a small dose is administered as a trial to examine its effects. If the child adequately tolerates the small dose, the dosage might be increased.

The problem behaviors of students with ADHD can be temporarily controlled with prescriptive stimulants (Swanson & others, 1993). For many other children with ADHD, a combination of medication, behavior management, effective teaching, and parental monitoring improves their behavior. However, not all children with ADHD respond positively to prescription stimulants, and some critics believe that physicians are too quick in prescribing stimulants for children with milder forms of ADHD (Clay, 1997).

Educational Issues Involving Children with Disabilities

The legal requirement that schools serve all children with a disability is fairly recent. Beginning in the mid 1960s to mid 1970s, legislatures, the federal courts, and the United States Congress laid down special educational rights for children with disabilities. Prior to that time, most children with a disability were either refused enrollment or inadequately served by schools. In 1975, **Public Law 94-142,** *the Education for All Handicapped Children Act, required that all students with disabilities be given a free, appropriate public education and be provided the funding to help implement this education.*

In 1983, Public Law 94-142 was renamed the **Individuals with Disabilities Education Act (IDEA).** *The IDEA spells out broad mandates for services to all children with disabilities. These include evaluation and eligibility determination, appropriate education and the individualized education plan (IEP), and the least restrictive environment (LRE)* (Martin, Martin, & Terman, 1996).

Evaluation and Eligibility Determination   Children who are thought to have a disability are evaluated to determine their eligibility for services under IDEA. Schools are prohibited from planning special education programs in advance and offering them on a space-available basis.

Children must be evaluated before a school can begin providing special services. Parents should be involved in the evaluation process. Reevaluation is required at least every three years (sometimes every year), when requested by parents, or when conditions suggest a reevaluation can obtain an independent evaluation, which the school is required to consider in providing special education services. If the evaluation finds that the child has a disability and requires special services, the school must provide them to the child.

The IDEA has many specific provisions that relate to the parents of a child with a disability. These include requirements that schools send notices to parents of

Public Law 94-142
The Education for All Handicapped Children Act, created in 1975, which requires that all children with disabilities be given a free, appropriate public education and which provides the funding to help with the costs of implementing this education.

Individuals with Disabilities Education Act (IDEA)
The IDEA spells out broad mandates for services to all children with disabilities (IDEA is a renaming of Public Law 98-142); these include evaluation and eligibility determination, appropriate education and the individualized education plan (IEP), and the least restrictive environment (LRE).

Education of Children Who Are Exceptional

Inclusion

The Council for Exceptional Children

Legal Issues and Disabilities

proposed actions, of attendance at meetings regarding the child's placement or individualized education plan, and of the right to appeal school decisions to an impartial evaluator.

The Individuals with Disabilities Education Act (IDEA), including its 1997 amendments, requires that technology devices and services be provided to students with disabilities if they are necessary to ensure a free, appropriate education (Lewis, 1998).

Two types of technology that can be used to improve the education of students with disabilities are instructional technology and assistance technology. **Instructional technology** *includes various types of hardware and software, combined with innovative teaching methods, to accommodate students' needs in the classroom.* This technology includes videotapes, computer-assisted instruction, and complex hypermedia programs in which computers are used to control the display of audio and visual images stored on videodisc. The use of telecommunication systems, especially the Internet and its World Wide Web, holds considerable promise for improving the education of students with or without a disability.

Assistive technology *consists of various services and devices to help students with disabilities function within their environment.* Examples include communication aids, alternative computer keyboards, and adaptive switches (Elkind, 2000). (see figure 17.4). To locate such services, educators can use computer databases, such as the Device Locator System (Academic Software, 1996).

Figure **17.4**
Special Input Devices
Special input devices can help students with physical disabilities use computers more effectively.

Appropriate Education and the Individualized Education Plan (IEP)

The IDEA requires that students with disabilities have an **individualized education plan (IEP),** *a written statement that spells out a program specifically tailored for the student with a disability. In general, the IEP should be (1) related to the child's learning capacity, (2) specially constructed to meet the child's individual needs and not merely a copy of what is offered to other children, and (3) designed to provide educational benefits.*

Least Restrictive Environment (LRE)

Under the IDEA, a child with a disability must be educated in the **least restrictive environment (LRE).** *This means a setting that is as similar as possible to the one in which children do not have a disability are educated.* This provision of the IDEA has given a legal basis to making an effort to educate children with a disability in the regular classroom (Crockett & Kaufmann, 1999). The term used to describe the education of children with a disability in the regular classroom used to be *mainstreaming.* However, that term has been replaced by the term **inclusion,** *which means educating a child with special education needs full-time in the general school program.* Today, **mainstreaming** *means educating a student with special education needs partially in a special education classroom and partially in a regular classroom.*

Not long ago, it was considered appropriate to educate children with disabilities outside the regular classroom. However, today, schools must make every effort to provide inclusion for children with disabilities (Heward, 2000; Wolery, 2000). These efforts can be very costly financially and very time consuming in terms of faculty effort.

The principle of least restrictive environment compels schools to examine possible modifications of the regular classroom before moving the child with a disability to a more restrictive placement. Also, regular classroom teachers often need specialized training to help some children with a disability, and state educational agencies are required to provide such training.

Many legal changes regarding children with disabilities have been extremely positive. Compared with several decades ago, far more children today are receiving competent, specialized services. For many children, inclusion in the regular classroom, with modifications or supplemental services, is appropriate (Kochhar, West, & Taymans, 2000; Turnbull & others, 1999). However, some experts believe that separate

instructional technology
Various types of hardware and software, combined with innovative teaching methods, to accommodate students' learning needs in the classroom.

assistive technology
Services and devices that help students with disabilities function within their environment.

individualized education plan (IEP)
A written statement that spells out a program tailored to a child with a disability. The plan should be (1) related to the child's learning capacity, (2) specially constructed to meet the child's individual needs and not merely a copy of what is offered to other children, and (3) designed to provide educational benefits.

least restrictive environment (LRE)
The concept that a child with a disability must be educated in a setting that is as similar as possible to the one in which children who do not have a disability are educated.

inclusion
Educating a child with special education needs full-time in the regular classroom.

mainstreaming
Educating a child with special education needs partially in a special education classroom and partially in a regular classroom.

programs may be more effective and appropriate for children with disabilities (Martin, Martin, & Terman, 1996).

At this point we have discussed many ideas about the education of children with disabilities. A review of these ideas is presented in summary table 17.3. Next, we will continue our exploration of schools by focusing on achievement.

ACHIEVEMENT

Need for Achievement

Extrinsic and Intrinsic Motivation

Attribution

Mastery Orientation

Ethnicity and Culture

Goal Setting, Planning, and Self-Monitoring

Self-Efficacy

Achievement

We are a species motivated to do well at what we attempt, to gain mastery over the world in which we live, to explore unknown environments with enthusiasm and curiosity, and to achieve the heights of success. We live in an achievement-oriented world, with standards that tell children success is important. The standards suggest that success requires a competitive spirit, a desire to win, a motivation to do well, and the wherewithal to cope with adversity and to persist until an objective is reached. Some developmentalists, though, believe that we are becoming a nation of hurried, "wired" people who are raising our children to become the same way—uptight about success and failure and far too worried about what we accomplish in comparison with others. It was in the 1950s that an interest in achievement began to flourish. The interest initially focused on the need for achievement.

Need for Achievement

Think about yourself and your friends for a moment. Are you more achievement-oriented than they are, or are you less so? If we were to ask you and your friends to tell stories about achievement-related themes, could we accurately determine which of you is the most achievement-oriented?

Some individuals are highly motivated to succeed and they expend a lot of effort, striving to excel. Other individuals are not as motivated to succeed and don't work as hard to achieve (Brophy, 1998). These two types of individuals vary in their **achievement motivation (need for achievement),** *the desire to accomplish something, to reach a standard of excellence, and to expend effort to excel.* David McClelland (1955) assessed achievement by showing individuals ambiguous pictures that were likely to stimulate achievement-related responses. The individuals were asked to tell a story about the picture, and their comments were scored according to how strongly they reflected achievement.

A host of studies have correlated achievement-related responses with different aspects of the individual's experiences and behavior (Winter, 2000). The findings are diverse, but they suggest that achievement-oriented individuals have a stronger hope for success than a fear of failure, are moderate rather than high or low in risk taking, and persist for appropriate lengths of time in solving difficult problems. Early research had indicated that independence training by parents promotes children's achievement, but more recent research reveals that parents, to increase achievement, need to set high standards for achievement, model achievement-oriented behavior, and reward their children for their achievements. And, in one study, the middle school students who had the highest grades were those whose parents, teachers, and schools were authoritative (Paulson, Marchant, & Rothlisberg, 1995).

Extrinsic and Intrinsic Motivation

We begin our coverage of extrinsic and intrinsic motivation by examining what they are, then turn to a number of ideas about how they work best in learning and achievement.

What Are Extrinsic and Intrinsic Motivation?   The behavioral perspective emphasizes the importance of extrinsic motivation in achievement. **Extrinsic motivation** *involves external incentives such as rewards and punishments.* The

achievement motivation
(need for achievement) The desire to accomplish something, to reach a standard of excellence, and to expend effort to excel.

extrinsic motivation
External incentives such as rewards and punishments.

SUMMARY TABLE 17.3
Children with Disabilities

Concept	Processes/Related Ideas	Characteristics/Description
Who Are Children with Disabilities?	Scope of Problems	• An estimated 10 percent of U.S. children with a disability receive special education services. • Slightly more than 50 percent of these children are classified as having a learning disability.
Learning Disabilities	Characteristics	• Children with learning disabilities are of normal intelligence or above, have difficulties in at least one academic area and usually several, and have a difficulty that is not attributable to another diagnosed problem. • About three times as many boys as girls have a learning disability. • The most common problem involves reading. Dyslexia is a severe impairment in the ability to read and spell. • Controversy surrounds the learning disability category with some experts believing it is overdiagnosed, others arguing that it is not.
	Intervention Strategies	• Many focus on improving the child's reading ability.
Attention Deficit Hyperactivity Disorder	Characteristics	• ADHD is a disability in which children consistently show problems in one or more of these areas: (1) ADHD with predominantly inattention, (2) ADHD with predominantly hyperactivity/impulsivity, or (3) ADHD with both of these categories present.
	Causes and Treatment	• Definitive causes have not been found. • Many experts recommend a combination of academic, behavioral, and medical interventions to help students with ADHD learn more effectively.
Educational Issues Involving Children with Disabilities	Legal Aspects	• A number of laws have been passed that spell out the rights for children with disabilities.
	Evaluation and Eligibility	• The IDEA spells out broad mandates for services to all children with disabilities. • Children must be evaluated before a school can begin providing special services.
	Appropriate Education and the Individualized Education Plan (IEP)	• An IEP consists of a written plan that spells out a program tailored to a child with a disability. • The concept of inclusion is contained in the IEP. Inclusion involves educating the child with a disability in setting that is as similar as possible to the one in which children without disabilities are educated.

humanistic and cognitive approaches stress the importance of intrinsic motivation in achievement. **Intrinsic motivation** *is based on internal factors such as self-determination, curiosity, challenge, and effort.* Some adolescents study hard because they want to make good grades or avoid parental disapproval (extrinsic motivation). Other adolescents study hard because they are internally motivated to achieve high standards in their work (intrinsic motivation).

intrinsic motivation
Internal factors such as self-determination, curiosity, challenge, and effort.

Self-Determination and Personal Choice
One view of intrinsic motivation emphasizes self-determination (deCharms, 1984; Deci & Ryan, 1994). In this view, adolescents want to believe that they are doing something because of their own will, not because of external success or rewards.

Researchers have found that giving adolescents some choice and providing opportunities for personal responsibility increases their internal motivation and intrinsic interest in school tasks (Stipek, 1996). For example, one study found that

The reward of a thing well done is to have done it.

Ralph Waldo Emerson
American Poet and Essayist, 19th Century

Motivation and Achievement
Intrinsic Motivation

high school science students who were encouraged to organize their own experiments demonstrated more care and interest in laboratory work than their counterparts who were given detailed instructions and directions (Rainey, 1965). In another study, which included mainly African American students from low-income backgrounds, teachers were encouraged to give the students more responsibility for their school program (deCharms, 1984). This consisted of opportunities to set their own goals, plan how to reach the goals, and monitor their progress toward the goals. Students were given some choice of activities to engage in and when they would do them. They also were encouraged to take personal responsibility for their behavior, including reaching the goals that they had set. Compared to a control group, students in the intrinsic motivation/self-determination group had higher achievement gains and were more likely to graduate from high school.

Effects of Rewards   In some situations, rewards can actually undermine learning. In one study, students who already had a strong interest in art spent more time drawing when they did not expect a reward than did their counterparts who also had a strong interest in art but knew they would be rewarded (Lepper, Greene, & Nisbett, 1973). Other researchers have found similar effects (Morgan, 1984).

However, classroom rewards can be useful (Eisenberger & Cameron, 1998). Two uses are (Bandura, 1982; Deci, 1975): (1) as an incentive to engage in tasks, in which case the goal is to control the student's behavior, and (2) as information about mastery. When rewards convey information about mastery, they are more likely to promote student feelings of competence. However, rewards used as incentives lead to perceptions that the student's behavior was caused by the external reward rather than by the student's own motivation to be competent.

To better understand the difference between using rewards to control students' behavior and using them to provide information about mastery, consider this example (Schunk, 1996). A teacher puts a reward system in place in which the more work students accomplish, the more points they will earn. Students will be motivated to work to earn points because the points can be exchanged for privileges, but the points also provide information about their capabilities. That is, the more points students earn, the more work they have accomplished. As they accumulate points, students are more likely to feel competent. In contrast, if points are provided simply for spending time on a task, the task might be perceived as a means to an end. In this case, because the points don't convey anything about capabilities, students are likely to perceive that the rewards control their behavior.

Thus, rewards convey information about students' mastery can increase intrinsic motivation by increasing their sense of competence. However, negative feedback, such as criticism, that carries information that students are *in*competent can undermine intrinsic motivation, especially if students doubt their ability to become competent (Stipek, 1996).

In the next section, our attention shifts to attribution. As you read about attribution, you will see that intrinsic and extrinsic motivation are often one set of causes that adolescents look to as they attempt to explain their behavior.

Attribution

Attribution theory *states that in their effort to make sense out of their own behavior or performance individuals are motivated to discover its underlying causes. Attributions are perceived causes of outcomes.* In a way, attribution theorists say, adolescents are like intuitive scientists, seeking to explain the cause behind what happens (Weary, 2000). For example, an adolescent asks "Why am I not doing well in this class?" "Did I get a good grade because I studied hard or because the teacher gave an easy test, or both?" The search for a cause or explanation is most likely to be initiated when unexpected and important events end in failure, such as when a good student gets a low grade (Graham & Weiner, 1996). Among the most frequently inferred causes of success and failure are ability, effort, task ease or difficulty, luck, mood, and help or hindrance from others.

Bernard Weiner (1986, 1992) identified three dimensions of causal attributions: (1) *Locus* refers to whether the cause is internal or external to the actor; (2) *stability* focuses on the extent to which the cause remains the same or changes; (3) *controllability* is the extent to which the individual can control the cause. For example, an adolescent might perceive his aptitude as being internal, stable, and uncontrollable. The adolescent might also perceive chance or luck as external to himself, variable, and uncontrollable. Figure 17.5 lists eight possible combinations of locus, stability, and controllability and how they match up with various common explanations of failure.

To see how attributions affect subsequent achievement strivings, consider these two adolescents (Graham & Weiner, 1996):

- Jane flunks her math test. She subsequently seeks tutoring and increases her study time.
- Susan also fails her math test but decides to drop out of school.

Jane's negative outcome (failing the test) motivated her to search for the reasons behind her low grade. She attributes the failure to herself, not blaming her teacher or bad luck. She also attributes the failure to an unstable factor—lack of preparation and study time. Thus, she perceives that her failure is due to internal, unstable, and also controllable factors. Because she sees the factors as unstable, Jane has a reasonable expectation that she can still succeed in the future. And because she sees the factors as controllable, she also feels guilty. Her expectations for success enable her to overcome her deflated sense of self-esteem. Her hope for the future results in renewed goal-setting and increased motivation to do well on the next test.

Susan's negative outcome (also failing the test) led her to drop out of school rather than resolve to study harder. Her failure also stimulates her to make causal attributions. Susan ascribes failure to herself and attributes her poor performance to lack of ability, which is internal, unstable, and uncontrollable. Because she sees the cause as internal, her self-esteem suffers. Because she sees it as stable, she sees failure in her future and has a helpless feeling that she can't do anything about it. And because she sees it as uncontrollable, she feels ashamed and humiliated. In addition, her parents and teacher tell her they feel sorry for her

attribution theory
The theory that, in their effort to make sense out of their own behavior or performance, individuals are motivated to discover its underlying causes. Attributions are perceived causes of outcomes.

Attribution
Effort, Expectations, and Motivation

When students fail or do poorly on a test or assignment, they often generate causal attributions in an attempt to explain the poor performance. The following explanations reflect eight combinations of Weiner's three main categories of attributions: locus (internal-external), stability (stable-unstable), and controllability (controllable-uncontrollable).

Combination of Causal Attributions	Reason Students Give for Failure
Internal-Stable-Uncontrollable	Low aptitude
Internal-Stable-Controllable	Never study
Internal-Unstable-Uncontrollable	Sick the day of the test
Internal-Unstable-Controllable	Did not study for this particular test
External-Stable-Uncontrollable	School has tough requirements
External-Stable-Controllable	The instructor is biased
External-Unstable-Uncontrollable	Bad luck
External-Unstable-Controllable	Friends failed to help

Figure **17.5**

Combinations of Causal Attributions and Explanations for Failure

Through the Eyes of Psychologists

Carol Dweck, *Columbia University*

"Mastery-oriented adolescents see failure as an interlude between past and future successes and as an opportunity for new learning and mastery."

helpless orientation
An orientation in which one seems trapped by the experience of difficulty and attributes one's difficulty to a lack of ability.

mastery orientation   An orientation in which one is task-oriented and, instead of focusing on one's ability, is concerned with learning strategies.

performance orientation
An orientation in which one focuses on achievement outcomes; winning is what matters most, and happiness is thought to result from winning.

Mastery Motivation
Exploring Self-Efficacy
Self-Efficacy Resources

self-efficacy
The belief that one can master a situation and produce favorable outcomes.

but don't provide any recommendations or strategies for success, furthering her belief that she is incompetent. With low expectations for success, low self-esteem, and a depressed mood, Susan decides to drop out of school.

What are the best strategies for teachers to use in helping students like Susan to change their attributions? Educational psychologists often recommend providing students with a planned series of experiences in achievement contexts in which modeling, information about strategies, practice, and feedback are used to help them (1) concentrate on the task at hand rather than worrying about failing, (2) cope with failures by retracing their steps to discover their mistake or analyzing the problem to discover another approach, and (3) attribute their failures to a lack of effort rather than lack of ability (Brophy, 1998; Dweck & Elliott, 1983).

With regard to modeling, rather than exposing adolescents to models who handle tasks with ease and demonstrate success, they should be presented with models who struggle to overcome mistakes before finally succeeding (Brophy, 1998). In this way, adolescents learn how to deal with frustration, persist in the face of difficulties, and constructively cope with failure.

Mastery Orientation

Closely related to an emphasis on intrinsic motivation, attributions of internal causes of behavior, and the importance of effort in achievement is a mastery orientation. Developmental psychologists Valanne Henderson and Carol Dweck (1990) have found that children show two distinct responses to difficult or challenging circumstances. Individuals with a **helpless orientation** *seem trapped by the experience of difficulty, and they attribute their difficulty to lack of ability.* They frequently say such things as "I'm not very good at this," even though they might earlier have demonstrated their ability through many successes. And, once they view their behavior as failure, they often feel anxious, and their performance worsens even further. Individuals with a **mastery orientation** *are task-oriented; instead of focusing on their ability, they are concerned about their learning strategies and the process of achievement rather than outcomes.* Mastery-oriented children often instruct themselves to pay attention, to think carefully, and to remember strategies that have worked for them in previous situations. They frequently report feeling challenged and excited by difficult tasks, rather than being threatened by them (Anderman, Maehr, & Midgley, 1996).

Another issue in motivation involves whether to adopt a mastery or a performance orientation. We have already described a mastery orientation. A **performance orientation** *involves being concerned with the achievement outcome; winning is what matters, and happiness is thought to result from winning.*

What sustains mastery-oriented individuals is the self-efficacy and satisfaction they feel from dealing effectively with the world in which they live. By contrast, what sustains performance-oriented individuals is winning. Although skills can be, and often are, involved in winning, performance-oriented individuals do not necessarily view themselves as having skills. Rather, they see themselves as using tactics, such as undermining others, to get what they want.

Does all of this mean that mastery-oriented individuals do not like to win and that performance-oriented individuals are not motivated to experience the self-efficacy that comes from being able to take credit for one's accomplishments? No. A matter of emphasis or degree is involved, though. For mastery-oriented individuals, winning isn't everything; for performance-oriented individuals, skill development and self-efficacy take a back seat to winning.

Self-Efficacy

Self-efficacy *is the belief that one can master a situation and produce favorable outcomes.* Albert Bandura (1994, 1997, 2000), whose social cognitive theory we described in chapter 2, "The Science of Child Development," believes that self-efficacy is a critical factor in whether or not students achieve ◀║║ P. 42. Self-efficacy has much in common with mastery motivation and intrinsic motivation. Self-efficacy is the belief that "I can"; helplessness is the belief that "I cannot" (Stipek, 1996). Students with high self-efficacy endorse such statements as "I know that I will be able to learn the material in this class" and "I expect to be able to do well at this activity."

Dale Schunk (1989, 1991) has applied the concept of self-efficacy to many aspects of students' achievement. In his view, self-efficacy influences a student's choice of activities. Students with low self-efficacy for learning may avoid many learning tasks, especially those that are challenging. By contrast, high-self-efficacy counterparts eagerly work at learning tasks. High-self-efficacy students are more likely to expend effort and persist longer at a learning task than low-self-efficacy students.

Bandura (1997) also addressed the characteristics of efficacious schools. School leaders seek ways to improve instruction. They figure out ways to work around stifling policies and regulations that impede academic innovations. Masterful academic leadership by the principal builds teachers' sense of instructional efficacy, while in low-achieving schools, principals function more as administrators and disciplinarians (Coladarci, 1991).

High expectations and standards for achievement pervade efficacious schools. Teachers regard their students as capable of high academic achievement, set challenging academic standards for them, and provide support to help them reach these high standards. In contrast, in low-achieving schools not much is expected academically of students, teachers spend less time actively teaching and monitoring students' academic progress, and they tend to write off a high percentage of students as unteachable (Brookover & others, 1979). Not surprisingly, students in such schools have low self-efficacy and a sense of academic futility.

They can because they think they can.

Virgil
Roman Poet, 1st Century B.C.

Goal Setting, Planning, and Self-Monitoring

Researchers have found that self-efficacy and achievement improve when individuals set goals that are specific, proximal, and challenging (Bandura, 1997; Schunk, 1996). A nonspecific, fuzzy goal is "I want to be successful." A more concrete, specific goal is "I want to make the honor roll by the end of the semester."

Individuals can set both long-term (distal) and short-term (proximal) goals. It is okay for individuals to set some long-term goals, such as "I want to graduate from high school" or "I want to go to college," but they also need to create short-term goals, which are steps along the way. "Getting an A on the next math test" is an example of a short-term, proximal goal. So is "Doing all of my homework by 4 P.M. Sunday." David McNally (1990), author of *Even Eagles Need a Push*, advises that when individuals set goals and plan, they should be reminded to live their lives one day at a time. Have them make their commitments in bite-size chunks. A house is built one brick at a time, a cathedral one stone at a time. The artist paints one stroke at a time. The student should also work in small increments.

Another good strategy is for individuals to set challenging goals. A challenging goal is a commitment to self-improvement. Strong interest and involvement in activities are sparked by challenges. Goals that are easy to reach generate little interest or effort. However, goals should be optimally matched to the individual's skill level. If goals are unrealistically high, the result will be repeated failures that lower the individual's self-efficacy.

Carol Dweck (1996; Dweck & Leggett, 1988) and John Nicholls (1979) define goals in terms of immediate achievement-related focus and definition of success. For example, Nicholls distinguishes between ego-involved goals, task-involved goals, and work-avoidant goals. Individuals who have ego-involved goals strive to maximize favorable evaluations and minimize unfavorable ones. For example, ego-involved individuals focus on how smart they will look and how effectively they can outperform others. In contrast, individuals who have task-involved goals focus on mastering tasks. They concentrate on how they can do the task and what they will learn. Individuals with work-avoidant goals try to exert as little effort as possible when faced with a task.

It is not enough just to get individuals to set goals. It also is important to encourage them to plan how they will reach their goals. Being a good planner means managing time effectively, setting priorities, and being organized.

Goal Setting

Individuals not only should plan their next week's activities but also monitor how well they are sticking to their plan. Once engaged in a task, they need to monitor their progress, judge how well they are doing on the task, and evaluate the outcomes to regulate what they do in the future (Eccles, Wigfield, & Schiefele, 1998). Researchers have found that high-achieving adolescents often are self-regulatory learners (Pressley & Wolosyhn, 1995; Schunk & Zimmerman, 1994; Zimmerman, 2000). For example, high-achieving adolescents self-monitor their learning more and systematically evaluate their progress toward a goal more than low-achieving students do (Pintrich, in press). Encouraging adolescents to self-monitor their learning conveys the message that adolescents are responsible for their own behavior and that learning requires active dedicated participation by the adolescent (Zimmerman, Bonner, & Kovach, 1996).

In sum, we have seen that a number of psychological and motivational factors influence children's achievement. Especially important in the child's ability to adapt to new academic and social pressures are achievement motivation, internal attributions of causes of behavior, intrinsic motivation, a mastery orientation and goal setting, planning, and self-regulation. Next, we examine the roles of ethnicity and culture in achievement.

Ethnicity and Culture

What is the nature of achievement in ethnic minority children? How does culture influence children's achievement?

Ethnicity   The diversity that exists among ethnic minority children is evident in their achievement. For example, many Asian American students have a strong academic achievement orientation, but some do not.

In addition to recognizing the diversity that exists within every cultural group in terms of their achievement, it also is important to distinguish between difference and deficiency. Too often, the achievement of ethnic minority students—especially African Americans, Latinos, and Native Americans—has been interpreted as *deficits* by middle-socioeconomic-status White standards, when they simply are *culturally different and distinct* (Jones, 1994).

At the same time, many investigations overlook the socioeconomic status of ethnic minority students. In many instances, when ethnicity *and* socioeconomic status are investigated in a study, socioeconomic status predicts achievement better than ethnicity does. Students from middle- and upper-income families fare better than their counterparts from low-income backgrounds in a host of achievement situations—for example, expectations for success, achievement aspirations, and recognition of the importance of effort (Gibbs, 1989).

Sandra Graham (1986, 1990) has conducted a number of studies that reveal not only stronger socioeconomic-status than ethnic differences in achievement but also the importance of studying ethnic minority student motivation in the context of general motivational theory. Her inquiries fall within the framework of attribution theory and focus on the causes that African American students give for their achievement orientation, such as why they succeed or fail. She is struck by how consistently middle-income African American students do not fit the stereotype of being unmotivated. Like their White middle-income counterparts, they have high achievement expectations and understand that failure is usually due to a lack of effort, rather than bad luck.

A special challenge for many ethnic minority students, especially those living in poverty, is dealing with racial prejudice, conflict between the values of their group and those of the majority group, and a lack of high-achieving adults in their cultural group who can serve as positive role models.

ADVENTURES FOR THE MIND

Personalizing Achievement

EXAMINE YOUR LIFE and the achievement-related experiences that you have had that you think convey some important messages about achievement. Especially think about experiences you had in middle school or high school. How did you handle the achievement challenges? Looking back, do you wish you had coped with these experiences differently?

It also is important to consider the nature of the schools that primarily serve ethnic minority students (Eccles, Wigfield, & Schiefele, 1998; Spencer, 1999). More than one third of all African American and almost one third of all Latino students attend schools in the 47 largest city school districts in the United States, compared with only 5 percent of all White and 22 percent of all Asian American students. Many of these ethnic minority students come from low-income families (more than one half are eligible for free or reduced-cost lunches). These inner-city schools are less likely than other schools to serve more advantaged populations or to offer high-quality academic support services, advanced courses, and courses that challenge students' active thinking skills. Even students who are motivated to learn and achieve may find it difficult to perform effectively in such contexts.

Asian grade schools intersperse studying with frequent periods of activities. This approach helps children maintain their attention and likely makes learning more enjoyable. Shown here are Japanese fourth-graders making wearable masks.

Culture   In the past decade, the poor performance of American children in math and science has become well publicized. For example, in one cross-national comparison of the math and science achievement of 9- to 13-year-old students, the United States finished 13th (out of 15) in science and 15th (out of 16) in math achievement (Educational Testing Service, 1992). In this study, Korean and Taiwanese students placed first and second, respectively.

Harold Stevenson's (1995; Stevenson, Hofer, & Randel, 2000; Stevenson & others, 1990) research explores reasons for the poor performance of American students. Stevenson and his colleagues have completed five cross-cultural comparisons of students in the United States, China, Taiwan, and Japan. In these studies, Asian students consistently outperform American students. And, the longer the students are in school, the wider the gap becomes between Asian and American students—the lowest difference is in the first grade, the highest in the eleventh grade (the highest grade studied).

To learn more about the reasons for these large cross-cultural differences, Stevenson and his colleagues spent thousands of hours observing in classrooms, as well as interviewing and surveying teachers, students, and parents. They found that the Asian teachers spent more of their time teaching math than did the American teachers. For example, more than one fourth of total classroom time in the first grade was spent on math instruction in Japan, compared with only one tenth of the time in the U.S. first-grade classrooms. Also, the Asian students were in school an average of 240 days a year, compared with 178 days in the United States.

In addition to the substantially greater time spent on math instruction in the Asian schools than the American schools, differences were found between the Asian and American parents. The American parents had much lower expectations for their children's education and achievement than did the Asian parents. Also, the American parents were more likely to believe that their children's math achievement was due to innate ability; the Asian parents were more likely to say that their children's math achievement was the consequence of effort and training. The Asian students were more likely to do math homework than were the American students, and the Asian parents were far more likely to help their children with their math homework than were the American parents (Chen & Stevenson, 1989).

Critics of the cross-national comparisons argue that, in many comparisons, virtually all U.S. children are being compared with a "select" group of children from other countries, especially in the secondary school comparisons. Therefore, they conclude, it is no wonder that American students don't fare so well. That criticism holds for some international comparisons. However, even when the top 25 percent of students in different countries were recently compared, U.S. students move up some, but not a lot (Mullis & others, 1998).

At this point we have studied a number of ideas about achievement. A review of these ideas is presented in summary table 17.4.

Harold Stevenson's Research

Through the Eyes of Psychologists

Harold Stevenson, *University of Michigan*

"We [the United States] accept performances in students that are nowhere near where they should be."

SUMMARY TABLE 17.4
Achievement

Concept	Processes/ Related Ideas	Characteristics/Description
Need for Achievement	The Achievement Motive	• Achievement motivation (need for achievement) is the desire to accomplish something, to reach a standard of excellence, and to expend effort to excel. • Links between parenting practices and children's achievement have been found.
Extrinsic and Intrinsic Motivation	Extrinsic Motivation	• This involves external incentives such as rewards and punishments.
	Intrinsic Motivation	• This is based on internal factors such as self-determination, curiosity, challenge, and effort. • Giving students some choice and providing opportunities for personal responsibility increase intrinsic motivation.
	Rewards	• In some situations, rewards can undermine motivation. When rewards are used, they should convey information about mastery rather than external control.
Attribution	Attribution Theory	• Attribution theory states that individuals are motivated to discover the underlying causes of behavior in an effort to make sense of the behavior.
	Weiner's View	• Weiner identified three dimensions of causal attribution: locus, stability, and controllability. Combinations of these dimensions produce different explanations of failure.
Mastery Orientation	Comparisons with Helpless and Performance Orientations	• A mastery orientation focuses on the task rather than ability, involves positive affect, and includes solution-oriented strategies. • A helpless orientation focuses on personal inadequacies, attributing difficulty to lack of ability. Negative affect (boredom, anxiety, for example) also is present. • A performance orientation involves being concerned with achievement outcome rather than achievement process. • Mastery orientation is the preferred achievement orientation.
Self-Efficacy	Its Nature	• This is the belief that one can master a situation and produce positive outcomes. Bandura believes that self-efficacy is a critical factor in whether students will achieve. • Schunk argues that self-efficacy influences a student's choice of tasks, with low-efficacy students avoiding many learning tasks.
Goal Setting, Planning, and Self-Monitoring	Goals	• Setting specific, proximal (short-term), and challenging goals benefits students' self-efficacy and achievement. • Dweck and Nicholls define goals in terms of immediate achievement-related focus and definition of success.
	Planning	• Being a good planner means managing time effectively, setting priorities, and being organized.
	Self-Monitoring	• Self-monitoring is a key aspect of self-regulation and benefits student learning.
Ethnicity and Culture	Ethnicity	• Too often, researchers have characterized minority groups in terms of deficits. • When studying ethnic minority children, it is important to consider their socioeconomic status.
	Culture	• American children are more achievement-oriented than children in many countries, but are less achievement-oriented than many children in Asian countries such as China, Taiwan, and Japan.

Chapter Review

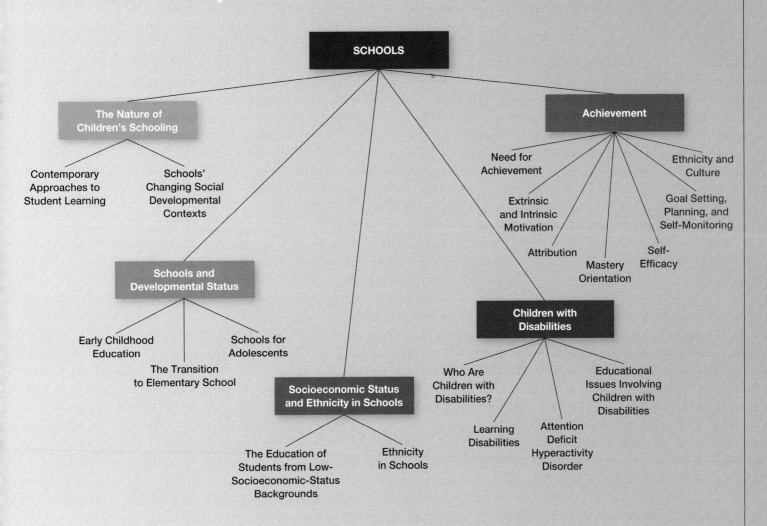

TO OBTAIN A DETAILED REVIEW OF THE CHAPTER, STUDY THESE FOUR SUMMARY TABLES:

Key Terms

Key People

Child Development Resources

Educational Psychology (2001)
    by John Santrock
    New York: McGraw-Hill

Read here about many aspects of schools, teaching, and learning.

Exceptional Children (8th ed.) (2000)
    by Daniel Hallahan and James Kaufmann
    Boston: Allyn & Bacon

This book gives in-depth coverage of learning disabilities, ADHD, and other disabilities.

Motivating Students to Learn (1998)
    by Jere Brophy
    New York: McGraw-Hill

Here you will find an in-depth exploration of many issues in motivation and schooling.

Motivation to Succeed (1998)
    by Jacquelynne Eccles, Alan Wigfield, and Ulrich Schiefle
    in W. Damon (Ed.), *Handbook of Child Psychology (5th Ed., Vol. 3)*
    New York: Wiley

Leading experts on achievement motivation and schools analyze many areas of research.

Taking It to the Net

1. Mark is going to teach high school mathematics. He has read that parents' involvement in their children's education is virtually nonexistent by the time the kids reach high school. What can Mark do as a teacher to encourage parental involvement.

2. Eight-year-old Grace has just been diagnosed with dyslexia. Her parents have no idea what causes the disorder or how to help her. What causes dyslexia? And what can be done to help Grace?

3. Karen is on a school board committee studying how the transition to middle school can decrease student motivation and lead to social and academic problems that might continue into high school. She wants to present an overview of the psychological research on this issue. What have psychologists found to be the negative roles that middle schools play in achievement and motivation?

Connect to *http://www.mhhe.com/santrockc9* to find the answers!

Chapter 18

CULTURE

Culture and Children's Development

The Nature of Culture

The Relevance of Culture to the Study of Children

Cross-Cultural Comparisons

Socioeconomic Status and Poverty

The Nature of Socioeconomic Status

Socioeconomic Variations in Families, Neighborhoods, and Schools

Poverty

Ethnicity

The Nature of Ethnicity

Ethnicity and Socioeconomic Status

Differences and Diversity

Prejudice, Discrimination, and Bias

Assimilation and Pluralism

America: A Nation of Blended Cultures

Technology

Television

Computers and the Internet

Culture

The Stories of Sonya's and Michael's Cultural Conflicts

SONYA, A 16-year-old Japanese American girl was upset over her family's reaction to her White American boyfriend. Her parents refused to meet him and more than once threatened to disown her. Her older brothers also reacted angrily to Sonya's dating a White American, warning that they were going to beat him up. Her parents were also disturbed that Sonya's grades, above average in middle school, were beginning to drop.

Generational issues contributed to the conflict between Sonya and her family (Nagata, 1989). Her parents had experienced strong sanctions against dating Whites when they were growing up and were legally prevented from marrying anyone but a Japanese. As Sonya's older brothers were growing up, they valued ethnic pride and solidarity. The brothers saw her dating a White as "selling out" her own ethnic group. Sonya's and her family members' cultural values obviously differ.

Michael, a 17-year-old Chinese American high school student, was referred to an outpatient adolescent crisis center by the school counselor for depression and suicidal tendencies (Huang & Ying, 1989). Michael was failing several subjects and was repeatedly absent or late for school. Michael's parents were successful professionals who told the therapist that there was nothing wrong with them or with Michael's younger brother and sister, so what, they wondered, was wrong with Michael? What was wrong was that the parents expected all of their children to become doctors. They were frustrated and angered by Michael's school failures, especially since he was the firstborn son, who in Chinese families is expected to achieve the highest standards of all siblings.

The therapist underscored the importance of the parents' putting less pressure for achievement on Michael and gradually introduced more realistic expectations for Michael (who was not interested in becoming a doctor and did not have the necessary academic record anyway). The therapist supported Michael's desire not to become a doctor and empathized with the pressure he had experienced from his parents. As Michael's school attendance improved, his parents noted his improved attitude toward school and supported a continuation of therapy. Michael's case illustrates how expectations that Asian American youth will be "whiz kids" can become destructive.

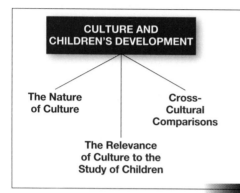

CULTURE AND CHILDREN'S DEVELOPMENT

The Nature of Culture

Cross-Cultural Comparisons

The Relevance of Culture to the Study of Children

culture
The behavior, patterns, beliefs, and all other products of a particular group of people that are passed on from generation to generation.

The Web of Culture
Global Internet Communication
The Global Lab Project
Worldwide Classroom

Through the Eyes of Psychologists

Richard Brislin, *East-West Center, Honolulu*

"A major difficulty in discussions of culture is that individuals rarely have the opportunity to examine the influence of their own cultural background on their behavior."

Culture and Children's Development

Sonya's and Michael's circumstances underscore the importance of culture in understanding children's development. The cultural heritage of the families had a strong influence on the conflict Sonya and Michael experienced in their families and on their behavior outside of the family—in Sonya's case, dating; in Michael's case, school. Of course, a family's cultural background does not always produce conflict between children and other family members, but the two cases described here reveal the importance of understanding a family's cultural values, especially those of ethnic minority families.

The Nature of Culture

In chapter 1, we defined **culture** *as the behavior, patterns, beliefs, and all other products of a particular group of people that are passed on from generation to generation.* The products result from the interaction between groups of people and their environment over many years ◀▥ P. 12.

The concept of culture is broad—it includes many components and can be analyzed in many ways (Berry, 2000). Already in previous chapters we have analyzed the nature of a number of sociocultural contexts in children's development—families, peers, and schools, for example. In this chapter, we will focus on these aspects of culture, including cross-cultural comparisons, socioeconomic status and poverty, ethnicity, and technology.

Cross-cultural expert Richard Brislin (1993) described a number of characteristics of culture:

- Culture is made up of ideals, values, and assumptions about life that guide people's behavior.
- Culture consists in those aspects of the environment that people make.
- Culture is transmitted from generation to generation, with the responsibility for the transmission resting on the shoulders of parents, teachers, and community leaders.
  - Culture's influence becomes noticed the most in well-meaning clashes between people from very different cultural backgrounds.
  - Despite compromises, cultural values still remain.
  - When their cultural values are violated or their cultural expectations are ignored, people react emotionally.
  - It is not unusual for people to accept a cultural value at one point in their lives and reject it at another point. For example, rebellious adolescents and young adults might accept a culture's values and expectations after having children of their own.

The Relevance of Culture to the Study of Children

If the study of child development is to be a relevant discipline in the twenty-first century, increased attention will need to be given to the study of culture and ethnicity (Greenfield, 2000; Greenfield & Suzuki, 1998; Rubin, 1998; Valsiner, 2000). The future will bring extensive contact between people from varied cultural and ethnic backgrounds. Schools and neighborhoods can no longer be the fortresses of one privileged group whose agenda is the exclusion of those with different skin colors or different customs. Immigrants, refugees, and ethnic minority individuals increasingly refuse to become part of a homogeneous melting pot, instead requesting that schools, employers, and governments honor many of their cultural customs. Adult refugees and immigrants might find more opportunities and better-paying jobs in the United States, but their children may learn attitudes in U.S. schools that challenge traditional authority patterns in the home (Brislin, 1993).

For the most part, the study of children has been ethnocentric, emphasizing American values, especially middle-socioeconomic-status, White, male values (Matsumoto, 1997). Cross-cultural psychologists point out that many of the assumptions about contemporary ideas in fields like child development were developed in Western cultures (Triandis, 1994). One example of **ethnocentrism**—*the tendency to favor one's own group over other groups*—is the American emphasis on the individual or self. Many Eastern countries, such as Japan, China, and India, are group oriented. So is Mexican culture. Shortly, we will further discuss the individual and group emphases in cultures.

Research by American psychologist Donald Campbell and his colleagues (Brewer & Campbell, 1976; Campbell & LeVine, 1968) revealed that people in all cultures tend to

- believe that what happens in their culture is "natural" and "correct" and that what happens in other cultures is "unnatural" and "incorrect"
- perceive their cultural customs as universally valid, that is, believe that "what is good for us is good for everyone"
- behave in ways that favor their cultural group
- feel hostile toward other cultural groups

Global interdependence is no longer a matter of belief or choice. It is an inescapable reality. Children and their parents are not just citizens of the United States, or Canada, or another country. They are citizens of the world, a world that, through advances in transportation and technology, has become increasingly interactive. By better understanding the behavior and values of cultures around the world, we may be able to interact more effectively with each other and make this planet a more hospitable, peaceful place in which to live (Brislin, 2000; Matsumoto, 2000).

Cross-Cultural Comparisons

Early in this century, overgeneralizations about the universal aspects of children were made based on data and experience in a single culture—the middle-class culture of the United States (Havighurst, 1976). For example, it was believed that adolescents everywhere went through a period of "storm and stress" characterized by self-doubt and conflict. However, when anthropologist Margaret Mead visited the island of Samoa, she found that adolescents of the Samoan culture were not experiencing such stress.

Mead (1928) studied adolescents on the South Seas island of Samoa. She concluded that the basic nature of adolescents is not biological, as G. Stanley Hall envisioned, but rather sociocultural. She argued that when cultures provide a smooth, gradual transition from childhood to adulthood, which is the way adolescence is handled in Samoa, little storm and stress are associated with the period. Mead's observations of Samoan adolescents revealed that their lives were relatively free of storm and stress. Mead concluded that cultures that allow adolescents to

©2000 Sidney Harris. Used by permission of Sidney Harris.

Anthropologist Margaret Mead (left) with a Samoan adolescent girl. Mead found that adolescence in Samoa was relatively stress-free, although recently her findings have been challenged. Mead's observations and analysis challenged G. Stanley Hall's biological, storm-and-stress view and called attention to the sociocultural basis of adolescence.

ethnocentrism
A tendency to favor one's group over other groups.

cross-cultural studies
Studies that compare a culture with one or more other cultures. Such studies provide information about the degree to which adolescent development is similar, or universal, across cultures or about the degree to which it is culture-specific.

individualism
Giving priority to personal goals rather than to group goals; emphasizing values that serve the self, such as feeling good, personal distinction and achievement, and independence.

Cross-Cultural Comparisons

observe sexual relations, see babies born, regard death as natural, do important work, engage in sex play, and know clearly what their adult roles will be promote a relatively stress-free adolescence. However, in cultures like the United States, in which children are considered very different from adults and where adolescence is not characterized by the aforementioned experiences, adolescence is more likely to be stressful.

More than half a century after Mead's Samoan findings, her work was criticized as being biased and error-prone (Freeman, 1983). The current criticism also states that Samoan adolescence is more stressful than Mead observed and that delinquency appears among Samoan adolescents just as it does among Western adolescents. In the current controversy over Mead's findings, some researchers have defended Mead's work (Holmes, 1987).

As we discovered in chapter 1, **cross-cultural studies** *involve the comparison of a culture with one or more other cultures, which provides information about the degree to which children's development is similar, or universal, across cultures, or the degree to which it is culture-specific* ◄‖‖ P. 12. The study of children has emerged in the context of Western industrialized society, with the practical needs and social norms of this culture dominating thinking about child development. Consequently, the development of children in Western cultures has evolved as the norm for all children of the human species, regardless of economic and cultural circumstances. This narrow viewpoint can produce erroneous conclusions about the nature of children. To develop a more global, cosmopolitan perspective on children, let us consider achievement behavior and rites of passage in different cultures.

Achievement   The United States is an achievement-oriented culture, and U.S. children are more achievement oriented than children are in many other countries ◄‖‖ P. 540. Many American parents socialize their children to be achievement oriented and independent. In one investigation of 104 societies, parents in industrialized countries like the United States placed a higher value on socializing children for achievement and independence than did parents in nonindustrialized countries like Kenya, who placed a higher value on obedience and responsibility (Bacon, Child, & Barry, 1963).

Anglo-American children are more achievement oriented than Mexican and Mexican American children are. For example, in one study, Anglo-American children were more competitive and less cooperative than their Mexican and Mexican American counterparts (Kagan & Madsen, 1972). In this study, Anglo-Americans were more likely to minimize the gains of other students when they could not reach the goals themselves. In other investigations, Anglo-American children were more individual centered, while Mexican children were more family centered (Holtzmann, 1982). Some developmentalists believe that the American culture is too achievement oriented for rearing mentally healthy children (Elkind, 1981).

While Anglo-American children are more achievement oriented than children in many other cultures, they are not as achievement oriented as many Japanese, Chinese, and Asian American children (Stevenson, 1995) ◄‖‖ P. 547. For example, as a group, Asian American children demonstrate exceptional achievement patterns. Asian American children exceed the national average for high school and college graduates. Eighty-six percent of Asian Americans, compared to 64 percent of White Americans, are in some higher-education program 2 years after high school graduation. Clearly, education and achievement are highly valued aspirations of many Asian American children.

Cross-cultural studies involve the comparison of a culture with one or more other cultures. Shown here is a 14-year-old !Kung girl who has added flowers to her beadwork during the brief rainy season in the Kalahari desert in Botswana, Africa. Delinquency and violence occur much less frequently in the peaceful !Kung culture than in most other cultures around the world.

Individualism and Collectivism   In cross-cultural research, the search for basic traits has extended to characteristics common to whole nations. In recent years, the most elaborate search for traits has focused on the dichotomy between individualism and collectivism (Hofstede, 1980; Triandis, 1994, 2000). **Individualism** *in-*

volves giving a priority to personal goals rather than to group goals; it emphasizes values that serve the self, such as feeling good, personal distinction and achievement, and independence. **Collectivism** emphasizes values that serve the group by subordinating personal goals to preserve group integrity, interdependence of the members, and harmonious relationships. Figure 18.1 summarizes some of the main characteristics of individualistic and collectivistic cultures. Many Western cultures, such as the United States, Canada, Great Britain, and the Netherlands, are described as individualistic; many Eastern cultures, such as China, Japan, India, and Thailand, are described as collectivistic.

Many of psychology's basic tenets have been developed in individualistic cultures like the United States. Consider the flurry of *self-* terms in psychology that have an individualistic focus: for example, *self-actualization, self-awareness, self-efficacy, self-reinforcement, self-criticism, self-serving, selfishness,* and *self-doubt* (Lonner, 1988).

Critics of the Western notion of psychology point out that human beings have always lived in groups, whether large or small, and have always needed one another for survival. They argue that the Western emphasis on individualism may undermine our basic species need for relatedness (Kagitcibasi, 1988, 1995). Some social scientists believe that many problems in Western cultures are intensified by the Western cultural emphasis on individualism. Individualistic cultures have higher rates than collectivistic cultures of suicide, drug abuse, crime, teenage pregnancy, divorce, child abuse, and mental disorders. Some critics believe that the pendulum might have swung too far toward individualism in many Western cultures. Regardless of their cultural background, people need a positive sense of *self* and *connectedness to others* to develop fully as human beings.

INDIVIDUALISTIC	COLLECTIVISTIC
Focuses on individuals	Focuses on groups
Self is determined by personal traits independent of groups; self is stable across contexts	Self is defined in in-group terms; self can change with context
Private self is most important	Public self is most important
Personal achievement, competition, power are important	Achievement is for the benefit of the in-group; cooperation is stressed
Cognitive dissonance is frequent	Cognitive dissonance is infrequent
Emotions (such as anger) are self-focused	Emotions (such as anger) are often relationship based
People who are the most liked are self-assured	People who are the most liked are modest, self-effacing
Values: pleasure, achievement, competition, freedom	Values: security, obedience, in-group harmony, personalized relationships
Many casual relationships	Few, close relationships
Save own face	Save own and other's face
Independent behaviors: swimming, sleeping alone in room, privacy	Interdependent behaviors: co-bathing, co-sleeping
Relatively rare mother-child physical contact	Frequent mother-child physical contact (such as hugging, holding)

Figure **18.1**
Characteristics of Individualistic and Collectivistic Cultures

collectivism
Emphasizing values that serve the group by subordinating personal goals to preserve group integrity, interdependence of members, and harmonious relationships.

rites of passage
Ceremonies or rituals that mark an individual's transition from one status to another, especially into adulthood.

Rites of Passage **Rites of passage** *are ceremonies or rituals that mark an individual's transition from one status to another, especially into adulthood.* Some societies have elaborate rites of passage that signal the adolescent's transition to adulthood; others do not. In many primitive cultures, rites of passage are the avenue through which adolescents gain access to sacred adult practices, knowledge, and sexuality (Sommer, 1978). These rites often involve dramatic practices intended to facilitate the adolescent's separation from the immediate family, especially the mother. The transformation usually is characterized by some form of ritual death and rebirth, or by means of contact with the spiritual world. Bonds are forged between the adolescent and the adult instructors through shared rituals, hazards, and secrets to allow the adolescent to enter the adult world. This kind of ritual provides a forceful and discontinuous entry into the adult world at a time when the adolescent is perceived to be ready for the change.

Africa, especially sub-Saharan Africa, has been the location of many rites of passage for adolescents. Under the influence of Western culture, many of the rites are disappearing today, although some vestiges remain. In locations where formal education is not readily available, rites of passage are still prevalent.

Americans do not have formal rites of passage that mark the transition from adolescence to adulthood. Some religious and social groups, however, have initiation ceremonies that indicate an advance in maturity—the Jewish bar mitzvah, the Catholic confirmation, and social debuts, for example.

School graduation ceremonies come the closest to being culturewide rites of passage in the United States. The high school graduation ceremony has become nearly universal for middle-SES adolescents and increasing numbers of adolescents from low-income backgrounds (Fasick, 1988). Nonetheless, high school graduation does not result in universal changes—many high school graduates continue to live with their parents, to be economically dependent on them, and to be undecided about career and lifestyle matters. Another rite of passage for increasing numbers of American adolescents is sexual intercourse (Halonen & Santrock, 1999). By the end of adolescence, more than 70 percent of American adolescents have had sexual intercourse.

The absence in America of clear-cut rites of passage makes the attainment of adult status ambiguous. Many individuals are unsure whether they have reached adult status. In Texas, the age for beginning employment is 15, but many younger adolescents and even children are employed, especially Mexican immigrants. The age for driving is 16, but when emergency need is demonstrated, a driver's license can be obtained at age 15. Even at age 16, some parents might not allow their son or daughter to obtain a driver's license, believing that 16-year-olds are too young for this responsibility. The age for voting is 18, and the age for drinking has recently been raised to 21. Exactly when adolescents become adults has not been as clearly delineated in America as it has been in some primitive cultures, where rites of passage are universal.

Socioeconomic Status and Poverty

Many subcultures exist within countries. For example, the values and attitudes of children growing up in an urban ghetto or rural Appalachia may differ from those of children growing up in a wealthy suburb.

The Nature of Socioeconomic Status

Socioeconomic status *refers to the grouping of people with similar occupational, educational and economic characteristics.* Socioeconomic status implies certain inequalities. Generally, members of a society have (1) occupations that vary in prestige, and some individuals have more access than others to higher-status occupations; (2) different levels of educational attainment, and some individuals have more access than others to better education; (3) different economic resources; and (4) different levels of power to influence a community's institutions. These differences in the ability to control resources and to participate in society's rewards produce unequal opportunities for adolescents.

The number of visibly different socioeconomic statuses depends on the community's size and complexity. In most investigators' descriptions of socioeconomic status, two categories, low and middle, are used, although as many as five categories are delineated. Sometimes low socioeconomic status is described as low-income, working class, or blue collar; sometimes the middle category is described as middle-income, managerial, or white collar. Examples of low-SES occupations are factory worker, manual laborer, welfare recipient, and maintenance worker. Examples of middle-SES occupations include skilled worker, manager, and professional (doctor, lawyer, teacher, accountant, and so on).

Socioeconomic Variations in Families, Neighborhoods, and Schools

The families, schools, and neighborhoods of children have socioeconomic characteristics. Some children have parents who have a great deal of money, and who work in prestigious occupations. These children live in attractive houses and neighborhoods, and attend schools where the mix of students is primarily from middle- and upper-SES backgrounds. Other children have parents who do not have very much money and who work in less prestigious occupations. These children do not live in very attractive houses and neighborhoods, and they attend schools where the mix of students is mainly from lower-SES backgrounds. Such variations in neighborhood settings can influence adolescents' adjustment (Lee, 2000; Leffert & Blyth, 1996; Sampson & Earls, 1995; Spencer, 2000). In one study, neighborhood crime and isolation were linked with low self-esteem and psychological distress in children (Roberts, Jacobson, & Taylor, 1996).

SOCIOECONOMIC STATUS AND POVERTY

The Nature of Socioeconomic Status

Poverty

Socioeconomic Variations in Families, Neighborhoods, and Schools

socioeconomic status (SES)
A grouping of people with similar occupational, educational, and economic characteristics.

In America and most Western cultures, socio-economic differences in child rearing exist (Hoff-Ginsberg & Tardif, 1995). Low-income parents often place a high value on external characteristics, such as obedience and neatness, whereas higher (middle- and upper-SES) parents often place a high value on internal characteristics, such as self-control and delay of gratification. SES differences in parenting behaviors also exist. Higher-SES parents are more likely to explain something, use verbal praise, accompany their discipline with reasoning, and ask their children questions. In contrast, low-SES parents are more likely to discipline children with physical punishment and criticize them (Heath, 1983).

SES differences also are involved in an important aspect of children's intellectual orientation. Most school tasks require children to use and process language. As a part of developing language skills, students must learn to read efficiently, write effectively, and give competent oral reports. Although variations exist, one study found that students from low-SES families read less and watched television more than their middle-SES counterparts (Erlick & Starry, 1973). Consequently, they may tend to develop weaker intellectual skills such as reading and writing that promote academic success. Although television involves some verbal activity, it is primarily a visual medium, which suggests that children from low-SES families prefer a visual medium over a verbal medium.

One recent study examined socioeconomic status, parenting, and skill-building activities in divorced families (DeGarmo, Forgatch, & Martinez, 1998). Each of three indicators of socioeconomic status—education, occupation, and income—were studied independently to determine their effects on achievement in elementary school boys. Each indica-

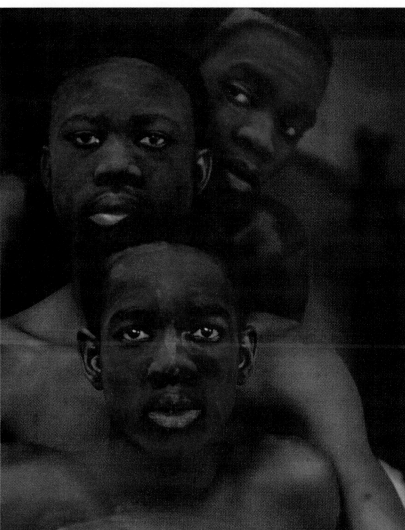

These Congolese Koto boys painted their faces as part of a rite of passage to adulthood. What kinds of rites of passage do American adolescents have?

tor was associated with better parenting in the divorced families. Especially noteworthy was the finding that the effects of maternal education on boys' achievement was mediated by the time the child spent reading, engaged in skill-building activities, and time not spent watching television.

Like their parents, children from low-SES backgrounds are at high risk for experiencing mental health problems (McLoyd, 1993, 1998, 2000). Social maladaptation and psychological problems, such as depression, low self-confidence, peer conflict, and juvenile delinquency, are more prevalent among children living in low-SES families than among economically advantaged children (Gibbs & Huang, 1989). Although psychological problems are more prevalent among adolescents from low-SES backgrounds, these adolescents vary considerably in intellectual and psychological functioning. For example, a sizable portion of children from low-SES backgrounds perform well in school; some perform better than many middle-SES students. When children from low-SES backgrounds are achieving well in school, it is not unusual to find a parent or parents making special sacrifices to provide the necessary living conditions and support that contribute to school success. One study found that, although positive times occurred in the lives of ethnically diverse children growing up in poverty, many of their negative experiences were worse than those of their middle-SES counterparts (Richards & others, 1994). These adversities involved physical punishment and lack of structure at home, violence in the neighborhood, and domestic violence in their buildings.

In chapter 17, "Schools," we read about schools in low-income neighborhoods having fewer resources than schools in higher-income neighborhoods. The schools in the low-income areas also are more likely to have more students with lower achievement test scores, lower rates of graduation, and smaller percentages of students going to college (Garbarino & Asp, 1981). For example, in one profile, 80 percent of urban disadvantaged students scored in the bottom half of standardized tests for reading and math (*The Research Bulletin,* 1991). In some instances, however, federal aid to schools has provided a context for enhanced learning in low-income areas.

Poverty

In a report on the state of America's children and adolescents, the Children Defense Fund (1992) described what life is like for all too many youth. When sixth-graders in a poverty-stricken area of St. Louis were asked to describe a perfect day, one boy said he would erase the world, then he would sit and think. Asked if he wouldn't rather go outside and play, the boy responded, "Are you kidding, out there?"

The world is a dangerous and unwelcoming place for too many of America's youth, especially those whose families, neighborhoods, and schools are low-income (Edelman, 1997). Some adolescents are resilient and cope with the challenges of poverty without any major setbacks, but too many struggle unsuccessfully. Each child of poverty who reaches adulthood unhealthy, unskilled, or alienated keeps our nation from being as competent and productive as it can be (Children's Defense Fund, 1992).

The Nature of Poverty
Poverty is defined by economic hardship, and its most common marker is the federal poverty threshold (Huston, McLoyd, & Coll, 1994). The poverty threshold was originally based on the estimated cost of food (a basic diet) multiplied by 3. This federal poverty marker is adjusted annually for family size and inflation.

Based on the U.S. government's criteria for poverty, the proportion of children under the age of 18 living in families below the poverty threshold has increased from approximately 15 percent in the 1970s to more than 20 percent in the late 1990s (Brooks-Gunn, Britto, & Brady, 1999). Approximately 14 million children (more than one in five) in the United States are living in families below the poverty threshold.

The U.S. figure of 20 percent of children living in poverty is almost twice as high as those from other industrialized nations. For example, Canada has a child poverty rate of 9 percent and Sweden has a rate of 2 percent. Poverty in the United States is demarcated along ethnic lines. Almost 50 percent of African American and 40 percent of Latino children live in poverty. Compared to White children, ethnic minority children are more likely to experience persistent poverty over many years and live in isolated poor neighborhoods where social supports are minimal and threats to positive development abundant (Jarrett, 1995) (see figure 18.2).

Why is poverty among American children so high? Three reasons are apparent (Huston, McLoyd, & Coll, 1994): (1) Economic changes have eliminated many blue-collar jobs that paid reasonably well, (2) the percentage of youth living in single-parent families headed by the mother has increased, and (3) government benefits were reduced during the 1970s and 1980s.

Poor children and their families are often exposed to poor health conditions, inadequate housing and homelessness, environmental toxins, and violent or unsupportive neighborhoods (BeShears & McLeod, 2000; Sheidow & others, 2000). Unlike income loss or unemployment due to job loss, poverty is not a homogeneous variable or distinct event. Also, unemployment, unstable work history, and income loss do not always push families into poverty.

Let's further consider some of the psychological ramifications of

Children, Youth, and Poverty
Poverty in Canada
Research on Poverty

Note: A distressed neighborhood is defined by high levels (at least one standard deviation above the mean) of (1) poverty; (2) female-headed families; (3) high school dropouts; (4) unemployment; and (5) reliance on welfare.

Figure **18.2**

Percentages of Youth Under 18 Who Are Living in Distressed Neighborhoods

living in poverty. First, the poor are often powerless. In occupations, they rarely are the decision makers. Rules are handed down to them in an authoritarian manner. Second, the poor are often vulnerable to disaster. They are not likely to be given notice before they are laid off from work and usually do not have financial resources to fall back on when problems arise. Third, their range of alternatives is often restricted. Only a limited number of jobs are open to them. Even when alternatives are available, the poor might not know about them or be prepared to make a wise decision, because of inadequate education and inability to read well. Fourth, being poor means having less prestige. This lack of prestige is transmitted to children early in their lives. The child in poverty observes that many other children wear nicer clothes and live in more attractive houses.

When poverty is persistent and long-standing, it can have especially damaging effects on children. In one study, the longer children lived in families with income below the poverty line, the lower was the quality of their home environments (Garrett, Ng'andu, & Ferron, 1994). Also in this study, improvements in family income had their strongest effects on the home environments of chronically poor children. In another study, children in families experiencing both persistent and occasional poverty had lower IQs and more internalized behavior problems than never-poor children, but persistent poverty had a much stronger negative effect on these outcomes than occasional poverty did (Duncan, Brooks-Gunn, & Klebanov, 1994).

A special concern is the high percentage of single mothers in poverty, more than one-third of whom are in poverty, compared to only 10 percent of single fathers. Vonnie McLoyd (1990, 1998) concludes that because poor, single mothers are more distressed than their middle-class counterparts are, they often show low support, nurturance, and involvement with their children. Among the reasons for the high poverty rate of single mothers are women's low pay, infrequent awarding of alimony payments, and poorly enforced child support by fathers. The term **feminization of poverty** *refers to the fact that far more women than men live in poverty. Women's low income, divorce, and the resolution of divorce cases by the judicial system, which usually leaves women with less money than they and their children need to adequately function, are the likely causes of the feminization of poverty.*

One recent trend in antipoverty programs is to conduct two-generation interventions (McLoyd, 1998). This involves providing both services for children (such as educational day care or preschool education) and services for parents (such as adult education, literacy training, and job skill training). Recent evaluations of the two-generation programs suggest that they have more positive effects on parents than they do on children (St. Pierre, Layzer, & Barnes, 1996). Also discouraging for children is that when the two-generational programs show benefits, these are more likely to be health benefits than cognitive gains.

At this point we have studied a number of ideas about culture, socioeconomic status, and poverty. A review of these ideas is presented in summary table 18.1. Next, we will explore the role of ethnicity in children's lives.

*W*hat happens to a dream deferred?
Does it dry up
like a raisin in the sun?

Langston Hughes
American Poet and Author, 20th Century

feminization of poverty
The fact that far more women than men live in poverty. Women's low income, divorce, and the resolution of divorce cases by the judicial system, which usually leaves women with less money than they and their children need to adequately function, are the likely causes.

Ethnicity

Children live in a world that has been made smaller and more interactive by dramatic improvements in travel and communication. Children also live in a world that is far more diverse in its ethnic makeup than in past decades. Ninety-three languages are spoken in Los Angeles alone! With these changes have come conflicts and concerns about what the future will bring.

- In 1992, riots broke out in Los Angeles after African American Rodney King was beaten by White police and a jury acquitted the police of any wrongdoing. The beating and the trial brought racial animosities to the surface.
- In 1993, in what was formerly Yugoslavia, children and adolescents experienced the renewal of ancient animosities as Serbs and Croats pummeled and killed each other. Even UN intervention and boycotts failed to stem the underlying ethnic hatred and the killing.

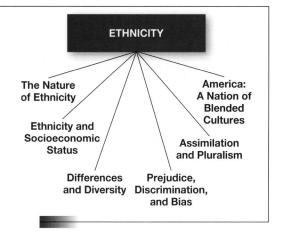

SUMMARY TABLE 18.1
Culture and Children's Development, and Socioeconomic Status and Poverty

Concept	Processes/ Related Ideas	Characteristics/Description
Culture and Children's Development	The Nature of Culture	• *Culture* refers to the behavior patterns, beliefs, and all other products of a particular group of people that are passed on from generation to generation.
	The Relevance of Culture	• If the study of children is to be a relevant discipline in the twenty-first century, there will have to be increased attention to culture.
	Cross-Cultural Comparisons	• These involve the comparison of one culture with one or more cultures, which provides information about the degree to which information is universal or culture-specific.
	Rites of Passage	• These are ceremonies that mark an individual's transition from one status to another, especially into adulthood. • In primitive cultures, rites of passage are well-defined, but in contemporary America they are not.
Socioeconomic Status and Poverty	The Nature of Socioeconomic Status	• Socioeconomic status (SES) is the grouping of people with similar occupational, educational, and economic characteristics. • SES often carries with it certain inequities.
	Socioeconomic Variations in Families, Neighborhoods, and Schools	• The families, neighborhoods, and schools of children have SES characteristics that are related to the child's development. • Parents from low-SES families are more likely to value external characteristics and to use physical punishment than their middle-SES counterparts.
	Poverty	• Poverty is defined by economic hardship. Its most common marker is the federal poverty threshold (based on the estimated cost of food multiplied by 3). • Based on this threshold, the percentage of American children living in poverty has increased from 15 percent in the 1970s to 20 percent in the late 1990s. • The subculture of the poor is often characterized not only by economic hardship but also by social and psychological difficulties. • When poverty is persistent and longlasting, it especially has adverse effects on children's development.

Exploring Diversity

Diversity Resources

Ethnic Groups

- In Germany, an increasing number of youth join the neo-Nazi movement. Some German-born citizens want an ethnic cleansing of their country; non-German-born immigrants have been beaten and killed.
- English is a problem for half of the population of Miami, Florida. That is a sharp increase from the 30 percent who said 10 years ago that they had problems communicating in English and reflects the influx of Latino and Creole-speaking Haitian immigrants.
- In the Middle East, Jews and Arabs live in separate communities, and many of them loathe each other. Territorial disputes and threats of war occur daily.
- In South Africa, oppression of Blacks by Whites has lessened since the elimination of apartheid, and the election of Nelson Mandela should mean improvements for the majority Black population. However, Blacks in South Africa are still poorly educated, live in extremely poor housing, and have inadequate access to health care.

One effort to improve the lives of adolescents living in poverty is called "El Puente," which is described in the Explorations in Child Development box. El Puente is a program that is primarily aimed at Latino adolescents living in low-income areas. Next, we further explore the role of ethnicity in development.

$\mathcal{E}$XPLORATIONS IN CHILD DEVELOPMENT
El Puente

EL PUENTE ("the bridge") was opened in New York City in 1983 because of community dissatisfaction with the health, education, and social services youth were receiving (Simons, Finlay, & Yang, 1991). El Puente emphasizes five areas of youth development: health, education, achievement, personal growth, and social growth.

El Puente is located in a former Roman Catholic church on the south side of Williamsburg in Brooklyn, a neighborhood made up primarily of low-income Latino families, many of which are far below the poverty line. Sixty-five percent of the residents receive some form of public assistance. The neighborhood has the highest school dropout rate for Latinos in New York City and the highest felony rate for adolescents in Brooklyn.

When the youths, aged 12 through 21, first enroll in El Puente, they meet with counselors and develop a 4-month plan that includes the programs they are interested in joining. At the end of 4 months, youth and staff develop a plan for continued participation. Twenty-six bilingual classes are offered in such subjects as the fine arts, theater, photography, and dance. In addition, a medical and fitness center, GED night school, and mental health and social services centers are also a part of El Puente.

El Puente is funded through state, city, and private organizations and serves about three hundred youth. The program has been replicated in Chelsea and Holyoke, Massachusetts, and two other sites in New York are being developed.

These adolescents participate in the programs of El Puente, located in a predominantly low-income Latino neighborhood in Brooklyn, New York. The El Puente program stresses five areas of youth development: health, education, achievement, personal growth, and social growth.

The Nature of Ethnicity

In chapter 1 we defined **ethnicity** *as based on cultural heritage, nationality characteristics, race, religion, and language.* Nowhere are cultural changes in the United States more dramatic than in the increasing ethnic diversity of America's children ◀llll P. 12.

Relatively high rates of minority immigration are contributing to the growth in the proportion of ethnic minorities in the U.S. population (McLoyd, 1998). Because immigrants often experience stressors uncommon to or less prominent among long-time residents (such as language barriers, disclocations and separations from support networks, dual struggle to preserve identity and to acculturate, and changes in SES status), intervention programs may need to be made more culturally sensitive when working with immigrant children and their immigrant families.

The United States has an increasing immigrant population, yet psychologists have been slow to study these families. One recent study looked at the cultural values and intergenerational value discrepancies in immigrant (Vietnamese, Armenian, and

ethnicity
A dimension of culture based on cultural heritage, nationality, race, religion, and language.

Mexican) and non-immigrant families (African American and European American) (Phinney, 1996). Family obligations were endorsed more by parents than adolescents in all groups, and the intergenerational value discrepancy generally increased with time in the United States.

Ethnicity and Socioeconomic Status

Much of the research on ethnic minority children has failed to tease apart the influences of ethnicity and socioeconomic status (SES). Ethnicity and SES can interact in ways that exaggerate the negative influence of ethnicity because ethnic minority individuals are overrepresented in the lower socioeconomic levels of American society (Spencer & Dornbusch, 1990). Consequently, too often researchers have given ethnic explanations of child development that were largely based on socioeconomic status rather than on ethnicity. For example, decades of research on group differences in self-esteem failed to consider the socioeconomic status of African American and White American children (Hare & Castenell, 1985). When the self-esteem of African American children from low-income backgrounds is compared with that of White American children from middle-class backgrounds, the differences are often large but not informative because of the confounding of ethnicity and SES (Bell-Scott & Taylor, 1989; Scott-Jones, 1995).

While some ethnic minority children are from middle-SES backgrounds, economic advantage does not entirely enable them to escape their ethnic minority status (Spencer & Dornbusch, 1990). Middle-SES ethnic minority children still encounter much of the prejudice, discrimination, and bias associated with being a member of an ethnic minority group. Often characterized as a "model minority" because of their strong achievement orientation and family cohesiveness, Japanese Americans still experience stress associated with ethnic minority status (Sue, 1990). Although middle-SES ethnic minority children have more resources available to counter the destructive influences of prejudice and discrimination, they still cannot completely avoid the pervasive influence of negative stereotypes about ethnic minority groups.

While not all ethnic minority families are poor, poverty contributes to the stressful life experiences of many ethnic minority children. Vonnie McLoyd (1990) concluded that ethnic minority children experience a disproportionate share of the adverse effects of poverty and unemployment in America today. Thus, many ethnic minority children experience a double disadvantage: (1) prejudice, discrimination, and bias because of their ethnic minority status, and (2) the stressful effects of poverty.

Differences and Diversity

Historical, economic, and social experiences produce legitimate differences between various ethnic minority groups, and between ethnic minority groups and the majority White group (Halonen & Santrock, 1999). Individuals living in a particular ethnic or cultural group adapt to the values, attitudes, and stresses of that culture. Their behavior, while possibly different from your own, is, nonetheless, often functional for them. Recognizing and respecting these differences is an important aspect of getting along with others in a diverse, multicultural world. Children, like all of us, need to take the perspective of individuals from ethnic and cultural groups that are different than their own and think, "If I were in their shoes, what kind of experiences might I have had?" "How would I feel if I were a member of their ethnic or cultural group?" "How would I think and behave if I had grown up in their world?" Such perspective taking often increases empathy and understanding of individuals from ethnic and cultural groups different from one's own.

Unfortunately, the emphasis often placed by our society and science on the differences between ethnic minority groups and the White majority in the United States has been damaging to ethnic minority individuals. Ethnicity has defined who will enjoy the privileges of citizenship and to what degree and in what ways (Jones, 1994).

*T*hrough the Eyes of Psychologists

Vonnie McLoyd, *Duke University*

"Poverty and stress are common in the lives of many ethnic minority women who are single parents, and too often this translates into stressful lives for their children."

Migration and Ethnic Relations

Immigration: Journals and Newsletter

Immigration and Ethnicity: Research Centers

Immigrant Families

I am here and you will know that I am the best and will hear me. The color of my skin or the kink of my hair or the spread of my mouth has nothing to do with what you are listening to.

Leontyne Price
American Operatic Soprano, 20th Century

An individual's ethnic background has determined whether the individual will be alienated, oppressed, or disadvantaged.

For too long, differences between any ethnic minority group and Whites were conceptualized as *deficits* or inferior characteristics on the part of the ethnic minority group. Indeed, research on ethnic minority groups often focused only on a group's negative, stressful aspects. For example, research on African American adolescent females invariably examined such topics as poverty, unwed mothers, and dropping out of school. These topics continue to be important areas of adolescent development much in need of research, but research on the positive aspects of African American adolescent females in a pluralistic society is also much needed and sorely neglected. The self-esteem, achievement, motivation, and self-control of children from different ethnic minority groups deserve considerable study.

The current emphasis on differences between ethnic groups underscores the strengths of various ethnic minority groups and is long overdue. For example, the extended-family support system that characterizes many ethnic minority groups is now recognized as an important factor in coping. And researchers are finding that African American males are better than Anglo-American males at nonverbal cues, multilingual/multicultural expression, improvised problem solving, and using body language in communication (Evans & Whitfield, 1988).

As we noted in chapter 1, there also is considerable diversity within each ethnic group (McHale, 1995; Wilson & Hall, 2000). Ethnic minority groups are not homogeneous; they have different social, historical, and economic backgrounds (Stevenson, 1995, in press). For example, Mexican, Cuban, and Puerto Rican immigrants are Latinos, but they had different reasons for migrating, came from varying socioeconomic backgrounds in their native countries, and experience different rates and types of employment in the United States (Coll & others, 1995). The U.S. federal government now recognizes the existence of 511 *different* Native American tribes, each having a unique ancestral background with differing values and characteristics. Asian Americans include the Chinese, Japanese, Filipinos, Koreans, and Southeast Asians, each group having a distinct ancestry and language. The diversity of Asian Americans is reflected in their educational attainment: Some achieve a high level of education, while many others have no education whatsoever. For example, 90 percent of Korean American males graduate from high school, but only 71 percent of Vietnamese American males do.

Sometimes, well-meaning individuals fail to recognize the diversity within an ethnic group (Sue, 1990). For example, a sixth-grade teacher went to a human relations workshop and was exposed to the necessity of incorporating more ethnicity into her instructional planning. Since she had two Mexican American adolescents in her class, she asked them to be prepared to demonstrate to the class on the following Monday how they danced at home. The teacher expected both of them to perform Mexican folk dances, reflecting their ethnic heritage. The first boy got up in front of the class and began dancing in a typical American fashion. The teacher said, "No, I want you to dance like you and your family do at home, like you do when you have Mexican American celebrations." The boy informed the teacher that his family did not dance that way. The second boy demonstrated a Mexican folk dance to the class. The first boy was highly assimilated into the American culture and did not know how to dance Mexican folk dances. The second boy was less assimilated and came from a Mexican American family that had retained more of its Mexican heritage.

This example illustrates the diversity and individual differences that exist within any ethnic minority group. Failure to recognize diversity and individual variations results in the stereotyping of an ethnic minority group (Bowser & Hunt, 1996).

Prejudice, Discrimination, and Bias

Prejudice *is an unjustified negative attitude toward an individual because of the individual's membership in a group.* The group toward which the prejudice is directed can be made up of people of a particular ethnic group, sex, age, religion, or other detectable difference. Our concern here is prejudice against ethnic minority groups.

Jason Leonard, age 15: "I want America to know that most of us black teens are not troubled people from broken homes and headed to jail. . . . In my relationships with my parents, we show respect for each other and we have values in our house. We have traditions we celebrate together, including Christmas and Kwanzaa."

Ethnic Minority Families
African Americans
Latinos and Native Americans
Asian Americans
Prejudice

*P*rejudice is the reason of fools.

Voltaire,
French Philosopher, 18th Century

prejudice
An unjustified negative attitude toward an individual because of her or his membership in a group.

DVENTURES FOR THE MIND

Reconstructing Prejudice

NO MATTER HOW well-intentioned children are, their life circumstances have probably given them some prejudices. If they don't maintain particular prejudices toward people with different cultural and ethnic backrounds, there might be other kinds of people who bring out prejudices in them. For example, prejudices can be developed about people who have certain religious beliefs or political convictions, people who are unattractive or too attractive, people with unpopular occupations (police officers, lawyers), people with a disability, and people from bordering towns.

Psychologist William James once observed that one function of education is to rearrange prejudices. How could adolescents' education rearrange prejudices like the ones we have listed? Consider prejudice toward ethnic minority groups, the main focus of our discussion of prejudice in this chapter. One strategy might be to adopt the jigsaw classroom concept involving cooperative learning, which was discussed in chapter 17. What other strategies might work?

assimilation
The absorption of ethnic minority groups into the dominant group, which often means the loss of some or virtually all of the behavior and values of the ethnic minority group.

pluralism
The coexistence of distinct ethnic and cultural groups in the same society.

Through the Eyes of Psychologists

James Jones, *University of Delaware*

"Prejudice narrows understanding by biasing our judgments and predetermining what will be discovered from exploring our environment."

Many ethnic minority individuals continue to experience persistent forms of prejudice, discrimination, and bias (Sue, 1990). Ethnic minority adolescents are taught in schools that often have a middle-SES, White bias and in classroom contexts that are not adapted to ethnic minority adolescents' learning styles. They are assessed by tests that are often culturally biased and are evaluated by teachers whose appreciation of their abilities may be hindered by negative stereotypes about ethnic minorities (Spencer & Dornbusch, 1990). Discrimination and prejudice continue to be present in the media, interpersonal interactions, and daily conversations. Crimes, strangeness, poverty, mistakes, and deterioration are often mistakenly attributed to ethnic minority individuals or foreigners.

As Asian American researcher Stanley Sue (1990) points out, people frequently have opposing views about discrimination and prejudice. On the one side are individuals who value and praise the significant strides made in civil rights in recent years, pointing to affirmative action programs as proof of these civil rights advances. On the other side are individuals who criticize American institutions, such as education, because they believe that many forms of discrimination and prejudice still characterize these institutions.

For several reasons, the "browning" of American portends heightened racial/ethnic prejudice and conflict, or at least sharper racial and ethnic cleavages (McLoyd, 1998). First, it is occurring against a backdrop of longstanding White privilege and an ingrained sense of entitlement and superiority among non-Latino Whites. Second, the youth of today's immigrants are less likely than their counterparts in the early twentieth century to believe that they must reject the values and ways of their parents' homeland to succeed in American society. Many espouse economic, but not cultural, assimilation into mainstream society. Third, today's immigrants often settle in inner-city neighborhoods where assimilation often means joining a world that is antagonistic to the American mainstream because of its experience of racism and economic barriers.

Progress has been made in ethnic minority relations, but discrimination and prejudice still exist, and equality has not been achieved. Much remains to be accomplished.

Assimilation and Pluralism

Assimilation *refers to the absorption of ethnic minority groups into the dominant group.* This often means the loss of some or virtually all of the behavior and values of the ethnic minority group. Individuals who favor assimilation usually advocate that ethnic minority groups should become more American. By contrast, **pluralism** *refers to the coexistence of distinct ethnic and cultural groups in the same society.* Individuals who advocate pluralism usually advocate that cultural differences should be maintained and appreciated (Leong, 2000).

For many years, assimilation was thought to be the best course for American society because the mainstream was believed to be superior in many ways. Even though many individuals today reject the notion that the mainstream culture is intrinsically superior to ethnic minority cultures, the assimilation approach is currently resurfacing with a more complex face. Advocates of assimilation now often use practical and functional arguments rather than intrinsic superiority arguments to buttress their point of view. For example, they say that educational programs for immigrant children (Mexican, Chinese, and so on) should stress the learning of English as early as possible, rather than bilingual education. Their argument is that spending time on any language other than English may be a handicap, especially since a second language is not functional in the classroom. By contrast, the advocates of pluralism argue that an English-only approach reasserts the mainstream-is-right-and-best belief. Thus, responses to the ethnic minority issue of bilingual education involve a clash of fundamental values. As Sue (1990) asks, how can one argue against the development of functional skills and to some degree the support of Americanization? Similarly, how can one doubt that pluralism, diversity, and respect for different cultures are valid? Sue believes that the one-sidedness of the issue is the main problem. Advocates of assimilation often overlook the fact that a consensus may be lacking on what constitutes functional skills or that a particular context may alter what skills are useful. For example, with an increasing immigrant population, the ability to speak Spanish or Japanese may be an asset, as is the ability to interact with and collaborate with diverse ethnic groups.

Sue believes that one way to resolve value conflicts about sociocultural issues is to conceptualize or redefine them in innovative ways. For example, in the assimilation/pluralism conflict, rather than assuming that assimilation is necessary for the development of functional skills, we could focus on the fluctuating criteria of what skills are considered functional or the possibility that developing functional skills does not prevent the existence of pluralism. For instance, the classroom instructor might use multicultural examples when teaching social studies, while also discussing culturally universal and culturally specific approaches to American and other cultures.

Consider the flowers of a garden: Though differing in kind, color, form, and shape, yet, inasmuch as they are refreshed by the waters of one spring, revived by the breath of one wind, invigorated by the rays of one sun, this diversity increases their charm and adds to their beauty. . . . How unpleasing to the eye if all the flowers and plants, the leaves and blossoms, the fruits, the branches, and the trees of that garden were all of the same shape and color! Diversity of hues, form, and shape enriches and adorns the garden and heightens its effect.

'Abdu'l Baha
Persian Baha'i Religious Leader, 19th/20th Century

America: A Nation of Blended Cultures

America has been and continues to be a great receiver of ethnic groups. It has embraced new ingredients from many cultures. The cultures often collide and cross-pollinate, mixing their ideologies and identities. Some of the culture of origin is retained, some of it lost, some of it mixed with the American culture. One after another, immigrants have come to America and been exposed to new channels of awareness and, in turn, exposed Americans to new channels of awareness. African American, Latino, Asian American, Native American, and other cultural heritages mix with the mainstream, receiving a new content and giving a new content. The ethnicity of Canadian children is discussed in the Explorations in Child Development box.

At this point, we have discussed many ideas about ethnicity. A review of these ideas is presented in summary table 18.2. Earlier in the chapter, we saw that children in low socioeconomic circumstances watch TV more and read less than their middle socioeconomic status counterparts. Next, we will explore further the roles of television and other technology in children's lives.

Technology

Few cultural changes have affected children's lives in the twentieth century more than technology. These changes are likely to continue throughout the twenty-first century. We will begin our exploration of technology's influence on children's development by focusing on television and then discussing technology, computers, and the Internet.

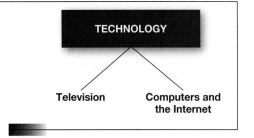

Television

Many children spend more time in front of the television set than they do with their parents. Although it is only one mass medium that affects children's behavior, television is the most influential (Huston & Wright, 1998). The persuasive capabilities of television are staggering; the 20,000 hours of television watched by the time the average American adolescent graduates from high school are more than the number of hours spent in the classroom.

Television and Children
Children's Television Workshop

$\mathcal{E}$XPLORATIONS IN CHILD DEVELOPMENT
Canada

CANADA IS A VAST and diverse country with a population of approximately 27 million people. Although Canada shares a number of similarities with the United States, there are some important differences (Majhanovich, 1998; Siegel & Wiener, 1993). Canada comprises a mixture of cultures that are loosely organized along the lines of economic power. The three main Canadian cultures include:

• Native peoples, or First Nations, who were Canada's original inhabitants
• Descendants of French settlers who came to Canada during the seventeenth and eighteenth centuries
• Descendants of British settlers who came to Canada during and after the seventeenth century, or from the United States after the American Revolution in the latter part of the eighteenth century

The late nineteenth century brought three more waves of immigrants:

• From Asia, mainly China, immigrants came to the west coast of Canada in the latter part of the nineteenth and early twentieth centuries.

• From various European countries, immigrants came to central Canada and the prairie provinces during the early twentieth century and following World War II.
• From countries in economic and political turmoil (in Latin America, the Caribbean, Asia, Africa, the Indian subcontinent, the former Soviet Union, and the Middle East), immigrants have come to many different parts of Canada.

Canada has two official languages—English and French. Primarily French-speaking individuals reside mainly in Quebec; primarily English-speaking individuals reside mainly in other Canadian provinces. In addition to its English- and French-speaking populations, Canada has a large multicultural community. In three large Canadian cities—Toronto, Montreal, and Vancouver—more than 50 percent of the children and adolescents come from homes in which neither English nor French is the native language (Siegel & Wiener, 1993).

Television is a medium of entertainment which permits millions of people to listen to the same joke at the same time, and yet remain lonesome.

T. S. Eliot
American-born English Poet, 20th Century

Television's Many Roles   Television can have a negative influence on children's development by taking them away from homework, making them passive learners, teaching them stereotypes, providing them with violent models of aggression, and presenting them with unrealistic views of the world. However, television can also have a positive influence on children's development by presenting motivating educational programs, increasing children's information about the world beyond their immediate environment, and providing models of prosocial behavior (Clifford, Gunter, & McAleer, 1995).

Television has been called many things, not all of them good. Depending on one's point of view, it may be a "window on the world," the "one-eyed monster," or the "boob tube." Television has been attacked as one of the reasons that scores on national achievement tests in reading and mathematics are lower now than in the past. Television, it is claimed, attracts children away from books and schoolwork. In one study, children who read printed materials, such as books, watched television less than those who did not read (Huston, Seigle, & Bremer, 1983). Furthermore, critics argue that television trains children to become passive learners; rarely, if ever, does television require active responses from the observer.

Television also is said to deceive; that is, it teaches children that problems are resolved easily and that everything always comes out right in the end. For example, TV detectives usually take only 30 to 60 minutes to sort through a complex array of clues to reveal a killer—and they *always* find the killer. Violence is a way of life on many shows. On TV it is all right for police to use violence and to break moral codes in their fight against evildoers. The lasting results of violence are rarely brought home to the viewer. A person who is injured on TV suffers for only a few seconds; in real life, the person might need months or years to recover, or might not recover at all.

SUMMARY TABLE 18.2
Ethnicity

Concept	Processes/ Related Ideas	Characteristics/Description
Ethnicity	Its Nature	• Ethnicity is based on cultural heritage, nationality characteristics, race, religion, and language.
Ethnicity and Socioeconomic Status	Research Implications	• Too often researchers have not teased apart ethnic and socioeconomic status effects when studying ethnic minority children.
	Poverty and Ethnicity	• Although not all ethnic minority families are poor, poverty contributes to the stress of many ethnic minority families and between ethnic minority groups and the White majority.
Differences and Diversity	Understanding the Nature of Differences	• Recognizing differences in ethnicity is an important aspect of getting along with others in a diverse, multicultural world. • Too often differences have been described as deficits on the part of ethnic minority individuals.
	Diversity	• Ethnic minority groups are not homogeneous. Failure to recognize this diversity results in stereotyping.
Prejudice, Discrimination, and Bias	Their Nature	• Prejudice is an unjustified negative attitude toward an individual because of the individual's membership in a group. • Progress has been made in ethnic minority relations, but discrimination and bias still exist.
Assimilation and Pluralism	Increased Pluralism	• For many years, assimilation was thought to be the best course for American society, but pluralism is increasingly being advocated.
America: A Nation of Blended Cultures	Its Nature	• America has been, and continues to be, a great receiver of ethnic immigrants.

Yet one out of every two first-grade children says that the adults on television are like adults in real life (Lyle & Hoffman, 1972).

Sesame Street demonstrates that education and entertainment can work well together (Green, 1995). Through *Sesame Street,* children experience a world of learning that is both exciting and entertaining. *Sesame Street* also follows the principle that teaching can be accomplished both directly and indirectly. Using the direct way, a teacher might tell children exactly what they are going to be taught and then teach them. However, in real life, social skills are often communicated in indirect ways. Rather than merely telling children, "You should cooperate with others," TV can show children so that they can figure out what it means to be cooperative and what the advantages are.

The Amount of Television Children Watch
Just how much television do young children watch? They watch a lot, and they seem to be watching more all the time. In the 1950s, 3-year-old children watched television for less than 1 hour a day; 5-year-olds watched just over 2 hours a day. In the 1970s, however, preschool children watched television for an average of 4 hours a day; elementary school children watched for as long as 6 hours a day (Friedrich & Stein, 1973). In the 1980s, children averaged 11 to 28 hours of television per week (Huston, Watkins, & Kunkel, 1989), which is more than for any other activity except sleep. As shown in figure 18.3, children in the United States watch considerably more television than their counterparts in other developed countries.

"Mrs. Horton, could you stop by school today?"

©1981 Martha F. Campbell.

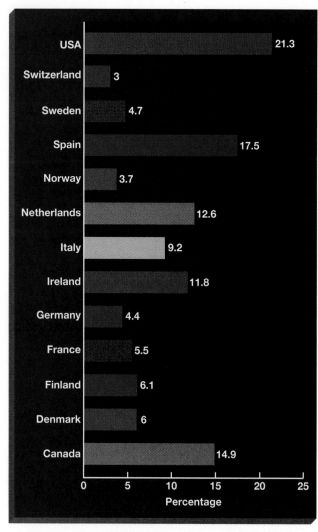

Figure **18.3**

Percentage of 9-Year-Old Children Who
Report Watching More Than 5 Hours of
Television per Weekday

Exploring Television Violence
Children, Youth, Media, and Violence
Culture and TV Violence

A special concern is the extent to which children are exposed to violence and aggression on television (Huston & Wright, 1998; Murray, 2000). Up to 80 percent of the prime-time shows include violent acts, including beatings, shootings, and stabbings. The frequency of violence increases on the Saturday-morning cartoon shows, which average more than 25 violent acts per hour.

The Effects of Television on Aggression and Prosocial Behavior

What are the effects of television violence on children's aggression? Does television merely stimulate a child to go out and buy a Star Wars ray gun, or can it trigger an attack on a playmate? When children grow up, can television violence increase the likelihood that they will violently attack someone?

In one longitudinal investigation, the amount of violence viewed on television at age 8 was significantly related to the seriousness of criminal acts performed as an adult (Huesmann, 1986). In another investigation, long-term exposure to television violence was significantly related to the likelihood of aggression in 1,565 boys 12 to 17 years old (Belson, 1978). Boys who watched the most aggression on television were the most likely to commit a violent crime, swear, be aggressive in sports, threaten violence toward another boy, write slogans on walls, or break windows. These investigations are *correlational*, so we can conclude from them not that television violence causes children to be more aggressive, but only that watching television violence is *associated with* aggressive behavior. In one experiment, children were randomly assigned to one of two groups: One watched television shows taken directly from violent Saturday-morning cartoon offerings on 11 different days; the second group watched television cartoon shows with all of the violence removed (Steur, Applefield & Smith, 1971). The children were then observed during play at their preschool. The preschool children who saw the TV cartoon shows with violence kicked, choked, and pushed their playmates more than the preschool children who watched nonviolent TV cartoon shows did. Because children were randomly assigned to the two conditions (TV cartoons with violence versus with no violence), we can conclude that exposure to TV violence *caused* the increased aggression in children in this investigation.

In an extensive study of television violence, a number of conclusions were reached (Federman, 1997). Television violence can have three harmful effects on viewers. A viewer can learn aggressive attitudes and behaviors from watching television violence, become sensitized to the seriousness of the violence, and feel frightened of becoming a victim of real-life violence. The effects are more likely to occur in certain types of violent portrayals. Contextual features of television violence, such as an attractive perpetrator, justification for violence, and violence that goes unpunished, can increase the risk of harmful effects. Other features, such as showing the harmful consequences, may reduce the likelihood of violence.

An example of a high-risk portrayal of violence on television involves a hostile motorcycle gang that terrorizes a neighborhood. In their harassment, they kidnap a well-known rock singer. A former boyfriend of the singer then tries to rescue her. He sneaks up on the gang and shoots six of them, one at a time. Some of the gunfire causes the motorcycles to blow up. The scene ends with the former boyfriend rescuing the tied-up singer.

This violence contains all of the features that encourage aggression in adolescents. The ex-boyfriend is young and good looking, and cast as a rugged hero. His attack on the gang is shown as justifiable—the gang members are ruthless and uncontrollable, and have kidnapped an innocent woman. The "hero" is never punished or disciplined,

Developmental Issues	What Children See on TV	What Children Should See
To establish a sense of *trust and safety.*	The world is dangerous; enemies are everywhere; weapons are needed to feel safe.	A world where people can be trusted and help each other, where safety and predictability can be achieved, where fears can be overcome.
To develop a sense of *autonomy with connectedness.*	Autonomy is equated with fighting and weapons. Connectedness is equated with helplessness, weakness, and altruism.	A wide range of models of independence within meaningful relationships and of autonomous people helping each other.
To develop a sense of *empowerment and efficacy.*	Physical strength and violence equals power and efficacy. Bad guys always return, and a range of ways to have an impact are *not* shown.	Many examples of people having a positive effect on their world without violence.
To establish *gender identity.*	Exaggerated, rigid gender divisions—boys are strong, violent, and save the world; girls are helpless, victimized and irrelevant to world events.	Complex characters with wide-ranging behaviors, interests, and skills; commonalities between the sexes overlapping in what both can do.
To develop an *appreciation of diversity* among people.	Racial and ethnic stereotyping. Dehumanized enemies. Diversity is dangerous. Violence against those who are different is justified.	Diverse peoples with varied talents, skills, and needs, who treat each other with respect, work out problems nonviolently, and enrich each other's lives.
To construct the foundations of *morality and social responsibility.*	One-dimensional characters who are all good or all bad. Violence is the solution to interpersonal problems. Winning is the only acceptable outcome. Bad guys deserve to be hurt.	Complex characters who act responsibly and morally toward others—showing kindness and respect, working out moral problems, taking other people's points of view.
To have opportunities for *meaningful play.*	Program content is far removed from children's experience or level of understanding. Toys are linked to programs promoting initiative, not to creative play.	Meaningful content to use in play, which resonates deeply with developmental needs; shows not linked to realistic toys so that children can create their own unique play.

Figure **18.4**

A Developmental Framework for Assessing Television

even though it appears that he has taken the law into his own hands. Serving as the ultimate reward, the young woman proclaims her love for him after he rescues her. Also, in spite of the extensive violence in this movie, no one is shown as being seriously hurt. The focus quickly shifts away from gang members after they have been shot, and viewers do not see anyone die or suffer.

Television can also teach children that it is better to behave in positive, prosocial ways than in negative, antisocial ways. Television researcher Aimee Leifer (1973) demonstrated that television is associated with prosocial behavior in young children; she selected a number of *Sesame Street* episodes that reflected positive social interchanges. She was especially interested in situations that taught children how to use their social skills. For example, in one interchange, two men were fighting over the amount of space available to them; they gradually began to cooperate and to share the space. Children who watched these episodes copied these behaviors, and, in later social situations, they applied the prosocial lessons they had learned. To read about ways to make television more developmentally appropriate, see figure 18.4.

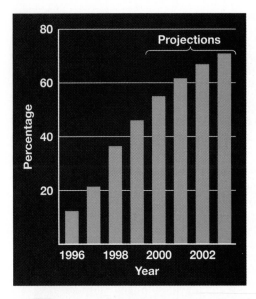

Figure **18.5**

Percentage of American Adolescents Who Go Online

Internet
The core of computer-mediated communication. The Internet system is worldwide and connects thousands of computer networks, providing an incredible array of information adolescents can access.

E-mail	83%
Search engine	78
Music sites	59
General research	58
Games	51
TV/movie sites	43
Chat room	42
Own Web page	38
Sports sites	35

Figure **18.6**

Percentage of American Adolescents Who Go Online Engaging in a Particular Activity

Television and Cognitive Development   Children bring various cognitive skills and abilities to their television viewing experience (Rabin & Dorr, 1995). Compared to older children, preschoolers and young children attend to television more, comprehend less central content and more incidental content, and have difficulty making inferences about content (Anderson & others, 1986). These youngest viewers have difficulty representing television content and often fill in their incomplete representations with stereotypes and familiar scripts derived from their limited general knowledge of television and the world (Meadowcroft & Reeves, 1989). They usually are not aware that some content is intended to sell them toys and breakfast cereal rather than to entertain and inform them. Older children have a better understanding in all of these areas, but they still process television information less effectively than adults do. Children's greater attention to television, and their less complete and more distorted understanding of what they view, suggest that they may miss some of the positive aspects of television and be more vulnerable to its negative aspects.

How does television influence children's creativity and verbal skills? Television is negatively related to children's creativity (Williams, 1986). Also, because television is primarily a visual modality, verbal skills—especially expressive language—are enhanced more by aural or print exposure (Beagles-Roos & Gat, 1983). Educational programming for young children can promote creativity and imagination, possibly because it has a slower pace and auditory and visual modalities are better coordinated. Newer technologies, especially interactive television, hold promise for motivating children to learn and become more exploratory in solving problems.

Computers and the Internet

Culture involves change, and nowhere is that change greater than in the technological revolution today's children are experiencing with increased use of computers and the Internet. For children to be adequately prepared for tomorrow's jobs, technology needs to become an integral part of their lives (Sharp, 1999). In a poll of seventh- through twelfth-graders jointly conducted by CNN and the National Science Foundation (1997), 82 percent predicted that they would not be able to make a good living unless they have computer skills and understand other technology. The technology revolution is part of the information society in which we now live.

People are using computers to communicate today the way they used to use pens, postage stamps, and telephones. The new information society still relies on some basic nontechnological competencies: good communication skills, the ability to solve problems, thinking deeply, thinking creatively, and having positive attitudes. However, how people pursue these competencies is being challenged and extended in ways and at a speed that few people had to cope with in previous eras (Bissell, Manring, & Rowland, 1999; Collis & Sakamoto, 1996).

The Internet   The **Internet** *is the core of computer-mediated communication. The Internet system is worldwide and connects thousands of computer networks, providing an incredible array of information adolescents can access.* In many cases, the Internet has more current, up-to-date information than books. In 1996, President Clinton proposed that every school in the United States should be wired for Internet access because of how it has revolutionized access to information. By 1998, 89 percent of public schools had been connected to the Internet. As indicated in figure 18.5, 47 percent of adolescents used the computer to go online in 1999, a figure that is expected to rise to more than 70 percent by 2002.

What do adolescents do when they are online? As shown in figure 18.6, sending and receiving e-mail is the activity they engage in most frequently. More than 40 percent of the adolescents who go online connect with a chat room.

EXPLORATIONS IN CHILD DEVELOPMENT
Using the Internet in the Classroom

FOLLOWING ARE SOME effective ways that the Internet can be used in classrooms.

- *To help students gather and integrate knowledge.* The Internet has huge databases of information that are organized in different ways. As students explore Internet sources, they can construct projects that integrate information from various sources that they otherwise could not access (Cafolla, Kauffman, & Knee, 1997).

- *To foster collaborative learning.* One of the most effective ways to use the Internet in your classroom is in project-centered activities for small groups. The Internet is so huge and has so many resources that teamwork improves the outcome of most Internet searches. One collaborative learning use of the Internet is to have a group of students conduct a survey on a topic (Maddux, Johnson, & Willis, 1997). Students can construct the survey, put it out on the Internet, and expect to get responses back from many parts of the world in just a few days. They can organize, analyze, and summarize the data from the survey and then share it with other classes around the world. Another type of collaborative learning project involves sending groups of students on Internet "scavenger hunts" to find out information and/or solve a problem.

- *To allow e-mail.* An increasing number of innovative educational projects include e-mail. In chapter 8,

"Information Processing," we examined Ann Brown and Joe Campione's program Fostering a Community of Learners (Brown, in press; Brown & Campione, 1996). Students in FCL can communicate with experts, which frees teachers from the burden of being the sole dispenser of knowledge and gives students access to a wider circle of knowledgeable people. This is sometimes called "electronic mentoring." Students also can communicate with each other. In the Global Lab project, classrooms around the world are interconnected so that students can communicate via e-mail with students in other countries (Berenfeld, 1994).

Students enjoy using e-mail to communicate with students in other schools, states, and countries. E-mail can especially be rewarding for shy students who become anxious and withdraw from face-to-face communicating.

- *To improve the teacher's knowledge and understanding.* An excellent Internet resource for teachers is the Eric Resource Information Center, which provides free information about a wide range of educational topics. You can send an e-mail inquiry to the AskERIC department (askeric@ericir.syr.edu) with the search's key words, and within 3 days they will e-mail you a list of citations. The AskERIC department also provides information about lesson plans and connections to other resources.

E-mail *stands for "electronic mail" and is another valuable way that the Internet can be used. Messages can be sent to and received from individuals as well as large numbers of people.* Explorations in Child Development discusses some ways that teachers can effectively use the Internet in classrooms.

Special concerns have emerged about children's and adolescents' access to information on the Internet, which has been largely unregulated. In many instances, adolescents can access adult sexual material, information about how to make bombs, and other inappropriate information.

With as many as 11 million American adolescents now online, more and more of adolescent life is taking place in a landscape that is inaccessible to many parents. Many adolescents have a computer in their bedroom, and most parents don't have any idea what information their adolescents are obtaining online. Some psychologists recommend putting the computer in the family room, where adults and adolescents have more opportunities to discuss what information is being accessed online. Every Web browser records what sites users visit. With just elementary computer knowhow, parents can monitor their adolescents' computer activities.

e-mail
Electronic mail. A valuable use of Internet. Messages can be sent to and received by individuals as well as large numbers of people.

Tips for Using the Internet
Webliography
Internet Pals
Critical Analysis of the Internet

How extensively are adolescents using the Internet? What are some of the Internet activities in which they participate?

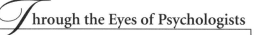
hrough the Eyes of Psychologists

Sandra Calvert, *Georgetown University*

"It is timely and important for our society to make the journey through the information age accessible and interesting to all youth, and to ensure them a safe passage during the journey."

Technology and Sociocultural Diversity

Technology brings with it certain social issues (Calvert, 1999). A special concern is whether increased use of technology (especially computers) in homes and schools will widen the learning gap between rich and poor, male and female students (Maddux, Johnson, & Willis, 1997). For example, in 1996, less than one-third of schools with a majority of students from low-income backgrounds had Internet access, whereas two-thirds of schools with students from primarily higher socioeconomic backgrounds had Internet access. There are gaps in computer availability across ethnic groups as well. In 1998, 49.3 percent of Whites had Internet access compared to 35.5 percent of African Americans (Hoffman & Novak, 1999). And families with a male child are more likely to own a computer than those with a female child (DeVillar & Faltis, 1991).

Technology and Education

The number of computers in schools has increased dramatically. Yet despite its potential for improving student learning, the use of technology in schools continues to lag behind other segments of society, such as business. Computers are still used too often for drill-and-practice activities rather than for constructive learning. In one survey, a majority of middle and high school students reported using computers only minimally over a 30-week period (Becker, 1994). In this survey, 1 of 11 students said they used school computers for English class, 1 of 15 for a math class, and only 1 of 40 for a social science class.

Many teachers do not have adequate training in using computers, and school districts have been slow to provide much needed technology workshops. And with rapidly changing technology, the computers that many schools purchase quickly become outdated. Other computers break and sit in need of repair.

Such realities mean that learning in schools has not yet been technologically revolutionized. Only when schools have technologically trained teachers and current, workable technologies will the technology revolution have an opportunity to truly transform classrooms.

It is important to keep in mind that technology itself does not improve a child's ability to learn. A number of conditions in combination are necessary to create learning environments that adequately support students' learning. These include vision and support from educational leaders, educators who are skilled in the use of technology for learning, access to contemporary technologies, and an emphasis on the child as an active, constructivist learner (International Society for Technology in Education, 1999).

At this point we have studied many ideas about technology and children's development. A review of these ideas is presented in summary table 18.3.

Technology and Education
Educational Technology Journal
Critical Issues in Technology and Education
Technology Standards in Education
Learning Technology Center

Just a step away is the creation of a global, interactive, multi-media database to make the most current information available to all teachers anywhere in the world.

Dee Dickinson
Contemporary American Teacher and Author

$\mathcal{S}$UMMARY $\mathcal{T}$ABLE 18.3
Technology

Concept	Processes/ Related Ideas	Characteristics/Description
Television	Television's Many Roles	• Although television can have a negative influence on children's development by taking them away from homework, making them passive learners, teaching them stereotypes, and presenting them with unrealistic views of the world, television also can have positive influences by presenting motivating educational programs, increasing children's information beyond their immediate environment, and providing models of prosocial behavior.
	The Amount of Television Children Watch	• Children watch huge amounts of TV. Preschool children watch an average of 4 hours a day. • U.S. children watch more TV than children in all other countries.
	The Effects of Television on Aggression and Prosocial Behavior	• Up to 80 percent of the prime-time TV shows have violent episodes. • TV violence is not the only cause of children's aggression, but most experts agree that it can induce aggression and antisocial behavior. • Prosocial behavior on TV is associated with increased positive behavior by children.
	Television and Cognitive Development	• Children's cognitive skills and abilities influence their TV viewing experiences. • TV viewing is negatively related to children's verbal skills and creativity.
Computers and the Internet	Their Influences on Children	• Today's children are experiencing a technological revolution through the dramatic increase in the use of computers and the Internet.
	The Internet	• The Internet is the core of computer-mediated communication, and it is worldwide. • A special concern is the largely unregulated aspects of the Internet that make it difficult for parents to monitor the information their children are accessing.
	Technology and Sociocultural Diversity	• One concern is whether increased technology will widen the gap between rich and poor, male and female students.
	Technology and Education	• The number of computers has significantly increased in America's schools, but many schools have not been technologically revolutionized. • Keep in mind that technology alone does not improve children's learning. A combination of other factors such as an emphasis on active, constructivist learning also is required.

Chapter Review

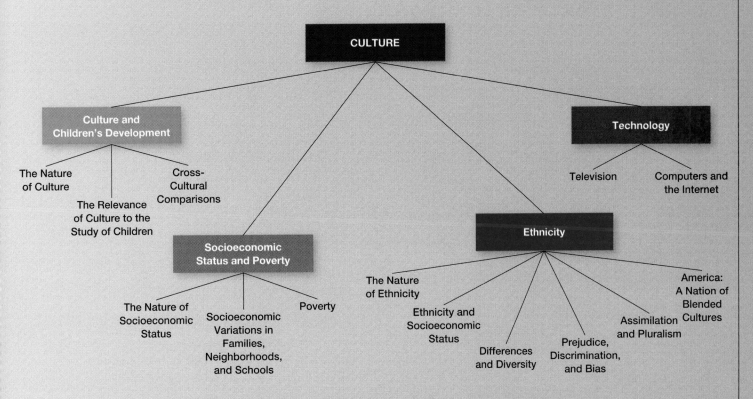

TO OBTAIN A DETAILED REVIEW OF THE CHAPTER, STUDY THESE THREE SUMMARY TABLES:

Key Terms

culture 554
ethnocentrism 556
cross-cultural studies 556
individualism 556
collectivism 557

rites of passage 557
socioeconomic status (SES) 558
feminization of poverty 561
ethnicity 563
prejudice 565

assimilation 566
pluralism 566
Internet 572
e-mail 573

Key People

Richard Brislin 554
Donald Campbell 555
Margaret Mead 555

Vonnie McLoyd 561
James Jones 566
Stanley Sue 566

Aimee Leifer 571
Sandra Calvert 574

Child Development Resources

Children's Journey Through the Information Age (1999)
    by Sandra Calvert
    New York: McGraw-Hill

This is an excellent, contemporary treatment of many dimensions of the information age, such as television and computers.

Cybereducator (1999)
    by Joan Bissell, Anna Manring, and Veronica Roland

A guide to using the Internet for K–12 education.

Studying Ethnic Minority Adolescents (1998)
    by Vonnie McLoyd & Laurence Steinberg (Eds.)
    Mahwah, NJ: Erlbaum

Read about a number of important research and practical issues regarding ethnic minority youth.

Working with Latino Youth (1999)
    by Joan Koss-Chioino and Louis Vargas
    San Francisco: Jossey-Bass

This book provides practical information about the special needs of Latino youth and strategies for helping them.

Taking It to the Net

1. Jeremy is attending college in California, where he is majoring in political science. For his senior thesis he is required to choose an area of social policy and develop a legislative agenda. Based upon recent news reports about the increasing number of low- and middle-income wage earners who don't make enough money for decent housing, food, and health care for their children, he decides to make the needs of these children his priority. What types of programs should he propose for the children of these families?

2. Mrs. Bernstein thinks that she ought to involve her fourth-grade students in a dialogue about racism and prejudice, because there are several ethnic groups represented in her class. But a colleague warned her that talking to kids about racism could backfire and actually cause prejudice. Is that possible?

3. Denise has heard about the "digital divide"—the concept that ethnic minorities and economically deprived populations are not participating in the Internet explosion. Denise is about to begin teaching third grade in an inner-city school, and she wonders if the school is likely to be as well equipped technologically as a school in a better neighborhood. What are the facts?

Connect to *http://www.mhhe.com/santrockc9* to find the answers!

Epilogue

CHILDREN: THE FUTURE OF SOCIETY

In the end the power behind development is life.

Erik Erikson
Danish-Born, American Psychoanalytic Theorist, 20ᵗʰ Century

In the twenty-first century, the well-being of children is one of our most important concerns. We all cherish the future of our children, for they are the future of any society. Children who do not reach their full potential, who are destined to make fewer contributions to society than society needs, and who do not take their place as productive adults diminish the power of that society's future. In this epilogue, we will summarize some of the most important concepts and issues that have been discussed in this book and present a montage of thoughts that convey the power, beauty, and complexity of children's development.

Our journey through childhood has been long and complex, and you have read about many different facets of children's lives. This is a good time to stand back and ask yourself what you have learned. What theories, studies, and ideas struck you as more important than others? What did you learn about your own development as an infant, a child, and an adolescent? Did anything you learn stimulate you to rethink how children develop? How you developed into the person you are today?

Themes in Children's Development

As we look back across the chapters of *Child Development*, some common themes emerge. Let's explore some of these main themes.

Knowledge About Children's Development Has Benefited from a Diversity of Theories and an Extensive Research Enterprise

A number of theories have made important contributions to our understanding of children's development. From the biological theory of ethology to the cognitive theories of Piaget and Vygotsky to the social theories of Erikson and Bronfenbrenner, each has contributed an important piece of the developmental puzzle. However, no single theory is capable of predicting, explaining, and organizing the rich, complex, multifaceted landscape of the child's developmental journey. The inability of a single theory to explain all of children's development should not be viewed as a shortcoming of a theory. Any theory that at-

tempts to explain all of children's development is too general. The field of child development has been moved forward by theories that are precise and zero in on key aspects of one or two dimensions of children's lives rather than by theories that try to do everything.

Knowledge about children's development has also benefited from a research effort that has greatly expanded over the last several decades. The science of child development has become a highly sophisticated field in which collecting evidence about children is based on well-defined rules, exemplary practices, mathematical procedures for handling the evidence, and drawing inferences from what has been found.

Children Benefit from Both Basic Research and Applied Research

Across the eighteen chapters of *Child Development*, we have discussed both basic research and applied research. Basic research, sometimes called pure research, is the study of issues to obtain knowledge for its own sake rather than for practical application. By contrast, applied research is the study of issues that have direct practical significance, often with the intent of changing human behavior. Social policy research is applied research rather than basic research.

A developmentalist who conducts basic research might ask: How is the cognitive development of children different from adolescents? By contrast, a developmentalist who conducts applied research might ask: How can knowledge about children's and adolescents' cognitive development be used to educate them more effectively or to help them cope more effectively with stress? A basic researcher might also ask: Can a nonhuman primate, such as a chimpanzee, learn to use sign language? An applied researcher might ask: Can strategies used to teach language to chimpanzees be applied to improve the language abilities of retarded children who do not speak?

Most developmentalists believe that both basic and applied research contribute to improving children's lives. Although basic research sometimes produces information that can be applied to improve the welfare of children, it does not guarantee this application. By contrast, insisting that research always be relevant is like trying to grow flowers by focusing only on the blossoms and not tending to the roots. Basic research is root research. Without the discovery of basic principles, we would have little information to apply (Wade & Tavris, 1993).

Children's Development Is Influenced by an Interaction of Heredity and Environment

Both heredity and environment are necessary even for children to exist. Heredity and environment operate together—or cooperate—to produce a child's height and weight, ability to shoot a basketball, intelligence, reading skills, temperament, and all other dimensions of the child's development.

In chapter 1, we discussed the nature-nurture controversy, the debate about whether development is primarily influenced by heredity and maturation (nature) or by environment and experience (nurture). The debate shows no signs of subsiding, but for now virtually all developmentalists are interactionists, accepting that children's development is determined by both heredity and environment. Behavior geneticists continue to specify more precisely the nature of heredity-environment interaction through such concepts as those of passive, evocative, and active genotype/environment interactions and shared and nonshared environmental influences.

Children's Development Involves Both Continuity and Discontinuity

Some developmentalists emphasize the continuity of development, the view that development involves gradual, cumulative change from conception to death. Others stress the discontinuity of development, the view that development consists of distinct stages in the life span.

Development involves both continuity and discontinuity. For example, while Piaget's stages reflect discontinuity in that they portray children as making a distinct change from preoperational to concrete operational thinking, researchers recently have found that young children's intelligence shows more continuity than was once believed. Who is right? Probably both. As Piaget envisioned, most preschool children are egocentric and center on the obvious physical characteristics of stimuli. Most concrete operational children do not think hypothetically and don't solve problems in a scientific manner. In these ways, children's development is stagelike, as Piaget proposed. However, as information-processing oriented researchers believe, children's thinking is not as stagelike as Piaget thought.

Children's Development Is Determined by Both Early and Later Experiences

While children's development is influenced by both early and later experiences, developmentalists still debate how strong the contributions of each type of experience are. The early-experience advocates argue that early experiences, especially in infancy, are more important than later experiences. They believe, for example, that warm, nurturant, sensitive caregiving in the first year of life is necessary for optimal later development. Later experiences are not as important in shaping the child's developmental path, they say.

By contrast, other developmentalists stress that later experiences are just as important as early experiences in children's development. That is, warm, nurturant, sensitive parenting is just as important in the elementary school years in shaping children's development as it is in infancy. People in Western cultures are stronger advocates of early experiences, those in Eastern cultures of later experiences. The debate goes on.

Children's Development Is Determined by an Interaction of Biological, Cognitive, and Socioemotional Processes

Biological processes involve changes in a child's physical nature, such as genes inherited from parents, development of the brain, prenatal and pubertal hormonal changes, and the development of motor skills. Cognitive processes involve changes in the child's thought, intelligence, and language, such as developing symbols for objects, memorizing a poem, solving a math problem, and putting together a sentence. Socioemotional processes involve changes in the child's relationships with other people, emotions, and personality, such as an infant's smile in response to her mother's touch, the intimate conversation of two friends, and a girl's development of assertiveness.

In many parts of the book, you read about how biological, cognitive, and socioemotional processes are intricately interwoven. For example, biology plays an important role in children's temperament, especially influencing how shy or gregarious children are. Inadequate parenting early in children's development can seriously undermine their intelligence. Cognitive changes substantially alter how children think about their parents and peers. Both theory and research involving children's development are becoming more integrated and less compartmentalized as links across different domains of development are sought.

Children's Development Involves Both Communalities with Other Children and Individual Variation

Every child develops in certain ways like all other children. Every child, unless afflicted by a serious handicap, walks by the age of 1 to 1½ years, talks by the age of 2 or 2½ years, engages in fantasy play in early childhood, is reared by adult caregivers who have more power and control than the child does, engages in mutual give-and-take in peer relations, goes to school, and becomes more independent and searches for an identity as an adolescent.

But children are not just like collections of geese; they are also unique, each child writing an individual history. One child may grow up in the well-groomed lawns of suburbia, another in the confines of an inner-city ghetto. One child may be short, another tall. One child may be a genius, another mentally retarded. One child may be abused, another lavished with love. And one child may be highly motivated to learn, another couldn't care less.

Children's Behavior Is Multiply Determined

An important aspect of thinking about the behavior of any child is that the child's behavior is multiply determined. When we think about what causes a child's behavior, we often lean toward explaining it in terms of a single cause. Consider a 7-year-old boy named Bobby. His teacher says that he is having trouble in school because he is from a father-absent home. The implication is that not having a father present in the home causes Bobby's poor academic performance. Not having a father might be one factor in Bobby's poor performance in school, but many others also influence his behavior. These factors include his genetic heritage and a host of environmental and sociocultural experiences, both in the past and the present. On closer inspection of Bobby's circumstances, we learn that not only has he been father-absent all of his life, never knowing his father, but that his extended-family support system has also been weak. We also learn that he lives in a low-income area with little community support for recreation, libraries, and child services. The school system Bobby is enrolled in has a poor record of helping low-achieving children and has little interest in developing programs for children from disadvantaged circumstances. We could find other factors that help explain Bobby's poor school achievement, but these examples illustrate the importance of going beyond accepting a single cause as *the* reason for a child's behavior. As with each of us, Bobby's behavior is multiply determined.

Children's Development Is Determined by Internal/External and Self/Other Influences

Controversy still surrounds whether children are architects of their own development (internal, self-determined) or whether their development is primarily orchestrated by the external forces of others. However, most experts on children recognize that development is not entirely internal and self-generated and, likewise, not entirely external and other-determined. Trying to tease apart internal/external and self/other influences is extraordinarily difficult because the child is always embedded in a social context with others. To be certain, children are not buffeted about helplessly by their environment. Children bring developmental capacities to any situation and act on the situation. At the same time, however, they interact with others who offer their own versions of the world, which children sometimes learn from and adopt for themselves. At times, children are solitary young scientists, crafting their own book of dreams and reality, as Piaget envisioned; at others, they are socially intertwined with skilled teachers and peers, as Vygotsky conceived.

America, especially male America, has had a history of underscoring the importance of self-determination and individu-

alism. Recently, however, females have challenged the status of self-determination as a more important human value than being connected to others and competent at relationships. And as psychologists have become more interested in cultures around the world, they have begun to recognize that many cultures, especially Eastern cultures, promote values that emphasize concern for others, interdependence, and harmonious relationships. It is important for us to raise a nation of children who not only value a separate "I"-ness, uniqueness, and self-determination but who also value connectedness with others, concern for others, and harmony in relationships.

We Need to Dramatically Reduce the Number of Children at Risk of Not Reaching Their Full Potential

Far too many children in America are not reaching their full potential because they are not being adequately reared by caregivers, adequately instructed in school, or adequately supported by society. Children who do reach their full potential and grow up to make competent contributions to their world invariably have been given considerable individual attention and support as they were growing up. Children need parents who are extensively involved with them, are sensitive to their needs, and have a sound understanding of their own and their children's development.

We also need schools that place a greater emphasis on a curriculum that is developmentally appropriate. This needs to be accomplished at all levels of education, especially in early childhood education, elementary school education, and middle school education. And we need to give more attention to our nation's social policy, especially in terms of ways to break through the poverty cycle that enshrouds more than 25 percent of the children in the United States. Our nation's political values need to reflect greater concern for the inadequate conditions in which far too many children live. And, to reduce the number of children at risk for not reaching their potential, we should focus our attention on the prevention of problems or early intervention in the problems.

Children Will Benefit from an Interdisciplinary Approach to Their Development

Some of you taking this class in child development are being taught by a child psychologist, others by someone who specialized in human development or family relationships, others by an educational psychologist or professor in an education department, others by a nurse or pediatrician, and yet others by professors from different disciplines. The field of child development has become more interdisciplinary. Our knowledge about children, and how to improve children's lives, has benefited, and will continue to benefit, from the contributions of scholars and professionals from a number of different disciplines, including developmental psychology, education and educational psychology, pediatrics and nursing, child clinical psychology and child psychiatry, sociology, anthropology, and law. The collaboration between child developmentalists and pediatricians/nurses is one example of this interdisciplinary cooperation, with the emerging area of how development influences children's health reflecting this cross-disciplinary trend. Another example is the interest in children's eyewitness testimony that links the fields of child development and law.

Children's Development Is Embedded in Sociocultural, Historical Circumstances

Throughout this book we have emphasized the importance of considering the contexts in which the child develops. Context refers to the setting in which development occurs, a setting that is influenced by historical, economic, social, and cultural factors. These contexts or settings include homes, schools, peer groups, churches, cities, neighborhoods, communities, university laboratories, the United States, Russia, France, Japan, Egypt, and many others—each with meaningful historical, economic, social, and cultural legacies.

In the twentieth century alone in the United States, successive waves of children have witnessed dramatic historical changes, including two world wars and their violence, the Great Depression and its economic woes, the advent of television and computers, increased levels of education, and altered gender roles. And as new generations of babies have been born, they have increasingly been babies with an ethnic minority heritage.

THE JOURNEY OF CHILDHOOD

I hope you can look back and say that you learned a lot in this course about children, not only other children, but yourself as a child and how your childhood contributed to who you are today. The insightful words of nineteenth-century Danish philosopher Søren Kierkegaard capture the importance of looking back to understand ourselves: "Life is lived forward but understood backwards." I also hope that those of you who become the parents of children or who work with children in some capacity—whether as teacher, as counselor, or as community leader—feel that you now have a better grasp of what children's development is all about.

Future generations depend on our ability to face our children. At some point in our adult lives, each one of us needs to examine the shape of our life and ask whether we have met the responsibility of competently and caringly carving out a better world for our children. Twenty-one centuries ago, Roman poet and philosopher Lucretius described one of adult life's richest meanings: grasping that the generations of living things pass in a short while and, like runners, pass on the torch of life. More than twenty centuries later, American writer James Agee captured yet another of life's richest meanings: In every child who is born, the potentiality of the human species is born again.

As we come to the end of this book, I leave you with the following montage of thoughts and images that convey the beauty and complexity of children's development.

The rhythm and meaning of human development involve beginnings, when questions of whence and whither, when and how are asked. How from so simple a beginning do endless forms develop and grow and mature? What was this organism, what is it now, and what will it become? Birth's fragile moment arrives, when the newborn is on a threshold between two worlds.

As newborns, we were not empty-headed organisms. We cried, kicked, coughed, sucked, saw, heard, and tasted. We slept a lot and occasionally we smiled, although the meaning of our first smiles was not entirely clear. We crawled and then we walked, a journey of a thousand miles beginning with a single step. With each forward step we left some ghost of ourselves behind. Sometimes we conformed, sometimes others conformed to us. Our development was a continuous creation of more-complex forms and our helpless kind demanded the "meeting eyes of love." We split the universe into two halves: "me" and "not me." And we juggled the need to curb our own will with becoming what we could will freely.

In early childhood, our greatest untold poem was being only 4 years old. We skipped, played, and ran all the day long, never again in our lives to be so busy, busy becoming something we had not quite grasped yet. Who knew our thoughts, which we worked up into small mythologies all our own? While our thoughts and feelings took wings, the blossoms of our heart no wind could touch. Our small world widened as we discovered new refuges and new people. When we said "I," we meant something totally unique, not to be confused with any other.

In middle and late childhood, we were on a different plane, belonging to a generation and feeling properly our own. It is the wisdom of human development that at no other time are we more ready to learn that at the end of early childhood's period of expansive imagination. Our thirst was to know and to understand. Our parents continued to cradle our lives, but our growth was also being shaped by successive choirs of friends. We did not think much about the future or the past, but enjoyed the present.

In no order of things was adolescence the simple time of life for us. We clothed ourselves with rainbows and went "brave as the zodiac," flashing from one end of the world to the other. We tried on one face after another, searching for a face of our own. We wanted our parents to understand us and hoped they would give us the privilege of understanding them. We wanted to fly but found that first we had to learn to stand and walk and climb and dance. In our most pimply and awkward moments we became acquainted with sex. We played furiously at adult games but were confined to a society of our own peers. Our generation was the fragile cable by which the best and the worst of our parents' generation were transmitted to the present. In the end, there were but two lasting bequests our parents could leave us—one being roots, the other wings.

Glossary

A

AB̄ error The Piagetian object-permanence concept in which an infant progressing into substage 4 makes frequent mistakes, selecting the familiar hiding place (A) rather than the new hiding place (B̄). 209

accommodation Piagetian concept of adjustment to new information. 205

acculturation Cultural change that results from continuous, firsthand contact between two distinctive cultural groups. Acculturative stress is the negative consequence of acculturation. 352

achievement motivation (need for achievement) The desire to accomplish something, to reach a standard of excellence, and to expend effort to excel. 540

active (niche-picking) genotype-environment correlations Correlations that exist when children seek out environments they find compatible and stimulating. 90

adaptive behavior Behavior that promotes the organism's survival in its habitat. 70

adolescence The developmental period of transition from childhood to early adulthood, entered at approximately 10 to 12 years of age and ending at 18 to 22 years of age. 16

adolescent egocentrism The heightened self-consciousness of adolescents, which is reflected in their belief that others are as interested in them as the adolescents are in themselves, and in adolescents' sense of personal uniqueness and vulnerability. 221

adoption study A study in which investigators seek to discover whether, in behavior and psychological characteristics, adopted children are more like their adoptive parents, who provided a home environment, or more like their biological parents, who contributed their heredity. Another form of the adoption study is to compare adoptive and biological siblings. 86

affordances The opportunities for interaction that an object offers us, allowing us to perform functional activities. 149

afterbirth The third stage of birth, when the placenta, umbilical cord, and other membranes are detached and expelled. 113

AIDS (acquired immune deficiency syndrome) A disease caused by a virus (HIV) that destroys the body's immune system. Consequently, germs that usually do not harm someone with a normal immune system produce devastating results and death. 185

algorithms Strategies that guarantee a solution to a problem. 259

alternate forms reliability Giving alternate forms of the same test on two different occasions. 283

altruism Unselfish interest in helping another person. 436

amniocentesis A prenatal medical procedure in which a sample of amniotic fluid is withdrawn by syringe and tested to discover if the fetus is suffering from any chromosomal or metabolic disorders. It is performed between the 12th and 16th weeks of pregnancy. 79

amnion The life-support system that is a bag or envelope that contains a clear fluid in which the developing embryo floats. 99

analgesia Drugs used to alleviate pain, such as tranquilizers, barbiturates, and narcotics. 114

androgens Hormones, the most important of which is testosterone, that promote the development of male genitals and secondary sex characteristics. 396

androgyny The presence of desirable masculine and feminine characteristics in the same person. 409

anesthesia Drugs used in late first-stage labor and during expulsion of the baby to block sensation in an area of the mother's body or to block the mother's consciousness. 114

anger cry A cry similar to the basic cry but with more air forced through the vocal cords (associated with exasperation or rage). 344

animism A facet of preoperational thought, the belief that inanimate objects have "lifelike" qualities and are capable of action. 212

anorexia nervosa An eating disorder that involves the relentless pursuit of thinness through starvation. 192

anoxia The insufficient availability of oxygen to the fetus or newborn. 113

Apgar Scale A widely used method to assess the health of newborns at 1 and 5 minutes after birth. The Apgar Scale evaluates infants' heart rate, respiratory effort, muscle tone, body color, and reflex irritability. 119

aphasia A language disorder, resulting from brain damage, that involves a loss of the ability to use words. 314

assimilation Piagetian concept of the incorporation of new information into existing knowledge. 205

assimilation The absorption of ethnic minority groups into the dominant group, which often means the loss of some or virtually all of the behavior and values of the ethnic minority group. 566

assistive technology Services and devices that help students with disabilities function within their environment. 539

associative play Play that involves social interaction with little or no organization. 496

attachment A close emotional bond between the infant and the caregiver. 358

attention Concentrating and focusing mental resources. 240

attention deficit hyperactivity disorder (ADHD) A disability in which children consistently show one or more of the following characteristics: (1) inattention, (2) hyperactivity, and (3) impulsivity. 536

attribution theory The theory that, in their effort to make sense out of their own behavior or performance, individuals are motivated to discover its underlying causes. Attributions are perceived causes of outcomes. 543

authoritarian parenting This is a restrictive, punitive style in which the parent exhorts the child to follow the parent's directions and to respect work and effort. Firm limits and controls are placed on the child, and little verbal exchange is allowed. This style is associated with children's socially incompetent behavior. 464

authoritative parenting This style encourages children to be independent but still places limits and controls on their actions. Extensive verbal give-and-take is allowed, and parents are warm and nurturant toward the child. This style is associated with children's socially competent behavior. 464

automaticity The ability to process information with little or no effort. 238

autonomous morality (Piaget) The second stage of moral development in Piaget's theory, displayed by older children (about 10 years of age and older). The child becomes aware that rules and laws are created by people and that, in judging an action, one should consider the actor's intentions as well as the consequences. 421

B

basal metabolism rate (BMR) The minimum amount of energy an individual uses in a resting state. 171

basic cry A rhythmic pattern usually consisting of a cry, a briefer silence, a shorter inspiratory whistle that is higher pitched than the main cry, and then a brief rest before the next cry. 344

basic-skills-and-phonetics approach An approach that emphasizes that reading instruction should teach phonetics and its basic rules for translating written symbols into sounds. 328

Bayley Scales of Infant Development Developed by Nancy Bayley, these scales are widely used in assessing infant development. The current version has three parts: Mental Scale, Motor Scale, and Behavior Rating Scale. 292

behavior genetics The study of the degree and nature of behavior's heredity basis. 86

behaviorism The scientific study of observable behavioral responses and their environmental determinants. 42

biological processes Changes in an individual's body. 15

blastocyst The inner layer of cells that develops during the germinal period. These cells later develop into the embryo. 98

bonding   Close contact, especially physical, between parents and their newborn in the period shortly after birth.   123

boundary ambiguity   The uncertainty in stepfamilies about who is in or out of the family and who is performing or responsible for certain tasks in the family system.   479

brainstorming   A technique in which participants are encouraged to come up with creative ideas in a group, play off each other's ideas, and say practically whatever comes to mind.   303

Brazelton Neonatal Behavioral Assessment Scale   A test given several days after birth to assess newborns' neurological development, reflexes, and reactions to people.   119

breech position   A baby's position in the uterus that causes the buttocks to be the first part to emerge from the vagina.   115

Broca's area   An area of the brain's left frontal lobe that directs the muscle movements involved in speech production.   314

bulimia   An eating disorder that involves a binge-and-purge sequence on a regular basis.   192

canalization   The process by which characteristics take a narrow path or developmental course. Apparently, preservative forces help to protect a person from environmental extremes.   85

care perspective   The moral perspective, emphasized by Carol Gilligan, that views people in terms of their connectedness with others and emphasizes interpersonal communication, relationships with others, and concern for others.   429

case study   An in-depth look at an individual.   53

centration   The focusing of attention on one characteristic to the exclusion of all others.   213

cephalocaudal pattern   The sequence in which the greatest growth occurs at the top—the head—with physical growth in size, weight, and feature differentiation gradually working from top to bottom.   130

cerebral cortex   An area of the forebrain that makes up about 80 percent of the brain's volume and plays critical roles in perception, language, thinking, and many other important functions.   131

cesarean delivery   A childbirth method in which the baby is removed from the mother's uterus through an incision made in her abdomen. This also is sometimes referred to as cesarean section.   115

character education   A direct approach that involves teaching students a basic moral literacy to prevent them from engaging in immoral behavior and doing harm to themselves or others.   440

child-centered kindergarten   Education that involves the whole child by considering both the child's physical, cognitive, and social development and the child's needs, interests, and learning styles.   519

chorionic villi sampling   A prenatal medical procedure in which a small sample of the

placenta is removed at a certain point in the pregnancy between the 8th and the 11th weeks of pregnancy.   79

chromosomes   Threadlike structures that come in 23 pairs, one member of each pair coming from each parent. Chromosomes contain the genetic substance DNA.   72

classical conditioning   The process in which a neutral stimulus becomes associated with a meaningful stimulus and acquires the capacity to elicit a similar response.   40

cliques   Smaller groups that involve greater intimacy among members and have more cohesion than crowds.   506

cognitive appraisal   Lazarus' term for children's interpretations of events in their lives as harmful, threatening, or challenging, and their determination of whether they have the resources to effectively cope with the event.   350

cognitive constructivist approaches   Approaches that emphasize the child's active, cognitive construction of knowledge and understanding; Piaget's theory is an example of this approach.   518

cognitive developmental theory of gender   In this view, children's gender-typing occurs after they have developed a concept of gender. Once they begin to consistently conceive themselves as male or female, children often organize their world on the basis of gender.   403

cognitive moral education   A concept based on the belief that students should learn to value things like democracy and justice as their moral reasoning develops.   440

cognitive processes   Changes in an individual's thought, intelligence, and language.   15

collectivism   Emphasizing values that serve the group by subordinating personal goals to preserve group integrity, interdependence of members, and harmonious relationships.   557

commitment   The part of identity development in which adolescents show a personal investment in what they are going to do.   386

concepts   Categories used to group objects, events, and characteristics on the basis of common properties.   255

concurrent validity   A form of criterion validity that assesses the relation of a test's scores to a criterion that is presently available (concurrent).   284

conduct disorder   The psychiatric diagnosis category used when multiple behaviors occur over a 6-month period. These behaviors include truancy, running away, fire setting, cruelty to animals, breaking and entering, excessive fighting, and others. When three or more of these behaviors co-occur before the age of 15 and the child or adolescent is considered unmanageable or out of control, the clinical diagnosis is conduct disorder.   443

connectedness   An important element in adolescent identity development. It consists of two dimensions: mutuality, sensitivity to and respect for others' views; and permeability, openness to others' views.   388

conservation   The idea that an amount stays the same regardless of how its container changes.   213

constructive play   Play that combines sensorimotor/practice repetitive activity with symbolic representation of ideas. Constructive play occurs when children engage in self-regulated creation or construction of a product or a problem solution.   498

constructivist view   Advocated by Piaget and the information-processing psychologists, this view states that perception is a cognitive construction based on sensory input plus information retrieved from memory. In this view, perception is a kind of representation of the world that builds up as the infant constructs an image of experiences.   148

content validity   The test's ability to test a broad range of the content that is to be measured.   283

context   The settings, influenced by historical, economic, social, and cultural factors, in which development occurs.   12

continuity of development   The view that development involves gradual, cumulative change from conception to death.   17

continuity view   A developmental view that emphasizes the role of early parent-child relationships in constructing a basic way of relating to people throughout the life span.   457

controversial children   Children who are frequently nominated both as someone's best friend and as being disliked.   491

conventional reasoning   The second, or intermediate, level in Kohlberg's theory of moral development. Internalization is intermediate. Individuals abide by certain standards (internal), but they are the standards of others (external), such as parents or the laws of society.   422

convergent thinking   Thinking that produces one correct answer and is characteristic of the kind of thinking required on conventional intelligence tests.   302

cooperative play   Play that involves social interaction in a group with a sense of group identity and organized activity.   496

coordination of secondary circular reactions   Piaget's fourth sensorimotor substage, which develops between 8 and 12 months of age. In this substage, several significant changes take place involving the coordination of schemes and intentionality.   207

correlational research   Research whose goal is to describe the strength of the relation between two or more events or characteristics.   54

creativity   The ability to think in novel and unusual ways and come up with unique solutions to problems.   302

crisis   A period of identity development during which the adolescent is choosing among meaningful alternatives.   386

criterion validity   The test's ability to predict an individual's performance when assessed by other measures, or criteria, of the attribute.   283

critical period   A period in which there is learning readiness. Beyond this period, learning is difficult or impossible.   315

critical thinking   Thinking reflectively and productively, and evaluating the evidence.   265

cross-cultural studies   Comparisons of one culture with one or more other cultures. These provide information about the degree to which children's development is similar, or universal, across cultures, and to the degree to which it is culture-specific.   12

cross-cultural studies   Studies that compare a culture with one or more other cultures. Such studies provide information about the degree to which adolescent development is similar, or universal, across cultures or about the degree to which it is culture-specific.   556

cross-sectional research   Research that studies people all at one time.   55

crowd   The largest and least personal of adolescent groups.   506

cultural-familial retardation   A mental deficit in which no evidence of organic brain damage can be found; individuals' IQs range from 55 to 70.   301

culture   The behavior patterns, beliefs, and all other products of a group that are passed on from generation to generation.   12

culture   The behavior, patterns, beliefs, and all other products of a particular group of people that are passed on from generation to generation.   554

culture-fair tests   Intelligence tests that are intended to not be culturally biased.   298

dating scripts   The cognitive models that adolescents and adults use to guide and evaluate dating interactions.   511

dependent variable   The factor that is measured as the result of an experiment.   55

deprivation dwarfism   A type of growth retardation caused by emotional deprivation; when children are deprived of affection, they experience stress, which alters the release of hormones by the pituitary gland.   164

development   The pattern of change that begins at conception and continues through the life cycle.   14

developmental biodynamics   The new perspective on motor development in infancy that seeks to explain how motor behaviors are assembled for perceiving and acting.   145

developmental construction views   Views sharing the belief that as individuals grow up, they acquire modes of relating to others. There are two main variations of this view. One emphasizes continuity and stability in relationships throughout the life span; the other emphasizes discontinuity and changes in relationships throughout the life span.   457

developmentally appropriate practice   Education that focuses on the typical developmental patterns of children (age appropriateness) and the uniqueness of each child (individual appropriateness). Such practice contrasts with developmentally inappropriate practice, which ignores the concrete, hands-on approach to learning. Direct teaching largely through abstract paper-and-pencil activities presented to large groups of young children is believed to be developmentally inappropriate.   521

developmental quotient (DQ)   An overall developmental score that combines subscores on motor, language, adaptive, and personal-social domains in the Gesell assessment of infants.   292

difficult child   A temperament style in which the child tends to react negatively and cry frequently, engages in irregular daily routines, and is slow to accept new experiences.   356

direct instruction approach   A teacher-centered approach that is characterized by teacher direction and control, mastery of academic material, high expectations for students' progress, and maximum time spent on learning tasks.   518

discontinuity of development   The view that development involves distinct stages in the life span.   17

discontinuity view   A developmental view that emphasizes change and growth in relationships over time.   459

dishabituation   Renewed interest in a stimulus.   241

dismissing/avoidant attachment   An insecure attachment category in which individuals deemphasize the importance of attachment. This category is associated with consistent experiences of rejection of attachment needs by caregivers.   470

divergent thinking   Thinking that produces many answers to the same question and is characteristic of creativity.   302

DNA   A complex molecule that contains genetic information.   72

dominant-recessive genes principle   If one gene of a pair is dominant and one is recessive (goes back or recedes), the dominant gene exerts its effect, overriding the potential influence of the recessive gene. A recessive gene exerts its influence only if both genes in a pair are recessive.   83

doula   A caregiver who provides continuous physical, emotional, and educational support to the mother before, during, and just after childbirth.   114

Down syndrome   A common genetically transmitted form of mental retardation, caused by the presence of an extra (47th) chromosome.   78

dyslexia   A category of learning disabilities involving a severe impairment in the ability to read and spell.   535

early childhood   The developmental period that extends from the end of infancy to about 5 to 6 years, sometimes called the preschool years.   16

early-later experience issue   The issue of the degree to which early experiences (especially infancy) or later experiences are the key determinants of the child's development.   17

easy child   A temperament style in which the child is generally in a positive mood, quickly establishes regular routines, and adapts easily to new experiences.   356

echoing   Repeating what a child says, especially if it is an incomplete phrase or sentence.   317

eclectic theoretical orientation   An approach that does not follow any one theoretical approach, but instead selects and uses whatever is considered the best in many different theories.   47

ecological theory   Bronfenbrenner's view of development, involving five environmental systems—microsystem, mesosystem, ecosystem, macrosystem, and chronosystem. These emphasize the role of social contexts in development.   45

ecological view   Advocated by the Gibsons, this view states that the purpose of perception is to detect perceptual invariants—those that remain stable—in a constantly changing world.   149

ectoderm   The outermost layer of cells, which becomes the nervous system, sensory receptors (ears, nose, and eyes, for example), and skin parts (hair and nails, for example).   98

egocentrism   A salient feature of preoperational thought, the inability to distinguish between one's own and someone else's perspective.   211

e-mail   Electronic mail. A valuable use of Internet. Messages can be sent to and received by individuals as well as large numbers of people.   573

embryonic period   The period of prenatal development that occurs 2 to 8 weeks after conception. During the embryonic period, the rate of cell differentiation intensifies, support systems for the cells form, and organs appear.   98

emotion   Feeling, or affect, that involves a mixture of physiological arousal and overt behavior.   340

emotional intelligence   A form of social intelligence that involves the ability to monitor one's own and others' feelings and emotions, to discriminate among them, and to use this information to guide one's thinking and action.   352

empathy   Reacting to another's feelings with an emotional response that is similar to the other person's feelings.   433

encoding   The mechanism by which information gets into memory.   238

endoderm   The inner layer of cells that develops into digestive and respiratory systems.   98

equilibration   A mechanism that Piaget proposed to explain how children shift from one stage of thought to the next. The shift occurs as children experience cognitive conflict or disequilibrium in trying to understand the world. Eventually, they resolve the conflict and reach equilibrium of thought.   205

Erikson's Theory   Erikson proposed eight stages of psychosocial development that unfold throughout the human life span. Each stage consists of a unique developmental task that confronts individuals with a crisis that must be faced.   33

estradiol   A hormone associated in girls with breast, uterine, and skeletal development.   181

estrogens   Hormones, the most important of which is estradiol, that influence the development of female physical sex characteristics and help regulate the menstrual cycle.   396

ethnic identity   A sense of membership in an ethnic group, based upon shared language, religion, customs, values, history, and race.   12

ethnic identity   An enduring, basic aspect of the self that includes a sense of membership in an ethnic group and the attitudes and feelings related to that membership.   388

ethnicity   A characteristic based on cultural heritage, nationality characteristics, race, religion, and language.   12

ethnicity   A dimension of culture based on cultural heritage, nationality, race, religion, and language.   563

ethnocentrism   A tendency to favor one's group over other groups.   554

ethology   An approach that stresses that behavior is strongly influenced by biology, tied to evolution, and characterized by critical or sensitive periods.   44

evocative genotype-environment correlations   Correlations that exist when the child's genotype elicits certain types of physical and social environments.   90

evolutionary psychology   The theory that emphasizes the importance of adaptation, reproduction, and "survival of the fittest" in explaining behavior.   70

expanding   Restating, in a linguistically sophisticated form, what a child has said.   317

experimental research   Research involving experiments that permit the determination of cause. A carefully regulated procedure in which one or more of the factors believed to influence the behavior being studied are manipulated and all other factors are held constant.   54

extrinsic motivation   External incentives such as rewards and punishments.   540

feminization of poverty   The fact that far more women than men live in poverty. Women's low income, divorce, and the resolution of divorce cases by the judicial system, which usually leaves women with less money than they and their children need to adequately function, are the likely causes.   561

fetal alcohol syndrome (FAS)   A cluster of abnormalities that appear in the offspring of mothers who drink alcohol heavily during pregnancy.   108

fetal period   The prenatal period of development that begins 2 months after conception and lasts for 7 months, on the average.   100

fine motor skills   Motor skills that involve more finely tuned movements, such as finger dexterity.   143

first habits and primary circular reactions   Piaget's second sensorimotor substage, which develops between 1 and 4 months of age. Infants learn to coordinate sensation and types of schemes or structures—that is, habits and primary circular reactions.   207

fragile X syndrome   A genetic disorder that results from an abnormality in the X chromosome, which becomes constricted and often breaks.   78

fraternal twins   Twins who develop from separate eggs and separate sperm, making them genetically no more similar than nontwin siblings.   86

frontal lobe   An area of the cerebral cortex involved in voluntary movement and thinking.   132

games   Activities engaged in for pleasure that include rules and often competition with one or more individuals.   499

gender   The sociocultural dimension of being male or female.   396

gender identity   The sense of being female or male, which most children acquire by the time they are 3 years old.   396

gender role   A set of expectations that prescribes how females and males should think, act, and feel.   396

gender-role transcendence   The belief that, when an individual's competence is at issue, it should be conceptualized not on the basis of masculinity, femininity, or androgyny but, rather, on a personal basis.   411

gender schema   A cognitive structure that organizes the world in terms of male and female.   404

gender schema theory   According to this theory, an individual's attention and behavior are guided by an internal motivation to conform to gender-based sociocultural standards and stereotypes.   404

gender stereotypes   Broad categories that reflect impressions and beliefs about what behavior is appropriate for females and males.   405

generalization   Generalizing or applying information to other problems or situations. This also has been discussed in the context of transfer.   238

genes   Units of hereditary information composed of DNA. Genes act as a blueprint for cells to reproduce themselves and manufacture the proteins that maintain life.   72

genetic epistemology   The study of how children's knowledge changes over the course of their development.   9

genotype   A person's genetic heritage; the actual genetic material.   84

germinal period   The period of prenatal development that takes place in the first 2 weeks after conception. It includes the creation of the zygote, continued cell division, and the attachment of the zygote to the uterine wall.   98

gifted   Having above-average intelligence (an IQ of 120 or higher) and/or superior talent for something.   301

grasping reflex   A neonatal reflex that occurs when something touches the infant's palms. The infant responds by grasping tightly.   142

gross motor skills   Motor skills that involve large muscle activities, such as walking.   143

habituation   Repeated presentation of the same stimulus, which causes reduced attention to the stimulus.   241

helpless orientation   An orientation in which one seems trapped by the experience of difficulty and attributes one's difficulty to a lack of ability.   544

heteronomous morality (Kohlberg)   The first stage in Kohlberg's theory. At this stage, moral thinking is often tied to punishment.   422

heteronomous morality (Piaget)   The first stage of moral development in Piaget's theory, occurring at 4 to 7 years of age. Justice and rules are conceived of as unchangeable properties of the world, removed from the control of people.   421

heuristics   Strategies or rules of thumb that can suggest a solution to a problem but don't guarantee a solution.   259

hidden curriculum   The moral atmosphere that is part of every school.   439

holophrase hypothesis   The theory that, in infants' first words, a single word is used to stand for a complete sentence.   321

horizontal décalage   Piaget's concept that similar abilities do not appear at the same time within a stage of development.   218

hypotheses   Specific testable assumptions and predictions that are derived from theories.   29

hypothetical-deductive reasoning   Piaget's formal operational concept that adolescents have the cognitive ability to develop hypotheses about ways to solve problems and can systematically deduce which is the best path to follow in solving the problem.   220

identical twins   Twins who develop from a single fertilized egg that splits into two genetically identical replicas, each of which becomes a person.   86

identification theory   A theory that stems from Freud's view that preschool children develop a sexual attraction to the opposite-sex parent, then at 5 to 6 years of age renounce the attraction because of anxious feelings, subsequently identifying with the same-sex parent and unconsciously adopting the same-sex parent's characteristics.   398

identity achievement   Marcia's term for an adolescent's having undergone a crisis and made a commitment.   386

identity diffusion   Marcia's term for the state adolescents are in when they have not yet experienced a crisis (that is, they have not yet explored meaningful alternatives) or made any commitments.   386

identity foreclosure   Marcia's term for the state adolescents are in when they have made a commitment but have not experienced a crisis.   386

identity moratorium Marcia's term for the state of adolescents who are in the midst of a crisis, but whose commitments either are absent or are only vaguely defined. 386

identity versus identity confusion Erikson's fifth developmental stage, which individuals experience during the adolescent years. At this time, adolescents examine who they are, what they are all about, and where they are going in life. 383

imaginary audience An adolescent's belief that others are as preoccupied with her as she is. 222

immanent justice Piaget's concept that if a rule is broken, punishment will be meted out immediately. 421

implantation The attachment of the zygote to the uterine wall, which takes place about 10 days after conception. 98

inclusion Educating a child with special education needs full-time in the regular classroom. 539

independent variable The manipulated, influential, experimental factor in an experiment. 55

index offenses Criminal acts, whether they are committed by juveniles or adults. They include such acts as robbery, aggravated assault, rape, and homicide. 443

individual differences The stable, consistent ways in which people are different from one another. 282

individualism Giving priority to personal goals rather than to group goals; emphasizing values that serve the self, such as feeling good, personal distinction and achievement, and independence. 556

individualism, instrumental purpose, and exchange The second Kohlberg stage of moral development. At this stage, individuals pursue their own interests but also let others do the same. 422

individuality An important element in adolescent identity development. It consists of two dimensions: self-assertion, the ability to have and communicate a point of view; and separateness, the use of communication patterns to express how one is different from others. 388

individualized education plan (IEP) A written statement that spells out a program tailored to a child with a disability. The plan should be (1) related to the child's learning capacity, (2) specially constructed to meet the child's individual needs and not merely a copy of what is offered to other children, and (3) designed to provide educational benefits. 539

Individuals with Disabilities Education Act (IDEA) The IDEA spells out broad mandates for services to all children with disabilities (IDEA is a renaming of Public Law 98-142); these include evaluation and eligibility determination, appropriate education and the individualized education plan (IEP), and the least restrictive environment (LRE). 538

induction A discipline technique in which a parent uses reason and explanation of the consequences for others of the child's actions. 438

indulgent parenting A style in which parents are highly involved with their children but place few demands or controls on them. This is associated with children's social incompetence, especially a lack of self-control. 465

infancy The developmental period that extends from birth to 18 to 24 months. 16

infinite generativity The ability to produce an endless number of meaningful sentences using a finite set of words and rules. 310

information processing How individuals process information about their world; how information enters the mind, how it is stored and transformed, and how it is retrieved to perform such complex activities as problem solving and reasoning. 38

information-processing approach The approach that focuses on the ways children process information about their world—how they manipulate information, monitor it, and strategize about it. 238

innate goodness view The idea, presented by Swiss-born philosopher Jean-Jacques Rousseau, that children are inherently good. 7

instructional technology Various types of hardware and software, combined with innovative teaching methods, to accommodate students' learning needs in the classroom. 539

intelligence Verbal ability, problem-solving skills, and the ability to adapt to and learn from life's everyday experiences. 282

intelligence quotient (IQ) Devised in 1912 by William Stern, this consists of an individual's mental age divided by chronological age multiplied by 100. 285

intermodal perception The ability to relate and integrate information about two or more sensory modalities, such as vision and hearing. 156

internalization The developmental change from behavior that is externally controlled to behavior that is controlled by internal standards and principles. 422

internalization of schemes Piaget's sixth sensorimotor substage, which develops between 18 and 24 months of age. In this substage, infants' mental functioning shifts from a purely sensorimotor plane to a symbolic plane, and they develop the ability to use primitive symbols. 208

Internet The core of computer-mediated communication. The Internet system is worldwide and connects thousands of computer networks, providing an incredible array of information adolescents can access. 572

intimacy in friendship Self-disclosure and the sharing of private thoughts. 502

intrinsic motivation Internal factors such as self-determination, curiosity, challenge, and effort. 541

intuitive thought substage The second substage of preoperational thought, occurring approximately between 4 and 7 years of age. Children begin to use primitive reasoning and want to know the answers to all sorts of questions. 212

involution The process by which the uterus returns to its prepregnant size. 122

justice perspective A moral perspective that focuses on the rights of the individual; individuals independently make moral decisions. 428

juvenile delinquency A broad range of behaviors, ranging from socially unacceptable behavior (such as acting out in school) to status offenses (such as running away) to criminal acts (such as burglary). 443

Klinefelter syndrome A genetic disorder in which males have an extra X chromosome, making them XXY instead of XY. 78

L

labeling Identifying the names of objects. 317

laboratory A controlled setting from which many of the complex factors of the real world have been removed. 52

language A form of communication, whether spoken, written, or signed, that is based on a system of symbols. 310

language acquisition device (LAD) Chomsky's theoretical concept of a biological endowment enables the child to detect certain language categories, such as phonology, syntax, and semantics. 315

lateralization Specialization of functions in one hemisphere of the cerebral cortex or the other. 132

learned helplessness Seligman's theory of depression—that it occurs when individuals are exposed to negative experiences, especially prolonged stress or pain, over which they have no control. 349

learning disability A disability that involves (1) having normal intelligence or above, (2) having difficulties in at least one academic area and usually several, and (3) having no other problem or disorder, such as mental retardation, that can be determined as causing the difficulty. 535

least restrictive environment (LRE) The concept that a child with a disability must be educated in a setting that is as similar as possible to the one in which children who do not have a disability are educated. 539

longitudinal research Research that studies the same people over a period of time, usually several years or more. 55

long-term memory A type of memory that holds enormous amounts of information for a long period of time in a relatively permanent fashion. 247

love withdrawal A discipline technique in which a parent withholds attention or love from the child. 437

low-birthweight infant   An infant born after a regular period of gestation (the length of time between conception and birth) of 38 to 42 weeks but weighs less than 5 1/2 pounds.   116

mainstreaming   Educating a child with special education needs partially in a special education classroom and partially in a regular classroom.   539

marasmus   A wasting away of bodily tissues in the infant's first year, caused by severe protein-calorie deficiency.   139

mastery orientation   An orientation in which one is task-oriented and, instead of focusing on one's ability, is concerned with learning strategies.   544

maternal blood test   A prenatal diagnostic technique that is used to assess blood alphaprotein level, which is associated with neural-tube defects. This technique is also called the alpha-fetoprotein test (AFP).   80

maturation   The orderly sequence of changes dictated by the individual's genetic blueprint.   16

Maximally Discriminative Facial Movement Coding System (MAX)   Izard's system of coding infants' facial expressions related to emotion. MAX coders watch slow-motion and stop-action videotapes of infants' facial reactions to stimuli.   344

mean length of utterance (MLU)   An index of language development based on the number of morphemes per sentence a child produces in a sample of about 50 to 100 sentences.   322

means-end analysis   A heuristic in which one identifies the goal (end) of a problem, assesses the current situation, and determines what needs to be done (means) in order to attain the goal.   259

meiosis   The process of cell doubling and separation of chromosomes in which each pair of chromosomes in a cell separates, with one member of each pair going into each gamete.   72

memory   The retention of information over time, involving encoding, storage, and retrieval.   240

menarche   First menstruation.   179

mental age (MA)   An individual's level of mental development relative to others.   285

mental retardation   A condition of limited mental ability in which the individual has a low IQ, usually below 70 on a traditional intelligence test, has difficulty adapting to everyday life, and has an onset of these characteristics during the so-called developmental period—by age 18.   300

mesoderm   The middle layer of cells, which becomes the circulatory system, bones, muscles, excretory system, and reproductive system.   98

metacognition   Cognition about cognition, or "knowing about knowing."   238

metacognitive activity   Using self-awareness to adapt to and manage strategies during problem solving and thinking.   269

metacognitive knowledge   Monitoring and reflecting on one's current or recent thoughts.   269

middle and late childhood   The developmental period that extends from about 6 to 11 years of age, approximately corresponding to the elementary school years, sometimes called the elementary school years.   16

mitosis   The process by which each chromosome in a cell's nucleus duplicates itself.   72

Montessori approach   An educational philosophy in which children are given considerable freedom and spontaneity in choosing activities and are allowed to move from one activity to another as they desire.   521

moral development   Age-related thoughts, feelings, and behaviors regarding rules, principles, and values that guide what people should do.   420

Moro reflex   A neonatal startle response that occurs in reaction to a sudden, intense noise or movement. When startled, the newborn arches its back, throws its head back, and flings out its arms and legs. Then the newborn rapidly closes its arms and legs to the center of the body.   142

morphology   Word formation.   311

motherese   The kind of speech often used by mothers and other adults to talk to babies—in a higher pitch than normal and with simple words and sentences.   317

multiple-factor theory   L. L. Thurstone's theory that intelligence consists of seven primary mental abilities: verbal comprehension, number ability, word fluency, spatial visualization, associative memory, reasoning, and perceptual speed.   288

mutual interpersonal expectations, relationships, and interpersonal conformity   Kohlberg's third stage of moral development. At this stage, individuals value trust, caring, and loyalty to others as a basis of moral judgments.   422

myelination   A process in which nerve cells are insulated with a layer of fat cells, which increases the speed at which information travels through the nervous system.   166

natural childbirth   A method of childbirth, developed in 1914 by Dick-Read, intended to reduce the mother's pain by decreasing her fear through education about childbirth and relaxation techniques during delivery.   115

naturalistic observation   Observations that take place out in the real world instead of in a laboratory.   52

natural selection   The evolutionary process that favors individuals of a species that are best adapted to survive and reproduce.   70

nature-nurture controversy   Nature refers to an organism's biological inheritance, nurture to environmental influences. The "nature" proponents claim biological inheritance is the most important influence on development; the "nurture" proponents claim that environmental experiences are the most important.   17

negative affectivity (NA)   Emotions that are negatively toned, such as anxiety, anger, guilt, and sadness.   340

neglected children   Children who are infrequently nominated as a best friend but are not disliked by their peers.   491

neglectful parenting   A style in which the parent is very uninvolved in the child's life. It is associated with children's social incompetence, especially a lack of self-control.   464

neo-Piagetians   Developmentalists who have elaborated on Piaget's theory, believing that children's cognitive development is more specific in many respects than he thought.   226

neuron   A nerve cell that handles information processing at the cellular level.   131

nonshared environmental experiences   The child's own unique experiences, both within the family and outside the family, that are not shared by another sibling. Thus, experiences occurring within the family can be part of the "nonshared environment."   90

normal distribution   A symmetrical distribution with a majority of the cases falling in the middle of the possible range of scores and few scores appearing toward the extremes of the range.   286

norms   Established standards of performance for a test. Norms are created by giving the test to a large group of individuals representative of the population for whom the test is intended. This allows the test constructor to determine the distribution of the test scores. Norms tell us which scores are considered high, low, or average.   284

object permanence   The Piagetian term for one of an infant's most important accomplishments: understanding that objects and events continue to exist even when they cannot directly be seen, heard, or touched.   208

occipital lobe   An area of the cerebral cortex involved in vision.   132

onlooker play   Play in which the child watches other children play.   496

operations   Internalized sets of actions that allow children to do mentally what before they had done physically.   211

oral rehydration therapy (ORT)   A treatment involving a range of techniques designed to prevent dehydration during episodes of diarrhea by giving children fluids by mouth.   175

organic retardation   Mental retardation caused by a genetic disorder or by brain damage; "organic" refers to the tissues or organs of the body, so there is some physical damage in organic retardation.   301

organization   Piaget's concept of grouping isolated behaviors into a higher-order, more smoothly functioning cognitive system; the grouping or arranging of items into categories. The use of organization improves long-term memory.   205

organogenesis   Organ formation that takes place during the first 2 months of prenatal development.   100

original sin view Advocated during the Middle Ages, the belief that children were born into the world as evil beings and were basically bad. 6

overextension The tendency of children to misuse words by extending one word's meaning to include objects that are not related to, or are inappropriate for, the word's meaning. 321

oxytocics Synthetic hormones designed to stimulate contractions. 114

pain cry A sudden appearance of loud crying without preliminary moaning and a long initial cry followed by an extended period of breath holding. 344

parallel play Play in which the child plays separately from others, but with toys like those the others are using or in a manner that mimics their play. 496

parietal lobe An area of the cerebral cortex involved in bodily sensations, such as touch. 132

passive genotype-environment correlations Correlations that exist when parents, who are genetically related to the child, provide a rearing environment for the child. 89

peers Children of about the same age or maturity level. 488

perception The interpretation of what is sensed. 148

performance orientation An orientation in which one focuses on achievement outcomes; winning is what matters most, and happiness is thought to result from winning. 544

personal fable An adolescent's sense of personal uniqueness and indestructibility. 222

perspective taking The ability to assume another person's perspective and understand his or her thoughts or feelings. 378, 491

phenotype The way an individual's genotype is expressed in observed and measurable characteristics. 84

phenylketonuria (PKU) A genetic disorder in which an individual cannot properly metabolize an amino acid. PKU is now easily detected but, if left untreated, results in mental retardation and hyperactivity. 78

phonology A language's sound system. 310

Piaget's theory The theory that children actively construct their understanding of the world and go through four stages of cognitive development. 35

placenta A life-support system that consists of a disk-shaped group of tissues in which small blood vessels from the mother and offspring intertwine. 98

play A pleasurable activity that is engaged in for its own sake. 495

play therapy Therapy that allows the child to work off frustrations and is a medium through which the therapist can analyze the child's conflicts and ways of coping with them. Children may feel less threatened and be more likely to express their true feelings in the context of play. 495

pluralism The coexistence of distinct ethnic and cultural groups in the same society. 566

polygenic inheritance The genetic principle that many genes can interact to produce a particular characteristic. 84

popular children Children who are frequently nominated as a best friend and are rarely disliked by their peers. 491

positive affectivity (PA) A range of positive emotions—from high energy, enthusiasm, and excitement to being calm, quiet, and withdrawn—that includes joy, happiness, and laughter. 340

possible self What an individual might become, what the person will be like, and what the person is afraid of becoming. 376

postconventional reasoning The highest level in Kohlberg's theory of moral development. Morality is completely internalized. 423

postpartum period The period after childbirth when the mother adjusts, both physically and psychologically, to the process of childbirth. This period lasts for about 6 weeks, or until her body has completed its adjustment and returned to a near prepregnant state. 120

power assertion A discipline technique in which a parent attempts to gain control over the child or the child's resources. 437

practice play Play that involves repetition of behavior when new skills are being learned or when physical or mental mastery and coordination of skills are required for games or sports. Sensorimotor play, which often involves practice play, is primarily confined to infancy, while practice play can be engaged in throughout life. 497

pragmatics The use of appropriate conversation and knowledge underlying the use of language in context. 312

preconventional reasoning The lowest level in Kohlberg's theory of moral development. The individual shows no internalization of moral values—moral reasoning is controlled by external rewards and punishment. 422

predictive validity A form of criterion validity that assesses the relation of a test's scores to the individual's performance at a point in the future. 284

prejudice An unjustified negative attitude toward an individual because of her or his membership in a group. 565

prenatal period The time from conception to birth. 16

preoccupied/ambivalent attachment An insecure attachment category in which adolescents are hypertuned to attachment experiences. This is thought to mainly occur because parents are inconsistently available to the adolescents. 470

prepared childbirth Developed by French obstetrician, Ferdinand Lamaze, this childbirth strategy is similar to natural childbirth but includes a special breathing technique to control pushing in the final stages of labor and a more detailed anatomy and physiology course. 115

pretend/symbolic play Play that occurs when a child transforms the physical environment into a symbol. 497

preterm infant An infant born prior to 38 weeks after conception. 116

primary appraisal Lazarus' concept that individuals interpret whether an event involves harm or loss that already has occurred, a threat that involves some future danger, or a challenge to be overcome. 350

primary circular reactions Schemes based on the infant's attempt to reproduce an interesting or pleasurable event that initially occurred by chance. 207

problem-based learning An approach that emphasizes solving authentic problems, like those that occur in daily life. 264

problem solving Finding an appropriate way to attain a goal. 258

Project Follow Through An adjunct to Project Head Start, in which the enrichment programs are carried through the first few years of elementary school. 524

Project Head Start Compensatory education designed to provide children from low-income families the opportunity to acquire the skills and experiences important for school success. 521

proximodistal pattern The sequence in which growth starts at the center of the body and moves toward the extremities. 130

psychoanalytic theory According to this theory, development is primarily unconscious and heavily colored by emotion, behavior is merely a surface characteristic, it is important to analyze the symbolic meanings of behavior, and early experiences are important in development. 31

psychosocial moratorium Erikson's term for the gap between childhood security and adult autonomy that adolescents experience as part of their identity exploration. 384

puberty A period of rapid skeletal and sexual maturation that occurs mainly in early adolescence. 180

Public Law 94-142 The Education for All Handicapped Children Act, created in 1975, which requires that all children with disabilities be given a free, appropriate public education and which provides the funding to help with the costs of implementing this education. 538

random assignment In experimental research, the assignment of participants to experimental and control groups by chance. 55

rapport talk The language of conversation and a way of establishing connections and negotiating relationships; more characteristic of females than of males. 407

reaction range The range of possible phenotypes for each genotype, suggesting the importance of an environment's restrictiveness or richness. 85

reading The ability to understand written discourse. 328

recasting Rephrasing a statement that a child has said, perhaps turning it into a question. 317

reciprocal socialization   The process by which children socialize parents just as parents socialize them.   456

reciprocal teaching   A teaching method in which students take turn leading small-group discussions.   266

reflexive smile   A smile that does not occur in response to external stimuli. It happens during the first month after birth, usually during irregular patterns of sleep, not when the infant is in an alert state.   345

rejected children   Children who are infrequently nominated as a best friend and are actively disliked by their peers.   491

reliability   The extent to which a test yields a consistent, reproducible measure of performance.   283

REM (rapid eye movement) sleep   A recurring sleep stage during which vivid dreams commonly occur.   135

report talk   Talk that conveys information; more characteristic of males than of females.   407

reproduction   The process that, in humans, begins when a female gamete (ovum) is fertilized by a male gamete (sperm).   72

retrieval   Taking information out of storage.   240

rites of passage   Ceremonies or rituals that mark an individual's transition from one status to another, especially into adulthood.   557

rooting reflex   A newborn's built-in reaction that occurs when the infant's cheek is stroked or the side of the mouth is touched. In response, the infant turns its head toward the side that was touched, in an apparent effort to find something to suck.   142

S

scaffolding   Changing the level of support over the course of a teaching session in which a more-skilled individual (teacher or more advanced peer of the child) adjusts the amount of guidance to fit the child's current performance level.   226

scaffolding   Parental behavior that supports children's efforts, allowing children to be more skillful than they would be if they relied only on their own abilities.   456

schema   A cognitive structure or network of associations that organizes and guides an individual's perception.   404

scheme (or schema)   The basic unit of an organized pattern of sensorimotor functioning.   207

scientific method   An approach that can be used to discover accurate information. It includes these steps: conceptualize the problem, collect data, draw conclusions, and revise research conclusions and theory.   29

secondary appraisal   Lazarus' concept that individuals evaluate their resources and determine how effectively they can cope with an event.   350

secondary circular reactions   Piaget's third sensorimotor substage, which develops between

4 and 8 months of age. Infants become more object oriented or focused on the world, moving beyond preoccupation with the self in sensorimotor interactions.   207

secure attachment   The infant uses the caregiver as a secure base from which to explore the environment. Ainsworth believes that secure attachment in the first year of life provides an important foundation for psychological development later in life.   360

self-concept   Domain-specific self-evaluations.   380

self-efficacy   The belief that one can master a situation and produce favorable outcomes.   544

self-esteem   The global evaluative dimension of the self; also called self-worth or self-image.   380

self-regulatory learning   Generating and monitoring thoughts, feelings, and behaviors to reach a goal.   270

self-understanding   A child's cognitive representation of the self, the substance and content of a child's self-conceptions.   372

semantics   The meanings of words and sentences.   312

sensation   Occurs when information interacts with the sensory receptors—the eyes, ears, tongue, nostrils, and skin.   148

sensorimotor play   Behavior engaged in by infants to derive pleasure from exercising their existing sensorimotor schemas.   497

sensory memory   The memory system that holds information from the world in its original sensory form for only an instant.   246

seriation   The concrete operation that involves ordering stimuli along a quantitative dimension (such as length).   218

service learning   A form of education that promotes social responsibility and service to the community.   441

sexual script   A stereotyped pattern of role prescriptions for how individuals should behave sexually.   184

shape constancy   The recognition that an object remains the same shape even though its orientation to us changes.   151

shared environmental experiences   Children's common environmental experiences that are shared with their siblings, such as their parents' personalities and intellectual orientation, the family's social class, and the neighborhood in which they live.   90

sickle-cell anemia   A genetic disorder that affects the red blood cells and occurs most often in people of African descent.   78

simple reflexes   Piaget's first sensorimotor substage, which corresponds to the first month after birth. The basic means of coordinating sensation and action is through reflexive behaviors, such as rooting and sucking, which infants have at birth.   207

size constancy   The recognition that an object remains the same size even though the retinal image of the object changes.   151

slow-to-warm-up child   A temperament style in which the child has a low activity level, is somewhat negative, shows low adaptability, and displays a low intensity of mood.   356

social cognitive theory   The theory that behavior, environment, and person/cognitive factors are important in understanding development.   42

social cognitive theory of gender   This theory emphasizes that children's gender development occurs through observation and imitation of gender behavior, and through rewards and punishments they experience for gender-appropriate and -inappropriate behavior.   398

social cognitive theory of morality   The theory that distinguishes between moral competence (the ability to perform moral behaviors) and moral performance (performing those behaviors in specific situations).   432

social constructivist approach   Emphasizes the social contexts of learning and that knowledge is mutually built and constructed.   229

social constructivist approaches   Approaches that focus on collaboration with others to produce knowledge and understanding; Vygotsky's theory is an example of this approach.   518

social contract or utility and individual rights   Kohlberg's fifth stage of moral development. At this stage, individuals reason that values, rights, and principles undergird or transcend the law.   423

social conventional reasoning   Thoughts about social consensus and convention.   429

social play   Play that involves social interactions with peers.   498

social policy   A national government's approach to influencing the welfare of its citizens.   12

social referencing   "Reading" emotional cues in others to help determine how to act in a particular situation.   345

social smile   A smile in response to an external stimulus, which, early in development, typically is in response to a face.   345

social system morality   The fourth stage in Kohlberg's theory of moral development. Moral judgments are based on understanding the social order, law, justice, and duty.   422

socioeconomic status (SES)   A grouping of people with similar occupational, educational, and economic characteristics.   558

socioemotional processes   Changes in an individual's relationships with other people, emotions, and personality.   15

solitary play   Play in which the child plays alone and independently of others.   495

split-half reliability   Dividing the items into two halves, such as the first half of the test and the second half of the test. Individuals' scores on the two halves of the test are compared to determine how consistently they performed.   283

standardization   Developing uniform procedures for administering and scoring a test, as well as creating norms for the test.   284

standardized tests   Commercially prepared tests that assess performance in different domains. A standardized test often allows a child's performance to be compared with the performance of other children at the same age, in many cases on a national level.   53

status offenses   Less serious acts (than index offenses). Status offenses include truancy, underage drinking, sexual promiscuity, and uncontrollability. They are performed by youth under a specified age, which make them juvenile offenses.   443

storage   The retention of information over time.   240

stranger anxiety   An infant's fear of and wariness toward strangers; it tends to appear in the second half of the first year of life.   345

Strange Situation   Ainsworth's observational measure of infant attachment to a caregiver that requires the infant to move through a series of introductions, separations, and reunions with the caregiver and an adult stranger in a prescribed order.   361

strategy construction   The process of discovering a new procedure for processing information.   238

stress   The response of individuals to the circumstances and events (called stressors) that threaten them and tax their coping abilities.   350

subgoaling   Setting intermediate goals that put one in a better position to reach the final goal or solution.   258

sucking reflex   A newborn's built-in reaction of automatically sucking an object placed in its mouth. The sucking reflex enables the infant to get nourishment before it has associated a nipple with food.   142

sudden infant death syndrome (SIDS)   A condition that occurs when an infant stops breathing, usually during the night, and suddenly dies without an apparent cause.   136

symbolic function substage   The first substage of preoperational thought, occurring roughly between the ages of 2 and 4. In this substage, the young child gains the ability to represent mentally an object that is not present.   211

syntax   The ways words are combined to form acceptable phrases and sentences.   311

tabula rasa view   The idea, proposed by John Locke, that children are like a "blank tablet."   6

telegraphic speech   The use of short and precise words to communicate; it characterizes young children's two- or three-word combinations.   321

temperament   An individual's behavioral style and characteristic emotional response.   356

temporal lobe   An area of the cerebral cortex involved in hearing.   132

teratogen   From the Greek word tera, meaning "monster." Any agent that causes a birth defect. The field of study that investigates the causes of birth defects is called teratology.   101

tertiary circular reactions   Schemes in which the infant purposely explores new possibilities with objects, continually changing what is done to them and exploring the results.   208

tertiary circular reactions, novelty, and curiosity   Piaget's fifth sensorimotor substage, which develops between 12 and 18 months of age. Infants become intrigued by the variety of properties that objects possess and by the

multiplicity of things they can make happen to objects.   208

testosterone   A hormone associated in boys with the development of genitals, an increase in height, and a change in voice.   181

test-retest reliability   The extent to which a test yields the same measure of performance when an individual is given the same test on two different occasions.   283

theory   An interrelated, coherent set of ideas that helps to explain and make predictions.   29

thinking   Manipulating and transforming information in memory.   255

top-dog phenomenon   The circumstance of moving from the top position in elementary school to the lowest position in middle or junior high school.   528

transitivity   In concrete operational thought, a mental concept that underlies the ability to logically combine relations to understand certain conclusions. It focuses on reasoning about the relations between classes.   218

triarchic theory   Sternberg's theory that intelligence consists of componential intelligence, experiental intelligence, and contextual intelligence.   290

trophoblast   The outer layer of cells that develops in the germinal period. These cells provide nutrition and support for the embryo.   98

Turner syndrome   A genetic disorder in which females are missing an X chromosome, making them XO instead of XX.   78

twin study   A study in which the behavioral similarity of identical twins is compared with the behavioral similarity of fraternal twins.   86

two-factor theory   Spearman's theory that individuals have both general intelligence, which he called *g*, and a number of specific intelligences, referred to as *s*.   288

type A babies   Infants who show insecurity by avoiding their caregiver (for example, by ignoring the caregiver, averting their gaze, or failing to seek proximity).   360

type B babies   Infants who use the caregiver as a secure base from which to explore the environment.   360

type C babies   Infants who show insecurity by resisting the caregiver (for example, by clinging to the caregiver but at the same time kicking and pushing away).   360

type D babies   Infants who show insecurity by being disoriented or afraid. This type of behavior is described as disorganized.   360

ultrasound sonography   A prenatal medical procedure in which high-frequency sound waves are directed into the pregnant woman's abdomen.   79

umbilical cord   A life-support system containing two arteries and one vein that connects the baby to the placenta.   99

underextension   A child's failure to apply a new word she is learning to a relevant object or event.   321

universal ethical principles   The sixth and highest stage in Kohlberg's theory of moral development. Individuals develop a moral standard based on universal human rights.   423

unoccupied play   Play in which the child is not engaging in play as it is commonly understood and might stand in one spot, look around the room, or perform random movements that do not seem to have a goal.   495

unresolved/disorganized attachment   An insecure category in which the adolescent has an unusually high level of fear and is disoriented. This may result from such traumatic experiences as a parent's death or abuse by parents.   470

validity   The extent to which a test measures what it is intended to measure.   283

values clarification   Helping people clarify what their lives are for and what is worth working for.   440

Vygotsky's theory   A sociocultural cognitive theory that emphasizes developmental analysis, the role of language, and social relations.   36

Wernicke's area   An area of the brain's left hemisphere that is involved in language comprehension.   315

whole-language approach   An approach that stresses that reading instruction should parallel children's natural language learning. Reading materials should be whole and meaningful.   328

working (short-term) memory   The limited-capacity memory system in which information is retained for as long as 30 seconds, unless the information is rehearsed, in which case it can be retained longer.   247

XYY syndrome   A genetic disorder in which males have an extra Y chromosome.   78

zone of proximal development (ZPD)   Vygotsky's term for the range of tasks that are too difficult for children to master alone but that can be mastered with the guidance and assistance of adults or more highly skilled children.   226

zygote   A single cell formed through fertilization.   72

A

Abbassi, V. (1998). Growth and normal puberty. *Pediatrics* (Supplement), *102* (2), 507–511.

Aber, J. L. (1993, March). *Poverty and child development: The policy implications of understanding causal mechanisms.* Paper presented at the biennial meeting of the Society for Research in Child Development, New Orleans.

Aboud, F., & Skerry, S. (1983). Self and ethnic concepts in relation to ethnic constancy. *Canadian Journal of Behavioral Science, 15,* 3–34.

Abramovitch, R., Corter, C., Pepler, D. J., & Stanhope, L. (1986). Sibling and peer interaction: A final follow-up and comparison. *Child Development, 47,* 217–229.

Abramson, L. Y., Metalsky, G. I., & Alloy, L. B. (1989). Hopelessness depression: A theory-based subtype of depression. *Psychological Bulletin, 96,* 358–372.

Academic Software, Inc. (1996). *Adaptive device locator system (computer program).* Lexington, KY: Author.

Acredolo, L. P., & Hake, J. L. (1982). Infant perception. In B. B. Wolman (Ed.), *Handbook of developmental psychology.* Englewood Cliffs, NJ: Prentice Hall.

Adams, G. R., Gulotta, T. P., & Montemayor, R. (Eds.). (1992). *Adolescent identity formation.* Newbury Park, CA: Sage.

Adams, R. J. (1989). Newborns' discrimination among mid- and long-wavelength stimuli. *Journal of Experimental Child Psychology, 47,* 130–141.

Adato, A. (1995, April). Living legacy? Is heredity destiny? *Life,* pp. 60–68.

Adler, T. (1991, January). Seeing double? Controversial twins study is widely reported, debated. *APA Monitor, 22,* 1, 8.

Ahn, N. (1994). Teenage childbearing and high school completion: Accounting for individual heterogeneity. *Family Planning Perspectives, 26,* 17–21.

Ainsworth, M. D. S. (1967). Infancy in Uganda: Infant care and the growth of love. In B. M. Caldwell & H. N. Riccuiti (Eds.), *Review of child development research* (Vol. 3). Chicago: University of Chicago Press.

Ainsworth, M. D. S. (1979). Infant-mother attachment. *American Psychologist, 34,* 932–937.

Alan Guttmacher Institute. (1995). *National survey of the American male's sexual habits.* New York: Author.

Alan Guttmacher Institute. (1998). *Teen sex and pregnancy.* New York: Author.

Alexander, A., Anderson, H., Heilman, P. C., & Others. (1991). Phonological awareness training and remediation of analytic decoding deficits in a group of severe dyslexics. *Annals of Dyslexia, 41,* 193–206.

Alexander, G. R., & Korenbrot, C. C. (1995). The role of prenatal care in preventing low birth weight. *Future of Children, 5,* (1), 103–120.

Aligne, C. A., & Stoddard, J. J. (1997). Tobacco and children: An economic evaluation of the medical effects of parental smoking. *Archives of Pediatric and Adolescent Medicine, 151,* 648–653.

Allen, J. P., & Hauser, S. T. (1994, February). *Adolescent-family interactions as predictors of qualities of parental, peer, and romantic relationships at age 25.* Paper presented at the meeting of the Society for Research on Adolescence, San Diego.

Allen, J. P., Hauser, S. T., & Borman-Spurrell, E. (1996). Attachment security and related sequelae of severe adolescent psychopathology: An eleven-year follow-up study. *Journal of Consulting and Clinical Psychology, 64,* 254–263.

Allen, J. P., & Kuperminc, G. P. (1995, March). *Adolescent attachment, social competence, and problematic behavior.* Paper presented at the meeting of the Society for Research in Child Development, Indianapolis.

Allen, J. P., Moore, C., Kuperminc, G., & Bell, K. (in press). Attachment and adolescent social functioning. *Child Development.*

Allen, M., Brown, P., & Finlay, B. (1992). *Helping children by strengthening families.* Washington, DC: Children's Defense Fund.

Amabile, T. M. (1993). Commentary. In D. Goleman, P. Kaufman, & M. Ray, *The creative spirit.* New York: Plume.

Amabile, T. M., & Hennesey, B. A. (1992). The motivation for creativity in children. In A. K. Boggiano & T. S. Pittman (Eds.), *Achievement and motivation.* New York: Cambridge University Press.

Amato, P. R., & Booth, A. (1996). A prospective study of divorce and parent-child relationships. *Journal of Marriage and the Family, 58,* 356–365.

Amato, P. R., & Keith, B. (1991). Parental divorce and the well-being of children: A meta-analysis. *Psychological Bulletin, 110,* 26–46.

America in Transition. (1989). Washington, DC: National Governors' Association Task Force on Children.

American Association for Protecting Children. (1986). *Highlights of official child neglect and abuse reporting: 1984.* Denver: American Humane Association.

American Association for the Advancement of Science. (1993). *Benchmarks for science literacy: Project 2061.* New York: Oxford University Press.

American Psychiatric Association. (1994). *Diagnostic and statistical manual of mental disorders* (4th ed.). Washington, DC: Author.

Amsterdam, B. K. (1968). *Mirror behavior in children under two years of age.* Unpublished doctoral dissertation, University of North Carolina, Chapel Hill.

Anastasi, A., & Urbina, S. (1996). *Psychological testing* (7th ed.). Upper Saddle River, NJ: Prentice Hall.

Anderman, E. M., Maehr, M. L., & Midgley, C. (1996). *Declining motivation after the transition to middle school: Schools can make a difference.* Unpublished manuscript, Lexington: University of Kentucky.

Anderson, D. R., Lorch, E., Field, D., Collins, P., & Nathan, J. (1986). Television viewing at home: Age trends in visual attention and time with TV. *Child Development, 52,* 151–157.

Anderson, E., Greene, S. M., Hetherington, E. M., & Clingempeel, W. G. (1999). The dynamics of parental remarriage. In E. M. Hetherington (Ed.), *Coping with divorce, single parenting, and remarriage.* Mahwah, NJ: Erlbaum.

Anderson, L. D. (1939). The predictive value of infant tests in relation to intelligence at 5 years. *Child Development, 10,* 202–212.

Anselmi, D. L. (1998). *Questions of gender.* New York: McGraw-Hill.

Appalachia Educational Laboratory. (1998). *ADHD—Building academic success.* Charleston, WV: Author.

Archer, S. L. (1989). The status of identity: Reflections on the need for intervention. *Journal of Adolescence, 12,* 345–359.

Archer, S. L. (Ed.). (1994). *Intervention for adolescent identity development.* Newbury Park, CA: Sage.

Archer, S. L., & Waterman, A. S. (1994). Adolescent identity development: Contextual perspectives. In C. Fisher & R. Lerner (Eds.), *Applied developmental psychology.* New York: McGraw-Hill.

Arehart, D. M., & Smith, P. H. (1990). Identity in adolescence: Influences on dysfunction and psychosocial task issues. *Journal of Youth and Adolescence, 19,* 63–72.

Ariès, P. (1962). *Centuries of childhood* (R. Baldrick, Trans.). New York: Knopf.

Armsden, G., & Greenberg, M. T. (1984). *The inventory of parent and peer attachment: Individual differences and their relationship to psychological well-being in adolescence.* Unpublished manuscript, University of Washington.

Arnold, M. L. (1989, April). *Moral cognition and conduct: A quantitative review of the literature.* Paper presented at the Society for Research in Child Development meeting, Kansas City.

Aronson, E. (1986, August). *Teaching students things they think they already know about: The case of prejudice and desegregation.* Paper presented at the meeting of the American Psychological Association, Washington, DC.

Asarnow, J. R., & Callan, J. W. (1985). Boys with peer adjustment problems: Social cognitive processes. *Journal of Consulting and Clinical Psychology, 53,* 80–87.

Asher, J., & Garcia, R. (1969). The optimal age to learn a foreign language. *Modern Language Journal, 53,* 334–341.

Aslin, R. (1987). Visual and auditory development in infancy. In J. Osofsky (Ed.), *Handbook of infant development* (2nd ed.). New York: Wiley.

Astin, A. W., Parrott, S. A., Korn, W. S., & Sax, L. J. (1997). *The American freshman: Thirty year trends.* Los Angeles, CA: Higher Education Research Institute, UCLA.

Astrid, N., & Debry, G. (1994). Potential teratogenic and neurodevelopmental consequences of coffee and caffeine exposure: A review of human and animal data. *Neurotoxicology and Teratology, 16,* 531–543.

Attie, I., & Brooks-Gunn, J. (1989). Development of eating problems in adolescent girls: A longitudinal study. *Developmental Psychology, 25,* 70–79.

Au, K., Carroll, J., & Scheu, J. (in press). *Balanced literacy instruction: A teacher's resource book.* Norwood, MA: Christopher-Gordon.

Bachman, J. G., Johnston, L. P., & O'Malley, P. M. (1987). *Monitoring the future.* Ann Arbor: University of Michigan, Institute of Social Research.

Bacon, M. K., Child, I. L., & Barry, H. (1963). A cross-cultural study of correlates of crime. *Journal of Abnormal and Social Psychology, 66,* 291–230.

Baddeley, A. (1990). *Human memory: Theory and practice.* Boston: Allyn & Bacon.

Baddeley, A. (1998). *Human memory* (rev. ed.). Boston: Allyn & Bacon.

Baer, J. S., Barr, H. M., Bookstein, F. L., Sampson, P. D., & Streissguth, A. P. (1998). Prenatal alcohol exposure and family history of alcoholism in the etiology of adolescent alcohol problems. *Journal of Studies on Alcohol, 59,* 533–543.

Bagwell, C. L., Newcomb, A. F., & Bukowski, W. M. (1994, February). *Early adolescent friendship as a predictor of adult adjustment: A twelve year follow-up investigation.* Paper presented at the biennial meeting of the Society for Research on Adolescence, San Diego.

Baillargeon, R. (1995). The object concept revisited: New directions in the investigation of infants' physical knowledge. In C. E. Granrud (Ed.), *Visual perception and cognition in infancy.* Hillsdale, NJ: Erlbaum.

Bakeman, R., & Brown, J. V. (1980). Early interaction: Consequences for social and mental development at three years. *Child Development, 51,* 437–447.

Baltes, P. B. (1987). Theoretical propositions of life-span developmental psychology: On the dynamics between growth and decline. *Developmental Psychology, 23,* 611–626.

Baltes, P. B., Lindenberger, U., & Staudinger, U. M. (1998). Life-span theory in developmental psychology. In W. Damon (Ed.), *Handbook of child psychology* (5th ed., Vol. 1). New York: Wiley.

Bandura, A. (1977). *Social learning theory.* Englewood Cliffs, NJ: Prentice Hall.

Bandura, A. (1982). Self-efficacy mechanism in human agency. *American Psychologist, 37,* 122–147.

Bandura, A. (1986). *Social foundations of thought and action: A social cognitive theory.* Englewood Cliffs, NJ: Prentice Hall.

Bandura, A. (1991). Social cognitive theory of moral thought and action. In W. M. Kurtines & J. Gewirtz (Eds.), *Handbook of moral behavior and development* (Vol. 1). Hillsdale, NJ: Erlbaum.

Bandura, A. (1994). *Self-efficacy: The exercise of control.* New York: W. H. Freeman.

Bandura, A. (1997). *Self-efficacy.* New York: W. H. Freeman.

Bandura, A. (1998, August). *Swimming against the mainstream: Accentuating the positive aspects of humanity.* Paper presented at the meeting of the American Psychological Association, San Francisco.

Bandura, A. (2000). Social cognitive theory. In A. Kazdin (Ed.), *Encyclopedia of psychology.* Washington, DC, & New York: American Psychological Association and Oxford U. Press.

Banks, E. C. (1993, March). *Moral education curriculum in a multicultural context: The Malaysian primary curriculum.* Paper presented at the biennial meeting of the Society for Research in Child Development, New Orleans.

Banks, J. A. (1995). *Multicultural education: Its effects on students' racial and gender role attitudes.* In J. A. Banks & C. A. M. Banks (Eds.), *Handbook of research on multicultural education.* New York: Macmillan.

Banks, J. A. (1997). Approaches to multicultural education reform. In J. A. Banks & C. A. M. Banks (Eds.), *Multicultural education.* Boston: Allyn & Bacon.

Banks, M. S., & Salapatek, P. (1983). Infant visual perception. In P. H. Mussen (Ed.), *Handbook of child psychology* (4th ed., Vol. 2). New York: Wiley.

Barker, R., & Wright, H. F. (1951). *One boy's day.* New York: Harper & Row.

Barnard, K. E., & Martell, L. K. (1995). Mothering. In M. H. Bornstein (Ed.), *Handbook of parenting* (Vol. 3). Hillsdale, NJ: Erlbaum.

Barnett, D., Ganiban, J., & Cicchetti, D. (1999). Maltreatment, negative expressivity, and the development of type D attachments from 12 to 24 months of age. In J. I. Vondra & D. Barnett (Eds.), *Monographs of the Society for Research in Child Development, 64,* No. 3, Serial No. 258, 97–118.

Baron, N. S. (1992). *Growing up with language.* Reading, MA: Addison-Wesley.

Barrett, D. E., Radke-Yarrow, M., & Klein, R. E. (1982). Chronic malnutrition and child behavior: Effects of calorie supplementation on social and emotional functioning at school age. *Developmental Psychology, 18,* 541–556.

Barron, B. J., Mayfield-Stewart, C., Schwartz, D., & Dzarnik, C. (1996, April). *Students' use of tools for formative assessment.* Paper presented at the meeting of the American Educational Research Association, New York.

Barton, L., Hodgman, J. E., & Pavlova, Z. (1999). Causes of death in the extremely low birth weight infant. *Pediatrics, 103,* 446–451.

Baskett, L. M., & Johnson, S. M. (1982). The young child's interaction with parents versus siblings. *Child Development, 53,* 643–650.

Bat-Chava, Y., Allen, L., Aber, J. L., & Seidman, E. (1997, April). *Racial and ethnic identity and the contexts of development.* Paper presented at the meeting of the Society for Research in Child Development, Washington, DC.

Bates, A. S., Fitzgerald, J. F., Dittus, R. S., & Wollinsky, F. D. (1994). Risk factors for underimmunization in poor urban infants. *Journal of the American Medical Association, 272,* 1105–1109.

Bates, E., & Thal, D. (1991). Associations and dissociations in language development. In J. Millder (Ed.), *Research on language disorders: A decade of progress.* Austin: Pro-Ed.

Bates, N. A., Rynn, M. A., Conway, D. H., Lischner, H. W., Hahnlen, N., & Bagarazzi, M. L. (1999, May). *Assessment of psychiatric comorbidity in children infected with human immunodeficiency virus, Type I.* Paper presented at the meeting of the Society for Pediatric Research, San Francisco.

Batson, C. D. (1989). Personal values, moral principles, and the three path model of prosocial motivation. In N. Eisenberg & J. Reykowski (Eds.), *Social and moral values.* Hillsdale, NJ: Erlbaum.

Baum, A. (2000). Genetic disorders. In A. Kazdin (Ed.), *Encyclopedia of psychology.* Washington, DC, & New York: American Psychological Association and Oxford U. Press.

Baumann, J. F., Hoffman, J. V., Moon, J., & Duffy-Hester, A. M. (1998). Where are teachers' voices in the phonics/whole language debate? Results from a survey of U.S. elementary classroom teachers. *Reading Teacher, 51,* 636–650.

Baumeister, R. F. (1991). Identity crisis. In R. M. Lerner, A. C. Petersen, & J. Brooks-Gunn (Eds.), *Encyclopedia of adolescence* (Vol. 1). New York: Garland.

Baumrind, D. (1971). Current patterns of parental authority. *Developmental Psychology Monographs, 4* (1, Pt. 2).

Baumrind, D. (1989, April). *Sex-differentiated socialization effects in childhood and adolescence.* Paper presented at the biennial meeting of the Society for Research in Child Development, Kansas City.

Baumrind, D. (1999, November). Unpublished review of J. W. Santrock's *Child Development,* 9th ed. (New York: McGraw-Hill).

Bayley, N. (1943). Mental growth during the first three years. In R. G. Barker, J. S. Kounin, & H. F. Wright (Eds.), *Child behavior and development.* New York: McGraw-Hill.

Bayley, N. (1969). *Manual for the Bayley Scales of Infant Development.* New York: Psychological Corp.

Bayley, N. (1970). Development of mental abilities. In P. H. Mussen (Ed.), *Manual of child psychology* (3rd ed., Vol. 1). New York: Wiley.

Beagles-Roos, J., & Gat, I. (1983). Specific impact of radio and television in children's story comprehension. *Journal of Educational Psychology, 75,* 128–137.

Beal, C. R. (1994). *Boys and girls: The development of gender roles.* New York: McGraw-Hill.

Bechtold, A. G., Busnell, E. W., & Salapatek, P. (1979, April.) *Infants' visual localization of visual and auditory targets.* Paper presented at the meeting of the Society for Research in Child Development, San Francisco.

Beck, A. T. (1973). *The diagnosis and management of depression.* Philadelphia: University of Pennsylvania Press.

Beck, A. T. (1993). Cognitive therapy: Past, present, and future. *Journal of Consulting and Clinical Psychology, 61,* 194–198.

Becker, H. J. (1994). *Analysis of trends of school use of new information technology.* Irvine, CA: University of California.

Bednar, R. L., Wells, M. G., & Peterson, S. R. (1995). *Self-esteem* (2nd ed.). Washington, DC: American Psychological Association.

Bell, C. C., & Clark, D. C. (1998). Adolescent suicide. *Pediatric Clinics of North America, 45,* 365–370.

Bell, M. A., & Fox, N. A. (1992). The relations between frontal brain electrical activity and cognitive development during infancy. *Child Development, 63,* 1142–1163.

Bell, S. M., & Ainsworth, M. D. S. (1972). Infant crying and maternal responsiveness. *Child Development, 43,* 1171–1190.

Bell-Scott, P., & Taylor, R. L. (1989). Introduction: The multiple ecologies of black adolescent development. *Journal of Adolescent Research, 4,* 117–118.

Belle, D. (1999). *The after school lives of children.* Mahwah, NJ: Erlbaum.

Belsky, J. (1989). Infant-parent attachment and day care: In defense of the strange situation. In J. S. Lande, S. Scarr, & N. Gunzenhauser (Eds.), *Caring for children: Challenge to America.* Hillsdale, NJ: Erlbaum.

Belson, W. (1978). *Television violence and the adolescent boy.* London: Saxon House.

Bem, S. L. (1977). On the utility of alternative procedures for assessing psychological androgyny. *Journal of Consulting and Clinical Psychology, 45,* 196–205.

Bem, S. L. (1981). Gender schema theory: A cognitive account of sex-typing. *Psychological Review, 88,* 354–364.

Bennett, W. (1993). *The book of virtues.* New York: Simon & Schuster.

Benson, P. (1993). *The troubled journey.* Minneapolis: Search Institute.

Bereiter, C., & Scardamalia, M. (1993). *Surpassing ourselves: An inquiry into the nature and implications of expertise.* Chicago: Open Court.

Berenfeld, B. (1994). Technology and the new model of science education. *Machine-Mediated Learning, 1,* 121–138.

Bergen, D. (1988). Stages of play development. In D. Bergen (Ed.), *Play as a medium for learning and development.* Portsmouth, NH: Heinemann.

Berk, S. F. (1985). *The gender factory: The apportionment of work in American households.* New York: Plenum.

Berko, J. (1958). The child's learning of English morphology. *Word, 14,* 150–177.

Berkowitz, M., & Gibbs, J. (1983). Measuring the developmental features of moral discussion. *Merrill-Palmer Quarterly, 29,* 399–410.

Berlin, L., & Cassidy, J. (2000). Understanding parenting: Contributions of attachment theory and research. In J. D. Osofsky & H. E. Fitzgerald

(Eds.), *WAIMH handbook of infant mental health* (Vol. 3). New York: Wiley.

Berlyne, D. E. (1960). *Conflict, arousal, and curiosity.* New York: McGraw-Hill.

Berndt, T. J. (1979). Developmental changes in conformity to peers and parents. *Developmental Psychology, 15,* 608–616.

Berndt, T. J. (1982). The features and effects of friendships in early adolescence. *Child Development, 53,* 1447–1460.

Berndt, T. J. (1999). Friends' influence on children's adjustment. In W. A. Collins & B. Laursen (Eds.), *Relationships as developmental contexts.* Mahwah, NJ: Erlbaum.

Berndt, T. J., & Perry, T. B. (1990). Distinctive features and effects of early adolescent friendships. In R. Montemayor (Ed.), *Advances in adolescent research.* Greenwich, CT: JAI Press.

Bertenthal, B. I. (1993). Infants' perception of biomechanical motions: Intrinsic image and knowledge-based constraints. In C. E. Granrud (Ed.), *Visual perception and cognition in infancy.* Hillsdale, NJ: Erlbaum.

Bialystok, E. (1993). Metalinguistic awareness: The development of children's representations in language. In C. Pratt & A. Garton (Eds.), *Systems of representation in children.* London: Wiley.

Bialystok, E. (1997). Effects of bilingualism and biliteracy on children's emerging concepts of print. *Developmental Psychology, 33,* 429–440.

Bialystok, E. (1999). Cognitive complexity and attentional control in the bilingual mind. *Child Development, 70,* 537–804.

Bier, J. B., Oliver, T. L., Ferguson, A., & Vohr, B. R. (1999, May). *Human milk reduces outpatient infections in low birth weight infants.* Paper presented at the meeting of the Society for Pediatric Research, San Francisco.

Bierman, K. L., Smoot, D. L., & Aumiller, K. (1993). Characteristics of aggressive-rejected, aggressive (nonrejected), and rejected (nonaggressive) boys. *Child Development, 64,* 139–151.

Bigler, R. S., & Liben, L. S. (in press). Cognitive mechanisms in children's gender stereotyping: Theoretical and educational implications of a cognitive-based intervention. *Child Development.*

Bigler, R. S., Liben, L. S., & Yekel, C. A. (1992, August). *Developmental patterns of gender-related beliefs: Beyond unitary constructs and measures.* Paper presented at the meeting of the American Psychological Association, Washington, DC.

Biller, H. B. (1993). *Fathers and families: Paternal factors in child development.* Westport, CT: Auburn House.

Billy, J. O. G., Rodgers, J. L., & Udry, J. R. (1984). Adolescent sexual behavior and friendship choice. *Social Forces, 62,* 653–678.

Bingham, C. R., & Crockett, L. J. (1996). Longitudinal adjustment patterns of boys and girls experiencing early, middle, and late sexual intercourse. *Developmental Psychology, 32,* 647–658.

Biological Sciences Curriculum Study. (1989). *Science for life and living: Integrating science, technology, and health. Third Annual Progress Report.* Dubuque, IA: Kendall Hunt.

Bissell, J., Manring, A., & Rowland, V. (1999). *Cybereducator.* New York: McGraw-Hill.

Bjorklund, D. F., & Harnishfeger, K. K. (1987). Developmental differences in the mental effort requirements for the use of an organizational strategy in free recall. *Journal of Experimental Child Psychology, 44,* 109–125.

Blachman, B. A., Ball, E., Black, R., & Tangel, D. (1994). Kindergarten teachers develop phoneme awareness in low-income inner-city classrooms: Does it make a difference? In B. A. Blachman (Ed.), *Reading and writing.* Mahwah, NJ: Erlbaum.

Black, M., & Matula, K. (1999). *Essentials of Bayley Scales of Infant Development II: Assessment.* New York: John Wiley.

Blair, C., & Ramey, C. (1996). Early intervention with low birth weight infants: The path to second generation research. In M. J. Guralnick (Ed.), *The effectiveness of early intervention.* Baltimore: Paul H. Brookes.

Blasi, A. (1988). Identity and the development of the self. In D. Lapsley & F. C. Power (Eds.), *Self, ego, and identity: Integrative approaches.* New York: Springer-Verlag.

Bloom, L. (1998). Language acquisition in its developmental context. In W. Damon (Ed.), *Handbook of child psychology* (5th ed., Vol. 2). New York: Wiley.

Blumenfeld, P. C., Pintrich, P. R., Wessles, K., & Meece, J. (1981, April). *Age and sex differences in the impact of classroom experiences on self-perceptions.* Paper presented at the biennial meeting of the Society for Research in Child Development, Boston.

Bohlin, G., & Hagekull, B. (1993). Stranger wariness and sociability in the early years. *Infant Behavior and Development, 16,* 53–67.

Bolen, J. C., Brand, S. D., & Sacks, J. J. (1999, April). *Injury prevention behaviors: Children's use of occupant restraints and bicycle helmets.* Paper presented at the meeting of the Society for Research in Child Development, Albuquerque.

Bonk, C. J., & Cunningham, D. J. (1999). Searching for learner-centered, constructivist, and sociocultural components of collaborative educational learning tools. In C. J. Bonk & K. S. King (Eds.), *Electronic collaborators.* Mahwah, NJ: Erlbaum.

Bonvillian, J. D., Orlansky, M. D., & Novack, L. L. (1983). Developmental milestones: Sign language and motor development. *Child Development, 54,* 1435–1445.

Booth, A., & Dunn, J. F. (Eds.). (1996). The effectiveness of providing social support for families of children at risk. In M. J. Guralnick (Ed.), *The effectiveness of early intervention.* Baltimore: Paul H. Brookes.

Bordelon, K. W. (1985). Sexism in reading materials. *Reading Teacher, 38,* 792–797.

Boring, E. G. (1950). *A history of experimental psychology.* New York: Appleton-Century-Crofts.

Bornstein, M. H. (1989). Stability in early mental development. In M. H. Bornstein & N. A. Krasnegor (Eds.), *Stability and continuity in mental development.* Hillsdale, NJ: Erlbaum.

Bornstein, M. H. (1999, April). *Culture, parents, and children: Intranational and international study.*

Paper presented at the meeting of the Society for Research in Child Development, Albuquerque.

Bornstein, M. H., & Arterberry, M. E. (1999). Perceptual development. In M. H. Bornstein & M. E. Lamb (Eds.), *Developmental psychology: An advanced textbook* (4th ed.). Mahwah, NJ: Erlbaum.

Bornstein, M. H., & Krasnegor, N. A. (1989). *Stability and continuity in mental development.* Hillsdale, NJ: Erlbaum.

Bornstein, M. H., & Sigman, M. D. (1986). Continuity in mental development from infancy. *Child Development, 57,* 251–274.

Botvin, G. J. (1999, June). *Impact of preventive interventions on protection for drug use, onset, and progression.* Paper presented at the meeting of the Society for Prevention Research, New Orleans.

Bouchard, T. J. (1995, August). *Heritability of intelligence.* Paper presented at the meeting of the American Psychological Association, New York City.

Bouchard, T. J., Lykken, D. T., McGue, M., Segal, N. L., & Tellegen, A. (1990). Source of human psychological differences: The Minnesota Study of Twins Reared Apart. *Science, 250,* 223–228.

Bower, B. (1985). The left hand of math and verbal talent. *Science News, 127,* 263.

Bower, T. G. R. (1966). Slant perception and shape constancy in infants. *Science, 151,* 832–834.

Bower, T. G. R. (1989). *The rational infant: Learning in infancy.* New York: W. H. Freeman.

Bower, T. G. R. (1996, January). Personal communication. Program in Psychology and Human Development, University of Texas at Dallas, Richardson, TX.

Bowlby, J. (1969). *Attachment and loss* (Vol. 1). London: Hogarth Press.

Bowlby, J. (1989). *Secure and insecure attachment.* New York: Basic Books.

Bowser, B. P., & Hunt, R. G. (Eds.). (1996). *Impacts of racism on White Americans.* Newbury Park, CA: Sage.

Boyes, M. C., Giordano, R., & Galperyn, K. (1993, March). *Moral orientation and interpretive contexts of moral deliberation.* Paper presented at the biennial meeting of the Society for Research in Child Development, New Orleans.

Boyum, L., & Parke, R. D. (1995). Family emotional expressiveness and children's social competence. *Journal of Marriage and the Family, 57,* 593–608.

Bracken, M. B., Eskenazi, B., Sachse, K., McSharry, J., Hellenbrand, K., & Leo-Summers, L. (1990). Association of cocaine use with sperm concentration, motility, and morphology. *Fertility and Sterility, 53,* 315–322.

Braham, P., Rattansi, A., & Skellington, R. (Eds.). (1992). *Racism and anti-racism.* Newbury Park, CA: Sage.

Bray, J. H., & Berger, S. H. (1993). Developmental Issues in Stepfamilies Research Project: Family relationships and parent-child interactions. *Journal of Family Psychology, 7,* 76–90.

Bray, J. M., Berger, S. H., & Boethel, C. L. (1999). Marriage to remarriage and beyond. In E. M. Hetherington (Ed.), *Coping with divorce, single parenting, and remarriage.* Mahwah, NJ: Erlbaum.

Brazelton, T. B. (1956). Sucking in infancy. *Pediatrics, 17,* 400–404.

Brazelton, T. B. (1983). *Infants and mothers: Differences in development.* New York: Delta.

Brazelton, T. B. (1998, September 7). Commentary. *Dallas Morning News,* p. C2.

Brazelton, T. B., Nugent, J. K., & Lester, B. M. (1987). Neonatal behavioral assessment scale. In J. D. Osofsky (Ed.), *Handbook of infant development* (2nd ed.). New York: Wiley.

Bredekamp, S. (1987). *Developmentally appropriate practice in early childhood programs serving children from birth through age 8.* Washington, DC: National Association for the Education of Young Children.

Bredekamp, S. (1993). Reflections on Reggio Emilia. *Young Children, 49,* 13–16.

Bredekamp, S. (1997). NAEYC issues revised position statement on developmentally appropriate practice in early childhood programs. *Young Children, 52,* 34–40.

Bredekamp, S., & Rosegrant, T. (1996). *Reaching potentials* (Vol. 2). Washington, DC: National Association for the Education of Young Children.

Bretherton, I., Stolberg, U., & Kreye, M. (1981). Engaging strangers in proximal interaction: Infants' social initiative. *Developmental Psychology, 17,* 746–755.

Breur, J. T. (1999). *The myth of the first three years.* New York: Free Press.

Brewer, M. B., & Campbell, D. T. (1976). *Ethnocentrism and intergroup attitudes.* New York: Wiley.

Brislin, R. (1993). *Understanding culture's influence on behavior.* Fort Worth, TX: Harcourt Brace.

Brody, G. H., & Shaffer, D. R. (1982). Contributions of parents and peers to children's moral socialization. *Developmental Review, 2,* 31–75.

Brodzinsky, D. M., Lang, R., & Smith, D. W. (1995). Parenting adopted children. In M. H. Bornstein (Ed.), *Handbook of parenting* (Vol. 3). Hillsdale, NJ: Erlbaum.

Brodzinsky, D. M., Schechter, D. E., Braff, A. M., & Singer, L. M. (1984). Psychological and academic adjustment in adopted children. *Journal of Consulting and Clinical Psychology, 52,* 582–590.

Brodzinsky, D. M., Schecter, M., & Hening, R. (1992). *Being adopted.* New York: Doubleday.

Bronfenbrenner, U. (1986). Ecology of the family as a context for human development: Research perspectives. *Developmental Psychology, 22,* 723–742.

Bronfenbrenner, U. (1995). Developmental ecology through space and time: A future perspective. In P. Moen, G. H. Elder, & K. Luscher (Eds.), *Examining lives in context.* Washington, DC: American Psychological Association.

Bronfenbrenner, U. (1995, March). *The role research has played in Head Start.* Paper presented at the meeting of the Society for Research in Child Development, Indianapolis.

Bronfenbrenner, U. (1999). Unpublished review of J. W. Santrock's *Life-span development,* 7th ed. (New York: McGraw-Hill).

Bronfenbrenner, U. (2000). Ecological systems theory. In A. Kazdin (Ed.), *Encyclopedia of psychology.* Washington, DC, & New York: American Psychological Association and Oxford U. Press.

Bronfenbrenner, U., & Morris, P. (1998). The ecology of developmental processes. In W. Damon (Ed.), *Handbook of child psychology* (5th ed., Vol. 1). New York: Wiley.

Brook, J. S., Brook, D. W., Gordon, A. S., Whiteman, M., & Cohen, P. (1990). The psychological etiology of adolescent drug use: A family interactional approach. *Genetic, Social, and General Psychology Monographs, 116,* 110–267.

Brookover, W. B., Beady, C., Flood, P., Schweitzer, U., & Wisenbaker, J. (1979). *School social systems and student achievement: Schools make a difference.* New York: Praeger.

Brooks, J. G., & Brooks, M. G. (1993). *The case for constructivist classrooms.* Alexandria, VA: Association for Supervision and Curriculum Development.

Brooks-Gunn, J., Britto, P. R., & Brady, C. (1999). Struggling to make ends meet: Poverty and child development. In M. E. Lamb (Ed.), *Parenting and child development in "nontraditional" families.* Mahwah, NJ: Erlbaum.

Brooks-Gunn, J., & Chase-Landsdale, P. L. (1995). Adolescent parenthood. In M. H. Bornstein (Ed.), *Children and parenting* (Vol. 3). Hillsdale, NJ: Erlbaum.

Brooks-Gunn, J., & Graber, J. A. (1999). *What's sex got to do with it? The development of health and sexual identities during adolescence.* Unpublished manuscript, Department of Psychology, Columbia University, New York City.

Brooks-Gunn, J., Klebanov, P. K., & Duncan, G. J. (1996). Ethnic differences in children's intelligence test scores: Role of economic deprivation, home environment, and maternal characteristics. *Child Development, 67,* 396–408.

Brooks-Gunn, J., Klebanov, P. K., & McCarton, C. (1997, April). *Neighborhood and family risk factors: Links to development in the first three years of life.* Paper presented at the meeting of the Society for Research in Child Development, Washington, DC.

Brooks-Gunn, J., & Matthews, W. S. (1979). *He and she: How children develop their sex role identity.* Englewood Cliffs, NJ: Prentice Hall.

Brooks-Gunn, J., & Paikoff, R. L. (1993). "Sex is a gamble, kissing is a game": Adolescent sexuality and health promotion. In S. P. Millstein, A. C. Petersen, & E. O. Nightingale (Eds.), *Promoting the health behavior of adolescents.* New York: Oxford University Press.

Brooks-Gunn, J., & Paikoff, R. L. (1997). Sexuality and developmental transitions during adolescence. In J. Schulenberg, J. Maggs, & K. Hurrelmann (Eds.), *Health risks and developmental transitions during adolescence.* New York: Cambridge University Press.

Brooks-Gunn, J., & Warren, M. P. (1989, April). *How important are pubertal and social events for different problem behaviors and contexts?* Paper presented at the biennial meeting of the Society for Research in Child Development, Kansas City.

Brophy, J. (1998). *Motivating students to learn.* New York: McGraw-Hill.

Broughton, J. M. (1978). Development of concepts of self, mind, reality, and knowledge. In W. Damon (Ed.), *Social cognition.* San Francisco: Jossey-Bass.

Broughton, J. M. (1983). The cognitive developmental theory of self and identity. In B. Lee & G. Noam (Eds.), *Developmental approaches to self.* New York: Plenum.

Brown, A. L. (1990). Domain-specific principles affect learning and transfer in children. *Cognitive Science, 14,* 107–133.

Brown, A. L. (1997). Transforming schools into communities of learners. *American Psychologist, 52,* 399–409.

Brown, A. L. (1998, April). *Reciprocal teaching.* Paper presented at the meeting of the American Educational Research Association, San Diego.

Brown, A. L. (1997). Transforming schools into communities of thinking and learning. *American Psychologist, 52,* 399–413.

Brown, A. L., & Campione, J. C. (1996). Psychological learning theory and the design of innovative environments. In L. Schauble & R. Glaser (Eds.), *Innovations in learning.* Mahwah, NJ: Erlbaum.

Brown, A. L., Kane, M. J., & Echols, K. (1986). Young children's mental models determine analogical transfer across problems with a common goal structure. *Cognitive Development, 1,* 103–122.

Brown, B. B. (1999). Measuring the peer environment of American adolescents. In S. L. Friedman & T. D. Wachs (Eds.), *Measuring environment across the life span.* Washington, DC: American Psychological Association.

Brown, B. B. (in press). "You're going with whom?!": Peer group influences on adolescent romantic relationships. In W. Furman, B. B. Brown, & C. Feiring (Eds.), *Contemporary perspectives on adolescent romantic relationships.* New York: Cambridge University Press.

Brown, B. B., & Huang, B.-H. (1995). Examining parenting practices in different peer contexts: Implications for adolescent trajectories. In L. J. Crockett & A. C. Crouter (Eds.), *Pathways through adolescence.* Hillsdale, NJ: Erlbaum.

Brown, B. B., Lambron, S. L., Mounts, N. S., & Steinberg, L. (1993). Parenting pactices and peer group affiliation in adolescence. *Child Development, 64,* 467–482.

Brown, B. B., & Lohr, M. J. (1987). Peer group affiliation and adolescent self-esteem: An integration of ego identity and symbolic interaction theories. *Journal of Personality and Social Psychology, 52,* 47–55.

Brown, B. B., & Mounts, N. S. (1989, April). *Peer group structures in single vs. multiethnic high schools.* Paper presented at the meeting of the Society for Research in Child Development, Kansas City.

Brown, B. B., Steinberg, L., Mounts, N., & Philipp, M. (1990, March). *The comparative influence of peers and parents on high school achievement: Ethnic differences.* Paper presented at the meeting of the Society for Research on Adolescence, Atlanta.

Brown, B. B., & Theobald, W. (1998). Learning contexts beyond the classroom: Extracurricular activities, community organizations, and peer groups. In K. Borman & B. Schneider (Eds.). *The adolescent years.* Chicago: University of Chicago Press.

Brown, J., & Allen, D. (1988). Hunger in America. *Annual Review of Public Health, 9,* 503–526.

Brown, J. S., & Burton, R. B. (1978). Diagnostic models for procedural bugs in basic mathematical skills. *Cognitive Science, 2,* 155–192.

Brown, L. M., & Gilligan, C. (1992). *Meeting at the crossroads: Women's and girls' development.* Cambridge, MA: Harvard University Press.

Brown, R. (1973). *A first language: The early stages.* Cambridge, MA: Harvard University Press.

Brown, R. (1986). *Social psychology* (2nd ed.). New York: Free Press.

Bruce, J. M., Olen, K., & Jensen, S. J. (1999, April). *The role of emotion and regulation in social competence.* Paper presented at the meeting of the Society for Research in Child Development, Albuquerque.

Bruck, M., & Ceci, S. J. (1999). The suggestibility of children's memory. *Annual Review of Psychology* (Vol. 50). Palo Alto, CA: Annual Reviews.

Bruer, J. T. (1999). *The myth of the first three years.* New York: Free Press.

Bruner, J. S. (1983). *Child talk.* New York: W. W. Norton.

Bruner, J. S. (1989, April). *The state of developmental psychology.* Paper presented at the meeting of the Society for Research in Child Development, Kansas City.

Bruner, J. S. (1996). *The culture of education.* Cambridge, MA: Harvard University Press.

Bruner, J. S. (1997, April). Discussant on symposium, *Social foundations of language development.* Society for Research in Child Development, Washington, DC.

Bryon, Y. J., Pang, S., Wei, L. S., Dickover, R., Diange, A., and Chen, I. S. Y. (1995). Clearance of HIV infection in a perinatally infected infant. *New England Journal of Medicine, 332,* 833–838.

Budwig, N. (1993). *A developmental functionalist approach to child language.* Hillsdale, NJ: Erlbaum.

Bugental, D. B., & Goodnow, J. J. (1998). Socialization processes. In W. Damon (Ed.), *Handbook of child psychology* (5th ed., Vol. 3). New York: Wiley.

Buhrmester, D. (1989). *Changes in friendship, interpersonal competence, and social adaptation during early adolescence.* Unpublished manuscript, Department of Psychology, UCLA.

Buhrmester, D. (1990). Friendship, interpersonal competence, and adjustment in preadolescence and adolescence. *Child Development, 61,* 1101–1111.

Buhrmester, D. (1993, March). *Adolescent friendship and the socialization of gender differences in social interaction styles.* Paper presented at the biennial meeting of the Society for Research in Child Development, New Orleans.

Buhrmester, D. (1999, January). Personal communication, Program in Psychology, University of Texas at Dallas, Richardson.

Buhrmester, D., & Carbery, J. (1992, March). *Daily patterns of self-disclosure and adolescent adjustment.* Paper presented at the biennial meeting of the Society for Research on Adolescence, Washington, DC.

Buhrmester, D., & Furman, W. (1987). The development of companionship and intimacy. *Child Development, 58,* 1101–1113.

Bukowski, W. M., Newcomb, A. F., & Hoza, B. (1987). Friendship conceptions among early adolescents: A longitudinal study of stability and change. *Journal of Early Adolescence, 7,* 143–152.

Bukowski, W. M., Sippola, L. K., & Boivin, M. (1995, March). *Friendship protects "at risk" children from victimization by peers.* Paper presented at the meeting of the Society for Research in Child Development, Indianapolis.

Burchinal, M. R., Roberts, J. E., Nabors, L. A., & Bryant, D. M. (1996). Quality of center child care and infant cognitive and language development. *Child Development, 67,* 606–620.

Burton, R. V. (1984). A paradox in theories and research in moral development. In W. M. Kurtines & J. L. Gewirtz (Eds.), *Morality, moral behavior, and moral development.* New York: Wiley.

Buss, D. M. (1995). Psychological sex differences: Origins through sexual selection. *American Psychologist, 50,* 164–168.

Buss, D. M. (1998). The psychology of human mate selection. In C. B. Crawford & D. L. Krebs (Eds.). *Handbook of evolutionary psychology.* Mahwah, NJ: Erlbaum.

Buss, D. M. (1999). *Evolutionary psychology: The new science of the mind.* Boston: Allyn & Bacon.

Buss, D. M. (2000). Evolutionary psychology. In A. Kazdin (Ed.), *Encyclopedia of psychology.* Washington, DC, & New York: American Psychological Association and Oxford U. Press.

Buss, D. M., & Kendrick, D. T. (1998). Evolutionary social psychology. In D. T. Gilbert, S. T. Fiske, & G. Lindzey (Eds.), *Handbook of social psychology* (4th ed., Vol. 2). New York: McGraw-Hill.

Buss, D. M., & Schmitt, D. P. (1993). Sexual strategies theory: An evolutionary perspective on human mating. *Psychological Review, 100,* 204–232.

Butterfield, L. J. (1999, May). *The Apgar legend lives.* Paper presented at the meeting of the Society for Pediatric Research, San Francisco.

C

CNN and the National Science Foundation. (1997). *Poll on technology and education.* Washington, DC: National Science Foundation.

Cabrera, N., Tamis-LeMonda, C. S., Bradley, R., Hofferth, S., & Lamb, M. (in press). Fatherhood in the 21st century. *Child Development.*

Cafolla, R., Kaufmann, D., & Knee, R. (1997). *World Wide Web for teachers.* Boston: Allyn & Bacon.

Cairns, R. B. (1983). The emergence of developmental psychology. In P. H. Mussen (Ed.), *Handbook of child psychology* (4th ed., Vol. 1). New York: Wiley.

Cairns, R. B. (1998). The making of developmental psychology.

Cairns, R. B., & Cairns, B. D. (1994). *Lifelines and risks: Pathways of youth in our time.* New York: Cambridge University Press.

Calabrese, R. L., & Schumer, H. (1986). The effects of service activities on adolescent alienation. *Adolescence, 21,* 675–687.

Calfee, R.C. (2000). Educational psychology. In A. Kazdin (Ed.), *Encyclopedia of psychology.* Washington, DC, & New York: American Psychological Association and Oxford U. Press.

Call, J. (1955, March). *Imitative learning as a problem-solving strategy in Orangutans (pono pygmaeus) and three- and four-year-old human children.* Paper presented at the meeting of the Society for Research in Child Development, Indianapolis.

Calvert, S. (1999). *Children's journeys through the information age.* New York: McGraw-Hill.

Cameron, J. R., Hansen, R., & Rosen, D. (1989). Preventing behavioral problems in infancy through temperament assessment and parental support programs. In W. B. Carey & S. C. McDevitt (Eds.), *Clinical and education applications of temperament research.* Amsterdam: Swets & Zeitlinger.

Campbell, C. Y. (1988, August 24). Group raps depiction of teenagers. *Boston Globe,* p. 44.

Campbell, D. T., & LeVine, R. A. (1968). Ethnocentrism and intergroup relations. In R. Abelson & others (Eds.), *Theories and cognitive consistency: A sourcebook.* Chicago: Rand-McNally.

Campbell, F. A., & Ramey, C. T. (1994). Effects of early intervention on intellectual and academic achievement: A follow-up study of children from low-income families. *Child Development, 65,* 684–698.

Campbell, L., Campbell, B., & Dickinson, D. (1999). *Teaching and learning through multiple intelligences* (2nd ed.). Boston: Allyn & Bacon.

Campos, J. (1994, spring). The new functionalism in emotions. *SRCD Newsletter,* pp. 1, 7, 9–11, 14.

Campos, J. J., Langer, A., & Krowitz, A. (1970). Cardiac responses on the visual cliff in prelocomotor human infants. *Science, 170,* 196–197.

Canfield, R. L., & Haith, M. M. (1991). Young infants' visual expectations for symmetric and asymmetric stimulus sequences. *Developmental Psychology, 27,* 198–208.

Carey, S. (1977). The child as word learner. In M. Halle, J. Bresman, & G. Miller (Eds.), *Linguistic theory and psychological reality.* Cambridge, MA: MIT Press.

Carey, S. (1988). Are children fundamentally different kinds of thinkers and learners than adults? In K. Richardson & S. Sheldon (Eds.), *Cognitive development to adolescence.* Hillsdale, NJ: Erlbaum.

Carey, S., & Gelman, R. (1991). *The epigenesis of mind.* Hillsdale, NJ: Erlbaum.

Carlson, C., Cooper, C., & Hsu, J. (1990, March). *Predicting school achievement in early adolescence: The role of family process.* Paper presented at the meeting of the Society for Research in Adolescence, Atlanta.

Carlson, K. S. (1995, March). *Attachment in sibling relationships during adolescence: Links to other familial and peer relationships.* Paper presented at the meeting of the Society for Research in Child Development, Indianapolis.

Carlson, V., Cicchetti, D., Barnett, D., & Braunwald, K. (1989). Disorganized/disoriented attachment relationships in maltreated infants. *Developmental Psychology, 25,* 525–531.

Carnegie Corporation. (1989). *Turning points: Preparing youth for the 21st century.* New York: Author.

Carnegie Corporation. (1996). *Report on education for children 3–10 years of age.* New York: Carnegie Foundation.

Carter, D. B., & Levy, G. D. (1988). Cognitive aspects of children's early sex-role development: The influence of gender schemas on preschoolers' memories and preference for sex-typed toys and activities. *Child Development, 59,* 782–793.

Carter-Saltzman, L. (1980). Biological and sociocultural effects on handedness: Comparison between biological and adoptive families. *Science, 209,* 1263–1265.

Case, R. (1985). *Intellectual development: Birth to adulthood.* New York: Academic Press.

Case, R. (1987). Neo-Piagetian theory: Retrospect and prospect. *International Journal of Psychology, 22,* 773–791.

Case, R. (1999). Conceptual development in the child and the field: A personal view of the Piagetian legacy. In E. K. Skolnick, K. Nelson, S. A. Gelman, & P. I. Miller (Eds.), *Conceptual development.* Mahwah, NJ: Erlbaum.

Case, R., Kurland, D. M., & Goldberg, J. (1982). Operational efficiency and the growth of short-term memory span. *Journal of Experimental Child Psychology, 33,* 386–404.

Caspi, A., Henry, B., McGee, R. O., Moffitt, T. E., & Silva, P. A. (1995). Temperamental origins of child and adolescent behavior problems: From age three to age fifteen. *Child Development, 66,* 55–68.

Cassell, C. (1984). *Swept away: Why women fear their own sexuality.* New York: Simon & Schuster.

Cassidy, J. (1999). The nature of the child's ties. In J. Cassidy & P. Shaver (Eds.), *Handbook of attachment.* New York: Guilford.

Cassidy, J., & Berlin, L. J. (1994). The insecure/ambivalent pattern of attachment: Theory and research. *Child Development, 65,* 971–991.

Cassidy, J., & Shaver, P. R. (Eds.). (1999). *Handbook of attachment.* New York: Guilford.

Cauffman, B. E. (1994, February). *The effects of puberty, dating, and sexual involvement on dieting and disordered eating in young adolescent girls.* Paper presented at the meeting of the Society for Research on Adolescence, San Diego.

Ceballo, R. E. (1999, April). *The psychological impact of children's perceptions of neighborhood danger and collective efficacy.* Paper presented at the meeting of the Society for Research in Child Development, Albuquerque.

Ceci, S. J., Rosenblum, T., de Bruyn, E., & Lee, D. Y. (1997). A bio-ecological model of intellectual development. In R. J. Sternberg & E. Grigorenko (Eds.), *Intelligence, heredity, and environment.* New York: Cambridge University Press.

Centers for Disease Control. (1988). HIV-related beliefs, knowledge, and behaviors among high school students. *Morbidity and Mortality Weekly Reports, 37,* 717–721.

Chall, J. S. (1979). The great debate: Ten years later with a modest proposal for reading stages. In L. B. Resnick & P. A. Weaver (Eds.), *Theory and practice of early reading.* Hillsdale, NJ: Erlbaum.

Chan, W. S. (1963). *A source book in Chinese philosophy.* Princeton, NJ: Princeton University Press.

Charlesworth, R. (1987). *Understanding child development* (2nd ed.). Albany, NY: Delmar.

Charlesworth, R. (1996). *Understanding child development* (4th ed.). Albany, NY: Delmar.

Chasnoff, I. J., Griffith, D. R., Freier, C., & Murray, J. (1992). Cocaine/polydrug use in pregnancy: Two-year follow-up. *Pediatrics, 89,* 284–289.

Chattin-McNichols, J. (1992). *The Montessori controversy.* Albany, NY: Delmar.

Chauhuri, J. H., & Williams, P. H. (1999, April). *The contribution of infant temperament and parental emotional availability to toddler attachment.* Paper presented at the meeting of the Society for Research in Child Development, Albuquerque.

Chen, C., & Stevenson, H. W. (1989). Homework: A cross-cultural examination. *Child Development, 60,* 551–561.

Cherlin, A. J., & Furstenberg, F. F. (1994). Stepfamilies in the United States: A reconsideration. In J. Blake & J. Hagen (Eds.), *Annual review of sociology.* Palo Alto, CA: Annual Reviews.

Cherlin, A. J., Furstenberg, F. F., Chase-Lansdale, P. L., Kiernan, K. E., Robins, P. K., Morrison, D. R., & Teitler, J. O. (1991). Longitudinal studies of effects of divorce in children in Great Britain and the United States. *Science, 252,* 1386–1389.

Chescheir, N. C., & Hansen, W. F. (1999). New in perinatology. *Pediatrics in Review, 20,* 57–63.

Chess, S., & Thomas, A. (1977). Temperamental individuality from childhood to adolescence. *Journal of Child Psychiatry, 16,* 218–226.

Chi, M. T. H. (1978). Knowledge structures and memory development. In R. S. Siegler (Ed.), *Children's thinking: What develops?* Hillsdale, NJ: Erlbaum.

Child Trends. (1996). *Facts at a glance.* Washington, DC: Author.

Children's Defense Fund. (1992). *The state of America's children, 1992.* Washington, DC: Author.

Chomitz, V. R., Cheung, L. W. Y., & Lieberman, E. (1995, Spring). The role of lifestyle in preventing low birth weight. *Future of Children, 5,* (1), 121–138.

Chomsky, N. (1957). *Syntactic structures.* The Hague: Mouton.

Cicagles, M., Field, T., Hossain, Z., Pelaez-Nogueras, M., & Gewirtz, J. (1996). Touch among children at nursery school. *Early Child Development and Care, 126,* 101–110.

Cicchetti, D., Ganiban, J., & Barnett, D. (1991). Contributions from the study of high risk populations to understanding the development of emotion regulation. In J. Garber & K. Dodge (Eds.), *The development of emotion regulation and dysregulation.* New York: Cambridge University Press.

Cicchetti, D., & Toth, S. (1998). Perspectives on research and practice in developmental psychopathology. In I. E. Sigel & K. A. Renninger (Eds.), *Handbook of child psychology* (5th ed., Vol. IV). New York: Wiley.

Cillessen, A. H. N., Van Ijzendoorn, H. W., Van Lieshout, C. F. M., & Hartup, W. W. (1992). Heterogeneity among peer-rejected boys: Subtypes and stabilities. *Child Development, 63,* 893–905.

Circirelli, V. G. (1994). Sibling relationships in cross-cultural perspective. *Journal of Marriage and the Family, 56,* 7–20.

Clark, E. V. (1983). Meanings and concepts. In P. H. Mussen (Ed.), *Handbook of child psychology* (4th ed., Vol. 4). New York: Wiley.

Clark, R. D., & Hatfield, E. (1989). Gender differences in receptivity to sexual offers. *Journal of Psychology and Human Sexuality, 2,* 39–55.

Clark, S. D., Zabin, L. S., & Hardy, J. B. (1984). Sex, contraception, and parenthood: Experience and attitudes among urban black young men. *Family Planning Perspectives, 16,* 77–82.

Clarke-Stewart, K. A., & Fein, G. G. (1983). Early childhood programs. In P. H. Mussen (Ed.), *Handbook of child psychology* (4th ed., Vol. 2). New York: Wiley.

Clay, R. A. (1997, December). Are children being over-medicated? *APA Monitor,*, pp. 1, 27.

Clement, J., Lockhead, J., & Soloway, E. (1979, March). *Translation between symbol systems: Isolating a common difficulty in solving algebra word problems.* COINS technical report No. 79–19. Amherst: University of Massachusetts, Department of Computer and Information Sciences.

Clifford, B. R., Gunter, B., & McAleer, J. L. (1995). *Television and children.* Hillsdale, NJ: Erlbaum.

Clifton, R. K., Morrongiello, B. A., Kulig, J. W., & Dowd, J. M. (1981). Developmental changes in auditory localization in infancy. In R. N. Aslin, J. R. Alberts, & M. R. Petersen (Eds.), *Development of perception* (Vol. 1). Orlando, FL: Academic Press.

Clifton, R. K., Muir, D. W., Ashmead, D. H., & Clarkson, M. G. (1993). Is visually guided reaching in early infancy a myth? *Child Development, 64,* 1099–1110.

Clinchy, B. M., Mansfield, A. F., & Schott, J. L. (1995, March). *Development of narrative and scientific modes of thought in middle childhood.* Paper presented at the meeting of the Society for Research in Child Development, Indianapolis.

Cognition and Technology Group at Vanderbilt. (1997). *Designing environments to reveal, support, and expand our children's potentials.* Paper presented at the meeting of the Society for Research in Child Development, Washington, DC.

Cognition and Technology Group at Vanderbilt. (1997). *The Jasper Project.* Mahwah, NJ: Erlbaum.

Cohen, H. J., Grosz, J., Ayooh, K., & Schoen, S. (1996). Early intervention for children with HIV infections. In M. J. Guralnick (Ed.), *The effectiveness of early intervention.* Baltimore: Paul H. Brookes.

Cohen, R. J., Swerdlik, M. E., & Phillips, S. M. (1996). *Psychological testing and assessment* (3rd

ed.). Mountain View, CA: Mayfield.

Cohen, S. E. (1994, February). *High school dropouts.* Paper presented at the meeting of the Society for Research on Adolescence, San Diego.

Cohn, J. F., & Tronick, E. Z. (1988). Mother-infant face-to-face interaction. Influence is bidirectional and unrelated to periodic cycles in either partner's behavior. *Developmental Psychology, 24,* 396–397.

Coie, J. (1999, November). Unpublished review of J. W. Santrock's *Child Development,* 9th ed. (New York: McGraw-Hill).

Coie, J. D., & Dodge, K. A. (1998). Aggression and antisocial behavior. In W. Damon (Ed.), *Handbook of child psychology* (5th ed., Vol. 3). New York: Wiley.

Coladarci, T. (1992). Teachers' sense of efficacy and commitment to teaching. *Journal of Experimental Education, 60,* 323–337.

Colby, A., Kohlberg, L., Gibbs, J., & Lieberman, M. (1983). A longitudinal study of moral judgment. *Monographs of the Society for Research in Child Development, 48* (21, Serial No. 201).

Cole, M. (1999). Culture in development. In M. H. Bornstein & M. E. Lamb (Eds.), *Developmental psychology: An advanced textbook* (4th ed.). Mahwah, NJ: Erlbaum.

Coleman, J. S. (1961). *The adolescent society.* New York: Free Press.

Coles, R. (1970). *Erik H. Erikson: The growth of his work.* Boston: Little, Brown.

Coll, C. T. G., Erkut, S., Alarcon, O., Garcia, H. A. V., & Tropp, L. (1995, March). *Puerto Rican adolescents and families: Lessons in construct and instrument development.* Paper presented at the meeting of the Society for Research in Child Development, Indianapolis.

Collins, W. A., Harris, M., & Susman, A. (1995, March). Parenting during middle childhood. In M. H. Bornstein (Ed.), *Handbook of parenting* (Vol. 1). Hillsdale, NJ: Erlbaum.

Collins, W. A., Hennighausen, K. H., & Sroufe, L. A. (1998, June). *Developmental precursors of intimacy in romantic relationships: A longitudinal analysis.* Paper presented at International Conference on Personal Relationships, Saratoga Springs, NY.

Collis, B. A., & Sakamoto, T. (1996). Children in the information age. In B. A. Collis, G. A. Knezek, K. W. Laid, W. J. Miyashita, W. J. Pelgrum, T. Plomp, & T. Sakamoto (Eds.), *Children and computers in schools.* Mahwah, NJ: Erlbaum.

Comer, J. P. (1988). Educating poor minority children. *Scientific American, 259,* 42–48.

Comer, J. P., Haynes, N. M., Joyner, E. T., & Ben-Avie, M. (1996). *Rallying the whole village: The Conner process for reforming urban education.* New York: Teachers College Press.

Committee on Developments in the Science of Learning. (1999). *How people learn.* Washington, DC: National Academic Press.

Compas, B. E., & Grant, K. E. (1993, March). *Stress and adolescent depressive symptoms: Underlying mechanisms and processes.* Paper presented at the biennial meeting of the Society for Research in Child Development, New Orleans.

Conger, R. D., & Chao, W. (1996). Adolescent depressed mood. In R. L. Simons (Ed.),

Understanding differences between divorced and intact families: Stress, interaction, and child outcome. Thousand Oaks, CA: Sage.

Conger, R. D., & Ge, X. (1999). Conflict and cohesion in parent-adolescent relations: Changes in emotional expression. In M. J. Cox & J. Brooks-Gunn (Eds.), *Conflict and cohesion in families.* Mahwah, NJ: Erlbaum.

Considine, R. V., Sinha, M. K., & Heiman, M. I. (1996). Serum immunoreactive–leptin concentrations in normal-weight and obese humans. *New England Journal of Medicine, 334,* 292–295.

Cook, M., & Birch, R. (1984). Infant perception of the shapes of tilted plane forms. *Infant Behavior and Development, 7,* 389–402.

Cooper, C. (in press). *The weaving of maturity: Cultural perspectives on adolescent development.* New York: Oxford University Press.

Cooper, C., Jackson, J. F., Azmitia, M., Lopez, E., & Dunbar, N. (1995). Bridging students' multiple worlds: African American and Latino youth in academic outreach programs. In R. F. Macias & R. G. Garcia-Ramos (Eds.), *Changing schools for changing students.* Santa Barbara: University of California Linguistic Minority Research Institute.

Cooper, C. R., & Ayers-Lopez, S. (1985). Family and peer systems in early adolescence: New models of the role of relationships in development. *Journal of Early Adolescence, 5,* 9–22.

Cooper, C. R., & Grotevant, H. D. (1989, April). *Individuality and connectedness in the family and adolescents' self and relational competence.* Paper presented at the meeting of the Society for Research in Child Development, Kansas City.

Cooper, C. R., Grotevant, H. D., Moore, M. S., & Condon, S. M. (1982, August). *Family support and conflict: Both foster adolescent identity and role taking.* Paper presented at the meeting of the American Psychological Association, Washington, DC.

Cooper, M. L., Shaver, P. R., & Collins, N. L. (1998). Attachment styles, emotional regulation, and adjustment in adolescence. *Journal of Personality and Social Psychology, 74,* 1380–1397.

Coopersmith, S. (1967). *The antecedents of self-esteem.* San Francisco: W. H. Freeman.

Cornell, D. (1998, April 6). Commentary. *Newsweek,* p. 24.

Corrigan, R. (1981). The effects of task and practice on search for invisibly displaced objects. *Developmental Review, 1,* 1–17.

Cote, J. E., & Levine, C. (1988). On critiquing the identity crisis paradigm: A rejoinder to Waterman. *Developmental Review, 8,* 209–218.

Coulton, C. J., & Korbin, J. E. (1995, March). *How do measures of community organization differ in African-American and European-American neighborhoods?* Paper presented at the meeting of the Society for Research in Child Development, Indianapolis.

Cowan, P. A., Powell, D., & Cowan, C. P. (1998). Parenting interventions: A family systems perspective. In W. Damon (Ed.), *Handbook of child psychology* (5th ed., Vol. 4). New York: Wiley.

Cowley, G. (1998, April 6). Why children turn violent. *Newsweek,* pp. 24–25.

Cox, M. J., Owen, M. T., Lewis, J. M., & Henderson, V. K. (1989). Marriage, adult adjustment, and early parenting. *Child Development, 60,* 1015–1024.

Craik, F. I. M., & Lockhart, R. S. (1972). Levels of processing: A framework for memory research. *Journal of Verbal Learning and Verbal Behavior, 11,* 671–684.

Crawford, C., & Krebs, D. L. (Eds.) (1998). *Handbook of evolutionary psychology.* Mahwah, NJ: Erlbaum.

Crnic, K. (1996). *Children, families, and stress.* Cambridge, MA: Blackwell.

Crockenberg, S. B. (1986). Are temperamental differences in babies associated with predictable differences in caregiving? In J. V. Lerner & R. M. Lerner (Eds.), *Temperament and social interaction during infancy and childhood.* San Francisco: Jossey-Bass.

Crockett, J. B., & Kauffman, J. M. (1999). *The least restrictive environment.* Mahwah, NJ: Erlbaum.

Cromer, R. (1987). Receptive language in the mentally retarded: Processes and diagnostic distinctions. In R. Schiefelbusch & L. Lloyd (Eds.), *Language perspectives: Acquisition, retardation, and intervention.* Baltimore: University Park Press.

Crump, A. D., Haynie, D., Aarons, S., & Adair, E. (1996, March). *African American teenagers' norms, expectations, and motivations regarding sex, contraception, and pregnancy.* Paper presented at the meeting of the Society for Research on Adolescence, Boston.

Culatta, R., & Tompkins, J. R. (1999). *Introduction to special education.* Columbus, OH: Merrill.

Cummings, E. M. (1987). Coping with background anger in early childhood. *Child Development, 58,* 976–984.

Cummings, E. M., & Cummings, J. L. (1988). A process-oriented approach to children's coping with angry behavior. *Developmental Review, 8,* 296–321.

Curtiss, S. (1977). *Genie.* New York: Academic Press.

Cushner, K. (1999). *Human diversity in action.* New York: McGraw-Hill.

Dabbs, J. M., Jr., Frady, R. I., Carr, T. S., & Besch, M. F. (1987). Saliva, testosterone, and criminal violence in young adult prison inmates. *Psychosomatic Medicine, 49,* 174–182.

Dabbs, J. M., Jr., & Morris, R. (1990). Testosterone, social class, and antisocial behavior in a sample of 4,462 men. *Psychological Science, 1,* 209–211.

Damon, W. (1988). *The moral child.* New York: Free Press.

Damon, W. (1991). Self-concept, adolescent. In R. M. Lerner, A. C. Petersen, & J. Brooks-Gunn (Eds.), *Encyclopedia of adolescence* (Vol. 2). New York: Garland.

Damon, W. (1995). *Greater expectations.* New York: Free Press.

Damon, W., & Hart, D. (1988). *Self-understanding in childhood and adolescence.* New York: Cambridge University Press.

D'Angelo, L. J., Belzer, M., Futterman, D., & Peralta, L. (2000). Response to the joint statement on HIV screening. *Pediatrics, 105,* 467–468.

Darwin, C. (1859). *On the origin of species.* London: John Murray.

Davidson, D. (1996). The effects of decision characteristics on children's selective search of predecisional information. *Acta Psychologica, 92,* 263–281.

Davis, K. (1996). *Families.* Pacific Grove, CA: Brooks/Cole.

Davis, S. M., Lambert, L. C., Gomez, Y., & Skipper, B. (1995). Southwest Cardiovascular Curriculum Project: Study findings for American Indian elementary students. *Journal of Health Education, 26,* S72–S81.

Day, R. H., & McKenzie, B. E. (1973). Perceptual shape constancy in early infancy. *Perception, 2,* 315–320.

DeCasper, A. J., & Spence, M. J. (1986). Prenatal maternal speech influences newborn's perception of speech sounds. *Infant Behavior and Development, 9,* 133–150.

deCharms, R. (1984). Motivation enhancement in educational settings. In R. Ames & C. Ames (Eds.), *Research on motivation in education* (Vol. 1). Orlando: Academic Press.

DeGarmo, D. S., Forgatch, M. S., & Martinez, C. R. (1998). *Parenting of divorced mothers as a link between social status and boys' academic outcomes: Unpacking the effects of SES.* Unpublished manuscript, Oregon Social Learning Center, University of Oregon, Eugene.

deHaan, M., & Nelson, C. A. (1999). Brain activity differentiates face and object processing in 6-month-old infants. *Development Psychology, 35,* 1113–1121.

DeLoache, J. S. (1984). Oh where, oh where: Memory-based searching by very young children. In C. Sophian (Ed.), *Origins of cognitive skills.* Hillsdale, NJ: Erlbaum.

DeLoache, J. S. (1989). The development of representation in young children. In H. W. Reese (Ed.), *Advances in child development and behavior* (Vol. 22, pp. 1–39). New York: Academic Press.

DeLoache, J. S., Cassidy, D. J., & Brown, A. L. (1985). Precursors of mnemonic strategies in very young children's memory. *Child Development, 56,* 125–137.

DeLoache, J. S., Cassidy, D. J., & Carpenter, C. J. (1987). The Three Bears are all boys: Mothers' gender labeling of neutral picture book characters. *Sex Roles, 17,* 163–178.

DeLoache. J. S., Miller, K. F., & Pierroutsakos, S. L. (1997). Reasoning and problem solving. In D. Kuhn & R. S. Siegler (Eds.), *Handbook of child psychology* (5th ed., Vol. 2). New York: Wiley.

DeMarie-Dreblow, D., & Miller, P. H. (1988). The development of children's strategies for selective attention: Evidence for a transitional period. *Child Development, 59,* 1504–1513.

DeVillar, R. A., & Faltis, C. J. (1991). *Computers and cultural diversity: Restructuring for school success.* Albany: State University of New York Press.

Deci, E. (1975). *Intrinsic motivation.* New York: Plenum Press.

Deci, E., & Ryan, R. (1994). Promoting self-determined education. *Scandinavian Journal of Educational Research, 38,* 3–14.

Degirmencioglu, S. M., Saltz, E., & Ager, J. W. (1995, March). *Early dating and "going steady": A retrospective and prospective look.* Paper presented at the meeting of the Society for Research in Child Development, Indianapolis.

DelCielo, D., Castaneda, M., Hui, J., & Frye, D. (1993, March). *Is theory of mind related to categorization?* Paper presented at the biennial meeting of the Society for Research in Child Development, New Orleans.

Deluca, P. (1999, April). *Does illness enhance children's understanding of the inside of the body, death, and illness contagion?* Paper presented at the meeting of the Society for Research in Child Development, Albuquerque.

Dempster, F. N. (1981). Memory span: Sources of individual and developmental differences. *Psychological Bulletin, 89,* 63–100.

Denham, S. A., Cook, M., & Zoller, D. (1992). Maternal emotional responsiveness to toddlers' social-emotional functioning. *Journal of Child Psychology and Psychiatry, 34,* 715–728.

de Villiers, J. (1996). Toward a rational empiricism: Why interactionism isn't behaviorism any more than biology is genetics. In M. Rice (Ed.), *Toward a genetics of language.* Hillsdale, NJ: Erlbaum.

de Villiers, J. G., & de Villiers, P. A. (1999). Language development. In M. H. Bornstein & M. E. Lamb (Eds.), *Developmental psychology: An advanced textbook* (4th ed.). Mahwah, NJ: Erlbaum.

Dewey, C. R. (1999, April). *Day care, family, and child characteristics: Their roles as predictors and moderators of language development.* Paper presented at the meeting of the Society for Research in Child Development, Albuquerque.

Dewey, J. (1933). *How we think.* Lexington, MA: D. C. Heath.

de Wolff, M. S., & van Ijzendoorn, M. H. (1997). Sensitivity and attachment: A meta-analysis on parental antecedents of infant attachment. *Child Development, 68,* 571–591.

Diamond, A. D. (1955, March). *Exciting new findings in development cognitive neuroscience.* Paper presented at the meeting of the Society for Research in Child Development, Indianapolis.

Diamond, A. D. (1985). Development of the ability to use recall to guide action, as indicated by infants' performance on AB. *Child Development, 56,* 868–883.

Diamond, A., & Goldman-Rakic, P. S. (1989). Comparison of human infants and rhesus monkeys on Piaget's AB search task: Evidence for dependence on dorsolateral prefrontal cortex. *Experimental Brain Research, 74,* 24–40.

Dickerscheid, J. D., Schwarz, P. M., Noir, S., & El-Taliawy, T. (1988). Gender concept development of preschool-aged children in the United States and Egypt. *Sex Roles, 18,* 669–677.

Didow, S. M. (1993, March). *Language and action: Toddlers' coordinated talk with a partner.* Paper presented at the meeting of the Society for Research in Child Development, New Orleans.

Dix, T. (1991). The affective organization of parenting: Adaptive and maladaptive processes. *Psychological Bulletin, 110,* 3–25.

Dixon, R. A., & Lerner, R. M. (1999). History and systems in developmental psychology. In M. H. Bornstein & M. E. Lamb (Eds.), *Developmental psychology: An advanced textbook* (4th ed.). Mahwah, NJ: Erlbaum.

Dobzhansky, T. G. (1977). *Evolution.* New York: W. H. Freeman.

Dodge, K. A. (1993). Social cognitive mechanisms in the development of conduct disorder and depression. *Annual Review of Psychology, 44,* 559–584.

Douvan, E., & Adelson, J. (1996). *The adolescent experience.* New York: Wiley.

Dowdy, B. B., & Kliewer, W. (1996, March). *Dating, parent-adolescent conflict, and autonomy.* Paper presented at the meeting of the Society for Research on Adolescence, Boston.

Downey, G., & Bonica, C. A. (1997, April). *Characteristics of early adolescent dating relationships.* Paper presented at the meeting of the Society for Research in Child Development, Washington, DC.

Downey, G., & Coyne, J. C. (1990). Children of depressed parents: An integrative review. *Psychological Bulletin, 108,* 50–76.

Doyle, A., Doehring, P., Tessier, O., de Lorimier, S., & Shapiro, S. (1992). Transitions in children's play: A sequential analysis of states preceding and following social pretense. *Developmental Psychology, 28,* 137–144.

Doyle, J. A., & Paludi, M. A. (1998). *Sex and gender* (4th ed.). New York: McGraw-Hill.

Dryfoos, J. G. (1990). *Adolescents at risk: Prevalence and prevention.* New York: Oxford University Press.

Dryfoos, J. G. (1995). Full service schools: Revolution or fad? *Journal of Research on Adolescence, 5,* 147–172.

DuBois, D. L., & Hirsch, B. J. (1990). School and neighborhood friendship patterns of Blacks and Whites in early adolescence. *Child Development, 61,* 524–536.

DuBois, D. L., Felner, R. D., & Brand, S. (1997, April). *Self-esteem profiles and adjustment in early adolescence: A two-year longitudinal study.* Paper presented at the meeting of the Society for Research in Child Development, Washington, DC.

DuRant, R. H. (1999, April). *Exposure to violence, depression, and substance use and abuse and the use of violence by young adolescents.* Paper presented at the meeting of the Society for Research in Child Development, Albuquerque.

Duck, S. W. (1975). Personality similarity and friendship choices by adolescents. *European Journal of Social Psychology, 5,* 351–365.

Duck, S. W. (1988). Child adolescent friendships. In P. Marsh (Ed.), *Eye to eye: How people interact.* Topsfield, MA: Salem House.

Duncan, G. J., Brooks-Gunn, J., & Klebanov, P. K. (1994). Economic deprivation and early childhood development. *Child Development, 65,* 296–318.

Duncker, K. (1945). On problem solving. *Psychological Monographs, 58* (Whole No. 270).

Dunkel-Schetter, C. (1998). Maternal stress and preterm delivery. *Prenatal and Neonatal Medicine, 3,* 39–42.

Dunkel-Schetter, C. (1999, August). *Is maternal stress a risk factor for adverse birth outcomes?* Paper presented at the meeting of the American Psychological Asssociation, Boston.

Dunkel-Schetter, C., Gurung, R. A. R., Lobel, M., & Wadhwa, P. D. (in press). Psychological, biological, and social processes in pregnancy: Using a stress framework to study birth outcomes. In A. Baum, T. Revenson, & J. Singer (Eds.), *Handbook of health psychology.* Mahwah, NJ: Erlbaum.

Dunn, J., & Brown, J. (1994). Affect expression in the family, children's understanding of emotions, and their interactions with others. *Merrill-Palmer Quarterly, 40,* 120–137.

Dunn, J., & Kendrick, C. (1982). *Siblings.* Cambridge, MA: Harvard University Press.

Dunn, L., & Kontos, S. (1997). What have we learned about developmentally appropriate education? *Young Children, 52* (2), 4–13.

Dunphy, D. C. (1963). The social structure of urban adolescent peer groups. *Society, 26,* 230–246.

Durkin, K. (1985). Television and sex-role acquisition: 1. Content. *British Journal of Social Psychology, 24,* 101–113.

Durkin, K., & Hutchins, G. (1984). Challenging traditional sex role stereotypes via career education broadcasts: The reactions of young secondary school pupils. *Journal of Educational Television, 10,* 25–33.

Dweck, C. (1996). Social motivation: Goals and social-cognitive processes. In J. Juvonen & K. R. Wentzel (Eds.), *Social motivation.* New York: Cambridge University Press.

Dweck, C., & Elliott, E. (1983). Achievement motivation. In P. Mussen (Ed.), *Handbook of child psychology* (4th ed., Vol. 4). New York: Wiley.

Dweck, C., & Leggett, E. (1988). A social cognitive approach to motivation and personality. *Psychological Review, 95,* 256–273.

E

Eagly, A. H. (1996). Differences between women and men. *American Psychologist, 51,* 158–159.

Eagly, A. H. (1997, August). *Social roles as an origin theory for sex-related differences.* Paper presented at the meeting of the American Psychological Association, Chicago.

Eagly, A. H., & Crowley, M. (1986). Gender and helping behavior: A meta-analytic review of the social psychological literature. *Psychological Bulletin, 100,* 283–308.

Eagly, A. H., & Wood, W. (1999). *The origins of sex differences in human behavior: Evolved dispositions versus social roles.* Unpublished manuscript, Department of Psychology, Northwestern University, Evanston, IL.

East, P., & Felice, M. E. (1996). *Adolescent pregnancy and parenting.* Hillsdale, NJ: Erlbaum.

Eccles, J. S. (1993, March). *Parents as gender-role socializers during middle childhood and adolescence.* Paper presented at the biennial meeting of the Society for Research in Child Development, New Orleans.

Eccles, J. S., & Roeser, R. W. (1999). School and community influences on human development. In M. H. Bornstein & M. E. Lamb (Eds.), *Developmental psychology: An advanced textbook* (4th ed.). Mahwah, NJ: Erlbaum.

Eccles, J. S., Wigfield, A., & Schiefele, U. (1998). Motivation to succeed. In W. Damon (Ed.), *Handbook of child psychology* (5th ed., Vol. 3). New York: Wiley.

Edelman, M. W. (1997, April). *Children, families and social policy.* Paper presented at the meeting of the Society for Research in Child Development, Washington, DC.

Educational Testing Service. (1992, February). *Cross-national comparison of 9–13 year olds' science and math achievement.* Princeton, NJ: Educational Testing Service, .

Edwards, C. P. (1987). Culture and the construction of moral values. In J. Kagan & S. Lamb (Eds.), *The emergence of morality in young children.* Chicago: University of Chicago Press.

Ehrhardt, A. A. (1987). A transactional perspective on the development of gender differences. In J. M. Reinisch, L. A. Rosenblum, & S. A. Sanders (Eds.), *Masculinity/femininity: Basic perspectives.* New York: Oxford University Press.

Eiferman, R. R. (1971). Social play in childhood. In R. Herron & B. Sutton-Smith (Eds.), *Child's play.* New York: Wiley.

Eiger, M. S. (1992). The feeding of infants and children. In R. A. Hoekelman, S. B. Friedman, N. M. Nelson, & H. M. Seidel (Eds.), *Primary pediatric care* (2nd ed.). St. Louis: Mosby Yearbook.

Eimas, P. (1995). The perception of representation of speech by infants. In J. L. Morgan & K. Demuth (Eds.), *Signal to syntax.* Hillsdale, NJ: Erlbaum.

Eisenberg, N. (Ed.). (1982). *The development of prosocial behavior.* New York: Wiley.

Eisenberg, N. (1998). Introduction. In N. Eisenberg (Ed.), *Handbook of child psychology* (5th ed., Vol 3). New York: Wiley.

Eisenberg, N., & Fabes, R. A. (1994). Emotional regulation and the development of social competence. In M. Clark (Ed.), *Review of personality and social psychology.* Newbury Park, CA: Sage.

Eisenberg, N., & Fabes, R. A. (1998). Prosocial development. In N. Eisenberg (Ed.), *Handbook of child psychology* (5th ed., Vol. 3). New York: Wiley.

Eisenberg, N., Martin, C. L., & Fabes, R. A. (1996). Gender development and gender effects. In D. C. Berliner & R. C. Calfee (Eds.), *Handbook of educational psychology.* New York: Macmillan.

Eisenberg, N., & Murphy, B. (1995). Parenting and children's moral development. In M. H. Bornstein (Ed.), *Children and parenting* (Vol. 4). Hillsdale, NJ: Erlbaum.

Eisenberg, N., Shea, C. I., Carolo, G., & Knight, G. P. (1991). Empathy-related responding and cognition: A chicken and egg dilemma. In W. M. Kurtines & J. Gewirtz (Eds.), *Moral behavior and development* (Vol. 2). Hillsdale, NJ: Erlbaum.

Eisenberger, R., & Cameron, J. (1998). Reward, intrinsic interest, and creativity: New findings. *American Psychologist, 53,* 676–678.

Elder, G. H. (1980). Adolescence in historical perspective. In J. Adelson (Ed.), *Handbook of adolescent psychology.* New York: Wiley.

Elder, G., Jr. (1999). Unpublished review of J. W. Santrock's *Life-span development,* 7th ed. (New York: McGraw-Hill).

Elias, M. (1998, June 23). For 50 years pediatrics has taken giant steps. *USA Today,* pp. 1, 2D.

Elicker, J. (1996). A knitting tale: Reflections on scaffolding. *Childhood Education, 72,* 29–32.

Elkind, D. (1961). Quantity conceptions in junior and senior high school students. *Child Development, 32,* 551–560.

Elkind, D. (1976). *Child development and education.* New York: Oxford University Press.

Elkind, D. (1978). Understanding the young adolescent. *Adolescence, 13,* 127–134.

Elkind, D. (1981). *The hurried child.* Reading, MA: Addison-Wesley.

Elkind, D. (1985). Reply to D. Lapsley and M. Murphy's *Developmental Review* paper. *Developmental Review, 5,* 218–226.

Elkind, D. (1988, January). Educating the very young: A call for clear thinking. *NEA Today,* pp. 22–27.

Ellis, H. C. (1987). Recent developments in human memory. In V. P. Makosky (Ed.), *The G. Stanley Hall lecture series.* Washington, DC: American Psychological Association.

Embretson, S. E., & Hershberger, S. L. (Eds.) (1999). *The new rules of assessment.* Mahwah, NJ: Erlbaum.

Emde, R. N., Gaensbauer, T. G., & Harmon, R. J. (1976). Emotional expression in infancy: A biobehavioral study. *Psychological Issues: Monograph Series, 10* (37).

Emery, R. E. (1994). *Renegotiating family relationships.* New York: Guilford Press.

Enger, E. D., Kormelink, R., Ross, F. C., & Otto, R. (1996). *Diversity of life.* Dubuque, IA: Wm. C. Brown.

Enright, R. D., Lapsley, D. K., Dricas, A. S., & Fehr, L. A. (1980). Parental influence on the development of adolescent autonomy and identity. *Journal of Youth and Adolescence, 9,* 529–546.

Erikson, E. H. (1950). *Childhood and society.* New York: W. W. Norton.

Erikson, E. H. (1962). *Young man Luther.* New York: W. W. Norton.

Erikson, E. H. (1968). *Identity: Youth and crisis.* New York: W. W. Norton.

Erikson, E. H. (1969). *Gandhi's truth.* New York: W. W. Norton.

Erlick, A. C., & Starry, A. R. (1973, June). *Sources of information for career decisions.* Report of Poll No. 98, Purdue Opinion Panel.

Erwin, E. J. (Ed.). (1996). *Putting children first.* Baltimore: Paul Brookes.

Etzel, R. (1988, October). *Children of smokers.* Paper presented at the meeting of the American Academy of Pediatrics, New Orleans.

Evans, B. J., & Whitfield, J. R. (Eds.). (1988). *Black males in the United States: An annotated bibliography from 1967 to 1987.* Washington, DC: American Psychological Association.

Evans, I. M., Cicchelli, T., Cohen, M., & Shapiro, N. (1995). *Staying in school.* Baltimore: Paul H. Brookes.

Eyler, F. D., Behnke, M., Conlon, M., Woods, N. S., & Wobie, K. (1998). Birth outcome from a prospective, matched study of prenatal crack/cocaine use: I. Interactive and dose effects on health and growth. *Pediatrics, 101,* 229–237.

Eyler, F. D., Behnke, M. L., & Stewart, N. J. (1990). *Issues in identification and follow-up of cocaine-exposed neonates.* Unpublished manuscript, University of Florida, Gainesville.

F

Fabes, R. A., Eisenberg, N., Jones, S., Smith, M., Gutherie, I., Poulin, R., Shepard, S., & Friedman, J. (1999). Regulation, emotionality, and preschoolers' socially competent peer interactions. *Child Development, 70,* 432–442.

Fabricius, W. V., & Hagen, J. W. (1984). Use of causal attributions about recall performance to assess metamemory and predict strategic memory behavior in young children. *Developmental Psychology, 20,* 975–987.

Fagot, B. I. (1995). Parenting boys and girls. In M. H. Bornstein (Ed.), *Handbook of parenting* (Vol. 1). Hillsdale, NJ: Erlbaum.

Falbo, T., & Poston, D. L. (1993). The academic, personality, and physical outcomes of only children in China. *Child Development, 64,* 18–35.

Famy, C., Streissguth, A. P., & Unis, A. S. (1998). Mental illness in adults with fetal alcohol syndrome or fetal alcohol effects. *American Journal of Psychiatry, 155,* 552–554.

Fantz, R. L. (1963). Pattern vision in newborn infants. *Science, 140,* 296–297.

Fasick, F. (1988). Patterns of formal education in high school as rites of passage. *Adolescence, 23,* 457–468.

Federman, J. (Ed.). (1997). *National television violence study* (Vol. 2). Santa Barbara: University of California.

Fein, G. G. (1986). Pretend play. In D. Görlitz & J. F. Wohlwill (Eds.), *Curiosity, imagination, and play.* Hillsdale, NJ: Erlbaum.

Feinman, S. (1981). Why is cross-sex-role behavior more approved for girls than for boys? A status characteristic approach. *Sex Roles, 7,* 289–299.

Feiring, C. (1995, March). *The development of romance from 15 to 18 years.* Paper presented at the meeting of the Society for Research in Child Development, Indianapolis.

Feiring, C. (1996). Concepts of romance in 15-year-old adolescents. *Journal of Research on Adolescence, 6,* 181–200.

Feldman, D. H., & Piirto, J. (1995). Parenting talented children. In M. H. Bornstein (Ed.), *Handbook of parenting* (Vol. 1). Hillsdale, NJ: Erlbaum.

Feldman, M. A. (1996). The effectiveness of early intervention for children of parents with mental retardation. In M. J. Guralnick (Ed.), *The effectiveness of early intervention.* Baltimore: Paul H. Brookes.

Feldman, S. S. (1999). Unpublished review of J. W. Santrock's *Adolescence,* 8th ed. (New York: McGraw-Hill).

Feldman, S. S., & Elliott, G. R. (1990). Progress and promise of research on normal adolescent development. In S. S. Feldman & G. Elliott (Eds.), *At the threshold: The developing adolescent.* Cambridge, MA: Harvard University Press.

Feldman, S. S., & Weinberger, D. A. (1994). Self-restraint as a mediator of family influences on boys' delinquent behavior: A longitudinal study. *Child Development, 65,* 195–211.

Fenson, L., Dale, P. S., Reznick, S. J., Bates, E., Thal, D. J., & Pethick, S. (1994). Variability in early communicative development. *Monographs of the Society for Research in Child Development,* Serial No. 242, Vol. 60, No. 5.

Ferguson, D. M., Harwood, L. J., & Shannon, F. T. (1987). Breastfeeding and subsequent social adjustment in 6- to 8-year-old children. *Journal of Child Psychology and Psychiatry, 28,* 378–386.

Ferrari, M., & Sternberg, R. J. (1998). The development of mental abilities. In D. Kuhn & R. S. Siegler (Eds.), *Handbook of child psychology* (5th ed., Vol. 2). New York: Wiley.

Field, T. (1990). *Infancy.* Cambridge, MA: Harvard University Press.

Field, T. (1992, September). Stroking babies helps growth, reduces stress. *Brown University Child and Adolescent Behavior Letter,* pp. 1, 6.

Field, T. (1995). Psychologically depressed parents. In M. H. Bornstein (Ed.), *Handbook of parenting* (Vol. 4). Hillsdale, NJ: Erlbaum.

Field, T. (1998). Maternal depression effects on infants and early interventions. *Preventive Medicine, 17,* 200–203.

Field, T., Grizzle, N., Scafidi, F., & Schanberg, S. (1996). Massage and relaxation therapies' effects on depressed adolescent mothers. *Adolescence, 31,* 903–911.

Field, T., Henteleff, T., Hernandez-Reif, M., Martines, E., Mavunda, K., Kuhn, C., & Schanberg, S. (1998). Children with asthma have improved pulmonary functions after massage therapy. *Journal of Pediatrics, 132,* 854–858.

Field, T., Hernandez-Reif, M., Seligman, S., Krasnegor, J., & Sunshine, W. (1997). Juvenile rheumatoid arthritis: Benefits from massage therapy. *Journal of Pediatric Psychology, 22,* 607–617.

Field, T., Hernandez-Reif, M., Taylor, S., Quintino, O., & Burman, I. (1997). Labor pain is reduced by massage therapy. *Journal of Psychosomatic Obstetrics and Gynecology, 18,* 286–291.

Field, T., Lasko, D., Mundy, P., Henteleff, T., Kabat, S., Talpins, S., & Dowling, M. (1997). Brief report: Autistic children's attentiveness and responsivity improve after touch therapy. *Journal of Autism and Developmental Disorders, 27,* 333–338.

Field, T., Quintino, O., Hernandez-Reif, M., & Koslosky, G. (1998). Adolescents with attention deficit hyperactivity disorder benefit from massage therapy. *Adolescence, 33,* 103–108.

Field, T., Sandberg, D., Quetel, T. A., Garcia, R., & Rosario, M. (1985). Effects of ultrasound feedback on pregnancy anxiety, fetal activity, and neonatal outcomes. *Obstetrics and Gynecology, 66,* 525–528.

Field, T., Scafidi, F., & Schanberg, S. (1987). Massage of preterm newborns to improve growth and development. *Pediatric Nursing, 13,* 385–387.

Field, T., Seligman, S., Scafidi, F., & Schanberg, S. (1996). Alleviating posttraumatic stress in children following Hurricane Andrew. *Journal of Applied Developmental Psycology, 17,* 37–50.

Field, T. M., Woodson, R., Greenberg, R., & Cohen, D. (1982). Discrimination and imitation of facial expressions by neonates. *Science, 218,* 179–181.

Fields, M. V., & Spangler, K. (2000). *Let's begin reading right: Developing appropriate beginning literacy.* Columbus, OH: Merrill.

Fields, R. (1998). *Drugs in perspective* (3rd ed.). New York: McGraw-Hill.

Finkel, D., Whitfield, K., & McGue, M. (1995). Genetic and environmental influences on functional age: A twin study. *Journal of Gerontology, 50B,* P104–P113.

Firlik, R. (1996). Can we adapt the philosophies and practices of Reggio Emilia, Italy, for use in American schools? *Young Children, 51,* 217–220.

Fisher-Thompson, D., Polinski, L., Eaton, M., & Hefferman, K. (1993, March). *Sex-role orientation of children and their parents: Relationship to the sex-typing of Christmas toys.* Paper presented at the biennial meeting of the Society for Research in Child Development, New Orleans.

Flavell, J. H. (1980, fall). A tribute to Piaget. *Society for Research in Child Development Newsletter,* p. 1.

Flavell, J. H. (1999). Cognitive development: Children's knowledge about the mind. *Annual Review of Psychology* (Vol. 50). Palo Alto, CA: Annual Reviews.

Flavell, J. H., Beach, D. R., & Chinksy, J. M. (1966). Spontaneous verbal rehearsal in a memory task as a function of age. *Child Development, 37,* 283–289.

Flavell, J. H., Flavell, E. R., & Green, F. L. (1983). Development of the appearance-reality distinction. *Cognitive Psychology, 15,* 95–120.

Flavell, J. H., Friedrichs, A., & Hoyt, J. (1970). Developmental changes in memorization processes. *Cognitive Psychology, 1,* 324–340.

Flavell, J. H., Green, F. L., & Flavell, E. R. (1995). Young children's knowledge about thinking. *Monographs of the Society for Research in Child Development, 60* (1).

Flavell, J. H., Green, F. L., Flavell, E. R., & Lin, N. T. (1999). Development of children's knowledge about unconsciousness. *Child Development, 70,* 396–412.

Flavell, J. H., Miller, P. H. (1998). Social cognition. In W. Damon (Ed.), *Handbook of child psychology* (5th ed., Vol. 2). New York: Wiley.

Flavell, J. H., Miller, P. H., & Miller, S. A. (1993). *Cognitive development* (3rd ed.). Englewood Cliffs, NJ: Prentice Hall.

Fleming, J. E., Boyle, M., & Offord, D. R. (1993). The outcome of adolescent depression in the Ontario child health study follow-up. *Journal of the American Academy of Child and Adolescent Psychiatry, 32,* 28–29.

Flynn, J. R. (1999). Searching for justice: The discovery of IQ gains over time. *American Psychologist, 54,* 5–20.

Fogel, A., Toda, S., & Kawai, M. (1988). Mother-infant face-to-face interaction in Japan and the United States: A laboratory comparison using 3-month-old infants. *Developmental Psychology, 24,* 398–406.

Folkman, S., & Lazarus, R. (1991). Coping and emotion. In N. Stein, B. L. Leventhal, & T. Trabasso (Eds.), *Psychological and biological approaches to emotion.* Hillsdale, NJ: Erlbaum.

Fordham, S., & Ogbu, J. U. (1986). Black students' school success: Coping with the burden of "acting white." *Urban Review, 18,* 176–206.

Forrest, J. D., & Singh, S. (1990). The sexual and reproductive behavior of American women, 1982–1988. *Family Planning Perspectives, 22,* 206–214.

Fox, N. (1997). *Attachment in infants and adults: A link between the two?* Paper presented at the meeting of the Society for Research in Child Development, Washington, DC.

Fraga, C. G., Motchnik, P. A., Shigenaga, M. K., Helbock, H. J., Jacob, R. A., & Ames, B. N. (1991). Ascorbic acid protects against endogenous oxidative DNA damage in human sperm. *Proceedings of the National Academy of Sciences of the United States, 88,* 11003–11006.

Fraiberg, S. (1959). *The magic years.* New York: Scribner's.

Francis, J., Fraser, G., & Marcia, J. E. (1989). *Cognitive and experimental factors in moratorium-achievement (MAMA) cycles.* Unpublished manuscript. Department of Psychology, Simon Fraser University, Burnaby, British Columbia.

Freeman, D. (1983). *Margaret Mead and Samoa.* Cambridge, MA: Harvard University Press.

Freeman, K. E., & Gehl, K. S. (1995, March). *Beginnings, middles, and ends: 24-month-olds' understanding of analogy.* Paper presented at the meeting of the Society for Research in Child Development, Indianapolis.

Freppon, P. A., & Dahl, K. L. (1998). Balanced instruction: Insights and considerations. *Reading Research Quarterly, 33,* 240–251.

Freud, A., & Dann, S. (1951). Instinctual anxiety during puberty. In A. Freud (Ed.), *The ego and its mechanisms of defense.* New York: International Universities Press.

Freud, S. (1917). *A general introduction to psychoanalysis.* New York: Washington Square Press.

Fried, P. A., & Watkinson, B. (1990). 36- and 48-month neurobehavioral follow-up of children prenatally exposed to marijuana, cigarettes, and alcohol. *Developmental and Behavioral Pediatrics, 11,* 49–58.

Friedman, D. S., Dietz, W. H., Srinivasan, S. R., & Berensen, G. S. (1999). The relation of overweight to cardiovascular risks among children and adolescents: The Bogalusa Heart Study. *Pediatrics, 103,* 1175–1182.

Friedrich, L. K., & Stein, A. H. (1973). Aggressive and prosocial TV programs and the natural behavior of preschool children. *Monographs of the Society for Research in Child Development, 38* (4, Serial No. 151).

Frost, J. L., & Wortham, S. C. (1988, July). The evolution of American playgrounds. *Young Children,* pp. 19–28.

Frye, D., Zelazo, P. D., Brooks, P. J., & Samuels, M. C. (1996). Inference and action in early causal reasoning. *Developmental Psychology, 32,* 120–131.

Fugger, E. F., Black, S. H., Keyvanfar, K., & Schulman, J. D. (1998). Birth of normal daughters after Microsort separation and intrauterine insemination, in-vitro fertilization, or intracycloplasmic sperm injection. *Human Reproduction, 13,* 2367–2370.

Fuller, M. (1984). Black girls in a London comprehensive school. In M. Hammersley & P. Woods (Eds.), *Life in school: The sociology of pop culture.* New York: Open University Press.

Furman, W., Brown, B. B., & Feiring, C. (Eds.) (in press). *Contemporary perspectives on romantic adolescent relationships.* New York: Cambridge University Press.

Furman, W., & Buhrmester, D. (1992). Age and sex differences in perceptions of networks of personal relationships. *Child Development, 63,* 103–115.

Furman, W., & Wehner, E. A. (in press). Adolescent romantic relationships: A developmental perspective. In S. Shulman & W. A. Collins (Eds.), *New directions for child development: Adolescent romantic relationships.* San Francisco: Jossey-Bass.

Furstenberg, F. F., Jr., & Nord, C. W. (1987). Parenting apart: Patterns of childrearing after marital disruption. *Journal of Marriage and the Family, 47,* 893–904.

Furth, H. G. (1973). *Deafness and learning: A psychosocial approach.* Belmont, CA: Wadsworth.

Furth, H. G., & Wachs, H. (1975). *Thinking goes to school.* New York: Oxford University Press.

G

Gadpaille, W. J. (1996). *Adolescent suicide.* Washington, DC: American Psychological Association.

Galambos, N. L., & Maggs, J. L. (1989, April). *The after-school ecology of young adolescents and self-reported behavior.* Paper presented at the biennial meeting of the Society for Research in Child Development, Kansas City.

Galambos, N. L., & Tilton-Weaver, L. (1996, March). *The adultoid adolescent: Too much, too soon.* Paper presented at the meeting of the Society for Research on Adolescence, Boston.

Galinsky, E., & David, J. (1988). *The preschool years: Family strategies that work—from experts and parents.* New York: Times Books.

Galotti, K. M., Kozberg, S. F., & Appleman, D. (in press). Younger and older adolescents' thinking about commitments. *Journal of Experimental Child Psychology.*

Galotti, K. M., Kozberg, S. F., & Farmer, M. C. (1990, March). *Gender and developmental differences in adolescents' conceptions of moral reasoning.* Paper presented at the meeting of the Society for Research in Adolescence, Atlanta.

Gandini, L. (1993). Fundamentals of the Reggio Emilia approach to early childhood education. *Young Children, 49,* 4–8.

Ganger, J. B., Baker, A. K., Chawla, S., & Pinker, S. (1999, April). *The contribution of heredity to early vocabulary and grammatical development: A twin study.* Paper presented at the meeting of the Society for Research in Child Development, Albuquerque.

Garbarino, J. (1976). The ecological correlates of child abuse: The impact of socioeconomic stress on mothers. *Child Development, 47,* 178–185.

Garbarino, J. (1999). *Lost boys: Why our sons turn violent and how we can save them.* New York: Free Press.

Garbarino, J., & Asp, C. E. (1981). *Successful schools and competent students.* Lexington, MA: Lexington Books.

Garcia, L., Hart, D., & Johnson-Ray, R. (1998). What do children and adolescents think about themselves? A developmental account of self-concept development. In S. Hala, (Ed.), *The development of social cognition.* London: University College of London Press.

Gardner, H. (1983). *Frames of mind.* New York: Basic Books.

Gardner, H. (1993). *Multiple intelligences.* New York: Basic Books.

Gardner, L. I. (1972). Deprivation dwarfism. *Scientific American, 227,* 76–82.

Garmezy, N. (1993). Children in poverty: Resilience despite risk. *Psychiatry, 56,* 127–136.

Garmon, L., Basinger, K. S., & Gibbs, J. C. (1995, March). *Gender differences in the expression of moral judgment.* Paper presented at the meeting of the Society for Research in Child Development, Indianapolis.

Garrett, P., Ng'andu, N., & Ferron, J. (1994). Poverty experiences of young children and the quality of their home environments. *Child Development, 65,* 331–345.

Garvey, C. (1977). *Play.* Cambridge, MA: Harvard University Press.

Gazzaniga, M. S. (1986). *The social brain.* New York: Plenum.

Geary, D. C., & Bjorklund, D. F. (2000). Evolutionary developmental psychology. *Child Development, 71,* 57–65.

Gelfand, D. M., Teti, D. M., & Fox, C. E. R. (1992). Sources of parenting stress for depressed and nondepressed mothers of infants. *Journal of Clinical Child Psychology, 21,* 262–272.

Gelman, R. (1969). Conservation acquisition: A problem of learning to attend to relevant attributes. *Journal of Experimental Child Psychology, 7,* 67–87.

Gelman, R., & Brenneman, K. (1994). Domain specificity and cultural variation are not inconsistent. In L. A. Hirschfeld & S. Gelman (Eds.), *Mapping the Mind: Domain specificity in cognition and culture.* New York: Cambridge University Press.

Gelman, R., & Williams, E. M. (1998). Enabling constraints for cognitive development and learning. In W. Damon (Ed.), *Handbook of child psychology* (5th ed., Vol. 4). New York: Wiley.

George, C., Main, M., & Kaplan, N. (1984). *Attachment interview with adults.* Unpublished manuscript, University of California, Berkeley.

Gergen, P. J., Fowler, J. A., Maurer, K. R., Davis, W. W., & Overpeck, M. D. (1998). The burden of environmental tobacco smoke exposure on the respiratory health of children 2 months through 5 years of age in the United States: Third National Health and Nutrition Examination Survey, 1988 to 1994. *Pediatrics, 101,* E8.

Gesell, A. L. (1928). *Infancy and human growth.* New York: Macmillan.

Gesell, A. L. (1934). *An atlas of infant behavior.* New Haven, CT: Yale University Press.

Gewirtz, J. (1977). Maternal responding and the conditioning of infant crying: Directions of influence within the attachment-acquisition process. In B. C. Etzel, J. M. LeBlanc, & D. M. Baer (Eds.), *New developments in behavioral research.* Hillsdale, NJ: Erlbaum.

Gibbs, J. T. (1989). Black American adolescents. In J. T. Gibbs & L. N. Huang (Eds.), *Children of color.* San Francisco: Jossey-Bass.

Gibbs, J. T., & Huang, L. N. (1989). A conceptual framework for assessing and treating minority youth. In J. T. Gibbs & L. N. Huang (Eds.), *Children of color.* San Francisco: Jossey-Bass.

Gibbs, P.R. (2000). Adoption. In A. Kazdin (Ed.), *Encyclopedia of psychology.* Washington, DC, & New York: American Psychological Association and Oxford U. Press.

Gibson, E. G. (1969). *The principles of perceptual learning and development.* New York: Appleton-Century-Crofts.

Gibson, E. J. (1982). The concept of affordances in development: The renaissance of functionalism. In W. A. Collins (Ed.), *Minnesota Symposium on Child Psychology* (Vol. 15). Hillsdale, NJ: Erlbaum.

Gibson, E. J. (1989). Exploratory behavior in the development of perceiving, acting, and the acquiring of knowledge. *Annual Review of Psychology, 39.* Palo Alto, CA: Annual Reviews.

Gibson, E. J., & Walk, R. D. (1960). The "visual cliff." *Scientific American, 202,* 64–71.

Gibson, E. J., Riccio, G., Schmuckler, M. A., Stoffregen, T. A., Rosenberg, D., & Taormina, J. (1987). Detection of the traversibility of surfaces by crawling and walking infants. *Journal of Experimental Psychology: Human Perception and Performance, 13,* 533–544.

Gibson, J. J. (1966). *The senses considered as perceptual systems.* Boston: Houghton Mifflin.

Gibson, J. J. (1979). *The ecological approach to visual perception.* Boston: Houghton Mifflin.

Gilligan, C. (1982). *In a different voice.* Cambridge, MA: Harvard University Press.

Gilligan, C. (1992, May). *Joining the resistance: Girls' development in adolescence.* Paper presented at the symposium on development and vulnerability in close relationships, Montreal, Quebec.

Gilligan, C. (1996). The centrality of relationships in psychological development: A puzzle, some evidence, and a theory. In G. G. Noam & K. W. Fischer (Eds.), *Development and vulnerability in close relationships.* Hillsdale, NJ: Erlbaum.

Gilligan, C., & Attanucci, J. (1988). Two moral orientations. In C. Gilligan, J. V. Ward, J. M. Taylor, & B. Bardige (Eds.), *Mapping the moral domain.* Cambridge, MA: Harvard University Press.

Gilligan, C., Brown, L. M., & Rogers, A. G. (1990). Psyche embedded: A place for body, relationships, and culture in personality theory. In A. I. Rabin, R. A. Zucker, R. A. Emmons, & S. Frank (Eds.), *Studying persons and lives.* New York: Springer.

Ginsburg, H. P., Klein, A., & Starkey, P. (1997). The development of children's mathematical thinking. In I. E. Sigel & K. A. Renninger (Eds.), *Handbook of child psychology* (5th ed., Vol. 4). New York: Wiley.

Gjerde, P. F., Block, J., & Block, J. H. (1991). The preschool family context of 18-year-olds with depressive symptoms: A prospective study. *Journal of Research on Adolescence, 1,* 63–92.

Gleason, J. B., & Ratner, N. (1998). *Psycholinguistics* (4th ed.). Ft. Worth: Harcourt Brace.

Gojdamaschko, N. (1999). Vygotsky. In M. A. Runco & S. Pritzker (Eds.), *Encyclopedia of creativity.* San Diego: Academic Press.

Goldfield, E. C., Kay, B. A., & Warren, W. H. (1993). Infant bouncing: The assembly and tuning of action systems. *Child Development, 64,* 1128–1142.

Goldin-Meadow, S. (1977). The development of language-like communication without a language model. *Science, 197,* 401–403.

Goldsmith, H. H. (1988, August). *Does early temperament predict late development?* Paper presented at the meeting of the American Psychological Association, Atlanta.

Goldsmith, H. H. (1994, Winter). The behavior-genetic approach to development and experience: Contexts and constraints. *SRCD Newsletter, 1* (6), 10–11.

Goldsmith, H. H., & Gottesman, I. I. (1981). Origins of variation in behavioral style: A longitudinal study of temperament in young twins. *Child Development, 52,* 91–103.

Goleman, D. (1995). *Emotional intelligence.* New York: Bantam Books.

Goleman, D., Kaufman, P., & Ray, M. (1993). *The creative spirit.* New York: Plume.

Golombok, S., Cook, R., Bish, A., & Murray, C. (1995). Families created by the new reproductive technologies: Quality of parenting and social and emotional development of the children. *Child Development, 66,* 285–298.

Gomel, J. N., Hanson, T. L., & Tinsley, B. J. (1999, April). *Cultural influences on parents' beliefs about the relations between health and eating: A domain analysis.* Paper presented at the meeting of the Society for Research in Child Development, Albuquerque.

Goodman, R. A., Mercy, J. A., Loya, F., Rosenberg, M. L., Smith, J. C., Allen, N. H., Vargas, L., & Kolts, R. (1986). Alcohol use and interpersonal violence: Alcohol detected in homicide victims. *American Journal of Public Health, 76,* 144–149.

Goodnow, J. J. (1995, March). *Incorporating "culture" into accounts of development.* Paper presented at the meeting of the Society for Research in Child Development, Indianapolis.

Gopnik, A. (1997, April). *How the child's theory of mind changes.* Paper presented at the meeting of the Society for Research in Child Development, Washington, DC.

Gopnik, A., & Meltzoff, A. (1997). *Words, thoughts, and theories.* Cambridge, MA: MIT Press.

Gorman, K. S., & Pollitt, E. (1996). Does schooling buffer the effects of early risk? *Child Development, 67,* 314–326.

Gottfried, A. E., Gottfried, A. W., & Bathurst, K. (1995). Maternal and dual-earner employment status and parenting. In M. H. Bornstein (Ed.), *Handbook of parenting* (Vol. 2). Hillsdale, NJ: Erlbaum.

Gottlieb, G. (1991). Experiential canalization of behavioral development theory. *Developmental Psychology, 27,* 4–13.

Gottlieb, G., Wahlsten, D., & Lickliter, R. (1998). The significance of biology for human development: A developmental psychobiological systems view. In W. Damon (Ed.), *Handbook of child psychology* (5th ed., Vol. 1). New York: Wiley.

Gottman, J. M., Katz, L. F., & Hooven, C. (1997). *Meta-emotion: How families communicate.* Mahwah, NJ: Erlbaum.

Gottman, J. M., & Parker, J. G. (Eds.). (1987). *Conversations with friends.* New York: Cambridge University Press.

Gould, S. J. (1981). *The mismeasure of man.* New York: W. W. Norton.

Gounin-Decarie, T. (1996). Revisiting Piaget, or the vulnerability of Piaget's infancy theory in the nineties. In G. G. Noam & K. W. Fischer (Eds.), *Development and vulnerability in close relationships.* Hillsdale, NJ: Erlbaum.

Graber, J. A., & Brooks-Gunn, J. (in press). "Sometimes I think that you don't like me": How mothers and daughters negotiate the transition to adolescence. In M. Cox & J. Brooks-Gunn (Eds.), *Conflict and closeness in families: Consequences for children and youth.* Mahwah, NJ: Erlbaum.

Graham, S. (1986, August). *Can attribution theory tell us something about motivation in blacks?* Paper presented at the meeting of the American Psychological Association, Washington, DC.

Graham, S. (1990). Motivation in Afro-Americans. In G. L. Berry & J. K. Asamen (Eds.), *Black students: Psychosocial issues and academic achievement.* Newbury Park, CA: Sage.

Graham, S. (1992). Most of the subjects were white and middle class. *American Psychologist, 47,* 629–637.

Graham, S., & Weiner, B. (1996). Theories and principles of motivation. In D. C. Berliner & R. C. Calfee (Eds.), *Handbook of educational psychology.* New York: Macmillan.

Grant, J. (1997). *State of the world's children.* New York: UNICEF and Oxford University Press.

Grant, J. P. (1993). *The state of the world's children.* New York: UNICEF and Oxford University Press.

Greenfield, P. M., & Suzuki, L. K. (1998). Culture and human development: Implications for parenting, education, pediatrics, and mental health. In W. Damon (Ed.), *Handbook of child psychology* (5th ed., Vol. 4). New York: Wiley.

Greeno, J. G., Collins, A. M., & Resnick, L. (1996). Cognition and learning. In D. C. Berliner & R. C. Chafee (Eds.), *Handbook of educational psychology.* New York: Macmillan.

Greenough, W. (2000). Brain development. In A. Kazdin (Ed.), *Encyclopedia of psychology.* Washington, DC, & New York: American Psychological Association and Oxford U. Press.

Greenough, W. T. (1997, April 21). Commentary in article, "Politics of biology." *U.S. News & World Report,* p. 79.

Greenough, W. T. (1999, April) *Experience, brain development, and links to mental retardation.* Paper presented at the meeting of the Society for Research in Child Development, Albuquerque.

Grodstein, F., Goldman, M. B., & Cramer, R. L. (1993). Relation of female infertility to consumption of caffeinated beverages. *American Journal of Epidemiology, 137,* 1353–1360.

Gross, R. T. (1984). Patterns of maturation: Their effects on behavior and development. In M. D. Levine & P. Satz (Eds.), *Middle childhood: Development and dysfunction.* Baltimore: University Park Press.

Grossmann, K., Grossmann, K. E., Spangler, G., Suess, G., & Unzner, L. (1995). Maternal sensitivity and newborns' orientation responses as related to quality of attachment in Northern Germany. In I. Bretherton & E. Waters (Eds.), Growing points of attachment theory and research. *Monographs of the Society for Research in Child Development, 50* (1–2, Serial No. 209).

Grotevant, H. D., & Cooper, C. R. (1985). Patterns of interaction in family relationships and the development of identity exploration in adolescence. *Child Development, 56,* 415–428.

Grotevant, H. D., & Cooper, C. R. (in press). Individuality and connectedness in adolescent development: Review and prospects for research on identity, relationships, and context. In E. Skoe & A. von der Lippe (Eds.), *Personality development in adolescence: A cross-national and life-span perspective.* London: Routledge.

Grotevant, H. D., & McRoy, R. G. (1990). Adopted adolescents in residential treatment: The role of the family. In D. M. Brodzinsky & M. D. Schechter (Eds.), *The psychology of adoption.* New York: Oxford University Press.

Guilford, J. P. (1967). *The structure of intellect.* New York: McGraw-Hill.

Gunnar, M. R., Malone, S., & Fisch, R. O. (1987). The psychobiology of stress and coping in the human neonate: Studies of the adrenocortical activity in response to stress in the first week of life. In T. Field, P. McCabe, & N. Scheiderman (Eds.), *Stress and coping.* Hillsdale, NJ: Erlbaum.

Gupta, S. (1999, February). *Stressful life events, stress hormones, and fetal growth.* Paper presented at the meeting of the Society for Behavioral Medicine, San Diego.

Gur, R. C., Mozley, L. H., Mozley, P. D., Resnick, S. M., Karp, J. S., Alavi, A., Arnold, S. E., & Gur, R. E. (1995). Sex differences in regional cerebral glucose metabolism during a resting state. *Science, 267,* 528–531.

Gustafson, G. E., Green, J. A., & Kalinowski, L. L. (1993, March). *The development of communicative skills: Infants' cries and vocalizations in social context.* Paper presented at the biennial meeting of the Society for Research in Child Development, New Orleans.

Guttentag, M., & Bray, H. (1976). *Undoing sex stereotypes: Research and resources for educators.* New York: McGraw-Hill.

H

Hack, M. H., Klein, N. K., & Taylor, H. G. (1995, Spring). Long-term developmental outcomes of low birth weight infants. *Future of Children, 5,* 176–196.

Hahn, W. K. (1987). Cerebral lateralization of function: From infancy through childhood. *Psychological Bulletin, 101,* 376–392.

Haidt, J. D. (1997, April). *Cultural and class variations in the domain of morality and the morality of conventions.* Paper presented at the meeting of the Society for Research in Child Development, Washington, DC.

Haight, W. L., & Miller, P. J. (1993). *Pretending at home.* Albany: State University of New York Press.

Haith, M. H. (1991, April). *Setting a path for the '90s: Some goals and challenges in infant sensory and perceptual development.* Paper presented at the meeting of the Society for Research in Child Development, Seattle.

Haith, M. M. (1993). Preparing for the 21st century: Some goals and challenges for studies of infant sensory and perceptual development. *Developmental Review, 13,* 354–371.

Haith, M. M., & Benson, J. B. (1998). Infant cognition. In W. Damon (Ed.), *Handbook of child psychology* (5th ed., Vol. 2). New York: John Wiley.

Haith, M. M., Hazen, C., & Goodman, G. S. (1988). Expectation and anticipation of dynamic visual events by 3.5 month old babies. *Child Development, 59,* 467–479.

Hakim-Larson, J. A. (1995, March). *Affective defaults: Temperament, goals, rules, and values.* Paper presented at the meeting of the Society for Research in Child Development, Indianapolis.

Hakuta, K., & Garcia, E. E. (1989). Bilingualism and education. *American Psychologist, 44,* 374–379.

Hale, S. (1990). A global developmental trend in cognitive processing speed. *Child Development, 61,* 653–663.

Hall, G. S. (1904). *Adolescence* (Vols. 1 & 2). Englewood Cliffs, NJ: Prentice Hall.

Hall, W. (1998, February 24). I.Q. scores are up, and psychologists wonder why. *Wall Street Journal,* pp. B11–12.

Hallahan, D. P., & Kaufmann, J. M. (2000). *Exceptional learners* (8th ed.). Boston: Allyn & Bacon.

Halonen, J., & Santrock, J. W. (1999). *Psychology: The contexts of behavior* (3rd ed.). New York: McGraw-Hill.

Hamburg, D. A. (1990). *Life skills training: Preventive interventions for young adolescents.* Washington, DC: Carnegie Council on Adolescent Development.

Hamburg, D. A. (1997). Meeting the essential requirements for healthy adolescent development in a transforming world. In R. Takanishi & D. Hamburg (Eds.), *Preparing adolescents for the 21st century.* New York: Cambridge University Press.

Hamburg, D. A., Millstein, S. G., Mortimer, A. M., Nightingale, E. O., & Petersen, A. C. (1993). Adolescent health promotion in the twenty-first century: Current frontiers and future directions. In S. G. Millstein, A. C. Petersen, & E. O. Nightingale (Eds.), *Promoting the health of adolescents.* New York: Oxford University Press.

Hamilton, M. C. (1991). *Preference for sons or daughters and the sex role characteristics of potential parents.* Paper presented at the meeting of the Association for Women in Psychology, Hartford, CT.

Hammen, C. (1993, March). *Risk and resilience in children and their depressed mothers.* Paper presented at the biennial meeting of the Society for Research in Child Development, New Orleans.

Hans, S. (1989, April). *Infant behavioral effects of prenatal exposure to methadone.* Paper presented at the biennial meeting of the Society for Research in Child Development, Kansas City.

Hare, B. R., & Castenell, L. A. (1985). No place to run, no place to hide: Comparative status and future prospects of black boys. In M. B. Spencer, G. K. Brookins, & W. R. Allen (Eds.), *Beginnings: The social and affective development of black children.* Hillsdale, NJ: Erlbaum.

Harkness, S., & Super, C. M. (1995). Culture and parenting. In M. H. Bornstein (Ed.), *Children and parenting* (Vol. 2). Hillsdale, NJ: Erlbaum.

Harlow, H. F., & Zimmerman, R. R. (1959). Affectional responses in the infant monkey. *Science, 130,* 421–432.

Harris, G., Thomas, A., & Booth, D. A. (1990). Development of salt taste in infancy. *Developmental Psychology, 26,* 534–538.

Harris, J. R. (1998). *The nurture assumption: Why children turn out the way they do: Parents matter less than you think and peers matter more.* New York: Free Press.

Harris, L., (1987, September 3). The latchkey child phenomena. *Dallas Morning News,* pp. 1A, 10A.

Harrist, A. W. (1993, March). *Family interaction styles as predictors of children's competence: The role of synchrony and nonsynchrony.* Paper presented at the biennial meeting of the Society for Research in Child Development, New Orleans.

Hart, B., & Risley, T. R. (1995). *Meaningful differences in the everyday experience of young American children.* Baltimore: Paul H. Brookes.

Hart, C. H., Charlesworth, R., Burts, D. C., & DeWolf, M. (1993, March). *The relationship of attendance in developmentally appropriate or inappropriate kindergarten classrooms to first-grade behavior.* Paper presented at the biennial meeting of the Society for Research in Child Development, New Orleans.

Hart, D. (1996). Unpublished review of J. W. Santrock's *Child Development,* 8th ed. (Dubuque, IA: Brown & Benchmark).

Hart, D., Field, N., Garfinkle, J., & Singer, J. (in press). Representations of self and other: A semantic space model. *Journal of Personality.*

Hart, D., & Karmel, M. P. (1996). Self-awareness and self-knowledge in humans, great apes, and monkeys. In A. Russon, K. Bard, & S. Parker (Eds.), *Reaching into thought.* New York: Cambridge University Press.

Harter, S. (1982). The Perceived Competence Scale for Children. *Child Development, 53,* 87–97.

Harter, S. (1985). *Self-Perception Profile for Children.* Denver: University of Denver, Department of Psychology.

Harter, S. (1986). Processes underlying the construction, maintenance, and enhancement of the self-concept of children. In J. Suls & A. Greenwald (Eds.), *Psychological perspective on the self* (Vol. 3). Hillsdale, NJ: Erlbaum.

Harter, S. (1989). *Self-Perception Profile for Adolescents.* Denver: University of Denver, Department of Psychology.

Harter, S. (1990). Self and identity development. In S. S. Feldman & G. R. Elliott (Eds.), *At the threshold: The developing adolescent.* Cambridge, MA: Harvard University Press.

Harter, S. (1998). The development of self-representations. In N. Eisenberg (Ed.), *Handbook of child psychology* (5th ed., Vol. 3). New York: Wiley.

Harter, S. (1999). *The construction of the self.* New York: Guilford.

Harter, S., Alexander, P. C., & Neimeyer, R. A. (1988). Long-term effects of incestuous child abuse in college women. Social adjustment, social cognition, and family characteristics. *Journal of Consulting and Clinical Psychology, 56,* 5–8.

Harter, S., & Lee, L. (1989). *Manifestations of true and false selves in adolescence.* Paper presented at the meeting of the Society for Research in Child Development, Kansas City.

Harter, S., & Marold, D. B. (1992). Psychological risk factors contributing to adolescent suicide ideation. In G. Noam & S. Borst (Eds.), *Child and adolescent suicide.* San Francisco: Jossey Bass.

Harter, S., Marold, D. B., Whitesell, N. R., & Cobbs, G. (1996). A model of the effects of perceived parent and peer support on adolescent false self behavior. *Child Development, 67,* 360–374.

Harter, S., & Monsour, A. (1992). Developmental analysis of conflict caused by opposing attributes in the adolescent self-portrait. *Developmental Psychology, 28,* 251–260.

Harter, S., Waters, P., & Whitesell, N. (1996, March). *False self behavior and lack of voice among adolescent males and females.* Paper presented at the meeting of the Society for Research on Adolescence, Boston.

Harter, S., Waters, P. L., Whitesell, N. R., & Kastelic, D. (1998). Level of voice among female and male high school students: Relational context, support, and gender orientation. *Developmental Psychology, 34,* 892–901.

Hartmann, D. P., & George, T. P. (1999). Design, measurement, and analysis in developmental research. In M. H. Bornstein & M. E. Lamb (Eds.), *Developmental psychology: An advanced textbook* (4th ed.). Mahwah, NJ: Erlbaum.

Hartshorn, K. (1998). *The effect of reinstatement on infant long-term retention.* Unpublished doctoral dissertation, Department of Psychology, Rutgers University, New Brunswick, NJ.

Hartshorne, H., & May, M. S. (1928–1930). *Moral studies in the nature of character: Studies in deceit* (Vol. 1); *Studies in self-control* (Vol. 2). *Studies in the organization of character* (Vol. 3). New York: Macmillan.

Hartup, W. W. (1976). Peer interaction and the development of the individual child. In E. Schopler & R. J. Reichler (Eds.), *Psychopathology and child development.* New York: Plenum.

Hartup, W. W. (1983). The peer system. In P. H. Mussen (Ed.), *Handbook of child psychology* (4th ed., Vol. 4). New York: Wiley.

Hartup, W. W. (1996). The company they keep: Friendships and their developmental significance. *Child Development, 67,* 1–13.

Hartup, W. W. (1999, April). *Peer relations and the growth of the individual child.* Paper presented at the meeting of the Society for Research in Child Development, Albuquerque.

Hartup, W. W., & Laursen, B. (1999). Relationships as developmental contexts: Retrospective themes and contemporary issues. In W. Andrew Collins & B. Laursen (Eds.), *Relationships as developmental contexts.* Mahwah, NJ: Erlbaum.

Harvey, E. (1999). Short-term and long-term effects of parental employment on children of the National Longitudinal Survey of Youth. *Developmental Psychology, 35,* 445–454.

Hauser, S. T., & Bowlds, M. K. (1990). Stress, coping, and adaptation. In S. S. Feldman & G. R. Elliott (Eds.), *At the threshold: The developing adolescent.* Cambridge, MA: Harvard University Press.

Hauser, S. T., Powers, S. I., Noam, G. G., Jacobson, A. M., Weisse, B., & Follansbee, D. J. (1984). Familial contexts of adolescent ego development. *Child Development, 55,* 195–213.

Havighurst, R. J. (1976). A cross-cultural view. In J. F. Adams (Ed.), *Understanding adolescence.* Boston: Allyn & Bacon.

Hawkins, J. A., & Berndt, T. J. (1985, April). *Adjustment following the transition to junior high school.* Paper presented at the biennial meeting of the Society for Research in Child Development, Toronto.

Hayden-Thomson, L., Rubin, K. M., & Hymel, S. (1987). Sex preferences in sociometric choices. *Developmental Psychology, 23,* 558–562.

Hayes, C. (Ed.). (1987). *Risking the future: Adolescent sexuality, pregnancy, and childbearing* (Vol. 1). Washington, DC: National Academy Press.

Hayman, L. L., Mahon, M. M., & Turner, J. R. (1999). *Health behavior in childhood and adolescence.* Mahwah, NJ: Erlbaum.

Heath, S. B. (1983). *Ways with words.* Cambridge, England: Cambridge University Press.

Heath, S. B. (1989). Oral and literate traditions among Black Americans living in poverty. *American Psychologist, 44,* 367–373.

Heath, S. B., & McLaughlin, M. W. (Eds.). (1993). *Identity and inner-city youth.* New York: Teachers College Press.

Hellige, J. B. (1990). Hemispheric asymmetry. *Annual Review of Psychology, 41.* Palo Alto, CA: Annual Reviews.

Henderson, J. M. T., & France, K. G. (1999, April). *Sleep patterns in the first year of life: Developmental pathways.* Paper presented at the meeting of the Society for Research in Child Development, Albuquerque.

Henderson, K. A., & Zivian, M. T. (1995, March). *The development of gender differences in adolescent body image.* Paper presented at the meeting of the Society for Research in Child Development, Indianapolis.

Henderson, V. L., & Dweck, C. S. (1990). Motivation and achievement. In S. S. Feldman & G. R. Elliott (Eds.), *At the threshold: The developing adolescent.* Cambridge, MA: Harvard University Press.

Henninger, M. L. (1999). *Teaching young children.* Columbus, OH: Merrill.

Herrnstein, R. J., & Murray, C. (1994). *The bell curve: Intelligence and class structure in modern life.* New York: Free Press.

Hess, L., Lonky, E., & Roodin, P. A. (1985, April). *The relationship of moral reasoning and ego strength to cheating behavior.* Paper presented at the meeting of the Society for Research in Child Development, Toronto.

Hetherington, E. M. (1989). Coping with family transitions: Winners, losers, and survivors. *Child Development, 60,* 1–14.

Hetherington, E. M. (1995, March). *The changing American family and the well-being of children.* Paper presented at the meeting of the Society for Research in Child Development, Indianapolis.

Hetherington, E. M. (1999). *Should we stay together for the sake of the children?* Unpublished manuscript, Dept. of Psychology, University of Virginia, Charlottesville.

Hetherington, E. M. (2000). Divorce. In A. Kazdin (Ed.), *Encyclopedia of psychology.* Washington, DC, & New York: American Psychological Association and Oxford U. Press.

Hetherington, E. M., Bridges, M., & Insabella, G. M. (1998). What matters? What does not? Five perspectives on the association between marital transitions and children's adjustment. *American Psychologist, 53,* 167–184.

Hetherington, E. M., & Clingempeel, W. G. (1992). Coping with marital transitions: A family systems perspective. *Monographs of the Society for Research in Child Development, 57* (2–3, Serial No. 227).

Hetherington, E. M., & Jodl, K. M. (1994). Stepfamilies as settings for child development. In A. Booth & J. Dunn (Eds.). *Stepfamilies: Who benefits? Who does not?* Hillsdale, NJ: Erlbaum.

Hetherington, E. M., Reiss, D., & Plomin, R. (Eds.). (1994). *Separate social worlds of siblings: The impact of nonshared environment on development.* Hillsdale, NJ: Erlbaum.

Heuwinkel, M. K. (1996). New ways of learning and new ways of teaching. *Childhood Education, 72,* 27–31.

Heward, W. L. (2000). *Exceptional children.* Columbus, OH: Merrill.

Hiebert, E. H., & Raphael, T. E. (1996). Psychological perspectives on literacy and extensions to educational practice. In D. C. Berliner & R. C. Calfee (Eds.), *Handbook of educational psychology.* New York: Macmillan.

Higgins, A., Power, C., & Kohlberg, L. (1983, April). *Moral atmosphere and moral judgment.* Paper presented at the biennial meeting of the Society for Research in Child Development, Detroit.

Hill, C. R., & Stafford, F. P. (1980). Parental care of children: Time diary estimate of quantity, predictability, and variety. *Journal of Human Resources, 15,* 219–239.

Hill, J. O., & Trowbridge, F. L. (1998). Childhood obesity: Future directions and research priorities. *Pediatrics, 101,* 570–574.

Hill, K., Battin-Pearson, S., Hawkins, J. D., & Jie, G. (1999, June). *The role of social developmental processes in facilitating or disrupting the link between early offending and adult crimes in males and females.* Paper presented at the meeting of the Society for Prevention Research, New Orleans.

Hillebrand, V., Phenice, A., & Hines, R. P. (2000). *Knowing and serving diverse families.* Columbus, OH: Merrill.

Hinde, R. A. (1992). Developmental psychology in the context of other behavioral sciences. *Developmental Psychology, 28,* 1018–1029.

Hines, M. (1982). Prenatal gonadal hormones and sex differences in human behavior. *Psychological Bulletin, 92,* 56–80.

Hines, M. (1990). Gonadal hormones and human cognitive development. In J. Balthazart (Ed.), *Hormones, brain, and behavior in vertebrates.* Basel: Karger.

Hirsch, B. J., & Rapkin, B. D. (1987). The transition to junior high school: A longitudinal study of self-esteem, psychological symptomatology, school life, and social support. *Child Development, 58,* 1235–1243.

Hobel, C. J., Dunkel-Schetter, C., Roesch, S. C., Castro, L. C., & Arora, C. P. (1999). Maternal plasma corticotropin-releasing hormone associated with stress at 20 weeks' gestation in pregnancies ending in preterm delivery. *American Journal of Obstetrics and Gynecology, 180,* S257–S263.

Hochschild, A. R. (1983). *The managed heart: Commercialization of feelings.* Berkeley, University of California Press.

Hodges, E. V. E., Boivin, M., Vitaro, F., & Bukowski, W. M. (1999). The power of friendship: Protection against an escalating cycle of peer victimization. *Developmental Psychology, 35,* 94–101.

Hodges, E. V. E., & Perry, D. G. (1999). Personal and interpersonal antecedents and consequences of victimization by peers. *Journal of Personality and Social Psychology, 76,* 677–685.

Hoff-Ginsberg, E. (1998, April). *What explains the SES-related difference in children's vocabularies and what does that tell us about the process of word learning?* Paper presented at the Conference on Language Learning, Boston.

Hoff-Ginsberg, E. (1999). *How children use input to acquire vocabulary: Evidence from a study of individual and group differences.* Unpublished manuscript, Division of Science, Florida Atlantic University.

Hoff-Ginsberg, E., & Lerner, S. (1999, April). *The nature of vocabulary differences related to socioeconomic status at two and four years.* Paper presented at the meeting of the Society for Research in Child Development, Albuquerque.

Hoff-Ginsberg, E., & Tardif, T. (1995). Socioeconomic status and parenting. In M. H. Bornstein (Ed.), *Children and parenting* (Vol. 2). Hillsdale, NJ: Erlbaum.

Hoffman, D., & Novak, T. (1999). *Computer access, socioeconomic status, and ethnicity.* Unpublished manuscript, Vanderbilt University, Nashville, TN.

Hoffman, L. W. (1989). Effects of maternal employment in two-parent families. *American Psychologist, 44,* 283–293.

Hoffman, L. W., & Youngblade, L. M. (1999). *Mothers at work: Effects on children's well-being.* New York: Cambridge.

Hoffman, M. L. (1970). Moral development. In P. H. Mussen (Ed.), *Manual of child psychology* (3rd ed., Vol. 2). New York: Wiley.

Hoffman, M. L. (1988). Moral development. In M. H. Bornstein & E. Lamb (Eds.), *Developmental psychology: An advanced textbook* (2nd ed.). Hillsdale, NJ: Erlbaum.

Hoffnung, M. (1984). Motherhood: Contemporary conflict for women. In J. Freeman (Ed.), *Women: A feminist perspective* (3rd ed.). Palo Alto, CA: Mayfield.

Hofstede, G. (1980). *Culture's consequences: International differences in work-related values.* Newbury Park, CA: Sage.

Hohnen, B., & Stevenson, J. (1999). The structure of genetic influences on general cognitive, language, phonological, and reading abilities. *Developmental Psychology, 35,* 590–603.

Hollins, E. R., & Oliver, E. I. (Eds.) (1999). *Pathways to success in school: Culturally responsive teaching.* Mahwah, NJ: Erlbaum.

Holmbeck, G. N. (1996). A model of family relational transformations during the transition to adolescence: Parent-adolescent conflict and adaptation. In J. A. Graber, J. Brooks-Gunn, & A. C. Petersen (Eds.), *Transitions through adolescence.* Hillsdale, NJ: Erlbaum.

Holmbeck, G. N., Paikoff, R. L., & Brooks-Gunn, J. (1995). Parenting adolescents. In M. H. Bornstein (Ed.), *Children and parenting* (Vol. 1). Hillsdale, NJ: Erlbaum.

Holmes, L. D. (1987). *Quest for the real Samoa: The Mead-Freeman controversy and beyond.* South Hadley, MA: Bergin & Garvey.

Holtzmann, W. (1982). Cross-cultural comparisons of personality development in Mexico and the United States. In D. Wagner & H. W. Stevenson (Eds.), *Cultural perspectives on child development.* San Francisco: W. H. Freeman.

Holtzman, W. H. (Ed.). (1992). *School of the future.* Austin, TX: American Psychological Association and Hogg Foundation for Mental Health.

Hones, D. E., & Cha, S. C. (1999). *Educating new Americans.* Mahwah, NJ: Erlbaum.

Honzik, M. P., MacFarlane, J. W., & Allen, L. (1948). The stability of mental test performance between two and eighteen years. *Journal of Experimental Education, 17,* 309–324.

Hopkins, J. R. (2000). Erikson, Erik H. In A. Kazdin (Ed.), *Encyclopedia of psychology.* Washington, DC, & New York: American Psychological Association and Oxford U. Press.

Horowitz, F. D. (1999, April). *Child development and the pits: Simple questions, complex answers, and developmental theory.* Presidential address at the meeting of the Society for Research in Child Development, Albuquerque.

Horowitz, F. D., & O'Brien, M. (1989). In the interest of the nation: A reflective essay on the state of knowledge and the challenges before us. *American Psychologist, 44,* 441–445.

Hort, B. E., & Leinbach, M. D. (1993, March). *Children's use of metaphorical cues in gender-typing of objects.* Paper presented at the biennial meeting of the Society for Research in Child Development, New Orleans.

Hotchner, T. (1997). *Pregnancy and childbirth.* New York: Avon.

Hoving, K. L., Spender, T., Robb, K. Y., & Schulte, D. (1978). Developmental changes in visual information processing. In P. A. Ornstein (Ed.), *Memory development in children.* Hillsdale, NJ: Erlbaum.

Howes, C. (1985, April). *Predicting preschool sociometric status from toddler peer interaction.* Paper presented at the meeting of the Society for Research in Child Development, Toronto.

Howes, C. (1992). *The collaborative construction of pretend: Social pretend play functions.* Albany: State University of New York Press.

Huang, L. N., & Gibbs, J. T. (1989). Future directions: Implications for research training, and practice. In J. T. Gibbs & L. N. Huang (Eds.), *Children of color.* San Francisco: Jossey-Bass.

Huang, L. N., & Ying, Y. (1989). Chinese American children and adolescents. In J. T. Gibbs & L. N. Huang (Eds.), *Children of color.* San Francisco: Jossey-Bass.

Hudson, L. M., Forman, E. R., & Brion-Meisels, S. (1982). Role-taking as a predictor of prosocial behavior in cross-age tutors. *Child Development, 53,* 1320–1329.

Huebner, A. M., & Garrod, A. C. (1993). Moral reasoning among Tibetan monks: A study of Buddhist adolescents and young adults in Nepal. *Journal of Cross-Cultural Psychology, 24,* 167–185.

Huesmann, L. R. (1986). Psychological processes promoting the relation between exposure to media violence and aggressive behavior by the viewer. *Journal of Social Issues, 42,* 125–139.

Hunt, C. E. (1999, May). *Sudden infant death syndrome (SIDS) in families: Risk factors for recurrence.* Paper presented at the meeting of the Society for Pediatric Research, San Francisco.

Hunt, M. (1974). *Sexual behavior in the 1970s.* Chicago: Playboy Press.

Hunt, R. R., & Ellis, H. C. (1999). *Fundamentals of cognitive psychology* (6th ed.). New York: McGraw-Hill.

Hunt, R. R., & Kelly, R. E. S. (1996). Accessing the particular from the general: The power of distinctiveness in the context of organization. *Memory and Cognition, 24,* 217–225.

Hurt, H., Malmud, E., Brodsky, N. L., & Giannetta, J. M. (1999, May). *What happens when the child with in utero cocaine-exposure (COC) goes to school?* Paper presented at the meeting of the Society for Pediatric Research, San Francisco.

Huston, A. C. (1983). Sex-typing. In P. H. Mussen (Ed.), *Handbook of child psychology* (4th ed., Vol. 4). New York: Wiley.

Huston, A. C., & Alvarez, M. (1990). The socialization context of gender-role development in early adolescence. In R. Montemayor, G. R. Adams, & T. P. Gulotta (Ed.), *From childhood to adolescence: A transitional period?* Newbury Park, CA: Sage.

Huston, A. C., McLoyd, V. C., & McColl, C. G. (1994). Children and poverty: Issues in contemporary research. *Child Development, 65,* 275–282.

Huston, A. C., Seigle, J., & Bremer, M. (1983, April). *Family environment and television use by preschool children.* Paper presented at the meeting of the Society for Research in Child Development, Detroit.

Huston, A. C., Watkins, B. A., & Kunkel, D. (1989). Public policy and children's television. *American Psychologist, 44,* 424–433.

Huston, A. C., & Wright, J. C. (1998). Mass media and children's development. In I. E. Siegel, & K. A. Renninger (Eds.), *Handbook of child psychology* (5th ed., Vol. 4). New York: Wiley.

Hutenlocher, P. (1997). *Developmental changes in synaptic connections in the visual cortex in infancy.* Unpublished manuscript, University of Chicago.

Huttenlocher, J., & Cymerman, E. (1999). Unpublished data on speech syntax. Chicago: University of Chicago.

Huttenlocher, J., Levine, S., & Vevea, J. (1998). Environmental input and cognitive growth: A study using time-period comparisons. *Child Development, 69,* 1012–1029.

Hyde, J. S. (1993). Meta-analysis and the psychology of women. In F. L. Denmark and M. A. Paludi (Eds.), *Handbook on the psychology of women.* Westport, CT: Greenwood.

Inagaki, K. (1995, March). *Young children's personifying and vitalistic biology.* Paper presented at the meeting of the Society for Research in Child Development, Indianapolis.

Infante-Rivard, C., Fernandez, A., Gauthier, R., David, M., & Rivard, G. E. (1993). Fetal loss associated with caffeine intake before and during pregnancy. *Journal of the American Medical Association, 270,* 2940–2943.

Ingersoll, E. W., & Thoman, E. B. (1999). Sleep/wake states of preterm infants: Stability, developmental change, diurnal variation, and relation with caregiving activity. *Child Development, 170,* 1–10.

Inoff-Germain, G., Arnold, G. S., Nottelmann, E. D., Susman, E. J., Cutler, G. B., & Chrousos, G. P. (1988). Relations between hormone levels and observational measures of aggressive behavior of young adolescents in family interactions. *Developmental Psychology, 24,* 129–139.

Institute for Families in Society. (1997). *Program to combat bullying in schools.* Columbia: University of South Carolina.

International Society for Technology in Education. (1999). *National educational technology standards for students document.* Eugene, OR: International Society for Technology in Education.

Izard, C. E. (1982). *Measuring emotions in infants and young children.* New York: Cambridge University Press.

Jaccos, J. K., Garnier, H. E., & Weisner, T. (1996, March). *The impact of family life on the process of dropping out of high school.* Paper presented at the meeting of the Society for Research on Adolescence, Boston.

Jalongo, M. R., & Isenberg, J. P. (2000). *Exploring your role: A practitioner introduction to early childhood education.* Columbus, OH: Merrill.

James, W. (1890/1950). *The principles of psychology.* New York: Dover.

Jarrett, R. L. (1995). Growing up poor: The family experiences of socially mobile youth in low-income African-American neighborhoods. *Journal of Adolescent Research, 10,* 111–135.

Jeans, P. C., Smith, M. B., & Stearns, G. (1955). Incidence of prematurity in relation to maternal nutrition. *Journal of the American Dietary Association, 31,* 576–581.

Jensen, L. A. (1995, March). *The moral reasoning of orthodox and progressivist Indians and Americans.* Paper presented at the meeting of the Society for Research in Child Development, Indianapolis.

Jensen, R. A. (1969). How much can we boost IQ and scholastic achievement? *Harvard Educational Review, 39,* 1–123.

Jessor, R., Turbin, M. S., & Costa, F. (1998). Protective factors in adolescent health behavior. *Journal of Personality and Social Psychology, 75,* 788–800.

Jessor, R., Turbin, M. S., & Costa, F. (in press). Risk and protection in successful outcomes among disadvantaged adolescents. *Applied Developmental Science.*

Ji, B. T., Shu, X.O., Linet, M. S., Zheng, W., Wacholde, S., Gao, Y. T., Ying, D. M., & Jin, F. (1997). Paternal cigarette smoking and the risk of childhood cancer among offspring of nonsmoking mothers. *Journal of the National Cancer Institute, 89,* 238–244.

Jiao, S., Ji, G., & Jing, Q. (1996). Cognitive development of Chinese urban only children and children with siblings. *Child Development, 67,* 387–395.

Johnson, D. W. (1990). *Teaching out: Interpersonal effectiveness and self-actualization.* Upper Saddle River, NJ: Prentice Hall.

Johnson, J. E., Christie, J. F., & Yawkey, T. D. (1987). *Play and early childhood development*. Glenview, IL: Scott, Foresman.

Johnson, J. S., & Newport, E. L. (1989). Critical period effects in second language learning. *Cognitive Psychology, 21*, 60–69.

Johnson, K., Strader, T., Berbaum, M., Bryant, D., Bucholtz, G., Collins, D., & Noe, T. (1996). Reducing alcohol and other drug use by strengthening community, family, and youth resiliency. *Journal of Adolescent Research, 11*, 36–37.

Johnson, M. H. (1998). The neural basis of cognitive development. In W. Damon (Ed.), *Handbook of child psychology* (5th ed., Vol. 2). New York: Wiley.

Johnson, M. H. (1999). Developmental neuroscience. In M. H. Bornstein & M. E. Lamb (Eds.), *Developmental psychology: An advanced textbook* (4th ed.). Mahwah, NJ: Erlbaum.

Johnson, M. K., Beebe, T., Mortimer, J. T., & Snyder, M. (1998). Volunteerism in adolescence: A process perspective. *Journal of Research on Adolescence, 8*, 309–332.

Johnston, J., Etteman, J., & Davidson, T. (1980). *An evaluation of "Freestyle": A television series to reduce sex-role stereotypes*. Ann Arbor: University of Michigan, Institute of Social Research.

Johnston, L. D., O'Malley, P. M., & Bachman, J. G. (1992, January 25). *Most forms of drug use decline among American high school and college students*. News release, Institute for Social Research, University of Michigan, Ann Arbor.

Johnston, L. D., O'Malley, P. M., & Bachman, J. G. (1995). *National survey results on drug use from the Monitoring the Future Study, Vol. 1: Secondary school students*. Ann Arbor: University of Michigan, Institute of Social Research.

Johnston, L. D., O'Malley, P. M., & Bachman, J. G. (1997, December). *Report of Monitoring the Future Project*. Ann Arbor: University of Michigan, Institute of Social Research.

Jones, B. F., Rasmussen, C. M., & Moffitt, M. C. (1997). *Real-life problem solving*. Washington, DC: American Psychological Association.

Jones, D. C., & Costin, S. E. (1997, April). *The friendships of African-American and European-American adolescents*. Paper presented at the meeting of the Society for Research in Child Development, Washington, DC.

Jones, E. R., Forrest, J. D., Goldman, N., Henshaw, S. K., Lincoln, R., Rosoff, J. I., Westoff, C. G., & Wulf, D. (1985). Teenage pregnancy in developed countries: Determinants and policy implications. *Family Planning Perspectives, 17*, 53–63.

Jones, J. M. (1994). The African American: A duality dilemma? In W. J. Lonner & R. Malpass (Eds.), *Psychology and culture*. Needham Heights, MA: Allyn & Bacon.

Jones, M. C. (1924). A laboratory study of fear: The case of Peter. *Journal of Genetic Psychology, 31*, 308–315.

Jones, M. C. (1965). Psychological correlates of somatic development. *Child Development, 36*, 899–911.

Jones, S. E. (2000). Ethics: An overview. In A. Kazdin (Ed.), *Encyclopedia of psychology*. Washington, DC, & New York: American Psychological Association and Oxford U. Press.

Joseph, C. L. M. (1989). Identification of factors associated with delayed antenatal care. *Journal of the American Medical Association, 81*, 57–63.

Josselson, R. (1994). Identity and relatedness in the life cycle. In H. A. Bosma, T. L. G., Graafsma, H. D. Grotevant, & D. J. De Levita (Eds.), *Identity and development*. Newbury Park, CA: Sage.

Juang, L. P., & Nguyen, H. H. (1997, April). *Autonomy and connectedness: Predictors of adjustment in Vietnamese adolescents*. Paper presented at the meeting of the Society for Research in Child Development, Washington, DC.

Jusczyk, P. (1999, March 19). Commentary in I. Wickelgren, Nurture helps mold able minds. *Science*, p. 1833.

Kagan, J. (1984). *The nature of the child*. New York: Basic Books.

Kagan, J. (1987). Perspectives on infancy. In J. D. Osofsky (Ed.), *Handbook on infant development* (2nd ed.). New York.

Kagan, J. (1992). Yesterday's premises, tomorrow's promises. *Developmental Psychology, 28*, 990–997.

Kagan, J. (1998). The biology of the child. In W. Damon (Ed.), *Handbook of child psychology* (5th ed., Vol. 3). New York: Wiley.

Kagan, J. (1998). *The power of parents*. Available on the World Wide Web: http://www.Psychplace.com.

Kagan, J., & Snidman, N. (1991). Temperamental factors in human development. *American Psychologist, 46*, 856–862.

Kagan, S., & Madsen, M. C. (1972). Experimental analysis of cooperation and competition of Anglo-American and Mexican children. *Developmental Psychology, 6*, 49–59.

Kagitcibasi, C. (1988). Diversity of socialization and social change. In P. R. Dasen, J. W. Berry, & N. Sartorious (Eds.), *Health and cross-cultural psychology: Toward applications*. Newbury Park, CA: Sage.

Kagitcibasi, C. (1995). Is psychology relevant to global human development issues? Experience from Turkey. *American Psychologist, 50*, 293–300.

Kagitcibasi, C. (1996). *Human development across cultures*. Hillsdale, NJ: Erlbaum.

Kail, R. (1993, March). *The nature of global developmental change in processing time*. Paper presented at the biennial meeting of the Society for Research in Child Development, New Orleans.

Kail, R., & Pellegrino, J. W. (1985). *Human intelligence*. New York: W. H. Freeman.

Kallio, K. S. (1999, April). *Changing conceptions of nature and nurture: Implications for theory*. Paper presented at the meeting of the Society for Research in Child Development, Albuquerque.

Kamerman, S. B. (1989). Child care, women, work, and the family: An international overview of child care services and related policies. In J. S. Lande, S. Scarr, & N. Gunzenhauser (Eds.), *Caring for children: Challenge to America*. Hillsdale, NJ: Erlbaum.

Kamii, C. (1985). *Young children reinvent arithmetic: Implications of Piaget's theory*. New York: Teachers College Press.

Kamii, C. (1989). *Young children continue to reinvent arithmetic*. New York: Teachers College Press.

Kandel, D. B. (1974). The role of parents and peers in marijuana use. *Journal of Social Issues, 30*, 107–135.

Katz, L., & Chard, S. (1989). *Engaging the minds of young children: The project approach*. Norwood, NJ: Ablex.

Katz, L. F. (1999, April). *Toward a family-based hypervigilance model of childhood aggression: The role of the mother's and the father's meta-emotion philosophy*. Paper presented at the meeting of the Society for Research in Child Development, Albuquerque.

Katz, P. A. (1987, August). *Children and social issues*. Paper presented at the meeting of the American Psychological Association, New York.

Keating, D. P., & Hertzman, C. (1999). Modernity's paradox. In D. P. Keating & C. Hertzman (Eds.), *Developmental health and the wealth of nations*. New York: Guilford Press.

Kee, D. W., & Howell, S. (1988, April). *Mental effort and memory development*. Paper presented at the meeting of the American Educational Research Association, New Orleans.

Keener, D. C., & Boykin, K. A. (1996, March). *Parental control, autonomy, and ego development*. Paper presented at the meeting of the Society for Research on Adolescence, Boston.

Keeney, T. J., Cannizzo, S. R., & Flavell, J. H. (1967). Spontaneous and induced verbal rehearsal in a recall task. *Child Development, 38*, 953–966.

Keil, F. C. (1989). *Concepts, kinds, and cognitive development*. Cambridge, MA: MIT Press.

Kelder, S. H., Perry, C. L., Peters, R. J., Lytle, L. L., & Klepp, K. (1995). Gender differences in the class of 1989 study: The school component of the Minnesota Heart Health Program. *Journal of Health Education, 26*, S36–S44.

Keller, A., Ford, L., & Meacham, J. (1978). Dimensions of self-concept in preschool children. *Developmental Psychology, 14*, 483–489.

Kellman, P. J. & Banks, M. S. (1998). Infant visual perception. In W. Damon (Eds.), *Handbook of child psychology* (5th ed., Vol. 2). New York: Wiley.

Kennell, J. H., & McGrath, S. K. (1999). Commentary: Practical and humanistic lessons from the third world for perinatal caregivers everywhere. *Birth, 26*, 9–10.

Kenney, A. M. (1987, June). Teen pregnancy: An issue for schools. *Phi Delta Kappan*, pp. 728–736.

Kessen, W., Haith, M. M., & Salapatek, P. (1970). Human infancy. In P. H. Mussen (Ed.), *Manual of child psychology* (3rd ed., Vol. 1). New York: Wiley.

Kimmel, A. (1996). *Ethical issues in behavioral research*. Cambridge, MA: Blackwell.

Kimura, D. (1989, November). How sex hormones boost—or cut—intellectual ability. *Psychology Today*, pp. 62–66.

King, N. (1982). School uses of materials traditionally associated with children's play. *Theory and Research in Social Education, 10,* 17–27.

Kinsey, A. C., Pomeroy, W. B., & Martin, C. E. (1948). *Sexual behavior in the human male.* Philadelphia: Saunders.

Kirk, R. E. (2000). Randomized experiments. In A. Kazdin (Ed.), *Encyclopedia of psychology.* Washington, DC, & New York: American Psychological Association and Oxford U. Press.

Kisilevsky, B. S. (1995). The influence stimulus and subject variables on human fetal responses to sound and vibration. In J-P Lecaunet, W. P. Fifer, M. A. Krasnegor, & W. P. Smotherman (Eds.), *Fetal development.* Hillsdale, NJ: Erlbaum.

Klaus, M., & Kennell, H. H. (1976). *Maternal-infant bonding.* St. Louis: Mosby.

Klaus, M. H., Kennell, J. H., & Klaus, P. H. (1993). *Mothering the mother.* Reading, MA: Addison-Wesley.

Klein, P. J., & Meltzoff, A. N. (1999). Long-term memory, forgetting, and deferred imitation in 12-month-old infants. *Developmental Science, 2,* 102–113.

Klish, W. J. (1998, September). Childhood obesity. *Pediatrics in Review, 19,* 312–315.

Klonoff-Cohen, H. S., Edelstein, S. L., Lefkowitz, E. S., Srinivasan, I. P., Kaegi, D., Chang, J. C., and Wiley, K. J. (1995). The effect of passive smoke and tobacco exposure through breast milk on sudden infant death syndrome. *Journal of the American Medical Association, 293,* 795–798.

Knight, M. (1999). The Darwinian algorithm and scientific inquiry. *Contemporary Psychology, 44,* 150–152.

Kobak, R. (1999). The emotional dynamics of disruptions in attachment relationships: Implications for theory, research, and clinical intervention. In J. Cassidy & P. Shaver (Eds.), *Handbook of attachment.* New York: Guilford.

Kochanska, G. (1999, April). *Applying a temperament model to the study of social development.* Paper presented at the meeting of the Society for Research in Child Development, Albuquerque.

Kochhar, C. A., West, L., & Taymans, J. M. (2000). *Handbook for successful inclusion.* Columbus, OH: Merrill.

Kohl, H. W., & Hobbs, K. E. (1998). Development of physical activity behaviors among children and adolescents. *Pediatrics, 101,* 549–554.

Kohlberg, L. (1958). *The development of modes of moral thinking and choice in the years 10 to 16.* Unpublished doctoral dissertation, University of Chicago.

Kohlberg, L. (1966). A cognitive-developmental analysis of children's sex-role concepts and attitudes. In E. E. Maccoby (Ed.), *The development of sex differences.* Palo Alto, CA: Stanford University Press.

Kohlberg, L. (1969). Stage and sequence: The cognitive-developmental approach to socialization. In D. A. Goslin (Ed.), *Handbook of socialization theory and research.* Chicago: Rand McNally.

Kohlberg, L. (1976). Moral stages and moralization: The cognitive-developmental approach. In T. Lickona (Ed.), *Moral development and behavior.* New York: Holt, Rinehart & Winston.

Kohlberg, L. (1986). A current statement on some theoretical issues. In S. Modgil & C. Modgil (Eds.), *Lawrence Kohlberg.* Philadelphia: Falmer.

Kohlberg, L., & Candee, D. (1979). *Relationships between moral judgment and moral action.* Unpublished manuscript, Harvard University.

Kohn, M. L. (1977). *Class and conformity: A study in values* (2nd ed.). Chicago: University of Chicago Press.

Kolbe, L. J., Collins, J., & Cortese, P. (1997). Building the capacity of schools to improve the health of the nation. *American Psychologist, 52,* 256–265.

Kopp, C. B. (1992, October). *Trends and directions in studies of developmental risk.* Paper presented at the 27th Minnesota Symposium on Child Psychology, University of Minnesota, Minneapolis.

Kortenhaus, C. M., & Demarest, J. (1993). Gender role stereotyping in children's literature: An update. *Sex Roles, 28,* 219–230.

Kostelecky, K. L. (1997, April). *Stressful life events, relationships, and distress during late adolescence.* Paper presented at the meeting of the Society for Research in Child Development, Washington, DC.

Kozol, J. (1991). *Savage inequalities.* New York: Crown.

Kozulin, A. (2000). Vygotsky, Lev. In A. Kazdin (Ed.), *Encyclopedia of psychology.* Washington, DC, & New York: American Psychological Association and Oxford U. Press.

Krauss, R. A., & Glucksberg, S. (1969). The development of communication: Competence as a function of age. *Child Development, 40,* 255–266.

Kreutzer, M., Leonard, C., & Flavell, J. H. (1975). An interview study of children's knowledge about memory. *Monographs of the Society for Research in Child Development, 40* (1, Serial No. 159).

Kuebli, J. (1994). Young children's understanding of everyday emotions. *Young Children, 49,* 36–47.

Kuhl, P. K. (1993). Infant speech perception: A window on psycholinguistic development. *International Journal of Psycholinguistics, 9,* 33–56.

Kuhn, D. (1998). Afterword to Volume 2: Cognition, perception, and language. In W. Damon (Ed.), *Handbook of child psychology* (5th ed., Vol. 2). New York: Wiley.

Kuhn, D. (1999). A developmental model of critical thinking. *Educational Researcher, 28,* 26–37.

Kuhn, D., Amsel, E., & O'Laughlin, M. (1988). *The development of scientific thinking skills.* Orlando, FL: Academic Press.

Kuhn, D., Garcia-Mila, M., Zohar, Z., & Anderson, C. (1995). Strategies for knowledge acquisition. *Monographs of the Society for Research in Child Development, 60* (4, Serial No. 245), 1–127.

Kuhn, D., Schauble, L., & Garcia-Mila, M. (1992). Cross-domain development of scientific reasoning. *Cognition and Instruction, 9,* 285–327.

Kupersmidt, J. B., & Coie, J. D. (1990). Preadolescent peer status, aggression, and school adjustment as predictors of externalizing problems in adolescence. *Child Development, 61,* 1350–1363.

Kurdek, L. A., & Fine, M. A. (1993). Parent and nonparent residential family members as providers of warmth, support, and supervision to young adolescents. *Journal of Family Psychology, 7,* 245–249.

Kurdek, L. A., & Krile, D. (1982). A developmental analysis of the relation between peer acceptance and both interpersonal understanding and perceived social self-competence. *Child Development, 53,* 1485–1491.

Kurtz, D. A., Cantu, C. L., & Phinney, J. S. (1996, March). *Group identities as predictors of self-esteem among African American, Latino, and White adolescents.* Paper presented at the meeting of the Society for Research on Adolescence, Boston.

Kutchinsky, B. (1992). The child sexual abuse panic. *Norsisk Sexoligi, 10,* 30–42.

Kwak, H. K., Kim, M., Cho, B. H., & Ham, Y. M. (1999, April). *The relationship between children's temperament, maternal control strategies, and children's compliance.* Paper presented at the meeting of the Society for Research in Child Development, Albuquerque.

L

LaVoie, J. (1976). Ego identity formation in middle adolescence. *Journal of Youth and Adolescence, 5,* 371–385.

Lackmann, G. M., Salzberger, U., Tollner, U., Chen, M., Carmella, S. G., & Hecht, S. S. (1999). Metabolites of a tobacco-specific carcinogen in urine from newborns. *Journal of the National Cancer Institute, 91,* 459–465.

Ladd, G. W. (1999). Peer relationships and social competence during early and middle childhood. *Annual Review of Psychology* (Vol. 50). Palo Alto, CA: Annual Reviews.

Ladd, G. W., & Hart, C. H. (1992). Creating informal play opportunities: Are parents' and preschoolers' initiations related to children's competence with peers? *Cognitive Psychology, 28,* 1179–1187.

Ladd, G. W., & Kochenderfer, B. J. (in press). Parenting behaviors and parent-child relationship: Correlates of peer victimization in kindergarten. *Developmental Psychology.*

Ladd, G. W., LeSeiur, K., & Profilet, S. M. (1993). Direct parental influences on young children's peer relations. In S. Duck (Ed.), *Learning about relationships* (Vol. 2). London: Sage.

Lamb, M. E. (1977). The development of mother-infant and father-infant attachments in the second year of life. *Developmental Psychology, 13,* 637–648.

Lamb, M. E. (1986). *The father's role: Applied perspectives.* New York: Wiley.

Lamb, M. E. (1994). Infant care practices and the application of knowledge. In C. B. Fisher & R. M. Lerner (Eds.), *Applied developmental psychology.* New York: McGraw-Hill.

Lamb, M. E. (1997). Fatherhood then and now. In A. Booth & A. C. Crouter (Eds.), *Men in families.* Mahwah, NJ: Erlbaum.

Lamb, M. E. (1998). Nonparental child care: Context, quality, correlates, and consequences. In W. Damon (Ed.), *Handbook of child psychology* (5th ed., Vol. 4). New York: Wiley.

Lamb, M. E., Frodi, A. M., Hwant, C. P., Frodi, M., & Steinberg, J. (1982). Mother- and father-infant interaction involving play and holding in traditional and nontraditional Swedish families. *Developmental Psychology, 18,* 215–221.

Lamb, M. E., Hwang, C. P., Ketterlinus, R. D., & Fracasso, M. P. (1999). Parent-child relationships: Development in the context of the family. In M. H. Bornstein & M. E. Lamb (Eds.), *Developmental psychology: An advanced textbook* (4th ed.). Mahwah, NJ: Erlbaum.

Lamb, M. E., & Sternberg, K. J. (1992). Sociocultural perspectives on nonparental child care. In M. E. Lamb, K. J. Sternberg, C. Hwang, & A. G. Broberg (Eds.), *Child care in context.* Hillsdale, NJ: Erlbaum.

Lamb, S. (1993). The beginnings of morality. In A. Garrod (Ed.), *Approaches to moral development.* New York: Teachers College Press.

Lambert, J. D. (1997, April). *Fathers as developing individuals: Investigating contemporary father-child relationships.* Paper presented at the meeting of the Society for Research in Child Development, Washington, DC.

Lambert, W. E., Genesee, F., Holobow, N., & Chartrand, L. (1993). Bilingual education for majority English-speaking children. *European Journal of Psychology of Education, 8,* 3–22.

Lane, H. (1976). *The wild boy of Aveyron.* Cambridge, MA: Harvard University Press.

Langer, L. L. (1991). *Holocaust testimonies: The ruins of memory.* New Haven: Yale University Press.

Lapsley, D. K. (1989). Continuity and discontinuity in adolescent social cognitive development. In R. Montemayor, G. Adams, & T. Gullota (Eds.), *Advances in adolescence research* (Vol. 2). Orlando, FL: Academic Press.

Lapsley, D. K. (1991). The adolescent egocentrism theory and the "new look" at the imaginary audience and personal fable. In R. M. Lerner, A. C. Petersen, & J. Brooks-Gunn (Eds.), *Encyclopedia of adolescence.* New York: Garland.

Lapsley, D. K. (1996). *Moral psychology.* Boulder, CO: Westview Press.

Lapsley, D. K., & Power, F. C. (Eds.). (1988). *Self, ego, and identity.* New York: Springer-Verlag.

Lapsley, D. K., & Quintana, S. M. (1985). Recent approaches in children's elementary moral and social education. *Elementary School Guidance and Counseling Journal, 19,* 246–251.

Lareau, A. (1996). Assessing parent involvement in schooling: A critical analysis. In K. L. Alexander & D. R. Entwisle (Eds.), *Schools and children at risk.* Mahwah, NJ: Erlbaum.

Larson, R., Csikszentmihalyi, M., & Graef, R. (1980). Mood variability and the psychosocial adjustment of adolescents. *Journal of Youth and Adolescence, 9,* 469–490.

Larson, R., Clore, G. L., & Wood, G. A. (in press). The emotions of romantic relationships. In W. Furman, B. B. Brown, & C. Feiring (Eds.), *Contemporary perspectives in romantic relationships.* New York: Cambridge University Press.

Larson, R., & Richards, M. (1994). *Divergent realities: The emotional lives of mothers, fathers, and adolescents.* New York: Basic Books.

Larson, R., & Richards, M. (in press). Waiting for the weekend: The development of Friday and Saturday nights as the emotional climax of the week. In R. W. Larson & A. C. Crouter (Eds.), *Temporal rhythms in the lives of adolescents: Themes and variations.* San Francisco: Jossey-Bass.

Lazar, L., Darlington, R., & Collaborators. (1982). Lasting effects of early education: A report from the consortium for longitudinal studies. *Monographs of the Society for Research in Child Development, 47.*

Lazarus, R. S. (1996). *Psychological stress and the coping process.* New York: McGraw-Hill.

LeMare, L. J., & Rubin, K. H. (1987). Perspective taking and peer interaction: Structural and developmental analyses. *Child Development, 58,* 306–315.

Learner-Centered Principles Work Group. (1997). *Learner-centered psychological principles: A framework for school reform and redesign.* Washington, DC: American Psychological Association.

Leffert, N., & Blyth, D. A. (1996, March). *The effects of community contexts on early adolescents.* Paper presented at the meeting of the Society for Research on Adolescence, Boston.

Leifer, A. D. (1973). *Television and the development of social behavior.* Paper presented at the meeting of the International Society for the Study of Behavioral Development, Ann Arbor, Michigan.

Lenneberg, E. (1967). *The biological foundations of language.* New York: Wiley.

Lenneberg, E. H., Rebelsky, F. G., & Nichols, I. A. (1965). The vocalization of infants born to deaf and hearing parents. *Human Development, 8,* 23–37.

Leong, F. T. L. (2000). Cultural pluralism. In A. Kazdin (Ed.), *Encyclopedia of psychology.* Washington, DC, & New York: American Psychological Association and Oxford U. Press.

Lepper, M., Greene, D., & Nisbett, R. R. (1973). Undermining children's intrinsic interest with extrinsic rewards: A test of the overjustification hypothesis. *Journal of Personality and Social Psychology, 28,* 129–137.

Lester, B. M., Freier, K., & LaGasse, K. (1995). Prenatal cocaine exposure and child outcome: How much do we really know? In M. Lewis & M. Bendersky (Eds.), *Mothers, babies, and cocaine.* Hillsdale, NJ: Erlbaum.

Lester, B. M., Tronick, E. Z. (1990). Introduction. In B. M. Lester & E. Z. Tronick (Eds.), *Stimulation and the preterm infant: The limits of plasticity.* Philadelphia: W. B. Saunders.

Leventhal, A. (1994, February). *Peer conformity during adolescence: An integration of developmental, situational, and individual characteristics.* Paper presented at the meeting of the Society for Research on Adolescence, San Diego.

Levesque, J., & Prosser, T. (1996). Service learning connections. *Journal of Teacher Education, 47,* 325–334.

Levin, J. (1980). *The mnemonics '80s: Keywords in the classroom.* Theoretical paper No. 86. Wisconsin Research and Development Center for Individualized Schooling, Madison.

Levy, G. D., & Carter, D. B. (1989). Gender schema, gender constancy, and gender-role knowledge: The roles of cognitive factors in preschoolers' gender-role stereotype attributions. *Developmental Psychology, 25,* 444–449.

Lewis, M. (1997). *Altering fate: Why the past does not predict the future.* New York: Guilford Press.

Lewis, M., & Brooks-Gunn, J. (1979). *Social cognition and the acquisition of the self.* New York: Plenum.

Lewis, M., Sullivan, M. W., Sanger, C., & Weiss, M. (1989). Self-development and self-conscious emotions. *Child Development, 60,* 146–156.

Lewis, M. D. (2000). The promise of dynamic systems approaches for an integrated account of human development. *Child Development, 71,* 36–43.

Lewis, R. (1997). With a marble and telescope: Searching for play. *Childhood Education, 36,* 346.

Lewis, R. (1999). *Human genetics* (3rd ed.). New York: McGraw-Hill.

Lewis, R. B. (1998). Assistive technology and learning disabilities: Today's realities and tomorrow's promises. *Journal of Learning Disabilities, 31,* 4–15.

Liben, L. S., & Signorella, M. L. (1993). Gender-schematic processing in children: The role of initial presentation of stimuli. *Developmental Psychology, 29,* 141–149.

Lieberman, E. E., Lang, J. M., Frigoletto, F. D., Heffner, L. J., & Cohen, A. (2000). Intrapartum maternal fever and neonatal outcome. *Pediatrics, 105,* 8–13.

Lieberman, E. E., Lang, J. M., Frigoletto, F., Richardson, D. K., Rengin, S. A., & Cohen, A. (1997). Epidural analgesic, intrapartum fever, and neonatal sepsis evaluation. *Pediatrics, 99,* 415–419.

Lifshitz, F., Pugliese, M. T., Moses, N., & Weyman-Daum, M. (1987). Parental health beliefs as a cause of nonorganic failure to thrive. *Pediatrics, 80,* 175–182.

Limber, S. P. (1997). Preventing violence among school children. *Family Futures, 1,* 27–28.

Limber, S. P., & Wilcox, B. L. (1996). Application of the U.N. convention on the rights of the child to the United States. *American Psychologist, 51,* 1246–1250.

Lindbohm, M. (1991). Effects of paternal occupational exposure in spontaneous abortions. *American Journal of Public Health, 121,* 1029–1033.

Lindner-Gunnoe, M. (1993). *Noncustodial mothers' and fathers' contributions to the adjustment of adolescent stepchildren.* Unpublished doctoral dissertation. University of Virginia.

Lipsitz, J. (1983, October). *Making it the hard way: Adolescents in the 1980s.* Testimony presented at the Crisis Intervention Task Force, House Select Committee on Children, Youth, and Families, Washington, DC.

Lipsitz, J. (1984). *Successful schools for young adolescents.* New Brunswick, NJ: Transaction.

Lively, W., & Bromley, D. (1973). *Person perception in childhood and adolescence.* New York: Wiley.

Locke, J. L., Bekken, K. E., Wein, D., & Ruzecki, V. (1991, April). *Neuropsychology of babbling: Laterality effects in the production of rhythmic manual activity.* Paper presented at the meeting of the Society for Research in Child Development, Seattle.

Lockman, J. J., & Thelen, E. (1993). Developmental biodynamics: Brain, body, behavior connections. *Child Development, 64,* 953–959.

Loebel, M., & Yali, A. M. (1999, August). *Effects of positive expectancies on adjustment to pregnancy.* Paper presented at the meeting of the American Psychological Association, Boston.

Loftus, E. F. (1993). The reality of repressed memories. *American Psychologist, 48,* 518–537.

Long, T., & Long, L. (1983). *Latchkey children.* New York: Penguin.

Lonner, W. J. (1988, October). *The introductory psychology text and cross-cultural psychology: A survey of cross-cultural psychologists.* Bellingham: Western Washington University, Center for Cross-cultural Research.

Lorenz, K. Z. (1965). *Evolution and the modification of behavior.* Chicago: University of Chicago Press.

Lovett, S. B., & Pillow, B. H. (1996). Development of the ability to distinguish between comprehension and memory: Evidence from goal-state evaluation tasks. *Journal of Educational Psychology, 88,* 546–562.

Lucey, J. F. (1999). Comments on a sudden infant death article in another journal. *Pediatrics, 103,* 812.

Luo, Q., Fang, X., & Aro, P. (1995, March). *Selection of best friends by Chinese adolescents.* Paper presented at the meeting of the Society for Research in Child Development, Indianapolis.

Luria, A., & Herzog, E. (1985, April). *Gender segregation across and within settings.* Paper presented at the biennial meeting of the Society for Research in Child Development, Toronto.

Luster, T. J., & Brophy-Herb, H. (2000). Adolescent mothers and their children. In J. D. Osofsky & H. E. Fitzgerald (Eds.), *WAIMH handbook of infant mental health* (Vol. 4). New York: Wiley.

Lutz, D. A., & Sternberg, R. J. (1999). Cognitive development. In M. H. Bornstein & M. E. Lamb (Eds.), *Developmental psychology: An advanced textbook* (4th ed.). Mahwah, NJ: Erlbaum.

Lyle, J., & Hoffman, H. R. (1972). Children's use of television and other media. In E. A. Rubenstein, G. A. Comstock, & J. P. Murray (Eds.), *Television and social behavior* (Vol. 4). Washington, DC: U.S. Government Printing Office.

Lynn, R. (1996). Racial and ethnic differences in intelligence in the U.S. on the Differential Ability Scale. *Personality and Individual Differences, 20,* 271–273.

Lyon, G. R. (1996). Learning disabilities. *Future of Children, 6* (1) 54–76.

Lyon, G. R., & Moats, L. C. (1997). Critical conceptual and methodological considerations in reading intervention research. *Journal of Learning Disabilities, 30,* 578–588.

Lyon, T. D., & Flavell, J. H. (1993). Young children's understanding of forgetting over time. *Child Development, 64,* 789–800.

Lyons, N. P. (1990). Listening to voices we have not heard. In C. Gilligan, N. P. Lyons, & T. J. Hanmer (Eds.), *Making connections.* Cambridge, MA: Harvard University Press.

M

Maas, J. B. (1998). *Power sleep.* New York: Villard.

MacFarlane, J. A. (1975). Olfaction in the development of social preferences in the human neonate. In *Parent-infant interaction.* Ciba Foundation Symposium No. 33. Amsterdam: Elsevier.

MacLean W. E. (2000). Down syndrome. In A. Kazdin (Ed.), *Encyclopedia of psychology.* Washington, DC, & New York: American Psychological Association and Oxford U. Press.

MacWhinney, B. (Ed.). (1999). *The emergence of language.* Mahwah, NJ: Erlbaum.

Maccoby, E. E. (1984). Middle childhood in the context of the family. In *Development during middle childhood.* Washington, DC: National Academy Press.

Maccoby, E. E. (1987, November). Interview with Elizabeth Hall: All in the family. *Psychology Today,* pp. 54–60.

Maccoby, E. E. (1992). Trends in the study of socialization: Is there a Lewinian heritage? *Journal of Social Issues, 48,* 171–185.

Maccoby, E. E. (1996). Peer conflict and intrafamily conflict: Are there conceptual bridges? *Merrill-Palmer Quarterly, 42,* 165–176.

Maccoby, E. E. (1997, April). Discussant on symposium, *Missing pieces in the puzzle: biological contributions to gender development.* Society for Research in Child Development, Washington, DC.

Maccoby, E. E. (1998). *The two sexes.* Cambridge, MA: Harvard University Press.

Maccoby, E. E. (1999). The uniqueness of the parent-child relationship. In W. A. Collins & B. Laursen (Eds.), *Relationships as developmental contexts.* Mahwah, NJ: Erlbaum.

Maccoby, E. E., & Jacklin, C. N. (1974). *The psychology of sex differences.* Palo Alto, CA: Stanford University Press.

Maccoby, E. E., & Martin, J. A. (1983). Socialization in the context of the family: Parent-child interaction. In P. H. Mussen (Ed.), *Handbook of child psychology* (4th ed., Vol. 4). New York: Wiley.

Maccoby, E. E., & Mnookin, R. H. (1992). *Dividing the child: Social and legal dilemmas of custody.* Cambridge, MA: Harvard University Press.

Maddux, C. D., Johnson, D. L., & Willis, J. W. (1997). *Educational computing.* Boston: Allyn & Bacon.

Maddux, J. E., Roberts, M. C., Sledden, E. A., & Wright, L. (1986). Developmental issues in child health psychology. *American Psychologist, 41,* 24–34.

Mader, S. (1999). *Biology* (6th ed.). New York: McGraw-Hill.

Madison, B. E., & Foster-Clark, F. S. (1996, March). *Pathways to identity and intimacy: Effects of gender and personality.* Paper presented at the meeting of the Society for Research on Adolescence, Boston.

Maggs, J. L., Schulenberg, J., & Hurrelmann, K. (1997). Developmental transitions in adolescence: Health promotion implications. In J. Schulenberg, J. L. Maggs, & K. Hurrelmann (Eds.), *Health risks and developmental transitions during adolescence.* New York: Cambridge University Press.

Magnusson, D. (1988). *Individual development from an interactional perspective: A longitudinal study.* Hillsdale, NJ: Erlbaum.

Main, M., & Solomon, J. (1990). Procedures for identifying infants as disorganized/disoriented during the Ainsworth Strange Situation. In M. Greenberg; D. Cicchetti, & E. M. Cummings (Eds.), *Attachment during the preschool years.* Chicago: University of Chicago Press.

Majhanovich, S. (1998, April). *Unscrambling the semantics of Canadian multiculturalism.* Paper presented at the meeting of the American Educational Research Association, San Diego.

Malinosky-Rummell, R., & Hansen, D. J. (1993). Long-term consequences of childhood physical abuse. *Psychological Bulletin, 114,* 68–79.

Malloy, M. H. (1999). Risk of previous very low birth weight and very preterm infants among women delivering a very low birth weight and very preterm infant. *Journal of Perinatology, 19,* 97–102.

Mandler, G. (1980). Recognizing: The judgment of previous occurrence. *Psychological Review, 87,* 252–271.

Mandler, J. M. (1990). A new perspective on cognitive development in infancy. *American Scientist, 78,* 236–243.

Mandler, J. M. (1992). The foundations of conceptual thought in infancy. *Cognitive Development, 7,* 273–285.

Mandler, J. M. (1998). Representation. In W. Damon (Ed.), *Handbook of child psychology* (5th ed., Vol. 2). New York: Wiley.

Maratsos, M. (1998). The acquisition of grammar. In D. Kuhn & R. S. Siegler (Eds.), *Handbook of child psychology* (5th ed., Vol. 2). New York: Wiley.

Marcia, J. E. (1980). Ego identity development. In J. Adelson (Ed.), *Handbook of adolescent psychology.* New York: Wiley.

Marcia, J. E. (1989). Identity in adolescence. *Journal of Adolescence, 12,* 401–410.

Marcia, J. E. (1987). The identity status approach to the study of ego identity development. In T. Honess & K. Yardley (Eds.), *Self and identity: Perspectives across the life-span.* London: Routledge & Kegan Paul.

Marcia, J. E. (1994). The empirical study of ego identity. In H. A. Bosma, T. L. G. Graafsma, H. D. Grotevant, & D. J. De Levita (Eds.), *Identity and development.* Newbury Park, CA: Sage.

Marcia, J. E. (1996). Unpublished review of J. W. Santrock's *Adolescence* 7th ed., (Dubuque, IA: Brown & Benchmark).

Marcus, D. L., Mulrine, A., & Wong, K. (1999, September 13). How kids learn. *U.S. News & World Report,* pp. 44–50.

Margolin, L. (1994). Child sexual abuse by uncles. *Child Abuse and Neglect, 18,* 215–224.

References **R–21**

Markstrom, C. A., & Tryon, R. J. (1997, April). *Resiliency, social support, and coping among poor African-American and European-American Appalachian adolescents.* Paper presented at the meeting of the Society for Research in Child Development, Washington, DC.

Markus, H. R., & Kittayama, S. (1994). The cultural construction of self and emotion: Implications for social behavior. In S. Kitayama & H. R. Markus (Eds.), *Emotion and culture.* Washington, DC: American Psychological Association.

Markus, H. R., Mullally, P. R., & Kittayama, S. (1999). *Selfways: Diversity in modes of cultural participation.* Unpublished manuscript, Department of Psychology, University of Michigan.

Markus, H. R., & Nurius, P. (1986). Possible selves. *American Psychologist, 41,* 954–969.

Marr, D. (1982). *Vision.* New York: W. H. Freeman.

Marten, L. A., & Matlin, M. W. (1976). Does sexism in elementary readers still exist? *Reading Teacher, 29,* 764–767.

Martin, C. L. (1990). Attitudes and expectations about children with nontraditional traditional gender roles. *Sex Roles, 22,* 151–165.

Martin, E. W., Martin, R., & Terman, D. L. (1996). The legislative and litigation history of special education. *Future of Children, 6* (1), 25–63.

Martin, N. C. (1997, April). *Adolescents' possible selves and the transition to adulthood.* Paper presented at the meeting of the Society for Research in Child Development, Washington, DC.

Martorano, S. (1977). A developmental analysis of performance on Piaget's formal operations tasks. *Developmental Psychology, 13,* 666–672.

Masten, A. S. (in press). Resilience comes of age: Reflections on the past and outlook for the next generation of research. In M. D. Glantz, J. Johnson, & L. Huffman (Eds.), *Resilience and development.* New York: Plenum Press.

Masten, A. S., & Coatsworth, J. D. (1995). Competence, resilience, and psychopathology. In D. Cicchetti & D. Cohen (Eds.), *Developmental psychopathology* (Vol. 2). New York: Wiley.

Masten, A. S., & Coatsworth, J. D. (1998). The development of competence in favorable and unfavorable environments. *American Psychologist, 53,* 205–220.

Matas, L., Arend, R. A., & Sroufe, L. A. (1978). Continuity in adaptation: Quality of attachment and later competence. *Child Development, 49,* 547–556.

Mathes, P. G., & Torgesen, J. K. (1999). All children can learn to read: Critical care for the prevention of reading failure. In J. W. Miller & M. C. McKenna (Eds.), *Literacy education in the 21st century.* Mahwah, NJ: Erlbaum.

Matlin, M. W. (1993). *The psychology of women* (2nd ed.). San Diego: Harcourt Brace Jovanovich.

Matsumoto, D. (1997). *Culture and modern life.* Pacific Grove, CA: Brooks/Cole.

Maurer, D., & Salapatek, P. (1976). Developmental changes in the scanning of faces by young infants. *Child Development, 47,* 523–527.

Mayer, J. D., Caruso, D., & Salovey, P. (in press). Competing models of emotional intelligence. In R. Sternberg (Ed.), *Handbook of human intelligence.* New York: Cambridge University Press.

Mayer, R. E. (1999). *The promise of educational psychology.* Upper Saddle River, NJ: Merrill.

McAdoo, H. P. (Ed.). (1999). *Family ethnicity* (2nd ed.). Newbury Park, CA: Sage.

McBride, B. A. (1991, April). *Variations in father involvement with preschool-aged children.* Paper presented at the biennial meeting of the Society for Research in Child Development, Seattle.

McCall, R. B., Applebaum, M. I., & Hogarty, P. S. (1973). Developmental changes in mental performance. *Monographs of the Society for Research in Child Development, 38* (Serial No. 150).

McCarty, M. E., & Ashmead, D. H. (1999). Visual control of reaching and grasping in infants. *Developmental Psychology, 35,* 620–631.

McClelland, D. C. (1955). Some social consequences of achievement motivation. In M. R. Jones (Ed.), *The Nebraska Symposium on Motivation.* Lincoln: University of Nebraska Press.

McCormick, C. B., & Pressley, M. (1997). *Educational psychology.* New York: Longman.

McDaniel, M. A., & Pressley, M. (1987). *Imagery and related mnemonic process.* New York: Springer-Verlag.

McFarlane, J., Parker, B., & Soeken, K. (1996). Abuse during pregnancy: Associations with maternal health and infant birth weight. *Nursing Research, 45,* 37–47.

McGrath, S., Kennell, J., Suresh, M., Moise, K., & Hinkley, C. (1999, May). *Doula support vs. epidural analgesia: Impact on cesarean rates.* Paper presented at the meeting of the Society for Pediatric Research, San Francisco.

McHale, J. L., Frosch, C. A., Greene, C. A., & Ferry, K. S. (1995, March). *Correlates of maternal and paternal behavior.* Paper presented at the meeting of the Society for Research in Child Development, Indianapolis.

McHale, S. M. (1995). Lessons about adolescent development from the study of African-American youth. In L. J. Crockett & A. C. Crouter (Eds.), *Pathways through adolescence.* Hillsdale, NJ: Erlbaum.

McLanahan, S., & Sandefur, G. (1994). *Growing up with a single parent: What hurts, what helps?* Cambridge, MA: Harvard University Press.

McLoyd, V. (1990). Minority children: An introduction to the special issue. *Child Development, 61,* 263–266.

McLoyd, V. C. (1982). Social class differences in sociodramatic play: A critical review. *Developmental Review, 2,* 1–30.

McLoyd, V. C. (1993, March). *Sizing up the future: Economic stress, expectations, and adolescents' achievement motivation.* Paper presented at the biennial meeting of the Society for Research in Child Development, New Orleans.

McLoyd, V. C. (1998). Children in poverty: Development, public policy, and practice. In W. Damon (Ed.), *Handbook of child psychology* (5th ed., Vol. 4). New York: Wiley.

McLoyd, V. C. (1999). Cultural influences in a multicultural society: Conceptual and methodological issues. In A. S. Masten (Ed.), *Cultural processes in child development.* Mahwah, NJ: Erlbaum.

McLoyd, V. C. (2000). Poverty. In A. Kazdin (Ed.), *Encyclopedia of psychology.* Washington, DC, & New York: American Psychological Association and Oxford U. Press.

McMillan, J. H. (2000). *Educational research* (3rd ed.). New York: HarperCollins.

McNally, D. (1990). *Even eagles need a push.* New York: Dell.

Mead, M. (1928). *Coming of age in Samoa.* New York: Morrow.

Mead, M. (1978, Dec. 30–Jan. 5). The American family: An endangered species. *TV Guide,* pp. 21–24.

Meadowcraft, J., & Reeves, B. (1989). Influence of story schema development on children's attention to television. *Communication Research, 16,* 352–374.

Mehler, J., Jusczyk, P. W., Lambertz, G., Halsted, N., Bertoncini, J., & Amiel-Tison, C. (1988). A precursor of language acquisition in young infants. *Cognition, 29,* 132–178.

Melby, J. N., & Vargas, D. (1996, March). *Predicting patterns of adolescent tobacco use.* Paper presented at the meeting of the Society for Research on Adolescence, Boston.

Meltzoff, A. (1995). What infant memory tells us about infantile amnesia: Long-term recall and deferred imitation. *Journal of Experimental Child Psychology, 59,* 497–515.

Meltzoff, A. N. (1988). Infant imitation and memory: Nine-month-old infants in immediate and deferred tests. *Child Development, 59,* 217–225.

Meltzoff, A. N. (1990, June). *Infant imitation.* Invited address at the University of Texas at Dallas.

Meltzoff, A. N., & Moore, M. K. (1999). A new foundation for cognitive development in infancy: The birth of the representational infant. In E. K. Skolnick, K. Nelson, S. A. Gelman, & P. H. Miller (Eds.), *Conceptual development.* Mahwah, NJ: Erlbaum.

Meltzoff, A. N., & Moore, M. K. (1999). Resolving the debate about early imitation. In A. Slater & D. Maurer (Eds.), *The Blackwell reader in developmental psychology.* Oxford, England: Blackwell.

Meltzoff, A., & Gopnik, A. (1997). *Words, thoughts, and theories.* Cambridge, MA: MIT Press.

Mercer, J. R., & Lewis, J. F. (1978). *System of multicultural pluralistic assessment.* New York: Psychological Corp.

Meredith, N. V. (1978). Research between 1960 and 1970 on the standing height of young children in different parts of the world. In H. W. Reece & L. P. Lipsitt (Eds.), *Advances in child development and behavior* (Vol. 12). New York: Academic Press.

Michel, G. L. (1981). Right-handedness: A consequence of infant supine head-orientation preference? *Science, 212,* 685–687.

Miller, G. A. (1981). *Language and speech.* New York: W. H. Freeman.

Miller, J. G. (1991). A cultural perspective on the morality of beneficence and interpersonal responsibility. In S. Ting-Toomey & F. Korzenny

(Eds.), *International and intercultural communication annual* (Vol. 15). Newbury Park, CA: Sage.

Miller, J. G. (1995, March). *Culture, context, and personal agency: The cultural grounding of self and morality.* Paper presented at the meeting of the Society for Research in Child Development, Indianapolis.

Miller, J. G., & Bersoff, D. M. (1993, March). *Culture and affective closeness in the morality of caring.* Paper presented at the biennial meeting of the Society for Research in Child Development, New Orleans.

Miller, J. W. (1999). Literacy in the 21st century: Emergent themes. In J. W. Miller & M. C. McKenna (Eds.), *Literacy education in the 21st century.* Mahwah, NJ: Erlbaum.

Miller, S. A., & Harley, J. P. (1999). *Zoology* (4th ed.). New York: McGraw-Hill.

Miller-Jones, D. (1989). Culture and testing. *American Psychologist, 44,* 360–366.

Mills, J. L., Holmes, L. B., Aarons, J. H., Simpson, J. L., Brown, Z. A., Jovanovic-Graubard, L. G., Conley, M. R., Graubard, B. I., Knopp, R. H., & Metzger, B. E. (1993). Moderage caffeine use and the risk of spontaneous abortion and intrauterine growth retardation. *Journal of the American Medical Association, 269,* 593–597.

Minnett, A. M., Vandell, D. L., & Santrock, J. W. (1983). The effects of sibling status on sibling interaction: Influence of birth order, age spacing, sex of the child, and sex of the sibling. *Child Development, 54,* 1064–1072.

Minuchin, P. P., & Shapiro, E. K. (1983). The school as a context for social development. In P. H. Mussen (Ed.), *Handbook of child psychology* (4th ed., Vol. 4). New York: Wiley.

Mischel, W. (1973). Toward a cognitive social learning reconceptualization of personality. *Psychological Review, 80,* 252–283.

Mischel, W. (1974). Process in delay of gratification. In L. Berkowitz (Ed.), *Advances in experimental social psychology* (Vol. 7). New York: Academic Press.

Mischel, W. (1987). *Personality* (4th ed.). New York: Holt, Rinehart & Winston.

Mischel, W. (1995, August). *Cognitive-affective theory of person-environment psychology.* Paper presented at the meeting of the American Psychological Association, New York City.

Mischel, W., & Mischel, H. (1975, April). *A cognitive social-learning analysis of moral development.* Paper presented at the meeting of the Society for Research in Child Development, Denver.

Mischel, W., & Patterson, C. J. (1976). Substantive and structural elements of effective plans for self-control. *Journal of Social and Personality Psychology, 34,* 942–950.

Mitchell, A. S. (1999, April). *The nature of sibling relationships in adolescence: A sequential analysis of verbal and nonverbal behaviors in twins and nontwins.* Paper presented at the meeting of the Society for Research in Child Development, Albuquerque.

Mize, J., Petit, G. S., & Brown, E. G. (1995). Mothers' supervision of their children's play: Relations with beliefs, perceptions, and knowledge. *Developmental Psychology, 31,* 311–321.

Moely, B. E., Olson, F. A., Halwes, T. G., & Flavell, J. H. (1969). Production deficiency in young children's clustered recall. *Developmental Psychology, 1,* 26–34.

Montemayor, R. (1982). The relationship between parent-adolescent conflict and the amount of time adolescents spend with parents, peers, and alone. *Child Development, 53,* 1512–1519.

Morelli, G. A., Rogoff, B., & Angelillo, C. (1992). *Cultural variation in young children's opportunities for involvement in adult activities.* Poster presented at the meeting of the American Anthropological Association, San Francisco.

Morgan, J. L., & Demuth, K. (Eds.). (1995). *Signal to syntax.* Hillsdale, NJ: Erlbaum.

Morgan, M. (1984). Reward-induced decrements and increments in intrinsic motivation. *Review of Educational Research, 54,* 5–30.

Morrison, F. J., Holmes, D. L., & Haith, D. L. (1974). A developmental study of the effects of familiarity on short-term visual memory. *Journal of Experimental Child Psychology, 18,* 412–425.

Morrison, G. S. (2000). *Fundamentals of early childhood education.* Columbus, OH: Merrill.

Morrongiello, B. A., Fenwick, K. D., & Chance, G. (1990). Sound localization acuity in very young infants: An observer-based testing procedure. *Developmental Psychology, 26,* 75–84.

Mortimer, E. A. (1992). Child health in the developing world. In R. E. Behrman, R. M. Kliegman, W. E. Nelson, & V. C. Vaughan (Eds.), *Nelson textbook of pediatrics* (14th ed.).

Mott, F. L., & Marsiglio, W. (1985, September/October). Early childbearing and completion of high school. *Family Planning Perspectives,* p. 234.

Mueller, N., & Silverman, N. (1989). Peer relations in maltreated children. In D. Cicchetti & V. Carlson (Eds.), *Child maltreatment.* New York: Cambridge University Press.

Mullis, I. V. S., Martin, M. O., Beaton, A. E., Gonzales, E. J., Kelly, D. L., & Smith, T. A. (1998). *Mathematics and science achievement in the final year of secondary school.* Chestnut Hill, MA: Boston College, TIMSS International Study Center.

Mumme, D. L., Fernald, A., & Herrera, C. (1996). Infant's responses to facial & emotional signals in a social referencing paradigm. *Child Development, 67,* 3219–3237.

Mundy, P., Seibert, J., & Hogan, A. (1984). Relationship between sensorimotor and early communication abilities in developmentally delayed children. *Merrill-Palmer Quarterly, 30,* 33–48.

Munroe, R. H., Himmin, H. S., & Munroe, R. L. (1984). Gender understanding and sex role preference in four cultures. *Developmental Psychology, 20,* 673–682.

Munsch, J., Woodward, J., & Darling, N. (1995). Children's perceptions of their relationships with coresiding and non-custodial fathers. *Journal of Divorce and Remarriage, 23,* 39–54.

Myers, D. L. (1999). *Excluding violent youths from juvenile court: The effectiveness of legislative waiver.* Doctoral dissertation, University of Maryland, College Park.

N

NAEYC. (1988). NAEYC position statement on developmentally appropriate practices in the primary grades, serving 5- through 8-year-olds. *Young Children, 43,* 64–83.

NICHD Early Child Care Research Network. (1996, April 20). Infant child care and attachment. *Child Development, 68,* 860–879.

Nagata, D. K. (1989). Japanese American children and adolescents. In J. T. Gibbs & L. N. Huang (Eds.), *Children of color.* San Francisco: Jossey-Bass.

Nahas, G. G. (1984). *Marijuana in science and medicine.* New York: Raven Press.

Nash, J. M. (1997, February 3). Fertile minds. *Time,* pp. 50–54.

National Advisory Council on Economic Opportunity. (1980). *Critical choices for the 80s.* Washington, DC: U.S. Government Printing Office.

National Assessment of Educational Progress. (1996). Gender differences in motivation and strategy use in science. *Journal of Research in Science Teaching, 33,* 393–406.

National Assessment of Educational Progress. (1997). *NAEP 1996 mathematics report card for the nation and the states.* Washington, DC: National Center for Education Statistics.

National Association for the Education of Young Children. (1986). Position statement on developmentally appropriate practice in programs for 4- and 5-year-olds. *Young Children, 41,* 20–29.

National Association for the Education of Young Children. (1996). NAEYC position statement: Responding to linguistic and cultural diversity. *Young Children, 51,* 4–12.

National Center for Education Statistics. (1998). *Violence and discipline problems in U.S. public schools.* Washington, DC: Author.

National Childhood Cancer Foundation. (1998). *Cancer in children.* Washington, DC: Author.

National Commission on Sleep Disorders. (1993, January). *Report of the National Commission on Sleep Disorders Research.* Washington, DC: U.S. Department of Health and Human Services.

National Community Service Coalition. (1995). *Youth volunteerism.* Washington, DC: Author.

National Research Council. (1999). *Starting out right: A guide to promoting children's reading success.* Washington, DC: National Academy Press.

Neemann, J., Hubbard, J., & Masten, A. S. (1995). The changing importance of romantic relationship involvement to competence from childhood to late adolescence. *Development and Psychopathology, 7,* 727–750.

Neimark, E. D. (1982). Adolescent thought: Transition to formal operations. In B. B. Wolman (Ed.), *Handbook of developmental psychology.* Englewood Cliffs, NJ: Prentice Hall.

Neisser, U., Boodoo, G., Bouchard, T. J., Boykin, A. W., Brody, N., Ceci, S. J., Halpern, D. F., Loehlin, J. C., Perloff, R., Sternberg, R. J., & Urbina, S. (1996). Intelligence: Knowns and unknowns. *American Psychologist, 51,* 77–101.

Nelson, C. (1999). Research description. *Institute of Child Development biennial report.* Minneapolis: Institute of Child Development.

Nelson, K. (1999). Levels and modes of representation: Issues for the theory of conceptual change and development. In E. K. Skolnick, K. Nelson, S. A. Gelman, & P. H. Miller (Eds.), *Conceptual development.* Mahwah, NJ: Erlbaum

Newcomb, M. D., & Bentler, P. M. (1988). Impact of adolescent drug use and social support on problems of young adults: A longitudinal study. *Journal of Abnormal Psychology, 97,* 64–75.

Newman, B. S., & Muzzonigro, P. G. (1993). The effects of traditional family values on the coming out process of gay male adolescents. *Adolescence, 28,* 213–226.

Newman, D. L., & Caspi, A. (1996, March). *Temperament styles observed at age 3 predict interpersonal functioning in the transition to adulthood.* Paper presented at the meeting of the Society for Research on Adolescence, Boston.

Newman, J. (1995). How breast milk protects newborns. *Scientific American, 273,* (6), 76–80.

Nezami, E. (2000). Standardized tests. In A. Kazdin (Ed.), *Encyclopedia of psychology.* Washington, DC, & New York: American Psychological Association and Oxford U. Press.

Nicholls, J. G. (1979). Development of perception of own attainment and causal attribution for success and failure in reading. *Journal of Educational Psychology, 71,* 94–99.

Nicklas, T. A., Webber, L. S., Jonson, C. S., Srinivasan, S. R., & Berenson, G. S. (1995). Foundations for health promotion with youth: A review of observations from the Bogalusa Heart Study. *Journal of Health Education, 26,* S18–S26.

Ninio, A., & Snow, C. E. (1996). *Pragmatic development.* Boulder, CO: Westview Press.

Nottlemann, E. D., Susman, E. J., Blue, J. H., Inoff-Germain, G., Dorn, L. D., Loriaux, D. L., Cutler, G. B., & Chrousos, G. P. (1987). Gonadal and adrenal hormone correlates of adjustment in early adolescence. In R. M. Lerner & T. T. Foch (Eds.), *Biological-psychological interactions in early adolescence.* Hillsdale, NJ: Erlbaum.

Nugent, K., & Brazelton, T. B. (2000). Preventive infant mental health: Uses of the Brazelton scale. In J. D. Osofsky & H. E. Fitzgerald (Eds.), *WAIMH Handbook of infant mental health* (Vol. 2). New York: Wiley.

Obler, L. K. (1993). Language beyond childhood. In J. B. Gleason (Ed.), *The development of language* (3rd ed.). New York: Macmillan.

Offer, D., Ostrov, E., Howard, K. I., & Atkinson, R. (1988). *The teenage world: Adolescents' self-image in ten countries.* New York: Plenum.

Office of Juvenile Justice and Prevention. (1998). *Arrests in the United States under age 18: 1997.* Washington, DC: Author.

Ogbu, J. U. (1989, April). *Academic socialization of Black children: An inoculation against future failure.* Paper presented at the meeting of the Society for Research in Child Development, Kansas City.

O'Hara, M. W. (2000). Pregnancy. In A. Kazdin (Ed.), *Encyclopedia of psychology.* Washington, DC, and New York: American Psychological Association and Oxford U. Press.

Okun, B. F., & Rappaport, L. J. (1980). *Working with families.* North Scituate, MA: Duxbury Press.

Olds, S. B., London, M. L., & Ladewig, P. A. (1988). *Maternal newborn nursing: A family-centered approach,* Menlo Park, CA: Addison-Wesley.

Oller, D. K. (1999, August). *Bilingual infants show neither advantages nor disadvantages over monolingual infants.* Paper presented at the meeting of the American Psychological Association, Boston.

Olson, H. C., & Burgess, D. M. (1996). Early intervention with children prenatally exposed to alcohol and other drugs. In M. J. Guralnick (Ed.), *The effectiveness of early intervention.* Baltimore: Paul H. Brookes.

Olson, M. (1999, May). *How will the sequencing of the human genome change biomedical research?* Paper presented at the meeting of the Society for Pediatric Research, San Francisco.

Olweus, D. (1980). Bullying among schoolboys. In R. Barnen (Ed.), *Children and violence.* Stockholm: Adaemic Litteratur.

Olweus, D. (in press). *Bullying at school: What we know and what we can do.* Oxford, England: Blackwell.

Overton, W. F., & Byrnes, J. P. (1991). Cognitive development. In R. M. Lerner, A. C. Petersen, & J. Brooks-Gunn (Eds.). *Encyclopedia of adolescence* (Vol. 1). New York: Garland.

Paivio, A. (1971). *Imagery and verbal processes.* Ft. Worth, TX: Harcourt Brace.

Paivio, A. (1986). *Mental representations: A dual coding approach.* New York: Oxford University Press.

Paludi, M. A. (1999). *The psychology of women.* Upper Saddle River, NJ: Prentice Hall.

Paneth, N. S. (1995, Spring). The problem of low birth weight. *Future of Children, 5,* (1), 19–34.

Panofsky, C. (1999, April). *What the zone of proximal development conceals.* Paper presented at the meeting of the Society for Research in Child Development, Albuquerque.

Parcel, G. S., Simons-Morton, G. G., O'Hara, N. M., Baranowski, T., Kolbe, L. J., & Bee, D. E. (1987). School promotion of healthful diet and exercise behavior: An integration of organizational change and social learning theory interventions. *Journal of School Health, 57,* 150–156.

Parcel, G. S., Tiernan, K., Nadar, P. R., & Gottlob, D. (1979). Health education and kindergarten children. *Journal of School Health, 49,* 129–131.

Paris, S. G., & Lindauer, B. H. (1982). The development of cognitive skills during childhood. In B. B. Wolman (Ed.), *Handbook of developmental psychology.* Upper Saddle River, NJ: Prentice Hall.

Parkay, F. W., & Stanford, B. H. (1999). *Becoming a teacher* (4th ed.). Boston: Allyn & Bacon.

Parke, R. D. (1972). Some effects of punishment on children's behavior. In W. W. Hartup (Ed.), *The young child* (Vol. 2). Washington, DC: National Association for the Education of Young Children.

Parke, R. D. (1977). Some effects of punishment on children's behavior—Revisited. In E. M. Hetherington & R. D. Parke (Eds.), *Readings in contemporary child psychology.* New York: McGraw-Hill.

Parke, R. D. (1993, March). *Family research in the 1990s.* Paper presented at the biennial meeting of the Society for Research in Child Development, New Orleans.

Parke, R. D., & Buriel, R. (1998). Socialization in the family. Ethnic and ecological perspectives. In W. Damon (Ed.), *Handbook of child psychology* (5th ed., Vol. 3). New York: Wiley.

Parker, F. L., Abdul-Kabir, S., Stevenson, H. G., & Garrett, B. (1995, March). *Partnerships between researchers and the community in Head Start.* Paper presented at the meeting of the Society for Research in Child Development, Indianapolis.

Parker, J. G., & Asher, S. R. (1987). Peer relations and later personal adjustment: Are low accepted children at risk? *Psychological Bulletin, 102,* 357–389.

Parker, S. J., & Barrett, D. E. (1992). Maternal Type A behavior during pregnancy, neonatal crying, and infant temperament: Do Type A women have Type A babies? *Pediatrics, 89,* 474–479.

Parten, M. (1932). Social play among preschool children. *Journal of Abnormal Social Psychology, 27,* 243–269.

Patterson, G. R., DeBaryshe, B. D., & Ramsey, E. (1989). A developmental perspective on antisocial behavior. *American Psychologist, 44,* 329–355.

Patterson, G. R., & Stouthamer-Loeber, M. (1984). The correlation of family management practices and delinquency. *Child Development, 55,* 1299–1307.

Patterson, S. J., Sochting, I., & Marcia, J. E. (1992). The inner space and beyond: Women and identity. In G. R. Adams, T. P. Gullotta, & R. Montemayor (Eds.), *Adolescent identity formation.* Newbury Park, CA: Sage.

Paul, E. L., & White, K. M. (1990). The development of intimate relationships in late adolescence. *Adolescence, 25,* 375–400.

Paulson, S. E., Marchant, G. J., & Rothlisberg, B. (1995, March). *Relations among parent, teacher, and school factors: Implications for achievement outcome in middle grade students.* Paper presented at the meeting of the Society for Research in Child Development, Indianapolis.

Paus, T., Zijdenbos, A., Worsley, K., Collins, D. L., Blumenthal, J., Giedd, J., Rapoport, J., & Evans, A. C. (1999). Structural maturation of neural pathways in children and adolescents: An in vivo study. *Science, 283,* 1908–1911.

Pavlov, I. P. (1927). In G. V. Anrep (Trans.), *Conditioned reflexes.* London: Oxford University Press.

Pentz, M. A. (1994). Primary prevention of adolescent drug abuse. In C. Fisher & R. Lerner (Eds.), *Applied developmental psychology.* New York: McGraw-Hill.

Perkins, D., & Tishman, S. (1997, March). Commentary in "Teaching today's pupils to think more critically." *APA Monitor,* p. 51.

Perry, C., Hearn, M., Murray, D., & Klepp, K. (1988). *The etiology and prevention of adolescent alcohol and drug abuse.* Unpublished manuscript, University of Minnesota.

Perry-Jenkins, M., Payne, J., & Hendricks, E. (1999, April). *Father involvement by choice or necessity: Implications for parents' well-being.* Paper presented at the meeting of the Society for Research in Child Development, Albuquerque.

Perusse, D. (1999, April). *Normal and abnormal early motor-cognitive development: A function of exposure to shared environmental risks.* Paper presented at the meeting of the Society for Research in Child Development, Albuquerque.

Peskin, H. (1967). Pubertal onset and ego functioning. *Journal of Abnormal Psychology, 72,* 1–15.

Petersen, A. C. (1993). Creating adolescents: The role of context and process in developmental trajectories. *Journal of Research on Adolescence, 3,* 1–18.

Petersen, A. C., Leffert, N., & Miller, K. (1993, March). *The role of interpersonal relationships in the development of depressed affect and depression in adolescence.* Paper presented at the biennial meeting of the Society for Research in Child Development, New Orleans.

Peterson, C. C., & Peterson, J. L. (1973). Preference for sex of offspring as a measure of change in sex attitudes. *Psychology, 10,* 3–5.

Peterson, K. S. (1997, September 3). In high school, dating is a world into itself. *USA Today,* pp. 1–2D.

Peth-Pierce, R. (1998). *The NICHD Study of Early Child Care.* Washington, DC: National Institute of Child Health and Human Development.

Pettit, G. S., Bates, J. E., Dodge, K. A., & Meece, D. W. (1999). The impact of after-school peer contact on early adolescent externalizing problems is moderated by parental monitoring, perceived neighborhood safety, and prior adjustment. *Child Development, 70,* 768–778.

Pfeffer, C. R. (1996). *Severe stress and mental disturbance in children.* Washington, DC: American Psychiatric Press.

Phillips, D., Friedman, S. L., Huston, A. C., & Weinraub, M. (1999, April). *The roles of work and poverty in the lives of families with young children.* Paper presented at the meeting of the Society for Research in Child Development, Albuquerque.

Phinney, J. (2000). Ethnic identity. In A. Kazdin (Ed.), *Encyclopedia of psychology.* Washington, DC, & New York: American Psychological Association and Oxford U. Press.

Phinney, J. S. (1989). Stages of ethnic identity development in minority group adolescents. *Journal of Early Adolescence, 9,* 34–49.

Phinney, J. S. (1996). When we talk about American ethnic groups, what do we mean? *American Psychologist, 51,* 918–927.

Phinney, J. S., & Alipura, L. L. (1990). Ethnic identity in college students from four ethnic groups. *Journal of Adolescence, 13,* 171–183.

Phinney, J. S., & Cobb, N. J. (1993, March). *Adolescents' reasoning about discrimination: Ethnic and attitudinal predictors.* Paper presented at the biennial meeting of the Society for Research in Child Development, New Orleans.

Phinney, J. S., & Devich-Navarro, M. (1997). Variations in bicultural identification among African American and Mexican American adolescents. *Journal of Research on Adolescence, 7,* 3–32.

Phinney, J. S., Ferguson, D. L., & Tate, J. D. (1997). Intergroup attitudes among ethnic minority adolescents: A causal model. *Child Development, 68,* 955–969.

Phinney, J. S., & Rosenthal, D. A. (1992). Ethnic identity in adolescence: Process, context, and outcome. In G. R. Adams, T. P. Gullotta, & R. Montemayor (Eds.), *Adolescent identity formation.* Newbury Park, CA: Sage.

Piaget, J. (1932). *The moral judgment of the child.* New York: Harcourt Brace Jovanovich.

Piaget, J. (1952a). Jean Piaget. In C. A. Murchison (Ed.), *A history of psychology in autobiography* (Vol. 4). Worcester, MA: Clark University Press.

Piaget, J. (1952b). *The origins of intelligence in children.* (M. Cook, Trans.). New York: International Universities Press.

Piaget, J. (1954). *The construction of reality in the child.* New York: Basic Books.

Piaget, J. (1962). *Play, dreams, and imitation in childhood.* New York: W. W. Norton.

Piaget, J. (1972). Intellectual evolution from adolescence to adulthood. *Human Development, 15,* 1–12.

Piaget, J., & Inhelder, B. (1969). *The child's conception of space* (F. J. Langdon & J. L. Lunzer, Trans.). New York: W. W. Norton. (Original work published 1948)

Pianta, R. (1999, August). *Promoting literacy before and after school entry: Classroom activities and transition practices.* Paper presented at the meeting of the American Psychological Association, Boston.

Pierce, K. M., Hamm, J. V., & Vandell, D. L. (1997, April). *Experiences in after-school programs and children's adjustment at school and at home.* Paper presented at the meeting of the Society for Research in Child Development, Washington, DC.

Pillow, D. R., Zautra, A. J., & Sandler, I. (1996). Major life events and minor stressors: Identifying mediational links in the stress process. *Journal of Personality and Social Psychology, 70,* 381–394.

Pinger, R. R., Payne, W. A., Hahn, D. B., & Hahn, E. J. (1998). *Drugs.* New York: McGraw-Hill.

Pinker, S. (1994). *The language instinct.* New York: William Morrow.

Pintrich, P. R. (in press). The role of goal orientation in self-regulated learning. In M. Boekaerts, P. R. Pintrich, & M. Zeidner (Eds.), *Handbook of self-regulation.* San Diego: Academic Press.

Piotrowski, C. C. (1997, April). *Mother and sibling triads in conflict: Linking conflict style and the quality of sibling relationships.* Paper presented at the meeting of the Society for Research in Child Development, Washington, DC.

Pipes, P. (1988). Nutrition in childhood. In S. R. Williams & B. S. Worthington-Roberts (Eds.), *Nutrition throughout the life cycle.* St. Louis: Times Mirror/Mosby.

Pleck, J. H. (1983). The theory of male sex role identity: Its rise and fall, 1936–present. In M. Levin (Ed.), *In the shadow of the past: Psychology portrays the sexes.* New York: Columbia University Press.

Pleck, J. H. (1995). The gender-role strain paradigm: An update. In R. F. Levant & W. S. Pollack (Eds.), *A new psychology of men.* New York: Basic Books.

Plomin, R. (1993, March). *Human behavioral genetics and development: An overview and update.* Paper presented at the biennial meeting of the Society for Research in Child Development, New Orleans.

Plomin, R. (1996, August). *Nature and nurture together.* Paper presented at the meeting of the American Psychological Association, Toronto.

Plomin, R. (1999). Commentary. In I. Wickelgren, Nurture helps to mold able minds. *Science, 283,* 1832.

Plomin, R., & DeFries, J. C. (1998). The genetics of abilities and disabilities. *Scientific American, 278,* 40–48.

Plomin, R., DeFries, J. C., & McClearn, G. E. (1990). *Behavioral genetics: A primer.* New York: W. H. Freeman.

Plomin, R., Reiss, D., Hetherington, E. N., & Howe, G. W. (1994). Nature and nurture: Contributions to measures of the family environment. *Developmental Psychology, 30,* 32–43.

Pollitt, E. P., Gorman, K. S., Engle, P. L., Martorell, R., & Rivera, J. (1993). Early supplementary feeding and cognition. *Monographs of the Society for Research in Child Development, 58* (7, Serial No. 235).

Polloway, E. A., Patton, J. R., Smith, R. E. C., & Buck, G. H. (1997). Mental retardation and learning disabilities: Conceptual and applied issues. *Journal of Learning Disabilities, 30,* 297–308.

Poole, D. A., & Lindsey, D. S. (1996). *Effects of parents' suggestions, interviewing techniques, and age on young children's event reports.* Presented at the NATO Advanced Study Institute, Port de Bourgenay, France.

Posner, J. K., & Vandell, D. L. (1994). Low-income children's after-school care: Are there benefits of after-school programs? *Child Development, 65,* 440–456.

Posner, M. I. (1999, April). *Relating mechanisms of cognitive and emotional regulation.* Paper presented at the meeting of the Society for Research in Child Development, Albuquerque.

Poulin-Doubois, D., & Shultz, T. R. (1988). The development of the understanding of human behavior: From agency to intentionality. In J. Astington, P. Harris, & D. Olson (Eds.), *Developing theories of mind.* Cambridge, MA: Cambridge University Press.

Poulton, S., & Sexton, D. (1996). Feeding young children: Developmentally appropriate considerations for supplementing family care. *Childhood Education, 73,* 66–71.

Povinelli, D. J. (1995). The unduplicated self. In P. Rochat (Ed.), *The self in infancy.* Amsterdam: North-Holland-Elsevier.

Povinelli, D. J., Perilloux, H. K., & Landau, K. R. (1996). Self-recognition in young children using delayed versus live feedback: Evidence of a developmental asynchrony. *Child Development, 67,* 1540–1554.

Povinelli, D. J., & Simon, B. B. (1998). Young children's reactions to briefly versus extremely delayed images of the self: Emergence of the autobiographical stance. *Developmental Psychology, 34,* 188–194.

Presidential Task Force on Psychology and Education. (1992). *Learner-centered psychological principles: Guidelines for school redesign and reform (draft).* Washington, DC: American Psychological Association.

Pressley, M. (1983). Making meaningful materials easier to learn. In M. Pressley & J. R. Levin (Eds.), *Cognitive strategy research: Educational applications* (pp. 239–266). New York: Springer-Verlag.

Pressley, M. (1995). More about the development of self-regulation: Complex, long-term, and thoroughly social. *Educational Psychologist, 30,* 207–212.

Pressley, M. (in press). *Effective reading instruction: The case for balanced teaching.* New York: Guilford Press.

Pressley, M., & Schneider, W. (1997). *Introduction to memory development during childhood and adolescence.* Mahwah, NJ: Erlbaum.

Pressley, M., & Woloshyn, V. (1995). *Cognitive strategy instruction that really improves children's academic performance.* Cambridge, MA: Brookline Books.

Prinstein, M. M., Fetter, M. D., & La Greca, A. M. (1996, March). *Can you judge adolescents by the company they keep?: Peer group membership, substance abuse, and risk-taking behaviors.* Paper presented at the meeting of the Society for Research on Adolescence, Boston.

Pueschel, S. M., Scola, P. S., Weidenman, L. E., & Bernier, J. C. (1995). *The special child.* Baltimore: Paul H. Brookes.

Quiggle, N. L., Garber, J., Panak, W. F., & Dodge, K. A. (1992). Social information processing in aggressive and depressed children. *Child Development, 63,* 1305–1320.

Rabin, B. E., & Dorr, A. (1995, March). *Children's understanding of emotional events on family television series.* Paper presented at the meeting of the Society for Research in Child Development, Indianapolis.

Rabiner, D. L., Gordon, L., Klumb, D., & Thompson, L. B. (1991, April). *Social problem solving deficiencies in rejected children: Motivational factors and skill deficits.* Paper presented at the meeting of the Society for Research in Child Development, Seattle.

Radke-Yarrow, M., Nottlemann, E., Martinez, P., Fox, M. B., & Belmont, B. (1992). Young children of affectively ill parents: A longitudinal study of psychosocial development. *Journal of the Academy of Child and Adolescent Psychiatry, 31,* 68–77.

Raikes, H. (1996). A secure base for babies: Applying attachment concepts to the infant care setting. *Young Children, 51,* 59–67.

Rainey, R. (1965). The effects of directed vs. non-directed laboratory work on high school chemistry achievement. *Journal of Research in Science Teaching, 3,* 286–292.

Raman, L. (1999, April). *Developmental differences in children's and adults' understanding of illness.* Paper presented at the meeting of the Society for Research in Child Development, Albuquerque.

Ramey, C. T., Bryant, D. M., Campbell, E. A., Sparling, J. J., & Wasik, B. H. (1988). Early intervention for high-risk children. The Carolina Early Intervention Program. In R. H. Price, E. L. Cowen, R. P. Lorion, & J. Ramos-McKay (Eds.), *14 ounces of prevention.* Washington, DC: American Psychological Association.

Ramey, C. T., & Campbell, F. A. (1984). Preventive education for high-risk children: Cognitive consequences of the Carolina Abecedarian Project. *American Journal of Mental Deficiency, 88,* 515–523.

Ramey, C. T., Campbell, F. A., Burchinal, M., Skinner, M. L., Gardner, D. M., & Ramey, S. L. (in press). Persistent effects of early intervention on high-risk children and their mothers. *Applied Developmental Science.*

Ramey, C. T., Campbell, F. A., & Ramey, S. L. (in press). Early intervention: Successful pathways to improving intellectual development. *Journal of Developmental Neuropsychology.*

Ramey, C. T., & Ramey, S. L. (1998). Early prevention and early experience. *American Psychologist, 53,* 109–120.

Ramsay, D. S. (1980). Onset of unimanual handedness in infants. *Infant Behavior and Development, 3,* 377–385.

Ratner, N. B. (1993). Atypical language development. In J. B. Gleason (Ed.), *The development of language* (3rd ed.). New York: Macmillan.

Ratner, N. B. (1993). Learning to speak. *Science, 262,* 260.

Reilly, R. (1988, August 15). Here no one is spared. *Sports Illustrated,* pp. 70–77.

Reinherz, H. Z., Giaconia, R. M., Silverman, A. B., & Friedman, A. C. (1994, February). *Early psychosocial risks for adolescent suicide ideation and attempts.* Paper presented at the meeting of the Society for Research on Adolescence, San Diego.

Remafedi, G., Resnick, M., Blum, R., & Harris, L. (in press). The demography of sexual orientation in adolescents. *Pediatrics.*

Reschly, D. (1996). Identification and assessment of students with disabilities. *Future of Children, 6* (1), 40–53.

Resnick, L., & Nelson-LeGall, S. (1997). Socializing intelligence. In L. Smith, J. Dockrell, & P. Tomlinson (Eds.), *Piaget, Vygotsky, and beyond.* London: Routledge Paul.

Resnick, L. B., & Chi, M. T. H. (1988). Cognitive psychology and science learning. In M. Druger (Ed.), *Science for the fun of it: A guide to informal science education.* Washington, DC: National Science Teachers Association.

Rest, J. (1995). *Concerns for the social-psychological development of youth and educational strategies: Report for the Kaufmann Foundation.* Minneapolis: University of Minnesota, Department of Educational Psychology.

Rest, J., Narvaez, D., Bebeau, M. J., & Thoma, S. J. (1999). *Postconventional moral thinking.* Mahwah, NJ: Erlbaum.

Rest, J. R. (1986). *Moral development: Advances in theory and research.* New York: Praeger.

Rest, J. R., Turiel, E., & Kohlberg, L. (1969). Relations between level of moral judgment and preference and comprehension of the moral judgments of others. *Journal of Personality, 37,* 225–252.

Reynolds, A. J. (1999, April). *Pathways to long-term effects in the Chicago Child-parent Center Program.* Paper presented at the meeting of the Society for Research in Child Development, Albuquerque.

Reynolds, D. (2000). School effectiveness and improvement. In A. Kazdin (Ed.), *Encyclopedia of psychology.* Washington, DC, & New York: American Psychological Association.

Rice, M. (Ed.). (1996). *Toward a genetics of language.* Hillsdale, NJ: Erlbaum.

Richards, M., Suleiman, L., Sims, B., & Sedeno, A. (1994, February). *Experiences of ethnically diverse young adolescents growing up in poverty.* Paper presented at the meeting of the Society for Research on Adolescence, San Diego.

Richards, M. H., Crowe, P. A., Larson, R., & Swarr, A. (1998). Developmental patterns and gender differences in the experience of peer companionship during adolescence. *Child Development, 69,* 154–163.

Richards, M. H., & Duckett, E. (1994). The relationship of maternal employment to early adolescent daily experiences with and without parents. *Child Development, 65,* 225–236.

Richards, M. H., & Larson, R. (1990, July). *Romantic relations in early adolescence.* Paper presented at the fifth International Conference on Personal Relations, Oxford University, Oxford, England.

Rickards, T. (1999). Brainstorming. In M. A. Runco & S. Pritzker (Eds.), *Encyclopedia of creativity.* San Diego: Academic Press.

Ridgeway, D., Waters, E., & Kuczaj, S. A. (1985). Acquisition of emotion-descriptive language: Receptive and productive vocabulary norms for ages 18 months to 6 years. *Developmental Psychology, 21*, 901–908.

Ritblatt, S. N. (1995, March). *Theory of mind in preschoolers: False beliefs, deception, and pretend play.* Paper presented at the meeting of the Society for Research in Child Development, Indianapolis.

Roberts, D., Jacobson, L., & Taylor, R. D. (1996, March). *Neighborhood characteristics, stressful life events, and African-American adolescents' adjustment.* Paper presented at the meeting of the Society for Research on Adolescence, Boston.

Roberts, J. E., Burchinal, M. R., & Durham, M. (1999). Parents' report of vocabulary and grammatical development of African American preschoolers. *Child Development, 70*, 92–106.

Roberts, W., & Strayer, J. (1996). Empathy, emotional expressiveness, and prosocial behavior. *Child Development, 67*, 471–489.

Robinson, D. P., & Greene, J. W. (1988). The adolescent alcohol and drug problem: A practical approach. *Pediatric Nursing, 14*, 305–310.

Rockhill, C. M., & Greener, S. M. (1999, April). *Development of the Meta-Mood Scale for elementary-school children.* Paper presented at the meeting of the Society for Research in Child Development, Albuquerque.

Rode, S. S., Chang, P., Fisch, R. O., & Sroufe, L. A. (1981). Attachment patterns of infants separated at birth. *Developmental Psychology, 17*, 188–191.

Rodin, J. (1984, December). Interview: A sense of control. *Psychology Today*, pp. 38–45.

Rodriguez, J. L., Diaz, R. M., Duran, D., & Espinosa, L. (1995). The impact of bilingual preschool education on the language development of Spanish-speaking children. *Early Childhood Research Quarterly, 10*, 475–490.

Rogers, A. (1987). *Questions of gender differences: Ego development and moral voice in adolescence.* Unpublished manuscript, Department of Education, Harvard University.

Rogers, C. R. (1950). The significance of the self regarding attitudes and perceptions. In M. L. Reymart (Ed.), *Feelings and emotions.* New York: McGraw-Hill.

Rogers, C. S., & Sawyers, J. K. (1988). *Play in the lives of children.* Washington, DC: National Association for the Education of Young Children.

Rogoff, B. (1990). *Apprenticeship in thinking.* New York: Oxford University Press.

Rogoff, B. (1998). Cognition as a collaborative process. In W. Damon (Ed.), *Handbook of child psychology* (5th ed., Vol. 2). New York: Wiley.

Rogosch, F. A., Cicchetti, D., Shields, A., & Toth, S. L. (1995). Parenting dysfunction in child maltreatment. In M. H. Bornstein (Ed.), *Handbook of parenting* (Vol. 4). Hillsdale, NJ: Erlbaum.

Rohner, R. P., & Rohner, E. C. (1981). Parental acceptance-rejection and parental control: Cross-cultural codes. *Ethnology, 20*, 245–260.

Roopnarine, J. L., & Johnson, J. E. (2000). *Approaches to early childhood education.* Columbus, OH: Merrill.

Rose, A. A., Feldman, J. F., McCarton, C. M., & Wolfson, J. (1988). Information processing in seven-month-old infants as a function of risk status. *Child Development, 59*, 489–603.

Rose, A. J., & Asher, S. R. (1999, April). *Seeking and giving social support within a friendship.* Paper presented at the meeting of the Society for Research in Child Development, Albuquerque.

Rose, H. A. (1997, April). *Bringing biology back in: A biopsychosocial model of gender development.* Paper presented at the meeting of the Society for Research in Child Development, Washington, DC.

Rose, H. A., & Martin, C. L. (1993, March). *Children's gender-based inferences about others' activities, emotions, and occupations.* Paper presented at the biennial meeting of the Society for Research in Child Development, New Orleans.

Rose, S., & Frieze, I. R. (1993). Young singles' contemporary dating scripts. *Sex Roles, 28*, 499–509.

Rose, S. A., Feldman, J. F., & Wallace, I. F. (1992). Infant information processing in relation to six-year cognitive outcomes. *Child Development, 63*, 1126–1141.

Rosenberg, M. (1979). *Conceiving the self.* New York: Basic Books.

Rosenberg, M. (1986). Self-concept from middle childhood through adolescence. In J. Suls & A. G. Greenwald (Eds.), *Psychological perspective on the self* (Vol. 3). Hillsdale, NJ: Erlbaum.

Rosenblith, J. F. (1992). *In the beginning* (2nd ed.). Newbury Park, CA: Sage.

Rosenstein, D., & Oster, H. (1988). Differential facial responses to four basic tastes in newborns. *Child Development, 59*, 1555–1568.

Rosenthal, R., & Jacobsen, L. (1968). *Pygmalion in the classroom.* Fort Worth: Harcourt Brace.

Rosenwalks, Z. (1998, September 10). Commentary. *USA Today*, p. 1A.

Rosenzweig, M. (2000). Ethology. In A. Kazdin (Ed.), *Encyclopedia of psychology.* Washington, DC, & New York: American Psychological Association and Oxford U. Press.

Rosenzweig, M. R. (1969). Effects of heredity and environment on brain chemistry, brain anatomy, and learning ability in the rat. In M. Monosevitz, G. Lindzey, & D. D. Thiessen (Eds.), *Behavioral genetics.* New York: Appleton-Century-Crofts.

Rosnow, R. L., & Rosenthal, R. (1996). *Beginning behavioral research* (2nd ed.). Upper Saddle River, NJ: Prentice Hall.

Rothbart, M. K. (1999, April). *Developing a model for the study of temperament.* Paper presented at the meeting of the Society for Research in Child Development, Albuquerque.

Rothbart, M. K., & Bates, J. E. (1998). Temperament. In W. Damon (Ed.), *Handbook of child psychology* (5th ed., Vol. 3). New York: Wiley.

Rothbart, M. K., Hanley, D., & Albert, M. (1986). Gender differences in moral reasoning. *Sex Roles, 15*, 645–653.

Rothbart, M. L. K. (1971). Birth order and mother-child interaction, *Dissertation Abstracts, 27*, 45–57.

Rothstein, R. (1998, May). Bilingual education: the controversy. *Phi Delta Kappan.* pp. 672–678.

Rovee-Collier, C. (1987). Learning and memory in children. In J. D. Osofsky (Ed.), *Handbook of infant development* (2nd ed.). New York: Wiley.

Rovee-Collier, C. (1997). Dissociations in infant memory: Rethinking the development of implicit and explicit memory. *Psychological Review, 104*, 467–498.

Rovee-Collier, C. (in press). The development of infant memory. *Current Directions in Psychological Science.*

Rovee-Collier, C., Hartshorn, K., & DiRubbio, M. (1999). *Long-term maintenance of infant memory.* Unpublished manuscript, Department of Psychology, Rutgers University, New Brunswick, NJ.

Rowe, D. C., & Jacobson, K. C. (1999, April). *Genetic and environmental influences on vocabulary IQ: Parental education as moderator.* Paper presented at the meeting of the Society for Research in Child Development, Albuquerque.

Rubin, D. H., Krasilnikoff, P. A., Levanthal, J. M., Weile, B., & Berget, A. (1986, August 23). Effect of passive smoking on birthweight. *Lancet*, 415–417.

Rubin, K. H. (1998). Social and emotional development from a cultural perspective. *Developmental Psychology, 34*, 611–615.

Rubin, K. H., Bukowski, W., & Parker, J. G. (1998). Peer interactions, relationships, and groups. In N. Eisenberg (Ed.), *Handbook of child psychology* (5th ed., Vol. 3). New York: Wiley.

Rubin, K. H., Fein, G. G., & Vandenberg, B. (1983). Play. In P. H. Mussen (Ed.), *Handbook of child psychology* (4th ed., Vol. 4). New York: Wiley.

Rubin, K. H., Maioni, T. L., & Hornung, M. (1976). Free play behaviors in middle and lower social class preschoolers: Parten and Piaget revisited. *Child Development, 47*, 414–419.

Rubin, K. H., Mills, R. S. L., & Rose-Krasnor, L. (1989). Maternal beliefs and children's competence. In B. Schneider, G. Attili, J. Nadel, & R. Weissberg (Eds.), *Social competence in developmental perspective.* Amsterdam: Kluwer Academic.

Rubin, Z., & Solman, J. (1984). How parents influence their children's friendships. In M. Lewis (Ed.), *Beyond the dyad.* New York: Plenum.

Ruble, D. (1983). The development of social comparison processes and their role in achievement-related self-socialization. In E. Higgins, D. Ruble, & W. Hartup (Eds.), *Social cognitive development: A social-cultural perspective.* New York: Cambridge University Press.

Ruble, D. N., Boggiano, A. K., Feldman, N. S., & Loebl, J. H. (1980). Developmental analysis of the role of social comparison in self-evaluation. *Developmental Psychology, 16*, 105–115.

Rumberger, R. W. (1983). Dropping out of high school: The influence of race, sex, and family background. *American Educational Research Journal, 20*, 199–220.

Rumberger, R. W. (1995). Dropping out of middle school: A multilevel analysis of students and schools. *American Educational Research Journal, 3*, 583–625.

Russo, N. F. (1990). Overview: Forging research priorities for women's mental health. *American Psychologist, 45,* 368–374.

Rutter, M. (1979). Protective factors in children's response to stress and disadvantage. In M. W. Kent & J. E. Rolf (Eds.), *Primary prevention in psychopathology* (Vol. 3). Hanover, NH: University of New Hampshire Press.

Rutter, M., & Garmezy, N. (1983). Developmental psychopathology. In P. H. Mussen (Ed.), *Handbook of child psychology* (4th ed., Vol. 4). New York: Wiley.

Ryan-Finn, K. D., Cauce, A. M., & Grove, K. (1995, March). *Children and adolescents of color: Where are you? Selection, recruitment, and retention in developmental research.* Paper presented at the meeting of the Society for Research in Child Development, Indianapolis.

Rymer, R. (1992). *Genie.* New York: HarperCollins.

Saarni, C. (1999). *The development of emotional competence.* New York: Guilford.

Saarni, C., Mumme, D. L., & Campos, J. J. (1998). Emotional development: Action, communication, and understanding. In W. Damon (Ed.), *Handbook of child psychology* (5th ed., Vol. 3). New York: Wiley.

Sadker, M., & Sadker, D. (1986, March). Sexism in the classroom: From grade school to graduate school. *Phi Delta Kappan,* pp. 512–515.

Sadker, M., & Sadker, D. (1994). *Failing at fairness.* New York: Touchstone.

Sagan, C. (1977). *The dragons of Eden.* New York: Random House.

Saigal, S., Hoult, L. A., Streiner, D. L., Stoskopf, B. L., & Rosenbaum, P. L. (2000). School difficulties at adolescence in a regional cohort of children who were extremely low birth weight. *Pediatrics, 105,* 325–331.

Sallis, J. F. (2000). Health promotion. In A. Kazdin (Ed.), *Encyclopedia of psychology.* Washington, DC, & New York: American Psychological Association and Oxford U. Press.

Salovy, P., & Mayer, J. C. (1990). Emotional intelligence. *Imagination, Cognition, and Personality, 9,* 185–211.

Salovy, P., & Woolery, A. (2000). Emotional intelligence: Categorization and measurement. In G. Fletcher & M. S. Clark (Eds.), *The Blackwell handbook of social psychology* (Vol. 2). Oxford, England: Blackwell.

Sameroff, A. (1999, September 13). Commentary in "How kids learn." *U.S. News & World Report,* p. 47.

Sameroff, A. J. (2000). Ecological perspectives on developmental risk. In J. Osofsky & H. E. Fitzgerald (Eds.), *WAIMH handbook of infant mental health* (Vol. 4). New York: Wiley.

Sameroff, A. J., & Bartko, W. T. (1997, April). *Neighborhood as a contributor to multiple risk scores for predicting adolescent competence.* Paper presented at the meeting of the Society for Research in Child Development, Washington, DC.

Sampson, R. J., & Earls, F. (1995, April). *Community social organization in the urban mosaic: Project on human development in Chicago neighborhoods.* Paper presented at the meeting of the Society for Research in Child Development, Indianapolis.

Samuels, M., & Samuels, N. (1996). *New well pregnancy book.* New York: Fireside.

Sanson, A., & Rothbart, M. K. (1995). Child temperament and parenting. In M. H. Bornstein (Ed.), *Handbook of parenting* (Vol. 4). Hillsdale, NJ: Erlbaum.

Santrock, J. W. (1999). *Life-span development* (7th ed.). New York: McGraw-Hill.

Santrock, J. W., & Sitterle, K. A. (1987). Parent-child relationships in stepmother families. In K. Pasley & M. Thinger-Tallman (Eds.), *Remarriage and stepparenting.* New York: Guilford Press.

Savin-Williams, R. C., & Rodriguez, R. G. (1993). A developmental, clinical perspective on lesbian, gay male, and bisexual youths. In T. P. Gullotta, G. R. Adams, & R. Montemayor (Eds.), *Adolescent sexuality.* Newbury Park, CA: Sage.

Sax, G. (1997). *Principles of educational and psychology measurement* (4th ed.). Belmont, CA: Wadsworth.

Sax, L. J., Astin, A. W., Korn, W. S., & Mahoney, K. M. (1999). *The American freshman: National norms for fall, 1999.* Los Angeles: Higher Education Research Institute, UCLA.

Scafidi, F., & Field, T. (1996). Massage therapy improves behavior in neonates born to HIV-positive mothers. *Journal of Pediatric Psychology, 21,* 889–897.

Scales, P. C. (1992). *A portrait of young adolescents in the 1990s: Implications for promoting healthy growth and development.* Carrboro, NC: Center for Early Adolescence.

Scarr, S. (1984, May). Interview. *Psychology Today,* pp. 59–63.

Scarr, S. (1993). Biological and cultural diversity: The legacy of Darwin for development. *Child Development, 64,* 1333–1353.

Scarr, S. (1996). Best of human genetics. *Contemporary Psychology, 41,* 149–150.

Scarr, S. (2000). Day care. In A. Kazdin (Ed.), *Encyclopedia of psychology.* Washington, DC, & New York: American Psychological Association and Oxford U. Press.

Scarr, S., & Weinberg, R. A. (1980). Calling all camps! The war is over. *American Sociological Review, 45,* 859–865.

Scarr, S., & Weinberg, R. A. (1983). The Minnesota Adoption Studies: Genetic differences and malleability. *Child Development, 54,* 253–259.

Schacter, D. L. (1996). *Searching for memory.* New York: Basic Books.

Schauble, L. (1996). The development of scientific reasoning in knowledge-rich contexts. *Developmental Psychology, 32,* 102–119.

Scher, M. S., Richardson, G., & Day, N. L. (2000). Effects of prenatal cocaine/crack and other drug exposure on electroencephalographic sleep studies at birth and one year. *Pediatrics, 105,* 39–48.

Schneider, W., & Bjorklund, D. F. (1998). Memory. In D. Kuhn & R. S. Siegler (Eds.), *Handbook of child psychology* (5th ed., Vol. 2). New York: Wiley.

Schneider, W., & Bjorklund, D. F. (1998). Memory. In W. Damon (Ed.), *Handbook of child psychology* (5th ed., Vol. 2). New York: Wiley.

Schneider, W., & Pressley, M. (1989). *Memory development between 2 and 20.* New York: Springer-Verlag.

Schneider, W., & Pressley, M. (1997). *Memory development from 2 to 20* (2nd ed.). Mahwah, NJ: Erlbaum.

Schoendorf, K. C., & Kiely, J. L. (1992). Relationship of sudden infant death syndrome to maternal smoking during and after pregnancy. *Pediatrics, 90,* 905–908.

Schunk, D. H. (1989). Self-efficacy and cognitive skill learning. In C. Ames & R. Ames (Eds.), *Research on motivation and education* (Vol. 3). Orlando: Academic Press.

Schunk, D. H. (1991). Self-efficacy and academic motivation. *Educational Psychologist, 25,* 71–86.

Schunk, D. H. (1996). *Learning theories* (2nd ed.). Englewood Cliffs, NJ: Prentice Hall.

Schunk, D. H., & Zimmerman, B. J. (Eds.). (1994). *Self-regulation of learning and performance: Issues and educational applications.* Mahwah, NJ: Erlbaum.

Schwartz, D., & Mayaux, M. J. (1982). Female fecundity as a function of age: Results of artificial insemination in nulliparous women with azoospermic husbands. *New England Journal of Medicine, 306,* 304–406.

Schweinhart, L. J. (1999, April). *Generalizing from High/Scope longitudinal studies.* Paper presented at the meeting of the Society for Research in Child Development, Albuquerque.

Scott-Jones, D. (1995, March). *Incorporating ethnicity and socioeconomic status in research with children.* Paper presented at the meeting of the Society for Research in Child Development, Indianapolis.

Scribner, S. (1977). Modes of thinking and ways of speaking: Culture and logic reconsidered. In P. N. Johnson-Laird & P. C. Wason (Eds.), *Thinking: Readings in cognitive science.* New York: Cambridge University Press.

Search Institute. (1999). Does service learning make a difference? *Search Institute Source, 15* (1), 1–2.

Seligman, M. E. P. (1975). *Learned helplessness.* San Francisco: W. H. Freeman.

Seligman, M. E. P. (1995). *The optimistic child.* Boston: Houghton Mifflin.

Selman, R. (1980). *The growth of interpersonal understanding.* New York: Academic Press.

Selman, R. L. (1976). Social-cognitive understanding. In T. Lickona (Ed.), *Moral development and behavior.* New York: Holt, Rinehart & Winston.

Selman, R. L. (1980). *The growth of interpersonal understanding.* New York: Academic Press.

Serbin, L. A., & Sprafkin, C. (1986). The salience of gender: The process of sex-typing in three- to seven-year-old children. *Child Development, 57,* 1188–1209.

Serow, R. C., Ciechalski, J., & Daye, C. (1990). Students as volunteers. *Urban Education, 25,* 157–168.

Shade, S. C., Kelly, C., & Oberg, M. (1997). *Creating culturally-responsive schools.* Washington, DC: American Psychological Association.

Sharma, A. R., McGue, M. K., & Benson, P. L. (1996, March). *The emotional and behavioral adjustment of United States adopted adolescents.*

Paper presented at the meeting of the Society for Research on Adolescent Development, Boston.

Sharp, V. (1999). *Computer education for teachers* (3rd ed.). New York: McGraw-Hill.

Shatz, M., & Gelman, R. (1973). The development of communication skills: Modifications in the speech of young children as a function of the listener. *Monographs of the Society for Research in Child Development, 38* (Serial No. 152).

Shaver, P. R. (1993, March). *Where do adult romantic attachment patterns come from?* Paper presented at the biennial meeting of the Society for Research in Child Development, New Orleans.

Shaw, S. M. (1988). Gender differences in the definition and perception of household labor. *Family Relations, 37,* 333–337.

Sheeber, L., Hops, H., Andrews, J. A., & Davis, B. (1997, April). *Family support and conflict: Prospective relation to adolescent depression.* Paper presented at the meeting of the Society for Research in Child Development, Washington, DC.

Sheffield, V. C. (1999, May). *Application of genetic strategies and human genome project resources for the identification of human disease genes.* Paper presented at the meeting of the Society for Pediatric Research, San Francisco.

Shields, S. A. (1991). Gender in the psychology of emotion: A selective research review. In K. T. Strongman (Ed.), *International review of studies on emotion* (Vol. 1). New York: Wiley.

Shields, S. A. (1998, August). *What Jerry Maguire can tell us about gender and emotion.* Paper presented at the meeting of the International Society for Research on Emotions, Würzburg, Germany.

Shiono, P. H., & Behrman, R. E. (1995, Spring). Low birth weight: Analysis and recommendations. *Future of Children, 5,* (1), 4–18.

Shirley, M. M. (1933). *The first two years.* Minneapolis: University of Minnesota Press.

Shneidman, E. (1996). *The suicidal mind.* New York: Oxford University Press.

Shorr, D. N., & Schorr, C. J. (1995, March). *Children's perceptions of kindness and anonymity in others' helping.* Paper presented at the meeting of the Society for Research in Child Development, Indianapolis.

Shulman, S., & Collins, W. A. (Eds.) (in press). *New directions for child development: Adolescent romantic relationships.* San Francisco: Jossey-Bass.

Shweder, R. A., Goodnow, J., Hatano, G., LeVine, R. A., Markus, H., & Miller, P. (1998). The cultural psychology of development. In R. M. Lerner (Ed.), *Handbook of Psychology* (5th ed., Vol. 1).

Shweder, R. A., Mahapatra, M., & Miller, J. (1987). Culture and moral development. In J. Kagan & S. Lamb (Eds.), *The emergence of morality in young children.* Chicago: University of Chicago Press.

Sieber, J. E. (2000). Ethics in research. In A. Kazdin (Ed.), *Encyclopedia of psychology.* Washington, DC, & New York: American Psychological Association and Oxford U. Press.

Siegel, L. S., & Wiener, J. (1993, Spring). Canadian special education policies: Children with disabilities in a bilingual and multicultural

society. *Social Policy Report, Society for Research in Child Development, 7,* 1–16.

Siegler, R. S. (1976). Three aspects of cognitive development. *Cognitive Psychology, 8,* 481–520.

Siegler, R. S. (1998). *Children's thinking* (3rd ed.). Upper Saddle River, NJ: Prentice Hall.

Siegler, R. S., & Robinson, M. (1982). The development of numerical understandings. In H. W. Reese & L. P. Litsitt (Eds.), *Advances in child development and behavior* (Vol. 12). New York: Academic Press.

Sigel, I. E. (1998). Practice and research: A problem in developing communication and cooperation. In W. Damon (Ed.). *Handbook of child psychology* (5th ed., Vol. 4). New York: Wiley.

Simmons, R. G., & Blyth, D. A. (1987). *Moving into adolescence.* Hawthorne, NY: Aldine.

Simons, J. M., Finlay, B., & Yang, A. (1991). *The adolescent and young adult fact book.* Washington, DC: Children's Defense Fund.

Simons, J., Finlay, B., & Yang, A. (1991). *The adolescent and young adult fact book.* Washington, DC: Children's Defense Fund.

Singer, J. L., & Singer, D. G. (1988). Imaginative play and human development: Schemas, scripts, and possibilities. In D. Bergen (Ed.), *Play as a medium for learning and development.* Portsmouth, NH: Heinemann.

Singer, L. T., Arendt, R., Fagan, J., Minnes, S., Salvator, A., Bolek, T., & Becker, M. (1999). Neonatal visual information processing in cocaine-exposed and non-exposed infants. *Infant Behavior and Development, 22,* 1–15.

Skinner, B. F. (1957). *Verbal behavior.* New York: Appleton-Century-Crofts.

Skoe, E. E., & Marcia, J. E. (1988). *Ego identity and care-based moral reasoning in college women.* Unpublished manuscript, Acadia University.

Slaughter, V. P. (1995, March). *Conceptual coherence in a child's theory of mind: Training children to understand belief.* Paper presented at the meeting of the Society for Research in Child Development, Indianapolis.

Slavin, R. E. (1999). Reading by nine: What will it take? In J. W. Miller & M. C. McKenna (Eds.), *Literacy education in the 21st century.* Mahwah, NJ: Erlbaum.

Slee, P. T., & Taki, M. (1999, April). *School bullying.* Paper presented at the meeting of the Society for Research in Child Development, Albuquerque.

Slusser, W., & Powers, N. G. (1997). Breastfeeding update 1: Immunology, nutrition, and advocacy. *Pediatrics in Review, 18:* (4), 111–114.

Smith, P. K., Morita, Y., Junger-Tas, J., Olweus, D., Catalano, R., & Slee, P. T. (Eds.). (1999). *The nature of school bullying: A cross-national perspective.* London: Routledge.

Snarey, J. (1987, June). A question of morality. *Psychology Today,* pp. 6–8.

Snow, C. (1999). Social perspectives on the emergence of language. In B. MacWhinney (Ed.), *The emergence of language.* Mahwah, NJ: Erlbaum.

Snow, C. E. (1996). Interactionist account of language acquisition. In M. Rice (Ed.), *Toward a genetics of language.* Hillsdale, NJ: Erlbaum.

Solomon, B., Powell, K., & Gardner, H. (1999). Multiple intelligence. In M. A. Runco & S.

Pritzker (Eds.), *Encyclopedia of creativity.* San Diego: Academic Press.

Sommer, B. B. (1978). *Puberty and adolescence.* New York: Oxford University Press.

Sophian, C. (1985). Perseveration and infants' search: A comparison of two- and three-location tasks. *Developmental Psychology, 21,* 187–194.

Sorensen, E. S. (1993). *Children's stress and coping.* New York: Guilford.

Spearman, C. E. (1927). *The abilities of man.* New York: Macmillan.

Spelke, E. (1999, October). Save Mozart for later. *Nature, 401,* 643–644.

Spelke, E. S. (1979). Perceiving bimodally specified events in infancy. *Developmental Psychology, 5,* 626–636.

Spelke, E. S. (1988). The origins of physical knowledge. In L. Weiskrantz (Ed.), *Thought without language.* New York: Oxford University Press.

Spelke, E. S. (1988). The origins of physical knowledge. In L. Weiskrantz (Ed.), *Thought without language.* New York: Oxford University Press.

Spelke, E. S. (1991). Physical knowledge in infancy: Reflections on Piaget's theory. In S. Carey & R. Gellman (Eds.), *The epigenesis of mind: Essays on biology and cognition.* Hillsdale, NJ: Erlbaum.

Spelke, E. S. (1991). Physical knowledge in infancy: Reflections on Piaget's theory. In S. Carey & R. Gelman (Eds.), *The epigenesis of mind: Essays on biology and cognition.* Hillsdale, NJ: Erlbaum.

Spelke, E. S., & Newport, E. L. (1998). Nativism, empiricism, and the development of knowledge. In W. Damon (Ed.), *Handbook of child psychology* (5th ed., Vol. 2). New York: Wiley.

Spelke, E. S., & Owsley, C. J. (1979). Intermodal exploration and knowledge in infancy. *Infant Behavior and Development, 2,* 13–28.

Spence, J. T., & Helmreich, R. (1972). The Attitudes Toward Women Scale: An objective instrument to measure the rights and roles of women in contemporary society. *JSAS Catalog of Selected Documents in Psychology, 2,* 66.

Spence, M. J., & DeCasper, A. J. (1987). Prenatal experience with low-frequency maternal voice sounds influences neonatal perception of maternal voice samples. *Infant Behavior and Development, 10,* 133–142.

Spencer, M. B. (1990). Commentary in Spencer, M. B., & Dornbusch, S. Challenges in studying ethnic minority youth. In S. S. Feldman & G. R. Elliott (Eds.), *At the threshold: The developing adolescent.* Cambridge, MA: Harvard University Press.

Spencer, M. B. (1999). Social and cultural influences on school adjustment: The application of an identity-focused cultural ecological perspective. *Educational Psychologist, 34,* 43–57.

Spencer, M. B. (1999). Social and cultural influences on school adjustment: The application of an identity-focused cultural ecological perspective. In K. Wentzel & T. Berndt (Eds.), *Social influences on school adjustment.* Mahwah, NJ: Erlbaum.

Spencer, M. B., & Dornbusch, S. M. (1990). Challenges in studying minority youth. In S. S. Feldman & G. R. Elliott (Eds.), *At the threshold:*

The developing adolescent. Cambridge, MA: Harvard University Press.

Spencer, M. B., & Dornbusch, S. M. (1990). Challenges in studying minority youth. In S. S. Feldman & G. R. Elliott (Eds.), *At the threshold: The developing adolescent.* Cambridge, MA: Harvard University Press.

Spring, J. (1998). *The intersection of cultures.* New York: McGraw-Hill.

Springer, K., & Keil, F. C. (1991). Early differentiation of causal mechanisms appropriate to biological and nonbiological kinds. *Child Development, 4,* 767–781.

Squire, L. (1987). *Memory and brain.* New York: Oxford University Press.

Sroufe, L. A. (1985). Attachment classification from the perspective of infant-caregiver relationships and infant temperament. *Child Development, 49,* 547–556.

Sroufe, L. A. (1996). *Emotional development.* New York: Cambridge University Press.

Sroufe, L. A., Egeland, B., & Carlson, E. A. (1999). One social world: The integrated development of parent-child and peer relationships. In W. A. Collins & B. Laursen (Eds.) *Minnesota symposium on child psychology* (Vol. 31). Mahwah, NJ: Erlbaum.

Sroufe, L. A., Schhork, E., Mottie, E., Lawroski, N., & LaFreniere, P. (1983). The role of affect in social competence. In J. Kaggan & R. B. Zajonc (Eds.), *Emotions, cognition, and behavior.* New York: Plenum.

Sroufe, L. A., & Warren, S. (1999). *Infant attachment and developmental psychopathology.* Unpublished data, Institute of Child Development, University of Minnesota, Minneapolis.

Sroufe, L. A., & Waters, E. (1976). The ontogenesis of smiling and laughter: A perspective on the organization of development in infancy. *Psychological Review, 83,* 173–198.

Sroufe, L. A., Waters, E., & Matas, L. (1974). Contextual determinants of infant affectional response. In M. Lewis & L. Rosenblum (Eds.), *Origins of fear.* New York: Wiley.

St. Pierre, R., Layzer, J., & Barnes, H. (1996). *Regenerating two-generation programs.* Cambridge, MA: Abt Associates.

Stallings, J. (1975). Implementation and child effects of teaching practices in Follow Through classrooms. *Monographs of the Society for Research in Child Development, 40* (Serial No. 163).

Stanhope, L., & Corter, C. (1993, March). *The mother's role in the transition to siblinghood.* Paper presented at the biennial meeting of the Society for Research in Child Development, New Orleans.

Stanley, K., Soule, B., & Copans, S. A. (1979). Dimensions of prenatal anxiety and their influence on pregnancy outcome. *American Journal of Obstetrics and Gynecology, 135,* 333–348.

Stanovich, K. (1998). *How to think straight about psychology* (5th ed.). New York: Longman.

Stattin, H., & Magnusson, D. (1990). *Pubertal maturation in female development: Paths through life* (Vol. 2). Hillsdale, NJ: Erlbaum.

Stechler, G., & Halton, A. (1982). Prenatal influences on human development. In B. B. Wolman (Ed.), *Handbook of developmental psychology.* Englewood Cliffs, NJ: Prentice Hall.

Steinberg, L. D. (1986). Latchkey children and susceptibility to peer pressure: An ecological analysis. *Developmental Psychology, 22,* 433–439.

Steinberg, L., & Levine, A. (1997). *You and your adolescent* (2nd ed.). New York: HarperCollins.

Steiner, J. E. (1979). Human facial expressions in response to taste and smell stimulation. In H. Reese & L. Lipsitt (Eds.), *Advances in child development and behavior* (Vol. 13). New York: Academic Press.

Stengel, R. (1996, April 22). Fly till I die. *Time,* pp. 34–40.

Stenhouse, G. (1996). *Practical parenting.* New York: Oxford University Press.

Stern, D. N., Beebe, B., Jaffe, J., & Bennett, S. L. (1977). The infant's stimulus world during social interaction: A study of caregiver behaviors with particular reference to repetition and timing. In H. R. Schaffer (Ed.), *Studies in mother-infant interaction.* London: Academic Press.

Sternberg, R. J. (1986). *Intelligence applied.* Ft. Worth, TX: Harcourt Brace.

Sternberg, R. J. (1997). Educating intelligence: Infusing the triarchic theory into instruction. In R. J. Sternberg & E. Grigorenko (Eds.), *Intelligence, heredity, and environment.* New York: Cambridge University Press.

Sternberg, R. J. (1999). Intelligence. In M. A. Runco & S. Pritzker (Eds.), *Encyclopedia of creativity.* San Diego: Academic Press.

Sternberg, R. J., & Lubart, T. I. (1995). *Defying the crowd: Cultivating creativity in a culture of conformity.* New York: Free Press.

Sternglanz, S. H., & Serbin, L. A. (1974). Sex-role stereotyping in children's television programming. *Developmental Psychology, 10,* 710–715.

Steur, F. B., Applefield, J. M., & Smith, R. (1971). Televised aggression and interpersonal aggression of preschool children. *Journal of Experimental Child Psychology, 11,* 442–447.

Stevenson, H. C. (1998). Raising safe villages: Cultural-ecological factors that influence the emotional adjustment of adolescents. *Journal of Black Psychology, 24,* 44–59.

Stevenson, H. C. (in press). The confluence of the "both-and" in Black racial identity theory. In R. Jones (Ed.), *Advances in black psychology.* Hampbon, VA: Cobb & Henry.

Stevenson, H. G. (1995, March). *Missing data: On the forgotten substance of race, ethnicity, and socioeconomic classifications.* Paper presented at the meeting of the Society for Research in Child Development, Indianapolis.

Stevenson, H. W. (1995). Mathematics achievement of American students: First in the world by the year 2000? In C. A. Nelson (Ed.), *Basic and applied perspectives on learning, cognition, and development.* Minneapolis: University of Minnesota Press.

Stevenson, H. W., Hofer, B. K., & Randel, B. (1999). *Middle childhood: Education and schooling.* Unpublished manuscript, Dept. of Psychology, University of Michigan, Ann Arbor.

Stevenson, H. W., Lee, S., Chen, C., Stigler, J. W., Hsu, C., & Kitamura, S. (1990). Contexts of achievement. *Monograph of the Society for Research in Child Development, 55* (Serial No. 221).

Stigler, J. W., Nusbaum, H. C., & Chalip, L. (1988). Developmental changes in speed of processing: Central limiting mechanism or skill transfer. *Child Development, 59,* 1144–1153.

Stillman, R. (1998, September 10). Commentary. *USA Today,* p. 1D.

Stipek, D. J. (1996). Motivation and instruction. In D. C. Berliner & R. C. Calfee (Eds.), *Handbook of educational psychology.* New York: Macmillan.

Stocker, C., & Dunn, J. (1990). Sibling relationships in adolescence: Links with friendships and peer relationships. *British Journal of Developmental Psychology, 8,* 227–244.

Stocker, C., & Dunn, J. (1991). Sibling relationships in adolescence. In R. M. Lerner, A. C. Petersen, & J. Brooks-Gunn (Eds.), *Encyclopedia of adolescence* (Vol. 2). New York: Garland.

Strahan, D. B. (1983). The emergence of formal operations in adolescence. *Transcendence, 11,* 7–14.

Strahan, D. B. (1987). A developmental analysis of formal reasoning in the middle grades. *Journal of Instructional Psychology, 14,* 67–73.

Streissguth, A. P., Martin, D. C., Sandman, B. M., Kirchner, G. L., & Darby, B. L. (1984). Intrauterine alcohol and nicotine exposure: Attention and reaction time in 4-year-old children. *Developmental Psychology, 20,* 533–543.

Streitmatter, J. (1993). Gender differences in identity development: An examination of longitudinal data. *Adolescence, 28,* 55–66.

Stringer, S., & Neal, C. (1993, March). *Scaffolding as a tool for assessing sensitive and contingent teaching: A comparison between high- and low-risk mothers.* Paper presented at the biennial meeting of the Society for Research in Child Development.

Sue, S. (1990, August). *Ethnicity and culture in psychological research and practice.* Paper presented at the meeting of the American Psychological Association, Boston.

Sullivan, H. S. (1953). *The interpersonal theory of psychiatry.* New York: W. W. Norton.

Sullivan, K., & Sullivan, A. (1980). Adolescent-parent separation. *Developmental Psychology, 16,* 93–99.

Suomi, S. J., Harlow, H. F., & Domek, C. J. (1970). Effect of repetitive infant-infant separations of young monkeys. *Journal of Abnormal Psychology, 76,* 161–172.

Sutton-Smith, B. (1985, October). The child at play. *Psychology Today,* pp. 64–65.

Swanson, D. P. (1997, April). *Identity and coping styles among African American females.* Paper presented at the meeting of the Society for Research in Child Development, Washington, DC.

Swanson, D. P., Spencer, M. B., & Petersen, A. (1998). Identity formation in adolescence. In K. Borman & B. Schneider (Eds.), *The adolescent years: Social influences and educational challenges.* Chicago: University of Chicago Press.

Swanson, J. M., McBrunett, K., Wigal, T., & Others. (1993). The effect of stimulant medication on

ADD children. *Exceptional Children, 60,* 154–162.

Swarr, A. E., & Richards, M. H. (1996). Longitudinal effects of adolescent girls' pubertal development, perceptions of pubertal timing, and parental relations. *Developmental Psychology, 32,* 636–646.

Tager-Flusberg, H. (Ed.). (1994). *Constraints on language acquisition.* Hillsdale, NJ: Erlbaum.

Takahashi, K. (1990). Are the key assumptions of the "Strange Situation" procedure universal? A view from Japanese research. *Human Development, 33,* 23–30.

Tamis-LeMonda, C. S., & Cabrera, N. (1999). Perspectives on father involvement: Research and policy. *Social Policy Report, Society for Research in Child Development, 13,* No. 2, 1–25.

Tannen, D. (1990). *You just don't understand!* New York: Ballantine.

Tappan, M. B. (1998). Sociocultural psychology and caring psychology: Exploring Vygotsky's "hidden curriculum." *Educational Psychologist, 33,* 23–33.

Tapper, J. (1996, March). *Values, lifestyles, and crowd identification in adolescence.* Paper presented at the meeting of the Society for Research on Adolescence, Boston.

Taskinin, H. (1989). Spontaneous abortions and congenital malformations among the wives of men exposed to organic solvents. *Scandinavian Journal of Work, Environment, and Health, 15,* 345–352.

Tavris, C., & Wade, C. (1984). *The longest war: Sex differences in perspective* (2nd ed.). San Diego: Harcourt Brace Jovanovich.

Taylor, H. G., Klein, N., & Hack, M. (1994). Academic functioning in <750 gm birthweight children who have normal cognitive abilities: Evidence for specific learning disabilities. *Pediatric Research 35,* 289A.

Taylor, J. H., & Walker, L. J. (1997). Moral climate and the development of moral reasoning: The effects of dyadic discussions between young offenders. *Journal of Moral Education, 26,* 21–43.

Temple, C., Nathan, R., Temple, F., & Burris, N. A. (1993). *The beginnings of writing* (3rd ed.). Boston: Allyn & Bacon.

Terman, D. L., Larner, M. B., Stevenson, C. S., & Behrman, R. E. (1996). Special education for students with disabilities: Analysis and recommendations. *Future of Children, 6* (1), 4–24.

Terman, L. (1925). *Genetic studies of genius: Vol. 1. Mental and physical traits of a thousand gifted children.* Stanford, CA: Stanford University Press.

Terman, L. H., & Oden, M. H. (1959). *Genetic studies of genius: Vol. 5. The gifted group at mid-life.* Stanford, CA: Stanford University Press.

Terr, L. C. (1988). What happens to early memories of trauma? *Journal of the American Academy of Child and Adolescent Psychiatry, 27,* 96–104.

Teti, D. M., Sakin, J., Kucera, E., Caballeros, M., & Corns, K. M. (1993, March). *Transitions to*

siblinghood and security of firstborn attachment: Psychosocial and psychiatric correlates of changes over time.* Paper presented at the biennial meeting of the Society for Research in Child Development, New Orleans.

Tetreault, M. K. T. (1997). Classrooms for diversity: Rethinking curriculum and pedagogy. In J. A. Banks & C. A. Banks (Eds.), *Multicultural education* (3rd ed.). Boston: Allyn & Bacon.

Tharp, G. R., & Gallimore, R. (1988). *Rousing minds to life: Teaching, learning, and schooling in social context.* New York: Cambridge University Press.

Tharp, R. G. (1994). Intergroup differences among Native Americans in socialization and child cognition: An ethogenetic analysis. In P. M. Greenfield & R. Cocking (Eds.), *Cross-cultural roots of minority child development.* Mahwah, NJ: Erlbaum.

The Research Bulletin. (1991, Spring). *Disadvantaged urban eighth graders.* Washington, DC: Hispanic Policy Development Project.

Thelen, E. (1995). Motor development: A new synthesis. *American Psychologist, 50,* 79–95.

Thelen, E., & Smith, L. B. (1998). Dynamic systems theories. In W. Damon (Ed.), *Handbook of child psychology* (5th ed., Vol. 1). New York: Wiley.

Thoman, E. B., Denenberg, V. H., Sievel, J., Zeidner, L., & Becker, P. T. (1981). State organization in neonates: Developmental inconsistency indicates risk for developmental dysfunction. *Neuropaediatrica, 12,* 45–54.

Thomas, A., & Chess, S. (1991). Temperament in adolescence and its functional significance. In R. M. Lerner, A. C. Petersen, & J. Brooks-Gunn (Eds.), *Encyclopedia of adolescence* (Vol. 2). New York: Garland.

Thomas, K. (1998, November 4). Teen cyberdating is a new wrinkle for parents, too. *USA Today,* p. 9D.

Thompson, L., & Walker, A. J. (1989). Gender in families: Women and men in marriage, work, and parenthood. *Journal of Marriage and the Family, 51,* 845–871.

Thompson, R. A. (1999). The individual child: Temperament, emotion, self, and personality. In M. H. Bornstein & M. E. Lamb (Eds.), *Developmental psychology: An advanced textbook* (4th ed.). Mahwah, NJ: Erlbaum.

Thurstone, L. L. (1938). *Primary mental abilities.* Chicago: University of Chicago Press.

Tinsley, B. (1992). Multiple influences of the acquisition and socialization of children's health attitudes and behavior: An integrative review. *Child Development, 63,* 1043–1069.

Tinsley, B. J., Finley, K. A., & Ortiz, R. V. (1999, April). *Parental eating socialization in middle childhood: A multi-ethnic perspective.* Paper presented at the meeting of the Society for Research in Child Development, Albuquerque.

Tomlinson-Keasey, C. (1972). Formal operations in females from 11 to 54 years of age. *Developmental Psychology, 6,* 364.

Tomlinson-Keasey, C. (1990). The working lives of Terman's gifted women. In H. W. Grossman & N. L. Chester (Eds.), *The experience and meaning of work in women's lives.* Hillsdale, NJ: Erlbaum.

Tomlinson-Keasey, C. (1993, August). *Tracing the lives of gifted women.* Paper presented at the

meeting of the American Psychological Association, Toronto.

Tomlinson-Keasey, C. A. (1997). *Gifted women: Themes in their lives.* Paper presented at the meeting of the Society for Research in Child Development, Washington, DC.

Tomlinson-Keasey, C., Warren, L. W., & Elliott, J. E. (1986). Suicide among gifted women: A prospective study. *Journal of Abnormal Psychology, 95,* 123–130.

Tompkins, G. (1997). *Literacy for the 21st century: A balanced approach.* Upper Saddle River, NJ: Prentice Hall.

Torgesen, J. K. (1999). Reading disabilities. In R. Gallimore, L. P. Bernheimer, D. L. MacMillan, D. L. Speece, & S. Vaughn (Eds.), *Developmental perspectives on children with learning disabilities.* Mahwah, NJ: Erlbaum.

Toth, S. K., Connor, P. D., & Streissguth, A. P. (1999, April). *Psychiatric/behavioral and learning and memory problems in young adults with fetal alcohol syndrome and fetal alcohol effects.* Paper presented at the meeting of the Society for Research in Child Development, Albuquerque.

Toth, S. L., Manley, J. T., & Cicchetti, D. (1992). Child maltreatment and vulnerability to depression. *Development and Psychopathology, 4,* 97–112.

Tousignant, M. (1995, April 11). Children's cure or adults' crutch? Rise of Ritalin prompts debate over the reason. *Washington Post,* p. B1.

Treffers, P. E., Eskes, M., Kleiverda, G., & van Alten, D. (1990). Home births and minimal medical interventions. *Journal of the American Medical Association, 246,* 2207–2208.

Trehub, S. E., Schneider, B. A., Thorpe, L. A., & Judge, P. (1991). Observational measures of auditory sensitivity in early infancy. *Developmental Psychology, 27,* 40–49.

Triandis, H. C. (1994). *Culture and social behavior.* New York: McGraw-Hill.

Trimble, J. E. (1989, August). *The enculturation of contemporary psychology.* Paper presented at the meeting of the American Psychological Association, New Orleans.

Troiano, R. P., & Flegal, K. M. (1998). Overweight children and adolescents: Description, epidemiology, and demographics. *Pediatrics, 101,* 497–504.

Tubman, J. G., & Windle, M. (1995). Continuity of difficult temperament in adolescence: Relations with depression, life events, family support, and substance abuse. *Journal of Youth and Adolescence, 24,* 133–152.

Tucker, L. A. (1987). Television, teenagers, and health. *Journal of Youth and Adolescence, 16,* 415–425.

Tuckman, B. W., & Hinkle, J. S. (1988). An experimental study of the physical and psychological effects of aerobic exercise on school children. In B. G. Melamed, K. A. Matthews, D. K. Routh, B. Stabler, & N. Schneiderman (Eds.), *Child health psychology.* Hillsdale, NJ: Erlbaum.

Tulving, E. (1972). Episode and semantic memory. In E. Tulving & W. Donaldson (Eds.), *Origins of memory.* San Diego: Academic Press.

Turecki, S., & Tonner, L. (1989). *The difficult child.* New York: Bantam.

Turiel, E. (1966). An experimental test of the sequentiality of developmental stages in the child's moral judgments. *Journal of Personality and Social Psychology, 3,* 611–618.

Turiel, E. (1998). The development of morality. In N. Eisenberg (Ed.), *Handbook of child psychology* (5th ed., Vol. 3). New York: Wiley.

Turnbull, A., Turnbull, R., Shank, M., & Leal, D. (1999). *Exceptional lives: Special education in today's schools.* Columbus, OH: Merrill.

Underwood, M. K., Kupersmidt, J. B., & Coie, J. D. (1996). Childhood peer sociometric status and aggression as predictors of adolescent childbearing. *Journal of Research on Adolescence, 6,* 201–223.

Unger, R., & Crawford, M. (2000). *Women and gender* (4th ed.). New York: McGraw-Hill.

Updegraff, K. A. (1999, April). *Mothers' and fathers' involvement in adolescents' peer relationships: Links to friendship adjustment and peer competence.* Paper presented at the meeting of the Society for Research in Child Development, Albuquerque.

Urberg, K. A., & Wolowicz, L. S. (1996, March). *Antecedents and consequents of changes in parental monitoring.* Paper presented at the meeting of the Society for Research on Adolescence, Boston.

U.S. Department of Education. (1996). *Number and disabilities of children and youth served under IDEA.* Washington, DC: Office of Special Education Programs, Data Analysis System.

U.S. Department of Health and Human Services. (1998). *Teen births decline.* Washington, DC: Author.

U.S. General Accounting Office. (1987, September). *Prenatal care: Medicaid recipients and uninsured women obtain insufficient care.* A report to the Congress of the United States, HRD-97–137. Washington, DC: Author.

Valsiner, J. (2000). Cultural psychology. In A. Kazdin (Ed.), *Encyclopedia of psychology.* Washington, DC, & New York: American Psychological Association and Oxford U. Press.

van Ijzendoorn, M. H., & Kroonenberg, P. M. (1988). Cross-cultural patterns of attachment: A meta-analysis of the Strange Situation. *Child Development, 59,* 147–156.

Vandell, D. L. (1985, April). *Relationship between infant-peer and infant-mother interactions: What have we learned.* Paper presented at the meeting of the Society for Research in Child Development, Toronto.

Vandell, D. L., & Pierce, K. M. (1999, April). *Can after-school programs benefit children who live in high-crime neighborhoods?* Paper presented at

the meeting of the Society for Research in Child Development, Albuquerque.

Vandell, D. L., & Wilson, K. S. (1988). Infants' interactions with mother, sibling, and peer: Contrasts and relations between interaction systems. *Child Development, 48,* 176–186.

VanLehn, K. (1986). Arithmetic procedures are induced from examples. In J. Hiebert (Ed.), *Conceptual and procedural knowledge: The case of mathematics.* Hillsdale, NJ: Erlbaum.

Ventura, S. J., Martin, J. A., Curtin, S. C., & Mathews, T. J. (1997, June 10). *Report of final natality statistics, 1995.* Washington, DC: National Center for Health Statistics.

Vidal, F. (2000). Piaget, Jean. In A. Kazdin (Ed.), *Encyclopedia of psychology.* Washington, DC, & New York: American Psychological Association and Oxford U. Press.

Villiani, S. L. (1997). *Motherhood at the crossroads.* New York: Plenum.

Von Beveren, T. T. (1999). *Prenatal development and the newborn.* Unpublished manuscript, University of Texas at Dallas, Richardson, TX.

Vygotsky, L. S. (1962). *Thought and language.* Cambridge, MA: MIT Press.

Waddington, C. H. (1957). *The strategy of the genes.* London: Allen & Son.

Wade, C., & Tavris, C. (1993). *Psychology,* 3rd ed. New York: HarperCollins.

Wadhwa, P. (1999, February). *Stress in pregnant women and fetal heart rate.* Paper presented at the meeting of the Society for Behavioral Medicine, San Diego.

Wagner, B. M., Cole, R. E., & Schwartzman, P. (1993, March). *Prediction of suicide attempts among junior and senior high school youth.* Paper presented at the meeting of the Society for Research in Child Development, New Orleans.

Wahlsten, D. (2000). Behavioral genetics. In A. Kazdin (Ed.), *Encyclopedia of psychology.* Washington, DC, & New York: American Psychological Association and Oxford U. Press.

Wakschlag, L. S., Chase-Lansdale, P. L., & Brooks-Gunn, J. (1996, March). *Not just "ghosts in the nursery": Contemporary intergenerational relationships and parenting in young African American families.* Paper presented at the meeting of the Society for Research on Adolescence, Boston.

Walden, T. (1991). Infant social referencing. In J. Garber & K. Dodge (Eds.), *The development of emotional regulation and dysregulation.* New York: Cambridge University Press.

Waldman, I. D., & Rhee, S. H. (1999, April). *Are genetic and environmental influences on ADHD of the same magnitude throughout the range of symptoms as at the disordered extreme?* Paper presented at the meeting of the Society for Research in Child Development, Albuquerque.

Walker, H. (1998, May 31). Youth violence: Society's problem. *Eugene Register Guard,* p. 1C.

Walker, L. (1982). The sequentiality of Kohlberg's stages of moral development. *Child Development, 53,* 1130–1136.

Walker, L. J. (1984). Sex differences in the development of moral reasoning. A critical review. *Child Development, 51,* 131–139.

Walker, L. J. (1996). Unpublished review of J. W. Santrock's *Child Development,* 8th ed. (New York: McGraw-Hill).

Walker, L. J., de Vries, B., & Trevethan, S. D. (1987). Moral stages and moral orientation in real-life and hypothetical dilemmas. *Child Development, 58,* 842–858.

Walker, L. J., Hennig, K. H., & Krettenauer, T. (in press). Parent and peer contexts for children's moral reasoning development. *Child Development.*

Walker, L. J., & Pitts, R. C. (1998). Naturalistic conceptions of moral maturity. *Developmental Psychology, 34,* 403–419.

Walker, L. J., & Taylor, J. H. (1991). Family interaction and the development of moral reasoning. *Child Development, 62,* 264–283.

Wall, J. A. (1993, March). *Susceptibility to antisocial peer pressure in Mexican-American adolescents in relation to acculturation.* Paper presented at the biennial meeting of the Society for Research in Child Development, New Orleans.

Waltzman, M. L., Shannon, M., Bowen, A. P., & Bailey, M. C. (1999). Monkeybar injuries: Complications of play. *Pediatrics, 103,* e58.

Wark, G. R., & Krebs, D. L. (1996). Gender and dilemma differences in real-life moral judgments. *Developmental Psychology, 32,* 220–230.

Warrick, P. (1992, March 1). The fantastic voyage of Tanner Roberts. *Los Angeles Times,* pp. E1, 12, 13.

Warshak, R. A. (1997, January 15). Personal communication, Department of Psychology, University of Texas at Dallas, Richardson, TX.

Waterman, A. S. (1985). Identity in the context of adolescent psychology. In A. S. Waterman (Ed.), *Identity in adolescence: Processes and contents.* San Francisco: Jossey-Bass.

Waterman, A. S. (1989). Curricula interventions for identity change: Substantive and ethical considerations. *Journal of Adolescence, 12,* 389–400.

Waterman, A. S. (1992). Identity as an aspect of optimal psychological functioning. In G. R. Adams, T. P. Gullotta, & R. Montemayor (Eds.), *Adolescent identity formation.* Newbury Park, CA: Sage.

Waterman, A. S. (1997). An overview of service-learning and the role of research and evaluation in service-learning programs. In A. S. Waterman (Ed.), *Service learning.* Mahwah, NJ: Erlbaum.

Waters, E., Merrick, S. K., Albersheim, L. J., & Treboux, E. (1995, March). *Attachment security from infancy to early adulthood: A 20-year longitudinal study.* Paper presented at the meeting of the Society for Research in Child Development, Indianapolis.

Watson, J. (1994). Detection of the self: The perfect algorithm. In S. T. Parker, R. W. Mitchell, & M. L. Boccia (Eds.), *Self-awareness in animals and humans: Developmental perspectives.* New York: Cambridge University Press.

Watson, J. B. (1928). *Psychological care of infant and child.* New York: W. W. Norton.

Weaver, C. (in press). *Reconsidering a balanced approach to reading.* Urbana, IL: National Council of Teachers of English.

Weaver, R. F., & Hedrick, P. W. (1999). *Genetics* (3rd ed.). New York: McGraw-Hill.

Webster, J., Lloyd, W. C., Pritchard, M. A., Burridge, C. A., Plucknett, L. E., & Byrne, A. (1999). Development of evidence-based guidelines in midwifery and gynaecology nursing. *Midwifery, 15,* 2–5.

Weikart, D. P. (1993). [Long-term positive effects in the Perry Preschool Head Start program]. Unpublished data, High Scope Foundation, Ypsilanti, MI.

Weikart, D. P. (1982). Preschool education for disadvantaged children. In J. R. Travers & R. J. Light (Eds.), *Learning from experience: Evaluating early childhood demonstration programs.* Washington, DC: National Academy Press.

Weincke, J. K., Thurston, S. W., Kelsey, K. T., Varkonyi, A., Wain, J. C., Mark, E. J., & Christiani, D. C. (1999). Early age at smoking initiation and tobacco carcinogen DNA damage in the lung. *Journal of the National Cancer Institute, 91,* 614–619.

Weiner, B. (1986). *An attributional theory of motivation and emotion.* New York: Springer.

Weiner, B. (1992). *Human motivation: Metaphors, theories, and research.* Newbury Park, CA: Sage.

Weiner, I. B. (1980). Psychopathology in adolescence. In J. Adelson (Ed.), *Handbook of adolescent psychology.* New York: Wiley.

Weiss, B., Dodge, K. A., Bates, J. E., & Pettit, G. S. (1992). Some consequences of early harsh discipline: Child aggression and a maladaptive social information processing style. *Child Development, 63,* 1321–1335.

Weiss, S. M. (2000). Health psychology: History of the field. In A. Kazdin (Ed.), *Encyclopedia of psychology.* Washington, DC, & New York: American Psychological Association and Oxford U. Press.

Weissberg, R. P., & Greenberg, M. T. (1998). School and community competence-enhancement and prevention programs. In W. Damon (Ed.), *Handbook of child psychology* (5th ed., Vol. 4). New York: Wiley.

Wellman, H. M. (1990). *The child's theory of mind.* Cambridge, MA: MIT Press.

Wellman, H. M. (1997, April). *Ten years of theory of mind: Telling the story backwards.* Paper presented at the meeting of the Society for Research in Child Development, Washington, DC.

Wellman, H. M., & Bartsch, R. (1988). Young children's reasoning about beliefs. *Cognition, 30,* 239–277.

Wellman, H. M., & Gelman, S. A. (1992). Cognitive development: Foundational theories of core domains. *Annual Review of Psychology, 43,* 337–375.

Wellman, H. M., & Gelman, S. A. (1998). Knowledge acquisition in foundational domains. In D. Kuhn & R. S. Siegler (Eds.), *Handbook of child psychology* (5th ed., Vol. 2). New York: Wiley.

Wellman, H. M., Ritter, R., & Flavell, J. H. (1975). Deliberate memory behavior in the delayed reactions of very young children. *Developmental Psychology, 11,* 780–787.

Wellman, H. M., & Wooley, J. D. (1990). From simple desires to ordinary beliefs: The early development of everyday psychology. *Cognition, 57,* 245–275.

Wentworth, R. A. L. (1999). *Montessori for the millennium.* Mahwah, NJ: Erlbaum.

Wentzel, K. R., & Asher, S. R. (1995). The academic lives of neglected, rejected, popular, and controversial children. *Child Development, 66,* 754–763.

Werker, J. F., & LaLonde, C. E. (1988). Cross-language speech perception: Initial capabilities and developmental change. *Developmental Psychology, 24,* 672–683.

Werner, E. E. (1979). *Cross-cultural child development: A view from planet Earth.* Pacific Grove, CA: Brooks/Cole.

Wertheimer, M. (1945). *Productive thinking.* New York: Harper.

Wertheimer, R. F. (1999, April). *Children in working poor families.* Paper presented at the meeting of the Society for Research in Child Development, Albuquerque.

Whitaker, R. C., Wright, J. A., Pepe, M. S., Seidel, K. D., & Dietz, W. H. (1997). Predicting obesity in young adulthood from childhood and parental obesity. *New England Journal of Medicine, 337,* 869–873.

White, B., Castle, P., & Held, R. (1964). Observations on the development of visually directed reaching. *Child Development, 35,* 349–364.

White, C. W., & Coleman, M. (2000). *Early childhood education.* Columbus, OH: Merrill.

White, S. H. (1995, March). *The children's cause: Some early organizations.* Paper presented at the meeting of the Society for Research in Child Development, Indianapolis.

Whiting, B. B., & Edwards, C. P. (1988). *Children of different worlds.* Cambridge, MA: Harvard University Press.

Wickelgren, I. (1999). Nurture helps to mold able minds. *Science, 283,* 1832–1834.

Wigfield, A., & Eccles, J. S. (1994). Middle grades schooling and early adolescent development: An introduction. *Journal of Early Adolescence, 14,* 102–106.

Wigfield, A., & Eccles, J. S. (1995). Middle grades schooling and early adolescent development. *Journal of Early Adolescence, 15,* 5–8.

Wilcox, B. L. (1999, April). *Youth policy.* Paper presented at the meeting of the Society for Research in Child Development, Albuquerque.

Wilfond, B. S. (1999, May). *Genetic testing in children: Ethics issues of research and clinical practice.* Paper presented at the meeting of the Society for Pediatric Research, San Francisco.

Willatts, P. (1990). The stage IV infant's solution of problems requiring the use of supports. *Infant Behavior and Development, 7,* 125–134.

William T. Grant Foundation Commission. (1988, February). *The forgotten half: Non-college bound youth in America.* Washington, DC: Author.

Williams, C. R. (1986). *The impact of television: A natural experiment in three communities.* New York: Academic Press.

Williams, C., & Bybee, J. (1994). What do children feel guilty about? Developmental and gender differences. *Developmental Psychology, 30,* 617–623.

Williams, F., LaRose, R., & Frost, F. (1981). *Children, television, and sex role stereotyping.* New York: Praeger.

Williams, J. E., & Best, D. L. (1982). *Measuring sex stereotypes: A thirty-nation study.* Newbury Park, CA: Sage.

Williams, J. E., & Best, D. L. (1989). *Sex and psyche: Self-concept viewed cross-culturally.* Newbury Park, CA: Sage.

Wilson, M. N. (2000). Cultural diversity. In A. Kazdin (Ed.), *Encyclopedia of psychology.* Washington, DC, & New York: American Psychological Association and Oxford U. Press.

Wilson, W. J., & Neckerman, K. M. (1986). Poverty and family structure: The widening gap between evidence and public policy issues. In S. Danziger & D. Weinberg (Eds.), *Fighting poverty.* Cambridge, MA: Harvard University Press.

Wilson-Shockley, S. (1995). *Gender differences in adolescent depression: The contribution of negative affect.* M.S. Thesis, University of Illinois at Urbana-Champaign.

Windle, W. F. (1940). *Physiology of the human fetus.* Philadelphia: Saunders.

Windridge, K. C., Cert, P. G., & Berryman, J. C. (1999). Women's experiences of giving birth after 35. *Birth, 26,* 16–23.

Winne, P. H. (1995). Inherent details in self-regulated learning. *Educational Psychologist, 30,* 173–187.

Winne, P. H. (1997). Experimenting to bootstrap self-regulated learning. *Journal of Educational Psychology, 89,* 397–410.

Winner, E. (1986, August.). Where pelicans kiss seals. *Psychology Today,* pp. 24–35.

Winner, E. (1996). *Gifted children: Myths and realities.* New York: Basic Books.

Winsler, A., Diaz, R. M., Espinosa, L., & Rodriquez, J. L. (1999). When learning a second language does not mean losing the first: Bilingual language development in low-income, Spanish-speaking children attending bilingual preschool. *Child Development, 70,* 349–362.

Winsler, A., Diaz, R. M., & Montero, I. (1997). The role of private speech in the transition from collaborative to independent task performance in young children. *Early Childhood Research Quarterly, 12,* 59–79.

Wintre, M. G., & Vallance, D. D. (1994). A developmental sequence in the comprehension of emotions: Intensity, multiple emotions, and valence. *Developmental Psyschology, 30,* 509–514.

Witkin, H. A., Mednick, S. A., Schulsinger, R., Bakkestrom, E., Christiansen, K. O., Goodenbough, D. R., Hirchhorn, K., Lunsteen, C., Owen, D. R., Philip, J., Ruben, D. B., & Stocking, M. (1976). Criminality in XYY and XXY men. *Science, 193,* 547–555.

Wolfe, W. S., Campbell, C., Fongillo, E. A., Haas, J. D., & Melnick, T. A. (1994). Overweight school children in New York State: Prevalence and characteristics. *American Journal of Public Health, 84,* 807–813.

Wolff, P. H. (1969). The natural history of crying and other vocalizations in early infancy. In B. M. Foss (Ed.), *Determinants of infant development* (Vol. 4). London: Methuen.

Wong, C. A. (1997, April). *What does it mean to be an African-American or European-American growing up in a multi-ethnic community?* Paper presented at the meeting of the Society for Research in Child Development, Washington, DC.

Wong, D. L. (2000). *Essentials of pediatric nursing* (6th ed.). St. Louis: Mosby.

Woodrich, D. L. (1994). *Attention-deficit hyperactivity disorder: What every parent should know.* Baltimore: Paul H. Brookes.

Woodward, A. L., & Markman, E. M. (1998). Early word learning. In D. Kuhn & R. S. Siegler (Eds.), *Handbook of child psychology* (5th ed., Vol. 2). New York: Wiley.

Work Group of the American Psychological Association's Board of Educational Affairs. (1995). *Learner-centered psychological principles: A framework for school redesign and reform (draft).* Washington, DC: American Psychological Association.

World Health Organization (January 28, 2000). *Adolescent health patterns around the world* [press release]. Geneva, Switzerland: Author.

World Health Organization (February 2, 2000). *Adolescent health behavior in 28 countries.* Geneva, Switzerland: World Health Organization.

Worobey, J., & Belsky, J. (1982). Employing the Brazelton scale to influence mothering: An experimental comparison of three strategies. *Developmental Psychology, 18,* 736–743.

Wright, M. R. (1989). Body image satisfaction in adolescent girls and boys. *Journal of Youth and Adolescence, 18,* 71–84.

Wroblewski, R., & Huston, A. C. (1987). Televised occupational stereotypes and their effects on early adolescents: Are they changing? *Journal of Early Adolescence, 7,* 283–297.

Wylie, R. (1979). *The self concept. Vol. 2.: Theory and research on selected topics.* Lincoln: University of Nebraska Press.

Xiaohe, X., & Whyte, M. K. (1990). Love matches and arranged marriages. *Journal of Marriage and the Family, 52,* 709–722.

Xu, F., & Carey, S. E. (1955, March). *Surprising failures in ten-month-old infants' object representation.* Paper presented at the meeting of the Society for Research in Child Development, Indianapolis.

Yang, E., Satsky, M. A., Tietz, J. A., Garrison, S., Debus, J., Bell, K. L., & Allen, J. P. (1996, March). *Adolescent-father trust and communication: Reflections of marital relations between parents.* Paper presented at the meeting of the Society for Research on Adolescence, Boston.

Yates, M. (1995, March). *Community service and political-moral discussions among Black urban adolescents.* Paper presented at the meeting of the Society for Research in Child Development, Indianapolis.

Yates, M. (1996, March). *Community service and political-moral discussions among Black urban adolescents.* Paper presented at the meeting of the Society for Research on Adolescence, Boston.

Yeung, W. J., Sandberg, J. F., Davis-Kearn, P. E., & Hofferth, S. L. (1999, April). *Children's time with fathers in intact families.* Paper presented at the meeting of the Society for Research in Child Development, Albuquerque.

Yin, Y., Buhrmester, D., & Hibbard, D. (1996, March). *Are there developmental changes in the influence of relationships with parents and friends on adjustment during early adolescence?* Paper presented at the meeting of the Society for Research on Adolescence, Boston.

Yip, R. (1995, March). *Nutritional status of U.S. children: The extent and causes of malnutrition.* Paper presented at the meeting of the Society for Research in Child Development, Indianapolis.

Young, K. T. (1990). American conceptions of infant development from 1955 to 1984: What the experts are telling parents. *Child Development, 61,* 17–28.

Young, S. K., & Shahinfar, A. (1995, March). *The contributions of maternal sensitivity and child temperament to attachment status at 14 months.* Paper presented at the meeting of the Society for Research in Child Development, Indianapolis.

Youniss, J. (1980). *Parents and peers in the social environment: A Sullivan Piaget perspective.* Chicago: University of Chicago Press.

Yussen, S. R. (1977). Characteristics of moral dilemmas written by adolescents. *Developmental Psychology, 13,* 162–163.

Zelazo, P. R., Potter, S., & Valiante, A. G. (1995, March). *Effects of fetal cocaine exposure on neonatal information processing.* Paper presented at the meeting of the Society for Research in Child Development, Indianapolis.

Zeskind, P. S., Klein, L., & Marshall, T. R. (1992). Adults' perceptions of experimental modifications of durations and expiratory sounds in infant crying. *Developmental Psychology, 28,* 1153–1162.

Zigler, E., & Styfco, S. J. (1994). Head Start: Criticisms in a constructive context. *American Psychologist, 49,* 127–132.

Zigler, E. F., & Finn-Stevenson, M. (1999). Applied developmental psychology. In M. H. Bornstein & M. E. Lamb (Eds.), *Developmental psychology: An advanced textbook* (4th ed.). Mahwah, NJ: Erlbaum.

Zigler, E. F., & Hall, N. W. (2000). *Child development and social policy.* New York: McGraw-Hill.

Zill, N., Morrison, D. R., & Coiro, M. J. (1993). Long-term effects of parental divorce on parent–child relationships, adjustment, and achievement in young adulthood. *Journal of Family Psychology, 7,* 91–103.

Zimmerman, B. J. (1998, April). *Achieving academic excellence: The role of self-efficacy and self-regulatory skill.* Paper presented at the meeting of the American Psychological Association, San Diego.

Zimmerman, B. J. (in press). Attaining self-regulation: A social cognitive perspective. In M. Boekaerts, P. Pintrich, & M. Seidner (Eds.), *Self-regulation: Theory, research, and application.* Orlando, FL: Academic Press.

Zimmerman, B. J., Bonner, S., & Kovach, R. (1996). *Developing self-regulated learners.* Washington, DC: American Psychological Association.

Zimmerman, R. S., Khoury, E., Vega, W. A., Gill, A. G., & Warheit, G. J. (1995). Teacher and student perceptions of behavior problems among a sample of African American, Hispanic, and non-Hispanic White students. *American Journal of Community Psychology, 23,* 181–197.

Zubay, G. L. (1996). *Origins of life on the earth and in the cosmos.* Dubuque, IA: Wm. C. Brown.

Credits

permission of the publisher; (bottom): Courtesy of Lois Bloom; **p. 318:** © John Carter/Photo Researchers; **p. 322:** © ABPL Image Library/Animals Animals; **p. 325:** © Rosanne Olson/Tony Stone Images; **p. 329:** Courtesy of International Business Machines Corporation. Unauthorized use not permitted; **p. 330:** Courtesy of Catherine Snow

CHAPTER 11

Opener: © Anthony A. Boccaccio/The Image Bank-Chicago; **p. 339:** © Andy Sacks/Tony Stone Images; **p. 340:** Courtesy of Nancy Eisenberg; **11.1:** © Joe McNally/Sygma; **p. 356:** © Michel Tcherevkoff/The Image Bank-Chicago; **11.5:** © Martin Rogers/Stock Boston; **p. 359** (bottom): © David Young-Wolff/Photo Edit; **p. 360:** Courtesy of Alan Sroufe/photo by Leo Kim; **p. 363:** © Penny Tweedie/Tony Stone Images

CHAPTER 12

Opener: © Myrleen Ferguson/Photo Edit; **12.1:** © Dennis Cox; **p. 376:** Courtesy of Susan Harter; **12.4:** © Eddie Adams/Time, Inc.; **p. 385:** Courtesy of James Marcia; **p. 389:** Courtesy of Catherine Cooper

CHAPTER 13

Opener: © Yellow Dog Productions/The Image Bank-Texas; **p. 395:** © Shooting Star; **p. 398:** Courtesy of Alice Eagly; **p. 400** (top): © Digital Stock; (bottom): Courtesy of Eleanor Mac Coby; **p. 401:** © Suzanne Szasz/Photo Researchers; **p. 412:** © Catherine Gehm

CHAPTER 14

Opener: © Incredible Kids/CORBIS CD; **p. 424:** © Arthur Tilley 1995/FPG International; **p. 425:** Courtesy of Darcia Narvaez; **p. 427:** © David Frazier Photo Library; **p. 428:** Courtesy of Carol Gilligan; **p. 442:** © Ronald Cortes; **p. 445:** Courtesy of George Patterson; **p. 446** (top): © Mark Richards/Photo Edit; (bottom): Courtesy of James Garbarino, photo by Nicola Kountoupes; **p. 447:** © SABA

CHAPTER 15

Opener: © Lori Adamski Peek; **p. 455:** © P. West/San Jose Mercury News/Sygma; **p. 461:** Courtesy of Ross Parke; **p. 464:** Courtesy of Diana Baumrind; **p. 466:** © Peter Correz/Tony Stone Images; **p. 478:** Courtesy of E. Mavis Hetherington; **p. 479:** © Karen Kasmauski/Woodfin Camp; **p. 481:** © Tim Bleber/The Image Bank-Chicago

CHAPTER 16

Opener: © Tony Freeman/Photo Edit; **p. 489** (top): Courtesy of Gary Ladd; **16.1:** © Erik Anderson/Stock Boston; **p. 491:** Courtesy of John Coie. © Duke University Photography photo by Jim Wallace; **p. 496:** © Richard Hutchings/Photo Edit; **p. 499:** © Bryan Peterson; **p. 502:** Courtesy of Willard Hartup; **p. 505:** © Michael Siluk/The Image Works; **p. 508:** © Jan Doyle; **p. 509** (top): © FPG International 1996; (bottom): © PhotoDisc, Inc.; **p. 510:** Courtesy of Candice Feiring

CHAPTER 17

Opener: © Bruce Ayres/Tony Stone Images; **17.2** (left): © Ken Fisher/Tony Stone Images; (right): © Jake Rajs/Image Bank-Texas; **p. 525:** © David De-

Lossy/The Image Bank-Texas; **p. 528:** © Marc Antman/Image Works; **p. 530:** Courtesy of "I Have a Dream" program; **p. 532:** © John S. Abbott; **p. 539:** © David Young-Wolff/Photo Edit; **p. 544:** Courtesy of Carol Dweck; **p. 538:** © Richard Hutchings/Photo Researchers; **Fig. 17.4:** © Bob Daemmrich/Stock Boston; (bottom): Courtesy of Harold W. Stevenson; **p. 547** (top): © Eiji Miyazawa/Black Star

CHAPTER 18

Opener: © Peter Correz/Tony Stone Images; **p. 554:** Courtesy of Richard Brislin; **p. 555:** Courtesy of Institute for Intercultural Studies, Inc., New York; **p. 556:** © Marjorie Shostak/Antro Photos; **p. 559:** © Daniel Laine; **p. 563:** Courtesy of El Puente Academy; **p. 564:** Courtesy of Vonnie C. McLoyd; **p. 565:** © USA Today Library, photo by H. Darr Beiser; **p. 566:** Courtesy of James M. Jones; **p. 574** (top): © David Young-Wolff/Tony Stone Images; **p. 574** (bottom): Courtesy of Sandra L. Calvert

EPILOGUE

Opener: © Tom Rosenthal/Super Stock; **p. 586:** Photo Lennart Nilsson/Albert Bonniers Forlag AB., *A Child is Born*, Dell Publishing Company; **p. 587:** © Niki Mareschal/Image Bank-Texas; **p. 588:** © Barbara Feigles/Stock Boston; **p. 589:** © Comstock; **p. 590:** © Joseph Devenney/The Image Bank-Chicago

FIGURE CREDITS

PROLOGUE

Excerpted from *Full Esteem Ahead* © 1994. Reprinted with permission of HJ Kramer/New World Library, Novato, CA. www.nwlib.com.

CHAPTER 1

Figure 1.4: From A. Masten & J.D. Coatsworth, "The development of competence in favorable and unfavorable environments," *American Psychologist*, 553, 1998, pp. 205-220. Copyright © 1998 by the American Psychological Association. Reprinted with permission. **Figure 1.6:** From Santrock, *Children*, 5/e. Copyright © 1997 by The McGraw-Hill Companies. Reproduced with permission of The McGraw-Hill Companies. **Figure 1.7:** From Santrock, *Children*, 5/e. Copyright © 1997 by The McGraw-Hill Companies. Reproduced with permission of The McGraw-Hill Companies.

CHAPTER 2

Figure 2.1: From Santrock, *Children*, 5/e. Copyright © 1997 by The McGraw-Hill Companies. Reproduced with permission of The McGraw-Hill Companies. **Figure 2.2:** From Santrock, *Children*, 5/e. Copyright © 1997 by The McGraw-Hill Companies. Reproduced with permission of The McGraw-Hill Companies. **Figure 2.3:** From Santrock, *Children*, 5/e. Copyright © 1997 by The McGraw-Hill Companies. Reproduced with permission of The McGraw-Hill Companies. **Figure 2.5:** From Santrock, *Children,* 5/e. Copyright © 1997 by The McGraw-Hill Companies. Reproduced with permission of The McGraw-Hill Companies. **Figure 2.8:** From Santrock, *Children,* 5/e. Copyright © 1997 by The McGraw-Hill Companies. Reproduced with permis-

sion of The McGraw-Hill Companies. **Figure 2.10:** From Kopp/Krakow, *The Child*, p. 648. Copyright © 1982. Reprinted by permission of Addison Wesley Educational Publishers Inc. **Figure 2.12:** From Santrock, *Children*, 5/e. Copyright © 1997 by The McGraw-Hill Companies. Reproduced with permission of The McGraw-Hill Companies. **Figure 2.13:** From Santrock, *Children*, 5/e. Copyright © 1997 by The McGraw-Hill Companies. Reproduced with permission of The McGraw-Hill Companies. **Figure 2.14:** From Santrock, *Children*, 5/e. Copyright © 1997 by The McGraw-Hill Companies. Reproduced with permission of The McGraw-Hill Companies.

CHAPTER 3

Figure 3.2: From Mader, *Biology*, 6/e. Copyright © 1997 by The McGraw-Hill Companies. Reproduced with permission of The McGraw-Hill Companies. **Figure 3.4:** From Lewis, *Human Genetics*, 3/e. Copyright © 1999 by The McGraw-Hill Companies. Reproduced with permission of The McGraw-Hill Companies. **Figure 3.8:** From Santrock, *Children*, 5/e. Copyright © 1997 by The McGraw-Hill Companies. Reproduced with permission of The McGraw-Hill Companies. **Figure 3.10:** From Mader, *Biology*, 6/e. Copyright © 1997 by The McGraw-Hill Companies. Reproduced with permission of The McGraw-Hill Companies. **Figure 3.11:** From Santrock, *Children*, 5/e. Copyright © 1997 by The McGraw-Hill Companies. Reproduced with permission of The McGraw-Hill Companies. **Figure 3.13:** From Santrock, *Children*, 5/e. Copyright © 1997 by The McGraw-Hill Companies. Reproduced with permission of The McGraw-Hill Companies. **Figure 3.14:** From Santrock, *Children*, 5/e. Copyright © 1997 by The McGraw-Hill Companies. Reproduced with permission of The McGraw-Hill Companies.

CHAPTER 4

Figure 4.3: From Charles Carroll and Dean Miller, *Health: The Science of Human Adaptation* 5th ed. Copyright © 1991 Times Mirror Higher Education Group, Inc., Dubuque, Iowa. All Rights Reserved. Reprinted by permission. **Figure 4.4:** From Santrock, *Children*, 5/e. Copyright © 1997 by The McGraw-Hill Companies. Reproduced with permission of The McGraw-Hill Companies. **Figure 4.5:** From K.L. Moore, *The Developing Human: Clinically Oriented Embryology*, 4/e. Copyright © 1988. Used by permission of W.B. Saunders Company. **Figure 4.7:** From Queenan and Queenan, *New Life: Pregnancy, Birth, and Your Child's First Year*. Copyright © 1986. Used by permission. **Figure 4.8:** From Santrock, *Children*, 5/e. Copyright © 1997 by The McGraw-Hill Companies. Reproduced with permission of The McGraw-Hill Companies. **Figure 4.9:** From Virginia Apgar, "A Proposal for a New Method of Evaluation of a Newborn Infant," *Anesthesia and Analgesia*, 32, 1975, pp. 260-267. Used by permission of Lippincott Williams & Wilkins. **Figure 4.10:** From: CULTURAL PERSPECTIVES ON CHILD DEVELOPMENT, Wagner & Stevenson ©1982 by W.H. Freeman and Company. Used with permission.

CHAPTER 5

Figure 5.1: From Santrock, *Children*, 5/e. Copyright © 1997 by The McGraw-Hill Companies. Reproduced with permission of The McGraw-Hill Companies. **Figure 5.2:** Reprinted by permission of the publisher from THE POSTNATAL DEVELOPMENT OF THE HUMAN CEREBRAL CORTEX. VOL I-VIII by Jesse LeRoy Conel, Cambridge, Mass. Harvard University Press. Copyright © 1939-1975 by the President and Fellows of Harvard College. **Figure 5.4:** From Santrock, *Children,* 5/e. Copyright © 1997 by The McGraw-Hill Companies. Reproduced with permission of The McGraw-Hill Companies. **Figure 5.7:** From Santrock, *Children,* 5/e. Copyright © 1997 by The McGraw-Hill Companies. Reproduced with permission of The McGraw-Hill Companies. **Figure 5.8:** From W.K. Frankenburg & J.B. Dodds, "The Denver Development Screening Test," *Journal of Pediatrics,* 71, pp. 181-191. Copyright © 1967. Used by permission of MOSBY, Inc., A Harcourt Health Sciences Company. **Figure 5.9:** Charlesworth, *Understanding Human Development,* 2/e. Delmar Press, Albany, NY 1987; and G.J. Schirmer (ed) *Performance Objectives for Preschool Children.* Adapt Press, Sioux Falls, SD, 1974. **Figure 5.12:** Adapted from Alexander Semenoick in R.L. Fantz, "The Origin of Form Perception," *Scientific American,* 1961.

CHAPTER 6

Figure 6.1: Source: National Center for Health Statistics, NHCS Growth Charts, "Monthly Vital Statistic Report." **Figure 6.2:** Adapted from *Human Biology and Economy* 2nd Edition, by Alan Damon, by permission of W.W. Norton and Company, Inc. **Figure 6.3:** From G.J. Schirmer (ed)*Performance Objectives for Preschool Children.* Adapt Press, Sioux Falls, SD, 1974. **Figure 6.4:** From G.J. Schirmer (ed)*Performance Objectives for Preschool Children.* Adapt Press, Sioux Falls, SD, 1974. **Figure 6.5:** Source: Food and Nutrition Board, 1980. **Figure 6.6:** From Santrock, *Children,* 5/e. Copyright © 1997 by The McGraw-Hill Companies. Reproduced with permission of The McGraw-Hill Companies. **Figure 6.7:** From C.A. Aligne & J.J. Stoddard, "Tobacco and Children: An economic evaluation of the medical effects of parental smoking," *Archives of Pediatric & Adolescent Medicine,* 151, 1997, pp. 648-653. Copyrighted 1997, American Medical Association. Used by permission. **Figure 6.8:** From Santrock, *Children,* 5/e. Copyright © 1997 by The McGraw-Hill Companies. Reproduced with permission of The McGraw-Hill Companies. **Figure 6.9:** From J.M. Tanner et al, "Standards from Birth to Maturity for Height, Weight, Height Velocity: British Children, 1965," *Archives of Diseases in Childhood,* 41. Copyright © 1966. Used by permission of BMJ Publishing Group. **Figure 6.10:** From the Alan Guttmacher Institute (1995) National Survey of Family Growth and (1995) Survey of Adolescent Males New York. Alan Guttmacher Institute. **Figure 6.11:** From Santrock, *Children,* 5/e. Copyright © 1997 by The McGraw-Hill Companies. Reproduced with permission of The McGraw-Hill Companies.

CHAPTER 7

Figure 7.3: From Santrock, *Children,* 5/e. Copyright © 1997 by The McGraw-Hill Companies. Reproduced with permission of The McGraw-Hill Companies. **Figure 7.4:** From Santrock, *Children,* 5/e. Copyright © 1997 by The McGraw-Hill Companies.

Reproduced with permission of The McGraw-Hill Companies. **Figure 7.5:** Reprinted courtesy of D. Wolf and J. Nove. **Figure 7.6:** From Santrock, *Children,* 5/e. Copyright © 1997 by The McGraw-Hill Companies. Reproduced with permission of The McGraw-Hill Companies. **Figure 7.7:** From Santrock, *Children,* 5/e. Copyright © 1997 by The McGraw-Hill Companies. Reproduced with permission of The McGraw-Hill Companies. **Figure 7.8:** From Santrock, *Children,* 5/e. Copyright © 1997 by The McGraw-Hill Companies. Reproduced with permission of The McGraw-Hill Companies. **Figure 7.12:** From Santrock, *Children,* 5/e. Copyright © 1997 by The McGraw-Hill Companies. Reproduced with permission of The McGraw-Hill Companies. **Figure 7.13:** From Santrock, *Children,* 5/e. Copyright © 1997 by The McGraw-Hill Companies. Reproduced with permission of The McGraw-Hill Companies. **Figure 7.14:** From Santrock, *Children,* 5/e. Copyright © 1997 by The McGraw-Hill Companies. Reproduced with permission of The McGraw-Hill Companies.

CHAPTER 8

Figure 8.1: From Santrock, *Psychology,* 5/e. Copyright © 1997 by The McGraw-Hill Companies. Reproduced with permission of The McGraw-Hill Companies. **Figure 8.4:** From Joel Levin et al. "The Keyword Method in the Classroom," *Elementary School Journal,* 80: 4. Copyright © 1980 University of Chicago Press. Reprinted by permission. **Figure 8.7:** From Frederick Reif, Cognitive Mechanisms Facilitating Human Problem-Solving in a Realistic Domain: The Example of Physics, printed at the University of California at Berkeley, October 19, 1979. Reprinted by permission of the author. **Figure 8.8:** From B. Murdock, Jr., *Human Memory: Theory and Data.* Copyright © 1974. Used by permission of the author. **Figure 8.10:** From Robert S. Siegler, *Four Rules for Solving the Balance Scale Task.* Copyright © Robert S.Siegler. Reprinted by permission. **Figure 8.11:** From Santrock, *Educational Psychology,* chapter 8. Copyright © 2000 by The McGraw-Hill Companies. Reproduced by permission of The McGraw-Hill Companies. **Figure 8.13:** After Zimmerman, Bonner, and Kovach, *Developing Self-Regulated Learners: Beyond Achievement to Self-Efficacy,* 1996, p. 11 (Figure 1). Copyright © 1996 by the American Psychological Association. Adapted with permission. **Figure 8.14:** Adapted from Zimmerman, Bonner, and Kovach, *Developing Self-Regulated Learners: Beyond Achievement to Self-Efficacy,* pp. 18-19, Copyright © 1996 by the American Psychological Association. Adapted with permission.

CHAPTER 9

Figure 9.1: From Santrock, *Psychology,* 5/e. Copyright © 1997 by The McGraw-Hill Companies. Reproduced with permission of The McGraw-Hill Companies. **Figure 9.2:** From Santrock, *Psychology,* 5/e. Copyright © 1997 by The McGraw-Hill Companies. Reproduced with permission of The McGraw-Hill Companies. **Figure 9.3:** From Santrock, *Psychology,* 5/e. Copyright © 1997 by The McGraw-Hill Companies. Reproduced with permission of The McGraw-Hill Companies. **Figure 9.4:** Wechsler Intelligence Scale for Children-Revised. Copyright © 1981, 1955 by The Psychological Corporation, a

Harcourt Assessment Company. Adapted and reproduced by permission. All rights reserved. "Wechsler Intelligence Scale for Children" and "WISC-R" are registered trademarks of The Psychological Corporation. **Figure 9.5:** Used by permission of Dr. Ulric Neisser. **Figure 9.6:** From Raven's *Standard Progressive Matrices,* Item A5. Used by permission of Campbell Thomson and McLaughlin Limited. **Figure 9.7:** From Raven's *Standard Progressive Matrices,* Item A5. Used by permission of Campbell Thomson and McLaughlin Limited.

CHAPTER 10

Figure 10.3: From BRAIN, MIND, AND BEHAVIORAL, 2/e by Floyd E. Bloom and Arlyne Lazerson. © 1985 and 1988 by Educational Broadcasting Corp. Used by permission of W.H. Freeman and Company.

CHAPTER 11

Figure 11.2: From Santrock, *Children,* 5/e. Copyright © 1997 by The McGraw-Hill Companies. Reproduced with permission of The McGraw-Hill Companies. **Figure 11.4:** Excerpts adapted from THE OPTIMISTIC CHILD: A Proven Program to Safeguard Children Against Depression and Build Lifelong Resilience. Copyright © 1995 by Martin E.P. Seligman, Ph.D., Karen Reivich, M.A., Lisa Jaycox, Ph.D., and Jane Gilham, Ph.D. Reprinted by permission of Houghton Mifflin Company, and Arthur Pine Associates, Inc. All rights reserved. **Figure 11.5:** From A.T. Ainsworth, "The development of Infant-mother attachment" in *Review of Child Developmental Research,* Vol. 3, by B. Caldwell and H. Riccint (eds.) Reprinted by permission of the University of Chicago Press. **Figure 11.6:** From Santrock, *Children,* 5/e, Copyright © 1997 by the McGraw-Hill Companies. Reproduced with permission of the McGraw-Hill Companies. **Figure 11.7:** From Santrock, *Children,* 5/e. Copyright © 1997 by The McGraw-Hill Companies. Reproduced with permission of The McGraw-Hill Companies. **Self & Identity:** From S. Harter, "Self and identity development," in S.S. Feldman & G.R. Elliott (eds.), *At the threshold: The developing adolescent,* pp. 352-353. Copyright © 1990. Reprinted by permission of Stanford University Press and the author.

CHAPTER 12

Figure 12.1: From M. Lewis and J. Brooks-Gunn, *Social Cognition and the Acquisition of the Self,* p. 64. Copyright © 1979. Used by permission of the Plenum Publishing Corporation, and the author. **Figure 12.3:** From Thomas E. Lickona, Ph.D., ed., *Moral Development and Behavior.* Copyright © 1976. Used by permission of Thomas E. Lickona, Ph.D. **Figure 12.4:** From Santrock, *Children,* 5/e. Copyright © 1997 by The McGraw-Hill Companies. Reproduced with permission of The McGraw-Hill Companies. **Figure 12.5:** From Santrock, *Children,* 5/e. Copyright © 1997 by The McGraw-Hill Companies. Reproduced with permission of The McGraw-Hill Companies.

CHAPTER 13

Figure 13.1: From Santrock, *Children,* 5/e. Copyright © 1997 by The McGraw-Hill Companies. Reproduced with permission of The McGraw-Hill Companies. **Figure 13.2:** From Santrock, *Psychology,*

Deci, E., 541, 542
DeFries, J. C., 86, 88
DeGarmo, D. S., 559
Degirmencioglu, S. M., 510
deHaan, M., 131
DelCielo, D., 255
DeLoache, J. S., 243, 262, 404
Deluca, P., 171
Demarest, J., 403
DeMarie-Dreblow, D., 243
Dempster, F. N., 246
Demuth, K., 310
Denham, S. A., 461
Detterman, D. K., 295, 300
Devich-Navarro, M., 389
DeVillar, R. A., 574
Dewey, C. R., 363
Dewey, J., 265, 439
DeWolf, M., 521
Diamond, A. D., 209
Diange, A., 105
Diaz, R. M., 228, 331
Dickerscheid, J. D., 412
Dickinson, D., 288
Dickover, R., 105
Didow, S. M., 313
Dietz, W. H., 176, 178
Digest of Education Statistics, 530
DiRubbio, 242
Dittus, R. S., 111
Dix, T., 462
Dixon, R. A., 7
Dobzhansky, T. G., 71
Dodge, K. A., 349, 445, 464, 475, 491, 492, 493
Domek, C. J., 488
Dorn, L. D., 181
Dornbusch, S. M., 388, 564, 566
Douvan, E., 390
Dowdy, B. B., 510
Dowling, M., 118
Downey, G., 349, 510
Doyle, A., 497
Doyle, J. A., 59
Dricas, A. S., 387
Dryfoos, J. G., 192, 194
DuBois, D. L., 381, 508
Duck, S. W., 491, 502
Duckett, E., 474
Duffy-Hester, A. M., 328
Dunbar, N., 377
Duncan, G. J., 295, 561
Duncker, K., 260
Dunkel-Schetter, C., 107
Dunn, J., 317, 342, 461, 468, 469
Dunn, J. F., 45
Dunn, L., 521
Dunphy, D. C., 507
Duran, D., 331
DuRant, R. H., 531
Durham, M., 324
Durkin, K., 402, 403
Dweck, C. S., 372, 544, 545
Dzarnik, C., 265

Eagly, A. H., 398, 408, 411
Earls, F., 558
East, P., 186
Eaton, M., 400
Eccles, J. S., 11, 402, 529, 546, 547
Echols, K., 262

Edelman, M. W., 11, 13, 560
Educational Testing Service, 547
Edwards, C. P., 427, 479
Egeland, B., 18, 360, 457, 458
Ehrhardt, A. A., 396
Eiferman, R. R., 499
Eiger, M. S., 138
Eimas, P., 310
Eisenberg, N., 340, 342, 407, 425, 433, 435, 437, 438, 461
Eisenberger, R., 542
Ekman, P., 340
Elder, G., Jr., 48
Elder, G. H., 460
Elias, M., 174
Elicker, J., 228
Elkind, D., 213, 215, 222, 223, 519, 556
Elkind, J., 539
Elliott, E., 544
Elliott, G. R., 195
Elliott, J. E., 191
Ellis, H. C., 243
El-Taliawy, T., 412
Embretton, S. E., 53, 283
Emde, R. N., 345
Emery, R. E., 478
Emshoff, 190
Enger, E. D., 70
Enright, R. D., 387
Erikson, E. H., 27, 33, 34, 359, 383, 384, 388, 390, 397, 445, 495
Erkut, S., 565
Erlick, A. C., 559
Erwin, E. J., 13
Eskenazi, B., 76
Eskes, M., 114
Espinosa, L., 331
Etteman, J., 402
Etzel, R., 171
Evans, A. C., 166
Evans, B. J., 565
Evans, I. M., 530
Eyler, F. D., 109

Fabes, R. A., 340, 342, 407, 435, 461
Fabricius, W. V., 243
Fagan, J., 109
Fagot, B. I., 400
Falbo, T., 469
Faltis, C. J., 574
Famy, C., 108
Fang, X., 503
Fantz, R. L., 150
Farmer, M. C., 429
Fasick, F., 557
Federman, J., 570
Fehr, B., 502
Fehr, L. A., 387
Fein, G. G., 497, 525
Feinman, S., 414
Feiring, C., 507, 510
Feldman, D. H., 301
Feldman, J. F., 86, 294
Feldman, M. A., 301
Feldman, N. S., 376
Feldman, S. S., 183, 187, 195, 445
Felice, M. E., 186
Felner, R. D., 381
Fenson, L., 322, 324
Fenwick, K. D., 153
Ferguson, A., 138

Ferguson, D. L., 389
Ferguson, D. M., 138
Fernald, A., 346
Fernandez, A., 108
Ferrari, M., 269
Ferron, J., 561
Ferry, K. S., 362
Fetter, M. D., 507
Field, D., 572
Field, N., 376
Field, T., 107, 118, 349, 361
Field, T. M., 263
Fields, M. V., 328
Fields, R., 112
Finch, C., 381
Fine, M. A., 475
Finkel, D., 90
Finlay, B., 140, 532
Finley, K. A., 171
Finn-Stevenson, M., 9
Firlik, R., 517
Fisch, R. O., 123, 155
Fisher-Thompson, D., 400
Fiske, S. T., 250
Fitzgerald, J. F., 111
Flavell, E. R., 256, 257
Flavell, J. H., 204, 226, 238, 242, 245, 256, 257, 268, 269
Flegal, K. M., 172
Fleming, J. E., 349
Flood, P., 545
Flynn, J. R., 295
Fogel, A., 456
Folkman, S., 352
Follansbee, D. J., 388
Fongillo, E. A., 176
Ford, L., 374
Fordham, S., 508
Forgatch, M. S., 559
Forman, E. R., 379
Forrest, J. D., 185
Foster-Clark, F. S., 390
Fowler, J. A., 171
Fox, C. E. R., 349
Fox, M. B., 349
Fox, N., 362
Fox, N. A., 132
Fracasso, M. P., 10
Frady, R. I., 397
Fraga, C. G., 112
Fraiberg, S., 142, 145
France, K. G., 135
Francis, J., 387
Fraser, G., 387
Freeman, D., 556
Freeman, K. E., 261
Freier, C., 109
Freier, K., 109
Freppon, P. A., 329
Freud, A., 488, 495
Freud, S., 7, 8, 9, 32
Fried, P. A., 108, 109
Friedman, D. S., 178
Friedman, J., 340, 342
Friedman, S. L., 531
Friedrich, L. K., 569
Friedrichs, A., 269
Frieze, I. R., 511
Frigoletto, F., 104, 114
Frodi, A. M., 363
Frosch, C. A., 362
Frost, F., 402
Frost, J. L., 171
Frye, D., 255, 275
Fugger, E. F., 73
Fuller, M., 508

Furman, W., 458, 501, 507, 509
Furstenberg, F. F., 476, 478
Furth, H. G., 218, 319
Futterman, D., 104

Gabriel, L. T., 300
Gadpaille, W. J., 191
Gaensbauer, T. G., 345
Galambos, N. L., 196, 475
Galinsky, E., 477
Gallimore, R., 229
Galotti, K. M., 428, 429
Galperyn, K., 426
Gandini, L., 517
Ganger, J. B., 86
Ganiban, J., 361, 467
Gao, Y. T., 112
Garbarino, J., 447, 466, 560
Garber, J., 349
Garcia, E. E., 331
Garcia, H. A. V., 565
Garcia, L., 372
Garcia, R., 107, 331
Garcia-Mila, M., 269, 275
Gardner, D. M., 296
Gardner, H., 281, 288, 289, 303
Gardner, L. I., 165
Garfinkle, J., 376
Garmezy, N., 14, 381
Garmon, L., 428
Garnier, H. E., 530
Garrett, B., 524
Garrett, P., 561
Garrison, S., 482
Garrod, A. C., 426
Garvey, C., 497
Gat, I., 572
Gauthier, R., 108
Gazzaniga, M. S., 314
Ge, X., 472
Geary, D. C., 71
Gehl, K. S., 261
Gelfand, D. M., 349
Gelman, R., 214, 226, 255, 325
Gelman, S. A., 255, 256
Genesee, F., 331
George, C., 470
George, T. P., 52
Gergen, P. J., 171
Gesell, A. L., 8, 147, 292
Gewirtz, J., 118, 345
Giannetta, J. M., 109
Gibbs, J., 423, 425
Gibbs, J. C., 428
Gibbs, J. T., 298, 352, 546, 559
Gibbs, P. R., 76
Gibson, E. G., 150
Gibson, E. J., 149, 150, 152, 210
Gibson, J. J., 149
Giedd, J., 166
Gilligan, C., 390, 407, 425, 428, 429, 487
Ginsburg, H. P., 272
Giordano, R., 426
Gjerde, P. F., 458
Gleason, J. B., 310, 319
Glucksberg, S., 492
Gojdamaschko, N., 229
Goldberg, J., 247
Goldfield, E. C., 147
Goldin-Meadow, S., 314, 320
Goldman, M. B., 108

Subject Index